Business Organizations

BUSINESS ORGANIZATIONS
Cases, Problems, and Case Studies

D. GORDON SMITH
Law School
The University of Wisconsin

CYNTHIA A. WILLIAMS
College of Law
The University of Illinois

PUBLISHERS

76 Ninth Avenue, New York, NY 10011
http:// lawschool.aspenpublishers.com

© 2004 Aspen Publishers, Inc.
A Wolters Kluwer Company
www.aspenpublishers.com

Aspen Publishers
Attn: Permissions Department
76 Ninth Avenue, 7th Floor
New York, NY 10011-5201

Printed in the United States of America

2 3 4 5 6 7 8 9 0

ISBN 0-7355-2603-6

Library of Congress Cataloging-in-Publication Data

Smith, D. Gordon.
    Business organizations : cases, problems, and case studies / D. Gordon Smith, Cynthia
A. Williams.—1st ed.
        p. cm.
    ISBN 0-7355-2603-6
    1. Business enterprises—Law and legislation—United States—Cases. I. Williams,
Cynthia A. II. Title.
    KF1355.A7S63 2004
    346.73'065—dc22   2004001034

About Aspen Publishers

Aspen Publishers, headquartered in New York City, is a leading information provider for attorneys, business professionals, and law students. Written by preeminent authorities, our products consist of analytical and practical information covering both U.S. and international topics. We publish in the full range of formats, including updated manuals, books, periodicals, CDs, and online products.

Our proprietary content is complemented by 2,500 legal databases, containing over 11 million documents, available through our Loislaw division. Aspen Publishers also offers a wide range of topical legal and business databases linked to Loislaw's primary material. Our mission is to provide accurate, timely, and authoritative content in easily accessible formats, supported by unmatched customer care.

To order any Aspen Publishers title, go to *www.aspenpublishers.com* or call 1-800-638-8437.

To reinstate your manual update service, call 1-800-638-8437.

For more information on Loislaw products, go to *www.loislaw.com* or call 1-800-364-2512.

For Customer Care issues, e-mail *CustomerCare@aspenpublishers.com*; call 1-800-234-1660; or fax 1-800-901-9075.

Aspen Publishers
A Wolters Kluwer Company

To Sue, for her unerring support, and to our fabulous
five—Laura, Drew, Eve, Christian, and Conrad
—*D. Gordon Smith*

To my Mother, who did a fantastic job instilling the
cognitive biases of optimism and over-confidence in me,
and to my daughters Emily and Caroline, who make
every day a joy.
—*Cynthia A. Williams*

Summary of Contents

Contents

CHAPTER 3

Hybrid Entities

CHAPTER 4

Organization and Structure of a Corporation

CHAPTER 8

Federal Regulation of Corporate Governance

CHAPTER 9

Control of the Closely Held Firm

CHAPTER 10

Directors' Duty of Care

CHAPTER 11
Directors' and Shareholders' Duty of Loyalty

CHAPTER 12
Litigation to Enforce Directors' Duties

CHAPTER 13
Oppression of Minority Shareholders

CHAPTER 14

Friendly Mergers and Acquisitions

CHAPTER 15

Defending Against Hostile Takeovers

CHAPTER 16

Fraud and Insider Trading Under Federal Securities Law

Preface

Twenty years ago, almost all law schools offered separate courses in "Corporations" and "Agency and Partnership." By the late 1980s, most law schools had combined those courses into a more comprehensive "Business Associations" or "Business Organizations" course. In a recent survey, teachers in this area estimated that about 90 percent of law students take the basic course.[1] Over 80 percent of law schools represented in the survey offered four or more credit hours of "Business Associations," either as a one-semester course or as two separate courses. Obviously, this is a field that both students and professors feel compelled to explore in some depth.

The most significant challenge in attempting to capture this subject in a single casebook is that the law relating to business associations has been expanding at an unprecedented rate. Over the past two decades, new business associations (such as limited liability companies, limited liability partnerships, and variations of the business trust) have been developed and have gained widespread acceptance in the business world. The law relating to corporations underwent a dramatic expansion and reconsideration during the hostile takeover era of the 1980s, and the repercussions of those changes continue to be worked out by courts, legislatures, and regulators. Modern business developments — particularly, the globalization of the economy and the increasing importance of joint ventures, venture capital, franchising, and cross-border governance structures — inevitably impose stress on legal rules designed to address the problems of a different time. Finally, there has been an explosion in agency law, as fundamental principles of common law are adapted to the modern regulatory state.

Despite the complexity surrounding business associations, we believe that (with limited exceptions) the legal principles central to the law of business associations are actually quite straightforward. Most issues in this course arise simply because one person has acted on behalf of another person. Whenever this occurs, there is a risk that the actor will not behave in accordance with

---

1. *See* Robert B. Thompson, *The Basic Business Associations Course: An Empirical Study of Methods and Content*, 48 J. Leg. Ed. 438, 438 (1998).

the other person's wishes. Hence the adage, "If you want something done right you have to do it yourself." But doing everything oneself is an onerous burden on all but the smallest of small business operators. In the business world, therefore, people attempt to structure their relationships in ways that minimize the risk of having others deviate from their wishes. The law relating to business associations may be viewed as providing legal rules to accomplish this goal.

Much of the difficulty (and fascination) for students, practicing attorneys, and scholars lies in applying the fundamental principles to complex factual situations, and in understanding the business contexts in which those legal principles operate. Because many students come into the basic course with little knowledge of business and finance, one of the major goals of this casebook, in addition to exploring the applicable legal principles, is to increase the business sophistication of the students. That goal significantly informs our pedagogical approach, which may be summarized in the following three principles:

First, we share a conviction that students learn this subject best by wrestling with real-world situations and materials. As a result, we have included discussion Problems based on actual problems faced by identified companies, as reported in decided cases or in the business press. Moreover, we include at various points excerpts from transactional and litigation documents. The premise underlying this approach is that "the law of business associations" is more than the words of the statutes or the holdings of the cases, but includes the practices of those who work in the field. One side benefit to this approach is that such materials provide an excellent opportunity to explore ethical issues faced by practicing attorneys.

Second, we have found that most students in the basic "Business Associations" course are uninterested in reading law review articles exploring the nuances of legal theory, but that they are nevertheless interested in constructing a theoretical framework to assist in understanding the law. As a result, we emphasize fundamental concepts in the textual materials that introduce the cases. In addition, we have structured the materials in a manner that is designed to evoke comparisons between the various sections on a conceptual level. More specifically, the materials relating to each major section explore formation, management, financial attributes, fiduciary duties, and termination/dissolution. Also, we have edited the materials in a manner that evokes discussion of legal theory in the context of problem solving.

Third, we find that the law governing business associations is most fascinating when viewed from many perspectives. In writing text and selecting cases and materials, therefore, we have consciously included historical, economic, progressive, comparative/international, sociological, and psychological perspectives.

This book begins with a section on the law of agency, which at one time was considered a fundamental common law topic (of nearly equal magnitude with contract law, property law, and tort law) and remains an area of heavy traffic among modern courts. Mysteriously, the law of agency is largely neglected at most modern law schools. The remainder of the casebook covers general partnerships, corporations, and hybrid entities (i.e., limited liability companies, limited partnerships, limited liability partnerships, and other business associations).

The laws governing business associations come from courts, legislatures, regulatory agencies, and business practice. While some of the cases in the book are "classics," many are recent cases that apply the legal principles being studied to modern business structures or "hot" industries to engage the students and increase their business sophistication. Although this book is full of cases, it is supplemented by a book of statutes and regulations. In most cases, judges endeavor to interpret the statutes and regulations. This book, therefore, may not be used effectively without delving into the statutes.

D. Gordon Smith
Cynthia A. Williams

March 2004

Acknowledgments

We thank the folks at Aspen — most notably, Carol McGeehan for believing that two then-untenured professors who showed some promise in the field of corporate law could produce the "next generation" Business Organizations casebook and Barbara Roth for her constant encouragement and near limitless patience. Throughout the writing of this book, they have been unfailingly gracious and unerringly helpful. We especially appreciate their diligence in putting the book through multiple peer reviews prior to publication. Of course, we thank those reviewers — whoever you are! — for the constructive comments that have improved this work immensely.

Several of our colleague in the academy deserve special mention. Larry Hamermesh has shaped our selection and treatment of Delaware cases. If anyone knows more about Delaware corporate law than Larry, we have yet to meet that person. We are grateful for his patience with naive questions as well as his appreciation of nuance that makes corporate law (almost) sublime.

We thank Doug Moll for numerous conversations about minority oppression and other topics. We appreciate his deep concern for effective teaching and his willingness to help us think through difficult pedagogical questions.

We reserve special gratitude for John Ohnesorge, who was brave enough to use the book for his Business Organizations course while it was still in draft form. His detailed and insightful comments have improved every aspect of the book.

The book has also benefitted greatly from several years of students at Lewis & Clark Law School, the University of Wisconsin Law School, and the University of Illinois College of Law, who waded through not-always-coherent photocopied drafts. Professor Smith deeply appreciates the support of Jim Huffman, who as Dean of Lewis & Clark Law School encouraged the writing of this book in every way.

Of course, many research assistants also have made valuable contributions to this volume. We express particular thanks to Ken Piumarta, Cornelia Dormire, and Valerie Kirkendall of Lewis & Clark Law School; Sheetal Shah and John Laubmeier of the University of Wisconsin Law School; and Irene Hubicki of the University of Illinois College of Law.

Business Organizations

CHAPTER

1

The Law of Agency

Generally speaking, an agent is any person who is authorized to act on behalf of another (known as the principal). The law of agency governs the interactions among principals, agents, and the third parties with whom agents deal on behalf of principals. In the preface to one of the first treatises on the law of agency, William Paley wrote: "The law of Principal and Agent appears at first view to be founded upon principles so few and simple, and in general so easy of application, that a treatise upon such a subject may seem altogether superfluous." William Paley, *A treatise on the law of principal and agent* at iii. Paley found sufficient justification for his treatise, however, in the "vast extension of modern commerce, [and] the novelty and variety of the channels through which it is carried on."

Today agency issues are, if anything, more pervasive than in Paley's day, and they are certainly more complicated than Paley's skeptics would have been willing to concede. Personal injury law, commercial law, and employment law — not to mention partnership law and corporate law — all involve issues of agency law. The following materials do not attempt to cover the entire breadth of agency law, but instead strive to explore the fundamental principles relating to creation of an agency relationship and the potential liabilities flowing from that relationship. These principles are the most essential to the transaction of business generally and to the understanding of the law of business associations covered in subsequent chapters.

The law of agency developed as part of the common law. In 1812 Paley wrote that "the decisions upon this branch of the law which are to be met with in the older reports are neither numerous nor important." In the nineteenth century, however, the law of agency came into full flower. As business transactions became increasingly complicated, the law of agency became concomitantly necessary to bring order and equity. Justice Joseph Story published his magnificent *Commentaries on the Law of Agency* in 1839, and it quickly became the leading authority on agency law cited by American courts. Although the last edition of Story's treatise (the ninth, published in 1882, as revised by Charles P. Greenough) was cited well into the twentieth century, it was largely displaced by Floyd R. Mechem's *A Treatise on the Law of Agency* in 1888. The second edition of Mechem's treatise, which appeared in 1914, was widely cited by American courts, especially before the publication of the first edition of the Restatement of the Law of Agency by the American Law Institute in 1933, but Mechem is still cited by modern courts.

The 900-pound gorilla in this field, however, is the Restatement. Originally published in 1933, the Restatement was again published in 1958 in the Restatement (Second) of the Law of Agency, and the American Law Institute is currently producing a Restatement (Third) of the Law of Agency. Although it is not binding on courts, the Restatement is cited in many modern decisions invoking agency law. The Restatement has helped to unify the law of agency among different states. Despite the apparent certainty that the Restatement conveys, however, underlying the principles are many challenging legal issues with which business lawyers and courts often struggle.

A. CREATION OF THE AGENCY RELATIONSHIP

Paley's treatise on agency law devoted only a single sentence to the creation of the agency relationship: "The authority of an agent is created either by deed, by simple writing, by parol, or by mere employment, according to the capacity of the parties, or the nature of the act to be done." *Id.* at 2. Restatement (Second) offers a more detailed exploration, stating initially that an agency relationship is a consensual relationship between a principal and an agent. The relationship is created when (1) the principal consents to have the agent act on the principal's behalf and under the principal's control, and (2) the agent consents so to act. Restatement (Second) of Agency §§1, 15. Restatement (Third) retains essentially the same structure.

Although the parties must agree to enter into the type of relationship described, no contract is required to form an agency relationship. Restatement (Second) of Agency §16. Indeed, the parties need not have an intent to enter into something called an agency relationship. As stated in Comment b to Restatement (Second) of Agency §1, "if the agreement results in the factual relation between [the parties] to which are attached the legal consequences of agency, an agency exists although the parties did not call it agency and did not intend the legal consequences of agency."

The "legal consequences of agency" will be explored more fully in subsequent sections. For present purposes, suffice it say that the creation of an agency relationship has — in the words of Restatement (Third) — both "inward-looking" and "outward-looking" consequences. Inward-looking consequences relate to the relationship between the principal and the agent and are largely governed by the contracts between the parties and by the law of fiduciary duties. Outward-looking consequences relate to the relationship among the principal, the agent, and a third party and are governed by the various "principles of attribution" examined in Section C.

Outward-looking consequences tend to be the primary focus in cases where the central issue is agency formation. The opinion below (*Basile*) is an example of a case where agency formation is the central issue, although it is the inward-looking consequences that are implicated.

BASILE v. H & R BLOCK, INC.

761 A.2d 1115
Supreme Court of Pennsylvania
November 22, 2000

CASTILLE, Justice.

This Court granted allocatur to address questions concerning the scope and contours of agency relationships under Pennsylvania law. Specifically, we must determine whether appellees produced sufficient evidence of an agency relationship between appellants H & R Block, Inc., H & R Block Eastern Tax Services, Inc. (collectively "Block") and appellants' Rapid Refund customers so that appellees' class action complaint that Block breached a fiduciary duty to those customers may survive summary judgment.

H & R Block, Inc., provides tax preparation services nationwide through a network of retail offices operated through subsidiaries, one of which is H & R Block Eastern Tax Services. As part of its service, Block offers a program known as "Rapid Refund," which involves electronic filing of tax returns with the Internal Revenue Service (IRS), resulting in quicker refunds than a taxpayer filing a paper return would receive. Block also arranged for Mellon Bank (DE) National Association (Mellon Bank) to provide a refund anticipation loan (RAL) program to Block's qualified Rapid Refund customers. Under the RAL program, Mellon Bank advanced to the customer the amount of the customer's anticipated tax refund, less a financing charge, within days of Block's filing of the return. Appellee Sandra Basile applied for, and received, such a loan in 1993.

[After having several federal claims dismissed in federal district court, Basile] filed a class certification motion in common pleas court, and the parties filed cross motions for summary judgment on the breach of fiduciary duty claim. . . . The court granted certification on the breach of fiduciary duty claim. . . .

The parties then filed renewed cross motions for summary judgment on the fiduciary duty claim. The trial judge, the Honorable Stephen E. Levin, granted Block's motion for summary judgment finding that Block was not appellees' agent because appellees did not exercise substantial control over Block's preparation of the tax returns and, further, that no confidential relationship otherwise existed between the parties. Appellees appealed Judge Levin's order granting summary judgment on the breach of fiduciary duty claim. . . . The Superior Court reversed Judge Levin's grant of summary judgment, [finding] "as a matter of fact" that the pleadings established a principal-agent relationship between Block and appellees giving rise to a fiduciary duty as to all matters within the scope of the agency. Basile v. H & R Block, Inc., 729 A.2d 574, 582 (Pa. Super. 1999). The court remanded to the trial court for "disposition of questions of fact concerning the extent to which Block's failure to disclose the nature of the Rapid Refund program and its participation in the profits generated by the RALs constituted a violation of Block's duty as an agent." Having found that a fiduciary duty existed as a result of an agency relationship, the court did not reach appellees' alternate theory of liability—*i.e.*, that a fiduciary duty arose as a result of a confidential relationship between Block and appellees. Block sought allocatur only on the agency issue, and this Court granted allocatur to consider the propriety of the Superior Court's conclusion that an agency relationship existed between appellees and Block such that appellees may pursue a claim that Block breached its fiduciary duties to them. . . .

The parties do not dispute the facts material to the issue of whether an agency relationship existed. In 1990, Block began offering its Rapid Refund program whereby its taxpayer customers could receive speedier refunds using one of three services: (1) electronic filing of the tax return for a fee; (2) electronic filing for a fee with direct deposit of the taxpayer's refund by the IRS to the taxpayer's bank account; or (3) electronic filing for a fee with a RAL arranged by Block with a lender such as Mellon Bank. The third option involving the RALs is the service at issue.

Block offered its RAL program through Mellon Bank to Block's Pennsylvania customers. Between 1990 and 1993, more than 600,000 Pennsylvania residents participated in the RAL program. Specifically, Block customers who filed their returns electronically and met the lender's eligibility requirements were informed of the availability of loans in the amount of their anticipated refunds from Mellon Bank. If the customer was interested in the loan, Block would simultaneously transmit the taxpayer's income tax return information to the IRS and Mellon Bank. Within a few days of the transmittal, the taxpayer, if approved, would receive a check in the amount of the loan minus a bank transaction fee. The taxpayer could also elect to have Block's tax preparation and electronic filing fees withheld by the lender from the RAL check so that the taxpayer would not have to advance any money. When the taxpayer's actual tax refund was ready, usually within a matter of weeks, the IRS would deposit the refund check into an account with Mellon Bank to repay the loan. In exchange for the RAL, the taxpayer paid to Mellon Bank a flat rate finance charge of $29.00 or $35.00, which Block employees presented to the taxpayer as a flat dollar amount rather than as a percentage interest rate on the short term loan.[8] Since the RAL is secured by the tax refund, and the tax refund is paid directly into a proprietary account at Mellon Bank, the lender bank takes on few risks with the program. Block did not disclose to its RAL customers that it received a payment from Mellon Bank for each loan, shared in the profits of the RALs in other ways, or that the taxpayer's endorsement on the back of the loan proceeds check constituted a signature on a loan agreement printed on the reverse of the check.

The positions of the parties are easily stated. Appellees claim, and the Superior Court found, that they produced sufficient evidence to establish that an agency relationship existed between Block and the taxpayers who participated in the Rapid Refund program and secured RALs. They further claim that Block breached its fiduciary duty to those taxpayers by failing to disclose the true nature of the program as a loan program and to inform them that Block received a percentage of the finance charge paid to Mellon Bank and indirectly benefited from the loans in other ways. Appellees note that Block holds itself out to the public as "America's tax team" and encourages consumer trust by utilizing slogans such as "Do what millions of Americans do, trust H & R Block" and that Block's success in the field of tax return preparation is due to the image of trustworthiness Block has created. Appellees claim that Block exploited this relationship with their clients by steering them into loans with exorbitant rates

8. Due to the short-term nature of these loans (approximately two weeks), the finance charges translate to interest rates as high as 151 percent, depending on the amount of the loan. Appellee Basile's actual interest rate was 77.3 percent.

of interest carrying little practical value other than a quick refund for their clients, but which further profited Block financially.

Block denies that it had an agency relationship with its customers, arguing that appellees did not exercise the requisite substantial control over Block's preparation and electronic filing of the tax returns and that Block did not have the legal authority to bind appellees to the RAL agreements. Accordingly, Block argues that it owed no fiduciary duty to its clients with respect to the RALs. Instead, referring to then-Chief Judge Cardozo's well-known formulation maxim, Block avers that it was free to conduct itself with its clients according to the "morals of the marketplace." Meinhard v. Salmon, 249 N.Y. 458, 464, 164 N.E. 545, 547 (1938) (Cardozo, C.J.).

The law is clear in Pennsylvania that the three basic elements of agency are: "'the manifestation by the principal that the agent shall act for him, the agent's acceptance of the undertaking and the understanding of the parties that the principal is to be in control of the undertaking.'" Scott v. Purcell, 490 Pa. 109, 117, 415 A.2d 56, 60 (1980), quoting Restatement (Second) of Agency §1, Comment *b* (1958). "[A]gency results only if there is an agreement for the creation of a fiduciary relationship with control by the beneficiary." Smalich v. Westfall, 440 Pa. 409, 413, 269 A.2d 476, 480 (1971). The burden of establishing an agency relationship rests with the party asserting the relationship. Scott, 490 Pa. at 117 n.8, 415 A.2d at 61 n.8. "An agency relationship is a fiduciary one, and the agent is subject to a duty of loyalty to act only for the principal's benefit." Sutliff v. Sutliff, 515 Pa. 393, 404, 528 A.2d 1318, 1323 (1987), citing Restatement (Second) of Agency §387 (1958). Thus, in all matters affecting the subject of the agency, the agent must act with the utmost good faith in furthering and advancing the principal's interests, including a duty to disclose to the principal all relevant information.

Other jurisdictions have considered the precise issue before this Court — whether, under the law of those jurisdictions, an agency relationship existed between Block and taxpayers participating in Block's Rapid Refund program who secured RALs — with mixed results. A single court, the Maryland Court of Appeals, has held that Block acted as its customers' agent with respect to the RALs. *See* Green v. H & R Block, Inc., 355 Md. 488, 735 A.2d 1039 (1999). There, the court found that Block acted as the taxpayers agent in preparing their income tax returns, and that the agency relationship included the process of securing RALs, because the taxpayers retained ultimate control over Block's actions in preparing and filing the tax returns and applying for the RALs.[10] The court based its finding of an agency relationship as to the RALs on the fact that Block "played an integral part in the customer's receipt of the bank loan, which indisputedly has legal ramifications for the H & R Block customer and the bank." *Id.* at 1053. In addition, the court emphasized that Block intended to create a scenario in which taxpayers would trust it to prepare and file their returns and obtain the most rapid refund possible resulting in the taxpayers' reasonable belief that Block was acting as their agent. That scenario, the Maryland court felt, made it reasonable for Block's customers to believe that Block was acting as their agent.

---

10. Block conceded at oral argument in *Green* that it acted as the agent for the taxpayers in preparing and filing returns, but asserted that it acted as the lender's agent rather than the taxpayers' agent in securing the RALs. Block argued that the two transactions should be treated distinctly. No such concession has been made here.

The weight of authority, however, is to the contrary. In Carnegie v. H & R Block, Inc., 269 A.D.2d 145, 703 N.Y.S.2d 27 (2000), Beckett v. H & R Block, Inc., 306 Ill. App. 3d 381, 239 Ill. Dec. 736, 714 N.E.2d 1033 (1999), and Peterson v. H & R Block Tax Services, Inc., 971 F. Supp. 1204 (N.D. Ill. 1997), the courts found that no agency relationship existed in connection with the RALs. In *Carnegie*, the court upheld the dismissal of the plaintiff's cause of action for breach of fiduciary duty holding that "Block was not acting as plaintiff's agent in soliciting her to enter into the RAL transaction, which plaintiff did by her own acts as principal." *Carnegie*, 703 N.Y.S.2d at 29 (citing *Beckett*). The *Beckett* court similarly held that "whether to enter into the RAL agreement was a decision the customer made by signing the loan check. Block did not have the power to enter into this agreement on the customer's behalf. Thus, Block was not the client's agent." *Beckett*, 239 Ill. Dec. 736, 714 N.E.2d at 1041. The federal district court in *Peterson*, meanwhile, granted Block's motion to dismiss the plaintiff's claim that Block was the plaintiff's agent on different grounds, *i.e.*, finding that the plaintiff's complaint was "devoid of facts demonstrating that [the plaintiff] controlled the 'manner or method' in which Block performed its services." *Peterson*, 971 F. Supp. at 1213.

We agree with the prevailing view. The pleadings here do not establish an agency relationship. With specific respect to the RALs, there is no showing that appellees intended Block to act on their behalf in securing the RALs. To the contrary, Block offered appellees the opportunity to file their tax returns electronically with the *three* options set forth above, only one of which involved RALs. Appellees were not required to apply for an RAL in order to have their returns prepared by Block or filed electronically through Block. It was appellees alone who decided to take advantage of that particular option. Block was neither authorized to, nor did it in fact, act on its customers' behalf in this regard. If a customer elected to apply for an RAL, Block simply facilitated the loan process by presenting appellees to Mellon Bank as viable loan candidates. Block neither applied for the loan on behalf of appellees nor determined that appellees should apply; appellees undertook that procedure themselves. The RAL program was merely another distinct and separate service offered by Block to its customers. Furthermore, it was a distinct service that Block's customers were fully aware came at a higher price, just as one would expect for an advance of money. Simply introducing appellees to a lender willing to provide a loan is not sufficient to create an agency relationship. Therefore, we hold that, as a matter of law, Block was not acting as appellees' agent in the RAL transactions, such that they were subject to a heightened, fiduciary duty.

We are aware that here, as in *Green*, Block could be said to have played an "integral part" in arranging the RALs. In our view, however, "integral" or not, Block's mere facilitation of . . . its customers' desire to pursue the loans, as one of the multiple services offered by Block, is not sufficient to establish an agency relationship under Pennsylvania law. The special relationship arising from an agency agreement, with its concomitant heightened duty, cannot arise from any and all actions, no matter how trivial, arguably undertaken on another's behalf. Rather, the action must be a matter of consequence or trust, such as the ability to actually bind the principal or alter the principal's legal relations. Indeed, implicit in the long-standing Pennsylvania requirement that the principal manifest an intention that the agent act on the principal's behalf is the notion that the agent has authority to alter the principal's relationships with third parties, such as binding the principal to a contract. Notably, the Restatement, which we have cited with approval in this area in the past, specifically recognizes as much. *See* Restatement (Second) of Agency §12 ("An agent or apparent agent holds a power to alter the legal relations between the principal and third persons and between the principal and himself.") . . .

Such power decidedly did not exist here with regard to facilitating the RALs, nor even to preparing and filing the tax returns. Block had no more authority to alter the legal relationship between its customers and the IRS than it had to bind those customers to a loan agreement with Mellon Bank. Block could not file a tax return without the customer's authorization and signature, nor could Block obligate the customer to pay any amount of income tax to the IRS without authorization and consent in the form of the customer's signature on the return. Therefore, no agency relationship existed between Block and its customers.

Our conclusion that there is no agency relationship here carries no judgment regarding Block's business practices. If Block's method of doing business is worthy of the condemnation that appellees suggest, presumably the marketplace will react to correct it. It is not our place to imbue the relationship between Block and appellees with heightened legal qualities that the parties did not agree upon.

> Before courts can infer and superimpose a duty of the finest loyalty, the contract and the relationship of the parties must be plumbed. We recognize that "[m]any forms of conduct permissible in a workaday world for those acting at arm's length, are forbidden to those bound by fiduciary ties." (Meinhard v. Salmon, 249 N.Y. 458, 464, 164 N.E. 545). . . . If the parties find themselves or place themselves in the milieu of the "workaday" mundane marketplace, and if they do not create their own relationship of higher trust, courts should not ordinarily transport them to a higher realm of relationship and fashion the stricter duty for them.

Northeast General Corp. v. Wellington Advertising, Inc., 82 N.Y.2d 158, 604 N.Y.S.2d 1, 624 N.E.2d 129, 131 (1993).

Here, the parties created no higher realm of relationship. Nor is the transaction at issue here even unusual in the workaday marketplace. Many providers of goods and services also make referrals to banks or agencies that will finance the purchase at issue. In all of these transactions, the purchaser is generally well aware that there are costs attendant to the financing. Nothing prevented appellees from questioning Block employees regarding the basis for the costs of the RALs and whether Block benefited from the financing service. If Block's response did not satisfy appellees, they were free to take their business elsewhere. That is the essence of our market economy. . . .

Accordingly, the order of the Superior Court is vacated, and the matter is remanded to that court for proceedings not inconsistent with this opinion.

NIGRO, Justice, dissenting.

I respectfully dissent, as I believe that an agency relationship existed between H & R Block and Appellees. . . . [D]irect evidence of specific authority is unnecessary. Rather, the relationship can be inferred from the circumstances of the case by looking at factors such as the relation of the parties and their conduct.

I believe that Appellees met their burden of establishing that an agency relationship existed. Here, the Superior Court found that Appellees "established that they visited the [H & R] Block offices in response to media promotions

of the Rapid Refund Program to engage [H & R] Block to achieve two results:
1) to complete and file their tax returns, and 2) to obtain a refund of any
overpayment of taxes they had made to the Internal Revenue Service [IRS]."
Basile v. H & R Block, Inc., 729 A.2d 574, 581 (Pa. Super. 1999). Appellees
remained at the office while H & R Block employees completed the tax forms.
After completion, the H & R Block employees requested that Appellees sign
the tax returns before H & R Block sent the returns to the IRS and the state
Department of Revenue. These facts indicate that: (1) Appellees manifested
that H & R Block, through its employees, compute their taxes and complete
and send their tax forms, thereby "rendering service but retaining control of
the manner of doing it;" (2) H & R Block, through its employees, accepted the
undertaking of completing and sending Appellees' tax forms; and (3) Appellees
remained in control, that is, they had to sign their own forms and the H & R
Block employees completed the forms pursuant to information given to them
by Appellees. For these reasons, I believe that an agency relationship existed
between Appellees and H & R Block with respect to the computation of their
taxes and the completion and submission of their tax returns to the taxing
authority. What remains is to determine whether agency extended to the Rapid
Refund portion of the transaction. I believe it does.

Evidence in this case establishes that when the H & R Block tax preparer
determined that a particular taxpayer was eligible for a refund, the preparer
offered the taxpayer one of three options. The taxpayer could choose between
(1) an electronic filing of the tax return for a fee; (2) an electronic filing of
the tax return for a fee with an electronic direct deposit by the IRS of the tax
return to the taxpayer's bank account; or 3) an electronic tax return filing for
a fee with a refund anticipation loan arranged by H & R Block with a lending
institution such as Mellon Bank, called a "Rapid Refund." The Rapid Refund
enabled the taxpayer to receive her "refund" within a few days, instead of the
typical four to six weeks it would take for the taxing authority's refund check to
arrive. Customers who chose the H & R Block Rapid Refund option were given
an application which they completed and submitted to Mellon Bank. Once the
bank approved the application, it issued a check to the taxpayer in an amount
equal to the taxpayer's anticipated refund less transaction fees. The taxpayer
would then sign over the entire amount of the check from the taxing authority
which would arrive a few weeks later.

H & R Block essentially contends that its relationship with the taxpayer is
concluded once the tax return is filed, and that once the tax preparer offers
her the application for the Rapid Refund, the taxpayer's relationship is a credi-
tor/debtor one with Mellon Bank. I disagree as I believe that H & R Block's role
in facilitating the Rapid Refund for the taxpayer is as the taxpayer's agent as all
three elements of agency exist. Here, (1) the taxpayer manifested her consent
to the tax preparer that she wished to participate or take advantage of H & R
Block's Rapid Refund program when it was offered; (2) the preparer facilitated
the process of obtaining a Rapid Refund by offering an application; and (3) the
preparer consented to act on the taxpayer's need by matching the taxpayer to
a source for the early refund, here, Mellon Bank. Accordingly, I also believe an
agency relationship existed between Appellees and H & R Block for purposes
of the Rapid Refund Program. . . .

As H & R Block was the agent through which the Rapid Refund was facilitated,
it had a duty to disclose the nature of its relationship with Mellon Bank in respect

to the Rapid Refund Program. As the majority noted, "Block did not disclose to its [refund application loan] customers that it received a payment from Mellon Bank for each loan, shared in the profits of the [refund application loans] in other ways, or that the taxpayer's endorsement on the back of the loan proceeds check constituted a signature on a loan agreement printed on the reverse of the check." I believe that this is a gross violation of H & R Block's fiduciary duty to Appellees. Since I believe that the evidence creates the inference that an agency relationship existed between H & R Block and Appellees for the entire tax return "package" offered and further, that H & R Block violated the fiduciary duty it owed to Appellees, I respectfully dissent.

SAYLOR, Justice, dissenting.

I agree with the majority that, to the extent that refund anticipated loans ("RALs") are viewed as discrete transactions, no agency relationship between Block and its customers would be discernible. Like the majority, I would not be inclined to conclude, extrinsic of an existing, underlying agency relationship, that a separate agency role is necessarily undertaken by one who merely facilitates a lending transaction. Nevertheless, I join that portion of Mr. Justice Nigro's analysis which concludes, as did the Superior Court, that an agency relationship existed between Block and Appellees for the purposes of preparing Appellees' tax returns, filing them with the IRS, and obtaining refunds. Indeed, I note that H & R Block conceded as much, at least for purposes of Maryland law, in Green v. H & R Block, Inc., 355 Md. 488, 735 A.2d 1039, 1049 (1999). I also believe that the fiduciary duties associated with such relationship may be viewed as sufficiently broad to compel disclosure of aspects of self-interest in a related loan transaction. Thus, I would affirm the order of the Superior Court remanding "for disposition of questions of fact concerning the extent to which Block's failure to disclose the nature of the Rapid Refund program and its participation in the profits generated by the RALs constituted a violation of Block's duty as an agent." Basile v. H & R Block, Inc., 729 A.2d 574, 582 (Pa. Super. 1999).

B. AGENT'S FIDUCIARY DUTIES TO PRINCIPAL

Principals and agents owe duties to each other within an agency relationship. *See* Restatement (Second) of Agency, ch. 13. The principal's primary duties are performance of contract obligations, good conduct, noninterference, cooperation, and indemnification under certain circumstances. The agent's duties include the duty of care, the duty of disclosure, the duty to obey, and the duty to act within the scope of authority. But the most important duty in the law of agency — and the focus of attention here — is the agent's duty of loyalty to the principal. The essence of this duty is that the agent must act "solely for the benefit of the principal in all matters connected with [the] agency." Restatement (Second) of Agency §387. The agent's duty of loyalty is multifaceted and includes a duty to keep information belonging to the principal confidential, a duty not to compete with the principal in any matter within the scope of the agency relationship, and a duty not to act as an agent for another with interests that conflict with the principal's interests. If the agent breaches the duty of loyalty, the principal's primary remedies are damages and disgorgement of profits, if any.

The following case introduces the duty of loyalty, which is a fundamental element of entity law, and as such will reappear in numerous permutations throughout this book.

FOOD LION, INC. v. CAPITAL CITIES/ABC, INC.
194 F.3d 505
United States Court of Appeals, Fourth Circuit
October 20, 1999

MICHAEL, Circuit Judge.

Two ABC television reporters, after using false resumes to get jobs at Food Lion, Inc. supermarkets, secretly videotaped what appeared to be unwholesome food handling practices. Some of the video footage was used by ABC in a PrimeTime Live broadcast that was sharply critical of Food Lion. The grocery chain sued Capital Cities/ABC, Inc., American Broadcasting Companies, Inc., Richard Kaplan and Ira Rosen, producers of PrimeTime Live, and Lynne Dale and Susan Barnett, two reporters for the program (collectively, "ABC" or the "ABC defendants"). Food Lion did not sue for defamation, but focused on how ABC gathered its information through claims for fraud, breach of duty of loyalty, trespass, and unfair trade practices. Food Lion won at trial, and judgment for compensatory damages of $1,402 was entered on the various claims. Following a substantial (over $5 million) remittitur, the judgment provided for $315,000 in punitive damages. The ABC defendants appeal the district court's denial of their motion for judgment as a matter of law, and Food Lion appeals the court's ruling that prevented it from proving publication damages. Having considered the case, we (1) reverse the judgment that the ABC defendants committed fraud and unfair trade practices, (2) affirm the judgment that Dale and Barnett breached their duty of loyalty and committed a trespass, and (3) affirm, on First Amendment grounds, the district court's refusal to allow Food Lion to prove publication damages.

I.

In early 1992 producers of ABC's PrimeTime Live program received a report alleging that Food Lion stores were engaging in unsanitary meat-handling practices. The allegations were that Food Lion employees ground out-of-date beef together with new beef, bleached rank meat to remove its odor, and re-dated (and offered for sale) products not sold before their printed expiration date. The producers recognized that these allegations presented the potential for a powerful news story, and they decided to conduct an undercover investigation of Food Lion. ABC reporters Lynne Dale (Lynne Litt at the time) and Susan Barnett concluded that they would have a better chance of investigating the allegations if they could become Food Lion employees. With the approval of their superiors, they proceeded to apply for jobs with the grocery chain, submitting applications with false identities and references and fictitious local addresses. Notably, the applications failed to mention the reporters' concurrent employment with ABC and otherwise misrepresented their educational and employment experiences. Based on these applications, a South Carolina Food Lion store hired Barnett as a deli clerk in April 1992, and a North Carolina Food Lion store hired Dale as a meat wrapper trainee in May 1992.

Barnett worked for Food Lion for two weeks, and Dale for only one week. As they went about their assigned tasks for Food Lion, Dale and Barnett used tiny cameras ("lipstick" cameras, for example) and microphones concealed on their bodies to secretly record Food Lion employees treating, wrapping and labeling meat, cleaning machinery, and discussing the practices of the meat department. They gathered footage from the meat cutting room, the deli counter, the employee break room, and a manager's office. All told, in their three collective weeks as Food Lion employees, Dale and Barnett recorded approximately 45 hours of concealed camera footage.

Some of the videotape was eventually used in a November 5, 1992, broadcast of PrimeTime Live. ABC contends the footage confirmed many of the allegations initially leveled against Food Lion. The broadcast included, for example, videotape that appeared to show Food Lion employees repackaging and redating fish that had passed the expiration date, grinding expired beef with fresh beef, and applying barbeque sauce to chicken past its expiration date in order to mask the smell and sell it as fresh in the gourmet food section. The program included statements by former Food Lion employees alleging even more serious mishandling of meat at Food Lion stores across several states. The truth of the PrimeTime Live broadcast was not an issue in the litigation we now describe.

Food Lion sued ABC and the PrimeTime Live producers and reporters. Food Lion's suit focused not on the broadcast, as a defamation suit would, but on the methods ABC used to obtain the video footage. The grocery chain asserted claims of fraud, breach of the duty of loyalty, trespass, and unfair trade practices, seeking millions in compensatory damages. Specifically, Food Lion sought to recover (1) administrative costs and wages paid in connection with the employment of Dale and Barnett and (2) broadcast (publication) damages for matters such as loss of good will, lost sales and profits, and diminished stock value. Punitive damages were also requested by Food Lion.

The district court, in a remarkably efficient effort, tried the case with a jury in three phases. At the liability phase, the jury found all of the ABC defendants liable to Food Lion for fraud and two of them, Dale and Barnett, additionally liable for breach of the duty of loyalty and trespass. Based on the jury's fraud verdict and its special interrogatory findings that the ABC defendants had engaged in deceptive acts, the district court determined that the ABC defendants had violated the North Carolina Unfair and Deceptive Trade Practices Act (UTPA). Prior to the compensatory damages phase, the district court ruled that damages allegedly incurred by Food Lion as a result of ABC's broadcast of PrimeTime Live — "lost profits, lost sales, diminished stock value or anything of that nature" — could not be recovered because these damages were not proximately caused by the acts (fraud, trespass, etc.) attributed to the ABC defendants in this case. Operating within this constraint, the jury in the second phase awarded Food Lion $1,400 in compensatory damages on its fraud claim, $1.00 each on its duty of loyalty and trespass claims, and $1,500 on its UTPA claim. (The court required Food Lion to make an election between the fraud and UTPA damages, and the grocery chain elected to take the $1,400 in fraud damages.) At the final stage the jury lowered the boom and awarded $5,545,750 in punitive damages on the fraud claim against ABC and its two producers, Kaplan and Rosen. The jury refused to award punitive damages against the reporters, Dale and Barnett. In post-trial proceedings the district court ruled that the punitive damages award was excessive, and Food Lion accepted a remittitur to a total of $315,000.

After trial the ABC defendants moved for judgment as a matter of law on all claims, the motion was denied, and the defendants now appeal. Food Lion cross-appeals, contesting the district court's ruling that the damages the grocery chain sought as a result of the PrimeTime Live broadcast were not recoverable in this action. We now turn to the legal issues.

II.

A. . . .

ABC argues that Dale and Barnett cannot be held liable for a breach of duty of loyalty to Food Lion under existing tort law in North and South Carolina. It is undisputed that both reporters, on behalf of ABC, wore hidden cameras to make a video and audio record of what they saw and heard while they were employed by Food Lion. Specifically, they sought to document, for ABC's PrimeTime Live program, Food Lion employees engaging in unsanitary practices, treating products to hide spoilage, and repackaging and redating out-of-date products. The jury found that Dale and Barnett breached their duty of loyalty to Food Lion, and nominal damages of $1.00 were awarded.

As a matter of agency law, an employee owes a duty of loyalty to her employer. . . . The courts of North and South Carolina have not set out a specific test for determining when the duty of loyalty is breached. Disloyalty has been described in fairly broad terms, however. Employees are disloyal when their acts are "inconsistent with promoting the best interest of their employer at a time when they were on its payroll," Lowndes Prods., Inc. v. Brower, 259 S.C. 322, 191 S.E.2d 761, 767 (S.C. 1972), and an employee who "deliberately acquires an interest adverse to his employer . . . is disloyal," Long v. Vertical Techs., Inc., 113 N.C. App. 598, 439 S.E.2d 797, 802 (N.C. Ct. App. 1994).

ABC is correct to remind us that employee disloyalty issues are usually dealt with in the context of the employment contract: unfaithful employees are simply discharged, disciplined, or reprimanded. Up to now, disloyal conduct by an employee has been considered tortious in North and South Carolina in three circumstances. First, the tort of breach of duty of loyalty applies when an employee competes directly with her employer, either on her own or as an agent of a rival company. Second, the tort applies when the employee misappropriates her employer's profits, property, or business opportunities. Third, the tort applies when the employee breaches her employer's confidences.

Because Dale and Barnett did not compete with Food Lion, misappropriate any of its profits or opportunities, or breach its confidences, ABC argues that the reporters did not engage in any disloyal conduct that is tortious under existing law. Indeed, the district court acknowledged that it was the first court to hold that the conduct in question "would be recognized by the Supreme Courts of North Carolina and South Carolina" as tortiously violating the duty of loyalty. Food Lion, Inc. v. Capital Cities/ABC, Inc., 964 F. Supp. 956, 959 n.2 (M.D.N.C. 1997). We believe the district court was correct to conclude that those courts would decide today that the reporters' conduct was sufficient to breach the duty of loyalty and trigger tort liability.

What Dale and Barnett did verges on the kind of employee activity that has already been determined to be tortious. The interests of the employer (ABC) to whom Dale and Barnett gave complete loyalty were adverse to the interests of Food Lion, the employer to whom they were unfaithful. ABC and Food Lion were not business competitors but they were adverse in a fundamental way. ABC's interest was to expose Food Lion to the public as a food chain that engaged in unsanitary and deceptive practices. Dale and Barnett served ABC's interest, at the expense of Food Lion, by engaging in the taping for ABC while they were on Food Lion's payroll. In doing this, Dale and Barnett did not serve Food Lion faithfully, and their interest (which was the same as ABC's) was diametrically opposed to Food Lion's. In these circumstances, we believe that the highest courts of North and South Carolina would hold that the reporters — in promoting the interests of one master, ABC, to the detriment of a second, Food Lion — committed the tort of disloyalty against Food Lion. *[HOLDING: *]*

Our holding on this point is not a sweeping one. An employee does not commit a tort simply by holding two jobs or by performing a second job inadequately. For example, a second employer has no tort action for breach of the duty of loyalty when its employee fails to devote adequate attention or effort to her second (night shift) job because she is tired. That is because the inadequate performance is simply an incident of trying to work two jobs. There is no intent to act adversely to the second employer for the benefit of the first. Because Dale and Barnett had the requisite intent to act against the interests of their second employer, Food Lion, for the benefit of their main employer, ABC, they were liable in tort for their disloyalty. *[ADD TO HOLDING.]*

We hold that, insofar as North and South Carolina law is concerned, the district court did not err in refusing to set aside the jury's verdict that Dale and Barnett breached their duty of loyalty to Food Lion.

An agent's fiduciary duty of loyalty to her principal ends the day the agency relationship ends, and thus the former agent may begin to compete with the former principal. Employers will often protect themselves from competition with their former employees by requiring their employees to sign agreements not to compete with the company after the employment relationship ends. Such agreements will be enforced in most states so long as they are "reasonable," which means so long as they are limited in time (three years or less, typically), and so long as there are sensible geographic boundaries to the noncompete agreement. The following problem, though, shows the difficulties a very highly placed agent had in negotiating a noncompete agreement that still permitted him to exploit the industry-specific knowledge he had gained from his employment. *[To protect afterwards employers will require the signing of noncompete agreements.]*

PROBLEM 1-1

Paul Stoneham worked in marketing for Proctor & Gamble (P&G) for 13 years and ultimately became responsible for international marketing of P&G's hair conditioning products. As part of international marketing, P&G obtained raw market research data and used it to develop models of consumers' preferences to determine the product areas that were most successful in different countries. Stoneham's particular expertise was international marketing — that is, determining which products to sell in which foreign countries, based upon marketing strategies and advertising claims. As a member of worldwide, multifunctional teams at P&G, just prior to leaving the company Stoneham developed a confidential ten-year global marketing plan for P&G's best-selling hair conditioning product, Pantene.

When Stoneham reached a certain level within the company he was offered stock options, as were approximately 10 percent of the company's top management employees. As a condition for getting the options, Stoneham was required to sign an agreement not to compete with P&G for three years after leaving the company. While the court hearing P&G's case against Stoneham found that agreeing to the covenant not to compete was "entirely voluntary," failing to agree would have required Stoneham to give up the stock options. Stoneham was also required to sign a confidentiality agreement when he was hired, as were all other P&G employees, in which he agreed not to disclose any of P&G's confidential information or trade secrets.

In 1998, Stoneham was offered the job of president of Alberto-Culver International, a company whose hair care products directly competed with P&G's. Soon after joining Alberto-Culver, P&G brought an injunctive action against Stoneham to enforce the covenant not to compete, claiming that Stoneham's knowledge of how P&G cross-indexed its market research (in order to be able to determine which products were most successful among which consumers in which countries) and how P&G organized its cross-functional product teams was confidential information and constituted a trade secret. Moreover, P&G claimed that Stoneham's position developing marketing strategies for Alberto-Culver's hair care products put him in direct competition with the P&G products for which he had recently developed marketing strategies. The trial court ruled in Stoneham's favor, finding this was not confidential information and refusing to enforce the covenant not to compete.

How should the court of appeals rule on P&G's appeal? How would you advise someone like Stoneham (in advance), who is being asked to sign a broad confidentiality agreement and covenant not to compete?

C. PRINCIPLES OF ATTRIBUTION

As stated above, the existence of an agency relationship has both inward-looking consequences, through the imposition of fiduciary duties, and outward-looking consequences. The outward-looking consequences come about because principals can be held liable for the tortious actions of their agents, and can be required to fulfill contracts into which their agents have entered. In this section, we will explore the factors used by courts to justify holding principals responsible for the consequences of their agents' actions.

The official comment to Restatement (Third) §1.01 states:

> The chief justifications for the principal's accountability for the agent's acts are the principal's ability to select and control the agent and to terminate the agency relationship, together with the fact that the agent has agreed expressly or implicitly to act on the principal's behalf.

Reduced to its simplest terms, this passage invokes the concepts of *control*, *benefit*, and *consent*, all of which are commonly found in the cases. The primary rationale for imposing liability based on the existence of control is neatly summarized by the ancient maxim, *"Qui facit per alium facit per se"* ("he who acts through another acts himself"). The rationale for imposing liability based on the existence of benefits to the principal is simply that those who gain from the actions of another should sometimes be held to answer for costs inflicted by those actions. In addition to control and benefit, courts also seem to rely at times on the notion of *consent* to justify liability. As noted above, consent is central to the determination of when an agency relationship exists, and thus when it is fair to impose liability on the principal for actions of the agent.

As you work through the materials in this section, consider what level of control is necessary to prompt a finding of liability, and think about why control, standing alone, is (usually) insufficient for such a finding. Similarly, the existence of benefits to the principal does not necessarily lead to liability for the agent's actions. It is useful, therefore, to identify the circumstances in which benefit seems to play an important role in a court's decision, and to try to determine whether benefit, standing alone, may be sufficient to justify the imposition of liability. In thinking about each of these issues, it is also useful to separate the rationales for imposing liability in the tort context from the rationales for holding principals responsible for fulfilling contracts into which their agents have entered.

The following sections examine several bases for holding one person or entity — the principal — responsible for the actions of another person — the agent. The doctrines of authority, both actual authority and apparent authority, are distinctive to agency law. In addition to these doctrines of attribution based on principles of authority, principals may incur liability for the actions of their agents based on the general doctrine of vicarious liability — *respondeat superior* — which is also briefly introduced below.

1.   Actual Authority

Actual authority is created by a manifestation from the principal to the agent that the principal consents to the agent taking actions on the principal's behalf. Restatement (Third) of Agency §3.01. Thus, in evaluating the actual authority of an agent, one would evaluate the communications from the principal to the agent. Actual authority may exist even though there is no written contract between a principal and an agent, although certain kinds of authority (such as the authority to sell real estate for another) must be in writing based on individual state law requirements.

An agent's actual authority typically includes both express and implied aspects. The "express actual authority" of an agent to act on a principal's behalf may be conveyed orally or in writing; the "implied actual authority" is the power to do those things necessary to fulfill the agency. Thus, the express actual authority to "run my used car business" would imply actual authority to buy used cars, presumably on credit; advertise the cars; hire additional employees as necessary; and enter binding contracts with customers. When potential liability arises from the actions of an agent, principals may seek to narrowly construe their agent's actual authority, both express and implied, as in the following case.

CASTILLO v. CASE FARMS OF OHIO, INC.

United States District Court, W.D. Texas
96 F. Supp. 2d 578
December 1, 1999

JUSTICE, Senior District Judge.

Th[is] civil action was filed on December 19, 1997, by a group of migrant farm workers, claiming violations of the Migrant and Seasonal Agricultural Worker Protection Act ("AWPA"), the Fair Labor Standards Act ("FLSA"), and various state laws. The primary defendant is Case Farms of Ohio, a chicken processing plant located in Winesburg, Ohio.

A bench trial in this civil action commenced on March 29, 1999, and was completed on April 1, 1999. In accordance with Federal Rule of Civil Procedure 52(a), the following memorandum opinion constitutes the court's findings of fact and conclusions of law in this civil action. . . .

INTRODUCTION

I. BACKGROUND

Defendant Case Farms of Ohio, Inc. ("Case Farms"), is a chicken processing plant in Winesburg, Ohio. At this facility, approximately 400,000 live chickens per week, year-round, are live-hung, slaughtered, eviscerated, cleaned, cut and deboned, and ultimately packaged for market. Case Farms employees perform a range of jobs, which include eviscerating, deboning, receiving, grading, wrapping, weighing, and washing chickens.

In consideration of its historically high turnover rate, Case Farms actively recruited workers for its processing plant during 1996 and 1997. Andy Cilona, primarily responsible for recruiting workers for Case Farms, served as Case Farms' Human Resources Director from his date of hire until February 1996, and as Case Farms' Director of Corporate Development, from February 1996 until mid-1997. During one of his recruiting trips in Florida, Cilona initiated contact with a labor agency for temporary employees, America's Tempcorps ("ATC"). In conformity with an unwritten agreement with Case Farms, ATC worked in Texas, recruiting and hiring a number of people to work at Case

Farms' chicken processing plant in Ohio. During this recruitment process, ATC gave some of its recruits the telephone number of Alvaro Hernandez, a Case Farms employee, and instructed them to call Hernandez upon their arrival in Ohio. ATC also usually gave its recruits a free bus ticket or other free transportation to Ohio, as well as $20.00 each in traveling expenses. Case Farms ceased doing business with ATC in February 1996. . . .

[The] plaintiffs generally claim that they were recruited in Texas to work at Case Farms' Winesburg facility, and that, upon arriving at Case Farms, they discovered that the actual terms and conditions of their employment, transportation, and housing in Ohio did not coincide with the promises made to them in Texas. At the trial of this case, plaintiffs testified to the inadequate housing conditions and transportation provisions they encountered upon arrival in Ohio.

Thus, the bases for this civil action are the defendants' alleged misrepresentations and mistreatment of the plaintiffs in the recruitment process in Texas, and, as well, the working and living conditions afforded them in Ohio. Plaintiffs contend that defendants violated a number of the statutory rights of employees created by the Migrant and Seasonal Agricultural Worker Protection Act ("AWPA"), 29 U.S.C. §1801 et seq., and the Fair Labor Standards Act ("FLSA"), 29 U.S.C. §216(b). Plaintiffs further allege that defendants were guilty of breach of contract, fraud, and negligent misrepresentation with regard to the bases of plaintiffs' claims.

Defendant Case Farms responded to these allegations with primarily legal defenses. Generally speaking, rather than refute the veracity of most of the plaintiffs' factual claims, Case Farms' primary defense at trial was that it cannot be held legally responsible for the plaintiffs' alleged mistreatment. . . .

PART I
AN OVERVIEW OF THE LAW

The Migrant and Seasonal Agricultural Worker Protection Act ("AWPA") is a broad-ranging network of migrant and seasonal worker protections that requires, in part, written and forthright disclosures, in the workers' language, of working conditions at the time of recruitment. It prohibits false and misleading representations concerning employment policies and practices, housing conditions, and transportation arrangements for workers. It also regulates housing and transportation standards for covered workers. . . .

The bulk of the plaintiffs' claims arise out of the AWPA's statutory protections. The specific statutory provisions of the AWPA that are at issue in this civil action are as follows:

(1) utilization of an unregistered farm labor contractor,
(2) failure to provide written disclosures,
(3) the use of false and misleading information,
(4) violations of the terms of the working agreement,
(5) failure to ensure that the housing met applicable health and safety codes,
(6) failure to secure certification that the housing met the applicable health and safety codes,
(7) failure to post or to provide a statement of the terms and conditions of housing,

(8)   failure to properly insure and inspect transportation vehicles,
(9)   failure to ensure that each plaintiff received a proper pay statement, and
(10) "wages owed when due" violations.

In the event of violation of these provisions, the AWPA provides for statutory or actual damages, or equitable relief, at the discretion of the court.

Plaintiffs also allege violations of the minimum wage, and overtime wage, provisions of the Fair Labor Standards Act. The FLSA establishes a minimum wage, maximum working hours, record keeping and reporting requirements, and child labor prohibitions, as well as a system of civil and criminal penalties for its violation.

The remainder of the plaintiffs' claims, for breach of contract, fraud, and negligent misrepresentation, are based on state law.

PART II

GENERAL APPLICABLE LIABILITY PRINCIPLES

The distressing and deplorable conditions allegedly encountered and endured by [the] plaintiffs upon arriving in Ohio stand largely unrefuted. Often with little more than the $20.00 they were given for food during the three day bus ride from the Rio Grande Valley, the majority of the plaintiffs left behind their homes and families in Texas for the promise of suitable work in Ohio. Once there, many of the plaintiffs found themselves sleeping on floors in bare houses or apartments, often with a dozen or more other workers. One young woman described the frightening experience of sleeping in a unfurnished, one-bathroom house with approximately seventeen other people, mostly men. From the stand, she expressed her gratitude to several other male recruits, whom she had met just days before living with them in Ohio, for their willingness to allow her to sleep between them and the wall for protection. Another plaintiff testified that he and his sister were forced to sleep outside their apartment on concrete steps to escape the stench of the raw sewage that was seeping into their apartment. Other plaintiffs described their unremitting encounters with cockroaches and rats. With harrowing detail, plaintiffs related the discomfort and dangerousness of traveling to work in an overcrowded van that not only had only boards laid on cement blocks in lieu of seats, but which also was filled with exhaust fumes. For the most part, these disturbing and unsettling accounts were uncontested by Case Farms.

There can be no doubt that such living and transportation conditions were appalling, and would be, in many contexts, illegal. The plaintiffs' express challenge in this civil action, however, was to establish Case Farms' liability for such conditions. That is, before considering each of the many statutory violations alleged by the plaintiffs, an important threshold issue must be resolved. Does the law allow the plaintiffs to recover for their maltreatment from Case Farms? Can the plaintiffs, recruited and purportedly "employed" by ATC, recover from Case Farms? . . .

B. An Agricultural Employer's Liability Under Common Law Agency Principles

The fact that Congress has created a statutory framework of protections for migrant workers in no way exempts agricultural employers, recruiters, and overseers from common law agency principles. Rather, the protections afforded by the AWPA are designed to supplement traditional common law principles. Thus, one theory under which the plaintiffs could prove that Case Farms itself committed the alleged violations would be to demonstrate that the ATC defendants' misdeeds were committed by ATC within the scope of its role as an agent of Case Farms.

ATC's Agency

Plaintiffs' supplementary theory of Case Farms liability is, therefore, based on traditional, pre-AWPA common law tenets of agency. Plaintiffs argue that an agency relationship existed between ATC and Case Farms, and that the scope of that relationship included both the express authority to recruit and hire people to work at Case Farms' plant, and the implied authority to do all things proper, usual, and necessary to exercise that authority. Case Farms responds that to the extent any agency relationship existed between ATC and Case Farms, the scope of that agency was limited solely to informing recruits about the availability of work in Ohio at Case Farms' processing plant.

The fundamental precepts of the law of agency are well settled. At common law, a principal may be held liable for the acts of its purported agent based on an actual agency relationship created by the principal's express or implied delegation of authority to the agent. Both forms of agency are at issue here. Express actual authority exists "where the principal has made it clear to the agent that he [or she] wants the act under scrutiny to be done." Pasant v. Jackson Nat'l Life Ins. Co., 52 F.3d 94, 97 (5th Cir. 1995). Further, giving an agent express authority to undertake a certain act also includes the implied authority to do all things proper, usual, and necessary to exercise that express authority.

Applying these principles, the plaintiffs assert that the scope of the agency relationship between Case Farms and ATC expressly authorized ATC to recruit and hire people to work at Case Farms' Ohio plant. Such a contention is certainly well-supported by the evidence. Former Case Farms' Director of Corporate Development, Andy Cilona, among others, testified that "the arrangement with ATC was for it to hire workers for Case Farms' production." Based on Case Farms' explicit agreement with ATC, it is found, by a preponderance of the evidence, that such an express agency relationship, the scope of which included recruiting and hiring migrant workers to perform jobs at Case Farms' plant, did exist between Case Farms and ATC.

A principal is liable for the actions of an agent only if those actions are taken in the scope of the agent's employment. While Case Farms acknowledges that ATC was expressly authorized to recruit and hire workers for its plant, the chicken processing company maintains that the scope of that relationship was extremely narrow, and that the vagueness of the plaintiffs' claim that ATC was Case Farms' agent glosses over the exact nature of the relationship between ATC and Case Farms.[16] The plaintiffs, on the other hand, argue that the scope of ATC's express authority to recruit and hire people to work at Case Farms' plant

16. This court again notes with some astonishment that the entire relationship between Case Farms and ATC was oral. No written contract or record of this agreement exists. Such an agreement, of course, would have been invaluable in the resolution of these issues.

included the implied authority to do all things proper, usual, and necessary to exercise that authority.

A preponderance of the evidence supports the plaintiffs' contention. Credible evidence, adduced at trial, reveals that housing and transportation issues were well within the class of activities proper, usual, and necessary to recruit and hire workers for Case Farms' Ohio processing plant. It is uncontested that the combination of its high turnover rate, and relative isolation from metropolitan areas, complicates Case Farms' recruitment process. For Case Farms, recruitment was, at all relevant times, an on-going, virtually nation-wide undertaking. The very fact that this Ohio chicken processing plant was recruiting workers in Florida and Texas attests to the difficulties it faces finding workers. Furthermore, once the workers arrived in Ohio, it was difficult for workers to find housing on their own because of language barriers, lack of personal transportation, and their unfamiliarity with the area. So, it was essential to the success of Case Farms' hiring practices to assist out-of-state workers with housing. Case Farms, before any relationship with ATC, actually did assist incoming workers with housing and transportation in Ohio. Furthermore, it was clear from the evidence adduced at trial that Case Farms meant for ATC to perform these duties. Thus, it is found that Case Farms knew that these duties were proper, usual, and necessary in order to recruit and retain a workforce primarily migrating from out-of-state.

Case Farms points out, and places much weight on the fact, that its representatives Cilona and Kohli both testified that ATC was not authorized to hire workers and make them full fledged "Case Farms" employees. Rather, under the arrangement with ATC, the workers would supposedly remain "ATC employees," despite the fact that they worked in the Case Farms plant, doing the same work, at the same rate of pay, under the supervision of the same supervisors, as Case Farms workers.

Whether or not a plaintiff would become a "full-fledged" Case Farms employee, however, cannot be dispositive of the agency issue at hand. At issue in this civil action is precisely the question of whether superficial differences (such as which company's name appeared on a plaintiff's pay stub) somehow immunize the company that owns and operates the plant from liability. Given the fact that housing and transportation were necessary components of Case Farms' recruitment process, ATC's actions in those arenas were within the scope of its relationship as an agent of Case Farms.

For the foregoing reasons, it is found that the ATC defendants were clearly acting as Case Farms' agent in all of their actions relating to the recruitment and hiring of workers for Case Farms' chicken processing plant in Winesburg, Ohio. And, under the AWPA, recruitment by an agricultural employer includes recruitment through an agent. Hence, ATC's interactions with the plaintiffs may be attributed to Case Farms for the purpose of assessing compliance with AWPA. . . .

C. Case Farms' Liability for the Actions of ATC . . .

It is against the background of these general principles of liability that the many claims brought by the plaintiffs in this civil action will be considered. . . . ATC's actions, under common law precepts of agency, can be attributed directly to Case Farms for the purpose of assessing compliance with the AWPA. . . .

[After a lengthy review of the law, the court concluded that "Case Farms violated the law in its treatment of the plaintiffs, in the manners and ways set forth herein, and that plaintiffs should be awarded judgment therefor."]

2.   *Apparent Authority and Estoppel*

One person may bind another in a transaction with a third person, even in the absence of actual authority, when the third person reasonably believes — based on "manifestations" by the purported principal — that the actor is authorized to act on behalf of the purported principal. We say "purported principal" because this "apparent authority" does not require the prior existence of an agency relationship. In other words, apparent authority may be the basis for liability in two situations: (1) where persons appear to be agents, even though they do not qualify under the definition discussed above (often referred to as "apparent agency"), and (2) where agents act beyond the scope of their actual authority.

The primary difficulties with the doctrine of apparent authority revolve around the notion of "manifestation." "Manifestation" was not defined in Restatement (Second), though the term appeared in many sections. The commentary on Restatement (Second) §27 provides the following examples:

> [Manifestations from the principal to a] third person may come directly from the principal by letter or by word of mouth, from authorized statements of the agent, from documents or other indicia of authority given by the principal to the agent, or from third persons who have heard of the agent's authority from authorized or permitted channels of communication. Likewise, as in the case of authority, apparent authority can be created by appointing a person to a position, such as that of manager or treasurer, which carries with it generally recognized duties; to those who know of the appointment there is apparent authority to do the things ordinarily entrusted to one occupying such a position, regardless of unknown limitations which are imposed on a particular agent.

One of the most important innovations in Restatement (Third) is the inclusion of a new section defining "manifestation":

> A person manifests consent or intention through written or spoken words or other conduct if the person has notice that another will infer such consent or intention from the words or conduct.

Restatement (Third) of Agency §1.02.

The Restatement (Third) definition was intended to broaden the concept of manifestation. As noted in the commentary to §1.02, "conduct may constitute a manifestation sufficient to create apparent authority even though it does not use the word 'authority' and even though it does not consist of words targeted specifically to a third party." The primary purpose behind broadening the scope of this concept was to eliminate the separate doctrine of inherent agency power, which is discussed later in this section.

Given the commentary on Restatement (Second) §27 quoted above — notably that manifestations may come "from third persons who have heard of the agent's authority" or merely from appointing a person to a position — one might be excused for wondering whether the concept of manifestation needed to be expanded. According to the drafters of the Restatement (Third), the most important implication of the new definition of "manifestation" is that communications from the principal need not be directed to third persons before apparent authority is created. The necessity of finding a direct link between the principal and third persons could reasonably be drawn from the Restatement (Second) definition of "apparent authority," which required "manifestations to such third persons," yet courts have traditionally not been so restrictive in requiring such manifestations prior to finding apparent authority. Consistent with what the courts have done, the Restatement (Third) now clearly permits the creation of apparent authority when manifestations reach the third party through an intermediary (as long as the manifestations are traceable to the principal) or simply by placing a person in a certain position. The importance of the new definition of "manifestation," therefore, probably lies in the fact that it has now made explicit in the primary sections of the Restatement what previously appeared only in the commentary, and that it endorses what courts were already doing.

In any event, there are two key points to finding apparent authority: (1) the manifestation (however defined) must emanate from the principal (or purported principal) and must be received (either directly or indirectly) by the third person; and (2) the scope of the agent's apparent authority depends on the third person's reasonable interpretation of that manifestation. Whether it was reasonable for a third person to believe that the agent with whom she transacted business had the authority to enter into a particular transaction has subjective and objective components. Courts consider prior dealings between the parties, customs that apply in the particular setting, and the nature of the proposed transaction (for example, whether the agent proposes a transaction that would benefit the purported principal). Reliance is not technically required to establish apparent authority — rather, it is an element of estoppel, which is discussed briefly below — though some courts inquire after reliance in some circumstances.

As with actual authority, the rationale for imposing liability based on apparent authority seems to implicate issues of *control, benefit,* and *consent.* With respect to *control,* the issue is not the principal's control of the agent, but rather the principal's control over the third party's expectations. As noted by the Restatement (Second), "there is a basic requirement that the principal be responsible for the information which comes to the mind of the third person, similar to the requirement for the creation of [actual] authority that the principal be responsible for the information which comes to the [mind of the] agent." Restatement (Second) of Agency §27, comment *a.*

The doctrine of apparent authority is partly based on the prospect of *benefit* to purported principals. By allowing third parties to act in reliance on manifestations from the principals — without requiring investigation into the scope of actual authority — the doctrine of apparent authority "greases the wheels of commerce."

The concept of *consent* may provide the most powerful justification of liability based on apparent authority. In an oft-cited article on the law of agency, Oliver Wendell Holmes noted that "it is plain good sense to hold people answerable for wrongs which they have intentionally brought to pass, and to recognize that it is just as possible to bring wrongs to pass through free human agents as through slaves, animals, or natural forces." Oliver W. Holmes, *Agency*, 4 Harv. L. Rev. 345, 347 (1891). Holmes was, however, troubled by the fact that the law of agency sometimes held a principal liable for acts that were not specifically commanded or were beyond the principal's actual control. In a response to Holmes, Harvard Law Professor Everett Abbott argued that Holmes "fails to recognize that the principal by his representations to others may render himself accountable to them for acts not commanded, or even for acts which, as between himself and his agent, he has forbidden. Such a liability is as plain good sense as that for commanded acts, and will explain many of the cases for which the learned writer failed to find an intelligible theory." Everett V. Abbott, *Of the Nature of Agency*, 9 Harv. L. Rev. 507, 519-520 (1896).

Estoppel is a non-agency doctrine that is similar to apparent authority in that both are created when the principal leads a third party to believe that an agent is authorized to act on the principal's behalf, even though no such actual authority has been granted. Two things distinguish estoppel from apparent authority: (1) estoppel requires the third party to change position in reliance on the principal, whereas a principal may be bound under apparent authority even in the absence of such detrimental reliance; and (2) estoppel allows the third party to hold the principal liable but does not give the principal any rights against the third party (although the principal can often cure that deficiency by ratifying the transaction).

Because estoppel and apparent authority are so similar, many courts treat them as synonymous and often use the terms interchangeably or impose a detrimental reliance requirement in cases decided on the basis of "apparent authority." Nevertheless, the Restatement (Third) of Agency retains the distinction between apparent authority and estoppel "to clarify the law, and, in particular, to make clear when and why it is necessary for a plaintiff to show detrimental reliance."

The doctrines of apparent authority and estoppel, as articulated by common law judges and the drafters of the Restatement (Second), technically required communication between the principal and the third party. Even in estoppel cases where the principal was held responsible for inaction, the doctrine presumes some connection between principal and third party (namely, that the principal knew of the third party's mistaken belief in the authority of the purported agent). In some cases decided under these doctrines, however, the principal and the third party have never interacted, except through the agent. In the well-known case Kidd v. Thomas A. Edison, Inc., 239 F. 405 (S.D.N.Y. 1917), Judge Learned Hand observed of such instances: "It is only a fiction to say that the principal is estopped, when he has not communicated with the third person and thus misled him."

Judge Hand's observation prompts the question: Why are courts willing to hold principals responsible for the acts of their agents in cases where the doctrinal requirements necessary to establish apparent authority or estoppel have not been met? The problem, according to Judge Hand, lies not with the imposition of liability, but rather with the articulation of the doctrines of apparent authority and estoppel. In attempting to base liability in *consent* of the principal, those doctrines lost the notion that principals could sometimes be held liable merely because of *status*. In these "cases of customary authority," courts will hold principals liable to the extent that custom would justify reliance by a third party. Judge Hand explained the policy rationale underlying this practice as follows:

> The considerations which have made the rule survive are apparent. If a man select another to act for him with some discretion, he has by that fact vouched to some extent for his reliability. While it may not be fair to impose upon him the results of a total departure from the general subject of his confidence, the detailed execution of his mandate stands on a different footing. The very purpose of delegated authority is to avoid constant recourse by third persons to the principal, which would be a corollary of denying the agent any latitude beyond his exact instructions. Once a third person has assured himself widely of the character of the agent's mandate, the very purpose of the relation demands the possibility of the principal's being bound through the agent's minor deviations. Thus, as so often happens, archaic ideas continue to serve good, though novel, purposes.

Kidd prompted the drafters of the Restatement (Second) to add a new section describing an agent's "inherent agency power." Relying on the notion of status, this §8A states that inherent agency power "is not derived from [actual] authority, apparent authority, or estoppel, but solely from the agency relation and exists for the protection of persons harmed by or dealing with a servant or other agent." The use of the word "power" rather than "authority" recognizes that the principal has not authorized the agent's action by manifesting consent to either the agent or the third party. Nevertheless, the principal is bound by the agent's action for reasons of "fairness":

> It is inevitable that in doing their work, either through negligence or excess of zeal, agents will harm third persons or will deal with them in unauthorized ways. It would be unfair for an enterprise to have the benefit of the work of its agents without making it responsible to some extent for their excesses and failures to act carefully. The answer of the common law has been the creation of special agency powers or, to phrase it otherwise, the imposition of liability upon the principal because of unauthorized or negligent acts of his servants and other agents.

Restatement (Second) of Agency §8A, comment *a*.

Despite the apparent utility of the concept, inherent agency power is infrequently used to decide agency cases and usually surfaces where courts must choose between imposing a loss on an innocent third party and an innocent principal.

The Restatement (Third) abandons inherent agency power, purporting to subsume all of the cases covered thereby with the expanded notion of apparent authority. Nevertheless, the drafters of Restatement (Third) appear to have missed at least one set of cases: those involving so-called "undisclosed principals." Courts and the Restatements have long distinguished between "disclosed principals" and "undisclosed principals."[1] This distinction is important because

---

1. Restatement (Third) §1.04(2) states:

   (a) *Disclosed principal.* A principal is disclosed if, when an agent and a third party interact, the third party has notice that the agent is acting for a principal and has notice of the principal's identity.

"apparent authority is not present when a third party believes that an interaction is with an actor who is a principal." In other words, apparent authority cannot exist in cases involving an undisclosed principal.

One of the best-known common law agency cases illustrates the usefulness of "inherent agency power" in undisclosed principal cases. Watteau v. Fenwick, 1 Q.B. 346 (1893) involved a "beerhouse" called Victoria Hotel. A man named Humble (no, we're not making this up) had owned and operated the establishment for "some years," but the case arose after he sold it. Despite the sale, Humble remained as the manager, and the business license and signage both bore his name. Nevertheless, his authority to operate the business was expressly limited by the new owners, and Humble "had no authority to buy any goods for the business except bottled ales and mineral waters." Humble accepted other items—including cigars and "bovril"—from suppliers on credit, and when he did not pay, the suppliers sued the new owners, who were undisclosed principals. The court upheld the claim, reasoning:

> [O]nce it is established that the defendant was the real principal, the ordinary doctrine as to the principal and agent applies—that the principal is liable for all the acts of the agent which are within the authority usually confided to an agent of that character, notwithstanding limitations, as between the principal and the agent, put upon that authority. It is said that it is only so where there has been a holding out of authority—which cannot be said of a case where the person supplying the goods knew nothing of the existence of a principal. But I do not think so. Otherwise, in every case of undisclosed principal, or at least in every case where the fact of there being a principal was undisclosed, the secret limitation of authority would prevail and defeat the action of the person dealing with the agent and then discovering that he was an agent and had a principal.

The following case involves a claim of liability under the doctrine of apparent authority. The court ruled against the plaintiff, finding no apparent authority. Considering the concepts of *control*, *benefit*, and *consent*, try to determine what was lacking in the plaintiff's claims, and also whether the plaintiff would have been more successful if the court had allowed it to add a claim of estoppel.

BETHANY PHARMACAL CO. v. QVC, INC.

241 F.3d 854
United States Court of Appeals, Seventh Circuit
February 23, 2001

RIPPLE, Circuit Judge.

Bethany Pharmacal Company, Inc. ("Bethany") brought this action against QVC, Inc. ("QVC"). It claimed that QVC had agreed to allow Bethany to appear on QVC's televised shopping program in order to sell its skin moisturizer.

(b) *Undisclosed principal.* A principal is undisclosed if, when an agent and a third party interact, the third party has no notice that the agent is acting for a principal.

The Restatement (Third) also defines "*Unidentified principal*" ("A principal is unidentified if, when an agent and a third party interact, the third party has notice that the agent is acting for a principal but does not have notice of the principal's identity."), but that concept is not important to our study of the law of agency.

QVC moved for summary judgment. Bethany responded to QVC's motion and also sought leave to amend its complaint to add a promissory estoppel claim against QVC. The district court denied Bethany's request for leave to amend and granted QVC's motion for summary judgment. Bethany now seeks review of both rulings. For the reasons set forth in the following opinion, we affirm the judgment of the district court.

I

BACKGROUND

A. Facts

QVC operates a televised home shopping network. In 1997, QVC conducted a tour that it titled "The Quest for America's Best — QVC's 50 in 50 Tour" ("the Tour"). The purpose of the Tour was to find local vendors in each of the fifty states to appear on QVC's televised broadcast in order to sell their products. QVC hired Network Trade Associates, Inc. ("NTA") to serve as its contact with economic development offices or agencies in each of the fifty states. NTA, in turn, contacted the Illinois Department of Commerce and Community Affairs' ("DCCA") for assistance in conducting the Illinois leg of the Tour. Roberta Janis was the DCCA employee responsible for the QVC/NTA project. Although Janis' responsibilities dealt primarily with the logistical aspects of the Tour, she self-titled herself the "QVC Project Manager" in her correspondence concerning this project. At no time, however, did QVC enter into a contract with either DCCA or Janis.

QVC held two trade shows in Illinois in April 1997. The purpose of the trade shows was to choose twenty Illinois vendors who would sell their products on QVC's broadcast. QVC also intended to choose five additional vendors as alternates. Prior to the trade shows, NTA gave Janis the names and addresses of several Illinois vendors. Janis sent those vendors a QVC solicitation packet; the information in this packet listed her as a contact person. In order to participate in the trade shows, vendors had to complete a product information sheet included in the solicitation packet. On that sheet, the vendor described the product that the vendor proposed to sell on QVC's program. The information sheet also included the following written disclaimer:

> The data provided on this sheet is for information purposes only. QVC's acceptance of your completed form does not constitute acceptance or agreement that the information you have provided is correct or complete. It is also not a waiver of any of QVC's rights, remedies or defenses with respect to you or your product. Any sales of the product to QVC shall be governed by a purchase order issued by QVC. An authorized QVC Purchase Order is the only valid contract. Verbal statements or discussions do not constitute a commitment to do business and should not be considered as such.

Bethany was one of the Illinois businesses that received a QVC solicitation packet. Bethany is a pharmaceutical company that manufactures a moisturizing skin lotion called Ti-Creme. Bethany's chairman, Jack J. Scott, Sr., completed a product information sheet describing Ti-Creme on behalf of Bethany, in which he indicated that Bethany had 15,000 to 50,000 jars of Ti-Creme available on hand. The product information sheet also asked Scott to indicate the "[m]anufacturer lead time required for $10,000 wholesale order"; Scott responded, "On Hand."

Scott represented Bethany at QVC's Springfield, Illinois, trade show in April 1997. Janis also attended the trade show and her DCCA business cards were on display at the registration desk. James Plutte and Julie Campbell, both buyers for QVC, were also at the trade show. Plutte and Campbell explained to the vendors that, if their products were selected, they would receive a purchase order from QVC and that the vendors should not do anything until they heard directly from QVC.

Following the trade show, NTA notified Janis that it would send her a list of the twenty vendors and five alternates from Illinois that QVC had selected to appear on its broadcast, but it told Janis not to contact any of the listed vendors until QVC had notified the vendors of their selection itself. Apparently, Janis did not receive this list right away. Janis may not have received the list until after QVC had contacted the selected vendors, although the record is not clear on this point. What is clear is that Janis thought QVC had already contacted the vendors by the time she received the list. She therefore prepared a letter that she sent to the twenty participants and the five alternates in which she gave them logistical information about the broadcast and alerted them to a potential shortage in hotel accommodations during the time of the broadcast ("the Janis letter").[2] The Janis letter was printed on DCCA stationery, was addressed to "QVC Participants," congratulated them on being selected to participate in QVC's broadcast, and concluded by stating, "See you at the Fair." Although the same letter was sent to both participants and alternates, Janis directed her subordinates to attach a "post-it note" to the letters sent to the alternates with the word "Alternate."

In selecting the program participants, QVC chose Bethany as an alternate vendor. However, although Bethany received the Janis letter, it did not receive the post-it note informing it that it was only an alternate rather than a confirmed participant. After receiving the Janis letter, Scott telephoned Janis to thank her

[handwritten margin note: After receiving a list of those selected, Janis sent congratulatory letters to winners - alternates - notes]

[handwritten margin note: >✳]

[handwritten margin note: Bethany didn't get the post-it note]

---

2. Given the importance of the Janis letter to this litigation, we set forth its text in full:

Dear QVC Participants:

Congratulations! We just received the news from QVC identifying the twenty companies who will be participating in the QVC broadcast in Springfield at the Illinois State Fair on August 9th.

The Department of Commerce and Community Affairs Small Business Division will be preparing a press release and distributing it statewide. When it is ready, we will provide a copy to you for your use.

The broadcast will be held on the first Saturday of the State Fair which usually draws close to 150,000 attendees that day. The broadcast itself will be three (3) hours in length. The actual time for the broadcast is yet to be determined. The site selected for the broadcast is a 40,000 square foot area within the Farm Expo area. The site is in direct proximity to the Fair's main entrance.

Hotel rooms will be filling up fast. A listing of some Springfield hotels is provided to assist you in locating accommodations. A map of the State Fairgrounds is also provided.

Look forward to assisting you during the broadcast. See you at the Fair!

Sincerely,
Roberta Janis QVC Project Manager

for notifying him that QVC had selected Bethany as a participant. The parties disagree as to the content of the conversation that followed. Scott claims that, in response to his call, Janis said, "We'll be seeing you at the show." Janis, however, claims that she told Scott that her records indicated that he was only an alternate and that she asked him whether he had received information from QVC indicating that he was a participant. The parties agree, however, that, in the course of the conversation, Janis did not say anything definitive that clearly would have dispelled Scott's misperception.

Scott claims that, in reliance on the Janis letter, he spent $100,000 to buy 60,000 units of Ti-Creme. This amount was what he predicted he would need on hand to meet the demand for Ti-Creme when QVC's broadcast aired. His calculation was based on a QVC press release describing the financial success of the vendors who had participated in the broadcasts. No one at QVC suggested to Scott that he should purchase additional product or that he would need more than the $10,000 worth of product that he already claimed to have on hand.

B. Earlier Proceedings

QVC eventually learned that Scott's receipt of the Janis letter had led him to believe that Bethany had been selected to participate in the broadcast, but it did not change Bethany's status from an alternate to a participant. Consequently, Bethany filed this breach of contract action against QVC. In Bethany's view, the Janis letter constituted a binding contract between Bethany and QVC; the letter constituted a promise that Bethany would be allowed to sell Ti-Creme on QVC's broadcast. Bethany sought to recover the $100,000 it spent to purchase additional product in reliance on QVC's alleged promise. QVC filed a motion for summary judgment. When Bethany replied to QVC's motion, it also filed a motion seeking leave to amend its complaint to add a promissory estoppel claim.

The district court granted QVC's motion for summary judgment. The court first considered whether Janis was QVC's apparent agent, which would allow her to bind QVC to a contract. The court held that Janis was not QVC's apparent agent because QVC had done nothing to indicate to Scott that Janis had any authority to act on QVC's behalf. The court determined that, because Janis had initiated her contact with the vendors, her conduct did not constitute a manifestation by QVC to third parties that Janis had the authority to transact business on QVC's behalf.

The district court further held that, even if Janis was QVC's apparent agent, there still was no valid contract between Bethany and QVC. It concluded that Scott's belief that the Janis letter was an offer to enter into a contract was not reasonable because the Janis letter did not specify the terms of the purported offer or the identities of the offeror and offeree. The court also concluded that, even if there was a valid contract, Bethany could not establish that the contract had been breached because it could not show that it suffered damages or had a reasonable basis for computing the damages it claimed to have suffered.

Finally, the court refused to allow Bethany to amend its complaint to include a promissory estoppel claim against QVC. The court determined that Bethany would be unable to succeed on such a claim because the Janis letter did not clearly promise that QVC would allow Bethany to appear on its broadcast to promote Ti-Creme. Additionally, the court believed that Bethany's promissory estoppel claim would fail because Bethany's reliance on the Janis letter in purchasing additional product was unreasonable, given that QVC never had indicated that this purchase would be necessary.

II
DISCUSSION

In appealing the district court's judgment, Bethany submits that the district court erred in concluding that Janis was not QVC's apparent agent and that the Janis letter could not form the basis of a binding contract. Bethany also argues that the district court abused its discretion in refusing to allow it to amend its complaint in order to add a promissory estoppel claim. We shall examine each of these contentions.

A. Breach of Contract . . .

Under Illinois' law of agency, an apparent agency exists if (1) the principal consents to or knowingly acquiesces in the agent's conduct, (2) the third party has a reasonable belief that the agent possesses authority to act on the principal's behalf, and (3) the third party relied to his detriment on the agent's apparent authority. An agent's apparent authority can only be determined by evaluating the principal's conduct toward the third party. Specifically, the principal must do something to lead the third party to believe that the agent is authorized to act on its behalf. The agent cannot unilaterally create an apparent agency through her own words or conduct. An apparent agency may arise, however, "from silence of the alleged principals when they knowingly allow another to act for them as their agent." Mateyka v. Schroeder, 504 N.E.2d 1289, 1295 (1987). In such a situation, the scope of the apparent agent's authority is determined by the authority that a reasonably prudent person might believe the agent to possess based on the actions of the principal.

Bethany maintains that QVC created the appearance that Janis was its agent by allowing her to correspond with vendors and to act as an intermediary between QVC and the vendors. Bethany further maintains that QVC should be responsible for the consequences of the Janis letter because it knew about the letter but never told Janis not to send it. QVC responds that Janis herself initiated the conduct to which Bethany points, and, therefore, the conduct cannot be attributed to any manifestation or authorization on QVC's part. Additionally, QVC maintains that Bethany's perception of Janis as a QVC agent with the authority to bind QVC to a contract was unreasonable, given QVC's statement on the product information sheet that the only valid contract with QVC was a purchase order.

We cannot accept Bethany's argument. Bethany has not established that QVC took any steps that would make a reasonable person believe that Janis had the authority to contract on its behalf. QVC consistently maintained that the only way in which it would enter a binding contract was through a purchase order issued by QVC. QVC clearly stated this principle in the product information sheet that it distributed to all interested vendors, including Bethany. QVC representatives again stated this principle to the vendors attending the trade show when they verbally reminded the vendors of the importance of a purchase order. Bethany has produced no evidence to demonstrate that QVC ever indicated that Janis or DCCA could contract on its behalf through some means other than a purchase order. Indeed, we can find no evidence in the appellate record that QVC ever indicated to any vendor that someone other than a QVC buyer had the authority to contract on QVC's behalf.

Bethany's argument that QVC created an apparent agency in Janis by allowing her to interact with the vendors on its behalf misses the mark. QVC did allow Janis to work with the vendors by providing logistical information about the trade shows and the broadcast; however, given QVC's repeated disclaimers regarding the need for a purchase order, that relationship cannot reasonably be interpreted as including the authority to contract on QVC's behalf. Moreover, QVC did not stand idly by and accept the benefits of contracts Janis allegedly had procured on its behalf. Instead, upon realizing that Bethany had misinterpreted the Janis letter, QVC notified Bethany of Janis' error and made clear that Bethany would not be allowed to appear on its broadcast. In short, QVC consistently stated to Bethany that a valid contract could be created only by a purchase order. Furthermore, after learning of Bethany's misperception because of Janis' mistake, QVC consistently maintained that Bethany was only an alternate. Under these circumstances, it was unreasonable for Bethany to believe that Janis had any authority to bind QVC to a contract with a vendor.

B. Bethany's Motion to Amend Its Complaint . . .

The district court determined that allowing Bethany to amend its complaint to add a promissory estoppel claim would be futile because Bethany would be unable to succeed on that claim. Bethany takes issue with this conclusion. It argues that the Janis letter constitutes an unambiguous promise by QVC to allow Bethany to appear on its broadcast and that Scott relied on this promise to Bethany's detriment by purchasing $100,000 worth of product in order to meet the anticipated demand for Ti-Creme following the broadcast. QVC responds that the Janis letter was not an unambiguous promise, that Bethany's reliance on the Janis letter was unreasonable, that Bethany delayed unduly in seeking the amendment, and that allowing the amendment in the face of Bethany's undue delay would prejudice QVC.

In order to succeed on its promissory estoppel claim, Bethany would have to prove that QVC made an unambiguous promise, that Bethany relied on that promise to its detriment, and that its reliance was reasonable and foreseeable by QVC. Bethany has failed to establish that the Janis letter was an unambiguous promise or that its reliance on that letter was reasonable. The Janis letter contains no words of promise or obligation; instead, it merely states that QVC notified DCCA of the vendors it had chosen to participate in the broadcast. Such a statement does not amount to an unambiguous promise on QVC's part to have Bethany promote Ti-Creme on its broadcast. More fundamentally, as we have discussed in the previous section, it was unreasonable for Scott to rely on the Janis letter in purchasing $100,000 worth of Ti-Creme after QVC had stated expressly to Scott and the other vendors that the sale of any product to QVC would be governed by a purchase order. The district court did not abuse its discretion in refusing to allow the amendment on the grounds that it would be futile. . . .

Conclusion

The district court properly granted summary judgment. It also acted well within its discretion in denying Bethany leave to amend its complaint to add a promissory estoppel claim. Accordingly, the judgment of the district court is affirmed.

PROBLEM 1-2

Robert and Margo Rebar lived in Alabama. They needed a termite control service. They called Cook's Pest Control (Cook's), who promptly sent a representative to the Rebars' home. After discussing the terms of service, the Rebars and the representative of Cook's signed a one-year contract, which contained a "Retreatment Guarantee," stating: "This Guarantee provides for the retreatment of the structure but does not provide for the repair of damage caused by wood destroying organisms." In addition, the contract contained a mandatory, binding arbitration provision. The contract was renewable upon the payment of a fee by the Rebars.

On September 27, 2000 — just months after signing the initial contract — the Rebars discovered a termite infestation in their home. The Rebars contacted Cook's and pursued remediation. Apparently dissatisfied with Cook's response to the termite infestation, the Rebars nevertheless mailed a renewal fee to Cook's just prior to the expiration of the contract. In the envelope containing the renewal fee, the Rebars included a document titled, "Addendum to Customer Agreement," which read:

To: Cook's Pest Control, Inc.

Please read this addendum to your Customer Agreement carefully as it explains changes to some of the terms shown in the Agreement. Keep this document with the original customer Agreement.

Arbitration.

Cook's agrees that any prior amendment to the Customer Agreement shall be subject to written consent before arbitration is required. In the event that a dispute arises between Cook's and Customer, Cook's agrees to propose arbitration if so desired, estimate the cost thereof, and describe the process (venue, selection of arbitrator, etc.).

Notwithstanding prior amendments, nothing herein shall limit Customer's right to seek court enforcement (including injunctive or class relief in appropriate cases) nor shall anything herein abrogate Customer's right to trial by jury. Arbitration shall not be required for any prior or future dealings between Cook's and Customer.

Future Amendments.

Cook's agrees that any future amendments to the Customer Agreement shall be in writing and signed by Customer and [an] authorized representative of Cook's.

Effective Date.

These changes shall be effective upon negotiation of this payment or the next service provided pursuant to the Customer Agreement, whichever occurs first.

Acceptance be [sic] Continued Use.

Continued honoring of this account by you acknowledges agreement to these terms. If you do not agree with all of the terms of this contract, as amended, you must immediately notify me of that fact.

This document and the renewal fee were mailed to a Cook's office in Birmingham, not to the corporate offices in Decatur, Alabama. The letterhead on which the contract was printed listed only the Decatur office, but the Birmingham office apparently serviced the Rebar account. There the check and Addendum were received by Erin Williams, the office administrator of the Birmingham office. She deposited the check in a bank on behalf of Cook's. What she did with the Addendum is unclear, but Cook's claims that it was never received. Erin Williams did not have express or implied authority to agree to the contract modification.

Two weeks after sending the renewal payment and Addendum, the Rebars sued Cook's for fraud, negligence, breach of contract, breach of warranty, negligent misrepresentation, unjust enrichment, failure to warn, and negligent training, supervision, and retention of employees. Cook's wants to compel arbitration. The case comes down to whether the contract was properly modified.

What evidence would the Rebars find most useful in showing that Williams had apparent authority to modify the pest control agreement? What arguments might Cook's use to counter that claim?

3. *Respondeat Superior*

Early commentators and some courts distinguished between principals and agents, on the one hand, and masters and servants, on the other. According to Professor Floyd Mechem, the distinction was along the following lines:

> The characteristic of the agent is that he is a business representative. His function is to bring about, modify, affect, accept performance of, or terminate contractual obligations between his principal and third persons. To the proper performance of his functions therefore, it is absolutely essential that there be third persons in contemplation between whom and the principal legal obligations are to be thus created, modified or otherwise affected by the acts of the agent.
>
> The function of the servant, on the other hand, as his name suggests, is the rendition of service, —not the creation of contractual obligations. He executes the commands of his master, chiefly in reference to things, but occasionally with reference to persons when no contractual obligation is to result.

Floyd R. Mechem, *A Treatise on the Law of Agency* 21-22 (2d ed. 1914).

This distinction was often ignored by courts and was obliterated by the Restatement, which treats the master-servant relationship as a type of principal-agent relationship. Restatement (Second) of Agency §2. "Servant" is the common law term that corresponds to what is known today as an employee.

Thus, the terms "master" and "servant" are usually understood to be the equivalent of the terms "employer" and "employee." Indeed, Restatement (Third) abandons the terms "master" and "servant" in favor of "employer" and "employee," and so shall we.

The main consequence of finding an employer-employee relationship is that an employer is liable for torts committed by an employee within the scope of employment. Restatement (Second) of Agency §219(1). This is the familiar doctrine of *respondeat superior*.

The justification for imposing liability on a principal under the doctrine of *respondeat superior* is multifaceted. The commentary to Restatement (Third) §2.04 bases the doctrine on the concept of *control*:

> Its scope is limited to the employment relationship, and to conduct falling within the scope of that relationship, because an employer has the right to control how work is done. This right is more detailed than the right to control possessed by all principals, whether or not employers. . . .
>
> As the location of work moved outside the household and into mercantile and industrial settings, the employer's responsibility for harm caused by employee activities followed the employer's right to control how work is done.

The Restatements also distinguish between "employees" and "independent contractors." Restatement (Second) of Agency §2. Independent contractors are people who act on behalf of another but are not employees. Independent contractors may or may not be agents, depending on the ability of the principal to control their actions. The Restatement (Second) of Agency §220(2) lists ten factors to be used in determining whether one acting for another is an employee or an independent contractor, including such things as where the work is done (at the principal's place of business or elsewhere), whose tools are used, who directs the specifics of the work, how the person is paid, and the like. Clearly this is a fact-specific inquiry, as the line between employees and independent contractors is not always capable of bright-line determination.

The two cases and Problem 1-3 below offer perspectives on various issues surrounding the doctrine of *respondeat superior*. Dias v. Brigham Medical Associates involves the frequently litigated issue of institutional liability for doctor malpractice. Hospitals and practice groups are often sued as part of a medical malpractice claim, as plaintiffs attempt to access the "deep pocket." In this case, the Supreme Judicial Court of Massachusetts discusses in some detail the rationales for *respondeat superior* liability and reflects the modern trend toward de-emphasizing particularized inquiries into control — at least in the context of admitted employment relationships.

Meyer v. Holley shows how agency principles are sometimes imported into statutes. The case also hints at a vexing tension between the doctrine of *respondeat superior* and the corporate law doctrine of limited liability for shareholders, which we discuss in Chapter 5. Generally, "limited liability" means that the shareholders of a corporation are not personally responsible for paying judgments against a corporation if the corporation does not have the resources to pay such a judgment. The fundamental issue is whether shareholders who control a corporation can be treated as the "principal" of the corporation ("agent") for purposes of *respondeat superior* analysis, and therefore made personally liable for torts committed by the corporation's employees. Corporate law tends to treat the issue of shareholder liability as *sui generis*, so the issue is rarely raised using these terms. But as you read *Meyer*, consider the following: what is it about being a shareholder that insulates a person from *respondeat superior* liability even if the degree of control she exercises over the corporation and its business would otherwise be sufficient to qualify the shareholder for such liability under a pure agency analysis?

Finally, Problem 1-3 deals with the distinction between employees and independent contractors and explores ethical considerations in connection with agency relationships.

DIAS v. BRIGHAM MEDICAL ASSOCIATES

780 N.E.2d 447
Supreme Judicial Court of Massachusetts
December 23, 2002

IRELAND, J.

The plaintiffs, Stella and Luis Dias, administrators of the estate of their son, Ethan Dias, claim that defendant Brigham Medical Associates, Inc. (BMA), is vicariously liable under the theory of *respondeat superior* for the alleged medical malpractice of one of its physician practice group members, Dr. Daniel Schlitzer. Dr. Schlitzer was the on-call obstetrician at St. Luke's Hospital who treated the pregnant Stella Dias (plaintiff), following a motor vehicle accident. A Superior Court judge granted summary judgment for BMA, concluding that to hold BMA vicariously liable for Dr. Schlitzer's negligence, the plaintiffs would have to show that the corporation exercised, or had the right to exercise, direction and control over his treatment decisions. The judge found that BMA did not and could not exercise such control over Dr. Schlitzer. The plaintiffs appealed, and we transferred the case to this court on our own motion.

Because we conclude that traditional *respondeat superior* liability applies to the employer of a physician, and that to establish such liability it is not necessary that the employer have the right or ability to control the specific treatment decisions of a physician-employee, we vacate the judgment and remand the case for further proceedings consistent with this opinion.

1. Facts

We summarize the facts relevant for disposition of this appeal. On May 19, 1995, the plaintiff, at the time thirty-two weeks pregnant, was involved in a motor vehicle accident that resulted in her emergency treatment at St. Luke's Hospital in New Bedford. After being examined in the emergency room, she was transferred to the labor and delivery department, where she was treated by Dr. Schlitzer. The plaintiffs contend that the care rendered by him was negligent and resulted in the stillbirth of their son.

BMA, a Massachusetts corporation, a so-called "medical practice group," was comprised entirely of physicians specializing in obstetrical medicine. The record is undisputed that Dr. Schlitzer, at the time of the incident, was an employee and officer of BMA. In fact, both Dr. Schlitzer and BMA admitted in their respective interrogatory answers that Dr. Schlitzer was an employee of BMA "during the period in question," and that Dr. Schlitzer was on staff at BMA "all times relevant hereto." The judge found that, "[a]s a member of BMA, [Dr.] Schlitzer had been assigned by BMA to, and was then responsible for 'on-call' coverage at St. Luke's Hospital, and was in fact working a conventional [24]-hour shift at the [h]ospital." As to this latter point, however, the record contains ambiguities regarding Dr. Schlitzer's on-call coverage obligations on the night in question, as more fully discussed below.

2. Discussion. . . .

Broadly speaking, *respondeat superior* is the proposition that an employer, or master, should be held vicariously liable for the torts of its employee, or servant, committed within the scope of employment. See Restatement (Third) of Agency §2.04 (Tent. Draft No.2 2001). In one of its earliest cases concerning *respondeat superior*, the court concluded that an employer could not be held liable on that theory where the employer was unable to give direction and control to the employee regarding the precise actions that resulted in the tort, in that case an employee's method of driving or choice of route while on an errand for his employer. Khoury v. Edison Elec. Illuminating Co., 265 Mass. 236, 238 (1928) ("the employee must be subject to control by the employer, not only as to the result to be accomplished but also as to the means to be used").

In 1969, however, in circumstances similar to those at issue in the *Khoury* case, this court broadened the scope of liability under the theory of *respondeat superior*, and held that an employer need not control the details of an employee's tasks in order to be held liable for the employee's tortious acts. *See* Konick v. Berke, Moore Co., 355 Mass. 463, 467, 468 (1969). The facts of *Konick* were similar to those of *Khoury*: both involved an employee who, it was alleged, was negligently driving an automobile while on an errand for the employer. In the *Khoury* case the employer was not liable for its employee's actions, while the employer in the *Konick* case was found to be liable for the employee's automobile accident, even though the employer was unable to control the precise manner and means of the employee's driving. The court declared that it "should no longer follow our cases to the extent that they indicate that a master-servant relationship does not exist unless the employer has a right to control the manner and means (the details, in other words)," of the allegedly negligent conduct. *Id.* at 468. Our *Konick* decision comported with the view of the vast majority of States. The doctrine of *respondeat superior* in the Commonwealth thus evolved to place the burden of liability on the party better able to bear that burden. *See* Kansallis Fin. Ltd. v. Fern, 421 Mass. 659, 664 (1996) ("as between two innocent parties — the principal-master and the third party — the principal-master who for his own purposes places another in a position to do harm to a third party should bear the loss").

While acknowledging these general rules, both the judge and BMA rely on Kelley v. Rossi, 395 Mass. 659, 662, 663 (1985), where we stated that the general rule is that a resident-physician is a servant (employee) of a hospital where she is employed, but also said that, "the very nature of a physician's function tends to suggest that in most instances he will act as an independent contractor." *Id.* at 662. The judge understandably pointed to this statement to support his conclusion that, in the absence of evidence that an employer of a physician reserved the right to direct and control a physician's treatment decisions, a physician is presumed to be an independent contractor. However, the *Kelley* court was required to determine as a preliminary matter whether a physician was a "public employee," as defined by the Massachusetts Torts Claim Act statute, G.L. c. 258, §1. Kelley v. Rossi, *supra* at 661. The point was significant because a public employee is not liable in tort for acts of negligence performed within the scope of his or her public employment. The critical language in the *Kelley* case on which the judge relied thus concerned whether a particular physician was a "public employee" as that term was used in a statute, not with the common-law analysis of *respondeat superior* that governs BMA's liability for the acts or omissions of its admitted "employee."

To prevail against BMA, the plaintiffs need only establish that (1) at the time of the alleged negligence Dr. Schlitzer was an employee of BMA, and (2) the alleged negligent treatment of the plaintiff occurred within the scope of Dr. Schlitzer's employment by BMA. Once employment is established, the only remaining issue is whether he was working for BMA at the time of the alleged negligent treatment, *i.e.*, whether his treatment of the plaintiff was within the scope of his employment by BMA. This comports with traditional agency law that "[a]n employer is liable for torts committed by employees while acting in the scope of their employment." Restatement (Third) of Agency §2.04 (Tent. Draft No.2 2001).

In order to determine whether an employer-employee relationship actually exists, a judge may consider a number of factors. See Restatement (Second) of Agency §220(2) (1958). These factors may include, but are not limited to, the method of payment (*e.g.*, whether the employee receives a W-2 form from the employer), and whether the parties themselves believe they have created an employer-employee relationship. While the point is not of import in this case where both BMA and Dr. Schlitzer admit the existence of the employer-employee relationship, we recognize that the task of determining what constitutes an employer-employee relationship is fact dependent, and that in cases where there is no clear admission of employment, a direction and control analysis may be useful to determine whether the relationship is that of employer-employee as opposed to that of an independent contractor. The right to direct and control the details of an alleged employee's actions "may be very attenuated," but remains an important factor that should be examined when the employer-employee relationship is contested. *See id.* at §220 comment *d*. Once an employer-employee relationship is established, however, any further analysis of the employer's right to direct and control is unnecessary.[8] All that remains to be determined is whether the tort occurred within the scope of employment.

Applying these principles, corporate liability for the negligence of physician employees is commonly recognized. *See* . . . Bing v. Thunig, 2 N.Y.2d 656, 163 N.Y.S.2d 3, 143 N.E.2d 3 (1957), cited in numerous jurisdictions as a turning point in holding hospitals liable for the malpractice of their physicians. The *Bing* case, and other cases across jurisdictions that have followed it, stand for the proposition that although a corporate entity may not control the precise treatment decisions of physicians, the entity should not be able to escape liability for physician malpractice.

---

8. Put differently, once the relationship has been determined to be that of employer-employee, the employer is deemed to have the requisite right to direct and control the employee's performance. *See* Konick v. Berke, Moore Co., 355 Mass. 463, 467-468, 245 N.E.2d 750 (1969), quoting Hinson v. United States, 257 F.2d 178, 181 (5th Cir. 1958) ("If the relationship of master and servant exists and if what the employee is doing is in the furtherance of the master's business, *i.e.* in the scope of his employment, the law gives the master the right of direction and control."

Because BMA admitted that Dr. Schlitzer is its employee, the judge erred in holding that, as a matter of law, BMA could not be held liable for his alleged negligent acts because of BMA's inability to exert direction and control over his clinical decisions. The judge's rationale, that such control is presumed absent unless there is evidence to the contrary, undercuts the evolved purpose of *respondeat superior* liability, and would create an exception for physicians not recognized for any other profession.[9]

There remains one point that requires further comment. Dr. Schlitzer was the employee of BMA on the date of the alleged negligent treatment, but the record is ambiguous as to whether he was acting as BMA's employee at the time he treated the plaintiff. Asked at his deposition for which practice group he was covering when he treated her, Dr. Schlitzer was unable to answer. Dr. Schlitzer did testify that he covered the labor and delivery department on behalf of BMA on a rotating basis, and that at least part of his twenty-four hour shift on May 19 was in fulfilment of his obligation as a BMA employee. Dr. Schlitzer also testified, however, that he had been asked to assume coverage for additional practice groups at some point during his twenty-four hour shift. If Dr. Schlitzer was under an obligation to BMA to be present at the hospital at the time he treated the plaintiff, his treatment of her would be within the scope of his employment by BMA, regardless of whether he had agreed to take on additional coverage shifts for other groups. If, however, he was providing coverage for some other group, under an arrangement independent of his relationship with BMA, at the time he treated the plaintiff, that treatment would not have been rendered within the scope of his BMA employment. Thus, while the record conclusively establishes that Dr. Schlitzer was an employee of BMA, the record before us is inadequate for any definitive determination whether Dr. Schlitzer's treatment of the plaintiff was within the scope of his employment by BMA.

We vacate the judgment entered in the Superior Court, and remand this case for further proceedings consistent with this opinion.

MEYER v. HOLLEY

537 U.S. 280
Supreme Court of the United States
January 22, 2003

Justice BREYER delivered the opinion of the Court.

The Fair Housing Act forbids racial discrimination in respect to the sale or rental of a dwelling. 82 Stat. 81, 42 U.S.C. §§3604(b), 3605(a). The question before us is whether the Act imposes personal liability without fault upon an

---

9. In his summary judgment memorandum of decision, the judge cites as a basis for his decision public policy reasons for encouraging the aggregation of physicians into physician practice groups, and that such groups would be discouraged were they to be held liable for the negligent treatment decisions of their member-employees. Nothing in today's opinion, however, constrains the manner in which physician practice groups may organize or the manner in which they may structure their relationships with the professionals who will actually render services to the patients. All that today's opinion does is confirm that when the relationship forged is that of employer-employee, the ordinary rule of *respondeat superior* liability will apply.

officer or owner of a residential real estate corporation for the unlawful activity of the *corporation's* employee or agent. We conclude that the Act imposes liability without fault upon the employer in accordance with traditional agency principles, *i.e.*, it normally imposes vicarious liability upon the corporation but not upon its officers or owners.

I

For purposes of this decision we simplify the background facts as follows: Respondents Emma Mary Ellen Holley and David Holley, an interracial couple, tried to buy a house in Twenty-Nine Palms, California. A real estate corporation, Triad, Inc., had listed the house for sale. Grove Crank, a Triad salesman, is alleged to have prevented the Holleys from obtaining the house—and for racially discriminatory reasons.

The Holleys brought a lawsuit in federal court against Crank and Triad. They claimed, among other things, that both were responsible for a fair housing law violation. The Holleys later filed a separate suit against David Meyer, the petitioner here. Meyer, they said, was Triad's president, [and] Triad's sole shareholder. . . . They claimed that Meyer was vicariously liable in one or more of these capacities for Crank's unlawful actions.

The District Court consolidated the two lawsuits. It dismissed all claims other than the Fair Housing Act claim on statute of limitations grounds. It dismissed the claims against Meyer in his capacity as officer of Triad because (1) it considered those claims as assertions of *vicarious* liability, and (2) it believed that the Fair Housing Act did not impose personal vicarious liability upon a corporate *officer*. The District Court stated that "any liability against Meyer as an officer of Triad would only attach to Triad," the corporation. The court added that the Holleys had "not urged theories that could justify reaching Meyer individually." . . .

The District Court certified its judgment as final to permit the Holleys to appeal its vicarious liability determinations. The Ninth Circuit reversed those determinations. 258 F.3d 1127 (2001). The Court of Appeals recognized that "under general principles of tort law corporate shareholders and officers usually are not held vicariously liable for an employee's action," but, in its view, "the criteria for the Fair Housing Act" are "different." That Act, it said, "specified" liability "for those who direct or control or have the right to direct or control the conduct of another"—even if they were not at all involved in the discrimination itself and even in the absence of any traditional agent/principal or employee/employer relationship. Meyer, in his capacity as Triad's sole owner, had "the authority to control the acts" of a Triad salesperson. Meyer, in his capacity as Triad's officer, "did direct or control, or had the right to direct or control, the conduct" of a Triad salesperson. And even if Meyer neither participated in nor authorized the discrimination in question, that "control" or "authority to control" is "enough . . . to hold Meyer personally liable." . . .

Meyer sought certiorari. We granted his petition to review the Ninth Circuit's holding that the Fair Housing Act imposes principles of strict liability beyond those traditionally associated with agent/principal or employee/employer relationships. We agreed to decide whether "the criteria under the Fair Housing

Act . . . are different, so that owners and officers of corporations" are automatically and "absolutely liable for an employee's or agent's violation of the Act" — even if they did not direct or authorize, and were otherwise not involved in, the unlawful discriminatory acts.

II

The Fair Housing Act itself focuses on prohibited acts. In relevant part the Act forbids "any person or other entity whose business includes engaging in residential real estate-related transactions to discriminate," for example, because of "race." 42 U.S.C. §3605(a). It adds that "[p]erson" includes, for example, individuals, corporations, partnerships, associations, labor unions, and other organizations. §3602(d). It says nothing about vicarious liability.

Nonetheless, it is well established that the Act provides for vicarious liability. This Court has noted that an action brought for compensation by a victim of housing discrimination is, in effect, a tort action. *See* Curtis v. Loether, 415 U.S. 189, 195-196 (1974). And the Court has assumed that, when Congress creates a tort action, it legislates against a legal background of ordinary tort-related vicarious liability rules and consequently intends its legislation to incorporate those rules.

It is well established that traditional vicarious liability rules ordinarily make principals or employers vicariously liable for acts of their agents or employees in the scope of their authority or employment. And in the absence of special circumstances it is the corporation, not its owner or officer, who is the principal or employer, and thus subject to vicarious liability for torts committed by its employees or agents. The Restatement §1 specifies that the relevant principal/agency relationship demands not only control (or the right to direct or control) but also "the manifestation of consent by one person to another that the other shall act *on his behalf*, and consent by the other so to act." (Emphasis added.) A corporate employee typically acts on behalf of the corporation, not its owner or officer.

The Ninth Circuit held that the Fair Housing Act imposed more extensive vicarious liability — that the Act went well beyond traditional principles. The Court of Appeals held that the Act made corporate owners and officers liable for the unlawful acts of a corporate employee simply on the basis that the owner or officer controlled (or had the right to control) the actions of that employee. We do not agree with the Ninth Circuit that the Act extended traditional vicarious liability rules in this way.

For one thing, Congress said nothing in the statute or in the legislative history about extending vicarious liability in this manner. And Congress' silence, while permitting an inference that Congress intended to apply *ordinary* background tort principles, cannot show that it intended to apply an unusual modification of those rules.

Where Congress, in other civil rights statutes, has not expressed a contrary intent, the Court has drawn the inference that it intended ordinary rules to apply. *See, e.g.*, Burlington Industries, Inc. v. Ellerth, 524 U.S. 742, 756 (1998) (deciding an employer's vicarious liability under Title VII based on traditional agency principles); Meritor Savings Bank, FSB v. Vinson, 477 U.S. 57, 72, 106 S. Ct. 2399, 91 L. Ed. 2d 49 (1986) ("Congress wanted courts to look to agency principles for guidance").

This Court has applied unusually strict rules only where Congress has specified that such was its intent. *See, e.g.,* United States v. Dotterweich, 320 U.S. 277, 280-281, 64 S. Ct. 134, 88 L. Ed. 48 (1943) (Congress intended that a corporate officer or employee "standing in responsible relation" could be held liable in that capacity for a corporation's violations of the Federal Food, Drug, and Cosmetic Act of 1938, 52 Stat. 1040, 21 U.S.C. §§301-392); United States v. Park, 421 U.S. 658, 673, 95 S. Ct. 1903, 44 L. Ed. 2d 489 (1975) (discussing, with respect to the Federal Food, Drug, and Cosmetic Act, congressional intent to impose a duty on "responsible corporate agents"); United States v. Wise, 370 U.S. 405, 411-414, 82 S. Ct. 1354, 8 L. Ed. 2d 590 (1962) (discussing 38 Stat. 736, currently 15 U.S.C. §24, which provides: "Whenever a corporation shall violate any of the . . . antitrust laws, such violation shall be deemed to be also that of the individual directors, officers, or agents of such corporation who shall have authorized, ordered, or done any of the acts constituting in whole or in part such violation"); *see also* 46 U.S.C. §12507(d) ("If a person, not an individual, is involved in a violation [relating to a vessel identification system], the president or chief executive of the person also is subject to any penalty provided under this section").

For another thing, the Department of Housing and Urban Development (HUD), the federal agency primarily charged with the implementation and administration of the statute, has specified that ordinary vicarious liability rules apply in this area. And we ordinarily defer to an administering agency's reasonable interpretation of a statute. Chevron U.S.A. Inc. v. Natural Resources Defense Council, Inc., 467 U.S. 837, 842-845, 104 S. Ct. 2778, 81 L. Ed. 2d 694 (1984); Skidmore v. Swift & Co., 323 U.S. 134, 140, 65 S. Ct. 161, 89 L. Ed. 124 (1944).

A HUD regulation applicable during the relevant time periods for this suit provided that analogous administrative complaints alleging Fair Housing Act violations may be filed

> "against any person who directs or controls, or has the right to direct or control, the conduct of another person with respect to any aspect of the sale . . . of dwellings . . . *if that other person, acting within the scope of his or her authority as employee or agent of the directing or controlling person* . . . has engaged . . . in a discriminatory housing practice." 24 CFR §103.20(b) (1999) (repealed) (emphasis added).

When it adopted the similar predecessor to this regulation, HUD explained that it intended to permit a "respondent" (defined at 42 U.S.C. §3602) to raise in an administrative proceeding any defense "that could be raised in court." 53 Fed. Reg., at 24185. It added that the underscored phrase was designed to make clear that "a complaint may be filed against a directing or controlling person with respect to the discriminatory acts of another only if the other person was acting within the scope of his or her authority as *employee or agent of the directing or controlling person.*" *Ibid.* (emphasis added). HUD also specified that, by adding the words "acting within the scope of his or her authority as employee or agent of the directing or controlling person," it disclaimed any "intent to impose absolute liability" on the basis of the mere right "to direct or control." *Ibid.*

Finally, we have found no convincing argument in support of the Ninth Circuit's decision to apply nontraditional vicarious liability principles — a decision that respondents do not defend and in fact concede is incorrect. The Ninth Circuit rested that decision primarily upon the HUD regulation to which we have referred. The Ninth Circuit underscored the phrase *"or has the right to direct or contro[l] the conduct of another person."* 258 F.3d, at 1130. Its opinion did not explain, however, why the Ninth Circuit did not read these words as modified by the subsequent words that limited vicarious liability to actions taken as "employee or agent of the directing or controlling person." Taken as a whole, the regulation, in our view, says that ordinary, not unusual, rules of vicarious liability should apply.

The Ninth Circuit also referred to several cases decided in other Circuits. The actual holdings in those cases, however, do not support the kind of nontraditional vicarious liability that the Ninth Circuit applied. *See* Chicago v. Matchmaker Real Estate Sales Center, Inc., 982 F.2d 1086 (C.A. 7 1992) (defendant corporation liable for the acts of *its* agents; shareholder directly, not vicariously, liable); Walker v. Crigler, 976 F.2d 900 (C.A. 4 1992) (owner of rental property liable for the discriminatory acts of agent, the property's manager); Marr v. Rife, 503 F.2d 735 (C.A. 6 1974) (real estate agency's owner liable for the discriminatory acts of his agency's salespersons, but without statement of whether agency was a corporation). Nor does the language of these cases provide a convincing rationale for the Ninth Circuit's conclusions.

The Ninth Circuit further referred to an owner's or officer's "non delegable duty" not to discriminate in light of the Act's "overriding societal priority." And it added that "[w]hen one of two innocent people must suffer, the one whose acts permitted the wrong to occur is the one to bear the burden."

"[A] nondelegable duty is an affirmative obligation to ensure the protection of the person to whom the duty runs." General Building Contractors Assn., Inc. v. Pennsylvania, 458 U.S. 375, 396, 102 S. Ct. 3141, 73 L. Ed. 2d 835 (1982) (finding no nondelegable duty under 42 U.S.C. §1981). Such a duty imposed upon a principal would "go further" than the vicarious liability principles we have discussed thus far to create liability "although [the principal] has himself done everything that could reasonably be required of him," W. Prosser, *Law of Torts* §71, p.470 (4th ed. 1971), and irrespective of whether the agent was acting with or without authority. The Ninth Circuit identifies nothing in the language or legislative history of the Act to support the existence of this special kind of liability — the kind of liability that, for example, the law might impose in certain special circumstances upon a principal or employer that hires an independent contractor. In the absence of legal support, we cannot conclude that Congress intended, through silence, to impose this kind of special duty of protection upon individual officers or owners of corporations — who are not principals (or contracting parties) in respect to the corporation's unlawfully acting employee.

Neither does it help to characterize the statute's objective as an "overriding societal priority." We agree with the characterization. But we do not agree that the characterization carries with it a legal rule that would hold every corporate supervisor personally liable without fault for the unlawful act of every corporate employee whom he or she has the right to supervise. Rather, which "of two innocent people must suffer," and just when, is a complex matter. We believe that courts ordinarily should determine that matter in accordance with traditional principles of vicarious liability — unless, of course, Congress, better able than courts to weigh the relevant policy considerations, has instructed the courts differently. We have found no different instruction here.

III . . .

Respondents also point out that, when traditional vicarious liability principles impose liability upon a corporation, the corporation's liability may be imputed to the corporation's owner in an appropriate case through a "'piercing of the corporate veil.'" United States v. Bestfoods, 524 U.S. 51, 63, n.9, 118 S. Ct. 1876, 141 L. Ed. 2d 43 (1998) (quoting United States v. Cordova Chemical Co. of Michigan, 113 F.3d 572, 580 (C.A. 6 1997)). The Court of Appeals, however, did not decide the application of "veil piercing" in this matter. . . . It falls outside the scope of the question presented on certiorari. And we shall not here consider it. The Ninth Circuit nonetheless remains free on remand to determine whether these questions were properly raised and, if so, to consider them.

The judgment of the Court of Appeals is vacated, and the case is remanded for further proceedings consistent with this opinion.

PROBLEM 1-3

One of the growing fields in today's business world is competitive intelligence, otherwise (somewhat rudely) known as corporate espionage. Among other implications of globalization, there is increasing world product competition, since firms can more easily and cheaply ship products all around the world using large containers, packed at factories and loaded directly onto trains, trucks, or ships, with computerized systems to keep track of which products are being shipped where. As a result, firms are under increasing pressure to extract every ounce of competitive advantage. As the chairman of Procter and Gamble (P&G) said in April 1999 in a speech to the Society of Competitive Intelligence Professionals, "I can't imagine a time in history when the competencies, the skills, and the knowledge of the men and women in competitive intelligence are more needed and more relevant to a company." Andy Serwer, *P & G's Covert Operation,* Fortune Magazine, 9/17/2001.

Most of the techniques used by competitive analysts are entirely above reproach, such as "combing through publicly-available news reports and records to create a profit and loss statement for a private rival." *Id.* P&G found itself embroiled in a public relations and legal nightmare, however, when a recent competitive intelligence campaign led P&G-hired analysts to comb through rival Unilever's trash, rather than its public news reports and records. According to reports in Fortune Magazine, competitive-analysis executives at P&G hired a general contractor, who in turn hired about a dozen subcontractors to spy on its competitors, in particular Dutch rival Unilever. The operation was run out of an office in Cincinnati, which is P&G's hometown, but not out of P&G's headquarters. In their dumpster-diving expeditions, either the contractors or subcontractors allegedly trespassed at Unilever's hair-care headquarters in Chicago and misrepresented themselves to Unilever employees, suggesting they were market analysts or journalists. As a result, P&G gained access to reams of competitively sensitive information, including plans for new products, profit margins, and data on sales and prices.

Assume that you are the general counsel of P&G. Your company has a strict written ethics policy, which this behavior violates. The policy states, in part:

1. We are committed to legal compliance and ethical business practices in all of our operations.

2. We choose business partners that we believe share the commitment.

3. In our contracts, we require our business partners to comply with all applicable laws and regulations.

4. If we find that a business partner has committed legal violations, we will take appropriate action, which may include cancelling the affected contract(s), terminating our relationship with the partner, commencing legal actions against the partner, or other actions as warranted.

5. We support law enforcement and cooperate with law enforcement authorities in the proper execution of their responsibilities.

6. We support educational efforts designed to enhance legal compliance on the part of U.S. industry.

You have just been informed of the above facts about the dumpster-diving. How would you classify the relationship between P&G and the general contractor? What additional facts do you need to gather before you can advise your client on how to proceed?

In the actual case, P&G immediately stopped the campaign, investigated the facts, fired three managers, and then contacted Unilever and told them about the problem. What are the advantages and disadvantages of this approach?

KRISPY KREME DOUGHNUTS: A CASE STUDY

In its prospectus for its initial public offering, Krisy Kreme Doughnuts, Inc., described itself as a "leading branded specialty retailer of premium quality doughnuts." For those who have tasted the doughnuts, this description is far too clinical. The usual response to the mention of Krispy Kreme is an extended groan of gluttonous yearning.

Krispy Kreme Doughnuts, Inc., is a North Carolina corporation based in Winston-Salem. Krispy Kreme sells doughnuts through several hundred retail stores — which it calls "doughnut factories" — in nearly every state. Each doughnut factory is equipped to produce 4,000 to 10,000 doughnuts per day.

A majority of Krisy Kreme's stores are owned by franchisees.[1] The Company claims to receive over 500 telephone calls a week requesting franchise information, but all major markets in the United States and Canada are already committed. The company is currently formulating a strategy for invading small markets (with populations of at least 150,000).

Krispy Kreme began expanding through the use of "area developers" in the mid-1990s. Area developers license territories, usually defined by metropolitan statistical areas, and agree to build numerous stores within that area. Area developers must enter into a development agreement with Krispy Kreme (which establishes the number of stores to be developed in an area) and a franchise

---

1. As of October 29, 2000, Krispy Kreme had 164 stores. Of these, 60 were company stores and 104 were owned by franchisees.

agreement for each store opened. Area developers typically pay franchise fees ranging from $20,000 to $40,000 for each store that they develop.

The franchise relationship is a contractual relationship and both franchisors (here Krispy Kreme) and franchisees contribute significantly to its success. The franchise agreement is the basic governance document for the franchising relationship. While the franchisor nominally determines the content of the franchise agreement, the need to attract franchisees requires franchisors to provide attractive terms. Both parties value uniformity within the system and strive to maintain the competitiveness of the system. The terms of a franchising agreement require a balance between predictability (to avoid opportunism) and flexibility (to respond to a changing business environment).

Franchisor's Contributions

Franchisors typically contribute three things to the franchising relationship:

(1) Trademarks and trade dress. Krispy Kreme uses numerous federally registered trademarks. These include "Krispy Kreme" and "Hot Doughnuts Now," as well as the logos associated with these marks. These trademarks are licensed to franchisees, who agree to use them as the "sole identification" of their store.

(2) Trade secrets, which are part of what is often referred to as the "System." The company has many trade secrets, most importantly its doughnut and coffee mixes.[2] In Krispy Kreme's franchise agreement, "System" is defined as "the products and services we authorize and approve and . . . our business formats, methods, procedures, signs, designs, layouts, doughnut mixes, equipment, standards and specifications and the [trademarks and service marks]." The franchise agreement also contains a long list of items that are designated "confidential information," including product recipes, doughnut mixes, site selection criteria, and marketing programs. Franchisees agree not to use any of this information, except to operate their stores.

(3) Services, often including site selection, training, promotion, bookkeeping, compliance with laws and system standards, and insurance. The services provided by the franchisor are an important part of maintaining system quality and uniformity. In some franchise relationships, the franchisor provides services for a fee, and in others, the franchisor's services are incorporated into the franchise relationship. Several of the Krispy Kreme franchisor's services are discussed in more detail below.

Franchisee's Contributions

Franchisees typically pay a one-time franchise fee and ongoing royalties. The initial fee for Krispy Kreme franchisees is $40,000. Royalties amount to 4.5 percent of gross sales for area developers and 3 percent of gross sales for associates. These payments are the source of conflict between the franchisor and franchisee. The franchisor's incentive is to maximize the amount of sales revenue, which may not require the same actions as those that would maximize *profits* for the franchisees.

In addition to the payment of royalties, the franchisee is usually required to pay for the development of the franchise store according to the franchisor's

---

2. In February 2001, Krispy Kreme purchased Digital Java Inc., a closely held company based in Chicago, with the intention of gaining more control over the sourcing and roasting of its coffee.

specifications. In 2003 Krispy Kreme estimated the costs associated with starting a Krispy Kreme franchise as follows:

Real Estate & Improvements
— Own $350,000 - $700,000
— Lease $25,000 - $75,000 per year
Building & Site Work $300,000 - $500,000
Equipment/Signage/Furniture/Fixtures $100,000 - $175,000
Off-Premises Equipment & Displays $0 - $65,000
Initial Inventory $10,000 - $20,000
Doughnut Production Equipment $250,000 - $300,000
Grand Opening PR & Marketing $5,000 - $10,000
Additional Funds $15,000 - $20,000

Finally, individual franchisees often make an enormous personal investment in the business. For many franchisees, the franchise is their primary occupation.

Importance of the Network

Franchise organizations are typically divided into two types. Product franchises market highly specialized goods through a system of approved dealers. This form of franchising was developed in the mid-nineteenth century to sell the McCormick reaper and Singer sewing machines, among other products. Product franchising continues today for automobiles and myriad other products. Business-format franchises contrast with product franchises in several respects, most importantly in that the franchisor sells complete small businesses rather than merely products. The most visible examples of business-format franchising in today's society are fast-food chains, such as McDonald's or Domino's Pizza. Krispy Kreme is a business-format franchise. A key component of this type of franchise is the network of franchisees.

The distinguishing attribute of business-format franchising is *uniformity within the franchise system.* Unlocking the secrets of the franchise relationship requires recognition that each such relationship is embedded in a franchise system that demands uniformity among hundreds or thousands of franchise relationships. This is an attribute of uniformity much different from that normally discussed in the franchising context. Marketing scholars have long recognized the benefits of uniformity in branding a product, but that is of only ancillary interest here. Uniformity is also a governance mechanism. Because each franchise outlet manufactures and sells the same products, the performance of each outlet can be measured against the others.

In-Term Covenants Not to Compete

Most franchisors, including Krispy Kreme, prohibit franchisees from engaging in a competing business during the term of the franchise agreement. In the case of Krispy Kreme, this restriction takes the following form:

You . . . agree that, during the term of this Agreement, neither you nor any of your owners (nor any of your or your owners' spouses or children) will:

   (1) have any direct or indirect interest as a disclosed or beneficial owner in a Competitive Business, located or operating:

(a) within 25 miles of the Store;

(b) within 5 miles of any other Krispy Kreme Store in operation or under construction during the term of this Agreement; or

(c) within the United States of America;

(2) perform services as a director, officer, manager, employee, consultant, representative, agent or otherwise for a Competitive Business, wherever located or operating; or

(3) recruit or hire any person who is our employee or the employee of any Krispy Kreme Store or who has been our employee or the employee of any Krispy Kreme Store within the past six (6) months without obtaining the prior written permission of that person's employer. If we permit you to hire any such person, then you agree to pay us a non-refundable Management Development Fee in the amount of $25,000 as of the date of hire.

The term "Competitive Business" as used in this Agreement means any business operating, or granting franchises or licenses to others to operate, a food service business that sells cake doughnuts, yeast raised doughnuts, any other types of customary or large size doughnut, miniature doughnuts or doughnut holes in any distribution channels to any consumer for consumption or resale and such sales comprise five percent (5%) or more of such business' revenues (other than a Krispy Kreme Store operated under a franchise agreement with us).

Equipment & Supplies

Franchisors have divergent views on the desirability of selling equipment and supplies directly to franchisees. Even where the franchisor does not act as a supplier, however, it usually specifies detailed requirements for the most important items to be used by franchisees. Krispy Kreme is the sole supplier of doughnut production equipment and doughnut mixes for its franchisees. In addition, Krispy Kreme specifies suppliers or brands for other equipment and supplies. Krispy Kreme also requires franchisees to purchase computerized cash registers and software that is approved by the company, with mandatory updates limited to $2,000 per year.

System Standards

The system standards are the requirements for operating the franchise outlet, usually contained in an operations manual. These requirements are notoriously detailed and wide-ranging. For instance, the Krispy Kreme franchise agreement provides for regulation of the following: design, layout, decor, appearance, and lighting; types, models and brands of required fixtures, furnishings, equipment, signs, delivery vehicles, materials, and supplies; production, presentation, packaging, and delivery of products; sales, marketing, advertising and promotional programs and materials and media used in such programs; development and operation of a website in connection with your operation of the store; qualifications, training, dress, and appearance of Store employees; days and hours of operation of the Store; bookkeeping, accounting, data processing, and record keeping systems and forms; types, amounts, terms and conditions of insurance coverage required to be carried for the store; regulation of such other aspects of the operation and maintenance of the Store that we determine from time to time to be useful to preserve or enhance the efficient operation, image or goodwill of the store and other Krispy Kreme stores.

Training

In the traditional franchise, each franchisee is an independent business owner who requires myriad skills to successfully operate a store. Franchisors usually offer extensive training. Krispy Kreme's franchise agreement provides for a training program for up to two store managers at Krispy Kreme's training facility or at an operating Krispy Kreme store. Krispy Kreme does not charge for the training, but the franchisee is responsible for the compensation of the managers during the training period and the travel and living expenses the managers incur in connection with training.

for up to two store managers.

Advertising and Public Relations

Franchisors are quite concerned with the manner in which its products are presented to the public, and franchise agreements typically reflect that concern. For example, Krispy Kreme's Franchise Agreement requires each new store to hold a "Grand Opening," which "will utilize the public relations and advertising programs and media and advertising materials we have developed or approved." The company provides a "grand opening public relations and marketing manual" that describes the program. In addition, Krispy Kreme requires each of its franchisees to spend not less than 2 percent of gross sales on advertising. In the franchise agreement, Krispy Kreme reserves the right to establish a public relations and advertising fund, requiring franchisees to contribute up to 1 percent of gross sales. The company currently operates such a fund for area developers, but not for associates.

Must have a grand opening

Monitoring

Franchisors typically have the right to inspect franchise outlets. Krispy Kreme's franchising agreement provides:

> To determine whether you and the Store are complying with this Agreement and all System Standards, we and our designated agents have the right at any time during your regular business hours, and without prior notice to you, to:
>
> (1) inspect the Store;
> (2) observe, photograph, and videotape the operations of the Store for such consecutive or intermittent periods as we deem necessary;
> (3) remove samples of any Products, materials, or supplies for testing and analysis;
> (4) interview personnel and customers of the Store; and
> (5) inspect and copy any books, records, and documents relating to your operation of the Store.
>
> You agree to cooperate with us fully in connection with any such inspections, observations, photographing, videotaping, product removal and interviews. You agree to present to your customers such evaluation forms that we periodically prescribe and to participate and/or request your customers to participate in any surveys performed by us or on our behalf.

In this digital age, most monitoring can be accomplished more easily electronically. Krispy Kreme requires each of its franchisees to establish a computer system and to allow the company to access sales information. In addition, each franchisee is required to furnish weekly, monthly, quarterly, and annual reports to Krispy Kreme. Finally, the company explicitly provides for a right to audit each franchisee's books.

Term and Termination

Most franchises are granted for multi-year terms, usually between five and 20 years. The standard term of a Krispy Kreme franchise is 15 years. Long terms encourage franchisees to make relationship-specific investments.

All franchise agreements (including Kripy Kreme's) allow the franchisor to terminate the franchise relationship upon a material breach by the franchisee. Franchise agreements are not terminable at will, but most provide ample possibilities for franchisor termination. The Krispy Kreme franchise agreement, for example, lists 16 potential grounds for termination.

The franchisee's right to terminate is often not specified in the franchise agreement, but the primary penalty for premature franchisee termination is simply loss of the amounts already invested. Under the Krispy Kreme franchise agreement, a franchisee who terminates "without cause" (i.e., absent a material breach of the agreement by the franchisor) is subject to the following covenant not to compete:

> [F]or a period of two (2) years commencing on the effective date of termination, neither you nor any of your owners will have any direct or indirect interest (e.g., through a spouse or child) as a disclosed or beneficial owner, investor, partner, director, officer, employee, consultant, representative or agent or in any other capacity in any Competitive Business (as defined in Section 7 above) located or operating on the effective date of termination:
>
> (a) at the Site;
> (b) within twenty-five (25) miles of the Site; or
> (c) within five (5) miles of any other Krispy Kreme Store in operation or under construction on the later of the effective date of the termination or the date on which a person restricted by this Subsection becomes subject to this Subsection.

Some states prohibit covenants not to compete in the franchise context, while others consider their reasonableness.

Relationship

Law reporters are filled with suits claiming that franchisors and franchisees are actually principal and agent. Most franchise agreements contain a provision similar to the following from Krispy Kreme's franchise agreement:

> You and we understand and agree that this Agreement does not create a fiduciary relationship between you and us, that we and you are and will be independent contractors and that nothing in this Agreement is intended to make either you or us a general or special agent, joint venturer, partner or employee of the other for any purpose. You agree to conspicuously identify yourself in all dealings with customers, suppliers, public officials, Store personnel and others as the owner of the Store under a franchise we have granted and to place such notices of independent ownership on such forms, business cards, stationery and advertising and other materials as we require from time to time.

QUESTIONS

(1) Does this last paragraph, entitled "Relationship," resolve the issue of agency between Krispy Kreme, Inc., and its franchisees? If not, what additional factors would you consider in determining the existence (or not) of an agency relationship?

(2) Should your analysis depend on whether the issue arises in a claim between the parties or a claim involving a third party?

(3) With respect to a claim of fiduciary duty between the parties, would your analysis change depending on whether the claim is that Krispy Kreme is a fiduciary for a franchisee or the other way around?

(4) With respect to claims involving third parties, should your analysis depend on whether the issue arises in the context of a tort claim or a contract claim?

(5) Would your answer depend on whether the franchisee is an individual or an area developer?

(6) Would you be more or less likely to find a franchisor liable for the franchisee's action if the claim related to an activity for which the franchisee had been trained by the franchisor?

CHAPTER
2
General Partnerships

General partnerships are plentiful in the United States. Despite the widespread availability of limited liability entities—including corporations, limited liability companies, and limited partnerships—general partnerships are a popular business entity. The primary virtues of general partnerships are simplicity and favorable tax treatment. As will be discussed in more detail below, general partnerships are simple to form and flexible in their organization. In addition, general partnerships are not taxed as separate business entities, unlike corporations.

Like the law of agency, partnership law first developed through common law. Several states codified partnership law in the second half of the nineteenth century, but the primary vehicle of standardization of partnership law in the United States was the Uniform Partnership Act (UPA), which was proposed by the National Conference of Commissioners on Uniform State Laws (NCCUSL) in 1914 and subsequently adopted, with minor amendments, by 49 states (Louisiana excepted).

At the time of the drafting of the UPA, there was much debate about the value of codification. After all, the United States was built on the tradition of the common law of England rather than the civil law tradition of the European continent. Nevertheless, the desire for uniformity was strong. Uniformity was not sought for its own sake but for the sake of business efficiency. As noted by William Draper Lewis, one of the principal draftsmen of the UPA, uniformity in partnership law was desirable because "a considerable proportion of existing partnerships do business in more than one state." William Draper Lewis, *The Desirability of Expressing the Law of Partnership in Statutory Form*, 60 U. Pa. L. Rev. 93, 95 (1911). Lewis contended that conflicts among state partnership laws induced confusion among partners and third parties.

Even more important than uniformity to Lewis, however, was the clarifying effect of a uniform partnership statute. He attributed the existing conflicts among states to "a confusion, and to what we may call a haziness, in respect to fundamental legal conceptions." *Id.* at 96. Lewis hoped the UPA would shed light on those fundamental concepts, thus revealing his view of the value of codification.

The most fundamental concept is the nature of the partnership: are partnerships treated as entities separate from the individual partners or merely as aggregations of individuals, with the partnership having no separate legal status? The answer to this question has profound implications for almost all legal rules that govern partnerships. Under the common law, partnerships usually were treated as aggregates. Nevertheless, courts often employed the entity theory. This equivocation caused Professor Scott Rowley, in his treatise on partnerships, to remark, "There is no other relation known to law which, in its nature, is so complicated as is partnership." Scott Rowley, *Rowley on Partnership* 15 (2d ed. 1960). Frustration over the crazy quilt of rules produced by the common law moved Judge Learned Hand to write in support of universal recognition of the entity theory:

> The whole subject of partnership has undoubtedly always been exceedingly confused, simply because our law has failed to recognize that partners are not merely joint debtors. It could be straightened out into great simplicity, and in accordance with business usages and business understanding, if the entity of the firm, through a fiction, were consistently recognized and enforced. Like the concept of a corporation, it is for many purposes a device of the utmost value in clarifying ideas and in making easy the solution of legal relations.

In re Samuels & Lesser, 207 Fed. 195, 198 (S.D.N.Y. 1913).

Although the drafters of the UPA claimed to embrace the aggregate theory of partnership, the UPA is schizophrenic on the issue of partnership personality. Some provisions suggest that partnerships have a separate legal existence (for example, UPA §9 provides that each partner is considered an agent of the partnership, not of the other partners) while other sections suggest that a partnership is merely an aggregation of partners (for example, UPA §15 imposes liability on partners individually for obligations of the partnership). This confusion within the UPA is partially explained by its drafting history. The initial drafting committee was charged with drafting a statute following the entity approach, and the first drafts of the UPA were prepared by Dean James Barr Ames of Harvard Law School, an enthusiastic advocate of the entity approach. When Ames died in 1910, he was replaced by Dean William Draper Lewis of the University of Pennsylvania Law School, who believed in an aggregate approach to partnership. Under Lewis's guidance, the drafting committee changed some provisions in the early drafts to reflect an aggregate approach, thus creating the mix of entity and aggregate provisions.

The utility of the entity theory, so obvious today, was not so obvious to the drafters of the UPA, and vigorous debates surrounded the issue. Recounting a meeting of the UPA drafting committee and commentators, Lewis explained that three reasons persuaded the group to unanimously recommend a statute based on the aggregate theory: (1) existing common law was based on the aggregate theory; (2) the aggregate theory better reflected the expectations of third persons dealing with the partnership (creditors expected to hold partners directly liable for partnership obligations); and (3) the draft before the committee had overcome the most serious objections to the aggregate theory (primarily those relating to ownership of partnership property). William Draper Lewis, *The Uniform Partnership Act—A Reply to Mr. Crane's Criticism*, 29 Harv. L. Rev. 158, 172-173 (1915). Interestingly, Lewis also noted: "[T]hose with the largest practical experience present were opposed to regarding the partnership as a 'legal person' because of the effect of the theory in lessening the partner's sense of moral responsibility for partnership acts." *Id.* at 173.

Although the UPA is still immensely important to partnership law in the United States, discontent with its provisions—largely the result of the incoherence of the aggregate view of the partnership — prompted Georgia and California to adopt substantial amendments to their versions of the UPA in the 1980s. In 1986 the American Bar Association (ABA) recommended changes to the UPA. Finally, in 1987 the NCCUSL created a drafting committee to draft a revision of the UPA. After years of work, the committee produced a "final" version of the new act in 1991. Following ABA objections, the committee produced several subsequent revisions to the act. The latest version of the Revised Uniform Partnership Act (RUPA) is dated 1994, but it contains amendments adopted in 1996 and 1997. So far about two/thirds of the states have adopted RUPA.

[margin: (RUPA) The Revised Uniform Partnership Act dated 1994, adopted two years later; about 2/3 of states have adopted it]

The committee that drafted RUPA did not begin with a mandate to treat the partnership as an entity or an aggregate. Over the course of drafting, however, the committee settled on the entity theory of partnership because it "provides simpler rules and is consistent with RUPA's attempt to give partnerships greater stability." As a result of this recognition, the committee added RUPA §201 to clarify that a "partnership is an entity distinct from its partners." Donald J. Weidner & John W. Larson, *The Revised Uniform Partnership Act: The Reporters' Overview*, 49 Bus. Law. 1, 3 (1993).

[margin: §201 clarifies that a partnership is an entity distinct from its partners.]

RUPA makes many important changes to the UPA, most of which can be traced to RUPA's commitment to the entity theory throughout. RUPA makes the following important changes, some of which will be explored in more detail in later sections of the book: (1) RUPA §203 makes partnership property the property of the entity, not of the individual partners. (2) RUPA does away with the UPA rule that the departure of a partner causes a dissolution of the partnership. This rule reflected the concept that every aggregation of partners is unique and any change causes a new partnership to be formed. The UPA did not account for the fact that some departures trigger the winding up of the partnership business and some simply trigger a buyout of the departing partner. RUPA has different rules for each of these situations, thus tracking business practice more closely. (3) RUPA provides for the merger or conversion of partnerships into limited partnerships. Mergers or conversions of partnership would be unthinkable under UPA because partnerships were not an entity.

[margin: from UPA to RUPA:]

A. FORMATION

The rules contained in the uniform partnership acts apply only to relationships that meet the definition of "partnership." UPA §6(1) and RUPA §202(a) both define "partnership" as an "association of two or more persons to carry on as co-owners a business for profit." Despite several centuries of judicial consideration — including over 80 years of experience with the foregoing statutory definition — partnership formation still poses some of the most challenging issues in partnership law. This is largely attributable to the fact that no formalities are required to form a partnership. Although people may create a partnership through formal agreement, the most difficult formation questions arise in the context of inadvertent partnerships. Courts often find that a

[margin: b/c no formalities needed to form a partnership.]

partnership has been <u>created</u> in the absence of a <u>written</u> agreement, con-scious intent to form a partnership, <u>or knowledge that a partnership has been</u> formed.

The UPA definition of "partnership" comports with prior common law definitions in all essential respects. Nevertheless, <u>no general definition of</u> <u>"partnership" can adequately explain all of the cases.</u> This difficulty is best understood by reflecting on the fact that <u>partnership formation issues are raised</u> <u>almost exclusively in cases where one person is attempting to avoid liability to</u> <u>another</u>—either to a purported partner or to a third party—where such lia-bility is founded on the existence of a partnership. Partnership liability rules will be examined in more detail in Section 2.D. For the present, it is sufficient to understand two general principles: (1) <u>one partner may be bound to third</u> <u>parties by the act of another partner;</u> and (2) <u>partners are personally liable</u> <u>for obligations of the partnership.</u> As a result of these principles, partnership formation issues take on great importance. The <u>finding of a partnership can</u> <u>impose personal liability on an individual who did not act or even know of the</u> action of another partner. Against this backdrop, <u>courts tend to strive for fair-</u> ness rather than doctrinal purity. The <u>definition of "partnership,"</u> therefore, is necessarily flexible.

Courts often state that the existence of a partnership ^{often} depends on whether <u>the partners had the requisite intent.</u> But what must the parties have intended? Consider Bass v. Bass, 814 S.W.2d 38, 41 (Tenn. 1991):

> [T]he existence of a partnership depends upon the intention of the parties, and the controlling intention in this regard is that ascertainable from the acts of the parties. Although a <u>contract of partnership, either express or implied, is</u> essential to the creation of partnership status, <u>it is not essential that the par-</u> <u>ties actually intend to become partners.</u> The <u>existence of a partnership is not</u> a <u>question of the parties' undisclosed intention</u> or even <u>the terminology they</u> use to describe their relationship, nor is it necessary that the parties have an understanding of the legal effect of their acts. <u>It is the intent to do the things</u> which constitute a partnership that determines whether individuals are part-ners, regardless if it is their purpose to create or avoid the relationship. Stated another way, <u>the existence of a partnership may be implied from the circum-</u> <u>stances where it appears that the individuals involved have entered into a business</u> <u>relationship for profit,</u> combining their <u>property,</u> <u>labor,</u> <u>skill,</u> <u>experience,</u> or money.

Courts are not bound by statements of parties disavowing an intention to enter into a partnership. Nevertheless, <u>expressions of intent by the parties are</u> probably highly persuasive. <u>Courts are most likely to override the expressed</u> <u>intentions of the parties where the rights of third parties are involved.</u>

As in other areas of the law, intent is difficult to discern from a distance. The <u>informality of most partnerships ensures that intent is rarely expressed in</u> <u>written form.</u> As a result, <u>most courts focus on a few indicia of partnership</u> in an attempt to ascertain whether the parties intended to enter into a partnership. The most important of these <u>indicia of partnership is whether a purported</u> partner receives a <u>share of the profits of the business.</u> UPA §7(4) states that "receipt by a person of a <u>share of profits of a business is prima facie evidence</u>

that he is a partner in the business." *Cf.* RUPA §202(c)(3) (receipt of profits raises a presumption of partnership).

This test originated in the well-known English case, Waugh v. Carver, 2 H. Bl. 235, 126 Eng. Rep. 525 (C.P.D., Nov. 23, 1793), in which Erasmus Carver and William Carver agreed with Archibald Giesler to cooperate in generating business. Under the agreement, each side would "take a moiety" — that is, one half — of the proceeds, but each side would bear its own losses. As to liability, the agreement explicitly stated that neither side would be liable for the acts of the other. The court characterized the moiety as "profit" and held that the parties had formed a partnership because they agreed to share profits. The rationale for this holding was "the principle that by taking a part of the profits, he takes from the creditors a part of that fund which is the proper security to them for the payment of their debts."

Waugh does not admit any possible exceptions to the general rule that sharing of profits results in the formation of a partnership vis-à-vis third parties. Nevertheless, courts readily recognized an exception for employees who are paid for their services out of the profits of the firm. Often, distinguishing between employees and partners is easier said than done. Similarly, if creditors receive payments from the profits of the firm, courts will refrain from finding that a partnership has been formed. The analysis in these cases is highly textured. Given that the sharing of profits is present, courts examine other aspects of the relationship closely.

The following case explores some of the difficult questions that surround partnership formation. As you consider the claim in *Holmes*, contemplate the difference (if any) between forming a partnership and preparing to incorporate a business. Moreover, try to identify why it matters whether a partnership has been formed.

HOLMES v. LERNER

Court of Appeal, First District, Division 1, California
74 Cal. App. 4th 442
August 20, 1999 (as modified Sept. 7, 1999)

MARCHIANO, J.

This case involves an oral partnership agreement to start a cosmetics company known as "Urban Decay." Patricia Holmes prevailed on her claim that Sandra Kruger Lerner breached her partnership agreement and that David Soward interfered with the Holmes-Lerner contract, resulting in Holmes's ouster from the business. Lerner and Soward appeal from the judgment finding them liable to Holmes for compensatory and punitive damages of over $1 million. . . .

We affirm the judgment against Lerner, primarily because we determine that an express agreement to divide profits is not a prerequisite to prove the existence of a partnership. We also determine that the oral partnership agreement between Lerner and Holmes was sufficiently definite to allow enforcement . . .

BACKGROUND . . .

Lerner extremely rich woman, friend of Holmes her horse trainer.

Sandra Lerner is a successful entrepreneur and an experienced business person. She and her husband were the original founders of Cisco Systems. When she sold her interest in that company, she received a substantial amount of money, which she invested, in part, in a venture capital limited partnership called "& Capital Partners." By the time of trial in this matter, Lerner was extremely wealthy. Patricia Holmes met Lerner in late 1993, when Lerner visited Holmes's horse training facility to arrange for training and boarding of two horses that Lerner was importing from England. Holmes and Lerner became friends, and after an initial six-month training contract expired, Holmes continued to train Lerner's horses without a contract and without cost.

In 1995, Lerner and Holmes traveled to England to a horse show and to make arrangements to ship the horses that Lerner had purchased. On this trip, Lerner decided that she wanted to celebrate her 40th birthday by going pub crawling in Dublin. Lerner was wearing what Holmes termed " alternative clothes" and black nail polish, and encouraged Holmes to do the same.[1] Holmes, however, did not like black nail polish, and was unable to find a suitable color in the English stores. At Lerner's mansion outside of London, Lerner gave Holmes a manicuring kit, telling her to see if she could find a color she would wear. Holmes looked through the kit, tried different colors, and eventually developed her own color by layering a raspberry color over black nail polish. This produced a purple color that Holmes liked. Holmes showed the new color to Lerner, who also liked it.

Holmes developed her own color by layering various nail polish colors.

On July 31, 1995, the two women returned from England and stayed at Lerner's West Hollywood condominium while they waited for the horses to clear quarantine. While sitting at the kitchen table, they discussed nail polish, and colors. Len Bosack, Lerner's husband, was in and out of the room during the conversations. For approximately an hour and a half, Lerner and Holmes worked with the colors in a nail kit to try to recreate the purple color Holmes had made in England so they could have the color in a liquid form, rather than layering two colors. Lerner made a different shade of purple, and Holmes commented that it looked just like a bruise. Holmes then said that she wanted to call the purple color she had made "Plague." Holmes had been reading about 16th-century England, and how people with the plague developed purple sores, and thought the color looked like the plague sores.[2] Lerner and Holmes discussed the fact that the names they were creating had an urban theme, and tried to think of other names to fit the theme. Starting with "Bruise" and "Plague," they also discussed the names "Mildew," "Smog," "Uzi," and "Oil Slick." Len Bosack walked into the kitchen at that point, heard the conversation about the urban theme, and said "What about decay?" The two women liked the idea, and decided that "Urban Decay" was a good name for their concept.[3]

Holmes later named the color.

1. There were references throughout the trial to Lerner's "alternative" look and to "alternative" culture. Lerner, who referred to herself as an "edgy cosmetics queen," described "alternative culture" as "not really mainstream," "edgy," and "fashion forward." As an example, she noted her own purple hair. She defined "edgy" as not trying to be cute, and being unconventional.

2. Plague is described as "rich violet with a blue sheen."

3. At the trial, Lerner testified that she had an idea prior to July of 1995 that there might be a market for unusual nail colors, but was missing a "unifying theme" to identify the concept.

Lerner said to Holmes: "This seems like a good [thing], it's something that we both like, and isn't out there. Do you think we should start a company?" Holmes responded: "Yes, I think it's a great idea." Lerner told Holmes that they would have to do market research, determine how to have the polishes produced, and that there were many things they would have to do. Lerner said: "We will hire people to work for us. We will do everything we can to get the company going, and then we'll be creative, and other people will do the work, so we'll have time to continue riding the horses." Holmes agreed that they would do those things. They did not separate out which tasks each of them would do, but planned to do it all together.

[handwritten margin note: Lerner called Soward, a general partner rather VC firm, where she invested.]

Lerner went to the telephone and called David Soward, the general partner of & Capital, and her business consultant. Holmes heard her say "Please check Urban, for the name, Urban Decay, to see if it's available and if it is, get it for us." Holmes knew that Lerner did not joke about business, and was certain, from the tone of her voice, that Lerner was serious about the new business. The telephone call to secure the trademark for Urban Decay confirmed in Holmes's mind that they were forming a business based on the concepts they had originated in England and at the kitchen table that day. Holmes knew that she would be taking the risk of sharing in losses as well as potential success, but the two friends did not discuss the details at that time. Lerner's housekeeper heard Lerner tell Holmes: "It's going to be our baby, and we're going to work on it together." After Holmes left, the housekeeper asked what gave Lerner the idea to go into the cosmetics business, since her background was computers. Lerner replied: "It was all Pat's idea over in England, but I've got the money to make it work." Lerner told her housekeeper that she hoped to sell Urban Decay to Estee Lauder for $50 million.

*[handwritten margin notes: > * ; Lerner told her housekeeper: > *]*

Although neither of the two women had any experience in the cosmetics business, they began work on their idea immediately. Holmes and Lerner did market research by going to stores, talking with people about nail polish, seeing what nail polishes were available, and buying samples to bring back to discuss with each other. They met frequently in August and September at Lerner's home, and experimented with nail colors. They took pictures of various color mixing sessions. In early August, they met with a graphic artist, Andrea Kelly, and discussed putting together a logo and future advertising work for Urban Decay.

Prior to the first scheduled August meeting, Holmes told Lerner she was concerned about financing the venture. Lerner told her not to worry about it because Lerner thought they could convince Soward that the nail polish business would be a good investment. She told Holmes that Soward took care of Lerner's investment money. Holmes and Lerner discussed their plans for the company, and agreed that they would attempt to build it up and then sell it. Lerner and Holmes discussed the need to visit chemical companies and hire people to handle the daily operations of the company. However, the creative aspect, ideas, inspiration, and impetus for the company came from Holmes and Lerner.

Lerner, Holmes, Soward, and Kelly attended the first scheduled meeting. The participants in these meetings referred to them as "board meetings," even though there was no formal organizational structure, and technically, no board. They discussed financing, and Soward reluctantly agreed to commit $500,000 towards the project. Urban Decay was financed entirely by & Capital, the

*[handwritten margin notes: Early mtgs called board mtgs. > *]*

venture capital partnership composed of Soward as general partner, and Lerner and her husband as the only limited partners. Neither Lerner nor Holmes invested any of their individual funds.

Lerner and Soward went to Kirker Chemical Company later in August of 1995 and learned about mixing and manufacturing nail polish colors. Lerner discouraged Holmes from accompanying them. Although Lerner returned to Kirker, she never took Holmes with her. At the second board meeting, in late August, Soward introduced Wendy Zomnir, a friend of Soward's former fiance, as an advertising and marketing specialist. After Zomnir and Kelley left the meeting, Holmes, Lerner and Soward discussed her presentation. Holmes was enthusiastic about Zomnir and they decided to hire her. At the conclusion of the September board meeting, after Holmes had left, Lerner and Soward secretly made Zomnir an offer of employment, which included a percentage ownership interest in Urban Decay. It wasn't until a couple of meetings later, when Lerner or Soward referred to Zomnir as the "Chief Operating Officer" of Urban Decay, that Holmes learned of the terms of the offer.

In early October, after Holmes learned of the secret offer to Zomnir, she asked Lerner to define her role at Urban Decay. Lerner responded: "Your role is anything you want it to be." When Holmes asked to discuss the issue in more detail, Lerner turned and walked away. Holmes believed that Lerner was nervous about an upcoming photo session, and decided to discuss it with Lerner at a later date. At their regular board meetings, Holmes participated with Soward, Lerner, Zomnir, Kelly and another person in discussing new colors, and deciding which ones they wanted to sell, and which names would be used.

In September of 1995, Soward signed an application for trademark registration as president of Urban Decay. In December of 1995, Urban Decay was incorporated. Holmes asked for a copy of the articles of incorporation, but was given only two pages showing the name and address of the company. On December 31, Holmes sent a fax to Lerner stating that it had been difficult to discuss her position in Urban Decay with Lerner. Holmes asked Lerner: "What are my responsibilities and obligations, and what are my rights or entitlements?" Holmes also asked: "What are my current and potential liabilities and assets?" She requested that Lerner provide the information in writing. At this point, Holmes wanted to memorialize the agreement she and Lerner had made on July 31.

Soward intercepted the fax and called Holmes, asking: "What's going on?" Holmes explained that she wanted a written agreement, and Soward apologized, telling her that Lerner had asked him to get "something . . . in writing" to Holmes. Soward told Holmes that no one in the company had a written statement of their percentage interest in the company yet. Soward asked: "What do you want, one percent, two percent?" When Holmes did not respond, he told her that 5 percent was high for an idea. Holmes told him: "I'm not selling an idea. I'm a founder of this company." Soward exclaimed: "Surely you don't think you have fifty percent of this company?" Holmes told him that it was a matter between herself and Lerner, and that Soward should speak to Lerner. Soward agreed to talk to Lerner.

On January 11, 1996, Lerner and Holmes met at a coffee shop to discuss the fax. Holmes explained that she wanted "something in writing" and an explanation of her interest and position in the company. Lerner responded that a start up business is "like a freight train . . . you can either run and catch up, and get on, and take a piece of this company and make it your own, or get out of the way." As a result of this conversation, Holmes decided to double her efforts on behalf of Urban Decay. Because she was most comfortable working at the warehouse, she focused on that aspect of the business.[4] Holmes was reimbursed for mileage, but received no pay for her work.

During January and February, Urban Decay was launching its new nail polish product. Publicity included press releases, brochures, and newspaper interviews with Lerner. An early press release stated: "The idea for Urban Decay was born after Lerner and her horse trainer, Pat Holmes, were sitting around in the English countryside." Lerner approved the press release. In February of 1996, an article was printed in the San Francisco Examiner containing the following quotes from Lerner. "Since we couldn't find good nail polish, in cool colors there must be a business opportunity here. Pat had the original idea. Urban Decay was my spin." The Examiner reporter testified at trial that the quote attributed to Lerner was accurate. Lerner was also interviewed in April by CNN. In that interview she told the story of herself and Holmes looking for unusual colors, mixing their own colors at the kitchen table, and that "we came up with the colors, and it just sort of suggested the urban thing."[5]

Lerner had always notified Holmes whenever there was a board meeting, and she sent Holmes an agenda for the February 20, 1996, meeting. Lerner also sent a memo stating that she thought they should have an "operations meeting" with the warehouse supervisor first. Lerner's memo continued: "and then have a regular board meeting, including [Zomnir], me, David, and Pat, and no one else." Holmes understood that the regular board meeting would be for the purpose of discussing general Urban Decay business. At the operations meeting, Holmes made a presentation regarding the warehouse operations. The financial report showed $205,000 in revenues and $431,000 in expenses. The "directors" thought this early sales figure was "terrific." Soward handed out an organizational chart, which showed Lerner, with the title "CEO" at the top, Soward, as "President" beneath her, and Zomnir, as "COO" beneath Soward. Holmes asked "Where am I?" Lerner responded by pointing to the top of the chart and telling Holmes that she was a director, and was at the top of the chart, above all the other names.

In March of 1996, Holmes received a document from Soward offering her a one percent ownership interest in Urban Decay. Soward explained that Urban Decay had been formed as a limited liability company, which was owned by its members. For the first time, Holmes realized that Lerner and Soward had produced an organizational document that did not include her, and she was

---

4. Holmes testified that her work at the warehouse included responding to requests for brochures, developing a system for handling increased telephone inquiries, and negotiating a contract with a skills center to assist with the mail order business. She had authority to hire and fire employees and to sign checks on the Urban Decay account. Only Holmes, Soward, Lerner, Zomnir and the warehouse manager were authorized to sign on the account. Only the manager's authority was limited to $1,500. Holmes was spending four to five days a week at the warehouse. Urban Decay accountant Sharon Land testified that Holmes "contributed a great deal" to Urban Decay, and directed the retail business. Soward, Lerner and Zomnir seldom came to the office. Soward told Land that Holmes was on the board of directors.

5. When asked at trial why she used the word "we," Lerner responded that she was stressed. Lerner testified that almost every statement she made in the CNN interview was false, and a result of stress.

now being asked to become a minor partner. When she studied the document, she discovered that it referred to an exhibit A, which was purported to show the distribution of ownership interests in Urban Decay. Soward had given Zomnir a copy of exhibit A when he offered her an ownership interest in Urban Decay. However, when Holmes asked Soward for a copy of exhibit A, he told her it did not exist.[10] By this time, Holmes was planning to consult an attorney about the document.

Despite the deterioration of her friendship with Lerner, and her strained relationship with Soward, Holmes continued to attend the scheduled board meetings, hoping that her differences with Lerner could be resolved. She also continued to work at the warehouse on various administrative projects and on direct mail order sales. As late as the April board meeting, Holmes was still actively engaged in Urban Decay business. She made a presentation on a direct mail project she had been asked to undertake. As a result of Holmes's attendance at a sales presentation when she referred to herself as a cofounder of Urban Decay, Lerner instructed Zomnir to draft a dress code and an official history of Urban Decay. Lerner told Zomnir that it was a "real error in judgment" to allow Holmes to attend the sales presentation because she did not project the appropriate image. The official history, proposed in the memo, omitted any reference to Holmes. Finally, matters deteriorated to the point that Soward told Holmes not to attend the July board meeting because she was no longer welcome at Urban Decay.

On August 27, 1996, Holmes filed a complaint against Lerner and Soward, alleging 10 causes of action, including breach of an oral contract, intentional interference with contractual relations, fraud, breach of fiduciary duty, and constructive fraud. Holmes eventually dismissed some of her claims and the court dismissed others, sending the case to the jury on the causes of action noted above. At the trial, cosmetic industry expert Gabriella Zuckerman testified that Urban Decay was not just a fad. In her opinion, Urban Decay had discovered and capitalized on a trend that was just beginning. She reviewed projected sales figures of $19.9 million in 1997, going up to $52 million in 2003, and found them definitely obtainable. Arthur Clark, Holmes's expert at valuing start-up businesses, valued Urban Decay under different risk scenarios. In Clark's opinion, the value of Urban Decay to a potential buyer was between $4,672,000 and $6,270,000. Lerner's expert, who had never valued a cosmetics company, testified that Urban Decay had $2.7 million in sales in 1996. He estimated the value of Urban Decay as approximately $2 million, but concluded that it was not marketable.

Lerner and Soward claimed that Holmes was never a director, officer, or even an employee of Urban Decay. According to Lerner, she was just being nice to Holmes by letting her be present during Urban Decay business. Lerner denied Holmes had any role in creating the colors, names, or concepts for Urban Decay. When Holmes asked Lerner about her assets and liabilities in Urban Decay, Lerner thought she was asking for a job. She explained her statements

---

10. Holmes was never given exhibit A, and did not see it until trial. It showed & Capital Partners, L.P. with a 92 percent interest, having contributed $489,900. It also showed Lerner and her husband with contributions of $5,050 each, and 1 percent apiece. Zomnir's contribution was listed as $5,050, but she had a 5 percent interest. None of the individuals actually paid in the listed contributions.

to the press regarding Urban Decay being Holmes's idea as misquotes or the product of her stress.

The jury found in favor of Holmes on every cause of action. The jury assessed $480,000 in damages against Lerner, and $320,000 against Soward. Following presentation of evidence as to net worth, the jury awarded punitive damages of $500,000 against Lerner and $130,000 against Soward. In the judgment, the court declined to add the two amounts together, but stated that the verdict of $320,000 was against Lerner and Soward, jointly and severally, and that the additional $160,000 verdict was against Lerner individually. Lerner and Soward moved for a judgment notwithstanding the verdict, which was denied on December 16, 1997. They appealed from the judgment and the order denying their postverdict motion. . . .

DISCUSSION

Lerner and Soward argue that there was no partnership agreement as a matter of law. . . .

I. THERE WAS NO ERROR IN THE DETERMINATION THAT A
PARTNERSHIP WAS FORMED

Holmes testified that she and Lerner did not discuss sharing profits of the business during the July 31, "kitchen table" conversation. Throughout the case, Lerner and Soward have contended that without an agreement to share profits, there can be no partnership. Lerner and Soward begin their argument on appeal by quoting a statement from Westcott v. Gilman (1915) [150 P. 777], that profit sharing is "an essential element of every partnership. . . ." They argue that nothing has changed since the "ancient truth" regarding profit sharing was expressed in *Westcott*. However, an important element supporting the *Westcott* decision has changed, because *Westcott* relied on the language of former section 2395 of the Civil Code. That statutory predecessor of the Uniform Partnership Act defined a partnership as: " . . . the association of two or more persons, for the purpose of carrying on business together, and dividing its profits between them." Civil Code former section 2395 was repealed and replaced with the UPA in 1949.

The applicable version of the UPA omitted the language regarding division of profits and defined a partnership as: "an association of two or more persons to carry on as co-owners a business for profit." When the Legislature enacts a new statute, replacing an existing one, and omits express language, it indicates an intent to change the original act. We can only conclude that the omission of the language regarding dividing profits from the definition of a partnership was an intentional change in the law.[13] The UPA relocated the provision regarding

13. The significance of the change in the definition of a partnership is noted in the article by Professor Wright, California Partnership Law and the Uniform Partnership Act (1921) 9 Cal. L. Rev. 117, 127-128, criticizing the Civil Code provision because it "emphasizes the division of profits unduly," and noting that deletion of the " 'dividing the profit between them' " language of the Civil Code would theoretically allow a partnership to be formed in which all profits went to one partner, or all profits were reinvested.

profits to former section 15007, subdivision (4), which provided that in determining whether a partnership exists, "[t]he receipt by a person of a share of the profits of a business is prima facie evidence that he is a partner. . . ." This relocation of the element of sharing the profits indicates that the Legislature intends profit sharing to be evidence of a partnership, rather than a required element of the definition of a partnership. The presence or absence of any of the various elements set forth in former section 15007, including sharing of profits and losses, is not necessarily dispositive. As explained in Cochran v. Board of Supervisors (1978) [149 Cal. Rptr. 304], the rules to establish the existence of a partnership in [former section] 15007 should be viewed in the light of the crucial factor of the intent of the parties revealed in the terms of their agreement, conduct, and the surrounding circumstances when determining whether a partnership exists.

The UPA provides for the situation in which the partners have not expressly stated an agreement regarding sharing of profits. Former section 15018 provided in relevant part: "The rights and duties of the partners in relation to the partnership shall be determined, subject to any agreement between them, by the following rules: (a) Each partner shall . . . share equally in the profits and surplus remaining after all liabilities, including those to partners, are satisfied." This provision states, subject to an agreement between the parties, partners "shall" share equally in the profits. Lerner and Soward argue that using former section 15018 to supply a missing term regarding profit sharing ignores the provision of former section 15007, subdivision (2). That section, headed "rules for determining existence of partnership," provided that mere joint ownership of common property "does not of itself establish a partnership, whether such co-owners do or do not share any profits made by the use of the property." Lerner and Soward are mistaken. The definition in former section 15006 provides that the association with the intent to carry on a business for profit is the essential requirement for a partnership. Following that definition does not transform mere joint ownership into the essence of a partnership. . . .

The trial court in this case refused to add additional elements to the statutory definition and properly instructed the jury in the language of former section 15006. We agree with the trial court's interpretation of the law. The actual sharing of profits (with exceptions which do not apply here) is prima facie evidence, which is to be considered, in light of any other evidence, when determining if a partnership exists. In this case, there were no profits to share at the time Holmes was expelled from the business, so the evidentiary provision . . . is not applicable. According to former section 15006, parties who expressly agree to associate as co-owners with the intent to carry on a business for profit, have established a partnership. Once the elements of that definition are established, other provisions of the UPA and the conduct of the parties supply the details of the agreement. Certainly implicit in the Holmes-Lerner agreement to operate Urban Decay together was an understanding to share in profits and losses as any business owners would. The evidence supported the jury's implicit finding that Holmes birthed an idea which was incubated jointly by Lerner and Holmes, from which they intended to profit once it was fully matured in their company.

II. THE AGREEMENT WAS SUFFICIENTLY DEFINITE

Lerner and Soward argue that the agreement between Lerner and Holmes was too indefinite to be enforced. . . .

The agreement between Holmes and Lerner was to take Holmes's idea and reduce it to concrete form. They decided to do it together, to form a company, to hire employees, and to engage in the entire process together. The agreement here, as presented to the jury, was that Holmes and Lerner would start a cosmetics company based on the unusual colors developed by Holmes, identified by the Urban theme and the exotic names. The agreement is evidenced by Lerner's statements: "We will do . . . everything," "[i]t's going to be our baby, and we're going to work on it together." Their agreement is reflected in Lerner's words: "We will hire people to work for us." "We will do everything we can to get the company going, and then we'll be creative, and other people will do the work, so we'll have time to continue riding the horses." The additional terms were filled in as the two women immediately began work on the multitude of details necessary to bring their idea to fruition. The fact that Holmes worked for almost a year, without expectation of pay, is further confirmation of the agreement. Lerner and Soward never objected to her work, her participation in board meetings and decisionmaking, or her exercise of authority over the retail warehouse operation. Even as late as the trial in this matter, when Lerner was claiming that everything Holmes said was a lie, Lerner admitted: "It was not only my intention to give Pat every opportunity to be a part of this, but I had hoped that she would." . . . Holmes was not seeking specific enforcement of a single vague term of the agreement. She was frozen out of the business altogether, and her agreement with Lerner was completely renounced. The agreement that was made and the subsequent acts of the parties supply sufficient certainty to determine the existence of a breach and a remedy. . . .

[T]he judgment and postjudgment order are affirmed. . . .

PROBLEM 2-1

When Hugh Brogan went to the T99 Telecom Fair in October 1999, he could not have envisioned the circuitous route that his company would travel over the ensuing three years. Brogan had founded Sendo Limited in Birmingham, England, just two months earlier, and suddenly he found himself in negotiations with Microsoft Corporation, which wanted to collaborate with Sendo on the development of a so-called "Smartphone" — that is, a telephone that could also access the Internet and serve as a personal digital assistant. Sendo was already developing a product called the Z100, and Microsoft was developing a software product with the code name "Stinger."[1]

After a year of negotiation, the parties entered into a strategic development and marketing agreement (SDMA) and various license agreements in

---

1. For more details on the Microsoft-Sendo relationship, see Andy Reinhardt & Jay Greene, *Death of a Dream*, Bus. Wk. 22 (Feb. 10, 2003).

October 2000. In a complaint filed after their relationship deteriorated, Sendo described the primary terms of the SDMA:

> The SDMA provided, in part, that: (1) the Sendo Z100 Smartphone would be a market leading product; (2) Microsoft would prioritize the Sendo Z100 Smartphone; (3) Microsoft would pay an amount of money plus a contribution to expenses towards development of the Z100; and (4) Microsoft would receive a substantial percentage share of the Net Revenue from sales of the Z100 as it had contributed to the development cost.[1]

In addition, Microsoft promised a future investment in Sendo. Microsoft made that investment of $12 million in May 2001. In exchange, Microsoft received the right to appoint a representative to Sendo's board of directors, which it did in the person of Marc Brown. Brown was not only a director of Sendo; he was head of Microsoft's Corporate Development and Strategy Group, which monitored the progress of the relationship under the SDMA. During the ensuing months, development of the Z100 lagged. According to Sendo's complaint, the delays were all part of Microsoft's plan:

> Microsoft's Secret Plan was to plunder the small company of its proprietary information, technical expertise, market knowledge, customers, and prospective customers. Microsoft had been unable to successfully access the wireless market because the major handset manufacturers would not use their software. So instead, . . . Microsoft used Sendo's knowledge and expertise to . . . gain direct entry into the burgeoning next generation phone market and then, after driving Sendo to the brink of bankruptcy, cut it out of the picture.[2]

According to Sendo's complaint, Microsoft's interest in Sendo was part of a "master plan" to dominate the market for mobile handsets. According to the complaint, Sendo was attractive to Microsoft for three reasons: (1) Sendo had employees who were experienced in the technology of mobile handsets; (2) Sendo had existing relationships with major companies who would be the major customers for such handsets; and (3) Sendo had experience with the technical requirements imposed by carriers (this was especially important because some of these requirements were not written down). In October 2002, Microsoft announced that it had teamed with High Tech Computer Corp. to produce a unit similar to the Z100 for Orange, a British telecommunications company. Like most new Microsoft offerings, the SPV (which stands for "Sound, Pictures, Video") was riddled with technical bugs, but Orange and Microsoft were working on new versions.

In November 2002, Sendo switched from Microsoft's software to a product made by Symbian Ltd., the other main competitor in this industry.[3] Symbian is a London-based consortium owned by the giants of the electronics industry: Nokia, Motorola, Ericsson, Sony-Ericsson, Samsung, Matsushita, Panasonic, Psion, and Siemens.

---

2. Sendo Complaint ¶16.
3. The Sendo alliance was Microsoft's third failed attempt to enter the mobile handset market. It was the primary investor in Teledesic, the satellite network that officially failed in 2002. Then, in 2001 Microsoft backed out of a joint venture with Qualcomm.

On December 20, 2002, Sendo filed a complaint in the U.S. District Court in Texarkana, Texas,[4] alleging misappropriation of trade secrets, unfair competition, fraud, breach of fiduciary duty, and breach of contract, among other things. Sounds bad. According to Microsoft, it sounds much worse than it is. In an Answer and Counterclaim, filed on February 3, 2003, Microsoft referred to Sendo's account as "fanciful" and claimed that the failure of the Z100 was the result of Sendo's many breaches of the SDMA. Moreover, Microsoft claimed that Sendo misled Microsoft about the true nature of Sendo's finances.

Is there any evidence that would support the conclusion that Sendo and Microsoft formed a general partnership? What is the strongest evidence contrary to that conclusion?

The relationship between Microsoft and Sendo was often referred to as a "partnership" in the trade press. If a third party had entered into transactions with Sendo on the assumption that Microsoft was its partner in a legal sense, would the third party have a claim against Microsoft based on the doctrine of apparent authority?

Sendo's complaint alleges the existence of a "fiduciary relationship":

> A confidential fiduciary relationship existed between Microsoft and Sendo as a result of the parties' business relationship and course of dealing, certain contractual agreements executed by the parties, and placement of Microsoft's employee/representative, Marc Brown, on the Sendo Board of Directors. During the parties' business relationship, Defendants obtained a blueprint of Sendo's mobile telephone manufacturing business, technical knowledge and operator information. Through Marc Brown's position as a Director on the Sendo Board, Defendants also gained knowledge, access and influence over Sendo's finances, and had a duty to disclose information to Sendo. Defendants' fiduciary duties to Sendo were breached. Defendants had a duty to act with fair[ness] and honesty, a duty of full disclosure and to refrain from self-dealing. Defendants used their special relationship with Sendo and Sendo's confidential proprietary information to Defendants' advantage and benefit and to Sendo's detriment.[5]

How does such a relationship differ from a partnership? What sort of evidence should Sendo's lawyers seek to sustain the claim of breach of fiduciary duty?

B. MANAGEMENT

Management issues concern decision making in the ongoing operations of the partnership. In the absence of an agreement to the contrary, all partners have equal rights in the management and conduct of the partnership business. UPA §18(e); RUPA §401(f). If partners disagree about ordinary matters within the scope of the partnership business, the vote of a majority of partners controls. UPA §18(h); RUPA §401(j).

---

4. Sendo's U.S. office is located in Irving, Texas. On February 3, 2003, Microsoft filed a motion to transfer venue to the Western District of Washington, Microsoft's home state.

5. Sendo Complaint ¶71.

The UPA requires the unanimous consent of partners to authorize amendments to the partnership agreement (UPA §18(h)) and to add new partners (UPA §18(g)) and lists certain extraordinary transactions in UPA §9(3) that require the unanimous consent of partners. But the UPA does not have a general provision covering authorization of extraordinary transactions. As a result, most courts have reasoned from the existing provisions that any extraordinary transaction requires the unanimous consent of partners. This unanimity requirement was codified by RUPA §401(j), which addresses "act[s] outside the ordinary course of business of a partnership."

One of the vexing problems in partnership law involves management rights in partnerships with only two partners. In the event of an internal dispute about a matter of partnership business, William Draper Lewis suggested that the UPA as written made the result clear: "A contract made by one of two partners against the protest of the other is not made by a majority. The implication from the section as worded, therefore, is that such a contract, the third person knowing of the protest, would not be a partnership contract." William Draper Lewis, *The Uniform Partnership Act—A Reply to Mr. Crane's Criticism*, 29 Harv. L. Rev. 291, 302 (1911). This view has not always prevailed in the courts. In the well-known case of National Biscuit Company, Inc. v. Stroud, 106 S.E.2d 692 (N.C. 1959), the Supreme Court of North Carolina faced this issue in the context of a partnership that operated a grocery store. One of the two partners (Stroud) decided that he no longer wanted to purchase bread from Nabisco, and he told Nabisco that he would not be personally liable for any future orders. When the other partner (Freeman) subsequently ordered bread, Nabisco delivered. Upon the failure of the partnership to pay for the bread, Nabisco sued Stroud for payment. The court held Stroud personally liable, reasoning:

> Freeman as a general partner with Stroud, with no restrictions on his authority to act within the scope of the partnership business so far as the agreed statement of facts shows, had under the Uniform Partnership Act "equal rights in the management and conduct of the partnership business." Under [UPA §18(h)], Stroud, his co-partner, could not restrict the power and authority of Freeman to buy bread for the partnership as a going concern, for such a purchase was an "ordinary matter connected with the partnership business," for the purpose of its business and within its scope, because in the very nature of things Stroud was not, and could not be, a majority of the partners. Therefore, Freeman's purchases of bread from plaintiff for Stroud's Food Center as a going concern bound the partnership and his co-partner Stroud. . . .

While this case neatly displays the tension between the rules governing management rights and the rules governing authority, cases involving third-party claims against divided two-person partnerships are fairly rare.[1] The following

---

1. The *Nabisco* case is often contrasted with Summers v. Dooley, 481 P.2d 318 (Idaho 1971), in which one partner hired an employee over the objection of another. When the employee attempted to recover wages from the dissenting partner, the court refused to uphold the claim, reasoning as follows:

> A careful reading of the statutory provision indicates that [UPA §18] bestows equal rights in the management and conduct of the partnership business upon all of the partners. The concept of equality between partners with respect to management of business affairs is a central theme and recurs throughout the Uniform Partnership law, which has been enacted in this jurisdiction. Thus the only reasonable interpretation of [UPA §18(h)] is that business

case illustrates a more common problem: one rogue partner acts in a manner that exposes other partners to liability. As you read the case, consider the possible justifications for holding partners responsible for fraudulent behavior that they did not condone. Problem 2-2, following the case, then takes up the issue of partnership management in the context of a large, modern law firm.

FIRST AMERICAN TITLE INSURANCE CO. v. LAWSON

798 A.2d 661
Superior Court of New Jersey, Appellate Division
June 4, 2002

PARRILLO, J.A.D.

Appellant Certain Underwriters at Lloyds, London (Lloyds) brought an action seeking a declaration that the professional liability insurance policy it issued to the law firm of Wheeler, Lawson & Snyder, L.L.P. (law firm) and its individual partners was rescinded or, alternatively, provided no coverage for claims of professional malpractice asserted by two title insurers, First American Title Insurance Company and Lawyers Title Insurance Corporation (collectively, "title insurers") against the law firm and its partners. The trial court denied Lloyds' motion for summary judgment, finding that Lloyds was not entitled, as a matter of law, to rescind its professional liability policy *ab initio* based upon material misrepresentations in the insurance application; that Lloyds' policy had not been effectively cancelled; and that Lloyds' policy is a policy of primary insurance and does not exclude coverage for claims of negligence against the law firm, as a separate legal entity, and one of its partners, Snyder, both as "innocent insureds." We granted leave to appeal and now reverse. We hold that, under the circumstances, where a partner, acting with authorization and on behalf of his law firm, makes a material misrepresentation on an insurance application, the insurer is entitled to rescission as a matter of law.

The facts are not really in dispute. Edward Lawson, Kenneth Wheeler, and Craig Snyder formed a law partnership and, on August 6, 1997, filed a certificate of registration with the New Jersey Secretary of State for a limited liability partnership, Wheeler, Lawson & Snyder, L.L.P. Wheeler was licensed to practice law in Connecticut and the District of Columbia, but not in New Jersey. Lawson, a New Jersey licensed attorney, and Wheeler, worked at the law firm's principal office in Guttenberg, New Jersey; Snyder, a New York-licensed attorney, worked at the law firm's Manhattan office. Wheeler was the listed registered agent at the partnership's principal address.

The law firm maintained both a business operating account and an attorney trust account, both at Summit Bank. Wheeler, Lawson, and Snyder were all

---

differences must be decided by a majority of the partners provided no other agreement between the partners speaks to the issues.

This case is usually rationalized with *Nabisco* with the notion that partners cannot change the status quo (their existing ordinary business practices), except by majority vote. In *Nabisco*, the dissenting partner wanted to change; in *Summers* the initiating partner wanted to change. In both instances, the court refused to honor the change.

signatories on the business account, but only Wheeler and Lawson were signatories on the law firm's trust account. Essentially, Wheeler was responsible for opening all the bank accounts and for maintaining the books and records of the law firm.

As early as December 1996, Wheeler engaged in the unauthorized practice of law in New Jersey in connection with a number of real estate transactions in the State. Around the same time, Wheeler began misappropriating client trust funds in connection with these real estate closings. Between January and August 1997, Wheeler wrote checks to himself from the law firm's trust accounts totaling at least $5900, and cashed them.

Wheeler's unauthorized practice of law in New Jersey continued through 1998 and into the early part of 1999. For instance, on March 26, 1998, while a partner at the law firm, Wheeler acted as the closing attorney on the refinance of Lawson's condominium in Guttenberg. The closing papers identify him as an attorney-at-law in New Jersey. On April 15, 1998, Wheeler acted as the closing attorney when a law firm client, Joseph Ellis, refinanced his home in Newark. In January 1999, Wheeler acted as the closing attorney for property that Lawson himself was purchasing in Mahwah, New Jersey. Wheeler signed the title closing statement for Lawson and his wife.

At the end of 1997 or beginning of 1998, Lawson discovered Wheeler's misappropriation of client funds, including those of Lawson's mother, Elaine Lawson. When confronted, Wheeler admitted his wrongdoing:

> [Wheeler] explained to me what was happening. That we weren't making any money, and his plan was to — and I adopted the plan to generate a large sum of money so that we could pay back all the trust accounts, including my mother's, and then we were going to disband the firm.

The two partners then devised a "kiting" scheme whereby monies from one client trust account would be transferred to pay the obligations of another client. Monies were also being transferred from client trust accounts to the law firm's business account to pay expenses of the law firm, including partners' draws. On occasion, Lawson also used client trust account funds, including those of his mother, for his own personal use. By all accounts, Snyder was neither privy, nor a party, to this scheme.

At the same time, on December 4, 1997, Wheeler, on behalf of the law firm, completed an application for professional liability insurance subscribed by Lloyds. The initial application included questions designed to determine whether the prospective insured had any potential or actual malpractice claims expected, threatened or pending against the law firm. The relevant inquiry is set forth below:

> After inquiry, is any attorney in your firm aware of:
>
> (a) Any professional liability claims made against the firm or any member of the firm within the past 12 months?
> (b) Any acts, error or omissions in professional services that may reasonably be expected to be the basis of a professional liability claim?
> (c) Have all claims and/or incidents been reported to CNA?
>
> If "Yes" to either 8a or b, please complete Supplemental Claim Form for each.

Wheeler responded in the negative to subparts (a) and (b) of this question, and left subpart (c) blank.

Thereafter, on April 30, 1998, Wheeler, on behalf of the law firm, also executed an "Acceptance and Warranty Statement," wherein he represented that the statements and information he provided in the application upon which Lloyds may rely were true and accurate. Based on Wheeler's representations in his application and warranty, a policy covering both the law firm and its individual partners was subscribed by Lloyds, effective April 19, 1998 to April 19, 1999. A certificate of insurance, dated May 8, 1998, named the Clerk of the Supreme Court as certificate holder. . . .

The law firm financed payment of the policy premium through Imperial Premium Finance, Inc. (Imperial), which was authorized to cancel the policy for non-payment of principal. After not having received a premium payment by December 19, 1998, the due date, Imperial purportedly mailed to the law firm a notice of intent to cancel and, when payment was still not made by the extended date, a notice of cancellation. The policy was thereafter reinstated upon both payment of outstanding premium installments and Wheeler's execution of a warranty providing that . . . he, as signatory principal, was not aware: (1) of any claims being made during [the] past five years against [the] firm or any of its past or present partners; or (2) [of] any circumstances, allegations, or contentions as to any incident that may result in a claim being made against the firm or any of its past or present partners.

Before Wheeler's execution of this warranty, the law firm was notified on or about January 8, 1999 that the Supreme Court's Office of Attorney Ethics (OAE) would be conducting an audit of the law firm's books as a result of three grievances received concerning the firm's handling of real estate transactions. When the law firm failed to produce the necessary records, OAE faxed over to the firm its petition for emergent relief on January 26, 1999 seeking the temporary suspension of Lawson from the practice of law. On that same day, the seller in the Mahwah real estate transaction involving Lawson and his wife filed an order to show cause and verified complaint regarding an outstanding mortgage that Wheeler allegedly failed to pay off at closing. One day earlier, Wheeler had received a verified complaint and order to show cause by a seller in another real estate transaction involving other clients of the law firm. On January 26, in the midst of these events, Wheeler faxed the warranty—certifying that he was not aware of any actual or putative claims against the law firm—to Lloyds' agent.

As a result of these and other claims, First American and Lawyers Title, pursuant to obligations under their closing protection letters and title insurance policies, each paid monies to defrauded clients of the law firm because of the misappropriations by Lawson and Wheeler. The title insurers then filed lawsuits against the law firm and its individual partners to recover the monies they expended. These lawsuits were consolidated with Lloyds' declaratory judgment action. Summary judgment motions were filed by both title insurers and by Lloyds. As to the former, the trial court bifurcated the issues of liability and damages . . . , severed the title insurers' claims against defendant Snyder . . . , and disposed of all liability claims in favor of the title insurers' and against defendants Lawson, Wheeler, and the law firm. As to the latter, as previously noted, the trial court denied Lloyds' motion for summary judgment, holding that Lloyds was not entitled as a matter of law to rescind its policy as void *ab initio* based on material misrepresentations in the insurance application; that the policy had not been effectively cancelled; and that, despite the intentional wrongdoing of two of the law firm's three partners, claims against the law firm based on direct and vicarious liability for negligent supervision were not excluded from coverage under Lloyds' policy.

For purposes of this appeal, the trial court, despite finding that the failure to disclose the willful misconduct of a partner constituted a material misrepresentation, nevertheless ruled that Lloyds was not entitled to rescission of its policy. It reasoned thus:

> In this case I say equitable relief is inappropriate. I'm going to rule that Lloyd's does not have a right to void the policy *ab initio* or rescind the policy premised on the misrepresentations, which there were, of Wheeler. There's a complete lack of, in my opinion, due diligence on the part of Lloyd's in getting the type of information.

Basically, the trial court found that rescission was not available because the policy provided only for cancellation as a prospective remedy; because the insurance application was incomplete and Lloyds failed to verify the representations therein, and because the material misrepresentations of one partner do not bind the law firm or other so-called "innocent insureds." We find each of these reasons wanting and hold that under the circumstances Lloyds was entitled to rescission as a matter of law. . . .

Rescission voids an insurance policy *ab initio*. It is well-settled that a party seeking rescission based on equitable fraud is required to prove (1) a material misrepresentation of a presently existing or past fact; (2) the maker's intent that the other party rely on it; and (3) detrimental reliance by the other party. In other words, an insurer "'may rescind a policy for equitable fraud when the false statements materially affected either the acceptance of the risk or the hazard assumed by the insurer.'" Ledley v. William Penn Life Ins. Co., 138 N.J. 627, 637-38, 651 A.2d 92 (1995). "In general, a representation by the insured, whether contained in the policy itself or in the application for insurance, will support the forfeiture of the insured's rights under the policy if it is untruthful, material to the particular risk assumed by the insurer, and actually and reasonably relied upon by the insurer in the issuance of the policy." Allstate Ins. Co. v. Meloni, 98 N.J. Super. 154, 158-59, 236 A.2d 402 (App. Div. 1967). In applying the doctrine of equitable fraud to an insured's answers to questions posed in insurance applications, when the question is subjective — as here where it asks whether the law firm is aware of any circumstances which may result in a claim being made against the firm — equitable fraud is present only if the answer was knowingly false.

There is no real dispute in this case that, at the time of the law firm's initial application for professional liability insurance on December 4, 1997, Wheeler's negative response to the above-framed question was knowingly false. [The Court recited the facts set out above.]

Nor is there any question, in our view, that Wheeler's failure to disclose constituted a material misrepresentation, as found by the trial judge himself, and one that was detrimentally relied upon by Lloyds. It seems clear that the very nature of the omission was such as to "naturally and reasonably influence the judgment of the underwriter in making the contract at all, or in estimating the degree or character of the risk, or in fixing the rate of premium." Massachusetts Mutual Life Ins. Co. v. Manzo, 122 N.J. 104, 115, 584 A.2d 190 (1991) (quoting Kerpchak v. John Hancock Mutual Life Ins. Co., 97 N.J.L. 196, 198, 117 A. 836 (1922)). It is equally clear that Lloyds would not have subscribed to the policy had Wheeler's criminal and fraudulent activities been known. Under the circumstances, therefore, Lloyds was entitled to rescission of the policy on the grounds of equitable fraud.

Most of the arguments advanced by the title insurers in opposition are lacking in merit and do not warrant full discussion. For instance, agreeing with respondents that rescission as an equitable remedy was not available to Lloyds as a matter of law, the trial judge placed significance on the allegation that Lloyds accepted an incomplete application and failed to conduct its own "due diligence" investigation into the insured's qualifications. In so ruling, the trial judge said:

> In this case [Wheeler] lied based on his own personal involvement. But who is going to bear the risk of loss? An insurance company that did not engage in due diligence. An insurance company who was content to sit back, accept a form of policy of CNA, a sub part of one question wasn't even answered. That shows the sloppiness.

The trial court was mistaken for a number of reasons. First, the application submitted by Wheeler on December 4, 1997 was not incomplete. Only one question was unanswered and that is because it was rendered moot by Wheeler's responses to the two immediately preceding questions on the application. Those two questions inquired as to the existence of actual and potential claims against the law firm, to which Wheeler's negative response obviated the need to respond further to the third question, which asked whether any such claims had been reported.

As to Lloyds' purported failure of due diligence, it is settled that "[c]ontracts of insurance are contracts of utmost good faith," Gallagher v. New England Mutual Life Ins. Co. of Boston, [19 N.J. 14, 20, 114 A.2d 857 (1955)], and "the applicant therefor is bound to deal fairly with the insurer in the disclosure of facts material to the risk." Locicero v. John Hancock Mutual Life Ins. Co., 32 N.J. Super. 300, 306, 108 A.2d 281 (App. Div. 1954). Consequently, an insurer's duty to investigate is limited. Even where an insurer does perform an investigation, however, the applicant's duty to candidly fill out an insurance application is not in any way abated. . . .

There is, however, one argument advanced by the title insurers that is worthy of further discussion, namely that Wheeler's knowing material misrepresentation does not bind the law firm on whose behalf the insurance application was made. The trial judge agreed:

> Counsel admitted they could have contractually provided for a voiding of the policy based upon material misrepresentation. They did not do so. There are cases that talk about equitable remedies of voiding of policies based on material misrepresentation of fact. Those cases, as I read them, deal with one-on-one or very similar to one-on-one situations where the insured who makes the material misrepresentation is the person who is harmed by the voiding. The insured is punished for the material misrepresentation, not multiple other insured or innocent [parties]. . . .

[In this case you] have multiple named insureds. None of the cases that were cited to me have dealt with a voiding of a policy as to an innocent insured who did not adopt, who did not participate, who did not ratify, who did not condone the misrepresentation or material misstatement or misstatement of fact or omission of material facts. To do so would harm very innocent people. In a multiple member law firm it could cause a catastrophe. This is apart from the rights of an innocent third party vis-à-vis risk takers.

We disagree. Under the circumstances of this case, the misrepresentations of Wheeler, as agent of the law firm authorized to act on its behalf in the procurement of professional liability insurance, bind the principal, subjecting it to the equitable remedy of rescission.

Here, there is no dispute that, in procuring professional liability insurance for the law firm partnership, Wheeler was acting as an agent of the law firm, in furtherance of partnership business, and with the express authorization of his two co-partners. Indeed, Wheeler's partners specifically authorized him to fill out and submit the insurance application. Clearly, "[i]n an action brought for rescission, an agent's false statements bind his principal if such agent was authorized to speak for the principal in the course of obtaining the particular contract." Equitable Life Assur. Soc. v. New Horizons, Inc., 28 N.J. 307, 314, 146 A.2d 466 (1958) (citing Restatement of Agency §162).

This view is entirely consistent with that of the Uniform Partnership Law, expressly made applicable by [the New Jersey statute] to limited liability partnerships for the practice of law, such as the law firm here. That statute, in pertinent part, provides:

> Every partner is an agent of the partnership for the purpose of its business, and the act of every partner, including the execution in the partnership name of any instrument, for apparently carrying on in the usual way the business of the partnership of which he is a member binds the partnership, unless the partner so acting has in fact no authority to act for the partnership in the particular matter, and the person with whom he is dealing has knowledge of the fact that he has no such authority.

Case law interpreting this provision specifically holds that partners acting within the scope of partnership business bind not only the partnership, but their co-partners as well.

It is simply no defense that Wheeler's partners may not have authorized him to lie on the application. The fact remains that Wheeler was specifically authorized to fill out and submit the insurance application on behalf of the firm and, in procuring professional liability insurance, certainly he was acting within the scope of his employment.

Further, the fact that the law firm or some of the partners may not have been aware of the misrepresentations is of no consequence.

Although rescission is an inherently discretionary remedy, the trial judge in this case acted under a misconception of the applicable law. As such, we need not give the usual deference. We instead must adjudicate the controversy in light of the applicable law in order that a manifest denial of justice be avoided. Accordingly, we hold that the trial judge erred in withholding the remedy of rescission under these facts, where two of the law firm's three members — and the only ones with signature authority on the firm's New Jersey attorney trust accounts — engaged in a course of willful and serious attorney misconduct that the initiating wrongdoer, as agent of the partnership, repeatedly failed to disclose on application documents for professional liability insurance specifically designed to uncover such information. Lloyds was entitled to rescission as a matter of law.

In light of this disposition, we need not decide the remaining issues. . . .

Reversed and remanded for entry of judgment consistent with this opinion.

PROBLEM 2-2

Sidley & Austin (Sidley) is a large and prominent law firm with hundreds of lawyers and offices in many major U.S. cities. A general partnership, the firm was managed by an executive committee, which exercised near plenary authority over firm affairs. The only issue in the past 25 years on which all of the partners had voted was the 2001 merger of Sidley with Brown & Wood, a firm whose primary presence was in New York City. Otherwise, the executive committee — sometimes working through various subcommittees — controlled every facet of firm life.

In 1999 Sidley demoted 32 partners, giving them the titles of "counsel" or "senior counsel." The Equal Employment Opportunity Commission investigated the demotions to determine whether Sidley had violated the Age Discrimination in Employment Act. This statute protects "employees" from age discrimination. It was in this word that Sidley tried to take refuge: partners are not "employees," but rather "employers," the firm claimed.[1]

While the former partners were clearly "partners" under the Illinois partnership statute, the issue arose whether state partnership law should control the meaning of "employee" under federal antidiscrimination law. The statute is silent on this issue. We can assume, for present purposes, that courts would make this judgment in close cases by considering whether the partner needs the protection of such a statute.

In this case, the partnership had over 500 partners, but the executive committee was comprised of only 36 members. The executive committee was not elected by the partners as a whole; it was self-perpetuating. The demoted partners served on various working committees, all appointed by and subject to supervision of the executive committee. At the time of their demotion, the former partners had other attributes of traditional partners, including authority to act as agents of the partnership, the right to share in profits of the firm, and unlimited personal liability.

Which facts would you consider most important in deciding whether the demoted partners should be classified as "employees" for purposes of federal antidiscrimination laws?

---

1. The ADEA defines "employee" as "an individual employed by any employer." 29 U.S.C. §1002(6).

C. FIDUCIARY DUTIES

Fiduciary duties traditionally have developed through common law. Although UPA §21 purports to contain a description of the fiduciary duties of partners, it is very narrow in its literal terms, providing only that partners must not steal from the partnership. Other sections of the UPA often are said to supplement this duty of loyalty. For example, UPA §19 provides for access to partnership records, UPA §20 requires partners to render "true and full information" about the partnership to the other partners, and UPA §22 gives partners the right to an accounting under certain specified circumstances as well as when "other circumstances render it just and reasonable." In addition to the weak duty of loyalty provisions, the UPA contains no provision for the duty of care, although some courts have implied a duty of care. The explicit duties in the UPA are flimsy indeed, compared with the expansive duties of an agent to a principal. Perhaps because UPA §4(3) explicitly incorporates the law of agency, courts have been very generous about imposing fiduciary duties on partners under the UPA.

RUPA goes far to change the statutory structure of fiduciary duties under partnership law. Under RUPA §404, partners owe duties of loyalty and care. RUPA attempts to narrow the broad duties imposed by courts under UPA, providing that the duty of loyalty "is limited to the following," and specifying three discreet duties: (1) an anti-theft duty that corresponds to the anti-theft duty in UPA §21, except that the word "formation" has been dropped to indicate that fiduciary duties arise only after the partnership is created; (2) a prohibition against self-dealing; and (3) a prohibition against competing against the partnership. RUPA §404(b). If these provisions were interpreted literally by courts, they would narrow the scope of a partner's duty of loyalty from most common law standards. Partners are allowed to narrow the duty of loyalty still further by contract, but they are not allowed to eliminate the duty of loyalty completely. RUPA §103(b)(3).

The duty of care in RUPA §404(c) establishes that conduct showing gross negligence, recklessness, intentional misconduct, or knowing violation of the law would violate the requisite standard of care. This default standard forces partners to share any losses resulting from the negligence of one of the partners. The RUPA Reporters believed that losses from negligence are perceived as an inevitable series of costs that over time will be imposed randomly and equally on all partners. This is because partners are open to unlimited liability and therefore have an incentive to exercise due care and to monitor the behavior of other partners. In addition, if the partners know of disparities in ability or attitude toward care, they are likely to contract to alter the default loss-sharing rule. Therefore, the Reporters argue, there is no need to allocate risk of loss from negligence among the partners. Gross negligence was the standard applied by courts that have implied a duty of care. Donald J. Weidner & John W. Larson, *The Revised Uniform Partnership Act: The Reporters' Overview*, 49 Bus. Law. 1, 22 (1993). While the partners may modify the duty of care by contract, they are not allowed to "unreasonably reduce the duty of care." RUPA §103(b)(4).

In addition to the duties of loyalty and care, RUPA adds an obligation of good faith and fair dealing. RUPA §404(d). This obligation was not expressly required in the UPA except in a single, narrowly defined clause dealing with expulsions, but courts often implied a duty of good faith and fair dealing. The RUPA obligation is expressly made nonwaivable (mandatory), except that the parties may "determine the standards by which performance is to be measured, if the standards are not manifestly unreasonable." RUPA §103(b)(5). By failing to define the meaning of good faith and fair dealing in the partnership context, it is uncertain how this broad obligation will be interpreted and applied. The drafting committee has made it clear that the omission of any definition of good faith and fair dealing in RUPA is not an oversight: "The meaning of 'good faith' is not defined nor is it firmly fixed under present law. . . . [The Drafting Committee] concluded that it would be preferable to leave the term undefined. . . ."

The following is perhaps the most-cited partnership case ever, although, as you will see, it is not a partnership case at all. Judge Cardozo's vaulting rhetoric has ensured Meinhard v. Salmon a prominent place among the great articulations of fiduciary duty. It is followed by a problem exploring the tension between management rights and fiduciary obligation and a more recent case that illustrates a modern approach to fiduciary duties in the context of a large law-firm partnership.

MEINHARD v. SALMON
249 N.Y. 458, 164 N.E. 545
Court of Appeals of New York
December 31, 1928

CARDOZO, C.J.

On April 10, 1902, Louisa M. Gerry leased to the defendant Walter J. Salmon the premises known as the Hotel Bristol at the northwest corner of Forty-Second street and Fifth avenue in the city of New York. The lease was for a term of 20 years, commencing May 1, 1902, and ending April 30, 1922. The lessee undertook to change the hotel building for use as shops and offices at a cost of $200,000. Alterations and additions were to be accretions to the land.

Salmon, while in course of treaty with the lessor as to the execution of the lease, was in course of treaty with Meinhard, the plaintiff, for the necessary funds. The result was a joint venture with terms embodied in a writing. Meinhard was to pay to Salmon half of the moneys requisite to reconstruct, alter, manage, and operate the property. Salmon was to pay to Meinhard 40 per cent of the net profits for the first five years of the lease and 50 per cent for the years thereafter. If there were losses, each party was to bear them equally. Salmon, however, was to have sole power to "manage, lease, underlet and operate" the building. There were to be certain pre-emptive rights for each in the contingency of death.

The two were coadventurers, subject to fiduciary duties akin to those of partners. As to this we are all agreed. The heavier weight of duty rested, however, upon Salmon. He was a coadventurer with Meinhard, but he was manager as well. During the early years of the enterprise, the building, reconstructed, was operated at a loss. If the relation had then ended, Meinhard as well as Salmon would have carried a heavy burden. Later the profits became large with the result that for each of the investors there came a rich return. For each the venture had its phases of fair weather and of foul. The two were in it jointly, for better or for worse.

When the lease was near its end, Elbridge T. Gerry had become the owner of the reversion. He owned much other property in the neighborhood, one lot adjoining the Bristol building on Fifth avenue and four lots on Forty-Second

Salmon solely managed the property, with 4 months on the lease being approached Salmon: a new very lucrative lease land development plan was signed. Meinhard was never informed.

street. He had a plan to lease the entire tract for a long term to someone who would destroy the buildings then existing and put up another in their place. In the latter part of 1921, he submitted such a project to several capitalists and dealers. He was unable to carry it through with any of them. Then, in January, 1922, with less than four months of the lease to run, he approached the defendant Salmon. The result was a new lease to the Midpoint Realty Company, which is owned and controlled by Salmon, a lease covering the whole tract, and involving a huge outlay. The term is to be 20 years, but successive covenants for renewal will extend it to a maximum of 80 years at the will of either party. The existing buildings may remain unchanged for seven years. They are then to be torn down, and a new building to cost $3,000,000 is to be placed upon the site. The rental, which under the Bristol lease was only $55,000, is to be from $350,000 to $475,000 for the properties so combined. Salmon personally guaranteed the performance by the lessee of the covenants of the new lease until such time as the new building had been completed and fully paid for.

The lease between Gerry and the Midpoint Realty Company was signed and delivered on January 25, 1922. Salmon had not told Meinhard anything about it. Whatever his motive may have been, he had kept the negotiations to himself. Meinhard was not informed even of the bare existence of a project. The first that he knew of it was in February, when the lease was an accomplished fact. He then made demand on the defendants that the lease be held in trust as an asset of the venture, making offer upon the trial to share the personal obligations incidental to the guaranty. The demand was followed by refusal, and later by this suit. A referee gave judgment for the plaintiff, limiting the plaintiff's interest in the lease, however, to 25 per cent. The limitation was on the theory that the plaintiff's equity was to be restricted to one-half of so much of the value of the lease as was contributed or represented by the occupation of the Bristol site. Upon cross-appeals to the Appellate Division, the judgment was modified so as to enlarge the equitable interest to one-half of the whole lease. With this enlargement of plaintiff's interest, there went, of course, a corresponding enlargement of his attendant obligations. The case is now here on an appeal by the defendants.

RULE:

is this is true when parties are bound by a fiduciary duty.

Joint adventurers, like copartners, owe to one another, while the enterprise continues, the duty of the finest loyalty. Many forms of conduct permissible in a workaday world for those acting at arm's length, are forbidden to those bound by fiduciary ties. A trustee is held to something stricter than the morals of the market place. Not honesty alone, but the punctilio of an honor the most sensitive, is then the standard of behavior. As to this there has developed a tradition that is unbending and inveterate. Uncompromising rigidity has been the attitude of courts of equity when petitioned to undermine the rule of undivided loyalty by the "disintegrating erosion" of particular exceptions.

Wendt v. Fischer

Wendt v. Fischer, 243 N.Y. 439, 444, 154 N.E. 303. Only thus has the level of conduct for fiduciaries been kept at a level higher than that trodden by the crowd. It will not consciously be lowered by any judgment of this court.

The owner of the reversion, Mr. Gerry, had vainly striven to find a tenant who would favor his ambitious scheme of demolition and construction. Baffled in the search, he turned to the defendant Salmon in possession of the Bristol, the keystone of the project. He figured to himself beyond a doubt that the man in possession would prove a likely customer. To the eye of an observer, Salmon

[handwritten margin note: Salmon held the Bristol as a fiduciary for himself & his partner.]

held the lease as owner in his own right, for himself and no one else. In fact he held it as a fiduciary, for himself and another, sharers in a common venture. If this fact had been proclaimed, if the lease by its terms had run in favor of a partnership, Mr. Gerry, we may fairly assume, would have laid before the partners, and not merely before one of them, his plan of reconstruction. The pre-emptive privilege, or, better, [the pre-emptive opportunity,' that was thus an incident of the enterprise, Salmon appropriated to himself in secrecy and silence. He might have warned Meinhard that the plan had been submitted, and that either would be free to compete for the award.' If he had done this, we do not need to say whether he would have been under a duty, if successful in the competition, to hold the lease so acquired for the benefit of a venture then about to end, and thus prolong by indirection its responsibilities and duties. The trouble about his conduct is that he excluded his coadventurer from any chance to compete, from any chance to enjoy the opportunity for benefit that had come to him alone by virtue of his agency. This chance, if nothing more, he was under a duty to concede. The price of its denial is an extension of the trust at the option and for the benefit of the one whom he excluded.

[handwritten margin notes: he should have told Meinhard or: The issue is his excluding his coadventure from the chance to compete.]

No answer is it to say that the chance would have been of little value even if seasonably offered. Such a calculus of probabilities is beyond the science of the chancery. Salmon, the real estate operator, might have been preferred to Meinhard, the woolen merchant. On the other hand, Meinhard might have offered better terms, or reinforced his offer by alliance with the wealth of others. Perhaps he might even have persuaded the lessor to renew the Bristol lease alone, postponing for a time, in return for higher rentals, the improvement of adjoining lots. We know that even under the lease as made the time for the enlargement of the building was delayed for seven years. All these opportunities were cut away from him through another's intervention. He knew that Salmon was the manager. As the time drew near for the expiration of the lease, he would naturally assume from silence, if from nothing else, that the lessor was willing to extend it for a term of years, or at least to let it stand as a lease from year to year. Not impossibly the lessor would have done so, whatever his protestations of unwillingness, if Salmon had not given assent to a project more attractive. At all events, notice of termination, even if not necessary, might seem, not unreasonably, to be something to be looked for, if the business was over and another tenant was to enter. In the absence of such notice, the matter of an extension was one that would naturally be attended to by the manager of the enterprise, and not neglected altogether. At least, there was nothing in the situation to give warning to any one that while the lease was still in being, there had come to the manager an offer of extension which he had locked within his breast to be utilized by himself alone. The very fact that Salmon was in control with exclusive powers of direction charged him the more obviously with the duty of disclosure, since only through disclosure could opportunity be equalized. If he might cut off renewal by a purchase for his own benefit when four months were to pass before the lease would have an end, he might do so with equal right while there remained as many years. He might steal a march on his comrade under cover of the darkness, and then hold the captured ground. Loyalty and comradeship are not so easily abjured. . . .

[handwritten margin note: Salmon's lack of info. & position as manager probably led Meinhard to believe that the lease had been extended.]

We have no thought to hold that Salmon was guilty of a conscious purpose to defraud. Very likely he assumed in all good faith that with the approaching end of the venture he might ignore his coadventurer and take the extension

[handwritten margin note: HOLDING:]

He probably thought that

for himself. He had given to the enterprise time and labor as well as money. He had made it a success. Meinhard, who had given money, but neither time nor labor, had already been richly paid. There might seem to be something grasping in his insistence upon more. Such recriminations are not unusual when coadventurers fall out. They are not without their force if conduct is to be judged by the common standards of competitors. That is not to say that they have pertinency here. Salmon had put himself in a position in which thought of self was to be renounced, however hard the abnegation. He was much more than a coadventurer. He was a managing coadventurer. For him and for those like him the rule of undivided loyalty is relentless and supreme. A different question would be here if there were lacking any nexus of relation between the business conducted by the manager and the opportunity brought to him as an incident of management. For this problem, as for most, there are distinctions of degree. If Salmon had received from Gerry a proposition to lease a building at a location far removed, he might have held for himself the privilege thus acquired, or so we shall assume. Here the subject-matter of the new lease was an extension and enlargement of the subject-matter of the old one. A managing coadventurer appropriating the benefit of such a lease without warning to his partner might fairly expect to be reproached with conduct that was underhand, or lacking, to say the least, in reasonable candor, if the partner were to surprise him in the act of signing the new instrument. Conduct subject to that reproach does not receive from equity a healing benediction.

The new lease was an extension of the subject-matter of the old one.

A question remains as to the form and extent of the equitable interest to be allotted to the plaintiff. The trust as declared has been held to attach to the lease which was in the name of the defendant corporation. We think it ought to attach at the option of the defendant Salmon to the shares of stock which were owned by him or were under his control. The difference may be important if the lessee shall wish to execute an assignment of the lease, as it ought to be free to do with the consent of the lessor. On the other hand, an equal division of the shares might lead to other hardships. It might take away from Salmon the power of control and management which under the plan of the joint venture he was to have from first to last. The number of shares to be allotted to the plaintiff should, therefore, be reduced to such an extent as may be necessary to preserve to the defendant Salmon the expected measure of dominion. To that end an extra share should be added to his half, . . .

Salmon should get ½ of the new deal plus one more; to preserve his expected dominion over the new agreement.

The judgment should be modified by providing that at the option of the defendant Salmon there may be substituted for a trust attaching to the lease a trust attaching to the shares of stock, with the result that one-half of such shares together with one additional share will in that event be allotted to the defendant Salmon and the other shares to the plaintiff, and as so modified the judgment should be affirmed with costs.

ANDREWS, J. (dissenting).

. . . Morton H. Meinhard was a woolen merchant. At some period during the negotiations between Mr. Salmon and Mrs. Gerry, so far as the findings show without the latter's knowledge, he became interested in the transaction. Before the lease was executed he advanced $5,000 toward the cost of the proposed alterations. Finally, on May 19th he and Salmon entered into a written agreement. "During the period of twenty years from the 1st day of May, 1902," the parties agree to share equally in the expense needed "to reconstruct, alter, manage and operate the Bristol Hotel property"; and in all payments required by the lease, and in all losses incurred "during the full term of the lease, *i.e.*, from the first day of May, 1902, to the 1st day of May, 1922." During the same term net profits are to be divided. Mr. Salmon has sole power to "manage, lease, underlet and operate" the premises. If he dies, Mr. Meinhard shall be consulted before any disposition is made of the lease, and if Mr. Salmon's representatives decide to dispose of it, and the decision is theirs, Mr. Meinhard is to be given the first chance to take the unexpired term upon the same conditions they could obtain from others.

The referee finds that this arrangement did not create a partnership between Mr. Salmon and Mr. Meinhard. In this he is clearly right. He is equally right in holding that while no general partnership existed the two men had entered into a joint adventure and that while the legal title to the lease was in Mr. Salmon, Mr. Meinhard had some sort of an equitable interest therein. Mr. Salmon was to manage the property for their joint benefit. He was bound to use good faith. He could not willfully destroy the lease, the object of the adventure, to the detriment of Mr. Meinhard. . . .

Were this a general partnership between Mr. Salmon and Mr. Meinhard, I should have little doubt as to the correctness of this result, assuming the new lease to be an offshoot of the old. Such a situation involves questions of trust and confidence to a high degree; it involves questions of good will; many other considerations. As has been said, rarely if ever may one partner without the knowledge of the other acquire for himself the renewal of a lease held by the firm, even if the new lease is to begin after the firm is dissolved. Warning of such an intent, if he is managing partner, may not be sufficient to prevent the application of this rule.

We have here a different situation governed by less drastic principles. I assume that where parties engage in a joint enterprise each owes to the other the duty of the utmost good faith in all that relates to their common venture. Within its scope they stand in a fiduciary relationship. I assume prima facie that even as between joint adventurers one may not secretly obtain a renewal of the lease of property actually used in the joint adventure where the possibility of renewal is expressly or impliedly involved in the enterprise. I assume also that Mr. Meinhard had an equitable interest in the Bristol Hotel lease. Further, that an expectancy of renewal inhered in that lease. Two questions then arise. Under his contract did he share in that expectancy? And if so, did that expectancy mature into a graft of the original lease? To both questions my answer is "No." . . .

What then was the scope of the adventure into which the two men entered? It is to be remembered that before their contract was signed Mr. Salmon had obtained the lease of the Bristol property. Very likely the matter had been earlier discussed between them. The $5,000 advance by Mr. Meinhard indicates that fact. But it has been held that the written contract defines their rights and duties. Having the lease, Mr. Salmon assigns no interest in it to Mr. Meinhard. He is to manage the property. It is for him to decide what alterations shall be made and to fix the rents. But for 20 years from May 1, 1902, Salmon is to make all advances from his own funds and Meinhard is to pay him personally on demand one-half of all expenses incurred and all losses sustained "during the full term of said lease," and during the same period Salmon is to pay him a part of the net profits. There was no joint capital provided.

It seems to me that the venture so inaugurated had in view a limited object and was to end at a limited time. There was no intent to expand it into a far greater undertaking lasting for many years. The design was to exploit a particular lease. Doubtless in it Mr. Meinhard had an equitable interest, but in it alone. This interest terminated when the joint adventure terminated. There was no intent that for the benefit of both any advantage should be taken of the chance of renewal — that the adventure should be continued beyond that date. Mr. Salmon has done all he promised to do in return for Mr. Meinhard's undertaking when he distributed profits up to May 1, 1922. . . .

The judgment of the courts below should be reversed and a new trial ordered, with costs in all courts to abide the event.

PROBLEM 2-3

Covalt and High jointly own a corporation called CSI Corporation. Covalt is a 25 percent owner (shareholder) of CSI, is an officer of the company, and works for CSI full time. High is a 75 percent owner (shareholder) of CSI, is an officer, and works for CSI full time. This is a classic closely held corporation, which some commentators called an "incorporated partnership," since it has the management and ownership features of a partnership. Unlike a partnership, however, corporate law provides for one share/one vote. Under this rule, High will outvote Covalt every time 75 votes to 25 votes.

In late 1971, after both Covalt and High had become corporate officers in CSI, they orally agreed to the formation of a separate partnership for the purpose of buying a parcel of real estate and constructing an office and warehouse building on the land. High became the managing partner for the partnership. In February 1973, the partnership leased the building to CSI for a five-year term. Following the expiration of the five-year term of the lease, CSI remained a tenant of the building; the corporation and the partnership orally agreed to certain rental increases from time to time.

On December 23, 1978, Covalt resigned his corporate position and began work for a competitor of CSI. Covalt, however, remained a shareholder of CSI and remained a partner with High in the ownership of the land and the building rented to CSI. (Presumably their holiday parties were a bit chilly that year.) On January 9, 1979, Covalt wrote to High demanding that the monthly rent for the partnership real estate leased to CSI be increased from $1,850 to $2,850 per month. (Testimony at a later trial indicated that $2,850 per month was the fair market value.) Upon receipt of the letter, High informed Covalt he would determine if the rent could be increased. Thereafter, however, High did not agree to the increased rent and took no action to renegotiate the amount of the monthly rent payable.

After dissolution of the partnership on August 27, 1980, Covalt sued High for lost profits. At trial, High testified that he felt CSI could not afford a higher rent and that the corporation had a poor financial status.

Did High breach a fiduciary duty to the Covalt-High partnership warranting an award of damages?

GIBBS v. BREED, ABBOTT & MORGAN

710 N.Y.S.2d 578
New York Supreme Court, Appellate Division
July 13, 2000

MAZZARELLI, J.

Plaintiffs Charles Gibbs and Robert Sheehan are former partners of Breed Abbott & Morgan ("BAM") who specialize in trust and estate law. They withdrew from BAM in July 1991 to join Chadbourne & Parke ("Chadbourne"), and brought this action for monies due to them under their BAM partnership agreement. Defendants asserted various counterclaims alleging that plaintiffs breached their fiduciary duty to BAM. The counterclaims were severed and tried without a jury. Plaintiffs appeal from the trial court's determination that, in the course of both partners' planning and eventually implementing their withdrawal from BAM, they breached their fiduciary duty to the partnership. Plaintiffs also appeal from the trial court's determination that $1,861,045 in damages resulted from these transgressions.

From January 1991 until July 1991, plaintiffs were the only partners in the Trusts and Estates department ("T/E") at BAM; plaintiff Gibbs was the head of the department. A third partner, Paul Lambert, had been the former head of the department, and he had obtained many, if not most of the department's clients. In 1989 he had left the firm to become the United States Ambassador to Ecuador and was still on leave in 1991. Lambert intended to return to the firm upon completion of his term as ambassador. The BAM trusts and estates department also employed three associate attorneys, Warren Whitaker (fifteenth year), Austin Wilkie (fourth year), and Joseph Scorese (first year); two accountants, Lois Wetzel and Ellen Furst; and two paralegals, Lee Ann Riley and Ruth Kramer.

Gibbs had become dissatisfied with BAM, and in January 1991 he began interviews to locate a new affiliation. He also approached Sheehan to persuade him to move with him. Sheehan and Gibbs subsequently conducted a number of joint interviews with prospective employers. In May 1991, Ambassador Lambert visited BAM, and Gibbs told him that he had been interviewing. Lambert relayed this information to the other partners. In early June, plaintiffs informed the executive committee that they had received an offer from two firms: McDermott, Will & Emory and Bryan Cave.

On June 19, 1991, both plaintiffs informed Stephen Lang, BAM's presiding partner, that they had accepted offers to join Chadbourne. Lang asked Gibbs not to discuss his departure with any of the T/E associates, and Gibbs agreed not to do so. On June 20, 1991, Lawrence Warble, a BAM partner who was named temporary head of the T/E department, met with its associates and non-legal personnel to inform them that plaintiffs were leaving the firm.

On June 24, 1991, Gibbs and Sheehan sent Chadbourne a memo listing the names of the personnel in the T/E department at BAM, their respective salaries, their annual billable hours, and the rate at which BAM billed out these employees to clients. The memo included other information about the attorneys, including the colleges and law schools they attended, and their bar admissions. This list had been prepared by Sheehan on April 26, 1991, months before the partners announced they were leaving. Sheehan specifically testified that the memo was prepared in anticipation of discussions with prospective firms, and both Gibbs and Sheehan testified at trial that the recruitment of certain associates and support personnel was discussed with different firms between March and May, as the partners were considering various affiliations. While Gibbs and Sheehan were still partners at BAM, Chadbourne interviewed four BAM employees that Gibbs had indicated he was interested in bringing to Chadbourne with him. On June 27, 1991, plaintiffs submitted their written resignations. Before Gibbs and Sheehan left BAM, they wrote letters to clients served by them, advising that they were leaving BAM and that other attorneys at BAM could serve them. These letters did not mention the fact that the two partners were moving to Chadbourne. Although the partnership agreement required 45 days notice of an intention to withdraw, BAM waived this provision upon plaintiffs' production of their final billings for work previously performed. Gibbs left BAM on July 9, 1991, and Sheehan left on July 11, 1991, both taking various documents, including their respective "chronology" or desk files. With the assistance of his chronology file, Gibbs began to contact his former clients on July 11, 1991. On July 11th, Chadbourne made employment offers to Whitaker, Wilkie, Wetzel, and Riley. Wilkie, Wetzel, and Riley accepted that same day; Whitaker accepted on July 15, 1991. In the following weeks, 92 of the 201 BAM T/E clients moved their business to Chadbourne.

After hearing all the testimony and the parties' arguments, the trial court determined that Gibbs' actions in persuading his partner Sheehan to leave BAM, "and the way in which the leave was orchestrated, were done, at least partially, with the intention of crippling BAM's Trusts and Estates ("T/E") department," and constituted a breach of loyalty to BAM. The court also found that Gibbs and Sheehan had breached their fiduciary duties to BAM by sending Chadbourne the April 26, 1991 memo detailing personal information about the individuals in the T/E Department at BAM, because this gave Chadbourne a competitive advantage in offering employment to other members of the department. Finally, the court found that Gibbs and Sheehan breached their fiduciary duties to BAM by taking their chronology files with them to Chadbourne. Specifically, the court concluded that by taking their respective chronology files, the partners "to a large degree hobbled their former partners in their effort to rebuild the Trusts and Estates department, in order to maintain a viable department, and in their ability to serve clients without undue disruption."

With respect to damages, the court concluded that both Gibbs and Sheehan were entitled to recover their share of BAM profits accruing until the end of July 1991, and that Sheehan was entitled to the remainder of his capital account with the firm. Although there was no evidence that the partners had improperly solicited former BAM clients, the court found that despite BAM's efforts to mitigate damages by hiring a new partner and two associates into the T/E Department, that department suffered financial losses as a result of plaintiffs' conduct, and concluded that it was entitled to recover lost profits for a reasonable period following plaintiffs' departure. The court directed that lost profits be calculated from July 1991, when the partners left the firm, to November 1993, when BAM dissolved. Gibbs and Sheehan were held jointly and severally liable for $1,861,045. The court also awarded defendants prejudgment interest and attorneys' fees. The court's liability finding should be modified, the damage award vacated, and the matter remanded for a determination of the financial loss, if any, occasioned by plaintiffs' disloyal act of supplying competitors with BAM's confidential employee data.

The members of a partnership owe each other a duty of loyalty and good faith. . . . According the trial court's findings on issues of fact and credibility appropriate deference, we uphold that portion of the court's liability determination which found that plaintiffs breached their fiduciary duty as partners of the firm they were about to leave by supplying confidential employee information to Chadbourne while still partners at BAM. However, we find no breach with respect to Gibbs' interactions with Sheehan, or with respect to either partner's removal of his desk files from BAM.

Defendants did not establish that Gibbs breached any duty to BAM by discussing with Sheehan a joint move to another firm, or that Sheehan's decision was based upon anything other than his own personal interests. In addition, while in certain situations "[A] lawyer's removal or copying, without the firm's consent, of materials from a law firm that do not belong to the lawyer, that are the property of the law firm, and that are intended by the lawyer to be used in his new affiliation, could constitute dishonesty, which is professional misconduct under [Model] Rule 8.4(c)" (D.C. Bar Legal Ethics Comm. Op. 273 at 192), here, the partners took their desk copies of recent correspondence with the good faith belief that they were entitled to do so.

Contrary to the finding of the trial court, and applying the principle that "[t]he distinction between motive and process is critical to a realistic application of fiduciary duties" [Robert Hillman, *Loyalty in the Firm: A Statement of General Principles on the Duties of Partners Withdrawing from Law Firms*, 55 Wash & Lee L. Rev. 997, 999 (1998)], we find no breach of duty in plaintiffs' taking their desk files. These were comprised of duplicates of material maintained in individual client files, the partnership agreement was silent as to these documents, and removal was apparently common practice for departing attorneys.

However, the record supports the court's finding that both partners committed a breach of their fiduciary duty to the BAM partners by supplying Chadbourne, and presumably the other partnerships they considered joining, with the April 26, 1991 memorandum describing the members of BAM's T/E department, their salaries, and other confidential information such as billing rates and average billable hours, taken from personnel files. Moreover, a closer examination of the record does not support the dissent's conclusion that these partners did not engage in surreptitious recruiting. The partners may not have discussed with firm employees the possibility of moving with them prior to June 20, 1991, but they indicated to Chadbourne the employees they were interested in prior to this date, and Gibbs specifically testified that he refrained from telling one of his partners, to whom he had a duty of loyalty, about his future plans to recruit specific associates and support staff from the partnership.

There is no evidence of improper client solicitation in this case, nor is it an issue on this appeal. Although the analogy could be useful in concluding that Gibbs did not breach his fiduciary duty to the partnership by working with Sheehan to find a new affiliation, the fiduciary restraints upon a partner with respect to client solicitation are not analogous to those applicable to employee recruitment. By contrast to the lawyer-client relationship, a partner does not have a fiduciary duty to the employees of a firm which would limit its duty of loyalty to the partnership. Thus, recruitment of firm employees has been viewed as distinct and "permissible on a more limited basis than . . . solicitation of clients" (Hillman, *supra* at 1031). Pre-withdrawal recruitment is generally allowed "only after the firm has been given notice of the lawyer's intention to withdraw" (*id.*).

However, here, Sheehan prepared a memo in April of 1991, well in advance of even deciding, much less informing his partners, of his intention to withdraw. There is ample support in the record for the trial court's finding that the preparation and sending of the April 26, 1991 memo, combined with the subsequent hiring of certain trusts and estates personnel, constituted an egregious breach of plaintiff's fiduciary duty to BAM. Moreover, it is not speculative to infer more widespread dissemination given Sheehan's trial testimony that the memo "was prepared in connection with talking to other firms," and that "he was sure the subject of staffing was discussed at firms other than Chadbourne." Sheehan's disclosure of confidential BAM data to even one firm was a direct breach of his duty of loyalty to his partners. Because the memo gave Chadbourne confidential BAM employment data as well as other information reflecting BAM's valuation of each employee, Chadbourne was made privy to information calculated to give it an unfair advantage in recruiting certain employees.

While partners may not be restrained from inviting qualified personnel to change firms with them, here Gibbs and Sheehan began their recruiting while still members of the firm and prior to serving notice of their intent to withdraw. They did so without informing their partners that they were disseminating confidential firm data to competitors. Their actions, while still members of the firm, were intended to and did place BAM in the position of not knowing which of their employees were targets and what steps would be appropriate for them to take in order to retain these critical employees. The dissent's analysis, that once the firm was notified of the partners' departure, there was no breach of fiduciary duty, is flawed. The breach occurred in April of 1991 and could not be cured by any after-the-fact notification by the fiduciary who committed the breach that he was withdrawing from the firm. Chadbourne still had the unfair advantage of the confidential information from the April 1991 memo, and still had the upper hand, which was manifested by its ability to tailor its offers and incentives to the BAM recruits.

Contrary to the dissent, I would characterize the memo distributed to prospective competitors as confidential. The data was obtained from BAM personnel files which Sheehan had unique access to as a BAM partner. The dissent's statement that such financial information is generally known to "headhunters" is without foundation. While the broad outlines of the partners' profits at a select number of large New York firms and the incremental increases in the base compensation of young associates at some firms are published in professional publications such as the New York Law Journal, or known to some recruitment firms, the available figures often vary substantially from the actual compensation received by specific individuals.

For example, the BAM partnership agreement, which is included in the record, reveals that the approximately 40 partners in the firm earn substantially different percentages of the firm's earnings. No professional publication would be privy to these financials. With respect to the specific associates and support staff whose compensation was disseminated in the April 1991 memo, the information disclosed to Chadbourne incorporated these individuals' bonuses. Bonus payments are confidential, often voted by the partnership, based upon the unique quality of an individual's work, the number of hours billed, and many other intangible factors. These lump sum payments often constitute a substantial portion of an associate's salary, and the payments are certainly not available to the public. Finally, support staff also receive bonuses paid to them at the discretion of the individual partners, from their personal accounts. This information is highly individualized and also privileged. Sheehan abused his fiduciary duty to the partnership by accessing personnel files to obtain the actual gross compensation of the associates and support staff he and Gibbs wished to bring with them, including bonuses, and disclosing this information to Chadbourne.

Moreover, the memo contained more than a list of salaries. It itemized each of the employees' annual billable hours, and the rates at which BAM billed these employees out to their clients, information which was not otherwise publically available. These facts go directly to a potential employee's value and were accessible only to members of the BAM partnership. Selected partners providing BAM's confidential information, which they were able to obtain by virtue of their position as fiduciaries, to Chadbourne was an act of disloyalty to their partnership. The confidential information placed Chadbourne, as a competing prospective employer, in the advantageous position of conducting interviews of the associates and support staff with more knowledge than any firm could obtain through independent research, as well as providing it with information BAM partners did not know it had, thereby prejudicing their own efforts to retain their associates and support staff.

The calculation of damages in cases such as this is difficult. "[B]reaches of a fiduciary relationship in any context comprise a special breed of cases that often loosen normally stringent requirements of causation and damages" (Milbank, Tweed, Hadley & McCloy v. Boon, 13 F.3d 537, 543 [2d Cir. 1994]). This is because the purpose of this type of action " 'is not merely to *compensate* the plaintiff for wrongs committed . . . [but also] to *prevent* them, by removing from agents and trustees all inducement to attempt dealing for their own benefit in matters which they have undertaken for others, or to which their agency or trust relates' " (Diamond v. Oreamuno, 24 N.Y.2d 494, 498 [emphasis in original]). However, the proponent of a claim for a breach of fiduciary duty must, at a minimum, establish that the offending parties' actions were "a substantial factor" in causing an identifiable loss.

A reasonable assessment of lost profits has been deemed an appropriate measure of damages in cases where there was evidence that the fiduciary improperly solicited clients to move with him or her, or where the fiduciary's acts could otherwise be connected to a subsequent loss of business. Here, the court based its damage award on what it believed to be a series of disloyal acts. Defendants did not establish how the only act of plaintiffs which this Court finds to be disloyal, that of supplying employee information to Chadbourne, in and of itself, was a substantial cause of BAM's lost profits. We therefore vacate the court's award to defendants of the total profits lost by BAM between the time of plaintiffs departure in July 1991 and BAM's dissolution in November 1993, and remand for consideration of the issue of whether plaintiff's disloyal act of sending Chadbourne the April 26, 1991 memorandum was a significant cause of any identifiable loss, and, if so, the amount of such loss.

Accordingly, the order, Supreme Court, New York County (Herman Cahn, J.), entered October 1, 1998, which, after a nonjury trial on defendants' counterclaims, determined that plaintiffs had breached their fiduciary duty to defendants, should be modified, on the law, to limit such conclusion to the act of disseminating confidential employee information, and otherwise affirmed, without costs.

SAXE, J. (concurring in part and dissenting in part).

Much has been written about the ethical and fiduciary obligations of attorneys upon withdrawal from their law firms, particularly with regard to their solicitation of firm clients. However, rather than involving the improper solicitation of former clients, this case concerns claims of wrongful "solicitation" or "taking" of a withdrawing attorney's own partners, associates, and support staff. We are also required to address the propriety of departing attorneys removing the duplicate copies of letters and memos in their possession that they personally prepared and issued over the preceding years, which plaintiffs term "desk chronology files" or "correspondence chronology files."

In view of the limited case authorities directly on point, resolution of this appeal requires a review of the general principles concerning client solicitation and attorneys' covenants not to compete, as well as the general policy considerations discussed in numerous scholarly articles concerning the competing interests in law firm breakups. The trial court's liability determination runs counter to these principles and policies and it is not supported by the evidence. Therefore, I would reverse the judgment in its entirety. To the extent the majority affirms one aspect of the liability determination, I dissent. As to the remainder of the majority opinion, I concur in the result, based upon the following discussion. . . .

The evidence before the trial court fails to support its findings that plaintiffs violated their fiduciary duty to their partners at Breed, Abbott. I agree with the majority's holding that Gibbs's pre-departure discussions with Sheehan cannot constitute a breach of Gibbs's fiduciary duty to Breed, Abbott, and that plaintiffs' removal of their desk chronology files breached no obligation to their former partners. However, I disagree with the conclusion that defendants are entitled to damages based upon plaintiffs having provided Chadbourne with information about other employees of the firm's trusts & estates department, which information was provided in the interests of bringing these employees along with them in their move to Chadbourne.

PERSUADING A PARTNER TO LEAVE THE FIRM AS A TEAM

Turning first to the trial court's finding that Gibbs "actively encouraged" or "persuaded" Sheehan to leave the firm with him, and "orchestrated" their move to cripple Breed, Abbott's trusts and estates department, there is no established fiduciary duty that can be stretched to cover Gibbs's conduct. The standard employed by the trial court, if applied generally, would too severely restrict attorneys' rights to change affiliations, compete with former partners, and offer clients full freedom of choice with respect to retaining counsel.

Initially, the "solicitation" of one's own partners to make a joint move simply does not qualify as a breach of fiduciary duty. . . .

The "solicitation" of one's own partners to make a joint move is fundamentally different than the solicitation of firm clients; the analysis which concludes that surreptitious solicitation of clients or secreting client files is improper is irrelevant to partners' conduct toward one another. "Soliciting" another member of one's firm does not involve the same concerns.

Although clients are not, technically, an "asset" or "property" of the firm, subject to possession, the rules regarding their solicitation treat them as something of an equivalent. The wrongfulness in preresignation solicitation of clients lies in directly and unfairly competing with the firm for business, while still a partner of it, taking unfair advantage of knowledge the firm lacks.

While it is arguable whether clients should be treated, for purposes of this analysis, as assets of the firm, it is clear that partners in a law firm cannot be treated as such.

Law partners "are bound by a fiduciary duty requiring 'the punctilio of an honor the most sensitive'" (see, Graubard Mollen Dannett & Horowitz v. Moskovitz, 86 N.Y.2d 112, 118, 629 N.Y.S.2d 1009, 653 N.E.2d 1179, *supra*, quoting Meinhard v. Salmon, 249 N.Y. 458, 464, 164 N.E. 545). Yet, neither this duty nor any rules of ethics prohibit partners in a law firm from leaving the firm, or from competing with their former firm immediately upon their departure, or even from making plans while still a member of the firm to compete with it following their departure. What is prohibited is actual competition with the firm while still a member of it.

An overall guiding principle limiting the conduct of departing partners is that the process must be handled properly and fairly, so that the withdrawing partner, while in possession of information that the firm lacks (namely, his impending departure), may not take unfair advantage of that information. Thus, where a partner surreptitiously approaches firm clients to obtain assurances that the clients will remain with him if he forms a new law firm, the partner has breached his duty to his partners and his firm. The prohibition against secretly soliciting clients, or removing client files, prior to one's resignation, is founded upon the prohibition against taking unfair advantage of the knowledge of his impending departure, while his partners are still unaware of it. It constitutes not a mere plan to compete in the future with his former law partners, but a present act of direct competition with those to whom he still owes a duty of loyalty. . . .

A partner planning a move necessarily makes numerous arrangements in anticipation of withdrawal, to ensure a smooth transition, including ensuring the capability of continuing to serve those former clients who choose to retain the departing partner. The same considerations apply equally when two partners plan a joint move. The fact that one partner conceived of the move first and approached the other with the idea, or even convinced an initially content colleague to embark upon a joint departure, cannot change the attorneys' right to leave their firm.

The observation of the trial court that plaintiffs' joint departure "denuded" Breed, Abbott's trusts and estates department is irrelevant to the issue of breach of fiduciary duty. Where a department of a law firm contains two active partners, a few associates and support staff, a decision by the two partners to withdraw from the firm will of necessity "denude" the department, and may indeed even "cripple" it, at least temporarily. However, it does not follow that the departure violates the duty owed by the departing partners to the firm. Partners' freedom to withdraw from a firm simply cannot be reconciled with a requirement that their departure be arranged in such a way as to protect the integrity of the department, and ensure its continued profit levels.

Partners who choose to leave a firm and join another presumably believe they will do better at their new affiliation. We can thus assume that as a result of the withdrawal, the old firm may well be economically damaged. Yet, the mere fact of such damage does not make it compensable.

ASSOCIATES AND OTHER STAFF

Once it is recognized that partners in law firms do not breach their duty to the other members of their firm by speaking to colleagues about leaving the firm, there is no logic to prohibiting partners from inviting selected employees to apply for a position at the new firm as well, absent contractual obligations not at issue here. Support staff, like clients, are not the exclusive property of a firm with which they are affiliated. . . .

Even assuming that a partner's duty of loyalty to the other members of his firm prohibits any recruitment of department support staff before the firm is notified of the partner's intended departure, here, there is no showing that members of the staff were contacted prior to the firm being notified. Once the firm is notified of the partners' planned withdrawal, both the firm and the departing partners are on equal footing in competing for these employees; the departing partners no longer have any unfair advantage.

Since plaintiffs were entitled to inform the department staff at issue of their move, and to invite these individuals to submit applications to Chadbourne themselves, there was no impropriety in the manner in which Chadbourne extended offers to members of plaintiffs' staff. The real damage to the firm, namely, the loss of the knowledgeable and experienced attorneys and support staff, was caused not by a breach of fiduciary duty, but simply by the departure of these people — an act that each one of them had an absolute right to do, despite the damage their joint departure would cause the firm.

THE APRIL 26, 1991 MEMO

Under the circumstances, plaintiffs' preliminary compilation of information regarding the salaries, billable hours and standard billing rates of the employees they sought to bring with them, and their providing it to Chadbourne after giving notice to Breed, Abbott, provides no support for a liability determination against them.

First of all, there is no showing, nor did the trial court find, that the purportedly confidential information was provided to Chadbourne — or any other firm — during the period that plaintiffs were interviewing, or at any time before they gave notice to Breed, Abbott. The April 26, 1991 memo was simply a compilation of information of which a lead partner of a practice group is normally aware as a matter of course. Testimony that "the subject of staffing was discussed" during plaintiffs' interviews with firms — a discussion which we must presume will occur any time partners inquire into the possibility of changing firm affiliations — in no way establishes that the April 26, 1991 memo was turned over at that time. The suggestion of the majority that plaintiffs disseminated this information prior to giving notice to Breed, Abbott is speculation.

Furthermore, although the salaries and bonuses paid to associates may be termed "confidential," in fact this information is often the greatest unkept secret in the legal profession. Unlike the earnings of law firm partners, which vary widely even within most firms, depending upon such factors as billable hours and "rainmaking" ability, the earnings of associates and support staff at large firms are relatively circumscribed, with each firm setting standard rates for both salaries and bonuses. Such information is widely known outside the firms themselves: the salary levels and bonuses paid to associates at large New York firms are regularly published in professional publications such as the New York Law Journal. Salary levels, bonuses and other financial information regarding employees' billing rates are well known to professional "headhunters," the agencies that specialize in recruiting and placing lawyers and law firm support staff, and associates' background information is available from sources such as the Martindale-Hubbell directory. . . .

I conclude that the information plaintiffs disclosed to Chadbourne should not be treated as a "trade secret" or "confidential matter" since if it were, a departing attorney might have a continuing obligation not to disclose it, even after leaving the firm.

It is only the partners' fiduciary duty, rather than the label "confidential information," that limits their right to disclose information about their present firm to members of a contemplated new affiliation, and this limitation applies only where disclosure of the information would constitute an act of direct competition with their present firm.

Finally, assuming that plaintiffs had a duty not to disclose financial information known to them concerning the department staff prior to June 19, 1991, I fail to see how Chadbourne obtained any unfair advantage in recruitment. Since no actual recruitment took place until Breed Abbott knew of plaintiffs' intentions, Breed Abbott's ability to take appropriate steps to attempt to retain the employees was in no way diminished. Consequently, no actionable damage can have been suffered by the disclosure of the information.

DESK CHRONOLOGY FILES

[The dissent agreed with the majority that there was no breach of fiduciary duty in the partners taking copies of their own chronology files, since these were duplicates of documents and letters the firm had in its central filing system.]

D. FINANCIAL ATTRIBUTES

Perhaps the most important consequence of the partnership formation determination discussed above is that partners are personally liable for all debts and obligations of the partnership. Of course, partners also are entitled to share in the profits of a partnership, but inadvertent sharing of profits is a rare and happy event. Inadvertent — or even anticipated — sharing of losses is a different matter. Issues relating to the financial attributes of the partnership can be broken down into two major parts: (1) How are profits and losses ultimately allocated among the partners? (2) Who is responsible to pay third parties for partnership liabilities? The following Sections begin with a brief introduction to partnership accounting, and then take up these two major issues.

1. Partnership Accounting

A brief introduction to partnership accounting is useful in understanding the legal rules governing partnerships. The fundamental concept of partnership accounting is the *capital account*. Roughly speaking, a capital account tracks each partner's ownership claim against the partnership. That ownership claim is determined by the following: (1) *contributions* made by each partner to the partnership; (2) each partner's share of *profits or losses* from partnership operations; (3) any *withdrawals* of funds from the partnership; and (4) each partner's *gains or losses* upon sale of the partnership or its assets. The capital account does not reflect loans made by partners to the partnership.

     — *Contributions.* Consider a restaurant with three partners: Andy, Beth, and Conrad. Upon formation of the partnership, each partner contributed $20,000 in cash. In addition, Andy loaned the partnership $50,000 for the purchase of kitchen equipment and restaurant furniture. Moreover, Conrad agreed to assume the additional responsibilities of managing the business affairs of the partnership.

     These contributions would result in a *credit* to each partner's capital account in the amount of $20,000. Andy's loan to the partnership would not be reflected in his capital account—that is, the loan would not be considered an ownership interest in the partnership—but it remains a separate obligation of the partnership. Even if Conrad's services required him to work more hours than his partners, he would not receive any increase in his capital account (though the partnership agreement may stipulate additional compensation for Conrad) because labor is not considered to be a capital contribution.

     — *Sharing of Profits and Losses.* The relative amount of capital contributions does not necessarily determine each partner's share of profits and losses from the ongoing business of the partnership. Equal sharing of profits and losses is the default rule under both the UPA (§18(a)) and RUPA (§401(b)), but partners often change that allocation by contract. In this restaurant business, the partners each contributed one-third of the capital of the partnership, but the partners may have agreed to allocate profits and losses as follows: Andy = 50%, Beth = 20%, and Conrad = 30%. Using this allocation and assuming that the business earned a profit of $300,000 in the first year of operation, the capital accounts of the partners would be credited with the following amounts:

Andy	$150,000
Beth	60,000
Conrad	90,000

Assuming that the partners had made no other contributions or withdrawals from the partnership, their capital accounts after one year would appear as follows:

Andy	$20,000	+	$150,000	=	$170,000		
Beth	20,000	+	60,000	=	80,000		
Conrad	20,000	+	90,000	=	110,000[1]		

To appreciate the importance of these numbers, assume that the partners sell their business at this point. According to both the UPA and RUPA, they must use the proceeds of that sale to pay any debts of the partnership (including Andy's $50,000 loan). Once the partnership's debts have been paid, any remaining amount — called the "surplus" — belongs to the partners. But how should the surplus be allocated? The capital accounts provide useful information to resolve this issue.

Assume for the sake of simplicity that the surplus exactly equals the amount of the total capital accounts. We will relax this assumption below when discussing gains and losses, but for the moment we will assume a surplus equal to $360,000. This money would be distributed to the partners according to the amounts in their capital accounts.

But what if the partners have a negative amount in their capital account? In our hypothetical partnership, this would require a loss following the initial capital contributions. Partners usually allocate losses in the same proportion as profits, following the default rule under both the UPA and RUPA. If we assume that, instead of a handsome profit, the partnership had incurred a $50,000 loss in its first year of operation, the capital accounts of the partners would be *charged* with the following amounts:

Andy	$25,000
Beth	10,000
Conrad	15,000

Assuming that the partners had made no other contributions or withdrawals from the partnership during the first year, their capital accounts after one year would appear as follows:

Andy	$20,000	−	$25,000	=	$(5,000)
Beth	20,000	−	10,000	=	10,000
Conrad	20,000	−	15,000	=	5,000

If the partnership is sold at this point and the surplus exactly equals the amount of the total capital accounts — that is, $10,000 — Beth and Conrad will receive payments of $10,000 and $5,000, respectively, but Andy will owe the partnership $5,000. Andy's obligation to the partnership arises from the fact that partners are personally liable for all obligations of the partnership (unlike shareholders, who have limited liability for the obligations of their corporation).

Withdrawals. As illustrated by the foregoing examples, the sharing of profits and losses is a bookkeeping transaction. The partners in our business did not receive any actual distributions of money until the business was sold. In most

---

1. Notice that none of the partners received interest on the amount of the initial capital contribution. While the partners can agree to pay interest, the default rules under the UPA and RUPA do not provide for interest payments.

partnerships, of course, the partners do not wait until a sale of the partnership before withdrawing funds. Instead, they take periodic distributions from the partnership in the form of *draws*. When made in regular installments (say, monthly), a draw is akin to a salary or wages. Although the amount of a partner's draw is determined by agreement among the partners — and can be more or less than the partner's share of partnership profits — most partnerships attempt to calibrate the amount of a partner's draw to the partner's share of partnership profits. As an actual outflow of cash, draws are *charged* to the capital account.

In the case of our business, assume that each of the partners withdraws $50,000 during a profitable first year of operation. The capital accounts of the partnership would reflect these withdrawals as follows:

Andy	$170,000	−	$50,000	=	$120,000
Beth	80,000	−	50,000	=	30,000
Conrad	110,000	−	50,000	=	60,000

The partners probably established the amount of the draws at the beginning of the year, and it is clear that the partnership earned more profits than the partners withdrew. The profits, therefore, might be viewed as earnings that are reinvested in the partnership. By contrast, the draws are earnings that are removed from the partnership. In many partnerships, the partners take a regular draw determined at the beginning of the year, then take an additional draw at year's end, the size of which depends on the profitability of the partnership. For example, following the highly successful first year, Andy may take an additional draw of $100,000, assuming the other partners or the partnership agreement permit him to make such a withdrawal. In that event, his capital account — that is, his claim against the partnership's assets — would be reduced to $20,000.

Gains and Losses Upon Sale or Liquidation. The amounts shown in the capital accounts do not necessarily correspond to the value of the partnership. For example, assume that the capital accounts of the partners in our hypothetical partnership show the following amounts:

Andy	$25,000
Beth	10,000
Conrad	15,000

In addition, assume that Andy's $50,000 loan is the only outstanding debt. If the partners sell their business for $130,000, they will have a surplus that exceeds the total capital accounts:

$130,000 (proceeds from sale) − $50,000 (Andy's loan) = $80,000 (surplus)

In this event, the sale of the partnership generated a "gain" (sometimes called a "profit") of $30,000:

$80,000 (surplus) − $50,000 (total of capital accounts) = $30,000 (gain)

Each partner would receive the amount in his or her capital account prior to the sale of the partnership *plus* an additional amount equal to his or her share of the gain. In this instance, the partners would receive the following amounts:

Andy	$25,000	+	$15,000	=	$40,000
Beth	10,000	+	6,000	=	16,000
Conrad	15,000	+	9,000	=	24,000

Notice that the total amount distributed to the partners is $80,000—the exact amount of the surplus.

If the surplus is less than the total capital accounts, the partnership is said to have a *loss* on the sale. That loss is allocated in that same way as operating losses. For example, in our hypothetical partnership, we will assume that the business is sold for $70,000, resulting in a surplus of only $20,000:

$70,000 (proceeds from sale) − $50,000 (Andy's loan) = $20,000 (surplus)

This, in turn, would result in a loss on the sale of $30,000:

$20,000 (surplus) − $50,000 (total of capital accounts) = $(30,000) (loss)

Each partner would receive the amount in his or her capital account prior to the sale of the partnership *minus* an amount equal to his or her share of the loss. In this instance, the partners would receive the following amounts:

Andy	$25,000	−	$15,000	=	$10,000
Beth	10,000	−	6,000	=	4,000
Conrad	15,000	−	9,000	=	6,000

Notice that the total amount distributed to the partners is $20,000—again, the exact amount of the surplus.

2.   *Sharing Profits and Losses Among Partners*

The allocation of profits and losses is determined by each partner's interest in the partnership. In the absence of a contrary agreement, partners share in profits equally, even if unequal amounts of capital have been contributed, and losses are shared in the same proportion as profits. UPA §18(a); RUPA §401(b). Partnerships often change the default rule of equal sharing, however, and provide for different sharing arrangements depending on each partner's partnership interest.

Partners are entitled to a repayment of any capital contributions or advances made to the partnership, UPA §18(a); RUPA §401(a) and (d), and the partnership must reimburse a partner for payments made and indemnify a partner for liabilities incurred in the ordinary course of partnership business or for preservation of the partnership's business or property. UPA §18(b); RUPA §401(c). Any partner who makes a payment or advance beyond the amount agreed to be contributed as capital is entitled to interest on the amount of the payment or advance. UPA §18(c); RUPA §401(e).

Profits from the partnership normally are paid out on a periodic basis, usually annually, during the life of the partnership. Capital contributions normally are repaid when a partner withdraws from the partnership or when the partnership terminates. Advances and indemnification for liabilities incurred often are paid during the course of the partnership, but if not, partners have a right to such amounts when the partnership terminates and the accounts of the partners are settled. The UPA does not expressly provide for partnership accounts, but RUPA §401(a) provides that each partner is deemed to have a capital account that is credited with contributions made and profits allocated and charged for any distributions from the partnership and losses allocated.

Assets of the partnership are used to pay liabilities of the partnership in the following order: (1) amounts owed to creditors of the partnership who are not partners; (2) amounts owed to partners other than for capital and profits; (3) amounts owing to partners for repayment of capital; and (4) amounts owing to partners for any remaining profits. If partnership assets are insufficient to cover any partnership liabilities, partners must contribute to the payment of those liabilities. UPA §40; RUPA §807.

The following case considers the sharing of profits and losses among partners in a so-called "service partnership" (that is, a partnership in which one of the partners provides only service — or human capital — not financial capital). Notice that *Kovacik* is at odds with the language of the UPA.

KOVACIK v. REED

315 P.2d 314
Supreme Court of California
September 20, 1957

SCHAUER, Justice.

In this suit for dissolution of a joint venture and for an accounting, defendant appeals from a judgment that plaintiff recover from defendant one half the losses of the venture. We have concluded that inasmuch as the parties agreed the plaintiff was to supply the money and defendant the labor to carry on the venture, defendant is correct in his contention that the trial court erred in holding him liable for one half the monetary losses, and that the judgment should therefore be reversed.

. . . From the "condensed statement of the oral proceedings" included in the settled statement, it appears that plaintiff, a licensed building contractor in San Francisco, operated his contracting business as a sole proprietorship under the fictitious name of "Asbestos Siding Company." Defendant had for a number of years worked for various building contractors in that city as a job superintendent and estimator.

Early in November, 1952, "Kovacik (plaintiff) told Reed (defendant) that Kovacik had an opportunity to do kitchen remodeling work for Sears Roebuck Company in San Francisco and asked Reed to become his job superintendent and estimator in this venture. Kovacik said that he had about $10,000.00 to invest in the venture and that, if Reed would superintend and estimate the jobs, Kovacik would share the profits with Reed on a 50-50 basis. Kovacik did not ask

Reed to agree to share any loss that might result and Reed did not offer to share any such loss. The subject of a possible loss was not discussed in the inception of this venture. Reed accepted Kovacik's proposal and commenced work for the venture shortly after November 1, 1952. . . . Reed's only contribution was his own labor. Kovacik provided all of the venture's financing through the credit of Asbestos Siding Company, although at times Reed purchased materials for the jobs in his own name or on his account for which he was reimbursed. . . .

"The venture bid on and was awarded a number of . . . remodeling jobs . . . in San Francisco. Reed worked on all of the jobs as job superintendent. . . . During . . . August, 1953, Kovacik, who at that time had had all of the financial records of the venture in his possession, . . . informed Reed that the venture had been unprofitable and demanded contribution from Reed as to amounts which Kovacik claimed to have advanced in excess of the income received from the venture. Reed at no time promised, represented or agreed that he was liable for any of the venture's losses and he consistently and without exception refused to contribute to or pay any of the loss resulting from the venture. . . . The venture was terminated on August 31, 1953."

Kovacik thereafter instituted this proceeding, seeking an accounting of the affairs of the venture and to recover from Reed one half of the losses. Despite the evidence above set forth from the statement of the oral proceedings, showing that at no time had defendant agreed to be liable for any of the losses, the trial court "found" more accurately, we think, concluded as a matter of law that "plaintiff and defendant were to share equally all their joint venture profits and losses between them," and that defendant "agreed to share equally in the profits and losses of said joint venture." Following an accounting taken by a referee appointed by the court, judgment was rendered awarding plaintiff recovery against defendant of some $4,340, as one half the monetary losses[1] found by the referee to have been sustained by the joint venture.

It is the general rule that in the absence of an agreement to the contrary the law presumes that partners and joint adventurers intended to participate equally in the profits and losses of the common enterprise, irrespective of any inequality in the amounts each contributed to the capital employed in the venture, with the losses being shared by them in the same proportions as they share the profits.

However, it appears that in the cases in which the above stated general rule has been applied, each of the parties had contributed capital consisting of either money or land or other tangible property, or else was to receive compensation for services rendered to the common undertaking which was to be paid before computation of the profits or losses. Where, however, as in the present case, one partner or joint adventurer contributes the money capital as against the other's skill and labor, all the cases cited, and which our research

---

1. The record is silent as to the factors taken into account by the referee in determining the "loss" suffered by the venture. However, there is no contention that defendant's services were ascribed any value whatsoever. It may also be noted that the trial court "found" that "neither plaintiff nor defendant was to receive compensation for their services rendered to said joint venture, but plaintiff and defendant were to share equally all their joint venture profits and losses between them." Neither party suggests that plaintiff actually rendered services to the venture in the same sense that defendant did. And, as is clear from the settled statement, plaintiff's proposition to defendant was that plaintiff would provide the money as against defendant's contribution of services as estimator and superintendent.

has discovered, hold that neither party is liable to the other for contribution for any loss sustained. Thus, upon loss of the money the party who contributed it is not entitled to recover any part of it from the party who contributed only services. The rationale of this rule, as expressed in Heran v. Hall[, 40 Ky. 159, 35 Am. Dec. 178 (1840),] and Meadows v. Mocquot, [110 Ky. 220, 61 S.W. 28, 22 Ky. Law. Rep. 1646 (1901)], is that where one party contributes money and the other contributes services, then in the event of a loss each would lose his own capital—the one his money and the other his labor. Another view would be that in such a situation the parties have, by their agreement to share equally in profits, agreed that the value of their contributions the money on the one hand and the labor on the other were likewise equal; it would follow that upon the loss, as here, of both money and labor, the parties have shared equally in the losses. Actually, of course, plaintiff here lost only some $8,680 or somewhat less than the $10,000 which he originally proposed and agreed to invest. . . .

It follows that the conclusion of law upon which the judgment in favor of plaintiff for recovery from defendant of one half the monetary losses depends is untenable, and that the judgment should be reversed. . . .

The judgment is reversed.

3. Liability of Partners to Third Parties

With respect to the responsibility of partners to third parties, it has always been the case that partners may be forced to fulfill the obligations of the partnership to third parties out of their personal funds. Although this aspect of the issue is beyond question, the details implementing that policy have engendered much debate. William Draper Lewis recalled that upon being appointed as the primary draftsman of the UPA, "[h]e found that his first problem was to determine the relation of the partners and the persons having claims on the partnership." William Draper Lewis, *The Uniform Partnership Act—A Reply to Mr. Crane's Criticism*, 29 Harv. L. Rev. 158, 165 (1915). Lewis was then operating under instructions from NCCUSL to adopt the entity theory of partnership. He concluded that under this theory, partners should be viewed as "contributors" to the partnership, "having an obligation to the partnership to furnish it with the necessary funds to meet its obligations to third persons, but that those having claims against the partnership have, as such claimants, no claims against the partners." *Id.* at 166. This view of partnership had, in Lewis's opinion, severe drawbacks because partnership creditors would be forced to first exhaust the assets of the partnership and then institute new proceedings to attach the claims of the partnership against the partners as contributors. In addition to being complicated, argued Lewis, this procedure would change existing partnership law rather dramatically, and would be based on a false assumption "that third persons dealing with a partnership do not deal directly with the partners as principals." *Id.* at 166.

Having rejected the entity approach to partner liability, Lewis drafted UPA §15, under which partners are jointly liable for all debts and other obligations of the partnership except wrongful acts (UPA §13) or breaches of trust (UPA §14) of one of the partners, for which the other partners are jointly and severally liable. "Joint liability," you may recall from your torts class, means that each partner could be responsible for paying an entire judgment against the partnership, assuming the partnership and other partners had no funds to pay, and that there were no insurance proceeds against which to satisfy a judgment. "Several liability" means that partners are responsible only for the portion of the liability their actions created. The liability of individual partners for obligations of the partnership may not be altered by agreement among the partners because it affects the rights of third parties. UPA §15 reveals its roots in the aggregate theory of partnership by making partners directly liable for partnership obligations. In addition, the provision does not require exhaustion of the partnership's assets prior to collection from individual partners.

Despite Lewis's efforts to avoid the exhaustion requirement by providing for direct liability of partners, many courts interpreting the UPA have required plaintiffs to exhaust partnership assets prior to seeking the personal assets of the partners. Traditionally, courts have imposed this exhaustion requirement only when the underlying claims create joint liability, allowing immediate suit against partners when the underlying claims create joint and several liability.

The drafters of RUPA perceived two main problems with the UPA's liability provisions. First, by providing for joint liability in some circumstances, UPA §15 creates practical problems for plaintiffs, who are required to join all partners as defendants in such litigation. Recognizing this problem, several states amended their version of the UPA to provide for joint and several liability of partners in all matters. Likewise, RUPA §306(a) makes all partnership liability joint and several. Note that, although this RUPA provision solves the practical problems engendered by joint liability, it retains direct personal liability of partners for obligations of the partnership and thus compromises the entity approach that RUPA elsewhere has explicitly embraced.

Second, omission of an exhaustion requirement was beneficial to creditors but inconvenient for the partners, who were required to pay an obligation out of their personal assets and then seek indemnification from the partnership. In the end, whether the exhaustion requirement is good policy probably depends on whether it accurately reflects the expectations of the parties. After all, both the UPA (implicitly) and RUPA (explicitly in §307(d)(3)) permit the parties to contract for whatever arrangement they desire.

The following case illustrates the effect of the partnership liability rules. As you read this case, consider the effect of rules holding Billauer and Ho'okano liable for actions of their partners. Is the result fair? What incentives do these rules produce?

In re KECK, MAHIN & CATE

274 B.R. 740
United States Bankruptcy Court, N.D. Illinois
March 6, 2002

CAROL A. DOYLE, Bankruptcy Judge.

This matter is before the court on plaintiff Jacob Brandzel's ("plaintiff") adversary complaint seeking a determination of defendants' liability under the Illinois Uniform Partnership Act ("IUPA"). The plaintiff is the plan administrator for the debtor Keck, Mahin & Cate ("Keck") pursuant to the chapter 11 plan ("Plan") confirmed by the bankruptcy court on December 16, 1999. The plaintiff seeks recovery for malpractice claims filed by Bank of Orange

County and Pacific Inland Bancorp (collectively, "Pacific Inland") and Wozniak Industries, Inc. ("Wozniak"), a claim filed by Citizens Commercial Leasing Corporation ("Citizens") and administrative claims allowed in the bankruptcy case as of December 16, 1999. Defendants Barbara P. Billauer and Thomas E. Ho'okano (collectively, "defendants") are former capital partners of Keck. Pursuant to the Plan, the plaintiff is the assignee of all allowed claims, and has the right to seek recovery from partners who did not participate in a settlement of partners' outstanding liabilities. Ms. Billauer and Mr. Ho'okano dispute any liability for allowed claims against Keck. For the reasons stated below, the court finds for the plaintiff regarding the Pacific Inland, Wozniak and administrative claims. The court finds for the defendants regarding the Citizens claim.

After holding a trial on the merits, the court makes the following findings of fact and conclusions of law:

A. BACKGROUND

Keck was an Illinois partnership whose partners engaged in the practice of law. On December 16, 1997, some of Keck's creditors filed an involuntary chapter 7 bankruptcy petition against the partnership. On December 31, 1997, the bankruptcy court granted Keck's motion to convert the case to chapter 11 of the Bankruptcy Code. The Plan was confirmed on December 16, 1999. Under the confirmation order ("Order"), Jacob Brandzel was appointed plan administrator.

Ms. Billauer and Mr. Ho'okano are former capital partners of Keck. Ms. Billauer was a partner from July 2, 1990 until August 31, 1993. Mr. Ho'okano was a partner from June 24, 1991 until March 26, 1993. Pursuant to the Plan, all Keck partners had the option to pay a specified settlement amount for partnership liabilities and become "participating partners," or to decline to pay the settlement amount and become "non-participating partners." Non-participating partners potentially faced maximum liability for Keck's obligations. Ms. Billauer and Mr. Ho'okano chose not to participate in the settlement and are being sued for their liability with regard to the Pacific Inland, Wozniak, Citizens and administrative claims, totaling $5,483,189.96.

B. ADMINISTRATIVE CLAIMS

The plaintiff seeks to hold the defendants liable for administrative claims allowed in the bankruptcy case as of December 16, 1999, in the amount of approximately $2.1 million. Under section 9.8 of the Plan and paragraph F of the Order, the plaintiff is entitled to recover allowed administrative claims as of December 16, 1999 from all non-participating partners. Neither Mr. Ho'okano nor Ms. Billauer dispute the validity of the Plan or Order granting the plaintiff the authority to recover administrative claims allowed as of December 16, 1999. They also have not contested the amount of administrative claims as of December 16, 1999. Therefore, the court finds for the plaintiff against both defendants with respect to the $2,177,787.73 in administrative claims allowed as of December 16, 1999.

C. PACIFIC INLAND, WOZNIAK AND CITIZENS CLAIMS

The plaintiff contends that the defendants are jointly and severally liable under section 13 of the IUPA, and the partnership agreement ("Agreement") for the Pacific Inland, Wozniak and Citizens claims. He asserts that each of these claims arose before or during the time the defendants were partners. Ms. Billauer and Mr. Ho'okano dispute any liability for the Pacific Inland, Wozniak and Citizens claims. Both Ms. Billauer and Mr. Ho'okano argue that: (1) the allowed claims were not in existence when they withdrew from the partnership; (2) Keck paid Citizens the full amount incurred while the defendants were partners; (3) the partnership dissolved upon their withdrawal and the new partnership assumed all prior debts, thereby terminating their liabilities; (4) liability is barred under the terms of the Agreement; . . . and (6) they are not liable because Keck was solvent when they left the partnership. Ms. Billauer also argues that (7) the Agreement is void as against public policy and (8) the doctrine of laches bars suit against her. Each of these defenses is discussed below.

1.   EXISTENCE OF WOZNIAK AND PACIFIC INLAND CLAIMS

Ms. Billauer and Mr. Ho'okano first argue that no obligations to Wozniak or Pacific Inland existed at the time they left Keck. They assert that they are liable under paragraph 8(a) of the Agreement only for "Firm Obligations" that arose before they left the partnership.[4] They further contend that the Wozniak and Pacific Inland malpractice claims did not become Firm Obligations until those claimants had a judgment entered against them or the malpractice claims were settled, which the defendants assert occurred after they left the partnership.

This argument is not persuasive. Sections 13 and 15 of the Illinois Uniform Partnership Act determine the scope of Ms. Billauer's and Mr. Ho'okano's liability to third parties (which includes the plaintiff in this case). That liability is not limited to "Firm Obligations" as that phrase is used in paragraph 8(a) of the Agreement. Section 13 of the Act provides that "[w]here, by any wrongful act or omission of any partner acting in the ordinary course of the business of the partnership, . . . loss or injury is caused to any person, . . . the partnership is liable therefor to the same extent as the partners so acting or omitting to act." Under the language of section 13, it is the "wrongful act or omission" of a partner that gives rise to the liability of all other partners. The only reasonable interpretation of this provision is that the liability of all partners arises at the time of "any wrongful act or omission" by any partner.

A partner cannot escape liability simply by leaving the partnership after the malpractice is committed but before the client wins or settles a malpractice claim. Courts have consistently held that, within the context of partnership dissolution, withdrawing partners remain liable for matters pending at the time

---

4. Neither Ms. Billauer nor Mr. Ho'okano contest that they are liable under the Agreement for partnership debts that arose before they joined the firm. Under the IUPA, partner liability for pre-existing partnership debts is generally limited to partnership assets. However, an incoming partner can be held personally liable where there is an express assumption of liability. Magrini v. Jackson, 150 N.E.2d 387, 392 (1958). In this case, the partnership agreement expressly provides for the assumption of pre-existing Firm Obligations by incoming partners.

of dissolution. These cases support the conclusion that liability under section 13 of the IUPA arises at the time of the offending conduct. . . .

[Applying that standard, the court found that the malpractice alleged in the Wozniack and Pacific Island claims was committed while Mr. Ho'okano and Ms. Billauer were still partners, but that the debt to Citizens on a line of credit was incurred after they withdrew from the partnership.]

3. DISSOLUTION OF PARTNERSHIP

Ms. Billauer and Mr. Ho'okano argue that they are not liable for the Pacific Inland and Wozniak claims because the partnership dissolved when they withdrew from the firm and a new partnership was formed. They contend that the new partnership assumed any debts from the old partnership, and that therefore no liabilities against them now exist. However, whether the partnership dissolved and a new partnership was formed, or the old partnership continued by virtue of paragraph 15(b) of the Agreement without the defendants, the result is the same. The general rule under Illinois law is that "dissolution of the partnership does not of itself discharge the existing liability of any partners." As noted earlier, that liability can stem from prior contractual obligations, including those that give rise to malpractice claims.

In addition, partners cannot release one another from liability to third parties. Illinois law requires consent by the third party itself to release the liability of any partner. This consent may be express or inferred based on the third party's course of conduct after it learned of the dissolution. Without this consent, partners cannot shield themselves from the rights of creditors. There is no evidence that either Wozniak or Pacific Inland consented to releasing Ms. Billauer and Mr. Ho'okano of their liability. Therefore, whether the partnership dissolved or the old partnership continued without the defendants, they are liable for debts incurred to the third-party claimants before their departure dates.

4. FIVE YEAR LIMITATION ON LIABILITY IN PARTNERSHIP AGREEMENT

Ms. Billauer and Mr. Ho'okano also argue that they can be pursued for partnership liabilities only during the first five years after they withdrew from the partnership. The defendants rely on paragraph 8(b)(2) of the Agreement, which attempts to reduce a partner's liability by twenty percent per year following a partner's departure from the firm. However, this provision does not absolve the defendants of liability under the Plan and Illinois law.

The Plan grants the plaintiff the authority to pursue the defendants for the full amount of the allowed claims at issue in this case. Section 9.8 of the Plan specifically states that "[i]n any legal action or proceeding of any kind against a Non-Participating Partner, the Plan Administrator shall have any and all rights available under applicable law to assert, and seek recovery for, . . . any amount up to the full amount of the Allowed Claims." Section 16.8 states that "[e]xcept as otherwise expressly provided [in the Plan], to the extent the Plan is inconsistent with any other documents, the provisions of the Plan shall be controlling." Therefore, the Plan grants the plaintiff the right to seek recovery for the full amount allowable under Illinois law, and the Plan controls over the terms of the partnership agreement to the extent there are any inconsistencies.

Under Illinois law and the Agreement, Ms. Billauer and Mr. Ho'okano are liable for claims arising before or during the time they were partners. Keck is a general partnership subject to Illinois law. Under Illinois law, partners are jointly and severally liable to creditors of the partnership. Illinois law does not limit this liability with respect to innocent co-partners. As noted above, partners cannot release their liability to third parties without their consent. There is no evidence of any such consent, so paragraph 8(b)(2) of the Agreement is not binding on claimants like Wozniak and Pacific Inland. Because the plaintiff stands in the shoes of these two creditors, the defendants cannot escape liability based on paragraph 8(b)(2) of the Agreement. . . .

D. Conclusion

For the foregoing reasons, the court finds that Mr. Ho'okano and Ms. Billauer are jointly and severally liable to the plaintiff in the amount of $775,000.00 for the Wozniak claim, $825,000.00 for the Pacific Inland claim and $2,177,787.73 for the administrative claims. The court finds for the defendants regarding the Citizens claim.

PROBLEM 2-4

Bobby Helpinstill and Mike Brown were partners in MBO Computers (MBO). After they opened a bank account in the name of the partnership at Longview National Bank (Longview), Brown developed a habit of writing checks for amounts exceeding the funds in the partnership's account and later covering the overdrafts with deposits. As some point, this relatively common and innocuous practice took a nefarious turn, as Brown embarked on a full-blown check-kiting scheme.

Check kiting is fraud, plain and simple. Here's how it works: MBO has $500 in its account with Longview, but Brown writes a check from that account for $1,000 and deposits the check in another bank. Brown knows that checks take some time to work their way through the banking system, and he attempts to take advantage of this lag. Before the check has circled back to Longview, Brown withdraws money from the second bank and deposits it in the Longview account. Then he starts the whole process over again. Ultimately, the goal of a person engaged in a check-kiting scheme is to withdraw a substantial amount of money and abscond.

Brown never got that far. He was caught, prosecuted, and sent to jail, leaving Longview with over $380,000 in losses. Unable to recover from Brown or MBO, Longview turned to Helpinstill, who was completely unaware of the check-kiting scheme.

Should Helpinstill be responsible to Longview for Brown's criminal activity? Is it relevant that Brown's activities were contrary to the company's express written financial policies?

E. DISSOLUTION

Dissolution has long been one of the most complex aspects of partnership law. William Draper Lewis attributed the complexity to a lack of precision in common law decisions: "The subject of dissolution and winding up of a partnership is involved in considerable confusion principally because of the various ways in which the word 'dissolution' is employed." William Draper Lewis, *The Uniform Partnership Act*, 24 Yale L.J. 617, 626-627 (1915). Courts used the term "dissolution" to refer variously to the departure of a partner from the partnership, the process of liquidating and winding up a partnership, or the completion of that process. Lewis's straightforward solution to this confusion was to codify the definitions of each stage of the process of ending a partnership.

"Dissolution" under the UPA means simply any "change in the relation of the partners caused by any partner ceasing to be associated in the carrying on as distinguished from the winding up of the business." UPA §29. The dissolution of a partnership is an event that triggers the process of winding up. As explained by the official comments, "[D]issolution designates the point in time when the partners cease to carry on the business together; termination is the point in time when all the partnership affairs are wound up; winding up, the process of settling partnership affairs after dissolution." Official Comment, Uniform Partnership Act §29. The dissolution of a partnership, therefore, does not result in its immediate termination. UPA §30. It is important to note that termination of a partnership as a legal entity is not the same as termination of the partnership business. Partners often elect to continue a partnership business by forming a new partnership or some other business entity.

The technical definition of "dissolution" emanates from the aggregate theory of partnership. If any partner departs from an existing partnership, the aggregation is altered and thus the partnership is dissolved. Note that dissolution occurs only when a partner ceases to be associated with the partnership, not when a partner is added. Although some courts have treated admission of a new partner as a dissolution, this view of dissolution isn't very useful, since the consequences of dissolution contemplate some breakup of the partnership.

Despite Lewis's confidence in the superiority of the UPA's approach to dissolution, subsequent cases have revealed that courts are often confused by the concept. In addition, strict adherence to the statutory definition of "dissolution" can lead to seemingly unjust results. The RUPA Reporters criticized the UPA definition as follows:

> The problem with the UPA's use of the term *dissolution* is . . . much more fundamental than the absence of a clear definition of the concept. The UPA's definition and use of the concept of dissolution is a bad idea because it reflects an aggregate concept of partnerships that fails to recognize the stability of many partnerships. The UPA unnecessarily destabilizes many partnerships, particularly those that have continuation agreements, and actually undercuts the attempts of partners to contract for stability. The UPA suggests that the partnership business is coming to a close when all that may be coming to a close is one partner's participation. In short, the UPA does not distinguish adequately a departure that triggers a winding up of the business from a departure that is governed by a buyout or continuation agreement.

Donald J. Weidner & John W. Larson, *The Revised Uniform Partnership Act: The Reporters' Overview*, 49 Bus. Law. 1, 5 (1993).

[Handwritten margin notes: "In order to find a definition for dissolution"; "an event that triggers winding up"; "this generally doesn't happen though when a new partner is added."; "RUPA committee's criticism of UPA dissolution definition"]

RUPA does away with the UPA rule that the departure of a partner causes a dissolution of the partnership and has different rules for continuation and winding up of the partnership business. Under RUPA the departure of a partner is called a "dissociation" in recognition of the fact that under RUPA the departure may or may not result in the winding up and termination of the partnership. RUPA Article 6 defines all "dissociations." Whether a dissociation results in a buyout of the dissociated partner and continuation of the partnership business or a winding up and termination of the partnership business depends on Article 8.

Within that Article, RUPA §801 lists all of the events that trigger a winding up, or liquidation, of the partnership business. The most common dissolution events are dissociations, but it is not necessary to have a dissociation to cause a dissolution and winding up. For example, a partnership may be dissolved by the express will of all of the partners (RUPA §801(2)(ii)) or by an event agreed to in the partnership agreement (RUPA §801(3)).

If a dissociation does not cause the dissolution and winding up of the partnership business, the dissociating partner must be bought out pursuant to Article 7. The main consequences of Article 7 are (1) the dissociated partner's interest must be purchased for "the greater of the liquidation value or the value based on a sale of the entire business as a going concern without the dissociated partner" (§701(c)); and (2) the dissociated partner's liability and ability to bind the partnership are terminated (§702).

With so many complex rules, disputes are inevitable. The following Sections explore some of the major issues that surround dissolution of a general partnership. Because RUPA is still young, relatively few cases have considered its provisions. Nevertheless, some of the results of the cases below that apply the UPA contrast with those that would adhere under RUPA.

1.   Liquidation Rights

One of the most important issues relating to dissolution relates to control over liquidation decisions. Liquidation is simply the process of turning partnership assets into cash, which is then used to pay any partnership liabilities. To the extent that cash remains after the liabilities are paid, it is distributed to the partners according to their ownership interests in the partnership. Liquidation rights are important because they may determine whether the partnership business continues, as in the following case. Moreover, the *right* to cause liquidation may be a very powerful bargaining chip when the time comes to divide the assets of the partnership.

CREEL v. LILLY

729 A.2d 385
Court of Appeals of Maryland
May 12, 1999

CHASANOW, Judge.

The primary issue presented in this appeal is whether Maryland's Uniform Partnership Act (UPA) permits the estate of a deceased partner to demand liquidation of partnership assets in order to arrive at the true value of the business. Specifically, Petitioner (Anne Creel) maintains that the surviving partners have a duty to liquidate all partnership assets because (1) there is no provision in the partnership agreement providing for the continuation of the partnership upon a partner's death and (2) the estate has not consented to the continuation of the business. Respondents (Arnold Lilly and Roy Altizer) contend that because the surviving partners wound up the partnership in good faith, in that they conducted a full inventory, provided an accurate accounting to the estate for the value of the business as of the date of dissolution, and paid the estate its proportionate share of the surplus proceeds, they are under no duty to liquidate the partnership's assets upon demand of the deceased partner's estate.

As discussed in more detail in Part II.A., *infra*, UPA, which has governed partnerships in this State for the past 80 years, has been repealed since this litigation commenced. The Act that now governs Maryland partnerships is the Revised Uniform Partnership Act (RUPA), which was adopted in July 1998 with a phase-in period. Therefore, until December 31, 2002, both UPA and RUPA will coexist, with §9A-1204 determining which Act applies to a particular partnership's formation, termination, and any other conflict that may arise.

At the outset we note there is a partnership agreement in the instant case that, while somewhat unclear, seems to provide for an alternative method of winding up the partnership rather than a liquidation of all assets. The circuit court and intermediate appellate court both found the agreement unclear as to dissolution and winding up of the business upon the death of a partner and correctly turned to UPA as an interpretative aid. In looking specifically at the trial court's order, the trial judge referred to the partnership agreement and UPA but was not explicit as to which one he primarily relied on in holding that a forced sale of all assets was not required in this case. Regardless, the trial judge's interpretation of the partnership agreement and holding are in conformity with UPA.

Due to our uncertainty as to whether the trial court's holding was based primarily on the partnership agreement or UPA, and also because clarification of the liquidation issue implicates other aspects of partnership law, we will examine not only the partnership agreement itself, but also Maryland's UPA and applicable case law, the cases in other jurisdictions that have interpreted the liquidation issue under UPA, and the newly adopted RUPA. For the reasons stated in this opinion, we concur in the finding of the courts below that Respondents are under no duty to "liquidate on demand" by Petitioner, as UPA does not mandate a forced sale of all partnership assets in order to ascertain the true value of the business. Winding up is not always synonymous with liquidation, which can be a harsh, drastic, and often unnecessary course of action. A preferred method in a good faith winding up, which was utilized in this case, is to pay the deceased partner's estate its proportionate share of the value of the partnership, derived from an accurate accounting, without having to resort to a full liquidation of the business. To hold otherwise vests excessive power and control in the deceased partner's estate, to the extreme disadvantage of the surviving partners. Thus, on this issue, we affirm the judgment of the Court of Special Appeals.

In this appeal, Petitioner also asks us to award the estate its share of the partnership profits generated by the Respondents' alleged continued use of the partnership assets for the period of time during which Petitioner claims the Respondents neither liquidated the business nor agreed to pay the estate its proper percentage share of the partnership. We reject Petitioner's request and agree with the courts below that there is no basis for damages because Good Ole Boys Racing (Good Ole Boys) is a successor partnership and not a continuation of Joe's Racing, which was properly wound up and terminated before the new partnership began operations.

I. Background

On approximately June 1, 1993, Joseph Creel began a retail business selling NASCAR racing memorabilia. His business was originally located in a section of his wife Anne's florist shop, but after about a year and a half he decided to raise capital from partners so that he could expand and move into his own space. On September 20, 1994, Mr. Creel entered into a partnership agreement — apparently prepared without the assistance of counsel — with Arnold Lilly and Roy Altizer to form a general partnership called "Joe's Racing." The partnership agreement covered such matters as the partnership's purpose, location, and operations, and stated the following regarding termination of the business:

7. Termination

(a) That, at the termination of this partnership a full and accurate inventory shall be prepared, and the assets, liabilities, and income, both in gross and net, shall be ascertained: the remaining debts or profits will be distributed according to the percentages shown above in the 6(e). . . .

(d) Upon the death or illness of a partner, his share will go to his estate. If his estate wishes to sell his interest, they must offer it to the remaining partners first.

The three-man partnership operated a retail store in the St. Charles Towne Center Mall in Waldorf, Maryland. For their initial investment in Joe's Racing, Mr. Lilly and Mr. Altizer each paid $6,666 in capital contributions, with Mr. Creel contributing his inventory and supplies valued at $15,000. Pursuant to the partnership agreement, Mr. Lilly and Mr. Altizer also paid $6,666 to Mr. Creel ($3,333 each) "for the use and rights to the business known as Joe's Racing Collectables." The funds were placed in a partnership bank account with First Virginia Bank-Maryland. All three partners were signatories to this account, but on May 19, 1995, unknown to Mr. Lilly and Mr. Altizer, Mr. Creel altered the account so that only he had the authority to sign checks. It was only after Mr. Creel's death that Mr. Lilly and Mr. Altizer realized they could not access the account funds, which were frozen by the bank upon Mr. Creel's passing. Moreover, on approximately February 20, 1995, Mr. Creel paid a $5,000 retainer to an attorney without his partners' knowledge. He wanted the attorney to prepare documents for the marketing of franchises for retail stores dealing in racing memorabilia.

Joe's Racing had been in existence for almost nine months when Mr. Creel died on June 14, 1995. Mrs. Creel was appointed personal representative of his estate. In this capacity, and acting without the knowledge of the surviving partners, Mrs. Creel and the store's landlord agreed to shorten the lease by one month so that it expired on August 31, 1995. June, July, and August's rent was paid by Mr. Lilly and Mr. Altizer.

In accordance with [UPA §31(4)], Joe's Racing was automatically dissolved upon Mr. Creel's death and because the partnership agreement did not expressly provide for continuation of the partnership nor did his estate consent to its continuation, the surviving partners were required under UPA to wind up the business. See [UPA §30 and §38(1)]. In order to pay debts and efficiently wind up the partnership affairs, Mr. Lilly and Mr. Altizer requested that Mrs. Creel and the bank release the funds in the partnership account ($18,115.93 as of July 13, 1995). Their request was refused and it was at this point that litigation commenced. We adopt the following procedural history of this case, as detailed in the unreported opinion of the Court of Special Appeals:

> Not receiving a favorable response, the surviving partners, on behalf of Joe's Racing, brought an action in the District Court against Mrs. Creel, individually and as personal representative of her late husband's estate, and First Virginia Bank-Maryland. Mrs. Creel filed a demand for a jury trial, which brought the case to the circuit court. By way of a counterclaim, the bank filed a complaint for interpleader. The court authorized the bank to deposit with the court the money in the partnership account, dismissed the bank from the suit, and ordered that the conflicting claims of the parties be transferred to the funds on deposit, with the case to proceed as one between the Joe's Racing partnership and Ann [sic] Creel, individually and as Personal Representative of the Estate of Joseph Creel. . . .
>
> Rejecting [Mrs. Creel's] request to refer the matter to an auditor for an accounting as (a) untimely (and therefore likely to delay final resolution of the case) and (b) unnecessary, the court[, after a four-day trial,] determined that Joseph Creel had a 52% interest in the partnership instead of a 36% interest as claimed by [Mr. Lilly and Mr. Altizer]; that Joseph Creel's expenditure of $5,000 of partnership funds for legal assistance was an expense chargeable to the partnership and did not justify reduction of his capital contribution by [$]5,000 as contended by [Mr. Lilly and Mr. Altizer]; and that effecting a change in the partnership bank account so that only he could sign checks was not a breach of fiduciary duty by Mr. Creel.
>
> The court also found that the surviving partners sought to wind up and close out the partnership and took all reasonable steps to do so, and that there was no breach by them of any fiduciary duty to the Estate. The lease on the store premises occupied by the partnership expired on 31 August 1995, and on that date Mr. Lilly conducted an inventory of all merchandise in the store. Based on that inventory, an accountant computed the value of the partnership business; Mrs. Creel was invited to review the books and records and retain her own accountant or appraiser if she questioned [Mr. Lilly or Mr. Altizer's] figures. *She declined to do so. After 31 August 1995, Messrs. Lilly and Altizer ceased doing business as Joe's Racing and began doing business together under the name "Good Ole Boys Racing."*
>
> *The court accepted the valuation prepared by [Mr. Lilly and Mr. Altizer's] accountant as the correct value of the partnership assets as of 31 August 1995, and found that the surviving partners fully disclosed and delivered to the Estate all records of the financial affairs of the Joe's Racing partnership up to 31 August 1995, which the court took to be the end of the winding up period. Rejecting [Mrs. Creel's] assertions (1) that [Mr. Lilly and Mr. Altizer] were obligated to liquidate the partnership assets in order to wind up the partnership; (2) that [Mr. Lilly and Mr. Altizer], instead of winding up the partnership by liquidating its assets, misappropriated partnership assets, i.e., inventory to make a profit, for which they were obligated to account;* and (3) that the Estate was entitled to 52% of such profits, the court declared that the Estate was entitled to a total of $21,631. . . .

On the basis of those findings, the court ordered that [Mrs. Creel] could withdraw the funds deposited in court by the bank and that [Mr. Lilly and Mr. Altizer]
should pay [Mrs. Creel] the difference between the amount of those funds and
$21,631.00. (Emphasis added.)

The Court of Special Appeals affirmed the judgment of the Circuit Court for
Charles County, finding that under UPA "winding up" does not always mean
"liquidate;" therefore, Joe's Racing had no duty to sell off all of its assets in a
liquidation sale. The court also held that Good Ole Boys was not a continuation
of Joe's Racing, and as such the Creel estate was not entitled to damages equal
to a share of the profits allegedly made by the successor partnership. Mrs. Creel
filed a petition for certiorari in May 1998, which we granted.

II.   Discussion and Analysis

A.

We begin our analysis by reviewing the law of partnership as it pertains to the
issues in this case. . . .

A partnership is either (1) for a definite term or a particular undertaking or
(2) at will, which means the business has no definite term or particular undertaking. An at-will partnership continues indefinitely and can be dissolved by the
express will of any partner or automatically by the happening of a specific event
as mandated by UPA, such as the death of a partner. Under UPA, partners may
avoid the automatic dissolution of the business upon the death of a partner by
providing for its continuation in their partnership agreement. Sophisticated
partnerships virtually always use carefully drafted partnership agreements to
protect the various partners' interests by providing for the continuation of the
business, the distribution of partnership assets, etc., in the face of various contingencies such as death. Less sophisticated partnerships, however, are often
operating under oral terms or a "homemade" agreement that does not contain
protections for the partners or the business.

While the death of a partner automatically dissolves the partnership unless
there is an agreement stating otherwise, the partnership is not terminated
until the winding-up process is complete. Winding up is generally defined as
"getting in the assets, settling with [the] debtors and creditors, and appropriating the amount of profit or loss [to the partners]." Comp. of Treas. v.
Thompson Tr. Corp., 121 A.2d 850, 856 (1956). The surviving partners have
the right to wind up the partnership or the deceased partner's representative
may obtain a winding up through the courts. [UPA §38] details the winding-up
procedures and whether Subsection [(1) or (2)] applies depends on whether
dissolution was caused in contravention of the partnership agreement or not,
wrongfully, etc. The winding-up procedure that applies in this case is found in
[UPA §38(1)]. . . .

Historically, under many courts and commentators' interpretation of UPA,
when a partner died and the partnership automatically dissolved because there
was no consent by the estate to continue the business nor was there a written
agreement allowing for continuation, the estate had the right to compel liquidation of the partnership assets. Reducing all of the partnership assets to cash

through a liquidation was seen as the only way to obtain the true value of the business. However, while winding up has often traditionally been regarded as synonymous with liquidation, this "fire sale" of assets has been viewed by many courts and commentators as a harsh and destructive measure. Consequently, to avoid the drastic result of a forced liquidation, many courts have adopted judicial alternatives to this potentially harmful measure. . . .

Over time, the UPA rule requiring automatic dissolution of the partnership upon the death of a partner, in the absence of consent by the estate to continue the business or an agreement providing for continuation, with the possible result of a forced sale of all partnership assets was viewed as outmoded by many jurisdictions including Maryland. The development and adoption of RUPA by the National Conference of Commissioners on Uniform State Laws (NCCUSL) mitigated this harsh UPA provision of automatic dissolution and compelled liquidation.

RUPA's underlying philosophy differs radically from UPA's, thus laying the foundation for many of its innovative measures. RUPA adopts the "entity" theory of partnership as opposed to the "aggregate" theory that the UPA espouses. Under the aggregate theory, a partnership is characterized by the collection of its individual members, with the result being that if one of the partners dies or withdraws, the partnership ceases to exist. On the other hand, RUPA's entity theory allows for the partnership to continue even with the departure of a member because it views the partnership as "an entity distinct from its partners." [RUPA §201(a).]

This adoption of the entity theory, which permits continuity of the partnership upon changes in partner identity, allows for several significant changes in RUPA. Of particular importance to the instant case is that under RUPA "a partnership no longer automatically dissolves due to a change in its membership, but rather *the existing partnership may be continued if the remaining partners elect to buy out the dissociating partner*." Will the Revised Uniform Partnership Act (1994) Ever Be Uniformly Adopted?, 48 Fla. L. Rev. at 579 (emphasis added). In contrast to UPA, RUPA's "buy-out" option does not have to be expressly included in a written partnership agreement in order for it to be exercised; however, the surviving partners must still actively choose to exercise the option, as "continuation is not automatic as with a corporation." [*Id.* at 579-580.] This major RUPA innovation therefore delineates two possible paths for a partnership to follow when a partner dies or withdraws: "[o]ne leads to the winding up and termination of the partnership and the other to continuation of the partnership and purchase of the departing partner's share." [*Id.* at 583.] Critically, under RUPA the estate of the deceased partner no longer has to consent in order for the business to be continued nor does the estate have the right to compel liquidation.

Like UPA, RUPA is a "gap filler" in that it only governs partnership affairs to the extent not otherwise agreed to by the partners in the partnership agreement. . . . There are certain RUPA provisions, however, that partners cannot waive, such as unreasonably restricting the right of access to partnership books and records, eliminating the duty of loyalty, unreasonably reducing the duty of care, and eliminating the obligation of good faith and fair dealing. [RUPA §103(b).]

Along with 18 other states, Maryland has adopted RUPA, effective July 1, 1998, with a phase-in period during which the two Acts will coexist. As of January 1, 2003, RUPA will govern all Maryland partnerships. In adopting

RUPA, the Maryland legislature was clearly seeking to eliminate some of UPA's harsh provisions, such as the automatic dissolution of a viable partnership upon the death of a partner and the subsequent right of the estate of the deceased partner to compel liquidation. In essence, the NCCUSL drafted RUPA to reflect the emerging trends in partnership law. RUPA is intended as a flexible, modern alternative to the more rigid UPA and its provisions are consistent with the reasonable expectations of commercial parties in today's business world.

B.

As discussed earlier, the traditional manner in which UPA allows for the continuation of the partnership upon the death of a partner is to either obtain the consent of the deceased partner's estate or include a continuation clause in the partnership agreement. There have been several cases in other jurisdictions, however, where neither of these conditions was met and the court elected another option under UPA instead of a "fire sale" of all the partnership assets to ensure that the deceased partner's estate received its fair share of the partnership. These jurisdictions have recognized the unfairness and harshness of a compelled liquidation and found other judicially acceptable means of winding up a partnership under UPA, such as ordering an in-kind distribution of the assets or allowing the remaining partners to buy out the withdrawing partner's share of the partnership.

    While the . . . cases have not involved the specific situation that we are faced with here — dissolution upon the death of a partner — the options the various courts have adopted to avoid a compelled liquidation of all partnership assets are equally applicable to the instant case. A dissolution is a dissolution and a winding-up process is a winding-up process, no matter what the underlying reason is for its occurrence. The reason for the dissolution is relevant when liabilities are being apportioned among partners, such as in a wrongful dissolution, but such is not the concern in the instant case. Many of these cases also involve a continued partnership, as opposed to a successor partnership like Good Ole Boys, but again the various courts' reasons for not compelling a sale of all assets in order to arrive at the true value of the business are equally applicable to the instant case. . . .

C.

In applying the law discussed in Part II.A. and B. to the facts of this case, we want to clarify that while UPA is the governing act, our holding is also consistent with RUPA and its underlying policies. The legislature's recent adoption of RUPA indicates that it views with disfavor the compelled liquidation of businesses and that it has elected to follow the trend in partnership law to allow the continuation of business without disruption, in either the original or successor form, if the surviving partners choose to do so through buying out the deceased partner's share.

    In this appeal, however, we would arrive at the same holding regardless of whether UPA or RUPA governs. Although our holding departs from the general UPA rule that the representative of the deceased partner's estate has a right to demand liquidation of the partnership, as we discuss in this subsection, *infra*, our position of "no forced sale" hardly represents a radical departure from traditional partnership law. . . . With that background, we turn to a discussion of the two issues Mrs. Creel raises in this appeal.

1. Compelled Liquidation Issue

The first issue is whether the Creel estate has the right to demand liquidation of Joe's Racing where its partnership agreement does not expressly provide for continuation of the partnership and where the estate does not consent to continuation. Before we move on to our analysis of the compelled liquidation issue, we point out that our finding that Good Ole Boys is a successor partnership, rather than a continuation of Joe's Racing, does not negate the need for a complete discussion of this issue. Unless there is consent to continue the business or an agreement providing for continuation, upon the death of a partner the accurate value of the partnership must be ascertained as of the date of dissolution and the proportionate share paid to the deceased partner's estate, no matter if we are dealing with a subsequent new partnership or a continuation of the original business. If a compelled liquidation of all partnership assets is seen as the only way to arrive at its true value, then property from the original partnership will have to be sold whether the present business is a continuation or a successor business; regardless, the potential harm of such a "fire sale" affects both equally. . . .

Because a partnership is governed by any agreement between or among the partners, we must begin our analysis of the compelled liquidation issue by examining the Joe's Racing partnership agreement. We reiterate that both UPA and RUPA only apply when there is either no partnership agreement governing the partnership's affairs, the agreement is silent on a particular point, or the agreement contains provisions contrary to law. . . . Thus, when conflicts between partners arise, courts must first look to the partnership agreement to resolve the issue. . . .

Even though the partnership agreement uses the word "termination," paragraph 7(a) is really discussing the dissolution of the partnership and the attendant winding-up process that ultimately led to termination. Paragraph 7(a) requires that the assets, liabilities, and income be "ascertained," but it in no way mandates that this must be accomplished by a forced sale of the partnership assets. Indeed, a liquidation or sale of assets is not mentioned anywhere in 7(a).

In this case, the winding-up method outlined in 7(a) was followed exactly by the surviving partners: a full and accurate inventory was prepared on August 31, 1995; this information was given to an accountant, who ascertained the assets, liabilities, and income of the partnership; and finally, the remaining debt or profit was distributed according to the percentages listed in 6(e).[6] As determined by the trial court, the interest of Joseph Cudmore, who never signed the partnership agreement, reverted to Joseph Creel, who was entitled to a 52 percent share. . . .

---

6. Paragraph 6(e) of the partnership agreement states "[t]hat the net profits or net losses be divided as follows:

Joseph Creel   28%
Arnold Lilly   24%
Joseph Cudmore   24%
Roy Altizer   24%"

Thus, when we look to the intention of the parties as reflected in 7(a) of the partnership agreement, the trial judge could conclude that the partners did not anticipate that a "fire sale" of the partnership assets would be necessary to ascertain the true value of Joe's Racing. Paragraph 7(a) details the preferred winding-up procedure to be followed, to include an inventory, valuation, and distribution of debt or profit to the partners. . . .

Assuming arguendo that the Joe's Racing partnership agreement cannot be interpreted as outlining an alternative to liquidation in winding up the partnership in the event of a dissolution caused by a partner's death, we still find that a sale of all partnership assets is not required under either UPA or RUPA in order to ascertain the true value of the business. Support for this is found in Maryland's recent adoption of RUPA, which encourages businesses to continue in either their original or successor form, and also the holdings of out-of-state cases where other options besides a "fire sale" have been chosen when a partnership is dissolved under UPA.

We agree with the trial court and the intermediate appellate court that there is nothing in Maryland's UPA, in particular [UPA §§37 and 38], or any of our case law that supports an unequivocal requirement of a forced sale in a situation akin to the instant case. . . .

2.   *Wrongful Dissolution*

In analyzing the effect of dissolution on the rights of the partners, the key issue is whether the dissolution was "rightful" or "wrongful," and resolution of that issue often depends on the nature of the partnership. A partnership can be a partnership for a specified term, a partnership for a particular undertaking, or a partnership at will. Generally speaking, a dissolution is rightful when it is accomplished without violating the agreement between the partners, which under the UPA occurs in five circumstances: (1) in a partnership for a specified term when the term expires; (2) in a partnership for a particular undertaking when the undertaking is accomplished; (3) in a partnership at will by the express will of any partner; (4) in a partnership for a specified term or for a particular undertaking by the express will of all partners; or (5) in any partnership, by the expulsion of any partner pursuant to the partnership agreement. UPA §31(1). A dissolution also is rightful in any partnership when any event makes it unlawful to carry on the business of the partnership, when any partner dies, when any partner or the partnership declares bankruptcy, or (sometimes) when a court declares the partnership dissolved. UPA §31(3)-(6). Generally speaking, a dissolution is wrongful when it is in contravention of the agreement of the partners, UPA §31(2), although some courts have found a wrongful dissolution of a partnership at will when the dissolution was accompanied by a breach of fiduciary duty.

As with dissolution under the UPA, dissociation under RUPA triggers different rights and responsibilities among the partners depending on whether it is rightful or wrongful. A partner may dissociate at any time. RUPA §602(a). If a partner dissociates in breach of the partnership agreement or, in a partnership for a definite term or for a particular undertaking, before the expiration of the term or completion of the undertaking (under specified circumstances), the dissociation has been wrongful, and the dissociating partner is liable to the partnership and the other partners for damages.

UPA §38 defines the rights of partners under both rightful and wrongful dissolution. If the dissolution is rightful, UPA §38(1) applies and gives each partner the power to force the partnership to pay all of its liabilities and distribute the surplus to the partners in cash—that is, to force liquidation of the partnership. If dissolution of the partnership is wrongful, UPA §38(2) applies. UPA §38(2)(a) gives each partner who did not wrongfully dissolve the partnership the liquidation right specified in UPA §38(1), plus two important additional rights: (1) the right to damages for breach of the partnership agreement from the partner who caused the wrongful dissolution (UPA §38(2)(a)(II)); and (2) the right to continue the business of the partnership without the partner who caused the wrongful dissolution (UPA §38(2)(b)). UPA §38(2)(c) provides that the partner who wrongfully dissolved the partnership would be entitled to a payment for his interest in the partnership (less any damages for breach of contract) and, if the business is continued, the right to be released from all existing liabilities of the partnership.

If the remaining partners choose to continue the partnership business under UPA §38(2)(b), they are allowed to postpone paying for the partnership interest of the partner who caused the wrongful dissolution. Under UPA §42, the wrongfully dissolving partner would be entitled to the value of his or her interest at the date of dissolution plus an additional payment equal to the interest on such amount from the time of dissolution to the time of payment or the profits attributable to the use of his or her property right during that time period. Only partners who have not wrongfully dissolved the partnership have the right to wind up the partnership's affairs. UPA §37.

Note that RUPA continues the regime established by UPA §38, under which a departing partner may force liquidation of the partnership, even though this widely criticized provision is routinely changed by agreement. Under RUPA §801(1), a partnership at will may be dissolved and wound up by the express will of the departing partner.

The following case examines the nature of wrongful dissolution under the UPA.

GOLDSTEIN v. 91ST STREET JOINT VENTURE

750 A.2d 602
Court of Special Appeals of Maryland
April 26, 2000

SALMON, Judge.

The origin of the dispute that gives rise to this appeal lies in the intense dislike that appellant, Edward S. Goldstein ("Goldstein"), has for Malcolm Berman ("Berman").[1] Both Berman and Goldstein own interests in a partnership that operates the Princess Royale Hotel and Convention Center located in Ocean

---

1. Berman and Goldstein have had prior disputes that landed in this Court. *See* 91st Street Joint Venture v. Goldstein, 114 Md. App. 561, 581, 691 A.2d 272 (1997), a case in which Berman and others attempted unsuccessfully to utilize a "charging order . . . to obtain a 'business divorce'" from Goldstein.

City, Maryland. The enmity between Goldstein and Berman ultimately led to a lengthy arbitration hearing, after which the arbitrator gave Berman and his cohorts the option of dissolving the partnership. The option to dissolve was exercised, and the arbitration award was confirmed by the Circuit Court for Baltimore County. Thereafter, the trial judge was called upon to decide whether Goldstein had a right to have the assets of the partnership liquidated. To make that determination, the court endeavored to interpret [UPA §38]. . . .

Reduced to its essentials, the major issue that concerned the trial court was whether Goldstein caused the dissolution of a partnership "in contravention of a partnership agreement" as that phrase is used in [§38]. If Goldstein did act "in contravention," then the "innocent" partners' rights are controlled by [§38(2)] of the UPA. In this case, Berman, and others, maintained that the "winding up" of partnership affairs was to be governed by [§38(2)] of the UPA. Accordingly, Goldstein's erstwhile partners had the property appraised, attempted to pay off Goldstein, and continued the business of the partnership, sans Goldstein.

Goldstein contends that the partnership[4] should have been dissolved pursuant to [§38(1)] by liquidating the assets of the partnership, paying off all partnership debt, and dividing the remaining proceeds between the partners according to their interests. If the partnership were liquidated, one of the consequences would be that Goldstein could collect immediately a $1.1 million development fee owed to him by the partnership. If [§38(2)] is applicable, Goldstein would not have the right to payment of the fee any time soon.

The trial judge ultimately ruled in favor of appellees . . . based upon his reading of the arbitrator's decision as well as his interpretation of [§38] of the UPA. Goldstein filed this timely appeal.

I. BACKGROUND FACTS

One of the appellees, 91st Street Joint Venture, is a Maryland general partnership, whose partners since 1988 have been Joint Venture Holding, Inc., and Princess Hotel Limited Partnership (collectively, the "Berman Partners") and Goldstein. Malcolm C. Berman controls the Berman Partners. The Berman Partners own more than a ninety-nine percent interest in 91st Street Joint Venture ("Joint Venture"). The appellees in this case are the Joint Venture along with the Berman Partners. Appellant Goldstein, at all times here pertinent, owned less than a one-fifth-of-one-percent interest in the Joint Venture. The fixed term of the Joint Venture was until September 30, 2040, or until the dissolution of the Joint Venture due to Goldstein's death.

In 1988, the Joint Venture commenced construction of the Princess Royale Hotel and Convention Center. Berman oversaw the construction and operation of the project.

The Joint Venture was governed by a "restated and amended 91st Street Joint Venture agreement" ("the Agreement"). The Agreement provides that the parties "are bound" by the Maryland UPA. Section 6.5 of the Agreement reads:

---

4. In this opinion, the terms "joint venture" and "partnership" are used interchangeably.

6.5   DEVELOPER'S FEE AND CERTAIN DISTRIBUTIONS

> Notwithstanding anything to the contrary contained herein, the $2.6 Million Dollars provided by the Partnership [Princess Hotel Limited Partnership] to the Joint Venture shall be paid to the Partnership prior to any other distributions being made hereunder. Thereafter, each of Goldstein and JVH [Joint Venture Holding, Inc.] shall be entitled to receive $1.1 Million Dollars as a Developer's Fee in connection with their services rendered to the Joint Venture in structuring and organizing the Joint Venture. Following distribution to the Partnership of its $2.6 Million Dollars *and $1.1 Million Dollars each to Goldstein and JVH*, any further distributions shall be made to the Joint Venturers in accordance with their capital accounts.

(Emphasis added.) The Agreement also provided for the submission to binding arbitration by the American Arbitration Association of all disputes arising out of the Agreement.

In 1996, the Berman partners decided to refinance the debt of the Joint Venture by taking out a loan from First Union Bank of Maryland ("First Union") and using the proceeds of the loan to pay off the existing lender, NationsBank, N.A. First Union agreed to lend the Joint Venture up to 12.5 million dollars with an interest rate of 7.125 percent per year. The agreement with First Union was very attractive to the Berman Partners because NationsBank charged the Joint Venture a significantly higher interest rate. The First Union agreement with the Joint Venture provided, *inter alia*, that payment of the $1.1 million developer's fee to Goldstein would be deferred for 12.5 years. The NationsBank loan had a somewhat similar provision that precluded the payment of the developer's fee until such time as NationsBank either consented to the $1.1 million payment or its loan was paid off. The Berman Partners sought Goldstein's consent to the proposed First Union loan, which required Goldstein to give his personal guaranty, albeit for only a small portion of the total loan. To secure Goldstein's consent, Malcolm Berman agreed to indemnify Goldstein completely from any potential exposure as a result of his guaranty. Nevertheless, Goldstein insisted that before making a decision he wanted his partners to supply him with a great deal of financial information concerning the operation of the Joint Venture. In addition, Goldstein informed his partners that he would not approve the First Union loan, or personally guaranty any portion of it, as long as there was a requirement that payment of his $1.1 million developer's fee be deferred.

In November of 1996, the Berman Partners filed with the American Arbitration Association a demand for arbitration of their claims that Goldstein had: (1) consented to the proposed refinancing with First Union or, alternatively, (2) breached a fiduciary duty to the Joint Venture by, *inter alia*, his failure to approve and guarantee a portion of the proposed First Union loan. Thereafter, the Berman Partners amended their arbitration demand to seek an additional ruling that Goldstein's conduct made him a defaulting partner pursuant to section 14.1 of the Agreement.

Section 14.1 lists numerous ways that a partner's conduct may constitute a default under the Agreement, one of which is if a partner breaches "any of the terms, provisions, covenants, or agreements contained in the Partnership Agreement." If a partner defaults under section 14.1, the non-defaulting partners have certain rights, including those set forth in section 14.2 of the Agreement. Section 14.2 reads:

Continuing the Joint Venture Business. Upon the election of a nondefaulting Joint Venturer to dissolve the Joint Venture pursuant to Section 14.1, the nondefaulting Joint Venturer shall have the right to continue the business of the Joint Venturer. The nondefaulting Joint Venturer shall purchase the defaulting Joint Venturer's interest at a purchase price determined by the appraisal procedures set forth in Section 19; provided, however, that any damages resulting from the breach by the defaulting Joint Venturer shall be deducted from the purchase price. Upon payment of the purchase price (minus damages), the interest of the defaulting Joint Venturer shall be transferred to the nondefaulting Joint Venturer upon the nondefaulting Joint Venturer's assumption of the obligations of the defaulting Joint Venturer under this Agreement. The purchase price (minus damages) must be paid in cash.

It should be noted that the rights of a non-defaulting partner under section 14.2 are quite similar to the rights granted to an "innocent" partner by [§38(2)] of the UPA.

For remedies, the Berman Partners asked the arbitrator to grant them (1) the right to dissolve the Joint Venture, (2) the right to continue the business of the Joint Venture, (3) the right to purchase Goldstein's interest in the Joint Venture, and (4) monetary damages. Goldstein filed a counterclaim in which he sought, *inter alia*, certain financial documents from the Joint Venture.

A six-day evidentiary hearing was held before the arbitrator, followed by post-hearing briefing and oral argument. The arbitrator, Jonathan A. Azrael, Esq., made his initial award on June 30, 1997. Azrael ruled that Goldstein had not breached his fiduciary duty to appellees nor had he breached any other obligation owed to his partners by withholding his consent to the proposed First Union loan, or by withholding his personal guaranty of that loan. The arbitrator also rejected appellees' contention that Goldstein had breached his fiduciary duty to the Joint Venture in several other ways.

In Paragraph 7 of the arbitrator's award it was stated:

7. The evidence clearly supports a finding that due to animosities on the part of [Goldstein] towards Malcolm Berman, [Goldstein] has so conducted himself in matters relating to the partnership that it is *not reasonably practicable to carry on the business in partnership with him, and further, that it is equitable to dissolve this partnership.* Upon application by Claimant, within fifteen (15) days from the date this Award is mailed to the parties, this Award will be modified to effect a dissolution of the Joint Venture under [§32(1)(d) and (f)] of the . . . Uniform Partnership Act. If Claimant does not make such application, no such dissolution will be ordered.

(Emphasis added.)

[The Berman partners then sought a modification of the arbitration award, seeking to continue the partnership pursuant to rights granted in section 14.2 of their partnership agreement.]

On August 25, 1997, the arbitrator issued a "modification, correction, and clarification of award" that rejected all the claims of the appellees, save one, which is not here relevant. Most significantly, the arbitrator said in his August 25, 1997, award:

4. The claim that the Award should be modified because [Goldstein] failed to cooperate in obtaining financing from NationsBank in 1994 and First Union in 1996 is DENIED.

5. The claim that the Award should be modified to find that [Goldstein] is a "defaulting partner" and that Joint Venture Holding, Inc. and Princess Hotel Limited Partnership have a right to continue the business of the Joint Venture is DENIED.

Shortly after the appellees received the "modification, correction and clarification of award," they applied to the arbitrator for "a modified award to effect a dissolution of the . . . Joint Venture under Section [32(1)(d) and (f)] of the [ ]UPA pursuant to Paragraph 7 of the initial award." This was not opposed by Goldstein. Several weeks later, on September 29, 1997, the arbitrator entered his "Second Modified Award," which stated in pertinent part: "[The Berman Partners] are ordered and directed to dissolve the Joint Venture in accordance with the Maryland Uniform Partnership Act."

On November 4, 1997, counsel for Goldstein wrote to appellees' counsel and said, in pertinent part:

> Having elected to dissolve the partnership, Joint Venture Holding, Inc. is obliged to liquidate the partnership's assets, pay the partnership debts and then distribute whatever is left among the partners in accordance with their percentage interests. Furthermore, I believe Mr. Goldstein has the right to be informed of and actually be a participant in the dissolution process.

About five months later, on April 14, 1998, counsel for appellees sent a letter to Goldstein's counsel and advised him that the Joint Venture had been dissolved in accordance with [§38(2)] of the UPA; that Goldstein's share of the Joint Venture was determined to be worth $12,941; and that the Berman Partners were buying him out and continuing the Joint Venture's business. . . .

All parties are in accord that the actions taken by appellees . . . were proper only if the dissolution of the partnership was caused by actions taken by Goldstein "in contravention of the partnership agreement" as that phrase is used in [§38] of the UPA. [The interpretive question the Court discussed at some length was whether Goldstein's animosity towards Berman, which was the basis for the arbitrator's order dissolving the partnership under section 32 of the UPA, was an action "in contravention of the partnership agreement" as that phrase is used in section 38, and therefore wrongful.]

. . . The question to be resolved is: What interpretation did the arbitrator give to section [38]?

The arbitrator was a lawyer well versed in the intricacies and nuances of the UPA. He undoubtedly understood the statutory construction problem . . . because one of the central points that the Berman Partners sought to prove in the arbitration proceeding was that they had a right to continue the partnership's business without the participation or presence of Goldstein. Although the arbitrator did not say so explicitly, it is clear from the negative implications that must be drawn from his rulings that he did not consider Goldstein to have acted "in contravention of the agreement" as that phrase is used in section [38]. Even if the arbitrator was wrong in his interpretation of the law, it would be too late now to second guess or otherwise overturn the arbitrator's ruling — since the arbitrator's award has already been confirmed by an enrolled judgment.

To discern the arbitrator's view of the law, we must examine what the appellees asked the arbitrator to do and how the arbitrator ruled on their requests. After appellees had already won the right to dissolve the partnership by virtue of the original award, the appellees asked the arbitrator for the right to continue the business of the partnership "in accordance with section 14.2" of the Agreement "and in accordance with section [38(2)(b)]" of the UPA. That request was explicitly denied by the arbitrator on August 25, 1997. If the arbitrator had harbored the belief that a dissolution caused by actions listed in section [32(1)(d) or (f)] was "wrongful" or "in contravention of the agreement," he would have had no possible alternative but to grant the Berman Partners' request to continue the partnership in "accordance with section [38(2)(b)]" of the UPA.

The trial judge, in his written opinion granting appellees' motion for summary judgment and motion to dismiss, makes no mention of the fact that the arbitrator explicitly denied appellees the right to continue the partnership business. Moreover, in their brief, appellees make no effort to explain (or circumvent in any way) the arbitrator's explicit denial of the right to continue the business even though this was one of the central points raised in Goldstein's brief.

We hold, based on the arbitrator's decision, that appellees had no right to wind up the affairs of the Joint Venture in accordance with section [38(2)]; instead, as Goldstein's lawyer pointed out to counsel for appellees in his letter of November 4, 1997, appellees were required to dissolve the partnership in accordance with section [38(1)]. Therefore, the trial judge erred in granting summary judgment in favor of appellees and in dismissing Goldstein's cross-petition to enforce consent order and judgment confirming arbitration award.

Judgment Reversed; Case Remanded to the Circuit Court for Baltimore County for Further Proceedings in Accordance with the Views Expressed in this Opinion. . . .

3. Expulsion

Partners sometimes wish to rid themselves of a troublesome colleague without dissolving the partnership. The process of expulsion is used in these situations where the partnership agreement provides for it. Under UPA §31(1), expulsion in good faith in accordance with the partnership agreement causes a rightful dissolution of the partnership. Similarly, RUPA §601(3) allows for dissociation pursuant to the partnership agreement, and such dissociation is not wrongful. *See* RUPA §602(b). In addition, RUPA §601(4) provides for limited circumstances in which the partners may work an expulsion by a unanimous vote of the other partners.

Where a partner has been rightfully expelled, the partner has no liquidation rights under UPA §38(1) as long as the partner is discharged from all partnership liabilities. Similarly, under RUPA §801 an expelled partner has no right to cause the liquidation of the partnership.

In some instances, expulsion may raise concerns regarding fiduciary duties. Where the remaining partners stand to benefit unfairly by the absence of the expelled partner, courts may intervene. The following problem raises this issue.

PROBLEM 2-5

Before joining the Washington D.C. office of Butler & Binion in 1986, Colette Bohatch had obtained valuable experience as deputy assistant general counsel for the Federal Energy Regulatory Commission (FERC). This experience seemed particularly well-tailored for her new practice: representing Pennzoil before FERC. After laboring as an associate for several years, working extensively on Pennzoil matters, Bohatch achieved partner status.

Bohatch had been recommended for partnership by John McDonald, the managing partner of the D.C. office. Shortly after obtaining her new status, however, Bohatch began to have concerns about her sponsor. Once she began receiving internal billing reports, Bohatch became concerned that McDonald was overbilling Pennzoil. Her concern was based completely on her personal observations of his work habits. She spoke with Richard Powers — the only other attorney in the office and also a partner, and they decided to investigate further. Together they secretly looked at McDonald's daily time diary and made a copy of it.

Although Bohatch never saw the actual bills to Pennzoil, she became convinced that McDonald was reporting too many hours. Moreover, she felt that she had an obligation under the District of Columbia Code of Professional Responsibility to report her concerns to the firm's management. On July 15, 1990, Bohatch contacted Louis Paine, Butler & Binion's managing partner in Texas. Paine promised to investigate.

The next day, McDonald met with Bohatch and told her that Pennzoil was dissatisfied with her work. He said that Pennzoil had asked that her work be supervised. Bohatch later testified that she had never before heard criticism of her work for Pennzoil. From that day forward, Bohatch never again received an assignment to work for Pennzoil.

Over the next month, the firm investigated Bohatch's charges. They reviewed the Pennzoil bills and found that in all but one instance fewer hours were billed than were shown on internal computer printouts as having been worked. A member of the firm's management committee also discussed the bills with John Chapman, one of Pennzoil's corporate counsel. Chapman — who had a long-standing relationship with McDonald — discussed the bills with his immediate superior and with Pennzoil's general counsel. The three of them reviewed Butler & Binion's bills for the preceding year and concluded that they were reasonable. After Chapman's superior discussed their conclusions with Pennzoil's president and chief executive officer, Chapman told Burns that Pennzoil was satisfied that the firm's bills were reasonable. Chapman also confirmed that he had complained to McDonald several months earlier about the quality of Bohatch's work.

During the investigation, Bohatch wrote to Paine that she believed McDonald had overcharged Pennzoil $20,000 to $25,000 per month for his work. In fact, in the preceding six months McDonald had billed Pennzoil on average less than $24,000 per month for his work. In August, Paine told Bohatch that the firm's investigation revealed no basis for her contentions, and he advised her to seek new employment.

The firm continued to pay Bohatch a monthly draw of $7,500 and provided her with an office and a secretary while she looked for a new position until halfway through 1991. Although the firm did not immediately expel her as a partner, it did not pay her any partnership distribution other than her draw. She finally found a new position in September 1991, and the firm voted formally to expel her from the partnership on October 21, 1991.

Assuming that the firm complied with the expulsion provision of the firm's partnership agreement (which provides for expulsion of any partner upon the vote of a majority of the partners), can Bohatch nevertheless prevail in a claim that the partners breached their fiduciary duties by expelling her?

MALL OF AMERICA ASSOCIATES: A CASE STUDY[1]

Jacob Ghermezian left Iran for Montreal, Canada, in 1959 and built a successful business importing Persian rugs. In the late 1960s, Jacob moved his family to Edmonton, Canada. Along with his sons — Raphael, Nader, Bahman, and Eskander — Jacob began purchasing substantial tracts of land in Edmonton. In 1981 the Ghermezians completed construction of the West Edmonton Mall, which contains over 800 stores and the world's largest indoor amusement park, featuring the Mindbender (a triple-loop roller coaster), a five-acre indoor waterpark, an ice skating rink, an 18-hole miniature golf course, a dolphin lagoon, and four real submarines that travel by a sunken ship, coral reefs, and colorful sea life. According to the Guinness Book of World Records, the West Edmonton Mall is the largest shopping center in the world, followed by the Mall of America, which is the subject of this case study.

The Mall of America

In 1986 the Ghermezians obtained rights to develop a mall in Bloomington, Minnesota. The site was the former location of Metropolitan Stadium, for many years the home of the Minnesota Vikings and Minnesota Twins. The Vikings and Twins moved to the Metrodome in downtown Minneapolis in 1982, and Metropolitan Stadium was demolished three years later.

From the beginning, the Mall of America encountered substantial local opposition. As one might expect, construction of the enormous retail center in a suburb of Minneapolis was strenuously opposed by regional malls and people who were attempting to revitalize downtown Minneapolis. In a letter written during the dispute that is described below, Eskander Ghermezian described some of the efforts that went into developing the Mall:

> Mall of America is part of the Ghermezian family. We worked very hard to identify and acquire the site, and after years of negotiations, we obtained approvals. It took two full years alone for my brothers and myself flying to Minnesota almost [non-stop] to convince the city and government officials both Democrats and Republicans, to come [to] Edmonton. We arranged for them to see the West Edmonton Mall. We even had to take steps like delivering a submarine that was made and tried in the Pacific Ocean in Canada, to Minneapolis for the people of the region to see what kind of plans we had for the Mall of America.

Even after acquiring political approval, the Ghermezians had difficulty attracting investors. During their search for financing, the Ghermezians met Melvin and Herbert Simon, part of a family well-known for its prowess in real estate development. The Simons in turn contacted the Teachers Insurance and

1. Special thanks to Roger Magnuson, Mitchell Granberg, and Chris Jensen of Dorsey & Whitney LLP for their assistance in collecting materials for this case study.

Annuity Association of America (TIAA), which agreed to finance the project, eventually investing over $650 million. In the middle of a later dispute with the Ghermezians, Herbert Simon reminded Eskander of the difficult financing environment that clouded the early development of the Mall:

The Simons said they were crucial in securing financing

> Eskander, if you had the ability to pull off this development without us, we would be only an interested bystander today. But the fact was that, notwithstanding all your Herculean efforts, you were faced with deadlines that circumstances prevented you from meeting. You came to us because we could provide what you could not. Maybe it was wrong that the financial marketplace failed, or refused, to recognize your family's ability to pull off this development but that was the case . . . you know it and I know it.
>   . . . You cannot deny that Mel and I put our company's assets, as well as our personal signatures, on the line to secure the financing required to get final approval for the development from the City of Bloomington, thereby preserving what you had worked two years to secure. You, of all people, recognize the problems we encountered in the late 80's and early 90's in the retail world that jeopardized all that the Simon family had worked 30 years to accumulate. Notwithstanding the financial ruin we faced, we persevered and completed the project and stood proudly at the grand opening. . . .

Construction on the Mall began on June 14, 1989, and the Mall opened to the public in August 1992. According to the Mall's Web site, the Mall has over 500 stores and receives between 35 and 42 million visitors annually.

The Partnership

Mall of America Associates (MOAA) was formed as a Minnesota general partnership by a 72-page Agreement of Partnership dated May 13, 1988. On the same date, the Simons and the Ghermezians created two other general partnerships: (1) the Mall of America Company, which owned the Mall property; and (2) Minntertainment Associates, which developed and operated entertainment facilities at the Mall. Each of these partnerships played an important role in future transactions, but the most important partnership for our purposes is MOAA. The partners of MOAA were Si-Minn Developers Limited Partnership (Si-Minn), representing the Simons, and Triple Five of Minnesota, Inc. (Triple Five), representing the Ghermezians. The structural terms of MOAA were as follows:

Term. MOAA was a partnership for a specified term, namely, until December 31, 2078, after which either partner could terminate the partnership upon 120 days' written notice.

Scope The purpose of the partnership was limited to "acquiring, owning, dividing and subdividing, developing, financing, encumbering, improving, operating, managing the [Mall] as an investment and selling it." The partnership agreement expressly provided that the partners would not be partners for any other purpose. Moreover, the partnership agreement expressly provided that the partners could engage in other businesses — even businesses that were "similar to or in competition with" MOAA's business — "without liability or accountability to the other Partner." The sole exception to this provision was that the partners were not allowed to engage in those businesses "which are involved in the development or operation" of the Mall. The agreement also provides:

> No Partner shall be liable to another Partner for failing to offer to the Partnership of the other Partner, or for appropriating or profiting from, any business opportunity, except for those which involve [the Mall].

Interests. The two partners each had a 50 percent interest in MOAA.

Management. Si-Minn was designated the "managing general partner," and Triple Five was the "non-managing general partner." As the managing general partner, Si-Minn was given "sole and exclusive power, authority, duty and responsibility to manage the business and affairs of the Partnership and to make all decisions regarding the Partnership and its business." Despite this broad grant of authority, Si-Minn was obligated to "consult regularly" with Triple Five.

Financial rights. The partnership agreement allocated various financial rights between the partners. A "development fee" of 6 percent of the total costs of development was to be divided equally between the two partners. A "leasing fee" of $3 per square foot was charged to tenants of the Mall, and this amount was to be allocated to the partners, with $2 per square foot going to the partner responsible for producing the tenant and the remaining $1 per square foot going to the other partner. The most important financial right was the "management fee," which was equal to 5 percent of all gross receipts of the Mall. As the managing partner, Si-Minn was entitled to 80 percent of this fee, and the remainder belonged to Triple Five.

Anti-dilution protection. Several provisions in the partnership agreement aim to ensure that the partners retained relatively equal claims on the business. For example, Triple Five could be forced by Si-Minn to reduce its ownership interest in MOAA for the purpose of admitting a new partner, but only if Si-Minn reduced its ownership interest by a proportionate amount.

Transfer restrictions. Both partners restricted the transfer of their partnership interests. If a third party offered to purchase one or more partnership interests, then the partner who did not receive the offer would have a right to prevent such sale by purchasing the other partner's interest at the offered price.

Liability. The partnership agreement expressly limited the liability of the partners to each other and to MOAA:

> No partner in this Partnership shall be liable to this Partnership, or to any Partner[,] for any act performed, or omitted to be performed, by it in the conduct of its duties as a Partner, if such act or omission is not performed or made fraudulently or with gross negligence.

Dissolution. MOAA was not an at-will partnership, and the partners had limited rights of dissolution. Indeed, the partnership provided for only three events of dissolution: (1) if one of the partners sold its partnership interest without the consent of the other partner, then that other partner was given an option to dissolve the partnership; (2) if one of the partners were dissolved or bankrupt, the other partner would receive an option to dissolve the partnership; and (3) by mutual written agreement of the partners.

I'm not correct in the head right now...

The Sale

TIAA converted its construction loan into an equity interest in the Mall on September 2, 1992. To effect this change, the parties formed a new Minnesota limited partnership called MOAC Limited Partnership (hereinafter referred to simply as the "Limited Partnership"). This limited partnership became the focus of a dispute between the Ghermezians and the Simons.

which became the focus of the dispute btwn. S & G

Every limited partnership must have at least one general partner and at least one limited partner. MOAA was the general partner of the Limited Partnership. There were two limited partners: TIAA and JV Minnesota One, Inc., a corporation formed by TIAA. Since TIAA provided most of the financing for the Mall, it is understandable that TIAA would want to obtain substantial ownership rights, and it accomplished this goal through the Limited Partnership, which was assigned a 99 percent interest in the Mall of America Company, the general partnership mentioned above that owned the Mall. In addition, TIAA was made a partner in Minntertainment Associates. TIAA was not a partner in MOAA.

TIAA earned money from the net income of the mall while:

Under the terms of the Limited Partnership, TIAA was paid a "cumulative preferred return" on its investment in the Mall. As a practical matter, given the income generated by the Mall to date, this return amounted to the entire net income of the Mall. As a result, the Simons and the Ghermezians earned income from the Mall only through the leasing and management fees described above.

The agreement of the Limited Partnership contains an extensive provision regulating the transfer of partnership interests. The agreement limits transfers for the first ten years following formation of the partnership (*i.e.*, until September 2, 2002). During that time, TIAA and JV Minnesota One may transfer their interests to another person, but only as long as they retain 50 percent of their total interest.

After ten years have elapsed, TIAA and JV Minnesota One may initiate a transfer, subject to a right of first refusal. Similarly, if a third party offers to purchase one of the partners' interests, the other partners would be allowed to match the third-party offer. If one of the partners in the Limited Partnership violates these transfer provisions, then the "purported transfer . . . shall be void."

In 1998 TIAA notified its partners in the Limited Partnership that it wanted to reduce or sell completely its interest in the Mall. (Apparently, TIAA was concerned about the size of its investment and wanted to limit its exposure.) Herbert Simon, acting on behalf of Si-Minn, wrote TIAA a letter on March 6, 1988, reminding TIAA of the transfer restrictions described above and suggesting that the sale of TIAA's limited partnership interest might trigger negative consequences to Si-Minn and Triple Five. Immediately following this communication, however, the Simons began to investigate the possibility of purchasing TIAA's limited partnership interest without informing the Ghermezians.

In a later letter to Eskander Ghermezian, Herbert Simon explained his desire to facilitate TIAA's sale of a portion of its limited partnership interest. According to Simon, "TIAA could trigger a shot gun buy/sell provision [in 2002] that could wipe out the interest of MOAA and lead to the termination of the management contract. . . ."[2] Purchasing half of the limited partnership

---

2. Simon's fear of "wipe out" was based on the fact that TIAA had a preferential claim of more than $680 million on the sale of the Mall. Under the terms of the Limited Partnership, TIAA was

interest immediately, he argued, would benefit both the Ghermezians and the Simons.

In April 1999 Herbert Simon (acting as chairman of Si-Minn) disclosed an agreement between Simon Property Group, Inc. (SPG), a publicly traded real estate investment trust (REIT) affiliated with the Simons, and TIAA for the purpose of allowing TIAA to extract cash from its investment in the Mall. The deal contemplated a $312 million mortgage on the Mall from Chase Manhattan Bank. Nearly all of the proceeds of the mortgage ($303.5 million) would be paid to TIAA. Of the remainder, $3.12 million was to be paid to SPG. At the same time, SPG agreed to purchase 50 percent of TIAA's interest in the Limited Partnership and Minntertainment Associates for a purchase price of $84.5 million.

The Ghermezians interpreted this announcement as a betrayal and immediately requested more information from the Simons. In a poignant letter, Eskander Ghermezian wrote to Herbert Simon:

> Herb, partner means partner; again, partner means partner. Partner means the highest good faith, the most honest, and complete disclosures of the greatest consideration. It means doing the right thing before God and man. As a partner we expect you to be faithful to us as difficult as that may be for you. We trusted you. You and your associates who have engaged in this [recent] harmful plan against us, should bear this in mind and immediately stop these damaging actions.
>
> Herb, don't do anything wrong to us, don't seek to bully us, don't go behind our back or make self-serving decisions that for generations to come, the Simon family will be ashamed of and regretful for what they have done to the Ghermezian family. My heart and the hearts of the entire Ghermezian family are tied to the Mall of America. Mall of America is part of our hearts and souls. You cannot destroy our souls. Be fair, be just and be truthful. We made a partnership with you . . . on Mall of America on a 50-50 basis, and we expect you to keep the agreement that we have together and honor our 50 percent interest in the Mall of America as we trusted you would.

Eskander concluded his letter by asking "for the tenth time" for information about the proposed deal, but the Simons did not provide the requested information. Instead, Herbert Simon wrote:

> We worked to structure a transaction that satisfied the immediate demands of TIAA, found financing to provide the bulk of the dollars needed and provided an investor that would put up substantial capital to come into the deal. In telephone conversations with Nader, Raphael and you, I offered that you could have ½ of the deal by putting up ½ of the equity dollars needed. . . . Your response to this was to suggest we had some obligation to find an investor that would put up the money through MOAA in exchange for 50% of the cash flow after debt service so that MOAA could enjoy 50% of the cash flow. You are privy to all of the numbers from Mall of America. Can you, in any degree of good faith, suggest that such an investor exists? And, if so, why have you not produced this investor?[3]

---

guaranteed the return of its capital contribution prior to any distributions to MOAA, the other partner in the Limited Partnership.

3. According to the Ghermezians, Herbert Simon's offer to allow Triple Five's participation in the deal was a sham because it required Triple Five to raise half of the purchase price — over $40 million — in less than one month. This was, allegedly, an impossible task for Triple Five.

During this time of great stress between the parties, the Simon family and its representatives repeatedly denied any obligation to negotiate for the purchase of TIAA's limited partnership interest on behalf of MOAA. Indeed, they claimed, the Ghermezians knew about TIAA's interest in selling and could have initiated such negotiations themselves.

when the mortgage transaction closed: The transactions closed on October 15, 1999.[4] Just after the closing, on October 26, 1999, Herbert Simon sent a letter to Eskander Ghermezian offering to purchase the Ghermezians' interest in MOAA and Minntertainment Associates for $20 million. Alternatively, he offered to allow the Ghermezians to continue as partners in MOAA upon signing an agreement ratifying the transactions and waiving all claims against the Simons. The Ghermezians declined to sign the agreement and did not accept Simon's offer.

The Lawsuit

The myriad contracts that shaped the relationships among the Ghermezians, the Simons, and TIAA did not expressly prohibit the sale of TIAA's limited partnership interest. Nevertheless, the Ghermezians felt aggrieved. They felt that the entire structure of the Mall partnerships evinced a desire to maintain their equal status with the Simons. According to the Ghermezians, the Simons had upset that balance by purchasing TIAA's limited partnership interest. As stated in their complaint, they felt that "the Simons misused their position as the managing partner in the Mall partnerships to commence secret negotiations with [TIAA] to divert this opportunity to other Simon-controlled entities, thereby depriving Triple Five of any of the potential benefits." In other words, the Ghermezians felt that the Simons should have obtained the limited partnership interest for MOAA rather than SPG.

The Simons responded by observing that MOAA had no contractual right to purchase TIAA's limited partnership interest. Perhaps more important, the Simons were unwilling to invest additional capital in MOAA for the purpose of this transaction. By contrast, SPG did not require an additional infusion of capital from the Simon family. As a publicly traded REIT, SPG had sufficient funds at its disposal to effect the transaction.

The Ghermezians brought claims for breach of fiduciary duty, breach of contract, violation of the Minnesota partnership statute, and other wrongs.

QUESTIONS

(1) Why did the Simons and the Ghermezians elect to form a general partnership (MOAA) to formalize their relationship?

(2) Professor Deborah DeMott of Duke University testified on behalf of Triple Five with respect to Si-Minn's conduct: "I would say that the conduct in this case would represent an extreme departure from the standards of conduct that I would think would reasonably be expected of a managing partner." Do you agree that Si-Minn breached a fiduciary duty to Triple Five when

---

4. During the time when the TIAA sale was being negotiated, TIAA and SPG announced a joint venture, ostensibly separate from their relationship through the Mall. The joint venture was announced on August 30, 1999, and it involved the investment of $1.7 billion in various mall properties in the northeast United States.

it purchased TIAA's partnership interests? What facts are most important in evaluating this question? Does the sale of TIAA's partnership interests represent a partnership opportunity for MOAA? To what extent do the contracts influence your view of the scope of Si-Minn's fiduciary duty?

(3) Would Si-Minn's actions described above constitute a violation of any statutory provisions in the Revised Uniform Partnership Act?

(4) Would Si-Minn's actions described above constitute a breach of the MOAA partnership agreement? If not, can you think of any provisions that you might propose for the Ghermezians in a future contract that would cover these actions?

(5) Would the MOAA partnership agreement effectively limit Si-Minn's liability for breach of fiduciary duty? Would Si-Minn's actions described above constitute fraud or gross negligence? If Si-Minn's actions do not constitute fraud or gross negligence, could a court nevertheless impose liability for breach of a fiduciary obligation?

CHAPTER
3

Hybrid Entities

General partnerships have many appealing attributes. They are easy to form and the default rules provided by the uniform partnership statutes—equal sharing of profits, direct participation in management, restrictions on the transfer of management rights, and easy dissolution or buyout—are attractive to many small businesses. Moreover, the default rules are easily adapted to each partnership's special needs simply by changing the terms of the partnership agreement. Indeed, the only major drawback of general partnerships is that the partners are personally liable for partnership obligations.

In this regard, corporations would seem to be more advantageous. Investors in a corporation have limited liability—that is, their responsibility for corporate obligations is limited to the amount of their investment. But this limited liability benefit comes at the cost of increased formality, and there is sometimes an awkward fit between corporate default rules and the needs of small businesses. In particular, the corporate norms of centralized management (through a board of directors), free transferability of voting rights, and difficulty dissolution are anathema to many small businesses. And unlike general partnerships, corporations are difficult to tailor to the particular needs of the owners because many changes to the default rules must be embodied in the corporation's charter, which may be amended only by board recommendation followed by shareholder approval and a public filing.

Corporations also suffer from the dreaded problem of "double" taxation—the notion that corporate profits are taxed once at the corporate level and then again at the level of the individual shareholder after payment of dividends. General partnerships avoid this negative tax treatment because the Internal Revenue Service does not treat general partnerships as separate entities for tax purposes. When a general partnership earns profits, therefore, those profits are allocated to the individual partners in the year that they are earned, even if the money is not actually distributed until a later time. Similarly, any losses incurred by the partnership will be available as tax deductions to the individual partners. Because of this tax treatment, general partnerships are said to be "pass-through" tax entities.

While some investors might prefer corporate tax treatment as a means of delaying the consequences of any taxable events until the time when the investment is sold, investors in businesses that distribute earnings on a regular basis usually prefer pass-through tax treatment. Subchapter S of the Internal Revenue Code offers relief from double taxation to corporations that meet its eligibility requirements. Among other things, such corporations (1) cannot have more than 75 shareholders; (2) must have only one class of stock (meaning that the corporation cannot have both common and preferred shares); and (3) may have as individual shareholders only U.S. citizens or resident aliens. Many corporations understandably find these restrictions unpalatable.

Hybrid entities are the result of a search for a business entity that combines the best feature of general partnerships, pass-through taxation, and the best feature of corporations, limited liability. In this chapter, we will examine three types of hybrid business entities: the limited liability partnership (LLP); the limited partnership (LP); and the limited liability company (LLC). We begin with LLPs because they are most similar to general partnerships. Indeed, the only difference is that they provide the partners with limited liability in certain circumstances. LPs are the oldest of the three hybrid entities, whose history in the United States dates to the early 1800s. Originally viewed as a narrow exception to the rule that limited liability was available only in the corporate form, LPs came to be valued during the last century primarily for their favorable tax treatment. To a large extent, the value of LPs has been eclipsed during the past decade by LLCs, which go the furthest of all hybrid entities in creating a corporation-like entity with pass-through tax treatment.

A. LIMITED LIABILITY PARTNERSHIPS

Limited liability partnerships (LLPs) are general partnerships that have registered with the state and as a result of such registration obtain a certain level of limited liability protection for the partners. The first LLPs were authorized under a Texas statute passed in 1991 at the behest of accountants and lawyers, all of whom traditionally practiced in general partnerships. The primary purpose of the early LLP statutes was to protect the personal assets of partners from the risk of negligence or malpractice by another partner. Under more recent statutes, partners in an LLP are not personally liable for any of the obligations of the partnership unless the partners become personally liable as a result of their own conduct or have participated in or supervised the wrongful conduct of another partner.

Like a general partnership, a limited liability partnership requires that two or more persons join to conduct a business activity for profit. To become an LLP, the partnership must file an application with the secretary of state and include information such as the name and address of the partnership, the number of partners, and a brief description of the nature of the partnership's business.

The following case study raises some fundamental issues relating to LLPs, including partner authority, partner liability, and fiduciary duty.

FRODE JENSEN & PILLSBURY WINTHROP, LLP: A CASE STUDY

When Frode Jensen announced his intention to leave Pillsbury Winthrop LLP (Pillsbury) for Latham & Watkins LLP (Latham) in August 2002, hardly anyone outside of the two firms took notice. But when Pillsbury issued a press release downplaying Jensen's productivity and stating that he had been the subject of a complaint alleging sexual harassment, suddenly everyone seemed interested.[1]

Frode Jensen was, by virtually all accounts, a solid if unspectacular corporate lawyer. He had begun his legal career as an associate with Davis Polk & Wardwell, a top New York law firm. After five years, he left Davis Polk for a smaller firm in Stamford, Connecticut, where he was elevated to partner within a year. A few years later, he moved again, this time to the Stamford office of Winthrop Stimson Putnam & Roberts.

Shortly after his arrival, Winthrop's biggest client in Stamford — the Singer Corporation — was acquired in a hostile takeover and moved its legal work to another firm. Jensen proceeded to build his stable of clients afresh, and ultimately came to represent Merck, Smith-Corona, and many less recognizable but substantial companies.[2] According to Jensen's complaint, filed in response to a Pillsbury press release, "During the period 1988 through 2001 his annual billings for the firm grew from approximately $1 million to a peak of approximately $10 million, and have averaged in excess of $5 million for the past six years. During several of those years his billings were the highest of any Winthrop partner in the firm."[3]

Jensen had enhanced his stature at Winthrop and, according to his complaint, he "took a central role" in merger talks with Pillsbury Madison & Sutro. The two firms merged in the fall of 2001. As of early 2003, the combined firm had approximately 800 attorneys in 17 offices, mostly in the United States, but also in London, Singapore, Sydney, and Tokyo. After the merger, Jensen sat on Pillsbury's managing board and was co-head of the international mergers and acquisitions practice.

Despite this apparent success, Jensen claims that he became dissatisfied with the firm after the merger. According to the complaint,

> he had serious concerns about the relentless, and, in his view, unrealistic focus of senior management at Pillsbury on achieving American Lawyer 100 "first quartile profitability," and the elevation within the firm of that goal over the goals of professional excellence and successfully serving the firm's clients. Moreover, the firm faced serious financial challenges, and upheaval in personnel . . . In addition, Jensen also became disappointed by Pillsbury's failure to appreciate the contributions of Pillsbury's Stamford office, where Jensen worked . . . Jensen also was disappointed by the firm's widespread morale problems, particularly amongst the firm's associates, due to decisions to lay off associates, due to incomplete or misleading statements made by Pillsbury's senior management to the firm's lawyers, as well as due to the firm's management style.

In August 2002, Jensen was offered a position with Latham, which would appear to most outsiders as a step up in the hierarchy of firms.[4] Jensen accepted

---

1. Reports on the ensuing events appeared in *The Wall Street Journal*, *The New York Times*, and many periodicals that cover the legal industry. For the most detailed account of Jensen's side of the story, see Carlyn Kolkere, *Take Down*, Am. Law. 68 (Feb. 2003).

2. For a discussion of Jensen's clients, see Thomas Scheffey, *Assessing Jensen's Book of Business*, Leg. Times 14 (Nov. 11, 2002).

3. Jensen's most successful year was 1999, when he billed $10 million, mostly as a result of his work in the Astra-Zeneca merger.

4. In the 2002 ranking of law firms by The American Lawyer, Latham ranks fourth in total revenues, while Pillsbury ranks 26th. Latham had 1,165 lawyers; Pillsbury had 733.

the position after notifying Pillsbury. Prior to announcing his departure publicly, Jensen negotiated the terms of his departure with John F. Pritchard, Pillsbury's vice chairperson. According to the complaint, "Pritchard specifically promised Jensen that his withdrawal would not be the subject of a negative or 'defensive' press statement by Pillsbury, and it was agreed and understood that there would be mutual non-disparagement."

On September 3, Latham issued a press release touting Jensen's hiring, calling him "a very capable lawyer [with] extensive contacts and experience in several industries, including the biotechnology sector." The next day, Pillsbury responded with a release of its own:

> Pillsbury Winthrop, in response to a press release issued by Latham & Watkins on September 3, 2002 announcing that Frode Jensen, a corporate securities partner in Pillsbury Winthrop's Stamford, Connecticut office is joining the New York Office of Latham & Watkins, would like to correct some possible misconceptions caused by the Latham release. Pillsbury Winthrop previously had intended not to comment on Mr. Jensen's departure in order to downplay the event. However, as a result of Latham's press release Pillsbury Winthrop Chair, Mary Cranston, explained that Mr. Jensen's departure comes on the heels of sexual harassment allegations involving Mr. Jensen and a significant decline in his productivity. According to Ms. Cranston, Mr. Jensen has been largely absent from the Stamford office since the start of this year. "Our firm values respect and integrity above all else. We investigated the harassment claims, concluded that there was a reasonable likelihood that harassment had occurred and responded with a variety of measures. It is always sad to lose a friend and colleague to another firm, however, under the circumstances of the past year, Mr. Jensen's move is probably in the best interest of all concerned, and we wish him well with his new firm." Ms. Cranston further stated that to her knowledge, Latham & Watkins did not contact anyone in Pillsbury Winthrop's management in connection with a reference check for Mr. Jensen.

While the charges of sexual harassment and productivity decline may have had some basis,[5] the press release was still shocking to most lawyers. Why would Pillsbury issue this press release? What did it have to gain? Surely, it was more

---

5. Jensen denies being unproductive, and as to the sexual harassment claims, the Complaint asserts: "These allegations are untrue in their entirety." Despite Jensen's protestations, it appears that his billings had declined from 1999, when he billed an extraordinary sum of $10 million. *See* Carlyn Kolkere, *Take Down*, Am. Law. 72-74 (Feb. 2003). In addition, Jensen admits in the Complaint that he, Pillsbury, and "a third-party" had entered into a "Separation Agreement, General Release of Claims and Covenant Not to Sue" on December 10, 2001. In addition, The American Lawyer reported that a female partner who was leaving the firm in December 2001 had complained about Jensen, alleging that Jensen had twice asked to kiss her, and that the firm paid the departing partner to release the firm and Jensen from liability and to keep the incidents confidential.

Jensen included a potentially explosive claim regarding sexual harassment in the Complaint:

> There are presently partners of Pillsbury who in the recent past have been charged with sexual harassment, which charges — unlike the false charges against Jensen — were founded, and which were settled by agreements that included confidentiality provisions that have been honored by Pillsbury. It is thus apparent that the only purpose of the public disclosure by Pillsbury regarding the unfounded allegations against Jensen was to destroy his relationship with Latham.

than spite. According to Jensen's complaint, his former firm was motivated by competition:

> 24. Particularly revealing, however, is that Pillsbury's conduct appears to have been motivated in part by the advice of a legal headhunter consulted by Pillsbury. On information and belief, on or about September 3, 2002, certain of the defendants consulted with a legal headhunter regarding Jensen's withdrawal and Latham's September 3 press release.
>
> 25. On information and belief, the headhunter advised defendants that Jensen's departure to Latham would be viewed in the legal community as a serious blow to Pillsbury, and that it would make it difficult for Pillsbury to recruit lateral partners from other law firms in the future, and that Pillsbury had to take some action to counter the consequences to Pillsbury of Jensen's departure. Defendant Park partially confirmed this set of events in an interview reported in "law.com Connecticut" on September 19, 2002 during which Park acknowledged that "Pillsbury also had received third-party feedback that perception of Jensen's departure could hurt the firm's ability to attract lateral partners."
>
> 26. It is plain that defendants feared that Jensen's move to Latham would impair Pillsbury's ability to attract lateral partners. Although Pillsbury throughout 2001 and 2002 identified the hiring of lateral partners as a key initiative for improving the firm's profitability, including in a study of the firm conducted by McKinsey & Co., Inc., it has experienced little, if any, success in this regard. When Jensen's departure was publicly received as a "coup" for Latham, Pillsbury lashed out in an unlawful and desperate manner because its senior management feared that Jensen's departure would make it even more difficult to attract lateral partners to the firm and, perhaps, serve to encourage other partners to leave.

Initially, Jensen assumed that he would maintain his partnership with Latham, but Latham was troubled that Jensen had not disclosed the sexual harassment charge during the interview process — a lapse that Jensen attributes to the confidentiality agreement signed in settlement of the claim. Moreover, Latham was concerned about the distractions Jensen was causing and the negative media attention the firm might receive if they decided to bring Jensen on board. On September 15, Jensen was forced to withdraw from Latham, leaving behind over $1 million in annual draw.[6] Considering his options, Jensen decided to sue Pillsbury, along with Mary Cranston, John Pritchard, Marina Park, and five "John or Jane Does," who are "outside advisors of defendants, including a headhunting firm and its principal, who conspired with defendants to cause injury to Jensen." The following are representative paragraphs from Jensen's complaint:

COUNT ONE
(Conspiracy — against all defendants) . . .

> 33. On or about September 4, 2002 defendants, together with John or Jane Does 1 through 5, including on information and belief a headhunting firm that encouraged and advised defendants, conspired together in person, by telephone

---

6. According to Jensen's court filings, he was making an annual draw of approximately $700,000 at Pillsbury.

and, on information and belief, by e-mail and other writings for the purpose of unlawfully defaming Jensen and interfering with his partnership contract at Latham.

34. In furtherance of that conspiracy, (i) Defendant Cranston issued the false and defamatory September 4 Release and caused it to be broadly disseminated amongst the legal and business community, and to the public generally, (ii) Defendant Park placed an unsolicited telephone call to Gordon and Davenport at Latham and read them the substance of the September4 Release for the sole purpose of undermining Jensen's partnership at Latham, (iii) Defendant Cranston stated publicly that Pillsbury "dragged [Jensen] through the mud", and (iv) on information and belief, Defendants John or Jane Does 1-5 encouraged Pillsbury's misconduct by advising Pillsbury that a failure to disparage Jensen would make Pillsbury's lateral partner acquisitions even more difficult. Defendant Park acknowledged and admitted the defendants' conspiracy by stating publicly that the September 4 Release "is out there and makes the point we [defendants] wanted to make."

35. By reason of the foregoing, the defendants are jointly and severally liable for conspiring to defame Jensen and to interfere with and destroy his partnership at Latham, in an amount not less than $15 million, the exact amount to be proven at trial.

36. Because of the willful, wanton and intentional nature of defendants' conduct, they also are liable for punitive damages in an amount to be determined at trial.

COUNT THREE
(Interference with Business Relations — against all defendants) . . .

45. On or about August 2002 Jensen was offered and accepted a partnership with Latham to commence October 1, 2002, and agreed to compensation of a minimum of $1,050,000 per year.

46. Each of the defendants was given notice of Jensen's acceptance of the Latham partnership.

47. On or about September 4, 2002, defendants sought to interfere with and destroy Jensen's business relations with Latham by (i) Cranston's issuing the defamatory September 4 Release and defendants causing it to be broadly disseminated to the public, (ii) Park's placing an unsolicited telephone call to Gordon and Davenport at Latham to read them the substance of the September 4 Release for the purpose of undermining Jensen's partnership at Latham, (iii) Cranston's and Park's continuing efforts to attack and defame Jensen in the media after the issuance of the September 4 Release and Park's telephone call to Latham, and (iv) on information and belief, Defendants John or Jane Does 1-5 encouraging Pillsbury's misconduct by advising Pillsbury that a failure to disparage Jensen would make Pillsbury's lateral partner acquisitions even more difficult.

48. By reason of the foregoing, defendants are jointly and severally liable for interfering with Jensen's business relations in an amount not less than $15 million, the exact amount to be determined at trial.

49. Because of the willful, wanton and intentional nature of defendants' conduct, they also are liable for punitive damages in an amount to be determined at trial.

COUNT FIVE
(Defamation per se, Defamation — against all defendants) . . .

56. On or about September 3, 2002 defendants together with John or Jane Does 1 through 5 acted to defame Jensen by, among other things, disparaging his skill and integrity as an attorney.

57. As part of their effort to defame Jensen, defendants made the following writings and statements: (i) Cranston issued the September 4 Release . . . which falsely disparages Jensen's integrity and his skills as an attorney, and falsely accuses Jensen of engaging in sexual harassment, and caused that Release to be broadly disseminated to the public through numerous media that Jensen presently is identifying, in addition to those set forth herein, (ii) Defendant Park telephoned Gordon and Davenport at Latham and read them the substance of the September 4 Release, (iii) Defendant Cranston publicly stated that Pillsbury "dragged [Jensen] through the mud", and (iv) on information and belief, Defendants John or Jane Does 1-5 encouraged Pillsbury's misconduct by advising Pillsbury that a failure to disparage Jensen would make Pillsbury's lateral partner acquisitions even more difficult. Defendant Park acknowledged and admitted that defendants intended to defame Jensen by stating publicly that the September 4 Release "is out there and makes the point we wanted to make."

58. The September 4 Release, and the other statements listed above and described throughout this pleading are false and were known, or should have been known, by defendants to be false. Defendants were not privileged to publish those statements, and the statements unlawfully disparage Jensen's skill and integrity as a lawyer, and his ability to function productively as a lawyer, and are calculated to cause injury to Jensen in his profession.

59. As a result of defendants' defamatory statements, Jensen was obliged to withdraw from his partnership at Latham.

60. By reason of the foregoing, the defendants are jointly and severally liable for defamation per se and defamation, in an amount not less than $15 million, the exact amount to be proven at trial.

61. Because of the willful, wanton and intentional nature of defendants' conduct, they also are liable for punitive damages in an amount to be determined at trial.

COUNT SEVEN
(Breach of Contract — against defendant Pillsbury) . . .

70. On or about December 10, 2001, Jensen, Pillsbury and a third-party entered into the Separation Agreement. The Separation Agreement includes a broad confidentiality clause, which provides in part as follows:

> The Firm, including, without limitation, Jensen, agrees to keep all information which it has concerning the Potential Claims and the terms of this Separation Agreement, as well as the terms of and the reason for your departure, confidential, except as is necessary to administer this Separation Agreement and as required by law.

71. Pillsbury breached the Separation Agreement by issuing the September 4 Release.

72. As a result of Pillsbury's breach of contract, Jensen has suffered substantial direct and consequential damage, including, but not limited to, the loss of

his partnership at Latham, the disparagement of his personal and professional reputation, and the severe impairment of his prospects for future employment.

73. By reason of the foregoing, Pillsbury is liable to Jensen for breach of contract in an amount of at least $15 million, the exact amount to be proven at trial.

COUNT EIGHT
(Breach of Contract — against defendants Pillsbury and Pritchard) . . .

75. On or about August 30, 2002 Pritchard, on behalf of Pillsbury, entered into a contract with Jensen concerning the terms and conditions of his departure. Among other things, Pritchard specifically approved the terms of the Latham press release announcing Jensen's partnership, and committed to Jensen that Pillsbury would not make any negative or "defensive" public statements regarding Jensen's departure and agreed to the terms of a draft press release to be released by Latham.

76. On or about August 30, 2002, Pritchard, on behalf of Pillsbury, sent an e-mail to Jensen stating "we're done": that the terms of his withdrawal were agreed.

77. Consistent with his agreement with Pritchard, Jensen formally withdrew from Pillsbury on August 31, 2002, and on or about September 3, 2002, Latham issued its press release, as approved by Pritchard, announcing Jensen's joining Latham.

78. By issuing the September 4 Release, by calling Gordon and Davenport and reading them the substance of the September 4 Release, and by the other defamatory public statements made by defendants, Pillsbury and Pritchard breached the terms of their agreement with Jensen.

79. As a result of the breach of contract by Pillsbury and Pritchard, Jensen has suffered substantial direct and consequential damages, including, but not limited to, the loss of his partnership at Latham, the disparagement of his personal and professional reputation, and the severe impairment of his prospects for future employment.

80. By reason of the foregoing, Pillsbury and Pritchard are liable to Jensen in an amount of at least $15 million, the exact amount to be proven at trial.

In addition to the $15 million in compensatory damages, Jensen asked the court for "punitive damages in an amount of at least $30 million, and such other and further relief as to the Court may be just and proper."

Pillsbury's initial reaction to the lawsuit was defiance. Pillsbury's general counsel, Ronald E. Van Buskirk, was quoted as saying, "Mr. Jensen is a disgruntled ex-partner making unjustified allegations. While we regret the filing of the lawsuit, we've thoroughly reviewed all the facts and absolutely stand by those individuals named in the case." *Law Firm Sued by Ex-Partner Over Statements*, N.Y. Times C8 (Oct. 9, 2002). Pillsbury's managing partner, Marina Park, stated flatly, "The press release is out there and makes the point we wanted to make."[7]

7. Jonathan D. Glater & Andrew Ross Sorkin, *Bitter Exchange by Law Firms Over the Hiring of a Lawyer*, N.Y. Times C2 (Sept. 9, 2002). Not long before the Jensen story broke, Ms. Park published a short advice column for lawyers on teamwork called "Hair of the Dog" in California Law Business (July 1, 2002). In that column, she wrote: "My colleague, Mary Cranston, likes to say that an important part of achieving one's vision is to learn to pat the obstacles on the head and move on."

The case took another turn in January 2003, when Jensen requested a $19 million prejudgment remedy lien.[8]According to this filing, Pillsbury was in "poor financial condition," evidenced by reduced revenues in 2002, coupled with attorney and staff layoffs, salary freezes, and buyouts.[9] Moreover, Jensen alleged that the firm did not have sufficient insurance to cover the damages that would result from his lawsuit. The parties settled the dispute on April 2, 2003. Pillsbury issued a statement recanting its previous statements about Jensen and calling him "a valued and respected member of the firm and . . . one of the firm's most productive corporate partners."

Pillsbury is a limited liability partnership registered in Delaware, despite the fact that it has no offices there. Mary Cranston works out of the San Francisco office; John Pritchard works out of the New York office; and Marina Park works out of the Silicon Valley office. Of course, Frode Jensen was based in Connecticut and brought his lawsuit there.

State limited liability partnership statutes are relevant to Jensen's claims in at least two ways. First, these statutes determine which state's laws apply. Many LLP statutes include an "internal affairs" rule to resolve difficult choice-of-law issues involving so-called "foreign" LLPs (that is, LLPs registered outside the state in which the relevant partners are located). Named after a comparable rule in state corporation law, the internal affairs rule would allow an LLP to be governed by the laws of the jurisdiction in which it is registered. Regardless of the rule embedded in the particular statute, choice-of-law provisions are mandatory and cannot be changed by the LLP's operating agreement. Connecticut's choice-of-law provision for foreign LLPs is a typical internal affairs provision:

> The internal affairs of a foreign registered limited liability partnership, including the liability of partners for debts, obligations and liabilities of or chargeable to the partnership, shall be subject to and governed by the laws of the state in which it is registered as a registered limited liability partnership.

Conn. Stat. §34-400.

So, too, with California: "The laws of the jurisdiction under which a foreign limited liability partnership is organized shall govern its organization and internal affairs and the liability and authority of its partners."

For matters that are not "internal affairs," states follow various choice-of-law rules. In this case, the choice-of-law rules of Connecticut would determine

---

8. The amount was calculated as follows:

Loss of 3 months of compensation from Latham	$262,500
Loss of 14 years of future compensation from Latham	22,400,000
Loss of 14 years of future bonuses and benefits from Latham	5,665,625
Loss of unfunded retirement benefits at Latham	2,500,000
Subtotal	$30,828,125
Present value (reduce total by multiplying by .7)	$21,579,687
Mitigation of damages (assuming Jensen has 50% chance of finding job equivalent to Pillsbury partnership)	.65
New subtotal	$14,026,796
Plus general damages for per se defamation	5,000,000
TOTAL	$19,026,796

9. Despite lower revenues, the firm increased profits per partner because it had ten fewer equity partners at the end of the year than at the beginning. *Red Scare: After Years in the Black, Bay Area Firms Saw Their Revenues Plummet in 2002*, The Recorder 1 (Jan. 6, 2003).

which state's laws would apply to the trial if it were to proceed since the case was brought there. Connecticut follows the "significant relationship" test advanced in the Restatement (Second) Conflicts of Law to determine choice-of-law issues in tort cases. *See* O'Connor v. O'Connor, 201 Conn. 632, 650, 519 A.2d 13, 16-23 (1986).

Under the significant relationship test, the applicable law is that of the state with the "most significant relationship to the occurrence and the parties." Restatement (Second) Conflicts of Law §145 (2002). The relevant contacts are (1) the place where the injury occurred; (2) the place where the conduct causing the injury occurred; (3) the domicile, residence, nationality, place of incorporation, and place of business of the parties; and (4) the place where the relationship, if any, between the parties is centered. *Id.* "[I]t is the significance, and not the number, of §145(2) contacts that determines the outcome of the choice of law inquiry under the Restatement approach." *O'Connor*, 201 Conn. 652-653.

A second way in which LLP statutes are relevant to Jensen's claims is that they determine the scope of partner liability. Generally speaking, the statutes may provide a "partial shield" or a "full shield." The partial shield statutes — also known as "first generation" statutes — provide limited liability for torts only. By contrast, the full shield — or "second generation" statutes — provide limited liability not only for torts, but also for contracts and any other liability incurred by the LLP.

Texas was the first state to adopt an LLP statute, and that statute retains a partial shield for partner liability:

> (a) Liability of Partner.
>
> (1) Except as provided in Subsection (a)(2), a partner in a registered limited liability partnership is not individually liable, directly or indirectly, by contribution, indemnity, or otherwise, for debts and obligations of the partnership incurred while the partnership is a registered limited liability partnership.
>
> (2) A partner in a registered limited liability partnership is not individually liable, directly or indirectly, by contribution, indemnity, or otherwise, for debts and obligations of the partnership arising from errors, omissions, negligence, incompetence, or malfeasance committed while the partnership is a registered limited liability partnership and in the course of the partnership business by another partner or a representative of the partnership not working under the supervision or direction of the first partner unless the first partner:
>
> > (A) was directly involved in the specific activity in which the errors, omissions, negligence, incompetence, or malfeasance were committed by the other partner or representative; or
> >
> > (B) had notice or knowledge of the errors, omissions, negligence, incompetence, or malfeasance by the other partner or representative at the time of occurrence and then failed to take reasonable steps to prevent or cure the errors, omissions, negligence, incompetence, or malfeasance.

Texas Civ. Stat. art. 6132b-3.08.

In contrast to the Texas statute, the Delaware statute provides a full liability shield:

> (c) An obligation of a partnership incurred while the partnership is a limited liability partnership, whether arising in contract, tort or otherwise, is solely the obligation of the partnership. A partner is not personally liable, directly or indirectly, by way of indemnification, contribution, assessment or otherwise, for such an obligation solely by reason of being or so acting as a partner.

6 Del. C. §15-306(c).

As with all limited liability entities, the owners of a Delaware LLP may become personally liable for their own actions:

> (e) Notwithstanding the provisions of subsection (c) of this section, under a partnership agreement or under another agreement, a partner may agree to be personally liable, directly or indirectly, by way of indemnification, contribution, assessment or otherwise, for any or all of the obligations of the partnership incurred while the partnership is a limited liability partnership.

Id., §15-306(e).

QUESTIONS

(1) Would the actions of Mary Cranston, John Pritchard, and Marina Park bind the LLP? Would it matter if Cranston, Pritchard, and Park had not been in management positions? What if they were associates rather than partners?
(2) If the actions of Cranston, Pritchard, or Park result in liability to the firm, would the other partners be entitled to bring claims for breach of fiduciary duty against the perpetrator?
(3) Assume that Pillsbury did not have sufficient assets to cover obligations that arose from Jensen's lawsuit. At the time of Jensen's lawsuit, Pillsbury had five partners located in Houston. Given the Texas partial-shield liability statute quoted above, would Jensen be able to collect any outstanding obligations personally from the Texas partners?

B.   LIMITED PARTNERSHIPS

Prior to the advent of the LLC, limited partnerships were the primary option for business planners attempting to combine the benefits of partnerships and corporations. The first limited partnership statutes in the United States were adopted in the early 1800s, providing an alternative investment vehicle to corporations, which at the time required special legislative action before they could be formed. As corporations became more accessible through the adoption of general incorporation statutes, the popularity of limited partnerships faded. Limited partnerships waged a comeback in the 1970s, however, when they were employed as tax shelters — investors used losses generated by the limited partnerships to "shelter" other income from federal taxation — but changes in federal income tax law have dramatically reduced this use of limited partnerships. Today limited partnerships remain a popular investment vehicle in certain industries (for example, venture capital funds are typically formed through limited partnerships), and the "family limited partnership" is used extensively in estate planning, but increasingly limited partnerships are being displaced by LLCs.

Most states have adopted a form of the Revised Uniform Limited Partnership Act (RULPA). The first Uniform Limited Partnership Act (ULPA) was promulgated in 1916, but its effectiveness was constrained by the fact that it viewed limited partnerships as small, local entities. As limited partnerships became popular vehicles for tax shelters, ULPA's shortcomings became apparent. This led to a major rewriting of ULPA in 1976 and the creation of RULPA. RULPA was further revised in 1985 and remains the most popular limited partnership statute today, having been adopted in 49 states (only Louisiana has not adopted RULPA). A new version of RULPA was promulgated in 2001, but state adoptions of the new statute have been slow to come, and unless otherwise indicated, references herein are to the 1985 version of RULPA.

Similar to other limited liability entities, limited partnerships are formed by the filing of a certificate of limited partnership with the state. RULPA §201. Like other such filings, the certificate of limited partnership contains minimal information about the limited partnership. Its primary purpose is to provide potential creditors with notice of its formation and the names and addresses of all general partners.

RULPA defines "limited partnership" as "a partnership formed by 2 or more persons under the laws of this State and having one or more general partners and one or more limited partners." RULPA §101(7). The key characteristics of a general partner are provided in RULPA §403, which states that a general partner has the rights, powers, and liabilities of "a partner in a partnership without limited partners." This is the most important example of how RULPA and the UPA/RUPA are connected.[1]

The key characteristic of a limited partner is provided in RULPA §303, which states that a limited partner "is not liable for the obligations of a limited partnership unless he is also a general partner or . . . he participates in the control of the business." The advantages of a limited partnership over a general partnership should be obvious from these provisions: while a general partnership subjects *all* partners to unlimited personal liability, limited partnerships require only one person to possess unlimited personal liability.

By creating a corporation to act as the general partner, business planners can effectively obtain limited liability for all participants in the limited partnership. Following the lead of many states, the drafters of the new ULPA (2001) have opened another avenue for universal limited liability: the limited liability limited partnership (LLLP). Under this version of the limited partnership, even general partners obtain limited liability to the same extent as general partners in an LLP. Under the new statute, LPs can register as LLLPs simply by including a statement to that effect in the certificate of limited partnership. Under ULPA

---

1. The new version of the ULPA (2001) has been "de-linked" from the uniform partnership acts, thus creating a much longer statute. According to the drafting committee, the primary motivation for de-linking the statutes was to eliminate ambiguity concerning which provisions of the general partnership statutes were relevant to limited partnership. This problem emerged when states adopted RUPA and repealed the UPA without serious consideration of how the new partnership statute would interface with the limited partnership statute.

(2001) §404(c), the effect of such a statement on the general partner's liability is as follows:

> An obligation of a limited partnership incurred while the limited partnership is a limited liability limited partnership, whether arising in contract, tort, or otherwise, is solely the obligation of the limited partnership. A general partner is not personally liable, directly or indirectly, by way of contribution or otherwise, for such an obligation solely by reason of being or acting as a general partner.

As a result of their long history, limited partnerships have developed a rich and textured law separate — but related to — the law governing general partnerships and the law governing corporations. As noted by the drafters of ULPA (2001), however, the importance of limited partnerships as a business entity is fading quickly:

> The new Act has been drafted for a world in which limited liability partnerships and limited liability companies can meet many of the needs formerly met by limited partnerships. This Act therefore targets two types of enterprises that seem largely beyond the scope of LLPs and LLCs: (i) sophisticated, manager-entrenched commercial deals whose participants commit for the long term, and (ii) estate planning arrangements (family limited partnerships).

In light of the waning relevance of limited partnership law to modern business practice, our discussion will be brief and will focus on insights we can gain from limited partnerships into the nature of limited liability. In the last Section, dealing with LLPs, we considered the effects that would flow from adding limited liability to the partnership form. In this Section, we consider a different aspect of limited liability — namely, the rationale for awarding or removing limited liability. Who gets limited liability? And why do they get it?

General partners typically have unlimited personal liability and limited partners have limited personal liability. There are several exceptions to limited liability for limited partners, the most important of which holds that a limited partner who "participates in the control of the business" is liable to persons who transact business with the limited partnership reasonably believing, based on the limited partner's conduct, that the limited partner is a general partner. This so-called "control rule" has been removed from the new ULPA (2001). Referring to the rule as an "anachronism" in the age of LLCs, LLPs, and LLLPs, the drafting committee included the following provision as ULPA (2001) §303:

> A limited partner is not personally liable, directly or indirectly, by way of contribution or otherwise, for an obligation of the limited partnership solely by reason of being a limited partner, even if the limited partner participates in the management and control of the limited partnership.

Despite this innovation, the control rule will remain an important feature of limited partnership law during the transition to full limited liability. Moreover, its existence suggests important insights about the nature of limited liability. As you read the following case, consider why courts and legislatures have traditionally removed limited liability from limited partners who participate in the control of the business. In addition, ask yourself why this rule has become an "anachronism." Is this a positive development?

ZEIGER v. WILF
755 A.2d 608
Superior Court of New Jersey, Appellate Division
July 19, 2000

LESEMANN, J.A.D.

This case offers a virtual primer in the Byzantine relationships among various forms of business organizations employed in a modern venture capital project. It includes a limited partnership, a corporation, a general partnership and several sophisticated individuals all involved in the proposed redevelopment of a hotel/office building in downtown Trenton. It also demonstrates the significance of limited individual liability which is a key reason for employing some of those entities, and the inevitable risk that anticipated rewards from such a venture may not be realized.

At issue here is an agreement by which plaintiff, a seller of the property to be renovated, was to receive a "consultant fee" of $23,000 per year for sixteen years. The payments, however, ceased after two years. A jury found the redevelopers (a limited partnership and a corporation) liable for those payments, and an appeal by those entities has now been abandoned. As a result, the matter now focuses on plaintiff's claim that Joseph Wilf, the individual who led the various defendant entities, should be held personally liable for the consultant payments and that such liability should also be imposed on a general partnership owned by Wilf and members of his family.

There is no claim that Wilf personally, or his general partnership, ever guaranteed the consultant payments or that plaintiff ever believed Wilf had made such guarantees. Nor is there a claim that plaintiff did not understand at all times that he was contracting only with a limited partnership and/or a corporation, and not with Wilf personally or with his general partnership. For those reasons, and also because we find no merit in various other theories of individual liability advanced by plaintiff, we affirm the summary judgment entered in favor of Wilf individually, and we reverse the judgment against Wilf's family-owned general partnership.

The property in question was a rundown hotel on West State Street in Trenton, located near several State government buildings. In or shortly before 1981, plaintiff Shelley Zeiger and his associate, Darius Kapadia, purchased the property with the intention of renovating and operating the hotel. They undertook some renovation and began operations but could not obtain sufficient financing to complete the project.

In or around March 1985, Steven Novick, an experienced developer, approached plaintiff concerning a possible purchase of the property. Novick believed the building could be successfully renovated and operated as an office building (with perhaps some hotel facilities included), particularly if he could lease some or all of the office space to the State. Richard Goldberger, another experienced developer, soon joined Novick in the project, as did another associate, said to have considerable contacts within the State government. Plaintiff was also well known in Trenton governmental and political circles.

As the negotiations proceeded, Novick brought defendant Joseph Wilf into the picture. Wilf was described as a "deep pocket partner," whose financial means could help insure the success of the project. He was also a well known and successful real estate developer and soon became the leader and primary spokesman for the purchasing group. Novick and Goldberger generally deferred to Wilf during the negotiations and structuring of the transaction.

On February 17, 1986, the negotiations culminated in a contract with a purchase price of $3,840,000 for the real estate, a liquor license, and miscellaneous assets connected with the hotel's operation. The contract was signed by a corporation formed by the purchasers, known as Goldberger, Moore & Novick, Trenton, No. 2, Inc. (hereinafter, "Trenton, Inc." or "the corporation").

As the deal was finally struck, the parties also agreed that plaintiff would receive a "consulting fee" of $27,000 per year, payable monthly for sixteen years. While plaintiff was to provide assistance when requested, it is clear that he was not expected to devote much time or effort to the project. The agreement specified he would not be required to spend more than two days per month in consultations. Plaintiff claims the consultation payments were, in reality, an additional part of the payment price, structured as they were to provide tax benefits to the Novick/Goldberger/Wilf group. In addition, plaintiff was to receive from the project two and one half percent of "annual net cash flow after debt service."

Closing took place on March 4, 1986. Trenton, Inc., was the purchaser and also signed the consultant agreement with plaintiff. The contract documents authorized the corporation to assign its property interests, as well as the consulting contract, to another entity, and on the day following closing the corporation did that by assignment to a limited partnership named Goldberger, Moore & Novick, Trenton, L.P. (hereinafter "Trenton L.P." or "the limited partnership").

The limited partnership then began the anticipated renovation and operation of the hotel/office building. Trenton, L.P. consisted of one general partner — the corporation just referred to (Trenton, Inc.), which owned 4.9 percent of the limited partnership. In addition, it had four limited partners: an entity known as Midnov, owned by Novick and Goldberger, which held a 42.7 percent interest; another entity known as Capitol Plaza Associates (CPA), controlled by Wilf and his family and described further below, which also owned 42.7 percent; George Albanese, a former State official, who held a 5.1 percent interest; and plaintiff Shelley Zeiger who owned a 4.9 percent interest.

The stock of Trenton, Inc., was owned fifty percent by Midnov (Novick and Goldberger's entity) and fifty percent by CPA (the Wilf family entity). Goldberger became president of Trenton, Inc.; Wilf was vice president; Novick was secretary/treasurer[;] and Bernadette Lynch was assistant secretary.

Thus, all of Wilf's interests in both the limited partnership and the corporation were held through his family entity, CPA. CPA was a general partnership and defendant Joseph Wilf was one of the general partners. While other family members were also general partners in CPA, Joseph Wilf was clearly its guiding and dominating force.

Shortly after closing, Trenton, L.P. began its attempts to secure both state leases for the property and a 9.5 million dollar mortgage to finance the required renovation. Wilf was the leader in that operation as he was in all aspects of the project. He maintains that in doing so, he was functioning as vice president of the corporation, which was the only general partner of the limited partnership. In substance, he claims that the limited partnership was operating (as it was required to do) through its general partner. Since that general partner was a corporation, the corporation was, in turn, operating in the only way that a corporation can operate: by the actions of its officers and agents. He maintains further that Goldberger and Novick soon abdicated most responsibility and simply stopped functioning as corporate officers — a claim not disputed by plaintiff. Thus, Wilf says, it was left to him to function as the responsible corporate officer.

Both the limited partnership and the corporation operated informally. There were few, if any, corporate meetings, resolutions or minutes. Wilf was less than meticulous in affixing his corporate title to documents or other papers which he says he signed as an officer of the corporate general partner. Significantly, however, plaintiff makes no claim that at any time he thought Wilf was operating in some other capacity, or that he believed Wilf or CPA were undertaking any personal responsibility or liability for any part of the project.

The limited partnership began making the monthly consultation payments to plaintiff in early 1986, and it continued to do so for approximately two years. In March 1988, however, the payments were stopped at Wilf's direction. An additional $12,000 was paid in May 1989 (which represented almost all the amount then due to plaintiff), but thereafter no further payments were made. Wilf said at the time that the money was needed for the renovation project and that (alone among all the participants), plaintiff was contributing nothing to the project. Plaintiff complained to Novick, and Novick promised to discuss the matter with Wilf. Novick did so, but Wilf continued to maintain that plaintiff should receive no further payments and thus, no further payments were made. Wilf subsequently acknowledged that he was not familiar with the terms of the consultation agreement or plaintiff's rights thereunder.

Trenton, L.P., did obtain its desired 9.5 million dollar renovation loan. However, by January 1987, those funds were exhausted and more money was needed. Wilf maintains that he invested an additional $565,000 in the project through his own company, and he then obtained a 2.8 million dollar mortgage loan from First Chicago Bank, which he, his brother and Goldberger personally guaranteed. Wilf subsequently paid off that mortgage but — presumably to repay his $565,000 investment and his payoff of the First Chicago loan — he took a $3,063,000 mortgage from Trenton, L.P., covering the office building/hotel.

Eventually, the project failed. The limited partnership and the corporation filed bankruptcy, as did Novick individually. On July 19, 1993, plaintiff sued Wilf, claiming that Wilf had become the "surviving partner and owner of the partnership assets" pertaining to the "purchase and transfer of" the hotel, and that he was in default respecting payment of plaintiff's consulting fees.

On July 30, 1993, shortly after plaintiff filed his complaint, the New Jersey Secretary of State revoked the corporate charter of Trenton, Inc. The record does not reveal the circumstances of or the reasons for the revocation. It indicates only that records in the Secretary of State's office showed the corporation as "void by proclamation," with a suspension date of July 30, 1993. However, on March 13, 1997, the Secretary of State issued a new certification, stating that the charter had been "voided in error for non-payment of State taxes by Proclamation on July 30, 1993," but that the corporation "was reinstated on March 13, 1997." There was no further indication of the "error" involved, nor, again, did the record indicate the circumstances of or reason for the initial revocation or the subsequent reinstatement.

On March 28, 1995, plaintiff filed an amended complaint naming as defendants Joseph Wilf; CPA; Trenton, L.P.; and Trenton, Inc. Approximately eighteen months later, after extensive discovery, Wilf moved for summary judgment dismissing the complaint as to him, which the motion judge granted on December 23, 1996. On January 24, 1997, that judge denied a motion for reconsideration.

On March 3, 1997, trial against the other defendants began before a different judge. While that trial was proceeding, the Secretary of State issued the aforesaid reinstatement certificate. On April 8, 1997, a jury returned a $456,801 verdict against the limited partnership and the corporation, to which sum the trial court added pre-judgment interest. However, while the trial court had submitted to the jury the liability issue as to the limited partnership and the corporation, it had withheld for determination by the court plaintiff's claim against CPA. On December 4, 1997, the court found that CPA was also liable to plaintiff for the aforesaid $456,801, and entered judgment against it for that amount.

This appeal was initially filed by plaintiff, seeking reversal of the judgment in favor of Joseph Wilf. A cross-appeal was then filed by CPA, by Trenton, L.P. and by Trenton, Inc. As noted however, because of the intervening bankruptcy proceedings, defendants have advised that no "useful purpose is served by continuing to process this appeal" on behalf of the limited partnership or the corporation. Thus, defendants have argued for reversal only as against CPA while, of course, also maintaining that the dismissal as to defendant Wilf should be affirmed. . . .

[P]laintiff claims the limited partnership statute imposes general partner liability on Wilf because he functioned as the operating head of the parties' renovation project. We find the claim inconsistent with both the policy and the language of the statute.

A basic principle of the Uniform Limited Partnership Law (1976), N.J.S.A. 42:2A-1 to -72, is a differentiation between the broad liability of a general partner for the obligations of a limited partnership, and the non-liability of a limited partner for such obligations. Preservation of that distinction and protection against imposing unwarranted liability on a limited partner has been a consistent concern of the drafters of the Uniform Act on which our New Jersey statute is based, and has been described as "the single most difficult issue facing lawyers who use the limited partnership form of organization." *See* Revised Unif. Limited Partnership Act, Prefatory Note preceding §101, U.L.A. (1976) (hereinafter "Commissioners' Report"). Indeed, the history of the Uniform Limited Partnership Act, and thus the evolution of our New Jersey statute, shows a consistent movement to insure certainty and predictability respecting the obligations and potential liability of limited partners. The framers of the Act have accomplished that by consistently reducing and restricting the bases on which a general partner's unrestricted liability can be imposed on a limited partner. Under the present version of the Uniform Act, the imposition of such liability (absent fraud or misleading) is severely limited. Our New Jersey statute (as discussed below) reflects that same philosophy in the provisions of N.J.S.A. 42:2A-27a.

The original version of the ULPA was adopted in 1916. That enactment dealt with the question of a limited partner's liability in one short provision. In

Section 7 it said,

> A limited partner shall not become liable as a general partner unless, in addition to the exercise of his rights and powers as a limited partner, he takes part in the control of the business.

In 1976, the original ULPA was substantially replaced by a revised version (on which the New Jersey statute is based) which "was intended to modernize the prior uniform law." *See* Commissioners Report Prefatory Note preceding Section 101. One of the ways that modernization was effected was by a new Section 303, which replaced the old Section 7, and was adopted virtually verbatim as Section 27 of the New Jersey statute. Section 303 reads as follows:

> [A] limited partner is not liable for the obligations of a limited partnership unless . . . , in addition to the exercise of his [or her] rights and powers as a limited partner, he [or she] takes part in the control of the business. However, if the limited partner's participation in the control of the business is not substantially the same as the exercise of the powers of a general partner, he [or she] is liable only to persons who transact business with the limited partnership with actual knowledge of his [or her] participation in control.

The Commissioners' Report in the comment to Section 303 states:

> Section 303 makes several important changes in Section 7 of the 1916 Act. . . . The second sentence of Section 303(a) reflects a wholly new concept. . . . It was adopted partly because . . . it was thought unfair to impose general partner's liability on a limited partner except to the extent that a third party had knowledge of his [or her] participation in control of the business . . . , but also (and more importantly) because of a determination that it is not sound public policy to hold a limited partner who is not also a general partner liable for the obligations of the partnership except to persons who have done business with the limited partnership reasonably believing, based on the limited partner's conduct, that he [or she] is a general partner.

Following that 1976 version, more limitations on a limited partner's liability came in 1988, with a series of "Safe Harbor" amendments, virtually all of which were adopted in New Jersey. *See* N.J.S.A. 42:2A-27b. The Commissioners' Report explained the reason for those additions to Section 303 of the Uniform Act:

> Paragraph (b) is intended to provide a "Safe Harbor" by enumerating certain activities which a limited partner may carry on for the partnership without being deemed to have taken part in control of the business. This "Safe Harbor" list has been expanded beyond that set out in the 1976 Act to reflect case law and statutory developments and more clearly to assure that limited partners are not subjected to general liability where such liability is inappropriate.

Although plaintiff argues that Section 27 of the New Jersey statute imposes a general partner's liability on Wilf (and CPA) because Wilf took "part in the control of the business," we are satisfied that the argument has no merit.[5] To accept it, and impose such liability on the facts presented here, would reverse the evolution described above and create precisely the instability and uncertainty that the drafters of the ULPA (and the New Jersey Act) were determined to avoid.

Plaintiff's argument rests on Wilf's key role in the renovation project. Wilf acknowledges that role, but argues that his actions were taken as a vice president of Trenton, Inc. — the corporation which was the sole general partner of Trenton, L.P. Wilf argues that since the corporation is an artificial entity, it can only function through its officers, and that is precisely what he was doing at all times when he acted concerning this enterprise. Wilf also points to the "Safe Harbor" provisions of N.J.S.A. 42:2A-27b to reinforce his claim that his actions here did not impose general partner liability upon him.

We agree with that analysis. As noted, the 1988 "Safe Harbor" provisions set out a number of activities which, under the statute, do not constitute participating in "the control of" a business so as to impose a general partner's liability on a limited partner. The provision to which Wilf particularly refers is subsection b(6) of section 27, which provides that,

> b. A limited partner does not participate in the control of the business within the meaning of subsection a. solely by[,]

> (6) Serving as an officer, director or shareholder of a corporate general partner;

That provision clearly applies here and essentially undercuts plaintiff's argument: while plaintiff claims that Wilf's activities constitute "control" of the activities of Trenton, L.P., the statute says, in just so many words, that those activities do *not* constitute the exercise of control.

In addition to the "Safe Harbor" protections, section 27a itself sharply limits the circumstances under which the exercise of "control" could lead to imposition of general partner liability on a limited partner. It first provides that if a limited partner's control activities are so extensive as to be "substantially the same as" those of a general partner, that control, by itself, is sufficient to impose liability: *i.e.*, if a limited partner acts "the same as" a general partner, he will be treated as a general partner. However, but for that extreme case, mere participation in control does not impose liability on a limited partner. Such liability may be imposed only as to "persons who," in essence, rely on the limited partner's participation in control and thus regard him as a general partner.

That limitation of liability to those who rely on a limited partner's exercise of control is critical to a sound reading of the statute. It is consistent with the series of amendments from 1916 to now, which have been designed to insure predictability and certainty in the use of the limited partnership form of business organization. To reject plaintiff's claim of liability would be consistent with that view of the statute. To accept the claim would inject precisely the instability and uncertainty which the statute is designed to avoid.

---

5. In reality, as noted above, Wilf was neither a limited partner in Trenton, L.P., nor a shareholder in Trenton, Inc. Both of those roles were filled by CPA, Wilf's family entity in which he was a general partner. In view of our resolution of the substantive issues of the case, we have treated Wilf and CPA interchangeably, although Wilf argues that any assumed finding of liability against CPA would not apply to him.

Here, there was none of the "reliance" which is a necessary basis for a limited partner's liability. It bears repeating that plaintiff, an insider in the project, does not claim he was ever misled as to the entities with whom he was dealing. Plaintiff is described as a sophisticated, experienced developer and businessman. He does not deny that description. He does not claim that he ever sought or obtained any individual guarantee or promise of payment from Wilf, and certainly not from CPA. Nor does plaintiff deny that he understood completely that he was dealing with a limited partnership and a corporation. He does not deny his understanding that those entities, by their very nature, provide limited resources and limited recourse for parties with whom they contract. *See* Frank Rizzo, Inc. v. Alatsas, 27 N.J. 400, 402, 142 A.2d 861 (1958), where the court, speaking of a corporation but employing language equally applicable to a limited partnership, noted that,

> [o]rdinarily we do not think in terms of the possibility of individual liability of corporate officers for obligations incurred by the entity in the usual course of business. Such personal liability is inconsistent with the existence of a body corporate at common law and can emanate only from some positive legislative fiat.

In short, there is no claim that plaintiff was misled, or that he relied on some impression that Wilf was a general partner of Trenton, L.P., and thus there is no basis for any finding of personal liability against Wilf under N.J.S.A. 42:2A-27a.

The only other possible statutory basis for imposing liability on Wilf is the provision which would impose such liability if Wilf's activities were "substantially the same as the exercise of the powers of a general partner" of Trenton, L.P. While that phrase is less than precise, and we are aware of no helpful decision interpreting or applying it, we see no basis for its application here.

First, recall that Wilf's activities as an officer of Trenton, Inc., are specifically sanctioned by the "Safe Harbor" provisions. With the other corporate officers having abrogated their responsibilities, it is difficult to see, first, what other choice was available to Wilf; and second, why his actions should have any adverse effect on him under the Limited Partnership Act.

Further, it is significant that plaintiff does not rest his argument so much on the powers and functions exercised by Wilf, as on the manner in which he exercised those functions. That is, the argument points mainly to Wilf's carelessness in not consistently and specifically identifying himself as an officer of Trenton, Inc., when he acted on behalf of Trenton, L.P. or signed documents on behalf of the limited partnership. The argument, in short, refers more to form than to substance. It lacks force because, regardless of Wilf's alleged carelessness, plaintiff was at all times fully aware of what Wilf was doing and how he was doing it. A failure to comply with some designated formality might have had some significance if, at any time or in any way, it misled plaintiff or prejudiced him. But, as we have noted several times, that is simply not the case.[7] . . .

---

7. The 1976 version of the Uniform Act was amended in 1985, to eliminate entirely the reference to a limited partner's control activities being "substantially the same as the exercise of the powers of a general partner." Thus, the present version projects liability on a limited partner *only* if an outsider "reasonably [believed], based upon the limited partner's conduct, that the limited partner is a general partner." The purpose of the amendment, quite clearly, is to make even clearer the points noted in the comments quoted above: it "is not sound public policy" to hold a

C.   LIMITED LIABILITY COMPANIES

The most important development in recent years in the area of business associations is the widespread acceptance of limited liability companies (LLCs) as an alternative entity for small businesses. The impetus for this rapid development was a 1988 revenue ruling providing that Wyoming LLCs would be treated as partnerships for tax purposes. That ruling sanctioned the use of an entity that combined limited liability and pass-through tax treatment for businesses that found LPs cumbersome or could not qualify for Subchapter S status (perhaps because they had more than the requisite number of investors or a financial structure more complicated than that permitted by the one class of stock requirement of Subchapter S).

The first LLC statute in the United States was adopted by Wyoming in 1977, but LLCs did not become widely popular until the passage of the Tax Reform Act of 1986, which increased the federal income tax rate on corporations and eliminated the so-called *General Utilities* doctrine (*see* General Utilities & Operating Co. v. Helvering, 296 U.S. 200 (1935)), which permitted a corporation to distribute appreciated property to its shareholders without realizing taxable gain, thus avoiding double taxation. Shortly thereafter, the IRS issued the revenue ruling discussed above, and the rush was on. States quickly adopted LLC statutes, and the popularity of LLCs has been increasing ever since.

Until the mid-1990s, the Internal Revenue Service evaluated each LLC separately in an attempt to discern whether the entity was more like a corporation or a partnership. This evaluation began with four of the so-called *Kintner* factors — centralized management, continuity of life, free transferability of ownership interests, and limited liability. These factors were named after United States v. Kintner, 216 F.2d 418 (9th Cir. 1954), and later embodied in an IRS regulation. According to the IRS, an entity could have any two of these characteristics and still be treated as a partnership for tax purposes. Of course, every entity wanted limited liability, and this left little room for flexibility in the remaining governance decisions.

Early LLC statutes were cut-and-paste productions, using provisions from state partnership, corporation, and limited partnership statutes to create a new entity whose primary goal was to allow for the combination of limited liability and partnership tax treatment. To ensure that all entities formed under the statute would obtain partnership tax treatment under the *Kintner* factors, many early statutes included numerous mandatory provisions. Before long, it became apparent that the *Kintner* factors were inhibiting the development of business forms, and the IRS decided to abandon individualized evaluation in favor of a system of election. Under the "check-the-box" regulation, which became effective in 1997, all unincorporated firms were allowed to select their tax classification. In other words, every LLC that wanted partnership tax treatment

---

limited partner to a general partner's liability, unless he has misled others into believing he was a general partner. *See Revised Unif. Limited Partnership Act, supra,* Prefatory Note preceding Section 101.

Although New Jersey has not (yet) adopted the 1985 amendment, neither has it rejected the proposal, and there is no reason to conclude that New Jersey's Section 27 is not consistent with both the presently existing Section 101 and its earlier version.

would obtain partnership tax treatment, even if the governance structure were effectively indistinguishable from a corporation.

LLC statutes now have been adopted in all 50 states and in the District of Columbia. The variety among LLC statutes is great. The National Conference of Commissioners on Uniform Laws has proposed the Uniform Limited Liability Company Act (ULLCA) in an attempt to unify the laws governing LLCs, but states have been slow to adopt it in full. Nevertheless, ULLCA has had an important influence on the evolution of LLC statutes.

Like other limited liability associations, LLCs are formed through a formal filing of articles of organization with the state. Like articles of incorporation, most articles of organization contain minimal information about the company. ULLCA §203. Agreements among the members of an LLC are typically contained in an operating agreement, which is analogous to a partnership agreement. If the articles of organization and the operating agreement conflict, under ULLCA §203(c) the operating agreement controls with respect to managers, members, and members' transferees; and the articles of organization control with respect to third parties who rely on them to their detriment. If the articles of organization or the operating agreement conflict with the statute, the statute prevails with respect to mandatory provisions (including the content of the Articles under ULLCA §203), and an agreement between the parties prevails with respect to nonmandatory provisions.

1. Limited Liability

Most LLC statutes adopt partnership default rules with respect to firm management. That is, every member of the LLC has equal management rights (member managed) unless the members provide for centralized management (manager managed) in their organizing documents. Whether the firm is member managed or manager managed, the members of an LLC are not personally liable for any obligation of the LLC simply because they are members or managers. Of course, members and managers of an LLC are responsible for their own acts or omissions and for obligations undertaken by agreement, but they are not personally responsible for the acts, omissions, or obligations of other members. The *Lanham* case, below, explores these principles.

WATER, WASTE & LAND, INC. v. LANHAM
955 P.2d 997
Supreme Court of Colorado (en banc)
March 9, 1998

Justice SCOTT delivered the Opinion of the Court.

This case requires us to decide whether the members or managers of a limited liability company (LLC) are excused from personal liability on a contract where the other party to the contract did not have notice that the members or managers were negotiating on behalf of a limited liability company at the time the contract was made. Because the county court found that the party dealing with the members or managers was unaware that they were acting as agents of a limited liability company when they negotiated the contract, and the evidence in the record supports the county court's findings, we see no legal basis to excuse the agents of the LLC from liability and therefore we reverse the judgment of the district court.

I.

Water, Waste & Land, Inc., the petitioner, is a land development and engineering company doing business under the name "Westec." At the time of the events in this case, Donald Lanham and Larry Clark were managers and also members of Preferred Income Investors, L.L.C. (Company or P.I.I.). The Company is a limited liability company organized under the Colorado Limited Liability Company Act (the LLC Act).

In March 1995, Clark contacted Westec about the possibility of hiring Westec to perform engineering work in connection with a development project which involved the construction of a fast-food restaurant known as Taco Cabaña. In the course of preliminary discussions, Clark gave his business card to representatives of Westec. The business card included Lanham's address, which was also the address listed as the Company's principal office and place of business in its articles of organization filed with the secretary of state. While the Company's name was not on the business card, the letters "P.I.I." appeared above the address on the card. However, there was no indication as to what the acronym meant or that P.I.I. was a limited liability company.

After further negotiations, an oral agreement was reached concerning Westec's involvement with the Company's restaurant project. Clark instructed Westec to send a written proposal of its work to Lanham and the proposal was sent in April 1995. On August 2, 1995, Westec sent Lanham a form of contract, which Lanham was to execute and return to Westec. Although Westec never received a signed contract, in mid-August it did receive verbal authorization from Clark to begin work. Westec completed the engineering work and sent a bill for $9,183.40 to Lanham. No payments were made on the bill.

Westec filed a claim in county court against Clark and Lanham individually as well as against the Company. At trial, the Company admitted liability for the amount claimed by Westec. The county court entered judgment in favor of Westec. The county court found that: (1) Clark had contacted Westec to do engineering work for Lanham; (2) it was "unknown" to Westec that Lanham had organized the Company as a limited liability company; and (3) the letters "P.I.I." on Clark's business card were insufficient to place Westec on notice that the Company was a limited liability company. Based on its findings, the county court ruled that: (1) Clark was an agent of both Lanham and the Company with "authority to obligate . . . Lanham and the Company"; (2) a valid and binding contract existed for the work; (3) Westec "did not have knowledge of any business entity" and only dealt with Clark and Lanham "on a personal basis"; and (4) Westec understood Clark to be Lanham's agent and therefore "Clark is not personally liable." Accordingly, the county court dismissed Clark from the suit, concluding he could not be held personally liable, and entered judgment in the amount of $9,183 against Lanham and the Company. Lanham appealed, seeking review in the Larimer County District Court (district court).

The district court reversed, concluding that "[t]he issue which the court must address is whether the County Court erred in holding Lanham, a member and primary manager of the company, personally liable for a debt of the company." In addressing that issue, the district court found that Westec was placed on notice that it was dealing with a limited liability company based on two factors: (1) the business card containing the letters "P.I.I."; and (2) the notice provision of section 7-80-208, of the LLC Act. Principally in reliance upon the LLC Act's notice provision, section 7-80-208, which provides that the filing of the articles of organization serve as constructive notice of a company's status as a limited liability company, the district court held that "the County Court erred in finding that Westec had no notice that it was dealing with an L.L.C." Contrary to the trial court's findings, the district court held that "evidence presented at trial was uncontradicted that Westec knew it was dealing with a business entity (P.I.I.) and §7-80- 208 imputes notice that the entity was an 'L.L.C.' in addition to any common law presumption of a duty to inquire." In the district court's view, the notice provision, as well as Westec's failure to investigate or request a personal guarantee, relieved Lanham of personal liability for claims against the Company. . . .

III.

A.

The district court interpreted the LLC Act's notice provision, *see* §7-80-208, as putting Westec on constructive notice of Lanham's agency relationship with the Company. In essence, this course of analysis assumed that the LLC Act displaced certain common law agency doctrines, at least insofar as these doctrines otherwise would be applicable to suits by third parties seeking to hold the agents of a limited liability company liable for their personal actions as agents.

We hold, however, that the statutory notice provision applies only where a third party seeks to impose liability on an LLC's members or managers simply due to their status as members or managers of the LLC. When a third party sues a manager or member of an LLC under an agency theory, the principles of agency law apply notwithstanding the LLC Act's statutory notice rules.

B.

Under the common law of agency, an agent is liable on a contract entered on behalf of a principal if the principal is not fully disclosed. In other words, an agent who negotiates a contract with a third party can be sued for any breach of the contract unless the agent discloses both the fact that he or she is acting on behalf of a principal *and* the identity of the principal. . . .

This somewhat counterintuitive proposition—that an agent is liable even when the third party knows that the agent is acting on behalf of an unidentified principal—has been recognized as sound by the courts of this state, and it is a well established rule under the common law. Thus, an agent is liable on contracts negotiated on behalf of a "partially disclosed" principal; that is, a principal whose existence — but not identity — is known to the other party.

C.

Whether a principal is partially or completely disclosed is a question of fact. On appeal from the county court, the district court had the power to find the facts independently by ordering a trial de novo. Instead, the district court exercised its authority to decide the case based on the record developed below. Having so decided, it was bound to accept the facts as found by the county court and its review was limited to the sufficiency of the evidence.

These precepts, then, lead us to conclude that the district court erred in substituting its own factual determinations for the findings of the county court. If the district court had held a trial de novo, its conclusion that the letters "P.I.I." on Clark's business card sufficiently alerted Westec's representatives to the fact of Clark's agency relationship with the Company and to the Company's identity would be entitled to deference if supported by evidence in the record. However, we see the evidence as sufficient to support the county court's finding to the contrary. Indeed, neither the business card nor the unsigned contract documents, both of which are of obvious significance in evaluating whether Westec knew the identity of the entity represented by Clark and Lanham, are in the record before us. We are, therefore, bound to accept the county court's finding that Westec did not know Clark was acting as an agent for the Company or that the letters "P.I.I." stood for "Preferred Income Investors," a limited liability company registered under Colorado law. For the same reason, the district court erred in concluding that Clark was not acting as Lanham's agent. The trial record was sufficient to support the county court's finding that Clark was an agent for Lanham and this conclusion should not have been disturbed by the district court.

D.

In light of the partially disclosed principal doctrine, the county court's determination that Clark and Lanham failed to disclose the existence as well as the identity of the limited liability company they represented is dispositive under the common law of agency. Still, if the General Assembly has altered the common law rules applicable to this case by adopting the LLC Act, then these rules must yield in favor of the statute. We conclude, however, that the LLC Act's notice provision was not intended to alter the partially disclosed principal doctrine.

Section 7-80-208, C.R.S. (1997) states:

> The fact that the articles of organization are on file in the office of the secretary of state is notice that the limited liability company is a limited liability company and is notice of all other facts set forth therein which are required to be set forth in the articles of organization.

In order to relieve Lanham of liability, this provision would have to be read to establish a conclusive presumption that a third party who deals with the agent of a limited liability company always has constructive notice of the existence of the agent's principal. We are not persuaded that the statute can bear such an interpretation.

Such a construction exaggerates the plain meaning of the language in the statute. Section 7-80-208 could be read to state that third parties who deal with a limited liability company are always on constructive notice of the company's limited liability status, without regard to whether any part of the company's name or even the fact of its existence has been disclosed. However, an equally plausible interpretation of the words used in the statute is that once the limited liability company's name is known to the third party, constructive notice of the company's limited liability status has been given, as well as the fact that managers and members will not be liable simply due to their status as managers or members.

Moreover, the broad interpretation urged by Lanham would be an invitation to fraud, because it would leave the agent of a limited liability company free to mislead third parties into the belief that the agent would bear personal financial responsibility under any contract, when in fact, recovery would be limited to the assets of a limited liability company not known to the third party at the time the contract was made. While Westec has not alleged that Clark or Lanham deliberately tried to conceal the Company's identity or status as a limited liability company, Lanham's construction would open the door to sharp practices and outright fraud. We may presume that in adopting section 7-80-208, the General Assembly did not intend to create a safe harbor for deceit. For this reason alone, a broad reading of the notice provision would be suspect.

In addition, statutes in derogation of the common law are to be strictly construed. For the reasons outlined above, the interpretation urged by Lanham would be a radical departure from the settled rules of agency under the common law. If the legislature had intended a departure of such magnitude, its desires would have been expressed more clearly.

Other LLC Act provisions reinforce the conclusion that the legislature did not intend the notice language of section 7-80-208 to relieve the agent of a limited liability company of the duty to disclose its identity in order to avoid personal liability. For example, section 7-80-201(1), 2 C.R.S. (1997), requires limited liability companies to use the words "Limited Liability Company" or the initials "LLC" as part of their names, implying that the legislature intended to compel any entity seeking to claim the benefits of the LLC Act to identify itself clearly as a limited liability company. By way of further support for our conclusion, section 7-80-107, 2 C.R.S. (1997), provides two bases of individual liability for members: (1) for "alleged improper actions," and (2) "the failure of a limited liability company to observe the formalities or requirements relating to the management of its business and affairs when coupled with some other wrongful conduct." . . .

Lanham received from Westec a form of contract demonstrating Westec's assumption that Lanham was the principal. At that point, he could have clarified his relationship to the Company. He did not do so. Hence, even if we were sympathetic to Lanham's plight, he had within his control the means to clearly state to Westec and the world that he was acting only for the limited liability company. Moreover, we must avoid straying from long established legal precepts and inserting uncertainty into accepted rules that govern business relationships.

In sum, then, section 7-80-208 places third parties on constructive notice that a fully identified company — that is, identified by a name such as "Preferred Income Investors, LLC," or the like — is a limited liability company provided that its articles of organization have been filed with the secretary of state. Section 7-80-208 is of little force, however, in determining whether a limited liability company's agent is personally liable on the theory that the agent has failed to disclose the identity of the company.

IV.

Under our interpretation, section 7-80-208 still offers significant protection to the members of a limited liability company. The notice provision protects the members from suit based on their *status* as members, as opposed to their *acts* as agents of the corporate entity. If a third party such as Westec had tried to pierce the corporate veil to hold Clark and Lanham personally responsible for the Company's contractual debt based on the fact that they were members of the LLC, section 7-80-208 would protect them from liability. The distinction between the use of an agency theory and the doctrine of piercing the corporate or limited liability company veil is significant. . . .

V.

For these reasons, we conclude that where an agent fails to disclose either the fact that he is acting on behalf of a principal or the identity of the principal, the notice provision of our LLC Act, section 7-80-208, cannot relieve the agent of liability to a third party. When a third party deals with an agent acting on behalf of a limited liability company, the existence and identity of which has been disclosed, the third party is conclusively presumed to know that the entity is a limited liability company and not a partnership or some other type of business organization. Where the third party does not know the identity of the principal entity, however, the situation is fundamentally different because the third party is without notice and the law does not contemplate that he has any way of finding the relevant records.

If Clark or Lanham had told Westec's representatives that they were acting on behalf of an entity known as "Preferred Income Investors, LLC" the failure to disclose the fact that the entity was a limited liability company would be irrelevant by virtue of the statute, which provides that the articles of organization operate as constructive notice of the company's limited liability form. The county court, however, found that Lanham and Clark did not identify Preferred Income Investors, LLC, as the principal in the transaction. The "missing link" between the limited disclosure made by Clark and the protection of the notice statute was the failure to state that "P.I.I.," the Company, stood for "Preferred Income Investors, LLC."

Accordingly, the judgment of the district court is reversed and this case is remanded to that court with instructions that it reinstate the judgment of the county court.

2. *Management*

The first and most important management issue regarding LLCs is whether they are to have centralized management (like a corporation) or decentralized management (like a partnership). LLC statutes provide for both types, with member management as the default rule. The ULLCA requires a statement in the articles of organization if the LLC is to be manager-managed. ULLCA §203(a)(6). Members in a member-managed LLC have equal management rights and decide all ordinary business matters by a majority of the members, each member having one vote. By contrast, members in manager-managed LLCs have limited powers; the managers have exclusive management rights and decide all ordinary business matters by a majority of the managers. All of these rules are subject to contrary agreement.

Another important issue relating to the management of LLCs is the extent of managers' authority. Managers (including member managers) of an LLC have actual and apparent authority to carry on business in the usual way. Members who are not managers, like shareholders in a corporation, have no inherent right to bind the LLC. Under ULLCA §301, members are not agents of an LLC merely by reason of being a member, but managers are agents of the LLC and have actual and apparent authority to carry on the business in the usual way. Extraordinary transactions are binding on the LLC only if actually authorized. Depending on the statute, that vote may require a majority of members or unanimous consent. The argument for unanimity is that LLCs are likely to be closely held; therefore, members are likely to want a veto power over extraordinary transactions, and the unanimity requirement is the easiest method of providing that. The arguments against are numerous: (1) obtaining consent may be costly because it may require individual negotiations; (2) the veto power may not be as justified in an LLC as it is in a general partnership because members cannot impose unlimited liability for their actions on each other; (3) a disgruntled member has the right to withdraw and be paid for his or her interest in the LLC.

The following case illustrates the ability of a manager in a manager-managed LLC to bind the entity in contract. More specifically, the case raises issues relating to the power of an LLC operating agreement to limit the authority of a manager to act on behalf of the LLC. As you read this case, consider ways in which the innocent members might have avoided exposing themselves to this sort of liability.

TAGHIPOUR v. JEREZ
52 P.3d 1252
Supreme Court of Utah
July 30, 2002

RUSSON, Justice.

On a writ of certiorari, Namvar Taghipour, Danesh Rahemi, and Jerez, Taghipour and Associates, LLC, seek review of the decision of the court of appeals affirming the trial court's dismissal of their causes of action against Mount Olympus Financial, L.C. ("Mt. Olympus"). We affirm.

BACKGROUND

Namvar Taghipour, Danesh Rahemi, and Edgar Jerez ("Jerez") formed a limited liability company known as Jerez, Taghipour and Associates, LLC (the "LLC"), on August 30, 1994, to purchase and develop a particular parcel of real estate pursuant to a joint venture agreement. The LLC's articles of organization designated Jerez as the LLC's manager. In addition, the operating agreement between the members of the LLC provided: "No loans may be contracted on behalf of the [LLC] . . . unless authorized by a resolution of the [m]embers."

On August 31, 1994, the LLC acquired the intended real estate. Then, on January 10, 1997, Jerez, unbeknownst to the LLC's other members or managers, entered into a loan agreement on behalf of the LLC with Mt. Olympus. According to the agreement, Mt. Olympus lent the LLC $25,000 and, as security for the loan, Jerez executed and delivered a trust deed that conveyed the LLC's real estate property to a trustee with the power to sell the property in the event of default. Mt. Olympus then dispensed $20,000 to Jerez and retained the $5,000 balance to cover various fees. In making the loan, Mt. Olympus did not investigate Jerez's authority to effectuate the loan agreement beyond determining that Jerez was the manager of the LLC.

After Mt. Olympus dispersed the funds pursuant to the agreement, Jerez apparently misappropriated and absconded with the $20,000. Jerez never remitted a payment on the loan, and because the other members of the LLC were unaware of the loan, no loan payments were ever made by anyone, and consequently, the LLC defaulted. Therefore, Mt. Olympus foreclosed on the LLC's property. The members of the LLC, other than Jerez, were never notified of the default or pending foreclosure sale.

On June 18, 1999, Namvar Taghipour, Danesh Rahemi, and the LLC (collectively, "Taghipour") filed suit against Mt. Olympus and Jerez. Taghipour asserted three claims against Mt. Olympus: (1) declaratory judgment that the loan agreement and subsequent foreclosure on the LLC's property were invalid because Jerez lacked the authority to bind the LLC under the operating agreement, (2) negligence in failing to conduct proper due diligence in determining whether Jerez had the authority to enter into the loan agreement, and (3) partition of the various interests in the property at issue. In response, Mt. Olympus moved to dismiss all three claims, asserting that pursuant to Utah Code section 48-2b-127(2), the loan agreement documents are valid and binding on the LLC since they were signed by the LLC's manager. This section provides:

> Instruments and documents providing for the acquisition, mortgage, or disposition of property of the limited liability company shall be valid and binding upon the limited liability company if they are executed by one or more managers of a limited liability company having a manager or managers or if they are executed by one or more members of a limited liability company in which management has been retained by the members.

The trial court granted Mt. Olympus' motion and dismissed Taghipour's claims against Mt. Olympus, ruling that under the above section, "instruments and documents providing for the mortgage of property of a limited liability company are valid and binding on the limited liability company if they are executed by the manager," that the complaint alleges that Jerez is the manager of the LLC, and that therefore the loan documents Jerez executed are valid and binding on the LLC.

Taghipour appealed to the Utah Court of Appeals. Taghipour argued that the trial court's interpretation of section 48-2b-127(2) was in error, inasmuch as it failed to read it in conjunction with Utah Code section 48-2b-125(2)(b), which provides that a manager's authority to bind a limited liability company can be limited by the operating agreement. That section provides in relevant part:

> If the management of the limited liability company is vested in a manager or managers, any manager has authority to bind the limited liability company, unless otherwise provided in the articles of organization or operating agreement.

The Utah Court of Appeals affirmed the trial court, concluding that the plain language of section 48-2b-127(2) provided no limitation on a manager's authority to execute certain documents and bind a limited liability company, and specifically stated such documents shall be valid and binding upon the limited liability company if executed by one or more managers. Further, the court of appeals concluded that this specific statute prevailed over the general statute, section 48-2b-125(2)(b), and that the loan documents executed by Jerez were therefore binding upon the LLC in this case. It also held that Mt. Olympus did all that it was required to do under section 48-2b-127(2) and that Taghipour waived the right to appeal the dismissal of the partition claim by failing to object to the dismissal of that claim. Taghipour petitioned this court for certiorari, which we granted.

Taghipour asks this court to reverse the court of appeals, arguing that (1) sections 48-2b-125(2)(b) and 48-2b-127(2) should be read in harmony to require that managers "be properly authorized to bind the limited liability company in all situations," and therefore Jerez lacked authority to bind the LLC under the operating agreement, and (2) a commercial lender has a due diligence obligation to determine the authority of a manager of a limited liability company before that manager can encumber the assets of the company, which Mt. Olympus failed to do by neglecting to determine whether Jerez had the authority to bind the LLC. In reply, Mt. Olympus contends that under Utah Code section 48-2b-127(2), Mt. Olympus could properly rely on Jerez's execution of the loan agreement as the manager of the LLC without further inquiry. . . .

ANALYSIS . . .

I. COMPETING STATUTORY PROVISIONS

To determine whether the loan agreement in this case is valid and binding on the LLC, it must first be determined whether this case is governed by section 48-2b-127(2), which makes certain kinds of documents binding on a limited liability company when executed by a manager, or section 48-2b-125(2)(b), which provides that a manager's authority to bind a limited liability company can be limited or eliminated by an operating agreement.

When two statutory provisions purport to cover the same subject, the legislature's intent must be considered in determining which provision applies. To determine that intent, our rules of statutory construction provide that "when two statutory provisions conflict in their operation, the provision more specific in application governs over the more general provision." Hall v. State Dep't of Corr., 2001 UT 34, ¶15, 24 P.3d 958.

In this case, the Utah Court of Appeals, affirming the trial court, concluded that section 48-2b-127(2) was more specific than section 48-2b-125(2)(b), and therefore took precedence over it. However, Taghipour contends that in determining which of the two provisions is more specific, the more restrictive clause is more specific because it is more limiting and "would require authority in all situations." Accordingly, Taghipour contends that section 48-2b-125(2)(b) is the more restrictive, and consequently, the more specific, provision.

The question of which statute the legislature intended to apply in this case is determined by looking to the plain language of the statutes that purport to cover the same subject. Section 48-2b-125(2)(b) provides in relevant part:

> If the management of the limited liability company is vested in a manager or managers, any manager has authority to bind the limited liability company, unless otherwise provided in the articles of organization or operating agreement.

Utah Code Ann. §48-2b-125(2)(b) (1998). In contrast, section 48-2b-127(2) provides:

> Instruments and documents providing for the acquisition, mortgage, or disposition of property of the limited liability company shall be valid and binding upon the limited liability company if they are executed by one or more managers of a limited liability company having a manager or managers or if they are executed by one or more members of a limited liability company in which management has been retained by the members.

Section 48-2b-127(2) is the more specific statute because it applies only to documents explicitly enumerated in the statute, *i.e.*, the section expressly addresses "[i]nstruments and documents" that provide "for the acquisition, mortgage, or disposition of property of the limited liability company." Thus, this section is tailored precisely to address the documents and instruments Jerez executed, *e.g.*, the trust deed and trust deed note. For example, a trust deed is similar to a mortgage in that it secures an obligation relating to real property, and a trust deed "is a conveyance" of title to real property, which is a disposition of property as contemplated by the statutory provision. Conversely, section 48-2b-125(2)(b) is more general because it addresses *every* situation in which a manager can bind a limited liability company.

Further, a statute is more specific according to the content of the statute, not according to how restrictive the statute is in application. Indeed, a specific statute may be either more or less restrictive than the statute more general in application, depending upon the intent of the legislature in enacting a more specific statute.

Moreover, if we were to hold that section 48-2b-125(2)(b) is the more specific provision, we would essentially render section 48-2b-127(2) "superfluous and inoperative," because section 48-2b-127(2) would simply restate section 48-2b-125(2)(b) and would therefore be subsumed by section 48-2b-125(2)(b).

Accordingly, the court of appeals correctly concluded that section 48-2b-127(2) is more specific, and therefore, the applicable statute in this case.

II.   VALID AND BINDING LOAN AGREEMENT DOCUMENTS

Section 48-2b-127(2) must be applied to the facts of this case to determine whether the documents are valid and bind the LLC. At the time relevant to this case, section 48-2b-127(2), the statute applicable to the issue in this case, provided:

> *Instruments and documents providing for the* acquisition, *mortgage,* or disposition *of property of the limited liability company shall be valid and binding upon the limited liability company if they are executed by one or more managers* of a limited liability company having a manager or managers or if they are executed by one or more members of a limited liability company in which management has been retained by the members.

Utah Code Ann. §48-26-127(2) (1998) (emphasis added). According to this section, the documents are binding if they are covered by the statute and if executed by a manager. There are no other requirements for such documents to be binding on a limited liability company.

In this case, as Taghipour acknowledges in the complaint and Taghipour's brief on appeal, Jerez was designated as the LLC's manager in the articles of organization. Jerez, acting in his capacity as manager, executed loan agreement documents, *e.g.*, the trust deed and trust deed note, on behalf of the LLC that are specifically covered by the above statute. As such, these documents are valid and binding on the LLC under section 48-2b-127(2). Therefore, the court of appeals correctly concluded that the LLC was bound by the loan agreement and, consequently, that Mt. Olympus was not liable to Taghipour for Jerez's actions. . . .

NEOCLONE BIOTECHNOLOGY INTERNATIONAL LLC: A CASE STUDY

Deven McGlenn first heard about NeoClone Biotechnology International in the fall of 1999. At the time, McGlenn was sitting in his Chicago office at Arthur Andersen — then one of the "Big Five" accounting firms — where McGlenn had begun his career as a consultant two years earlier. On the other end of the telephone call was Allen Clark, a Professor of Anatomy of the University of Wisconsin Medical School. Dr. Clark's first contact with McGlenn had nothing to do with business — Clark was a neighbor and friend of the parents of McGlenn's wife — but now Clark was seeking some business advice. He had become interested in a new technology developed at the University of Wisconsin, and he wanted McGlenn to assist in building a business around the technology.

The technology was a patented method of producing monoclonal antibodies. Antibodies are proteins produced naturally by the body to fight antigens, such as disease-causing bacteria and viruses. Each antibody is tailored to attack a specific antigen, and some antibodies — once activated — provide ongoing protection against future invasions by the same type of antigen (for example, antibodies created by having the measles produce an immunity against future infections). This immunizing attribute of antibodies makes them useful in developing vaccines. Antibodies are also used to diagnose various diseases.

Developing vaccines and diagnostic tools requires a large number of antibodies for use in research. Traditionally, scientists would produce antibodies by injecting laboratory animals with an antigen and harvesting the antibodies from the animal's blood. This method is slow and the resulting product is often contaminated by other substances in the animal's blood.

Monoclonal antibody technology represented a great advance over the traditional method. Simply understood, this technology required scientists to combine cells that produce antibodies naturally with cells that grow continually in a cell culture. The resulting cell (called a "hybridoma") produces antibodies continually. Because the antibodies are produced from a single cell (the hybridoma), they are called "monoclonal." These antibodies are purer and more accurately targeted to specific antigens than the antibodies produced using the traditional process.

The technology Clark described to McGlenn was a method of producing monoclonal antibodies even more quickly than had previously been done, in some instances at double the speed. Of course, the value of such a process lies primarily in the cost savings associated with quicker production cycles. While McGlenn knew next to nothing about the science of monoclonal antibody production, he knew a profitable business opportunity when he saw it, and this looked like it had some potential. NeoClone, as the company came to be called, would manufacture and sell antibodies — some "off the shelf" from NeoClone's catalogue and others custom made.

At the time, the business consisted of three founders. Donal Kaehler and David Largaespada were part of the research team that developed and patented the new production process in the laboratory of a University of Wisconsin professor, Dr. Rex Risser. The third founder, Mark Jackson, was an expert in laboratory personnel and materials management, and he had worked in Risser's laboratory after the process had been developed.

Patents relating to the new process were held by the Wisconsin Alumni Research Foundation (WARF) — a legendary leader in technology transfer. Founded in 1925,[1] WARF is a nonprofit organization that patents technologies developed at the University of Wisconsin-Madison.[2] Mark Jackson negotiated the license of two patents from WARF on behalf of NeoClone.

Since all three founders of NeoClone were working at the University of Wisconsin, they decided to set up shop in Madison, which has an up-and-coming biotechnology industry, anchored by Promega Corporation and Third

---

1. The impetus for WARF's founding was Professor Harry Steenbock's discovery that vitamin D could be artificially manufactured and stored in foods. Steenbock recognized that his research could lead to the elimination of rickets, and he sought the creation of WARF to ensure that his discovery — and others like it — would reach the public. After receiving a series of patents based on Steenbock's research, WARF granted its first license in 1927. Quaker Oats used the license to supplement its breakfast cereals.

2. Here's how it works. A researcher discloses an invention to WARF, and the WARF staff evaluates its patentability and commercial potential. If the invention is accepted, WARF provides an attorney to assist the researcher in preparing and prosecuting the patent application. In exchange, the professor assigns ownership of the future patent to WARF.

Once a patent is awarded, WARF licenses the technologies. The inventor receives 20 percent of any license revenues, and the remainder are used to support further research at the university. The University of Wisconsin, through WARF, remains consistently among the top universities in the United States in patent awards. According to WARF's Web site, nearly 100 companies based on technology developed by the University of Wisconsin are currently in operation.

Wave Technologies and encouraged by various University initiatives.[3] McGlenn worked with the founders of NeoClone occasionally over the next two and a half years, but he kept his day job at Andersen. NeoClone hired Amy Davison Clark (Allen Clark's daughter) as its first full-time employee in April 2000, but didn't add a second employee for another year. By the spring of 2002, NeoClone was beginning to develop, and the need for a full-time manager was becoming more apparent. At the same time, life at Andersen had taken a dramatic turn for the worse for McGlenn, as the firm was enveloped by the collapse of Enron Corporation. In June of 2002, McGlenn left Andersen and joined NeoClone as the Chief Executive Officer.

McGlenn immediately set to work preparing for expansion of the company. He had brought on Jeff Moore as Chief Operating Officer for this very purpose. Moore — who describes himself as a "recovering lawyer"[4] — had seven years of start-up experience with MicroCoating Technologies in Atlanta, Georgia.

Although NeoClone was generating revenues from the sale of antibodies, it needed some additional capital quickly. By the middle of October, Moore and McGlenn had successfully negotiated a $90,000 investment by a group of angel investors[5] in Madison. Although the group had begun their discussions around the idea of an equity investment, they were unable to agree on an appropriate valuation for the company.[6] Ultimately, they were able to come to terms on an investment involving convertible debt, which provides investors with the priority associated with debt in the event the company liquidates but also comes with the prospect of obtaining common stock at some time in the future. Like most early-stage investors, these angels were willing to invest only if they had the potential to participate in the upside of the company through equity. Straight debt holds out the prospect of steady returns, but early-stage investors recognize that many of their investments will fail completely. They hope to compensate for those large failures with large successes, and the interest available from straight debt investments simply cannot reach the levels necessary to obtain such results.

In this instance, the angel investors created a company called NEOCL Investment LLC (NILLC) for the sole purpose of investing in NeoClone. In exchange for its $90,000 investment, NILLC received a Convertible Note due October 14,

---

3. In addition to WARF, these initiatives include a Biotechnology Center, founded in 1984 by Richard Burgess, NeoClone's current Chairman. Also, the Office of Corporate Relations has extensive programs devoted to technology transfer.

4. Although internal operations are, for the most part, beyond the scope of this case study, McGlenn credits Moore with turning NeoClone into a professional operation. Moore's background in law enabled him to take the lead on the company's contract negotiations and to deal with many other issues that otherwise would have fallen to McGlenn.

5. "Angel investor" is a term used to identify wealthy individuals who invest privately in developing firms. McGlenn cited several reasons for pursuing an angel investment as opposed to institutional venture capital: (1) angels tend to perform less "due diligence"; (2) angels are willing to take bigger risks at early stages in a company's development; and (3) angels do not require changes in the business structure. While these characterizations may not be universal, McGlenn claims that he has observed these differences across a number of investors.

6. Angel investors tend to have fewer resources at their disposal than institutional venture capitalists. As a result, negotiations over valuation can often be conducted with relatively little information. In this instance, the Madison angel investors had financial statements from NeoClone, and they called two of NeoClone's current customers. Otherwise, their approach to valuation was rather informal. In some instances, angel investors will hire an independent company to perform due diligence and provide investment advice.

2006 (exactly four years from the date of the investment). The Note would bear simple interest at a fixed rate of 12 percent, but NeoClone would not be required to make periodic cash payments. Instead, the interest would accrue and become due upon maturity of the Note.

Prior to maturity, one of four things might result in the extinguishment of the loan:

(1) An action by NILLC to collect, prompted by an event of default by Neo-Clone. Usual events of default include the failure to make principal or interest payments—and those are included among the events of default in the Note Purchase Agreement here—but in this case, no payments of principal or interest prior to maturity were contemplated. The other events of default listed in the Note Purchase Agreement might prove more meaningful: the failure of NeoClone to observe any covenant,[7] the making of any materially untrue representation or warranty;[8] the acceleration of senior secured loans; and any voluntary or involuntary bankruptcy of NeoClone.

(2) A "Qualified Financing" of NeoClone's shares. The term "Qualified Financing" is defined as follows:

> (A) transaction closing on or prior to October 14, 2006 with each of the following characteristics:
>
> > (i) the Company (or its successor) issues equity securities in a single financing or a series of related financings;
> > (ii) for at least $1,500,000 in cash proceeds;
> > (iii) to one or more accredited investors (as defined in Regulation D under the Securities Act).

In all likelihood, the first financing that would meet this definition would be an investment by venture capitalists.[9] NeoClone will probably raise additional funds from angel investors prior to seeking venture capital, but angel investments tend to be at amounts less than $1,500,000. In addition, Neo-Clone has obtained bank financing, but the definition of "Qualified Financing" is expressly limited to equity securities, thus excluding bank loans.

Upon the occurrence of a "Qualified Financing," the balance due on the Note is converted into stock of NeoClone that is "identical to the equity securities issued in the Qualified Financing except that if such securities are a senior series of a class of securities that is preferred with respect to liquidation or dividends, the Conversion Stock may be a junior series of the same class of preferred securities."

---

7. Most of the covenants should be relatively easy to maintain. Under the Note Purchase Agreement, NeoClone is required to furnish the angel investors with periodic financial statements, file appropriate tax returns, maintain its existence, provide notice of any actions by members, and reserve sufficient equity securities to cover the conversion of the Note. The covenant with the most important control implications is one requiring NeoClone to ensure the election of a representative of NILLC to the "Board of Advisors" (*i.e.*, the Management Committee) of NeoClone.

8. The representations and warranties included in the Note Purchase Agreement appear entirely typical for this sort of transaction. Generally speaking, NeoClone makes such representations and warranties to assure the investors that everything is as it appears with the company. For example, NeoClone represents that it is a Wisconsin LLC, that the Note Purchase Agreement has been duly authorized, that the company owns its intellectual property, and that NeoClone has no undisclosed liabilities.

9. According to McGlenn, the first venture financing will likely occur in 2004 at the earliest.

The conversion under this provision is accomplished by giving NILLC a number of shares equal to the principal balance of the Note, plus any accrued interest, divided by the "Conversion Price" (which is set in the note at 60 percent of the price per share paid in the Qualified Financing). Here's how it would work: assume that one year from the date of the angel investment, venture capitalists purchased 150,000 shares at $10 per share. The angel investors would receive $90,000 (principal) + $10,800 (one year's interest) = $100,800 ÷ $6 (that is, 60% of the $10 price paid by venture capitalists) = 16,800 shares.

(3) The sale of NeoClone. Upon the occurrence of a "Sale Event" — defined in the Note as "a sale of all or substantially all of the assets of the Company or a merger, consolidation or sale of equity interests (or stock) by the Company's members (or shareholders) immediately after which more than 50% of the equity securities of the Company are held by persons who were not members of the Company prior to such transaction" — NeoClone has the option of pre-paying the Note without premium or penalty. Alternatively, the angel investors have the option of converting their debt claim into equity on the same terms as those available in a "Qualified Financing," except that the "Conversion Price" is established at "60% of the pre-conversion valuation of 100% of the Company's common equity implied by the Sale Event transaction price."

(4) An "Interim Equity Issuance" by NeoClone. The term "Interim Equity Issuance" is defined as follows:

> [T]he issuance and sale by the Company of its equity securities at any time after the Company has issued, on a cumulative basis, equity securities with an aggregate purchase price of $510,000 after the date of this Note, excluding the issuance or sale of equity securities to employees or consultants of the Company.[10]

Unlike the conversion that occurs upon the completion of a "Qualified Financing," conversion under this provision is optional on the part of the angel investors. The transaction contemplated by this provision was an additional angel investment,[11] and the terms of the conversion would be the same as the conversion under the "Qualified Financing" provision, except that the "Conversion Price" is established at "60% of the price per share paid to the Company by the purchaser in the Interim Equity Issuance."

In addition to the foregoing provisions, the Note allows for optional conversion upon maturity. The basic idea of conversion remains the same — turning debt into equity — but the valuation in this instance cannot be tied to a "Qualified Financing," "Sale Event," or "Interim Equity Issuance." To overcome

---

10. The aggregate purchase price in this provision is not completely arbitrary. Another section of the Operating Agreement allows the company to issue additional interests, anticipating more angel investments on terms similar to the first investment:

> The Members, by Majority Vote, must approve the issuance by the Company of any additional Interests except for . . . interests issuable upon conversion of up to $600,000 (original principal balance) of convertible notes in the form attached as Schedule 3.1(a)(i), of which convertible notes $90,000 principal amount is outstanding and $510,000 principal balance may be issued from and after the date of this Agreement with the approval of the Management Committee under section 5.8.

11. According to McGlenn, NeoClone will raise additional angel financing after the initial angel investment and prior to the first venture financing.

this problem, the parties simply assert that the conversion will be based on a specified valuation:

> The conversion price per share applicable to a conversion of the Note pursuant to this section 5(d) (the "Optional Conversion Stock Conversion Price") shall be an amount determined based on a $5 million pre-money valuation[12] of 100% of the Company's common equity on the date of conversion under this section 5(d) (the "Optional Conversion Date"). (For example, if there are 100,000 units of Company common equity issued and outstanding, the Optional Conversion Stock Conversion Price shall be $50.)

Given the current number of outstanding membership units (865,000, including outstanding options), the price for each additional unit would be $5.78. At this price, the angel investors would obtain just over 23,000 units,[13] which is less than 3 percent of the total equity ownership of the company.

The founders of NeoClone formed a Wisconsin LLC on July 9, 1999, and they still own a substantial majority of the membership units in NeoClone. Control of the company is specified primarily under a detailed Operating Agreement, which has been signed by all eight individual members—the three founders, Deven McGlenn, Allen Clark, Richard Burgess,[14] Nancy Thompson,[15] and Amy Davison Clark. In addition, the Operating Agreement has been signed by NeoClone's two institutional members—WARF and Breakthrough Development Co. LLC, a Madison company that provided strategic development services to NeoClone in exchange for a small equity share.

It is worth noting that the angel investors are not parties to the Operating Agreement. According to McGlenn, the angel investors were not interested in having an active involvement in the operation of NeoClone. While most of the angel investors have had long and successful business careers, they are not usually eager to spend their days running a start-up company.

The capital structure of NeoClone consists of two major categories of claimants: members, who have equity claims, and creditors, who have debt claims. The three founders of NeoClone own 72 percent of the outstanding membership units, ignoring options and units issuable upon the conversion of a note. The creditors include banks and the angel investors discussed above. The bank extended a $75,000 equipment line of credit and a $100,000 general operating line of credit in the fall of 2000. In each instance, these loans were personally guaranteed by Mark Jackson, Donal Kaehler, Allen Clark, Richard Burgess, and Deven McGlenn.

---

12. "Pre-money valuation" refers to the value of the company prior to the investment contemplated. If the angel investors elect to convert their debt claim into equity, they would be effectively investing an additional $133,200 (the principal amount plus four years' interest on the note), and this amount would be added to the pre-money valuation when determining the valuation of the company after the investment ("post-money").

13. The principal amount plus four years' interest on the note would be $133,200. The amount, divided by $5.78 per share equals approximately 23,045 units.

14. Burgess is a prominent researcher at the University of Wisconsin. He obtained a Ph.D in Biochemistry and Molecular Biology with Dr. James Watson at Harvard University, and he has since received numerous awards—including a Guggenheim Fellowship. He also serves as Chairman of the Board of NeoClone.

15. Thompson is an employee of Richard Burgess's laboratory who provides expertise on certain NeoClone products.

Like most LLCs, NeoClone has some attributes that resemble a corporation and others that resemble a partnership. When analyzing the attributes of a business entity, it is common to think about "control rights" and "financial rights." While there may be some overlap — control can dictate access to the money, and financial rights can provide leverage — these are useful categories to the extent that they help to organize the many attributes of the relationship.

Control Rights

Control rights include: (1) the composition and powers of the management committee; (2) the right to bind the company as an agent; (3) the right to determine membership; and (4) voting rights.

Management Committee. The Operating Agreement creates a Management Committee, which is comprised of up to seven members. The Management Committee functions somewhat like a board of directors in a corporation, except that it does not possess general management authority over the LLC. Instead, all of the functions of NeoClone's Management Committee are defined in the Operating Agreement. Most important, the Management Committee must approve any fundamental transaction (for example, merger, dissolution, or sale of all or substantially all of the assets of the LLC), any amendment to the Operating Agreement, any purchase or sale of membership interests, any agreement between the LLC and a member, and any incurrence of indebtedness in excess of $100,000. In addition, the Management Committee has authority over certain ordinary business matters, such as a change in the company's principal place of business, a decision to expand the business beyond Wisconsin, allocations of profits and losses to member capital accounts, distributions to members of cash from operations, and approval of any transfers of membership interests. Finally, the Management Committee has the power to remove or replace "Managers."[16]

The Operating Agreement does not specify annual elections of the Management Committee, though such a result might be the negative implication of the Operating Agreement's statement that Managers of the LLC "shall not stand for annual election." The Operating Agreement designated Richard Burgess, Mark Jackson, Donal Kaehler, Deven McGlenn, and a representative selected by NILLC as the initial members of the Management Committee. Interestingly, as of six months after the investment, NILLC still had not found a suitable representative, and its place on the Management Committee remained vacant.

Power to Bind. Under the default rules of partnership law, each partner is an agent of the partnership and can bind the partnership when acting within the ordinary course of business. Shareholders, on the other hand, are not agents of the corporation simply by virtue of holding shares. Like most LLC statutes, the Wisconsin LLC statute embraces the partnership rule for member-managed firms and the corporate rule for manager-managed firms. Wis. Stat. §183.0301.

---

16. Note that "Managers" are different from members of the Management Committee — which the Operating Agreement refers to as "Representatives" — and are discussed more thoroughly below.

NeoClone is a manager-managed LLC,[17] and the Operating Agreement understandably invokes the corporate rule, providing that the Managers and agents authorized by the Managers are the only people who may bind the LLC.[18] In acting on behalf of the LLC, both Managers and members — and presumably the Representatives on the Management Committee — owe fiduciary duties to the LLC. Wis. Stat. §183.0402.

As noted above, these Managers are distinct from the Management Committee. The Operating Agreement provides for one to four Managers, who appear to be similar to officers in a corporation. Managers are not elected annually,[19] but serve at the pleasure of the Management Committee and the members. The Operating Agreement designated Mark Jackson, Donal Kaehler, and Deven McGlenn as the initial managers of the LLC, and Jeff Moore has since been added.

Membership. Membership in the LLC is regulated through a web of interlocking provisions in the Operating Agreement. The default rule under partnership law would require a vote of all partners to admit a new partner, while corporate law would allow free transfer of shares. NeoClone's Operating Agreement requires a majority vote prior to the issuance of any additional membership units, thus restricting the admission of new members to some degree, but permitting the addition of a new member with less than unanimous approval. Membership is also controlled by the classic transfer restriction, a right of first refusal. While these are not common in partnerships — where the only transferable interest in the partnership is financial and a right of first refusal is seen as unnecessary — they are *de rigueur* in closely held corporations. The right of first refusal provides that if a member receives from a third party a bona fide offer to purchase a membership interest, NeoClone retains a right to purchase the membership interest on the same terms offered by the third party. The Operating Agreement adds a partnership-like twist to this otherwise ordinary provision, in that it specifies that a nonmember purchaser of the membership interest may not exercise control rights — even after a valid purchase — unless the Management Committee of the LLC approves.[20]

The Operating Agreement also strictly regulates the withdrawal of members, providing that any voluntary withdrawal is considered a breach of the Operating Agreement. This portion of the agreement has a distinctly partnership feel, as it refers to "dissociation" from and "dissolution" of the LLC.[21] In most instances, the withdrawal of a member does not result in dissolution of the LLC;[22] moreover, the withdrawing member is not entitled to a buyout from the

---

17. Under the Wisconsin LLC statute, the default rule requires member management. LLCs that want to be manager-managed must make that election in the articles of organization, Wis. Stat. §183.0401, which NeoClone has done.

18. In deciding "any matter connected with the business of" NeoClone, the Managers are required to act by majority consent. Wis. Stat. §183.0404(1)(b).

19. Wis. Stat. §183.0401 (providing that each manager "[s]hall hold office until a successor is elected and qualified, or until prior death, resignation or removal").

20. The Wisconsin LLC statute requires unanimous consent of the members, unless the operating agreement provides otherwise. Wis. Stat. §183.0706.

21. This follows the Wisconsin LLC statute, which uses the same sort of partnership language. Wis. Stat. §183.0802.

22. Indeed, the Operating Agreement lists only four events that result in dissolution: (a) the sale of all or substantially all of the company's assets; (b) the majority vote of the members to

LLC.[23] Instead, the successor of the dissociated member is entitled to "receive the distributions and to share in the allocations of profits and losses to which the dissociated Member would have been entitled," but the successor cannot exercise any control rights.

Voting Rights. Under statutory default rules, partners are entitled to one vote per partner, while shareholders are entitled to as many votes as shares they own. NeoClone has embraced the corporate rule. As noted above, members of the LLC elect the Management Committee, remove or replace Managers, and exercise joint control rights with the Management Committee over such matters as the issuance of additional membership interests and the approval of fundamental transactions (just as corporate shareholders exercise joint control with boards of directors over similar matters).[24]

Financial Rights

Financial rights include: (1) the right to share in profits (and the corresponding obligation to share in losses); (2) the right to a return of capital; (3) the right to distributions; and (4) limited liability.

Sharing Profits and Losses. NeoClone's allocation of profits and losses takes cues from both partnerships and corporations. Under the statutory default rules, general partnerships allocate profits and losses equally among the partners. Even if the equal-sharing rule is altered by contract, pass-through taxation requires the use of capital accounts to allocate profits and losses to the individual partners. By contrast, the default rules of corporate law do not provide for any allocation of profits and losses to common shareholders. Any profits or losses belong to the corporation itself, and common shareholders possess a claim against the residual assets of the corporation (that is, those assets that remain once all of the other obligations of the corporation have been paid). A shareholder's claim against such residual assets is based on the level of the shareholder's investment, as opposed to the equal-sharing rule of general partnerships. Of course, any losses incurred by the corporation would reduce the capital of the shareholders, but losses in excess of capital contributions are capped through the rule of limited liability.

The default rule of Wisconsin's LLC statute states that "profits and losses . . . shall be allocated among the members in the manner provided in an operating agreement."[25] Under the Operating Agreement, NeoClone's members have agreed to a complex sharing of profits and losses that follows generally

---

dissolve; (c) the happening of any event that would make it unlawful to conduct the company's business; or (d) the entry of a decree of dissolution under the relevant section of the Wisconsin LLC statute. The Operating Agreement expressly provides that a dissociation does not lead to dissolution of the LLC unless the members vote to dissolve. Under the default rules in the Wisconsin LLC statute, NeoClone would dissolve after any dissociation unless all of the remaining members voted to continue. Wis. Stat. §183.0901(4).

23. This changes the default rule under the Wisconsin LLC statute, which provides: "if not otherwise provided in the operating agreement, within a reasonable time after dissociation, the dissociating member is entitled to receive a distribution in complete redemption of the fair value of the member's interest in the limited liability company as of the date of dissociation. . . . " Wis. Stat. §183.0604.

24. The right of members to vote on fundamental transactions is granted in the Wisconsin LLC statute. Wis. Stat. §183.0404(2).

25. Wis. Stat. §183.0503. In the absence of an operating agreement, profits and losses are allocated "on the basis of value, as stated in the [LLC's] records." *Id.*

the investment level of the members (corporate rule), but uses capital accounts like those found in general partnerships.[26] The basic allocation provisions read as follows:

4.1 PROFITS AND LOSSES

(a) Profits. Profits shall be allocated as follows:

(i) First, to the Interest Holders, pro rata based on the Losses allocated to them pursuant to section 4.1(b)(iii) hereof until each Interest Holder has been allocated an amount of Profits pursuant to this section 4.1(a)(i) in the current and previous fiscal years that equals the Losses allocated to that Interest Holder pursuant to section 4.1(b)(iii) hereof in the previous fiscal years;

(ii) Second, to the Interest Holders, pro rata based on the Losses allocated to them pursuant to section 4.1(b)(ii) hereof until each Interest Holder has been allocated an amount of Profits pursuant to this section 4.1(a)(ii) in the current and previous fiscal years that equals the Losses allocated to that Interest Holder pursuant to section 4.1(b)(ii) hereof in the previous fiscal years; and

(iii) Thereafter, to all the Interest Holders, pro rata in accordance with the number of Interests held by each Interest Holder.

(b) Losses. Losses shall be allocated as follows:

(i) First, to the Interest Holders, pro rata based on the Profits allocated to them pursuant to sections 4.1(a)(iii) hereof until each Interest Holder has been allocated an amount of Losses pursuant to this section 4.1(b)(i) in the current and previous fiscal years equal to the Profits allocated to that Interest Holder pursuant to section 4.1(a)(iii) hereof in the previous fiscal years.

(ii) Second, to the Interest Holders based on their respective positive Capital Accounts, until each Interest Holder has been allocated an amount of Losses pursuant to this section 4.1(b)(ii) in the current and previous fiscal years to reduce that Interest Holder's Capital Account to zero;

(iii) Thereafter, to all the Interest Holders, pro rata based in accordance with the number of Interests held by such Interest Holder.

Return of Capital. Partners are entitled to a return of any capital contributions, but shareholders are not. Although NeoClone employs capital accounts to keep track of each member's contributions, the Operating Agreement expressly foreswears any obligation to return capital contributions. Nevertheless, capital contributions increase a member's capital account, and the capital account

26. The capital accounts are described in the Operating Agreement as follows:

A separate Capital Account shall be maintained for each Interest Holder. Each such Capital Account shall be increased by (a) the amount of money and the fair market value of property contributed by the Interest Holder to the Company (net of liabilities secured by such property which the Company is considered to assume or take subject to pursuant to Section 752 of the Code) and (b) allocations to the Interest Holder of Profits, and shall be decreased by (c) the amount of money and fair market value of property distributed to the Interest Holder by the Company (net of liabilities secured by such property which the Interest Holder is considered to assume or take subject to . . . Section 752 of the Code), and (d) allocations to the Interest Holder of Losses, and shall be increased or decreased by (e) special allocations of income, gain, loss or deduction as provided in sections 4.4, 4.5, 4.6, 4.7 and 4.8 of this Agreement, and (f) any other allocation or adjustment as provided under Treasury Regulations Section 1.704-1(b).

is the basis for distribution upon liquidation of the LLC. As a result, capital contributions count.

Distributions. The differences between partnerships and corporations with respect to the rules governing distributions during the life of the firm are minimal. In most instances, the decision to distribute assets to equity claimants is left to the discretion of the firm's managers, whether those managers are partners or directors. The same holds true under most LLC statutes.[27] NeoClone does not break any new ground here, as it grants the Management Committee power to determine whether a distribution is in order.[28] Once the decision to make a distribution is made, it is done in accordance with each member's ownership interest.[29]

Separate distribution questions arise upon liquidation of the firm. As noted above, the use of capital accounts ensures that partners are given credit for capital contributions, while such contributions are not considered for shareholders, who receive an amount commensurate with their ownership percentage regardless of the amounts contributed to obtain that percentage. NeoClone's Operating Agreement includes a partnership-like distribution provision:

> Following the winding up of the Company, . . . the cash and other assets of the Company shall be applied first to the payment of all debts and liabilities of the Company including any loans from a Member (which for such purpose shall be treated the same as all other Company liabilities) and all expenses of liquidation, and the remainder shall be distributed to the Interest Holders in accordance with the positive balances in their Capital Accounts. . . .

Limited Liability. Obviously, one of the primary motivations for choosing an LLC over a general partnership is limited liability. NeoClone's Operating Agreement states flatly: "No Member shall be liable for the debts, obligations and liabilities of the Company except as expressly provided by the [Wisconsin LLC] Act."[30] In addition, the provision describing distributions upon liquidation of the LLC are intended to ensure that members will enjoy limited liability:

> If following the dissolution and liquidation of the Company, the Company's assets remaining after payment and discharge of the liabilities, obligations and expenses of the Company, including any liabilities to any one or more of the Members, are insufficient to return any amount to a Member, such Member shall have no recourse or further right or claim against any other Member by reason of such insufficiency. No Member shall be obligated to eliminate any deficit balance in such Member's Capital Account.

27. *See, e.g.,* Wis. Stat. §183.0601 (allowing interim distributions in accordance with the operating agreement, or, in the absence of an operating agreement, as determined by the managers).
28. The one exception here is that NeoClone follows the common practice of general partnerships in providing for an annual distribution sufficient for the payment of any tax liabilities arising from an allocation of profits.
29. *Cf.* Wis. Stat. §183.0602 (deferring to the operating agreement, but in the absence of an operating agreement, distributions to be allocated in the same manner as profits).
30. The section of the Wisconsin LLC statute providing for limited liability (Wis. Stat. §183.0304) expressly identifies two instances in which a member might incur personal liability. Members are responsible to follow through on promised contributions (Wis. Stat. §183.0502), and both members and managers are responsible for wrongful distributions (Wis. Stat. §183.0608).

Despite these provisions, members of NeoClone could be personally liable under the doctrine of "piercing the veil." Like many of its counterparts in other states, the Wisconsin LLC statute provides that "nothing in this chapter shall preclude a court from ignoring the limited liability company entity under principles of common law that are similar to those applicable to business corporations and shareholders in this state." Wis. Stat. §183.0304(2).

QUESTIONS

(1) According to McGlenn, venture capitalists have told him that the company would need to become a corporation before receiving venture capital. Can you imagine why venture capitalists would make such a demand? Why did NeoClone's founders decide to form an LLC?

(2) Business planners have long sought to combine limited liability with pass-through taxation and have used limited partnerships and S Corporations to accomplish that purpose. LLCs provide a simple mechanism for achieving the same result. Can you see any reasons to embrace the LLC aside from this favorable combination of attributes? In other words, do the default rules in the Wisconsin LLC statute, discussed above, provide a combination of attributes that is difficult to replicate with other business forms?

(3) Why did NeoClone adopt a three-tiered management structure consisting of Managers, a Management Committee, and Members?

CHAPTER
4

Organization and Structure of a
Corporation

We now turn to the subject that will occupy our attention throughout the remainder of the book—corporate governance. In its driest form, corporate governance can be conceived as the study of forces—both legal and nonlegal—that regulate the powers and duties of directors, officers, and shareholders. Yet, that definition misses as much as it includes, leaving out the sense of drama and conflict that imbues the study of corporate governance today. In the materials that follow, we will encounter troubling human character flaws—greed, pride, dishonesty, selfishness, and laziness—as well as some inspiring virtues. Our principal task is to explore the capacity of legal rules to encourage cooperation and constrain destructive behavior among the various participants in a corporate enterprise. Although we tend to focus on legal rules, the limits of law will become clear fairly early in our study. Markets, reputational constraints, trust, altruism, and norms pick up much of the slack. In the end, the study of corporate governance is the study of human relations. The trick is to construct a system under which the participants cooperate for mutual benefit. As you may know from your own experience, that is easier said than done.

In thinking about corporate governance, we begin by identifying the *dramatis personae*. The American conception of corporate governance traditionally focuses on three roles: officer, director, and shareholder. Many countries outside the United States have a broader conception of corporate governance, placing creditors, employees, communities, and society at large among the relevant constituencies of corporate law. While this broader "stakeholder" conception of the corporation has occasionally prevailed in the United States, especially in the context of debates about hostile takeovers, the traditional "shareholder" conception still dominates.

Officers (with titles such as Chief Executive Officer, President, and Chief Financial Officer) are in charge of the day-to-day operations of the corporation. These are the most senior employees of the corporation, and they make many of the decisions that define a corporation's activities. Perhaps surprisingly, corporate law has little to say about officers. Instead, the law of corporations concentrates on directors and shareholders. The top officers in the corporation typically are also members of the board of directors, which may partially explain that gap.

Directors are elected by shareholders to supervise the officers. In short, directors are the shareholders' representatives within the corporation. For this

171

reason, some people understand corporate governance as a species of political theory that analyzes the distribution of power within the corporation. Directors typically have no authority to act as individuals. Instead, they act as a collective body known as a board of directors. Many of the issues that arise under corporate law relate to conflicts between the board of directors and the shareholders.

Shareholders are sometimes referred to as the "owners" of the corporation, though exactly what that means has been heavily debated. We will pursue a more textured understanding of the shareholder role by examining the rights and obligations of shareholders in some detail. For the moment, it will suffice to say that shareholders possess important control rights — including the right to elect directors and to vote on fundamental transactions, such as mergers — as well as the right to all of the assets of the corporation once the corporation's creditors have been paid in a liquidation. Unlike partners in a general partnership, shareholders are not personally liable for the obligations of the corporation; they have limited liability.

This brief description of officers, directors, and shareholders risks portraying the corporate governance system in deceptively simple terms. Indeed, the basic principles underlying the corporate governance system are fairly easy to state, but these general principles do not capture the myriad ways in which these players interact. It is in these interactions that we find most of the complexity and intrigue associated with corporate governance.

Perhaps the most important factor in determining the nature of the interaction among officers, directors, and shareholders is ownership structure. While much of corporate law applies to all corporations regardless of ownership structure, courts, legislatures, and commentators often distinguish between "public corporations" — whose shares are owned by a large number of investors and are traded in the public securities markets — and "closely held corporations" — whose shares are owned by a small number of shareholders without access to the public securities markets.

The distinction between public and closely held corporations is fundamental for a number of reasons. First, the ownership structure often determines the identities of officers, directors, and shareholders. In a public corporation, officers, directors, and shareholders typically are three distinct groups of people. While some overlap is common — for example, the chief executive officer of a public corporation is usually a director (often the chairman of the board of directors), and large shareholders sometimes have representatives on the board of directors — the distinction among these groups is the source of many of corporate law conflicts. By contrast, in a closely held corporation, overlapping roles are the norm, not the exception. It is not uncommon for one person to be simultaneously a shareholder, a director, and an officer of a close corporation.

The difference in the composition of shareholders, directors, and officers of public and close corporations elicits different mechanisms of control in the two types of corporation. In a public corporation, for example, the formal mechanisms of control are exercised primarily by the board of directors, which has the statutory power to manage the affairs of the corporation. Shareholders control the directors, if at all, through annual elections of directors and through voting on specific proposals, when allowed. Shareholder oversight in public corporations traditionally has been weak, although the increased power of institutional investors (such as state pension funds, private pension funds, or mutual funds more generally) recently has begun to change the dynamics of public corporations. Thus, it has been observed that there is a separation of ownership (the shareholders) and control (the management) in public corporations, even given activist shareholder institutional investors. In close corporations, on the other hand, the formal mechanisms of control are exercised primarily by the shareholders, who often govern by prior agreement embodied in contracts among themselves rather than by rules embodied in the corporation statutes. So dominant are shareholders in the close corporation that many states permit them to eliminate the board of directors.

A second reason that the distinction between public and closely held corporations is fundamental is that public corporations are subject to a demanding set of disclosure requirements under federal securities law. With the exception of prohibitions against fraud, which apply to all sales of securities, federal securities law is largely silent in the context of closely held corporations. The invocation of federal securities law in the public corporation context raises interesting issues of federalism (the intersection of federal and state law), which we examine in subsequent chapters.

Federal securities law requires public reporting companies to provide to the markets quarterly and annual disclosure of large quantities of specified information, including financial results, significant business risks and contingencies, financial relationships with managers and directors, significant litigation, aspects of executive compensation, information on managers' and directors' experience, and the like. Not only does this mandatory securities disclosure provide one mechanism of accountability within the corporation, but it may shape the kinds of decisions managers make (perhaps to emphasize short-term financial results over longer-term investments), and it certainly informs the investment and voting decisions shareholders make. Given the important overlay of federal securities regulation onto state corporation statutes, we emphasize federal securities regulation from the beginning in this study of corporate governance.

A third important distinction between public and closely held corporations relates to the so-called "market for corporate control." Public corporations are subject to the threat of being taken over by another company gaining control of a majority of the corporation's outstanding stock. The mechanisms for such takeovers will be studied below, but for the present, it is enough to understand that the threat of a hostile takeover is a major factor that shapes corporate law. Indeed, today many of the most important cases examining the fiduciary duties of managers and directors involve battles for control, as do many cases about shareholder voting powers, the structure of articles of incorporation and corporate bylaws (the documents that set out the rules of the corporation and the distribution of powers between directors or officers and shareholders), and even such seemingly prosaic issues as whether a special directors' meeting was properly called. Given the importance of the market for corporate control, we will emphasize that aspect of many of the cases below.

Now that we have become acquainted with the principal players in our drama and have acquired a basic understanding of the importance of ownership structure, it is time to say a word about the sources of corporate law. Corporation statutes govern the relations among shareholders, directors, and officers of a corporation. Like general partnership statutes, corporation statutes have been adopted by all of the 50 states. Because of the so-called "internal affairs doctrine," the rules governing the relations between officers, directors, and shareholders are taken from the state of incorporation.

Delaware has long been the most popular state of incorporation for public corporations, which are said to select a state of incorporation based primarily on the sophistication of the state's corporation law, including not only the corporation statute, but also common law decisions in the state. As a result, the Delaware General Corporation Law (DGCL) is an important source of corporation law.

Closely held corporations tend to be less concerned with the sophistication of a state's corporation law because the issues resolved by a highly sophisticated system of corporation law — for example, the fiduciary standards applicable to directors in a hostile takeover — usually do not arise in a close corporation context. Founders of closely held corporations, therefore, tend to be motivated more by the initial costs of incorporation and the annual costs of maintaining the corporate form. These costs are often lowest when the incorporation occurs in the state where the business is located. Many states outside Delaware have adopted versions of the Model Business Corporation Act (Model Act), which was prepared by the Committee on Corporation Laws of the Business Law Section of the American Bar Association. As a result, in our study of corporate law we will often look at both Delaware provisions and at the provisions of the Model Act.

A. INCORPORATION

Unlike general partnerships under the UPA, corporations are without question legal entities with identities separate from the owners (shareholders) of the corporation. The process by which the separate legal entity is created is called incorporation. This Section briefly discusses the mechanics of incorporation and covers certain aspects of organizing a corporation that follow incorporation.

Incorporation today is a simple process, although it was not always so. Prior to the widespread adoption of general incorporation statutes in the mid-1800s, corporations in the United States were formed only by legislative action, usually by a state legislature. This process allowed the state legislatures to exert significant control over the businesses within their respective states. Although legislatures rarely granted monopoly powers to corporations expressly, it was not uncommon for corporations to have implicit monopolies for public works projects, such as building bridges, canals, or roads. In such cases, the legislature would simply grant a charter to only one corporation, thus ensuring a monopoly. This process sometimes led to corruption, as people bribed legislatures to obtain grants of monopoly power.

During the Jacksonian period of American politics, populism swept the United States and corporate law was a prime target. The old system was displaced through the passage of general incorporation statutes — "general" because any eligible person could form a corporation without a special act of the legislature. Over time the requirements for incorporation have become exceedingly simple. Most statutes require only one person to form a corporation. Traditionally at least three incorporators and three directors were required. Although many states retain the requirement of three directors, most states allow only one incorporator. The corporation comes into existence when articles of incorporation are filed with the state, unless a later effective date is specified.

The organizing document that is used to incorporate a company is called either the "articles of incorporation" or, in Delaware, the "certificate of incorporation." We will use the term "charter," which is a generic term that refers either to the articles of incorporation or to the certificate of incorporation, whichever is the name of the organizing document in a particular state. Charters are required to include certain provisions, including the name of the corporation, the number of authorized shares of stock, and the name and address of a registered agent in the state of incorporation. *See generally* DGCL §102(a); Model Act §2.02(a). Under Delaware law, the charter must also include the purpose of the corporation, which can be as general as "to engage in any lawful purpose for which a corporation may be organized." DGCL §102(a)(3).

In addition to the required provisions, most well-advised corporations include some of the following additional provisions:

Initial Directors. Many charters provide the names and addresses of the corporation's initial directors. If initial directors are not named in the articles of incorporation, the incorporators must hold an organizational meeting after incorporation and elect the directors. The initial directors of the corporation typically complete the organization of the corporation, which includes the appointment of officers of the corporation, the sale of shares of capital stock of the corporation, and various other administrative tasks.

Corporate Purposes. A charter under the Model Act may contain a statement of the purposes of the corporation, Model Act §2.02(b)(2)(i), and as stated above, under Delaware law the charter must contain a statement of the corporate purpose. DGCL §102(a)(3). During the 1800s and early 1900s, a statement of purposes was important to defining the limits of a corporation's activity. When corporations were created by state legislatures, their charters typically had narrow purpose clauses, and if a corporation exceeded the purposes stated in its charter, it was said to be acting "*ultra vires*," which means literally "beyond powers." Over time corporations were allowed to list multiple purposes in the corporate charter. By the turn of the century, most newly formed corporations listed hundreds of purposes in the charter to prevent the possibility of acting *ultra vires*. Modern incorporation statutes eliminate most cases in which *ultra vires* could be used as a claim by the corporation or any party doing business with the corporation to avoid contractual commitments.

Corporation statutes eventually permitted corporations to include a provision in the charter stating that the corporation may engage in any lawful business. Although common today, such provisions did not obtain immediate acceptance. Even today, some corporate charters limit the extent of the corporation's actions. This occurs most often because the corporation is limited by some other regulation (for example, banks and insurance companies are subject to other state and federal regulation of their activities) or because one of the founders of the corporation desires to restrict the activities of the corporation. When a limitation is expressed in the corporation's charter, there are three means of enforcing it: (1) a shareholder suit against the corporation; (2) a suit by the corporation against directors or officers for actions beyond the purpose; or (3) an involuntary judicial dissolution proceeding by the attorney general.

Management Provisions. A charter may include provisions for managing the business and regulating the affairs of the corporation. Well-written charters usually contain some such provisions. Although many management provisions are statutory or are contained in the corporation's bylaws (see below), some provisions are placed in charters to insulate them from change by the shareholders. Since under the controlling statutes only the directors may propose changes to the charter (which must be approved by the shareholders to be effective), *see* DGCL §242(b)(1); Model Act §10.03(a), putting management provisions in the charter protects them from shareholder-initiated changes. So, for instance, the charter may require "cause" for a director to be removed from the board at any time other than the annual shareholders' meeting. Such a "for cause" limitation on removal makes it more difficult for an outsider to take control of the firm by buying a controlling block of shares and calling a special meeting to replace the board. Other provisions are placed in the charter because the statute requires it. For example, a provision placing exclusive power to amend the bylaws with the shareholders must appear in the charter.

Bylaw Provisions. The articles of incorporation may include any provision required or permitted to be in the bylaws. The purpose of placing such a provision in the charter rather than in the bylaws is to prevent the amendment of the provision without approval by both the board of directors and the shareholders.

Director Liability. Most modern charters limit the liability of directors for money damages, subject to certain enumerated exceptions. This type of provision, called an "exculpatory provision," first appeared in corporation statutes in the mid-1980s after the Delaware Supreme Court decided in *Smith v. Van Gorkom*, 488 A.2d 858 (1985), that the directors of a publicly held corporation were personally liable for breach of the duty of care in a merger context. The *Van Gorkom* decision sent shock waves through boardrooms, as directors feared personal liability on a scale never before contemplated. In most states, an exculpatory provision eliminating director liability is optional, not self-executing. (Self-executing statutes appear in a few states, such as Florida, Indiana, Ohio, Maine, and Wisconsin.) A "self-executing" exculpatory statute limits director liability even absent a provision in the articles of incorporation. Even in states with optional statutes, most charters now routinely include an exculpatory provision limiting director liability.

Indemnification. Indemnification is another method of protecting directors from personal liability in their capacity as directors. Modern incorporation statutes allow a corporation to offer mandatory indemnification, subject to certain exceptions.

In addition to required and optional provisions in the corporate charter, modern incorporation statutes are notable for the things that they *do not* require. The following two types of provisions at one time were required in corporate charters:

Duration. Corporation statutes sometimes require the charter to set forth the duration of the corporation's existence and allow the duration to be perpetual. Reflecting the modern trend, Model Act §3.02 presumes that the corporation is perpetual unless the articles of incorporation provide otherwise.

Initial Capital. Corporation statutes sometimes require the charter to set forth a certain minimum amount of capital, usually $1,000. The Model Act reflects the modern trend toward the elimination of all minimum capital requirements.

The act of incorporating seems simple enough. Indeed, it is a ministerial action that does not require specialized training. Nevertheless, corporate law is high on formality. The detailed work that accompanies an incorporation may have profound effects on the future of the company, as demonstrated in the following case. In addition to the importance of formal rules, notice the actions of the law firm. Who was the firm's client before the conflict manifested itself? Did the firm act properly in the face of conflict?

GRANT v. MITCHELL
2001 WL 221509 (unpublished)
Delaware Court of Chancery
February 23, 2001

STRINE, Vice Chancellor.

Plaintiff Ralph Grant brings this action under 8 Del. C. §225 to determine the proper directors and officers of nominal defendant, Epasys, Inc. Grant contends that he is the sole director of Epasys, under authority of an incorporator's consent he executed on August 24, 2000.

Defendant Julee Mitchell denies Grant's contention and argues that Grant had earlier exercised his authority as sole incorporator to create a two-person board comprised of Mitchell and himself. In support of that argument, Mitchell points out that Grant signed a sworn "Foreign Corporation Certificate" on January 7, 2000 that identified Epasys's directors and officers. The Foreign Corporation Certificate identified Grant and Mitchell as the directors.

In this post-trial opinion, I conclude that it is more likely than not that Grant named an initial board of directors comprised of Mitchell and himself at or around the time Epasys was incorporated. The most reliable evidence in the record—the Foreign Corporation Certificate and documents created by the lawyers Grant chose to represent Epasys—supports this conclusion.

As a result, Grant's attempt to name himself as sole director in August 2000 was invalid and Mitchell is entitled to judgment in her favor.

I.
FACTUAL BACKGROUND

A. THE GENESIS OF EPASYS

This case requires this court to address a small sliver of a much larger dispute among the founders of Epasys. The founders of Epasys were plaintiff Grant, defendant Mitchell, and non-party Jack Meltzer.

The founders began their relationship in 1998. At that time, Mitchell and Meltzer were seeking to bring a computer software program, "Monitor," to market. Monitor was designed to help businesses keep track of the federal and state environmental requirements (*e.g.*, discharge limits) that apply to their facilities and operations. Grant was then working for a systems integration business, and had cash resources he could invest.

The founders agreed to try to develop Monitor into a commercially viable program under the rubric of a business named Phoenix Environmental, LLC

[handwritten margin note: Company started as an Arizona LLC in order to sell computer environmental requirement software for businesses.]

("Phoenix"), an Arizona limited liability company. Grant agreed to invest $500,000 as an initial matter, in exchange for one-third of Phoenix's stock. Mitchell and Meltzer, who are romantic as well as business partners, held the remaining two-thirds interest.

In 1999, Grant invested another $500,000 into Phoenix. In exchange, he was given 9% more stock and the right to use all of the tax losses generated by Phoenix. Thus, as of that time, Grant owned 42% of Phoenix's equity, and Mitchell and Meltzer held 29% apiece.

Later in 1999, the founders began the process of converting Phoenix from an LLC into a corporation. It was the intention of the founders to seek venture capital financing for the new corporation and to add representatives of the investors to the new corporation's board of directors. The founders were apparently optimistic that they could obtain such outside financing in a relatively short time. The founders also decided to relocate the business from Phoenix, Arizona to Boston, Massachusetts.

B. THE FOUNDERS SEEK THE ADVICE OF MCDERMOTT, WILL & EMERY

[handwritten margin note: Their corporate attorney John.]

To assist them in the task of forming a new corporation, the founders consulted with John Egan, a corporate partner at the Boston office of McDermott, Will & Emery. According to Egan, he informed the founders that it was typical for a party like Grant, who was putting in cash equity, to get a preferred or priority equity position, and for sweat equity investors like Mitchell and Meltzer to get equity positions that were earned over time. The rationale for this distinction was that venture capitalists who would want to invest in the business would want assurance that the sweat equity was actually delivered before Mitchell and Meltzer became vested in their ownership positions.

Egan claims that the founders discussed the fact that Grant would have control of the corporation until the new investors came on board. Egan also says that the founders discussed the fact that Grant would be the incorporator of the new corporation, which the founders agreed to call Epasys.

Egan also testified that the founders discussed the composition of Epasys's board of directors. He says that the founders agreed that there would eventually be a five-person board comprised of Grant, Mitchell, and three representatives of the new outside investors.

Grant's recollection of the meeting is substantially similar to Egan's. Grant claims that it was agreed that he would have control, and that he would have the sole right to select the board as the incorporator.

Mitchell, however, denies that she was advised by Egan that Grant was to have sole power to select the board by virtue of his status as incorporator. And while she admits that Egan did discuss the priority often given to cash investors, she contends that she and Meltzer never assented to giving such priority to Grant and never would have.

C. EPASYS IS INCORPORATED

After the meeting with Egan, the founders proceeded with the creation of Epasys. On December 23, 1999, Epasys's certificate of incorporation was filed with the Secretary of State's office. The certificate named Ralph Grant as incorporator.

McDermott, Will also prepared two other documents dated December 23, 1999. One of the documents was a "Unanimous Written Consent of the Directors in Lieu of an Organizational Meeting." The directors' consent purported to adopt the second of the documents, a set of bylaws. The directors' consent also elected Ralph Grant as President, and Julee Mitchell as Treasurer and Secretary of Epasys. Finally, the directors' consent purported to ratify actions taken by Grant as incorporator in a consent dated December 22, 1999.

The directors' consent had signature lines for Grant and Mitchell, thus signifying that the creator of the document believed that they were the two initial directors of Epasys selected by Grant as incorporator. The directors' consent, however, was never executed. Nor has the incorporator's consent of December 22, 1999 emerged.

In his deposition testimony, however, Grant recalled receiving the bylaws at the time Epasys was incorporated. Grant assumed that he signed the bylaws and that the bylaws were valid.

D. THE FOUNDERS' DIVERGENT TESTIMONY ABOUT THE COMPOSITION OF EPASYS'S BOARD

Grant contends that before Epasys began doing business, he and the other founders discussed two critical subjects: (1) what equity stakes each would hold in the company; and (2) the composition of the Epasys board. As to the first subject, Grant says that the founders agreed that the initial equity stakes would be the same as their final equity positions in Phoenix. As to the composition of Epasys's board, Grant testified as follows:

Q: Now, prior to the formation of EpaSys, did you have any discussions with Ms. Mitchell, Mr. Meltzer, or both of them, about who would be on the board of directors of EpaSys?

A: Yes.

Q: Please relate those discussions.

A: We—I said that following John Egan's advice, it probably should be a board consisting of five people—three at the minimum, but more likely five—and that we wanted to attract people of some substance—that is, people who would give us credibility in either the marketplace or credibility with venture capitalists—and that we didn't have that credibility at that time. I wanted to wait until such time as we had something that would attract people of some stature on to the board.

Q: At any time did you ever discuss with Ms. Mitchell or Mr. Meltzer, or both of them, about putting either or both of them on the board of directors of EpaSys?

A: Yes.

Q: Please relate those discussions.

A: I indicated that I thought it would be appropriate for one, not both, to be on the board, and at such time as we had three or more people that were going to be on the board.

Q: Why did you think it appropriate for only one, but not both of them, to be put on the board?

A: Because I thought that our interests at that time were close to equal, our equity interests, and that it would be inappropriate to have two of them with voting rights on the board, compared to my one vote.

Q: This discussion with Ms. Mitchell and Mr. Meltzer about putting one but not both on the board when the board of directors was five, when did that occur, if you recall?

A: I can't recall whether it was prior to EpaSys — it was either immediately prior to or shortly after EpaSys began operations.

Mitchell has a far different recollection. She claims that the founders had discussed the board composition issue many times and that it was agreed that all three of the founders would be on the board. Mitchell also said that the founders discussed adding outside members at some later time, but denies Grant's contention that no board was to be formed until outside investors were identified. She also claims never to have agreed to permitting Grant to be sole incorporator, and to have questioned Grant's status as sole incorporator with him when it came to her attention. Grant allegedly told her that McDermott, Will had said that it was only possible to have one incorporator.

E. GRANT SIGNS A FOREIGN CORPORATION CERTIFICATE IDENTIFYING MITCHELL AND HIMSELF AS THE DIRECTORS OF EPASYS

On January 7, 2000, the McDermott, Will firm delivered a Massachusetts Foreign Corporation Certificate to the offices of Epasys for signature by Grant and Mitchell. Grant was to sign in his purported capacity as President. Mitchell was to sign as Treasurer and Secretary.

The Foreign Corporation Certificate was required as a condition for Epasys to do business in Massachusetts. By law, the Foreign Corporation Certificate must identify the directors and officers of the corporation and must be signed under penalties of perjury. The Certificate identifies the officers and directors of Epasys as follows:

11. The name and business address of the officers and the directors of the corporation are as follows:

	Name	Business Address
President:	Ralph Grant	163 West Newton St., Boston MA 02118
Treasurer:	Julee Mitchell	163 West Newton St., Boston MA 02118
Secretary:	Julee Mitchell	163 West Newton St., Boston MA 02118
Directors:	Ralph Grant	163 West Newton St., Boston MA 02118
	Julee Mitchell	163 West Newton St., Boston MA 02118

Grant signed the document. So did Mitchell.

Both have strikingly different recollections about doing so. Grant says he was rushed to sign it, did not read it carefully, and failed to pick up the fact that the document listed himself and Mitchell as directors. Had he seen that part of the document, Grant claims he would not have signed it because it was not correct. Grant says he knew that there was no board at that point because he was the incorporator and had not named a board. Grant further contends that he did not give McDermott, Will any information about the officers and directors of Epasys from which to prepare the Certificate and has no idea who did.

Mitchell testified that the Certificate upset her because it did not list Meltzer as a director. Mitchell claims that she raised this issue with Grant either later that same day or the next day. When confronted with this fact, Grant allegedly said that he did not know why Meltzer was not listed as a director. After discussing the issue with Meltzer privately, Mitchell says they elected not to rock the boat and to live with only herself being a director along with Grant.

F. EPASYS BEGINS OPERATING

when doing business:

Epasys then began to do business. The founders each held themselves out to be officers of the company when dealing with third-parties.

Consistent, however, with the lack of documentation that characterized their dealings, the founders did not issue stock to themselves in amounts reflecting their agreement as to their respective equity stakes. And while the founders met to discuss business on a regular basis, there is no evidence that Grant and Mitchell ever met formally as a board of directors.

Initially, Epasys operated out of a Boston townhouse in which Mitchell and Meltzer were living (the "Townhouse"). Grant procured a Boston apartment, which Epasys paid for.

Consistent with their prior arrangement at Phoenix, Grant provided continuing cash infusions into the company while the company sought outside investors. Because he would have simply been paying himself, Grant took no salary as President. Mitchell and Meltzer did receive salaries of $160,000 each, far more than either had ever made in a previous job.

Epasys began hiring other staff and offering them stock options. This was problematic, of course, because the founders had not even issued stock to themselves. McDermott, Will was asked to draft the stock option plan. It also worked on drafts of the documents necessary to grant equity to the founders.

Grant says that he was comfortable proceeding to fund the business while the company's equity ownership was still undocumented because it was understood that he would eventually receive additional equity in exchange for the cash he was contributing to fund Epasys's operations. In fact, Grant claims that the other founders eventually agreed that he would receive an additional 5% equity for every million dollars he put into the business.

Mitchell denies that this was the arrangement. Instead, she says that Grant agreed to provide interim funding as a low-interest rate loan until such time as Epasys could secure venture capital financing.

Neither Grant's nor Mitchell's version of what Grant was to receive for his cash support of the business is corroborated by documentary evidence or the testimony of other witnesses.

G. THE RELATIONSHIP AMONG THE FOUNDERS FALL APART AND GRANT ACTS TO REMOVE MITCHELL AND MELTZER FROM THEIR OFFICES

During the late spring and summer of 2000, the working relationship among the founders deteriorated. The company had not secured outside financing and its product development efforts were not as advanced as the founders wished.

According to Mitchell, Grant began to make decisions in isolation from her and Meltzer. Moreover, Grant appeared to be preoccupied with minor issues such as the need for a corporate dress code. For his part, Grant believed that Mitchell and Meltzer were not working hard and were causing morale problems among the company's other employees. After the company moved its offices out of the Townhouse, Grant says that Mitchell and Meltzer would often remain at the Townhouse during the workday and not come to Epasys's offices. Grant alleges that Mitchell and Meltzer were far behind in writing the necessary text to help Epasys's software development team update the Monitor software.

By August, Grant was set on removing Mitchell and Meltzer from their offices. As part of his justification, Grant claimed that Mitchell and Meltzer had improperly awarded themselves bonuses earlier in the year, which they had used to buy a new car. Grant also alleges that Mitchell "forged" Grant's name on a renewal of the Townhouse lease.

Grant enlisted the help of the McDermott, Will firm in August 2000 to aid him in removing Mitchell and Meltzer. McDermott, Will considered a number of issues in that regard. Most notably, the firm fixated on the question of whether Grant could remove Mitchell from the board. The documentary evidence supports the conclusion that McDermott, Will believed that Mitchell was a board member.[12]

If McDermott, Will had not earlier believed that a two-person board had been formed, it seems likely that one of the many attorneys working on the matter would have raised the issue with the founders or have instructed McDermott, Will paralegal Renee Carson to correct the documents she had prepared listing Grant and Mitchell as directors. In this regard, it is notable that the corporate notebook that McDermott, Will prepared for itself and Epasys included the unsigned directors' consent that listed Mitchell and Grant as board members. This notebook was the compilation of the company's official documents, including its charter, the December 23, 1999 bylaws, and the Foreign Corporation Certificate.

The founders engaged in some efforts to resolve their differences, which did not bear fruit. In the end, McDermott, Will and Grant decided to take an approach premised on the theory that no board of Epasys had been named as of August, 2000. Using this premise, McDermott, Will prepared a written consent of the sole incorporator in which Grant named himself as the sole director. Grant then executed a later consent as sole director naming himself to all the

---

12. The billing records and notes of McDermott, Will attorneys support the inference that the firm's lawyers came upon the argument that Mitchell was never a director as an afterthought. The primary emphasis of the firm in working with Grant at that time seemed to be on whether it was possible for Grant to remove Mitchell as a director for cause. For example, the billing records of McDermott, Will attorney Sam Webb state that he was assigned to: "Review organizational issues in light of potential Director conflict; review Restricted Stock Agreements and related documents and consider MWE's duties in the event of a conflict between Directors on a board of 2 with no stocks [sic] issued." JX 36 (8/15/00 time entry for MWE attorney Webb); *see also id.* (8/17/00 time entry for MWE attorney Webb referring to research on board "deadlock"). Even more revealing are the notes taken by a McDermott, Will attorney of a strategy meeting firm lawyers held about how to assist Grant in removing Mitchell and Meltzer from their positions at Epasys. The meeting notes suggest that McDermott, Will attorneys started from the premise that Mitchell was a director and brainstormed their way into the idea that she had never been put on the board in the first place. These excerpts from the notes show the backdoor way in which the idea that Mitchell had never been appointed crept into their discussion: Issues to be resolved: 1) Corp. Issues—Remove Julee as member of BoD . . . Legal Issues re BD (board of directors) stalemate . . .—No clear way to break logjam under DE law . . . SW [WME Attorney Webb]—Comfortable that it is in the best interests of the Company to remove directors . . . Corp. Options 1) Seek receivership in Delaware Chancery Court 2) Dissolve Entity 3) Remove Julee from BoD, Ralph Takes Control of BoD and Company (or Julee never on the BoD) (will result in litigation) . . . ? Delaware law—Can Company remove Board of Directors member for cause? Breach of Fiduciary Responsibility—Who can remove Board of Directors member? JX 46 (notes of MWE attorney Mahoney of strategy meeting in 8/21/00). Although McDermott, Will attorneys ascribe their research into removing Mitchell as an examination of options that Grant had in the event that Mitchell claimed to be a director, the record is, on balance, more supportive of the view that the relevant McDermott, Will attorneys believed that a two-person board had been formed earlier, but then seized on the lack of documentation of that formation to come up with a creative argument for their client to use to achieve his ends.

statutory offices at Epasys. He thereafter removed Mitchell and Meltzer from their jobs.

A flurry of litigation then ensued. Mitchell and Meltzer sued Grant in Massachusetts seeking, among other relief, a determination that they collectively owned a majority of Epasys's stock and a compulsory annual meeting. Acting as members of Phoenix, Mitchell and Meltzer removed Grant as managing director of that LLC, and demanded that Epasys cease using the Monitor software, which Mitchell and Meltzer contended was still owned by Phoenix.

Grant sought to have Epasys put into bankruptcy, under terms which would have effectively assured his control of the company. When that strategy stalled, Grant initiated this action seeking a declaration that he is the sole director of Epasys. He also filed suit in Arizona for a declaration that Phoenix was dissolved and that its assets were transferred to Epasys as of the time of Epasys's creation.

II.
The Limited Purpose of This Proceeding

It is important to keep in mind the limited utility of this action in the larger scheme of the fight among Epasys's founders. Epasys is overdue for an annual meeting. As a result, any declaration I make is necessarily ephemeral.

Notably, I am not being asked to decide who owns what equity interest in Epasys. I am only being asked to decide who were the members of Epasys's initial board of directors.

Because of my limited mandate, I will endeavor to write my opinion as narrowly as possible. I am sensitive to the fact that a judicial colleague in Massachusetts will soon be asked to determine the more important issue of who owns what equity in Epasys, and I therefore do not intend to make findings of fact regarding that issue.

With that in mind, I turn to my resolution of this dispute.

III.
Legal Analysis

This case does not turn on complicated questions of law, but on a single question of fact: when did Grant first exercise his authority as incorporator to name Epasys's board?

As sole incorporator, Grant had the limited but important authority spelled out in §108(a) and (c) of Title 8:

§108. Organization meeting of incorporators or directors named in certificate of incorporation.

(a) After the filing of the certificate of incorporation an organization meeting of the incorporator or incorporators, or of the board of directors if the initial directors were named in the certificate of incorporation, shall be held, either within or without this State, at the call of a majority of the incorporators or directors, as the case may be, for the purposes of adopting bylaws, electing directors (if the meeting is of the incorporators) to serve or hold office until the first annual meeting of stockholders or until their successors are elected and qualify, electing officers if the meeting is of the directors, doing any other or further acts to perfect the organizations of the corporation, and transacting such other business as may come before the meeting. . . .

(c) Any action permitted to be taken at the organization meeting of the incorporators or directors, as the case may be, may be taken without a meeting if each incorporator or director, where there is more than 1, or the sole incorporator or director where there is only 1, signs an instrument which states the action so taken.

This case turns on when Grant first exercised his authority as an incorporator. He says he did not do so until August 2000. Mitchell claims Grant did so at the latest on January 7, 2000 when he executed the Foreign Corporation Certificate.

After considering the record evidence carefully, I am persuaded that it is more probable than not that Grant acted as incorporator on or around the date of Epasys's creation to name himself and Mitchell as the initial directors of Epasys. Although it is odd to think of a single incorporator holding a meeting with himself, §108 does not preclude a single incorporator from meeting with himself to make such a decision. Indeed, the first sentence of §108(a) explicitly contemplates a meeting of "the incorporator." It is not inconceivable to think that a single incorporator could decide on the initial board of directors but fail to document that decision immediately. That is what most likely occurred here. In my view, Grant's sworn signature on the Foreign Corporation Certificate is the most reliable evidence of his actions. While this factual conclusion is not free from doubt, several reasons convince me it is the correct one.

First, Grant's contention that Mitchell and Meltzer would have consented to allowing him free rein to name a board without either of them on it is not convincing. Grant was making progress over the status quo at Phoenix by forming an initial Epasys board on which he would have equal say and would not be outnumbered by Mitchell and Meltzer. By even his own testimony, Grant admits that he told Mitchell and Meltzer that one of them would be on the board at the time Epasys was formed.

Second, I do not find Egan's testimony about the supposed initial deal among the founders to be particularly helpful. Grant's own testimony suggests that the founders did not follow Egan's supposed advice, because Grant himself admits that the equity interests of the founders were to be identical to those they held in Phoenix. Furthermore, Egan's testimony that Mitchell and Meltzer were mere sweat investors ignores the fact they were the ones that had developed the Monitor software that was the heart of Epasys's business plan. This software was a tangible capital contribution that was not dependent on future sweat. Most fundamentally, however, Egan simply does not shed light on what transpired between his initial meeting with the founders and the December 23, 1999 formation of Epasys.

Third, it is clear that something transpired at or around Epasys's formation that made employees of McDermott, Will believe that a two-person board comprised of Grant and Mitchell was formed. What is striking about this belief is that the record shows that it was Grant, rather than Mitchell or Meltzer, who was in contact on a regular basis with McDermott, Will.

What is also striking is that Grant says that McDermott, Will got the officer designations correct on the Foreign Corporation Certificate. That is, Grant says that it is correct that he was to be the President and Mitchell was to be the Treasurer and Secretary. But Grant claims it was not correct that he and Mitchell were to be the directors.

It is improbable that McDermott, Will would have gotten the officers correct and the directors incorrect by sheer luck. It is also improbable that McDermott, Will would have prepared an initial consent of the directors identifying Grant and Mitchell as the directors without client input. It is much more likely that the firm received the necessary information to prepare these documents from Grant himself.

Moreover, it is clear that employees at McDermott, Will who were working on Epasys matters harbored the belief that Grant and Mitchell were directors well into the year 2000. Employees of the firm prepared various draft corporate documents identifying the two of them as the directors.

If McDermott, Will believed that Epasys had not formed a board of directors, it is somewhat difficult to imagine that the firm would not have written a memorandum to the founders suggesting the need for the company to do so promptly. After all, McDermott, Will was in the process of drafting stock option plans and the documents necessary for Epasys to issue stock to the founders. That is, the firm was drafting documents involving corporate actions typically performed by boards of directors, not incorporators. Instead of urging the formation of a board, the McDermott, Will employees involved in that process seem to have believed that Grant and Mitchell were the two directors.[17]

Furthermore, I give very little weight to McDermott, Will's after-the-fact discovery in August, 2000 that Grant did not name directors upon the formation of Epasys. For whatever reason, McDermott, Will decided to treat Grant as their sole client contact and to rely exclusively upon his word in determining what advice to give. Contrary to Grant's assertion, the record is clear that McDermott, Will undertook to represent Grant personally and aggressively against the other founders and only withdrew from that representation when the founders complained that McDermott, Will had a conflict of interest.[18]

McDermott, Will's opinion that Grant never acted as incorporator before August 2000 is the one that would be expected from lawyers who then saw themselves as zealous advocates of Grant's personal position. That creative lawyers would take such a position in the absence of a signed incorporator's minute is also to be expected. But that opinion is undercut by the pre-August 2000 evidence from McDermott, Will's own files that reflects the firm's belief that Grant had formed a board of Grant and Mitchell.

Fourth, I do not rest my decision in any way on whether Grant or Mitchell was the more credible witness. Quite candidly, parts of the testimony of each struck me as unlikely to be true. Without denigrating the basic integrity of either Grant

17. The extent to which an incorporator can refuse to name a board of directors until the first annual meeting and manage the corporation pursuant to the powers granted by 8 Del. C. §107 has never been decided. Most of the learned commentators wisely counsel the rapid formation of a board whenever the new corporation intends to commence genuine business activity.

18. Numerous documents illustrate the extent to which McDermott, Will aligned itself with Grant personally. The firm's lawyers counseled with Grant on how to negotiate with the other founders and considered the extent to which the threat of criminal liability could be implicitly used to induce the other founders to settle with Grant on terms favorable to him. ("Negotiating Strategy—Threaten individual claim by Ralph based on forgery. Imply criminal case also but don't raise it explicitly. Part of consideration for settlement."). For example, McDermott, Will attorney Webb's notes reflect the importance Grant placed on "scaring the pants off" Mitchell and Meltzer in order to get them to compromise. Indeed, Grant ultimately asked McDermott, Will to negotiate with the other founders on his behalf, which the firm began to do. . . . McDermott, Will only withdrew from its role once Mitchell's attorney raised a conflict concern.

or Mitchell, it is clear that this dispute has engendered deep feelings of ill-will on both sides, feelings that do little to instill confidence in either's recitation of the facts. If there were no documentary evidence, it would be almost impossible to decide this case.

But it is in precisely these circumstances that it is appropriate for a court to look to some more reliable indicator of what actually happened as the basis for its decision. In this case, that indicator is the Foreign Corporation Certificate. Grant signed that official document under penalty of perjury. The Foreign Corporation Certificate is a simple, easy-to-read form. It is much harder to miss the part of the document identifying the directors than it is to see it.

Fifth, I note that there is no contradiction between the formation of an initial two-person board and the founders' desire to add additional outsiders later. As the sole owners of equity in Epasys, the founders could obviously expand the board, and the bylaws drafted by McDermott, Will permitted the board to be expanded to five members without additional stockholder approval. Put simply, it was a rational business strategy to form an initial board that could be expanded, especially because the company intended to undertake initiatives, such as the creation of an employee stock option plan, that required a board's approval.

Finally, I reject Grant's inconsistent reliance on formalism as a defense. Grant insists that he could not have acted as an incorporator in December or January because he did not sign a formal written consent. He also insists he did not take a meeting with himself and make the decision to name himself and Mitchell as directors. But when confronted with his own signature under penalty of perjury on an official document identifying himself and Mitchell as directors, Grant claims that the document is not a valid recordation of his actions as incorporator because he signed it as an officer of Epasys and not as incorporator.

In this regard, it is worth noting that McDermott, Will provided Epasys with a corporate notebook comprised of the company's key documents. This notebook included not only Epasys's charter, but also the Foreign Corporation Certificate, the unsigned directors' consent, and the December 23, 1999 bylaws. Thus, the company's own compilation of its key corporate records suggested that a two-person board had been created.

Grant's current litigation posture therefore emerges as a lawyer-generated strategy based on Grant's own failure to formally execute an incorporator's minute, and Grant's and Mitchell's joint failure to sign the initial directors' consent prepared by McDermott, Will. These lapses in documentation were seized upon as support for an argument that Grant never named an initial board as incorporator in December 1999 or January 2000.

The Foreign Corporation Certificate, however, as well as all the other documentary evidence suggests otherwise. All of that evidence suggests that: (1) Grant formed a two-person board of Mitchell and Grant, and (2) that the board by informal means appointed Grant as President and Mitchell as Treasurer and Secretary.

Because I conclude that Grant named an initial board of directors comprised of himself and Mitchell, his later August, 2000 attempt to name himself as sole director of Epasys was invalid. As a natural consequence, any actions he took as sole director of Epasys are equally invalid as against Mitchell and Meltzer.

This ruling leaves neither party a winner. Since August 2000, Grant has continued to provide substantial funding to Epasys. Upon this determination, Grant may well decide to stop doing so, which could force the company into bankruptcy. One hopes that the parties will consider their predicament at this point, rationally and not emotionally. It is in all of the founders' interests to work out their disputes amicably or, at the very least, promptly obtain a definitive ruling regarding their respective ownership interests in Epasys.

IV.

CONCLUSION

For the foregoing reasons, Mitchell is entitled to a judgment in her favor. Counsel shall present an implementing order, agreed upon as to form, within seven days of this opinion.

B.   PROMOTER CONTRACTS

A promoter is a person who founds and organizes a business. If the business is to be incorporated, the promoter is responsible for seeing that the corporation is legally formed. As a general rule, a promoter is personally liable on a contract for a projected corporation unless the other party to the contract knows that the corporation is not yet in existence and agrees to look to the corporation for performance. The agreement by a third party to look to the corporation for performance may be express or implied.

Promoters have a fiduciary obligation (that is, a duty of loyalty) to deal fairly with the corporations that they form. The duty may be enforced by subsequent creditors of or investors in the corporation, co-promoters, or the corporation itself (after it has come under the control of others).

A corporation may become a party to contracts made before its formation if it "adopts" the contracts, either expressly or implicitly. Adoption does not relieve the promoter of liability unless the parties to the contract so agree. Adoption is preferable to "ratification" because, technically speaking, a corporation cannot ratify promoter contracts. Ratification presumes that the corporation was in existence at the time the contracts were made, and corporations are, by definition, not existing at the time of promoter contracts. Despite the technical unavailability of ratification, courts often refer to ratification in discussing promoter contracts. Corporations also may become parties to promoter contracts under the doctrine of "novation," which relieves the promoter of further liability and replaces the promoter with the corporation as a party to the contract.

PROBLEM 4-1

The American Legacy Foundation (ALF) is a nonprofit corporation that was formed pursuant to the Master Settlement Agreement (the MSA) between large tobacco companies and 46 of the United States. The express goal of the ALF is to reduce tobacco use by America's youth through research and education. ALF is funded by contributions from the tobacco companies. The contributions include $250,000,000 in 1999, and $300,000,000 per year for the next four years "for the benefit" of ALF's National Public Education Fund (NPEF). In addition, the tobacco companies were required to make "base foundation" payments of $25,000,000 per year for nine years. As part of the MSA, the states agreed that the NPEF should not be used to vilify the tobacco companies:

> The National Public Education Fund shall be used only for public education and advertising regarding the addictiveness, health effects, and social costs related to the use of tobacco products and shall not be used for any personal attack on, or vilification of, any person (whether by name or business affiliation), company, or governmental agency, whether individually or collectively. [ALF] shall work to ensure that its activities are carried out in a culturally and linguistically appropriate manner.

The MSA also provides that ALF's organizational documents "shall specifically incorporate the provisions of this Agreement relating to" ALF. In accordance with this instruction, ALF's bylaws were drafted to include the foregoing "anti-vilification" provision. In a similar fashion, ALF's charter included provisions from other sections of the MSA (including prohibitions on political activity and a requirement that ALF's activities be carried out in a culturally and linguistically appropriate manner). Finally, ALF's bylaws prohibit amendments to the bylaws or charter that are inconsistent with the MSA. Indeed, one section of ALF's bylaws expressly recognizes that the MSA is binding on ALF.

As part of one of its advertising campaigns, ALF showed people stacking body bags outside the headquarters of Phillip Morris USA, one of the tobacco companies that signed the MSA. When Philip Morris complained, the attorney general of North Carolina contacted the attorneys general of the other states involved in the MSA and expressed his concern about the commercials. In response to the complaints, ALF temporarily discontinued the commercials.

But this commercial was not the only objectionable advertising, according to the tobacco companies. Lorillard Tobacco Company (Lorillard), the oldest tobacco company in the United States and signatory to the MSA, objected to a radio commercial entitled "Dog Walker." In this spot, a man walking a dog calls two employees of Lorillard and offers to sell them some dog urine. After all, the man reasons, urea is "one of the chemicals you guys put into cigarettes." Lorillard wrote a letter to ALF complaining about the commercials and referencing the anti-vilification provision of the MSA.

When this dispute landed in the Delaware courts, ALF claimed that Lorillard had no grounds for suing ALF under the MSA because ALF was not a party to the MSA. Indeed, ALF was formed pursuant to an agreement in the MSA. Assuming no rules of unique application to nonprofit corporations, under what conditions (if any) should ALF be bound by a contract that it did not sign?

C. CAPITAL STRUCTURE

The capital structure of a corporation is the combination of claims sold by the corporation. Those claims generally can be divided into two types — equity claims and debt claims. Shareholders own stock, and stock is an equity claim against a corporation. "Equity" connotes a power to control, usually by voting, and the right to receive the fruits of the business through dividends, distributions, and liquidation, if necessary. "Debt" connotes some fixed obligation of repayment independent of the success or failure of the business.

Equity. The articles of incorporation *authorize* the issuance of equity interests in the corporation by defining the type and number of equity interests that the corporation is allowed to sell. In some corporations, all equity holders have the same rights. Such corporations have one *class* of equity holders. If it is desirable to have equity holders with different rights—for example, if some equity holders are to receive dividends before other equity holders—the corporation will have multiple classes of equity. Sometimes people want to make distinctions within a class of equity holders, and these distinctions are accomplished by creating separate *series* within the class.

All of the equity interests of a corporation together are called the corporation's "capital stock." The individual units of capital stock are called "shares," and ownership in a corporation is quantified by saying that someone owns a certain number of shares of a certain class of capital stock of that corporation. Of course, the raw number of shares does not say anything about our shareholder's ownership relative to other shareholders. To know that would require additional knowledge about (1) what percentage of shares of the entire class our stockholder owns; and (2) what the rights are of that class of shares.

Shares are *issued* when they are sold. Shares are *outstanding* as long as shareholders hold them. If the corporation repurchases the shares, the corporation may continue to hold them as "treasury shares" (which are *issued but not outstanding*). Treasury shares are not voted by the corporation, and they may be resold for any price determined by the board, even if the price is below par value.[1] The Model Act eliminates the concept of treasury shares, providing that shares acquired by the corporation are authorized but unissued.

The articles of incorporation must set forth the total number of shares the corporation is authorized to issue, and if the articles authorize more than one class of shares, they must prescribe the classes and the number of shares in each class. The articles of incorporation also must prescribe a distinguishing designation for each class, and prior to the issuance of the shares, the preferences, limitations, and relative rights of that class must be described in the articles. Typical rights described in the charter are rights to dividends, liquidation rights, voting rights, conversion rights, redemption rights, and preemptive rights.

Articles of incorporation usually designate shares as "common shares" or "preferred shares." Common shares have two fundamental characteristics: (1) unlimited voting rights (including especially the right to vote for directors); (2) the right to the residual assets of the corporation (after payment of all corporate liabilities). The corporation must at all times have at least one share having each of the rights of common stock.

---

1. Many states (including Delaware) require the articles to specify a "par value" for the shares. Originally, the concept of par value evolved from the practice of financing the start-up of a corporation through pre-incorporation subscription agreements, but the meaning of "par value" gradually dissipated in the late 1800s, and it remains an anachronism today. Indeed, the Model Act has eliminated the concept entirely. For more discussion of par value and related concepts, see Chapter 5.A.

Preferred shares are shares that have some preference or priority in payment over common shares. The terms of the preferred shares are set out in the articles or in a separate certificate of designations. Examples of these attributes are listed in Model Act §6.01(c) and DGCL §151. If the articles so provide, the board of directors may designate the attributes of a class or series of shares in an amendment to the articles not requiring shareholder approval. Such shares are usually preferred shares, and are referred to as "blank check preferred."

Debt. Unlike equity, debt is not described in the articles of incorporation. The terms applying to debt securities are laid out in contracts. Many corporations borrow money and incur indebtedness by issuing "bonds" — a promise to repay a specific sum of money at a definite time, with periodic payments of interest. The bond usually refers the holder to a contract called an "indenture" for more complete information.

The indenture is entered into by the corporation and a trustee, who acts on behalf of the bondholders. It describes the procedures for issuance, payment, redemption, and discharge. It also contains extensive covenants, which are promises by the corporation to perform certain actions (for example, to make payments on time, to preserve the corporation's existence, to pay its taxes, to maintain its properties), to refrain from certain actions (for example, making certain distributions of the corporation's money, allowing the corporation to drop below a certain net worth). An indenture also specifies the "events of default," which are certain events (for example, nonpayment of principal and interest) that will allow the bondholders to accelerate payment. Finally, the indenture defines any special terms of the debt (for example, redemption, conversion). The following are some important terms of corporate bonds:

> *Registered versus Bearer.* The corporation makes periodic interest payments to the holders of its debt securities. "Registered securities" have the holder's name and address in a registry, and payments are made to whomever is listed in the registry (transfers of ownership must be recorded). "Bearer securities" have coupons attached, and payments are made to whoever presents the coupons.
>
> *Redemption.* Debt securities are usually, but not always, subject to redemption at the option of the issuing corporation. This means that the corporation may repurchase the debt securities from the owners at a price specified in the indenture. This right is referred to as the right to "call" the bonds. Companies prefer to issue bonds that are callable, since if interest rates decline the company can borrow money at a lower interest rate and use that money to call its outstanding higher-interest bond. If the corporation wants to get rid of debt securities that are not redeemable, it must make a tender offer, usually at a substantial premium, to the owners of the securities.
>
> *Priority.* Indentures define the payment priority of the debt securities in relation to existing and future debt securities. They may be "senior," "subordinated," or "senior subordinated."
>
> *Conversion.* Debt securities may be convertible into capital stock of the corporation at a price and at times specified in the indenture. This is a method of allowing investors to have the protection of debt (that is, regular repayments and priority upon dissolution) while having the option of participating in the growth of the corporation.
>
> *Ratings.* Debt securities issued to the public are rated by various private ratings organizations, such as Moody's and Standard & Poor's. If the securities are rated Baa or higher by Moody's or BBB or higher by Standard & Poor's (that is, if they are "medium grade obligations . . . [being] neither highly protected nor poorly

secured. Such bonds have outstanding investment characteristics and in fact have speculative characteristics as well."), they are referred to as investment-grade debt. Any securities below investment grade are referred to as "junk bonds."

Given that issuing debt reduces a company's financial flexibility, since the interest payments on debt must be paid every quarter or year, as stated in the bond indenture agreement, or the company will be in default, it is logical to ask why a company ever issues debt instead of equity. One part of the answer is that debt has tax advantages over equity, including that: (1) interest payments on debt are deductible to the company, but dividends the company pays to stockholders are not; (2) repayment of principal is a nontaxable return of capital to an investor, but dividends are ordinary income to the investor; (3) if the company fails, bad debt may be an ordinary loss but loss of stock is a capital loss to the investor. The primary risk of debt is that it requires repayment of fixed amounts at fixed intervals regardless of the success or failure of the business. By comparison, equity requires payment of dividends only when the business is successful.

Shareholders often have contrary views about debt. On the one hand, the use of debt enables the company to *leverage* the shareholders' investment. Leverage refers to the notion that borrowers may use borrowed money to generate returns greater than the cost of borrowing. In this event, the excess earnings increase the return on equity. On the other hand, borrowed money must be repaid, and the repayment obligation increases the risks associated with owning equity. Whether an additional amount of indebtedness will create benefits in excess of costs requires detailed analysis, and shareholders sometimes contract for special control rights with respect to any decisions about debt.

The following case highlights the centrality of capital structure to corporate governance. *Grimes* emphasizes the importance of capital structure by affirming the importance of the board of directors in defining the terms of stock issuances.

GRIMES v. ALTEON INC.

804 A.2d 256
Supreme Court of Delaware
July 19, 2002

VEASEY, Chief Justice.

The issue in this case is whether an alleged oral promise made to a stockholder by the CEO of a corporation to sell 10% of the corporation's future private stock offering to the stockholder, when coupled with a corresponding oral promise by the stockholder to buy that 10%, is enforceable where there has been no approval of the agreement by the board of directors and the agreement is not memorialized in a written instrument. The Court of Chancery held that the oral agreement between the stockholder and the CEO is unenforceable. We agree.

We so conclude on several grounds that are consistent with the holding of the Court of Chancery that the bilateral oral agreement creates a "right" to require the corporation to issue stock to the plaintiff within the meaning of Section 157 of the Delaware General Corporation Law, and is invalid under that section for lack of board approval and a writing. The relevant statutory scheme, including Section 157 and other provisions of the Corporation Law, establishes a policy that commitments regarding the issuance of stock must be approved in writing by the board of directors. This policy seeks to preserve the board's broad authority over the corporation and to protect the certainty of investors' expectations regarding stock.

Thus, based on the statutory structure of the Corporation Law as a whole, we affirm the judgment of the Court of Chancery.

FACTS

Alteon Inc., defendant below and appellee, is a pharmaceutical company specializing in drugs for cardiovascular and renal diseases. Charles L. Grimes, plaintiff below and appellant, is a lawyer and an investor who, along with his wife, Jane Gillespie Grimes, often purchases large blocks of stock (but below 10% to avoid insider obligations) in small technology-based companies. Grimes and his wife had held approximately 9.9% of Alteon's stock at the time of the events that have given rise to this litigation. Those events, as set forth in the complaint, may be summarized as follows.

Kenneth I. Moch, the President and Chief Executive Officer of Alteon, told Grimes that Alteon needed additional funds, and that Alteon was considering a private placement stock offering. Grimes told Moch that he was concerned about his holdings being diluted, and that he would buy 10% of any such offering. According to Grimes, Moch promised orally that he would offer Grimes 10% of the offering. In return, Grimes promised orally to buy 10% of the offering. Grimes admits that there is no writing memorializing these promises. He also admits that Alteon's board did not approve this transaction.

Subsequently, Alteon publicly announced a private placement offering. It did not allow Grimes to participate in this private placement, which presumably was fully taken by other purchasers. The stock market reacted positively to the placement, and Alteon's stock price increased from $3 to as high as $5⁵⁄₁₆ per share.

DECISION OF THE COURT OF CHANCERY

Grimes sued Alteon in the Delaware Court of Chancery for damages and specific performance of the oral agreement between Grimes and Moch. Alteon moved to dismiss the complaint under Court of Chancery Rule 12(b)(6) for failure to state a claim on which relief may be granted. The motion made three arguments. First, Alteon argued that any agreement between Grimes and Moch constituted a "right" under 8 Del. C. §157, and is thus invalid because it is not written and was not approved by the board of directors. Second, Alteon argued that the agreement was a "preemptive right" under 8 Del. C. §102(b)(3) and is thus invalid because it was not expressly provided in Alteon's certificate of incorporation. Third, Alteon argued that the agreement is too indefinite as to time, quantity, and price to constitute an enforceable contract. The Court of Chancery accepted the first ground and granted the motion to dismiss on that basis. The Court rejected the second ground, but stated that it is "highly questionable whether or not this would constitute a valid common law contract."

Because of our disposition of this case, we need not reach the second and third issues.

The Vice Chancellor's rationale is expressed in a brief bench ruling holding that the agreement constituted a "right" within the meaning of 8 Del. C. §157, and thus fails for lack of board approval and a written document evidencing it. The essence of the Vice Chancellor's bench ruling is as follows:

> I do agree with the defendants, however, that the right that is sought to be enforced here is a "right" within the meaning of Section 157. I am also satisfied that the intent of Section 157 — that is, that the overall statutory scheme that's contemplated by Section 157 and also by Section 161 — is that whenever investors are contracting to invest capital in a company or to purchase stock either directly or rights or options in stock, that the statutory scheme requires board approval and that there be a written instrument that evidences those arrangements. The reason is that where the overall capital structure of the corporation is concerned, it is a vitally important command of the law that the corporation know precisely what its capital stock is and what the potential calls on that capital will be. And it is for that reason the statute elevates that type of transaction to the level of requiring board approval and of requiring a writing. Only then will everyone know what claims on the capital will be, who has rights to invest capital, and what rights the corporation has with respect to actual or potential investors — that is, investors who have entered into contracts with the company.

Grimes has appealed to this Court the judgment of the Court of Chancery dismissing his complaint. We agree with the essential holding of the Court of Chancery that the agreement is invalid because it was not approved by the board of directors and was not memorialized in a written instrument. We do so based on the statutory scheme of the Corporation Law pertaining to stock issuance, with particular emphasis on Sections 152 and 157.

STOCK ISSUANCE AND THE DELAWARE GENERAL CORPORATION LAW STATUTORY SCHEME

Grimes argues that his arrangement with Moch does not constitute a "right" within the meaning of 8 Del. C. §157 and, therefore, need not be approved by the board or evidenced by a written instrument as required by that statute. Alteon argues that it does. Grimes argues that Section 157 applies only to options and "option like" rights. The fatal defect in Grimes' claim is that the agreement purports to grant a right that was not expressly approved by the board of directors as required by the statutory scheme of the Delaware General Corporation Law exemplified by Section 152 and Section 157.

The agreement purports to bind the corporation to issue to Grimes 10% of a future issuance of stock. Grimes' right to require the issuance of stock to him arises only if and when there is a public or private offering of newly issued stock. Because Grimes claims a right to require the issuance to him of 10% of any such offering, the Corporation Law applies and requires that the agreement and the issuance of the stock must be approved by the board of directors and evidenced by a written instrument.

One must read *in pari materia* the relevant statutory provisions of the Corporation Law. First there is the fundamental corporate governance principle set forth in 8 Del. C. §141(a) that the "business and affairs of every corporation . . . shall be managed by and under the direction of" the board of directors. One then turns to the board's role in stock issuance set forth in the relevant sections of Subchapter V of Title 8. The provisions in this Subchapter relate to the issuance of capital stock, subscriptions for additional shares, options and rights agreements. Taken together, they are calculated to advance two fundamental policies of the Corporation Law: (1) to consolidate in its board of directors the exclusive authority to govern and regulate a corporation's capital structure; and (2) to ensure certainty in the instruments upon which the corporation's capital structure is based.

As this Court has stated in requiring strict adherence to statutory formality in matters relating to the issuance of capital stock, the "issuance of corporate stock is an act of fundamental legal significance having a direct bearing upon questions of corporate governance, control and the capital structure of the enterprise. The law properly requires certainty in such matters."[7] Delaware's statutory structure implements these policies through a "clear and easily followed legal roadmap" of statutory provisions.[8] This statutory scheme consistently requires board approval and a writing.

Various provisions in Subchapter V set forth the formal requirements for the issuance of capital stock, the establishment of classes of stock, the consideration for the issuance of stock, and formalities regarding rights, options and subscriptions relating to capital stock. The statutes relating to the issuance of stock that provide the policy context that is relevant here are 8 Del. C. §§151, 152, 153, 157, 161 and 166. Taken together, these provisions confirm the board's exclusive authority to issue stock and regulate a corporation's capital structure. To ensure certainty, these provisions contemplate board approval and a written instrument evidencing the relevant transactions affecting issuance of stock and the corporation's capital structure.

Section 151(a), relating to classes and series of stock, states that "the resolution or resolutions providing for the issue of such stock [must be] adopted by the board of directors pursuant to authority expressly vested in it by the provisions of its certificate of incorporation." Section 152, relating to the issuance of stock, states, "The consideration . . . for subscriptions to, or the purchase of, the capital stock to be issued by a corporation shall be paid in such form and in such manner as the board of directors shall determine." Section 153, relating to the consideration for the issuance of stock, requires that such consideration shall be determined from time to time by the board of directors. Section 157, relating to rights and options respecting stock, requires board approval and a written instrument to create such rights or options. Section 161, relating to the issuance of additional stock, allows the directors to "issue or take subscriptions for additional shares of its capital stock up to the amount authorized in its certificate of incorporation." Section 166, relating to the formalities required of stock subscriptions, provides that subscription agreements are not enforceable against the subscriber unless in writing and signed by the subscriber.

The requirement of board approval for the issuance of stock is not limited to the act of transferring the shares of stock to the would-be stockholder, but

---

7. STAAR Surgical Co. v. Waggoner, 588 A.2d 1130, 1136 (Del. 1991); *accord Kalageorgi* [v. Victor Kamkin, Inc., 750 A.2d 531, 538 (Del. Ch. 1999)].

8. *Kalageorgi*, 750 A.2d at 538.

includes an antecedent transaction that purports to bind the corporation to do so. As noted, Section 152 requires the directors to determine the "consideration . . . for subscriptions to, or the purchase of, the capital stock" of a corporation. Thus, director approval of the transaction fixing such consideration is required. Moreover, it is well established in the case law that directors must approve a sale of stock. This duty is considered so important that the directors cannot delegate it to the corporation's officers.

Grimes argues that the contract provides "only that *if* Alteon's board should exercise its authority to issue additional Alteon stock in a future private placement (as it did here in the private placement of 2,834,088 shares of common stock), *then* Mr. and Mrs. Grimes were obligated to purchase a certain percentage of that stock at whatever price Alteon's board set. That contract does not give Mr. and Mrs. Grimes the ability to force Alteon to issue additional stock (at any price), and thus does not implicate the board's right to regulate the company's capital structure."

This argument begs the fundamental policy question behind the statutory scheme requiring director approval for steps taken in connection with stock issuance. If the corporation is required by the Grimes agreement to issue to Grimes 10% of an offering to sell stock, the board's business judgment is or may be significantly encumbered. For example, the board would not be able to sell 91%-100% of the stock it chooses to issue to another willing purchaser or purchaser in a private placement or otherwise. It may offer those purchasers only 90% of the offering. That constraint may limit the universe of prospective investors to those who would be content to have only 90% of the stock to be issued.

An agreement that binds a company to allow a 10% stockholder to remain at a 10% holding level may be a considerable sacrifice for a corporation, or it may be a good business decision for the board to consider. Focusing, however, on the problematic aspect of such a business decision, it would seem that a 10% holding in a corporation is large enough that the investor may have considerable leverage over the corporation. Such an agreement is tantamount to an agreement to permit Grimes to have a continuing influence over the future direction of the corporation. Moreover, potential investors might be deterred from investing in a corporation that had made such a commitment. Therefore, the agreement might actually decrease the capital potentially available to a company in a future stock offering. A business decision weighing the advantages and disadvantages of the Grimes transaction would be within the discretion of the board of directors. But that choice lies only in the board's province, not that of the CEO without express board approval.

There is an important policy basis for this requirement. Shares of stock are "a species of property right" that is of "foundational importance . . . to our economic system."[12] Thus, it is "critical that the validity of those securities, especially those that are widely traded, not be easily or capriciously called into question."[13] Explicit board approval of a stock issuance or a commitment to issue stock makes it more likely that the board will have considered thoroughly the reasons for and against the issuance. Thus, director approval

---

12. *Kalageorgi*, 750 A.2d at 538.
13. *Id.*

of stock issuance or agreements affecting the respective rights of the corporation and a putative purchaser of stock reduces later disputes about their propriety and enhances corporate stability and certainty. This policy can be demonstrated by focusing on two of the applicable provisions in the statutory scheme of Subchapter V of the Corporation Law, Sections 152 and 157.

SECTION 152

This transaction fixed the "form" and "manner" of the consideration Alteon could receive from Grimes, thereby implicating 8 Del. C. §152. That provision states, "The consideration . . . for subscriptions to, or the purchase of, the capital stock to be issued by a corporation shall be paid in such form and in such manner as the board of directors shall determine." Regardless of what label is put on the transaction entered into between Grimes and Moch, the transaction contemplated that Grimes would eventually "purchase" the "capital stock" of Alteon, and the agreement constrains the board's determination of the consideration for the issuance of the stock.

This transaction has two features fixing "consideration." First, Alteon bound itself to offer 10% of its stock to Grimes as part of any offering. Second, Alteon could not charge Grimes any more for this 10% than it charged other investors for the remainder.

Both of these features of the transaction served to "cap" the value of the cash consideration Grimes was to give Alteon on the transfer of the stock. This transaction restricted the manner of payment of consideration for Alteon's stock, because it required that it come from Grimes. Because Grimes was a 10% stockholder already, such a commitment could well have tangible negative effects for Alteon's raising of capital from sources other than Grimes. In essence, the promise to Grimes cost Alteon a certain freedom in raising capital, and could well have lowered the ultimate price Alteon could have charged for its capital stock. Section 152 mandates board approval for such promises relating to consideration, and that approval was absent in this case.

SECTION 157

Section 157(a) permits a corporation to "create and issue, whether or not in connection with the issue and sale of any shares of stock or other securities of the corporation, rights or options entitling the holders thereof to purchase from the corporation any shares of its stock," provided that "such rights or options [are] evidenced by or in such instrument or instruments as shall be approved by the board of directors." Because it is indisputable that Alteon's board of directors never passed any such resolution approving this transaction, this agreement is invalid if it is a "right" or an "option."

The predecessor provision to Section 157 was first passed in 1929, the first statute in the nation expressly to authorize the issuance of options. Although the Delaware Court of Chancery had recognized the validity of options before the enactment of that provision, the statute was intended to ensure that validity. From the origin of the provision, it was worded to authorize the creation and issuance of "rights or options. . . . " Later revisions have not made any changes to the provisions that are relevant to the present issue.

Delaware courts have put various types of transactions within the framework provided by Section 157. One common use of options is to compensate officers, directors, and employees of the corporation. Section 157(c) specifically addresses this use of the option. The Court of Chancery has observed that "stock option plans are an acceptable and necessary means by which corporations gain the services of new employees and retain the services of valued employees."[22] The Grimes agreement is not, however, an option.

This Court has also found the authority to adopt a shareholders' rights plan within Section 157. In Moran v. Household International, Inc.,[23] the appellants argued that Section 157 was merely a "corporate financing" statute. We declined to so limit Section 157, noting that the General Assembly did not expressly limit Section 157 to such a purpose. We observed that " 'corporate law is not static,' " but " 'must grow and develop in response to, indeed in anticipation of, evolving concepts and needs.' "[26]

In arguing that this transaction did not bestow upon Grimes a "right," Grimes cites commentary that defines an option by "the right of the optionee to buy or not to buy at the optionee's election." Section 157, however, does not concern only "options." It also concerns "rights." Thus options and rights in Section 157 must have two different meanings. This Court will avoid interpreting terms as mere surplusage. The term "right" has a plain English meaning that is broader than the term "option." A right is "[s]omething that is due to a person by just claim [that is] legally enforceable" according to one dictionary definition;[29] an option is more narrowly focused, requiring the power of choice. Thus, even if the power to choose the time of exercise is an integral component of an "option," by including the term "rights" in Section 157 the drafters of that statute presumably intended for other transactions to be included.

In a similar vein, Grimes argues that the term "rights" includes only options or option-like transactions. We rejected this argument in *Moran*. In that case, the appellants argued that a shareholder rights plan was not permitted under Section 157, labeling Section 157 as merely "a corporate financing statute. . . . " This Court, however, refused "to impose such a limitation upon the section that the legislature has not."[32]

Alteon urges us to adopt a definition of "right," as a "legally enforceable claim that another will do or will not do a given act. . . . "[33] Grimes responds that this broad definition of right logically includes any transaction that includes as a component an obligation to sell. We need not decide that such a broad definition is appropriate. Accordingly we express no opinion whether the term "rights" would include, for example, an executory stock purchase or a subscription. Even at the time Section 157 was first enacted, in 1929, there were provisions governing both types of transactions. When interpreting provisions dealing with a series of discrete transactions, it is reasonable that this Court will not interpret one provision to overlap others without some indication that the legislature intended such treatment. We therefore do not decide anything beyond the narrow issue presented here: Is the agreement that Grimes relies

---

22. Michelson v. Duncan, 386 A.2d 1144, 1150 (Del. Ch. 1978).
23. 500 A.2d 1346 (Del. 1985).
26. *Id*. (quoting Unocal Corp. v. Mesa Petroleum Co., 493 A.2d 946 (Del. 1985)).
29. Black's Law Dictionary 1322 (7th ed. 1999).
32. *Id*. at 1352.
33. Black's Law Dictionary 1322 (7th ed. 1999).

on to purchase 10% of a future stock offering a "right" under Section 157? We agree with the Court of Chancery that it is, and we expressly do not go beyond that holding to define "rights" under Section 157 any more broadly or for any other purpose.

Grimes' argument on appeal is based on the contention that his transaction does not fall within any of the categories the Delaware General Corporation Law has created for stock transactions, such as "purchase" or "subscription." If the transaction is not a "subscription," a "purchase," or any other commonly-known type of transaction involving stock, it does not follow that it is valid under the General Corporation Law. We cannot conclude that the General Assembly intended that the use of the broad term "rights" in Section 157 would have such a cramped meaning that it would exclude the Grimes transaction. Accordingly, we conclude that an agreement, like the one in question here, is a "right" under Section 157 if it purports to grant the obligee (Grimes) the ability to require the obligor (Alteon) to issue 10% of a stock offering to the obligee — even though the corporation's obligation is conditioned upon the correlative duty on the part of the obligee to buy 10% of the offering.

This reading of Section 157, to require all stock transactions not specifically dealt with in other provisions of the Corporation Law to require board approval under Section 157, serves two complementary purposes that Delaware Courts have found in the statutory scheme of our Corporation Law. The first is that the corporation should have the freedom to enter into new and different forms of transactions. Indeed, that was exactly the purpose for which Section 157 was originally created. The second is that, to the extent such transactions obligate the board concerning stock issuance, the board must approve them in writing. Certainty in investor expectations emphasizes the need for written board approval of any such transaction. Grimes' contention that his transaction, because of its *sui generis* nature, need not receive board approval does not comport with this policy.

CONCLUSION

We agree with the conclusion of the Court of Chancery that the Grimes agreement is unenforceable for lack of both board approval and a written agreement. One must read together the various statutes in Subchapter V, particularly Sections 152 and 157, because the statutory scheme of the Delaware General Corporation Law requires board approval and a written instrument evidencing an agreement obligating the corporation to issue stock either unconditionally or conditionally.

PROBLEM 4-2

When Marriott Corporation sold $400 million in senior notes in the spring of 1992,[1] the noteholders thought they knew what they were getting. The bonds

1. The notes came in two flavors: 10 percent Series L Senior Notes, due May 1, 2012, and 9½ percent Series M Senior Notes, due May 1, 2002.

were rated at investment grade, and the company operated a prosperous management services business and owned a fair amount of real estate. In October 1992, Marriott unveiled a surprise: it was splitting the company into two separate companies. Marriott International would take over the highly profitable management services end of the business, while Host Marriott would take the less profitable real estate business—as well as most of the company's debt.

The effect of this transaction was immediate, as the notes were dropped to "junk" status. Protests by the noteholders yielded some concessions from Marriott, but the noteholders were still injured, and some of them sued.

The Marriott transaction was widely perceived as a transfer of wealth from the bondholders to the shareholders of Marriott Corporation.[2] Perhaps the most famous transaction in this mold was the leveraged buyout (LBO) of RJR Nabisco, which was compellingly chronicled in *Barbarians at the Gate*. In that transaction—led by the LBO firm of Kohlberg, Kravis & Roberts—the $24 billion purchase price was financed primarily through junk bonds, which were to be repaid from earnings generated by RJR Nabisco. The effect on RJR Nabisco's outstanding public debt was to reduce its rating from investment grade to junk status. Unfortunately for the bondholders, the bond indenture did not explicitly prohibit the transaction, so the bondholders asked a court to rule that it was a breach of the implied covenant of good faith and fair dealing. The court turned a cold shoulder to this claim:

> Any attempt by this Court to create contractual terms *post hoc* . . . not only finds no basis in the controlling law and undisputed facts of this case, but also would constitute an impermissible invasion into the free and open operation of the marketplace.[3]

Given the lack of protection afforded creditors in the face of contractual ambiguity, why are investors still willing to purchase debt securities? Do you agree with the hands-off approach of the court in the RJR Nabisco case? Some people have suggested that directors should owe fiduciary duties to bondholders. Do you believe that the imposition of fiduciary duties in this context would be wise?

2. *See, e.g.,* F. John Stark, III, et al., *"Marriott Risk": A New Model Covenant to Restrict Transfers of Wealth from Bondholders to Stockholders*, 1994 Colum. Bus. L. Rev. 503.
3. Metropolitan Life Ins. Co. v. RJR Nabisco, Inc., 716 F. Supp. 1504, 1508 (S.D.N.Y. 1989).

CHAPTER
5

Financial Rights of Shareholders

The following discussion of the financial rights of shareholders of a corporation covers two majors areas: (1) the section on dividends and distributions covers the methods by which the corporation distributes money to shareholders and the limits on the power of the board to distribute money to shareholders at the expense of debtholders and other creditors; and (2) the section on limited liability and piercing the corporate veil addresses one of the main differences between general partnerships and corporations — the corporate rule that limits the liability of shareholders to the amount of capital they have invested in the corporation — and discusses circumstances when that rule is overcome by "piercing the veil" of limited liability.

A. DIVIDENDS AND DISTRIBUTIONS

This Section addresses the most common methods corporations use to distribute money to their shareholders and the legal rules governing such distributions. The most familiar method of distributing money to shareholders is through issuing dividends. A dividend is simply a payment, usually in cash, from a corporation to its shareholders. The timing and amount of dividends are determined by the board of directors in their discretion.

An alternative method of distributing money to shareholders is through share repurchases. When a corporation repurchases its own stock, it pays money to shareholders and gets nothing of value in return. Unlike the redemption of debt, which reduces the outstanding claims against the corporation, the redemption of shares simply reduces the number of outstanding shares but does not change the fact that the shares that remain outstanding own 100 percent of the residual value of the corporation.

Regardless of the form of distribution, corporation statutes limit the amount of distributions. The limits on distributions typically take two forms: a solvency test and a balance sheet test. Both are described below.

Solvency test. Most statutes (Delaware being the notable exception) impose a solvency restriction on distributions that would prohibit distributions that would result in insolvency (that is, a condition in which the corporation is unable to pay its debts as they become due in the ordinary course of business). The payment of dividends in such a circumstance also runs afoul of fraudulent conveyance laws, and creditors of the corporation will be able to avoid the payment.

Balance sheet tests. While solvency tests depend on the operations of the corporation, balance sheet tests are measured by concepts from the corporation's financial statements. The following are two different balance sheet tests:

> *"Impairment of capital" test.* Some statutes (*e.g.*, DGCL §170) permit distributions out of "surplus," which is defined in DGCL §154 to mean all capital in excess of the aggregate par values (for discussion of "par value," see below) of the issued shares plus any amounts the board has elected to add to its capital account.

> *Technical insolvency test.* Model Act §6.40(c)(2) prohibits distributions that would result in total assets being insufficient to pay the sum of the corporation's liabilities and any liquidation preferences that would be owing if the corporation dissolved at the time of distribution.

It is useful to recognize why there are limits on the board's ability to issue dividends to shareholders. Debtholders have priority if a business fails and there is a bankruptcy proceeding. That priority means that debtholders will be fully paid before shareholders receive any money back. If a corporation approaching bankruptcy distributes all of its remaining cash or other liquid assets to its shareholders as it approaches bankruptcy, then the relative priorities of debtholders and shareholders are effectively reversed. So limits on dividends are part of a system designed to protect creditors, including debtholders, from such reversals.

Unfortunately, this relatively simple concept led to some fairly complicated rules using the concept of "legal capital." The story of legal capital begins with "par value"—a term that initially was equivalent to the sales price of shares. Legal capital is simply the par value per share times the number of shares outstanding. Distributions can only be made out of "surplus," which is all capital in excess of the legal capital. Distributions that exceed surplus result in an "impairment of capital." Today the par value of shares has no relationship to the sales price. Indeed, it is not uncommon to set the par value of shares at a penny a share, so that all of the money raised in selling shares is available as "surplus," except for the one cent per share. While the legal capital account would therefore seem to be not much of a limitation on the issuance of dividends, it is possible under DGCL §154 to sell "no par" stock. If that is done, the board of directors must specify the amount of legal capital (called "stated capital") or all of the money raised in a no-par stock issuance would be treated as the legal capital.

The following case illustrates the legal capital system at work. Although the Model Act has eliminated legal capital, it is still an important part of the Delaware statute. *Klang* shows, however, that the board of directors has an immense amount of discretion in determining the accounting treatment for assets on their books, and thus can work within the legal capital system to accomplish their goals. One must ask, therefore, whether the goal of protecting creditors and debtholders from unwarranted preferences to the shareholders could be accomplished in a more straightforward way, perhaps as in the Model Act.

KLANG v. SMITH'S FOOD & DRUG CENTERS, INC.
702 A.2d 150
Supreme Court of Delaware
November 7, 1997

Veasey, Chief Justice.

This appeal calls into question the actions of a corporate board in carrying out a merger and self-tender offer. Plaintiff in this purported class action alleges that a corporation's repurchase of shares violated the statutory prohibition against the impairment of capital. . . .

No corporation may repurchase or redeem its own shares except out of "surplus," as statutorily defined, or except as expressly authorized by provisions of the statute not relevant here. Balance sheets are not, however, conclusive indicators of surplus or a lack thereof. Corporations may revalue assets to show surplus, but perfection in that process is not required. Directors have reasonable latitude to depart from the balance sheet to calculate surplus, so long as they evaluate assets and liabilities in good faith, on the basis of acceptable data, by methods that they reasonably believe reflect present values, and arrive at a determination of the surplus that is not so far off the mark as to constitute actual or constructive fraud.

We hold that, on this record, the Court of Chancery was correct in finding that there was no impairment of capital and there were no disclosure violations. Accordingly, we affirm.

Facts

Smith's Food & Drug Centers, Inc. ("SFD") is a Delaware corporation that owns and operates a chain of supermarkets in the Southwestern United States. Slightly more than three years ago, Jeffrey P. Smith, SFD's Chief Executive Officer, began to entertain suitors with an interest in acquiring SFD. At the time, and until the transactions at issue, Mr. Smith and his family held common and preferred stock constituting 62.1% voting control of SFD. Plaintiff and the class he purports to represent are holders of common stock in SFD.

On January 29, 1996, SFD entered into an agreement with The Yucaipa Companies ("Yucaipa"), a California partnership also active in the supermarket industry. Under the agreement, the following would take place:

(1) Smitty's Supermarkets, Inc. ("Smitty's"), a wholly-owned subsidiary of Yucaipa that operated a supermarket chain in Arizona, was to merge into Cactus Acquisition, Inc. ("Cactus"), a subsidiary of SFD, in exchange for which SFD would deliver to Yucaipa slightly over 3 million newly-issued shares of SFD common stock;

(2) SFD was to undertake a recapitalization, in the course of which SFD would assume a sizable amount of new debt, retire old debt, and offer to repurchase up to fifty percent of its outstanding shares (other than those issued to Yucaipa) for $36 per share; and

(3) SFD was to repurchase 3 million shares of preferred stock from Jeffrey Smith and his family.

SFD hired the investment firm of Houlihan Lokey Howard & Zukin ("Houlihan") to examine the transactions and render a solvency opinion. Houlihan eventually issued a report to the SFD Board replete with assurances that the transactions would not endanger SFD's solvency, and would not impair SFD's capital in violation of 8 Del. C. §160. On May 17, 1996, in reliance on the Houlihan opinion, SFD's Board determined that there existed sufficient surplus to consummate the transactions, and enacted a resolution proclaiming as much. On May 23, 1996, SFD's stockholders voted to approve the transactions, which closed on that day. The self-tender offer was over-subscribed, so SFD repurchased fully fifty percent of its shares at the offering price of $36 per share. . . .

PLAINTIFF'S CAPITAL-IMPAIRMENT CLAIM

A corporation may not repurchase its shares if, in so doing, it would cause an impairment of capital, unless expressly authorized by Section 160. A repurchase impairs capital if the funds used in the repurchase exceed the amount of the corporation's "surplus," defined by 8 Del. C. §154 to mean the excess of net assets over the par value of the corporation's issued stock.

Plaintiff asked the Court of Chancery to rescind the transactions in question as violative of Section 160. As we understand it, plaintiff's position breaks down into two analytically distinct arguments. First, he contends that SFD's balance sheets constitute conclusive evidence of capital impairment. He argues that the negative net worth that appeared on SFD's books following the repurchase compels us to find a violation of Section 160. Second, he suggests that even allowing the Board to "go behind the balance sheet" to calculate surplus does not save the transactions from violating Section 160. In connection with this claim, he attacks the SFD Board's off-balance-sheet method of calculating surplus on the theory that it does not adequately take into account all of SFD's assets and liabilities. Moreover, he argues that the May 17, 1996 resolution of the SFD Board conclusively refutes the Board's claim that revaluing the corporation's assets gives rise to the required surplus. We hold that each of these claims is without merit.

SFD's balance sheets do not establish a violation of 8 Del. C. §160.

In an April 25, 1996 proxy statement, the SFD Board released a pro forma balance sheet showing that the merger and self-tender offer would result in a deficit to surplus on SFD's books of more than $100 million. A balance sheet the SFD Board issued shortly after the transactions confirmed this result. Plaintiff asks us to adopt an interpretation of 8 Del. C. §160 whereby balance-sheet net worth is controlling for purposes of determining compliance with the statute. Defendants do not dispute that SFD's books showed a negative net worth in the wake of its transactions with Yucaipa, but argue that corporations should have the presumptive right to revalue assets and liabilities to comply with Section 160.

Plaintiff advances an erroneous interpretation of Section 160. We understand that the books of a corporation do not necessarily reflect the current values of its assets and liabilities. Among other factors, unrealized appreciation or depreciation can render book numbers inaccurate. It is unrealistic to hold that a corporation is bound by its balance sheets for purposes of determining compliance with Section 160. . . .

It is helpful to recall the purpose behind Section 160. The General Assembly enacted the statute to prevent boards from draining corporations of assets to the detriment of creditors and the long-term health of the corporation. That a corporation has not yet realized or reflected on its balance sheet the appreciation of assets is irrelevant to this concern. Regardless of what a balance sheet that has not been updated may show, an actual, though unrealized, appreciation reflects real economic value that the corporation may borrow against or that creditors may claim or levy upon. Allowing corporations to revalue assets and liabilities to reflect current realities complies with the statute and serves well the policies behind this statute.

The SFD Board appropriately revalued corporate assets to comply with 8 Del. C. §160.

Plaintiff contends that SFD's repurchase of shares violated Section 160 even without regard to the corporation's balance sheets. Plaintiff claims that the SFD Board was not entitled to rely on the solvency opinion of Houlihan, which showed that the transactions would not impair SFD's capital given a revaluation of corporate assets. The argument is that the methods that underlay the solvency opinion were inappropriate as a matter of law because they failed to take into account all of SFD's assets and liabilities. In addition, plaintiff suggests that the SFD Board's resolution of May 17, 1996 itself shows that the transactions impaired SFD's capital, and that therefore we must find a violation of 8 Del. C. §160. We disagree, and hold that the SFD Board revalued the corporate assets under appropriate methods. Therefore the self-tender offer complied with Section 160, notwithstanding errors that took place in the drafting of the resolution.

On May 17, 1996, Houlihan released its solvency opinion to the SFD Board, expressing its judgment that the merger and self-tender offer would not impair SFD's capital. Houlihan reached this conclusion by comparing SFD's "Total Invested Capital" of $1.8 billion — a figure Houlihan arrived at by valuing SFD's assets under the "market multiple" approach — with SFD's long-term debt of $1.46 billion. This comparison yielded an approximation of SFD's "concluded equity value" equal to $346 million, a figure clearly in excess of the outstanding par value of SFD's stock. Thus, Houlihan concluded, the transactions would not violate 8 Del. C. §160.

Plaintiff contends that Houlihan's analysis relied on inappropriate methods to mask a violation of Section 160. Noting that 8 Del. C. §154 defines "net assets" as "the amount by which total assets exceeds total liabilities," plaintiff argues that Houlihan's analysis is erroneous as a matter of law because of its failure to calculate "total assets" and "total liabilities" as separate variables. In a related argument, plaintiff claims that the analysis failed to take into account all of SFD's liabilities, *i.e.*, that Houlihan neglected to consider current liabilities in its comparison of SFD's "Total Invested Capital" and long-term debt. Plaintiff contends that the SFD Board's resolution proves that adding current liabilities into the mix shows a violation of Section 160. The resolution declared the value of SFD's assets to be $1.8 billion, and stated that its "total liabilities" would not exceed $1.46 billion after the transactions with Yucaipa. As noted, the $1.46 billion figure described only the value of SFD's long-term debt. Adding in SFD's $372 million in current liabilities, plaintiff argues, shows that the transactions impaired SFD's capital.

We believe that plaintiff reads too much into Section 154. The statute simply defines "net assets" in the course of defining "surplus." It does not mandate a "facts and figures balancing of assets and liabilities" to determine by what amount, if any, total assets exceeds total liabilities. The statute is merely definitional. It does not require any particular method of calculating surplus, but simply prescribes factors that any such calculation must include. Although courts may not determine compliance with Section 160 except by methods that fully take into account the assets and liabilities of the corporation, Houlihan's methods were not erroneous as a matter of law simply because they used Total Invested Capital and long-term debt as analytical categories rather than "total assets" and "total liabilities."

We are satisfied that the Houlihan opinion adequately took into account all of SFD's assets and liabilities. Plaintiff points out that the $1.46 billion figure that approximated SFD's long-term debt failed to include $372 million in current liabilities, and argues that including the latter in the calculations dissipates the surplus. In fact, plaintiff has misunderstood Houlihan's methods. The record shows that Houlihan's calculation of SFD's Total Invested Capital is already net of current liabilities. Thus, subtracting long-term debt from Total Invested Capital does, in fact, yield an accurate measure of a corporation's net assets.

The record contains, in the form of the Houlihan opinion, substantial evidence that the transactions complied with Section 160. Plaintiff has provided no reason to distrust Houlihan's analysis. In cases alleging impairment of capital under Section 160, the trial court may defer to the board's measurement of surplus unless a plaintiff can show that the directors "failed to fulfill their duty to evaluate the assets on the basis of acceptable data and by standards which they are entitled to believe reasonably reflect present values." In the absence of bad faith or fraud on the part of the board, courts will not "substitute [our] concepts of wisdom for that of the directors." Here, plaintiff does not argue that the SFD Board acted in bad faith. Nor has he met his burden of showing that the methods and data that underlay the board's analysis are unreliable or that its determination of surplus is so far off the mark as to constitute actual or constructive fraud.[12] Therefore, we defer to the board's determination of surplus, and hold that SFD's self-tender offer did not violate 8 Del. C. §160.

On a final note, we hold that the SFD Board's resolution of May 17, 1996 has no bearing on whether the transactions conformed to Section 160. The record shows that the SFD Board committed a serious error in drafting the resolution: the resolution states that, following the transactions, SFD's "total liabilities" would be no more than $1.46 billion. In fact, that figure reflects only the value of SFD's long-term debt. Although the SFD Board was guilty of sloppy work, and did not follow good corporate practices, it does not follow that Section 160 was violated. The statute requires only that there exist a surplus after a repurchase, not that the board memorialize the surplus in a resolution. The statute carves out a class of transactions that directors have no authority to execute, but does not, in fact, require any affirmative act on the part of

---

12. We interpret 8 Del. C. §172 to entitle boards to rely on experts such as Houlihan to determine compliance with 8 Del. C. §160. Plaintiff has not alleged that the SFD Board failed to exercise reasonable care in selecting Houlihan, nor that rendering a solvency opinion is outside Houlihan's realm of competence. *Compare* 8 Del. C. §141(e) (providing that directors may rely in good faith on records, reports, experts, etc.).

the board. The SFD repurchase would be valid in the absence of any board resolution. A mistake in documenting the surplus will not negate the substance of the action, which complies with the statutory scheme. . . .

The judgment of the Court of Chancery is affirmed.

B.   LIMITED LIABILITY AND PIERCING THE CORPORATE VEIL

Limited liability and piercing the corporate veil have long been among the most controversial topics in corporate law. Scholars still do not agree about the origins of limited liability in the United States. Although some corporations received limited liability in their special charters, many special charters provided for unlimited shareholder liability. Even when special charters did not provide for direct shareholder liability, they often allowed for unlimited assessments against shareholders, thus creating indirect shareholder liability. Otherwise, the status of limited liability in late eighteenth century America is unclear because no reported cases address the issue. It is clear, however, that the policy of limited liability for shareholders was not widely established by courts in the United States until some time into the nineteenth century. Beginning in the early 1810s, states began to adopt limited liability statutes, but attempts to revive unlimited liability persisted, and state legislatures did not consistently adopt a policy of limited liability until the 1840s. Nevertheless, by the time Joseph Angell and Samuel Ames published their famous corporate law treatise in 1832, they confidently asserted: "No rule of law we believe is better settled, than that, in general, the individual members of a private corporate body are not liable for the debts, either in their persons or in their property, beyond the amount of property which they have in stock."

Although the historical record is unclear, it appears that the availability of limited liability was a major factor in the decision to seek incorporation for many businesses in eighteenth century America. During the early 1800s, there was a public outcry at what was perceived as a state-sanctioned method of avoiding responsibility for one's actions. Later, during the Jacksonian period, making limited liability accessible to the masses became a driving inspiration behind the promulgation of general incorporation statutes. Despite initial reservations, therefore, limited liability has endured; indeed, it has thrived, especially in the past decade as state legislatures continue to create new entities offering limited liability protection to investors. See Chapter 3. Nevertheless, the existence and recent expansion of limited liability remain one of the most talked about issues in corporate law. The following paragraphs briefly describe the justifications for limited liability and examine the situations in which the protection of limited liability is removed. Like limited liability itself, the common law doctrine of piercing the corporate veil has generated much controversy, mainly for its apparent indeterminacy.

The primary advantages of limited liability are most pronounced in public corporations, not close corporations. For example, many commentators have argued that limited liability enables shareholders to diversify more efficiently because investors made fully liable for the debts of a corporation would expose themselves to too much risk. Under this reasoning, diversification under unlimited liability actually increases risk. Investors in close corporations usually do not invest to diversify, but rather because the corporation is also their source of employment.

The previous justification for limited liability is closely related to another — namely, that limited liability permits the free transfer of shares in the public markets. If shareholders risked incurring personal liability every time they purchased shares, trading in the public markets would be severely impaired. Even if this justifies limited liability for public corporations, it says nothing about close corporations, which by definition are not publicly traded.

Another oft-cited justification for limited liability is that it reduces monitoring costs in two ways: (1) it decreases the need to monitor managers (the more risk investors bear, the more closely they monitor their "agents"); and (2) it reduces costs of monitoring other shareholders (the greater the wealth of other shareholders, the lower the probability of any one shareholder's assets being taken to satisfy a judgment). These advantages of limited liability are much less pronounced in close corporations, where shareholders and managers often are the same people.

Regardless of whether limited liability is justified, its effects are apparent. First, limited liability increases the cost of debt and decreases the cost of equity to the corporation. In other words, shareholders must pay creditors to assume some of the risk of business failure. Limited liability increases the cost of debt by reducing the creditors' sources of payment and increasing business risk (because limited liability owners have less incentive than personally liable owners to act consistently with creditor interests). Voluntary creditors will charge the firm in advance for bearing this risk.

The major potential social cost of limited liability is that people who have limited liability have an incentive to engage in riskier than optimal activities because they are not forced to bear the total costs of such behavior. This increased risk is known as "moral hazard." Moral hazard does not impose social costs in every type of transaction involving a corporation. In transactions involving the corporation and voluntary creditors (particularly lenders, but possibly including employees, consumers, and trade creditors), for example, the firm will be forced to pay for the freedom to engage in risky activities; therefore, society theoretically will bear no extra costs from limited liability. If the firm cannot make credible promises to refrain from taking excessive risks, it must pay higher interest rates. If the price that must be paid to third parties for engaging in a particular activity exceeds the benefits to the firm, the activity will not be undertaken, regardless of the liability rule.

With respect to involuntary creditors (that is, tort victims), on the other hand, there probably is some social cost to limited liability (that is, there are some costs that the corporation does not internalize but instead imposes on tort victims). Insurance may internalize some of these costs, but not all. It is for this reason that Professors Hansmann of Yale University and Kraakman of Harvard University have argued for pro rata, unlimited shareholder liability in the tort law context. *See* Henry Hansmann & Renier Kraakman, *Toward Unlimited Shareholder Liability for Corporate Torts*, 100 Yale L.J. 1879 (1991).

Special problems arise in trying to justify limited liability within corporate groups, such as a parent company and its wholly owned subsidiaries. A whollyowned subsidiary is a legal entity separately incorporated from the parent corporation, but where the parent owns 100 percent of the stock of the subsidiary. In this context it is not so clear that the various business entities should be treated as separate, rather than looking at the enterprise as one related entity. The separate legal status of parent and subsidiary corporations is respected in the majority of cases, and the "whole enterprise" theory of liability for corporate groups in the parent/subsidiary context has been soundly rejected. Problem 5-1 at the end of this section explores this issue in more detail.

Notwithstanding the usual rule of limited liability, in some instances courts will require shareholders to pay the entire amount of a contract or a judgment on a tort law claim, beyond the amount of the shareholders' investments. This is referred to as "piercing the corporate veil," for reasons shrouded in the mists of history. The common law doctrine of piercing the corporate veil has fascinated corporate law scholars over the years, as they have attempted to break the code used by courts to decide when to "pierce" and when to retain limited liability. One well-reasoned attempt to make sense of the piercing cases was put forward by Judge Frank Easterbrook and Professor Daniel Fischel, who contend that piercing the corporate veil cases may be understood simply as rough attempts to balance the benefits of limited liability against its costs. Based on this notion of piercing, they make the following predictions about how the cases should come out:

Close corporations versus public corporations. In close corporations, those who supply the capital are usually the same people who manage the firm; therefore, there is no need to incur monitoring costs, and one of the major benefits of limited liability is gone. In addition, the costs of limited liability (that is, increased risk taking) will be more pronounced in close corporations, where the managers will capture more of any potential gains. Easterbrook and Fischel predict, therefore, that courts will often pierce in a close corporation context but not in a public corporation context.

Parent corporation versus individual shareholder. Easterbrook and Fischel predict that courts are more likely to pierce when the shareholder is a corporation than when the shareholder is an individual because allowing creditors to reach the assets of parent corporations does not create unlimited liability for any individual; therefore, the benefits of limited liability remain largely intact. In addition, the moral hazard (that is, increased risk taking) will be more pronounced where a corporation is allowed to form a subsidiary to perform especially risky activities.

Contract cases versus tort cases. Easterbrook and Fischel assert that courts are more likely to pierce in tort cases than in contract cases. This prediction is based on the assumption that corporations pay for risk *ex ante* under contracts but not under torts and that courts, therefore, should be more likely to force payment *ex post* in tort cases.

Undercapitalization. Easterbrook and Fischel assert that undercapitalization is a common source of piercing, especially in tort cases because the high transaction costs preclude *ex ante* negotiation. The rationale is obvious: the lower the amount of the firm's capital, the greater the incentive to engage in risky activities.

Shortly after Easterbrook and Fischel published their analysis, Professor Robert Thompson published the results of an empirical study of 1,583 piercing cases. See Robert Thompson, *Piercing the Corporate Veil: An Empirical Study,*

76 Cornell L. Rev. 1036 (1991). Among Thompson's conclusions were the following:

Close corporations versus public corporations. Consistent with Easterbrook and Fischel's analysis, *no case* concerned piercing the veil in a public corporation context. Stated another way, piercing the corporate veil is a doctrine reserved exclusively for close corporations.

Parent corporation versus individual shareholder. Contrary to Easterbrook and Fischel's expectations, cases involving an individual shareholder resulted in piercing 50 percent of the time, while cases involving a parent corporation resulted in piercing 28 percent of the time.

Contract cases versus tort cases. Again contrary to Easterbrook and Fischel's expectations, courts pierced more often in contract cases (42%) than in tort cases (31%).

Undercapitalization. Again contrary to Easterbrook and Fischel, undercapitalization did not seem to play a role in a large number of piercing cases. It appeared as a factor in only 19 percent of the contract cases and 13 percent of the tort cases studied.

Of course, Thompson's study is subject to many limitations, which he acknowledges, by virtue of the fact that his data are reported cases and may not represent the total cases decided (because many decisions are not reported) or filed (since most cases are settled) and do not take account of potential cases that are not filed because the litigants are deterred by their assessment of probable outcomes. Nevertheless, the findings do cast doubt on attempts to rationalize the cases using the factors selected by Easterbrook and Fischel.

Perhaps the best one can do is to trust that the courts do what they say they are doing. The following framework is explicitly used by many courts and explains many, although certainly not all, piercing the corporate veil cases:

Direct liability. When analyzing a claim seeking to pierce the corporate veil, a threshold question is whether liability may attach to the shareholder directly by reason of the shareholder's own actions instead of recognizing the liability as a *corporate* liability that must be paid by the shareholder personally because of the piercing analysis.

Corporate formalities. If there is no personal liability, the first question under the piercing analysis is whether corporate formalities have been carefully observed (for example, if the corporation has a separate bank account, there is no commingling of personal and corporate funds, regular meetings of directors and shareholders, or corporate records). If the formalities have been followed, few courts will pierce.

If the corporate formalities have not been observed, the analysis becomes murky. Some courts will pierce based on lack of corporate formalities alone on the theory that if the shareholder ignored the separate existence of the corporation, it would be unjust to force a creditor to respect it. But there is no logical reason to pierce the corporate veil simply because shareholders have failed to follow corporate formalities because the harm at issue in the lawsuit usually bears no relation to corporate formalities.

Fairness. Beyond a showing that the corporate formalities were not maintained, most courts require a showing of injustice or unfairness to link the wrongdoing to the harm. Two types of injustice are most common: (1) where the disregard of the corporate entity has been visible to a third party and that third party has reason to be confused about whether he or she was dealing with a corporation or an individual; (2) where the shareholder has disregarded the separateness of the corporation's funds and treated them as her own (such as through unauthorized withdrawals). Thus, if the shareholder herself seems to think it fair to treat the corporation's funds as interchangeable with her personal funds, it seems fair for the courts to do the same.

The following case examines the doctrine of piercing the corporate veil. It is based on a tort claim. The court cites precedent for the notion that "the concept of piercing the corporate veil is applied in Georgia to remedy injustices which arise where a party has overextended his privilege in the use of a corporate entity in order to defeat justice." Consider the evidence used to support the piercing claim and ask yourself whether piercing in this instance really accomplishes that purpose.

SOERRIES v. DANCAUSE
546 S.E.2d 356
Court of Appeals of Georgia
March 2, 2001

ELLINGTON, Judge.

In this dram shop liability case, William A. Soerries appeals from a jury verdict that pierced the corporate veil and held him personally liable for damages. Because we find that the evidence presented supported the jury's verdict, we affirm.

The facts, viewed in a light most favorable to the jury's verdict, show that Soerries was the sole shareholder of Chickasaw Club, Inc., which operated a popular nightclub in Columbus for 23 years until it closed in 1999. At approximately 11:45 P.M. on July 31, 1996, 18-year-old Aubrey Lynn Pursley was intoxicated when she entered the Chickasaw Club. Although a Columbus ordinance prohibits individuals under 21 years old from entering nightclubs, it is undisputed that club employees did not check Pursley's identification to establish her age. A friend testified that Pursley already was intoxicated when she arrived at the club. Even so, friends testified that Pursley drank additional alcohol at the club and was visibly intoxicated when she left at approximately 3:00 A.M. on August 1, 1996. Security videotapes showed that she left the club with a beer in her hand. Shortly thereafter, Pursley was killed when she lost control of her car and struck a tree.

Joseph Dancause, Pursley's stepfather, sued Chickasaw Club, Inc. and Soerries individually for the cost of the car and for punitive damages. Following a trifurcated jury trial, the trial court entered judgment on the jury's verdict, which pierced the corporate veil and found Soerries jointly liable with the corporation for $6,500 in compensatory damages and solely liable for $187,500 in punitive damages. Soerries appeals from this judgment.

Soerries argues that Dancause presented insufficient evidence to justify piercing the corporate veil. We disagree. As we have held:

> The concept of piercing the corporate veil is applied in Georgia to remedy injustices which arise where a party has overextended his privilege in the use of a corporate entity in order to defeat justice, perpetrate fraud or to evade contractual or tort responsibility. Because the cardinal rule of corporate law is that a

corporation possesses a legal existence separate and apart from that of its officers
and shareholders, the mere operation of corporate business does not render one
personally liable for corporate acts. Sole ownership of a corporation by one person or another corporation is not a factor, and neither is the fact that the sole
owner uses and controls it to promote his ends. There must be evidence of abuse
of the corporate form. Plaintiff must show that the defendant disregarded the separateness of legal entities by commingling on an interchangeable or joint basis or
confusing the otherwise separate properties, records or control. In deciding this
enumeration of error, we are confronted with two maxims that sometimes conflict.
On the one hand, we are mindful that great caution should be exercised by the
court in disregarding the corporate entity. On the other, it is axiomatic that when
litigated, the issue of piercing the corporate veil is for the jury, unless there is no
evidence sufficient to justify disregarding the corporate form.

J-Mart Jewelry Outlets v. Standard Design, 462 S.E.2d 406 (1995).

In this case, the jury heard testimony from Larry Jones, who managed the
Chickasaw Club for 20 years. Jones testified that the club was open four nights a
week and regularly admitted an average of 250 people who paid cover charges
of $3 to $4 each. Additional patrons were also admitted, so that the club sometimes exceeded its capacity of 477 people. According to Jones, he and the other
employees were paid each night in cash by Soerries out of the proceeds of the
club. Although Jones testified that 1996 was a "bad year" for the corporation
and that he was paid between $10,000 and $12,000, corporate payroll records
reported his earnings as only $5,690. Jones admitted that Soerries sometimes
paid him extra cash that was not reported to the club's bookkeeper.

It is undisputed that Soerries paid his employees, suppliers, and entertainers
in cash and not from existing corporate checking accounts. One employee
admitted he was paid "under the table." The employee never appeared on
corporate payroll records, although Soerries admitted giving him money to
help out around the club.

Corporate tax returns showed that, even though the Chickasaw Club was
a busy nightclub, it regularly declared business losses. On cross-examination,
Soerries failed to explain the substantial difference between reported income
on corporate and individual tax returns and evidence regarding cash proceeds from cover charges and alcohol sales. When asked how the club paid
its employees and other operating expenses while operating at a loss, Soerries explained that he often paid the corporate expenses out of his personal
funds.

Soerries owned the property on which the Chickasaw Club was located and
testified that he paid his $4,830 monthly mortgage note from the club's cash
proceeds. Although Soerries claimed that the club's payments were rent that he
then used to pay the note, personal tax returns showed that he received only
$34,173 in rent in 1996, even though the corporation reported paying $43,000
in rent in its 1996 corporate tax return. Further, both figures are significantly
less than the $57,960 in rent that would have been due from the corporation,
based upon 12 months of $4,830 rental payments. Additional evidence showed
that Soerries also owned other rental property in 1996 that would have paid
$3,150 per month, making the disparity between his alleged rental earnings
and his reported income even greater.

A jury could construe this evidence to demonstrate that Soerries commingled individual and corporate assets by personally assuming the corporation's financial liabilities, waiving corporate rental payments, or using corporate funds to directly pay his personal mortgage notes and other expenses. As such, the totality of the evidence presented raised a jury issue on whether Soerries

> disregarded the separateness of legal entities by commingling and confusion of properties, records, control, etc. It is obvious that if the individual who is the principal shareholder or owner of the corporation conducts his private and corporate business on an interchangeable or joint basis as if they were one, then he is without standing to complain when an injured party does the same. Under such circumstances, the court may disregard the corporate entity.

Abbott Foods of Ga. v. Elberton Poultry Co., 327 S.E.2d 751.

On appeal, we construe all the evidence most strongly in support of the verdict, and if there is evidence to sustain the verdict, we cannot disturb it. We find that the evidence presented was sufficient to support the jury's decision to pierce the corporate veil.

PROBLEM 5-1

One example, among many, of a company using multiple separately incorporated entities is the Royal Dutch Shell Group, a global oil-producing company that describes its corporate structure as follows on its Web site:

> The Royal Dutch/Shell Group of Companies has grown out of an alliance made in 1907 between Royal Dutch Petroleum Company and The Shell Transport and Trading Company, p.l.c., by which the two companies agreed to merge their interests on a 60:40 basis while keeping their separate identities. The Royal Dutch/Shell Group is made up of three parts — the three Group Holding Companies, the Service Companies and the Operating Companies. The parent Companies directly or indirectly own all of the shares in the Group Holding Companies but are not themselves part of the Royal Dutch/Shell Group of Companies. They appoint Directors to the Boards of the Group Holding Companies, from which they receive income in the form of dividends. Royal Dutch holds 60% of the interest in the Group, with 40 percent owned by Shell Transport. The main business of the Service Companies is to provide advice and services to other Group and associated companies, excluding Shell Petroleum Inc. and its subsidiaries. The Operating Companies are engaged in various activities related to oil and natural gas, chemicals, power generation, renewable resources and other businesses throughout the world. Each Operating Company is responsible for the performance and long-term viability of its own operations, but can draw on the experience of the Service Companies and, through them, of other Operating Companies. The individual Operating Companies run their own oil products businesses, and as such, it would be inappropriate to use the term "the Group's Oil Product Business" as if there was a single, centrally directed business.

On November 8, 1996, litigation was brought in the Southern District of New York against the Netherlands holding company, Royal Dutch Petroleum, and the British holding company, Shell Transport, alleging that Royal Dutch Shell's indirectly owned Nigerian subsidiary violated plaintiffs Ken Saro-Wiwa and John Kpuinen and their next of kin's human rights by recruiting the Nigerian military to suppress political opposition to Shell's oil development activity in the Ogoni region of Nigeria. Plaintiffs allege that in order to suppress that political opposition led by Saro-Wiwa and Kpuinen, at the behest of and under the direction of Shell, the Nigerian military arrested Saro-Wiwa and Kpuinen and tortured them. The military then tried Saro-Wiwa and Kpuinen for murder in front of a special military tribunal, convicted them on fabricated evidence, and hung them. Plaintiffs allege also that others of Saro-Wiwa's family were illegally detained and beaten.

Subject matter jurisdiction was based on the Alien Torts Claims Act (ATCA), which has been used increasingly over the past ten years to try to bring cases in the United States to challenge corporate action abroad (such as the alleged environmental degradation caused by the Texaco company in Equador or the alleged forcible resettlement of villages and use of forced labor by the UNOCAL company in Burma). The ATCA provides subject matter jurisdiction in the United States to non-U.S. citizens ("aliens") to challenge alleged violations of well-recognized international human rights, even where those challenges are brought against non-U.S. defendants. Assuming that there is a basis for personal jurisdiction in the United States, will plaintiffs be able to pierce the corporate veil from the Nigerian subsidiary up to the British and Netherlands holding company? What additional facts would you need to develop in litigation to address that question? Should the plaintiffs be able to pierce the corporate veil in these parent/subsidiary contexts? *Unfortunately not here but yes.*

people on the ground? who dealt w/ ogoni people or who did they see?

Business chart - Royal Dutch / Shell Group

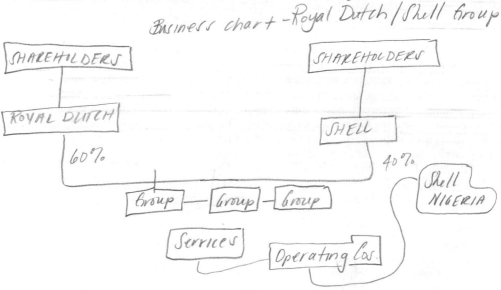

CHAPTER
6

State Regulation of Corporate Governance

The management of a corporation is divided among three groups: shareholders, directors, and officers. In a public corporation, the formal mechanisms of control are exercised primarily by the board of directors, which has the statutory power to manage the affairs of the corporation, while the actual, day-to-day control resides in the top executive officers. Shareholders control the directors, if at all, through annual director elections and through voting on specific proposals, when allowed.

The discussion in the following materials is divided between directors and shareholders. Although officers exercise the most practical control over a corporation on a daily basis, there are few corporation statutes that regulate the exercise of such control. The law focuses, instead, on directors and shareholders, both of which monitor the performance of officers, at least in theory.

Our main focus in this chapter is the structure of state laws applicable to shareholder voting. Still, it is impossible to understand the shareholders' powers, and statutory and practical limitations on those powers, without first having some appreciation of the statutory powers of the board of directors and some practical understanding of how directors exercise their power. We will start with the directors, then, and move from there to the structure of state laws regulating shareholders' powers to vote to elect directors in the first place. We'll then look at an emerging area of law that involves state law disclosure requirements that seek to ensure that shareholders have accurate information prior to voting.

A. DIRECTORS

Role of the board. The statutory power to manage the corporation rests with the board of directors. Each public corporation must have a board of directors, while closely held corporations can do away with the board of directors by agreement among the shareholders. Model Act §§8.01(a) and 7.32; Delaware General Corporation Law (DGCL) §§141(a) and 351. Although the charter or bylaws of a corporation may prescribe qualifications of directors (for example, they may require that the directors hold stock in the corporation or be residents of the state of incorporation), modern corporation statutes do not prescribe such qualifications. Model Act §8.02; DGCL §141(b). Traditionally, corporations were required to have at least three directors. Modern corporation statutes usually allow boards to have only one director, with the exact number or a range to be specified in the charter or bylaws. Model Act §8.03(a); DGCL §141(b).

Generally speaking, the role of the board of directors is to manage or supervise the management of the corporation. Model Act §8.01(b); DGCL §141(a). In a public corporation, this role includes hiring, advising, supervising, and (when necessary) firing the chief executive officer of the corporation. Boards of public corporations typically meet anywhere from four to ten times a year and tend to be nominated by and supportive of management. As a result, most boards of public corporations play a limited role in the management of the corporation except in times of crisis.

Inside versus outside directors. In talking about directors, we generally distinguish "inside" directors from "outside" directors. Inside directors are people who are employed full time by the corporation as corporate officers, in addition to their roles on the board of directors. Inside directors on the board always include the chief executive officer (CEO), and may include various other top corporate officers, such as the chief financial officer (CFO); the chief operating officer (COO); and the general counsel. Outside directors are people who don't work for the corporation, other than as members of the board. If outside directors do not have any other financial relationship with the company, they are termed "independent." So an architect who has designed theme parks for the Disney Corporation would not be considered an independent director at Disney (although an outsider), while the headmaster of a private school where the Disney CEO's children used to go to school would be considered independent. One-third of the directors of companies listed on major exchanges are the CEOs of other companies. Other board members will typically include lawyers, university presidents, former senators, ambassadors or generals, accounting professors, and even the occasional law professor. In start-up companies and high-technology companies it is typical that venture capitalists have seats on the board, but in established companies the percentage of bankers on the board has dropped sharply over the last decade, perhaps because of concerns about conflicts of interest.

During various periods of concern about corporate governance and the integrity of companies' financial and other disclosure, such as during 2001-2002's "post-Enron" period, regulators such as the New York Stock Exchange, the SEC, and Congress have emphasized the importance of having a majority of outside, independent directors on the board. It is thought that by having a majority of outside directors, the quality of boards' decisionmaking will be enhanced, there will be greater monitoring of officers' performance, greater independence in decisionmaking and fewer conflict-of-interest situations. Whether this will turn out to be true is debatable. Surveys of board members themselves show that they are aware of the difficulty of defining "independence" clearly enough: a majority of board members surveyed in 2002 thought 25 percent of their "independent" colleagues were not truly independent. Moreover, 45 percent of board members thought that they themselves didn't spend enough time on the job to be able to truly understand a company's value drivers and the risks the company faces — in other words, its business. Given the limitations of time and information inherent in a part-time job, it is inevitable that outside directors, even if theoretically "independent," will necessarily be dependent upon inside directors and other consultants for knowledge about the companies on which they sit. Also, one-third of directors are typically CEOs of other companies. There is a shared understanding that might be termed "cultural" among CEOs; and thus again there are questions about how much independence we can expect from even independent outside directors.

Terms of office. All directors are elected by the shareholders at an annual shareholders' meeting, unless their terms are staggered, Model Act §8.03(c); DGCL §211(b), or a vacancy in a directorship occurs mid-term. The terms "staggered" and "classified" refer to a board that allows for classes of directors to be elected for multiple-year terms. The structure of staggered boards is such that there is always a majority of directors who are continuing without need for re-election. If, for instance, a nine-person board is divided into three classes, with three-year terms, then every year, three of the directors would be elected (or re-elected) for a three-year term, and six of the directors would remain on the board without needing to be re-elected.

Having a staggered board acts as a powerful anti-takeover device. One way to take control of a public corporation where the target corporation's board is unwilling to approve the "business combination" (merger or acquisition) is to change the composition of the board through a proxy contest — that is, for an "insurgent" to nominate its own slate of nominees for the board. For reasons that will become clear in our discussion of hostile takeovers (see Chapter 15), the insurgent in such a proxy contest would typically purchase 10 to 15 percent of the firm's outstanding shares prior to the shareholder vote, and would attempt to recruit other shareholders to support its position. It would make clear in its proxy solicitation that its nominees are committed to the business combination being proposed. If a board is staggered, an insurgent would be required to win two annual elections to gain a majority of seats on the board. Given the amount of time during which the insurgent would not have control of the company but would have a large financial stake, companies with staggered boards are not often successful targets of attempted hostile takeovers.

Model Act §8.05 specifies that each director holds office until the annual meeting following his or her election unless terms are staggered. DGCL §141(b) states the term of directors differently: under that section, each director holds office until his or her successor is elected and qualified or until his or her earlier resignation or removal.

Removal of directors. Generally speaking, directors may be removed from the board by shareholders, with or without cause, unless the charter provides that directors may be removed only for cause. Model Act §8.08(a); DGCL §141(k). One important consequence of having a staggered board in Delaware is that directors may only be removed for cause, unless the charter provides otherwise. DGCL §141(k). In other words, having a staggered board in Delaware shifts the default rule from one in which a "for cause" limitation on removal must be specified in the charter to a default rule in which there is a "for cause" limitation on removal unless the charter provides otherwise. In addition to removal by shareholders, Model Act §8.09 provides that directors may be removed by a judicial proceeding for fraudulent or dishonest conduct or gross abuse of authority.

Vacancies. Vacancies on the board of directors may occur because of the resignation, death, or removal of a director or by the creation of a new directorship. Directors may resign at any time, usually by delivering a written notice of resignation. Model Act §8.07(a); DGCL §141(b). Vacancies may be filled by the remaining directors or by the shareholders. Model Act §8.10(a); DGCL §223(a)(1). The power of the directors to create new directorships and then fill them can be used for strategic reasons by the board or a majority faction of the board where different factions of the board disagree about an important decision.

Board meetings and directors' action on consent. Traditionally, all actions by directors had to be taken at duly called meetings of the board. Although corporation statutes at one time required boards to meet within the state of incorporation, modern statutes have eliminated that requirement. Model Act §8.20(a); DGCL §141(g). In a further accommodation of modern practices, corporation statutes now permit directors to be considered "present" at a meeting — even if not physically present — if the director participates in the meeting by telephone or other similar communications device that allows the directors to hear each other. Model Act §8.20(b); DGCL §141(i).

Modern corporation statutes also permit directors to act without holding a meeting. Model Act §8.21 and DGCL §141(f) allow such action by written consent if all of the directors consent to the action, as long as the charter or bylaws of the corporation do not provide otherwise. Actions by written consent are particularly common in close corporations, where informal contacts among directors are common.

Directors may act at meetings that may be held regularly, as specified in the bylaws, or at a special meeting, which requires a notice of the date, time, and place of the meeting, but not the purpose (unless the charter or bylaws so require). Model Act §8.22. Directors may waive notice of a meeting, either in writing or simply by participating in the meeting. Model Act §8.23. A majority of directors being present satisfies statutory quorum requirements, but the charter or bylaws of the corporation may alter the quorum requirement to specify more or less than a majority. Model Act §8.24(a) and (b); DGCL §141(b). Once the directors are properly assembled, a majority vote of the directors present is required to act, unless the charter or bylaws prescribe a greater number. Model Act §8.24(c); DGCL §141(b).

Committees of the board. The board may act through committees comprised of directors. Model Act §8.25(a) (which allows committees of two or more directors); DGCL §141(c) (which authorizes committees of one or more members). In public corporations, the trend is toward companies having a number of powerful committees composed primarily or exclusively of outside directors. These committees include the audit committee, which is responsible for financial controls and risk assessment in the company; the nominating committee, which is responsible for nominating people to the board and to the committees; and the compensation committee, which is responsible for determining the compensation and other benefits of the top executive officers. In 2002 the New York Stock Exchange (NYSE) adopted corporate governance requirements for companies listed on the NYSE. These requirements substantially increased the responsibilities of these committees, including requirements that the audit and nominating committees be composed entirely of independent outside directors.

The rules governing meetings of the whole board of directors also govern meetings of the committees of the board. Model Act §8.25(c). Actions taken by committees of the board may carry the same weight as actions by the whole board of directors, Model Act §8.25(d); DGCL §141(c), but the corporation statutes place some limits on the matters that may be delegated to a committee. Model Act §8.25(e); DGCL §141(c). Generally, actions that will need to be put to a shareholder vote may not be delegated to a board committee, nor may a committee adopt, amend, or repeal bylaws of the corporation. Model Act §8.25(e); DGCL §141(c)(2). Nor, in a Model Act jurisdiction, may a committee fill vacancies on the board or authorize dividends, except pursuant to formulas the whole board has adopted. Model Act §8.25(e).

While the statutory provisions set out above are straightforward, they become problematic in cases where there is a crisis facing the corporation or there are conflicts among various groups on the board. The following cases not only offer a startling introduction to the rough and tumble world of battles for corporate control but highlight the striking contrast between the informality that pervades partnership law and the formality that permeates corporate law.

ADLERSTEIN v. WERTHEIMER

2002 WL 205684 (slip opinion)
Court of Chancery of Delaware
January 25, 2002

LAMB, Vice Chancellor.

I.

This is an action pursuant to Section 225 of the Delaware General Corporation Law ("DGCL") brought by Joseph Adlerstein, the former Chairman and CEO of SpectruMedix Corporation ("SpectruMedix" or "the Company"), a Delaware corporation. SpectruMedix is in the business of manufacturing and selling instruments to the genetics and pharmaceutical industries and is headquartered in State College, Pennsylvania. Adlerstein's complaint is against the Company and three individuals who claim to be the current directors of the Company: Steven N. Wertheimer, Judy K. Mencher, and Ilan Reich.

At issue in the Complaint are a series of actions taken on July 9, 2001, at or in conjunction with a purported meeting of the SpectruMedix board of directors held at the New York City offices of McDermott, Will & Emery ("MW & E").[1] First, a board majority (consisting of Wertheimer and Mencher) voted to issue to the I. Reich Family Limited Partnership ("Reich Partnership"), an entity affiliated with Reich, a sufficient number of shares of a new class of supervoting preferred stock to convey to the Reich Partnership a majority of the voting power of the Company's stock. Second, the same majority voted to remove Adlerstein for cause as Chief Executive Officer of the Company, to strip him of his title as Chairman of the Board, and to appoint Reich to serve as Chief Executive Officer and as Chairman of the Board. Third, immediately after the board meeting, the Reich Partnership executed and delivered to SpectruMedix

[handwritten margin notes: board voted to give Reich Partners enough preferred stock to make them the majority voting bloc. voted to remove Adlerstein as CEO, for cause. —Reich was made CEO & chairman.]

---

1. Over the years Adlerstein was represented in various personal capacities by Stephen Selbst, a partner in MW & E's New York City office. Eventually Selbst also began to serve as counsel to SpectruMedix. Selbst was present at the July 9 meeting and, as counsel to SpectruMedix, schemed with Wertheimer, Mencher, and Reich to engineer Adlerstein's ouster.

a written consent in lieu of stockholders meeting purporting to remove Adlerstein as a director. When the dust settled, the board consisted of Wertheimer, Mencher, and Reich; the Reich Partnership had replaced Adlerstein as holder of majority voting control; and Reich had replaced Adlerstein as Chairman and CEO.

Adlerstein seeks a determination that the July 9 meeting was not properly convened and, therefore, all actions taken at or in conjunction with that meeting are null and void. Adlerstein also contends that, even if the meeting was duly noticed and convened, the actions taken at the meeting by Wertheimer and Mencher were the product of a breach of the fiduciary duties they owed to him in his capacity as a director and the controlling stockholder.

II.

Adlerstein is a scientist and entrepreneur. He has a Ph.D. in physics and was involved with the funding and management of a number of start-up technology companies before founding SpectruMedix (originally named Premier American Technologies Company) in 1992.

Wertheimer, an investment banker, was introduced to Adlerstein by Selbst and was elected to the board by Adlerstein on January 1, 2000. Mencher is a money manager with an expertise in high yield and distressed investments. On Wertheimer's recommendation, Adlerstein elected Mencher to the board on March 22, 2000.

In 1997, SpectruMedix completed an initial public offering of its common stock, raising net proceeds of $4.67 million, more than half of which was used to repay existing indebtedness. SpectruMedix experienced substantial net losses over the next several years, "burning" through all of the cash raised in the IPO.

In July 1999, SpectruMedix entered into a series of agreements with Applied Biosystems, Inc. and certain of its affiliates. As a result of these agreements SpectruMedix received $5 million in cash in exchange for a sublicense to certain technology licensed by SpectruMedix, shares of SpectruMedix Series A Preferred Stock, and a consulting agreement. Following this transaction, apart from a small amount of revenue from the sale of instruments and related disposable products, SpectruMedix received no other funds between July 31, 1999 and July 9, 2001.

In 1999, to avoid a liquidity crisis, Adlerstein loaned SpectruMedix $500,000. In exchange, SpectruMedix gave Adlerstein a note that was convertible (at Adlerstein's option) into shares of a new Series B Preferred Stock of SpectruMedix that voted with the common and carried 80,000 votes per share. In January 2000, Adlerstein converted approximately $103,000 outstanding under this loan agreement into shares of Series B Preferred Stock. As a result, although Adlerstein owned only 21.41% of the equity of SpectruMedix, he controlled 73.27% of the voting power of the Company.

Late in 1999, before joining the board, Wertheimer convinced Adlerstein to hire Manus O'Donnell, an independent management consultant, to study and report on the status of the Company's management and finances. O'Donnell conducted his study and delivered a report dated January 2, 2000, in which he concluded that, unless the Company began making sales of instruments, it had sufficient cash and cash equivalents to continue operations only until September 2001.

During September 2000, as a result of increasing concern over Spectru-Medix's deteriorating financial condition, Wertheimer and Mencher convinced Adlerstein to re-hire O'Donnell. On September 15, 2000, O'Donnell updated his report, shortening the period during which sufficient cash reserves were forecasted. He stated:

> [S]ince my last forecast in December, the company burn rate has increased substantially . . . mainly due to increased headcount expense. As a result cash would last until May 2001 if grant money is received as predicted (at 115K per month from October onward). If grants are not received, then cash would be exhausted in January 2001.

As O'Donnell noted, the change in forecast was due in large part to Adlerstein's decision to increase staffing levels from 23 to 51. This headcount increase resulted in an escalation of the annual payroll by just over 100%. O'Donnell concluded by telling the board of directors that, at the then-current level of fixed expenses, SpectruMedix needed to sell and get paid for one machine per month in order to maintain an adequate cash position.

On March 28, 2001, a sexual harassment complaint was made against Adlerstein asserting that he threatened an employee's job because she objected to his inappropriate behavior toward her. An independent consultant was hired who, after an investigation, concluded that Adlerstein had been guilty of sexual harassment as defined in the Company's policy and had been less than candid in connection with the investigation. The consultant made an oral report of this conclusion to Wertheimer and Mencher on May 14, 2001. Because Adlerstein failed to pay the consultant's bill, a written report detailing the investigation was not delivered to the Company until September 2001.

On April 11, 2001, a meeting of the SpectruMedix board was held. At that meeting Adlerstein represented to the board, and the minutes of the meeting state, that three instruments had been purchased and shipped during the quarter ending March 31, 2001 and the Company was projecting sales of six to nine instruments for the quarter ending June 30, 2001. In fact, according to uncontroverted testimony, the Company sold only one instrument during the quarter ending March 31, 2001 and that sale was made on the condition that SpectruMedix would further develop the instrument to a commercially viable level of functionality.

During April 2001, Wertheimer and Mencher convinced Adlerstein to again hire O'Donnell to generate an updated report on the financial condition of the Company. The resulting report, which projected a cash balance of $66,000 for the Company as of May 31, 2001, was discussed at an April 30, 2001 meeting of the board. As reflected in the board's minutes for that meeting Adlerstein on the one hand and Wertheimer and Mencher on the other had very different reactions to the Company's financial state:

> [Adlerstein] did not regard the situation as quite as desperate as the other directors. He said that the Company had previously faced similar cash crises and had weathered them. He said that he had found money to keep the Company alive in the past, and if required to do so again, he would find the resources. Mr. Wertheimer and Ms. Mencher lauded him for his past efforts to save the Company,

but said that the[y] were seeking to bring the Company to a cash neutral or profitable position as promptly as possible. The point, Ms. Mencher said, was to put the Company in a position where Dr. Adlerstein wouldn't be required to keep the Company afloat personally in the future.

This divergence in perspective continued through the July 9 meeting.

The board met again on May 25, 2001. Adlerstein reported that the Company was "low on cash" but delivered an upbeat report on the status of discussions he was having with several potential strategic partners. Wertheimer and Mencher remained concerned about the Company's deteriorating financial condition and began to question seriously the information Adlerstein was providing to them. As Mencher testified:

> [I]t became clear that we were not getting the entire picture of what was going on with the company and that the company was quickly heading . . . toward a major liquidity crisis — if it wasn't already in one — and that the company needed a crisis manager, just for somebody to get in and tell the board what was really going on and how long the company had to survive.

Thus, Wertheimer and Mencher suggested that the Company should again hire O'Donnell's firm to help the Company in reducing expenses and improving the instrument manufacturing process. Adlerstein agreed, and the entire board unanimously resolved to do so. O'Donnell and his colleague, Gordon Mason, agreed to take on such an assignment provided SpectruMedix execute a written consulting agreement.

During the month of June 2001, O'Donnell and members of his firm began to play a hands-on role at the Company's headquarters, reducing the number of employees while improving the instrument manufacturing process. Among other things, they drew up an organizational chart that defined lines of authority and responsibility in the Company, something Adlerstein had refused to do. These changes were met enthusiastically by the Company's senior employees.

Adlerstein conducted a rearguard action against O'Donnell's restructuring efforts. Most notably, he refused to sign a written contract with O'Donnell, notwithstanding the direction of the board that he do so. He also was frequently away from headquarters in State College during June but, when he did appear, acted to undo changes that had been implemented. Eventually, O'Donnell and Mason stopped working. Wertheimer and Mencher concluded that Adlerstein was intentionally impeding the progress of the consultants and resolved to investigate the situation at SpectruMedix for themselves.

Wertheimer contacted three of the four department heads at the Company and learned that these individuals were planning to quit their jobs with SpectruMedix if organizational and other changes implemented by the consultants were not kept in place. On July 2, 2001, O'Donnell forwarded a report to Wertheimer and Mencher which concluded that Adlerstein was "the central problem" at the Company, because "he is totally lacking in managerial and business competence and has demonstrated an unwillingness to accept these shortcomings." O'Donnell further opined: "For SpectruMedix to have any chance, [Adlerstein] must be removed from any operating influence within the company."

In June 2001, Wertheimer contacted Reich to discuss involving him as both an investor and manager of SpectruMedix. Wertheimer knew that Reich had the personal wealth and managerial experience to take on a restructuring of SpectruMedix.[7] As he testified at trial: "Ilan was the only guy I knew that had money and had the skills to go in and . . . pull this out of the fire. . . . No institutional investor would go anywhere near a company like this. It had to be somebody that liked to get his hands dirty, who liked to go into a company and basically try and make something out of something that was in a lot of trouble."

On June 27, 2001, Reich met with Selbst and O'Donnell to discuss the business of SpectruMedix. Adlerstein was unaware of this meeting. The next day, Reich and Adlerstein met in New York. Reich testified that he then determined that he would only be willing to invest in SpectruMedix if he, and not Adlerstein, were in charge of the Company. Reich thereafter executed a confidentiality agreement and received non-public information in due diligence.

On June 30, Reich sent an e-mail to Selbst that referred to an upcoming meeting between Selbst and Wertheimer for the purpose of discussing Adlerstein's Series B Preferred shares. Adlerstein was not copied on this e-mail and was not aware of this meeting. Also on June 30, Wertheimer had a discussion with Reich about firing Adlerstein.

On July 2, 2001, Reich participated in a conference call with Wertheimer and Mencher and later that day met with Wertheimer to discuss his potential investment. At that meeting, the option of firing Adlerstein for cause from his position as CEO due to his sexual harassment of a Company employee was discussed, as was Adlerstein's voting control over the Company. Adlerstein had no idea this meeting was taking place. But by this time Reich knew he would have an opportunity to take over SpectruMedix.

On July 3, 2001, Reich met with various department heads of the Company during a due diligence visit to the SpectruMedix headquarters. Aware of this visit, Adlerstein acted to discourage senior officials at State College from cooperating fully with Reich. As he e-mailed one of the Company's principal scientists:

> I am not willing to have you spend an inordinate amount of time satisfying [Reich's] . . . requests at the risk of exposing our innards (*i.e.* technologies, analysis) to someone . . . who, in the final analysis, is by no means a sure thing to invest in [SpectruMedix].

A. SPECTRUMEDIX'S INSOLVENCY

By the beginning of July 2001, if not earlier, SpectruMedix was either insolvent or operating on the brink of insolvency.[10] The Company had very little cash (or cash equivalents) and no material accounts receivable due. At the same time, the Company had substantial and increasing accounts payable, Adlerstein was not communicating with creditors, and key parts vendors were refusing to make deliveries unless paid in cash. Indisputably, SpectruMedix did not have

---

7. Wertheimer was aware that in the mid-1980s Reich had pleaded guilty to federal charges of trading on inside information while he was a partner in a prominent New York City law firm and served a one-year prison sentence. Nevertheless, he also knew that, from 1998 to 2000, Reich was employed as the President and CEO of Inamed Corporation, a publicly traded company, and had accomplished a significant turnaround of that company. Wertheimer knew that Reich had left Inamed in 2001 and might be interested in a new challenge.

10. According to [the defendants' exhibits], an unaudited balance sheet as of June 30, 2001, SpectruMedix had $89,293 in cash and certificates of deposit and $2,404,135 in accounts payable.

sufficient cash on hand to meet its next employee payroll on July 13, 2001, and had <u>no realistic expectation of receiving</u> sufficient funds to do so from <u>its operations</u>. Moreover, <u>the Company's auditors were unwilling to issue the opinion letter necessary for it to file an annual report with the SEC, which was due to be filed on July 10th</u>.

B. THE JULY 9, 2001 BOARD MEETING

1. Notice

<u>Wertheimer testified that,</u> on or about July 5, 2001, he and Adlerstein spoke <u>on the telephone about the deteriorating financial condition of the Company and matters relating to a significant arbitration involving SpectruMedix</u>.[11] In that proceeding, <u>MW & E had</u> <u>moved to withdraw as counsel to Spec-truMedix, as a result, among other things,</u> of disputes over non-payment of <u>fees and expenses</u>. Wertheimer and Adlerstein may have discussed the fact that the arbitrator planned to hold a conference on the motion to withdraw on Monday, July 9, and wished to be able to speak to Adlerstein by telephone. Wertheimer testified that, during this conversation, <u>Adlerstein agreed to convene a meeting of the board of directors at 11 A.M. on July 9, 2001, at MW & E's New York City offices</u>. Wertheimer further testified that Adlerstein was aware that the topics to be discussed at the meeting would be (i) SpectruMedix's dire financial condition and immediate need for cash, (ii) the arbitration, including the need to retain new counsel, (iii) the formal execution of an agreement to retain O'Donnell, and (iv) the Company's certified public accountants' refusal to issue an audit opinion. <u>Adlerstein maintains that, while he agreed to meet with Wertheimer on July 9 in MW & E's offices, the only purpose of that meeting was to be available to speak to the arbitrator about the motion to withdraw. He denies that he ever agreed to call a board meeting for that time or knew that one was to be held</u>.

The trial record contains plainly divergent testimony on the subject of whether Adlerstein called the July 9 meeting or was given notice of it. <u>Mencher, Reich, and Selbst all support Wertheimer's testimony, although they all learned about the meeting from Wertheimer</u>. Thus, <u>while their testimony is corroborative of his, it provides no independent evidence of Adlerstein's state of knowledge</u>. Adlerstein's trial testimony was undermined by Karl Fazler, the Company's business manager, who spoke with Adlerstein on the morning of July 9, and remembered <u>Adlerstein telling him that he was on his way to MW & E's offices in order to meet with the board of directors</u>. At the same time, <u>Adlerstein's testimony is buttressed</u>, to some degree, by the fact that none of the directors received written notice of a meeting although, the evidence suggests, SpectruMedix usually <u>circulated notice and a proposed agenda by e-mail</u>.

2. Adlerstein was kept in the dark about the Reich proposal

Mencher's notes show that Reich first proposed terms for an acquisition of SpectruMedix no later than July 5. On that date, she had a teleconference with Wertheimer and Reich in which they discussed the outline of the transaction

---

11. The other party to the arbitration was Iowa State University Research Foundation, the licensor of core technologies used in SpectruMedix's instrumentation. The arbitration posed a substantial risk to the future viability of SpectruMedix.

and the need to terminate Adlerstein. Her notes contain the entry "fire Joe + negotiate a settlement," followed by a summary of terms for his separation.

The documents necessary for a transaction with Reich were in draft form by July 6, 2001. Selbst sent these documents by e-mail to Wertheimer, Mencher, and Reich. He did not send them to Adlerstein, who was deliberately kept unaware that Reich had made a proposal until the July 9 meeting. At trial, Wertheimer was asked whether "[b]etween the time you got the proposal from Mr. Reich — until the time you walked in to the board meeting on July 9th, did you tell Doctor Adlerstein that you were negotiating a proposal with Ilan Reich . . . [?]" He responded that he had not:

> *A.* Because I wanted to save the company at that point. . . . So, no, I didn't tell him that this was going on, because I had no faith that he would — that he would, first of all, you know, go along with the deal; but secondly, I was also worried that he would do something to scare off the investor.

Although Adlerstein argues that the Reich proposal was finalized on Friday, July 6, the record supports the conclusion that Reich and Wertheimer were still negotiating some terms of the deal on the morning of July 9 and that final documents were not ready until that time. The deal finally negotiated provided, subject to board approval, that the Reich Partnership would invest $1 million in SpectruMedix, Reich would assume the active management of SpectruMedix, and SpectruMedix would issue shares of its Series C Preferred Stock to the Reich Partnership carrying with them voting control of the Company.

3. The meeting occurs

Adlerstein arrived late at MW & E's New York City offices to find Selbst and Wertheimer waiting for him. He inquired about the conference with the arbitrator and was told that the matter had been postponed. Mencher was hooked in by phone and, according to Wertheimer, Adlerstein called the meeting to order and "wanted to talk about lawyers and the arbitration." Wertheimer then interrupted and said that they needed to talk about finances. He then told Adlerstein that there was a proposal from Reich and handed him a term sheet showing the material elements of the deal.

After reviewing it, Adlerstein told Wertheimer and Mencher that he was not interested in the Reich proposal because it would dilute his shares in the Company and result in him losing voting control. He has since testified that his lack of interest was also because he believed the price of $1 million to be insufficient for control of SpectruMedix. He did not, however, voice this concern at the time.

In response to the objection that he did voice, Wertheimer and Mencher explained that in their judgment the Company was in immediate need of funds and the investment by Reich was needed to avoid liquidation. Wertheimer asked Adlerstein directly if he was personally in a position to provide the needed funds. Adlerstein responded that he was not.

Wertheimer and Mencher tried to engage Adlerstein in further discussion about the Reich proposal, but Adlerstein sat silent. He testified that the reason for his silence was advice given to him by Selbst in the past: "when in doubt about what to do in a situation like this, keep your mouth shut." Because

[handwritten margin note: when presented w/ a vote on the Reich proposal Adlerstein said nothing he said The others say he voted no.]

he and Mencher could not get Adlerstein to engage in any dialogue regarding the proposed transaction, Wertheimer moved the transaction for a vote. Wertheimer testified:

> There was no use in talking about it, because [Adlerstein] wouldn't talk. . . . So the fact that the discussion didn't go any longer, the finger should not be pointed at us, it should be pointed at the person that cut off the discussion. That is Doctor Adlerstein.

Adlerstein has testified that when the vote on the transaction was called he did not participate. The minutes of the meeting reflect that he voted "no." Each of the others present at the meeting—Wertheimer, Mencher, and Selbst—confirms the statement in the minutes.

[handwritten margin note: They then moved to remove him for cause.]

The board then took up the question of removing Adlerstein "for cause" from his office as CEO and Chairman of SpectruMedix. The elements of "cause" assigned were mismanagement of the Company, misrepresentations to his fellow board members as to its financial situation, and sexual harassment in contravention of his employment contract. After the meeting, the Reich Partnership executed and delivered a stockholder's written consent removing Adlerstein as a director of SpectruMedix. Reich was chosen to replace him.

Some months after July 9, Adlerstein executed a written consent purporting to vote his Series B Preferred shares to remove Wertheimer and Mencher from the board. Adlerstein initiated this Section 225 action on September 11, 2001.

[handwritten margin note: ouch!]

III.

The general purpose of Section 225 is to provide "a quick method of review of the corporate election process in order to prevent a corporation from being immobilized by controversies as to who are its proper officers and directors."[20] Because it is summary in nature, a Section 225 proceeding is limited to those issues that must necessarily be considered in order to resolve a disputed corporate election process. A Section 225 action focuses narrowly on the corporate election at issue and is not an appropriate occasion to resolve matters ancillary or secondary to that election.

[handwritten margin note: it focuses on corporate elections & is not to be used to resolve ancillary or secondary issues!]

Here, the question is whether the meeting held on July 9 was a meeting of the board of directors or not. If it was not, Adlerstein continues to exercise a majority of the voting power and is now the sole lawful director. If it was, I must then address a welter of arguments advanced by Adlerstein to prove that the actions taken at the July 9 meeting ought to be invalidated because Wertheimer and Mencher (and Selbst) all operated in secret to negotiate terms with Reich while keeping Adlerstein deliberately uninformed about their plan to present the Reich proposal at the July 9 meeting. The more persuasive of these arguments are predicated largely on the decisions of the Court of Chancery in VGS, Inc. v. Castiel[23] and Koch v. Stearn.[24]

[handwritten margin note: If the July 9 mtg wasn't valid, Adlerstein holds majority voting power & now is the sole lawful director.]

[handwritten margin note: also:]

Finally, if all else fails, Adlerstein argues that Wertheimer and Mencher violated their fiduciary duties of care and loyalty to SpectruMedix in approving the

---

20. Bossier v. Connell, 1986 Del. Ch. LEXIS 471, at *5 (Del. Ch. Oct. 7, 1986).
23. 2000 Del. Ch. LEXIS 122 (Del. Ch. Aug. 31, 2000).
24. 1992 Del. Ch. LEXIS 163 (Del. Ch. July 28, 1992).

Reich transaction with inadequate information and on terms that were unfair to the Company and its stockholders. He asks for an order canceling the shares and disregarding any effort by Reich to vote them.

For the reasons next discussed, I conclude that, although the meeting of July 9 was called as a board meeting, the actions taken at it must be invalidated. Thus, it is unnecessary to reach the last issue presented by Adlerstein.

HOLDING:
> *
thus no need to look at the fiduciary duty issue.

A. THE CALL OF THE MEETING

On balance, the evidence at trial indicates that Adlerstein called the July 9 meeting. The procedure for giving notice of a board meeting is typically set forth in a Company's certificate or bylaws. The bylaws of SpectruMedix provide that special meetings of the board "may be called by the president on two (2) days' notice to each director by mail or forty-eight (48) hours notice to each director either personally or by telegram. . . ." I credit Wertheimer's account of his July 5 telephone call with Adlerstein. There is no reason to believe that Adlerstein would not have agreed to convene a board meeting on July 9, in view of the many urgent problems confronting SpectruMedix at that time. Fazler's testimony that Adlerstein called him on the morning of the meeting and said that he was on his way to a board meeting provides additional support for Wertheimer on this point. . . .

Notice for special mtg is set out in the bylaws; can be called by pres. w/ 2 days' no tice to each director. Mtg seems to comply.

B. THE VALIDITY OF THE ACTIONS TAKEN AT THE JULY 9 MEETING

A more difficult issue is whether the decision of Wertheimer, Mencher, and Selbst (no doubt with the knowledge of Reich) to keep Adlerstein uninformed about their plan to present the Reich proposal for consideration at the July 9 meeting invalidates the board's approval of that proposal at the meeting.

Weighing against invalidating:

There are several factors that weigh against a finding of invalidity. The first is the absence from SpectruMedix's bylaws of any requirement of prior notice of agenda items for meetings of the board of directors, coupled with the absence of any hard and fast legal rule that directors be given advance notice of all matters to be considered at a meeting. Second, is the good faith belief of Wertheimer and Mencher that Adlerstein should be removed from management and that, if they had told him about the Reich proposal ahead of time, he would have done something to kill the deal. Third, is the fact of SpectruMedix's insolvency and the argument that the exigencies created by that insolvency gave Wertheimer and Mencher legal warrant to "spring" the Reich proposal on Adlerstein without warning.

[1]
*[2] * that he would have sabotaged that deal.*
[3] company's insolvency.

Ultimately, I am unable to agree that these factors, either singly or in the aggregate, provide legal justification for the conduct of the July 9 meeting. Instead, I conclude that in the context of the set of legal rights that existed within SpectruMedix at the time of the July 9 meeting, Adlerstein was entitled to know ahead of time of the plan to issue new Series C Preferred Stock with the purposeful effect of destroying his voting control over the Company. This right to advance notice derives from a basic requirement of our corporation law that boards of directors conduct their affairs in a manner that satisfies minimum standards of fairness.

These factors are not enough to justify the July 9th mtg:

Here, the decision to keep Adlerstein in the dark about the plan to introduce the Reich proposal was significant because Adlerstein possessed the contractual power to prevent the issuance of the Series C Preferred Stock by executing a written consent removing one or both of Wertheimer and Mencher from the board. He may or may not have exercised this power had he been told about the plan in advance. But he was fully entitled to the opportunity to do so and the machinations of those individuals who deprived him of this opportunity were unfair and cannot be countenanced by this court.[28] . . .

Wertheimer and Mencher argue that SpectruMedix's dire financial circumstances and actual or impending insolvency justify their actions because, they believe, it was necessary to keep Adlerstein uninformed in order for them to "save the Company." From the record at trial, it is fair to conclude that SpectruMedix was insolvent as of July 9, 2001, in the sense that it was unable to meet its obligations as they came due. This was already true of ordinary supply contracts and fees for its attorneys and consultants. It was also about to be true for a payroll due a few days after the July 9 meeting. Nevertheless, I conclude that these facts do not alter the outcome of the case. Quite the opposite, it is in such times of dire consequence that the well established rules of good board conduct are most important.

While it is true that a board of directors of an insolvent corporation or one operating in the vicinity of insolvency has fiduciary duties to creditors and others as well as to its stockholders, it is not true that our law countenances, permits, or requires directors to conduct the affairs of an insolvent corporation in a manner that is inconsistent with principles of fairness or in breach of duties owed to the stockholders. . . .

There is authority in this court suggesting the possibility that a board of directors could, "consistent with its fiduciary duties, issue a dilutive option in order to protect the corporation or its minority shareholders from exploitation by a controlling shareholder who was in the process of threatening to violate his fiduciary duties to the corporation."[34] Nevertheless, neither this nor any other authority suggests that directors could accomplish such action through trickery or deceit, and I am not prepared to hold otherwise.[35] . . .

28. The outcome in this case flows from the fact the Adlerstein was both a director and a controlling stockholder, not from either status individually. In the absence of some special contractual right, there is no authority to support the argument that Adlerstein's stockholder status entitled him to advance notice of actions proposed to be taken at a meeting of the board of directors. The actions may be voidable if improperly motivated. Condec v. Lunkenheimer, 230 A.2d 769, 775 (Del. Ch.1967). But the absence (or presence) of notice is not a critical factor. Similarly, in the absence of a bylaw or other custom or regulation requiring that directors be given advance notice of items proposed for action at board meetings, there is no reason to believe that the failure to give such notice alone would ordinarily give rise to a claim of invalidity. Dillon v. Berg, 326 F. Supp. 1214, 1221 (D. Del.), aff'd, 453 F.2d 876 (3d Cir. 1971). Nevertheless, when a director either is the controlling stockholder or represents the controlling stockholder, our law takes a different view of the matter where the decision to withhold advance notice is done for the purpose of preventing the controlling stockholder/director from exercising his or her contractual right to put a halt to the other directors' schemes.

34. Mendel v. Carroll, 651 A.2d 297, 306 (Del. Ch. 1994).

35. Of course, as Chancellor Allen noted in Mandel, "if the principal motivation for such dilution is simply to maintain corporate control . . . it would violate the norm of loyalty." 651 A.2d at 304. This principle was firmly established in Condec, 230 A.2d 769. The corollary proposition would appear to be equally true: i.e., an action taken primarily to divest a stockholder of control and transfer that control to another would also seem afoul of "the norm of loyalty."

PROBLEM 6-1

Bigmar, Inc. is a Delaware corporation that manufactures and markets generic pharmaceuticals in Europe. The company was founded by John Tramontana, who served as chairman and chief executive officer. When Bigmar needed additional capital in 1999, Tramontana decided to explore U.S. capital markets, and Bigmar's New York-based attorney introduced Tramontana to Cynthia May and her father, Harold Baldauf. Tramontana would come to rue this day.

In their interactions with Tramontana, May and Baldauf described themselves as "wealthy people" having "connections with the investment community." In addition, May represented herself as having "many degrees" and claimed to be running an investment fund called Marathon. In fact, she did not graduate from college and her work experience was limited. Her only management experience prior to her association with Bigmar was in connection with a failed pharmaceutical company. As the company's president, May had been sued for breach of fiduciary duty. Moreover, May and Baldauf had virtually no significant connections with the investment community. Their only access to financing was through their long-standing relationship with Citizens Bank, a local Saginaw, Michigan, retail bank.

Nevertheless, Tramontana was impressed by their initial meeting. He eventually allowed May and Baldauf to invest in Bigmar. Tramontana also reciprocated by investing in Jericho II, LLC, a company formed by May and Baldauf that later invested heavily in Bigmar stock.

Over time, the relationship between May and Bigmar became more involved. While she had started as a passive investor, by November 2001 she was sitting on Bigmar's board and serving as its President. She had moved all of Bigmar's financial records to her home office, and had become the lead representative of Bigmar in all financing negotiations. Finally, she had obtained from Tramontana a Delegation of Authority that authorized her to vote all of Jericho's Bigmar shares.

The Delegation of Authority appears to have been obtained through deceit. Jericho had taken out $6.7 million of loans from Citizens Bank to purchase Bigmar shares, and in May 2000, May told Tramontana that the loans were in default. (She never provided written evidence of the default.) This surprised Tramontana, who had been making payments to Jericho for the purpose of servicing these loans. When Tramontana was unable to provide sufficient funds to cure the default, May suggested a loan from Baldauf. According to May, however, her father would make such a loan only if she were given exclusive authority to vote Jericho's Bigmar shares. Believing that he had no alternative, Tramontana acceded to this condition. When combined with the shares already owned by May and Baldauf, these shares owned by Jericho gave May voting control of Bigmar.

Meanwhile, Bigmar was running out of money again. May entered into negotiations with venture capitalists, but she was using unrealistic financial projections. One venture capitalist told May that he was impressed with the company's products and operations, but he felt that "Bigmar is out of control." At the end of October 2001, May wrote an e-mail to Tramontana to explain that Bigmar was unable to pay its debts. She concluded, "I hope you can raise the money needed quickly, I am at a dead end here."

Shortly thereafter, Bigmar received a funding proposal from a venture capitalist, but the proposal was contingent on May relinquishing control. The venture capitalist "had serious concerns as to her understanding of finance and her ability to manage this company to success." Understandably, May turned her back on this proposal, favoring instead a proposal from another venture investor (Fusion Capital Partners) that—according to all of the Bigmar directors other than May—would not solve Bigmar's cash problems and would result in significant dilution of the existing investors. Nevertheless, through a series of artful misrepresentations and omissions, May was able to convince the directors to consent to the deal. Tramontana and the other directors thought that they were consenting to the negotiation of a term sheet—as opposed to entering into a definitive contract—and when Tramontana later insisted that Bigmar should explore other options, May sent him the following e-mail:

> I wish for God's sake that you would GROW [UP] just a little . . . I can't move. WE DO NOT HAVE THE AGREEMTS SIGNED AND BACK. . . . . . you've F–ed the banking up here in Sweden so I can't get the money that I made [arrangements] for . . . I could care less that you don't have any money in Switzerland . . . The STORY HAS NEVER CHANGED, except you always f. it up . . . by not following up on the details . . . and not listening . . . you can't follow a straight line without having your ego and little hissy fits . . . because it's easier to make fun of Cindy than do the work needed. . . . Get off the play ground . . . before the big boys beat you up. . . .

Then Cindy May started sending crazy e-mails.

In response, Tramontana sent May an e-mail asking her to resign as President and Secretary of Bigmar. Apparently, May never responded to this request.

Shortly thereafter, another proposal for financing emerged, this time from an existing Bigmar investor (Banca del Gottardo) and the same venture capitalist whose proposal May rejected earlier. That venture capitalist sent the following e-mail to Tramontana:

> As a start, I believe that we are in agreement as to the need to address the situation at Bigmar. Though we have different motivations for solving the Bigmar problem (yours relating to the need to protect you[r] current investors and ours involving the belief that Bigmar represents a tremendous oppurtunity [sic] if it can be correctly positioned), I believe that we both understand the need to take immediate, dramatic action. As we both heard, John is currently spending 40+% of his time simply dealing with the issues surrounding Cindy's combative attitude and lack of experience in both Pharmaceuticals as well as finance. This, coupled with numerous examples of factual misstatement and outright deception have made it clear to us that the only way that this company can move forward is to break Cindy's de facto control of the board of directors through the 4-4 split that currently exists and the control block she holds on the common stock. Specific examples of improper behavior are: a. No minutes being kept of any board meetings even though Cindy is the Secretary of the corporation. b. Cindy forcing John to surrender his voting rights on the Jehrico [sic] shares even though he guarantees 50% of the note used to purchase the stock. c. Cindy continuing to use patently false financial information in her road shows, even after being expressly told that it was false and being instructed to remove it. d. Cindy pushing her way through board votes with John being forced to abstain after being

told that as Chairman he could vote if their [*sic*] was a tie. e. Cindy forcing off a director from the board by saying that as a majority share holder [*sic*] she had the right to do so without a vote. f. Cindy pushing through a consulting contract for her father of $1,500,000 over three years (basically $70,000 per month) for fund raising and strategic advise [*sic*]—none of which has been performed. The list goes on.

To resolve their problems with May, the venture capitalist suggested having the Bank exercise its contractual right to appoint two additional directors to the board. The board could then embrace the new financing proposal and terminate May's employment with Bigmar. The Bank agreed with this suggestion. Before they could carry out the plan, however, May presented Tramontana with a signed agreement for an investment by Fusion Capital Partners.

Tramontana decided to call a board meeting. On November 14, 2001, Tramontana sent an electronic notice for a special meeting of the board of directors to be held on November 16. The notice explained that the meeting would be held by teleconference "at 10:00 A.M., Eastern Daylight time (GMT-05:00)" to discuss "the illiquidity situation of the corporation," "the sale of $2,000,000 of shares of Bigmar to [the Bank]," and "such other matters as may be properly brought before the meeting." The notice also stated, in capital letters, "IT IS VERY IMPORTANT THAT YOU WILL BE AVAILABLE FOR THE FOLLOWING MEETING. PLEASE SUPPLY YOUR CONTACT NUMBERS AS SOON AS POSSIBLE TO GIANMARIA ALIPPI AT [e-mail address and telephone number]." All of the directors received the notice.

On November 16, Tramontana gathered or called all of the directors who had provided contact information, as requested in the notice. May and the three directors associated with her did not provide contact information and did not participate in the meeting. That left five directors to participate in the meeting. Assume that these directors unanimously resolved to expand the size of the board from nine to eleven members, and to fill the two newly created positions with two nominees of the Bank. In addition, assume that these five directors approved the financing proposal from the Bank. Finally, assume the directors voted to remove May as President and Secretary of Bigmar, and to amend the bylaws to require a vote of 66⅔ percent of the shareholders to remove a director.

Was the board meeting validly convened? In considering this question, note that the bylaws of Bigmar require all notices of board meetings to be sent by the company's secretary (that would have been May at the time of the notice) and to name the place of the meeting.

What if the board meeting never actually occurred? In a strange twist, May claimed that Tramontana and the other directors never actually met. They produced minutes of a meeting, and all but one of the five directors who claimed to have been present testified at a trial that the meeting took place. Nevertheless, the minutes were actually written by Bigmar's lawyer, who was not present at the meeting; and there were no independent witnesses or other corroborating evidence that the meeting occurred. Indeed, telephone records that could have substantiated the occurrence of such a meeting were not produced. Assume for the sake of argument that the meeting did not actually occur. Should the actions of the five directors be invalidated?

B. SHAREHOLDERS

As we have seen, owners of common stock of a corporation have economic rights to the residual assets of a corporation, as well as the right to be free from personal liability for the obligations of the corporation in most circumstances. In addition, common shareholders have some control rights in the corporation, which they exercise mainly by voting—for the election or removal of directors, on charter amendments or amendments to the bylaws, and on other fundamental changes to the corporation, such as a merger. Shareholders also have the power to bring suits to prevent or remedy mismanagement by the directors or officers of the corporation. The following materials cover shareholder meetings and voting. Chapter 12 discusses the shareholders' power with respect to initiating litigation.

Keep in mind that the powers to vote and sue do not exhaust the full range of shareholders' powers. In a public corporation, shareholders always have another important option: the power to follow the "Wall Street Rule" and sell their shares. This option presumably keeps members of management focused on demonstrating to its shareholders, quarter by quarter, that the company is being well-managed and that share values are going up.

1. Shareholder Voting

State rules governing shareholder voting in corporations are quite simple:

(1) Each share of common stock carries one vote. DGCL §212(a); Model Act §7.21(a).

(2) Shareholders vote on the election of directors (DGCL §211(b); Model Act §§8.03, 8.08), and on certain fundamental transactions: (A) Amending the corporation's charter: DGCL §242(b); Model Act §10.03; (B) Amending the by-laws: DGCL §109(a); Model Act §10.20(a); (C) Approving a merger: DGCL §251(c); Model Act §11.03; (D) Approving the sale of assets not in the ordinary course of business, i.e., selling all or substantially all of the assets of the company: DGCL §271; Model Act §12.02; and (E) Approving the dissolution of the company. DGCL §275(b); Model Act §14.02. Finally, shareholders may vote to ratify conflict-of-interest transactions: DGCL §144(a)(2); Model Act §8.61(b)(2).

(3) Shareholders may vote at a shareholders' meeting either in person or by proxy. DGCL §212(b); Model Act §7.22(a).

(4) Majority vote wins except in director elections, when only a plurality is required. DGCL §§216 (2) and (3); Model Act §7.28 (a).

Most of these rules may be altered within prescribed limits by provisions in the corporation's charter or bylaws. In addition, the law provides that shareholders may aggregate their votes in a shareholders' agreement or a voting trust, which are control devices used in closely held corporations but not public corporations.

Proxy Voting. At common law, all shareholder votes were required to be cast in person. Modern statutes allow shareholders to vote their shares either in person or by proxy. DGCL §212(b); Model Act §7.22(a). A "proxy" is the authorization given by a shareholder to another person to vote the shareholder's shares.

The holder of a proxy is an agent subject to the control of the shareholder and having fiduciary duties to the shareholder. Although proxies may be used occasionally for voting in close corporations, especially as a control allocation device, voting by proxy is clearly the norm in public corporations. And because voting is the primary mechanism by which shareholders exert influence over the corporation, proxy voting has been a battleground in the struggle for control of public corporations.

Voting Rules. Generally, voting for directors is done by "straight voting," under which a majority voting coalition will win every seat on the board. Voting in a corporation is different from voting in a polity, because under straight voting, each shareholder votes all of his or her shares with respect to each open seat on the board. So if a person owns 100 shares of Company A and there are nine open seats on a nine-person board of directors, that person can vote 100 shares for each of the nine people nominated. Thus, if one shareholder or a voting coalition owns 51 percent of the shares of a company, under straight voting that majority block will elect each director, since they will be able to outvote the other shareholders 51 percent to 49 percent with respect to each nominee for each open seat. (Recall, however, that the overwhelming majority of board elections are uncontested and simply engender a "vote of confidence" for the nominees that the board's nominating committee has proposed.)

Another system, called "cumulative voting," allows shareholders to concentrate their voting power by "cumulating" all of the votes associated with their shares and voting them in a block for a limited number of nominees. The effect of cumulative voting is to assure minority shareholders' representation on the board in proportion to their voting strength. Thus, in the above example our hypothetical shareholder could vote her 100 shares times nine (the number of open seats), or 900 votes, and cast all 900 votes for one nominee, or she could distribute them among multiple nominees. Based on a simple mathematical formula, one can determine the maximum voting power a shareholder would have for a given number of shares and the number of open seats, and thus how many seats on the board she could be assured of winning.[1] In both the Delaware statute and the Model Act, the default rule is straight voting, while companies have the power to opt in to cumulative voting in the charter or bylaws. (DGCL §214; Model Act §7.28(b)). Cumulative voting is more common in close corporations as a control device than it is in public corporations. A study in 2001 of 350 companies going public for the first time in the 1990s showed that 13 percent of them had bylaw provisions providing for cumulative voting, so it is clearly a minority of public companies that use this voting device. *See* John C. Coates, IV, *Explaining Variation in Takeover Defenses: Blame the Lawyers*, 89 C.L.R. 1301 (2001).

---

1. To elect N number of directors, a shareholder would need $SN/(D+1)+1$ shares, where S is the number of shares voting, and D is the number of directors to be elected. As the number of directors to be elected goes down, as in a small board or a classified board, the number of shares that a minority shareholder would need to hold to be assured of board representation goes up.

2. *Shareholder Meetings*

Annual Meeting. The traditional method by which shareholders act is through voting at the annual meeting or by proxy in conjunction with the annual meeting. Corporation statutes provide for annual meetings for the election of directors, and unless directors are elected by written consent instead of at an annual meeting, which would be unusual in a public corporation outside of a contest for control, corporation statutes require that companies hold an annual meeting. DGCL §211(b); Model Act §7.01. The shareholders are given the power to seek a judicial order setting a date for the annual meeting if there has been a failure to hold the annual meeting as required. DGCL §211(c); Model Act §7.03(a)(1).

Special Meetings. Corporations statutes also permit the calling of special meetings to vote on particular issues that may arise between annual meetings. DGCL §211(d); Model Act §7.02. Special meetings are often called to replace the directors as part of a hostile takeover attempt or to seek the shareholders' approval of a friendly takeover or merger proposal. ("Hostile" takeovers are those that do not have the support of the board of the "target" company to be taken over. "Friendly" takeovers are the merger of two companies or the acquisition of one company by another in which the boards of both companies support the business combination. The lines can blur, since in some cases a "friendly" deal is chilly, but the target board goes along with it because of the power of the acquirer to replace the board and do a hostile takeover.) In Delaware, the board has the power to call a special meeting; the shareholders may have this power if it is granted to them in the charter or bylaws. DGCL §211(d). In a Model Act jurisdiction, the board or a 10 percent shareholder has the power to call a special meeting. Model Act §7.02(2). Clearly, the power of the shareholders to call a special meeting, as provided for in the Model Act and in some corporation's charters or bylaws, has important implications for how power is allocated in a company between the shareholders and the directors.

Acting on Consent. Traditionally shareholders were not allowed to act except at a shareholders' meeting that had been duly noticed and at which a quorum of shareholders were present, either in person or by proxy. Modern statutes allow shareholders to act without a meeting, by written consent, unless the charter takes away that power. DGCL §§228, 275(c) (allowing shareholders to act by the consent of the number of shareholders that would be necessary to approve an action at a meeting, unless the articles of incorporation take away the power to act on consent); Model Act §7.04(a) (requiring unanimous consent). These consent provisions were designed to make action by shareholders in closely held corporations easier, and yet today about half of all public corporations permit actions by shareholder consent as well. Under Delaware law, this power can be extremely useful to shareholders or to an entity seeking to take control of another company, since it means a majority coalition of shareholders can act, such as to replace the board, without having to ask the board to call a special meeting, set a meeting date, and notify shareholders of the special meeting. Thus, it means a majority coalition of shareholders can act without being subject to the board's tactical decisions to delay calling a special meeting. (You will see an example of this type of strategic delay by a board in Blasius Industries, Inc. v. Atlas Corporation, below.) In a Model Act jurisdiction the power to act on consent is not very important because it requires unanimous shareholder consent, and it would be an extremely rare action that could garner unanimous consent.

Notice of Meetings. The process for calling a special meeting and for deciding the time and place of either a special meeting or the annual meeting appears in the charter or bylaws of a corporation. All shareholder meetings must be preceded by notice to the shareholders that specifies the business to be transacted at the meeting. DGCL §222(a); Model Act §7.05. If notice is insufficient, actions taken at the meeting are voidable by shareholders who did not attend. Attendance at a meeting, unless it is for the purpose of objecting to the notice, constitutes a waiver of improper notice.

Setting the Record Date. In a public corporation, where shares of stock are constantly being bought and sold, even the day before the annual meeting, special procedures have been developed to determine who has a right to vote. Notice of a meeting is provided to all shareholders who own shares as of a "record date," which is fixed by the board of directors. DGCL §213(a); Model Act §7.07(a). In Delaware, the record date cannot be more than 60 days before the meeting date, nor less than 10 days before the meeting date. DGCL §213(a). In an Model Act jurisdiction, the record date cannot be more than 70 days before the meeting date. Model Act §7.07(b). Thus, the statutes provide limits within which the board must act in determining the timing of meetings and the relationship between the record date and the meeting date. The Delaware statute also contains provisions for setting the record date for determining the shareholders eligible to be counted when they purport to act on consent. DGCL §213(b).

Quorum Requirements. Unless the charter or bylaws provide otherwise, shareholders holding a majority of shares must be present (in person or by proxy) to constitute a quorum. DGCL §216; Model Act §7.25(a).

The following opinion in Blasius Industries v. Atlas Corporation was written by Chancellor Allen, an extremely well-respected corporate law judge formerly on the Delaware Court of Chancery. In this case, you will see the use of a consent solicitation in a power struggle within the corporation, as well as important equitable limits on the board's ability to use its powers to thwart shareholder democracy — even when the board is acting within the technical requirements of the corporation statute. *Blasius* reappears in our study of hostile takeovers in Chapter 15, and remains an important case today.

BLASIUS INDUSTRIES, INC. v. ATLAS CORP.

564 A.2d 651
Court of Chancery of Delaware
July 25, 1988

ALLEN, Chancellor.

Two cases pitting the directors of Atlas Corporation against that company's largest (9.1%) shareholder, Blasius Industries, have been consolidated and tried together. Together, these cases ultimately require the court to determine who is entitled to sit on Atlas' board of directors. Each, however, presents discrete and important legal issues.

The first of the cases was filed on December 30, 1987. As amended, it challenges the validity of board action taken at a telephone meeting of December 31, 1987 that added two new members to Atlas' seven member board. That action was taken as an immediate response to the delivery to Atlas by Blasius the previous day of a form of stockholder consent that, if joined in by holders of a majority of Atlas' stock, would have increased the board of Atlas from seven to fifteen members and would have elected eight new members nominated by Blasius.

As I find the facts of this first case, they present the question whether a board acts consistently with its fiduciary duty when it acts, in good faith and with appropriate care, for the primary purpose of preventing or impeding an unaffiliated majority of shareholders from expanding the board and electing a new majority. For the reasons that follow, I conclude that, even though defendants here acted on their view of the corporation's interest and not selfishly, their December 31 action constituted an offense to the relationship between corporate directors and shareholders that has traditionally been protected in courts of equity. As a consequence, I conclude that the board action taken on December 31 was invalid and must be voided. The basis for this opinion is set forth . . . below.

The second filed action was commenced on March 9, 1988. It arises out of the consent solicitation itself (or an amended version of it) and requires the court to determine the outcome of Blasius' consent solicitation, which was warmly and actively contested on both sides. The vote was, on either view of the facts and law, extremely close. For the reasons set forth . . . below, I conclude that the judges of election properly confined their count to the written "ballots" (so to speak) before them; that on that basis, they made several errors, but that correction of those errors does not reverse the result they announced. I therefore conclude that plaintiffs' consent solicitation failed to garner the support of a majority of Atlas shares. . . .

I.

BLASIUS ACQUIRES A 9% STAKE IN ATLAS.

Blasius is a new stockholder of Atlas. It began to accumulate Atlas shares for the first time in July, 1987. On October 29, it filed a Schedule 13D with the Securities Exchange Commission disclosing that, with affiliates, it then owed 9.1% of Atlas' common stock. It stated in that filing that it intended to encourage management of Atlas to consider a restructuring of the Company or other transaction to enhance shareholder values. It also disclosed that Blasius was exploring the feasibility of obtaining control of Atlas, including instituting a tender offer or seeking "appropriate" representation on the Atlas board of directors.

Blasius has recently come under the control of two individuals, Michael Lubin and Warren Delano, who after experience in the commercial banking industry, had, for a short time, run a venture capital operation for a small investment banking firm. Now on their own, they apparently came to control Blasius with the assistance of Drexel Burnham's well noted junk bond mechanism. Since then, they have made several attempts to effect leveraged buyouts, but without success.

In May, 1987, with Drexel Burnham serving as underwriter, Lubin and Delano caused Blasius to raise $60 million through the sale of junk bonds. A portion of these funds were used to acquire a 9% position in Atlas. According to its public filings with the SEC, Blasius' debt service obligations arising out of the sale of the junk bonds are such that it is unable to service those obligations from its income from operations.

The prospect of Messrs. Lubin and Delano involving themselves in Atlas' affairs, was not a development welcomed by Atlas' management. Atlas had a new CEO, defendant Weaver, who had, over the course of the past year or so, overseen a business restructuring of a sort. Atlas had sold three of its five divisions. It had just announced (September 1, 1987) that it would close its once important domestic uranium operation. The goal was to focus the Company on its gold mining business. By October, 1987, the structural changes to do this had been largely accomplished. Mr. Weaver was perhaps thinking that the restructuring that had occurred should be given a chance to produce benefit before another restructuring (such as Blasius had alluded to in its Schedule 13D filing) was attempted, when he wrote in his diary on October 30, 1987:

> 13D by Delano & Lubin came in today. Had long conversation w/MAH & Mark Golden [of Goldman Sachs] on issue. All agree we must dilute these people down by the acquisition of another Co. w/stock, or merger or something else.

THE BLASIUS PROPOSAL OF A LEVERAGE RECAPITALIZATION OR SALE.

Immediately after filing its 13D on October 29, Blasius' representatives sought a meeting with the Atlas management. Atlas dragged its feet. A meeting was arranged for December 2, 1987 following the regular meeting of the Atlas board. Attending that meeting were Messrs. Lubin and Delano for Blasius, and, for Atlas, Messrs. Weaver, Devaney (Atlas' CFO), Masinter (legal counsel and director) and Czajkowski (a representative of Atlas' investment banker, Goldman Sachs).

At that meeting, Messrs. Lubin and Delano suggested that Atlas engage in a leveraged restructuring and distribute cash to shareholders. In such a transaction, which is by this date a commonplace form of transaction, a corporation typically raises cash by sale of assets and significant borrowings and makes a large one time cash distribution to shareholders. The shareholders are typically left with cash and an equity interest in a smaller, more highly leveraged enterprise. Lubin and Delano gave the outline of a leveraged recapitalization for Atlas as they saw it.

Immediately following the meeting, the Atlas representatives expressed among themselves an initial reaction that the proposal was infeasible. On December 7, Mr. Lubin sent a letter detailing the proposal. In general, it proposed the following: (1) an initial special cash dividend to Atlas' stockholders in an aggregate amount equal to (a) $35 million, (b) the aggregate proceeds to Atlas from the exercise of option warrants and stock options, and (c) the proceeds from the sale or disposal of all of Atlas' operations that are not related to its continuing minerals operations; and (2) a special non-cash dividend to Atlas' stockholders of an aggregate $125 million principal amount of 7% Secured Subordinated Gold-Indexed Debentures. The funds necessary to pay the initial cash dividend were to principally come from (i) a "gold loan" in the amount of $35,625,000, repayable over a three to five year period and secured by 75,000 ounces of gold at a price of $475 per ounce, (ii) the proceeds from the sale of the discontinued Brockton Sole and Plastics and Ready-Mix Concrete businesses, and (iii) a then expected January, 1988 sale of uranium to the Public Service Electric & Gas Company. (DX H.)

ATLAS ASKS ITS INVESTMENT BANKER TO STUDY THE PROPOSAL.

This written proposal was distributed to the Atlas board on December 9 and Goldman Sachs was directed to review and analyze it. The proposal met with a cool reception from management. On December 9, Mr. Weaver issued a press release expressing surprise that Blasius would suggest using debt to accomplish what he characterized as a substantial liquidation of Atlas at a time when Atlas' future prospects were promising. He noted that the Blasius proposal recommended that Atlas incur a high debt burden in order to pay a substantial one time dividend consisting of $35 million in cash and $125 million in subordinated debentures. Mr. Weaver also questioned the wisdom of incurring an enormous debt burden amidst the uncertainty in the financial markets that existed in the aftermath of the October crash.

Blasius attempted on December 14 and December 22 to arrange a further meeting with the Atlas management without success. During this period, Atlas provided Goldman Sachs with projections for the Company. Lubin was told that a further meeting would await completion of Goldman's analysis. A meeting after the first of the year was proposed.

THE DELIVERY OF BLASIUS' CONSENT STATEMENT.

On December 30, 1987, Blasius caused Cede & Co. (the registered owner of its Atlas stock) to deliver to Atlas a signed written consent (1) adopting a precatory resolution recommending that the board develop and implement a restructuring proposal, (2) amending the Atlas bylaws to, among other things, expand the size of the board from seven to fifteen members — the maximum number under Atlas' charter, and (3) electing eight named persons to fill the new directorships. Blasius also filed suit that day in this court seeking a declaration that certain bylaws adopted by the board on September 1, 1987 acted as an unlawful restraint on the shareholders' right, created by Section 228 of our corporation statute, to act through consent without undergoing a meeting.

The reaction was immediate. Mr. Weaver conferred with Mr. Masinter, the Company's outside counsel and a director, who viewed the consent as an attempt to take control of the Company. They decided to call an emergency meeting of the board, even though a regularly scheduled meeting was to occur only one week hence, on January 6, 1988. The point of the emergency meeting was to act on their conclusion (or to seek to have the board act on their conclusion) "that we should add at least one and probably two directors to the board . . ." (Tr. 85, Vol. II). A quorum of directors, however, could not be arranged for a telephone meeting that day. A telephone meeting was held the next day. At that meeting, the board voted to amend the bylaws to increase the size of the board from seven to nine and appointed John M. Devaney and Harry J. Winters, Jr. to fill those newly created positions. Atlas' Certificate of Incorporation creates staggered terms for directors; the terms to which Messrs. Devaney and Winters were appointed would expire in 1988 and 1990, respectively.

THE MOTIVATION OF THE INCUMBENT BOARD IN EXPANDING THE BOARD AND
APPOINTING NEW MEMBERS.

In increasing the size of Atlas' board by two and filling the newly created positions, the members of the board realized that they were thereby precluding the holders of a majority of the Company's shares from placing a majority of new directors on the board through Blasius' consent solicitation, should they want to do so. Indeed the evidence establishes that that was the principal motivation in so acting.

The conclusion that, in creating two new board positions on December 31 and electing Messrs. Devaney and Winters to fill those positions the board was principally motivated to prevent or delay the shareholders from possibly placing a majority of new members on the board, is critical to my analysis of the central issue posed by the first filed of the two pending cases. If the board in fact was not so motivated, but rather had taken action completely independently of the consent solicitation, which merely had an incidental impact upon the possible effectuation of any action authorized by the shareholders, it is very unlikely that such action would be subject to judicial nullification. *See, e.g.,* Frantz Manufacturing Company v. EAC Industries, Del. Supr., 501 A.2d 401, 407 (1985); Moran v. Household International, Inc., Del. Ch., 490 A.2d 1059, 1080, *aff'd*, Del. Supr., 500 A.2d 1346 (1985). The board, as a general matter, is under no fiduciary obligation to suspend its active management of the firm while the consent solicitation process goes forward.

There is testimony in the record to support the proposition that, in acting on December 31, the board was principally motivated simply to implement a plan to expand the Atlas board that preexisted the September, 1987 emergence of Blasius as an active shareholder. I have no doubt that the addition of Mr. Winters, an expert in mining economics, and Mr. Devaney, a financial expert employed by the Company, strengthened the Atlas board and, should anyone ever have reason to review the wisdom of those choices, they would be found to be sensible and prudent. I cannot conclude, however, that the strengthening of the board by the addition of these men was the principal motive for the December 31 action. . . . The timing of these events is, in my opinion, consistent only with the conclusion that Mr. Weaver and Mr. Masinter originated, and the board immediately endorsed, the notion of adding these competent, friendly individuals to the board, not because the board felt an urgent need to get them on the board immediately for reasons relating to the operations of Atlas' business, but because to do so would, for the moment, preclude a majority of shareholders from electing eight new board members selected by Blasius. As explained below, I conclude that, in so acting, the board was not selfishly motivated simply to retain power.

There was no discussion at the December 31 meeting of the feasibility or wisdom of the Blasius restructuring proposal. While several of the directors had an initial impression that the plan was not feasible and, if implemented, would likely result in the eventual liquidation of the Company, they had not yet focused upon and acted on that subject. Goldman Sachs had not yet made its report, which was scheduled to be given January 6.

THE JANUARY 6 REJECTION OF THE BLASIUS PROPOSAL.

On January 6, the board convened for its scheduled meeting. At that time, it heard a full report from its financial advisor concerning the feasibility of the Blasius restructuring proposal. The Goldman Sachs presentation included a summary of five year cumulative cash flows measured against a base case and the Blasius proposal, an analysis of Atlas' debt repayment capacity under the Blasius proposal, and pro forma income and cash flow statements for a base case and the Blasius proposal, assuming prices of $375, $475 and $575 per ounce of gold.

After completing that presentation, Goldman Sachs concluded with its view that if Atlas implemented the Blasius restructuring proposal (i) a severe drain on operating cash flow would result, (ii) Atlas would be unable to service its long-term debt and could end up in bankruptcy, (iii) the common stock of Atlas would have little or no value, and (iv) since Atlas would be unable to generate sufficient cash to service its debt, the debentures contemplated to be issued in the proposed restructuring could have a value of only 20 to 30% of their face amount. Goldman Sachs also said that it knew of no financial restructuring that had been undertaken by a company where the company had no chance of repaying its debt, which, in its judgment, would be Atlas' situation if it implemented the Blasius restructuring proposal. Finally, Goldman Sachs noted that if Atlas made a meaningful commercial discovery of gold after implementation of the Blasius restructuring proposal, Atlas would not have the resources to develop the discovery.

The board then voted to reject the Blasius proposal. Blasius was informed of that action. The next day, Blasius caused a second, modified consent to be delivered to Atlas. A contest then ensued between the Company and Blasius for the votes of Atlas' shareholders. The facts relating to that contest, and a determination of its outcome, form the subject of the second filed lawsuit to be now decided. That matter, however, will be deferred for the moment as the facts set forth above are sufficient to frame and decide the principal remaining issue raised by the first filed action: whether the December 31 board action, in increasing the board by two and appointing members to fill those new positions, constituted, in the circumstances, an inequitable interference with the exercise of shareholder rights.

II.

Plaintiff attacks the December 31 board action as a selfishly motivated effort to protect the incumbent board from a perceived threat to its control of Atlas. Their conduct is said to constitute a violation of the principle, applied in such cases as Schnell v. Chris Craft Industries, Del. Supr., 285 A.2d 437 (1971), that directors hold legal powers subjected to a supervening duty to exercise such powers in good faith pursuit of what they reasonably believe to be in the corporation's interest. The December 31 action is also said to have been taken in a grossly negligent manner, since it was designed to preclude the recapitalization from being pursued, and the board had no basis at that time to make a prudent determination about the wisdom of that proposal, nor was there any emergency that required it to act in any respect regarding that proposal before putting itself in a position to do so advisedly.

Defendants, of course, contest every aspect of plaintiffs' claims. They claim the formidable protections of the business judgment rule. *See, e.g.*, Aronson v. Lewis, Del. Supr., 473 A.2d 805 (1983); Grobow v. Perot, Del. Supr., 539 A.2d 180 (1988); In re J.P. Stevens & Co., Inc. Shareholders Litigation, Del. Ch., 542 A.2d 770 (1988).[2]

They say that, in creating two new board positions and filling them on December 31, they acted without a conflicting interest (since the Blasius proposal did not, in any event, challenge *their* places on the board), they acted with due care (since they well knew the persons they put on the board and did not thereby preclude later consideration of the recapitalization), and they acted in good faith (since they were motivated, they say, to protect the shareholders from the threat of having an impractical, indeed a dangerous, recapitalization program foisted upon them). Accordingly, defendants assert there is no basis to conclude that their December 31 action constituted any violation of the duty of the fidelity that a director owes by reason of his office to the corporation and its shareholders.

Moreover, defendants say that their action was fair, measured and appropriate, in light of the circumstances. Therefore, even should the court conclude that some level of substantive review of it is appropriate under a legal test of fairness, or under the intermediate level of review authorized by Unocal Corp. v. Mesa Petroleum Co., Del. Supr., 493 A.2d 946 (1985) [with respect to defending against being taken over], defendants assert that the board's decision must be sustained as valid in both law and equity.

III.

One of the principal thrusts of plaintiffs' argument is that, in acting to appoint two additional persons of their own selection, including an officer of the Company, to the board, defendants were motivated not by any view that Atlas' interest (or those of its shareholders) required that action, but rather they were motivated improperly, by selfish concern to maintain their collective control over the Company. That is, plaintiffs say that the evidence shows there was no policy dispute or issue that really motivated this action, but that asserted policy differences were pretexts for entrenchment for selfish reasons. If this were found to be factually true, one would not need to inquire further. The action taken would constitute a breach of duty. Schnell v. Chris Craft Industries, Del. Supr., 285 A.2d 437 (1971); Guiricich v. Emtrol Corp., Del. Supr., 449 A.2d 232 (1982).

---

2. As we will see shortly, the Delaware courts define the "business judgment" rule as a rebuttable presumption that a board of directors acted in good faith, in an informed manner, and without any conflicts of interest in making a contested decision. So long as plaintiffs do not introduce facts to rebut that presumption, the courts will not second-guess the wisdom of business decisions that boards make. If, however, there is reason to wonder about whether at least some directors acted to advance their own financial interests (that is, they acted under a conflict of interest), or if the directors were grossly uninformed or acted in bad faith, then the courts will scrutinize transactions more carefully to see if they were fair to the shareholders. — EDS.

In support of this view, plaintiffs point to the early diary entry of Mr. Weaver (. . . *supra*), to the lack of any consideration at all of the Blasius recapitalization proposal at the December 31 meeting, the lack of any substantial basis for the outside directors to have had any considered view on the subject by that time — not having had any view from Goldman Sachs nor seen the financial data that it regarded as necessary to evaluate the proposal — and upon what it urges is the grievously flawed, slanted analysis that Goldman Sachs finally did present.

While I am satisfied that the evidence is powerful, indeed compelling, that the board was chiefly motivated on December 31 to forestall or preclude the possibility that a majority of shareholders might place on the Atlas board eight new members sympathetic to the Blasius proposal, it is less clear with respect to the more subtle motivational question: whether the existing members of the board did so because they held a good faith belief that such shareholder action would be self-injurious and shareholders needed to be protected from their own judgment.

On balance, I cannot conclude that the board was acting out of a self-interested motive in any important respect on December 31. I conclude rather that the board saw the "threat" of the Blasius recapitalization proposal as posing vital policy differences between itself and Blasius. It acted, I conclude, in a good faith effort to protect its incumbency, not selfishly, but in order to thwart implementation of the recapitalization that it feared, reasonably, would cause great injury to the Company.

The real question the case presents, to my mind, is whether, in these circumstances, the board, even if it *is* acting with subjective good faith (which will typically, if not always, be a contestable or debatable judicial conclusion), may validly act for the principal purpose of preventing the shareholders from electing a majority of new directors. The question thus posed is not one of intentional wrong (or even negligence), but one of authority *as between the fiduciary and the beneficiary* (not simply legal authority, *i.e.*, as between the fiduciary and the world at large).

IV.

It is established in our law that a board may take certain steps — such as the purchase by the corporation of its own stock — that have the effect of defeating a threatened change in corporate control, when those steps are taken advisedly, in good faith pursuit of a corporate interest, and are reasonable in relation to a threat to legitimate corporate interests posed by the proposed change in control. *See* Unocal Corp. v. Mesa Petroleum Co., Del. Supr., 493 A.2d 946 (1985); Kors v. Carey, Del. Ch., 158 A.2d 136 (1960); Cheff v. Mathes, Del. Supr., 199 A.2d 548 (1964); Kaplan v. Goldsamt, Del. Ch., 380 A.2d 556 (1977). Does this rule — that the reasonable exercise of good faith and due care generally validates, in equity, the exercise of legal authority even if the act has an entrenchment effect — apply to action designed for the primary purpose of interfering with the effectiveness of a stockholder vote? Our authorities, as well as sound principles, suggest that the central importance of the franchise to the scheme of corporate governance, requires that, in this setting, that rule not be applied and that closer scrutiny be accorded to such transaction.

1. WHY THE DEFERENTIAL BUSINESS JUDGMENT RULE DOES NOT APPLY TO BOARD ACTS
TAKEN FOR THE PRIMARY PURPOSE OF INTERFERING WITH A STOCKHOLDER'S VOTE,
EVEN IF TAKEN ADVISEDLY AND IN GOOD FAITH.

A. The question of legitimacy.

The shareholder franchise is the ideological underpinning upon which the legitimacy of directorial power rests. Generally, shareholders have only two protections against perceived inadequate business performance. They may sell their stock (which, if done in sufficient numbers, may so affect security prices as to create an incentive for altered managerial performance), or they may vote to replace incumbent board members.

It has, for a long time, been conventional to dismiss the stockholder vote as a vestige or ritual of little practical importance. It may be that we are now witnessing the emergence of new institutional voices and arrangements that will make the stockholder vote a less predictable affair than it has been. Be that as it may, however, whether the vote is seen functionally as an unimportant formalism, or as an important tool of discipline, it is clear that it is critical to the theory that legitimates the exercise of power by some (directors and officers) over vast aggregations of property that they do not own. Thus, when viewed from a broad, institutional perspective, it can be seen that matters involving the integrity of the shareholder voting process involve consideration not present in any other context in which directors exercise delegated power.

B. Questions of this type raise issues of the allocation of authority as between the board and the shareholders.

The distinctive nature of the shareholder franchise context also appears when the matter is viewed from a less generalized, doctrinal point of view. From this point of view, as well, it appears that the ordinary considerations to which the business judgment rule originally responded are simply not present in the shareholder voting context. That is, a decision by the board to act for the primary purpose of preventing the effectiveness of a shareholder vote inevitably involves the question who, as between the principal and the agent, has authority with respect to a matter of internal corporate governance. That, of course, is true in a very specific way in this case which deals with the question who should constitute the board of directors of the corporation, but it will be true in every instance in which an incumbent board seeks to thwart a shareholder majority. A board's decision to act to prevent the shareholders from creating a majority of new board positions and filling them does not involve the exercise of *the corporation's power* over its property, or with respect to *its* rights or obligations; rather, it involves allocation, between shareholders as a class and the board, of effective power with respect to governance of the corporation. This need not be the case with respect to other forms of corporate action that may have an entrenchment effect — such as the stock buybacks present in *Unocal, Cheff* or Kors v. Carey. Action designed principally to interfere with the effectiveness of a vote inevitably involves a conflict between the board and a shareholder majority. Judicial review of such action involves a determination of the legal and equitable obligations of an agent towards his principal. This is not, in my opinion, a question that a court may leave to the agent finally to decide so long as he does so honestly and competently; that is, it may not be left to the agent's business judgment.

Plaintiff argues for a rule of per se invalidity once a plaintiff has established that a board has acted for the primary purpose of thwarting the exercise of a shareholder vote. . . . A per se rule that would strike down, in equity, any board action taken for the primary purpose of interfering with the effectiveness of a corporate vote would have the advantage of relative clarity and predictability. It also has the advantage of most vigorously enforcing the concept of corporate democracy. The disadvantage it brings along is, of course, the disadvantage a per se rule always has: it may sweep too broadly.

In two recent cases dealing with shareholder votes, this court struck down board acts done for the primary purpose of impeding the exercise of stockholder voting power. In doing so, a per se rule was not applied. Rather, it was said that, in such a case, the board bears the heavy burden of demonstrating a compelling justification for such action.

In Aprahamian v. HBO & Company, Del. Ch., 531 A.2d 1204 (1987), the incumbent board had moved the date of the annual meeting on the eve of that meeting when it learned that a dissident stockholder group had or appeared to have in hand proxies representing a majority of the outstanding shares. The court restrained that action and compelled the meeting to occur as noticed, even though the board stated that it had good business reasons to move the meeting date forward, and that that action was recommended by a special committee. The court concluded as follows:

> The corporate election process, if it is to have any validity, must be conducted with scrupulous fairness and without any advantage being conferred or denied to any candidate or slate of candidates. In the interests of corporate democracy, those in charge of the election machinery of a corporation must be held to the highest standards of providing for and conducting corporate elections. The business judgment rule therefore does not confer any presumption of propriety on the acts of directors in postponing the annual meeting. Quite to the contrary. When the election machinery appears, at least facially, to have been manipulated those in charge of the election have the burden of persuasion to justify their actions.

Aprahamian, 531 A.2d at 1206-07.

In Phillips v. Insituform of North America, Inc., Del. Ch., C.A. No. 9173, Allen, C. (Aug. 27, 1987), the court enjoined the voting of certain stock issued for the primary purpose of diluting the voting power of certain control shares, [stating] . . .

> I conclude that no justification has been shown that would arguably make the extraordinary step of issuance of stock for the admitted purpose of impeding the exercise of stockholder rights reasonable in light of the corporate benefit, if any, sought to be obtained. Thus, whether our law creates an unyielding prohibition to the issuance of stock for the primary purpose of depriving a controlling shareholder of control or whether, as *Unocal* suggests to my mind, such an extraordinary step might be justified in some circumstances, the issuance of the Leopold shares was, in my opinion, an unjustified and invalid corporate act.

Phillips v. Insituform of North America, Inc., *supra* at 23-24. Thus, in *Insituform*, it was unnecessary to decide whether a per se rule pertained or not.

In my view, our inability to foresee now all of the future settings in which a board might, in good faith, paternalistically seek to thwart a shareholder vote, counsels against the adoption of a per se rule invalidating, in equity, every board action taken for the sole or primary purpose of thwarting a shareholder vote, even though I recognize the transcending significance of the franchise to the claims to legitimacy of our scheme of corporate governance. It may be that some set of facts would justify such extreme action. This, however, is not such a case.

3. DEFENDANTS HAVE DEMONSTRATED NO SUFFICIENT JUSTIFICATION FOR THE ACTION OF DECEMBER 31 WHICH WAS INTENDED TO PREVENT AN UNAFFILIATED MAJORITY OF SHAREHOLDERS FROM EFFECTIVELY EXERCISING THEIR RIGHT TO ELECT EIGHT NEW DIRECTORS.

The board was not faced with a coercive action taken by a powerful shareholder against the interests of a distinct shareholder constituency (such as a public minority). It was presented with a consent solicitation by a 9% shareholder. Moreover, here it had time (and understood that it had time) to inform the shareholders of its views on the merits of the proposal subject to stockholder vote. The only justification that can, in such a situation, be offered for the action taken is that the board knows better than do the shareholders what is in the corporation's best interest. While that premise is no doubt true for any number of matters, it is irrelevant (except insofar as the shareholders wish to be guided by the board's recommendation) when the question is who should comprise the board of directors. The theory of our corporation law confers power upon directors as the agents of the shareholders; it does not create Platonic masters. It may be that the Blasius restructuring proposal was or is unrealistic and would lead to injury to the corporation and its shareholders if pursued. Having heard the evidence, I am inclined to think it was not a sound proposal. The board certainly viewed it that way, and that view, held in good faith, entitled the board to take certain steps to evade the risk it perceived. It could, for example, expend corporate funds to inform shareholders and seek to bring them to a similar point of view. *See, e.g.*, Hall v. Trans-Lux Daylight Picture Screen Corporation, Del. Ch., 171 A. 226, 227 (1934); Hibbert v. Hollywood Park, Inc., Del. Supr., 457 A.2d 339 (1982). But there is a vast difference between expending corporate funds to inform the electorate and exercising power for the primary purpose of foreclosing effective shareholder action. A majority of the shareholders, who were not dominated in any respect, could view the matter differently than did the board. If they do, or did, they are entitled to employ the mechanisms provided by the corporation law and the Atlas certificate of incorporation to advance that view. They are also entitled, in my opinion, to restrain their agents, the board, from acting for the principal purpose of thwarting that action.

I therefore conclude that, even finding the action taken was taken in good faith, it constituted an unintended violation of the duty of loyalty that the board owed to the shareholders. I note parenthetically that the concept of an unintended breach of the duty of loyalty is unusual but not novel. *See* Lerman v. Diagnostic Data, *supra*; AC Acquisitions Corp. v. Anderson, Clayton & Co.,

Del. Ch., 519 A.2d 103 (1986). That action will, therefore, be set aside by order of this court. . . .

V.

I turn now to a discussion of the second case which is a Section 225 case designed to determine whether the nominees of Blasius were elected to an expanded Atlas board pursuant to the consent procedure.

On March 6, 1988, after several rounds of mailings by each side, Blasius presented consents to the corporation purporting to adopt its five proposals. The corporation appointed an independent fiduciary (Manufacturers Hanover Trust Company) to act as judge of the stockholder vote. It reported a final tally report on March 17 and issued a Certificate of the Stockholder Vote on March 22. That certificate stated that the vote had been exceedingly close and that, as calculated by Manufacturer's Hanover, none of Blasius' proposals had succeeded. In order to be adopted by a majority of shares entitled to vote, each proposition needed to garner 1,486,293 consents. Each was about 45,000 shares short (about 1.5% of the total outstanding stock). [The Court ultimately upheld the Certification, even though there were errors in the counting process, since it found that the errors did not affect the outcome.] . . .

3.   *Bylaw Proposals*

One of the few powers shareholders have within the corporation that is proactive, rather than reactive to directors, is the power to initiate changes to the bylaws. Under Delaware law, the shareholders must have that power. While the charter can also give concurrent power to the board to initiate changes to the bylaws, doing so does not take that power away from the shareholders. DGCL §109. The Model Act goes further, providing that the shareholders can amend a bylaw and expressly state that the directors cannot then amend, repeal, or reinstate that bylaw. Model Act §10.20(b)(2).

The shareholders' power with respect to the bylaws is in sharp contrast to their powers with respect to the charter. There, the directors must initiate any changes, which the shareholders then have the opportunity to vote upon. DGCL §242(b); Model Act §10.03(a). As a result of the directors' exclusive control over initiating changes to the charter, any provisions in the charter are impervious to shareholder-initiated changes unless a shareholders' group gains control over the board of directors.

The shareholders' power is not unlimited with respect to the bylaws, however. Significantly, since the board has the statutory authority to manage the corporation, under DGCL §141(a) and Model Act §8.01(b), shareholder-initiated changes to the bylaws cannot take away power from the directors, nor may the shareholders *require* the directors to do anything. Recently, as institutional investors have become more active in corporate governance and have begun to initiate shareholder proposals on such topics as classified boards (against them), poison pills (against them), and super-majority voting rules (generally against them), the issue of which bylaws proposals undermine the directors' management power has become heated. Moreover, as you will see below, directors still have the ability to maintain control over when a bylaw proposal will be acted upon, unless the shareholders act by written consent. Directors have that ability by their power to fix the dates of either an annual or special meeting so long as they act "equitably." Through this seemingly innocuous power to fix the dates of meetings, directors can often undermine shareholders' actions attempting to exert control through a bylaw amendment. Such a case, Stahl v. Apple Bancorp, is presented immediately below.

Stahl shows the importance of shareholders' power with respect to bylaws in a contest for control, as well as showing the board's strategic response using its power to set the date for the annual meeting. In reading this case, pay attention as well to the court's analysis of the fiduciary duties of the board of directors, since that is the subject to which we will next turn in our study of corporate law.

STAHL v. APPLE BANCORP
579 A.2d 1115
Court of Chancery of Delaware
May 18, 1990

ALLEN, Chancellor.

On March 28, 1990 Stanley Stahl, who is the holder of 30% of the outstanding common stock of Apple Bancorp, Inc. ("Bancorp"), announced a public tender offer for all of the remaining shares of Bancorp's stock. Mr. Stahl had earlier informed Bancorp's board of an intention to conduct a proxy contest for the election of directors to the company's board. On April 10 Bancorp's board of directors elected to defer the company's annual meeting, which it had intended to call for mid-May, and announced it would explore the advisability of pursuing an extraordinary transaction, including the possible sale of the company. Mr. Stahl filed this action on April 12.

The complaint seeks an order requiring the directors of Bancorp to convene the annual meeting of the stockholders on or before June 16, 1990. The suit is not brought under Section 211 of the Delaware General Corporation Law which creates a right in shareholders to compel the holding of an annual meeting under certain circumstances. Rather, the theory of the complaint is that the directors of Bancorp had intended to convene an annual meeting in May or June—and had gone so far as to fix April 17 as the record date for the meeting—but dropped that plan when it appeared that a proxy contest by plaintiff was likely to succeed. This change in plans is said, in the circumstances, to constitute inequitable conduct because it seeks to protect no legitimate interest of the corporation but is designed principally to entrench defendants in office.

Defendants are the members of the board of directors of Bancorp. They answer the complaint by saying that in not scheduling the 1990 annual meeting in the Spring of the year as has been the practice, they are behaving responsibly in the best interests of the corporation and its shareholders. They claim that their decision to delay the annual meeting was not a response to a proxy contest by plaintiff but was a response to the announcement of plaintiff's tender offer which they conclude is coercive and at an inadequate price. . . .

I.

The facts as they appear from the affidavits and depositions are as follows.

Bancorp is a Delaware corporation headquartered in New York. Since September 29, 1989, Bancorp has been the holding company of Apple Bank for Savings ("Apple Bank"), a savings bank chartered in New York. Pursuant to a reorganization on that date, all outstanding shares of Apple Bank were converted into shares of common stock of Bancorp. As of December 31, 1989, Bancorp had $3.41 billion in total deposits, $3.84 billion in total assets and $253.8 million of stockholders' equity. Bancorp's shares are listed on the New York Stock Exchange.

Each director of the company is named as a defendant. Mr. McDougal is chairman of the board and chief executive officer of the company. Mr. Brown is the company's president and its chief operating officer. All other directors of the company appear to be outside directors.

Mr. Stahl, who is Bancorp's largest shareholder, began acquiring shares of Apple Bank in 1986. Gradually he increased his holdings through open market purchases and privately negotiated transactions. Upon effectuation of the reorganization in September 1989, Stahl became the owner of approximately 20% of the then outstanding shares of Bancorp. By November 7, 1989, he owned approximately 30.3% of the outstanding Bancorp shares. As Stahl's proportionate share of Bancorp stock rose above 20%, Bancorp's financial advisor, and a large stockholder, each expressed concern to Mr. McDougal that Stahl might obtain control of the company without paying a control premium.

On November 15, 1989, the company's board of directors met to consider what action, if any, should be taken with respect to Stahl's stock accumulation. Two proposals were suggested: negotiating a standstill agreement with Stahl and adopting a stock purchase rights plan (a "rights plan") [also known as a "poison pill"]. The board authorized the preparation of the rights plan.

On November 16, McDougal informed Stahl of the board's intention to adopt a rights plan. McDougal suggested that one way of addressing the situation might be for Stahl to make a bid for the entire company at book value. Mr. Stahl indicated that he was unwilling to do so.

On November 17, the board adopted the rights plan. Stahl responded on November 22, 1989, by delivering to the company a proposal to be submitted to a vote at the next annual meeting of stockholders, calling for an amendment to the company's bylaws increasing the number of directors of the company from 12 to 21. In the proposal Stahl nominated 13 individuals (including himself) to be named to the board if his bylaw proposal were approved.[3] He nominated four individuals to be elected if his bylaw proposal were defeated. Later, Stahl stated in a Schedule 13D filing that he would solicit proxies in favor of his proposal and for the election of his nominees to the board. That filing also stated that, if elected, Stahl intended to recommend to the full board that the rights under the rights plan be redeemed and that the board evaluate the performance of

---

3. Apple has a staggered board. Under the company's certificate of incorporation and bylaws, only 4 seats are open for election this year. Thus, in order for Stahl to gain majority control of the board, the bylaw proposal must be approved.

management and make any changes it deemed necessary to improve overall management performance.

On March 19, 1990 the board fixed April 17, 1990 as the record date for determining the shareholders entitled to vote at the company's 1990 annual meeting. While no date for the annual meeting was fixed, it was anticipated that the meeting would be held in May 1990. Section 213 of the Delaware General Corporation Law provides that the record date for an annual meeting shall not be less than 10 or more than 60 days before the date the meeting is held. Thus, the latest date at which an annual meeting could be held with an April 17 record date would be June 16.

On March 28, 1990, Stahl commenced a tender offer to purchase any and all outstanding shares of common stock of the company at $38 cash per share. The offer is conditioned upon the expansion of the company's board of directors to 21 members and the election of Stahl's 13 nominees to serve on the board. The offer is also conditioned upon the stock purchase rights being redeemed or Stahl otherwise being satisfied that the rights are invalid. It is not conditioned upon the tender of any minimum number of shares or the receipt of financing or the obtaining of any regulatory approvals. In his tender offer documents, Stahl reiterated his intent to solicit proxies in support of his proposal to expand the company's board and to elect his nominees as directors. He also expressed an intent to cash out non-tendering stockholders in a second step merger as soon as practicable after completion of the tender offer. He did not, however, commit to do that or to use his best efforts to assure that such a transaction would occur. The tender offer stated that it was possible that a second step merger might not be proposed.

On April 9 and 10, the company's board of directors held a special meeting. The company's proxy solicitor informed the board that it was likely if the board did not present the stockholders with an economic alternative to Stahl's offer that Stahl would prevail in a proxy fight by a significant margin. The company received from its financial advisors a written opinion that Stahl's offer, which represented a 17% premium over the prior market price, was inadequate and unfair to the stockholders from a financial point of view. The financial advisors advised the board that greater value for the stockholders could be obtained through certain alternative strategies. They further advised the board that adequate exploration of those alternatives would require more time than was available before the meeting, if the record date stood at April 17.

The board resolved to recommend to Bancorp's stockholders that they reject Stahl's offer. It further resolved to withdraw the April 17 record date in order to allow itself more time to pursue alternatives to the Stahl offer. The directors decided that "it is not in the best interest of the company and its stockholders to hold the annual meeting until the company has had a fair opportunity to explore and pursue alternatives to the Stahl offer which would enable the company to maximize stockholder value." These alternatives included the sale of the company or the merger of the company with another financial institution.

On May 9 Mr. Stahl sent out proxy solicitation materials to Bancorp's stockholders even though no meeting was at that time scheduled. The pending motion was presented on May 14.

II.

Stahl asserts and it is not denied that defendants intended to hold Bancorp's 1990 annual meeting in May 1990. He claims that by requiring shareholders to submit matters to be voted upon at the annual meeting by November 1989 (which the board interpreted Bancorp's bylaws to do) and by fixing an April 17 record date, the defendants have initiated the proxy contest process. It is argued that the withdrawal of the record date is essentially a postponement of Bancorp's 1990 annual meeting, and that the postponement was effected in order to avoid the defeat the incumbent directors anticipated that they would suffer if the election of directors were held in May. Stahl argues that the board's action constitutes an impermissible manipulation of the corporate machinery having the effect of disenfranchising the company's stockholders and entrenching the incumbent directors. Stahl argues, citing Blasius Industries, Inc. v. Atlas Corp., Del. Ch., 564 A.2d 651 (1988), that the board is required to present a compelling justification for its actions in rescinding the April 17 record date. This plaintiff asserts it cannot do.

Defendants do not dispute that the board originally intended to hold the 1990 annual meeting in late May. They point out, however, that no meeting date had been set, and under neither 8 Del. C. §211 nor Bancorp's bylaws, was one required until September of 1990. Thus, it is said, the board's withdrawal of the April 17 record date was not an action that impeded a shareholder vote. Defendants assert that unlike the actions struck down in Blasius and in Lerman v. Diagnostic Data, Inc., Del. Ch., 421 A.2d 906 (1980), the withdrawal of the April 17 record date did not render a shareholder vote ineffective, but simply delayed it. Defendants assert that the record date was withdrawn not as a response to a proxy contest by Stahl, but rather as a response to Stahl's tender offer. The appropriate standard for evaluating the board's action, say defendants, is that articulated in Unocal Corp. v. Mesa Petroleum Co., Del. Supr., 493 A.2d 946 (1985), i.e., whether the board's withdrawal of the April 17 record date was a reasonable response to a reasonably perceived threat to corporate or shareholder interests. Defendants claim to have satisfied that standard. . . .

IV.

Turning to the merits of plaintiff's claim that the directors' decision to postpone the annual meeting violated their fiduciary duties of loyalty owed to the corporation and its shareholders, one first confronts the question [of] what is the appropriate legal standard against which the defendants' action is to be measured. Two approaches, which in the end become quite similar, are possible: the fiduciary duty analysis employed by cases dealing with board action designed to impact on the shareholder vote; or the modified business judgment test of *Unocal* and later cases which apply its test to board actions taken in the face of a threat to corporate control. The first approach is treated in this section of this opinion; the second in the next, concluding section.

Plaintiff contends that the deferral of the annual meeting and the rescission of the record date together constitutes a direct and intended interference with the exercise of the shareholders' right of franchise. It is said that to be sustained this action requires the directors to establish a compelling justification, which, plaintiff asserts, defendants cannot do. Plaintiff invokes the authority of a series of cases in support of his position: *e.g.*, Aprahamian v. HBO & Co., Del. Ch., 531 A.2d 1204 (1987); Blasius Industries, Inc. v. Atlas Corp., Del. Ch., 564 A.2d 651 (1988); Gintel v. Xtra Corp., Del. Ch., C.A. No. 11422, Allen, C. (February 27, 1990) (oral ruling).

For the reasons that follow I am unable to accept plaintiff's argument. Explaining why this is so is helped by placing the "compelling justification" language of Blasius Industries, Inc. v. Atlas Corp., which plaintiff invokes, into its larger doctrinal context.

It is an elementary proposition of corporation law that, where they exist, fiduciary duties constitute a network of responsibilities that overlay the exercise of even undoubted legal power. Thus it is well established, for example, that where corporate directors exercise their legal powers for an inequitable purpose their action may be rescinded or nullified by a court at the instance of an aggrieved shareholder. The leading Delaware case of Schnell v. Chris-Craft Industries, Inc., Del. Supr., 285 A.2d 437 (1971) announced this principle and applied it in a setting in which directors advanced the date of an annual meeting in order to impede an announced proxy contest.

Under this test the court asks the question whether the directors' purpose is "inequitable." An inequitable purpose is not necessarily synonymous with a dishonest motive. Fiduciaries who are subjectively operating selflessly might be pursuing a purpose that a court will rule is inequitable. Thus, for example, there was no inquiry concerning the board's subjective good faith in Condec Corporation v. Lunkenheimer Company, Del. Ch., 230 A.2d 769 (1967) where this court held that the issuance of stock for the principal purpose of eliminating the ability of a large stockholder to determine the outcome of a vote was invalid as a breach of loyalty. Nor was there such an inquiry in Canada Southern Oils, Ltd. v. Manabi Exploration Co., Inc., Del. Ch., 96 A.2d 810 (1953). . . .

Each of these cases dealt with board action with a principal purpose of impeding the exercise of stockholder power through the vote. They could be read as approximating a per se rule that board action taken for the principal purpose of impeding the effective exercise of the stockholder franchise is inequitable and will be restrained or set aside in proper circumstances.

Consistent with these authorities, in *Blasius* and in *Aprahamian* this court held that action designed primarily to impede the effective exercise of the franchise is not evaluated under the business judgment form of review:

> Action designed principally to interfere with the effectiveness of a vote inevitably involves a conflict between the board and a shareholder majority. Judicial review of such action involves a determination of the legal and equitable obligations of an agent towards his principal. This is not, in my opinion, a question that a court may leave to the agent finally to decide so long as he does so honestly and competently; that is, it may not be left to the agent's business judgment.

Blasius, 564 A.2d at 660. *See also Aprahamian*, 531 A.2d at 1207 ("The business judgment rule . . . does not confer any presumption of propriety on the acts of the directors in postponing the annual meeting.") These statements are simply restatements of the principle applied in *Schnell*. *Blasius* did, however, go on to reject the notion of per se invalidity of action taken to interfere with the effective exercise of the corporate franchise; it admitted the possibility that in some circumstances such action might be consistent with the director[']s equitable obligations. It was suggested, however, that such circumstances would have to constitute "compelling justification," given the central role of the stockholder franchise. Thus, *Blasius'* reference to "compelling justification" reflects only the high value that the prior cases had placed upon the exercise of voting rights and the inherently particularized and contextual nature of any inquiry concerning fiduciary duties. Neither it nor *Aprahamian* represent new law.

Thus the fundamental question when the motion is evaluated under these cases may be expressed as whether the defendants have exercised corporate power inequitably. In answering that question, it is necessary to ask, in the context of this case, whether they have taken action for the purpose of impairing or impeding the effective exercise of the corporate franchise and, if they have, whether the special circumstances are present (compelling justification) warranting such an unusual step.

In my opinion one employing this method of analysis need not inquire into the question of justification in this instance, for I cannot conclude that defendants have taken action for the primary purpose of impairing or impeding the effective exercise of the corporate franchise. I reach this conclusion understanding that the Bancorp board had planned to call the annual meeting of stockholders for May and that it changed that plan in response to the risk that the combination of the proposed Stahl proxy contest and tender offer would result in a change in board control and the sale of the company.

For these purposes I do not accept that the Stahl tender offer, conditioned on the outcome of a stockholder vote, would have a coercive effect on that vote, nor do I rest my opinion on the ground that a board may always postpone a meeting for a substantial period on the eve of an annual meeting if it concludes that it will lose a proxy contest and thus decides to authorize a significant new development, such as the sale of the company.

Rather, I place my opinion on the narrow ground that the action of deferring this company's annual meeting where no meeting date has yet been set and no proxies even solicited does not impair or impede the effective exercise of the franchise to any extent. To speak of the effective exercise of the franchise is to imply certain assumptions concerning the structure and mechanism that define the vote and govern its exercise. Shares are voted at meetings; meetings are generally called as fixed in bylaws. While the refusal to call a shareholder meeting when the board is not obligated to do so might under some imaginable circumstance breach a fiduciary duty, such a decision does not itself constitute an impairment of the exercise of the franchise that sparked the close judicial scrutiny of *Schnell*, *Blasius*, etc.

In no sense can the decision not to call a meeting be likened to kinds of board action found to have constituted inequitable conduct relating to the vote. In each of these franchise cases the effect of the board action — to advance (*Schnell*) or defer (*Aprahamian*) a meeting; to adopt a bylaw (*Lerman*); or to fill board vacancies (*Blasius*) — was practically to preclude effective stockholder action (*Schnell*, *Blasius*, *Lerman*) or to snatch victory from an insurgent slate on the eve of the noticed meeting (*Aprahamian*). Here the election process will go forward at a time consistent with the company's bylaws and with Section 211 of our corporation law. Defendant's decision does not preclude plaintiff or any other Bancorp shareholder from effectively exercising his vote, nor have proxies been collected that only await imminent counting. Plaintiff has no legal right to compel the holding of the company's annual meeting under Section 211(c) of the Delaware General Corporation Law, nor does he, in my opinion, have a right in equity to require the board to call a meeting now.

This view may be criticized as placing undue emphasis on the formal act of fixing the date of the annual meeting. However, that is an act of some dignity and significance. *See* Gries v. Eversharp, Inc., Del. Supr., 69 A.2d 922 (1949). Once fixed[,] that date may be postponed at least in some circumstances. *Compare* MAI Basic Four, Inc. v. Prime Computer, Inc., Del. Ch., C.A. No. 10868 Hartnett, V.C., 1989 WL 63900 (June 13, 1989) with Aprahamian v. HBO & Co., Del. Ch., 531 A.2d 1204 (1987). But, while postponement of a noticed meeting will in some circumstances constitute an inequitable manipulation, I can in no event see that the franchise process can be said to be sufficiently engaged before the fixing of this meeting date to give rise to that possibility. . . .

C. FIDUCIARY DUTY OF DISCLOSURE

An important requirement protecting the shareholders' power to vote is that they must be adequately and accurately informed by the directors prior to voting. The duty of disclosure — sometimes called the "duty of candor" — occupies an important niche in the panoply of director duties. As discussed in Chapters 7 and 16, the mandatory disclosure system under federal securities law determines in large part the scope and substance of corporate disclosure obligations, at least with respect to public companies. Nevertheless, the Delaware courts guard jealously the place of state fiduciary law in regulating disclosure. Indeed, beginning with Lynch v. Vickers Energy Corp., 383 A.2d 278 (Del. 1977), the Delaware courts developed an expansive notion of the fiduciary duty of disclosure that began to compete with federal disclosure rules.

Lynch was far from the first case to articulate a fiduciary duty of disclosure,[1] but its description of a duty of "complete candor" prompted widespread interest among litigants. *Lynch* involved a classic conflict of interest — a tender offer by a majority shareholder for the shares held by the minority shareholders — and thus fit comfortably under a fairly conventional and well-established "ratification" theory. Ratification will be treated more thoroughly in Chapter 11, but for the moment, it will suffice to note that a *fully informed* vote of shareholders "cleanses" a transaction tainted by conflict of interest. To the extent that *Lynch* was describing a duty to provide full information in such a context, it was completely unremarkable. Indeed, for the next several years, application of the duty of candor was limited to cases involving conflict-of-interest transactions.

The turning point for the duty of disclosure was Smith v. Van Gorkom, 488 A.2d 858 (Del. 1985), a case typically cited for other reasons. The Delaware Supreme Court's discussion of the duty of disclosure is important because *Van Gorkom* did not involve a conflict-of-interest transaction. Nevertheless, the court held that the directors of Trans Union breached their fiduciary duty of disclosure "by their failure to disclose all material information such as a

---

1. For an excellent history of the duty of disclosure in Delaware, see Lawrence A. Hamermesh,*Calling Off the Lynch Mob: A Corporate Director's Fiduciary Disclosure Duty*, 49 Vand. L. Rev. 1087 (1996).

reasonable stockholder would consider important" in voting on the merger proposal. *Id.* at 893.

Van Gorkom opened whole new possibilities for the duty of disclosure, and the Delaware courts soon found themselves attempting to cage this new duty. By the time of Stroud v. Grace, 606 A.2d 75 (Del. 1992), decided seven years after *Van Gorkom,* the Delaware Supreme Court was comfortable asserting that the duty of candor "represents nothing more than the well-recognized proposition that directors of Delaware corporations are under a fiduciary duty to disclose fully and fairly all material information within the board's control when it seeks shareholder action." *Id.* at 84. But the *Stroud* court went one step further, holding that "in the absence of a proxy solicitation," corporate managers have a duty of disclosure contiguous with the requirements of the DGCL, and those requirements are fairly flimsy. In the context of charter amendments to be approved at an annual meeting — the issue in *Stroud* — the only state statutory disclosure requirements are a duty to provide notice of the meeting (DGCL §222(a)) and a duty to set forth and summarize the proposed amendment (DGCL §242(b)(1)).

Stroud was expressly "limited to non-public, privately-held corporations," *id.* at 86, and thus did not raise questions regarding the interface of federal and state disclosure duties. Defining the intersection of those two regulatory regimes became more urgent in 1995, when Congress adopted the Private Securities Litigation Reform Act (PSLRA), which raised the pleading standards for disclosure actions in federal courts. By increasing the burdens on federal disclosure claims, PSLRA necessarily made state disclosure claims more attractive. This was particularly true of Delaware disclosure claims, which did not require proof of reliance, causation, or quantifiable monetary damages. In short, they carried a "virtual per se rule of damages for breach of the fiduciary duty of disclosure." In re Tri-Star Pictures, Inc. Litigation, 634 A.2d 319, 333 (Del. 1993).

Sensing that the PSLRA was being undermined by increasing state litigation, Congress responded by passing the Securities Litigation Uniform Standards Act of 1998 (SLUSA). The purpose of the statute was to preempt state securities fraud class actions, but it explicitly preserved some of those actions through a provision tagged as the "Delaware carve-outs":

> (A) Actions preserved. — . . . [A] covered class action described in subparagraph (B) of this paragraph that is based upon the statutory or common law of the State in which the issuer is incorporated . . . may be maintained in a State or Federal court by a private party.
> (B) Permissible actions. — A covered class action is described in this subparagraph if it involves:
>> (i) the purchase or sale of securities by the issuer or an affiliate of the issuer exclusively from or to holders of equity securities of the issuer; or
>> (ii) any recommendation, position, or other communication with respect to the sale of securities of the issuer that —
>>> (I) is made by or on behalf of the issuer or an affiliate of the issuer to holders of equity securities of the issuer; and
>>> (II) concerns decisions of those equity holders with respect to voting their securities, acting in response to a tender or exchange offer, or exercising dissenters' or appraisal rights.

Securities Act of 1933, §16, 15 U.S.C. §77 (2003).

This provision played a central role in Malone v. Brincat, 722 A.2d 5 (Del. 1998), the Delaware Supreme Court's attempt to clarify the respective domains of federal and state securities law. *Malone* considered a claim by shareholders of Mercury Finance Company (Mercury), which became infamous for massive accounting fraud. Once unearthed, the fraud led to the quick demise of the company — a loss of approximately $2 billion in shareholder value. The distinguishing feature of the *Malone* claim is that the plaintiffs had not purchased or sold securities in reliance on the misstatements, nor were they claiming to have taken a particular action that was influenced by the misstatements.

The Court of Chancery dismissed the complaint on the ground that federal securities law — not state fiduciary law — was responsible for "ensur[ing] the timely release of accurate information into the marketplace." From the plaintiffs' perspective, the problem with this holding was that they did not qualify for a federal securities law claim. As will be discussed in more detail in Chapter 16, one of the elements of such a claim is that the plaintiff be a purchaser or seller of securities. In *Malone* the plaintiffs were shareholders who had purchased prior to the fraudulent disclosures and held throughout the relevant time periods.

The Delaware Supreme Court was less willing to cede ground. While stopping short of imposing a duty of continuous disclosure, the court held that general fiduciary principles require honest disclosure:

> The shareholder constituents of a Delaware corporation are entitled to rely upon their elected directors to discharge their fiduciary duties at all times. Whenever directors communicate publicly or directly with shareholders about the corporation's affairs, with or without a request for shareholder action, directors have a fiduciary duty to shareholders to exercise due care, good faith and loyalty. It follows *a fortiori* that when directors communicate publicly or directly with shareholders about corporate matters the *sine qua non* of directors' fiduciary duty to shareholders is honesty.

Malone, 722 A.2d at 10. The court then proceeded to define the respective domains of federal and state disclosure obligations.

Federal Securities Law. We will discuss federal regulation of corporate disclosure in some detail in Chapter 16. In *Malone*, the Delaware Supreme Court articulated a rather narrow view of its unique place in disclosure regulation:

> In deference to the panoply of federal protections that are available to investors in connection with the purchase or sale of securities of Delaware corporations, this Court has decided not to recognize a state common law cause of action against the directors of Delaware corporations for "fraud on the market." Here, it is to be noted, the claim appears to be made by those who did not sell and, therefore, would not implicate federal securities laws which relate to the purchase or sale of securities.

Malone, 722 A.2d at 13.

State Fiduciary Law: Action Requested. Delaware courts had long recognized a duty of disclosure in the context of a request for shareholder action. As noted above, this became the standard description of the domain of the duty of disclosure by the time of *Stroud*. *Malone* affirmed this tradition and stated that requests for shareholder action are the *only* contexts in which plaintiffs may assert a "duty of disclosure":

The duty of disclosure is, and always has been, a specific application of the general fiduciary duty owed by directors. The duty of disclosure obligates directors to provide the stockholders with accurate and complete information material to a transaction or other corporate event that is being presented to them for action.

The issue in this case is not whether Mercury's directors breached their duty of disclosure. It is whether they breached their more general fiduciary duty of loyalty and good faith by knowingly disseminating to the stockholders false information about the financial condition of the company. The directors' fiduciary duties include the duty to deal with their stockholders honestly.

Malone, 722 A.2d at 10.

As these paragraphs make clear, the "duty of disclosure" in Delaware is a term of art that does not cover all cases in which disclosure is at issue. In some instances — notably in *Malone* itself — failures of disclosure are dealt with under the more general rubrics of duty of loyalty or duty of care.

State Fiduciary Law: No Action Requested. Perhaps *Malone*'s most important holding was that directors do, in fact, owe a fiduciary duty, even when no shareholder action is requested. There appears to be some overlap with federal securities law here, but the court affirmed the continuing vitality of state fiduciary duties in this context:

When the directors disseminate information to stockholders when no stockholder action is sought, the fiduciary duties of care, loyalty and good faith apply. Dissemination of false information could violate one or more of those duties.

Malone, 722 A.2d at 12.

While the SLUSA did not apply to the transactions in *Malone*, which occurred prior to the passage of the statute, the court was mindful of its message and its apparent accommodation of overlap between federal and state claims. Still, the court commented, "The historic roles played by state and federal law in regulating corporate disclosures have been not only compatible but complementary." *Malone*, 722 A.2d at 13.

Despite the Court's efforts in *Malone* to clarify the line between federal and state disclosure actions, questions remained. The following cases explore this next generation of questions. *Millenco* considers whether directors can have more stringent disclosure obligations under state law than under federal law in areas where the two overlap, and *Lazar* considers the scope of the Delaware carve-outs.

MILLENCO L.P. v. meVC DRAPER FISHER JURVETSON FUND I, INC.

824 A.2d 11
Court of Chancery of Delaware
December 19, 2002

LAMB, Vice Chancellor.

I.

The plaintiff in this action is Millenco L.P., a privately owned company engaged in the business of investing for profit. Millenco is the largest stockholder of the defendant meVC Draper Fisher Jurvetson Fund I, Inc. (the "Fund"), owning over 6.3% of the Fund shares, purchased on the open market for a total purchase price of more than $10 million. Millenco has owned those shares continuously since before the record date of the Fund's 2001 Annual Meeting of Stockholders ("2001 Annual Meeting").

The Fund is a Delaware corporation organized as a closed-end mutual fund that has elected to be treated as a business development company under Section 54 the Investment Company Act of 1940 (the "1940 Act"). The Fund's stated investment objective is long-term capital appreciation from venture capital investments in information technology companies. In March 2000, the Fund conducted an initial public offering of its stock at $20 per share, realizing $311,650,000 of net proceeds. As of August 30, 2001, the closing price of the Fund's stock on the New York Stock Exchange had declined to $7.85 per share and the Fund's net asset value had declined to $12.35 per share.

The other defendants in this action are Larry J. Gerhard, Harold E. Hughes, Jr., Chauncey F. Lufkin and John Grillos, who are the current members of the Fund's board of directors. Before the IPO, the founders of the Fund appointed a five-member board of directors, consisting of the four individual defendants and Peter S. Freudenthal. Two of the five directors were representatives of the two Fund advisers: Freudenthal was a principal of MeVC Advisers, Inc. ("meVC Advisers") and defendant Grillos is a principal of Draper Fisher Jurvetson MeVC Management Co., LLC ("Draper Advisers"). Freudenthal was the Fund's President until he resigned in June 2002. Grillos has, at all times relevant to the complaint, been the Fund's CEO. Section 56(a) of the 1940 Act requires that a majority of the Fund's directors be independent. Gerhard, Hughes, and Lufkin were appointed to serve as the Fund's independent, disinterested directors. These three disinterested directors also comprised the Fund's three-member Audit Committee.

The directors' terms of office were staggered, with Freudenthal and Grillos designated to stand for reelection to three-year terms in 2001, Gerhard in 2002, and Hughes and Lufkin in 2003. Freudenthal and Grillos were reelected at the Fund's 2001 Annual Meeting. Gerhard was reelected in 2002.

II.

This action was begun on April 3, 2002. In the second amended complaint, Millenco seeks, among other things, to invalidate the elections of directors at the 2001 and 2002 Annual Meetings on grounds that the proxy solicitations conducted in connection therewith were materially false and misleading. At the heart of this claim lies the Fund's failure to disclose the existence of certain relationships between and among Grillos, an inside director, and Gerhard and Hughes, two nominally independent directors. These relationships arise out of the involvement of all three (*i.e.*, Grillos, Gerhard and Hughes) in an enterprise known as eVineyard, Inc. Millenco contends that full and accurate disclosure of the nature of those relationships was necessary for Fund stockholders to make an informed judgment about the "independence" of both Gerhard and Hughes.

A. GRILLOS'S INVOLVEMENT IN EVINEYARD

The business relationship of Grillos and Gerhard goes back for some years to a time when Grillos hired Gerhard as CEO of a company known as Test Systems Strategy, Inc. In 1999, Gerhard solicited Grillos to be an initial investor in eVineyard. Eventually, Grillos invested $256,000 personally, another $1,474,000 through iTech which Grillos managed as a principal, as well as additional sums as a limited partner in Osprey Ventures which invested approximately $1,500,000 in eVineyard.

In May 1999, Grillos was named to the eVineyard board of directors and also appointed as both Chairman of the Board and Chairman of the Compensation Committee. Pursuant to the eVineyard by-laws, the Chairman of the Board is an executive officer of the corporation. Moreover, Section 3.4 of those by-laws provides that "if the chief executive officer [*i.e.*, Gerhard] is not also the chairman of the board, then the chief executive officer [Gerhard] shall report to the chairman of the board [*i.e.*, Grillos]." Grillos continued to serve in these roles through November 6, 2001, when he resigned as Chairman of the Board, and January 28, 2002, when he resigned as a director and as Chairman of the Compensation Committee, but retained board visitation rights. While he was Chairman of the Board and Chairman of the Compensation Committee, eVineyard entered into a revised employment agreement with Gerhard. Grillos testified that he "took the lead" in terms of negotiating this contract with Gerhard.

Gerhard is a director of eVineyard and served as its CEO at all relevant times. Hughes is also a director of eVineyard and, for a time in 2001, served as COO/President. They are both substantial eVineyard stockholders.

B. GRILLOS AND GERHARD PROPOSE A FUND INVESTMENT IN EVINEYARD

On November 7, 2001, the day after Grillos's resignation as Chairman of eVineyard, Grillos and Gerhard proposed a transaction that Paul Wozniak, a principal of MeVC Advisers and CFO of the Fund, described as one in which "the [F]und would wind up owning eVineyard stock in a deal that essentially boils down to a straight purchase of eVineyard stock [for $1 million] despite the machinations created to make it look otherwise." Wozniak also noted: "Even if this transaction proves technically legal (which is questionable at this juncture), the appearance of conflict is so great that we at meVC Advisors do not wish for this deal to move forward."

C. 2001 PROXY AND ELECTION

In 2001, Grillos and Freudenthal were up for reelection to the Board at the annual shareholders meeting. On March 1, 2001, the Fund filed a proxy statement with the SEC that included the Board's recommendation for the reelection of these two directors. The proxy statement disclosed Grillos's and Freudenthal's status as "interested persons" of the Fund due to their affiliation with the Fund's investment advisers. It also disclosed that Gerhard, Hughes and Lufkin were the Fund's "disinterested" directors. Grillos's biography included a description of his positions with the Fund and its sub-adviser and certain other positions he had held or was holding at the time. It did not disclose his positions with or investment in eVineyard or his relationships with Gerhard and Hughes. Grillos and Freudenthal ran unopposed and on April 21, 2001 were reelected to three-year terms.

D. 2002 PROXY AND ELECTION

On February 25, 2002, the Fund filed with the SEC the proxy statement for the 2002 annual shareholders meeting. The proxy included two Board-recommended proposals for shareholder approval: (i) new advisory agreements with the Fund's investment adviser and sub-adviser, and (ii) Gerhard's reelection to the Board. The proxy statement disclosed that Gerhard was not an "interested" person of the Fund. His biography included his position as Chairman of the Board of eVineyard (having succeeded Grillos), as well as his prior positions as President and CEO of that company. It did not, however, disclose Grillos's relationship to eVineyard. Gerhard ran unopposed and was reelected.

Millenco opposed the ratification of the new advisory agreements and successfully conducted a campaign to defeat them.

III.

The parties have cross-moved for summary judgment on Millenco's claim seeking to invalidate the 2001 and 2002 elections of directors on grounds of breach of the directors' duty of disclosure. . . .

It is undisputed that no information relating to Grillos's association with eVineyard, Gerhard and Hughes was ever disclosed to the Fund's shareholders. Instead, the Fund's proxy statements have both disclosed that Gerhard, Hughes and Lufkin are "Independent Directors" who are not "interested persons" within the meaning of the 1940 Act. While the 2002 proxy statement discloses that Gerhard and Hughes are both affiliated with eVineyard, it does not disclose Grillos's past or current relationships with that company.

Millenco makes a plain and powerful argument that the omitted information about the Grillos/eVineyard connection was material. First, under Delaware law, the fiduciary duties of directors require that they disclose fully and with complete candor all material facts when they solicit proxies from stockholders. Second, that duty is "best discharged through a broad rather than a restrictive approach to disclosure,"[10] and mere technical compliance with a statutory mandate or relevant regulations does not create a safe harbor from liability for deceptive disclosures or material omissions. Third, "[a]n omitted fact is material if there is a substantial likelihood that a reasonable investor would consider it important in deciding how to vote."[12] Finally, where, as here, the omitted information goes to the independence or disinterest of directors who are identified as the company's "independent" or "not interested" directors, the "relevant inquiry is not whether an actual conflict of interest exists, but rather whether full disclosure of potential conflicts of interest has been made."[13] Applied to the facts presented, Millenco argues that the failure of either proxy statement to

---

10. Zirn v. VLI Corp., 621 A.2d 773, 779 (Del. 1993).
12. Rosenblatt v. Getty Oil Co., 493 A.2d 929, 944 (Del. 1985).
13. Wilson v. Great American Industries, Inc., 855 F.2d 987, 994 (2d Cir. 1988).

disclose or describe Grillos's relationship to eVineyard renders the proxy statements materially misleading and incomplete. A fund stockholder, Millenco suggests, would certainly have regarded the omitted information material in deciding how to vote on the election of directors in both 2001 and 2002.

The defendants make two arguments to avoid the result urged by Millenco. First, they argue that because the directors do not meet the definition of interestedness under the 1940 Act, the omitted information is immaterial as a matter of law. Second, the defendants argue that disclosure of the omitted information was not required because, when viewed in the context of the totality of information regarding Grillos's relationship to eVineyard, the omitted information does not bear materially on Gerhard's and Hughes's independence. These arguments are untenable.

[With respect to the first argument, the court held that the SEC had stressed the importance of the independent directors as "watchdogs" of investors' interests in mutual funds, and thus that the information would need to be disclosed under federal law. The court went on to hold that]:

Even if the relationships of the defendants did not fit perfectly within the ambit of Section 14A requirements, nondisclosure of the relationships is not excused under federal law. The SEC emphasized as much when it noted that the disclosure requirements of Schedule 14A were minimum requirements and not safe harbor determinations of materiality:

> [W]e wish to emphasize that a fund's independent directors can vigilantly represent the interests of shareholders only when they are truly independent of those who operate and manage the fund. To that end, we encourage funds to examine any circumstances that could potentially impair the independence of independent directors, whether or not they fall within the scope of our disclosure requirements.[17]

. . . Finally, it must be said that a discussion of whether the supposedly independent directors were in fact independent under the 1940 Act is only of passing significance to the court's analysis. The real issue is whether the omission of the information in question violated the defendants' disclosure duties under Delaware law. In that sense, disclosure is necessary if a stockholder would have considered the information important in deciding how to vote. As the foregoing discussion illustrates, the omitted information would almost certainly be considered important in the context of an election of directors, especially in the context of a registered investment company.

Given the chance, the Fund's stockholders could have reasonably inferred, either from Grillos's de jure powers at eVineyard or from his de facto exercise of such powers, that his roles at eVineyard gave Grillos actual or potential influence over Gerhard and/or Hughes, which influence could be viewed as affecting their judgment as independent directors of the Fund. Further, the defendants' frequent references to Gerhard and Hughes as "independent" or "disinterested" directors of the Fund strongly implies that they were free to act with complete and undivided loyalty to the Fund. The Fund's stockholders were entitled to know the omitted information in order to judge for themselves Gerhard's and Hughes's independence and disinterestedness.

17. 66 F.R. 3734, at *3743.

The defendants' second argument is that, even if the omitted information tended to show a lack of director independence, a complete understanding of Grillos's relationship with eVineyard shows that the undisclosed relationships could not have interfered with or diminished Gerhard's and Hughes's ability to act independently. This argument misconstrues the legal test to be applied. "Materiality is to be assessed from the viewpoint of the 'reasonable' stockholder, not from a director's subjective perspective."[20] In other words, it does not matter whether Gerhard and Hughes each strongly held his ability to act independently of Grillos or whether the other defendants shared this view. What matters is how a reasonable stockholder would have regarded disclosure of the facts relating to Grillos's relationships to eVineyard, Gerhard and Hughes. Millenco correctly argues that the facts surrounding these relationships bore on the directors' independence and, because there is a substantial likelihood a reasonable investor would have wanted to know about these facts in deciding how to vote on the elections of each of Grillos, Freudenthal, and Gerhard, needed to be disclosed in the 2001 and 2002 proxy materials.

The defendants' efforts to explain away the omitted information by pointing to additional information that softens or mitigates the impact of the omission merely reinforces the conclusion that the Fund stockholders should have been given the chance to decide for themselves how things looked. The possibility that, with the benefit of complete disclosure, the stockholders would have allowed these men to run unopposed for election can hardly justify the omission of any information at all.

In the end, the defendants cannot escape the conclusion that they should have presented their explanations about the various relationships in the proxy statements in which they solicited votes for the election of directors at the 2001 and 2002 Annual Meetings. They were free to explain why they believed that the eVineyard relationships did not have the potential to impair the independence of either Gerhard or Hughes as directors of the Fund. Had they done so, the stockholders would have been able to decide for themselves what significance to attribute to such facts and the accompanying explanations. What defendants were not free to do was to take the position that the stockholders had no right to know this information because they, the defendants, had determined it was not important.

IV.

In view of the court's conclusion that the election of directors at both the 2001 and 2002 Annual Meetings was procured by the use of materially false and misleading proxy materials, the appropriate remedy is to order new elections to fill the three director seats that were up for election at those meetings. The record reflects that, if Millenco had been furnished with the omitted information in 2001 or 2002, it would have acted to oppose the elections. The courts of this state "have long held that inequitable conduct by directors that interferes with a fair voting process may be set aside in equity."[24] Moreover, the "right of

20. [Arnold v. Society for Savings Bancorp, Inc., 650 A.2d 1270, 1277 (Del. 1994).]
24. Linton v. Everett, 1997 WL 441189 at *9 (Del. Ch. July 31, 1997).

shareholders to participate in the voting process includes the right to nominate an opposing slate."[25]

The only remaining issue is whether to order a new election in advance of the 2003 annual meeting of stockholders. The answer to that question will turn on when that meeting is or will be scheduled to be held. If the court receives assurances that such a meeting will be held within 60 days of the date of this opinion, the court will be inclined to the view that only a single meeting needs to be conducted. If not, the court will order the convening of a special meeting no later than February 15, 2003 for the purpose of electing 3 directors.

V.

For the foregoing reasons, Millenco's motion for summary judgment is granted, and the defendants' cross-motion for summary judgment is denied. Counsel for Millenco shall submit an order in conformity with this opinion no later than December 30, 2002, on notice.

LAZAR v. GREGERSON
2002 WL 535405
United States District Court, N.D. California
April 8, 2002

ILLSTON, J.

On April 5, 2002, the Court heard argument on plaintiff's motion for remand and defendants' motion to dismiss. Having considered the arguments of counsel and the papers submitted, and for the reasons set forth below, the Court hereby grants plaintiff's motion, remands this action to the San Francisco Superior Court where it was filed, and denies defendants' motion to dismiss as moot.

BACKGROUND

This putative class action lawsuit was brought on behalf of former holders of stock in PeerLogic, Inc. ("PeerLogic") against PeerLogic's former chairman, Daniel Gregerson, following the acquisition of PeerLogic by Critical Path, Inc. ("Critical Path"). The complaint, filed on November 9, 2001 in San Francisco Superior Court, alleges causes of action of breach of fiduciary duty and breach of the duty of candor and full disclosure. Class actions on behalf of an overlapping class of plaintiffs were also filed in federal court, commencing in February, 2001.

On February 6, 2002, defendants removed this action pursuant to the Securities Litigation Uniform Standards Act of 1998 ("SLUSA" or "the Act"). Thereafter, defendants filed a motion to dismiss, arguing that plaintiff's claims are preempted by SLUSA; and plaintiffs moved to remand, arguing that removal under SLUSA was improper. Both motions are presently before this Court. . . .

25. *Id.* (also noting that "[t]o set aside the election results on the basis of inequitable manipulation of the corporate machinery, it is not required that *scienter, i.e.,* actual subjective intent to impede the voting process be shown").

DISCUSSION

Defendants argue that plaintiff's claims are preempted by federal securities laws, and that dismissal is therefore required. Plaintiff argues that defendants' removal of this action was improper, because plaintiff's complaint only alleges violations of state law, and because the claims fall under a provision of SLUSA excepting certain actions from preemption.

In 1995, Congress enacted the Private Securities Litigation Reform Act ("PSLRA"), which imposed heightened procedural and substantive standards on class action plaintiffs in private securities actions in federal courts. Three years later, to prevent circumvention of the PSLRA by bringing securities lawsuits in state rather than federal courts, Congress enacted SLUSA. SLUSA provides as follows: [the court quotes the Delaware carve-outs.]

If an action is a "covered class action" that does not fall under this exemption, it is properly removed and dismissed. If a covered action is determined to be "preserved" under the so-called "Delaware carve-out" exemption provision of SLUSA, it must be remanded to state court. Neither party seriously argues that this is not a "covered class action" under SLUSA. The sole issue presented by the parties' motions is, therefore, whether plaintiffs' complaint falls within the scope of the "Delaware carve-out" exemption.

Turning to the complaint itself, it alleges that Gregerson and the Doe defendants breached their duties of loyalty, due care and candor to plaintiff by failing to ensure that the acquisition agreement reached between PeerLogic and Critical Path was fair and in the best interests of PeerLogic's shareholders; failing to ensure that merger materials disseminated to the class did not contain material misrepresentations of fact; and failing to conduct a reasonable investigation prior to the acquisition. Plaintiff alleges that "Defendants' willingness to ignore Critical Path's fraudulent accounting practices and false financial statements" resulted from their desire "to obtain significant payments for themselves via lucrative 'employment contracts,' 'severance agreements,' 'non-compete contracts' and/or 'consulting' agreements which were contemporaneously negotiated by defendants for their own benefit."

Specifically, the complaint alleges that on August 8, 2000, Critical Path and PeerLogic issued a joint statement announcing that an acquisition would occur and stating that the acquisition did not impact Critical Path's "commitment to fourth quarter 2000 profitability." The complaint alleges that defendants were provided with Critical Path financial information in the course of due diligence in preparation for the acquisition, and that defendants "failed to confirm the accuracy of the figures, assumptions or estimates provided by Critical Path." It alleges that, on the day after the acquisition, Critical Path issued a release touting the strengths of the new combination.

The complaint further alleges that the merger materials disseminated to PeerLogic shareholders incorporated false financial data provided by Critical Path to the PeerLogic board. This information included Critical Path's financial statements, a statement for the combined companies for a one year period, and documents filed with the SEC stating that the financial statements were prepared in accordance with GAAP and fairly represented Critical Path's financial condition. The complaint alleges that, by releasing these materials, PeerLogic's board exposed its shareholders to undisclosed risks and uncertainties. The complaint also alleges that PeerLogic's board of directors falsely stated that the acquisition was in the best interests of the company and its shareholders.

Finally, the complaint describes the loss of 55% of the value of Critical Path stock when, on January 19, 2001, Critical Path announced a loss for the forth quarter of 2000 and projected losses into 2001. Critical Path formed a committee to investigate its financial disclosures, and on February 15, 2001, admitted that its fourth quarter 2000 results were false. On April 5, 2001, Critical Path admitted that its third quarter 2000 revenues were overstated. The complaint alleges that these third and forth quarter statements violated GAAP principles. Based on these factual allegations, the complaint asserts causes of action for breach of the fiduciary duties of due care and loyalty, and breach of the duty of candor and full disclosure, against PeerLogic CEO Gregerson and 100 Doe defendants.

The complaint thus "is based upon the statutory or common law" of California, which is the state in which PeerLogic was incorporated. It is undisputed that no federal question appears on the face of the complaint. The complaint seeks relief based on common law duties, not federal securities law. SLUSA establishes federal courts' exclusive jurisdiction over actions brought "to enforce any liability or duty created by [the Securities Exchange Act of 1934] or the rules and regulations thereunder." Even though the complaint alleges false statements and omissions made by defendants in connection with the acquisition, plaintiff is not seeking to "enforce any liability or duty" arising under federal securities law.

Defendants argue that the Court should look behind the claims to find that the "gravamen of the complaint is that Critical Path made misrepresentations to PeerLogic and its shareholders." Although the factual basis for plaintiff's claims undeniably involves actions taken by Critical Path, the Court finds that, on the whole, the gravamen of the complaint concerns alleged wrongdoing by PeerLogic's board. Specifically, plaintiff alleges that Gregerson failed sufficiently to inquire into Critical Path's financial state, disseminated false information about the acquisition to PeerLogic shareholders, and falsely advised them that the acquisition was in their "best interests," all to secure personal benefits from the transaction. The Court therefore rejects defendants' invitation to recast plaintiff's complaint as a federal securities action.

Plaintiff's claims, moreover, fall directly under the explicit exclusionary language of §77p(d). Plaintiff and other former holders of PeerLogic stock claim that defendants breached their duties to PeerLogic shareholders, and that this breach occurred in defendants' communications concerning a proposed acquisition. Under SLUSA, such a claim is not removable. Defendants' argument to the contrary is essentially the same as their argument concerning the gravamen of the complaint, namely, that plaintiff's claims are fundamentally that she was harmed by Critical Path's alleged misstatements, not PeerLogic's. . . .

For the foregoing reasons, plaintiff's motion to remand is hereby granted and this action is remanded to the San Francisco Superior Court. Defendants' motion to dismiss is denied as moot.

CHAPTER
7

Federal Regulation of Shareholder Voting

As discussed in Chapter 5, the owners of common stock of a corporation may receive periodic dividends throughout the life of the firm. In addition, they have the right to receive any residual assets of the corporation if it is sold or goes bankrupt. Moreover, common stockholders have the right to be free from personal liability for the obligations of the corporation in most circumstances. These financial rights, although important, do not comprise the total bundle of stockholder rights. As discussed in Chapter 6, common stockholders also have voting rights. We examine federal regulation of voting rights in this chapter. Another important shareholder right, the right to initiate litigation is the focus of Chapter 12.

In a public corporation, a shareholder's management rights — also called the right to a "voice" — are exercised primarily through the right to vote. Each share of common stock carries with it one vote. The shareholders' voting power is exercised primarily through the election or removal of directors (usually at an annual meeting of shareholders), amendments to the articles of incorporation and other fundamental transactions (such as a merger with another company), and changes to the corporation's bylaws. As will be discussed below, shareholders can also have a voice in the company through their power to bring proposals for board action forward in the annual meeting (called "shareholder resolutions"). This latter power has become increasingly important — and contested — in reaction to the corporate governance concerns raised in 2002 and 2003 by problems at Enron, WorldCom, and the like, which will be discussed in detail in the next chapter.

While these voting rights may appear substantial, serious practical limitations impede the exercise of shareholder voice. Professors Adolf Berle and Gardiner Means recognized the shareholders' effective inability to control important decisions in the public corporation in 1932 in an extremely influential book, *The Modern Corporation and Private Property*. Berle and Means described one of the defining features of a public corporation as a separation of share ownership from effective control. That is, while the shareholders are understood by many to be the owners of the corporation, their powers of control over the corporation are limited compared to other types of ownership. Even where shareholders have power — for example, the power to elect the board of directors — that power is reactive: in the overwhelming majority of cases, shareholders react to the nominees presented by managers rather than bringing forth their own nominees. As we will see below, shareholders may nominate their own candidates for the board of directors, but this right is rarely exercised. In 2001, there were only 24 shareholder-initiated contests for seats on the board of directors of America's 14,200 public companies. Instead, control is exercised by the management of the corporation, who collectively might own a very low percentage of shares of the company.

Since Berle and Means highlighted this issue, the separation of ownership from control has been a defining issue in debates about state corporate law and federal securities law. Distilled to its essence, the issue is this: managers of large public corporations have the power to make almost all of the decisions in the corporation, from what pencils to buy to what companies to buy. Clearly, centralized power is necessary if anything at all is to be accomplished on a daily basis, since it would be impossible to put every decision that needs to be made to a shareholder referendum. Moreover, centralized power ensures that someone with management expertise and knowledge in the relevant field is making decisions. And yet, what ensures that managers are making decisions that are in the corporation's best interest or in the shareholders' best interest, rather than in the manager's best interest? When a company buys private jets for its executives or hangs an original Van Gogh in the company's headquarters, is that decision ultimately going to be reflected in increased productivity or profitability, or is it ultimately going to be reflected in an increased sense of executive self-worth, or some mixture of both? Given the broad discretion allocated to managers and directors, what assurance is there that they will be accountable to the corporation and its shareholders, and even, perhaps, to society at large? That is the question that Berle and Means posed in 1932, and it is a question that is still at the core of the study of corporate law.

One mechanism of accountability applicable to public corporations is found in the federal securities laws, including the Securities Act of 1933 and the Securities Exchange Act of 1934, both of which were passed in the shadow of Berle and Means' book. In these statutes, Congress explicitly sought to require companies to provide more information to investors and the market on a regular basis so that investors could make informed investment and voting decisions and exercise what power they had with full and accurate information.

Another mechanism of accountability applicable to both public and closely held corporations is the power of shareholders to vote to elect and remove directors and to approve or reject fundamental transactions. These two mechanisms of accountability are the subject of this chapter. Other mechanisms of corporate accountability, such as the market for corporate control (takeovers), the fiduciary duties of managers and directors, and litigation to enforce shareholders' rights and directors' duties, will be discussed in subsequent chapters.

In a public corporation, shareholder voting occurs in the direct intersection of federal securities law and state corporate law. Thus, state corporate law defines the decisions about which shareholders have voting rights, while federal securities law sets out the procedures by which those votes occur and prescribes the information that shareholders must be provided with prior to voting. The next Section of this chapter describes that intersection of federal and state law, and the subsequent Section introduces federal securities regulation more fully. Shareholders' voting powers, and how they are exercised pursuant to federal regulation, as well as the practical limitations on them, are discussed in the final Sections of this chapter.

A.   SHAREHOLDER VOTING

As a general matter, state corporate law identifies the types of issues on which shareholders may or must vote, and for public corporations, federal law sets out the procedures by which voting occurs and explains what information must be provided to shareholders prior to their votes. As you saw previously, under state law common shareholders have a number of voting rights, including the right to determine who will be on the board of directors, the right to vote on fundamental transactions, the right to vote on amendments to the charter or the bylaws, and the right to vote on shareholders' proposals.

The procedure by which voting occurs in a public company today is called the "proxy process." A "proxy" is the authorization given by a shareholder to another person to vote the shareholder's shares. Most often, in a public corporation shareholders' proxies are successfully sought by incumbent management, which means that management has the right to cast most shareholders' votes! Yet, based on federal securities law, management must indicate to shareholders how they will vote on every item coming up on the agenda as part of the process of soliciting proxy authority, so shareholders know how their votes will be cast when they delegate authority to management. The process of soliciting proxies takes place well before the shareholder meeting, and the logistics are handled by a proxy solicitation firm. If there is a contested election or shareholder vote, almost all of the important persuasion and discussion takes place prior to the vote by different factions sending out competing packets of information (proxy solicitations). An example of such a vote was the 2002 vote by shareholders of the Hewlett Packard company (HP) about whether to acquire the Compaq Computer Corporation. In a somewhat unusual development, one of HP's directors, Walter Hewlett, voted for the acquisition as a member of the board, and then, on further consideration, changed his mind and led a proxy battle against the acquisition. Although his efforts were ultimately unsuccessful, it was a highly pitched campaign played out in the pages of the Wall Street Journal and other leading business publications, leading to a razor-thin margin of victory in favor of the merger and the strategic vision of HP's CEO and chairman of the board, Carly Fiorina.

B.   FEDERAL SECURITIES REGULATION AND CAPITAL MARKETS

The proxy solicitation process is regulated under the federal securities laws. Prior to 1933, there was no federal regulation of the sale of securities. Rather, 47 states regulated such sales within their own borders under state "blue sky laws," named after the oft-repeated comment of a Kansas legislator that "some securities swindlers were so barefaced they 'would sell building lots in the blue sky.'" Joel Seligman, *The Transformation of Wall Street: A History of the Securities and Exchange Commission and Modern Corporation Finance* (2d ed. 1995). The New York Stock Exchange, where the majority of securities were bought and sold, was privately owned by its member stock brokers (as it is today) and subject to self-regulation (as it is today, though the Securities and Exchange Commission (SEC) now exercises oversight over the Exchange's self-regulation).

As you probably know, in the early 1930s the United States, and the world, suffered through a serious economic depression. While it is typical to talk of the "stock market crash" as part of the Great Depression, it is more historically accurate to talk of the stock market's "slow but steady decline." Thus, from September of 1929 through July of 1932, the aggregate value of all of the stocks traded on the New York Stock Exchange declined by more than 80 percent. In the context of great economic insecurity and loss, Wall Street, fairly or unfairly, became synonymous with the economic problems facing the nation and a favored target for Franklin Roosevelt to attack on the campaign trail. Once elected in November 1932, President Roosevelt identified the enactment of new federal laws to regulate the securities markets as one of his top priorities.

Congress agreed with President Roosevelt and enacted seven major securities statutes between 1933 and 1940 to address concerns about the management of U.S. companies and the workings of the capital markets. The two most important of these statutes are the Securities Act of 1933 (the "'33 Act") and the Securities Exchange Act of 1934 (the "'34 Act"). The '33 Act is a transaction-specific statute that regulates sales of stocks or bonds to the public in primary market transactions — that is, transactions in which a company sells stocks or bonds to the public, which usually happens with the assistance of an underwriter. (An underwriter is a securities firm that buys a new batch of stocks or bonds from a company, called the issuer, and resells them to the public at a profit.) The '33 Act primarily defines the kinds of information that must be available about companies, about the new securities being offered, and about the underwriting arrangements prior to sales to the public being allowed. In addition, the '33 Act sets out onerous liability provisions whenever issuers or underwriters participate in sales that involve material misstatements or material omissions of fact, including provisions mandating strict liability for issuers.

The '34 Act is a much more comprehensive statute that generally regulates secondary market transactions — that is, purchases and sales of securities among investors in the trading markets and exchanges. The '34 Act regulates the Exchanges, such as the New York Stock Exchange, the American Stock Exchange, and eight regional exchanges. Today the '34 Act also regulates computerized trading mechanisms, such as the NASDAQ trading market and electronic bulletin boards. The '34 Act both regulates the actions of brokers and dealers in those trading venues with respect to some trading practices and delegates authority to the SEC to regulate other aspects of broker/dealer conduct. The '34 Act also regulates certain actions in the markets, such as buying securities "on margin" (on credit) or "short-swing" sales of securities (buying and then reselling, or selling and then repurchasing, securities within six months) by company insiders and prohibits other activities, such as market manipulation or fraud. The '34 Act also delegates power to the SEC to regulate the proxy process, and, as amended in 1978, regulates tender offers for shares of stock. ("Tender offers" are offers to buy a control block of shares of a public company — generally 51 percent of the shares — in order to take control of that company.) The '34 Act also identifies the kinds of information public reporting companies are required to disclose to the market on a regular basis — quarterly, annually, and whenever there are significant corporate developments, such as the resignation of the CEO or the company's accountants, or the purchase or sale of significant assets, such as a subsidiary. ("Public reporting companies" are defined as companies with securities listed on a national securities exchange (sections 12(a) and 12(g) of the Securities Exchange Act of 1934), or with common stock held by more than 750 shareholders and with assets of $10 million or more (*id.*, as further developed by Rule 12g-1), or with bonds listed on an exchange and held by more than 300 people. *Id.*, §15(d).)

As can be seen, Congress used a number of regulatory approaches in the securities acts, from outright prohibitions of certain actions to standard setting for acceptable conduct with respect to other types of actions. But the regulatory approach that applies most directly to our corporate governance triumvirate — officers, directors, and shareholders — is mandatory disclosure. Congress sought to ensure that full, accurate information about public companies would be available to the markets and shareholders on a regular basis — whenever companies issued new stocks or bonds; in periodic disclosure, quarterly, and annually; when there are significant corporate developments; and in proxy disclosure whenever shareholders were being asked to vote on anything, from the annual elections of directors to extraordinary transactions such as a merger.

In adopting disclosure as a primary regulatory mandate, Congress rejected the idea of directly regulating the merits of companies' actions, so long as shareholders and potential shareholders were fully informed of the risks entailed. The SEC does not review whether a company should issue new securities, given its capital structure, or even whether a company is at risk for not being able to pay on its bond obligations. Rather, when SEC staff members review disclosure documents, they are looking to see if the risks of an investment are adequately disclosed. For instance, consider a company trying to raise money by selling stock in order to drill for oil or gas. Assume the company doesn't own the land on which it wants to drill; doesn't have a lease on the land; doesn't know if it can get a lease on the land; hasn't done geological tests to see if there is oil and gas beneath the surface; and doesn't know if it would be commercially feasible to extract that oil or gas if it were there. Raising money for such a speculative project is fine under the federal securities laws, so long as the rather substantial uncertainties are clearly described in the offering document (called a "prospectus") under the '33 Act.

Two general points should be emphasized about mandatory disclosure under the federal securities laws. First, for public companies disclosure is a continuous process, being required at fixed times throughout the year and upon the occurrence of important transactions. This disclosure is meant to provide mechanisms of accountability to the shareholders that Congress thought were lacking in the 1920s and early 1930s, so that shareholders would know what managers are doing with their company and could react accordingly. Second, while much of the required disclosure is financial information, there is also a lot of pure corporate governance information that is required to be disclosed — not only who the managers and directors are and what their financial compensation is from the company, but also information about significant conflicts of interest that might exist between the company and its officers. In this sense it is accurate to say that corporate governance today is a matter of significant federal as well as state concern. In fact, the "federalization" of corporate governance has increased substantially with the Sarbanes-Oxley Act of 2002, to be discussed in Chapter 8.

C. FEDERAL PROXY REGULATION

Having set out an overview of federal securities regulation generally, we now turn more specifically to federal proxy regulation. The purpose of this regulation is to provide shareholders with the information necessary for them make informed choices when voting. Toward that end, there is a disclosure document, called a "proxy statement," that must be provided directly to the shareholders (or to the people who will be exercising voting power for institutional investors, such as mutual fund or pension fund managers) whenever the shareholders have the right to vote and thus whenever the shareholder's proxy is being "solicited." The requirements for the proxy statement are set out in Schedule 14A, promulgated under the authority of §14(a) of the '34 Act. Section 14(a) is a broad delegation of authority to the SEC to regulate the proxy process, which states:

> It shall be unlawful for any person . . . in contravention of such rules and regulations as the Commission may prescribe as necessary or appropriate in the public interest or for the protection of investors, to solicit or to permit the use of his name to solicit any proxy or consent or authorization in respect of any security [issued by a public reporting company].

The proxy solicitation process typically occurs in preparation for the annual meeting required under state law. *See* Delaware General Corporation Law (DGCL) §211(b); Model Business Corporation Act (Model Act) §7.01. Proxies can also be solicited as part of an extraordinary transaction outside the context of an annual meeting, such as the approval of a merger in those situations where the shareholders have voting rights, or the removal of existing directors in the context of a hostile takeover attempt. Since the overwhelming majority of shareholders who vote do so in advance by giving their proxy (legal authority) to a delegee to vote their shares on the basis of the proxy statement, the proxy solicitation process in a public corporation is the voting process, and the focus of regulatory activity is in ensuring that the proxy statement is comprehensive and accurate.

At the annual meeting, the major item of business is to elect the directors for the next year, or for the next term of years in a company with a staggered board. Other important items of business on the agenda typically include approving the accountants for the next year, and approving any executive compensation packages.[1] Moreover, there may be proposals by the board of directors to amend the certificate of incorporation for some reason, such as to authorize the issuance of new shares of stock or to adopt anti-takeover devices. Directors might also have the power to propose amendments to the bylaws under a particular company's certificate of incorporation; if so, director proposals to

---

1. While the shareholders don't have a right to approve executive compensation packages under state law, under federal tax law there are financial advantages to the company if the shareholders have approved performance-based executive compensation packages, such as granting stock options geared to the performance of the company. Also, in 2002 the New York Stock Exchange adopted rules to expand the types of stock-based executive compensation plans that must be approved by the shareholders in firms listed on the Exchange.

amend the bylaws might be on the agenda for the annual meeting.[2] Each of these agenda items must be fully and accurately described in the proxy statement, examples of which are easily accessible in the database of public filings at the SEC, the Electronic Data Gathering and Retrieval System (EDGAR). *See* *http://www.sec.gov/edgar.shtml.*

In addition, shareholders can propose items of business for the agenda of the annual meeting. If a particular group of shareholders wants to initiate a change to the bylaws, for instance, or suggest that the board study a particular issue, they would send a "shareholders' resolution" and 500-word supporting statement to the company well in advance of the annual meeting and ask the company to include the resolution and supporting statement in the company's proxy statement. The company will do so, reluctantly in most cases, if the resolution meets the procedural and substantive requirements that the SEC has established. Over the last few years shareholders have become increasingly active in putting shareholder resolutions on the agenda, challenging everything from executive compensation to the structure of the CEO's position to environmental compliance. This development is discussed in Section 3, below. If there are shareholders' resolutions on the agenda, these too will be described by both management and the shareholder proponents, and the resolution, and both parties' descriptions, will be included in the company's proxy statement. (Clearly, though, management will give reasons for a no vote on the resolution, and will make it clear that if shareholders give their proxy power to management it will be used to vote against the shareholders' resolution, while the shareholder proponents will identify reasons to vote yes on their resolution.)

The following sections of this chapter describe the most important aspects of federal regulation of the proxy solicitation process.

1.   *Definition of "Proxy Solicitation"*

Federal proxy regulations promulgated pursuant to section 14(a) of the '34 Act apply only to shareholder communications that are defined as "proxy solicitations." Thus, only those communications that seek voting authority are regulated under section 14(a). In general, once a communication is identified as a proxy solicitation, Rules 14a-3 to 14a-15 apply, requiring the party engaging in a proxy solicitation to send a "proxy statement" with specified information to the shareholders being solicited. These rules regulate the information that must be provided to shareholders (Rule 14a-3, as further specified in Schedule 14A); the format for the actual proxy card that shareholders are asked to fill out (Rule 14a-4); and the format for the presentation of information (Rule 14a-5). In addition, Rule 14a-6 requires anyone soliciting a proxy to file a preliminary proxy statement with the SEC, followed by the filing of a definitive proxy statement, which is also sent to shareholders.

---

2. Under Delaware law, shareholders always have the power to initiate changes to the bylaws, notwithstanding the particular company's charter, which might also give a concurrent power to the board to initiate changes to the bylaws. DGCL §109(a). The Model Act contains a similar structure of potentially concurrent power but allows the articles of incorporation to reserve the power to change the bylaws exclusively to the shareholders. Model Act §10.20 (b)(1).

Rules 14a-7 and 14a-8 are particularly concerned with shareholders' resolutions. Rule 14a-7 concerns the obligation of companies either to provide interested shareholders with a shareholders' list so that the shareholders can communicate directly with other shareholders concerning a resolution or to mail soliciting materials directly to shareholders at the soliciting shareholders' expense. Rule 14a-8 sets out the procedural and substantive requirements under which companies will be required to include shareholder proposals and supporting material in the company's definitive proxy statement. The most important part of Rule 14a-8 sets out the reasons that companies can exclude shareholder proposals from the company's proxy statement. Given that shareholders would far prefer their materials to be included in the company's proxy statement and thus mailed at the company's expense, much of the debate and legal wrangling over shareholder proposals takes place in the context of Rule 14a-8.

Rule 14a-9 sets out a cause of action for false or misleading statements in a proxy statement. Because Rule 14a-9 sets out the primary cause of action for liability for a misleading proxy communication, we discuss it in more detail below. Rule 14a-10 prohibits certain solicitations; Rule 14a-12 identifies exceptions to the general requirement to send a written proxy statement prior to engaging in a proxy solicitation; Rule 14a-13 covers the procedure for communicating with banks, brokerage firms, or other entities that hold securities for investors; and Rules 14a-14 through 14a-16 cover specific situations and transactions.

None of these rules apply, though, unless a communication is a proxy solicitation. The definition of "proxy solicitations" under Rule 14a-1 is broad, however, as it reaches both direct communications requesting voting authority and indirect communications that may have an impact on voting decisions. Thus, Rule 14a-1(*l*) defines "solicitation" as follows:

> (1) The terms "solicit" and "solicitation" include:
>   (i) Any request for a proxy whether or not accompanied by or included in a form of proxy;
>   (ii) Any request to execute or not to execute, or to revoke, a proxy; or
>   (iii) The furnishing of a form of proxy or other communication to security holders under circumstances reasonably calculated to result in the procurement, withholding or revocation of a proxy.

This last subparagraph in particular has been broadly construed by the courts. In the following case, Long Island Lighting Co. v. Barbash, the Second Circuit considered whether newspaper advertisements published in the midst of a public debate over the construction of a nuclear power plant could be considered a "proxy solicitation." As you will see, the *Barbash* court employs an expansive definition of "solicitation," over the vigorous dissent of Judge Winter. The major implication of a communication being held to be a proxy solicitation is that usually the party making it must send a proxy statement (as defined in Rule 14a-3 and Schedule 14A) to all of the shareholders being solicited.

In response to *Barbash*, and to other concerns expressed by institutional investors about communications among fund managers being construed as "proxy solicitations," the SEC amended its proxy rules in 1992 to allow more communications among shareholders free of a need to distribute a written proxy statement. In particular, Rule 14a-2(b) was amended to create exemptions from the proxy statement delivery requirements where a person (other than a member of management or of the board of a registrant, or a person with a substantial financial interest in a matter on the agenda) simply wants to communicate about a matter of corporate governance or about proposals on the agenda without seeking proxy authority. These amendments are intended to allow large institutional shareholders to communicate more freely among themselves about corporate performance and about the quality of management, in response to a growing "shareholder rights" movement in the 1990s among institutional investors. Whether these exemptions to the requirements to send a written proxy statement go far enough in allowing vibrant shareholder communications is a subject of continuing debate. As you read *Barbash*, consider whether the communications at issue in the case would fall within the exemptions in SEC Rule 14a-2(b), and thus whether the result would be any different today than when *Barbash* was decided.

LONG ISLAND LIGHTING CO. v. BARBASH
United States Court of Appeals, Second Circuit
779 F.2d 793
December 13, 1985

CARDAMONE, Circuit Judge.

A Long Island utility furnishing that area with power has scheduled a stockholders meeting for Thursday December 12, 1985. It has been embroiled in public controversy over its construction of the Shoreham Nuclear Power Plant and adverse publicity intensified recently because of extended loss of service to customers arising from damages to the transmission system caused by Hurricane Gloria.

In this setting, the company, believing that several groups had begun to solicit proxies during October in anticipation of the upcoming stockholders meeting, brought suit to enjoin them. The district court judge first slowed the matter by adjourning the case until the fall election was over, and then speeded it up by directing discovery to be completed in one day. Such handling only demonstrates again that in the law it is wise — even when expeditious action is required — to make haste slowly.

Long Island Lighting Company (LILCO) brings this expedited appeal from a November 8, 1985 order of the United States District Court for the Eastern District of New York (Weinstein, Ch. J.) that granted summary judgment dismissing LILCO's complaint against the Steering Committee of Citizens to Replace LILCO (the Citizens Committee), John W. Matthews and Island Insulation Corp. LILCO brought this action to enjoin defendants' alleged violations of §14(a) of the Securities Exchange Act of 1934 and Rules 14a-9, 17 C.F.R. §240.14a-9 and 14a-11, 17 C.F.R. 240.14a-11, promulgated under that statute, that govern proxy solicitations. The complaint alleges that defendants have committed such violations by publishing a false and misleading advertisement in connection with a special meeting of LILCO's shareholders scheduled for the purpose of electing a new LILCO Board of Directors. For the reasons explained below, this matter is remanded to the district court.

I

Plaintiff LILCO is a New York electric company serving Nassau and Suffolk Counties on Long Island, New York. Its common and preferred stocks are registered in accordance with Section 12(b) of the Securities Exchange Act and are traded on the New York Stock Exchange. Defendant John W. Matthews was an unsuccessful candidate for Nassau County Executive in the election held November 5, 1985. During the campaign he strongly opposed LILCO and its operation of the Shoreham Nuclear Power Plant. As an owner of 100 shares of LILCO's preferred stock and a manager of an additional 100 shares of common stock held by his company, Island Insulation Corp., Matthews initiated a proxy contest for the purpose of electing a majority of LILCO's Board of Directors. The stated purpose of the other defendants, the Citizens Committee, is to replace LILCO with a municipally owned utility company. The Citizens Committee was formed prior to this litigation, in order to challenge LILCO's construction of the Shoreham atomic energy plant, its service and its rates.

LILCO filed its complaint on October 21, 1985 alleging that defendants published a materially false and misleading advertisement in Newsday, a Long Island newspaper, and ran false and misleading radio advertisements throughout the New York area. The ads criticized LILCO's management and encouraged citizens to replace LILCO with a state-run company. The complaint sought an injunction against further alleged solicitation of LILCO shareholders until the claimed false and misleading statements had been corrected and a Schedule 14B had been filed. The district court granted LILCO an expedited hearing on its appeal from Magistrate Scheindlin's decision denying expedited discovery and also set for hearing defendants' motions to dismiss the complaint pursuant to Fed. R. Civ. P. 12(b)(6).

On October 30, 1985 Chief Judge Weinstein adjourned the hearing until November 6 in order to prevent interference with Matthews' political campaign. The district court directed the defendants to bring the requested documents to the hearing on that date and told Matthews and others whom LILCO wished to depose to be available for such discovery. At the November 6 hearing the district judge directed LILCO's counsel to question Matthews under oath and overruled counsel's objections that he was unprepared to examine Matthews and that he had no prior opportunity to review the defendants' documents. The trial court also refused LILCO's request to question other defendants and told counsel that it must limit its questions to the alleged "conspiracy" between Matthews and the other defendants. Two days after this hearing the district court issued its Preliminary Memorandum Dismissing Complaint. Treating defendant's motion to dismiss as one for summary judgment, the district court granted summary judgment in favor of defendants on the ground that the proxy rules did not apply to the advertisements. This appeal followed.

II

LILCO argues first, that in view of the necessity in every case to determine whether a communication constitutes a "solicitation" under the proxy rates, the district court abused its discretion by limiting LILCO's opportunity for discovery. Second, LILCO asserts that the district court erroneously held that communications to shareholders through general and indirect publications can in no circumstances constitute "solicitations" under the proxy rules. Finally, LILCO contests the district court's view that this construction of the proxy rules is necessary to render them compatible with the First Amendment. . . .

B. RULES GOVERNING PROXY SOLICITATION

In our view the district court further erred in holding that the proxy rules cannot cover communications appearing in publications of general circulation and that are indirectly addressed to shareholders. Regulation 14(a) of the Securities Exchange Act governs the solicitation of proxies with respect to the securities of publicly held companies, with enumerated exceptions set forth in the rules. 17 C.F.R. §240.14a-1 *et seq.* Proxy rules promulgated by the Securities Exchange Commission (SEC) regulate as proxy solicitations:

> (1) any request for a proxy whether or not accompanied by or included in a form of proxy;
> (2) any request to execute or not to execute, or to revoke, a proxy; or
> (3) the furnishing of a form of proxy or other communications to security holders under circumstances reasonably calculated to result in the procurement, withholding or revocation of a proxy.

Rule 14a-1(l), 17 C.F.R. §240.14a-1(l).

These rules apply not only to direct requests to furnish, revoke or withhold proxies, but also to communications which may indirectly accomplish such a result or constitute a step in a chain of communications designed ultimately to accomplish such a result. Securities and Exchange Commission v. Okin, 132 F.2d 784, 786 (2d Cir. 1943) (letter to shareholders was within the scope of the proxy rules where it was alleged that it was "a step in a campaign whose purpose it was to get [defendant] elected an officer of the company; it was to pave the way for an out-and-out solicitation later.")

The question in every case is whether the challenged communication, seen in the totality of circumstances, is "reasonably calculated" to influence the shareholders' votes. *See id.*; Trans. World Corp. v. Odyssey Partners, 561 F. Supp. 1311, 1320 (S.D.N.Y. 1983). Determination of the purpose of the communication depends upon the nature of the communication and the circumstances under which it was distributed. Brown v. Chicago, Rock Island & Pacific R.R., 328 F.2d 122 (7th Cir. 1964). In Studebaker Corporation v. Gittlin, 360 F.2d 692, 694 (2d Cir. 1966), the defendant solicited authorizations from shareholders to obtain a shareholder list in the course of a proxy fight. Because the authorizations were sought only for the purpose of seeking future proxies, the court held that the authorizations were also covered by the proxy rules. *Id.* at 696.

Deciding whether a communication is a proxy solicitation does not depend upon whether it is "targeted directly" at shareholders. *See* Rule 14a-6(g), 17 C.F.R. §240.14a-6(g) (requiring that solicitations in the form of "speeches, press releases, and television scripts" be filed with the SEC). As the SEC correctly notes in its amicus brief, it would "permit easy evasion of the proxy rules" to exempt all general and indirect communications to shareholders, and this is true whether or not the communication purports to address matters of "public interest." *See* Medical Comm. for Human Rights v. SEC, 432 F.2d 659 (D.C. Cir. 1970) (applying proxy rules to shareholder's proposal to prohibit company from manufacturing napalm during the Vietnam War). The SEC's authority to regulate proxy solicitations has traditionally extended into matters of public interest.

C. FIRST AMENDMENT CONCERNS

The extent to which the activities of the defendants amount to a solicitation of the proxies of shareholders of LILCO may determine whether or not their actions are protected by the First Amendment. Therefore, it is unnecessary to express an opinion on any claim of privilege under the First Amendment until there has been a determination of the "solicitation" issue as a result of further proceedings in the district court.

III

Because discovery here was so abbreviated and the district court's determination was predicated on a mistaken notion of what constitutes a proxy solicitation and on the relationship between the proxy rules and the First Amendment, the case must be remanded to the district court. LILCO represented during oral argument before us that — if given the opportunity — its discovery could be swiftly completed. We suggest that on remand the district court limit LILCO's discovery to an appropriate period. Even this expedited schedule will obviously conflict with the scheduled stockholders meeting of December 12. LILCO advised the Court by letter dated November 22, 1985 that after reasonable discovery it also wanted an opportunity to move for a preliminary injunction. Thus, in light of its request the meeting should probably be postponed and, if necessary, stayed by order of the district court. Finally, this panel retains jurisdiction over this matter to the extent that after the district court has had an opportunity to conduct its proceedings and rule on the merits, we will address the issues raised on appeal.

   In consideration of the time constraints, the mandate of the Court shall issue forthwith.

   WINTER, Circuit Judge, dissenting.
   In order to avoid a serious First Amendment issue, I would construe the federal regulations governing the solicitation of proxies as inapplicable to the newspaper advertisement in question. *See* Lowe v. Securities and Exchange Commission, 472 U.S. 181, 105 S. Ct. 2557, 86 L. Ed. 2d 130 (1985). Further discovery would then be unnecessary, and I therefore respectfully dissent.

I

First, the facts. The Long Island Lighting Company (LILCO) is a state-regulated public utility. It is currently the subject of controversy in its service area concerning the safety of a nuclear power plant, the cost of constructing that plant, the level of electricity rates, and service difficulties resulting from a recent hurricane.

One of LILCO's principal antagonists is John W. Matthews, a defendant in this litigation. During the fall of 1985, Matthews was the Democratic candidate for County Executive in Nassau County and appears to have focused much of his campaign upon LILCO issues. During this campaign, Matthews purchased a sufficient number of shares of LILCO's preferred stock to force a special shareholders' meeting pursuant to its Charter. On October 9, 1985, he made a demand for such a meeting. The next day, a corporation that is controlled by Matthews and owns LILCO common stock asked to inspect and copy LILCO's list of common stockholders. The stated purpose of this request was to enable it and Matthews to communicate with LILCO shareholders with regard to the election of LILCO's Board and to whether LILCO should be sold to Nassau and Suffolk Counties.

Another group of antagonists are the other individual defendants, who constitute a group styled "Citizens to Replace LILCO." On October 15 the Citizens to Replace LILCO published the newspaper advertisement that has given rise to the present litigation. That advertisement accused LILCO of mismanagement and of attempting to pass through to ratepayers needless costs relating to construction of the nuclear power plant. It also noted that a publicly owned power authority would not have to pay dividends to stockholders. The advertisement argued strenuously that ratepayers would be better off if a Long Island Power Authority were created to replace LILCO as a supplier of power. It asked readers to join the Committee and to give it financial support.

LILCO's complaint alleges that Matthews and the defendant members of the Citizens to Replace LILCO acted in a concerted fashion to publish this advertisement in order to influence the exercise of proxies by LILCO shareholders. It alleges that the advertisement was false and misleading in numerous respects relating to alleged advantages for ratepayers in the creation of a public power authority. Claiming a violation of federal proxy regulations, LILCO asked for an injunction prohibiting the defendants from soliciting proxies until they make appropriate filings with the Securities and Exchange Commission and correct the false and misleading statements in the ad. The relief requested would prevent further publication of the ad.

After the truncated discovery described by my colleagues, the district judge denied the injunction and granted summary judgment for the defendants. He stated that in his view: "Even if defendants did conspire to influence the outcome of the proxy fight . . . this fact would be irrelevant." The case as framed on appeal thus raises two issues. First is the question, fully briefed and argued by the parties and *amici*, whether the federal regulation of proxy materials applies to newspaper advertisements such as the one at issue and, if so, whether those regulations so applied do not violate the First Amendment. Second is the question whether, assuming that the proxy regulations do apply and pass constitutional muster, the case should be remanded for further discovery.

It is clear, of course, that the second issue — the need for further discovery — cannot be determined until the relationship of the proxy regulations to the First Amendment has been resolved. If, for example, the First Amendment protects such advertisements regardless of the motive of those who purchase them, further discovery would be irrelevant. My colleagues, asserting that "the district court's determination was predicated on a mistaken notion . . . on the relationship between the proxy rules and the First Amendment," believe such motives are relevant. I respectfully disagree.

II

The content of the Committee's advertisement is of critical importance. First, it is on its face addressed solely to the public. Second, it makes no mention either of proxies or of the shareholders' meeting demanded by Matthews. Third, the issues the ad addresses are quintessentially matters of public political debate, namely, whether a public power authority would provide cheaper electricity than LILCO. Claims of LILCO mismanagement are discussed solely in the context of their effect on its customers. Finally, the ad was published in the middle of an election campaign in which LILCO's future was an issue.

On these facts, therefore, LILCO's claim raises a constitutional issue of the first magnitude. It asks nothing less than that a federal court act as a censor, empowered to determine the truth or falsity of the ad's claims about the merits of public power and to enjoin further advocacy containing false claims. We need not resolve this constitutional issue, however.

Where advertisements are critical of corporate conduct but are facially directed solely to the public, in no way mention the exercise of proxies, and debate only matters of conceded public concern, I would construe federal proxy regulation as inapplicable, whatever the motive of those who purchase them. This position, which is strongly suggested by relevant case law, *see infra,* maximizes public debate, avoids embroiling the federal judiciary in determining the rightness or wrongness of conflicting positions on public policy, and does not significantly impede achievement of Congress' goal that shareholders exercise proxy rights on the basis of accurate information.

It is of course true that LILCO shareholders may be concerned about public allegations of mismanagement on LILCO's part. However, shareholders are most unlikely to be misled into thinking that advertisements of this kind, particularly when purchased in the name of a committee so obviously disinterested in the return on investment to LILCO's shareholders, are either necessarily accurate or authoritative sources of information about LILCO's management. Such advertisements, which in no way suggest internal reforms shareholders might bring about through the exercise of their proxies, are sheer political advocacy and would be so recognized by any reasonable shareholder.

To be sure, the fact that a corporation has become a target of political advocacy might well justify unease among shareholders. No one seriously asserts, however, that the right to criticize corporate behavior as a matter of public concern diminishes as shareholders' meetings become imminent.

III

Potential conflicts between First Amendment values and federal regulatory goals have arisen before and have been resolved by the Supreme Court by construing the particular regulatory scheme not to reach activities which clearly implicate the First Amendment. These decisions pay heed to the precepts counselling against unnecessary adjudication of constitutional issues. *See* Ashwander

v. TVA, 297 U.S. 288, 346-48, 56 S. Ct. 466, 482-83, 80 L. Ed. 688 (1936) (Brandeis, J., concurring); United States v. Curcio, 712 F.2d 1532, 1541 n.14 (2d Cir. 1983). "Thus, if a case can be decided on either of two grounds, one involving a constitutional question, the other a question of statutory construction or general law, the Court will decide only the latter." *Ashwander*, 297 U.S. at 347, 56 S. Ct. at 483. . . .

. . . I believe the advertisement in question is not subject to federal proxy regulation regardless of Matthews' participation in its publication or the motives of its authors. Further discovery is irrelevant in my view, and I would affirm.

2. *Liability for Misleading Proxy Disclosure*

As stated above, Congress adopted mandatory disclosure as its preferred regulatory approach to protect shareholders' voting rights. And yet, if the information that a company discloses is not complete, or is not fully accurate, then it is worse than useless in empowering shareholders in the corporate governance relationship. As a result, in Rule 14a-9 the SEC has defined a cause of action for false or misleading proxy statements, and shareholders have an implied private right of action to bring claims under that Rule. *See* J.I. Case Co. v. Borak, 377 U.S. 426 (1964).

In general, it is a violation of Rule 14a-9 for a company to make a false statement of material fact or to omit to state material facts in its proxy statements. The key concept, then, is whether misstatements or omissions were of "material" facts. "Materiality" is an intellectual workhorse in securities regulation, defining both issuers' disclosure obligations *ex ante* and causes of action for securities fraud *ex post.* The definition of a "material fact" was set out in the leading case of TSC Industries v. Northway, 426 U.S. 438 (1976), as information "a reasonable shareholder would consider important in deciding how to vote." As the Court stated, "[p]ut another way, there must be a substantial likelihood that the disclosure of the omitted fact would have been viewed by the reasonable investor as having significantly altered the 'total mix' of information made available." *TSC Indus.*, 426 U.S. at 449. Whether a misstatement or omission is of a "material fact" is an inherently fact-specific inquiry, since it is necessary to examine the total mix of information available at any given time to answer the question.

In general, financial facts concerning the value of securities or the value of a transaction are material. Moreover, while it is generally true that facts concerning companies' environmental policies or social practices (such as their use of sweatshop labor or of bribes to get business) have not routinely been held to be material, today, with a growing number of investors screening their investments for such social and environmental practices, even these social and political facts can be held to be material, as in United Paperworkers International Union v. International Paper Co., 985 F.2d 1190 (2d Cir. 1993). The following case shows the difficulty of trying to simplify the concept of "materiality" into a bright-line rule. Discussions with securities lawyers confirm that making decisions on whether information is material or not, and thus needs to be disclosed, is the most difficult part of their job. Indeed, often the problem is difficult because the lawyer views the information as material and counsels disclosing it, which the client resists because of concerns over the business impact of disclosure: showing that the information is likely to be considered significant to a reasonable shareholder, and thus is material.

UNITED PAPERWORKERS INTERNATIONAL UNION v. INTERNATIONAL PAPER CO.

985 F.2d 1190
United States Court of Appeals, Second Circuit
February 12, 1993

KEARSE, Circuit Judge.

Defendant International Paper Company ("Paper Co." or the "Company") appeals from a final judgment of the United States District Court for the Southern District of New York, Charles L. Brieant, Chief Judge, (1) declaring that a Paper Co. proxy statement, in opposition to a shareholder proposal submitted for consideration at the Company's 1992 annual meeting, contained misleading statements and omitted material facts, in violation of §14(a) of the Securities Exchange Act of 1934 ("1934 Act" or the "Act"), 15 U.S.C. §78n(a) (1988), and Rule 14a-9, 17 C.F.R. §240.14a-9 (1992), promulgated thereunder by the Securities and Exchange Commission ("SEC"), and (2) enjoining the Company to resubmit the shareholder proposal at its 1993 annual meeting. On appeal, Paper Co. contends principally that the district court erred in ruling that the proxy statement was misleading in light of the total mix of information available to shareholders. . . . For the reasons below, we reject the contentions of Paper Co., and we conclude that the judgment should be modified to require the Company to allow the sponsor of the resolution to include a fair description of the judgment in the proxy materials to be mailed by the Company.

I. BACKGROUND

The events and statements are not in dispute. Paper Co., a corporation whose shares are traded on the New York Stock Exchange, is a major manufacturer of paper and paper products. In connection with the Company's annual meeting scheduled for May 12, 1992, the Presbyterian Church (USA) of Louisville, Kentucky (the "Church"), which owned some 31,000 shares of the Company's stock, and the Sisters of Saint Dominic of Blauvelt, New York (collectively the "Sponsors"), sought to have the Company's shareholders adopt a resolution dealing with corporate accountability for issues concerning the environment. The resolution called for the adoption of the so-called "Valdez Principles" developed by the Coalition for Environmentally Responsible Economies ("CERES"), which called on corporations to, *inter alia,* reduce waste matter and provide for its safe treatment, market safe products and services, and provide redress for environmental damage. The Company printed the proposed resolution ("Valdez Resolution" or "proposal # 6"), together with the Sponsors' supporting statement, in its 1992 Proxy Statement ("Proxy Statement") mailed to shareholders on March 31, 1992. The resolution read as follows:

 RESOLVED, that shareholders request our company to:
  1. sign and actively implement the Valdez Principles; and

2. engage with shareholders, CERES, and affected communities in a continuing process to achieve a genuine and publicly trusted measure of public environmental accountability.

The Sponsors' supporting statement expressed, *inter alia*, the belief that "the growing significance of environmental issues and the impact of our company's environmental practices demand a comprehensive policy and commitment to public environmental accountability."

In the Proxy Statement, Paper Co. opposed the resolution, stating that the Company had already addressed environmental matters "in an appropriate and timely manner" and indeed was in the "forefront" with respect to environmental protection; that certain of the Valdez Principles "may not be applicable to the Company"; and that implementation of the Valdez Resolution "would not provide any greater environmental protection than now exists." Paper Co. stated that its Board had adopted a comprehensive statement of Environmental, Health and Safety Principles ("Company Principles"), which it described as "the most recent articulation of the Company's longstanding commitment to the protection of the environment, which has been an explicit Company policy for many years." The Proxy Statement continued by stating that:

the Company's environmental conduct code in fact is both more stringent and more industry specific than the Valdez Principles. In the areas of waste disposal, air emissions and groundwater, the Company has invested hundreds of millions of dollars ($110 million in 1991 alone) in technology, equipment, facilities and personnel to be at the forefront in the enhancement and protection of the environment. An environmental staff was formed by the Company many years ago to maintain compliance with environmental laws and regulations as well as Company policy. The Company regularly audits each operating unit for compliance with the letter and the spirit of those rules. A committee of the Board, the Environment, Health & Technology Committee, meets regularly to review environmental, safety and health policies and programs throughout the Company, and advise the Board of the effectiveness of these policies and programs.

The Board believes the Valdez Principles, though well-intentioned, are in many respects ambiguous and certain of them may not be applicable to the Company. The Board does not believe, for example, that the Company and its shareholders should be burdened with duplicative independent audit requirements and costs associated with additional reports, as called for by the Principles. Moreover, the Board believes that the Principles, calling as they do for the selection of one director "qualified to represent environmental interests," are inappropriate since there are many and varied interests which shareholders have that should be the concern of all directors. Finally, the Board believes that implementation of the proposal would not provide any greater environmental protection than now exists and could be significantly more costly.

In summary, the Board believes that protection of the environment is critical to any business today, but that the environmental affairs of the Company and the interests of our shareholders are already being addressed in an appropriate and timely manner.

Approval of Item No. 6 requires the affirmative vote of the holders of a majority of the shares voting on this proposal.

THE BOARD OF DIRECTORS RECOMMENDS A VOTE **AGAINST** THIS ITEM NO. 6

The Company Principles, which were appended to the Proxy Statement, stated, *inter alia,* that "International Paper is dedicated to safe and environmentally sound products, packaging and operations"; that "[e]nvironmental steward-ship has always been an important part of International Paper's business"; that "[t]he principles are consistent with International Paper's long-standing poli-cies on environment, health and safety"; and that the Company had a "strong environmental compliance program."

Prior to mailing the proxy materials to shareholders, Paper Co. had, as required by SEC regulations, submitted its response to the resolution's Sponsors. The Sponsors had not objected to it.

In April 1992, however, the Union, which in recent years had had an unusu-ally tense relationship with the Company and which owned 25 shares of the Company's stock, commenced the present action, contending that the Com-pany's Proxy Statement response to the Valdez Resolution contained false and misleading representations and omissions. As discussed in greater detail below, the Union alleged that, as revealed in Paper Co.'s 10-K Report, which was filed with the SEC but not distributed to shareholders, [and as described in its annual report, which was sent to the shareholders], the Company had been accused of numerous environmental offenses, had pleaded guilty to felonies, had agreed to pay huge fines, and had been the target of numerous administrative complaints. . . .

[The District Court denied a preliminary injunction that sought to delay the annual meeting and then granted summary judgment to the plaintiff, holding that the company's description of its environmental record was materially — and intentionally — misleading:]

> [The Company] cannot argue with any rationality that the Board's response to the shareholder proposal was anything but a calculated attempt to mislead the shareholders and induce them to cast a negative vote. The Board was pre-sumptively and constructively aware of all relevant details of the Company's environmental record; rather than portraying that record accurately, or remain-ing silent, it chose instead to engage in flowery corporate happy-talk in order to defeat the proposal. The undisputed evidence compels a finding that the Board acted with the requisite knowledge and intent in making the misstatements and omissions detailed above.

Id. at 1144. . . .

II. THE RULING THAT THE PROXY STATEMENT WAS MISLEADING

On its appeal, Paper Co. contends principally that the district court erred in finding a violation of §14(a) and Rule 14a-9 because (a) the Proxy Statement, either standing alone or read in conjunction with the annual report, was not materially misleading, and (b) in any event, those two documents read with the 10-K Report and press reports adequately disclosed all material facts. We find no merit in these contentions. . . .

Section 14(a) of the Act makes it unlawful to solicit proxies in contravention of any rule or regulation promulgated by the SEC. 15 U.S.C. §78n(a). Rule

14a-9 promulgated thereunder prohibits the inclusion in a proxy statement of:

> any statement which, at the time and in the light of the circumstances under which it is made, is false or misleading with respect to any material fact, *or which omits to state any material fact necessary in order to make the statements therein not false or misleading.*

17 C.F.R. §240.14a-9 (emphasis added). A fact is material for purposes of Rule 14a-9 " 'if there is a substantial likelihood that a reasonable shareholder would consider it important in deciding how to vote.' " Virginia Bankshares, Inc. v. Sandberg, 501 U.S. 1083, 1090, 111 S. Ct. 2749, 2757, 115 L. Ed. 2d 929 (1991) (quoting TSC Industries, Inc. v. Northway, Inc., 426 U.S. 438, 449, 96 S. Ct. 2126, 2132, 48 L. Ed. 2d 757 (1976)). . . .

In the present case, Paper Co. responded to the shareholder proposal in the Proxy Statement with a rather glowing description of the Company's environmental spirit, performance, and sense of responsibility. Plainly, a reasonable shareholder would consider the Company's actual record important in assessing the merits of the Company's response to the shareholder proposal. The response was, therefore, misleading absent a description of the Company's record of environmental derelictions or non-compliance.

In considering a claim of material omission in violation of Rule 14a-9, however, the court ordinarily should not consider the proxy statement alone. To succeed on such a claim, the plaintiff must show that there was "a substantial likelihood that the disclosure of the omitted fact would have been viewed by the reasonable investor as having significantly altered the 'total mix' of information made available." TSC Industries, Inc. v. Northway, Inc., 426 U.S. at 449, 96 S. Ct. at 2132.

A. "TOTAL MIX" AND THE 10-K AND PRESS REPORTS

The "total mix" of information may include data sent to shareholders by a company in addition to its proxy materials, *see, e.g.*, Ash v. LFE Corp., 525 F.2d 215, 219 (3d Cir. 1975) (proxy statements need not "duplicate the financial data furnished to shareholders in the corporation's annual reports"), as well as other information "reasonably available to the shareholders," Rodman v. Grant Foundation, 608 F.2d 64, 70 (2d Cir. 1979). However, "not every mixture with the true will neutralize the deceptive," Virginia Bankshares, Inc. v. Sandberg, 501 U.S. at 1083, 111 S. Ct. at 2760, and even information actually sent to shareholders need not be considered part of the total mix reasonably available to them if "the true" is "buried" in unrelated discussions, *see, e.g.*, Rodman v. Grant Foundation, 608 F.2d at 70 (proxy statement deemed adequate in part because information "was not 'buried' by being disbursed among or immersed in irrelevant data"). The mere fact that a company has filed with a regulatory agency documents containing factual information material to a proposal as to which proxies are sought plainly does not mean that the company has made adequate disclosure to shareholders under Rule 14a-9. Corporate documents that have not been distributed to the shareholders entitled to vote on the proposal should rarely be considered part of the total mix of information reasonably available to those shareholders.

The "total mix" of information may also include "information already in the public domain and facts known or reasonably available to the shareholders."

Rodman v. Grant Foundation, 608 F.2d at 70; *see* Seibert v. Sperry Rand Corp., 586 F.2d 949, 952 (2d Cir.1978). Thus, when the subject of a proxy solicitation has been widely reported in readily available media, shareholders may be deemed to have constructive notice of the facts reported, and the court may take this into consideration in determining whether representations in or omissions from the proxy statement are materially misleading. . . .

In the present case, the district court properly rejected Paper Co.'s contention that public press reports and its 10-K Report should be viewed as part of the total mix of information reasonably available to shareholders. Though the Company argued that news articles should be considered, the articles were few in number, narrow in focus, and remote in time. The Company pointed to only eight articles, and they apparently dealt only with the Company's litigation in the states of Maine and Mississippi, reporting its plea of guilty in the former and ongoing lawsuits in the latter. Further, these articles were not published in the context of this proxy contest. Rather, they spanned more than a year; the latest of them had appeared more than two months before the Company's Proxy Statement was even issued; and all but one had appeared more than six months earlier. These articles were properly considered not to be part of the information that was reasonably available to shareholders.

Nor was the Company's 10-K Report part of the reasonably available mix. That report was filed with the SEC, not distributed to shareholders. Nothing in any of the documents sent to shareholders highlighted the 10-K Report. The Proxy Statement did not mention it at all; and the annual report made no reference to it in its description of the Company's environmental record. . . .

We conclude that the district court correctly ruled that the press reports and the Company's 10-K Report to the SEC were not part of the total mix of information reasonably available to shareholders about to vote on the Valdez Resolution.

B. THE PROXY STATEMENT AND THE ANNUAL REPORT

There can be no serious question here that the Proxy Statement standing alone was materially misleading with respect to the Company's environmental record. The stated purpose of the Valdez Principles was to "achieve a genuine and publicly trusted measure of public environmental accountability." The Company's representations, in opposition, that it had a longstanding commitment to the protection of the environment, that it was a leader in environmental protection, that it had a vigorous compliance program, and that it had addressed such issues appropriately, conveyed an impression that was entirely false.

The annual report, which the district court treated as part of the total mix reasonably available to shareholders, presents its own special problems. Had the Company's misleadingly self-laudatory statements not been made, and had the disclosures made in the annual report appeared in the Proxy Statement, we would likely consider the disclosures not to be materially incomplete. On the other hand, given the unqualifiedly glowing statements that were actually made in the Proxy Statement, we consider it a close question whether such disclosures as were made in the annual report should be deemed part of the total mix available to shareholders or should instead be deemed buried in a part of the report where one seeking environmental information, might not think to look. . . .

We need not decide, however, whether the annual report should have been ruled not part of the total mix here, for we agree with the district court that even such disclosures as could be found in that report were not sufficient in light of the pristine picture painted by the Proxy Statement. Shareholders could have viewed the disclosures made in the annual report as not being inconsistent with the Company's "achieve[ment of] a genuine and publicly trusted measure of public environmental accountability" had they read only the Proxy Statement and the information disclosed in the annual report. For example, reading only the annual report, they could have believed that the five pleas of guilty were for minor infractions that did not bespeak a lack of corporate responsibility; they would likely have viewed the Company's statements in a different light had they known that the charges were not minor but felonies, that the $2.2 million fine was the second largest ever assessed for violation of hazardous-waste laws, and that some of the felonies involved falsification of required environmental reports. They would undoubtedly have been considerably enlightened as to the sincerity of the Company's claimed explicit policy and firm long-standing commitment for protection of the environment had they known the facts, undisclosed by the annual report, that the Company had falsified environmental reports and breached the settlement agreement it had reached in the Maine civil litigation. Shareholders could have believed the Company's claimed "strong compliance program" was not belied by the mere fact that the Company had been sued in "some" of "several" lawsuits as described in the annual report; they would have had a decidedly different picture had they also known facts not disclosed in that report, including that there were 43 such suits charging the Company with having dumped chemically contaminated waste in three rivers in one state alone, that the Company had been named in more than 50 administrative proceedings to enforce federal and state laws governing treatment of hazardous wastes, and that the Company's record was such that the EPA was seeking to prohibit it from doing business with the federal government for three years.

In sum, the disclosures contained in the annual report failed to cure the materially misleading representations and omissions in the Proxy Statement. The district court properly ruled that the Company had violated §14(a) and Rule 14a-9. . . .

PROBLEM 7-1

In early 1997, the Greater New York Bank Savings Bank (Greater New York) was not in an enviable condition. One of the primary ways that a bank makes money is by lending money to individuals and commercial entities, and charging interest. Some percentage of a bank's customers have trouble repaying their loans, which are then termed "nonperforming." In 1997, 19.69 percent of Greater New York's loans were nonperforming, compared to a 3.38 percent mean and 1.52 percent median for comparable companies. Since outstanding loans are also one of a bank's primary assets, this weakness was reflected in Greater New York's 7.9 percent of nonperforming assets, compared to 1.6 percent mean and 0.86 percent median for comparables.

Notwithstanding this discouraging statistical picture, Greater New York president Gerald Keegan was approached in early 1997 by top officers at Astoria

Federal Savings and Loan (Astoria), and asked whether Greater New York was interested in being acquired. Astoria indicated that it would be willing to pay $18 per share for all of Greater New York's outstanding stock, subject to the usual due diligence. ("Due diligence" is a process where a buying company examines the selling company's books and records and interviews numerous employees of the selling company to assure itself that the company is worth buying, and at what price. Due diligence is done after a confidentiality agreement is negotiated so that the potential buying company cannot misuse the information it gathers.)

The next day, Keegan received a phone call from Thomas O'Brian, vice chairman of North Fork Bancorporation (North Fork). O'Brian indicated that North Fork was also interested in acquiring Greater New York, for approximately $19 per share, using an exchange of shares transaction, subject to the usual due diligence. (The exchange of shares means that North Fork would pay for the acquisition by giving every Greater New York shareholder shares in North Fork, based on an exchange ratio that constituted $19.00 per share to each Greater New York shareholder.) Keegan told O'Brian that Greater New York was not planning to merge and that he was unwilling to talk to O'Brian under any circumstances. The same day Keegan informed the Greater New York board about the Astoria offer and the North Fork expression of interest; the board authorized him to continue discussions with Astoria. Thus, Keegan continued to negotiate with Astoria, including on the terms of a confidentiality order for the due diligence process, and on future employment for himself and other members of the board if the transaction went forward.

Eventually Astoria solidified its offer at $18.94 per share, and Greater New York prepared proxy documents to conduct a shareholder vote on the merger proposal. (The selling company's shareholders always have a right to vote in a merger; the buying company's shareholders may or may not have voting rights, depending on the structure of the transaction.) During the two to three weeks that had elapsed, North Fork had written numerous letters indicating its interest in a potential acquisition at $19.00 per share, conditioned on due diligence. One day before the Greater New York board voted to accept Astoria's offer, North Fork was contacted by Greater New York's investment bank and asked if $19.00 per share was its best offer, to which North Fork replied, "yes, until such time as we would be allowed to go in and conduct due diligence."

The proxy statement that went out to the shareholders for their approval of the merger with Astoria described the $18.94 per share Astoria offer as a fair price. (At that time Greater New York stock was trading at approximately $12.00 per share.) The proxy statement also described negotiations with "another organization," and stated that the other organization's offer price (based on a fixed exchange ratio of its stock to Greater New York's, valued on March 27, 1997), was $18.53; that Greater New York had asked the other organization to increase its price "and it declined to do so." The proxy statement failed to state that:

    1. The other organization (North Fork) was a serious, motivated institution that already owned a substantial stake in Greater New York and had the financial ability to compete with Astoria on a level playing field if allowed to; and

2. The board may have preferred Astoria to North Fork because North Fork was not prepared to offer employment to Greater New York board members, including Keegan, and Astoria was.

Do the shareholders have a cause of action for material misstatements or omissions under Rule 14a-9?

3.   Shareholder Proposals: Rule 14a-8

As was seen in United Paperworkers International Union v. International Paper Co., shareholders have the power to require companies to include their proposals, called "shareholder resolutions," in the company's proxy statement, and thus to force a vote on such proposals. Some of these proposals are referred to as "social activist proposals," asking boards of directors to study or disclose whether a company uses sweatshop labor in its production facilities or purchases goods from contractors or subcontractors who do, for instance; or asking a company to study and report on energy use or the company's commitment to environmentally sustainable policies. Most social activist shareholder proposals are brought by members of the "socially responsible investment" (SRI) community. SRI investors seek to screen the companies they invest in based on products or practices to avoid (typically some combination of cigarettes, gambling, alcohol, and military weapons; and some screen out contraceptives or abortifacients) or products or practices to promote (such as renewable energy, environmental sustainability, or a commitment to diversity in employment). Many SRI investors are members of religious communities or are fund managers who invest the pension funds of ministers, priests, and nuns; others are members of labor unions or environmental organizations. Each of the big "fund families" (such as Fidelity, Magellan, and Vanguard) now has SRI funds. Altogether, assets in socially screened investment portfolios under professional management rose by more than a third from 1999 to 2001 to $2.034 trillion, comprising about 12 percent of money under professional management.

Other shareholder proposals are referred to as "corporate governance proposals," seeking changes in company's bylaws to do away with "poison pills," for instance (provisions that give boards power to resist unwanted takeovers), or seeking to separate the jobs of the chief executive officer from the chairman of the board of directors. These proposals are generally brought by the non-SRI institutional investment community, such as mutual fund managers or public pension fund managers like the California Public Employees Retirement System (CALPERS). Labor organizations, such as the AFL-CIO's Center for Working Capital, have been active in bringing both corporate governance proposals and pro-labor social proposals. Generally, corporate governance "shareholder activists" seek to promote management policies that maximize a firm's value and to promote corporate governance arrangements that allow a robust takeover market.

The shareholder proposal rule has been in force since the early 1940s, but the modern use of shareholder proposals began in 1968, when religious investors and antiwar groups introduced a proxy resolution at the Dow Chemical Company asking it to amend its articles of incorporation to ensure that any napalm the company sold would not be used in the war in Vietnam. *See* Medical Comm. for Human Rights v. SEC, 432 F.2d 659, 661-662 (D.C. Cir. 1970), *vacated as moot*, 404 U.S. 403 (1972). Social activists soon saw the potential power of this technique for "working from within" the corporation to encourage greater social accountability, and so the number of such proposals introduced each year gradually increased. For decades social proposals generally got votes of between 2 and 3 percent, and corporate governance proposals did not fare much better. Yet shareholder activists justified continuing to bring the proposals as a means to engage top management in discussions about various social and corporate governance issues and as the only means to raise such issues with other shareholders. The leverage of withdrawing a potentially embarrassing proposal has been used in many cases to get companies to agree to various changes at the company or to produce information to activists.

The last few years have seen a dramatic change, however, in part in reaction to numerous well-publicized corporate governance failures (such as at Enron, WorldCom, Tyco, and HealthSouth), and in part as a result of shareholder activists' increasing sophistication. More proposals are being brought every year: in the 2003 proxy season, there were 893 shareholder resolutions on the ballot, compared to 802 during the 2002 proxy season. Three-quarters of the resolutions were corporate governance proposals, and one-quarter were social and environmental proposals. The more dramatic change, though, is in the percentage of shares voting in support of resolutions. Twenty percent of corporate governance proposals passed in 2002, particularly proposals to split the CEO/chairman of the board position or to remove anti-takeover devices. And while only one social activist proposal passed in 2002 (asking the Cracker Barrel company to institute a policy forbidding discrimination on the basis of sexual orientation), that proposal had a particularly interesting history: it received 58 percent support, notwithstanding the opposition of management, and closed a ten-year campaign to get the Cracker Barrel company to institute a gay-rights policy.[3] Moreover, the average support for social issue proposals climbed to 9.4 percent, and 14 percent of the proposals got at least 15 percent support. For instance, at Exxon-Mobil 20 percent of shares in 2002 were voted in favor of having the company issue a report on its strategic initiatives to produce sustainable energy. Given that Exxon-Mobil has 6 billion shares outstanding, a 20 percent vote represents 1.2 billion shares.

Since the 2002 proxy season was affected by Enron's meltdown, but not any of the other celebrated frauds and defalcations, voting trends in 2003 and subsequent years are more indicative of the changing relationship between management and activist shareholders. In the 2003 proxy voting season, a majority of resolutions seeking to limit executive compensation or to eliminate staggered boards received majority votes. During the same proxy season, some

---

3. Indeed, Cracker Barrel's initial decision in 1992 to exclude a gay-rights proposal led to the SEC holding in a no-action letter that the proposal could be excluded as "ordinary business." This decision landed the SEC in court for changing its position on what constitutes "ordinary business." *See* New York City Employees' Retirement Sys. v. SEC, 45 F.3d 7 (2d Cir. 1995) (SEC's change in position did not need to be accomplished by notice and comment rule-making).

social and environmental shareholder proposals have achieved votes in the 20 to 40 percent range, which may indicate the beginning of a convergence of voting between SRI investors and other types of institutional investors.

Moreover, in 2003 the SEC promulgated a new rule under the Investment Company Act of 1940, Rule 30b1-4, requiring mutual fund managers by August 31, 2004, to disclose how they voted on every shareholder proposal at every company in their portfolio. This rule for proxy transparency was fiercely fought by the large fund families (Fidelity, Magellan, TIAA-CREF, and Vanguard, for instance), presumably in part because many previously undisclosed conflicts of interest will now be subject to scrutiny. That is, many mutual funds earn a significant part of their revenue managing the pensions of individual companies in their portfolios. Thus, it is unlikely that the funds will vote against management's interests on shareholder proposals, since the companies can threaten to take their pension business elsewhere. So, rather than acting like shareholders' agents in voting, many mutual fund managers vote with a company's management. As proxy voting disclosure creates transparency, these conflicts of interest will be exposed, and it is likely that the trend toward higher votes on shareholder proposals will continue — certainly on corporate governance proposals. Thus, shareholders' developing power within the corporate governance relationship will continue to increase.

Given companies' understandable preference for maintaining control of the agenda and the message at the annual meeting, the major battleground for shareholder proposals is whether the shareholders can force the company, under Rule 14a-8, to include their proposal and supporting statement in the company's proxy statement. If a shareholder group is unsuccessful in forcing the company to include its proposal in the company's proxy materials, the shareholder group can use Rule 14a-7 to gain access to the shareholder list and mail its proposal out separately, but this costs a huge amount of money, so it is not a realistic option in most cases. Thus, inclusion under Rule 14a-8 is critical. Rule 14a-8 contains a number of procedural requirements. For example, a shareholder proponent must own at least $2,000 worth of stock, or 1 percent of outstanding shares, whichever is less, and must have owned that amount of stock for at least one year prior to submitting a proposal. Rule 14a-8, Question 2. There are also timing requirements, so that a shareholder's resolution must reach the company 120 days before the date of the company's proxy statement released to shareholders in connection with the previous year's annual meeting. Rule 14a-8, Question 5. This timing requirement is structured to allow the company time to determine whether to include a proposal, and if it decides to exclude the proposal, to give the company time to seek a no-action letter from the SEC. (See below for a discussion of the no-action procedure.) The core of Rule 14a-8 is set out in Rule 14a-8(i), Question 9, which identifies 13 reasons that companies can lawfully use to exclude shareholder proposals. Some of the most important reasons companies use include:

(1) *The proposal is improper under state law*: Shareholders may not command directors to do something; they must recommend or suggest action. This limitation arises because state law provides that a public company must be managed by or under the directors, so infringements on the scope of their managerial authority are not permitted.

(5) *The proposal is not relevant*: If a proposal relates to less than 5 percent of a company's total assets or less than 5 percent of its net earnings or gross sales, it can be excluded, unless it raises significant social policy issues related to the company's business. Thus, in Lovenheim v. Iroquois Brands, Ltd., 618 F. Supp. 554 (D. C. 1985), the District Court for the District of Columbia held that the Iroquois Brands food-importing company could not exclude a resolution asking the company to stop importing pate de fois gras, given concerns for the way the geese were force-fed to produce the pate, even though Iroquois Brands had pate sales of $79,000, on which it had a net loss of $3,121, as compared to annual revenues of $141 million, with $6 million in annual profits. The court ruled as it did because the ethical treatment of animals raised important social policy concerns that were related to a product the company sold, so the proposal could not be excluded.

(7) *The proposal relates to ordinary business/management functions*: If a proposal relates to operational details of how to run the business, it can be excluded, but proposals raising important public policy issues may not be excluded on this basis. The line between these two categories is constantly shifting, depending on which issues are currently a matter of public debate. For instance, while hiring decisions are ordinary business, a company's policy of discrimination on the basis of sexual preference in hiring would not be ordinary business today (but was for a time under the Cracker Barrel no-action letter, since repudiated by the SEC). This reason for excluding proposals is one of the most frequently used, and fought over, as you will see in the following case.

(8) *The proposal relates to elections*: Companies may exclude proposals nominating candidates to the board or relating to elections. Some shareholder activists have been quite critical of this reason to exclude shareholder proposals, claiming that it further entrenches unresponsive management and self-perpetuating boards of directors. As a result of an increasing number of institutional investors that have tried to get election-related proposals on the agenda, such as proposed bylaw amendments to change the nomination process for the board, the SEC began a study in 2003 of the nominating and elections process.

The following case discusses a fairly unusual type of shareholder proposal, but it includes a discussion of the meaning of the more usual reasons companies use to exclude proposals. In the following materials, you will also see the SEC's no-action procedure in action. A no-action procedure is a method by which SEC staff members provide guidance to companies on the SEC's interpretation of its rules. The procedure works as follows. A company will write to the appropriate office in the SEC, describe an action it seeks to take (such as not including a shareholder activist's proposal in its proxy materials), and explain to the SEC its rationale for why the company believes such an action is proper under the applicable securities laws, rules, and regulations. If the SEC staff member who handles the letter agrees with the company's rationale, he or she will write back that "based on the facts as described, we will recommend no enforcement action be taken" against your company. No-action letters are technically not precedents on which parties can rely, even in the same case in which the letter was sought, because they are the actions of SEC staff members, not of the Commission acting as a whole. Yet no-action letters are collected in electronic databases, discussed in leading securities treatises, and cited in judicial opinions. Thus, no-action letters occupy a unique, and important, position in the practice of securities law.

NEW YORK CITY EMPLOYEES' RETIREMENT SYSTEM v. DOLE FOOD CO.

795 F. Supp. 95
United States District Court, Southern District of New York
April 24, 1992

CONBOY, District Judge.

Proceeding by an order to show cause, the New York City Employees' Retirement System ("NYCERS") brings this action for a preliminary injunction that would enjoin defendant Dole Food Company, Inc. ("Dole") from the solicitation of shareholder proxies for Dole's upcoming annual meeting without informing shareholders of NYCERS' shareholder proposal. In the alternative, NYCERS seeks inclusion of the proposal on a supplemental mailing prior to the annual meeting.

I. BACKGROUND

NYCERS is a public pension fund that owns approximately 164,841 shares of common stock in Dole Food Company, Inc. ("Dole"). On December 12, 1991, New York City Comptroller Elizabeth Holtzman, in her capacity as the custodian of NYCERS' assets, wrote to the executive vice president of Dole, requesting Dole to include the following proposal ("the NYCERS proposal") in its proxy statement prior to its annual meeting:

NEW YORK CITY EMPLOYEES' RETIREMENT SYSTEM SHAREHOLDER RESOLUTION ON HEALTH CARE TO DOLE FOOD COMPANY, INC.

WHEREAS: The Dole Food Company is concerned with remaining competitive in the domestic and world marketplace, acknowledging the positive relationship between the health and well being of its employees and productivity, and the resulting effect on corporate growth and financial stability; and

WHEREAS: Sustained double-digit increases in health care costs have put severe financial pressure on a company attempting to continue to provide adequate health care for its employees and their dependents; and

WHEREAS: The company has a societal obligation to conduct its affairs in a way which promotes the health and well being of all;

BE IT THEREFORE RESOLVED: That the shareholders request the Board of Directors to establish a committee of the Board consisting of outside and independent directors for the purpose of evaluating the impact of a representative cross section of the various health care reform proposals being considered by national policy makers on the company and their [sic] competitive standing in domestic and international markets. These various proposals can be grouped in three generic categories; the single payor model (as in the Canadian plan), the limited payor (as in the Pepper Commission Report) and the employer mandated (as in the Kennedy-Waxman legislation).

Further, the aforementioned committee should be directed to prepare a report of its findings. The report should be prepared in a reasonable time, at a reasonable cost and should be made available to any shareholder upon written request.

SUPPORTING STATEMENT

Our nation is now at a crossroads on health care. Because of cutbacks in public programs, jobs that offer no benefits and efforts by employers to shift health care costs to workers, 50 million Americans have health care coverage that is inadequate to meet their needs and another 37 million have no protection at all.

The United States spends $2 billion a day, or eleven percent of its gross national product, on health care. As insurance premiums increase 18 to 30 percent a year, basic health care has moved well beyond the reach of a growing number of working families. This increase also places heavy pressure on employer labor costs. There is no end in sight to this trend.

As a result and because of the significant social and public policy issues attendant to operations involving health care, we urge shareholders to SUPPORT the resolution.

On January 16, 1992, J. Brett Tibbitts, deputy general counsel of Dole Food Company, Inc., wrote to the office of chief counsel of the Securities & Exchange Commission's ("SEC") division of corporation finance and stated Dole's position that Dole could exclude the NYCERS proposal from its proxy statement because the proposal concerned employee benefits, an assertedly "ordinary business operation," and both SEC regulations and the law of the Dole's state of incorporation relegate such ordinary business operations to management, not shareholder, control.

On February 10, 1992, John Brousseau, special counsel to the SEC's division of corporation finance, responded to Tibbitts' letter with the following written statement:

The proposal relates to the preparation of a report by a Committee of the Company's Board of Directors to evaluate various health-care proposals being considered by national policy makers.

There appears to be some basis for your view that the proposal may be excluded pursuant to rule 14a-8(c)(7) because the proposal is directed at involving the Company in the political or legislative process relating to an aspect of the Company's operations. Accordingly, we will not recommend enforcement action to the Commission if the proposal is omitted from the Company's proxy materials. In reaching a position, the staff has not found it necessary to address the alternative basis for omission on which the Company relies.

On March 19, 1992, Brousseau reported to NYCERS that the SEC had denied NYCERS' request for the SEC to review the SEC staff determination on the NYCERS proposal. On April 9, 1992, NYCERS brought the instant action. In conjunction with NYCERS' request for an order to show cause, NYCERS submitted an affidavit of Theodore R. Marmor, a professor of political science and public policy at Yale University. In his affidavit, Professor Marmor averred, *inter alia,* that (1) at least 37 million Americans have no health insurance; (2) the United States spends more on health per capita than any other developed nation; (3) health care expenditures in 1989 represented 56 percent of pretax company profits in 1989, as compared to 8 percent in 1985; and (4) the national average cost for health care per employee is $3,200, and some large companies pay $5,000 or more per employee. Professor Marmor also defined and explained the three major categories of national health care proposals pending in Congress:

14. First, there is the so-called "play or pay" model. The Kennedy-Waxman bill pending in Congress adopts this approach. Under this plan, American businesses would be required either to offer health coverage to their employees or to pay a premium to a centralized pool. The pool would be used to ensure that all Americans not covered by their employer would receive some form of health care coverage.

15. Another approach is a unitary funding arrangement, the so-called "single payor" system, and there are proposals pending in Congress modeled on the Canadian health care system. The system creates a single pool of dollars (or its equivalent) that is publicly accountable and that is created through a form of tax or fee. Each year it is determined roughly how much will be spent on health care, and then negotiations take place with physicians, hospitals and other medical institutions over how much they will be paid. Further, a set of comprehensive medical benefits is established, which allows all residents to receive treatment for any medically necessary procedure. This results in less administrative overhead. The plans tend to minimize out-of-pocket expenses from patients, instead of paying for health care out of one pool of funds.

16. A third model is the "limited-payor" approach. This approach was suggested by the Pepper Commission, a bi-partisan congressional commission which issued a five-year health care reform plan in September, 1990. The plan would provide small employers with various kinds of tax deductions and credits for purchasing health plans from existing health insurance carriers. For large employers, it would adopt a "play or pay" approach, requiring employers to provide coverage for their employees after purchasing health plans from insurance carriers or by paying for coverage by the federal government. The federal government also would provide coverage for the unemployed and the poor by replacing and expanding the role currently performed by states through the Medicaid program. When job-based coverage and the federal program are fully implemented and in place, all individuals would be required to obtain health care coverage either from their employers or the federal program. For both public and private coverage, the Pepper Commission recommended a federally-specified minimum benefit package. Individuals would be responsible for a share of premiums and service costs on all preventative service up to a minimum and subject to their ability to pay. Lower income workers and nonworkers would receive subsidies to keep their contributions low.

II. DISCUSSION

A party seeking a preliminary injunction must normally establish a) irreparable harm and b) either a substantial likelihood of success on the merits, or sufficiently serious questions on the merits to make them fair grounds for litigation with a balance of hardships tipping decidedly toward the moving party. In this case, NYCERS must prove a substantial likelihood of success on the merits because NYCERS requests a so-called mandatory injunction, *i.e.*, one that disturbs the status quo, and the relief that NYCERS seeks from the preliminary injunction is identical to that sought as the ultimate relief in the action.

A. SUBSTANTIAL LIKELIHOOD OF SUCCESS ON THE MERITS

The federal securities regulation that governs proposals of securities holders is 17 CFR §240.14a-8 ("Rule 14a-8"). Rule 14(a)-8(a) states in pertinent part:

If any security holder of a registrant notifies the registrant of his intention to present a proposal for action at a forthcoming meeting of the registrant's security holders, the registrant shall set forth the proposal in its proxy statement. . . .

However, Rule 14(a)-8(c) allows a corporation to omit a shareholder proposal from its proxy statement because of certain enumerated circumstances. In substance, Dole argues that the instant matter fits within the "ordinary business operations," "insignificant relation," and "beyond power to effectuate" exceptions enumerated in Rule 14(a)-8(c).

The corporation has the burden to show that a proposal fits within an exception to Rule 14(a)-8(a). Our determination on this matter also takes into account NYCERS' own burden, as discussed above, of demonstrating a "substantial" likelihood of success on the merits.

On April 16, this Court held a hearing pursuant to NYCERS' request for a mandatory injunction. At the hearing, counsel for both parties elaborated on the legal arguments that they had submitted in their papers, but neither party produced any witnesses, or any proof by affidavit of the nature of Dole's employee health care programs, coverage, costs, union agreements or insurance contracts. Indeed, the argument and the parties' briefs were largely abstract in nature. Nevertheless, for the reasons stated below, we find that NYCERS has met its burden of showing that it is substantially likely that Dole would fail to show on the merits that the proposal falls within one of the enumerated exceptions.

1. Rule 14a-8(c)(7): "Ordinary Business Operations"

Rule 14a-8(c)(7) states that a corporation may exclude a shareholder proposal from a proxy statement

> [i]f the proposal deals with a matter relating to the conduct of the ordinary business operations of the registrant.

The term "ordinary business operations" is neither self-explanatory nor easy to explain. The exception does not elaborate on whether "business operations" encompass merely certain routine internal functions or whether they can extend to cost-benefit analyses or profit-making activity. The SEC's commentary on the current version of the "ordinary business operations" exception states, "[W]here proposals involve business matters that are mundane in nature *and* do not involve any substantial policy or other considerations, the sub-paragraph may be relied upon to omit them." Adoption of Amendments Relating to Proposals by Security Holders, 41 Fed. Reg. 52,994, 52,998 (1976) (emphasis added). This commentary indicates that even if the proposal touches on the way daily business matters are conducted, the statement may not be excluded if it involves a significant strategic decision as to those daily business matters, *i.e.*, one that will significantly affect the manner in which a company does business. One Court has held that the purpose of the "ordinary business exception" is to prevent shareholders from seeking to "assert the power to dictate the minutiae of daily business decisions." Grimes v. Centerior Energy Corp., 909 F.2d 529, 531 (D.C. Cir. 1990), *cert. denied*, 498 U.S. 1073, 111 S. Ct. 799, 112 L. Ed. 2d 860 (1991).

While we give due deference to the SEC staff opinion letter in this case and other similar cases, we find that NYCERS has shown under that the proposal does not relate to "ordinary business operations." If one aspect of "ordinary business operations" is certain, it is that the outcome of close cases such as the instant one are largely fact-dependent. Nevertheless, Dole has not provided the Court with any information on (1) whether Dole has a health insurance program; (2) if such a program exists at Dole, how it operates; and (3) the amount of corporate financial resources that Dole devotes to health insurance. Instead, Dole argues, "To the extent [the NYCERS proposal] relates to Dole's business at all, it relates to its employee relations and health care benefits, a matter traditionally within the 'ordinary business' category." In support of its position, Dole cites several SEC "No-Action" letters relating to proposals similar to the instant one. However, the SEC "No-Action" letters contain scarcely any analysis, and, while they are entitled to deference, they do not bind this Court. We note that the SEC itself has changed its reasoning as to why proposals relating to national employee health insurance relate to "ordinary business relations." The SEC has shifted rationales for rejecting proposals such as this one, initially stressing the "employee relations" aspect of national health insurance and then emphasizing its "political [and] legislative" dimensions.

We further find that the principal cases relied upon by Dole are distinguishable from the instant case. Austin v. Consolidated Edison Co. of New York, 788 F. Supp. 192 (S.D.N.Y. 1992) involved an internal, relatively mundane plan to change the eligibility criteria of a company's specific retirement benefits policy, a subject of union collective bargaining. As Professor Marmor's affidavit demonstrates, however, the proposals in the instant case relate to a strategic policy choice as to the prospect of a major outlay to the federal treasury, as well as possible internal changes that may affect the entire scope of Dole's employee health insurance policy. The question of which plan, if any, that Dole should support, and how Dole would choose to function under the plans (e.g., "pay or play") could have large financial consequences on Dole. The instant case is also distinguishable from New York City Employees' Retirement System v. Brunswick Corporation, 789 F. Supp. 144 (S.D.N.Y. 1992). In Brunswick, NYCERS submitted a vague proposal that the company 1) study the national health plans in those countries in which the company had subsidiaries and 2) describe any aspect of these foreign health plans that should be included in the development of a national health insurance plan in the United States. Unlike the proposal in Brunswick, the proposal in the instant case does not seek to involve the corporation in making abstract political proposals but rather requests the corporation to study existing, concrete plans before Congress that affect the scope of Dole's health insurance operations.

The proposed report primarily relates to Dole's policy making on an issue of social significance that, while not relating to a specific health care policy at Dole, nevertheless relates to a distinct type of operations that Dole has undoubtedly grappled with in the past. Accordingly, we do not find that the instant proposal relates to "ordinary business operations."

2. Rule 14a-8(c)(5): "Insignificant Relationship" Exception

Rule 14a-8(c)(5) states that a corporation may exclude a shareholder proposal from a proxy statement

> [i]f the proposal relates to operations which account for less than 5 percent of the registrant's total assets at the end of its most recent fiscal year, and for less than 5

percent of its net earnings and gross sales for its most recent fiscal year, *and* is not otherwise significantly related to the registrant's business. (emphasis supplied).

Dole does not dispute that the clear language of the NYCERS proposal in large part relates to national health insurance's impact on Dole. Without specific reference to Rule 14a-8(c)(5), Dole argues that the NYCERS proposal lacked a discrete nexus to Dole's distinct line of business, presumably the manufacture of food products. Dole's argument is essentially made under the exception referred to in the last phrase of Rule 14a-8(c)(5), *i.e.*, that the proposal is "not otherwise significantly related to the registrant's business."

We need not address Dole's "nexus" argument because we find the activity addressed by the NYCERS proposal relates to activities that likely occupy outlays of more than five percent of Dole's income. It is substantially likely that Dole's health insurance outlays constitute more than five percent of its income. Dole has offered no information on the percentage of its income that it devotes to employee health insurance. In his affidavit, Professor Marmor stated that nationwide, 1989 health care expenditures represented 56 percent of pre-tax company profits. We find it substantially likely that this figure applies to Dole to a greater or lesser extent. Because the subject of the proposed study likely relates to a significant aspect of Dole's business, we find that the proposal does not fall within the exception stated in Rule 14(a)-8(c)(5).

3. Rule 14(a)-8(c)(6): "Beyond Power to Effectuate" Exception

Rule 14(a)-8(c)(6) states that a corporation need not include a shareholder proposal on a proxy statement

[i]f the proposal deals with a matter beyond the registrant's power to effectuate."].

Dole argues, "The NYCERS proposal requests the analysis of, and implicitly suggests that Dole should attempt to influence the selection of, national health care reform proposals." However, Dole does not point to any language that suggests that a necessary consequence of the proposal is political lobbying. While couched in language that clearly supports a national solution to the problems of growing health insurance costs, the NYCERS proposal merely calls for the commission of a research report on national health insurance proposals and their impact on Dole's competitive standing. Moreover, we fail to see why such a study necessarily "deals with a matter beyond the registrant's power to effectuate." For example, a decision that Dole's interests mandate a choice to "pay" rather than "play" under two of the three major proposals would clearly be within Dole's power to effectuate if these proposals are enacted. Moreover, Dole might conceivably find that it is in its interests to draft such a proposal and lobby for its enactment. For the reasons stated above, we disagree with Dole's argument that the political aspect of this proposal means that it does not relate to Dole's business in a substantial way.

B. IRREPARABLE HARM

The exclusion of the NYCERS proposal from the upcoming annual shareholder vote would mean that NYCERS would not be able to bring its proposal to Dole shareholders for another year. We find that Dole has established the required element of irreparable harm. *Cf.* NYCERS v. American Brands Inc., 634 F. Supp. 1382, 1388 (S.D.N.Y. 1986).

Having found that the required showing has been met, this Court directs Dole to include in its proxy materials for its June 4, 1992 annual meeting NYCERS' shareholder proposal submitted to Dole by letter dated December 12, 1991.

HOLDING

PROBLEM 7-2

The following shareholder proposal, titled "Shareholder Proposal on Majority Votes Co-Sponsored by the Connecticut Retirement and Trust Funds Submitted on behalf of the New York City Pension Funds by William C. Thompson, Jr., Comptroller, City of New York," was submitted to the Gillette Corporation in 2003 for inclusion in the company's proxy statement. On what bases might Gillette argue that the proposal is excludable? As a tactical matter, should the company seek a no-action position, or should they negotiate with the shareholders and seek withdrawal of the proposal?

WHEREAS, in 2002, Congress, the SEC, and the stock exchanges, recognizing the urgent need to restore public trust and confidence in the capital markets, acted to strengthen accounting regulations, to improve corporate financial disclosure, independent oversight of auditors, and the independence and effectiveness of corporate boards; and

WHEREAS, we believe these reforms, albeit significant steps in the right direction, have not adequately addressed shareholder rights and the accountability of directors of corporate boards to the shareholders who elect them; and

WHEREAS, we believe the reforms have not addressed a major concern of institutional investors — the continuing failure of numerous boards of directors to adopt shareholder proposals on important corporate governance reforms despite being supported by increasing large majorities of the totals of shareholder votes cast for and against the proposals;

NOW, THEREFORE, BE IT RESOLVED: That the shareholders request the Board of Directors to adopt a policy that establishes a process and procedures for adopting shareholder proposals that are presented in the company's proxy statement, and are supported by more than fifty percent of the combined total of shares voted FOR and AGAINST such proposals, at an annual meeting of the company.

At minimum, the policy should require the Board of Directors to take the following actions:

(1) Following the official tabulation and certification of the votes, the Board of Directors will communicate directly with the proponents of such proposals to pursue constructive dialogue and agreement on the proposals. If no agreement is reached with the proponents, sixty days prior to the deadline set by the company for receiving shareholder proposals for the next annual meeting, the board will act on the proposals as follows:

(i) With respect to proposals on corporate governance reforms that would require amendments to the certificate of incorporation or bylaws, the board will propose such amendments, in the company's proxy statement, for the consideration and vote of the shareholders at the next annual meeting.

(ii) If approval of the amendments to the certificate of incorporation or bylaws require more than a simple majority vote, the board of directors will propose, for the consideration and vote for the shareholders, amendments lowering the required vote thresholds to a simple majority of the votes case for and against.

(iii) If the amendments, as presented by the Board, are supported by more than fifty percent of the combined totals of the shares voted FOR and AGAINST, the Board, at that annual meeting, will adopt the amendments.

(iv) With respect to shareholder proposals that sought the Board's adoption of governance or social policy reforms that the Board can adopt without violating the company's certificate of incorporation or bylaws, the board will adopt such shareholder proposals before the next annual meeting of the company.

PROBLEM 7-3

The following is a shareholder proposal and supporting statement that was sent to the Dow Chemical Company in 2003. On what basis can the company argue against including the proposal? What would the shareholders' arguments be? How ought the SEC to rule on Dow's no-action request?

DOW CHEMICAL SHAREHOLDER PROPOSAL POLICIES ON DIOXIN AND PERSISTENT TOXICS

Whereas:

Some of Dow's operations and products result in the production and/or release of persistent bioaccumulative toxic (PBT) compounds during their life cycle, notably dioxin.

Dow's Midland, Michigan headquarters currently has regulatory permits to release dioxin to air, land and water. The surrounding city and watershed are contaminated with dioxin, with levels detected in the floodplain downriver, as high as 80 times the state's residential cleanup standard.

According to several scientific agencies, including the Agency for Toxic Substances and Disease Registry:

- Dioxin is harmful in minuscule amounts and has been linked, in animal studies, to endometriosis, immune system impairment, diabetes, neurotoxicity, birth defects, miscarriages, various harms to reproductive system functioning, and cancer.
- Dioxin can affect insulin, thyroid and steroid hormones.
- Developing babies are considered most susceptible to many of these dangers.
- The Environmental Protection Agency's draft dioxin reassessment suggests that some people may be harmed at levels of dioxin currently found in human bodies, and identified potentially highly exposed groups including nursing infants, consumers of contaminated fish or livestock, and residents near dioxin sources.

Canadian and U.S. governments have signed the Great Lakes Water Quality Agreement, establishing a goal to "virtually eliminate the input of persistent toxic substances [to the Great Lakes]" using the philosophy of "zero discharge."

More than 150 nations have signed the Stockholm Convention on Persistent Organic Pollutants (POPs) that, once ratified, would commit ratifying countries to eliminate certain intentionally produced POPs and ultimately eliminate certain POPs byproducts (including dioxin) where feasible.

Dow's Environmental, Health and Safety policy includes a commitment to "prevention of adverse environmental and health impacts," and Dow has recognized the importance of PBT reduction through its 2005 environmental goals.

   RESOLVED: Shareholders request that the Board of Directors issue a report by October 2003, at reasonable cost and excluding confidential information, summarizing the company's plans to remediate existing dioxin contamination sites and to phase out products and processes leading to emissions of persistent organic pollutants and dioxins.

SUPPORTING STATEMENT:

   Shareholders believe that such report should include:

1.   A list of current and future Dow Chemical products and waste treatment facilities creating or emitting dioxin or PBTs at any point in their life cycle.
2.   Timetables and benchmarks to meet phase-out goals of the treaties.
3.   Annual expenditures for each year from 1995-2002 summarizing funds spent on attorney's fees, expert fees, lobbying, and public relations/media expenses relating to the potential health and environmental consequences of dioxin releases or exposures at all Dow sites, as well as actual expenditures on remediation of dioxin contaminated sites.
4.   A list of the company's major reservoir sources of dioxin (concentrated deposits in the environment which may disperse into the ambient environment) at Dow-owned facilities in the U.S. and globally.
5.   A description of any major controversies involving community and environmental stakeholders concerning the remediation of particular sites, including Michigan, and reasonable projections of any material liabilities for cleanup or otherwise related to the contamination.

KMART CORPORATION: A CASE STUDY

The first Kmart discount store opened in Garden City, Michigan, in 1962. Originally a creation of S.S. Kresge Co, Kmart stores flourished, and Kresge changed its name to Kmart Corporation in 1977. By 1990, Kmart had overtaken Sears as the largest retailer in the United States. The person at the top when Kmart reached the pinnacle was Joe Antonini, who began his career with Kmart as an assistant store manager in 1964. He worked his way up to president of the apparel division in 1984, where he successfully introduced a more fashionable line of women's clothing using actress Jaclyn Smith as a spokeswoman. Antonini was elevated to the offices of president and chief operating officer in 1986 and was named chairman and chief executive officer in 1987.

   In his first letter to shareholders in Kmart's 1988 Annual Report, Antonini reported record sales and earnings for the previous year but conceded that, despite the records, Kmart's "sales plans were not met." Antonini then described "a number of important programs to improve the sales and profitability of the Kmart discount department store business and to make Kmart the store of choice among shoppers in America." In addition to internal restructuring and increased advertising, Antonini announced "a heavy capital investment in a number of retail automation programs, the most important of which is the installation of Point-of-Sale systems in our stores."

The goal of this automation was to improve inventory control and decrease labor costs, something that Kmart's main competitor, Wal-Mart, had already achieved. Despite extensive efforts to automate during Antonini's tenure, Kmart's inventory control problems persisted and were cited by observers as one of the primary causes of Antonini's downfall.

The other primary concern for Antonini relating to Kmart's discount store operations was the age and condition of Kmart's discount stores. When Antonini assumed the helm, the average age of the approximately 2,200 Kmart discount stores was 15 years. Many of those stores had "water-warped floors, broken light fixtures, shelves placed too close together and cheap displays set in the middle of aisles." As of early 1990 — shortly after Antonini announced a "renewal program" to relocate, expand, or refurbish virtually all existing Kmart discount stores in the United States — only 10 percent of Kmart stores were less than three years old, while more than 40 percent of stores at both Target and Wal-Mart were less than three years old.

Antonini's original renewal plan called for Kmart to relocate 280 stores, expand 620 stores, refurbish 1,260 stores, and close 30 stores, at a cost of approximately $2.3 billion. In January 1994, the board of directors revised the renewal program to provide for relocation of an additional 500 stores previously slated for expansion or refurbishment, after deciding that larger-format discount stores would be more productive and competitive than the smaller stores contemplated by the original renewal plan. The costs of the renewal program escalated to over $3.5 billion.

Despite Antonini's efforts, same-store sales at Kmart stores rose an average of only 3 percent during Antonini's first four years at the helm, as compared to Wal-Mart's average of 24 percent. One retail economist commented that "Wal-Mart is eating Kmart's breakfast, lunch, dinner and midnight snack."

In addition to the problems of inventory control and store renewal in the discount store operations, Antonini struggled throughout his tenure to develop Kmart's specialty retail operations. When Antonini came to power, Kmart owned three specialty retailers in the United States — Walden Book Company, Inc. (book stores), Pay Less Drug Stores Northwest, Inc. (super drugstores), and Builders Square, Inc. (home improvement stores). Kmart also owned Bargain Harold's Discount Limited, a Canadian retailer. Moreover, in 1987 Kmart entered into joint ventures with Bruno's, Inc., a leading food retailer in the southeast United States, to develop a combination discount and grocery store called "American Fare," and with Makro, Inc., owner of four warehouse clubs in Cincinnati, Washington, D.C., Philadelphia, and Atlanta, selling groceries, apparel, and hardline products. Finally, Kmart owned substantial equity investments in subsidiaries of Melville Corporation, which operated Kmart's domestic footwear departments, and in Coles Myer Ltd., the largest retailer in Australia.

Just months before Antonini's ascension to the top posts at Kmart, his predecessor, Bernard Fauber, had cited "saner diversification" as one of the keys to Kmart's future success. When he assumed the top posts, however, Antonini seized on the vision of creating a combination of discount and specialty retailer by developing and acquiring other specialty retailers. In March 1988 Kmart purchased a 51 percent share of Makro and took full ownership a year later, when Kmart purchased PACE Membership Warehouse, Inc. and announced plans to convert all Makro stores into Pace Warehouse Clubs. In the fall of 1988,

Kmart opened two Office Square stores in the Chicago area. Office Square, a warehouse office supply business, grew to five stores before being sold to Office-Max, Inc., which subsequently was acquired by Kmart. In January 1989, Kmart opened the first American Fare store in Atlanta, Georgia, and had plans for another in Charlotte, North Carolina. Kmart viewed these stores as "laboratories for developing a working food and general merchandise combination concept," and eventually converted them into Super Kmart Centers, a format combining the traditional Kmart discount store with a supermarket's food offerings. Kmart opened two Sports Giant stores in the Detroit metropolitan area in 1989. In March 1990, Kmart acquired The Sports Authority, Inc., an operator of a chain of eight large-format sporting goods stores, and later that year converted the Sports Giant stores into Sports Authority stores. In 1992 Kmart added the Borders Inc. bookstore chain in the United States, six discount stores in the Czech Republic, and seven discount stores in Slovakia. Kmart further expanded its international operations in 1994 by opening new discount stores in Mexico and Singapore. Antonini's vision for Kmart apparently would have dotted the world with Kmart Power Centers: shopping centers featuring Kmart discount stores surrounded by Kmart-owned specialty stores, including PACE Membership Warehouse, Builders Square, PayLess Drug Store, Waldenbooks, The Sport Authority, OfficeMax, and Borders.

Antonini's efforts to automate and renew Kmart's discount stores and expand and improve Kmart's specialty stores required significant amounts of capital. Contending that Kmart's common stock was undervalued, Antonini announced a plan in January 1994 to raise capital by creating and issuing separate classes of common stock whose terms would be tied to four of Kmart's subsidiaries: The Sports Authority, Builders Square, Borders, and OfficeMax. The proposal was known as the "targeted stock proposal." "Targeted stock" (now typically called "tracking stock") is the name given by Wall Street bankers to a separate class or series of a company's common stock with returns tied to the performance of a certain subsidiary or other division of the company.

Under the terms of the targeted stock proposal, shareholders were asked to authorize the amendment of Kmart's Restated Articles of Incorporation to provide for the issuance of shares of common stock in series to be created by the board of directors. Each of the series would be common stock of Kmart but would be designed to reflect separately the performance of a specialty retail subsidiary. The common stock outstanding at the time targeted stock was to be issued would still constitute Kmart common stock and would reflect Kmart's discount stores, any retained interest in the specialty retail subsidiaries (Kmart intended to retain about 70 percent to 80 percent interest in each subsidiary), and any other businesses of Kmart. The timing, sequence, and size of each offering of targeted stock would be determined by the board of directors without further vote of the shareholders.

By the time Antonini announced the targeted stock proposal, investors and analysts had already begun to suggest that Kmart's foray into specialty retailing was a mistake and that Kmart should sell all of its specialty retail holdings. Indeed, in early 1993 Kmart itself had floated the idea of divesting itself of the specialty retailers. Shortly after announcement of the targeted stock proposal, the State of Wisconsin Investment Board (SWIB) issued a statement urging shareholders to vote against the targeted stock proposal and against five incumbent Kmart directors who were up for reelection. SWIB criticized

Kmart's performance during Antonini's tenure and argued that Kmart's acquisition of specialty retail stores had "distracted Kmart from its core discount business." SWIB's opposition to the targeted stock proposal was quickly joined by other investors.

Also after the announcement of the targeted stock proposal, both Moody's Investors Service Inc. and Standard & Poor's Ratings Group lowered their ratings of Kmart outstanding indebtedness because of concern over the profitability of Kmart's discount stores. In a particularly pointed statement, Standard & Poors noted that Kmart's financial performance had been "slowly deteriorating since 1988," the first full year of Antonini's tenure.

Both Kmart and its investment bankers felt the targeted stock proposal was the best way to maximize shareholder value, even after shareholders rejected the idea. Furthermore, even among those who opposed the proposal, reasons for the opposition differed. Some investors wanted Kmart to sell all of the specialty retailing operations, arguing that they were a distraction from Kmart's main business of discount retailing. Other investors wanted the company to create a tax-free spin-off of the specialty retailers to shareholders. Still others believed that the stock market would not value targeted stock appropriately and wanted Kmart to sell its own common stock instead. Institutional investors may have opposed the proposal because they were not allowed to vote to authorize so many new shares for issuance or because they could not vote for a plan that allowed employees to buy stock at a discount. Some investors appeared to oppose the proposal simply to cast an emotional vote against Kmart's management.

The fact that Kmart's proposal for raising money by issuing securities to the public came before the shareholders was unusual and its defeat by shareholders was "one of the most astonishing investor rebellions in corporate history." The shareholder vote was unusual because most corporations access the capital markets through the issuance of additional securities upon approval of the board of directors only. Kmart could have taken this course, except that Kmart's management perceived the trading price of Kmart common stock to be below its "true" value. Antonini and the board, therefore, followed the counsel of investment bankers at Lehman Brothers, who advised that Kmart could maximize the proceeds of a public offering by issuing targeted stock. Because Kmart's charter did not allow for the issuance of targeted stock, Kmart was required to seek approval of shareholders to amend the corporate charter before accessing the capital markets.

Investor rejection of the targeted stock proposal was shocking because shareholder approval of management-proposed charter amendments normally is pro forma. In this instance, the rules regulating voting on the amendment were contained in the Michigan Business Corporation Act, which requires "the affirmative vote of a majority of the outstanding shares" for approval of any charter amendment. Of the 416 million shares outstanding, 108.6 million (26.1 percent) were voted against the proposal, including many of the 19 million shares held by employees. An additional 28 percent abstained. When the voting was over, John Wilcox, chairman of Georgeson & Co., Kmart's proxy solicitor, took the prize for understatement, saying: "It was worse than we predicted."

Immediately after the proxy contest, SWIB representative James Severance seemed to gloat: "We wanted to force this company to rethink their direction. . . . Either you replace the strategy or the strategist." But Antonini seemed intent on accomplishing the substance of the targeted stock proposal without shareholder approval. He suggested that the vote was a "misunderstanding," while outside director (later chairman) Donald Perkins labelled it "a communications problem." Antonini hired Professor John Pound of the Kennedy School of Government at Harvard to act as an intermediary for Kmart in its relations with about 20 institutional investors that together held more than 15 percent of Kmart stock. Unfortunately for Antonini, after conducting interviews with representatives of each of the investors, Pound concluded that the institutions all wanted Kmart to sell the specialty retail subsidiaries.

After hearing Pound's report, Antonini agreed to adopt the strategy advocated by dissident shareholders and announced plans to sell the specialty retail subsidiaries. In November 1994, Kmart executed highly successful initial public offerings of OfficeMax ($642 million) and The Sports Authority ($233.7 million) and sold its entire stake in Coles Myer for approximately $928 million. In addition, Kmart announced its intention to sell the Borders Group and Builders Square. Also after the proxy contest, Antonini appointed four new executive vice presidents from outside the company, perhaps in an attempt to answer critics who claimed that he was too loyal to long-time Kmart employees who could not get the job done.

Although the shareholder vote had appeared to give directors "a clear mandate to shake up top management," several candidates considered by Kmart's board reportedly were nervous about the prospect of working under Antonini without some assurance about when they would assume leadership of the company. Six months after the shareholder vote, having failed to find a successor for Antonini and still facing pressure from shareholders, Kmart's board of directors removed Antonini as chairman of the board and named Donald Perkins — a respected former chairman of Jewel Companies, Inc. — as his temporary successor. Commenting on Antonini's removal as chairman, James Severance of SWIB, a public pension fund and Antonini's most visible antagonist, said, "The board was too passive. If this represents the board asserting itself, then that's good news."

Antonini's removal as chairman, however, appears to have been less a signal of the board's resolve than an attempt to ward off shareholder pressure. Perkins later admitted that he had hoped his appointment as chairman would buy Antonini some time as CEO. And in February the board of directors appeared to have given up the search to replace Antonini as CEO. But Kmart's shareholders were restless. Perkins commented that, after being named chairman, he had "a number of discussions" with shareholders about Antonini's continued role with the company. SWIB's Severance promised, "We are going to continue to keep Joe's and the board's feet to the fire." On March 20, 1995, major Kmart shareholders met with Perkins. Although Perkins expressed confidence in Antonini, the shareholders' message was simple: "Joe has to go." The next day, Kmart's board of directors unanimously agreed to ask Antonini to resign.

QUESTIONS

Kmart is widely perceived as one of the first "success stories" for the SEC's policy of encouraging more shareholder involvement in corporate governance, which was implemented in part through the 1992 amendments to the proxy rules discussed above. Do you think shareholder participation in corporate governance should be encouraged, or should shareholders follow the "Wall Street Rule" by simply purchasing shares of well-managed companies and selling shares of badly managed companies, but otherwise remaining distant from corporate decision making?

What factors led Kmart's shareholders to conclude that Antonini was incompetent? It is worth remembering that Antonini was widely respected as a marketing genius before taking the reins as Kmart's CEO. Among other things, Antonini initiated Kmart's successful relationship with Martha Stewart. After Antonini's termination, Kmart continued to struggle and eventually filed for bankruptcy in 2002. In light of these facts, does it bother you that Kmart's investors forced the board of directors to fire Antonini?

As noted above, Kmart's shareholders were allowed to vote on the targeted stock proposal only because it required an amendment to Kmart's articles of incorporation. Do you believe that shareholders should be allowed to vote as a matter of course (and not only in the few instances where state corporation law requires a shareholder vote) on strategic decisions, such as whether Kmart should pursue specialty retailing? If the shareholders of Kmart wanted to influence the company's specialty retail strategy, could they have used a shareholder proposal? How might they have structured such a proposal?

CHAPTER

8

Federal Regulation of Corporate Governance

Prior to 2002, the conventional wisdom among many corporate law professors was that the regulation of the relationship among directors, managers, and shareholders was primarily a matter of state law and that federal securities law had only a minor role to play. As described in Chapter 7, this conventional wisdom is not quite accurate, since one purpose of federal securities disclosure is to inform shareholders of directors' actions, including conflict-of-interest transactions between directors and the companies that they direct. Another purpose was to enhance the power of shareholders in the corporation through federal proxy regulation. Thus, the federal securities laws have always had a role to play in regulating the corporate governance relationship. Yet, prior to 2002, the federal role was largely indirect; most direct regulation of corporate governance was left to state law.

The summer of 2002 brought the beginnings of a potential shift in this balance of federal versus state power, in the form of the Sarbanes-Oxley Act of 2002 (SOX). SOX was passed 99-0 in the Senate and 423-3 in the House of Representatives after a feverish month of legislative activity and was signed into law on July 30, 2002. Various bills had been introduced in both the Senate and the House in late 2001 and early 2002 in response to the accounting fraud (described below) and subsequent bankruptcy of the Enron Corporation, an energy company that prior to its bankruptcy was the seventh largest U.S. company by market capitalization, and which became the largest bankruptcy in U.S. history in December of 2001. Yet, despite Enron's dramatic fall from grace, the legislation languished and may have died but for the announcement on June 25, 2002, that the telecommunications company WorldCom had overstated its earnings by more than $3.8 billion in five quarters, an announcement rapidly followed by World Com's bankruptcy. In the context of indictments that same summer of the CEOs of Tyco International, Imclone, and Adelphia Communications for fraud (Adelphia), looting the company and tax evasion (Tyco), and insider trading (Imclone); as well as major accounting restatements and SEC inquiries at such stalwart companies as Coca-Cola, Xerox, and AOL/Time Warner, Congress was compelled to act to show that it was serious about corporate fraud. How Congress acted, and how the legislation it passed affects the balance of power between the federal government and state government with respect to corporate governance, is best appreciated by looking carefully at the colorful facts of one of the defining corporate frauds, that of the Enron Corporation. The rest of the Sections in this chapter look at a number of "gate-keepers" whose roles in corporate governance have been particularly criticized, and therefore emphasized, post-Enron: independent directors, accountants, and lawyers.

ENRON CORPORATION AND THE SARBANES-OXLEY ACT: A CASE STUDY

Once admired as one of the most innovative companies in America, Enron Corporation now has a legacy as one of the most spectacular frauds in business history. The rapid collapse of Enron in late 2001 resulted not only in the displacement of thousands of Enron employees and the loss of some $68 billion in stock market value, but also in significant collateral damage. Most visibly, the Enron debacle led to the implosion of Arthur Andersen, Enron's auditor and at that time one of the so-called "Big Five" accounting firms. When other firms followed in Enron's wake—the most notorious being Global Crossing and WorldCom—policymakers seized the opportunity to enact major regulatory reforms. While it is far too early to assess Enron's legacy, its collapse has already changed the legal landscape significantly. For our purposes, the most important of the post-Enron reforms was SOX. This case study will recount briefly the story of Enron Corporation[1] and will summarize the major reforms embodied in SOX.[2]

Seeds of Disaster. Enron began its corporate life as an energy company, a producer of natural gas. The company was the product of a merger of two natural gas companies in 1985,[3] and Kenneth Lay was selected to run the combined company. He immediately began the process of transforming the company into an energy trading firm. In that role, Enron was not merely an industry leader, but an industry creator.

Lay's vision for Enron did not focus on natural gas production but rather on financial intermediation. In other words, he wanted Enron to facilitate trades between energy producers and consumers. This was a radical notion in the mid-1980s, when electricity and natural gas production were monopolized by regulated utilities. Under Lay's leadership, Enron promoted deregulation of these industries.

Of course, an essential part of its business plan involved the lobbying of state and federal politicians. Naturally, in this context, Lay became as well known for his political ties as for his business savvy. When Enron later entered

---

1. The accounts of Enron's rise and fall are legion, but for background facts, we rely heavily on the first account to appear in the law reviews, the excellent article by Prof. William Bratton. *See* William W. Bratton, *Enron and the Dark Side of Shareholder Value*, 76 Tul. L. Rev. 1275 (2002). For interesting insider accounts of Enron, *see* Brian Curver, *Anatomy of Greed: The Unshredded Truth from an Enron Insider* (2002) and Mimi Swartz & Sherron Watkins, *Power Failure: The Inside Story of the Collapse of Enron* (2003).

2. One purpose of this case study is to illustrate the legal reaction to a real-world crisis. As a result, the focus will be on SOX, rather than on subsequent developments that have arisen in the implementation of SOX. To the extent that such developments are relevant to our study of business organizations, they will be described in subsequent sections of this book.

3. Initially, the firm was to be called "Enteron," but when someone pointed out that this word means "intestine," the name was changed to Enron. Frank Partnoy, *Infectious Greed: How Deceit and Risk Corrupted the Financial Markets* 298 (2003).

the quicksand that ultimately lead to its demise, Lay attempted to call on his political allies for assistance, but his former friends did not respond.

Two people who became crucial pieces of the Enron puzzle were added to the company in 1990. The first was Jeffrey Skilling, then a partner with the consulting firm of McKinsey & Company, who agreed to join the executive ranks at Enron. The second was Andrew Fastow, recently graduated from Northwestern University's MBA program, who joined the company's finance group. Both contributed substantially to Enron's growth — as we will see below, not always in a legitimate fashion — and both were promoted in 1997: Skilling to president and chief operating officer (COO) and Fastow to vice president of finance.

Once installed as president and COO, Skilling created a culture based on high-powered incentives. His most notorious innovation was the "rank and yank" system, described colorfully by William Bratton:

> Enron's whiz kid recruits entered a perpetual tournament. . . . Each got to pick ten other employees to rank his or her perfomance. But the system also allowed coworkers to make unsolicited evaluations into an online datebase. At year's end, Skilling threw everybody's results onto a bell curve, and those on the wrong end of the curve [the bottom 15 percent] were terminated. Those who remained scratched and clawed to get or stay in the winner's circle. Winners got million dollar bonuses and were privileged to accompany Skilling for glacier hiking in Patagonia or Land Cruiser racing in Australia.

Bratton, *supra* note 1, at 1293.

Under the influence of Lay and Skilling — with more than a small assist from the less visible Fastow, as it turns out — Enron became one of the largest corporations in the world, at least by accounting measures.[4] But the quickly constructed empire began to unravel even more quickly on October 16, 2001, when Enron announced "after-tax non-recurring charges" of $1.01 *billion* for the third quarter of the fiscal year. A week later, Fastow was placed on a leave of absence.

On October 31, William Powers, Dean of the University of Texas Law School, joined the Enron board. Powers was assigned to chair the Special Investigative Committee, whose task was to plow through Enron's records and produce a report for the directors, who wanted to know how this mess could have happened.[5] In particular, the directors wanted an explanation of various transactions between Enron and related parties, some of which are described below.

Just over a week later, Enron restated its financial statements for 1997 through the first two quarters of 2001, reducing net income from the prior statements by $586 million. On November 19, Enron filed its third-quarter Form 10-Q with the SEC. This was the document that contained financial statements showing the effects of a $1.01 billion charge. Enron's creditors were nervous. On the same day, Enron officers met with its major creditors at the Waldorf Astoria in New York City. Although Enron was then in the midst of a proposed merger

---

4. *See* "The 500 Largest U.S. Corporations," Fortune, April 16, 2001, at F.1 (listing Enron as the seventh largest corporation according to total revenues).

5. With the assistance of Wilmer, Cutler & Pickering, a Washington, D.C. law firm, the report — called the Report of Investigation by the Special Investigative Committee of the Board of Directors of Enron Corp. (the Powers Report) — was published on February 1, 2002.

with Dynegy,[6] what the creditors heard shook them. As noted later by the court-appointed examiner in Enron's bankruptcy case,

> During this meeting, Enron informed its bankers that while the debt reflected on its third quarter 2001 balance sheet under GAAP [generally accepted accounting principles] was $12.978 billion, Enron's "debt" (as set forth in the presentation) was $38.094 billion. Thus, as Enron noted, $25.116 billion of debt was "off balance sheet," or in some cases, on the balance sheet as a liability, but classified as something other than a debt.

In re Enron Corp., First Interim Report of Neal Batson, Court-appointed Examiner (S.D.N.Y. Sept. 21, 2002).

During this time, information about the "off balance sheet" related-party transactions began to emerge, and the markets lost confidence in Enron. Enron filed for bankruptcy protection on December 2, 2001.

Accounting Problems. Enron will be remembered most as a failure of the U.S. accounting system.[7] In the wake of Enron, there seemed to be plenty of blame to go around: Enron's board of directors, its top officers (Lay, Skilling, and Fastow), its accountants, its lawyers, Wall Street analysts, the financial press, and government regulators have all been questioned. While the number of illegal transactions at Enron precludes a thorough treatment here, the following illustrate the type of accounting tricks devised by Fastow and his minions to improve the appearance of Enron's financial statements.

1. Special purpose entities (SPEs). The Enron scandal introduced laypeople to SPEs for the first time, as news reports told of the creation of entities by Fastow with names based on *Star Wars*: Joint Energy Development Investments, L.P. (also known as JEDI) and Chewco (named after Chewbacca, the famously incoherent Wookie). Widely used by corporations for many purposes, many of which are legal, SPEs were employed illegally by Enron for the purpose of improving their financial statements.

JEDI was a limited partnership formed by Enron as general partner, with the California Public Employee Retirement System (CalPERS), as limited partner. Each invested $250 million in JEDI. Enron's investment was in the form of Enron stock while CalPERS invested cash. Each had a 50 percent interest in the partnership. JEDI was established for the purpose of making energy investments. Under U.S. accounting rules, Enron did not have to include JEDI on the Enron consolidated financial statements because it did not own a controlling interest in the firm.

When Enron asked CalPERS to invest in a larger partnership in 1997, CalPERS agreed, but only if its interest in JEDI were liquidated. Enron tried to locate a substitute investor for JEDI but was unsuccessful. As a result, Enron

---

6. Dynegy eventually backed away from Enron because of undisclosed liabilities. Enron sued Dynegy for wrongful termination of the merger agreement, and the parties settled in August 2002.

7. For an excellent description of the accounting problems at Enron, *see* George J. Benston & Al L. Hartgraves, *Enron: What Happened and What Can We Learn from It*, 21 J. Acct. & Pub. Poly. 105 (2002).

replaced CalPERS with SPE Chewco. According to the Powers Report, the formation of Chewco was the "first time Enron's Finance group (under Fastow) used an SPE run by an Enron employee to keep a significant investment partnership outside of Enron's financial statements." Power Report, *supra* note 5, at 41.

Chewco had three sources of financing: (1) a $240 million loan from Barclay's Bank, which was guaranteed by Enron; (2) a $132 million advance from JEDI, which was itself owned by Enron and Chewco; and (3) an $11.5 million equity investment from Michael J. Kopper—an Enron employee who reported to Fastow.[8] Kopper did not have $11.5 million of his own money, so he borrowed all but $125,000 from Barclay's Bank. As with the loan to Chewco, that loan was guaranteed by Enron. The executive committee of Enron's board of directors approved the Chewco investment after presentations by Skilling and Fastow. According the Powers Report, Fastow did not explain that Kopper's "equity investment" was really a loan from Barclay's Bank. *Id.* at 46.

Why did Enron go to all of this trouble? The goal was to keep JEDI's indebtedness—which was substantial, at over $1.6 billion—off Enron's financial statements. As long as Enron owned less than a majority of JEDI, GAAP did not require consolidation—that is, including JEDI's liabilities and assets on Enron's balance sheet and combining the two firms' income. The problem with Enron's decision not to consolidate JEDI was Chewco. If Enron controlled Chewco, then Enron controlled JEDI, and both Chewco and JEDI would need to be consolidated with Enron.

Whether Enron was deemed to be in control of Chewco would depend on various accounting rules, including an accounting policy adopted by the SEC known as the "three percent rule." Under this rule, at least 3 percent of an SPE's total capital must come from an outside equity investor. In addition, the person who owns that equity must have the ability to dispose of the SPE's assets. In other words, the outside equity holder, although representing only 3 percent of the SPE's total capital, must hold a majority of the SPE's total equity, showing just how "leveraged" the capital structure of the SPE can be. In the case of Chewco, Kopper was purported to be the outside investor. But, of course, the money for Kopper's investment came from Barclay's Bank in transactions that were characterized as "equity loans." Enron attempted to structure the transactions in a manner that allowed Barclay's to treat them as loans while allowing Chewco to treat them as equity. While such a structure was apparently a common practice for SPEs, it did not satisfy the conditions of the SEC accounting policy. *Id.* at 50.

In the end, the structure of the JEDI-Chewco transaction came to light, and Enron was forced to restate its financials to reflect the consolidation of those two companies. This restatement had the effect of reducing Enron's earnings

---

8. Fastow originally proposed himself as manager of Chewco, but Enron's law firm, Vinson & Elkins, said that such an arrangement would require disclosure in the company's proxy statement. In addition, Enron's Code of Conduct of Business required approval of Fastow's appointment by the chairman and CEO of Enron. Because Kopper was not a senior officer of Enron, his participation did not require disclosure in the proxy statement, though approval of the chairman and CEO was still required. According to the Powers Report, Ken Lay was both chairman and CEO at the time of the Chewco transaction, and he denied knowing Kopper. Although Skilling acknowledged approving Kopper's participation in Chewco, Skilling served as the COO at the time, and his approval was ineffective under the Code of Conduct.

by $405 million, and its indebtedness was increased by $628 million for the period from 1997 through the middle of 2001.[9]

2. *Fraudulent Asset Sales.* GAAP typically requires assets to be recorded at their historical cost. In some instances, however, firms can "mark assets to market" — that is, change the value of assets to more fully reflect current market values. One circumstance in which mark-to-market accounting would be justified is a third-party sale. When assets are sold to a third party in an arm's length transaction, their market price is thereby established. If the seller retains similar assets, it can revalue those assets in accordance with the price established by the third-party sale. Apparently, Enron engaged in numerous transactions designed to enable this sort of revaluation, but the transactions did not involve true third-party sales.

One example involved another well-publicized Enron SPE known as LJM Cayman L.P. (LJM1).[10] Acting through a limited liability company of which he was the sole member, Fastow was the general partner of LJM1. He raised $15 million from two outside investors. In September 1999, LJM1 used a large chunk of that money to purchase a 13 percent interest in a Brazilian power plant. The sale was valued at $11.3 million.

The power plant was actually owned by a Brazilian company, of which Enron owned 65 percent. Because the plant was "experiencing significant construction problems," Powers Report *supra*, at 136, Enron wanted to sell some of its interest but could not find a buyer. Enter Fastow: he negotiated the sale of part of Enron's interest in the Brazilian company to LJM1. Enron claimed that this sale eliminated its control position over the Brazilian company,[11] thus allowing Enron to move the badly performing company off Enron's financial statements. In addition, one of Enron's subsidiaries had a gas supply contract with the Brazilian company, and Enron used the phoney sales price to revalue the contract, booking $65 million in marked-to-market income in the second half of 1999.

Meanwhile, the power plant continued to experience construction problems. Nevertheless, nearly two years after the original transaction, Enron repurchased the interest from LJM1 for $14.4 million. According to the Powers Report, "[t]he price was calculated to provide LJM1 its maximum possible rate of return." *Id.* at 137. Apparently, this sort of transaction was not unique.

3. *Derivative Transactions.* Many of Enron's problems stemmed from derivative transactions. Indeed, Frank Partnoy has asserted, "Enron was, in reality, a derivatives-trading firm, not an energy firm." Partnoy, *supra* note 3, at 297.[12]

---

9. Frank Partnoy has observed: "Enron's dealings in JEDI and Chewco later horrified many individual investors, but the truth was that they were arguably legal, not especially unusual, mostly disclosed, and largely irrelevant to Enron's collapse." Partnoy, *supra* note 3, at 312.

10. The initials LJM represented Fastow's wife and two daughters.

11. How Enron could plausibly take this position is not clear. *See* Benston & Hartgraves, *supra* note 7, at 113 ("Considering that 65% less 13% equals 52%, it is not clear why Andersen did not make Enron consolidate [the Brazilian company] and allowed it to record an additional gain of $65 million by marking to market a portion of a gas supply contract. . . . ").

12. More surprisingly, Partnoy claims:

Enron's core business of derivatives trading was actually highly profitable, so profitable, in fact, that Enron almost certainly would have survived if the key parties had understood the details of its business. Instead, in late 2001, Enron was hoist with its own petard,

A "derivative" is simply a financial instrument whose value is derived from some other asset. For example, the value of an option to purchase stock is derived from the value of the underlying stock. As the value of the stock increases, the option to purchase that stock becomes more valuable. And vice versa.

A simple illustration of Enron's use of derivatives is provided by Enron's dealings with Chase Manhattan Bank (which later merged with J.P. Morgan and continued the types of transactions described herein). Enron wanted a loan from Chase but did not want to recognize the liability on its financial statements. To avoid this undesirable result, the two companies devised a complicated set of transactions that had the effect of a loan but the appearance of a sale. In the first set of transactions, Enron sold forward gas commodity contracts to Mahonia, Ltd., a company formed under the laws of Jersey, one of the Channel Islands. These contracts obligated Enron to sell gas to Mahonia at future dates for specified prices. In the second set of transactions, Enron purchased offsetting contracts from another Jersey company known as Stoneville Aegean Ltd. These contracts obligated Enron to buy gas from Stoneville at future dates for specified prices. Both Mahonia and Stoneville were connected to Chase.

Now comes the tricky part. Enron did not account for these mirror transactions symmetrically. It recorded the sales to Mahonia as revenues but did not count the purchases from Stoneville as expenses. Moreover, Enron collected the discounted present value of the Mahonia contracts but did not pay immediately on the Stoneville contracts. Mahonia raised the money to pay Enron by selling the forward contracts to Chase. The difference between the discounted value Enron received from Mahonia and the undiscounted value Enron would be required to pay to Stoneville was approximately equal to the interest on a 7 percent loan.

These transactions are called "prepaid swaps," and their beneficial effect on Enron's financial statements is obvious. When they were later brought to the attention of the U.S. Senate, Senator Carl Levin was astonished that these simple loans could be treated in any way other than as indebtedness. He called the transactions "phoney." But, as noted by Frank Partnoy:

> These deals might have been phony, but they were both common and, arguably, legal. Numerous companies used prepaid swaps to borrow money off balance sheet, and prepaid swaps . . . were part of mainstream corporate life, even though few investors had heard of them. Yes, these deals did not fit economic reality, but in a world governed by accounting standards, economic reality was barely relevant.

Partnoy, *supra* note 3, at 338.

The Fall. As noted above, the public markets widely acknowledged Enron's troubles when the company took a massive "non-recurring" charge on its third-quarter 2001 financial statements, and shortly thereafter restated earlier financial statements. But the first hint of trouble came earlier, on August 14,

---

collapsing — not because it wasn't making money — but because institutional investors and credit-rating agencies abandoned the company when they learned that Enron's executives had been using derivatives to hide the risky nature of their business.

Id.

when Skilling unexpectedly resigned for "personal" reasons only six months after taking the position of CEO.

Shortly after Skilling's resignation, Sherron Watkins—a former Arthur Andersen accountant and then vice president of corporate development at Enron—wrote a now-famous memo to Ken Lay expressing her concern about unusual accounting transactions like those described above.[13] Lay met personally with Watkins, then had the board of directors instruct Enron's attorneys at the Houston firm of Vinson & Elkins to investigate Watkins' charges. (This despite Watkins' specific warning that Vinson & Elkins would not be able to objectively review the transactions on which they had earlier issued favorable opinions.[14]) In an October 15 report, Vinson & Elkins concluded, "facts disclosed through our preliminary investigation do not, in our judgement, warrant a further widespread investigation by independent counsel and auditors."

Despite this report, pressure on Arthur Andersen increased. On October 23, David Duncan, the Andersen partner in charge of the Enron account, called a staff meeting, where he stressed the importance of the firm's "document retention" policy. While Duncan later testified that he did not realize his remark would lead to widespread destruction of Enron-related documents, that is exactly what happened. Over the next three days, over a ton of documents were shredded (more than is usually shredded in an entire year), and over 30,000 emails were deleted. Flynn McRoberts, *Ties to Enron Blinded Andersen*, Chi. Trib. 1 (Sept. 3, 2002). Andersen was later charged and found guilty of obstruction of justice, though the jurors in post-trial interviews said that the document destruction was not the basis for their verdict. Instead, they pointed the finger at Andersen's attorney, Nancy Temple, who wrote a memo to David Duncan suggesting that she knew of the SEC's interest in Enron and was trying to keep information away from investigators. In any event, Andersen was completely destroyed as a firm.

Regulatory Response. The corporate governance system relies on a collection of intermediaries to act as watchdogs over corporate officers. Most directly, every company has a board of directors that is charged with supervising the management of the corporation. In addition, professionals outside the corporation—including accounting firms, law firms, investment bankers, institutional investors, stock analysts, and government regulators—combine to monitor corporate activity from various viewpoints. Somehow, all of these controls managed to break down in the case of Enron. This lead to a widespread belief that the system of corporate governance was broken.

Initially, it appeared that Enron would pass, like so many business failures before it, without much more than a prolonged glance from investors

---

13. As a result of this memo, Watkins became known as the "Enron whistleblower." She was subsequently chosen as one of three "Persons of the Year" by Time Magazine. *See* Time, *Persons of the Year 2002: Cynthia Cooper, Coleen Rowley, and Sherron Watkins* (Dec. 22, 2002).

14. Two days after Watkins' meeting with Lay, Vinson & Elkins delivered an e-mail entitled "Confidential Employee Matter" to Lay. The message read in part: "Per your request, the following are some bullet thoughts on how to manage the case with the employee who made the sensitive report. . . . Texas law does not currently protect corporate whistleblowers. The Supreme Court has twice declined to create a cause of action for whistleblowers who are discharged. . . ." *See* Time, *Persons of the Year 2002: Party Crasher* (Dec. 22, 2002).

and regulators. When in June 2002 Global Crossing, WorldCom, and other firms revealed similar accounting problems, however, the public demanded a response, and Congress delivered in the form of SOX. The following paragraphs briefly summarize the major provisions of SOX.

1. Public Company Accounting Oversight Board: The Public Company Accounting Oversight Board was established to regulate the accounting profession. Its mission is to "oversee the audit of public companies . . . to protect the interests of investors and further the public interest in the preparation of informative, accurate, and independent audit reports." The board is not a government agency; rather, it is a nonprofit corporation subject to oversight by the SEC. The board has authority with respect to establishing rules for audits, but it specifically has the power to adopt standards suggested by professional organizations. *See* SOX §103(a), codified at 15 U.S.C. §7213. The board has five members appointed by the SEC, each for a five-year term. Each of the members must serve the board full-time, and two of the members must be certified public accountants. SOX §101(e), 15 U.S.C. §7211.

The board was seen as potentially one of the most important reforms in SOX because it seemed to indicate more searching oversight of how the accounting industry exercised its self-regulation. It got off to a rough start, however, when the SEC nominated William Webster—former head of the FBI and CIA—as the first board chairman. The nomination was the result of a split vote (3-2) by the SEC. The dissenting Commissioners wanted someone who would be tougher on industry than Webster was expected to be. Already reeling from a series of scandals, SEC Chairman Harvey Pitt was soon forced to resign when it was revealed that Webster had been on the audit committee of U.S. Technologies when it had been charged with accounting fraud, that Chairman Pitt had known of Webster's "accounting issue" and had failed to disclose this information to the White House prior to Webster's nomination.

2. Auditor independence: The statutory provisions attempting to encourage greater auditor independence are another important aspect of SOX. Outside auditors are understood to be important gatekeepers in the capital markets. The theory is that an independent evaluation has been done of the systems being used to generate a company's financial statements, and that based on that evaluation the auditor can say that the financial statements the company produces presents the company's financial status fairly, according to GAAP. By 2000, only about 25 percent of the "Big Five" accounting firms' income came from audit fees, however, and the balance was from non-audit services such as designing and implementing financial information systems, management consulting, bookkeeping, human resources outsourcing, and tax consulting. An important part of an audit is for the auditor to "test" the reliability of the company's information systems to see how much confidence one can have in the accuracy of the numbers being produced. If the auditor's accounting firm has set up those systems, it is impossible for the testing to be "independent," which is one of the core purposes of an audit. Moreover, if the auditor's accounting firm has given tax advice, it is impossible for that same firm independently to evaluate the amount of money being "reserved" to pay for potential taxes, or potential tax penalties and interest if questionable deductions are disallowed, for instance.

For some years prior to 2000, the SEC had been concerned about the proliferation of non-audit services by accounting firms and had been encouraging them and the AICPA (American Institute of Certified Public Accountants, one of the industry's self-regulatory agencies) to address the potential conflicts of interest and effects on auditor independence of non-audit services. Yet, the AICPA failed to act (as did Congress). Given the spectacular audit failures at Enron, World Com, Xerox, Global Crossing, and other companies, though, action on this issue became inevitable. SOX contained a number of provisions to try to encourage greater auditor independence, in general by prohibiting auditors from providing most non-audit services. *See* SOX §201, 15 U.S.C. §78j. Yet, audit companies may still provide tax-consulting services, and that is arguably the largest part of the problem of auditor non-independence: one-third of an audit firm's fees are estimated to come from tax consulting. Moreover, the board of directors may make specific exemptions to non-audit bans so long as the exemption is consistent with the protection of investors. *See id.* SOX also requires auditors to change the lead audit partner with primary responsibility for a client engagement every five years, again to try to encourage independence, although there is no requirement to change accounting firms. *See* SOX §203, 15 U.S.C. §78(j).

While the above provisions do not represent a shift of authority from the states to the federal government, since the SEC has had authority to regulate accountants since the 1930s (authority it has primarily delegated to accounting firms' self-regulatory organizations), many of the other provisions of SOX represent a shift in regulatory authority, leading to much greater federal involvement in corporate governance. Among the corporate governance provisions in SOX are the following:

3. Composition of Audit Committee: Every public company must have an audit committee comprised exclusively of "independent directors" responsible for hiring the auditors, and supervising their work. *See* SOX §301, 15 U.S.C. §78(j). "Independent" is defined as not having any affiliation with the audited company other than as a board member (that is, the director may not be an inside director or a major shareholder), and also not receiving any business income or consulting fees from the audited company other than income related to being a board and committee member. *See id.* SOX also directed the SEC to promulgate rules to require disclosure of whether the audit committee has at least one financial expert, and if not, why not. SOX §407, 15 U.S.C. §7265. (The New York Stock Exchange (NYSE) went even further and proposed changes to its listing standards to require that a majority of a company's board of directors be independent for a company to be listed on the NYSE.)

4. CEO Certification: SOX requires CEOs and chief financial officers (CFOs) of reporting companies to certify to the accuracy of their company's financial statements and that they have evaluated the effectiveness of their internal financial controls and have confidence in them. SOX §302, 15 U.S.C. §7241. SOX requires the SEC to develop regulations for companies to disclose, on an annual basis, how the effectiveness of internal financial controls has been evaluated. SOX §404, 15 U.S.C. §7262.

5. Restatement of financial results: In the event that a company is required to restate its financial results because of "misconduct," SOX requires the CEO

and CFO to reimburse the company for any bonus or other incentive-based compensation (including stock options) earned during a 12-month period following the issuance of the financial statements to be restated. SOX §304(a), 15 U.S.C. §7243. It also requires the CEO or CFO to reimburse the company for any profits he or she realized on the sale of company stock received during that same 12-month time. *See id.* This provision was a response to the increasing number of companies that were restating their financial statements downward during this period of time: while there were, on average, 49 restatements per year in the years 1990 to 1997, by 2000 there were 156. (Still, one must keep in mind that there were approximately 14,600 public companies in 2000, so it is not the number of restatements that suggested a need to act, but the prominence of the companies involved: Xerox, Lucent, Qualcomm, Coca-Cola, IBM, and GE, for instance.)

6. Code of Ethics: SOX directs the SEC to issue rules requiring each public reporting company to state whether it has a code of ethics for senior financial officers, and if not, why not. This section of SOX also directs the SEC to promulgate rules to require disclosure within two business days of any change in the code of ethics or waiver for senior financial officers. *See* SOX §406, 15 U.S.C. §7264. This latter provision was a direct response to the involvement of Michael Kopper (CFO Fastow's underling) in "investing" in the Chewco transaction. As set out in the facts above, Kopper was chosen as the person to "invest" in Chewco because his involvement would not need to be disclosed under then-existing securities regulations because he was not a senior officer of Enron.

7. Conflict-of-Interest Transactions: SOX prohibits public reporting companies from extending credit or arranging for the extending of credit, directly or indirectly, for personal loans to its executive officers or directors. SOX §402, 15 U.S.C. §78(m). This provision was presumably a direct response to some of the gross excesses described in the press at the Tyco Company, where the company had "loaned" CEO Dennis Kozlowski the money for not one but two multi-million dollar estates in Boca Raton, Florida. Tyco also "loaned" Kozlowski the money to purchase an apartment on Fifth Avenue in New York, to decorate the apartment with fine French antiques and (in facts that became notorious) a $6,500 shower curtain; and had paid half of the $2 million tab for a birthday party for his wife on the Italian island of Sardinia, just to begin to describe the company largesse to which Mr. Kozlowski helped himself. Mr. Kozlowski, the CFO, and Tyco's general counsel were soon charged with looting the company of over $600 million, so this may not have been an example of improper company loans after all, but the facts were just beginning to be reported during the summer of 2002, and seemingly had a great impact on this provision of SOX.

8. Officers and Directors' Removal: SOX expands the SEC's ability to seek the removal of officers and directors and to seek to ban them from similar positions, due to their "unfitness." SOX §305(a)(1), 15 U.S.C. §78(u)(d)(2). Previously the SEC had to show "substantial unfitness" in order to remove officers or directors or to ban them from similar positions.

In addition to these provisions directed to accountants and directors or top officers, SOX also addressed the responsibility of lawyers as gatekeepers:

9. Lawyers' Responsibilities: Specifically, SOX directed the SEC to adopt rules requiring attorneys who appear before it to report "evidence" of securities laws

violations, fiduciary breaches, or similar misconduct to a reporting company's chief legal counsel or CEO and, if those officers fail to act "appropriately," to the company's audit committee, its independent directors, or the board of directors as a whole. SOX §307, 15 U.S.C. §7245. While this provision might seem uncontroversial — after all, it is the company that hires a lawyer, so it is the company that is a lawyer's client, not the executive officers — it has spawned a storm of criticism and concern. Part of the storm arose because the SEC's first proposed rules envisioned "noisy withdrawal" — that is, a lawyer being required to notify the SEC of his or her withdrawal from representing a company if the board failed to act in response to a lawyer's report of securities law violations, fiduciary breaches, or similar violations. But even after the SEC withdrew its "noisy withdrawal" proposal and returned to "board reporting," §307 remains controversial. Lawyers understand that "client development" often means being particularly compatible with the CEO and other top executives with whom they've developed working relationships, and such compatibility is certainly undermined by reporting differences of opinion between the CEO and lawyer to the board. Moreover, this is much more direct federal regulation of the legal profession than previously obtained, which is another source of controversy.

A number of the other provisions of SOX relate directly to required securities disclosure and regulation of the markets:

10. Real time disclosure: SOX amends §13 of the Securities Exchange Act of 1934, the section establishing periodic disclosure, to require reporting companies to make "real time" disclosure of material changes in their financial condition or operations. SOX §409, 15 U.S.C. §78(m)(1). Previously, companies could usually wait until their next quarterly report to discuss material changes or trends affecting their financial results or operations, unless those changes were events specifically identified in Form 8-K for more immediate disclosure (such as signing a merger agreement or selling a major subsidiary). Thus, post-SOX, companies must disclose material changes "on a rapid and current basis."

11. Off-balance sheet transactions disclosure: SOX directs the SEC to promulgate rules that require disclosure of all material off-balance sheet transactions, an obvious response to the Enron off-balance sheet transactions. SOX §401, 15 U.S.C. §7261(c)(1). (Recall that the debt reflected on Enron's third-quarter 2001 balance sheet was $12.978 billion, while its actual debt was $39.095 billion, meaning that there was $25.116 billion of off-balance sheet debt.) Section 401(c) also directs the SEC to study the use of SPEs and their relationship to off-balance sheet transactions, and report back to Congress on whether further regulation is necessary to ensure that there is adequate financial transparency of the material risks facing companies from the use of SPEs. *See id.*

12. Whistleblower Protection: One of the ways that information was forced into the public domain at Enron was through the action of "whistleblower" Sherron Watkins. Yet, as you saw in the facts above, "whistleblowers" are often not protected under state law causes of action for wrongful discharge if they are discharged for their efforts. SOX §806 establishes protection for whistleblowers and establishes a private right of action on behalf of whistleblowers for compensatory damages for violations. SOX §806(a), 18 U.S.C. §1514A.

13. Securities Analysts' Independence: SOX requires the SEC to adopt rules governing the independence and objectivity of securities analysts. SOX §501,

15 U.S.C. §78o-6(a). While the Enron and WorldCom corporate governance debacles were unfolding, another series of unfortunate events began to attract public and regulatory attention, which involved conflicts of interest within securities firms. Large securities firms employ research analysts to evaluate companies and provide ideas to their clients about good stocks to buy. Large securities firms also compete to "underwrite" new stock offerings, which means to sell the offerings to the public. While the firms are supposed to ensure that the recommendations of the stock analysts are not affected by the securities offerings in which the company is involved, events in the summer of 2002 showed that any purported separation between the interests of underwriting departments and the recommendations of stock analysts was paper-thin. Thus, stocks that analysts termed "dogs" and "losers" were being touted to clients when the firm was underwriter for the companies issuing such dogs and losers. Indeed, the conflicts of interest went deeper than that. Attorney General of New York Elliott Spitzer took the lead to investigate and found numerous instances in many firms where securities analysts were told to rewrite their research reports or be fired. In one particularly colorful instance, a star telecommunications analyst was alleged to have agreed to issue favorable reports on a company his securities firm was underwriting in exchange for his firm making a $1 million contribution to a private nursery school in New York so that his twin children might receive favorable consideration in their kindergarten application. (A subsequent article in the New York Times haughtily implied that such bribery would never be effective and went on to describe many, many instances of contributions to private nursery schools well in excess of $1 million — leaving the impression that it might not have been the bribery that was the problem, but that it had been attempted on the cheap.)

14. Enhanced Criminal Penalties: In addition to all of the above (and other provisions) of SOX, the statute also enhances criminal penalties for destruction of documents and for securities fraud, leading to potential penalties of 25 years' imprisonment for securities fraud. SOX §805, 28 U.S.C. §994 (U.S. Sentencing Guidelines). Whether any prosecutor will ever seek such a penalty is uncertain, but clearly it will operate as a strong deterrent to intentional securities fraud of the Enron and WorldCom varieties.

A.   DIRECTOR INDEPENDENCE

One of the perennial questions asked when there are corporate debacles is "Where were the directors?," a question often followed by reforms that seek to enhance the monitoring role of outside, independent directors. Starting with the bankruptcy of the Penn Central corporation in 1972, then the sixth largest company in the United States, a number of whose directors were quoted as saying they had first heard about the bankruptcy by reading the morning newspaper, there have been reform efforts aimed at getting rid of rubber-stamping boards. As one of our colleagues has written, over the last 20 years there have been corporate governance recommendations aimed at creating independent monitoring boards by the American Bar Association's Committee on Corporate Laws, the SEC, the New York Stock Exchange, and the American Law

Institution's Principles of Corporate Governance project, among others. *See* Larry E. Ribstein, *Market v. Regulatory Responses to Corporate Fraud: A Critique of the Sarbanes-Oxley Act of 2002*, 28 J. Corp. L. 1 (2002). Sarbanes-Oxley also added fuel to the independent director fire. And yet, as discussed in Chapter 6, strategies that rely upon independent directors to exercise keen, critical oversight of management can be frustrated by the fact that non-employee directors are involved only part-time in the business of the company. Moreover, since they are part-time, non-employee directors are dependent on the management of the company for their information about the company, thereby reducing their potential effectiveness.

Another concern with reform efforts aimed at creating truly independent monitoring boards is the fact that board members serve, essentially, at the pleasure of management, since top management usually suggests the names of board nominees when there is a vacancy. (And vacancies are rare, given that board members at a large public company can expect to earn upwards of $90,000 per year for attendance at a few board meetings a year, in addition to other perks such as retirement benefits, stock options, meeting fees of $1,000 per board or committee meeting, and even the occasional pair of tickets to the U.S. Open Golf Tournament or similar sporting events.) A study in 1991 concluded that 82 percent of board vacancies were filled as a result of recommendations by the CEO. As noted institutional shareholder activists Robert Monks and Nell Minow have stated, to understand the context of corporate governance in the United States at the beginning of the 21st century, one has to think seriously about the implications of having "self-perpetuating" boards.

In light of the dramatic events of late 2001 and 2002, efforts are afoot by institutional investors to change the self-perpetuating nature of board membership by changing companies' bylaws to permit shareholder groups to nominate board members. The following series of letters concerns a shareholder proposal toward that end. While you are reading these letters, recall the materials in Chapter 7 to inform your views about whether the SEC should concur in a no-action position or not.

AOL TIME WARNER INC.
2003 WL 942784
SEC No-Action Letter
Publicly Available February 28, 2003

PROPOSAL

RESOLVED, that the stockholders of AOL Time-Warner, Inc. ("AOLTW" or the "Company") urge the board of directors to take the necessary steps to amend the Bylaws of AOLTW to establish a procedure by which a Nominating Stockholder (defined below) may ensure the inclusion of a Qualified Nominee (defined below) in AOLTW's proxy statement and on AOLTW's proxy card.

The procedure should require the Nominating Stockholder to provide to AOLTW in writing, a reasonable length of time before the annual or special meeting, a notice containing the same information about both the Nominating Stockholder and the Qualified Nominee as is required regarding other nominees and participants in a solicitation pursuant to Schedule 14A (the "Disclosure"). . . .

A Nominating Stockholder should be defined as one or more stockholders that hold in the aggregate 3% or more of AOLTW's outstanding common stock. A Qualified Nominee is a person who has consented to being named in the proxy statement and to serving as a director if elected, and who, in accordance with AOLTW's policy, is under 72 years of age.

SUPPORTING STATEMENT

Stockholders currently have no meaningful control over the process by which candidates are selected for election to company boards of directors. AOLTW's bylaws state that stockholders may suggest candidates, but there is no requirement that the candidates be placed on the ballot. Indeed, there is no indication in either of the proxy statements since AOLTW was formed that any stockholder nominee was considered.

We believe that direct access to the proxy for purposes of electing a director nominated by stockholders is the most effective mechanism for ensuring diverse opinions and promoting independent oversight. Now is an appropriate time to facilitate such stockholder participation, in light of the business and compliance challenges facing AOLTW.

As detailed in an October 14, 2002 article in The New York Times, AOLTW's credibility has been damaged by revelations regarding questionable revenue recognition practices and the refusal to abandon unrealistic financial projections. The SEC and Justice Department are investigating the accounting practices of the Company's AOL unit, and the Company announced in October 2002 that it would restate two years of financial results. AOLTW's stock closed at $14.75 on October 31, 2002, down over 73% from its closing price of $56.60 just 17 months earlier on May 21, 2001.

We urge shareholders to vote FOR this proposal.
December 20, 2002

LETTER TO SEC

December 26, 2002
Securities and Exchange Commission
Division of Corporation Finance
Office of Chief Counsel
450 Fifth Street, N.W.
Washington, D.C. 20549

Re: AOL Time Warner Inc. — Proposal Submitted by the American Federation of State, County and Municipal Employees ("AFSCME") Employees Pension Plan

Ladies and Gentlemen:
This letter respectfully requests that the staff of the Division of Corporation Finance (the "Staff") of the Securities and Exchange Commission (the "SEC") advise AOL Time Warner Inc. (the "Company") that it will not recommend any enforcement action to the SEC if the Company omits from its proxy statement and proxy to be filed and distributed in connection with its 2003 annual meeting

of shareholders (the "Proxy Materials") the proposal (the "Proposal") it received from the AFSCME Employees Pension Plan (the "Proponent"). . . .

II. Grounds for Omission.

A. The Proposal relates to the election for membership on the Company's Board of Directors and, therefore, may be omitted from the Company's Proxy Materials pursuant to Rule 14a-8(i)(8).

Rule 14a-8(i)(8) permits exclusion of shareholder proposals and supporting materials "[i]f the proposal relates to an election for membership on the company's board of directors." Regarding Rule 14a-8(i)(8), formerly Rule 14a-8(c)(8), the SEC has stated that "the principle purpose of this provision is to make clear, with respect to corporate elections, that Rule 14a-8 is not the proper means for conducting campaigns or effecting reforms in elections of that nature." Release No. 34-12598 (July 7, 1976). In fact, the SEC has established a separate regulatory scheme, including Rule 14a-12, for shareholders to propose additional directors and conduct such campaigns.

The Staff has consistently agreed that shareholder proposals that establish procedures that may result in contested elections to the Board of Directors, rather than relating to nomination or qualification generally, are excludable pursuant to Rule 14a-8(i)(8). *See, e.g.,* BellSouth Corp. (January 24, 2000) ("BellSouth"); Ford Motor Company (January 24, 2000) ("Ford"); Storage Technology Corp. (March 22, 2002) and (March 11, 1998) ("Storage Technology"); Unocal Corp. (February 8, 1991) ("Unocal"). In *Unocal*, the Staff permitted the exclusion of a shareholder proposal seeking to amend company by-laws to require the inclusion in proxy materials of shareholder nominees to the Board of Directors in the same manner as other nominees because it may result in contested elections. Similarly, in *Storage Technology*, the Staff found that a proposal requesting that the Board of Directors include in the proxy statement a list of shareholder nominees, each selected by at least three shareholders cumulatively holding 3,000 shares of stock, could be excluded under Rule 14a-8(c)(8) because it would "establish a procedure that may result in contested elections of directors." Furthermore, as in the current Proposal, the Staff has permitted the omission of shareholder proposals seeking to allow shareholders of a certain size access to a company's proxy materials for purposes of seeking election of a director. For example, in *BellSouth*, a proposal urging the company to take all necessary steps to include information in the proxy materials regarding nominees to the Board of Directors proposed by three percent shareholders was properly excluded since it may result in contested elections. . . .

Rather than establishing general nomination or qualification procedures, the Proposal here would establish a procedure for inclusion of shareholder nominees in the proxy statement of the Company that would result in contested elections. The Staff has consistently stated that the shareholder proposal process is not the proper means for conducting contests for elections of directors. The Proposal is, therefore, properly omitted from the Company's Proxy Materials pursuant to Rule 14a-8(I)(8). . . .

For the foregoing reasons, the Company respectfully requests that the Staff confirm that it would not recommend enforcement action if the Company omits the Proposal from its Proxy Materials. If you have any questions or if the Staff is unable to concur with our conclusions without additional information or discussions, we respectfully request the opportunity to confer with members of the Staff prior to the issuance of any written response to this letter. Please do not hesitate to call the undersigned at (212) 484-7350.

Please acknowledge receipt of this letter and its attachments by stamping the enclosed copy of the first page of this letter and returning it in the self-addressed stamped envelope provided for your convenience.

Very truly yours,
Susan A. Waxenberg
Assistant General Counsel and Assistant Secretary
AOL Time Warner Inc.
75 Rockefeller Plaza, 25-18 · New York, NY 10019
tel 212 484 7350

LETTER TO SEC FROM PROPONENT

January 24, 2003
Securities and Exchange Commission
Division of Corporation Finance
Office of Chief Counsel
450 Fifth Street, NW
Washington, DC 20549

Re: Stockholder proposal of AFSCME Employees Pension Plan; no-action request by AOL Time Warner Inc.

Dear Sir/Madam:

Pursuant to Rule 14a-8 under the Securities Exchange Act of 1934, the AFSCME Employees Pension Plan (the "Plan") submitted to AOL Time Warner Inc. ("AOLTW" or the "Company") a stockholder proposal (the "Proposal") urging AOLTW's board to amend the Company's bylaws to establish a procedure by which a Nominating Stockholder (as defined in the Proposal) may ensure the inclusion of a Qualified Nominee (also defined in the Proposal) in AOLTW's proxy statement and on AOLTW's proxy card.

In a letter to the Commission dated December 26, 2002, AOLTW stated that it intends to omit the Proposal from its proxy materials being prepared for the 2003 annual meeting of stockholders. . . . As discussed more fully below and in the attached opinion of Grant & Eisenhofer, P.A., AOLTW has failed to meet its burden of establishing entitlement to [exclude the proposal]. Accordingly, its request for no-action relief should be denied.

Rule 14a-8(i)(8): Relates to an Election for Membership on the Company's Board of Directors

Rule 14a-8(i)(8) permits exclusion of a proposal if it "relates to an election for membership on the company's board of directors or analogous governing body." (For simplicity, this exclusion is referred to herein as the "Election Exclusion.") AOLTW contends that the Proposal falls within this exclusion because it would foster contested elections of directors. AOLTW is correct that the SEC staff has, in recent years, excluded proposals similar to the Proposal on the ground that they were likely to lead to contested director elections. We believe that the Election Exclusion should not be applied to allow blanket exclusion of all proposals seeking stockholder access to management's proxy, and we respectfully request that the position be reconsidered. Specifically, we urge the SEC staff to permit such proposals that, like the Proposal, would not permit circumvention of the Commission's proxy rules governing election contests or the disclosure requirements contained in Schedule 14A.

The language of the Election Exclusion provides little guidance regarding its scope. Because of the breadth of its language, it could be construed as permitting exclusion of all proposals touching on the election of directors. However, the SEC staff has not interpreted the Election Exclusion so broadly, and has required companies to include in their proxy statements many different proposals that concern the election of directors, including proposals asking companies to declassify their board, *see, e.g.,* Boeing Co. (Feb. 23, 1999); adopt cumulative voting, *see, e.g.,* Archer Daniels Midland (June 20, 1996); adopt director tenure limits or mandatory retirement ages, *see, e.g.,* LSB Industries (Feb. 17, 1997); and nominate two candidates for each open board seat, *see, e.g.,* SBC Communications Inc. (Jan. 31, 2001; review denied, Mar. 16, 2001). . . .

Stockholder Access Proposals

Proposals seeking stockholder access to management's proxy statement (hereinafter, "Stockholder Access Proposals"), however, have met with an inconsistent response from the SEC staff, and, as AOLTW points out, the most recent letters have uniformly permitted exclusion.

Although the precise formulation may vary, Stockholder Access Proposals generally provide that shareholders — often only those holding more than a threshold amount of stock — may nominate a candidate to serve on a company's board, and require the company to include the nominee's name and certain other information on the company proxy statement and proxy card. Here, the Proposal urges AOLTW's board to amend the Company's bylaws to establish a procedure by which any holder or group of holders owning 3% or more of AOLTW's outstanding common stock (the "Nominating Stockholder") may nominate a single candidate (a "Qualified Nominee") for inclusion in AOLTW's proxy statement and card. The Proposal would require that the information required by Schedule 14A with respect to both the Nominating Stockholder and the Qualified Nominee be provided to AOLTW at the time of the nomination. The Proposal also provides that the Nominating Stockholder must agree to abide by all applicable legal requirements, including, without limitation, Rule 14a-12, to the extent soliciting materials other than the Company's proxy statement are used.

The Proposal is designed to improve AOLTW's corporate governance by providing a substantial stockholder or group of stockholders with a cost-effective way to participate meaningfully in the director nomination and election processes. Currently, the incumbent board has exclusive access to management's proxy statement for the purpose of nominating director candidates. A stockholder that wishes to sponsor a board candidate must shoulder all of the expenses associated with such a campaign, including costs associated with preparing, printing and mailing a separate proxy statement and tabulating a separate proxy card, which can total hundreds of thousands of dollars.

Because the cost is so high, director campaigns are typically waged only by those seeking control of the company. Providing a more level playing field with respect to the nomination of director candidates is a logical outgrowth of the principle that stockholders have the exclusive power to elect directors, and that providing access to management's proxy will enable stockholders to fulfill their monitoring role more effectively.

The "Contested Election" Rationale and the Commission's Proxy Rules

In permitting exclusion of Stockholder Access Proposals, the SEC staff has reasoned that such proposals, "rather than establishing procedures for nomination or qualification generally, would establish a procedure that may result in contested elections of directors." *See, e.g.,* United Road Services, Inc. (May 5, 2000); The Black & Decker Corp. (Jan. 18, 2000); The Coca-Cola Company (Jan. 24, 2000). In some cases, the staff has explained further that the establishment of such a procedure "is a matter more appropriately addressed under Rule 14a-11 [now 14a-12]." *See, e.g.,* Unocal Corp. (Feb. 8, 1990); Bell-South Corp. (Feb. 4, 1998). AOLTW relies on these decisions to urge that it be permitted to exclude the Proposal.

The Plan believes that the "contested election" rationale has been inconsistently applied to proposals dealing with election procedures, in ways that undermine rather than bolster the Commission's current disclosure regime, and that there is no basis for the distinction in the history of the Election Exclusion. Further, public policy considerations militate against the exclusion of Stockholder Access Proposals simply because they might result in challenges to incumbent directors in management's proxy statement.

The SEC staff has supported its use of the contested election rationale by quoting language from a 1976 release proposing minor changes to the Election Exclusion. In that release, the Commission stated, "[T]he principal purpose of the provision is to make clear, with respect to corporate elections, that Rule 14a-8 is not the proper means for conducting campaigns or effecting reforms in elections of that nature, since other proxy rules, including Rule 14a-11 [now 14a-12], are applicable thereto." Exchange Act Rel. No. 12598 (July 7, 1976). That statement does not directly address the propriety of Stockholder Access Proposals. It does, however, contain two principles useful in interpreting the Election Exclusion: first, that Rule 14a-8 should not be used as a mechanism to conduct a campaign in favor of or against a particular candidate for the board; and second, that the SEC staff is concerned that certain proposals reforming the election process could interfere with the Commission's regulation of proxy solicitations.

The Plan agrees that the shareholder proposal rule itself should not be used to nominate director candidates or oppose one or more candidates nominated by the board. There has been little controversy over the SEC staff's invocation of the Election Exclusion to allow exclusion of self-nominating proposals, for example, or proposals urging stockholders to vote against one or more incumbent directors. The Proposal does neither of these things.

The Proposal does, however, seek to reform the process by which directors are nominated and elected at AOLTW. It is possible to construe "effecting reforms in elections of that nature" as referring to — and thus supporting exclusion of — all proposals aimed at reforming the corporate election process. However, the

SEC staff has not taken this position: rather, it has determined that certain election procedure proposals — those that do not result in a "contested election" — are not excludable, while Stockholder Access Proposals may be excluded.

The basis for this distinction is difficult to discern, especially in light of the SEC staff's treatment of recent proposals asking companies to nominate two or more persons for each open board seat and include information about all nominees in the proxy statement and on the proxy card ("Double Nominee Proposals"). Double Nominee Proposals, like Stockholder Access Proposals, would bring about a major change to the process for electing directors. With respect to the Double Nominee Proposals, a contested election would surely occur because the incumbent board could recommend that stockholders vote for only half (or fewer) of the candidates. Nonetheless, the SEC staff has not allowed companies to exclude these proposals. *See, e.g.*, General Electric Company (Jan. 12, 2001) (rejecting argument that Double Nominee Proposal created contested election, justifying exclusion under Rule 14a-8(i)(8)); General Motors Corp. (Apr. 10, 2000) (same).

The SEC staff's concern regarding circumvention of the other proxy rules, evident in Release 12598, may explain its inconsistent treatment of Double Nominee Proposals and Stockholder Access Proposals. Specifically, the SEC staff may believe that because under the Double Nominee Proposals all candidates are nominated by the incumbent board, violations of the other proxy rules could not occur. The Double Nominee Proposals do require all "SEC-required declarations" — presumably referring to the information about the nominees required by Schedule 14A — to be included in management's proxy statement. However, the Double Nominee Proposals do not prohibit candidates from among the slate not recommended by the incumbent board from sending out their own solicitation materials or even circulating a separate proxy card without complying with the proxy rules. Indeed, if such candidates were serious about winning the election, they would likely engage in at least some solicitation activity.

By contrast, the procedure established pursuant to the Proposal would ensure that Nominating Stockholders and Qualified Nominees do comply fully with all of the Commission's proxy rules. As an initial matter, the proxy rules do not require that the specified disclosure regarding candidates not nominated by the incumbent board appear in a separate document from management's proxy statement or that stockholders shoulder all of the substantial financial burden of sponsoring a candidate for a company's board. Rule 14a-3(a) provides that "No solicitation subject to this regulation shall be made unless each person solicited is concurrently furnished or has previously been furnished with a publicly-filed preliminary or definitive proxy statement containing the information specified in Schedule 14A. . . ." Management's proxy statement, so long as it contained the Schedule 14A information with respect to the Qualified Nominee and the Nominating Stockholder, would satisfy this requirement. . . .

The purpose of the proxy rules — complete and accurate disclosure of information regarding matters to be voted on by stockholders — can be served as well under a stockholder access regime as under the current system. Stockholders, who have limited control rights under our governance system, must rely on directors — their elected representatives — to safeguard their interests. Stockholders thus have a vital interest in ensuring that the procedures used to nominate and elect directors result in an effective and vigilant board; they should be permitted to express their opinions on whether a stockholder access regime is preferable to the current system in this regard. These public policy considerations thus support the inclusion of the Proposal in AOLTW's proxy statement, despite the fact that it may make contested director elections more likely. . . .

To conclude, the Proposal sets forth a stockholder right of access to management's proxy statement that has been carefully designed to enhance the participation of substantial stockholders in AOLTW's corporate governance while ensuring compliance with the Commission's proxy rules. The Proposal does not violate Delaware law or contain false or misleading statements. Accordingly, we urge the SEC staff not to permit AOLTW to exclude the Proposal in reliance on the Election Exclusion, Rule 14a-8(i)(1), (i)(2) or (i)(3).

If you have any questions or need additional information, please do not hesitate to call me at (202) 429-1007.

Very truly yours,
Charles J. Jurgonis
Plan Secretary

SEC LETTER

February 28, 2003
Re: AOL Time Warner Inc.
Incoming letter dated December 26, 2002

The proposal amends the bylaws to require that AOL Time Warner include the name, along with certain disclosures and statements, of any person nominated for election to the board by a stockholder who beneficially owns 3% or more of AOL Time Warner's outstanding stock.

There appears to be some basis for your view that AOL Time Warner may exclude the proposal under rule 14a-8(i)(8), as relating to an election for membership on its board of directors. It appears that the proposal, rather than establishing procedures for nomination or qualification generally, would establish a procedure that may result in contested elections of directors. Accordingly, the Division will not recommend enforcement action to the Commission if AOL Time Warner omits the proposal from its proxy materials in reliance on rule 14a-8(i)(8). In reaching this position, we have not found it necessary to address the alternative bases for omission upon which AOL Time Warner relies.

Sincerely,
Jennifer Bowes
Attorney-Advisor

Although the AOL Time Warner shareholders were frustrated in these efforts, the final chapter of this story has not yet been written. On April 14, 2003, the SEC announced that it had asked the Division of Corporation Finance to formulate possible changes in the proxy rules and regulations regarding procedures for the election of corporate directors. As stated in the press release, the review will include an examination of the rules concerning shareholder proposals, the corporate director nomination process, elections of directors, and the solicitation of proxies for director elections. On November 19, 2003, the SEC adopted rules that would expand disclosure about the nominating committee of the board, including what provisions the committee has for shareholders to nominate candidates, and what communications, generally, occur between shareholders and the nominating committee. On October 14, 2003, the SEC proposed direct access rules that would, in certain circumstances, require companies to include shareholders' nominees for director in company proxy materials. The proposed triggering circumstances include instances where a prior nominee to the board received "withhold" votes from 35% or more of the shareholders, or cases in which a shareholder proposal suggesting this direct access procedure received a majority vote.

B. ACCOUNTING CONTROLS

As set out above, the Sarbanes-Oxley Act attempts to encourage greater auditor independence, both by prohibiting accounting firms from providing certain kinds of non-audit services to their audit clients, at least without a waiver from the board, and by establishing requirements for the composition and responsibilities of the audit committee. Still, some shareholders have sought to go beyond these provisions, as the following series of communications indicates.

VERIZON COMMUNICATIONS INC.
2003 WL 262457
SEC No-Action Letter
Publicly Available January 23, 2003

AUDITOR CONFLICTS PROPOSAL

RESOLVED, that the shareholders of Verizon Communications, Inc. ("Company") request that the Board of Directors adopt a policy stating that the public accounting firm retained by our Company to provide audit services, or any affiliated company, should not also be retained to provide any management consulting services to our Company.

Statement of Support: The role of independent auditors in ensuring the integrity of the financial statements of public corporations is fundamentally important to the efficient and effective operation of the financial markets. The U.S. Securities and Exchange Commission recently stated:

> Independent auditors have an important public trust. Investors must be able to rely on issuers' financial statements. It is the auditor's opinion that furnishes investors with critical assurance that the financial statements have been subjected to a rigorous examination by an objective, impartial, and skilled professional, and that investors, therefore, can rely on them. If investors do not believe that an auditor is independent of a company, they will derive little confidence from the auditor's opinion and will be far less likely to invest in that public company's securities. Final Rule: Revision of the

Commission's Auditor Independence Requirements, Release No. 33-7919, Feb. 5, 2001.

We believe that today investors seriously question whether auditors are independent of the company and corporate management that retain them. A major reason for this skepticism, we believe, is that management of once admired companies such as Enron, Tyco, and WorldCom have misled investors and their auditors have either been complicit or simply inept. Over the last year hundreds of billions of dollars in market value have vanished as investors have lost confidence in the integrity of our markets. A key reason for this lack of confidence is the distrust investors have in companies' financial statements.

The U.S. Congress has attempted to respond to this crisis of confidence through passage of the Sarbanes-Oxley Act of 2002 (the "Sarbanes Act"). The Sarbanes Act prohibits a company's auditors from performing a wide range of defined non-audit services. These prohibitions, in turn, track the defined non-audit services in Rule 2-01(c)(4) of the SEC's Final Rule: Revision of the Commission's Auditor Independence Requirements, Release No. 33-7919, Feb. 5, 2001.

However, the Sarbanes Act fails to prohibit auditors from providing management consulting services, which we believe represents a significant loophole. While the Act does require that the audit committee of the board preapprove these non-audit services, we do not believe that is enough. We believe that management consulting represents a significant source of potential revenue to auditors and poses serious conflict of interest issues. For this reason, we think the better course is for companies not to engage their auditors to perform any management consulting services.

Many companies, including ours, either continue to engage their auditors to provide management consulting or provide inadequate disclosure in their proxy statements to ascertain whether they continue to engage their auditors for management consulting services. We urge your support for this resolution asking the board to cease engaging auditors for management consulting.

LETTER TO COMPANY FROM PROPONENT

November 1, 2002
Marianne Drost
Corporate Secretary
Verizon Communications, Inc.
1095 Avenue of the Americas
New York, New York 10036

Re: Shareholder Proposal

Dear Ms. Drost:
On behalf of the Massachusetts Carpenters Pension & Annuity Funds ("Funds"), I hereby submit the enclosed shareholder proposal ("Proposal") for

inclusion in the Verizon Communications, Inc. ("Company") proxy statement to be circulated to Company shareholders in conjunction with the next annual meeting of shareholders. The Proposal relates to the issue of auditor independence. The Proposal is submitted under Rule 14(a)-8 (Proposals of Security Holders) of the U.S. Securities and Exchange Commission proxy regulations.

The Funds are the beneficial owner of approximately 60,520 shares of the Company's common stock that have been held continuously for more than a year prior to this date of submission. The Funds and other Carpenter pension funds are long-term holders of the Company's common stock.

The Funds intend to hold the shares through the date of the Company's next annual meeting of shareholders. The record holder of the stock will provide the appropriate verification of the Funds' beneficial ownership by separate letter. Either the undersigned or a designated representative will present the Proposal for consideration at the annual meeting of shareholders.

If you have any questions or wish to discuss the Proposal, please contact our Corporate Governance Advisor, Edward J. Durkin, at (202) 546-6206 ext. 221. Copies of correspondence or a request for a "no-action" letter should likewise be forwarded to Mr. Durkin at United Brotherhood of Carpenters, Carpenters Corporate Governance Project, 101 Constitution Avenue, NW, Washington D.C. 20001 or faxed to 202-543-4871.

Sincerely,
Thomas J. Harrington
Fund Chairman

LETTER TO SEC

December 16, 2002
Office of the Chief Counsel
Division of Corporation Finance
Securities and Exchange Commission
450 Fifth Street, NW
Washington, DC 20549

Re: Verizon Communications Inc.
Commission File No. 1-8606

Rule 14a-8, Shareholder Proposal of Massachusetts State Carpenters Pension & Annuity Funds
Ladies and Gentlemen:
Verizon Communications Inc. (the "Corporation") received a letter, dated November 1, 2002, from the Massachusetts State Carpenters Pension & Annuity Funds (the "Proponent"), requesting that the Corporation submit a proposal (the "Proposal") to the Corporation's 2003 Annual Meeting of Shareholders. The Proposal requests that the Corporation's Board of Directors adopt a policy restricting the Corporation's outside auditors from providing "management consulting services" to the Corporation. . . .

On behalf of the Corporation, I hereby notify the Securities and Exchange Commission (the "Commission") and the Proponent of the Corporation's intention to omit the Proposal from the Corporation's Proxy Materials in connection with the 2003 Annual Meeting of Shareholders for the reasons hereinafter set forth. In accordance with Rule 14a-8(j) under the Securities Exchange Act of 1934, as amended, I enclose for filing five additional copies of this letter and the Exhibit hereto.

Rule 14a-8(i)(3) and Rule 14a-9: Misleading Statements in Violation of Proxy Rules

Rule 14a-8(i)(3) states that a shareholder proposal may be omitted if it is "contrary to any of the Commission's proxy rules", including Rule 14a-9's prohibition on materially false or misleading statements in proxy materials. The Proposal requests the Board of the Corporation to adopt a policy that the Corporation's independent auditor should not also be retained to provide "management consulting services" to the Corporation. The Proposal is fundamentally flawed in that the central term on which it depends, "management consulting services," has no generally accepted definition or meaning under the securities laws, auditor independence standards, the Commission's current rules on qualification of accountants, or the Commission's recently proposed rules on auditor independence pursuant to the Sarbanes-Oxley Act of 2002 (Securities Exchange Act Release No. 34-46934 (December 2, 2002)). Indeed, the Proponent appears to acknowledge that there is no such term in the Sarbanes-Oxley Act.

It is also not clear from the Proposal whether the requested prohibition concerning "any affiliated company" refers to affiliates of the "Company" or to affiliates of "the public accounting firm." Again, this is a material ambiguity. Neither the shareholders who would be asked to vote on the Proposal nor the Board which would be asked to act on the Proposal would be able to determine the scope of the requested prohibition.

The Commission Staff has previously found stockholder proposals to be misleading within the meaning of Rule 14-8(i)(3), and in numerous no-action letters has permitted the exclusion of such proposals, when they were "vague and indefinite" and subject to differing determinations by shareholders voting on the proposal and the company's board in implementing the proposal, with the result that any action ultimately taken by the company could be significantly different from the action envisioned by the shareholders voting on the proposal. Exxon Corporation (January 2, 1997). The Staff has permitted exclusion when proposals were "inherently so vague and indefinite that neither the shareholders voting on the proposal, nor the Company in implementing the proposal (if adopted), would be able to determine with any reasonable certainty exactly what actions or measures the proposal requires," *e.g.*, Philadelphia Electric Company (July 30, 1992); *e.g.*, NYNEX Corporation (January 12, 1990).

Accordingly, since the Proposal is vague and misleading, it may be omitted from the Corporation's Proxy Materials under Rule 14a-8(i)(3).

Rule 14a-8(i)(7): Ordinary Business Operations

Under Rule 14a-8(i)(7), a proposal is excludable from a company's proxy materials if it deals with a matter relating to the conduct of the ordinary business operations of the company. Although as noted above, the Proposal is inherently vague and ambiguous, it would appear to operate to restrict management in its ability to consult with the audit firm on day-to-day matters. Thus, the Proposal would interfere with the conduct of the Company's ordinary business operations. The Proposal would also operate, in effect, to restrict the Board in its selection of an audit firm. In a line of no-action letters, the Commission Staff has consistently taken the position that shareholder proposals relating to the selection and qualification of a company's independent auditors may be omitted from a company's proxy materials pursuant to Rule 14a-8(i)(7). *See, e.g.,* Community Bancshares, Inc. (March 15, 1999); Excalibur Technology Corporation (May 4, 1998); Occidental Petroleum Corporation (December 11, 1997); Transamerica Corporation (March 8, 1996); LTV Corporation (December 30, 1996). More recently, the Staff reaffirmed its longstanding position that shareholder proposals dealing with the selection of a company's independent auditors may be excluded from a company's proxy materials pursuant to Rule 14a-8(i)(7) because such proposals related to the company's ordinary business operations. SONICblue Incorporated (March 23, 2001).

In SONICblue, a shareholder submitted a proposal mandating that the company's auditor be selected annually by shareholder vote. The shareholder argued that because the Commission had recently revised its Auditor Independence Requirements, the selection of the auditor was not an ordinary business matter entirely within the discretion of the company's management. The Staff, however, concurred in SONICblue's opinion that the proposal could be excluded from the proxy materials under Rule 14a-8(i)(7) "as relating to SONICblue's ordinary business operations (i.e., the method of selecting independent auditors)."

The Corporation's decision whether to limit the services of its auditor to an extent greater than required by already comprehensive statutes, Commission rules, and stock exchange rules is within the purview of the ordinary business judgement of the Corporation and its management and not within the purview of a shareholder proposal. The Staff has permitted exclusion on ordinary business grounds of a proposal that addresses a topic on which the Commission has promulgated a rule, but which seeks to require a company to do something beyond that which the rule requires. For example, when a proposal seeks to require a company to make a financial disclosure that goes beyond the financial statement disclosures which are required by the rules of the Commission or stock exchange, the Staff has permitted the company to exclude the proposal under Rule 14a-8(i)(7). In Santa Fe Southern Pacific Corporation (January 30, 1986), the Staff allowed the exclusion of a proposal requiring the preparation and disclosure of certain financial statements to which the company objected under Rule 14a-8(c)(7) (predecessor to Rule 14-8(i)(7)) "since it appears to deal with a matter relating to the conduct of the Company's ordinary business operations (*i.e.*, the determination to make financial disclosure not required by law)."

The Proposal thus addresses "tasks so fundamental to management's ability to run the company on a day-to-day basis that they could not, as a practical matter, be subject to direct shareholder oversight" and it seeks to "micro-manage" a company "by probing too deeply into matters of a complex nature which shareholders, as a group, would not be in a position to make an informed judgement." Securities Exchange Act Release No. 34-40018 (May 21, 1998).

In light of the foregoing, in my opinion, the Proposal may be omitted from the Corporation's Proxy Materials under Rule 14a-8(i)(7).

For each of the above reasons, it is my opinion that the Proposal may properly be omitted from the Proxy Materials for the Corporation's 2003 Annual Meeting of Shareholders. I respectfully request your confirmation that the Commission Staff will not recommend any enforcement action to the Commission if the Proposal is omitted from the Proxy Materials for the Corporation's 2003 Annual Meeting of Shareholders.

Kindly acknowledge receipt of the letter by stamping and returning the extra enclosed copy of this letter in the enclosed self-addressed, stamped envelope. If you have any questions with respect to this matter, please telephone me at (212) 395-6299.

Very truly yours,
Darlene D. Kleiner
Assistant General Counsel
Verizon
1095 Avenue of the Americas
Room 3869
New York, NY 10036
Tel 212 395-6299

SEC LETTER

January 23, 2003
Re: Verizon Communications Inc.
Incoming letter dated December 16, 2002

The proposal requests that the board of directors adopt a policy "stating that the public accounting firm retained by our Company to provide audit services, or any affiliated company, should not also be retained to provide any management consulting services to our Company."

We are unable to concur in your view that Verizon may exclude the proposal under rule 14a-8(i)(3). Accordingly, we do not believe that Verizon may omit the proposal from its proxy material in reliance on rule 14a-8(i)(3).

We are unable to concur in your view that Verizon may exclude the proposal under rule 14a-8(i)(7). That provision permits the omission of a proposal that deals with a matter relating to the ordinary business operations of a registrant. In view of the widespread public debate concerning the impact of non-audit services on auditor independence and the increasing recognition that this issue raises significant policy issues, we do not believe that Verizon may omit the proposal from its proxy materials in reliance on rule 14a-8(i)(7).

Sincerely,
Alex Shukhman
Attorney-Advisor

C. ATTORNEY RESPONSIBILITY

Section 307 of Sarbanes-Oxley, titled "Rules of Professional Responsibility for Attorneys" SOX §307, 15 U.S.C. §7245, requires the SEC to "develop minimum standards of professional conduct for attorneys appearing before or practicing before the Commission in any way." One rule that Sarbanes-Oxley specifically directed the SEC to promulgate could require attorneys to "report evidence of a material violation of securities law or breach of fiduciary duty" by the company or any agent thereof to the chief legal counsel or executive officer, and if those persons fail to act, to report evidence of the violation or breach to the audit committee, to any other committee composed entirely of independent directors, or to the board as a whole. *See id.* In response, the SEC promulgated Rule 205, which requires such "up the ladder" reporting. Rule 205 also permits (but does not require) lawyers to disclose confidential client information to the SEC to prevent the client from committing a material violation that is likely to cause substantial injury to the financial interests of the issuer or investors. At the time it promulgated Rule 205, August of 2003, the SEC indicated it was still considering its so-called "noisy withdrawal" proposal, which would permit or require lawyers in some circumstances to notify the SEC that they had withdrawn from the representation of the issuer (presumably because the issuer was about to violate the securities laws), and to report evidence of material violations to the SEC. Section 307 came about as a result of concerns over the involvement of members of respected law firms in enabling Enron to misstate its financial results, as the following case illustrates. When reading this case, consider the extent to which the procedures developed by Section 307 would — or would not — have made a difference at Enron.

IN RE ENRON CORP. SECURITIES, DERIVATIVE & ERISA LITIGATION

235 F. Supp. 2d 549
United States District Court, S.D. Texas
December 19, 2002

HARMON, District Judge.

The above referenced putative class action, brought on behalf of purchasers of Enron Corporation's publicly traded equity and debt securities during a proposed federal Class Period from October 19, 1998 through November 27, 2001, alleges securities violations (1) under Sections 11 and 15 of the Securities Act of 1933 ("1933 Act"); [and] (2) under Sections 10(b), 20(a), and 20A of the Securities Exchange Act of 1934 ("Exchange Act" or "the 1934 Act"), and Rule 10b-5 promulgated thereunder by the Securities and Exchange Commission ("SEC").

Pending before the Court *inter alia* are motions to dismiss . . . filed by [two] law firms. . . .

In essence Lead Plaintiff's consolidated complaint alleges that these and other named Defendants "are liable for (i) making false statements, or failing to disclose adverse facts while selling Enron securities and/or (ii) participating in a scheme to defraud and/or a course of business that operated as a fraud or deceit on purchasers of Enron's public securities during the Class Period. . . . "

Applicable Law

The rapid collapse of Enron Corporation ("Enron") and the resulting scope, variety, and severity of losses are unprecedented in American corporate history. It is not surprising that this consolidated action raises a number of novel and/or controversial issues that the law has thus far not addressed or about which the courts are in substantial disagreement. Lead Plaintiff Regents of the University of California's claims are grounded in securities statutes, but judicial construction of those statutes spans the full spectrum of possibilities. After a careful review of frequently divergent case law and extensive deliberation, the Court applies the following law to the allegations in the consolidated complaint and, where appropriate, explains the bases for its selection. . . .

II. FEDERAL SECURITIES LAW

A. SECTION 10(B) OF THE 1934 ACT AND RULE 10B-5

. . . One objective underlying the enactment of §10(b) following the 1929 stock market crash was "to insure honest securities markets and thereby promote investor confidence." United States v. O'Hagan, 521 U.S. at 658. Furthermore Congress tried " 'to substitute a philosophy of full disclosure for the philosophy of *caveat emptor* and thus to achieve a high standard of business ethics in the securities industry.' " Affiliated Ute Citizens of Utah v. United States, 406 U.S. 128, 150 (1972), *quoting* SEC v. Capital Gains Research Bureau, Inc., 375 U.S. 180, 186 (1963). The Supreme Court has indicated that the statute should be "construed 'not technically and restrictively, but flexibly to effectuate its remedial purposes.' " Affiliated Ute Citizens of Utah v. United States, 406 U.S. at 151, *quoting* SEC v. Capital Gains Research Bureau, Inc., 375 U.S. at 195. . . .

C. PROFESSIONAL CONDUCT/DUTY TO NONCLIENT INVESTORS

1. Attorneys

The issue of attorney liability involving a duty to disclose nonmisleading information to nonclients and third parties is a thorny one, complicated by tension between the need to provide remedy to parties suffering monetary loss because of a lawyer's conduct and the attorney-client relationship with its attendant confidentiality, loyalty and zealous representation requirements and policy concerns.

Ethical rules of conduct such as disciplinary rules do not create corresponding legal duties nor constitute standards for imposition of civil liability on lawyers. They do, however, reflect public policy concerns.

ABA Model Rule of Professional Conduct 1.6 (2001) states, "A lawyer shall not reveal information relating to representation of a client unless the client consents after consultation," except that the lawyer may, but does not have to, reveal confidential information (1) to the extent that the lawyer reasonably believes is necessary to prevent the client from committing a criminal act which the lawyer believes is likely to result in imminent death or substantial bodily harm,[37] or (2) to establish a claim or defense by the lawyer in a controversy between the lawyer and the client, or to establish a defense to a criminal or civil charge against the lawyer based on conduct in which the client was involved, or to answer any allegations in any proceeding about the lawyer's representation of the client.

Pursuant to ABA Model Rule of Professional Conduct 1.2(d) an attorney "shall not counsel a client to engage, or assist a client in, conduct that the lawyer knows is criminal or fraudulent . . . ,"[38] but the attorney may discuss the legal consequences of any proposed conduct and help the client make a good faith effort to determine the application of the law to that proposed conduct. Comment 6 to the rule states, "The fact that a client uses advice in the course of action that is criminal or fraudulent does not, of itself, make a lawyer party to the course of action. However, a lawyer may not knowingly assist a client in criminal or fraudulent conduct. There is a critical distinction between presenting an analysis of legal aspects of questionable conduct and recommending the means by which a crime or fraud might be committed with impunity."

If the attorney learns that his client is involved in ongoing criminal or fraudulent acts, under ABA Model Rule 1.16 (2001),

> (a) Except as stated in paragraph (c), a lawyer shall . . . withdraw from the representations of a client if: (1) the representation will result in violation of the rules of professional conduct or other law; . . .
>
> (b) Except as stated in paragraph (c) a lawyer may withdraw from representing a client . . . if: (1) the client persists in a course of action involving the lawyer's services that the lawyer reasonably believes is criminal or fraudulent; (2) the client has used the lawyer's services to perpetrate a crime or fraud; and . . .
>
> (c) When ordered to do so by a tribunal, a lawyer shall continue representation notwithstanding good cause for terminating the representation.
>
> (d) Upon termination of representation, a lawyer shall take steps to the extent reasonably practicable to protect a client's interests, such as giving reasonable notice to the client, allowing time for employment of other counsel, surrendering papers and property to which the client is entitled. . . .

After withdrawal the lawyer must also refrain from disclosing the client's confidences except as allowed under Rule 1.6.

Model Rule 1.07 also bars a lawyer from representing a party where there is a substantial risk that the lawyer's representation would be materially and adversely affected by the lawyer's or his law firm's own interest.

The Texas Rules of Professional Conduct have similar but not identical provisions. [The court quotes Rule 1.02(d) of the Texas Rules of Professional Conduct (1990), which states: "When a lawyer has confidential information clearly establishing that a client is likely to commit a criminal or fraudulent act *that is likely to result in substantial injury to the financial interests or property of another,* the lawyer shall promptly make reasonable efforts under the circumstances to dissuade the client from committing the crime or fraud."] . . .

37. Economic harm is not identified as a basis for the exception.
38. The Terminology section defines "knows" as "actual knowledge of the fact in question" and states that a "person's knowledge may be inferred from circumstances."

The common law regarding attorney liability to nonclients for misstatements that are attributed specifically to him has been evolving steadily to address increasing concerns about attorney accountability or the lack thereof.

The Fifth Circuit has only twice addressed the issue of an attorney's duty to disclose information accurately to a third party in the context of alleged securities violations. In 1988, the Fifth Circuit, in a suit challenging the accountability of an underwriter's counsel for the alleged inaccuracy of the underwriter's offering statement to the investing public, reaffirmed the traditional rule that "lawyers are accountable only to their clients for the sufficiency of their legal opinions" because "any significant increase in attorney liability to third parties could have a dramatic effect upon our entire system of legal ethics," established to require the attorney to avoid conflicting duties, "remain loyal to the client," and "keep attorney client confidences." Abell v. Potomac Ins. Co., 858 F.2d 1104, 1124 & nn.18 and 19 (5th Cir. 1988), *vacated on other grounds*, 492 U.S. 914 (1989). . . . The Fifth Circuit did concede that an attorney who prepared a signed opinion letter for use by a third party might be liable under Rule 10b-5, but otherwise declined to depart from the traditional rule because it found "no binding authority creating a special rule in the field of securities law." *Id.* at 1124-25.

Nevertheless, in Trust Company of Louisiana v. N.N.P., 104 F.3d 1478 (5th Cir. 1997), which makes only passing reference to *Abell*, the Fifth Circuit concluded that the plaintiff, a non-client and the payee of notes . . . purportedly secured by the Government National Mortgage Association certificates ("GNMAs"), had satisfied all the elements of proof to show that the attorney and his firm owed the payee a duty under Louisiana law for negligent misrepresentation and for the imposition of primary liability under Rule 10b-5 (*i.e.*, that the lawyer knowingly and with scienter made material misstatements in connection with the purchase of a security upon which the plaintiff justifiably relied and suffered injury). Specifically the attorney had assured the plaintiff that his firm had possession of and was the custodian for the GNMAs when counsel knew that the law firm did not have the certificates, but only assignments of interest in the certificates.

[The court then reviews several decisions in other Circuits. For example, the court describes Klein v. Boyd, Fed. Sec. L. Rep. (CCH) ¶¶90,136; 90,323 (3d Cir.) as follows: "[T]he Third Circuit panel concluded that although the firm may not have a duty to blow the whistle on its client, once it chooses to speak, a law firm does have a duty to speak truthfully, to make accurate or correct material statements, even where the document does not indicate that the attorney authored it." The court found a similar holding in Rubin v. Schottenstein, Zox & Dunn, 143 F.3d 263 (6th Cir. 1998).]

In Texas, it has long been established that a lawyer may be liable if he knowingly commits a fraudulent act or enters into a conspiracy with his client to defraud a third person. In the instant action, Lead Plaintiff alleges that Enron's lawyers, accountants, and underwriters participated together with Enron in a Ponzi scheme to enrich themselves, which, in a significant and essential part of the plan, defrauded third-party investors in Enron securities to keep funds flowing into the corporation. . . .

This Court concludes that professionals, including lawyers and accountants, when they take the affirmative step of speaking out, whether individually or as essentially an author or co-author in a statement or report, whether identified or not, about their client's financial condition, do have a duty to third parties not in privity not to knowingly or with severe recklessness issue materially misleading statements on which they intend or have reason to expect that those third parties will rely. . . . Moreover, with respect to the element of reliance, for purposes of §10(b) as well as the tort of fraudulent misrepresentation, the Court is concerned about avoiding the danger of opening the professional liability floodgates to any and every potential investor or foreseeable user of the allegedly misleading information who might obtain and rely on the statement. Therefore this Court finds that a restrictive approach with respect to the group to which the attorney or accountant owes the duty and which thus should have standing to sue . . . is appropriate and necessary. In this suit, Lead Plaintiff has alleged as a crucial part of the Ponzi scheme that at least some fraudulent misrepresentations were made by Vinson and Elkins & Arthur Andersen and were aimed at investors to attract funds into Enron, as well as at credit rating agencies to keep Enron's credit rating high and bank loans flowing. Therefore the "limited group" that the attorneys or accountants allegedly intended, or might reasonably have expected, to rely on their material misrepresentations, and who allegedly did rely and suffered pecuniary loss, included Plaintiffs in this suit. . . .

2. Law Firms

The consolidated complaint claims that Vinson & Elkins, Enron's outside general counsel during the Class Period, and Kirkland & Ellis participated in writing, reviewing, and approving Enron's SEC filings, shareholder reports and financial press releases, and in creating Chewco, JEDI, LJM1, LJM2, and nearly all the related SPEs' transactions. They knew that LJM2's principal purpose was to engage in transactions with Enron and that Enron insiders Fastow, Kopper and Glisan were operating on both sides of the transactions, to virtually insure lucrative returns for the entities' partners.

a. Vinson & Elkins L.L.P.

Enron was Vinson & Elkins' largest client, accounting for more than 7% of the firm's revenues. Over the years more than twenty Vinson & Elkins lawyers have left the firm and joined Enron's in-house legal department.

The complaint recites a long history of alleged improprieties by Vinson & Elkins as part of the elaborate Ponzi scheme.

The complaint asserts that Vinson & Elkins participated in the negotiations for, prepared the transactions for, participated in the structuring of, and approved the illicit partnerships (Chewco/JEDI and the LJMs) and the SPEs (Raptors/Condor, etc.) with knowledge that they were manipulative devices, not independent third parties and not valid SPEs, designed to move debt off Enron's books, inflate its earnings, and falsify Enron's reported financial results and financial condition at crucial times. Vinson & Elkins repeatedly provided "true sale" and other opinions that were false and were indispensable for the sham deals to close and the fraudulent scheme to continue. Vinson & Elkins also allegedly drafted and/or approved the adequacy of Enron's press releases, shareholder reports, and SEC filings, including Form 10Ks and Registration Statements that Vinson & Elkins knew were false and misleading. Vinson & Elkins also drafted the disclosures about the related party transactions, which it also knew were false and misleading because they concealed material facts. It also was involved in structuring and providing advice about the bogus commodity trades utilized by JP Morgan and Enron with the involvement of Mahonia. Moreover, the firm continually issued false opinions about the illegitimate business transactions, such as that they were "true sales." When the scheme began to collapse in August 2001 and Skilling resigned, whistle-blower Sherron Watkins sent her August 9, 2001 memorandum warning Kenneth Lay not to use Vinson & Elkins to handle an investigation of her voiced concerns about Enron's accounting practices because Vinson & Elkins had a conflict in that "they provided some 'true sale' opinions on some of the [Condor and Raptor] deals." Despite Watkins's warning, Vinson & Elkins was called and allegedly conducted a whitewash investigation of what it knew were accurate allegations of fraudulent misconduct that also involved Vinson & Elkins. Vinson & Elkins received over $100 million in legal fees from Enron.

Specifically, the complaint asserts that Vinson & Elkins provided advice in structuring virtually every Enron off-balance sheet transaction and prepared the transaction documents, including opinions, for deals . . . used to defraud investors and the securities markets. . . . Vinson & Elkins allegedly had to know about and joined in the fraudulent Ponzi scheme because of its continuing, intimate involvement in the formation of and transactions with these blatantly fraudulent entities, created solely to cook Enron's books.

For instance, Lead Plaintiff points to Vinson & Elkins' involvement in the eleventh-hour formation of Chewco in late 1997 when JEDI's outside investor withdrew and JEDI had to be restructured or Enron would have to consolidate JEDI on its books, carry JEDI's debt on its balance sheet, and lose its ability in the future to continue to generate profits from an independent SPE. Vinson & Elkins prepared the documents for Chewco's financing and falsified them to make it appear that Chewco was independent of Enron. Because the arrangement had to be completed by year's end, Vinson & Elkins with Kirkland & Ellis drafted a side agreement, dated December 30, 1997, providing for Enron to give the required $6.6 million in cash to fund Chewco by means of clandestine reserve accounts for Big River Funding and Little River Funding. Furthermore, to avoid disclosure of the arrangement, because making Fastow manager of Chewco would necessitate disclosing that interest in Enron's SEC filings and potentially expose the non-arm's-length nature of the whole transaction, Vinson & Elkins, with Fastow, arranged for Michael Kopper to be the manager and thus conceal Enron's financial relationship with Chewco from Enron shareholders. Kopper allegedly objected that there was a conflict of interest because Kopper was also an Enron employee, but the two law firms disregarded his concern. Neither law firm insisted on disclosure of the arrangement in Enron's SEC filings even though the impropriety was obvious. Moreover, Enron continued to use Chewco/JEDI to generate sham profits from 1997 through 2001 in transactions that Vinson & Elkins participated in structuring and providing bogus "true sale" opinions to facilitate, all for the same purpose.

[The court proceeds to detail other similar misdeeds by Vinson & Elkins in connection with the accounting frauds perpetrated by Enron and described in the case study above.]

More specifically, the complaint states that in Enron's Reports on Form 10-K for year-end 1997-2000, Vinson & Elkins approved a description of JEDI as an unconsolidated affiliate only 50% owned by Enron. In its Report on Form 10-K filed 3/30/00, Vinson & Elkins drafted and approved the following disclosure:

"At December 31, 1999 JEDI held approximately 12 million shares of Enron Corp. common stock. The value of the Enron Corp. common stock has been hedged. In addition, an officer of Enron has invested in the limited partner of JEDI and from time to time acts as agent on behalf of the limited partner's management." These purported disclosures were false and misleading because Chewco, which was not independent of Enron, was not capitalized with outside equity at risk, but was capitalized by JEDI and an Enron guaranty. Enron did not disclose that Chewco was a limited partner of JEDI until Enron announced its catastrophic restatement on 11/8/01. Nor was it disclosed that JEDI's transactions were not true commercial, economic transactions comparable to those of independent third-parties in arm's-length bargains.

The complaint speaks to Vinson & Elkins' alleged false and misleading disclosures about JEDI/Chewco. In March 2001, Enron paid Michael Kopper and his domestic partner, William Dodson, $35 million in a "purchase" of Chewco's limited partnership interest in JEDI so that Kopper could buy Fastow's interest in the LJM partnerships. The deceptive disclosure about the buyout, drafted and approved by Vinson & Elkins for inclusion in Enron's reports on Form 10-Q filed on 5/15/01 and 8/14/01, never stated that it was a deal among some Enron officers, Kopper and Fastow or that it included the $2.6 million gift to Kopper and Dodson. Moreover, the buyout was erroneously characterized as having a net positive effect on Enron's financial statements, when in actuality the consolidation of JEDI resulted in a massive reduction in Enron's reported net income and shareholders' equity and a massive increase in its reported debt. . . .

Tracking the language in the Powers' report, the complaint asserts that common to all Enron related-party disclosures, drafted and approved by Vinson & Elkins, was concealment of the following material matters known to Vinson & Elkins: (1) that the transactions were not true commercial, economic transactions comparable to those with independent third parties; (2) the "disclosures" concealed the real substance and effect of the transactions on Enron and on its financial statements, e.g., that the transactions should have been consolidated on Enron's financial statements; and (3) they failed to disclose Fastow's actual financial interest in or compensation from the LJM partnerships. Instead the disclosures in SEC filings through the Class Period gave the impression that each transaction was fair to the company, not contrived, but made at arm's length as it would have been if made with an independent third party. In actuality the transactions, which were controlled only by Enron, Fastow or Kopper through the LJM entities, were bogus, contrived to enrich individual Defendants, and, according to the Powers-led special investigative committee, designed "to accomplish financial results, not achieve bona fide economic objectives or to transfer risk." In nearly every transaction, Fastow or Kopper made millions of dollars while bearing little or no risk, and Enron obtained favorable financial-statement results while bearing all the risk. . . .

The complaint points out that although Sherron Watkins' August 2001 letter to Ken Lay represented that Vinson & Elkins had been involved in the fraud and had a clear conflict of interest, Lay still turned to top Vinson & Elkins partners to find out how to cover up the allegations. Furthermore, Vinson & Elkins, despite this obvious conflict, agreed to conduct an investigation into the charges and to issue a letter or report dismissing the allegations of fraud that Vinson & Elkins knew were true. Vinson & Elkins also agreed not to "second guess" the accounting work or judgments of Arthur Andersen and to limit its inquiry to top level executives at Enron. Vinson & Elkins' review took place between August 15 and October 15, 2001. . . .

During its investigation, according to the complaint, Vinson & Elkins only interviewed top level executives that Vinson & Elkins knew were involved in the fraud and would deny it. On October 15, 2001 the law firm issued a letter to Enron dismissing all of Sherron Watkins' allegations even though Vinson & Elkins knew they were true from its own involvement. . . .

The complaint recites that although Lay wanted to fire Watkins, he and Vinson & Elkins agreed that discharge would be a mistake and would lead to a wrongful termination suit, disclosing Watkins' allegations about transactions at Enron. So she was shifted to another position at Enron where she would have less exposure to information damaging to Enron.

b. Kirkland & Ellis

The complaint alleges that Kirkland & Ellis actively engaged in the scheme to defraud and course of business that operated as a fraud on Enron investors. Kirkland & Ellis began working with Fastow, Enron, and Vinson & Elkins in the early '90's to create and use off balance sheet investment partnerships and SPEs that allowed Enron to engage in transactions designed to increase or maintain its credit rating by artificially inflating its profits and moving debt off of its balance sheet. The law firm's relationship with Fastow began in the 1980's when Fastow worked for Continental Bank in Chicago and intensified during the Class Period at Enron; in light of this close relationship, Jordon Mintz, Vice President and General Counsel of Enron Global Finance, referred to the firm as "Fastow's attorneys."

Lead Plaintiff asserts that Enron hand-picked Kirkland & Ellis to provide ostensibly "independent" representation for Chewco, JEDI, LJM1, LJM2, and other SPEs, but in actuality that the firm was selected by Fastow because it was willing to take direction from Fastow and Enron. Along with Arthur Andersen, Vinson & Elkins, and Enron's banks, Kirkland & Ellis under Enron's direction participated in structuring the manipulative devices at the heart of the scheme, including the partnerships and SPEs (LJM1 and 2, Chewco and the Raptors) and their related transactions to present a false picture of Enron's financial condition and results, with the law firm's full knowledge of that purpose. In addition to structuring the entities, Kirkland & Ellis allegedly participated in the monetization of assets, in the preparation of partnership and loan agreements for Chewco, LJM1, and LJM2, and in the offering and sale of partnership interests in LJM2 through private placement memoranda. The firm also allegedly generated false legal opinions about the structure, legality and bona fides of the SPEs and their transactions, representing that these were legitimate business deals. The complaint charges that Kirkland & Ellis issued opinions related to numerous transactions and entities. . . . The firm's opinions were essential for effecting the transactions. Nevertheless, because the transactions were shams to inflate Enron's financial performance while favored insiders siphoned off Enron's assets and because the transactions were conducted on terms inconsistent with disclosures being made to investors by Enron, Vinson & Elkins, the banks, and Arthur Andersen, Kirkland & Ellis' opinions were also false. Kirkland & Ellis knew that the SPEs were contrived, manipulative devices that were not independent of Enron, but, like Kirkland & Ellis, acting under the

control and direction of Fastow, Kopper, Skilling, Lay and other Enron officials. These Enron insiders directed the SPEs without regard for the legal or
economic interests or rights of the SPEs, in whose behalf Kirkland & Ellis was
purportedly served as independent counsel. Kirkland & Ellis received tens of
millions of dollars in fees for its work, and most of that money was paid directly
to it by Enron, even though the law firm was supposed to be representing
entities independent of Enron and with economic interests adverse to those of
Enron.

More specifically, the complaint asserts that when Enron was unable to find
a legitimate buyer for the outside investor's interest in JEDI in 1997 in time
for year-end reporting, Kirkland & Ellis, directed by Fastow and Enron, along
with Vinson & Elkins, Fastow and Kopper, created Chewco (controlled by Enron
and Michael Kopper), Big River Funding and Little River Funding to purchase
that stake in JEDI. Kirkland & Ellis did so even though it was supposed to
be providing independent representation of Chewco and its equity investors.
Kirkland & Ellis knew that Chewco lacked an independent outside investor with
a 3% stake, required for independent third-party status for Chewco, and that
Barclays' loan of $240 million to Chewco (guaranteed by Enron) and loans to
straw parties by means of a $6 million cash deposit with Barclays to provide
the money for the equity investment in Chewco, were an improper effort to
circumvent that requirement for a valid SPE. Kirkland & Ellis and Vinson &
Elkins prepared the documentation for Chewco's financing and falsified the
documents to make it appear that Chewco was independent. They also prepared
a side agreement, dated 12/30/97, reflecting that Enron would provide the
necessary cash to fund Chewco through clandestine reserve accounts for Big
River Funding and Little River Funding. The Kopper/Enron side agreement
drawn up by the two firms indicates that no outside equity was used to fund
Chewco and therefore it was not a viable SPE, but merely a manipulative device
to further the fraud.

Kirkland & Ellis did more to conceal the real situation. If, as originally
intended, Fastow were to have managerial control of Chewco, that interest
would have to be disclosed in Enron's SEC filings and the non-arm's-length
nature of the deal would be revealed. Kirkland & Ellis therefore arranged for
Kopper, Fastow's subordinate, to manage the SPE.

In addition, during December 1997, Kirkland & Ellis restructured the transaction to avoid disclosure of Enron's financial relationship to Chewco at year
end. Kirkland & Ellis converted the general partner of Chewco from a limited liability company to a limited partnership and made Kopper the manager
of the general partner instead of Fastow. Although Kopper expressed concern about the conflict of interest because he was simultaneously an Enron
employee and the owner of both Chewco's general partner and of the equity
of limited partner Big River Funding, Kirkland & Ellis went ahead anyway.
Furthermore, Kirkland & Ellis, with Arthur Andersen, Fastow, Kopper and
Vinson & Elkins, participated in the concealment of Kopper's managerial position with Chewco by "transferring" Kopper's ownership interest in Big River
Funding and Little River Funding to Kopper's domestic partner, Dodson, and
completing the purchase of the 50% interest in JEDI by Chewco. Kirkland
& Ellis knew that Chewco/JEDI was not a valid SPE, should have been consolidated, and was now available for Enron to use in more non-arm's-length
transactions, which the law firm would also help structure from 1998-2001, to

create billions of dollars of sham profits for Enron and conceal the true nature of its indebtedness.

[The court proceeds to detail similar misdeeds by Kirkland in various other Enron transactions.]

b. The Law Firms

(i) Vinson & Elkins

Contrary to Vinson & Elkins' contention, the situation alleged in the consolidated complaint is not one in which Vinson & Elkins merely represented and kept confidential the interests of its client, which has "the final authority to control the contents of the registration statement, other filing, or prospectus" [quoting Vinson & Elkins' motion to dismiss]. Instead, the complaint alleges that the two were in league, with others, participating in a plan, with each participant making material misrepresentations or omissions or employing a device, scheme or artifice to defraud, or engaging in an act, practice or course of business that operated as a fraud, in order to establish and perpetuate a Ponzi scheme that was making them all very rich.

Vinson & Elkins was necessarily privy to its client's confidences and intimately involved in and familiar with the creation and structure of its numerous businesses, and thus, as a law firm highly sophisticated in commercial matters, had to know of the alleged ongoing illicit and fraudulent conduct. Among the complaint's specific allegations of acts in furtherance of the scheme are that the firm's involvement in negotiation and structuring of the illicit partnerships and off-the-books SPEs, whose formation documentation it drafted, as well as that of the subsequent transactions of these entities. It advised making Kopper manager of Chewco so that Enron's involvement in and control of the SPE would not have to be disclosed, drafted "true sales" opinions that Lead Plaintiff asserts were essential to effect many of the allegedly fraudulent transactions. Vinson & Elkins was materially involved in the New Power IPO, and it structured and provided advice on the Mahonia trades, all actions constituting primary violations of §10(b). In other words, it "effected the very" deceptive devices and contrivances that were the heart of the alleged Ponzi scheme. SEC v. U.S. Environmental, 155 F.3d at 112. According to the allegations in the complaint, Vinson & Elkins chose to engage in illegal activity for and with its client in return for lucrative fees. Contrary to the Rules of Professional Conduct, it did not resign and thereby violated its professional principles and ethics. Nevertheless, had Vinson & Elkins remained silent publicly, the attorney/client relationship and the traditional rule of privity for suit against lawyers might protect Vinson & Elkins from liability to nonclients for such alleged actions on its client's (and its own) behalf.

But the complaint goes into great detail to demonstrate that Vinson & Elkins did not remain silent, but chose not once, but frequently, to make statements to the public about Enron's business and financial situation. Moreover in light of its alleged voluntary, essential, material, and deep involvement as a primary violator in the ongoing Ponzi scheme, Vinson & Elkins was not merely a drafter, but essentially a co-author of the documents it created for public consumption, concealing its own and other participants' actions. Vinson & Elkins made the alleged fraudulent misrepresentations to potential investors, credit agencies, and banks, whose support was essential to the Ponzi scheme, and Vinson & Elkins deliberately or with severe recklessness directed those public statements toward them in order to influence those investors to purchase more securities, credit agencies to keep Enron's credit high, and banks to continue providing loans to keep the Ponzi scheme afloat. Therefore Vinson & Elkins had a duty to be accurate and truthful. Lead Plaintiff has alleged numerous inadequate disclosures by Vinson & Elkins that breached that duty.

Vinson & Elkins protests that its purported "whitewash" investigation and report in the wake of Sherron Watkins' August 1999 memorandum were not disclosed to the public until after Enron waived the attorney/client privilege and produced the report for Congressional hearings in 2002, after the Class Period ended, and thus cannot be the basis of a §10(b) misrepresentation claim by the investors. Nevertheless the investigation and report can serve as the basis of a §10(b) and Rule 10b-5(a) or (c) claim alleging use of a device, scheme or artifice to defraud or engagement in an act, practice or course of business that operated as a fraud in the perpetuation of the Ponzi scheme.

Furthermore, the complaint references, summarizes, and quotes from the Powers' investigative committee report the negatively critical findings about Vinson & Elkins' substantial and dubious role in the events of the Class Period, as delineated in the complaint, which support Lead Plaintiff's allegations.

For these reasons the Court finds that Lead Plaintiff has stated claims under §10(b) against Vinson & Elkins.

(ii) Kirkland & Ellis

The Court agrees with Kirkland & Ellis that Lead Plaintiff has only alleged that Kirkland & Ellis represented some of the illicit Enron-controlled, non-public SPEs and partnerships that Enron, but not Kirkland & Ellis, used for transactions (devices or contrivances) to hide its debt and record sham profits, disguising its true financial condition, and performed legal services on their and Enron's behalf. The complaint does not allege that Kirkland & Ellis invested in any partnership or profited from any dealings with Enron other than performing routine legal services for the partnerships. All the assertions against the firm are conclusory and general. While the allegations against Kirkland & Ellis may indicate that it acted with significant conflicts of interests and breached professional ethical standards, unlike its claims against Vinson & Elkins, Lead Plaintiff has not alleged that Kirkland & Ellis' activities would be protected by an attorney-client relationship and the traditional rule that only a client can sue for malpractice because it never made any material misrepresentations or omissions to investors or the public generally that might make it liable to non-clients under §10(b). Any documents that it drafted were for private transactions between Enron and the SPEs and the partnerships and were not included in or drafted for any public disclosure or shareholder solicitation. Any opinion letters that the firm wrote are not alleged to have reached the plaintiffs nor been drafted for the benefit of the plaintiffs. It was not Enron's counsel for either its securities filings or its SEC filings. Thus the Court grants Kirkland & Ellis' motion to dismiss.

CHAPTER
9

Control of the Closely Held Firm

Shareholders in closely held corporations often decide to vary the default rules contained in corporation statutes. Because the number of shareholders is — by definition — small, highly tailored arrangements allocating control are often feasible. The following Sections describe myriad ways in which shareholders can structure control rights in a closely held corporation.

A. SHAREHOLDER AGREEMENTS

One of the most common methods of allocating control in a closely held corporation is to set up a simple contract among the shareholders. The usual thrust of such a contract is to provide protection to minority shareholders. After all, majority shareholders exercise control through the default rules of corporate law, so a contract is unnecessary to protect their interests.

Minority shareholders often seek representation on the board of directors through a so-called "vote pooling" agreement. Simply stated, these agreements obligate shareholders to vote together as a single block. Courts have long enforced such agreements, and modern corporation statutes expressly provide for pooling agreements. *See, e.g.,* Model Business Corporation Act (Model Act) §7.31.

The more controversial shareholder agreements are those that attempt to control the actions of the directors. Unless a minority shareholder has enough clout to obtain a majority of the director seats, representation alone offers little protection. As a result, minority shareholders frequently bargain for rights with respect to specified corporate transactions. In some instances, these are affirmative rights, such as the right to name certain corporate officers, the right to employment, or the right to certain salaries or dividends. In other instances, the protective provisions come in the form of negative covenants — rights to veto certain corporate transactions.

At one time, courts were very skeptical of shareholder agreements in which the parties attempted to make decisions otherwise vested in the board of directors. Perhaps the best known case of this kind is McQuade v. Stoneham, 189 N.E. 234 (N.Y. App. 1934), which involved the owners of the New York Giants, a professional baseball club. Charles Stoneham was the majority owner of the

National Exhibition Company, which owned the Giants. Upon the sale of a minority interest in the company to Francis McQuade, Stoneham, McQuade, and John McGraw — the Hall of Fame manager of the Giants, who was also a minority shareholder of the company — entered into a shareholder agreement pursuant to which they agreed to "use their best endeavors for the purpose of continuing as directors of said Company and as officers thereof" each of the other parties. In addition, the agreement specified each of their salaries. When the board of directors — all of whom, other than McQuade, were allegedly under Stoneham's control — terminated McQuade as treasurer of the company, and when Stoneham and McGraw subsequently failed to vote for McQuade as a director (thus resulting in his ouster from the board), McQuade sued to enforce the shareholder agreement. The court declined to enforce the agreement, however, reasoning:

> [T]he stockholders may not, by agreement among themselves, control the directors in the exercise of the judgment vested in them by virtue of their office to elect officers and fix salaries. Their motives may not be questioned so long as their acts are legal. The bad faith or the improper motives of the parties does not change the rule. Directors may not by agreements entered into as stockholders abrogate their independent judgment.

Over time, this sort of reasoning has fallen out of favor. Courts in many states have approved shareholder agreements on their own, while others have done so after being prompted by a state legislature. In either circumstance, the effect has been to allow for greater contracting freedom among shareholders.

Model Act §7.32 is an example of the legislation that validates shareholders' agreements even when they limit board powers in certain enumerated ways. Although the power of the board may be limited in many ways, the comment to §7.32(a)(8) suggests that an agreement providing that directors have no duty of care or loyalty would be against public policy. Other important provisions in Model Act §7.32 include the following:

- Model Act §7.32(b)(1) requires that agreements be unanimous and provides that they must be included in the charter or bylaws of the corporation or in a separate agreement.
- Model Act §7.32(b)(3) limits the duration of shareholders' agreements to ten years.
- Model Act §7.32(c) requires a legend on the share certificate to notify transferees of the shareholders' agreement.
- Model Act §7.32(d) limits the availability of this section to close corporations.
- Model Act §7.32(f) provides that shareholders will not have personal liability even if the effect of the agreement is to create a partnership.

You will notice that many of the control devices covered by this chapter are contained in shareholder agreements.

The following case construes a shareholders' agreement. As you read the case, try to determine if the requirements for a valid shareholders' agreement, as set out in Model Act §7.32, actually exist. How compelling is the court's rationale? And does the court address the plaintiffs' construction of the agreement in a persuasive fashion? Given the problems this badly drafted agreement created, how might the parties have better expressed what they were trying to accomplish in this agreement?

RONNEN v. AJAX ELECTRIC MOTOR CORP.

648 N.Y.S.2d 422
Court of Appeals of New York
July 9, 1996

LEVINE, Judge.

The opposing parties to this litigation are brother and sister who, with their children, collectively hold a bare majority of the issued and outstanding shares of the capital stock of Ajax Electric Motor Corp., a closely held corporation based in Rochester. Respondent Neil Norry has been the chief executive officer of Ajax. The immediate matter in dispute is the validity of the election of the board of directors of the corporation at its annual shareholders' meeting held March 13, 1995.

Central to that dispute is a March 5, 1982 shareholders' agreement between Norry (and his two sons) and his sister, appellant Deborah Ronnen, on behalf of herself and as custodian for her children. The shareholders' agreement granted Norry certain rights to vote Ronnen's stock and that of her children.

The March 13, 1995 shareholders' meeting began in acrimony between Ronnen and Norry, who initially chaired the meeting. Immediately prior to the meeting, Ronnen served Norry with a temporary restraining order prohibiting him from voting the Ronnen shares regarding proposed amendments to the Ajax bylaws and certificate of incorporation, which were on the agenda for the meeting. When the meeting convened, Ronnen's attorney had the proceedings videotaped, without prior notice to Norry. In response to these actions, Norry announced that the meeting was being adjourned. Over Ronnen's protest, [Norry] voted the Ronnen shares with the Norry shares for a combined majority vote to adjourn and left the meeting. In his absence, Ronnen and the remaining shareholders of Ajax, including appellants Bruce Lipsky and Joseph Livingston, elected a slate of directors.

Norry then brought a proceeding . . . to invalidate the election of directors in his absence and for an order directing a new election. Ronnen, Lipsky and Livingston petitioned . . . to confirm the election. Supreme Court interpreted the shareholders' agreement as giving Norry the right to vote the Ronnen shares in any election of a board of directors. This factor, together with the hostile atmosphere permeating the March 13, 1995, meeting, led Supreme Court to conclude that a new election should be held. The Appellate Division affirmed the order for a new election of directors, with two Justices dissenting on the ground that the shareholders' agreement did not transfer Ronnen's voting rights to Norry for board of directors elections and that the election was in other respects properly conducted. Ronnen, Lipsky and Livingston appeal as of right on the basis of the double dissent.

We now affirm. The parties are not in dispute over the circumstances leading up to the March 5, 1982 agreement between the Norry shareholders and Ronnen. Ajax had been a highly prosperous distributor of electric motors nationwide, founded by Irving Norry (the father of Neil Norry and Deborah Ronnen), Sydney Gilbert and David Lipsky. Irving Norry and his wife had, by 1980, transferred by gift or sale all of their shareholdings in Ajax to their two children and their families. Friction developed between Norry and Ronnen regarding, among other things: Norry's acquisition for his children of his mother's Ajax shares, upsetting the equality of the Norry siblings' interests in the corporation; Ronnen's displeasure over an irrevocable option her brother had been granted in 1967 to acquire her Ajax shares under what she considered an inadequate price formula; the level Norry had fixed for his compensation and other alleged financial self-dealing in Ajax and in Norry Electric Co., a separate family business; and Ronnen's objection to not being kept informed of financial decisions Norry made in connection with the management of both corporations. Ronnen wished to ensure that her interest in Ajax could be passed on to her children free of interference by Norry. Norry expressed willingness to accommodate Ronnen, provided he was guaranteed continued managerial control of Ajax and was given the opportunity to acquire the Ronnen shares in Ajax before they could be sold to an outsider. He also wished to buy out his sister's interest in Norry Electric Co. These various objectives of the parties were implemented in the shareholders' agreement and other contemporaneous transactions.

The shareholders' agreement recited as one of its purposes "to provide for the vote of [the Norry and Ronnen families'] Shares in order to provide for continuity in the control and management of Ajax." The primary voting control provision was set forth in paragraph 8 of the agreement. Subparagraph 8(a) provided that the Ronnen shareholders "agree that Neil Norry shall exercise voting rights over the Shares owned by them . . . with respect to any and all matters *relating to Ajax's day-to-day operations and corporate management*" (emphasis supplied). Norry was also given the right to vote the Ronnen shares regarding any sale of substantially all of Ajax's assets or stock to an outside party, provided that the transaction treated the Norry and Ronnen interests equivalently. The agreement, however, reserved to Ronnen the right to vote the Ronnen shares "[i]n connection with other major corporate policy decisions," and listed as examples of such major decisions, "other types of corporate reorganizations" and other similar actions. Subparagraph 8(b) gave Norry an irrevocable proxy to vote the Ronnen shares as provided in the preceding subparagraph.

The unambiguous words of paragraph 8 and the recital purpose clause of the agreement present an issue of pure contract interpretation for the court, and admit of no construction other than the conferral to Norry of the right to vote the Ronnen shares in any election of a board of directors of Ajax. The undisputed background facts support this interpretation as well. The parties have not cited to any provision of the Ajax certificate of incorporation transferring corporate management decisions from the board of directors to the shareholders. Therefore, management of the business of Ajax was, by statute, exclusively "under the direction of its board of directors" (Business Corporation Law §701).

We have held that "the law in force at the time [an] agreement is entered into becomes as much a part of the agreement as though it were expressed or referred to therein, for it is presumed that the parties had such law in contemplation when the contract was made and the contract will be construed in the light of such law" (Dolman v. United States Trust Co., 2 N.Y.2d 110, 116, 157 N.Y.S.2d 537, 138 N.E.2d 784). Thus, without the right to vote the Ronnen shares to elect the directors of the corporation, the transfer of voting rights regarding "corporate management" under subparagraph 8(a) of the agreement would be essentially meaningless since management control was vested in the directors and not the shareholders. We have long and consistently ruled against any construction which would render a contractual provision meaningless or without force or effect.

The reservation to Ronnen of the right to vote the Ronnen shares "[i]n connection with . . . major corporate policy decisions" is consistent with the parties' intent to confer on Norry the right to vote the Ronnen shares in the election of board of directors, since major corporate decisions, such as corporate mergers, connote extraordinary change while director elections are the ordinary subject matter of a shareholder meeting. It, therefore, follows that by agreeing to transfer to Norry the right to vote the Ronnen shares "with respect to any and all matters relating to Ajax's . . . corporate management," the parties must have intended, on the facts of this case, to give Norry the right to vote the shares to elect a board of directors.

By the same token, in the absence of having an irrevocable proxy to vote their cumulative majority interests for the election of directors, the shareholders' agreement's recited purpose to ensure "continuity in the control and management of Ajax" could not be achieved. We should not adopt a construction of subparagraph 8(a) which would frustrate one of the explicit central purposes of the agreement.

Ronnen, however, points to the language of paragraphs 10, 12 and 14 of the shareholders' agreement as negating any inference that Norry was given the right to vote the Ronnen shares in elections of the board of directors. Paragraph 10 of the agreement recites that "[t]he parties agree that . . . they shall vote the Shares" to ensure a seat on the board of directors for Deborah Ronnen. Paragraph 12 provides that "[t]he parties agree that . . . they shall vote the Shares in the election of Directors" to ensure Ronnen's access to all reports concerning the management of Ajax, and paragraph 14 similarly requires the "parties" to "vote the Shares in the election of Directors" so as to generally cap Norry's total executive compensation at $125,000 a year.

Ronnen, thus, argues that the literal language of paragraphs 10, 12 and 14 militates against an interpretation of the agreement ceding the right of Ronnen, "a party" to the agreement, to vote the Ronnen shares for the election of directors, and that such an interpretation would deprive those provisions of any force or effect. Ronnen further argues that the use of the plural, "parties," in those paragraphs was ignored by the courts below, who rewrote the clauses in question as an agreement that, singularly, "Neil Norry shall vote the Shares" in accordance with the substantive requirements of paragraphs 10, 12 and 14. We disagree.

As we have already discussed, subparagraph 8(a) of the shareholders' agreement unequivocally guarantees the right of Norry to vote a majority block of shares on all matters "relating to . . . corporate management" of Ajax, which in this case necessarily entails majority voting rights to elect a board of directors favorable to the continuation of his corporate policies. Construing paragraphs 10, 12 and 14 literally, to permit Ronnen to vote the Ronnen shares in board of directors elections to form a majority with shareholders possibly unfavorable to Norry's management role would, thus, take away from Norry the bargained for management rights and privileges promised in paragraph 8. We have previously applied the principle that a contract which confers certain rights or benefits in one clause will not be construed in other provisions completely to undermine those rights or benefits.

Contrary to Ronnen's contention, a transfer of Ronnen's voting rights to Norry on election of a board of directors will not render paragraphs 10, 12 and 14 meaningless. These three provisions were manifestly intended to suit the purposes of Ronnen, guaranteeing her a seat on the board of directors and requiring the three Norry shareholders (Neil Norry and his sons) to vote the majority block of shares for directors who will be favorable to her position on access to corporate information and on imposing a ceiling on Norry's compensation. Thus, the pluralized language in paragraphs 10, 12 and 14 that "[t]he parties agree that . . . they shall vote the Shares" in board of directors elections can readily be construed to refer to the three Ronnens who were parties to the agreement, all of whose shares would be necessary to form a majority voting block with the Ronnen shares. That interpretation should be favored, as it would reconcile paragraphs 10, 12 and 14 with paragraph 8 of the agreement and effectuate all of the parties' objectives in entering into the agreement.

For all the foregoing reasons, we hold that the courts below properly construed the shareholder's agreement as giving Neil Norry the right to vote the Ronnen shares in board of directors elections. The position on appeal of appellants Lipsky and Livingston that, as thus construed, the shareholders' agreement is void as against public policy is unpreserved and, hence, has not been considered.

Finally, in view of the irrevocable proxy Ronnen gave Norry to vote the Ronnen shares in any election of directors, together with the other circumstances surrounding the March 13, 1995 shareholders' meeting alluded to by Supreme Court, the ordering of a new board of directors election in this case was within that court's discretionary equity powers under Business Corporation Law §619 to "confirm the election, order a new election, or take such other action *as justice may require*" (emphasis supplied).

Accordingly, the order of the Appellate Division should be affirmed, with costs.

B. TRANSFER RESTRICTIONS

Transfer restrictions are widely used to control selection of business associates, to provide certainty in estate planning, and to ensure that the corporation complies with close corporation statutes, S corporation regulations, or securities act exemptions. They are imposed in the charter or bylaws of the corporation or in a separate agreement among shareholders or between shareholders and the corporation. Delaware General Corporations Law (DGCL) §202(b); Model Act §6.27(a).

Transfer restrictions are valid if they pass a two-part test. First, the restrictions must comply with the formal requirements relating to adoption of the restriction and must be conspicuously noted on the share certificates. DGCL §202(a) and (b); Model Act §6.27(a) and (b). Second, the restrictions must be for a proper purpose. The general test for a proper purpose is "reasonableness." General types of transfer restrictions are laid out in DGCL §202(c) and

Model Act §6.27(d): (1) the shareholder must offer the corporation or other shareholders the option to purchase the shares, either at a price specified by prior agreement or at the price offered by the prospective third-party purchaser (an "option"); (2) the corporation or other shareholders are obligated to purchase the shares (a "buy-sell" agreement); (3) the corporation or other shareholders must approve the transfer of the shares (a "prior approval" or "consent" requirement); (4) the shareholder is simply prohibited from transferring to certain persons or classes of persons. Options and buy-sell agreements are common forms of transfer restrictions and are usually enforced by courts. Prior approvals normally are enforceable as long as approval may not be unreasonably withheld. Flat prohibitions on transfer are viewed very skeptically by courts and usually would be struck down as unreasonable. It is important to note that all transfer restrictions may not affect shares issued before the restriction is adopted unless the holders vote in favor of the restriction. DGCL §202(b); Model Act §6.27(a).

The most common transfer restrictions are buy-sell agreements. Buy-sell agreements solve many problems in close corporations: (1) they provide liquidity for shareholders who wish to withdraw; (2) they determine the price of the shares at a time when none of the parties to the agreement knows which of them will be the sellers and which will be the purchasers (thus providing an incentive to all to provide for a "fair" price); and (3) they allow the principals of the corporation to plan with some certainty.

Prices in a buy-sell agreement take one of four forms: (1) fixed price, which must be updated constantly to reflect the current value of the shares; (2) book value, the most popular measure because of ease of determination, but it is based on historical costs and may not reflect true underlying values; (3) appraisal, which has the potential to be very good, but the parties should decide beforehand on what basis the business should be appraised; and (4) formula, which suffers from being very complicated.

The following Problem provides a useful illustration of transfer restrictions, and why a party might want a buy-sell agreement, but it also illustrates the perils of unforeseen consequences.

PROBLEM 9-1

Henry Harper and Christopher Kosachuk formed LatinAdvisor.com as a Delaware corporation in October 1999. The initial directors were Harper, Kosachuk, and Violy McCausland, Harper's mother. The first item of business for the company was to develop a Web site, and for this task, Harper and Kosachuk contracted with Contrasena, a company controlled by Harper's uncle. LatinAdvisor paid for Contrasena's services with stock. After this transaction, the outstanding shares of LatinAdvisor were as follows:

Henry Harper	48 shares
Christopher Kosachuk	48 shares
Contrasena	4 shares

In February 2000, McCausland talked to Harper about the need for a stockholder agreement containing restrictions on the transfer of Kosachuk's shares.

A member of the board of advisors of McCausland's investment bank had told her that LatinAdvisor would need such an agreement before it could attract venture capital. Harper was receptive to this suggestion, as he had already developed concerns about Kosachuk's work ethic. Harper then asked Wachtell, Lipton, Rosen & Katz, a elite New York law firm, to prepare a stockholders agreement.

Harper presented the Stockholders Agreement to Kosachuk on March 2, 2000, and demanded that Kosachuk sign it immediately. Kosachuk reviewed the agreement for a few minutes and then signed it. The Stockholders Agreement contained the following paragraph:

> 1. The Employees agree that upon termination of employment of either of the Employees with the Company for any reason whatsoever (including without limitation, resignation, termination by the Company with or without cause, death or disability), the other Employee whose employment has not been terminated shall have the right exercisable within 30 days of such termination to elect to purchase, all or a portion of the Callable Shares (as defined below) of the Employee whose employment has been terminated (the "Terminated Employee") at a price of $10 per share. . . . [1]

Two weeks after the agreement was signed, Harper invited Kosachuk to a meeting. Kosachuk thought that the purpose of the meeting was to discuss a possible investment in LatinAdvisor, but he soon learned otherwise. Harper, accompanied by several friends, handed Kosachuk a package of documents, including: (1) a stockholders' consent, signed by Harper and a representative of Contrasena, removing Kosachuk as a director; and (2) a directors' consent, signed by Harper and McCausland, removing Kosachuk as an officer and an employee.

Although Harper then had the right under the Stockholders Agreement to purchase 95 percent of Kosachuk's shares for a total of $456, he offered to pay Kosachuk $50,000 within 15 days of his resignation and an additional $50,000 within four months. When Kosachuk refused to sign the Termination Agreement, Harper deposited $456 in Kosachuk's bank account and notified Kosachuk of his intention to enforce the stockholders agreement.

Assume that within one week of Kosachuk's termination Harper negotiated a venture capital investment on behalf of LatinAdvisor.com pursuant to which the venture capitalists were willing to pay $10 million for a 40 percent interest in the company. Does Kosachuk have any basis for claiming that the Stockholder Agreement is unenforceable by Harper?

---

1. "The *'Callable Shares'* shall mean a number of shares of Common Stock and other securities of the Company equal to the percentage of all shares of Common Stock and other securities of the Company owned by the Terminated Employee on the date of termination of his employment and corresponding to the number of full calendar months of employment of the Terminated Employee with the Company prior to his termination (the *'Employment Term'*) as set forth below." The Stockholder Agreement also includes a table detailing the pro rata percentage of the Terminated Employee's Common Stock which the other Employee may purchase. If the employee was terminated within three months, the percentage allowed was 95 percent. This percentage declined every three months until twenty-four months, at which time the other Employee would have no right to purchase the shares.

C. VOTING TRUSTS

DGCL §218 and Model Act §7.30 are examples of modern statutes that authorize the use of voting trusts. Voting trusts long were frowned upon by courts as instruments of deceit. Historically, they are associated with the robber barons who gained control over large corporations by assembling votes in voting trusts. As a result of this historical skepticism of voting trusts, even modern statutes routinely limit their duration to no longer than ten years and impose various formal requirements to prevent abuse. For example, voting trusts must be in writing and must be filed with the corporation. Litigants have often attempted to characterize agreements among shareholders as de facto voting trusts in an attempt to invalidate them; if an agreement is determined to be a de facto voting trust, the agreement inevitably will have failed to comply with the formal requirements of voting trusts and will, therefore, be invalid.

Voting trusts were created to overcome rules against irrevocable proxies.[1] Unlike proxies, in which the shareholder retains ownership of the shares but simply directs the proxy holder to vote the shares, in a voting trust, legal title to shares is transferred from the shareholders to the voting trustees. Although shareholders retain the financial rights belonging to the shares, the trustees possess exclusive voting power over the shares. The voting trustees typically issue voting trust certificates to the beneficial owners of the shares. These certificates usually can be traded.

The purposes of voting trusts are varied. Generally speaking, voting trusts work to ensure continuity of management. By placing control in the hands of a trustee, shareholders are assured of consistent voting. Voting trusts are often implemented as part of a reorganization plan or to prevent dissension among various factions of stockholders.

Courts have evolved in their treatment of voting trusts. Early courts validated voting trusts only if they accomplished a legitimate purpose. The modern judicial view of voting trusts is that they are enforceable unless contrary to public policy.

PROBLEM 9-2

California Pizza Kitchen (CPK) is a restaurant that "combine[s] fresh, distinctive ingredients on premium pizzas to create innovative tastes that consumers could easily identify with, yet had never previously associated with

---

1. As noted in Chapter 6.B.1, a proxy is the authorization given by a shareholder to another person to vote the shareholder's shares. Proxies are revocable unless they are "coupled with an interest." The law traditionally had a strong presumption against irrevocability and usually would enforce an irrevocable proxy only if the interest were a charge, lien, or some property right in the shares themselves or if the shareholder had given a security interest in the shares to protect the proxy holder under a loan. More recent cases suggest that courts will enforce irrevocable proxies any time the proxy is given for the protection of the proxy holder or to ensure that the shareholder will perform some duty to the proxy holder. Despite liberalization of the common law rules governing irrevocable proxies, courts still struggle to draw the line. Model Act §7.22 defines "coupled with an interest" in great detail in an attempt to eliminate some of the confusion over the scope of irrevocable proxies. Cf. DGCL §212(e).

pizza."[2] Its offerings include BBQ Chicken Pizza, Thai Chicken Pizza, Philly Cheesesteak Pizza, Havana Chicken Pizza and Grilled Garlic Shrimp Pizza. Founded in 1985 by Richard Rosenfield and Larry Flax, the company quickly expanded, and by 1992, it was operating 23 restaurants in seven states.

CPK's rapid growth attracted the attention of PepsiCo Inc., which purchased a controlling interest in CPK in 1992. This led to even greater expansion: the company opened 60 restaurants in five years. In 1997, PepsiCo decided to divest itself of all restaurant businesses, and CPK sold a majority stake to a group led by Bruckmann, Rosser, Sherrill & Co., L.P. (BRS).

Although the investment group led by BRS purchased 67.4 percent of CPK, BRS itself held a minority of the shares. Other investors — including the private equity investment firm of Furman Selz — owned substantial blocks of CPK's shares. Moreover, Rosenfield and Flax, the founders of CPK, owned most of the shares not owned by the BRS investment group. Control over CPK was allocated partially through a Securities Holders Agreement and partially through a Voting Trust Agreement.

The Securities Holders Agreement contained various control provisions, including stock transfer restrictions and registration rights in the event of a public offering of shares by the company. The most important control provision, however, was the following paragraph, which allocated positions on the board of directors:

> Each Investor . . . agrees that it shall take, at any time and from time to time, all action necessary . . . to ensure that the Board of Directors of the Company is composed at all times of at least five persons (with the exact number to be determined by BRS from time to time) as follows: (a) prior to the third anniversary of the Closing Date, Richard L. Rosenfield (who during such time period shall also be a Co-Chairman of the Board of Directors of the Company), so long as he is a stockholder of the Company, Larry S. Flax (who during such time period shall also be a Co-Chairman of the Board of Directors of the Company), so long as he is a stockholder of the Company, and the balance of the members designated by BRS; and (b) on and after the third anniversary of the Closing Date, one individual designated jointly by Richard L. Rosenfield and Larry S. Flax (but only so long as Messrs. Rosenfield and Flax together then own or have voting power over $16\frac{2}{3}\%$ or more of the then outstanding Common Stock of the Company) and the balance of the members designated by BRS.

Under the Voting Trust Agreement, the investors in the BRS group contributed their shares to a Trust, and Harold O. Rosser and Stephen F. Edwards, both affiliated with BRS, were appointed as Trustees. During the ten-year term of the Voting Trust Agreement, the Trust was irrevocable except in accordance with limited termination events, one of which is described below. The Voting Trust Agreement contained the following provision entitled "Voting Discretion":

> [T]he Voting Trustees shall possess and shall be entitled in their discretion, not subject to any review, to exercise in person or by proxy, in respect of any and all shares of Common Stock at any time deposited under this Agreement, all rights and powers of every name and nature, including the right to vote thereon or to

2. California Pizza Kitchen, Prospectus dated August 2, 2000.

consent to any and every act of the Company, in the same manner and to the same extent as if the Voting Trustees were the absolute owners of such stock in their own right.

The Voting Trust Agreement also contained the following termination provision:

> [T]his Agreement shall terminate in the event of a sale by the Company, pursuant to an effective registration statement . . . under the Securities Act of 1933, as amended, of any stock for gross offering proceeds of at least $20 million.

Why would BRS want a voting trust in addition to the Securities Holders Agreement, which gives them control over the board of directors? If the other investors wanted to monitor the voting trustees more closely, how would they draft the "Voting Discretion" section? Why would the parties who created the Trust provide for termination in the event of an initial public offering?

D. CLASSIFIED SHARES

Corporations statutes allow corporations to create more than one class of shares, with each class having unique rights. DGCL §151; Model Act §6.01. The primary purpose of classifying shares is to allocate control among the various classes of shareholders. The ways in which control may be allocated by assigning different rights to different classes of shares are infinite; they include giving a class a veto power over all decisions, giving a class no voting power (only financial rights), allowing a class to vote only on certain matters, or providing the right to board representation to certain classes.

Multiple classes of stock invite conflict. The following case provides a stark reminder of the need to define with a great deal of precision the rights of the various class. *Benchmark* involves a venture capital investment and is a rare example of a venture capitalist who is on the short end of an investment contract. For a more detailed examination of venture capital contracts, see the case study of Red Hat, Inc. that concludes this chapter.

BENCHMARK CAPITAL PARTNERS IV, L.P. v. VAGUE*
2002 WL 1732423 (unpublished)
Court of Chancery of Delaware
July 15, 2002

NOBLE, Vice Chancellor.

* The Delaware Supreme Court affirmed this Chancery Court opinion, stating: "the Court having considered this matter after oral argument and on the briefs filed by the parties has determined that the final judgment of the Court of Chancery should be affirmed on the basis of and for the reasons assigned by the Court of Chancery in its opinion dated July 15, 2002." Benchmark Capital Partners IV, L.P. v. Juniper Financial Corp., 2003 WL 1904669 (Apr. 16, 2003).

I. INTRODUCTION

This is another one of those cases in which sophisticated investors have negotiated protective provisions in a corporate charter to define the balance of power or certain economic rights as between the holders of junior preferred stock and senior preferred stock. These provisions tend to come into play when additional financing becomes necessary. One side cannot or will not put up more money; the other side is willing to put up more money, but will not do so without obtaining additional control or other diminution of the rights of the other side. In short, these cases focus on the tension between minority rights established through the corporate charter and the corporation's need for additional capital.

In this case, Plaintiff Benchmark Capital Partners IV, L.P. ("Benchmark") invested in the first two series of the Defendant Juniper Financial Corp.'s ("Juniper") preferred stock. When additional capital was required, Defendant Canadian Imperial Bank of Commerce ("CIBC") was an able and somewhat willing investor. As a result of that investment, Benchmark's holdings were relegated to the status of junior preferred stock and CIBC acquired a controlling interest in Juniper by virtue of ownership of senior preferred stock. The lot of a holder of junior preferred stock is not always a happy one. Juniper's Fifth Amendment and Restated Certificate of Incorporation (the "Certificate") contains several provisions to protect the holders of junior preferred stock from abuse by the holder of senior preferred stock. Two of those provisions are of particular importance here. The Certificate grants the junior preferred stockholders a series vote on corporate actions that would "[m]aterially adversely change the rights, preferences and privileges of the [series of junior preferred stock]." In addition, the junior preferred stockholders are entitled to a class vote before Juniper may "[a]uthorize or issue, or obligate itself to issue, any other equity security . . . senior to or on a parity with the [junior preferred stock]."

The Certificate provides that those provisions protecting the rights of the junior preferred stockholders may be waived by CIBC.[4] CIBC may not, however, exercise this power "if such amendment, waiver or modification would . . . diminish or alter the liquidation preference or other financial or economic rights" of the junior preferred stockholders or would shelter breaches of fiduciary duties.

Juniper now must seek more capital in order to satisfy regulators and business requirements, and CIBC, and apparently only CIBC, is willing to provide the necessary funds. Juniper initially considered amending its charter to allow for the issuance of another series of senior preferred stock. When it recognized that the protective provisions of the Certificate could be invoked to thwart that strategy, it elected to structure a more complicated transaction that now consists principally of a merger and a sale of Series D Preferred Stock to CIBC. The merger is scheduled to occur on July 16, 2002 with a subsidiary merging with and into Juniper that will leave Juniper as the surviving corporation, but with a restated certificate of incorporation that will authorize the issuance of a new

---

4. The protective rights at issue here may be waived by a majority vote of a class consisting of the holders of the Series A, Series B and Series C Preferred shares on an as-converted to common stock basis. Because of CIBC's holdings of Series C Preferred Stock, it is able to cast a majority of the votes of this class on its own. Thus, the waiver is referred to as the "Series C Trump." Benchmark has invested in the two series of junior preferred stock, the Series A Preferred and Series B Preferred.

series of senior preferred stock and new junior preferred stock with a reduced liquidation preference and will cause a number of other adverse consequences or limitations to be suffered by the holders of the junior preferred. As part of this overall financing transaction, Juniper, after the merger, intends to issue a new series of preferred, the Series D Preferred Stock, to CIBC in exchange for a $50 million capital contribution. As the result of this sequence of events, the equity holdings of the junior preferred stockholders will be reduced from approximately 29% to 7%. Juniper will not obtain approval for these actions from the holders of the junior preferred stock. It contends that the protective provisions do not give the junior preferred stockholders a vote on these plans and, furthermore, in any event, that CIBC has the right to waive the protective provisions through the Series C Trump.[6]

Benchmark, on the other hand, asserts that the protective provisions preclude Juniper's and CIBC's heavy-handed conduct and brings this action to prevent the violation of the junior preferred stockholder's fundamental right to vote on these corporate actions as provided in the Certificate and to obtain interim protection from the planned evisceration of its equity interest in Juniper. Because of the imminence of the merger and the issuance of the new senior preferred stock, Benchmark has moved for a preliminary injunction to stop the proposed transaction. This is the Court's decision on that motion.

II. The Parties

Benchmark, a Delaware limited partnership based in Menlo Park, California, is a venture capital firm specializing in preferred stock investments. It manages more than $2 billion and has made approximately 50 preferred stock investments in the preceding 5 years.

Juniper is a Delaware corporation with its principal place of business in Wilmington, Delaware, where it has more than 300 employees. It is a financial services enterprise with the issuance of credit cards as its core business. Juniper Bank is Juniper's wholly-owned state-chartered banking subsidiary.

CIBC is a Canadian bank based in Toronto and controls Juniper through a subsidiary as the result of a $145 million investment in 2001.

The individual defendants are directors of Juniper. Defendants Richard Vague and James Stewart are founders and officers of Juniper. Defendant John Tolleson is a member of the special committee appointed by the board of Juniper to review the Series D Preferred financing.

III. Factual Background

A. Benchmark and CIBC Invest in Juniper

Benchmark became the initial investor in Juniper when in June 2000, it invested $20 million and, in exchange, was issued Series A Preferred Shares. Juniper raised an additional $95.5 million in August 2000 by issuing its Series B Preferred Shares. Benchmark contributed $5 million in this effort. It soon became

---

6. Juniper concedes that CIBC does not have the power to waive any junior preferred stockholder's right to vote with respect to a diminished liquidation preference.

necessary for Juniper to obtain even more capital. Efforts to raise additional funds from existing investors and efforts to find new potential investors were unavailing until June 2001 when CIBC and Juniper agreed that CIBC would invest $27 million in Juniper through a mandatory convertible note while CIBC evaluated Juniper to assess whether it was interested in acquiring the company. CIBC also agreed to provide additional capital through a Series C financing in the event that it chose not to acquire Juniper and if Juniper's efforts to find other sources for the needed funding were unsuccessful.

In July 2001, CIBC advised Juniper that it would not seek to acquire Juniper. After reviewing its options for other financing, Juniper called upon CIBC to invest the additional capital. The terms of the Series C financing were negotiated during the latter half of the summer of 2001. A representative of Benchmark, J. William Gurley, and its attorney were active participants in these negotiations. Through the Series C Transaction, which closed on September 18, 2001, CIBC invested $145 million (including the $27 million already delivered to Juniper). With its resulting Series C Preferred holdings, CIBC obtained a majority of the voting power in Juniper on an as-converted basis and a majority of the voting power of Juniper's preferred stock. CIBC also acquired the right to select six of the eleven members of Juniper's board. As required by Juniper's then existing certificate of incorporation, the approval of the holders of Series A Preferred and Series B Preferred Stock, including Benchmark, was obtained in order to close the Series C Transaction.[8]

B. THE CERTIFICATE'S PROTECTIVE PROVISIONS

In the course of obtaining that consent, CIBC had extensive negotiations regarding the provisions of Juniper's charter designed to protect the rights and interests of the holders of Series A Preferred and Series B Preferred Stock. For example, CIBC had sought the power to waive, modify or amend certain protective provisions held by the Series A Preferred and Series B Preferred stockholders. As the result of those discussions, the Certificate was adopted. CIBC obtained the right to waive certain protective voting provisions, but the right was not unlimited. A review of the Certificate's protective provisions directly involved in the pending dispute follows.

Juniper's Certificate protects the holders of Series A Preferred and Series B Preferred from risks associated with the issuance of any additional equity security that would be senior to those shares by requiring their prior approval through a separate class vote as prescribed in Section C.6.a(i):

> So long as any shares of Series A Preferred Stock or Series B Preferred Stock remain outstanding, the Corporation shall not, without the vote or written consent by the holders of at least a majority of the then outstanding shares of the Series A Preferred Stock and Series B Preferred Stock, voting together as a single class; *provided, however,* that the foregoing may be amended, waived or modified pursuant to Section C.4.c: (i) Authorize or issue, or obligate itself to issue, any

---

8. The facts giving rise to this dispute are generally uncontested. One exception is the assertion of Mr. Gurley, who, as noted, was actively involved on Benchmark's behalf in negotiating the Series C Transaction, that Juniper and CIBC promised that the Series C financing would provide Juniper with sufficient funding to implement its business plan and that no additional capital would be needed in order to achieve profitability. . . . Others, however, dispute that recollection.

other equity security (including any security convertible into or exercisable for any equity security) senior to or on a parity with the Series A Preferred Stock or Series B Preferred Stock as to dividend rights or redemption rights, voting rights or liquidation preferences (other than the Series C Preferred Stock and Series C Prime Preferred Stock sold pursuant to, or issued upon the conversion of the shares sold pursuant to, the Series C Preferred Stock Purchase Agreement . . .)

Under Section C.6.a(ii), Juniper also must provide the holders of the junior preferred stock with a class vote before it may proceed to dispose of all or substantially all of its assets or to "consolidate or merge into any other Corporation (other than a wholly-owned subsidiary Corporation)." Furthermore, this right to a class vote also applies to efforts to increase the number of Juniper's directors.

Because CIBC was investing a substantial sum in Juniper, it insisted upon greater control than it would have obtained if these voting provisions (and other comparable provisions) could be exercised without limitation by the holders of Series A Preferred and Series B Preferred shares as a class. Thus, it sought and obtained a concession from the Series A Preferred and Series B Preferred holders that it could amend, waive, or modify, *inter alia,* the protective provisions of Section C.6.a. The right of CIBC to waive the voting rights of the Series A Preferred and Series B Preferred holders was limited by excluding from the scope of the waiver authority any action that "would (a) diminish or alter the liquidation preference or other financial or economic rights, modify the registration rights, or increase the obligations, indemnities or liabilities, of the holders of Series A Preferred Stock, Series A Prime Preferred Stock or Series B Preferred Stock or (b) authorize, approve or waive any action so as to violate any fiduciary duties owed by such holders under Delaware law."

Another protection afforded the holders of both the Series A Preferred and Series B Preferred Stock was set forth in Sections C.6.c(ii) & C.6.d(ii) of the Certificate. Those provisions require a vote of the holders of each series, provided that the requirement for a series vote was not amended or waived by CIBC in accordance with Section C.4.c, if that corporate action would "[m]aterially adversely change the rights, preferences and privileges of the Series A Preferred [and Series B] Preferred Stock."

C. ADDITIONAL FINANCING BECOMES NECESSARY

By early 2002, Juniper was advising its investors that even more capital would be necessary to sustain the venture. Because Juniper is in the banking business, the consequences of a capital shortage are not merely those of the typical business. Capital shortfall for a banking entity may carry the potential for significant and adverse regulatory action. Regulated not only by the Federal Reserve Board and the Federal Deposit Insurance Corporation but also by the Delaware Banking Commissioner, Juniper is required to maintain a "well-capitalized" status. Failure to maintain that standard (or to effect a prompt cure) may result in, among other things, regulatory action, conversion of the preferred stock into a "senior common stock" which could then be subjected to the imposition of additional security through the regulatory authorities, and the loss of the right to issue Visa cards and to have its customers serviced through the Visa card processing system.

Juniper, with the assistance of an investment banking firm, sought additional investors. The holders of the Series A Preferred and Series B Preferred Stock, including Benchmark, were also solicited. Those efforts failed, thus leaving CIBC as the only identified and viable participant available for the next round of financing, now known as the Series D Transaction.

D. THE SERIES D PREFERRED TRANSACTION

Thus, Juniper turned to consideration of CIBC's proposal, first submitted through a term sheet on March 15, 2002, to finance $50 million through the issuance of Series D Preferred Stock that would grant CIBC an additional 23% of Juniper on a fully-diluted basis and reduce the equity interests of the Series A Preferred and Series B Preferred holders from approximately 29% to 7%.

The board, in early April 2002, appointed a special committee to consider the CIBC proposal.[14] As the result of the negotiations among Juniper, the special committee, and CIBC, the special committee was able to recommend the Series D Transaction with CIBC. The terms of the Series D Transaction are set forth in the "Juniper Financial Corp. Series D Preferred Stock Purchase Agreement" and the "Agreement and Plan of Merger and Reorganization by and Between Juniper Financial Corp. and Juniper Merger Corp."

In general terms, the Series D Transaction consists of the following three steps:

1. Juniper will carry out a 100-1 reverse stock split of its common stock.
2. Juniper Merger Corp., a subsidiary of Juniper established for these purposes, will be merged with and into Juniper which will be the surviving corporation. The certificate of incorporation will be revised as part of the merger.
3. Series D Preferred Stock will be issued to CIBC (and, at least in theory, those other holders of Series A, B and C Preferred who may exercise preemptive rights) for $50 million.

Each share of existing Series A Preferred and each share of existing Series B Preferred will be converted into one share of new Series A Preferred or Series B Preferred, respectively, and the holders of the existing junior preferred will also receive, for each share, a warrant to purchase a small fraction of a share of common stock in Juniper and a smaller fraction of a share of common stock in Juniper.[19] A small amount of cash will also be paid. Juniper will receive no capital infusion as a direct result of the merger. Although the existing Series A Preferred and Series B Preferred shares will cease to exist and the differences between the new and distinct Series A Preferred and Series B Preferred

---

14. The special committee consisted of Mr. Tolleson, who Benchmark challenges as a friend and colleague of Mr. Vague, and two directors who were appointed to the board by the Series A Preferred and the Series B Preferred stockholders in accordance with the Prior Investors' Rights Agreement. Benchmark has not challenged the independence of these two directors. Benchmark, however, does challenge the authority and the performance of the special committee, but Benchmark has not advanced those arguments in support of its pending application for a preliminary injunction.

19. Benchmark asserts that both the warrants and the common stock are essentially worthless at this time, a contention which Juniper does not dispute. Juniper seeks to justify the warrants and the common stock as providing the Series A Preferred and Series B Preferred holders with an opportunity to participate in the future success of Juniper.

shares will be significant,[20] the resulting modification of Juniper's certificate of incorporation will not alter the class and series votes required by Section C.6. The changes to Juniper's charter as the result of the merger include, *inter alia,* authorization of the issuance of Series D Preferred Shares, which will be senior to the newly created Series A Preferred and Series B Preferred Stock with respect to, for example, liquidation preferences, dividends, and as applicable, redemption rights. Also the Series D Stock will be convertible into common stock at a higher ratio than the existing or newly created Series A Preferred and Series B Preferred Stock, thereby providing for a currently greater voting power. In general terms, the equity of the existing Series A Preferred and Series B Preferred holders will be reduced from approximately 29% before the merger to approximately 7% after the Series D financing, and CIBC will hold more than 90% of Juniper's voting power.

Juniper intends to proceed with the merger on July 16, 2002 and to promptly thereafter consummate the Series D financing. It projects that, without the $50 million infusion from CIBC, it will not be able to satisfy the "well-capitalized" standard as of July 31, 2002. That will trigger, or so Juniper posits, the regulatory problems previously identified and business problems, such as the risk of losing key personnel and important business relationships. Indeed, Juniper predicts that liquidation would ensue and, in that event (and Benchmark does not seriously contest this), that the holders of Series A Preferred and Series B Preferred Stock would receive nothing (or essentially nothing) from such liquidation.

IV. CONTENTIONS OF THE PARTIES

Benchmark begins its effort to earn a preliminary injunction by arguing that the junior preferred stockholders are entitled to a vote on the merger on a series basis under Sections C.6.c(ii) & C.6.d(ii) because the merger adversely affects, *inter alia,* their liquidation preference and dividend rights and on a class basis under Section C.6.a(i) because the merger, through changes to Juniper's capital structure as set forth in its revised certificate of incorporation, will authorize the issuance of a senior preferred security. Benchmark also invokes its right to a class vote to challenge the Series D Purchase Agreement under Section C.6.a(i) because that agreement obligates Juniper to issue a senior preferred security. Similarly, Benchmark challenges the issuance of the new Series D Preferred Stock after the merger because it will be issued without a class vote by the holders of either the old or the new Series A Preferred Stock and the new Series B Preferred Stock.

---

20. For example, the holders of the newly created Series A Preferred and Series B Preferred Stock will have an aggregate liquidation preference of $15 million as compared to the liquidation preference of the existing Series A Preferred and Series B Preferred holders of approximately $115 million. Moreover, "[t]he dividend payable . . . to the holders of the New Series A Stock will be reduced from $0.1068 per share to $0.020766 per share and the dividend payable . . . to the holders of the New Series B Preferred Stock will be reduced from $0.23 per share to $0.030268 per share." The redemption rights and other preferences of the existing Series A Preferred and Series B Preferred holders will similarly be compromised by the conversion to the New Series A Preferred and New Series B Preferred Stock as a result of the merger. Finally, the New Series A Preferred and New Series B Preferred Stock will be subordinate to another series of preferred stock, the Series D Preferred Stock.

In response, Juniper and CIBC argue that the junior preferred stockholders are not entitled to a class or series vote on any aspect of the Series D financing, particularly the merger. The adverse effects of the transaction arise from the merger and not from any separate amendment of the certificate of incorporation, which would have required the exercise of the junior preferred stockholders' voting rights.[24] Juniper and CIBC emphasize that none of the junior preferred stock protective provisions expressly applies to mergers. Finally, Juniper and CIBC assert that the Series C Trump allows for the waiver of all of the voting rights at issue (except for the diminishment of the liquidation preference accomplished by the merger). Benchmark, as one might expect, maintains that the exercise of the Series C Trump is precluded because the "economic or financial rights" of the holders of the junior preferred will be adversely affected and, therefore, the limitation on CIBC's right to exercise the Series C Trump is controlling. . . .

V. ANALYSIS . . .

1. General Principles of Construction

Certificates of incorporation define contractual relationships not only among the corporation and its stockholders but also among the stockholders. Thus, the Certificate defines, as a matter of contract, both the relationship between Benchmark and Juniper and the relative relationship between Benchmark, as a holder of junior preferred stock, and CIBC, as the holder of senior preferred stock. For these reasons, courts look to general principles of contract construction in construing certificates of incorporation. . . .

These principles also apply in construing the relative rights of holders of different series of preferred stock.

2. Challenges to the Merger . . .

a. Merger as Changing the Rights, Preferences and Privileges

Benchmark looks at the Series D Preferred financing and the merger that is integral to that transaction and concludes that the authorization of the Series D Preferred Stock and the other revisions to the Juniper certificate of incorporation accomplished as part of the merger will materially adversely affect the rights, preferences, and privileges of the junior preferred shares. Among the adverse affects to be suffered by Benchmark are a significant reduction in its right to a liquidation preference, the authorization of a new series of senior preferred stock that will further subordinate its interests in Juniper, and a reduction

---

24. Juniper focuses on the separate statutory regimes for amendments of certificates of incorporation and for mergers. A corporation may amend its certificate of incorporation to reclassify its authorized stock, 8 Del. C. §242(a)(3), or to create a new class of stock with rights and preferences superior to other classes of stock, 8 Del. C. §242(a)(5). By 8 Del. C. §242(b)(2), "[t]he holders of the outstanding shares of a class shall be entitled to vote as a class upon a proposed amendment, whether or not entitled to vote thereon by the certificate of incorporation, if the amendment would increase or decrease the aggregate number of authorized shares of such class, increase or decrease the par value of the shares of such class, or alter or change the powers, preferences, or special rights of the shares of such class so as to affect them adversely." Mergers, by contrast, are accomplished in accordance with 8 Del. C. §251. A merger agreement, in accordance with 8 Del. C. §251(b)(3), and a certificate of merger, in accordance with 8 Del. C. §253(c)(4), shall state: "[I]n the case of a merger, such amendments or changes in the certificate of incorporation of the surviving corporation as are desired to be effected by the merger. . . . "

in other rights such as dividend priority. These adverse consequences will all be the product of the merger. Benchmark's existing Series A Preferred and Series B Preferred shares will cease to exist as of the merger and will be replaced with new Series A Preferred Stock, new Series B Preferred Stock, warrants, common stock, and a small amount of cash. One of the terms governing the new junior preferred stock will specify that those new junior preferred shares are not merely subordinate to Series C Preferred Stock, but they also will be subordinate to the new Series D Preferred Stock. Thus, the harm to Benchmark is directly attributable to the differences between the new junior preferred stock, authorized through the merger, and the old junior preferred stock as evidenced by the planned post-merger capital structure of Juniper.

Benchmark's challenge is confronted by a long line of Delaware cases which, in general terms, hold that protective provisions drafted to provide a class of preferred stock with a class vote before those shares' rights, preferences and privileges may be altered or modified do not fulfill their apparent purpose of assuring a class vote if adverse consequences flow from a merger and the protective provisions do not expressly afford protection against a merger. This result traces back to the language of 8 Del. C. §242(b)(2), which deals with the rights of various classes of stock to vote on amendments to the certificate of incorporation that would "alter or change the powers, preferences, or special rights of the shares of such class so as to affect them adversely." That language is substantially the same as the language ("rights, preferences and privileges") of Sections C.6.c(ii) & C.6.d(ii). Where the drafters have tracked the statutory language relating to charter amendments in 8 Del. C. §242(b), courts have been reluctant to expand those restrictions to encompass the separate process of merger as set forth in 8 Del. C. §251, unless the drafters have made clear the intention to grant a class vote in the context of a merger. . . .

The range of Sections C.6.c(ii) and C.6.d(ii) is not expressly limited to changes in the Certificate. However, given the well established case law construing the provisions of certificates of incorporations and the voting rights of classes of preferred stockholders, I am satisfied that the language chosen by the drafters (*i.e.*, the "rights, preferences, and privileges") must be understood as those rights, preferences and privileges which are subject to change through a certificate of incorporation amendment under the standards of 8 Del. C. §242(b) and not the standards of 8 Del. C. §251. . . .

b. Authorization of Series D Preferred Shares Through the Merger Process

Benchmark's straightforward argument that it is entitled to a class vote on the authorization of the Series D Preferred Stock through the merger can easily be set forth. By Section C.6.a(i) of the Certificate, the holders of the Series A Preferred and Series B Preferred Stock have the right, unless that right is properly waived by CIBC, to a class vote on the authorization of a senior preferred security. The Series D Preferred Stock will be on parity with the Series C Preferred Stock and, thus, will be senior to be the existing junior preferred and the newly created junior preferred that will be created as part of the merger.[39] The

---

39. I avoid, for the moment, consideration of Juniper's argument that the Series D Preferred shares will never be senior to the existing Series A Preferred and Series B Preferred Stock because the junior preferred shares will have been extinguished by the merger when the Series D Preferred Stock are authorized.

protective provisions of the Certificate do not distinguish between authorization through amendment of the Certificate under 8 Del. C. §242(b) and those changes in the Certificate resulting from a recapitalization accompanying a merger pursuant to 8 Del. C. §251. Thus, according to Benchmark, it matters not how the result is achieved. Moreover, Section C.6.a(i) does not track or even resemble the "privileges, preferences and special rights" language of 8 Del. C. §242(b)(2) that was important to the [last issue]. Benchmark thus argues that the clear and unambiguous words of Section C.6.a(i) guarantee (at least in the absence of an effective waiver by CIBC) it and the other holders of Series A Preferred and Series B Preferred shares a class vote before the Series D Preferred Stock may be authorized. While Benchmark has advanced an appealing and rational analysis, I conclude, for the reasons set forth below, that it has failed to demonstrate a reasonable probability of success on the merits of this argument.

In ascertaining whether a class of junior preferred stockholders has the opportunity to vote as a class on a proposed corporate action, the words chosen by the drafters must be read "against the background of Delaware precedent."[40] For example, Sullivan Money Management, Inc. v. FLS Holdings, Inc. involved the question of whether a class vote was required in order to change critical rights of preferred shareholders " 'by amendment to the Certificate of Incorporation of [FLS Holdings, Inc.] or otherwise.' " In interpreting the charter of FLS Holdings, Inc., the Court was urged to treat the phrase "or otherwise" as including mergers. The Court, in rejecting this contention, set forth the following:

> The word "merger" is nowhere found in the provision governing the Series A Preferred Stock. The drafters' failure to express with clarity an intent to confer class voting rights in the event of a merger suggests that they had no intention of doing so, and weighs against adopting the plaintiffs' broad construction of the words "or otherwise."

Here, the authorization of the Series D Preferred Stock results from the merger and the restatement of Juniper's certificate of incorporation as part of that process. [Warner Communications, Inc. v. Chris-Craft Indus., Inc., 583 A.2d 962 (Del. Ch. 1989), *aff'd*, 567 A.2d 419 (Del. 1989),] and the cases following it . . . demonstrate that certain rights of the holders of preferred stock that are secured by the corporate charter are at risk when a merger leads to changes in the corporation's capital structure. To protect against the potential negative effects of a merger, those who draft protective provisions have been instructed to make clear that those protective provisions specifically and directly limit the mischief that can otherwise be accomplished through a merger under 8 Del. C. §251.

In sum, Benchmark complains of the harm which will occur because of alterations to Juniper's capital structure resulting from modifications of the certificate of incorporation emerging from the merger. General language alone granting preferred stockholders a class vote on certain changes to the corporate charter (such as authorization of a senior series of stock) will not be read to require a class vote on a merger and its integral and accompanying modifications to the corporate charter and the corporation's capital structure.

---

40. Elliot Assocs., L.P. v. Avatex Corp., 715 A.2d 843, 852 (Del. 1998).

To reach the result sought by Benchmark, the protective rights " 'must . . . be clearly expressed and will not be presumed.' " Unfortunately for Benchmark, the requirements of a class vote for authorization of a new senior preferred stock through a merger was not "clearly expressed" in the Certificate. . . .

3. Obligation to Issue and Issuance of Series D Preferred Shares

Under Section C.6.a(i), Juniper is also required to obtain class approval, unless effectively waived by CIBC, from its junior preferred holders before it can issue or obligate itself to issue a senior preferred stock. Juniper plans to issue its Series D Preferred Stock after the merger and at a time when the new Series A Preferred shares and the new Series B Preferred shares will be outstanding. The shares will not be issued as the result of the merger, but instead will be issued pursuant to the Purchase Agreement between CIBC and Juniper. Because the merger is not implicated by the issuance of the shares, there is no "background" precedent against which this act must be evaluated in the same sense as the case law addressing the consequences of mergers. These facts bring Juniper's proposed issuance of its Series D Preferred Stock squarely within the scope of the restrictions imposed by Section C.6.a(i) of the post-merger certificate. Specifically, to paraphrase that provision, so long as any shares of the new Series A Preferred or Series B Preferred are outstanding, Juniper may not, without the class vote or class consent of the new Series A Preferred and Series B Preferred stockholders, issue any senior equity security. While the restrictions of Section C.6.a(i) may be subject to the Series C Trump and, thus, may yet not prevent the issuance of the Series D Preferred Stock without the approval of the holders of the junior preferred stock, I am satisfied that Section C.6.a(i) applies, from the plain and unambiguous language of its text, to the issuance of Series D Preferred Stock when and as planned by Juniper. . . .

All of the class voting rights conferred upon the junior preferred holders by Section C.6.a(i) are subject to waiver by CIBC through the proper exercise of its Series C Trump. The Series C Trump is broad and (for present purposes) is restricted in application only if the corporate action for which the class vote is waived would "diminish or alter the liquidation preference or other financial or economic rights" of the holders of the junior preferred stock. Issuance of the Series D Preferred Stock will not "diminish or alter" Benchmark's liquidation preference — that was accomplished through the merger. The question thus becomes one of whether the issuance of a previously authorized senior preferred security "diminish[es] or alter[s]" the junior preferred shares' "financial or economic rights."

In some very general sense, when shares of a security with a higher priority are issued, the financial and economic rights of the holders of junior securities are adversely affected. On the other hand, that broad of a reading of "financial or economic rights" would make it difficult to find a valid waiver under the Certificate because all of the rights at issue — liquidation preferences, dividend rights, redemption rights, and even voting rights — in some sense implicate financial or economic rights and interests. In this analysis, the Court, of course, must seek to give meaning to all of the relevant provisions of the Certificate and to interpret the Certificate "as a whole."

One approach to interpreting the critical language can be drawn from the line of cases addressing the vexing issues associated with authorization of a new senior security without a class vote under 8 Del. C. §242 such as whether that creation of a new security with priority can be construed to alter or change the preferences, special rights or powers given to any particular class of stock through the certificate of incorporation and whether that creation of a new senior security also can be deemed to affect such class adversely. Under the analytical approach suggested by these cases, the issuance of shares of a security that has priority will not adversely affect the preferences or special rights of a junior security. The argument, in general, is that the terms and powers of that particular class of junior security have not themselves been changed. That another security with priority has been issued is said to "burden" it, but its particular rights have not been modified, and thus those rights are not perceived as having been "diminished or altered." I tend toward this reading because it does interpret the preferred stock protective provisions against the "background of Delaware precedent" and because "financial and economic rights" appear in a list with other items such as liquidation preferences and registration rights which are more fairly viewed as technical and specific (as opposed to broad and general) rights.

On the other hand, "financial and economic rights" can easily be given the broad interpretation suggested by Benchmark. Moreover, if one places too much emphasis on the [aforementioned] cases for interpretive assistance, the carefully negotiated hierarchy here (right to class vote, but first subject to waiver which in turn is subject to exception) might not be fully acknowledged. Thus, the potential shortcoming of interpreting this language . . . is that the rights of the holders of the junior security in those cases are so limited that it is fair to question whether rights that narrow were intended by the parties here.

Therefore, the meaning to be given to the exception to Series C Trump or waiver is not free of ambiguity. There is no ambiguity in the actual grant of the Series C Trump to CIBC. Both sides agree that the Series C Trump, absent the exception, would provide CIBC with the authority it claims. Accordingly, the effectiveness of any exercise of the Series C Trump in this context depends upon the scope to be given to the exception. Benchmark suffers, in this context, because it must rely on the exception; terms of preferred shareholders' protective provisions "must . . . be clearly expressed and will not be presumed"; and it bears the burden as the moving party on its motion for a preliminary injunction.

A preliminary injunction necessarily involves an initial determination on [a] less than complete record and that limitation precludes a detailed consideration of extrinsic evidence. In light of the foregoing, I conclude that Benchmark has not demonstrated a reasonable probability of success on the merits of its claim that the waiver should not be available to CIBC. . . .

E. CUMULATIVE VOTING

Cumulative voting is a method of counting shareholder votes in director elections in which each shareholder is entitled to cast a number of votes equal to the product of the number of such shareholder's shares times the number of directors to be elected. Unlike "straight" voting, under cumulative voting a shareholder may cast all of his or her votes in favor of a single director rather than allocating them among the candidates. For example, if a corporation has three directors and one of the shareholders owns 500 shares of common stock, under a system of cumulative voting the shareholder is entitled to a total of 1,500 votes, which he or she may allocate among as many or as few director candidates as he or she chooses. Under straight voting, the shareholder could vote a maximum of 500 shares on any one director candidate.

The purpose of cumulative voting is to increase minority participation on the board of directors. Under straight voting, the holders of a majority of the shares would be able to elect all of the directors, but under cumulative voting, minority shareholders may be able to elect one or more directors despite the best efforts of the majority. Other methods of ensuring minority representation on the board of directors are shareholders' agreements or special classes of stock entitled to elect a certain number of directors. Model Act §7.28(b) and DGCL §214 provide that shareholders do not have the right to cumulate their votes for directors unless the articles of incorporation provide otherwise. These are "opt in" provisions. Many states have "opt out" provisions, and six states still have mandatory cumulative voting.

To calculate the number of shares required to elect one director under cumulative voting, the following formula is useful:

$$[\text{Shares Voting}/(\text{Directors to be Elected} + 1)] + 1 = \text{Shares Required}$$

To illustrate the use of this formula, we assume a corporation with 1,800 shares of stock outstanding, all of which will be voted at the annual meeting in which three directors will be elected. The number of shares required to elect one of the three directors is as follows:

$$1,800/4 + 1 = 451$$

In other words, a shareholder would need *at least* 451 shares to ensure that he or she could elect one director. If a shareholder desires to elect more than one director, the following calculations are relevant:

Number of Directors to be elected			Number of shares needed
2 directors:	3,600/4 + 1	=	901
3 directors:	5,400/4 + 1	=	1,351

The shareholder described above has sufficient shares (500) to elect one director, but he does not have enough shares to elect two directors. The holders of the remaining shares (1,300) have enough to elect only two directors. As illustrated by the foregoing example, cumulative voting can be confusing to the uninitiated.

Staggering the board may defeat the effect of cumulative voting. For example, in the corporation in the example, the three directors might have staggered

1. Model Act §8.06 refers to the process of dividing the board into different classes to be elected in alternating years as "staggering" the board. DGCL §141(d) allows "classes" of directors. What most people called a "staggered board," therefore, becomes a "classified board" in Delaware.

terms of three years each; in other words, one director is elected each year. Even with cumulative voting, the shareholder who owns 500 shares would not be able to elect any directors without obtaining a majority of the outstanding shares. The formula for cumulative voting confirms that when only one director position is being filled, a majority of the shares voting is required to assure victory: 1800/2 + 1 = 901.

PROBLEM 9-3

Hartmarx was founded on the ashes of the Great Chicago Fire in 1872. Long known as Hart Schaffner & Marx, it was associated for many years with golfer Jack Nicklaus, who was its celebrity spokesperson. More recently, the company has fallen on hard times, and in 2001 it was briefly the target of a takeover proposal. In 2002, one of the company's shareholders proposed that the company adopt cumulative voting for director elections. The following is an excerpt from the company's 2002 Proxy Statement:

SHAREHOLDER PROPOSAL

Cy Peiser, 5415 North Sheridan Road, Chicago, IL 60640, consultant with the Executive Corps of Chicago and representing to be the beneficial owner of 11,221 shares of the Company's common stock, has given notice that he intends to present the following proposal for consideration at the Annual Meeting. The directors disclaim any responsibility for the contents of the proposal or the statement in support, both of which are presented as received from Mr. Peiser.

Resolved: That the stockholders of Hartmarx Corporation hereby request its Board of Directors to take all the necessary steps to amend immediately the Company's Restated Certificate of Incorporation, By-Laws and related governing instruments in order to provide for cumulative voting in the election of directors, so that each stockholder shall have as many votes as are equal to the number of shares owned, multiplied by the number of directors to be elected, and may cast all of such votes for one or more candidates.

The following statement was submitted by Mr. Peiser in support of the resolution:

Many corporations have adopted cumulative voting, and many states have made it mandatory. California law requires that all shares held by state pension and state college funds be voted in favor of cumulative voting proposals. The National Bank Act provides for cumulative voting for bank company boards.

In addition to this recognition of its importance, cumulative voting increases the possibility of electing directors with diverse viewpoints more likely to broaden the perspectives of the Board, particularly those independent of the management. It will help to achieve the objective of the Board representing all the shareholders, which includes providing a voice for minority holdings, while not interfering with corporate governance by the voting majority of the Board. Only cumulative voting gives proportionate weight to votes by such stockholders whose holdings are sufficiently significant to elect some but not all the directors.

It is worth noting that previous proxy statements had stated that two of the directors were elected "pursuant to the provisions of a Stockholder's

Agreement entered into by the Corporation and Traco International, N.V. in conjunction with Traco's December 31, 1992 acquisition of 5,714,286 shares of the Corporation's Common Stock at $5.25 per share" and that such shares controlled by Mr. Bakhsh are an exception to the 15% poison pill limit. With good reason, the Board accordingly provided for these two directors, now comprising 20% of the Board, to match his holdings. This is exactly what cumulative voting accomplishes for any holdings, and to be fair, for example, 10% of the shareholdings also should be permitted to elect one director by cumulative voting.

It is important that you mark your proxy FOR this resolution as it most certainly is beneficial to stockholders.

COMPANY STATEMENT

THE BOARD OF DIRECTORS RECOMMENDS A VOTE AGAINST THIS PROPOSAL.

The Board of Directors has considered this advisory proposal and recommends a vote against this proposal. The Company's current system for election of directors, like that of the overwhelming majority of publicly-traded corporations, allows all stockholders to vote on the basis of their share ownership. To serve on the Board of Directors, each director must have been elected by the holders of a plurality of the Company's outstanding shares of common stock. The Board of Directors believes this method is the fairest and is most likely to produce a board of directors that will effectively represent the interests of all of the Company's stockholders.

In the opinion of the Board of Directors, cumulative voting would allow a relatively small group of stockholders to elect a director who would not have the support of the holders of most of the outstanding shares of common stock. Cumulative voting introduces the possibility of a director being committed to serve the special interests of the small fraction of stockholders responsible for the director's election rather than the best interests of the stockholders as a whole.

Further, each director has a fiduciary duty to represent all of the Company's stockholders and to advance the best interests of the Company. By permitting a relatively small group of stockholders to pool their votes and elect a director, cumulative voting could, in the opinion of the Board of Directors, produce a conflict between a director's duty to represent all the stockholders and a director's allegiance to his or her narrow constituency. The resulting inability of one or more directors to exercise independent judgment can cause a board of directors to become partisan and disrupt the ability of the members of a board to work effectively. The Board of Directors believes that the directors should work toward the common goal of advancing the best interests of the Company and not be divided by competing special interest groups.

Finally, Section 214 of the General Corporation Law of the State of Delaware states that a certificate of incorporation may provide for cumulative voting. Therefore, in order to effect cumulative voting, stockholders of the Company must vote to amend the Company's Restated Certificate of Incorporation. No such proposal has been placed before the stockholders, but if it were, it would require the favorable vote of the holders of shares representing at least a majority of the issued and outstanding common stock.

In summary, the Board of Directors believes the Company's current method of electing directors is the fairest and most efficient way to ensure that each director serves the interests of the Company and all its stockholders rather than the interests of special groups. Accordingly, the Board of Directors recommends a vote AGAINST the proposal.

The shareholder proposal passed with 51 percent of the vote, but Hartmarx did not accede to the shareholders' request to implement cumulative voting. If Hartmarx were a closely held corporation, would the arguments for and against cumulative voting be the same as those offered in the Hartmarx proxy statement?

F. SUPERMAJORITY REQUIREMENTS

An easy way to ensure a minority voice in corporate affairs is to provide for supermajority quorum requirements and voting. This changes the normal corporate model of majority rule. In effect, supermajority requirements give a minority shareholder veto power over corporate decisions without offending corporate norms because corporation statutes allow high quorum and voting requirements. DGCL §216 (if specified in the charter or bylaws); Model Act §§7.27 (if specified in the charter).

Under Delaware law, supermajority requirements can be adopted through a simple majority vote. *See, e.g.,* DGCL §242(b)(4) (requiring a supermajority vote only when an existing supermajority voting provision is to be "altered, amended, or repealed"). By contrast, the Model Act provides that "any amendment to the articles of incorporation that adds . . . a greater quorum or voting requirement must meet the same quorum requirement and be adopted by the same vote" as required by the proposed provision. Model Act §7.27(b).

The rules for amending or repealing supermajority requirements can be equally complex. In Delaware, the rules depend on whether the supermajority requirements appear in the charter or bylaws. When supermajority *voting* requirements appear in the charter, they can be amended or repealed only by the greater vote specified in the charter provision. DGCL §242(b)(4). Surprisingly, there is no such statutory restriction on the amendment or repeal of supermajority voting requirements in the bylaws.[1] As a result, supermajority voting requirements that appear in the bylaws may be amended or repealed by a mere majority unless the bylaws themselves dictate that such an amendment requires a greater vote. Also, Delaware has no provision governing the amendment or repeal of supermajority quorum requirements.

Under the Model Act, the amendment or repeal of supermajority provisions requires a supermajority vote, Model Act §7.27(b).

Supermajority provisions also may be applied to actions of the board of directors. DGCL §141(b) (if specified in the charter or bylaws); Model Act §8.24 (if specified in charter or bylaws). In close corporations, supermajority provisions often appear in shareholders' agreements. Model Act §7.32.

---

1. The statutory provision governing the amendment of charter provisions was inspired by Sellers v. Joseph Bancroft & Sons Company, 2 A.2d 108 (Del. Ch. 1938), which said that an attempt to reduce super-majority voting requirements by the vote of a mere majority was "quite contrary to the evident purpose of the percentage provisions. If it be permissible, the protection to the preferred stockholders who invested their money on the faith of those percentage safeguards, was utterly illusory." *Id.* at 112. Although the Delaware legislature embraced this holding by adopting DGCL §242(b)(4), it never adopted a similar provision for bylaw amendments.

Supermajority provisions may apply to certain transactions — for example, mergers or sales of all or substantially all of the assets of the corporation — or to all transactions. Of course, if supermajority provisions apply to all transactions, the possibility of deadlock increases. A common use of supermajority requirements is to protect against change in other negotiated allocations of control. For example, if the shareholders of a corporation agree to board representation of a minority shareholder and that agreement is embodied in the corporation's charter, that provision in the charter should also provide for change only upon the vote of a supermajority; in effect, changes to the provision should be subject to a minority shareholder's veto.

PROBLEM 9-4

In 1969 Sam J. Frankino founded Agency Rent-a-Car, which later changed its name to National Auto Credit, Inc. (NAC). Frankino successfully guided the company through a public offering of stock in 1983, but he resigned as chairman of the board of directors in 1998 under a cloud caused by alleged financial improprieties. Even after his resignation, he remained in control of 55 percent of NAC's shares.

Following Frankino's departure, the directors who remained amended NAC's bylaws by adding the following provision to Article IX:

> The provisions contained in Sections 1 through 12 of Article III of these Bylaws shall not be amended, altered or repealed except (a) by the affirmative vote of the holders of at least eighty percent (80%) of each class of stock outstanding and entitled to vote at any meeting of the stockholders, provided notice of the proposed amendment, alteration or repeal shall have been given in the notice of such meeting or (b) by the board of directors. . . .

In an attempt to regain control over the board of directors, Frankino signed a written consent deleting the sentence above that required an 80 percent supermajority vote to amend Article III. He then amended Article III to expand the board of directors from six to thirteen members and elected seven new directors.

The directors who opposed Frankino claimed that his actions were invalid because he should not have been allowed to remove a supermajority voting provision with less than a supermajority vote. Frankino counters by pointing to Article II, §8 of NAC's bylaws, which provides that a simple majority vote is effective to resolve any issue unless a different vote is required by "express provision of the statutes or of the Certificate of Incorporation or . . . these Bylaws."

Should Frankino's actions be upheld?

G. PREEMPTIVE RIGHTS

Preemptive rights are the rights of a shareholder to subscribe to the portion of any increase in a corporation's capital stock necessary to maintain the shareholder's relative voting power as against other shareholders. If a shareholder owns 10 percent of a corporation's shares, therefore, a preemptive right would entitle the shareholder to purchase 10 percent of a subsequent issuance of shares. Up through the first part of the 20th century, preemptive rights were treated as an inherent attribute of capital stock. Preemptive rights no longer are considered inherent in capital stock, but they may be granted or denied by the articles of incorporation.

Both the DGCL and the Model Act provide for an "opt in" to preemptive rights, meaning that the default rule is against preemptive rights but that a corporation may provide for preemptive rights by including a provision to that effect in the articles of incorporation. Most state corporation statutes include an "opt out" provision for preemptive rights. The "opt in" provision reflects skepticism about the value of preemptive rights and a recognition that from the corporation's standpoint, preemptive rights simply complicate the issuance of new shares.

Because preemptive rights complicate the issuance of shares, public companies rarely have such provisions. By contrast, preemptive rights are very common in closely held corporations. The following case involves the use of preemptive rights (rights of first refusal) in the venture capital context. As you read this case, consider the incentives produced by the rights and the reasons for allowing a forced waiver of such rights.

KIMBERLIN v. CIENA CORPORATION
1998 WL 603234
United States District Court, Southern District of New York
September 11, 1998

SOTOMAYOR, D.J.

Plaintiff Kevin Kimberlin complains to this Court that he is a victim of newer and larger investor defendants who have improperly denied the initial investor plaintiffs full participation in the growth potential of defendant Ciena Corporation. Plaintiff paints a portrait of the defendants as "the big boys repeatedly trampling the rights of the little guy who was there first." . . .

BACKGROUND

The following facts are those reasonably supported by the evidence presented, read in the light most favorable to the non-moving parties. Plaintiff Kevin Kimberlin is a New York investment banker who owns controlling or sole interests in three of the other four plaintiffs — Spencer Trask Holdings, Inc., a New York-based venture capital firm; INNO Co., a New York-based investment company; and Kevin Kimberlin L.P., a limited partnership set up by Kimberlin to hold Ciena stock. Laura McNamara, the fifth plaintiff, is a managing director of Spencer Trask.

Ciena is a manufacturer of fiber optic technology incorporated in Delaware and based in Maryland. Formerly known as Hydralite, the company's product line centers upon technology developed by its founder and Chief Technical Officer, Dr. David Huber to enable current users of fiber optic technology (e.g., long-distance telephone service providers) to expand their bandwidth — that is, in effect, to create a greater data-handling capacity—without the expense of installing new fiber optic cable.

The relationship between Kimberlin and Ciena began in 1993, when Kimberlin provided Ciena with $190,000 in seed capital pursuant to a stock purchase agreement, plus a $300,000 letter of credit. At the same time, Ciena and Spencer Trask entered into a Private Placement Agreement (the "Placement Agreement") for a future capitalization effort. As Ciena grew, it attracted more investor interest, and in April 1994 Ciena issued its first series of preferred stock (the "Series A" stock issue). Spencer Trask did not, however, underwrite the Series A issue as specified in the Placement Agreement, but rather Sevin Rosen Funds, a larger venture capital firm, handled the Series A offering. Sevin Rosen had been introduced to Ciena in late 1993 and was apparently instrumental in installing defendant Patrick Nettles as director and CEO of Ciena in February 1994.

In compensation for failing to use Spencer Trask for the Series A placement, Ciena agreed to modify the Placement Agreement so that Ciena would offer its Series B preferred stock through Spencer Trask. The modified Placement Agreement contained a liquidated damages clause which stated that if Ciena did not use Spencer Trask to underwrite the Series B offering, Spencer Trask would receive a warrant for 150,000 shares of Series A stock. In addition, Kimberlin purchased (partially for himself, partially for INNO) 421,520 shares of Series A preferred stock.

In December 1995, Ciena issued its second round of private financing, the Series B preferred stock offering. The offering was made, again not through Spencer Trask, but through Charles River Ventures, another venture capital firm. When Kimberlin, through his attorneys, objected that this violated the modified Placement Agreement, Ciena forwarded the stock warrant provided for in the liquidated damages clause. Kimberlin continued to object, and ultimately a settlement was reached on February 10, 1995, which terminated the Placement Agreement and gave Kimberlin a warrant for 300,000 shares of Series B Stock. This warrant was ultimately distributed by Kimberlin as follows: Kevin Kimberlin, L.P.—250,000 shares; Spencer Trask—45,000 shares; and Laura McNamara—5,000 shares. In addition, the Series B offering, which closed on December 22, 1994 without Kimberlin and INNO (both holders of Series A shares), was reopened that same day to allow Kimberlin to purchase 131,733 shares of Series B preferred stock.

During 1995, Ciena was involved in negotiations for a rather large supply contract with Sprint Corporation, a contract of significant value to Ciena. As a result of capital needs created by the contract, Ciena determined that a new round of financing, the Series C preferred stock offering, would be required. It is this Series C offering that forms the crux of the dispute in this case.

The negotiations with Sprint were included in monthly reports from Ciena at least as early as the August 1995 report (which was dated September 8). Further progress reports were included in the monthly reports for subsequent months, with the October report (dated November 9, 1995) indicating that "it appears that a contract [with Sprint] should be signed next month," and the November report (dated December 8, 1995) indicating "Sprint Contract Negotiations near completion." The Company also published a 1996-1998 Business Plan, dated October 16, 1995, which, while not mentioning Sprint by name, indicated repeatedly that revenues for 1996 were projected from Ciena's first and sole customer and also indicated net sales in 1996 of $50 M. Although the monthly reports and the business plan were apparently distributed to the major investors, Kimberlin did not receive this information until he had a phone conversation sometime in early November with Dr. Nettles in which Kimberlin complained of the lack of information. Kimberlin subsequently received the August and October monthly reports as well as the October 16 Business Plan described above.

On October 13, 1995, the Ciena board agreed to pursue a third round of capital financing, the Series C preferred stock issue. By this point, the board of directors included the individual named defendants in this case: Jon W. Bayless, a senior executive of Sevin Rosen Funds; Michael J. Zak, a general partner of Charles River Ventures; and H. Berry Cash, a senior executive of InterWest Partners, another venture capital firm. In early November, Bayless proceeded to call the Series A and B holders to determine their interest in participating in the Series C. Kimberlin received one of these calls, informing him that Ciena was targeting a raise of $8 M from the existing investors, and that Kimberlin's prorata share (based on his percentage of Series A & B stock) would be 68,437 shares. Kimberlin informed Bayless that he would take his full prorata portion of Series C. On November 2, 1995, Bayless had put together a tentative list of prior investors' participation which indicated an expected purchase by the prior investors of $7.25 M-$11.5 M, but which had next to Kimberlin's name nothing but question marks. Kimberlin, in his affidavit, does not state whether his conversation with Bayless took place prior to November 2.

By November 16, 1995, agreement had apparently been reached with Weiss, Peck and Greer, a venture capital firm, to be the lead investors in the Series C round, and a term sheet was circulated to the potential investors. The term sheet showed a total financing of $15-25 M. Although Nettles asserts otherwise, Kimberlin claims he never received this term sheet. In addition, on December 8, 1995, a term sheet and a draft Series C agreement were sent to potential investors; however, the distribution list showed that Kimberlin was not included in the mailing.

Apparently, for planning purposes, Ciena used a target amount of $10 M to be raised from the existing investors, which translated into a prorata share for Kimberlin of 72,533 shares.[2] On December 15, 1995, Kimberlin faxed a letter to Joseph Chinnici, the Chief Financial Officer of Ciena, informing Chinnici that he had heard that the total Series C financing was now going to be $25 M, and that Kimberlin wished to purchase his prorata share (which, including his warrants, he calculated at 6.035%) of the entire Series C offering (not just the portion reserved for the existing investors), which he calculated as 251,526 shares, not the 72,533 already discussed. During a phone conversation with Nettles that same day, Kimberlin claims that Nettles told him that changing the stock allocations at that point would destroy the financing scheme and that if he insisted on taking his full prorata share of the entire Series C, he would in fact get nothing at all. Ultimately, says Kimberlin, he was assured by Nettles

2. $10 M at the target price of $7/share results in 1,428,571 shares. Kimberlin's beneficial ownership (*i.e.*, including INNO, of which Kimberlin owned 100%) of Series A and B shares totaled 553,253 shares out of 10,896,612 shares outstanding, resulting in a percentage ownership of 5.077%. Multiplying this percentage by 1,428,571 shares results in a prorata share of 72,533 shares of Series C.

that if he agreed to waive his prorata rights of first refusal, Kimberlin would be treated "like all the other existing investors," that the 72,533 shares of Series C reflected this, and that in the event of an initial public offering (IPO) of Ciena, Kimberlin would be listed as a major stockholder of the company even if his ownership at the time were less than 5% (the threshold for required reporting under SEC rules).

On that same day the Ciena board of directors met and the directors were informed that the contract with Sprint, upon which the Series C financing depended, had been executed the day prior, on December 14, 1995. The information and a copy of the contract had also been given out to some of the Series C investors, but not to Kimberlin. At the December 15 meeting, the Ciena board gave its final approval to the Series C financing. Also at this meeting, it was determined that Bessemer Ventures, one of the existing investors, would receive an additional $1 M of Series C stock, thus raising the entire Series C to its final amount of $26 M.

On December 18, 1995, the Series C Purchase Agreement was sent to all investors, including Kimberlin. The Series C agreement shows all of the existing stockholders in Ciena and also all of the Series C purchasers, including the number of shares which they would purchase at closing. Kimberlin says he "does not recall" receiving this information with the Series C agreement on December 18. Kimberlin signed and returned the signature page for the Series C agreement, which closed on December 21, 1995.

Kimberlin and his co-plaintiffs filed this suit on November 19, 1996. . . .

DISCUSSION . . .

II. THE VALIDITY OF THE TERMINATION OF THE SERIES B PREEMPTIVE RIGHTS

At the heart of all of the plaintiffs' various claims is the assertion that plaintiffs had a right under the prior stock purchase agreements to purchase a larger share of Ciena stock in the Series C offering than was actually made available by Ciena, and that this lost opportunity was caused by the defendants' wrongful conduct. Defendants counter that any such rights to a given share of Ciena stock were terminated by the vote of the other stockholders. It is clear that this question must be resolved at the outset, for if the defendants are correct, the plaintiffs could not have been damaged by the loss of their preemptive rights because there were no longer any such rights to lose. The Court agrees with defendants that the termination of the Series B preemptive rights was valid.

The Series B stock purchase agreement states as follows:

> 7.10. Right of First Refusal. The Company hereby grants to each Investor the right of first refusal to purchase, pro-rata, all (or any part) of (x) New Securities . . . that the Company may, from time to time, propose to sell and issue. . . . The Investor's pro rata share shall be the ratio of the number of Preferred Shares then held by the Investor as of the date of the Rights Notice . . . to the sum of the total number of Preferred Shares then held by all Investors . . . as of such date.

Included within the definition of "New Securities" are preferred stock issues such as the Series C stock issue in dispute here (but not the later IPO).

The Series B agreement also, however, provides for the termination of these rights of first refusal:

> 14. Modifications: Waiver. (a) ... [A]ny provision of this Agreement may be amended and the observance of such provision may be waived (either generally or in a particular instance and either retroactively or prospectively) with (but only with) the written consent of (i) the Company, ... (iii) in the case of any modification of [Section 7] the holders of at least 67% of the Investor Shares ... acting together as a single class.

"Investor Shares" includes both Series A and Series B preferred stock. The new Section 7 of the Series B purchase agreement also superseded nearly identical provisions in the Series A agreement.

The effect of the above provisions gave each of the Series B investors (including all of the plaintiffs) the right to purchase a prorata share of any future rounds of stock issuance, including of course the Series C. However, it also gave the power to the holders of 67% of the combined Series A/Series B preferred shares to nullify those rights of first refusal at any time.

The key portion of the Series C purchase agreement is as follows:

> 19. Prior Agreements. ... By execution of this Agreement, (a) the Prior Investors ... hereby consent to the amendment of the Prior Agreements as contemplated herein, and (b) the Prior Investors waive the rights of first refusal under Section 7.10 of the Prior Agreements in respect of the issuances of Series C Preferred hereunder, such waiver to be effective on behalf of all the Investors referred to in the Prior Agreements pursuant to Section 14 thereof.

There is no dispute that both Ciena and all of the Prior Investors executed the Series C agreement which included this waiver provision, well above the 67% required to make the provision effective. The plaintiffs, of course, claim that their waivers were procured fraudulently and should not count, a proposition with which this Court agrees for purposes of this motion. However, the Kimberlin plaintiffs only held 5% of the necessary shares—close to 8% if they exercised their warrants to purchase more Series B stock—and so excluding their votes still left at least 92% voting to waive the rights of first refusal. Thus, unless this waiver vote was ineffective for some reason, plaintiffs' Series B rights of first refusal terminated as of the signing of the Series C agreement by the other investors.

The plaintiffs make two arguments in response. First, they argue that the 67% requirement has not been met because certain of the prior investors' votes should not be counted. Second, they argue that even if the 67% threshold has been crossed, the Series B purchase agreement should be interpreted as prohibiting any allocation of new stock issue which does not at least preserve each prior investor's right to purchase a pro rata share of that amount of stock which is not allocated to new investors. Neither of these contentions, however, is correct.

A. WAS THE 67% THRESHOLD MET?

The plaintiffs assert that certain investors' waivers should not count because their votes were tainted, and that without these votes, the necessary 67% of

Prior Investors' shares did not vote to waive the prorata allocation. The plaintiffs' arguments boil down to the assertion that certain "favored investors" were "bribed" into voting to waive the rights of first refusal because they knew that they would receive more than their prorata share of the existing investors' portion of the Series C offering. Plaintiffs contend that therefore these investors' shares "cannot legally, logically or fairly be counted" towards the 67% threshold, but precisely why this is so is unfortunately left for the Court to divine.

To the extent that, as asserted in the Complaint, the plaintiffs complain about those directors of Ciena who voted themselves a greater allocation of Series C shares, the Court assumes that plaintiffs mean to suggest that their shares should not count because this constitutes impermissible self-dealing in breach of their fiduciary duties as directors. Whether these directors had a fiduciary duty to the plaintiffs (as opposed to Ciena), whether voting their shares in such a manner breached that duty, and whether the remedy for such a breach would be the disqualification of their votes are issues which are all far from self-evident but which the Court need not reach, because of the three directors named as defendants in this case, only one wound up with a larger percentage of the existing investors' portion than his percentage ownership of Series A and B stock. . . .

InterWest and Charles River would actually, by insisting upon maintaining at least their prorata share of the Series C shares allocated to the existing investors, have wound up with more Series C stock, and thus any assertion of self-dealing on their part is simply unsupportable. . . . Thus, under the "self-dealing" theory, only Sevin Rosen's shares (along with the Kimberlin plaintiffs') should not be counted, which amounts to at most about 25% of the voting shares (Sevin Rosen's 17% plus the Kimberlin plaintiffs' 8% if they exercised their warrants). This still leaves some 75% of the existing investors waiving their rights of first refusal, and thus the waiver is still valid. . . .

[T]here are, in addition to Sevin Rosen, two other groups of prior investors, not represented on Ciena's board, who received a percentage of the Series C offering allocated to the existing investors which was higher than their percentage of Series A/B ownership: Bessemer and SVE. If these votes were not counted, along with those of Sevin Rosen and Kimberlin, then the total percentage vote for waiver would be approximately 60%, just shy of the necessary threshold for waiving the rights of first refusal.

However, the plaintiffs can point to no legal reason why the votes of SVE and Bessemer should not be counted. These shareholders had no representation on the board such that the self-dealing question raised earlier is presented. Moreover, as shareholders—and not majority or controlling shareholders—they had no fiduciary duty towards their fellow shareholders, and certainly no duty to vote their shares contrary to their own interests. Nor have the plaintiffs alleged wrongdoing of any sort on the part of these two entities. It appears from the evidence that they did no more than express an interest to the Ciena officers in receiving a larger share of Series C. Even if the Ciena board had, as the plaintiffs allege, a plan to drive out Kimberlin and his associates—and further assuming that such a plan would be impermissible in some unspecified way—the Court fails to see why such a plan should be held to deprive SVE and Bessemer—"favored investors" though they may be—of their right to vote their shares as they saw fit.

The plaintiffs' position, were it to be upheld, would require this Court to find that no prior investor could, as a matter of law, receive a larger share of the Series C offering vis-à-vis other prior investors than their holding of Series A & B. Such a position would, however, be untenable and illogical, given the plaintiffs' own admission that it was perfectly proper — even desirable — to waive the rights of first refusal to allow in new investors to Series C. After all, these new investors received a substantially — in fact, infinitely — greater share of Series C because they of course had no Series A & B shares to begin with. Plaintiffs' position would thus mean that while new investors could come in and purchase essentially any amount the Ciena board chose to sell them, the old investors — simply by virtue of their having invested in Ciena at an earlier, even less certain time — would be forever limited by their previous percentage ownership. It is difficult if not impossible to imagine a justification for such a holding. The Court thus finds that there is no fact issue as to whether the 67% level needed to waive the rights of first refusal under the Series B purchase agreement was reached.

B. DID THE SERIES B AGREEMENT RESTRICT THE POWER TO WAIVE FIRST REFUSAL RIGHTS?

Having determined that the 67% threshold was reached, the Court turns to plaintiffs' next argument — namely, that even if the threshold was reached, the power of 67% of the prior investor shares to waive the right of first refusal was limited. Plaintiffs argue that, although the prorata rights of first refusal could be waived to allow in new investors, each prior investor had a right to purchase his or her prorata percentage of those shares reserved for the prior investors — a right which could not be waived by a vote of the prior investors. Plaintiffs make two arguments in this regard: (1) the Series B agreement should be interpreted this way in light of trade usage and course of dealing; and (2) such a nonwaivable right is implicit in the duty of good faith and fair dealing that is part of the Series B agreement. The Court will address each contention in turn.

1. Trade Usage and Course of Dealing

Plaintiffs' first argument urges this Court to interpret the waiver provisions in the Series B agreement to allow only a limited power of waiver — that is, while the prorata right of first refusal may be waived to allow new investors in, every prior investor maintains a right to purchase his prorata portion of those shares sold to the existing investors — a right not subject to a vote of 67% of the prior investors. Plaintiffs assert, through their expert John Mahar, that it is standard industry practice to include waivers and that such waivers "are intended to permit new investors into the financing while the remaining 'existing investors are allowed to participate in that part of the total investment that has been earmarked for them according to the pro rata calculation.'" This, the plaintiffs assert, constitutes evidence of trade usage which should be used to interpret the waiver provisions. Moreover, say plaintiffs, when the Series B offering was made, the prior investors' shares were calculated precisely in this manner, thus establishing a course of dealing which also must be used to interpret the Series B agreement.

Contrary to the plaintiffs' contentions, under Delaware law, course of dealing and trade usage are applicable to interpreting the waiver and prorata provisions of the Series B agreement only upon a threshold finding that these provisions are ambiguous. . . .

There is no ambiguity in the waiver and prorata provisions of the Series B agreement. Section 14(a) of the agreement clearly states that "any provision of this Agreement may be amended and the observance of any such provision may be waived (either generally or in a particular instance and either retroactively or prospectively" by the vote of 67% of the prior investors' shares. There is no limitation on this waiver power to be found either in Section 14 or in Section 7.10, the section granting the prorata rights, and no reasonable person could read such a limitation into this language. This is particularly true in light of the extensive and detailed nature of the stock purchase agreement, which is some 53 single-spaced pages long, and of section 7.10 in particular, which runs for several paragraphs and sets out the operation of the first refusal rights in detail. Surely such an important and easily draftable provision, if intended, would have been expressly provided for. Moreover, there is at least one provision of the Series B agreement (Section 14) which, like the plaintiffs' asserted right, is made expressly nonwaivable except by unanimous consent, so it is clear that the drafters of the purchase agreement contemplated nonwaivable provisions but did not consider the prorata rights to be one. In light of the unambiguous language of the Series B agreement, the Court cannot, and does not, consider the plaintiffs' evidence of trade usage and course of dealing.

2. Duty of Good Faith and Fair Dealing

The Series B agreement, as does every contract, carries with it an implied covenant of good faith and fair dealing. The thrust of this duty is to "require[ ] a party in a contractual relationship to refrain from arbitrary or unreasonable conduct which has the effect of preventing the other party to the contract from receiving the fruits of the contract." Wilgus v. Salt Pond Inves. Co., 498 A.2d 151, 159 (Del. Ch. 1985). However, "the duty arises only where it is clear from what the parties expressly agreed, that they would have proscribed the challenged conduct as a breach of the implied covenant of good faith had they thought to negotiate with respect to the matter." [Dave Greytak Enters. v. Mazda Motors of Am., 622 A.2d 14, 22-23 (Del. Ch.), aff'd, 609 A.2d 668 (Del. 1992).] "It follows that where the subject at issue is expressly covered by the contract, or where the contract is intentionally silent as to that subject, the implied duty to perform in good faith does not come into play." Greytak, 622 A.2d at 23.

In other words, the duty of good faith cannot be relied upon to alter the terms of the contract itself. As stated earlier, the Court finds the waiver provisions of the Series B agreement to be unambiguous. It is implausible, given the detailed and extensive nature of the agreement, to say that the parties simply did not consider the issue of whether waiver of the first refusal rights was limited in the way plaintiffs suggest. That the prior investors might choose to waive the prorata first refusal rights in the future was hardly unforeseen — in fact, as noted by plaintiffs' expert, such waivers are routine. Rather, it is clear that the parties chose not to place any restrictions on the right of two-thirds of the shareholders to waive these first refusal rights. To allow the plaintiffs to add this provision would be to rewrite the purchase agreement under the guise of the duty of good faith, which is plainly not consonant with principles of Delaware contract law.

In sum, then, the plaintiffs have failed to show any factual or legal basis for finding that the waiver of prorata first refusal rights from the Series B agreement was ineffective as of the execution of the Series C agreement. . . .

For the foregoing reasons, [t]he plaintiffs' contract claims . . . are dismissed without prejudice.

H. DEADLOCK

Deadlocks occur when the shareholder vote is evenly divided. While deadlocks usually arise from a failure to allocate control in advance, occasionally business planners intentionally provide opportunities for deadlocks. The rationale for such planning is that some business relationships should not proceed unless there is unanimous assent to the action.

A deadlock usually leads to dissolution of a corporation. As with all fundamental decisions involving a corporation, the decision to dissolve typically requires approval by the directors and the shareholders. After dissolution is authorized, the corporation may dissolve by filing articles of dissolution with the secretary of state.

In some instances, however, shareholders cannot even agree to dissolve. When this happens, the corporation may be judicially dissolved upon a showing of deadlock. The following case involves such a dissolution. Notice that the court assigns a date of dissolution that is prior to the commencement of the lawsuit. Is this a reasonable approach in light of the statutory provisions governing judicial dissolution?

CONKLIN v. PERDUE
2002 WL 31421763 (slip opinion)
Superior Court of Massachusetts
September 17, 2002

ALLAN VAN GESTEL, Justice of the Superior Court.

This matter is before the Court for findings of fact, rulings of law and an order for judgment following a jury-waived trial.

FINDINGS OF FACT

The plaintiff, Jeffrey M. Conklin ("Conklin"), at the time of the start of the trial on June 18, 2002, was unemployed. He is a graduate of Boston College and holds a J.D. degree from Villanova University and an M.B.A. degree from Duke University.

Conklin worked for a number of years, from 1979 to 1993, at Digital Equipment Corporation ("DEC"). He started at DEC as a contract negotiator and advanced through a position as legal counsel for international purchasing to legal counsel for international matters in the financial area.

The defendant, Beth A. Perdue ("Perdue"), is a graduate of Case Western Reserve University and has a law degree from the University of Michigan. She also worked for a number of years at DEC, in the purchasing and contracts department.

While at DEC, Conklin met Perdue. They developed a personal, as well as business, relationship that included some international overlap.

Perdue left DEC in 1992, and Conklin resigned from DEC on June 4, 1993. In 1993, the two then determined to join together and establish a consulting firm to advise businesses on strategic alliances. "Strategic alliances" was a catch phrase that covered a range of activities designed to establish more positive relationships between businesses or between businesses and markets. Conklin and Perdue hoped to capitalize on their experience at DEC in understanding the intricacies of negotiating international agreements and on their knowledge of international markets, particularly in south Asia.

The entity that they formed eventually became CPInternational, Inc. ("CPI"). The "CP" stood for *C*onklin and *P*erdue.

CPI was a Massachusetts corporation which, for taxing purposes, made an election to be treated as a Subchapter S corporation. Conklin and Perdue were each directors, officers and 50% shareholders of CPI. Perdue was the president, and Conklin was the treasurer. CPI, with its two shareholders, an absence of any market for its stock, and its essentially total shareholder participation in management was a classic closely held corporation of the kind described in Donahue v. Rodd Electrotype Company of New England, Inc., 367 Mass. 578 (1975).

CPI had no capital in the beginning and, although it earned small amounts of money on a few contracts, was basically financed by Conklin, either personally or with money he borrowed from his parents. Perdue made essentially no capital contributions to CPI.

Each of Conklin and Perdue reimbursed themselves for expenses, the largest amount of which seemed to be related to international travel to countries in south Asia. Conklin and Perdue also each took from CPI what they called a "draw." One of the issues in dispute in this case is whether that draw should actually be considered a loan. The Court finds, however, that CPI's final Federal tax return, for the year 1997, includes a Schedule K-1 in the name of Perdue, listing "Property distributions (including cash) . . . reported to [her] on Form 1099" of $112,434. This $112,434 amount is the "draw" in contest. Perdue produced her own individual tax return establishing that she paid taxes on this amount.

In October of 1994, Conklin was invited to make a speech in India before the U.S./India Business Council. The U.S. Secretary of Commerce, the late Ron Brown, led the United States delegation to India in connection with the program. It being customary to give symbolic gifts in connection with such trade mission affairs, Conklin and Perdue suggested that the gift be an Internet web-page to the people of India; the web-page would demonstrate ways in which American and Indian businesses could locate, communicate and collaborate with each other. The idea was accepted, and CPI set about creating a demonstration web-page.

Because CPI had no funds to create such a web-page, it put together a consortium of four American Companies — IBM, BBN, Sun Microsystems and Bay Networks — to fund the creation of the demonstration web-page. The total funding was about $60,000. What was created was an example of how the sponsoring companies' products could be used in India. The demonstration piece had no interactive functions. The program ultimately became known at CPI as "TradeInfo."

The trade mission to India was not a success. It came at the time of a fundraising scandal implicating the Secretary of Commerce. CPI got no follow-on consulting business from this program.

CPI did, however, make contact with the Confederation of Indian Industries ("CII"). The two entities entered into a promotional agreement whereby the CII membership list was to be put on the CPI TradeInfo program. The idea was that American companies would use the TradeInfo program with the CII database to make business-to-business contacts in India. CPI hoped that once those contacts were made, it would then be engaged by the American companies for consulting work in their negotiations of agreements with the Indian companies. In a direct sense, this program between CPI and CII was non-revenue generating and actually cost CPI some money.

In the summer of 1995, CPI started on the TradeInfo project with the CII database by beginning to create another canned demonstration similar to that used in the Indian trade mission program. CPI, which was running out of money at the time, engaged a small company in New York named Cyber House Publishing ("Cyber House") to create a web site. The web site was intended to permit U.S. companies to search the CII database for Indian companies and then call CPI for assistance in getting together.

This clearly was not a large project. Cyber House's billings only totaled $4,800. But, as an example of CPI's strained financial circumstances, even that amount was not fully paid.

What Cyber House created, however, could be accessed only by contacting Cyber House. It was, basically, a low-level prototype with no Internet address. It had no software systems, nor was it interactive or able to perform business-to-business communications.

By the end of 1995, CPI was essentially out of money, and it had only one customer, a company called HCL, which was overdue on its payments. Tensions arose between Conklin and Perdue. Conklin continued to be the sole source of money to finance CPI, and he was concerned that Perdue was not focusing adequately on the financial end of the business, nor was she contributing to it. In fact, Conklin was concerned that Perdue was an economic drain on the company.

Also by the end of 1995, CPI was located in leased space at 36 Newbury Street in Boston's Back Bay. The rent was $1,650 per month, and Conklin alone was on the lease as a guarantor.

Conklin claims — and Perdue denies the claim — that in the summer of 1995 he had her sign a promissory note reflecting the indebtedness she owed the company for the draw money she was taking. Conklin says that the note was provided to him by the company's accountants and that Perdue executed two copies thereof. He testified that he then put the two signed copies of the note in a manila envelope which he thereafter kept in a drawer of his desk. No such promissory note, nor any copy thereof, was produced at trial.

By late December 1995, Conklin concluded that CPI was not economically sustainable and had no good future prospects. He also decided that working with Perdue was difficult; and he was tired of all of the traveling.

Thus, on December 29, 1995, Conklin called Perdue and told her things were not working out; that he was in debt, and there was no security for it; and that CPI had no revenue prospects. He further told her that the 50/50 arrangement was not working out and said that he would sit down and discuss the matter with her on the day after New Year's Day.

Perdue's response was that she was "shocked." To which Conklin responded: "How can you be shocked?"

Conklin then went away for the New Year's weekend. When he returned home from the weekend, there was a voice-mail message from Perdue. It said: "I'm not going to meet. I took some records. I'll copy them and return them."

Conklin then called Perdue, and they had a brief, five-minute conversation. In the conversation, Perdue insisted that she had a legal right to do what she did. This time it was Conklin who said he was "stunned."

Conklin went to the CPI office the next day and met with the office manager, Astrid Mueller. He described the office as appearing as if it had been ransacked and looking like it had been broken into. Folders were all over the place, a computer printer was missing, and computer tapes had been taken. He also says he discovered that the promissory notes and his tax returns were no longer there.

Conklin then called Perdue and demanded that she bring everything back. She refused. He then proceeded to have the locks changed on the office doors.

However, Perdue describes the visit to the office on the New Year's weekend, and the removal of materials, somewhat differently. She says that she went to the office on Saturday, December 30, 1995, the morning after the telephone conversation with Conklin. She says that she first started to do a back-up of the computer system. She then started going through files, wondering what to take to protect the company. She says she left notes of what she had done. She specifically denies, however, taking any promissory notes—insisting that she never signed any in the first place.

Perdue concedes that on December 30, 1995, she had help from a man named Lawrence Hartford ("Hartford") in removing the files and other materials from the CPI office.

Hartford also testified about the New Year's weekend incidents—he says there were two—when he assisted Perdue in removing things from the CPI office. His story strained credulity. He described himself as a "decorative painter" who met Perdue in 1992. He evidently worked from time to time at Perdue's home, doing what sounded like interior decorating work. Hartford says he became friends with Perdue socially.

Hartford claims he received a call from Perdue on the Friday starting New Year's weekend,[3] asking for help in removing her "stuff" from the CPI office because she was going to be locked out. Hartford then says that he picked Perdue up at her home in the South End and drove to Newbury Street, arriving there at about 10:00 P.M. He then alleges that they entered the building and went up the elevator to the CPI office. There, he claims, Perdue unlocked the

---

3. The Court takes judicial notice of the fact that in 1995, the last Friday of the month was December 29, 1995, and New Year's Day was Monday January 1, 1996.

door, and the two of them went in. He also testified that, at Perdue's insistence, they did not put on any lights in the office because she did not want Conklin to know she was there. Then, according to Hartford, in the dark of a winter night in Boston, he and Perdue examined materials on her desk and on a secretary's desk, but Perdue took nothing therefrom, including such highly personal things as photographs of Perdue's nieces and a radio headset. Then, still in pitch dark, Hartford claims to have gone over to Conklin's desk and found a manila envelope containing two identical pages headed "promissory note." He says that he then said to Perdue: "Isn't this it?" To which he says she responded: "We should go"; and, presumably, taking nothing but the manila envelope and its contents, they left.

Hartford then says that he received a second call from Perdue on Saturday morning, as a result of which they again went to the CPI offices and removed the materials that Perdue also described in her testimony as having been removed on December 30, 1995. The materials removed on Saturday were taken by Hartford and Perdue to "Office Max" at the South Bay Center for copying. They were signed in under the name "J. Hartford" rather than Perdue in order to further conceal their whereabouts from Conklin. Eventually, Hartford says that he and [Perdue] picked up the copied materials from Office Max and took them to her home in the South End. They used two cars this time because of the documents' bulk after copying.

The Court does not credit Hartford's testimony about the dark-of-night visit to the CPI office on Friday, December 29, 1995.

From the time of the New Year's weekend on, there initially was some effort by Conklin and Perdue to reach agreement on resolving the break-up of their relationship and resolving the affairs of CPI. Except for a few conversations and exchanges of correspondence regarding dissolution in early January 1996, however, there were no apparent efforts by either Conklin or Perdue — both law school graduates — to comply with the legal particulars regarding the winding-up of CPI's corporate affairs.

Conklin, at the same time, began a new venture on his own. On January 4, 1996, he incorporated Emerging Markets, Inc., known sometimes as Emerging Markets Business Information Services, Inc., later as TradeAccess, Inc., and now as Ozro, Inc. (herein "TradeAccess"). Conklin says the initial incorporation was simply to keep track of what he was going to do.

In an exchange of correspondence on January 15, January 17 and January 19, 1996, Conklin and Perdue reached the point where each was doing little but making accusations about the other regarding the business of CPI, and each was refusing to consent to any action by the other regarding the ongoing business of CPI or its winding-up. Also, on January 15, 1996, the small paid staff of CPI was laid off. This was the beginning of a process when each of Conklin and Perdue made allegations against the other, both in the nature of causing harm to CPI and in the nature of breaching fiduciary duties to each other. The business divorce had begun in earnest and eventually found its way, as most divorces do, into the hands of a judge for resolution of issues colored much more by emotion than economic or business reality.

The principal disagreements between Conklin and Perdue related to his allegations that Perdue's draw money was in fact a loan from the corporation and her's that Conklin, in his new venture, effectively stole corporate opportunities that belonged to CPI. Both of these issues are really derivative claims of CPI, the corporation, not of Conklin or Perdue as individuals.

For about two years thereafter, Conklin worked to make his new entity, TradeAccess, succeed. He failed, however. In the process, there was no credible evidence that he took or used materials or opportunities that belonged to CPI. He was, of course, technically still a shareholder and officer of CPI and had whatever duties that status conveyed upon him, assuming CPI remained active for such purposes.

Perdue, despite the aggressive tone in her January 1996 letters, remained remarkably passive, to the state of being essentially inactive, in any attempt to move forward with the business of CPI. Conklin, having moved on with TradeAccess, for all intents and purposes abandoned CPI to Perdue.

To be sure, of course, there were the frictions that came from communications between Conklin and entities with which he, while at CPI, had been involved. These problems mostly produced suspicions and accusations on Perdue's part that Conklin's attempts to explain his noninvolvement with CPI after January of 1996 were really attempts to destroy CPI and steal its business. This Court does not see them in such a dark light. Obviously, the parties could have accomplished the split-up much better and much more smoothly. But it was their emotional reactions to each other, not their exercise of business thievery or breaches of fiduciary duties, that were in play.

Similar suspicions were what drove the accusations that Conklin, through TradeAccess, was interfering with CPI's contractual and other advantageous relationships. As a matter of fact, there was nothing that amounted to such interference, and CPI had essentially no contracts to interfere with. TradeAccess, for one thing, was not in the same business as CPI; and, more importantly, there was no evidence that TradeAccess ever succeeded in the marketplace, except possibly for the time when it sought and received patents for its new product.

In the middle of 1998, long after CPI was in a state of total inactivity and final exhaustion, Conklin, with TradeAccess, came up with a new idea: the ability to negotiate complex business arrangements over the Internet. He then conceived of and had devised a mock-up of how this could be done. He described it as "iterative, multivariate negotiations." Through the use of this product, businesses would be able to contact each other and effectively negotiate complex transactions over the Internet. Eventually, after reducing his ideas to practice, he — and two others who worked with him — sought and received, starting in October of 2000, four patents on the process. This enabled him to attract some outside financing and seemingly to infuse life into his new business. However, this business too seems to have turned out to be an economic failure.

Significantly for this case, this Court does not find that anything in the patented process developed by Conklin and his associates, starting in 1998 and thereafter, was acquired from or was a continuation of anything that CPI was doing when it was an active corporation prior to the end of 1995. CPI never had a real product, and it certainly never had anything that allowed business-to-business iterative, multivariate negotiations over the Internet. The Patent Office's examination of prior art, and its conclusion that Conklin and his associates were entitled to four patents, enables a presumption that the patents were valid, and belies any idea that the inventors copied anything from CPI.

RULINGS OF LAW

Much turns on the status of CPI at various times, particularly in early 1996, and the consequent relationships thereto, and to each other, of CPI's two 50% shareholders, two directors and sole officers, each of the latter of which are Conklin and Perdue. Consequently, the Court first addresses the legal status of CPI as a Massachusetts corporation in January of 1996. In so doing, the Court has been made aware of a decision in the Delaware Chancery Court dealing with somewhat similar issues involving a Delaware corporation with shareholder, director and officerships quite similar to that of CPI. See Dionisi et al. v. DeCampli et al., 1995 Del. Ch. LEXIS 88 (June 28, 1995).

In *Dionisi*, Vice-Chancellor Steele was faced with the break-up of a closely held corporation basically involving two graphic designers who, after previous employment at E.I. du Pont de Nemours & Co., got together to form a small, start-up graphic design business. The entity was incorporated under Delaware law, but the parties treated it much like a joint venture. After a short few years, with very marginal economic success, the two founders had a falling out. Just as in this case, the parties in *Dionisi* sued each other for a wide array of breaches of fiduciary duties, unfair business practices, interference with contractual relations, and the like. Also, just as in this case, the parties in *Dionisi* did not avail themselves of the provisions of Delaware corporate law to effect the formal dissolution of the entity.

Vice-Chancellor Steele, in *Dionisi*, took it upon himself to dissolve the entity in the way that either of the parties could have, but failed to do. . . .

This Court finds itself in much the same position as the Delaware Chancery Court in *Dionisi*. CPI has two 50% shareholders, Conklin and Perdue. Conklin and Perdue, unlike the two shareholders in *Dionisi*, were lawyers, not graphic artists. The two shareholders here are also the only two directors and the only two executive officers of CPI. Since at least mid-January 1996, Conklin and Perdue have been deadlocked in the management of the corporate affairs of CPI and, as shareholders, have been unable to break the deadlock.

Mass. G.L. c. 156B, Sec. 99, provides in material part as follows:

> A petition for dissolution of a corporation may be filed in the supreme judicial court in the following cases: . . .
> (b) Such a petition may be filed by the holder or holders of not less than forty per cent of all the shares of its stock outstanding and entitled to vote thereon, treating all classes of stock entitled to vote as a single class for the purpose of determining whether the petition is brought by the holders of not less than forty per cent of the outstanding shares as aforesaid, if: . . .
>
> > (1) the directors are deadlocked in the management of corporate affairs, and the shareholders are unable to break the deadlock; . . .
>
> After such notice as the court may order and after hearing, the court may decree a dissolution of the corporation, notwithstanding the fact that the business of the corporation is being conducted at a profit, if it shall find that the best interests of the stockholders will be served by such dissolution. Upon such dissolution, the existence of the corporation shall cease, subject to the provisions of sections one hundred and two, one hundred and four and one hundred and eight.

Section 102 of c. 156B is the provision that provides that dissolution under Sec. 99 shall not prevent the corporation from continuing as a body corporate for a period of three years "for the purpose of prosecuting and defending suits by and against it and/or enabling it gradually to settle and close its affairs, to dispose of and convey its property to any person and to make distributions to its stockholders of any assets remaining after payment of its debts and obligations, *but not for the purpose of continuing the business for which it was established.*" (Emphasis added.)

Can this Court, like the Delaware Chancery Court in *Dionisi*, seize upon G.L. c. 156B, Sec. 99, as a vehicle provided by the Legislature that enables the Court to do what the parties themselves did not: dissolve CPI because of the deadlock by the directors in the management of the corporation and the inability of the shareholders to break that deadlock? . . .

By the Acts of 1964, Chapter 723, the Commonwealth adopted a new Business Corporation Law, which represented the first general overhaul of the Massachusetts corporate laws since 1903. See Hosmer, *New Business Corporation Law,* 11 Ann. Survey of Massachusetts Law 1. Mr. Hosmer, Chairman of the Boston Bar Association Committee that drafted the new business corporation laws, noted that "Chapter 156B [in sec. 99] clarifies the deadlock situation for voluntary dissolution by adopting the definitions of the A.B.A. Model Act and deals with the determination of the vote required in case more than one class of stock is outstanding."

The significance of the new c. 156B to the situation before this Court was presaged, perhaps unknowingly, in Rizzuto v. Onset Cafe, Inc., [330 Mass. 595, 597-98 (1953)]. There the court said:

> The dissolution of corporations, like their creation, is primarily and fundamentally a matter of legislative and not judicial cognizance. . . . *The allegations of the bill or the findings of the judge do not bring this case within the scope of any statute authorizing judicial dissolution of corporations.* (Emphasis added.)

Here, of course, the findings and rulings of this Court do reveal that, given the deadlock between Conklin and Perdue, the situation does fall within the scope of a statute authorizing judicial dissolution — a statute that was enacted after *Rizzuto* and was a new provision in the General Laws.

The dissolution of a corporation under c. 156B, Sec. 99 calls for the Court to apply its equitable powers. Prior to the adoption of the Massachusetts Rules of Civil Procedure in 1974, corporate dissolution proceedings generally were brought by a bill in equity. Indeed, Sec. 99 states that the result of a proceeding thereunder is for the Court to "*decree* a dissolution of the corporation." (Emphasis added.) At the time that c. 156B was enacted, "decrees" were the vehicle for resolution of matters on the equity side of the court, just as "judgments" were the vehicle on the law side. Further, the Massachusetts Rules of Civil Procedure do not apply "to proceedings pertaining to the dissolution of corporations and distribution of their assets." Mass. R. Civ. P. Rule 81(a)(1) 6.

Given all of the foregoing, this Court, believing it to be within its equitable powers, will proceed here, like the Chancery Court in *Dionisi*, to address the dissolution of CPI, as Conklin or Perdue should have done, under G.L. c. 156B, Sec. 99. In doing so, the Court must first determine when the requisite deadlock between the directors and shareholders first occurred.

As noted in the findings, there was a period from December 29, 1995 through mid-January 1996, when Conklin and Perdue — although in great discord and disarray emotionally, physically, legally and otherwise—seemed to be coming to grips with the termination of their relationship and the dissolution of CPI. Those efforts, however, erupted and imploded with the exchange of correspondence on January 15, January 17 and January 19, 1996. In that exchange, the efforts at resolution metamorphosed into recriminations and accusations, with each of Conklin and Perdue telling the other that he or she would not consent to any action the other took with regard to CPI, its business or its dissolution. The requisite deadlock had arrived, and Conklin and Perdue—CPI's sole 50% shareholders—were unable to break the deadlock. Thus, this Court, acting pursuant to its inherent equitable powers and the authority vested in G.L. c. 156B, Sec. 99, hereby determines that January 19, 1996 is the day that Conklin and Perdue were first in total deadlock regarding the management of CPI and, therefore, the date upon which the corporation is to be deemed dissolved. . . .

The Court now turns to each of the specific claims and their resolution.

Conklin makes four claims against Perdue: he charges her with money lent (Count I); money had and received (Count II); breach of contract (Count III); and breach of fiduciary duty (Count IV).

The first three claims are not Conklin's personally, but rather derivative claims of the corporation, CPI. All three relate to the issue of whether Perdue's draw was in reality a loan. On the evidence presented, this Court rules that the draw was compensation and not a loan. While a different conclusion may have been compelled if some written evidence of a loan was presented, or its absence convincingly accounted for, but it was not. Further, the fact that for S corporation tax purposes certain items needed particular handling and characterization does not change the fact. Indeed, the treatment of the K-1 for Perdue on the CPI final 1997 tax return, the issuance to her of a tax Form 1099, and her ultimate payment of income tax on the draw demonstrates quite the contrary. Counts I, II and III must be dismissed.

Count IV charges Perdue with breach of her fiduciary duties in the December 30, 1995 removal of corporate files and materials from the office. Given her position as a 50% shareholder, and Conklin's December 29, 1995 telephone call threat to the effect that CPI was over as a going operation, the charge of a breach is a close one. It need not be resolved, however, because there was no satisfactory evidence of any damage to Conklin or CPI, all of the records ultimately having been returned and always having been in the custody and control of a 50% shareholder, director and corporate officer. Indeed, it is Conklin's claim—and a major part of his defense to Perdue's claims—that CPI was effectively without any business or any prospects of business on December 29, 1995. As such, neither he nor the corporation had much, if anything, to lose.

Perdue asserts [various] claims against Conklin [, including] breach of fiduciary duty. . . .

Any fiduciary duty on Conklin's part ended on January 19, 1996, the date that this Court has ruled was the date of dissolution of the closely held corporation from which those duties flow. . . . Here, there is no showing that Conklin, prior to January 19, 1996, took any opportunity of CPI's that was not first known to and not pursued by it. Nor is there any showing that after January 19, 1996, CPI did, or purported to do, any business, or that Conklin took anything belonging to it thereafter. . . .

What is left after all of the foregoing is that neither Conklin, Perdue nor CPI are entitled to anything from the other, except that Conklin and Perdue have a theoretical right each to share one-half of the net book value of CPI as of January 19, 1996. There was, however, no evidence presented as to what that net book value might have been. Indeed, the only credible evidence presented led to the inference that it was essentially zero. . . .

RED HAT, INC.: A CASE STUDY

Marc Ewing was only 24 years old in 1993 when he founded a company redundantly called "ACC Corp., Inc." to develop an oddly named software program called Red Hat Linux. The "Red Hat" was purportedly inspired by a Cornell University lacrosse cap Ewing received from his grandfather. "Linux" is the computer operating system originally developed in 1991 by Linus Torvalds of Finland but subsequently improved by software developers all over the world. In 1995, Ewing met Bob Young, whose many years of finance and marketing experience in computer leasing and software distribution fit nicely with Ewing's technical expertise. The two joined forces to create Red Hat Software, Inc., based in Research Triangle Park, North Carolina, with Young serving as president and Ewing as chief technology officer.

In August 1999 — after shortening the company name to Red Hat, Inc. — both Ewing and Young became multimillionaires when the company they founded sold shares of common stock to the public at a price of $14 per share. The shares began trading on Wednesday, August 11, 1995, and by Friday of the same week the price had skyrocketed to $85.25, an increase of over 500 percent.

At the height of what has come to be known as the "Internet Bubble" in December 1999, Red Hat's shares sold for over $300 apiece. That price was so high that the company decided to split the shares in January 2000; that is, the company turned every existing share into two shares, thus reducing the price to a more manageable level. Of course, the stock market subsequently reduced the stock price to a *much more* manageable level. At the beginning of 2003, Red Hat's shares were selling for just over $6.00. This brief case study examines the investment contracts of Red Hat to examine the relationship between investors and managers of the company.

Venture Financing of Red Hat

Red Hat sold 6 million shares of common stock in the IPO. Before the IPO the company had over 60 million shares outstanding (assuming the conversion of all series of preferred stock). In addition to Young and Ewing, who together owned 18 million shares at the time of the IPO, the largest shareholders of Red Hat stock were an "angel" investor (Frank Batten, Jr.), two venture capital firms (Greylock and Benchmark), and a strategic partner (Intel). Red Hat sold shares of preferred stock to these outside investors in three separate transactions: Series A Preferred Stock (August 15, 1997); Series B Preferred Stock (September 29, 1998); and Series C Preferred Stock (February 25 through April 1, 1999).

The process of financing a company over time through multiple offerings of preferred stock is known as "staged financing," and it is an important aspect of venture capital financing. Each series of preferred stock had a similar package of financial and control rights, which were largely determined in the first round and repeated in later rounds. Although public information on the point is not available, the price of each round of financing is negotiated by a "lead investor," who typically has no prior investment in the company. The terms of Red Hat's preferred stock—which appeared in the company's Second Amended and Restated Certificate of Incorporation—included the following:

Dividends. Dividends can be a powerful constraint on managerial opportunism, at least in companies that generate free cash flow (that is, an amount of money in excess of the amount that the company can profitably invest). In such companies, dividends deplete the funds available to managers, thus eliminating the cushion between success and failure. The incentive to perform at a high level follows naturally. In the context of a high-growth company, however, free cash flow is almost never an issue, as reflected in Red Hat's position on dividends: "We have never paid any cash dividends on our common stock and do not anticipate paying any cash dividends in the foreseeable future."

Even in the absence of free cash flow, the rules governing dividends may constrain opportunism by determining the allocation of funds in the event a dividend is declared. For example, many venture capital financings provide cumulative dividend rights for the investors. These rights provide venture capitalists with a certain fixed return on investment, which may become important when the preferred stock is converted into common stock or upon the occurrence of certain fundamental transactions, such as a merger or public offering.

Despite the stated policy of the company not to pay dividends, as a legal matter the board of directors has unilateral power to declare or refrain from declaring dividends, within the expansive limits established by fiduciary duty law. Another important issue relating to dividends, therefore, is whether the board of directors can favor one group of investors over another. One means of restricting the power of the board in this area is to specify dividend rights among the preferences granted to preferred stock. Red Hat's preferred stock enjoyed the following dividend preference:

> The Corporation shall not declare or pay any dividends on shares of Common Stock . . . until the holders of the Series A Preferred Stock, Series B Preferred Stock and Series C Preferred Stock then outstanding shall have first received, or simultaneously receive, a distribution on each outstanding share of Series A Preferred Stock, Series B Preferred Stock and Series C Preferred Stock in an amount at least equal to the product of (i) the per share amount, if any, of the dividends to be declared, paid or set aside for the Common Stock, multiplied by (ii) the number of whole shares of Common Stock into which such share of Series A Preferred Stock, Series B Preferred Stock and Series C Preferred Stock is then convertible. The Corporation shall not declare or pay any dividends on any shares of Preferred Stock unless, at the same time, a dividend in a like amount per share shall be paid upon, or declared and set apart for, all shares of Preferred Stock then outstanding.

The effect of this provision is to ensure that the holders of all three series of preferred stock—the angel investors, the venture capitalists, and the strategic partners—are treated equally in the payment of dividends, and that the preferred stock is at least equal to the common stock—held by the founders—in the amount of dividends paid. Red Hat's preferred shareholders would not necessarily receive any "preference" in the sense of being paid before the common shareholders, but the preferred shareholders are at least assured that the common shareholders cannot distribute the assets of the company without sharing.

Liquidation. The term "liquidation" is normally associated with the sale of a company's assets and the subsequent distribution of proceeds (if any) to investors. Used in this sense, liquidation is typically viewed as the necessary culmination of a business failure, and the only issue for investors is who receives the largest portion of the residue. To protect as much of the "principal amount" of their investment as possible, holders of preferred stock usually demand a liquidation preference—that is, the right to be repaid the original amount of the investment prior to any payment made to holders of common stock in the event of a liquidation. By requiring the return of the original investment to preferred shareholders, liquidation rights remove any incentive that might otherwise tempt the common shareholders to liquidate opportunistically.

As expected, the venture capitalists who invested in Red Hat received a liquidation preference, but with a twist. As in most venture capital contracts, the term "liquidation" has a broader meaning than the one suggested above. The term also includes mergers, acquisitions, and sales of all or substantially all of the assets of the company in a merger-like transaction. In short, "liquidation" may be an extremely positive event for both entrepreneurs and venture capitalists. Accordingly, many venture capitalists demand "participating preferred stock," which receives not only a liquidation preference but also a share of the assets remaining after payment of the liquidation preference. While participating preferred stock is frequently used in venture capital financings, nonparticipating preferred stock is especially attractive to the entrepreneurs, who are usually the largest common shareholders.

The holders of Red Hat preferred stock negotiated liquidation rights that fall somewhere between fully participating and nonparticipating preferred stock. They negotiated an option to receive *the greater of* the amount that they would receive if they were converted into common stock or a fixed payment worth slightly more than the original purchase price of the preferred stock.

Voting. Voting rights are the most obvious means of controlling opportunism in the corporate setting. Venture capitalists usually receive general voting rights and targeted voting rights. The term "general voting rights" designates rights shared among all equity holders and the term "targeted voting rights" designates rights over specified transactions that are reserved to the venture capitalists. The targeted voting rights are typically framed as negative covenants, thus empowering venture capitalists to veto certain transactions, but not allowing the venture capitalists to initiate transactions. Taken together, the general and targeted voting rights provide venture capitalists with substantial influence over the portfolio company.

The holders of Red Hat preferred stock were entitled to vote as a single class with holders of common stock. Each share of preferred stock had votes equal to the number of shares of common stock into which it could have been converted at the time of the vote. Somewhat surprisingly, the terms of the preferred stock did not provide the preferred stockholders with a certain number of directors, though the board has always had representatives of the outside investors.

Even though the preferred stockholders did not control the board of directors, they exerted substantial influence over company decision making by virtue of the "Negative Covenants" contained in the charter:

> So long as at least 25% of the shares of Series A Preferred Stock, Series B Preferred Stock and Series C Preferred Stock outstanding on the Series C Original Issue Date (such numbers to be proportionately adjusted in the event of any stock splits, stock dividends, recapitalizations or similar events) are outstanding, the Corporation shall not, without the prior written consent of the holders of shares of Series A Preferred Stock, Series B Preferred Stock and Series C Preferred Stock representing not less than 66⅔% of the shares of Common Stock into which all outstanding shares of such Preferred Stock are then convertible:
>
> > (a) merge or consolidate into or with another corporation (except a merger or consolidation in which the holders of capital stock of the Corporation immediately prior to such merger or consolidation continue to hold at least 50% by voting power of the capital stock of the surviving or acquiring corporation), or sell all or substantially all the assets of the Corporation;
> > (b) acquire (whether by merger, stock purchase, asset purchase or otherwise) all or substantially all of the properties, assets or stock of any other corporation or entity;
> > (c) amend the Certificate of Incorporation (including through the filing of a Certificate of Designation) of the Corporation to authorize any additional shares of Common Stock or Preferred Stock or to authorize or designate any other class or series of stock in addition to Common Stock and Preferred Stock;
> > (d) declare or pay any dividends or distributions on Common Stock (other than dividends payable solely in Common Stock and repurchases of Common Stock for a price equal to its original purchase price pursuant to restricted stock agreements);
> > (e) voluntarily liquidate or dissolve; . . .

Most venture capital investments in the United States contain a similarly long list of negative covenants, often called "protective provisions." Depending on the scope of these covenants, they may provide a fairly close substitute for majority control of the board of directors. In the case of Red Hat, the covenants focus on major transactions with the potential to transfer wealth away from the preferred shareholders.

Conversion. The preferred stock issued in venture capital financings is almost always convertible into common stock of the portfolio company. Optional conversion provisions allow the venture capitalists to convert at their discretion, usually when the company is a party to a merger or acquisition and the proceeds to common shareholders are more attractive than the liquidation preference. Automatic conversion provisions require the venture capitalists to convert in specified circumstances, the most important of which is an IPO. Bernard Black and Ronald Gilson have argued that automatic conversion is part of an implicit contract over control between the entrepreneur and the venture capitalists. That contract requires venture capitalists to forfeit control rights when the company meets a predefined measure of success (for example, an IPO at a specified stock price or aggregate dollar amount).

Working together, optional and automatic conversion provide the entrepreneur with incentives to create a successful company and preclude actions that would disadvantage the venture capitalist. It is not surprising, therefore, that Red Hat's contracts contain both types of provisions. In Red Hat, as in most venture capital financings, the initial conversion rate is set at 1:1, but the need to protect the preferred shareholders against dilution requires that this rate be adjustable. To see the potential problems caused by dilution, consider a simple stock split. In preparation for the IPO, Red Hat's board of directors approved a 2-for-1 stock split in June 1999. Prior to the stock split, the holders of preferred stock were entitled to convert their shares into 16,972,726 shares of common stock (one-for-one conversion rate). At the same time, there were approximately 13,444,826 outstanding shares of common stock. Using these figures, we can see that the holders of preferred stock are entitled to approximately 55.8 percent of the residual assets of the company.[1] The purpose of anti-dilution protection in the terms of the preferred stock is to ensure that the claim is not diminished when the company issues shares for consideration that is less than the conversion price. In the case of the stock split described, the number of shares of common stock doubles, but the assets of the company remained unchanged, so the preferred stockholders want to ensure that they retain their claim to 55.8 percent of those assets. The charter contains a special conversion provision relating to stock splits:

> If the Corporation shall at any time or from time to time after the Series C Original Issue Date effect a subdivision of the outstanding Common Stock, the Series A Conversion Price, Series B Conversion Price and Series C Conversion Price then in effect immediately before that subdivision each shall be proportionately decreased. . . .

This provision required Red Hat to reduce the Conversion Price for each series of preferred stock by half. As a result, at the time of the IPO, the 16,972,726 shares of Red Hat preferred stock were converted into 33,945,452 shares of common stock. In other words, each share of preferred stock was converted into two shares of common stock. The number of shares of common stock outstanding also doubled from 13,444,826 to 26,889,652. The result is that the preferred stockholders retained their claim to 55.8 percent of the company's assets.

The conversion rate is one of the most important features of these securities because venture capital investments are structured to result in conversion if the company executes an IPO. Unlike the optional conversion provision discussed above, the holders of preferred stock have no choice in this instance. Thus, these provisions are usually called "mandatory conversion" provisions. Red Hat's charter contains a mandatory conversion provision triggered by Red Hat's IPO, and all of the holders of preferred stock became holders of common stock when the IPO was complete. In the process, they lost all of the other rights associated with the preferred stock (except registration rights, discussed below, which are not an attribute of the preferred stock but rather are granted by separate contract).

Redemption. "Redemption" is a general term that covers several different provisions. These provisions are united by the fact that each involves the repurchase of shares by the company for an amount specified in the contract.

---

1. This is simply the number of shares of common stock into which the outstanding shares of preferred stock could be converted (16,972,726) divided by the total number of shares of common stock assuming such conversion (30,417,552).

Venture capital contracts often contain provisions giving the venture capitalists an option to force the repurchase of their shares. Such an option — commonly known as a "put" — usually takes effect only after the passage of several years from the date of the investment, and the redemption price is often the same as the original issue price, though it may contain a small premium. Venture capital agreements sometimes — though rarely — give the company the right to redeem the shares owned by the venture capitalists. Such a provision — known as a "call" — allows the entrepreneur to exit, presuming that it is able to muster the necessary funds. Because call provisions would allow entrepreneurs to redeem the venture capitalists' shares when the company is very successful, venture capitalists typically will not enter into investments that contain a call provision.

Red Hat did not have the right to "call" the shares of preferred stock, but the Red Hat preferred shareholders bargained for limited put rights. The rights were limited because they could not be asserted until 2004, and even then they would be phased in according to a schedule providing for redemption of one-third of the shares every year for three years. Like so many other provisions in the contracts, these redemption rights are designed to protect the venture capitalists from potential abuse by the entrepreneur. The staggered nature of the redemption may limit its effectiveness, but it is rare for these provisions to be invoked. Instead, they serve as leverage in negotiations with the entrepreneur because they are accompanied by an implicit threat that the venture capitalists will withdraw if the entrepreneur does not behave properly.

Registration Rights. Among the various potential means of exit, venture capitalists typically earn the highest financial and reputational returns from investments in firms that go public. Most venture investors, however, do not sell their shares in IPOs. Instead, they typically exit investments within a few years after the IPO, either by selling the shares or distributing them to their fund investors. Any offering or sale of securities in the United States — including sales by venture capitalists — must be registered with the SEC unless the offering or sale is exempt from the registration requirements. Ostensibly to ensure their ability to sell shares into the public capital markets, venture capitalists typically contract for so-called "registration rights," which require portfolio companies to register the offering of shares by venture capitalists under specified conditions.

Rights of First Refusal. The rights of first refusal granted to venture capitalists are a crucial control mechanism when used in conjunction with staged financing. The following provision shows how the outside investors in Red Hat maintain their level of investment in the company through several rounds of financing:

> The Company shall deliver to each Investor a written notice of any proposed or intended issuance, sale or exchange of [the Company's securities, which notice shall] . . . (iv) offer to issue and sell to or exchange with such Investor (A) a pro rata portion of the [s]ecurities determined by dividing the aggregate number of shares of Common Stock then held by such Investor (giving effect to the conversion of all shares of convertible preferred stock then held) by the total number of shares of Common Stock then outstanding (giving effect to the conversion of all outstanding shares of convertible preferred stock and the exercise of all vested options) (the "Basic Amount"), and (B) any additional portion of the Offered Securities attributable to the Basic Amounts of other Investors as such Investor

shall indicate it will purchase or acquire should the other Investors subscribe for less than their Basic Amounts (the "Undersubscription Amount").

Control and Governance of Red Hat

Prior to the IPO, the company had 80 common stockholders of record holding 26,889,652 shares. These shares of common stock were held primarily by three executive officers. Ewing (9,088,476), Young (9,081,826), and Matthew Szulik (1,063,678), Red Hat's president, collectively owned 19,233,980 shares, or 31.6 percent of the total shares (assuming conversion of the preferred stock into common stock). Perhaps more significantly, however, the outside investors held a majority of the company's stock. Its four largest outside investors — Batten (15,005,888), Greylock (8,723,866), Benchmark (5,815,910), and Intel (3,005,058) — collectively held 32,550,722 shares, or 53.5 percent of the total shares (again, assuming conversion).

In addition to the shares of common and preferred stock, the company had issued stock options and warrants for the purchase of shares of common stock. Options allow the holder to purchase a designated number of shares of stock at a fixed price. Typically, the price is set as the fair market value of the company's common stock on the date of the grant. If the value of the common stock increases with the passage of time, the holder of the option benefits. The warrants issued by Red Hat are similar to nonqualified stock options and have a nominal exercise price of $.0001 per share. As of July 31, 1999, there were outstanding stock options for the purchase of 5,762,188 shares of common stock and outstanding warrants for the purchase of 3,197,450 shares of common stock. The stock options have been issued primarily to employees, and the warrants were issued early in the company's life to three of its employees. Perhaps surprisingly, neither Young nor Ewing received stock options from the company prior to the IPO.

At the time of the IPO, Red Hat had a board of directors comprised of three insiders (Young, Ewing, and Szulik) and three outsiders (Frank Batten, Jr., William S. Kaiser, and Eric Hahn). Kaiser represents Greylock and Hahn is a partner in another venture capital firm. Each of the outside investors was added in connection with an investment in the company. Szulik was added in April 1999 — the same time as Hahn — perhaps to maintain balance between insiders and outsiders.

Executive compensation is determined by the compensation committee of the board of directors, which was comprised of the three outside directors. Only Young and Ewing earned over $100,000 in the fiscal year prior to the IPO. Young earned a salary of $161,458 and a bonus of $25,000, while Ewing earned a salary of $145,125 and a bonus of $20,000.

QUESTIONS

Prior to the IPO, would the entrepreneurs or the investors (or both) make the following decisions:

- Expanding Red Hat's product offerings?
- Merging with Microsoft? *ent/not investors*
- Selling shares by the venture capitalists?

- Converting preferred stock into common stock?
- Paying dividends? (Amount?) *neither*
- Expanding the size of the board of directors? *if 50% proportional w/ insiders & outsiders*
- Replacing Marc Ewing as a director? *neither*
- Replacing Marc Ewing as an officer? *neither*
- Increasing Bob Young's salary? *entr., not directors*

If the entrepreneurs want to get rid of the venture capitalists, how can they accomplish that?

Under what circumstances would the venture capitalists want to redeem their shares? *company doing well but not doing IPO.*

Under what circumstances would venture capitalists exercise their right of first refusal when a company issues additional shares? When wouldn't they?

CHAPTER
10

Directors' Duty of Care

Directors' duties were first developed by courts as a matter of common law. Only within the past 30 years have those duties been defined in most incorporation statutes. The Model Business Corporation Act (Model Act) first included a statement of the duty of care in 1974. *Report of Committee on Corporate Laws: Changes in the Model Business Corporation Act*, 30 Bus. Law. 501, 504-505 (1975). The Delaware General Corporation Law (DGCL) still does not contain any general statement of directors' duties. In Delaware such duties are strictly judge-made. This chapter explores the directors' duty of care.

Directors are subject to a duty of care that on the surface is similar to the duty of care imposed in tort law because it flows from the same fundamental principle — namely, that a person who undertakes an action that places others at risk of injury is under a duty to act carefully and is liable for the failure to do so. As Judge Ralph Winter has observed, however, the "business judgment rule" significantly limits the force of the duty of care in the corporate context:

> While it is often stated that corporate directors and officers will be liable for negligence in carrying out their corporate duties, all seem agreed that such a statement is misleading. Whereas an automobile driver who makes a mistake in judgment as to speed or distance injuring a pedestrian will likely be called upon to respond in damages, a corporate officer who makes a mistake in judgment as to economic conditions, consumer tastes or production line efficiency will rarely, if ever, be found liable for damages suffered by the corporation. Whatever the terminology, the fact is that liability is rarely imposed upon corporate directors or officers simply for bad judgment and this reluctance to impose liability for unsuccessful business decisions has been doctrinally labeled the business judgment rule.

Joy v. North, 692 F.2d 880, 885 (2d Cir. 1982).

But why would courts be reluctant to impose liability in the corporate context? Common justifications for the business judgment rule are that it avoids judicial interference in areas where judges have no expertise, and it encourages directors to serve by limiting their exposure to liability. These rationales for the business judgment rule are not entirely persuasive. Consider other contexts: the law does not limit the liability of doctors whose treatment decisions turn out badly by presuming that they are not practicing medicine negligently, or of home builders whose buildings collapse by presuming that they are not building negligently. Implicit in the business judgment rule is a policy judgment that permitting shareholders to enforce liability against directors for breach of the duty of care is not a good idea. But why not?

Chancellor Allen presents his view in the following case. Chancellor Allen wrote the *Gagliardi* opinion just before he left the bench to become a faculty member at the New York University School of Law. With the exception of the classic Dodge v. Ford Motor Co. case, discussed in the last Section of this chapter, all of the cases in this chapter were decided in Delaware. Over the past two decades, many states have adopted a statutory statement of the duty of care based on the Model Act. Although the Model Act first included such a statement in 1974, it did not attempt to codify the business judgment rule until 1998, when it bifurcated the standards applicable to corporate directors between "standards of conduct" (the duty of care) and "standards of liability" (the business judgment rule). *See* Model Act §§8.30-8.31. Cases arising under the Model Act have traditionally been analyzed in a manner similar to the Delaware cases, and they often cite major Delaware cases as precedents. Thus, the effect of the recent amendments to the Model Business Corporation Act (which have not yet been adopted by any state) is unclear.

GAGLIARDI v. TRIFOODS INTERNATIONAL, INC.

683 A.2d 1049
Court of Chancery of Delaware
July 19, 1996

ALLEN, Chancellor.

Currently before the Court is a motion to dismiss a shareholders action against the directors of TriFoods International, Inc. and certain partnerships and individuals that own stock in TriFoods. In broadest terms the motion raises the question what must a shareholder plead in order to state a derivative claim to recover corporate losses allegedly sustained by reason of "mismanagement" unaffected by directly conflicting financial interests?

Plaintiff, Eugene Gagliardi, is the founder of the TriFoods, Inc. and in 1990 he induced certain persons to invest in the company by buying its stock. In 1993 he was removed as Chairman of the board and his employment with the company terminated. He continues to own approximately 13% of the company's common stock. The business of the company has, according to the allegations of the complaint, deteriorated very badly since Mr. Gagliardi's ouster. . . .

COUNT IV: NEGLIGENT MISMANAGEMENT

This count, which is asserted against all defendants, alleges that "implementation of their grandiose scheme for TriFoods' future growth . . . in only eighteen months destroyed TriFoods." Plaintiff asserts that the facts alleged, which sketch that "scheme" and those results, constitute mismanagement and waste.

The allegations of Count IV are detailed. They assert most centrally that prior to his dismissal Gagliardi disagreed with Hart [Former President of Trifoods] concerning the wisdom of TriFoods manufacturing its products itself and disagreed strongly that the company should buy a plant in Pomfret, Connecticut and move its operations to that state. Plaintiff thought it foolish (and he alleges that it was negligent judgment) to borrow funds . . . for that purpose.

Plaintiff also alleges that Hart caused the company to acquire and fit-out a research or new product facility in Chadds Ford, Pennsylvania, which "duplicated one already available and under lease to Designer Foods [the predecessor name of TriFoods], and which was, therefore, a further waste of corporate assets."

Next, it is alleged that "defendants either acquiesced in or approved a reckless or grossly negligent sales commission to build volume."

Next, it is alleged that "Hart and the other defendants caused TriFoods to purchase [the exclusive rights to produce and sell a food product known as] Steak-umms from Heinz in April 1994." The price paid compared unfavorably with a transaction in 1980 in which this product had been sold and which earlier terms are detailed. "Defendants recklessly caused TriFoods to pay $15 million for Steak-umms alone (no plant, no equipment, etc.) which was then doing annual sales of only $28 million."

Next, it is alleged that "Hart caused TriFoods . . . to pay $125,000 to a consultant for its new name, logo and packaging."

Next, it is alleged that Hart destroyed customer relationships by supplying inferior products.

Next, it is alleged that "Hart refused to pay key manufacturers and suppliers . . . thus injuring TriFoods' trade relations." . . .

Do these allegations of Count IV state a claim upon which relief may be granted? In addressing that question, I start with what I take to be an elementary precept of corporation law: in the absence of facts showing self-dealing or improper motive, a corporate officer or director is not legally responsible to the corporation for losses that may be suffered as a result of a decision that an officer made or that directors authorized in good faith. There is a theoretical exception to this general statement that holds that some decisions may be so "egregious" that liability for losses they cause may follow even in the absence of proof of conflict of interest or improper motivation. The exception, however, has resulted in no awards of money judgments against corporate officers or directors in this jurisdiction and, to my knowledge, only the dubious holding in this Court of Gimbel v. Signal Companies, Inc., (Del. Ch.), 316 A.2d 599, aff'd (Del. Supr.) 316 A.2d 619 (1974), seems to grant equitable relief in the absence of a claimed conflict or improper motivation. Thus, to allege that a corporation has suffered a loss as a result of a lawful transaction, within the corporation's powers, authorized by a corporate fiduciary acting in a good faith pursuit of corporate purposes, does not state a claim for relief against that fiduciary no matter how foolish the investment may appear in retrospect.

The rule could rationally be no different. Shareholders can diversify the risks of their corporate investments. Thus, it is in their economic interest for the corporation to accept in rank order all positive net present value investment projects available to the corporation, starting with the highest risk adjusted rate of return first. Shareholders don't want (or shouldn't rationally want) directors to be risk averse. Shareholders' investment interests, across the full range of their diversifiable equity investments, will be maximized if corporate directors and managers honestly assess risk and reward and accept for the corporation the highest risk adjusted returns available that are above the firm's cost of capital.

But directors will tend to deviate from this rational acceptance of corporate risk if in authorizing the corporation to undertake a risky investment, the directors must assume some degree of personal risk relating to ex post facto claims of derivative liability for any resulting corporate loss.

Corporate directors of public companies typically have a very small proportionate ownership interest in their corporations and little or no incentive compensation. Thus, they enjoy (as residual owners) only a very small proportion of any "upside" gains earned by the corporation on risky investment projects. If, however, corporate directors were to be found liable for a corporate loss from a risky project on the ground that the investment was too risky (foolishly risky! stupidly risky! egregiously risky!—you supply the adverb), their liability would be joint and several for the whole loss (with I suppose a right of contribution). Given the scale of operation of modern public corporations, this stupefying disjunction between risk and reward for corporate directors threatens undesirable effects. Given this disjunction, only a very small probability of director liability based on "negligence", "inattention", "waste", etc., could induce a board to avoid authorizing risky investment projects to any extent! Obviously, it is in the shareholders' economic interest to offer sufficient protection to directors from liability for negligence, etc., to allow directors to conclude that, as a practical matter, there is no risk that, if they act in good faith and meet minimal proceduralist standards of attention, they can face liability as a result of a business loss.

The law protects shareholder investment interests against the uneconomic consequences that the presence of such second-guessing risk would have on director action and shareholder wealth in a number of ways. It authorizes corporations to pay for director and officer liability insurance and authorizes corporate indemnification in a broad range of cases, for example. But the first protection against a threat of sub-optimal risk acceptance is the so-called business judgment rule. That "rule" in effect provides that where a director is independent and disinterested, there can be no liability for corporate loss, unless the facts are such that no person could possibly authorize such a transaction if he or she were attempting in good faith to meet their duty. Saxe v. Brady, Del. Ch., 184 A.2d 602 (1962).

Thus, for example, it does not state a claim to allege that: (1) Hart caused the corporation to pay $125,000 to a consultant for the design of a new logo and packaging. On what possible basis might a corporate officer or director be put to the expense of defending such a claim? Nothing is alleged except that an expenditure of corporate funds for a corporate purpose was made. Whether that expenditure was wise or foolish, low risk or high risk is of no concern to this Court. What is alleged certainly does not bring the allegation to within shouting distance of the Saxe v. Brady principle. (2) Nor does an allegation that defendants acquiesced in a reckless commission structure "in order to build volume" state a claim; it alleges no conflicting interest or improper motivation, nor does it state facts that might come within the Saxe v. Brady principle. It alleges only an ordinary business decision with a pejorative characterization added. (3) The allegation of "duplication" of existing product research facilities similarly simply states a matter that falls within ordinary business judgment; that plaintiff regards the decision as unwise, foolish, or even stupid in the circumstances is not legally significant; indeed that others may look back on it and agree that it was stupid is legally unimportant, in my opinion. (4) That the terms of the purchase of "Steak-umms" seem to plaintiff unwise (especially when compared to the terms of a 1980 transaction involving that product) again fail utterly to state any legal claim. No self-interest, nor facts possibly disclosing improper motive or judgment satisfying the waste standard are alleged. Similarly, (5) the allegations of corporate loss resulting from harm to customer relations by delivery of poor product and (6) harm to supplier relations by poor payment practices, again state nothing that constitutes a legal claim. Certainly these allegations state facts that, if true, constitute either mistakes, poor judgment, or reflect hard choices facing a cash-pressed company, but where is the allegation of conflicting interest or suspect motivation? In the absence of such, where are the facts that, giving the pleader all reasonable inferences in his favor, might possibly make the Saxe v. Brady principle applicable? There are none. Nothing is alleged other than poor business practices. To permit the possibility of director liability on that basis would be very destructive of shareholder welfare in the long-term . . .

HOLDING:
poor business
judgment can
not & is not a
cause of action

Finally, . . . there is the allegation that despite warnings from plaintiff and despite the alleged fact that the Pomfret facility "was not reasonably fit" for the purpose, the directors authorized the purchase of the facility at a "grossly excessive" price in order to implement a business plan that would have the company manufacture some or all of its food products and that defendants caused the company to borrow substantial funds to accomplish that task. Once more there is no allegation of conflict of interest with respect to this transaction, nor is there any allegation of improper motivation in authorizing the transactions. There is, in effect, only an allegation that plaintiff believes the transaction represents poor business judgment and the conclusion that "no reasonable business person would have engaged in it." Thus this claim does attempt to plead the Saxe v. Brady test of corporate waste. . . .

For the foregoing reason Count IV of the amended complaint will be dismissed. . . .

A.   THE DECISION MAKING CONTEXT

The duty of care is primarily a procedural duty—that is, a duty to make decisions in good faith and in an informed manner. Except in extreme cases characterized as "waste," courts rarely challenge the substance of a board decision. The following case illustrates the application of the duty of care and the business judgment rule to decision making in the context of a fundamental transaction, here the sale of a company. This is one of the few cases anywhere that imposes liability on board members based on breach of the duty of care, and it is therefore well known in corporate boardrooms.

SMITH v. VAN GORKOM
488 A.2d 858
Supreme Court of Delaware (en banc)
January 29, 1985

HORSEY, Justice (for the majority).

This appeal from the Court of Chancery involves a class action brought by shareholders of the defendant Trans Union Corporation ("Trans Union" or "the

Company"), originally seeking rescission of a cash-out merger of Trans Union into the defendant New T Company ("New T"), a wholly-owned subsidiary of the defendant, Marmon Group, Inc. ("Marmon"). . . .

We hold: (1) that the Board's decision, reached September 20, 1980, to approve the proposed cash-out merger was not the product of an informed business judgment; (2) that the Board's subsequent efforts to amend the Merger Agreement and take other curative action were ineffectual, both legally and factually; and (3) that the Board did not deal with complete candor with the stockholders by failing to disclose all material facts, which they knew or should have known, before securing the stockholders' approval of the merger.

I. . . .

Trans Union was a publicly-traded, diversified holding company, the principal earnings of which were generated by its railcar leasing business. During the period here involved, the Company had a cash flow of hundreds of millions of dollars annually. However, the Company had difficulty in generating sufficient taxable income to offset increasingly large investment tax credits (ITCs). Accelerated depreciation deductions had decreased available taxable income against which to offset accumulating ITCs. The Company took these deductions, despite their effect on usable ITCs, because the rental price in the railcar leasing market had already impounded the purported tax savings.

In the late 1970's, together with other capital-intensive firms, Trans Union lobbied in Congress to have ITCs refundable in cash to firms which could not fully utilize the credit. During the summer of 1980, defendant Jerome W. Van Gorkom, Trans Union's Chairman and Chief Executive Officer, testified and lobbied in Congress for refundability of ITCs and against further accelerated depreciation. By the end of August, Van Gorkom was convinced that Congress would neither accept the refundability concept nor curtail further accelerated depreciation. . . .

On August 27, 1980, Van Gorkom met with Senior Management of Trans Union. Van Gorkom reported on his lobbying efforts in Washington and his desire to find a solution to the tax credit problem more permanent than a continued program of acquisitions. Various alternatives were suggested and discussed preliminarily, including the sale of Trans Union to a company with a large amount of taxable income.

Donald Romans, Chief Financial Officer of Trans Union, stated that his department had done a "very brief bit of work on the possibility of a leveraged buy-out." This work had been prompted by a media article which Romans had seen regarding a leveraged buy-out by management. The work consisted of a "preliminary study" of the cash which could be generated by the Company if it participated in a leveraged buy-out. As Romans stated, this analysis "was a very first and rough cut at seeing whether a cash flow would support what might be considered a high price for this type of transaction."

On September 5, at another Senior Management meeting which Van Gorkom attended, Romans again brought up the idea of a leveraged buy-out as a "possible strategic alternative" to the Company's acquisition program. Romans and Bruce S. Chelberg, President and Chief Operating Officer of Trans Union, had been working on the matter in preparation for the meeting. According to

Romans: They did not "come up" with a price for the Company. They merely "ran the numbers" at $50 a share and at $60 a share with the "rough form" of their cash figures at the time. Their "figures indicated that $50 would be very easy to do but $60 would be very difficult to do under those figures." This work did not purport to establish a fair price for either the Company or 100% of the stock. It was intended to determine the cash flow needed to service the debt that would "probably" be incurred in a leveraged buy-out, based on "rough calculations" without "any benefit of experts to identify what the limits were to that, and so forth." These computations were not considered extensive and no conclusion was reached.

At this meeting, Van Gorkom stated that he would be willing to take $55 per share for his own 75,000 shares. He vetoed the suggestion of a leveraged buy-out by Management, however, as involving a potential conflict of interest for Management. Van Gorkom, a certified public accountant and lawyer, had been an officer of Trans Union for 24 years, its Chief Executive Officer for more than 17 years, and Chairman of its Board for 2 years. It is noteworthy in this connection that he was then approaching 65 years of age and mandatory retirement. . . .

Van Gorkom decided to meet with Jay A. Pritzker, a well-known corporate takeover specialist and a social acquaintance. However, rather than approaching Pritzker simply to determine his interest in acquiring Trans Union, Van Gorkom assembled a proposed per share price for sale of the Company and a financing structure by which to accomplish the sale. Van Gorkom did so without consulting either his Board or any members of Senior Management except one: Carl Peterson, Trans Union's Controller. Telling Peterson that he wanted no other person on his staff to know what he was doing, but without telling him why, Van Gorkom directed Peterson to calculate the feasibility of a leveraged buy-out at an assumed price per share of $55. Apart from the Company's historic stock market price,[5] and Van Gorkom's long association with Trans Union, the record is devoid of any competent evidence that $55 represented the per share intrinsic value of the Company.

Having thus chosen the $55 figure, based solely on the availability of a leveraged buy-out, Van Gorkom multiplied the price per share by the number of shares outstanding to reach a total value of the Company of $690 million. Van Gorkom told Peterson to use this $690 million figure and to assume a $200 million equity contribution by the buyer. Based on these assumptions, Van Gorkom directed Peterson to determine whether the debt portion of the purchase price could be paid off in five years or less if financed by Trans Union's cash flow as projected in the Five Year Forecast, and by the sale of certain weaker divisions identified in a study done for Trans Union by the Boston Consulting Group ("BCG study"). Peterson reported that, of the purchase price, approximately $50-80 million would remain outstanding after five years. Van Gorkom was disappointed, but decided to meet with Pritzker nevertheless.

Van Gorkom arranged a meeting with Pritzker at the latter's home on Saturday, September 13, 1980. Van Gorkom prefaced his presentation by stating to

---

5. The common stock of Trans Union was traded on the New York Stock Exchange. Over the five year period from 1975 through 1979, Trans Union's stock had traded within a range of a high of $39½ and a low of $24¼. Its high and low range for 1980 through September 19 (the last trading day before announcement of the merger) was $38¼-$29½.

Pritzker: "Now as far as you are concerned, I can, I think, show how you can pay a substantial premium over the present stock price and pay off most of the loan in the first five years. . . . If you could pay $55 for this Company, here is a way in which I think it can be financed."

Van Gorkom then reviewed with Pritzker his calculations based upon his proposed price of $55 per share. Although Pritzker mentioned $50 as a more attractive figure, no other price was mentioned. However, Van Gorkom stated that to be sure that $55 was the best price obtainable, Trans Union should be free to accept any better offer. Pritzker demurred, stating that his organization would serve as a "stalking horse" for an "auction contest" only if Trans Union would permit Pritzker to buy 1,750,000 shares of Trans Union stock at market price which Pritzker could then sell to any higher bidder. After further discussion on this point, Pritzker told Van Gorkom that he would give him a more definite reaction soon.

On Monday, September 15, Pritzker advised Van Gorkom that he was interested in the $55 cash-out merger proposal and requested more information on Trans Union. Van Gorkom agreed to meet privately with Pritzker, accompanied by Peterson, Chelberg, and Michael Carpenter, Trans Union's consultant from the Boston Consulting Group. The meetings took place on September 16 and 17. Van Gorkom was "astounded that events were moving with such amazing rapidity."

On Thursday, September 18, Van Gorkom met again with Pritzker. At that time, Van Gorkom knew that Pritzker intended to make a cash-out merger offer at Van Gorkom's proposed $55 per share. Pritzker instructed his attorney, a merger and acquisition specialist, to begin drafting merger documents. There was no further discussion of the $55 price. However, the number of shares of Trans Union's treasury stock to be offered to Pritzker was negotiated down to one million shares; the price was set at $38 — 75 cents above the per share price at the close of the market on September 19. At this point, Pritzker insisted that the Trans Union Board act on his merger proposal within the next three days, stating to Van Gorkom: "We have to have a decision by no later than Sunday [evening, September 21] before the opening of the English stock exchange on Monday morning." Pritzker's lawyer was then instructed to draft the merger documents, to be reviewed by Van Gorkom's lawyer, "sometimes with discussion and sometimes not, in the haste to get it finished."

On Friday, September 19, Van Gorkom, Chelberg, and Pritzker consulted with Trans Union's lead bank regarding the financing of Pritzker's purchase of Trans Union. The bank indicated that it could form a syndicate of banks that would finance the transaction. On the same day, Van Gorkom retained James Brennan, Esquire, to advise Trans Union on the legal aspects of the merger. Van Gorkom did not consult with William Browder, a Vice-President and director of Trans Union and former head of its legal department, or with William Moore, then the head of Trans Union's legal staff.

On Friday, September 19, Van Gorkom called a special meeting of the Trans Union Board for noon the following day. He also called a meeting of the Company's Senior Management to convene at 11:00 A.M., prior to the meeting of the Board. No one, except Chelberg and Peterson, was told the purpose of the meetings. Van Gorkom did not invite Trans Union's investment banker, Salomon Brothers or its Chicago-based partner, to attend.

Of those present at the Senior Management meeting on September 20, only Chelberg and Peterson had prior knowledge of Pritzker's offer. Van Gorkom disclosed the offer and described its terms, but he furnished no copies of the proposed Merger Agreement. Romans announced that his department had done a second study which showed that, for a leveraged buy-out, the price range for Trans Union stock was between $55 and $65 per share. Van Gorkom neither saw the study nor asked Romans to make it available for the Board meeting.

Senior Management's reaction to the Pritzker proposal was completely negative. No member of Management, except Chelberg and Peterson, supported the proposal. Romans objected to the price as being too low;[6] he was critical of the timing and suggested that consideration should be given to the adverse tax consequences of an all-cash deal for low-basis shareholders; and he took the position that the agreement to sell Pritzker one million newly-issued shares at market price would inhibit other offers, as would the prohibitions against soliciting bids and furnishing inside information to other bidders. Romans argued that the Pritzker proposal was a "lock up" and amounted to "an agreed merger as opposed to an offer." Nevertheless, Van Gorkom proceeded to the Board meeting as scheduled without further delay.

Ten directors served on the Trans Union Board, five inside (defendants Bonser, O'Boyle, Browder, Chelberg, and Van Gorkom) and five outside (defendants Wallis, Johnson, Lanterman, Morgan and Reneker). All directors were present at the meeting, except O'Boyle, who was ill. Of the outside directors, four were corporate chief executive officers and one was the former Dean of the University of Chicago Business School. None was an investment banker or trained financial analyst. All members of the Board were well informed about the Company and its operations as a going concern. They were familiar with the current financial condition of the Company, as well as operating and earnings projections reported in the recent Five Year Forecast. The Board generally received regular and detailed reports and was kept abreast of the accumulated investment tax credit and accelerated depreciation problem.

Van Gorkom began the Special Meeting of the Board with a twenty-minute oral presentation. Copies of the proposed Merger Agreement were delivered too late for study before or during the meeting. He reviewed the Company's ITC and depreciation problems and the efforts theretofore made to solve them. He discussed his initial meeting with Pritzker and his motivation in arranging that meeting. Van Gorkom did not disclose to the Board, however, the methodology by which he alone had arrived at the $55 figure, or the fact that he first proposed the $55 price in his negotiations with Pritzker.

Van Gorkom outlined the terms of the Pritzker offer as follows: Pritzker would pay $55 in cash for all outstanding shares of Trans Union stock upon completion of which Trans Union would be merged into New T Company, a subsidiary wholly-owned by Pritzker and formed to implement the merger; for a period

---

6. Van Gorkom asked Romans to express his opinion as to the $55 price. Romans stated that he "thought the price was too low in relation to what he could derive for the company in a cash sale, particularly one which enabled us to realize the values of certain subsidiaries and independent entities."

of 90 days, Trans Union could receive, but could not actively solicit, competing offers; the offer had to be acted on by the next evening, Sunday, September 21; Trans Union could only furnish to competing bidders published information, and not proprietary information; the offer was subject to Pritzker obtaining the necessary financing by October 10, 1980; if the financing contingency were met or waived by Pritzker, Trans Union was required to sell to Pritzker one million newly-issued shares of Trans Union at $38 per share.

Van Gorkom took the position that putting Trans Union "up for auction" through a 90-day market test would validate a decision by the Board that $55 was a fair price. He told the Board that the "free market will have an opportunity to judge whether $55 is a fair price." Van Gorkom framed the decision before the Board not as whether $55 per share was the highest price that could be obtained, but as whether the $55 price was a fair price that the stockholders should be given the opportunity to accept or reject.

Attorney Brennan advised the members of the Board that they might be sued if they failed to accept the offer and that a fairness opinion was not required as a matter of law.

Romans attended the meeting as chief financial officer of the Company. He told the Board that he had not been involved in the negotiations with Pritzker and knew nothing about the merger proposal until the morning of the meeting; that his studies did not indicate either a fair price for the stock or a valuation of the Company; that he did not see his role as directly addressing the fairness issue; and that he and his people "were trying to search for ways to justify a price in connection with such a [leveraged buy-out] transaction, rather than to say what the shares are worth." Romans testified:

> I told the Board that the study ran the numbers at 50 and 60, and then the subsequent study at 55 and 65, and that was not the same thing as saying that I have a valuation of the company at X dollars. But it was a way — a first step towards reaching that conclusion.

Romans told the Board that, in his opinion, $55 was "in the range of a fair price," but "at the beginning of the range."

Chelberg, Trans Union's President, supported Van Gorkom's presentation and representations. . . .

The Board meeting of September 20 lasted about two hours. Based solely upon Van Gorkom's oral presentation, Chelberg's supporting representations, Romans' oral statement, Brennan's legal advice, and their knowledge of the market history of the Company's stock, the directors approved the proposed Merger Agreement. However, the Board later claimed to have attached two conditions to its acceptance: (1) that Trans Union reserved the right to accept any better offer that was made during the market test period; and (2) that Trans Union could share its proprietary information with any other potential bidders. While the Board now claims to have reserved the right to accept any better offer received after the announcement of the Pritzker agreement (even though the minutes of the meeting do not reflect this), it is undisputed that the Board did not reserve the right to actively solicit alternate offers.

The Merger Agreement was executed by Van Gorkom during the evening of September 20 at a formal social event that he hosted for the opening of the

Chicago Lyric Opera. Neither he nor any other director read the agreement prior to its signing and delivery to Pritzker. . . .

On Monday, September 22, the Company issued a press release announcing that Trans Union had entered into a "definitive" Merger Agreement with an affiliate of the Marmon Group, Inc., a Pritzker holding company. Within 10 days of the public announcement, dissent among Senior Management over the merger had become widespread. Faced with threatened resignations of key officers, Van Gorkom met with Pritzker, who agreed to several modifications of the Agreement. Pritzker was willing to do so provided that Van Gorkom could persuade the dissidents to remain on the Company payroll for at least six months after consummation of the merger.

Van Gorkom reconvened the Board on October 8 and secured the directors' approval of the proposed amendments — sight unseen. The Board also authorized the employment of Salomon Brothers, its investment banker, to solicit other offers for Trans Union during the proposed "market test" period.

The next day, October 9, Trans Union issued a press release announcing: (1) that Pritzker had obtained "the financing commitments necessary to consummate" the merger with Trans Union; (2) that Pritzker had acquired one million shares of Trans Union common stock at $38 per share; (3) that Trans Union was now permitted to actively seek other offers and had retained Salomon Brothers for that purpose; and (4) that if a more favorable offer were not received before February 1, 1981, Trans Union's shareholders would thereafter meet to vote on the Pritzker proposal.

It was not until the following day, October 10, that the actual amendments to the Merger Agreement were prepared by Pritzker and delivered to Van Gorkom for execution. As will be seen, the amendments were considerably at variance with Van Gorkom's representations of the amendments to the Board on October 8; and the amendments placed serious constraints on Trans Union's ability to negotiate a better deal and withdraw from the Pritzker agreement. Nevertheless, Van Gorkom proceeded to execute what became the October 10 amendments to the Merger Agreement without conferring further with the Board members and apparently without comprehending the actual implications of the amendments. . . .

Salomon Brothers' efforts over a three-month period from October 21 to January 21 produced only one serious suitor for Trans Union — General Electric Credit Corporation ("GE Credit"), a subsidiary of the General Electric Company. However, GE Credit was unwilling to make an offer for Trans Union unless Trans Union first rescinded its Merger Agreement with Pritzker. When Pritzker refused, GE Credit terminated further discussions with Trans Union in early January.

In the meantime, in early December, the investment firm of Kohlberg, Kravis, Roberts & Co. ("KKR"), the only other concern to make a firm offer for Trans Union, withdrew its offer under circumstances hereinafter detailed.

On December 19, this litigation was commenced and, within four weeks, the plaintiffs had deposed eight of the ten directors of Trans Union, including Van Gorkom, Chelberg and Romans, its Chief Financial Officer. On January 21, Management's Proxy Statement for the February 10 shareholder meeting was mailed to Trans Union's stockholders. On January 26, Trans Union's Board met and, after a lengthy meeting, voted to proceed with the Pritzker merger. The Board also approved for mailing, "on or about January 27," a Supplement to its Proxy Statement. The Supplement purportedly set forth all information relevant to the Pritzker Merger Agreement, which had not been divulged in the first Proxy Statement. . . .

On February 10, the stockholders of Trans Union approved the Pritzker merger proposal. Of the outstanding shares, 69.9% were voted in favor of the merger; 7.25% were voted against the merger; and 22.85% were not voted.

II.

We turn to the issue of the application of the business judgment rule to the September 20 meeting of the Board.

The Court of Chancery concluded from the evidence that the Board of Directors' approval of the Pritzker merger proposal fell within the protection of the business judgment rule. The Court found that the Board had given sufficient time and attention to the transaction, since the directors had considered the Pritzker proposal on three different occasions, on September 20, and on October 8, 1980 and finally on January 26, 1981. On that basis, the Court reasoned that the Board had acquired, over the four-month period, sufficient information to reach an informed business judgment on the cash-out merger proposal. . . .

The Court of Chancery made but one finding; *i.e.*, that the Board's conduct over the entire period from September 20 through January 26, 1981 was not reckless or improvident, but informed. This ultimate conclusion was premised upon three subordinate findings, one explicit and two implied. The Court's explicit finding was that Trans Union's Board was "free to turn down the Pritzker proposal" not only on September 20 but also on October 8, 1980 and on January 26, 1981. The Court's implied, subordinate findings were: (1) that no legally binding agreement was reached by the parties until January 26; and (2) that if a higher offer were to be forthcoming, the market test would have produced it, and Trans Union would have been contractually free to accept such higher offer. However, the Court offered no factual basis or legal support for any of these findings; and the record compels contrary conclusions. . . .

We think the concept of gross negligence is . . . the proper standard for determining whether a business judgment reached by a board of directors was an informed one.

In the specific context of a proposed merger of domestic corporations, a director has a duty under 8 Del. C. §251(b), along with his fellow directors, to act in an informed and deliberate manner in determining whether to approve an agreement of merger before submitting the proposal to the stockholders. Certainly in the merger context, a director may not abdicate that duty by leaving to the shareholders alone the decision to approve or disapprove the agreement. . . .

III.

. . . [T]he defendants contend that what the directors did and learned subsequent to September 20 and through January 26, 1981, was properly taken into account by the Trial Court in determining whether the Board's judgment was an informed one. We disagree with this *post hoc* approach.

The issue of whether the directors reached an informed decision to "sell" the Company on September 20, 1980 must be determined only upon the basis of the information then reasonably available to the directors and relevant to their decision to accept the Pritzker merger proposal. This is not to say that the directors were precluded from altering their original plan of action, had they done so in an informed manner. What we do say is that the question of whether the directors reached an informed business judgment in agreeing to sell the Company, pursuant to the terms of the September 20 Agreement presents, in reality, two questions: (A) whether the directors reached an informed business judgment on September 20, 1980; and (B) if they did not, whether the directors' actions taken subsequent to September 20 were adequate to cure any infirmity in their action taken on September 20. . . .

-A-

On the record before us, we must conclude that the Board of Directors did not reach an informed business judgment on September 20, 1980 in voting to "sell" the Company for $55 per share pursuant to the Pritzker cash-out merger proposal. Our reasons, in summary, are as follows:

The directors (1) did not adequately inform themselves as to Van Gorkom's role in forcing the "sale" of the Company and in establishing the per share purchase price; (2) were uninformed as to the intrinsic value of the Company; and (3) given these circumstances, at a minimum, were grossly negligent in approving the "sale" of the Company upon two hours' consideration, without prior notice, and without the exigency of a crisis or emergency.

As has been noted, the Board based its September 20 decision to approve the cash-out merger primarily on Van Gorkom's representations. None of the directors, other than Van Gorkom and Chelberg, had any prior knowledge that the purpose of the meeting was to propose a cash-out merger of Trans Union. No members of Senior Management were present, other than Chelberg, Romans and Peterson; and the latter two had only learned of the proposed sale an hour earlier. . . .

Without any documents before them concerning the proposed transaction, the members of the Board were required to rely entirely upon Van Gorkom's 20-minute oral presentation of the proposal. No written summary of the terms of the merger was presented; the directors were given no documentation to support the adequacy of $55 price per share for sale of the Company; and the Board had before it nothing more than Van Gorkom's statement of his understanding of the substance of an agreement which he admittedly had never read, nor which any member of the Board had ever seen.

Under 8 Del. C. §141(e), "directors are fully protected in relying in good faith on reports made by officers." The term "report" has been liberally construed to include reports of informal personal investigations by corporate officers. However, there is no evidence that any "report," as defined under §141(e), concerning the Pritzker proposal, was presented to the Board on September 20. Van Gorkom's oral presentation of his understanding of the terms of the proposed Merger Agreement, which he had not seen, and Romans' brief oral statement of his preliminary study regarding the feasibility of a leveraged buy-out of Trans Union do not qualify as §141(e) "reports" for these reasons: The former lacked substance because Van Gorkom was basically uninformed as to the essential provisions of the very document about which he was talking. Romans' statement was irrelevant to the issues before the Board since it did not purport to be a valuation study. At a minimum for a report to enjoy the status conferred by §141(e), it must be pertinent to the subject matter upon which a board is called to act, and otherwise be entitled to good faith, not blind, reliance. . . .

The defendants rely on the following factors to sustain the Trial Court's finding that the Board's decision was an informed one: (1) the magnitude of the premium or spread between the $55 Pritzker offering price and Trans Union's current market price of $38 per share; (2) the amendment of the Agreement as submitted on September 20 to permit the Board to accept any better offer during the "market test" period; (3) the collective experience and expertise of the Board's "inside" and "outside" directors; and (4) their reliance on Brennan's legal advice that the directors might be sued if they rejected the Pritzker proposal. We discuss each of these grounds seriatim:

(1)

A substantial premium may provide one reason to recommend a merger, but in the absence of other sound valuation information, the fact of a premium alone does not provide an adequate basis upon which to assess the fairness of an offering price. Here, the judgment reached as to the adequacy of the premium was based on a comparison between the historically depressed Trans Union market price and the amount of the Pritzker offer. Using market price as a basis for concluding that the premium adequately reflected the true value of the Company was a clearly faulty, indeed fallacious, premise, as the defendants' own evidence demonstrates.

The record is clear that before September 20, Van Gorkom and other members of Trans Union's Board knew that the market had consistently undervalued the worth of Trans Union's stock, despite steady increases in the Company's operating income in the seven years preceding the merger. . . .

The parties do not dispute that a publicly-traded stock price is solely a measure of the value of a minority position and, thus, market price represents only the value of a single share. Nevertheless, on September 20, the Board assessed the adequacy of the premium over market, offered by Pritzker, solely by comparing it with Trans Union's current and historical stock price.

Indeed, as of September 20, the Board had no other information on which to base a determination of the intrinsic value of Trans Union as a going concern. As of September 20, the Board had made no evaluation of the Company designed to value the entire enterprise, nor had the Board ever previously considered selling the Company or consenting to a buy-out merger. Thus, the adequacy of a premium is indeterminate unless it is assessed in terms of other competent and sound valuation information that reflects the value of the particular business.

Despite the foregoing facts and circumstances, there was no call by the Board, either on September 20 or thereafter, for any valuation study or documentation of the $55 price per share as a measure of the fair value of the Company in a cash-out context. . . .

We do not imply that an outside valuation study is essential to support an informed business judgment; nor do we state that fairness opinions by independent investment bankers are required as a matter of law. Often insiders familiar with the business of a going concern are in a better position than are outsiders to gather relevant information; and under appropriate circumstances, such directors may be fully protected in relying in good faith upon the valuation reports of their management. . . .

The record also establishes that the Board accepted without scrutiny Van Gorkom's representation as to the fairness of the $55 price per share for sale of the Company—a subject that the Board had never previously considered. The Board thereby failed to discover that Van Gorkom had suggested the $55 price to Pritzker and, most crucially, that Van Gorkom had arrived at the $55 figure based on calculations designed solely to determine the feasibility of a leveraged buy-out.[19] No questions were raised either as to the tax implications of a cash-out merger or how the price for the one million share option granted Pritzker was calculated. . . .

None of the directors, Management or outside, were investment bankers or financial analysts. Yet the Board did not consider recessing the meeting until a later hour that day (or requesting an extension of Pritzker's Sunday evening deadline) to give it time to elicit more information as to the sufficiency of the offer, either from inside Management (in particular Romans) or from Trans Union's own investment banker, Salomon Brothers, whose Chicago specialist in merger and acquisitions was known to the Board and familiar with Trans Union's affairs.

(2)

This brings us to the post-September 20 "market test" upon which the defendants ultimately rely to confirm the reasonableness of their September 20 decision to accept the Pritzker proposal. In this connection, the directors present a two-part argument: (a) that by making a "market test" of Pritzker's $55 per share offer a condition of their September 20 decision to accept his offer, they cannot be found to have acted impulsively or in an uninformed manner on September 20; and (b) that the adequacy of the $17 premium for sale of the Company was conclusively established over the following 90 to 120 days by the most reliable evidence available—the marketplace. . . .

Again, the facts of record do not support the defendants' argument. There is no evidence: (a) that the Merger Agreement was effectively amended to give the Board freedom to put Trans Union up for auction sale to the highest bidder; or (b) that a public auction was in fact permitted to occur. . . .

(3)

The directors' unfounded reliance on both the premium and the market test as the basis for accepting the Pritzker proposal undermines the defendants' remaining contention that the Board's collective experience and sophistication was a sufficient basis for finding that it reached its September 20 decision with informed, reasonable deliberation. . . .

---

19. As of September 20 the directors did not know: that Van Gorkom had arrived at the $55 figure alone, and subjectively, as the figure to be used by Controller Peterson in creating a feasible structure for a leveraged buy-out by a prospective purchaser; that Van Gorkom had not sought advice, information or assistance from either inside or outside Trans Union directors as to the value of the Company as an entity or the fair price per share for 100% of its stock; that Van Gorkom had not consulted with the Company's investment bankers or other financial analysts; that Van Gorkom had not consulted with or confided in any officer or director of the Company except Chelberg; and that Van Gorkom had deliberately chosen to ignore the advice and opinion of the members of his Senior Management group regarding the adequacy of the $55 price.

(4)

Part of the defense is based on a claim that the directors relied on legal advice rendered at the September 20 meeting by James Brennan, Esquire, who was present at Van Gorkom's request. Unfortunately, Brennan did not appear and testify at trial even though his firm participated in the defense of this action. . . .

Several defendants testified that Brennan advised them that Delaware law did not require a fairness opinion or an outside valuation of the Company before the Board could act on the Pritzker proposal. If given, the advice was correct. However, that did not end the matter. Unless the directors had before them adequate information regarding the intrinsic value of the Company, upon which a proper exercise of business judgment could be made, mere advice of this type is meaningless; and, given this record of the defendants' failures, it constitutes no defense here. . . .

We conclude that Trans Union's Board was grossly negligent in that it failed to act with informed reasonable deliberation in agreeing to the Pritzker merger proposal on September 20; and we further conclude that the Trial Court erred as a matter of law in failing to address that question before determining whether the directors' later conduct was sufficient to cure its initial error. . . .

-B-

We now examine the Board's post-September 20 conduct for the purpose of determining . . . whether it was informed and not grossly negligent. . . .

(1)

The public announcement of the Pritzker merger resulted in an "en masse" revolt of Trans Union's Senior Management. The head of Trans Union's tank car operations (its most profitable division) informed Van Gorkom that unless the merger were called off, fifteen key personnel would resign.

Instead of reconvening the Board, Van Gorkom again privately met with Pritzker, informed him of the developments, and sought his advice. Pritzker then made the following suggestions for overcoming Management's dissatisfaction: (1) that the Agreement be amended to permit Trans Union to solicit, as well as receive, higher offers; and (2) that the shareholder meeting be postponed from early January to February 10, 1981. In return, Pritzker asked Van Gorkom to obtain a commitment from Senior Management to remain at Trans Union for at least six months after the merger was consummated.

Van Gorkom then advised Senior Management that the Agreement would be amended to give Trans Union the right to solicit competing offers through January, 1981, if they would agree to remain with Trans Union. Senior Management was temporarily mollified; and Van Gorkom then called a special meeting of Trans Union's Board for October 8. . . .

In a brief session, the directors approved Van Gorkom's oral presentation of the substance of the proposed amendments, the terms of which were not reduced to writing until October 10. But rather than waiting to review the amendments, the Board again approved them sight unseen and adjourned, giving Van Gorkom authority to execute the papers when he received them. . . .

The next day, October 9, and before the Agreement was amended, Pritzker moved swiftly to off-set the proposed market test amendment. First, Pritzker informed Trans Union that he had completed arrangements for financing its acquisition and that the parties were thereby mutually bound to a firm purchase and sale arrangement. Second, Pritzker announced the exercise of his option to purchase one million shares of Trans Union's treasury stock at $38 per share — 75 cents above the current market price. Trans Union's Management responded the same day by issuing a press release announcing: (1) that all financing arrangements for Pritzker's acquisition of Trans Union had been completed; and (2) Pritzker's purchase of one million shares of Trans Union's treasury stock at $38 per share.

The next day, October 10, Pritzker delivered to Trans Union the proposed amendments to the September 20 Merger Agreement. Van Gorkom promptly proceeded to countersign all the instruments on behalf of Trans Union without reviewing the instruments to determine if they were consistent with the authority previously granted him by the Board. . . .

The October 10 amendments to the Merger Agreement did authorize Trans Union to solicit competing offers, but the amendments had more far-reaching effects. The most significant change was in the definition of the third-party "offer" available to Trans Union as a possible basis for withdrawal from its Merger Agreement with Pritzker. Under the October 10 amendments, a better offer was no longer sufficient to permit Trans Union's withdrawal. Trans Union was now permitted to terminate the Pritzker Agreement and abandon the merger only if, prior to February 10, 1981, Trans Union had either consummated a merger (or sale of assets) with a third party or had entered into a "definitive" merger agreement more favorable than Pritzker's and for a greater consideration — subject only to stockholder approval. Further, the "extension" of the market test period to February 10, 1981 was circumscribed by other amendments which required Trans Union to file its preliminary proxy statement on the Pritzker merger proposal by December 5, 1980 and use its best efforts to mail the statement to its shareholders by January 5, 1981. Thus, the market test period was effectively reduced, not extended.

(2)

Next, as to the "curative" effects of the Board's post-September 20 conduct, we review in more detail the reaction of Van Gorkom to the KKR proposal and the results of the Board-sponsored "market test."

The KKR proposal was the first and only offer received subsequent to the Pritzker Merger Agreement. . . .

. . . Romans' group worked with KKR to develop a proposal. It did so with Van Gorkom's knowledge and apparently grudging consent. On December 2, Kravis and Romans hand-delivered to Van Gorkom a formal letter-offer to purchase all of Trans Union's assets and to assume all of its liabilities for an aggregate cash consideration equivalent to $60 per share. The offer was contingent upon completing equity and bank financing of $650 million, which Kravis represented as 80% complete. The KKR letter made reference to discussions with major banks regarding the loan portion of the buy-out cost and stated that KKR was "confident that commitments for the bank financing . . . can be obtained within two or three weeks." The purchasing group was to include certain named key members of Trans Union's Senior Management, excluding

Van Gorkom, and a major Canadian company. Kravis stated that they were willing to enter into a "definitive agreement" under terms and conditions "substantially the same" as those contained in Trans Union's agreement with Pritzker. The offer was addressed to Trans Union's Board of Directors and a meeting with the Board, scheduled for that afternoon, was requested.

Van Gorkom's reaction to the KKR proposal was completely negative; he did not view the offer as being firm because of its financing condition. It was pointed out, to no avail, that Pritzker's offer had not only been similarly conditioned, but accepted on an expedited basis. Van Gorkom refused Kravis' request that Trans Union issue a press release announcing KKR's offer, on the ground that it might "chill" any other offer. Romans and Kravis left with the understanding that their proposal would be presented to Trans Union's Board that afternoon.

Within a matter of hours and shortly before the scheduled Board meeting, Kravis withdrew his letter-offer. He gave as his reason a sudden decision by the Chief Officer of Trans Union's rail car leasing operation to withdraw from the KKR purchasing group. Van Gorkom had spoken to that officer about his participation in the KKR proposal immediately after his meeting with Romans and Kravis. However, Van Gorkom denied any responsibility for the officer's change of mind.

At the Board meeting later that afternoon, Van Gorkom did not inform the directors of the KKR proposal because he considered it "dead." Van Gorkom did not contact KKR again until January 20, when faced with the realities of this lawsuit, he then attempted to reopen negotiations. KKR declined due to the imminence of the February 10 stockholder meeting. . . .

In the absence of any explicit finding by the Trial Court as to the reasonableness of Trans Union's directors' reliance on a market test and its feasibility, we may make our own findings based on the record. Our review of the record compels a finding that confirmation of the appropriateness of the Pritzker offer by an unfettered or free market test was virtually meaningless in the face of the terms and time limitations of Trans Union's Merger Agreement with Pritzker as amended October 10, 1980.

(3)

Finally, we turn to the Board's meeting of January 26, 1981. The defendant directors rely upon the action there taken to refute the contention that they did not reach an informed business judgment in approving the Pritzker merger. . . .

The Board's January 26 meeting was the first meeting following the filing of the plaintiffs' suit in mid-December and the last meeting before the previously-noticed shareholder meeting of February 10. All ten members of the Board and three outside attorneys attended the meeting. . . .

The Board could not remain committed to the Pritzker merger and yet recommend that its stockholders vote it down; nor could it take a neutral position and delegate to the stockholders the unadvised decision as to whether to accept or reject the merger. Under §251(b), the Board had but two options: (1) to proceed with the merger and the stockholder meeting, with the Board's recommendation of approval; or (2) to rescind its agreement with Pritzker, withdraw its approval of the merger, and notify its stockholders that the proposed shareholder meeting was cancelled. There is no evidence that the Board gave any consideration to these, its only legally viable alternative courses of action.

But the second course of action would have clearly involved a substantial risk — that the Board would be faced with suit by Pritzker for breach of contract based on its September 20 agreement as amended October 10. . . .

Upon the basis of the foregoing, we hold that the defendants' post-September conduct did not cure the deficiencies of their September 20 conduct. . . .

V.

The defendants ultimately rely on the stockholder vote of February 10 for exoneration. The defendants contend that the stockholders' "overwhelming" vote approving the Pritzker Merger Agreement had the legal effect of curing any failure of the Board to reach an informed business judgment in its approval of the merger. . . .

[T]his Court [has] held that corporate directors owe to their stockholders a fiduciary duty to disclose all facts germane to the transaction at issue in an atmosphere of complete candor. We defined "germane" in the tender offer context as all "information such as a reasonable stockholder would consider important in deciding whether to sell or retain stock." In reality, "germane" means material facts.

Applying this standard to the record before us, we find that Trans Union's stockholders were not fully informed of all facts material to their vote on the Pritzker Merger and that the Trial Court's ruling to the contrary is clearly erroneous. We list the material deficiencies in the proxy materials:

(1) The fact that the Board had no reasonably adequate information indicative of the intrinsic value of the Company, other than a concededly depressed market price, was without question material to the shareholders voting on the merger. . . .

(2) We find false and misleading the Board's characterization of the Romans report in the Supplemental Proxy Statement. The Supplemental Proxy stated:

> At the September 20, 1980 meeting of the Board of Directors of Trans Union, Mr. Romans indicated that while he could not say that $55.00 per share was an unfair price, he had prepared a preliminary report which reflected that the value of the Company was in the range of $55.00 to $65.00 per share.

Nowhere does the Board disclose that Romans stated to the Board that his calculations were made in a "search for ways to justify a price in connection with" a leveraged buy-out transaction, "rather than to say what the shares are worth," and that he stated to the Board that his conclusion thus arrived at "was not the same thing as saying that I have a valuation of the Company at X dollars." . . .

(3) We find misleading the Board's references to the "substantial" premium offered. . . . [T]he Board did not disclose its failure to assess the premium offered in terms of other relevant valuation techniques, thereby rendering questionable its determination as to the substantiality of the premium over an admittedly depressed stock market price. . . .

For the foregoing reasons, we conclude that the director defendants breached their fiduciary duty of candor by their failure to make true and correct disclosures of all information they had, or should have had, material to the transaction submitted for stockholder approval.

VI.

To summarize: we hold that the directors of Trans Union breached their fiduciary duty to their stockholders (1) by their failure to inform themselves of all information reasonably available to them and relevant to their decision to recommend the Pritzker merger; and (2) by their failure to disclose all material information such as a reasonable stockholder would consider important in deciding whether to approve the Pritzker offer. . . .

On remand, the Court of Chancery shall conduct an evidentiary hearing to determine the fair value of the shares represented by the plaintiffs' class, based on the intrinsic value of Trans Union on September 20, 1980. . . . Thereafter, an award of damages may be entered to the extent that the fair value of Trans Union exceeds $55 per share. . . .

Reversed and remanded for proceedings consistent herewith.

McNeilly, Justice, dissenting.

The majority opinion reads like an advocate's closing address to a hostile jury. And I say that not lightly. Throughout the opinion great emphasis is directed only to the negative, with nothing more than lip service granted the positive aspects of this case. . . .

The majority has spoken and has effectively said that Trans Union's Directors have been the victims of a "fast shuffle" by Van Gorkom and Pritzker. That is the beginning of the majority's comedy of errors. The first and most important error made is the majority's assessment of the directors' knowledge of the affairs of Trans Union and their combined ability to act in this situation under the protection of the business judgment rule.

Trans Union's Board of Directors consisted of ten men, five of whom were "inside" directors and five of whom were "outside" directors. . . . At the time the merger was proposed the inside five directors had collectively been employed by the Company for 116 years and had 68 years of combined experience as directors. [With one exception, the "outside" directors] were all chief executive officers of Chicago based corporations that were at least as large as Trans Union. The five "outside" directors had 78 years of combined experience as chief executive officers, and 53 years cumulative service as Trans Union directors. . . .

Directors of this caliber are not ordinarily taken in by a "fast shuffle." I submit they were not taken into this multi-million dollar corporate transaction without being fully informed and aware of the state of the art as it pertained to the entire corporate panorama of Trans Union. True, even directors such as these, with their business acumen, interest and expertise, can go astray. I do not believe that to be the case here. These men knew Trans Union like the back of their hands and were more than well qualified to make on the spot informed business judgments concerning the affairs of Trans Union, including a 100% sale of the corporation. Lest we forget, the corporate world of then and now operates on what is so aptly referred to as "the fast track." These men were at the time an integral part of that world, all professional business men, not intellectual figureheads. . . .

PROBLEM 10-1

Ziff-Davis describes itself as a "technology media" company. It publishes magazines like Macworld, PC Computing, and PC Magazine. But Ziff-Davis also has a popular Web site called ZDNet, and the company felt that its stock price was not fully reflecting the value of that asset. The solution? Ziff-Davis created two classes of common stock: "ZDNet Stock" has financial attributes that track the performance of the company's Internet assets (thus, ZDNet Stock is known as a "tracking stock") and "ZD Stock" represents the traditional publishing business and an 84 percent retained interest in the Web-based business. ZDNet has separate financial statements, but the terms for ZDNet stock are found in Ziff-Davis's charter.

On March 31, 1999, Ziff-Davis sold 10 million shares of ZDNet stock to the public for $19 a share. On the first day of trading, the price of ZDNet shares soared to $36 a share at the closing of the markets. (Also on that day, the price of ZD stock fell from $29 a share to $21.50.) The prospectus issued in conjunction with the sale of ZDNet stock contained the following "risk factor":

> Our charter does not contain any provisions governing how consideration received in connection with a merger or consolidation involving Ziff-Davis Inc. is to be allocated between holders of ZD stock and holders of ZDNet stock. Neither holders of ZD stock nor holders of ZDNet stock will have a separate class vote in any merger or consolidation so long as we divide the type and amount of consideration between holders of ZD stock and holders of ZDNet stock in a manner we determine, in our sole discretion, to be fair. In any such merger or consolidation, the different ways we may divide the consideration might have materially different results. As a result, the consideration to be received by holders of ZDNet stock in any such merger or consolidation may be materially less valuable than the consideration they would have received if they had a separate class vote on such merger or consolidation.

Assume that Ziff-Davis is considering a merger and that you are advising the board of directors. The directors want to allocate the proceeds of the merger among ZD stockholders and ZDNet stockholders fairly. They also want to insulate their decision from subsequent attack by qualifying for the business judgment rule. Who should make the allocation decision? Does it matter whether some directors hold a greater percentage of ZD stock than ZDNet stock?

B.   THE OVERSIGHT CONTEXT

As noted in the previous Section, the duty of care is primarily a procedural duty — that is, a duty to make decisions in a well-informed, careful manner. Part of the duty of care, though, is a duty to be informed about what is happening within the corporation — that is, to provide oversight. Although managers are making decisions about how to monitor the affairs of the corporation as part of their oversight duties, modern courts still distinguish between "decision making" and "oversight" cases. The new amendments to the Model Act codify the distinction. Although the standard of conduct under Model Act §8.30 is the same for both classes of cases (that is, to "discharge their duties with the care that a person in a like position would reasonably believe appropriate under similar circumstances"), the oversight function merits a unique standard of liability under new Model Act §8.31:

A director shall not be liable to the corporation or its shareholders for any decision to take or not to take action, or any failure to take any action, as a director, unless the party asserting liability in a proceeding establishes that . . . the challenged conduct consisted or was the result of . . . a sustained failure of the director to be informed about the business and affairs of the corporation, or other material failure of the director to discharge the oversight function.

Oversight cases often arise where employees of the corporation have engaged in illegal activities, and the corporation ultimately is forced to pay large penalties to the government or judgments or settlements to third parties arising from those illegal activities. Derivative plaintiffs then bring cases alleging that the directors breached their duty of care by failing to ensure that the corporation had an effective law compliance system and that the directors' failure caused the economic losses to the corporation. *Caremark*, which appears below, is an example of such a case. Other oversight cases arise because managers are "asleep at the wheel" while the corporation crashes. For example, the directors of Enron, WorldCom, Tyco, Qwest, and Imclone — spectacular corporate governance and financial failures of the year 2002 — were sued for a breach of the duty of care (among other claims) for failing to provide necessary oversight.

In the worst instances of neglect, a "figurehead director" lends his or her name to a corporation but assumes no responsibility for the affairs of the corporation. The now-classic example of such a case is Francis v. United Jersey Bank, 432 A.2d 814 (N.J. 1981), in which a director who was the widow of the company's founder paid on attention to the company, which allowed her two sons (the other directors) to misappropriate funds from the corporation. When the company went bankrupt and shareholders' stock became worthless, shareholders sought to recover money from the widow's estate, on the theory that her neglect of her corporate duties caused their loss. In the defense mounted by her estate, it was argued that the director "was old, was grief-stricken at the loss of her husband, sometimes consumed too much alcohol and was psychologically overborne by her sons." The court rejected the view that any of these facts mattered and found her to have violated her duty of care: "Because directors are bound to exercise ordinary care, they cannot set up as a defense lack of the knowledge needed to exercise the requisite degree of care." In fact, the duties the *Francis* court imposed as part of a director's oversight duties were not onerous: the court suggested a director should read board materials, particularly financial statements; attend board meetings; and ask questions. In the modern context, directors' oversight duties seem primarily to be ensuring that financial information gets to the board on a timely basis so that directors can determine if the company is "on target" financially; ensuring that there is reason to believe the company's financial reporting is accurate (that is, that the procedures in place make sense); and ensuring that the company has a functioning law compliance structure.

The following case became an instant classic when Chancellor Allen decided to revisit the law relating to oversight cases (again, just before he left the bench). The decision was quite controversial in corporate boardrooms, because it seemed to portend a new source of liability. Nevertheless, Chancellor Allen notes that the plaintiffs in this case probably would not have prevailed after a trial. You should consider whether the standards enunciated by Chancellor Allen impose substantial new burdens on directors. Also, an important aspect of the case is Chancellor Allen's interpretation of the Graham v. Allis-Chalmers case, 188 A.2d 125 (Del. 1963), which remains the Delaware Supreme Court standard for board-oversight cases.

In re CAREMARK INTERNATIONAL INC. DERIVATIVE LITIGATION

698 A.2d 959
Court of Chancery of Delaware
September 25, 1996

ALLEN, Chancellor.

Pending is a motion pursuant to Chancery Rule 23.1 to approve as fair and reasonable a proposed settlement of a consolidated derivative action on behalf of Caremark International, Inc. ("Caremark"). The suit involves claims that the members of Caremark's board of directors (the "Board") breached their fiduciary duty of care to Caremark in connection with alleged violations by Caremark employees of federal and state laws and regulations applicable to health care providers. . . .

Legally, evaluation of the central claim made entails consideration of the legal standard governing a board of directors' obligation to supervise or monitor corporate performance. For the reasons set forth below I conclude, in light of the discovery record, that there is a very low probability that it would be determined that the directors of Caremark breached any duty to appropriately monitor and supervise the enterprise. . . .

I. BACKGROUND

For these purposes I regard the following facts, suggested by the discovery record, as material. Caremark, a Delaware corporation with its headquarters in Northbrook, Illinois, was created in November 1992 when it was spun-off from Baxter International, Inc. ("Baxter") and became a publicly held company listed on the New York Stock Exchange. The business practices that created the problem pre-dated the spin-off. During the relevant period Caremark was involved in two main health care business segments, providing patient care and managed care services. As part of its patient care business, which accounted for the majority of Caremark's revenues, Caremark provided alternative site health care services, including infusion therapy, growth hormone therapy, HIV/AIDS-related treatments and hemophilia therapy. Caremark's managed care services included prescription drug programs and the operation of multi-specialty group practices.

A. EVENTS PRIOR TO THE GOVERNMENT INVESTIGATION

A substantial part of the revenues generated by Caremark's businesses is derived from third party payments, insurers, and Medicare and Medicaid reimbursement programs. The latter source of payments are subject to the terms of the Anti-Referral Payments Law ("ARPL"), which prohibits health care providers from paying any form of remuneration to induce the referral of Medicare or Medicaid patients. From its inception, Caremark entered into a variety of agreements with hospitals, physicians, and health care providers for advice and services, as well as distribution agreements with drug manufacturers, as had its predecessor prior to 1992. Specifically, Caremark did have a practice of entering into contracts for services (e.g., consultation agreements and research grants) with physicians at least some of whom prescribed or recommended services or products that Caremark provided to Medicare recipients and other patients. Such contracts were not prohibited by the ARPL but they obviously raised a possibility of unlawful "kickbacks."

As early as 1989, Caremark's predecessor issued an internal "Guide to Contractual Relationships" ("Guide") to govern its employees in entering into contracts with physicians and hospitals. The Guide tended to be reviewed annually by lawyers and updated. Each version of the Guide stated as Caremark's and its predecessor's policy that no payments would be made in exchange for or to induce patient referrals. But what one might deem a prohibited quid pro quo was not always clear. Due to a scarcity of court decisions interpreting the ARPL, however, Caremark repeatedly publicly stated that there was uncertainty concerning Caremark's interpretation of the law. . . .

B. GOVERNMENT INVESTIGATION AND RELATED LITIGATION

In August 1991, the [United States Department of Health and Human Services (HHS)] Office of the Inspector General ("OIG") initiated an investigation of Caremark's predecessor. Caremark's predecessor was served with a subpoena requiring the production of documents, including contracts between Caremark's predecessor and physicians (Quality Service Agreements ("QSAs")). Under the QSAs, Caremark's predecessor appears to have paid physicians fees for monitoring patients under Caremark's predecessor's care, including Medicare and Medicaid recipients. Sometimes apparently those monitoring patients were referring physicians, which raised ARPL concerns.

In March 1992, the Department of Justice ("DOJ") joined the OIG investigation and separate investigations were commenced by several additional federal and state agencies.

C. CAREMARK'S RESPONSE TO THE INVESTIGATION

During the relevant period, Caremark had approximately 7,000 employees and ninety branch operations. It had a decentralized management structure. By May 1991, however, Caremark asserts that it had begun making attempts to centralize its management structure in order to increase supervision over its branch operations.

The first action taken by management, as a result of the initiation of the OIG investigation, was an announcement that as of October 1, 1991, Caremark's predecessor would no longer pay management fees to physicians for services to Medicare and Medicaid patients. Despite this decision, Caremark asserts that its management, pursuant to advice, did not believe that such payments were illegal under the existing laws and regulations.

During this period, Caremark's Board took several additional steps consistent with an effort to assure compliance with company policies concerning the ARPL and the contractual forms in the Guide. . . .

Although there is evidence that inside and outside counsel had advised Care-mark's directors that their contracts were in accord with the law, Caremark recognized that some uncertainty respecting the correct interpretation of the law existed. In its 1992 annual report, Caremark disclosed the ongoing gov-ernment investigations, acknowledged that if penalties were imposed on the company they could have a material adverse effect on Caremark's business, and stated that no assurance could be given that its interpretation of the ARPL would prevail if challenged.

Throughout the period of the government investigations, Caremark had an internal audit plan designed to assure compliance with business and ethics policies. . . .

The Board appears to have been informed about . . . efforts to assure compliance with the law. . . .

D. FEDERAL INDICTMENTS AGAINST CAREMARK AND OFFICERS

On August 4, 1994, a federal grand jury in Minnesota issued a 47 page indict-ment charging Caremark, two of its officers (not the firm's chief officer), an individual who had been a sales employee of Genentech, Inc., and David R. Brown, a physician practicing in Minneapolis, with violating the ARPL over a lengthy period. According to the indictment, over $1.1 million had been paid to Brown to induce him to distribute Protropin, a human growth hormone drug marketed by Caremark. The substantial payments involved started, according to the allegations of the indictment, in 1986 and continued through 1993. Some payments were "in the guise of research grants", and others were "consulting agreements." The indictment charged, for example, that Dr. Brown performed virtually none of the consulting functions described in his 1991 agreement with Caremark, but was nevertheless neither required to return the money he had received nor precluded from receiving future funding from Caremark. In addi-tion the indictment charged that Brown received from Caremark payments of staff and office expenses, including telephone answering services and fax rental expenses.

In reaction to the Minnesota Indictment and the subsequent filing of this and other derivative actions in 1994, the Board met and was informed by manage-ment that the investigation had resulted in an indictment; Caremark denied any wrongdoing relating to the indictment and believed that the OIG investi-gation would have a favorable outcome. Management reiterated the grounds for its view that the contracts were in compliance with law.

Subsequently, five stockholder derivative actions were filed in this court and consolidated into this action. . . .

On September 21, 1994, a federal grand jury in Columbus, Ohio issued another indictment alleging that an Ohio physician had defrauded the Medi-care program by requesting and receiving $134,600 in exchange for referrals of patients whose medical costs were in part reimbursed by Medicare in violation of the ARPL. Although unidentified at that time, Caremark was the health care provider who allegedly made such payments. The indictment also charged that the physician, Elliot Neufeld, D.O., was provided with the services of a regis-tered nurse to work in his office at the expense of the infusion company, in addition to free office equipment.

An October 28, 1994 amended complaint in this action added allegations concerning the Ohio indictment as well as new allegations of over billing and inappropriate referral payments in connection with an action brought in Atlanta, Booth v. Rankin. . . .

E. SETTLEMENT NEGOTIATIONS

. . . Caremark began settlement negotiations with federal and state government entities in May 1995. In return for a guilty plea to a single count of mail fraud by the corporation, the payment of a criminal fine, the payment of substantial civil damages, and cooperation with further federal investigations on matters relating to the OIG investigation, the government entities agreed to negotiate a settlement that would permit Caremark to continue participating in Medicare and Medicaid programs. On June 15, 1995, the Board approved a settlement ("Government Settlement Agreement") with the DOJ, OIG, U.S. Veterans Administration, U.S. Federal Employee Health Benefits Program, federal Civilian Health and Medical Program of the Uniformed Services, and related state agencies in all fifty states and the District of Columbia. No senior officers or directors were charged with wrongdoing in the Government Settlement Agreement or in any of the prior indictments. In fact, as part of the sentencing in the Ohio action on June 19, 1995, the United States stipulated that no senior executive of Caremark participated in, condoned, or was willfully ignorant of wrongdoing in connection with the home infusion business practices. . . .

Settlement negotiations between the parties in this action commenced in May 1995 as well, based upon a letter proposal of the plaintiffs, dated May 16, 1995. These negotiations resulted in a memorandum of understanding ("MOU"), dated June 7, 1995, and the execution of the Stipulation and Agreement of Compromise and Settlement on June 28, 1995, which is the subject of this action. The MOU, approved by the Board on June 15, 1995, required the Board to adopt several resolutions, discussed below, and to create a new compliance committee. The Compliance and Ethics Committee has been reporting to the Board in accord with its newly specified duties. . . .

F. THE PROPOSED SETTLEMENT OF THIS LITIGATION

In relevant part the terms upon which these claims asserted are proposed to be settled are as follows:

1. That Caremark undertakes that it and its employees and agents not pay any form of compensation to a third party in exchange for the referral of a patient to a Caremark facility or service or the prescription of drugs marketed or distributed by Caremark for which reimbursement may be sought from Medicare, Medicaid, or a similar state reimbursement program;

2. That Caremark undertakes for itself and its employees and agents not to pay to or split fees with physicians, joint ventures, any business combination in which Caremark maintains a direct financial interest, or other health care providers with whom Caremark has a financial relationship or interest, in exchange for the referral of a patient to a Caremark facility or service or the prescription of drugs marketed or distributed by Caremark for which reimbursement may be sought from Medicare, Medicaid, or a similar state reimbursement program;

3. That the full Board shall discuss all relevant material changes in government health care regulations and their effect on relationships with health care providers on a semi-annual basis;

4. That Caremark's officers will remove all personnel from health care facilities or hospitals who have been placed in such facility for the purpose of providing remuneration in exchange for a patient referral for which reimbursement may be sought from Medicare, Medicaid, or a similar state reimbursement program;

5. That every patient will receive written disclosure of any financial relationship between Caremark and the health care professional or provider who made the referral;

6. That the Board will establish a Compliance and Ethics Committee of four directors, two of which will be non-management directors, to meet at least four times a year to effectuate these policies and monitor business segment compliance with the ARPL, and to report to the Board semi-annually concerning compliance by each business segment; and

7. That corporate officers responsible for business segments shall serve as compliance officers who must report semi-annually to the Compliance and Ethics Committee and, with the assistance of outside counsel, review existing contracts and get advanced approval of any new contract forms.

II. LEGAL PRINCIPLES

A. PRINCIPLES GOVERNING SETTLEMENTS OF DERIVATIVE CLAIMS

[T]his Court is now required to exercise an informed judgment whether the proposed settlement is fair and reasonable in the light of all relevant factors. On an application of this kind, this Court attempts to protect the best interests of the corporation and its absent shareholders, all of whom will be barred from future litigation on these claims if the settlement is approved. The parties proposing the settlement bear the burden of persuading the court that it is in fact fair and reasonable.

B. DIRECTORS' DUTIES TO MONITOR CORPORATE OPERATIONS

The complaint charges the director defendants with breach of their duty of attention or care in connection with the on-going operation of the corporation's business. The claim is that the directors allowed a situation to develop and continue which exposed the corporation to enormous legal liability and that in so doing they violated a duty to be active monitors of corporate performance. The complaint thus does not charge either director self-dealing or the more difficult loyalty-type problems arising from cases of suspect director motivation, such as entrenchment or sale of control contexts. The theory here advanced is possibly the most difficult theory in corporation law upon which a plaintiff might hope to win a judgment. . . .

[This case belongs to a] class of cases in which director liability for inattention is theoretically possible [when] a loss eventuates not from a decision but, from unconsidered inaction. Most of the decisions that a corporation, acting through its human agents, makes are, of course, not the subject of director attention. Legally, the board itself will be required only to authorize the most significant corporate acts or transactions: mergers, changes in capital structure, fundamental changes in business, appointment and compensation of the CEO, etc. As the facts of this case graphically demonstrate, ordinary business decisions that are made by officers and employees deeper in the interior of the organization can, however, vitally affect the welfare of the corporation and its ability to achieve its various strategic and financial goals. . . . Financial and organizational disasters such as these raise the question, what is the board's responsibility with respect to the organization and monitoring of the enterprise to assure that the corporation functions within the law to achieve its purposes?

Modernly this question has been given special importance by an increasing tendency, especially under federal law, to employ the criminal law to assure corporate compliance with external legal requirements, including environmental, financial, employee and product safety as well as assorted other health and safety regulations. In 1991, pursuant to the Sentencing Reform Act of 1984, the United States Sentencing Commission adopted Organizational Sentencing Guidelines which impact importantly on the prospective effect these criminal sanctions might have on business corporations. The Guidelines set forth a uniform sentencing structure for organizations to be sentenced for violation of federal criminal statutes and provide for penalties that equal or often massively exceed those previously imposed on corporations. The Guidelines offer powerful incentives for corporations today to have in place compliance programs to detect violations of law, promptly to report violations to appropriate public officials when discovered, and to take prompt, voluntary remedial efforts.

In 1963, the Delaware Supreme Court in Graham v. Allis-Chalmers Mfg. Co., addressed the question of potential liability of board members for losses experienced by the corporation as a result of the corporation having violated the anti-trust laws of the United States. There was no claim in that case that the directors knew about the behavior of subordinate employees of the corporation that had resulted in the liability. Rather, as in this case, the claim asserted was that the directors ought to have known of it and if they had known they would have been under a duty to bring the corporation into compliance with the law and thus save the corporation from the loss. The Delaware Supreme Court concluded that, under the facts as they appeared, there was no basis to find that the directors had breached a duty to be informed of the ongoing operations of the firm. In notably colorful terms, the court stated that "absent cause for suspicion there is no duty upon the directors to install and operate a corporate system of espionage to ferret out wrongdoing which they have no reason to suspect exists." The Court found that there were no grounds for suspicion in that case and, thus, concluded that the directors were blamelessly unaware of the conduct leading to the corporate liability.

How does one generalize this holding today? Can it be said today that, absent some ground giving rise to suspicion of violation of law, that corporate directors have no duty to assure that a corporate information gathering and reporting system[] exists which represents a good faith attempt to provide senior management and the Board with information respecting material acts, events or conditions within the corporation, including compliance with applicable statutes and regulations? I certainly do not believe so. I doubt that such a broad generalization of the *Graham* holding would have been accepted by the Supreme Court in 1963. The case can be more narrowly interpreted as standing for the proposition that, absent grounds to suspect deception, neither corporate boards nor senior officers can be charged with wrongdoing simply for assuming the integrity of employees and the honesty of their dealings on the company's behalf.

A broader interpretation of Graham v. Allis-Chalmers — that it means that a corporate board has no responsibility to assure that appropriate information and reporting systems are established by management — would not, in any event, be accepted by the Delaware Supreme Court in 1996, in my opinion. In stating the basis for this view, I start with the recognition that in recent years the Delaware Supreme Court has made it clear — especially in its jurisprudence concerning takeovers, from Smith v. Van Gorkom through Paramount Communications v. QVC — the seriousness with which the corporation law views the role of the corporate board. Secondly, I note the elementary fact that relevant and timely information is an essential predicate for satisfaction of the board's supervisory and monitoring role under Section 141 of the Delaware General Corporation Law. Thirdly, I note the potential impact of the federal organizational sentencing guidelines on any business organization. Any rational person attempting in good faith to meet an organizational governance responsibility would be bound to take into account this development and the enhanced penalties and the opportunities for reduced sanctions that it offers.

In light of these developments, it would, in my opinion, be a mistake to conclude that our Supreme Court's statement in *Graham* concerning "espionage" means that corporate boards may satisfy their obligation to be reasonably informed concerning the corporation, without assuring themselves that information and reporting systems exist in the organization that are reasonably designed to provide to senior management and to the board itself timely, accurate information sufficient to allow management and the board, each within its scope, to reach informed judgments concerning both the corporation's compliance with law and its business performance.

Obviously the level of detail that is appropriate for such an information system is a question of business judgment. And obviously too, no rationally designed information and reporting system will remove the possibility that the corporation will violate laws or regulations, or that senior officers or directors may nevertheless sometimes be misled or otherwise fail reasonably to detect acts material to the corporation's compliance with the law. But it is important that the board exercise a good faith judgment that the corporation's information and reporting system is in concept and design adequate to assure the board that appropriate information will come to its attention in a timely manner as a matter of ordinary operations, so that it may satisfy its responsibility.

Thus I am of the view that a director's obligation includes a duty to attempt in good faith to assure that a corporate information and reporting system, which the board concludes is adequate, exists, and that failure to do so under some circumstances may, in theory at least, render a director liable for losses caused by non-compliance with applicable legal standards. . . .

III. ANALYSIS OF THIRD AMENDED COMPLAINT AND SETTLEMENT

A. THE CLAIMS

On balance, after reviewing an extensive record in this case, including numerous documents and three depositions, I conclude that this settlement is fair and reasonable. In light of the fact that the Caremark Board already has a functioning committee charged with overseeing corporate compliance, the changes in corporate practice that are presented as consideration for the settlement do not impress one as very significant. Nonetheless, that consideration appears fully adequate to support dismissal of the derivative claims of director fault asserted, because those claims find no substantial evidentiary support in the record and quite likely were susceptible to a motion to dismiss in all events.

In order to show that the Caremark directors breached their duty of care by failing adequately to control Caremark's employees, plaintiffs would have to show either (1) that the directors knew or (2) should have known that violations of law were occurring and, in either event, (3) that the directors took no steps in a good faith effort to prevent or remedy that situation, and (4) that such failure proximately resulted in the losses complained of. . . .

1. Knowing violation of statute: Concerning the possibility that the Caremark directors knew of violations of law, none of the documents submitted for review, nor any of the deposition transcripts appear to provide evidence of it. . . . [T]he Board appears to have been informed by experts that the company's practices, while contestable, were lawful. There is no evidence that reliance on such reports was not reasonable. . . .

2. Failure to monitor: Since it does appear that the Board was to some extent unaware of the activities that led to liability, I turn to a consideration of the other potential avenue to director liability that the pleadings take: director inattention or "negligence." Generally where a claim of directorial liability for corporate loss is predicated upon ignorance of liability-creating activities within the corporation, as in *Graham* or in this case, in my opinion only a sustained or systematic failure of the board to exercise oversight — such as an utter failure to attempt to assure a reasonable information and reporting system exits — will establish the lack of good faith that is a necessary condition to liability. Such a test of liability — lack of good faith as evidenced by sustained or systematic failure of a director to exercise reasonable oversight — is quite high. But, a demanding test of liability in the oversight context is probably beneficial to corporate shareholders as a class, as it is in the board decision context, since it makes board service by qualified persons more likely, while continuing to act as a stimulus to good faith performance of duty by such directors.

Here the record supplies essentially no evidence that the director defendants were guilty of a sustained failure to exercise their oversight function. . . .

IV. Attorneys' Fees

The various firms of lawyers involved for plaintiffs seek an award of $1,025,000 in attorneys' fees and reimbursable expenses. . . .

In this case no factor points to a substantial fee, other than the amount and sophistication of the lawyer services required. There is only a modest substantive benefit produced; in the particular circumstances of the government activity there was realistically a very slight contingency faced by the attorneys at the time they expended time. . . .

In these circumstances, I conclude that an award of a fee determined by reference to the time expended at normal hourly rates plus a premium of 15% of that amount to reflect the limited degree of real contingency in the undertaking, is fair. Thus I will award a fee of $816,000 plus $53,000 of expenses advanced by counsel.

PROBLEM 10-2

Milan Panic was the founder and chief executive officer of ICN Pharmaceuticals (ICN), a large international manufacturer and distributor of pharmaceuticals. He was also a world-renowned chemist. In the early 1990s, Panic had served as prime minister of Yugoslavia. He was also a defendant in numerous sexual harassment lawsuits by ICN employees. According to an article in U.S. News & World Report, a female employee of ICN reported Panic's unwelcome advances to a senior ICN officer as early as 1990. Miriam Horn, *Sex and the CEO*, U.S. News and World Report (July 6, 1998). Over the next several years, ICN paid millions to settle multiple harassment suits against Panic. (The company reportedly paid $3.5 million in one case alone.)

Panic — whose name is pronounced "PAH-neesh" — denied allegations of sexual harassment, and company officials claimed that the lawsuits were attempts at extortion. The women who worked for Panic, however, told a different story. At least five women had filed complaints with the California Department of Fair Housing and Employment, and four of those filed lawsuits against ICN. Each of the complaints alleged that Panic has propositioned women employees for sex and retaliated against those who refused him.

When the board of directors first learned of the allegations is a matter of some dispute, but one director who was interviewed for the U.S. News story claimed that the board was unaware until January 1995, when the first lawsuit was filed. The board, comprised exclusively of men, formed a special committee to investigate the harassment claims, and that committee hired its own lawyers. The directors on the special committee did not personally speak with any employees, but in 1997 the committee concluded that the board of directors should take a more active role in enforcing the company's sexual harassment policy.

Panic is said to have developed a "cult of personality" at ICN. Indeed, according to the U.S. News story, one of the directors felt that the best way to fulfill his fiduciary duty to shareholders was to ensure that Panic did not get into trouble. Barbara Howar, a former correspondent for CBS news, described ICN's other managers as "obsequious and subservient to Panic." Bernard J. Wolfson, *A magnetic, maddening giant exiting O.C. stage*, Orange County Register (June 19, 2002). In short, Panic was the star CEO around which the company was built.

What additional facts relating to the foregoing situation would a shareholder plaintiff find most useful in mounting a case against the directors of ICN based on a breach of the duty of oversight?

C.   THE WASTE STANDARD

To this point, we have focused on procedural aspects of the duty of care — that is, what procedures the board must adopt when making decisions or monitoring events at the corporation. But are there instances in which the substance of a board decision is so awful that directors may be liable for breach of the duty of care? Even if the decisions were not motivated by self-interest? Even where there is no evidence that the managers failed to gather information? Courts often discuss this prospect by invoking the concept of "waste" of the corporation's assets. Other courts speak in terms of the rationality of the decision. An influential formulation by the Delaware Supreme Court states that "[a] board of directors enjoys a presumption of sound business judgment, and its decisions will not be disturbed if they can be attributed to any rational business purpose." Sinclair Oil Corp. v. Levien, 280 A.2d 717, 720 (Del. 1971).

Today this claim of "waste" often comes up in the context of executive compensation. Over the past few decades, the levels of executive compensation in the United States increased dramatically. Between 1960 and 1992, average CEO compensation in the United States grew from 50 times the average worker's salary to about 150 times that salary. These levels became politically controversial during the recessionary years of the early 1990s, leading the SEC to require companies to disclose more specific information on compensation of the CEO and the four most highly compensated executives, including deferred compensation such as stock options. Ironically, this disclosure may have led to even higher CEO salaries, as compensation experts and consultants used the increased financial transparency to convince CEOs that they were underpaid compared to other executives in the same field. The IRS has also tried to limit companies' incentives to pay exorbitant salaries by limiting the deductability of compensation over $1 million, unless the compensation is tied to performance goals. 26 U.S.C. §162m (1999). Despite these legislative efforts, a recent survey of executive compensation showed that CEOs of 350 large U.S. companies had a median salary and bonuses in excess of $1.5 million annually. When stock options are added, the figures become truly eye-popping, with some CEOs reaping hundreds of millions of dollars.

Executive compensation levels in the United States are also much higher than those in Europe or Japan, where the highest-paid executives typically earn only 20 to 30 times the lowest-paid workers in the company. By comparison, by 2002 many top executives in the United States earned over 500 times the lowest-paid workers in their companies. Indeed, executive compensation became an important issue in the 1998 merger between Daimler-Benz of Germany and Chrysler Corporation of the United States because the Chrysler CEO was paid a total compensation of about $11 million per year — about 200 times the average Chrysler worker — while his German counterpart, Jürgen Schrempp, was paid about one-fifth of that amount — only about 20 times the average Daimler-Benz worker.[1]

Increasing levels of executive compensation have been widely attributed to the desire of boards to retain proven (if not spectacular) executives in the face of a relative scarcity of top corporate managers. Given pliant boards, derivative plaintiffs have recently entered the fray, claiming that "excessive" salaries are a waste of corporate assets and thus a breach of the directors' duty of care. Such a claim was at issue in the litigation at the Disney Corporation, as described in the following case. In that litigation, plaintiffs challenged the terms of an employment agreement with Michael Ovitz as president of the Disney Corporation, under which Mr. Ovitz ultimately collected remuneration valued at

1. For more on the merger of Daimler and Chrysler, see the Case Study in Chapter 14.

$140 million (including stock options) for 14 months' employment. In February 2000 the Delaware Supreme Court upheld most of the Court of Chancery's first opinion dismissing the claims against the board for breach of the duty of care with respect to the decision-making process, waste, and breach of the duty of loyalty, but dismissed with leave to amend. The court did not find the case to be an easy one, stating that:

> This is potentially a very troubling case on the merits. On the one hand, it appears from the Complaint that: (a) the compensation and termination payout for Ovitz were exceedingly lucrative, if not luxurious, compared to Ovitz' value to the Company; and (b) the processes of the boards of directors in dealing with the approval and termination of the Ovitz Employment Agreement were casual, if not sloppy and perfunctory. On the other hand, the Complaint is so inartfully drafted that it was properly dismissed under our pleading standards for derivative suits. From what we can ferret out of this deficient pleading, the processes of the Old Board [approving the employment agreement] and the New Board [approving Ovitz's termination on favorable grounds] were hardly paradigms of good corporate governance practices. Moreover, the sheer size of the payout to Ovitz, as alleged, pushes the envelope of judicial respect for the business judgment of directors in making compensation decisions. Therefore, both as to the processes of the two Boards and the waste test, this is a close case.
>
> But our concerns about lavish executive compensation and our institutional aspirations that boards of directors of Delaware corporations live up to the highest standards of good corporate practices do not translate into a holding that these plaintiffs have set forth particularized facts [necessary] . . . under our law and our pleading requirements [for derivative litigation, which is the process by which fiduciary duty claims are brought].

Brehm v. Eisner, 746 A.2d 244, 249 (Del. 2000).
   With respect to the waste claim, the Court described its analysis as follows:

> The Complaint, in sum, contends that the Board committed waste by agreeing to the very lucrative payout to Ovitz under the non-fault termination provision because it had no obligation to him [since it could have terminated him "for cause"], thus taking the Board's decision outside the protection of the business judgment rule. Construed most favorably to plaintiffs, the Complaint contends that, by reason of the New Board's available arguments of resignation and good cause, it had the leverage to negotiate Ovitz down to a more reasonable payout than that guaranteed by his Employment Agreement. But the Complaint fails on its face to meet the waste test because it does not allege with particularity facts tending to show that no reasonable business person would have made the decision that the New Board made under these circumstances.

Brehm, 746 A.2d at 262.
   Still, the Court dismissed with leave to amend, while it was seemingly skeptical about whether the shareholder plaintiffs would be able to overcome the formidable protections of the business judgment rule regarding the terms of compensation. As you will see below, the Court of Chancery's most recent opinion, issued in 2003, suggests a more critical approach toward the actions of the Disney board. Much of this criticism was clearly fueled by the facts that plaintiffs uncovered and included in their Amended Complaint, but some of it was likely caused by the more searching inquiry being given to boards' actions generally

after Enron and WorldCom and similar instances of passive boards and failing companies. The Court of Chancery opinion now de-emphasizes waste, because other approaches for alleging and ultimately proving breaches of the duty of care have become viable.

In re THE WALT DISNEY COMPANY DERIVATIVE LITIGATION

825 A.2d 275
Court of Chancery of Delaware
May 28, 2003

CHANDLER, Chancellor.

In this derivative action filed on behalf of nominal defendant Walt Disney Company, plaintiffs allege that the defendant directors breached their fiduciary duties when they blindly approved an employment agreement with defendant Michael Ovitz and then, again without any review or deliberation, ignored defendant Michael Eisner's dealings with Ovitz regarding his non-fault termination. Plaintiffs seek rescission and/or money damages from defendants and Ovitz, or compensation for damages allegedly sustained by Disney and disgorgement of Ovitz's unjust enrichment. . . .

As will be explained in greater detail below, I conclude that plaintiffs' new complaint sufficiently pleads a breach of fiduciary duty by the Old and the New Disney Board of Directors[2] so as to withstand a motion to dismiss under Chancery Rules 23.1 and 12(b)(6). Stated briefly, plaintiffs' new allegations give rise to a cognizable question whether the defendant directors of the Walt Disney Company should be held personally liable to the corporation for a knowing or intentional lack of due care in the directors' decision-making process regarding Ovitz's employment and termination. It is rare when a court imposes liability on directors of a corporation for breach of the duty of care, and this Court is hesitant to second-guess the business judgment of a disinterested and independent board of directors. But the facts alleged in the new complaint do not implicate merely negligent or grossly negligent decision making by corporate directors. Quite the contrary; plaintiffs' new complaint suggests that the Disney directors failed to exercise *any* business judgment and failed to make *any* good faith attempt to fulfill their fiduciary duties to Disney and its stockholders. Allegations that Disney's directors abdicated all responsibility to consider appropriately an action of material importance to the corporation puts directly in question whether the board's decision-making processes were employed in a good faith effort to advance corporate interests. In short, the new complaint alleges facts implying that the Disney directors failed to "act in good faith and meet minimal proceduralist standards of attention." Based on the facts asserted in the new complaint, therefore, I believe plaintiffs have stated cognizable claims for which demand is excused and on which a more complete factual record is necessary.

2. The Disney Board of Directors changed from the time Ovitz was hired to the time of his non-fault termination. Therefore, the board at the time Ovitz was hired is referred to as the "Old Board," and the board at the time of the non-fault termination is the "New Board."

I. Procedural and Factual Background

As mentioned, this case involves an attack on decisions of the Walt Disney Company's board of directors, approving an executive compensation contract for Michael Ovitz, as well as impliedly approving a non-fault termination that resulted in an award to Ovitz (allegedly exceeding $140,000,000) after barely one year of employment. After the Supreme Court's remand regarding plaintiffs' first amended complaint, plaintiffs used the "tools at hand," a request for books and records as authorized under 8 Del. C. §220, to obtain information about the nature of the Disney Board's involvement in the decision to hire and, eventually, to terminate Ovitz. Using the information gained from that request, plaintiffs drafted and filed the new complaint, which is the subject of the pending motions. The facts, as alleged in the new complaint, portray a markedly different picture of the corporate processes that resulted in the Ovitz employment agreement than that portrayed in the first amended complaint. For that reason, it is necessary to set forth the repleaded facts in some detail. The facts set forth hereafter are taken directly from the new complaint and, for purposes of the present motions, are accepted as true. Of course, I hold no opinion as to the actual truth of any of the allegations set forth in the new complaint; nor do I hold any view as to the likely ultimate outcome on the merits of claims based on these asserted facts. I determine here *only* that the facts, if true, arguably support all three of plaintiffs' claims for relief, as asserted in the new complaint, and are sufficient to excuse demand and to state claims that warrant development of a full record.

A. THE DECISION TO HIRE OVITZ

Michael Eisner is the chief executive officer ("CEO") of the Walt Disney Company. In 1994, Eisner's second-in-command, Frank Wells, died in a helicopter crash. Two other key executives—Jeffrey Katzenberg and Richard Frank—left Disney shortly thereafter, allegedly because of Eisner's management style. Eisner began looking for a new president for Disney and chose Michael Ovitz. Ovitz was founder and head of CAA, a talent agency; he had never been an executive for a publicly owned entertainment company. He had, however, been Eisner's close friend for over twenty-five years.

Eisner decided unilaterally to hire Ovitz. On August 13, 1995, he informed three Old Board members—Stephen Bollenbach, Sanford Litvack, and Irwin Russell (Eisner's personal attorney)—of that fact. All three protested Eisner's decision to hire Ovitz. Nevertheless, Eisner persisted, sending Ovitz a letter on August 14, 1995, that set forth certain material terms of his prospective employment. Before this, neither the Old Board nor the compensation committee had ever discussed hiring Ovitz as president of Disney. No discussions or presentations were made to the compensation committee or to the Old Board regarding Ovitz's hiring as president of Walt Disney until September 26, 1995.

Before informing Bollenbach, Litvack, and Russell on August 13, 1995, Eisner collected information on his own, through his position as the Disney CEO, on the potential hiring of Ovitz. In an internal document created around July 7, 1995, concerns were raised about the number of stock options to be granted to Ovitz. The document warned that the number was far beyond the normal standards of both Disney and corporate America and would receive significant public criticism. Additionally, Graef Crystal, an executive compensation expert, informed board member Russell, via a letter dated August 12, 1995, that, generally speaking, a large signing bonus is hazardous because the full cost is borne immediately and completely even if the executive fails to serve the full term of employment. Neither of these documents, however, were submitted to either the compensation committee or the Old Board before hiring Ovitz. Disney prepared a draft employment agreement on September 23, 1995. A copy of the draft was sent to Ovitz's lawyers, but was not provided to members of the compensation committee.

The compensation committee, consisting of defendants Ignacio Lozano, Jr., Sidney Poitier, Russell, and Raymond Watson, met on September 26, 1995, for just under an hour. Three subjects were discussed at the meeting, one of which was Ovitz's employment. According to the minutes, the committee spent the least amount of time during the meeting discussing Ovitz's hiring. In fact, it appears that more time was spent on discussions of paying $250,000 to Russell for his role in securing Ovitz's employment than was actually spent on discussions of Ovitz's employment. The minutes show that several issues were raised and discussed by the committee members concerning Russell's fee. All that occurred during the meeting regarding Ovitz's employment was that Russell reviewed the employment terms with the committee and answered a few questions. Immediately thereafter, the committee adopted a resolution of approval.

No copy of the September 23, 1995 draft employment agreement was actually given to the committee. Instead, the committee members received, at the meeting itself, a rough summary of the agreement. The summary, however, was incomplete. It stated that Ovitz was to receive options to purchase five million shares of stock, but did not state the exercise price. The committee also did not receive any of the materials already produced by Disney regarding Ovitz's possible employment. No spreadsheet or similar type of analytical document showing the potential payout to Ovitz throughout the contract, or the possible cost of his severance package upon a non-fault termination, was created or presented. Nor did the committee request or receive any information as to how the draft agreement compared with similar agreements throughout the entertainment industry, or information regarding other similarly situated executives in the same industry.

The committee also lacked the benefit of an expert to guide them through the process. Graef Crystal, an executive compensation expert, had been hired to provide advice to Disney on Eisner's new employment contract. Even though he had earlier told Russell that large signing bonuses, generally speaking, can be hazardous, neither he nor any other expert had been retained to assist Disney regarding Ovitz's hiring. Thus, no presentations, spreadsheets, written analyses, or opinions were given by any expert for the compensation committee to rely upon in reaching its decision. Although Crystal was not retained as a compensation consultant on the Ovitz contract, he later lamented his failure to intervene and produce a spreadsheet showing the potential costs of the employment agreement.

The compensation committee was informed that further negotiations would occur and that the stock option grant would be delayed until the final contract was worked out. The committee approved the general terms and conditions of the employment agreement, but did not condition their approval on being able to review the final agreement. Instead, the committee granted Eisner the authority to approve the final terms and conditions of the contract as long as they were within the framework of the draft agreement.

Immediately after the compensation committee met on September 26, the Old Board met. Again, no expert was present to advise the board. Nor were any documents produced to the board for it to review before the meeting regarding the Ovitz contract. The board did not ask for additional information to be collected or presented regarding Ovitz's hiring. According to the minutes, the compensation committee did not make any recommendation or report to the board concerning its resolution to hire Ovitz. Nor did Russell, who allegedly secured Ovitz's employment, make a presentation to the board. The minutes of the meeting were fifteen pages long, but only a page and a half covered Ovitz's possible employment. A portion of that page and a half was spent discussing the $250,000 fee paid to Russell for obtaining Ovitz. According to the minutes, the Old Board did not ask any questions about the details of Ovitz's salary, stock options, or possible termination. The Old Board also did not consider the consequences of a termination, or the various payout scenarios that existed. Nevertheless, at that same meeting, the Old Board decided to appoint Ovitz president of Disney. Final negotiation of the employment agreement was left to Eisner, Ovitz's close friend for over twenty-five years.

B. NEGOTIATION OF THE EMPLOYMENT AGREEMENT

Ovitz was officially hired on October 1, 1995, and began serving as Disney's president, although he did not yet have an executed employment agreement with Disney. On October 16, 1995, the compensation committee was informed, via a brief oral report, that negotiations were ongoing with Ovitz. The committee was not given a draft of the employment agreement either before or during the meeting. A summary similar to the one given on September 26, 1995, was presented. The committee did not seek any further information about the negotiations or about the terms and conditions of Ovitz's agreement, nor was any information proffered regarding the scope of the non-fault termination provision. And, as before, no expert was available to advise the committee as to the employment agreement.

Negotiations continued among Ovitz, Eisner, and their attorneys. The lawyers circulated drafts on October 3, October 10, October 16, October 20, October 23, and December 12, 1995. The employment agreement was physically executed between Michael Ovitz and the Walt Disney Company on December 12, 1995. The employment agreement, however, was backdated to October 1, 1995, the day Ovitz began working as Disney's president. Additionally, the stock option agreement associated with the employment agreement was executed by Eisner (for Disney) on April 2, 1996. Ovitz did not countersign the stock option agreement until November 15, 1996, when he was already discussing his plans to leave Disney's employ. Neither the Old Board nor the compensation committee reviewed or approved the final employment agreement before it was executed and made binding upon Disney.

C. THE FINAL VERSION OF OVITZ'S EMPLOYMENT AGREEMENT

The final version of Ovitz's employment agreement differed significantly from the drafts summarized to the compensation committee on September 26, 1995, and October 16, 1995. First, the final version caused Ovitz's stock options to be "in the money" when granted. The September 23rd draft agreement set the exercise price at the stock price on October 2, 1995, the day after Ovitz began as president. On October 16, 1995, the compensation committee agreed to change the exercise price to the price on that date (October 16, 1995), a price similar to that on October 2nd. The agreement was not signed until December 12, 1995, however, at which point the value of Disney stock had increased by eight percent — from $56.875 per share on October 16th to $61.50 per share on December 12th. The overall stock market, according to the Dow Jones Industrial Average, had also increased by about eight percent at the same time. By waiting to sign the agreement until December, but not changing the date of the exercise price, Ovitz had stock options that instantly were "in the money." This allowed Ovitz to play a "win-win" game at Disney's expense — if the market price of Disney stock had fallen between October 16 and December 12, Ovitz could have demanded a downward adjustment to the option exercise price; if the price had risen (as in fact it had) Ovitz would receive "in the money" options.

Another difference in the final version of Ovitz's employment agreement concerned the circumstances surrounding a non-fault termination. The September 23rd draft agreement stated that non-fault termination benefits would only be provided if Disney wrongfully terminated Ovitz, or Ovitz died or became disabled. The October 16th draft contained a very similar definition. These were the only two drafts of which the compensation committee was made aware. The final version of the agreement, however, offered Ovitz a non-fault termination as long as Ovitz did not act with gross negligence or malfeasance. Therefore, instead of protecting Ovitz from a wrongful termination by Disney, Ovitz was able to receive the full benefits of a non-fault termination, even if he acted negligently or was unable to perform his duties, as long as his behavior did not reach the level of gross negligence or malfeasance. Additionally, a non-compete clause was not included within the agreement should Ovitz leave Disney's employ.

The employment agreement had a term of five years. Ovitz was to receive a salary of $1 million per year, a potential bonus each year from $0 to $10 million, and a series of stock options (the "A" options) that enabled Ovitz to purchase three million shares of Disney stock at the October 16, 1995 exercise price. The options were to vest at one million per year for three years beginning September 30, 1998. At the end of the contract term, if Disney entered into a new contract with Ovitz, he was entitled to the "B" options, an additional two million shares. There was no requirement, however, that Disney enter into a new contract with Ovitz.

Should a non-fault termination occur, however, the terms of the final version of the employment agreement appeared to be even more generous. Under a non-fault termination, Ovitz was to receive his salary for the remainder of the contract, discounted at a risk-free rate keyed to Disney's borrowing costs. He was also to receive a $7.5 million bonus for each year remaining on his contract, discounted at the same risk-free rate, even though no set bonus amount was guaranteed in the contract. Additionally, all of his "A" stock options were to vest immediately, instead of waiting for the final three years of his contract for them to vest. The final benefit of the non-fault termination was a lump sum "termination payment" of $10 million. The termination payment was equal to the payment Ovitz would receive should he complete his full five-year term with Disney, but not receive an offer for a new contract. Graef Crystal opined in the January 13, 1997, edition of California Law Business that "the contract was most valuable to Ovitz the sooner he left Disney."

D. OVITZ'S PERFORMANCE AS DISNEY'S PRESIDENT

Ovitz began serving as president of Disney on October 1, 1995, and became a Disney director in January 1996. Ovitz's tenure as Disney's president proved unsuccessful. Ovitz was not a good second-in-command, and he and Eisner were both aware of that fact. Eisner told defendant Watson, via memorandum, that he (Eisner) "had made an error in judgment in who I brought into the company." Other company executives were reported in the December 14, 1996 edition of the New York Times as saying that Ovitz had an excessively lavish office, an imperious management style, and had started a feud with NBC during his tenure. Even Ovitz admitted, during a September 30, 1996 interview on "Larry King Live," that he knew "about 1% of what I need to know."

Even though admitting that he did not know his job, Ovitz studiously avoided attempts to be educated. Eisner instructed Ovitz to meet weekly with Disney's chief financial officer, defendant Bollenbach. The meetings were scheduled to occur each Monday at 2 P.M., but every week Ovitz cancelled at the last minute. Bollenbach was quoted in a December 1996 issue of Vanity Fair as saying that Ovitz failed to meet with him at all, "didn't understand the duties of an executive at a public company[,] and he didn't want to learn."

Instead of working to learn his duties as Disney's president, Ovitz began seeking alternative employment. He consulted Eisner to ensure that no action would be taken against him by Disney if he sought employment elsewhere. Eisner agreed that the best thing for Disney, Eisner, and Ovitz was for Ovitz to gain employment elsewhere. Eisner wrote to the chairman of Sony Japan that Ovitz could negotiate with Sony without any repercussions from Disney. Ovitz and Sony began negotiations for Ovitz to become head of Sony's entertainment business, but the negotiations ultimately failed. With the possibility of having another company absorb the cost of Ovitz's departure now gone, Eisner and Ovitz began in earnest to discuss a non-fault termination.

E. THE NON-FAULT TERMINATION

Ovitz wanted to leave Disney, but could only terminate his employment if one of three events occurred: (1) he was not elected or retained as president and a director of Disney; (2) he was assigned duties materially inconsistent with his role as president; or (3) Disney reduced his annual salary or failed to grant his stock options, pay him discretionary bonuses, or make any required compensation payment. None of these three events occurred. If Ovitz resigned outright, he might have been liable to Disney for damages and would not have received the benefits of the non-fault termination. He also desired to protect his reputation when exiting from his position with Disney. Eisner agreed to help Ovitz depart Disney without sacrificing any of his benefits. Eisner and Ovitz worked together as close personal friends to have Ovitz receive a non-fault termination. Eisner stated in a letter to Ovitz that: "I agree with you that we must work together to assure a smooth transition and deal with the public relations brilliantly. I am committed to make this a win-win situation, to keep our friendship intact, to be positive, to say and write only glowing things. . . . Nobody ever needs to know anything other than positive things from either of us. This can all work out!"

Eisner, Litvack, and Ovitz met at Eisner's apartment on December 11, 1996, to finalize Ovitz's non-fault termination. The new complaint alleges that the New Board was aware that Eisner was negotiating with Ovitz the terms of his separation. Litvack sent a letter to Ovitz on December 12, 1996, stating that, by "mutual agreement," (1) Ovitz's term of employment would end on January 31, 1997; and (2) "this letter will for all purposes of the Employment Agreement be given the same effect as though there had been a 'Non-Fault Termination,' and the Company will pay you, on or before February 5, 1997, all amounts due you under the Employment Agreement, including those under Section 11(c) thereof. In addition, the stock options granted pursuant to Option A, will vest as of January 31, 1997 and will expire in accordance with their terms on September 30, 2002." On December 12, 1996, Ovitz's departure from Disney became public. Neither the New Board of Directors nor the compensation committee had been consulted or given their approval for a non-fault termination. In addition, no record exists of any action by the New Board once the non-fault termination became public on December 12, 1996.

On December 27, 1996, Litvack sent Ovitz a new letter superseding the December 12th letter. The December 27th letter stated that Ovitz's termination would "be treated as a 'Non-Fault Termination.'" This differed from the December 12th letter, which treated Ovitz's termination "as though there had been a 'Non-Fault Termination.'" It also made the termination of Ovitz's employment and his resignation as a Disney director effective as of the close of business on December 27th, instead of on January 31, 1997, as in the December 12th letter. Additionally, it listed the amount payable to Ovitz as $38,888,230.77, and stated that the "A" options to purchase three million shares of Disney vested on December 27th, instead of January 31, 1997, as in the December 12th letter. Both Eisner and Litvack signed the letter. Again, however, neither the New Board nor the compensation committee reviewed or approved the December 27th letter. No record exists of any New Board action after the December 27th letter became public, nor had any board member raised any questions or concerns since the original December 12th letter became public.

According to the new complaint, Disney's bylaws required board approval for Ovitz's non-fault termination. Eisner and Litvack allegedly did not have the authority to provide for a non-fault termination without board consent. No documents or board minutes currently exist showing an affirmative decision by the New Board or any of its committees to grant Ovitz a non-fault termination. The New Board was already aware that Eisner was granting the non-fault termination as of December 12, 1996, the day it became public. No record of any action by the New Board affirming or questioning that decision by Eisner either before or after that date has been produced. There are also no records showing that alternatives to a non-fault termination were ever evaluated by the New Board or by any of its committees. . . .

III. ANALYSIS

The primary issue before the Court is whether plaintiffs' new complaint survives the Rule 23.1 motion to dismiss under the second prong of Aronson v. Lewis. In order for demand to be excused under the second prong of *Aronson*, plaintiffs must allege particularized facts that raise doubt about whether the challenged transaction is entitled to the protection of the business judgment rule. Plaintiffs may rebut the presumption that the board's decision is entitled to deference by raising a reason to doubt whether the board's action was taken on an informed basis or whether the directors honestly and in good faith believed that the action was in the best interests of the corporation. Thus, plaintiffs must plead particularized facts sufficient to raise (1) a reason to doubt that the action was taken honestly and in good faith or (2) a reason to doubt that the board was adequately informed in making the decision.

Defendants contend that the new complaint cannot be read reasonably to allege any fiduciary duty violation other than, at most, a breach of the directors' duty of due care. They further assert that even if the complaint states a breach of the directors' duty of care, Disney's charter provision, based on 8 Del. C. §102(b)(7), would apply and the individual directors would be protected from personal damages liability for any breach of their duty of care. A §102(b)(7) provision in a corporation's charter does not "eliminate or limit the liability of a director: (i) [f]or any breach of the director's duty of loyalty to the corporation or its stockholders; (ii) for acts or omissions not in good faith or which involve intentional misconduct or a knowing violation of the law; (iii) under §174 of this title; or (iv) for any transaction from which the director derived an improper personal benefit." A fair reading of the new complaint, in my opinion, gives rise to a reason to doubt whether the board's actions were taken honestly and in good faith, as required under the second prong of *Aronson*. Since acts or omissions not undertaken honestly and in good faith, or which involve intentional misconduct, do not fall within the protective ambit of §102(b)(7), I cannot dismiss the complaint based on the exculpatory Disney charter provision.

Defendants also argue that Ovitz's employment agreement was a reasonable exercise of business judgment. They argue that Ovitz's previous position as head of CAA required a large compensation package to entice him to become Disney's president. As to the non-fault termination, defendants contend that that decision was reasonable in that the board wished to avoid protracted litigation with Ovitz. The Court is appropriately hesitant to second-guess the business judgment of a disinterested and independent board of directors. As alleged in the new complaint, however, the facts belie any assertion that the New or Old Boards exercised *any* business judgment or made *any* good faith attempt to fulfill the fiduciary duties they owed to Disney and its shareholders.

A. THE OLD AND NEW BOARDS

According to the new complaint, Eisner unilaterally made the decision to hire Ovitz, even in the face of internal documents warning of potential adverse publicity and with three members of the board of directors initially objecting to the hiring when Eisner first broached the idea in August 1995. No draft employment agreements were presented to the compensation committee or to the

Disney board for review before the September 26, 1995 meetings. The compensation committee met for less than an hour on September 26, 1995, and spent most of its time on two other topics, including the compensation of director Russell for helping secure Ovitz's employment. With respect to the employment agreement itself, the committee received only a summary of its terms and conditions. No questions were asked about the employment agreement. No time was taken to review the documents for approval. Instead, the committee approved the hiring of Ovitz and directed Eisner, Ovitz's close friend, to carry out the negotiations with regard to certain still unresolved and significant details.

The Old Board met immediately after the committee did. Less than one and one-half pages of the fifteen pages of Old Board minutes were devoted to discussions of Ovitz's hiring as Disney's new president. Actually, most of that time appears to have been spent discussing compensation for director Russell. No presentations were made to the Old Board regarding the terms of the draft agreement. No questions were raised, at least so far as the minutes reflect. At the end of the meeting, the Old Board authorized Ovitz's hiring as Disney's president. No further review or approval of the employment agreement occurred. Throughout both meetings, no expert consultant was present to advise the compensation committee or the Old Board. Notably, the Old Board approved Ovitz's hiring even though the employment agreement was still a "work in progress." The Old Board simply passed off the details to Ovitz and his good friend, Eisner.

Negotiation over the remaining terms took place solely between Eisner, Ovitz, and attorneys representing Disney and Ovitz. The compensation committee met briefly in October to review the negotiations, but failed again to actually consider a draft of the agreement or to establish any guidelines to be used in the negotiations. The committee was apparently not otherwise involved in the negotiations. Negotiations with Eisner continued until mid-December, but Ovitz had already started serving as Disney's president as of October 1, 1995.

Eisner and Ovitz reached a final agreement on December 12, 1995. They agreed to backdate the agreement, however, to October 1, 1995. The final employment agreement also differed substantially from the original draft, but evidently no further committee or board review of it ever occurred. The final version of Ovitz's employment agreement was signed (according to the new complaint) without *any* board input beyond the limited discussion on September 26, 1995.

From the outset, Ovitz performed poorly as Disney's president. In short order, Ovitz wanted out, and, once again, his good friend Eisner came to the rescue, agreeing to Ovitz's request for a non-fault termination. Disney's board, however, was allegedly never consulted in this process. No board committee was ever consulted, nor were any experts consulted. Eisner and Litvack alone granted Ovitz's non-fault termination, which became public on December 12, 1996. Again, Disney's board did not appear to question this action, although affirmative board action seemed to be required. On December 27, 1996, Eisner and Litvack, without explanation, accelerated the effective date of the non-fault termination, from January 31, 1997, to December 27, 1996. Again, the board apparently took no action; no questions were asked as to why this was done.

Disney had lost several key executives in the months before Ovitz was hired. Moreover, the position of president is obviously important in a publicly owned corporation. But the Old Board and the compensation committee (it is alleged) each spent less than an hour reviewing Ovitz's possible hiring. According to the new complaint, neither the Old Board nor the compensation committee reviewed the actual draft employment agreement. Nor did they evaluate the details of Ovitz's salary or his severance provisions. No expert presented the board with details of the agreement, outlined the pros and cons of either the salary or non-fault termination provisions, or analyzed comparable industry standards for such agreements. Notwithstanding this alleged information vacuum, the Old Board and the compensation committee approved Ovitz's hiring, appointed Eisner to negotiate with Ovitz directly in drafting the unresolved terms of his employment, never asked to review the final terms, and were never voluntarily provided those terms.

During the negotiation over the unresolved terms, the compensation committee was involved only once, at the very early stages in October 1995. The final agreement varied significantly from the draft agreement in the areas of both stock options and the terms of the non-fault termination. Neither the compensation committee nor the Old Board sought to review, nor did they review, the final agreement. In addition, both the Old Board and the committee failed to meet in order to evaluate the final agreement before it became binding on Disney. To repeat, no expert was retained to advise the Old Board, the committee, or Eisner during the negotiation process.

The new complaint, fairly read, also charges the New Board with a similar ostrich-like approach regarding Ovitz's non-fault termination. Eisner and Litvack granted Ovitz a non-fault termination on December 12, 1996, and the news became public that day. Although formal board approval appeared necessary for a non-fault termination, the new complaint alleges that no New Board member even asked for a meeting to discuss Eisner's and Litvack's decision. On December 27, 1996, when Eisner and Litvack accelerated Ovitz's non-fault termination by over a month, with a payout of more than $38 million in cash, together with the three million "A" stock options, the board again failed to do anything. Instead, it appears from the new complaint that the New Board played no role in Eisner's agreement to award Ovitz more than $38 million in cash and the three million "A" stock options, all for leaving a job that Ovitz had allegedly proven incapable of performing.

The New Board apparently never sought to negotiate with Ovitz regarding his departure. Nor, apparently, did it consider whether to seek a termination based on fault. During the fifteen-day period between announcement of Ovitz's termination and its effective date, the New Board allegedly chose to remain invisible in the process. The new complaint alleges that the New Board: (1) failed to ask why it had not been informed; (2) failed to inquire about the conditions and terms of the agreement; and (3) failed even to attempt to stop or delay the termination until more information could be collected. If the board had taken the time or effort to review these or other options, perhaps with the assistance of expert legal advisors, the business judgment rule might well protect its decision. In this case, however, the new complaint asserts that the New Board directors refused to explore any alternatives, and refused to even attempt to evaluate the implications of the non-fault termination—blindly allowing

Eisner to hand over to his personal friend, Ovitz, more than $38 million in cash and the three million "A" stock options.

These facts, if true, do more than portray directors who, in a negligent or grossly negligent manner, merely failed to inform themselves or to deliberate adequately about an issue of material importance to their corporation. Instead, the facts alleged in the new complaint suggest that the defendant directors *consciously and intentionally disregarded their responsibilities*, adopting a "we don't care about the risks" attitude concerning a material corporate decision. Knowing or deliberate indifference by a director to his or her duty to act faithfully and with appropriate care is conduct, in my opinion, that may not have been taken honestly and in good faith to advance the best interests of the company. Put differently, all of the alleged facts, if true, imply that the defendant directors *knew* that they were making material decisions without adequate information and without adequate deliberation, and that they simply did not care if the decisions caused the corporation and its stockholders to suffer injury or loss. Viewed in this light, plaintiffs' new complaint sufficiently alleges a breach of the directors' obligation to act honestly and in good faith in the corporation's best interests for a Court to conclude, if the facts are true, that the defendant directors' conduct fell outside the protection of the business judgment rule.

. . . Where a director consciously ignores his or her duties to the corporation, thereby causing economic injury to its stockholders, the director's actions are either "not in good faith" or "involve intentional misconduct." Thus, plaintiffs' allegations support claims that fall *outside* the liability waiver provided under Disney's certificate of incorporation.

B. OVITZ

Defendant Ovitz contends that the action against him should be dismissed because he owed no fiduciary duty not to seek the best possible employment agreement for himself. Ovitz did have the right to seek the best employment agreement possible for himself. Nevertheless, once Ovitz became a fiduciary of Disney on October 1, 1995, according to the new complaint, he also had a duty to negotiate honestly and in good faith so as not to advantage himself at the expense of the Disney shareholders. He arguably failed to fulfill that duty, according to the facts alleged in the new complaint.

Ovitz and Eisner had been close friends for over twenty-five years. Ovitz knew when he became president of Disney on October 1, 1995, that his unexecuted contract was still under negotiation. Instead of negotiating with an impartial entity, such as the compensation committee, Ovitz and his attorneys negotiated directly with Eisner, his close personal friend. Perhaps not surprisingly, the final version of the employment agreement differed significantly from the draft version summarized to the board and to the compensation committee on September 26, 1995. Had those changes been the result of arms-length bargaining, Ovitz's motion to dismiss might have merit. At this stage, however, the alleged facts (which I must accept as true) suggest that Ovitz and Eisner had almost absolute control over the terms of Ovitz's contract.

The new complaint arguably charges that Ovitz engaged in a carefully orchestrated, self-serving process controlled directly by his close friend Eisner, all designed to provide Ovitz with enormous financial benefits. The case law cited by Ovitz in support of his position suggests that an officer may negotiate his or her own employment agreement *as long as the process involves negotiations performed in an adversarial and arms-length manner.* The facts, as alleged in the new complaint, belie an adversarial, arms-length negotiation process between Ovitz and the Walt Disney Company. Instead, the alleged facts, if true, would support an inference that Ovitz may have breached his fiduciary duties by engaging in a self-interested transaction in negotiating his employment agreement directly with his personal friend Eisner.

The same is true regarding the non-fault termination. In that instance, Ovitz was also serving as a member of the Disney board of directors. The Supreme Court recently held in *Telxon Corp. v. Meyerson* that "directoral self-compensation decisions lie outside the business judgment rule's presumptive protection, so that, where properly challenged, the receipt of self-determined benefits is subject to an affirmative showing that the compensation arrangements are fair to the corporation." According to the facts alleged in the new complaint, Ovitz did not advise the Disney board of his decision to seek a departure that would be fair and equitable to all parties. Instead, he went to his close friend, Eisner, and, working together, they developed a secret strategy that would enable Ovitz to extract the maximum benefit from his contract, all without board approval.

Although the strategy was economically injurious and a public relations disaster for Disney, the Ovitz/Eisner exit strategy allegedly was designed principally to protect their personal reputations, while assuring Ovitz a huge personal pay-off after barely a year of mediocre to poor job performance. These allegations, if ultimately found to be true, would suggest a faithless fiduciary who obtained extraordinary personal financial benefits at the expense of the constituency for whom he was obliged to act honestly and in good faith. Because Ovitz was a fiduciary during both the negotiation of his employment agreement and the non-fault termination, he had an obligation to ensure the process of his contract negotiation and termination was both impartial and fair. The facts, as pleaded, give rise to a reasonable inference that, assisted by Eisner, he ignored that obligation.

IV. CONCLUSION

It is of course true that after-the-fact litigation is a most imperfect device to evaluate corporate business decisions, as the limits of human competence necessarily impede judicial review. But our corporation law's theoretical justification for disregarding honest errors simply does not apply to intentional misconduct or to egregious process failures that implicate the foundational directoral obligation to act honestly and in good faith to advance corporate interests. Because the facts alleged here, if true, portray directors consciously indifferent to a material issue facing the corporation, the law must be strong enough to intervene against abuse of trust. Accordingly, all three of plaintiffs' claims for relief concerning fiduciary duty breaches and waste survive defendants' motions to dismiss.

The practical effect of this ruling is that defendants must answer the new complaint and plaintiffs may proceed to take appropriate discovery on the merits of their claims. To that end, a case scheduling order has been entered that will promptly bring this matter before the Court on a fully developed factual record.

PROBLEM 10-3

Michael Ovitz's "golden parachute" has not been the only executive compensation issue to ruffle feathers in Disney's Magic Kingdom. The compensation package for Michael Eisner, chairman of the board and chief executive officer of Disney (and codefendant with Ovitz in the case above), has also been severely criticized by shareholders. In the year ended September 30, 1998, Eisner realized paper profits of $569.8 million after exercising options to acquire 22 million shares of Disney stock. That options package was part of an executive compensation plan for Mr. Eisner that had been controversial when adopted. The shareholders were asked to vote on the plan to comply with the shareholder approval requirements of §162(m) of the Internal Revenue Code. Eight percent of shareholders casting votes opposed the package, while 3.2 percent abstained.

In addition to shareholder proxy votes against Mr. Eisner's compensation package, social activist shareholders filed a resolution in 1997 seeking to tie Mr. Eisner's compensation to the social and political aspects of Disney's activities, both in the United States and around the world. The proxy resolution included the following language:

> Whereas: We believe that financial, social and environmental criteria should be taken into account in setting compensation for corporate officers. Public scrutiny on compensation is intensifying, with serious concerns being expressed about the widening chasm between salaries of top corporate officers and their employees as well as contract workers. . . .
>
> RESOLVED: shareholders request that the Board institute an Executive Compensation Review, and prepare a report available to shareholders by October 1997 with a summary of the results and recommended changes in practice. The review shall cover pay, benefits, perks, stock options, and special arrangements in the compensation packages for all top officers.
>
> The review will address:
>
> 1. Ways to link our company's executive compensation more closely to financial performance and social and environmental criteria.
> 2. Comparison of compensation packages for company officers with both the lowest and average wages for Disney contract workers in the U.S. and three low wage countries, including Haiti.
> 3. Whether a cap should be placed on compensation packages for officers to prevent our company from paying excessive compensation.

This resolution was defeated, but 14.8 percent of Disney shares (approximately 47 million shares) voted in favor of it.

Assume that shareholders are regrouping to reconsider how they might constrain the board of directors in compensating Mr. Eisner. What avenues seem productive for the shareholders? Does the fact that nearly 15 percent of shares were voted to connect Mr. Eisner's executive compensation to the social performance of the firm indicate any potential leverage for shareholders? Would you recommend that shareholders seek to pass a binding bylaw amendment requiring a specified increase in the value of Disney's stock or a specified social performance prior to Mr. Eisner being paid any bonuses?

D.   STATUTORY EXCULPATION FROM LIABILITY

In addition to weak standards of care and the protection of the business judgment rule, more recently directors are protected from personal liability for breaches of the duty of care by exculpation clauses often found in the articles of incorporation. DGCL §102(b)(7) and Model Act §2.02(b)(4) allow corporations to limit director liability for money damages for certain types of breach of the duty of care. Under the Model Act, the articles of incorporation may "eliminate or limit the liability of a director to the corporation or its shareholders for money damages for any action taken, or any failure to take any action" in breach of the duty of care, including breaches that constitute an intentional violation of civil law. Model Act §2.02(b)(4)(D). The articles may not exculpate directors for receiving financial benefits to which they are not entitled, for approving improper dividends, for intentionally harming the corporation, or for intentional violations of criminal law. Model Act §2.02(b)(4). DGCL §102(b)(7) permits similar exculpation, although under Delaware law the corporation may not exculpate its directors for breaches of the duty of loyalty, or for "acts or omission not in good faith or which involve intentional misconduct or a knowing violation of law." Exculpation clauses do not prevent a stockholder from pursuing other remedies, for example, an injunction, if the directors have breached their duty of care. These statutes were passed in the wake of Smith v. Van Gorkom and have been criticized by those who believe that directors should be more accountable to shareholders. Moreover, the Model Act standards have been criticized as demonstrating an insufficient concern with law compliance, since directors may be exculpated even for intentional violations of civil law.

The procedural impact of exculpation provisions under Delaware law has been discussed by the Delaware Supreme Court in numerous cases. The following case describes the use of this mechanism to dismiss complaints alleging a breach of the duty of care.

MALPIEDE v. TOWNSON

780 A.2d 1075
Supreme Court of Delaware
August 27, 2001

VEASEY, Chief Justice.

In this appeal, we affirm the holding of the Court of Chancery . . . granting of a motion to dismiss the plaintiffs' due care claim [in the context of a merger] on the ground that the exculpatory provision in the charter of the target corporation authorized by 8 Del. C. §102(b)(7), bars any claim for money damages against the director defendants based solely on the board's alleged breach of its duty of care. Accordingly, we affirm the judgment of the Court of Chancery dismissing the amended complaint.

With respect to the dismissal based on the exculpatory effect of the Section 102(b)(7) charter provision, we had an initial concern about the propriety of the trial court's consideration of the exculpatory charter provision on a Rule 12(b)(6) motion to dismiss because it is a matter outside the complaint.

Although presentation of matters outside the pleadings required the court to convert the Defendants' motion to dismiss into a motion for summary judgment, the failure to do so was not reversible error. Because the plaintiffs do not contest the existence, terms, validity or authenticity of the Frederick's exculpatory charter provision, we hold that the charter provision was properly before the Court of Chancery, which correctly held that the plaintiffs' due care claim was barred. Accordingly, we affirm the judgment of the Court of Chancery.

FACTS

Frederick's of Hollywood ("Frederick's") is a retailer of women's lingerie and apparel with its headquarters in Los Angeles, California. This case centers on the merger of Frederick's into Knightsbridge Capital Corporation ("Knightsbridge") under circumstances where it became a target in a bidding contest. Before the merger, Frederick's common stock was divided into Class A shares (each of which has one vote) and Class B shares (which have no vote). As of December 6, 1996, there were outstanding 2,995,309 Class A shares and 5,903,118 Class B shares. Two trusts created by the principal founders of Frederick's, Frederick and Harriet Mellinger (the "Trusts"), held a total of about 41% of the outstanding Class A voting shares and a total of about 51% of the outstanding Class B non-voting shares of Frederick's.

On June 14, 1996, the Frederick's board announced its decision to retain an investment bank, Janney Montgomery Scott, Inc. ("JMS"), to advise the board in its search for a suitable buyer for the company. In January 1997, JMS initiated talks with Knightsbridge. Four months later, in April 1997, Knightsbridge offered to purchase all of the outstanding shares of Frederick's for between $6.00 and $6.25 per share. At Knightsbridge's request, the Frederick's board granted Knightsbridge the exclusive right to conduct due diligence.

On June 13, 1997, the Frederick's board approved an offer from Knightsbridge to purchase all of Frederick's outstanding Class A and Class B shares for $6.14 per share in cash in a two-step merger transaction. The terms of the merger agreement signed by the Frederick's board prohibited the board from soliciting additional bids from third parties, but the agreement permitted the board to negotiate with third party bidders when the board's fiduciary duties required it to do so.[6] The Frederick's board then sent to stockholders a Consent Solicitation Statement recommending that they approve the transaction, which was scheduled to close on August 27, 1997.

On August 21, 1997, Frederick's received a fully financed, unsolicited cash offer of $7.00 per share from a third party bidder, Milton Partners ("Milton"). Four days after the board received the Milton offer, Knightsbridge entered into an agreement to purchase all of the Frederick's shares held by the Trusts for $6.90 per share.[7] Under the stock purchase agreement, the Trusts granted Knightsbridge a proxy to vote the Trusts' shares, but the Trusts had the right

---

6. In the event that the Frederick's board terminated the merger agreement in order to accept a superior proposal by a third party bidder, the agreement entitled Knightsbridge to liquidated damages of $1.8 million.

7. As noted earlier, the Trusts held about 40% of the Class A shares and 50% of the Class B shares. Knightsbridge also extended its $6.90 offer price to all outstanding Frederick's shares.

to terminate the agreement if the Frederick's board rejected the Knightsbridge offer in favor of a higher bid.

On August 27, 1997, the Frederick's board received a fully financed, unsolicited $7.75 cash offer from Veritas Capital Fund ("Veritas"). In light of these developments, the board postponed the Knightsbridge merger in order to arrange a meeting with the two new bidders. On September 2, 1997, the board sent a memorandum to Milton and Veritas outlining the conditions for participation in the bidding process. The memorandum required that the bidders each deposit $2.5 million in an escrow account and submit, before September 4, 1997, a marked-up merger agreement with the same basic terms as the Knightsbridge merger agreement. Veritas submitted a merger agreement and the $2.5 million escrow payment in accordance with these conditions. Milton did not.[9]

On September 3, 1997, the Frederick's board met with representatives of Veritas to discuss the terms of the Veritas offer. According to the plaintiffs, the board asserts that, at this meeting, it orally informed Veritas that it was required to produce its "final, best offer" by September 4, 1997. The plaintiffs further allege that the board did not, in fact, inform Veritas of this requirement.

The same day that the board met with Veritas, Knightsbridge and the Trusts amended their stock purchase agreement to eliminate the Trusts' termination rights and other conditions on the sale of the Trusts' shares. On September 4, 1997, Knightsbridge exercised its rights under the agreement and purchased the Trusts' shares. Knightsbridge immediately informed the board of its acquisition of the Trusts' shares and repeated its intention to vote the shares against any competing third party bids.

One day after Knightsbridge acquired the Trusts' shares, the Frederick's board participated in a conference call with Veritas to discuss further the terms of the proposed merger. During this conference call, Veritas representatives suggested that, if the board elected to accept the Veritas offer, the board could issue an option to Veritas to purchase authorized but unissued Frederick's shares as a means to circumvent the 41% block of voting shares that Knightsbridge had acquired from the Trusts. Frederick's representatives also expressed some concern that Knightsbridge would sue the board if it decided to terminate the June 15, 1997 merger agreement. In response, Veritas agreed to indemnify the directors in the event of such litigation.

On September 6, 1997, Knightsbridge increased its bid to match the $7.75 Veritas offer, but on the condition that the board accept a variety of terms designed to restrict its ability to pursue superior offers.[10] On the same day, the Frederick's board approved this agreement and effectively ended the bidding process. Two days later, Knightsbridge purchased additional Frederick's Class

---

9. Milton apparently discontinued its efforts to acquire Frederick's after Veritas submitted its higher bid.

10. The terms included: a provision prohibiting any Frederick's representative from speaking to third party bidders concerning the acquisition of the company (the "no-talk" provision); a termination fee of $4.5 million (about 7% of the value of the transaction); the appointment of a non-voting Knightsbridge observer at Frederick's board meetings; and an obligation to grant Knightsbridge any stock option that Frederick's granted to a competing bidder. The revised merger agreement did not expressly permit the Frederick's board to pursue negotiations with third parties where its fiduciary duties required it to do so.

A shares on the open market, at an average price of $8.21 per share, thereby acquiring a majority of both classes of Frederick's shares.

On September 11, 1997, Veritas increased its cash offer to $9.00 per share. Relying on (1) the "no-talk" provision in the merger agreement, (2) Knightsbridge's stated intention to vote its shares against third party bids, and (3) Veritas' request for an option to dilute Knightsbridge's interest, the board rejected the revised Veritas bid. On September 18, 1997, the board amended its earlier Consent Solicitation Statement to include the events that had transpired since July 1997. The deadline for responses to the consent solicitation was September 29, 1997, the scheduled closing date for the merger.

Before the merger closed, the plaintiffs filed in the Court of Chancery the purported class action complaint that is the predecessor of the amended complaint before us. The plaintiffs also moved for a temporary restraining order enjoining the merger. The Court of Chancery denied the requested injunctive relief.

The plaintiffs then amended their complaint to include a class action claim for damages caused by the termination of the auction in favor of Knightsbridge and the rejection of the higher Veritas offer. The amended complaint alleged that the Frederick's board had breached its fiduciary duties in connection with the sale of the company and had misstated and omitted material information in the Consent Solicitation Statement. The plaintiffs also sued Knightsbridge, alleging that it aided and abetted the board's breach of fiduciary duties and it tortiously interfered with the stockholders' prospective business relations (that is, the $9.00 Veritas bid).

The Court of Chancery granted the directors' motion to dismiss the amended complaint under Chancery Rule 12(b)(6), concluding that: (1) the complaint did not support a claim of breach of the board's duty of loyalty, (2) the exculpatory provision in the Frederick's charter precluded money damages against the directors for any breach of the board's duty of care, and (3) any misstatements or omissions in the Consent Solicitation Statement were immaterial as a matter of law. [Only the duty of care claim is discussed in this excerpted opinion.]

THE DUE CARE CLAIM

Having concluded that the complaint was properly dismissed under Chancery Rule 12(b)(6) for failure to state a claim on which relief may be granted on other fiduciary duty claims, we now turn to the due care claim. The primary due care issue is whether the board was grossly negligent, and therefore breached its duty of due care, in failing to implement a routine defensive strategy that could enable the board to negotiate for a higher bid or otherwise create a tactical advantage to enhance stockholder value.

In this case, that routine strategy would have been for the directors to use a poison pill to ward off Knightsbridge's advances and thus to prevent Knightsbridge from stopping the auction process. Had they done so, plaintiffs seem to allege that the directors could have preserved the appropriate options for an auction process designed to achieve the best value for the stockholders.

Construing the amended complaint most favorably to the plaintiffs, it can be read to allege that the board was grossly negligent in immediately accepting the Knightsbridge offer and agreeing to various restrictions on further negotiations without first determining whether Veritas would issue a counteroffer. Although the board had conducted a search for a buyer over one year, plaintiffs seem to contend that the board was imprudently hasty in agreeing to a restrictive merger agreement on the day it was proposed — particularly where other bidders had recently expressed interest. Although the board's haste, in itself, might not constitute a breach of the board's duty of care because the board had already conducted a lengthy sale process, the plaintiffs argue that the board's decision to accept allegedly extreme contractual restrictions impacted its ability to obtain a higher sale price. Recognizing that, at the end of the day, plaintiffs would have an uphill battle in overcoming the presumption of the business judgment rule, we must give plaintiffs the benefit of the doubt at this pleading stage to determine if they have stated a due care claim. Because of our ultimate decision, however, we need not finally decide this question in this case.

We assume, therefore, without deciding, that a claim for relief based on gross negligence during the board's auction process is stated by the inferences most favorable to plaintiffs that flow from these allegations. The issue then becomes whether the amended complaint may be dismissed upon a Rule 12(b)(6) motion by reason of the existence and the legal effect of the exculpatory provision of Article TWELFTH of Frederick's certificate of incorporation, adopted pursuant to 8 Del. C. §102(b)(7). That provision would exempt directors from personal liability in damages with certain exceptions (*e.g.*, breach of the duty of loyalty) that are not applicable here.[45]

A. THE EXCULPATORY CHARTER PROVISION WAS PROPERLY BEFORE THE COURT OF CHANCERY

The threshold inquiry is whether Article TWELFTH of the Frederick's certificate of incorporation was properly before the Court of Chancery. In their brief in support of their motion to dismiss in the Court of Chancery, the director defendants interposed the Section 102(b)(7) charter provision as a bar to plaintiffs' claims based on an alleged breach of the duty of care.

This provision, which appeared for the first time in the director defendants' brief in the Court of Chancery, was placed before the court without any authentication or supporting affidavit. The existence and authenticity of this provision was never questioned by plaintiffs, however. The trial court therefore tacitly accepted it as authentic without defendants formally asking the court to take judicial notice of its existence, which could easily be found in the public files in the Secretary of State's office and could properly be noticed judicially by the court.

---

45. Article TWELFTH provides:

> TWELFTH. A director of this Corporation shall not be personally liable to the Corporation or its shareholders for monetary damages for breach of fiduciary duty as a director, except for liability (i) for any breach of the director's duty of loyalty to the Corporation or its shareholders, (ii) for acts or omissions not in good faith or which involve intentional misconduct or a knowing violation of law (iii) under Section 174 of the Delaware General Corporation Law, or (iv) for any transaction for which the director derived an improper personal benefit.

Because the charter provision is not found within the four corners of the complaint, it is a "matter outside the pleading." Accordingly, on a Rule 12(b)(6) motion to dismiss, if

> matters outside the pleading are presented to and not excluded by the Court the motion shall be treated as one for summary judgment and disposed of as provided in Rule 56, and all parties shall be given a reasonable opportunity to present all material made pertinent to such a motion by Rule 56.

Under Rule 56 in this context, there *may* be an opportunity for either side to submit affidavits or engage in discovery to explore the "matter outside the pleadings [that had been] . . . presented to and not excluded by the Court."

Simply because a matter outside the pleading has been presented under Rule 12(b)(6) and thereby must be "treated as one for summary judgment" with "all parties . . . given a reasonable opportunity to present all material made pertinent to such a motion by Rule 56," it does not follow that the "floodgates of discovery" have to be opened. The Rule 56 opportunity to present affidavits or engage in discovery is not absolute. It is necessarily circumscribed by the discretion of the trial court in determining the scope of the "matters outside the pleading" that had been presented in connection with the Rule 12(b)(6) motion. Indeed, plaintiffs here do not contend that simply because defendants invoked the Section 102(b)(7) charter provision they are thereby invited to go on a fishing expedition. Accordingly, when matters outside the pleading — such as a Section 102(b)(7) charter provision — are presented, the trial court should carefully limit the discovery sought to a scope that is coextensive with the issue necessary to resolve the motion. Here, there was apparently no discovery issue.

When the issue is confined to the legal effect of a Section 102(b)(7) charter provision, it is difficult to envision what discovery would be implicated. To be sure, in a due care case where a Section 102(b)(7) charter provision is invoked, a plaintiff could theoretically contest the validity of the charter provision. In such a case, the plaintiff must have a proper basis to claim that the Section 102(b)(7) charter provision presented by the defendants on the Rule 12(b)(6) motion is not authentic, was improperly adopted by the stockholders, or the like.

Plaintiffs make no such claim here. Although plaintiffs contend that under *Emerald Partners*[55] the burden is on the defendants to produce evidence to support a Section 102(b)(7) defense, they do not contest the existence or authenticity of Frederick's 102(b)(7) charter provision. There being no Rule 56 avenue of discovery or affidavits that would be relevant to the narrow issue before the trial court in this case, we conclude that the plaintiffs were not deprived of any important procedural right arising from the fact that the trial court considered Frederick's 102(b)(7) charter exculpation provision in connection with the Rule 12(b)(6) motion to dismiss. Although it would have been preferable for the trial court to have observed the precise provisions of the rules and to have expressly treated the motion as one for summary judgment once the Section 102(b)(7) charter provision was interposed by the director defendants, we find no reversible error in failing to do so. The provision was properly

55. 726 A.2d 1215 (Del. 1999).

before the Court of Chancery in deciding on the director defendants' motion to dismiss.

As guidance for future cases, we observe that there are several methods available to the defense to raise and argue the applicability of the bar of a Section 102(b)(7) charter provision to a due care claim. The Section 102(b)(7) bar may be raised on a Rule 12(b)(6) motion to dismiss (with or without the filing of an answer), a motion for judgment on the pleadings (after filing an answer), or a motion for summary judgment (or partial summary judgment) under Rule 56 after an answer, with or without supporting affidavits.

In the case of a Rule 12(b)(6) motion, as here, if the Section 102(b)(7) charter provision is raised for the first time in the motion or brief in support of the motion, it is a matter outside the pleading. If not excluded by the court, the existence of such matter means that the motion will be converted, by clear force of the pleading rules, into a motion for summary judgment under Rule 56 and should be handled as we have noted above.

B. APPLICATION OF *EMERALD PARTNERS*

We now address plaintiffs' argument that the trial court committed error, based on certain language in *Emerald Partners*, by barring their due care claims. Plaintiffs' arguments on this point are based on an erroneous premise, and our decision here is not inconsistent with *Emerald Partners*.

In *Emerald Partners*, we made two important points about the raising of Section 102(b)(7) charter provisions. First we said: "[T]he shield from liability provided by a certificate of incorporation provision adopted pursuant to 8 Del. C. §102(b)(7) is in the nature of an affirmative defense." Second, we said:

> [W]here the factual basis for a claim *solely* implicates a violation of the duty of care, this court has indicated that the protections of such a charter provision may properly be invoked and applied. Arnold v. Society for Savings Bancorp., Del. Supr., 650 A.2d 1270, 1288 (1994); Zirn v. VLI Corp., Del. Supr., 681 A.2d 1050, 1061 (1996).

Based on this language in *Emerald Partners*, plaintiffs make two arguments. First, they argue that the Court of Chancery in this case should not have dismissed their due care claims because these claims are intertwined with, and thus indistinguishable from, the duty of loyalty and bad faith claims. Second, plaintiffs contend that the Court of Chancery incorrectly assigned to them the burden of going forward with proof.

1. The Court of Chancery Properly Dismissed Claims Based Solely on the Duty of Care

Plaintiffs here, while not conceding that the Section 102(b)(7) charter provision may be considered on this Rule 12(b)(6) motion nevertheless, in effect, conceded in oral argument in the Court of Chancery and similarly in oral argument in this Court that if a complaint unambiguously and solely asserted only a due care claim, the complaint is dismissible once the corporation's Section 102(b)(7) provision is invoked. This concession is in line with our holding in *Emerald Partners* quoted above.

Plaintiffs contended vigorously, however, that the Section 102(b)(7) charter provision does not apply to bar their claims in this case because the amended complaint alleges breaches of the duty of loyalty and other claims that are not barred by the charter provision. As a result, plaintiffs maintain, this case cannot be boiled down solely to a due care case. They argue, in effect, that their complaint is sufficiently well-pleaded that — *as a matter of law* — the due care claims are so inextricably intertwined with loyalty and bad faith claims that Section 102(b)(7) is not a bar to recovery of damages against the directors.

We disagree. It is the plaintiffs who have a burden to set forth "a short and plain statement of the claim showing that the pleader is entitled to relief." The plaintiffs are entitled to all reasonable inferences flowing from their pleadings, but if those inferences do not support a valid legal claim, the complaint should be dismissed without the need for the defendants to file an answer and without proceeding with discovery. Here we have assumed, without deciding, that the amended complaint on its face states a due care claim. Because we have determined that the complaint fails properly to invoke loyalty and bad faith claims, we are left with only a due care claim. Defendants had the obligation to raise the bar of Section 102(b)(7) as a defense, and they did. As plaintiffs conceded in oral argument before this Court, if there is only an unambiguous, residual due care claim and nothing else — *as a matter of law* — then Section 102(b)(7) would bar the claim. Accordingly, the Court of Chancery did not err in dismissing the plaintiffs due care claim in this case.

2. The Court of Chancery Correctly Applied the Parties' Respective Burdens of Proof

Plaintiffs also assert that the trial court in the case before us incorrectly placed on plaintiffs a pleading burden to negate the elements of the 102(b)(7) charter provision. Plaintiffs argue that this ruling is inconsistent with the statement in *Emerald Partners* that "the shield from liability provided by a certificate of incorporation provision adopted pursuant to 8 Del. C. §102(b)(7) is in the nature of an affirmative defense. . . . Defendants seeking exculpation under such a provision will normally bear the burden of establishing each of its elements."

The procedural posture here is quite different from that in *Emerald Partners*. There the Court stated that it was incorrect for the trial court to grant summary judgment on the record in that case because the defendants had the burden *at trial* of demonstrating good faith if they were invoking the statutory exculpation provision. In this case, we focus not on trial burdens, but only on pleading issues. A plaintiff must allege well-pleaded facts stating a claim on which relief may be granted. Had plaintiff alleged such well-pleaded facts supporting a breach of loyalty or bad faith claim, the Section 102(b)(7) charter provision would have been unavailing as to such claims, and this case would have gone forward.

But we have held that the amended complaint here does not allege a loyalty violation or other violation falling within the exceptions to the Section 102(b)(7) exculpation provision. Likewise, we have held that, even if the plaintiffs had stated a claim for gross negligence, such a well-pleaded claim is unavailing because defendants have brought forth the 102(b)(7) charter provision that bars such claims. This is the end of the case.

And rightly so, as a matter of the public policy of this State. Section 102(b)(7) was adopted by the Delaware General Assembly in 1986 following a directors and officers insurance liability crisis and the 1985 Delaware Supreme Court decision in Smith v. Van Gorkom. The purpose of this statute was to permit stockholders to adopt a provision in the certificate of incorporation to free directors of personal liability in damages for due care violations, but not duty of loyalty violations, bad faith claims and certain other conduct. Such a charter provision, when adopted, would not affect injunctive proceedings based on gross negligence. Once the statute was adopted, stockholders usually approved charter amendments containing these provisions because it freed up directors to take business risks without worrying about negligence lawsuits.

Our jurisprudence since the adoption of the statute has consistently stood for the proposition that a Section 102(b)(7) charter provision bars a claim that is found to state only a due care violation. Because we have assumed that the amended complaint here does state a due care claim, the exculpation afforded by the statute must affirmatively be raised by the defendant directors. The directors have done so in this case, and the Court of Chancery properly applied the Frederick's charter provision to dismiss the plaintiffs' due care claim. . . .

PROBLEM 10-4

Columbia/HCA Healthcare Corporation (HCA) had a profound effect on health care in the United States. As the largest operator of for-profit hospitals, HCA brought an aggressive acquisitions strategy and business mindset to hospital administration. It spurred industry consolidation that has since been blamed for increased health care costs. But perhaps its most lasting impression is that it was the subject of the longest and costliest health care fraud investigation ever. As of early 2003, HCA had paid $840 million in fines relating to fraudulent Medicare billing. While the company survived, it had been trimmed to 200 hospitals (from over 300 at its peak) and appears to have become a much tamer competitor.

Among all of the various legal proceedings that emanated from the fraud charges were claims against HCA's directors for breach of fiduciary duty. According to the plaintiffs in one such suit, the fraudulent practices included the following:

> (1) "upcoding" by providers, which refers to billing for services under DRG (diagnosis related group) codes for illnesses with a higher degree of complexity and severity than a patient's condition actually warranted; (2) improper cost reporting, such as seeking reimbursement for advertising and marketing costs, "grossing up" outpatient revenues, allocating costs from one division to another, and structuring transactions to disguise acquisition costs as reimbursable management fees; (3) offering financial incentives to physicians to increase referrals of Medicare patients to Columbia's facilities (*i.e.*, equity interests, fees, rents, or other perquisites); and (4) acquisition practices that offered inducements to executives of target companies and interfered with existing physician relationships.

The plaintiffs rely on *Caremark* and accuse the directors of "reckless and intentional breach of the duty of care" in exercising their oversight responsibilities. More specifically, the plaintiffs argued that the fraudulent practices described above raised certain "red flags" that should have attracted the directors' attention, but "intentional ignorance" and "willful blindness" prevented them from acting. The defendants respond by claiming that they are immune from liability under *Caremark* because of the following provision in HCA's Certificate of Incorporation:

A director of the Corporation shall not be personally liable to the Corporation or its stockholders for monetary damages for breach of fiduciary duty as a director; *provided, however,* that the foregoing shall not eliminate or limit the liability of a director (i) for any breach of the director's duty of loyalty to the Corporation or its stockholders, (ii) for acts or omissions not in good faith or which involve intentional misconduct or a knowing violation of law, (iii) under Section 174 of the Delaware General Corporation Law, as amended or (iv) for any transaction from which the director obtained an improper personal benefit.

As you can see, this provision closely tracks the language of DGCL §102(b)(7). Would a court in Delaware grant a motion to dismiss the plaintiffs' claims for monetary damages asserted against HCA's directors?

E.   INSURANCE AND INDEMNIFICATION

Another way that companies protect directors from personal liability for their actions as directors is by providing insurance, referred to as directors and officers insurance (or usually just "D&O insurance"). As with any insurance, on public policy grounds the company cannot insure against losses arising out of intentional misconduct or dishonesty; nor will insurance companies write policies to insure against directors' breaches of loyalty. Moreover, companies maintain "reimbursement insurance" to provide reimbursement to the company for any payments to third parties or the government (penalties, judgments, settlements, and the costs of the company defending itself) arising from actions of their directors and employees. Both D&O policies and the company's reimbursement policy will typically require the insurance company to defend its insureds (the company and the directors and officers) when a lawsuit is brought that states a claim for an "insurable event." Unfortunately, insurance companies and their insureds often disagree about whether a lawsuit states a claim for an insurable event. Thus, one stage in many complex commercial litigations is a declaratory judgment action between the insurance company and its insured about the potential scope of coverage and the insurance company's "duty to defend" its insured.

In addition to providing its directors and officers with insurance, companies will enter into indemnification agreements with top executives and its board of directors, typically by specifying such parties' indemnification rights in its bylaws. In typical bylaw provisions, the company agrees to pay ("indemnify") the directors and officers for any losses arising out of their service to the corporation (including the costs of defending lawsuits), subject to specified limitations, usually the limits provided in the jurisdiction's controlling statutes. Such agreements or bylaw provisions supplement common law principles of agency law, under which a principal is generally obligated to indemnify an agent against losses that arise out of the agency relationship, assuming the agent's actions were authorized and taken in good faith. See Restatement (Second) of Agency §§438-440. From the perspective of directors and officers, whether they are indemnified by the company or insured against losses by insurance policies the company pays for is important if the company's future solvency is problematic (such as in a Silicon Valley start-up with excellent prospects but no actual products to market at the time of incorporation). Prudent directors and officers seek — and typically get — both types of protection.

As might be anticipated, both the Delaware General Corporation Law and the Model Business Corporation Act specify indemnification rights and the limits thereto. Neither makes for scintillating reading, but because these issues are a part of most complex corporate litigation, it is important to have at least a glancing familiarity with the provisions. In general, the key issue that determines indemnification rights is whether the directors, officers, employees, or agents (DOEA) acted in good faith and in a manner reasonably anticipated to be in (or not opposed to) the corporation's best interest. 8 DGCL §145; Model Act §§8.51-8.57. If the DOEA are successful on the merits, then the company must indemnify them for their attorneys' fees and expenses.

A final type of agreement that often comes into play in litigation challenging the legality of actions of the directors or employees of a company is seen in the case below, here called a "forbearance agreement," and often called a "standstill agreement." The need for these agreements arises from a conflict between the corporation and the DOEA. Remember that the corporation can act only through its agents, including its board of directors and its employees. If these agents are alleged to have violated the law, the corporation as well as the agents will potentially be liable to third parties or to the government based on the doctrine of *respondent superior* — *even* where the agent's actions were against explicit company policy.

Such vicarious liability creates a dilemma for the corporation in litigation: while wanting to assert to third parties or to the government that there were no violations of law, the corporation may want to maintain its ability to seek compensation (maintain its right of "contribution") against its directors or employees if there is ultimately a settlement or judgment that costs the company money, particularly where the corporation views the directors' or employees' actions with disfavor. Conversely, the directors or employees want to protect their rights to indemnification and insurance but recognize that it may not be strategically smart to have the company litigating their good faith (on which insurance and indemnification rights depend) at the beginning of the legal proceedings. In such situations, the company and its directors or employees will often sign a "standstill agreement." Such an agreement typically freezes each party's claims against the other for a specified period of time and provides other protection (such as providing that neither party will raise statute of limitations defenses in any subsequent litigation or making explicit provision for advancing defense costs subject to a right of reimbursement). Through such an agreement, the company and the directors or employees can present a more united front against third parties or the government without unduly compromising their claims against each other. You can see the interaction of various of the above types of protection in Problem 10-5.

PROBLEM 10-5

When the Sunbeam Corporation, which manufactures home appliances and other consumer products, was languishing in 1996, it turned to Albert J. Dunlap. Dunlap had earned the nickname "Chainsaw Al" based on his penchant for downsizing troubled companies, and his initial actions at Sunbeam were predictable. He fired half of the company's 12,000 employees, trimmed its product lines, and consolidated management. When Dunlap took the reins in July 1996, Sunbeam stock was trading at $12.50 a share. Within two years, the company's stock had ascended to $53 a share. Dunlap's strategy seemed to be working. Then Sunbeam unexpectedly reported a loss in the first quarter of 1998, and the stock price fell by more than 50 percent. In June 1998, Barron's offered this scathing assessment of Sunbeam's financial statements:

> Sunbeam's financials under Dunlap look like an exercise in high-energy physics, in which time and space seem to fuse and bend. They are a veritable cloud chamber. Income and costs move almost imperceptibly back and forth between the income statement and balance sheet like charged ions, whose vapor trail has long since dissipated by the end of any quarter, when results are reported. There are also some signs of other accounting shenanigans and puffery, including sales and related profits booked in periods before the goods were actually shipped or payment received. . . .

More specifically, the primary problem identified by Barron's had to do with Sunbeam's revenue recognition policies—an area of accounting that can easily be manipulated. It was alleged that Sunbeam was shipping large quantities of its products to its dealers and then "recognizing" revenue on its books from the eventual sales. The problem with this accounting technique is that excess shipping in any retail industry causes inventory buildups, which dealers routinely address by offering deep discounts to customers to promote sales. Under generally accepted accounting principles (GAAPs), since it is probable that the company will need to offer such discounts, the company is obligated to "book" reserves to reflect the reasonably estimable amounts of the discounts. ("Booking" the reserve simply means including it as an accounting entry to be subtracted from the revenue that is recognized. By booking a reserve, and subtracting it, the amount of revenue that is recognized is not inflated.)

When the Barron's article was published, Dunlap is alleged to have denied to both stock analysts and his board of directors that accounting "management" was behind Sunbeam's turnaround. The next week, Sunbeam's board of directors—all handpicked by Dunlap—fired him. The firing was ironic because Dunlap had ridden into Sunbeam advocating a new approach to corporate governance, which he described in his autobiographical book, *Mean Business*: if you pay corporate directors in stock, Dunlap said, they won't put up with ineffective executives. By the time the company restated its financials in October 1998, the stock was trading around $8 per share. Predictably, a spate of shareholder lawsuits (and an SEC investigation) followed.

As pressure on Dunlap mounted, he entered into a forbearance agreement with Sunbeam in August 1988. Under that agreement, both Dunlap and Sunbeam agreed to freeze any litigation against each other for 180 days. Nevertheless, other litigation proceeded, and Dunlap's legal bills began to mount quickly. In December 1998, Sunbeam paid a law firm $123,548 for services rendered to Dunlap and Russell A. Kersh, Sunbeam's executive vice president for finance and administration. A few month later, however, Sunbeam's board of directors voted to refuse further requests for advances. In considering the propriety of the board's actions, read section 8.1 of Sunbeam's bylaws:

> To the extent permitted by law, as the same exists or may hereafter be amended (but, in the case of such amendment, only to the extent that such amendment

permits the Corporation to provide broader indemnification rights than said law permitted to the Corporation prior to such amendment) the Corporation shall indemnify any person against any and all judgments, fines, amounts paid in settling or otherwise disposing of threatened, pending or completed actions, suits or proceedings, whether by reason of the fact that he, his testator or intestate representative, is or was a director or officer of (or a plan fiduciary or plan administrator of any employee benefit plan sponsored by) the Corporation or of (or by) any other corporation of any type or kind, domestic or foreign, which he served in any capacity at the request of the corporation. Expenses so incurred by any such person in defending or investigating a threatened or pending civil or criminal action or proceedings shall at his request be paid by the Corporation in advance of the final disposition of such action or proceeding upon receipt of an undertaking by or on behalf of such director or officer to repay such amount if it shall be ultimately determined that such person is not entitled to be indemnified by the Corporation as authorized by this Article VIII. The foregoing right of indemnification shall in no way be exclusive of any other rights of indemnification to which any such person may be entitled, under any By-law, agreement, vote of shareholders or disinterested directors or otherwise, and shall inure to the benefit of the heirs, executors and administrators of such person.

In addition to the foregoing, consider the following Paragraph 3 of the forbearance agreement:

> Sunbeam agrees to advance to the Individuals [Dunlap and Kersh] their out-of-pocket expenses, costs and legal fees incurred by them in connection with: (i) certain litigations in which they are named as defendants by reason of the fact that they were officers and/or directors of Sunbeam, which litigations are identified in Schedule A to this agreement, and any future litigations in which they are named as defendants by reason of the fact that they were officers and/or directors of Sunbeam or The Coleman Company, Inc. ("Coleman"), and (ii) the investigation of Sunbeam currently being carried out by the Division of Enforcement of the Securities and Exchange Commission ("SEC") and any future investigation relating in any way to the Individuals' performance of their duties at Sunbeam which may be carried out by the SEC or any other governmental agency in accordance with and subject to limitations of reasonableness contained in any employment agreements entered into between the Individuals and Sunbeam, Sunbeam's by-laws, and Delaware law. Such advancement shall be subject to the receipt by Sunbeam of an appropriate undertaking by each of the Individuals to repay any amounts so advanced if it shall be ultimately determined that the Individual is not entitled to be indemnified by Sunbeam for such expenses, costs or fees (the "Undertaking"). Nothing in this Agreement shall constitute a waiver by Sunbeam of any claim for recoupment or repayment of any amounts so advanced, nor shall anything in this Agreement constitute a waiver by the Individuals or a limitation on the individuals with respect to any right to be indemnified by Sunbeam in accordance with applicable law, the By-Laws of Sunbeam, or the Individuals' respective Employment Agreements or to have continued coverage under Sunbeam's Directors' and Officers' Liability Insurance Policy. Sunbeam hereby acknowledges that it has received the Undertaking from the Individuals.

In light of these provisions and the underlying statutes, must Sunbeam advance expenses to Dunlap?

F. SHAREHOLDER PRIMACY NORM

We conclude our study of the duty of care by looking at the question, "To whom do directors owe their duty of care?" The Model Act requires directors to make decisions in the interests of "the corporation," and many cases state that the duty is owed to "the corporation and its shareholders." Despite the implication that "the corporation" is something more than just "the shareholders," courts have often concluded that "the shareholders" are the primary beneficiaries of the duty of care. This aspect of the duty of care is often called the "shareholder primacy norm."

The most commonly quoted judicial statement of the shareholder primacy norm was set out by the Michigan Supreme Court in Dodge v. Ford Motor Co., 170 N.W. 668 (Mich. 1919). This case involved a dispute between Henry Ford and two of the minority shareholders in the Ford Motor Company, John and Horace Dodge. The Dodge brothers owned a Detroit machine shop that supplied parts to the Ford Motor Company and had been instrumental in the early success of Ford's Model T automobile. In exchange for their contributions to the company, the brothers had been awarded 10 percent of the stock, on which they were paid millions of dollars in dividends over a period of about four years. In 1913 the Dodge brothers decided to stop supplying Ford Motor with parts and to begin building competing automobiles.

In an effort to raise capital for their venture, they attempted to sell their shares in the Ford Motor Company, but Henry Ford owned 58 percent of the stock. As with most closely held corporations, there was no market for a minority stake, especially since the majority owner was perceived as being quite eccentric. Further complicating matters for the Dodge brothers, Henry Ford decided to discontinue any special dividends to the shareholders. Ford justified the decision on grounds that he wanted to reduce the price of the Model T (even though he was selling cars as fast as he could manufacture them) and to dedicate large amounts of money to a massive expansion of the company's manufacturing capabilities. In his own words, he wanted to "employ still more men, to spread the benefits of the industrial system to the greatest possible number." Following board approval of Ford's plans, the Dodge brothers sued to force payment of dividends and to enjoin the plans to expand production and cut the prices of Ford's cars. The resulting decision favored the Dodge brothers on the dividend issue, and the court articulated its now famous version of the shareholder primacy norm:

> The difference between an incidental humanitarian expenditure of corporate funds for the benefit of the employees, like the building of a hospital for their use and the employment of agencies for the betterment of their condition, and a general purpose and plan to benefit mankind at the expense of others, is obvious. There should be no confusion (of which there is evidence) of the duties which Mr. Ford conceives that he and the stockholders owe to the general public and the duties which in law he and his codirectors owe to protesting, minority stockholders. A business corporation is organized and carried on primarily for the profit of the stockholders. The powers of the directors are to be employed for that end. The discretion of directors is to be exercised in the choice of means to attain that

end, and does not extend to a change in the end itself, to the reduction of profits, or to the nondistribution of profits among stockholders in order to devote them to other purposes.

At the same time, the court left intact Ford's plan to cut the price of the Model T and expand the company's production facilities. *Dodge* and similar cases have been widely interpreted as suggesting that directors must favor the interests of shareholders over nonshareholders (such as employees of the corporation and the public). Yet, given the business judgment rule, directors clearly have discretion to consider nonshareholder interests in decision making, so long as there is some connection with long-term shareholder interests involved in their exercise of discretion.

Given the shareholder primacy norm, capitalism in the United States and Great Britain is sometimes referred to as "shareholder capitalism," meaning that the overriding goal of the company, beyond producing needed goods and services, is to maximize shareholder wealth. In contrast, continental European and Japanese versions of capitalism are sometimes referred to as "stakeholder capitalism," because the managers of companies are understood to have broader obligations to balance shareholders' interests with the interests and concerns of employees, the community, and society as a whole. In stakeholder capitalism, these broader obligations are implemented as a part of statutory law, such as in the German system of codetermination, which gives employees places on the supervisory boards of public corporations, or as in the French corporate code, which directs managers to operate companies in the "general social interest."

The modern operation of the shareholder primacy norm in the United States is nicely illustrated in the following case, which shows that the connection between board action and long-term shareholder interests can be quite attenuated. The case involves a large charitable contribution by the Occidental Petroleum Corporation. The facts bear close attention, for you can see in them how a large transaction gets structured, what kinds of advisers are involved, and how a board protects itself from future challenges to its decisionmaking.

KAHN v. SULLIVAN

Delaware Supreme Court
594 A.2d 48
January 10, 1992

HOLLAND, Justice.

This is an appeal from the approval of the settlement of one of three civil actions brought in the Court of Chancery by certain shareholders of Occidental Petroleum Corporation ("Occidental"). Each civil action challenged a decision by Occidental's board of directors (the "Board"), through a special committee of Occidental's outside directors ("the Special Committee"), to make a charitable donation. The purpose of the charitable donation was to construct and fund an art museum. . . .

We have concluded that the decision of the Court of Chancery must be affirmed.

Occidental is a Delaware corporation. According to the parties, Occidental has about 290 million shares of stock outstanding which are held by approximately 495 thousand shareholders. For the year ending December 31, 1988, Occidental had assets of approximately twenty billion dollars, operating revenues of twenty billion dollars and pre-tax earnings of $574 million. Its corporate headquarters are located in Los Angeles, California.

At the time of his death on December 10, 1990, Dr. [Armand] Hammer was Occidental's chief executive officer and the chairman of its board of directors. Since the early 1920's, Dr. Hammer had been a serious art collector. When Dr. Hammer died, he personally and The Armand Hammer Foundation (the "Foundation"), owned three major collections of art (referred to in their entirety as "the Art Collection"). The Art Collection, valued at $300-$400 million included: "Five Centuries of Art," more than 100 works by artists such as Rembrandt, Rubens, Renoir and Van Gogh; the Codex Hammer, a rare manuscript by Leonardo da Vinci; and the world's most extensive private collection of paintings, lithographs and bronzes by the French satirist Honore Daumier.

For many years, the Board has determined that it is in the best interest of Occidental to support and promote the acquisition and exhibition of the Art Collection. Through Occidental's financial support and sponsorship, the Art Collection has been viewed by more than six million people in more than twenty-five American cities and at least eighteen foreign countries. The majority of those exhibitions have been in areas where Occidental has operations or was negotiating business contracts. Occidental's Annual Reports to its shareholders have described the benefits and good will which it attributes to the financial support that Occidental has provided for the Art Collection.

Dr. Hammer enjoyed an ongoing relationship with the Los Angeles County Museum of Art ("LACMA") for several decades. In 1968, Dr. Hammer agreed to donate a number of paintings to LACMA, as well as funds to purchase additional art. For approximately twenty years thereafter, Dr. Hammer both publicly and privately expressed his intention to donate the Art Collection to LACMA. However, Dr. Hammer and LACMA had never entered into a binding agreement to that effect. Nevertheless, LACMA named one of its buildings the Frances and Armand Hammer Wing in recognition of Dr. Hammer's gifts.

Occidental approved of Dr. Hammer's decision to permanently display the Art Collection at LACMA. In fact, it made substantial financial contributions to facilitate that display. In 1982, for example, Occidental paid two million dollars to expand and refurbish the Hammer Wing at LACMA.

In 1987, Dr. Hammer presented Daniel N. Belin, Esquire ("Belin"), the president of LACMA's Board of Trustees, with a thirty-nine page proposed agreement which set forth the terms upon which Dr. Hammer would permanently locate the Art Collection at LACMA. LACMA and Dr. Hammer tried, but were unable to reach a binding agreement. Consequently, Dr. Hammer concluded that he would make arrangements for the permanent display of the Art Collection at a location other than at LACMA. On January 8, 1988, Dr. Hammer wrote a letter to Belin which stated that he had "decided to create my own museum to house" the Art Collection.

On January 19, 1988, at a meeting of the executive committee of Occidental's board of directors ("the Executive Committee"), Dr. Hammer proposed that Occidental, in conjunction with the Foundation, construct a museum for the Art Collection. After discussing Occidental's history of identification with the Art Collection, the Executive Committee decided that it was in Occidental's best interest to accept Dr. Hammer's proposal. The Executive Committee approved the negotiation of arrangements for the preliminary design and construction of an art museum. It would be located adjacent to Occidental's headquarters, on the site of an existing parking garage used by Occidental for its employees. The Executive Committee also decided that once the art museum project was substantially defined, a final proposal would be presented to the Board or the Executive Committee for approval and authorization.

The art museum concept was announced publicly on January 21, 1988. On February 11, 1988, the Board approved the Executive Committee's prior actions. Occidental informed its shareholders of the preliminary plan to construct The Armand Hammer Museum and Cultural Center of Art ("the Museum") in its 1987 Annual Report. In accordance with the January 19, 1988 resolutions passed by the Executive Committee, construction of a new parking garage for Occidental began in the fall of 1988. The Board approved a construction bond on November 10, 1988.

On December 15, 1988, the Board was presented with a detailed plan for the Museum proposal. The Board approved the concept and authorized a complete study of the proposal. Following the December 15th Board meeting, the law firm of Dilworth, Paxson, Kalish & Kauffman ("Dilworth") was retained by the Board to examine the Museum proposal and to prepare a memorandum addressing the issues relevant to the Board's consideration of the proposal. [At the time of its selection, Dilworth also represented Dr. Hammer personally.] The law firm of Skadden, Arps, Slate, Meagher & Flom ("Skadden Arps") was retained to represent the new legal entity which would be necessitated by the Museum proposal. Occidental's public accountants, Arthur Andersen & Co. ("Arthur Andersen"), were also asked to examine the Museum proposal.

On or about February 6, 1989, ten days prior to the Board's prescheduled February 16 meeting, Dilworth provided each member of the Board with a ninety-six page memorandum. It contained a definition of the Museum proposal and the anticipated magnitude of the proposed charitable donation by Occidental. It reviewed the authority of the Board to approve such a donation and the reasonableness of the proposed donation. The Dilworth memorandum included an analysis of the donation's effect on Occidental's financial condition, the potential for good will and other benefits to Occidental, and a comparison of the contribution by Occidental to the charitable contributions of other corporations.

The advance distribution of the Dilworth memorandum was supplemented on February 10, 1989 by a tax opinion letter from Skadden Arps. That same day, the Board also received a consulting report from the Duncan Appraisal Corporation. The latter document addressed the option price for the Museum's purchase of Occidental's headquarters building, museum facility and parking garage in thirty years as contemplated by the Museum proposal.

During the February 16 Board meeting, a Dilworth representative personally presented the basis for that law firm's analysis of the Museum proposal, as set forth in its February 6 written memorandum. The presentation reviewed again the directors' standard of conduct in considering the Museum proposal, as well as the financial and tax consequences to Occidental as a result of the donation. Following the Dilworth presentation, the Board resolved to appoint the Special Committee, comprised of its eight independent and disinterested outside directors, to further review and to act upon the Museum proposal. . . .

On February 16, 1989, following the adjournment of the Board meeting, the Special Committee met to consider the proposal presented to the full Board for establishing the Museum. The Special Committee requested the representatives of Dilworth to attend the meeting to respond to any questions relating to its February 6, 1989 opinion letter and memorandum. The Special Committee also asked representatives from Skadden Arps and Arthur Andersen to attend its meeting to address questions concerning the proposed charitable contribution.

The minutes of the February 16, 1989 meeting of the Special Committee outline its consideration of the Museum proposal. Those minutes reflect that many questions were asked by members of the Special Committee and were answered by the representatives of Dilworth, Skadden Arps, or Arthur Andersen. As a result of its own extensive discussions, and in reliance upon the experts' opinions, the Special Committee concluded that the establishment of the Museum, adjacent to Occidental's corporate offices in Los Angeles, would provide benefits to Occidental for at least the thirty-year term of the lease. The Special Committee also concluded that the proposed museum would establish a new cultural landmark for the City of Los Angeles.

On February 16, 1989, the Special Committee unanimously approved the Museum proposal, subject to certain conditions. The proposal approved by the Special Committee included the following provisions:

(1) Occidental would construct a new museum building, renovate portions of four floors of its adjacent headquarters for use by the Museum, and construct a parking garage beneath the museum for its own use for a total cost of approximately $50 million;

(2) Occidental would lease the Museum building and the four floors of its headquarters to the Museum rent-free for a term of thirty years. Occidental would continue to pay the property taxes, and the Museum would pay the utilities and maintenance expenses;

(3) Occidental would purchase a thirty-year annuity at an estimated cost of $35.6 million to provide for the funding of the Museum's operations during its initial years;

(4) Occidental would grant the Museum an irrevocable option to purchase the Museum building, the parking garage, and the Occidental headquarters building in thirty years for $55 million;

(5) Dr. Hammer and the Foundation would transfer the Art Collection entirely to the Museum;

(6) The Museum would be named for Dr. Hammer — The Armand Hammer Museum of Art and Cultural Center;

(7) Occidental would have representation on the board of directors of the Museum;

(8) Occidental would receive public recognition for its role in establishing the Museum, for example, by the naming of the courtyard, library, or auditorium for Occidental and Occidental would have the right to use the Museum, and be entitled to "corporate sponsor" rights. . . .

The Special Committee decided to present requests for expenditures to carry out the foregoing resolutions to the Board in the form of Authorization for Expenditures ("AFE's"). The AFE's proposed by the Special Committee were unanimously approved by the Board when it reconvened on February 16, 1989.

On April 25, 1989, Occidental reported the Special Committee's approval of the Museum proposal to its shareholders in the proxy statement for its annual meeting to be held May 26, 1989. On May 2, 1989, the first shareholder action ("the Kahn action") was filed, challenging Occidental's decision to establish and fund the Museum proposal. The Sullivan [shareholder] action was filed on May 9, 1989. . . .

Settlement negotiations were entered into almost immediately between Occidental and the attorneys for the plaintiffs in the Sullivan action. The attorney for the plaintiffs in the Kahn action was invited to attend the settlement negotiations. After the parties to the Sullivan action were in substantial agreement, the attorney for the plaintiffs in the Kahn action said it was up to his clients whether to accept the settlement, but that he was not going to recommend it.

On June 3, 1989, the parties to the Sullivan action signed a Memorandum of Understanding ("MOU") that set forth a proposed settlement in general terms. The proposed settlement was subject to the right of the plaintiffs to engage in additional discovery to confirm the fairness and adequacy of the proposed settlement.

On June 9, 1989, the plaintiffs in the Kahn action moved for a preliminary injunction to enjoin the proposed settlement in the Sullivan action and also for expedited discovery. An order granting limited expedited discovery on the motion was entered over the defendants' objection. The motion for a preliminary injunction was denied by the Court of Chancery on July 19, 1989. In denying the motion for injunctive relief, the Court of Chancery found that Kahn would suffer no irreparable harm if a proposed settlement in Sullivan was subsequently finalized and submitted for approval since Kahn, as a stockholder of Occidental, would have the opportunity to appear and object to the settlement. The Court of Chancery also identified six issues to be addressed at any future settlement hearing:

> (1) the failure of the Special Committee appointed by the directors of Occidental to hire its own counsel and advisors or even to formally approve the challenged acts; (2) the now worthlessness of a prior donation by Occidental to the Los Angeles County Museum; (3) the huge attorney fees which the parties have apparently decided to seek or not oppose; (4) the egocentric nature of some of Armand Hammer's objections to the Los Angeles County Museum being the recipient of his donation; (5) the issue of who really owns the art; and (6) the lack of any direct substantial benefit to the stockholders.

[Over the course of the next few months, Occidental's board delegated full authority to the Special Committee to settle the litigation. The Special Committee then hired independent counsel with no prior relationship with Occidental to advise it. Pursuant to its delegated authority, the Special Committee entered into a stipulation of settlement in the Sullivan action.]

[Thus,] the parties to the Sullivan action presented the Court of Chancery with a fully executed Stipulation of Compromise, Settlement and Release agreement ("the Settlement") on January 24, 1990. This agreement was only slightly changed from the June 3, 1989 Memorandum of Understanding. The Settlement, *inter alia*, provided:

(1) The Museum building shall be named the "Occidental Petroleum Cultural Center Building" with the name displayed appropriately on the building.

(2) Occidental shall be treated as a corporate sponsor by the Museum for as long as the Museum occupies the building.

(3) Occidental's contribution of the building shall be recognized by the Museum in public references to the facility.

(4) Three of Occidental's directors shall serve on the Museum's Board (or no less than one-third of the total Museum Board) with Occidental having the option to designate a fourth director.

(5) There shall be an immediate loan of substantially all of the art collections of Dr. Hammer to the Museum and there shall be an actual transfer of ownership of the collections upon Dr. Hammer's death or the commencement of operation of the Museum — whichever later occurs.

(6) All future charitable contributions by Occidental to any Hammer-affiliated charities shall be limited by the size of the dividends paid to Occidental's common stockholders. At current dividend levels, Occidental's annual contributions to Hammer-affiliated charities pursuant to this limitation could not exceed approximately three cents per share.

(7) Any amounts Occidental pays for construction of the Museum in excess of $50 million and any amounts paid to the Foundation upon Dr. Hammer's death must be charged against the agreed ceiling on limitations to Hammer-affiliated charities.

(8) Occidental's expenditures for the Museum construction shall not exceed $50 million, except that an additional $10 million may be expended through December 31, 1990 but only if such additional expenditures do not enlarge the scope of construction and if such expenditures are approved by the Special Committee. Amounts in excess of $50 million must be charged against the limitation on donations to Hammer-affiliated charities.

(9) Occidental shall be entitled to receive 50% of any consideration received in excess of a $55 million option price for the Museum property or 50% of any consideration the Museum receives from the assignment or transfer of its option or lease to a third party.

(10) Plaintiffs' attorneys' fees in the Sullivan action shall not exceed $1.4 million. . . .

On April 4, 1990, the settlement hearing in the Sullivan action was held. A number of shareholders appeared or wrote letters objecting to the Settlement. The Objectors argued that the decision of the Special Committee on February 16 to approve the charitable donation to fund the Museum proposal was neither informed nor deliberate and was not cured by any subsequent conduct. Therefore, the Objectors argued that the actions by the Special Committee were not entitled to the protection of the business judgment rule. The Objectors also argued that the charitable donation to the Museum proposal constituted a waste of Occidental's corporate assets. Consequently, in view of the merits of the claims being compromised, the Objectors submitted that the benefits of the proposed Settlement in the Sullivan action were inadequate.

On August 7, 1990, the Court of Chancery found the Settlement to be reasonable under all of the circumstances. The Court of Chancery concluded that the claims asserted by the shareholder plaintiffs would likely be dismissed before or after trial. While noting its own displeasure with the Settlement, the Court of Chancery explained that its role in reviewing the proposed Settlement was restricted to determining in its own business judgment whether, on balance, the Settlement was reasonable. The Court opined that although the benefit to be received from the Settlement was meager, it was adequate considering all the facts and circumstances.

CLAIMS AND DEFENSES

Initially, we will review the Court of Chancery's examination of the nature of the shareholder plaintiffs' claims and the possible defenses thereto, in the context of the legal and factual circumstances presented. The proponents of the Settlement argued that the business judgment rule could undoubtedly have been invoked successfully by the defendants as a complete defense to the shareholder plaintiffs' claims. The business judgment rule "creates a presumption 'that in making a business decision the directors of a corporation acted on an informed basis, in good faith and in the honest belief that the action taken was in the best interests of the corporation.'" The Objectors presented several alternative arguments in support of their contention that the shareholder plaintiffs would have been able to rebut the defense based on the protection which the presumption of the business judgment rule provides. Each of those arguments was based, at least in part, upon this Court's decision in Smith v. Van Gorkom, Del. Supr., 488 A.2d 858 (1985). . . .

[T]he Objectors argued that the presumption of the business judgment rule would have been overcome because the Special Committee proceeded initially without retaining independent legal counsel. In fact, that was a concern identified by the Court of Chancery in its July 19, 1989 opinion. However, in approving the Settlement, the Court of Chancery noted that the Special Committee had retained independent counsel, and "subsequently, and for the first time, formally approved the challenged charitable contributions." Thus, the Court of Chancery specifically found that the Special Committee had the advice of independent legal counsel before it finally approved the Museum proposal.

In this appeal, with respect to the aforementioned finding, the Objectors submit that the Court of Chancery's eventual approval of the Settlement was based upon its mistaken belief that a major judicial concern, *i.e.*, the failure of the Special Committee to retain independent counsel prior to its formal approval of the Museum proposal, had been rectified. In particular, the Objectors contend that the Special Committee formally approved the Museum proposal at its July 20, 1989 meeting. The parties all agree that the Special Committee retained its independent legal counsel on August 4, 1989. Therefore, the Objectors argue that the Court of Chancery's conclusion that the business judgment rule would apply was based upon an erroneous premise.

In response to that argument by the Objectors, the proponents of the Settlement submit the record reflects that the Special Committee reviewed and ratified all of its prior actions on September 20, 1989, after retaining independent legal counsel. Accordingly, the proponents of the Settlement contend that, whether the September 20, 1989 action by the Special Committee is characterized as the first final approval of the Museum proposal or as a re-approval of its action taken on July 20, 1989, the Special Committee's ultimate decision to proceed with the Museum proposal was based upon the advice of independent counsel.

The Objectors' third argument in the Court of Chancery, challenging the viability of the business judgment rule as a successful defense, was based upon *Van Gorkom* and contended that the Special Committee and other directors were grossly negligent in failing to inform themselves of all material information reasonably available to them.[25] Thus, the Objectors argued that even if, arguendo, the Special Committee was itself independent and formally approved the Museum proposal after its retention of independent legal counsel, such approval would not have cured the Special Committee's prior failure to exercise due care. The Court of Chancery found the record showed that the Special Committee had given due consideration to the Museum proposal and rejected the Objectors' argument to the contrary. . . .

Following its analysis and conclusion that the business judgment rule would have been applicable to any judicial examination of the Special Committee's actions, the Court of Chancery considered the shareholder plaintiffs' claim that the Board and the Special Committee's approval of the charitable donation to the Museum proposal constituted a waste of Occidental's corporate assets. In doing so, it recognized that charitable donations by Delaware corporations are expressly authorized by 8 Del. C. §122(9). It also recognized that although §122(9) places no limitations on the size of a charitable corporate gift, that section has been construed "to authorize any reasonable corporate gift of a charitable or educational nature." Thus, the Court of Chancery concluded that the test to be applied in examining the merits of a claim alleging corporate waste "is that of reasonableness, a test in which the provisions of the Internal Revenue Code pertaining to charitable gifts by corporations furnish a helpful guide." We agree with that conclusion.

The Objectors argued that Occidental's charitable contribution to the Museum proposal was unreasonable and a waste of corporate assets because it was excessive.[26] The Court of Chancery recognized that not every charitable gift constitutes a valid corporate action. Nevertheless, the Court of Chancery concluded, given the net worth of Occidental, its annual net income before taxes, and the tax benefits to Occidental, that the gift to the Museum was within the range of reasonableness. . . . Therefore, the Court of Chancery found that it was "reasonably probable" that plaintiffs would fail on their claim of waste. That finding is supported by the record and is the product of an orderly and logical deductive process. . . .

CONCLUSION

The reasonableness of a particular class action settlement is addressed to the discretion of the Court of Chancery, on a case by case basis, in light

---

25. The Objectors submit that, *inter alia*, the Special Committee was apparently uninformed as to potential tax consequences of the charitable donation, the value of the Art Collection, how much of the Art Collection had been purchased with donations from Occidental, and what the cost for the Museum's rent-free use of the property would be to Occidental.

26. The Objectors also argued that the Museum project duplicated facilities previously funded by Occidental; served no social need; was designed primarily to enhance the personal reputation of Dr. Hammer; and resulted in damage (not good will) to Occidental. The Court of Chancery concluded that these concerns were ones about which reasonable minds could differ. That conclusion is also supported by the record and is the product of an orderly deductive process. . . .

of all of the relevant circumstances. In this case, we find that all of the Court of Chancery's factual findings of fact are supported by the record. We also find that all of the legal conclusions reached by the Court of Chancery were based upon a proper application of well established principles of law. Consequently, we find that the Court of Chancery did not abuse its discretion in deciding to approve the Settlement in the Sullivan action. . . .

SALOMON BROTHERS: A CASE STUDY

The U.S. Treasury Department generally sells its bills (less than one years' maturity); notes (one to five years' maturity); and bonds (over five years' maturity) using a closed-bid, multiple-price auction system and holding more than 150 auctions a year. Under that system, the U.S. government does not set a price for the securities it is selling. Rather, the government announces the quantity and maturity of securities it intends to sell (for instance, $9 billion of five-year U.S. Treasury notes), and potential purchasers submit bids indicating the quantity of securities they want to purchase and the price that they would be willing to pay for those securities. Prior to 1990, if auctions were oversubscribed, the Treasury Department had a policy of limiting sales to any one purchaser to 35 percent of the securities being auctioned. In such cases, the Department would recognize bids above 35 percent but fill the bids it had received by prorating each bidder's total bid. Under the pre-July 1990 rules, bidders might thus decide to submit a bid for more than 35 percent of the total being auctioned to increase their chances of getting the full number of securities they wanted, after proration.

In 1990, Salomon Brothers' managing director, Paul M. Mozer, who was the head of Salomon's Government [Bond] Trading Desk, became particularly aggressive in bidding for more than 35 percent of securities being auctioned. Indeed, in one July 1990 auction Mozer bid for more than 100 percent of the securities being auctioned, prompting a call from a senior Treasury official, Michael Basham, who asked Mozer not to be so aggressive in his bidding.

Mozer was noncommital in his response to Basham, which is odd enough in a relationship between the regulated and a top regulator, but then bid for more than 100 percent of the securities being auctioned in the very next auction. When Basham tried to call Mozer to criticize the aggressive bidding in this auction, Mozer refused to return Basham's phone call. The next day, the Treasury Department changed its rules, stating that in future auctions no bidder could bid (either for its own account or for a customer) at any one price for more than 35 percent of the securities being auctioned. Mozer was publicly critical of both the rule change and of Michael Basham, including being quoted in the New York Times as saying that the rule change was unnecessary and that the Treasury Department did not understand the market. On Wall Street, the rule became known as the "Mozer/Basham" rule.

Privately, Mozer took other actions in response to the rule change. Beginning in December 1990, Mozer began occasionally submitting unauthorized customer bids for more than 35 percent of securities being auctioned. In a number of auctions, Mozer submitted bids allegedly for Salomon's customers, without the customers' knowledge or authorization, and then "sold" the securities purchased through the unauthorized bids to Salomon Brothers for the

Government Trading Desk's own account (securities Salomon owned for investment or resale). According to standard Salomon procedures, the submission of the bid, the purchase from the Treasury Department, and the subsequent "sale" to Salomon all should have generated customer confirmations — that is, a written notice to the customer of the activity in its account. Mozer, who was a highly placed Salomon employee, was able to ensure that no confirmation was sent at any of these three points in the transaction by issuing "Do Not Confirm" instructions for the unauthorized trades. Between July 1990 and July 1991, Mozer submitted partially or wholly unauthorized customer bids, and engaged in other trading irregularities, in seven auctions. Each unauthorized customer bid submitted by Mozer to the Treasury Department was a crime by virtue of 18 U.S.C. §1001, which prohibits knowingly making false statements to the government.

One of the auctions in which Mozer submitted unauthorized bids and suppressed customer confirmations was an auction on February 21, 1991, of $9 billion of five-year U.S. Treasury notes. In that auction, Mozer submitted a bid for $3.15 billion of the notes (35 percent) for Salomon's account, at a yield of 7.51 percent to maturity. Thus, according to the Treasury Department rules, Salomon was prohibited from submitting any other bids at 7.51 percent. Mozer, however, submitted two additional unauthorized $3.15 billion bids at 7.51 percent in the name of two of its established customers: the Quantum Fund, and Mercury Asset Management (Mercury). The Federal Reserve Bank of New York (the Fed), which administered the auction, prorated each of the $3.15 billion bids at 54 percent, awarding $1.701 billion of the securities on each bid. Since each of the bids was actually Mozer's bid for Salomon's account, Salomon ended up with a total of $5.103 billion of the notes, or 56.7 percent of the securities being auctioned.

In the February 21, 1991 auction just described, a primary dealer named S.G. Warburg also submitted a bid at 7.51 percent for $100 million of securities. S.G. Warburg and Mercury Asset Management were both subsidiaries of the same holding company, S.G. Warburg, PLC, so if their bids were aggregated they had bid over the 35 percent limit, in violation of the new Treasury Department rules. On February 21, 1991, the Fed notified the Treasury Department of this fact, but employees of the Treasury Department decided not to reduce the amount of either bid for purposes of determining the results of the auction, in particular since proration in the auction was so significant. At the same time, the Treasury Department decided to investigate Warburg and Mercury's corporate relationship to determine if their bids should be aggregated for purposes of the 35 percent rule in the future. Ultimately concluding that aggregation was appropriate, the Treasury Department wrote a letter on April 17, 1991, to Warburg, PLC, discussing the February 21, 1991, bids by S.G. Warburg and Mercury, and informing Warburg, PLC that in the future S.G. Warburg and Mercury's bids would be aggregated for determining compliance with the 35 percent rule. Copies of the letter were sent to Mercury and to Mozer.

The Treasury Department letter clearly presented a problem for Mozer, since Mercury had not actually submitted a bid in the February 21 auction. Mozer first called a managing director at Mercury, said that a clerk at Salomon Brothers had made a mistake and had incorrectly placed Mercury's name on a bidding sheet, that the problem had been corrected internally and that Mozer would be grateful if the Mercury director would keep the matter confidential.

Mozer then went to the office of his boss, John Meriwether, and showed Meriwether the Treasury Department letter. John Meriwether was a vice-chairman of Salomon Brothers in charge of the firm's fixed income (bond) and proprietary trading (trading for Salomon's own account). When Meriwether finished reading the letter, Mozer told him that Mercury had not bid in the auction nor authorized the bid, and that the bid had been for Salomon Brothers. Meriwether was shocked at Mozer's confession, and told Mozer that the incident was "career-threatening" and that Meriwether would have to immediately discuss the matter with Thomas Strauss, the president of Salomon Brothers. Meriwether asked Mozer if Mozer had ever submitted other unauthorized customer bids, and Mozer incorrectly said no.

Over the course of the following days, a number of conversations took place between John Meriwether, Thomas Strauss, John Gutfreund (chairman and CEO of Salomon), and Salomon's chief legal officer, Donald Feuerstein. (Gutfreund and Strauss were both directors of Salomon, as well as being top executive officers.) Feuerstein's legal advice, in summary, was that the unauthorized bid was a crime and that while there was probably no legal duty to report the unauthorized bid (based on existing securities law doctrine), Salomon Brothers should report it to the government as a matter of good judgment. Meriwether, Strauss, Gutfreund, and Feuerstein came away from the discussions with the sense that a decision had been made to report the unauthorized bid to the government but no clear sense of who was going to make the report, and to whom the report would be made. As the SEC put it in their eventual consent settlement of the matter:

> Meriwether stated that he believed that Strauss would make an appointment to report the matter to Gerald Corrigan, the President of the Federal Reserve Bank of New York. Feuerstein stated that he believed that Gutfreund wanted to think further about how the bid should be reported . . . [but] that [Feuerstein] believed the report should be made to the Federal Reserve Bank of New York, which could then, if it wanted, pass the information on to the Treasury department. Strauss stated that he believed that he and Gutfreund would report the matter in a personal visit with Corrigan. . . . Gutfreund stated that he believed that a decision had been made that he and Strauss, either separately or together, would speak to Corrigan about the matter.

In re John H. Gutfreund, Thomas W. Strauss and John. W. Meriwether, 51 S.E.C. 93 (1992).

Over the next few months, Feuerstein and Gutfreund had occasional conversations about the matter, but no report was made to the government.

During the course of the April discussions, there was no discussion of undertaking further investigations of Mozer's actions, nor of putting limits on his authority to submit bids in future U.S. Treasury auctions. After Mozer's disclosure to his superiors of one unauthorized customer bid in the February 21 auction, he submitted two additional unauthorized bids. These additional bidding irregularities, as well as the other previous unauthorized customer bids, only came to light after other conduct by Mozer (alleged antitrust violations with respect to the securities sold in the May 22, 1991, Treasury auction) prompted an internal investigation of Mozer's actions.

In early July, Salomon Brothers engaged an outside law firm to conduct an investigation into Mozer's activities with respect to the May 22, 1991, auction, since by then it was clear that the government was investigating alleged antitrust problems. By mid-July, the law firm suggested broadening the scope of the investigation, because they had begun to get information about unauthorized customer bids. That investigation concluded in early August, by which point the law firm had uncovered evidence of bidding irregularities by Mozer in five Treasury auctions. The results of the investigation were reported to Feuerstein on August 6, 1991, and to Gutfreund, Strauss, and Meriwether on August 7. After consultation with counsel and public relations advisors, Salomon issued a press release on Friday, August 9, stating that it had "uncovered irregularities and rule violations in connection with its submission of bids in certain auctions of Treasury securities." The press release described the bidding violations and stated that Salomon had "suspended two managing directors on the Government Trading Desk and two other employees," with pay, until further facts were known. The August 9 press release made no mention of Gutfreund, Strauss, Meriwether, and Feuerstein's knowledge for four months of one unauthorized customer bid.

Late in the evening of Thursday, August 8, as the press release was being drafted, Strauss and Feuerstein arranged to have a telephone conversation with a Salomon board member and major stockholder, who ultimately became quite important to keeping Salomon Brothers alive: Warren Buffett. Buffett, who is sometimes referred to as the "Oracle of Omaha" (because he lives in Omaha, Nebraska, and because of his ability to pick winning investments), is one of the country's wealthiest individuals, with a reputation for tough-minded honesty. His company, Berkshire Hathaway, is a holding company that owns various other companies (including textile, insurance, and financial services companies). Berkshire Hathaway often seeks to buy companies outright, but occasionally it will take a major stake in a company, as it did in 1987 when it invested $700 million in Salomon in return for 9 percent preferred stock that was convertible into a 12 percent stake in the company. Buffett also got a seat on Salomon's board of directors. When Buffett spoke with Strauss and Feuerstein on the night of August 8, he was told in general terms about Mozer's actions, and was read the press release. Based on that phone conversation, Buffett thought the problem was being handled appropriately and that the press release was adequate.

Buffett's business partner, Charlie Munger, who is a lawyer, heard things differently that Thursday night, as the press release was being drafted. Munger had been told in a telephone conversation with Feuerstein that "one part of the problem had been known since April," and Munger immediately wanted to know what had been known, and by whom. When he was told that Gutfreund, Strauss, Meriwether, and Feuerstein had known of one unauthorized bid since April and had failed to notify the Fed, Munger argued that the press release must make that fact clear. Feuerstein disagreed, stating that Salomon's management was concerned that disclosure of those facts, not clearly required by securities law precedent, could have a negative impact on Salomon's ability to fund its ongoing operations. However, Munger was on vacation on an island in Minnesota and was unable to talk to Buffett until after the press release was issued. Thus, the strategy that was developed and implemented was for Salomon to call its directors and regulators on August 9, as it issued the press release, and tell them that management had known of one unauthorized customer bid since April but not to include that fact in the press release.

Hindsight shows that Salomon's August 9 press strategy was a disaster. Various Treasury Department and Federal Reserve Bank officials were furious that top managers had known since April of one of Mozer's unauthorized bids and had not told the government immediately about the problem. (This fury was exacerbated by the fact that Gutfreund had met with top Treasury officials in June to discuss the antitrust allegations about the May 22, 1991, auction, and had not brought up the subject of the unauthorized customer bid.) Thus, when reporters called administration officials on August 9 to get reactions to the press release, all they heard about was that "management had known about this," which set off a wild round of press accounts speculating about whether top management had been involved in the illegality or whether the facts that were known were just the tip of the iceberg of what would be discovered to be widespread illegality (neither of which proved to be the case).

By early the next week, it was clear that Salomon would need to disclose further facts, given all the press speculation. Moreover, once Buffett and Munger had had an opportunity to talk, Buffett began to press for further disclosure. Thus, Salomon scheduled a board of directors meeting for Wednesday, August 14, and at that meeting a more descriptive press release was approved. The August 14 press release included specific details about each of the bidding violations that had been uncovered and stated that certain top managers had known of one unauthorized bid since April 1991 and had failed to disclose it to the government. At the same time, the board was not told that on the previous day, the Fed had delivered a letter to Gutfreund calling into question whether Salomon could continue to submit bids for its customers in Treasury auctions and asking for a complete report within ten days of all of the "irregularities, violations, and oversights" of which Salomon was aware. Carol J. Loomis, *Warren Buffett's Wild Ride at Salomon*, Fortune, Oct. 27, 1997, at 114. As Buffett interpreted these events, Fed president Corrigan expected the letter to be given to the board and also expected that the board would recognize that top management needed to be ousted based on the seriousness with which the regulators viewed their lack of disclosure. When the board failed to act to force Gutfreund's resignation, according to Buffett, "[u]nderstandably, the Fed felt at this point that the directors had joined with management in spitting in its face."

Two days later, Gutfreund and Strauss resigned under pressure, and Buffett agreed to take on the role of interim chairman of Salomon, Inc., for the princely sum of $1 per year. (At the time of Gutfreund and Strauss's resignation, Meriwether's continued employment at Salomon was uncertain. Meriwether determined a few days after Buffett took over that it would be best for the firm for Meriwether to resign, which he did. Soon after, Feuerstein was forced to resign.) Buffett's actions are generally credited with having been critical in Salomon's survival. He has tremendous credibility with regulators, with Congress (which immediately began investigations of the matter, given the importance to the national interest of the integrity of the market for U.S. Treasury securities), with market participants, and with the press. Moreover, Buffett acted immediately and decisively to distance himself and the new management team from the problems of the past management team, calling their delay in notifying regulators of Mozer's illegal conduct "inexcusable and inexplicable"; implementing new procedures to prohibit overriding the customer confirmation system; and promising—and delivering—full cooperation with the government in fully investigating the extent of Mozer's wrongdoing. To emphasize the extent of his commitment to ethical business, Buffett sent a memo to each of Salomon's 8,000 employees soon after he took over indicating that there would be no tolerance for unethical misconduct:

> If you lose money for the firm by bad decisions, I will be very understanding. If you lose reputation for the firm, I will be ruthless. There is plenty of money to be made — and I want to make it — playing straight down the center of the court. I don't want anyone playing close to the line.

The memo concluded by saying that Buffett wanted to know of any ethical or legal violations, with the exception of minor traffic violations, and underlining the seriousness of his commitment by including his home telephone number.

These events, lavishly reported in the press (particularly since August is typically a slow news month), had a predictable effect on Salomon's stock price: it dropped. From a high of $36 dollars per share prior to the first press release, the stock fell 25 percent to $27 per share after the second release. There were other effects as well: the Fed suspended Salomon's ability to bid in auctions for customers; large institutional investors, such as state pension funds, suspended their dealings with Salomon Brothers; Salomon's underwriting business dried up; and Salomon's bond ratings were downgraded by Moody's and other bond rating companies. The stock price drop, combined with these corollary effects, had another predictable effect: it led to litigation. First, Salomon's stockholders brought federal securities litigation challenging the accuracy of Salomon's press disclosures. Next, Salomon's stockholders brought derivative litigation challenging Gutfreund, Strauss, Meriwether, and Mozer's exercise of their duty of care. The derivative plaintiffs made the following assertions in their Amended Consolidated Derivative Complaint:

> ¶4. As set forth in greater detail below, the head of Salomon's Government Trading Desk, Paul Mozer, aided and abetted by his closest associates and assistants, implemented a campaign to wrongfully manipulate the trading of United States Treasury securities in at least eight different treasury auctions in and prior to 1991. The violations included placing bids in the names of customers that were actually intended for Salomon's own account and maintaining false books and records intended to avoid detection by proper governmental authorities. These manipulations enabled Salomon to receive more than 35% of the securities offered at some Treasury auctions in violation of applicable laws and regulations, and in one case, enabled Salomon to receive 94% of the securities available at an auction. Mozer and others under his control sought to take advantage of Salomon's resulting market power by negotiating unfairly favorable terms on transactions involving the Treasury securities that Salomon acquired so as to increase the profits generated through their trading activities and thereby increase their compensation and their status both within the firm and outside.
>
> ¶5. Salomon's then most senior executives, including defendants John Gutfreund (Chairman of the Board and CEO), Thomas Strauss (then Vice-Chairman) and John Meriwether (chief of Salomon's fixed-income securities trading), were advised of Mozer's misconduct by Mozer no later than late April 1991 and determined that disclosure to appropriate government authorities should be promptly made. In breach of their fiduciary obligations, and contrary to the best interests of Salomon and its shareholders, these senior executives wrongfully delayed advising relevant government officials, misinformed government officials of the true facts and took no steps to prevent or investigate the underlying wrongdoing

or discipline the known perpetrators. The Individual Defendants failed to reveal these facts to government regulators, the investing public and the full Salomon board until disclosure was forced by the inquiries of government officials and the results of a confidential investigation by outside counsel which they had no role in initiating.

¶6. Largely as a result of the wrongful failures by Gutfreund, Strauss and Meriwether to promptly investigate, discipline, report and prevent the wrongful bidding practices, and their affirmative concealment of the underlying misconduct from senior government officials, Salomon, upon public revelation of the facts, was threatened by total expulsion from the Treasury bidding market which, if such penalty had been exacted, would have had devastating consequences for the totality of its business and potentially forced the Company into bankruptcy. As it was, the Company suffered a major and costly suspension of [its ability to enter bids for customers for close to a year], and, in addition, the image and reputation of Salomon was severely damaged and Salomon has incurred over $290 million in civil fines, penalties and payments and has suffered other serious loss of business and commercial or financial repercussions, among other resulting injuries.

¶19. By reason of their positions and because of their ability to control the business and corporate affairs of Salomon Brothers at all relevant times, the Individual Defendants owed . . . fiduciary obligations of fidelity, trust, loyalty, and due care and were and are required to use their utmost ability to control, supervise and manage Salomon and its subsidiaries in a fair, just and equitable manner and to act in furtherance of the best interests of Salomon and its stockholders and to exercise due care and loyalty in the management and administration of the affairs of Salomon Brothers and in the use and preservation of their properties and assets.

¶21. The Individual Defendants, because of their positions of control and authority as officers and senior executives of Salomon Brothers, were able to and did, directly or indirectly, control the operations of Salomon's Government Trading Desk and the reporting of misdeeds by Mozer and others to the Federal Reserve, Treasury and other relevant government agencies. The Individual Defendants participated in the alleged wrongdoing, in part, in order to (i) conceal and cover up their own prior misconduct and mismanagement of Salomon and avoid being held responsible therefor; (ii) protect their executive positions and the substantial compensation they obtained thereby; (iii) obtain enhanced and/or bonus compensation pursuant to management incentive plans; and/or (iv) inflate and maintain the price of Salomon's securities which the Individual Defendants owned or had options to purchase at favorable prices.

As members of the board or senior officers, Gutfreund, Strauss and Meriwether were covered by Salomon's D&O insurance policy, and indemnified "to the full extent of Delaware law." Thus, Salomon's Certificate of Incorporation stated that:

> To the extent permitted by law, as the same exists or may hereafter be amended (but, in the case of such amendment, only to the extent that such amendment permits the Corporation to provide broader indemnification rights than said law permitted to the Corporation prior to such amendment) the Corporation shall indemnify any person against any and all judgments, fines, amounts paid in settling or otherwise disposing of threatened, pending or completed actions, suits or proceedings, whether by reason of the fact that he, his testator or intestate representative, is or was a director or officer of (or a plan fiduciary or plan administrator of any employee benefit plan sponsored by) the Corporation or of (or by) any other corporation of any type or kind, domestic or foreign, which he

served in any capacity at the request of the corporation. The foregoing right of indemnification shall in no way be exclusive of any other rights or indemnification to which any such person may be entitled, under any By-law, agreement, vote of shareholders or disinterested directors or otherwise, and shall inure to the benefit of the heirs, executors and administrators of such person.

QUESTIONS

(1)   Analyze the plaintiffs' duty of care claim against Gutfreund, Strauss and Meriwether. If you represented Salomon Brothers, what arguments would you make? How would you advise the Company to proceed in this litigation?

(2)   Soon after the litigation ensued, Gutfreund, Strauss and Meriwether, each represented by separate counsel, sought a commitment from Salomon Brothers that it would advance the costs of defending them in the litigation, pursuant to the Articles of Incorporation. As part of its "new broom sweeps clean" strategy, the board of directors wanted to deny those requests in order to emphasize the differences between the philosophies of the new management team versus the old one and to signal that it was no longer "business as usual" at Salomon. How would you advise the board on this issue?

(3)   If you represented the plaintiffs and wanted to bring a claim against the board as a whole, instead of against individual officers, how would you structure the complaint? What additional facts would you need to investigate? What are the difficulties in bringing such a claim?

(4)   What advice would you give the board on changes they could make with respect to structure and functioning to give greater emphasis to law compliance at the board level? What additional facts do you need to investigate prior to making recommendations? What are the risks to the board from implementing a changed law compliance structure?

CHAPTER
11

Directors' and Shareholders' Duty of Loyalty

Any time a director or manager participates in a transaction involving a conflict of interest — that is, a transaction in which the director or manager may be motivated not only by the interests of the corporation but also by self-interest — the duty of loyalty is implicated. For example, when a board of directors approves a stock option plan under which the directors receive options, the directors have divided loyalties. On the one hand, as fiduciaries for the corporation, they should be interested in issuing the smallest number of options possible while ensuring that their compensation packages remain competitive with those of other companies. On the other hand, as recipients of the options, the directors may want to award the most generous options package possible. As a general rule, the duty of loyalty requires that directors serve the interests of the corporation over their self-interest, but this general rule does not resolve many of the real cases, which can be very complicated. Because of the complexity of the subject, courts have tended to analyze duty of loyalty claims differently in different contexts: general self-dealing, the fiduciary duties of majority shareholders, and expropriation of corporate opportunities are the categories of cases most often used. Each of these is explored in more detail below.

A. GENERAL SELF-DEALING

Although perhaps all director transactions with a corporation run the risk of exploiting the corporation for the benefit of the director, the law tolerates some amount of conflict simply because the benefits of such transactions often are so high. For example, a director of a closely held corporation may in some instances be the only individual willing to enter into a transaction with the corporation. In such a circumstance, a court could rightly be accused of overzealousness if it prohibited a transaction that would benefit all associated with the corporation. In public corporations, most directors are successful business people with financial interests in multiple companies. To the extent that directors are involved in multiple companies that do business with each other or have "corporate relationships" such as parent/subsidiary relationships,

471

conflicts are endemic. To prohibit all conflict-of-interest transactions in this context might sharply limit the pool of people who would be willing to serve as directors of America's public companies. Instead, corporate law attempts to identify "bad" transactions — those that are unfair to the company and its shareholders — while allowing "good" transactions — those that are fair — to go forward. This winnowing of fair from unfair is done using a collection of substantive and procedural rules under corporate law. By way of contrast, securities law focuses primarily on accurate disclosure of conflict-of-interest transactions.

At one time courts dealt with the possible harms inherent in self-interested transactions by making such transactions void or voidable by the corporation or a complaining shareholder. But this posture introduced a high degree of uncertainty into the binding effect of conflict-of-interest transactions, and eventually it was abandoned in favor of a narrower rule. Modern statutes like the former Modern Business Corporations Act (Model Act) §8.31 (which has been replaced by Subchapter F of the Model Act but still is in force in many states) and Delaware General Corporation Law (DGCL) §144 provide that conflict-of-interest transactions are not void or voidable if: (1) the material facts are disclosed to the board of directors or shareholders, *and* (2) either the disinterested directors or the disinterested shareholders authorize, approve, or ratify the transaction. Alternatively, conflict-of-interest transactions are not void or voidable if they are fair to the corporation. Although the statutes are disjunctive — implying that conflict-of-interest transactions are not void or voidable if they are *either* procedurally *or* substantively fair — most courts require some evidence of substantive fairness even when the procedural requirements have been met, particularly where the transaction is between the corporation and a controlling shareholder, as will be seen below. The substantive fairness of a conflict-of-interest transaction is demonstrated by showing both fair price and fair dealing.

In the mid-1990s, the Model Act was amended to clarify the implications of approval by disinterested directors or shareholders, but the amended provision is complex, and few states have adopted it. The amended Model Act applies only to "director's conflicting interest transactions," a term that is defined to include any transaction in which the beneficial financial interest of a director is of such financial significance to the director that the interest "would reasonably be expected to exert an influence on the director's judgment if [he or she] were called upon to vote on the transaction." Under Model Act §8.61, interested transactions may not be enjoined if (a) the board approves the transaction in accordance with Model Act §8.62; (b) the shareholders approve the transaction in accordance with Model Act §8.63; or (c) the transaction is fair to the corporation at the time it is authorized. The first two are *procedural* protections designed to remove the taint of self-interest. The third is a *substantive* protection designed to allow fair transactions even if they have never been approved by disinterested parties. Note that if approval were obtained in accordance with the statute, this would not necessarily validate the transaction; it would simply eliminate the interested-director cloud. The decision would still be subject to the business judgment rule and the duty of care.

The following case is a decision of the Delaware Supreme Court that illustrates a "classic" conflict-of-interest situation in a relatively simple fact pattern. It discusses the impact of approval of a conflict-of-interest transaction under Delaware law (DGCL §144) by a disinterested committee of directors or by disinterested shareholders. It also discusses the impact of an exculpation pro-vision authorized by §102(b)(7) on a duty of loyalty claim. In this opinion the court remands for further proceedings. While this opinion was not the last word in this litigation, it does provide a good overview of Delaware's statutory approach to conflict-of-interest transactions.

EMERALD PARTNERS v. BERLIN

726 A.2d 1215
Supreme Court of Delaware
March 16, 1999

WALSH, Justice.

In this appeal from the Court of Chancery, we review the grant of summary judgment in favor of the defendant corporation and its directors, on the ground that the plaintiffs, in their attack on a merger, had not sufficiently pled claims of entire fairness and best price. We conclude that the entire fairness claim was fairly pleaded and is intertwined with disclosure violation claims. Accordingly, we reverse as to the director defendants. . . .

I.

The appellant, Emerald Partners, a New Jersey limited partnership [and a minority shareholder of defendant May Petroleum, Inc. ("May")], filed this action on March 1, 1988, to enjoin the consummation of a merger between May, a Delaware corporation and thirteen corporations owned by Craig Hall ("Hall"), the Chairman and Chief Executive Officer of May. Also joined as defendants were May's directors, Ronald P. Berlin, David L. Florence, Rex A. Sebastian, and Theodore H. Strauss (collectively the "director defendants"). . . .

In October, 1987, Hall, at that time a holder of 52.4% of May's common stock, proposed a merger of May and thirteen sub-chapter S corporations owned by Hall that were primarily engaged in the real estate service business. The board of directors of May consisted of Hall and Berlin, the inside directors, and Florence, Sebastian and Strauss, the outside directors.

The outside directors authorized the engagement of Bear Stearns & Company ("Bear Stearns") to act as investment advisor and render a fairness opinion to the board and the May stockholders. On the basis of company valuations and the Bear Stearns fairness letter, the transaction, as eventually crafted, contem-plated that Hall would receive twenty-seven million May common shares in exchange for the merger of the Hall corporations with May, increasing Hall's shareholding to 73.5% of May's outstanding common stock as reflected in the post-merger entity.

May and the Hall corporations entered into a proposed merger agreement on November 30, 1987. On February 1, 1988, effective January 29, 1988, Hall reduced his beneficial interest in May to 25% of the outstanding com-mon stock by transferring shares to independent irrevocable trusts created for the benefit of his children. This transfer took place before the record date and prior to the stockholder vote on the merger. The merger agreement was reaffirmed by the board on February 13, 1988 with the only change reflecting the reduction in Hall's ownership. On February 16, 1988, May issued a proxy statement to shareholders that described May, the Hall corporations and the proposed merger terms. The May shareholders approved the merger on March 11, 1988, despite the pendency of the Emerald Partners' request for injunctive relief. . . . [Emerald Partners' request to enjoin the merger was granted by the Chancery Court on the basis that there wasn't a quorum voting, and then reversed by the Delaware Supreme Court.]

[T]he merger was completed on August 15, 1988.

Despite the consummation of the merger, Emerald Partners continued its class and derivative claims and these efforts are reflected in several subsequent rulings in the Court of Chancery. The present appeal stems from decisions of the Court of Chancery, which granted summary judgment in favor of both individual and corporate defendants. . . .

II.

A.

Emerald Partners claims that the Court of Chancery erred in refusing to consider its entire fairness and best price claims directed against the merger and then granting summary judgment based on May's certificate of incorporation provision, which tracks the language of 8 Del. C. §102(b)(7) — Delaware's director exculpation statute. . . .

As a matter of substantive law, the circumstances attendant upon the events leading to the negotiation of the merger would appear to implicate the entire fairness standard. Hall, as Chairman and Chief Executive Officer of both May and the Hall corporations and sole owner of the Hall corporations, clearly stood on both sides of the transaction. Additionally, at the time the parties entered the proposed merger agreement in November of 1987, Hall owned 52.4% of May common stock. Also, a breach of any one of the board of directors' triad of fiduciary duties, loyalty, good faith or due care, sufficiently rebuts the business judgment presumption and permits a challenge to the board's action under the entire fairness standard.

The Court of Chancery acknowledged that Emerald Partners' complaint and briefs cited facts that "might raise a question as to the judgment and care of the defendant directors" regarding their proxy statement disclosure decisions connected with the merger. While this statement by the court was not a finding that the director defendants had breached their duty of care, Emerald Partners has made a sufficient showing through factual allegations that entire fairness should be the standard by which the directors' actions are reviewed. Such a showing shifts to the director defendants the burden to establish that the challenged transaction was entirely fair.

B.

The Court of Chancery refused to consider Emerald Partners' entire fairness claim [finding it] ill-pleaded and examined the disclosure claims, standing alone. We conclude that the entire fairness and disclosure claims under these circumstances were intertwined and should not have been separately considered.

Emerald Partners contends that the February 16, 1988 proxy statement distributed in connection with, and seeking shareholder approval of, the proposed merger, contained misstatements about the merger negotiation process and misstatements or omissions regarding an investment. Specifically Emerald Partners challenges the following individual recitals in the proxy statement:

i) "[i]n connection with the Merger, the Non-Affiliated Directors have frequently held separate deliberations and have relied extensively on the advice of its independent legal counsel;"

ii) "[t]he terms of the Merger, including the exchange ratio of May Common Stock for shares of the Hall Corporations, were the result of arm's-length negotiations between representatives of the Hall Corporations and the Non-Affiliated Directors;" and

iii) the lack of disclosure regarding May's participation in the acquisition of the Singer Company.

The Court of Chancery held that the director defendants could not be found liable as a matter of law regardless of the materiality of these alleged omissions or misstatements. The court found that, throughout the relevant time period, a provision in May's certificate of incorporation protected the directors from liability for money damages for the proxy statement claims when "acting in honest pursuit of the best interests of the corporation." The court agreed with the defendants that Emerald Partners "failed to allege or reveal facts to support a conclusion that the directors acted in a manner which excepted them from the protections" of the charter provision "in deciding upon the appropriate extent of disclosure to be made in the proxy statement."

As previously noted, the Court of Chancery performed a separate analysis of both the entire fairness standard and the disclosure claim. Once the entire fairness standard has been implicated, as here, the defendants, at least initially, bear the burden of demonstrating the two basic aspects of fair dealing and fair price. Kahn v. Lynch Communication Systems, Inc., 638 A.2d 1110, 1115 (Del. 1994). The burden of proof on the issue of fairness may shift. This Court has identified two scenarios that can provide the basis for shifting the burden to the plaintiff to demonstrate that the transaction complained of was not entirely fair. First, an approval of the transaction by an independent committee of directors who have real bargaining power that can be exerted in dealings with a majority shareholder who does not dictate the terms of the merger may supply the necessary basis for shifting the burden. Kahn v. Lynch, 638 A.2d at 1118-19; Kahn v. Tremont Corp., 694 A.2d 422, 428 (Del. 1997); see also 8 Del. C. §144(a)(1). "It is the care, attention and sense of individual responsibility to the performance of one's duties . . . that generally touches on independence." Aronson v. Lewis, 473 A.2d 805, 816 (Del. 1984). Second, the approval of the transaction by a fully informed vote of a majority of the minority shareholders will shift the burden, Rosenblatt v. Getty Oil Co., 493 A.2d 929, 937 (Del. 1985); see also DGCL §144(a)(2). In all events, "[a] condition precedent to finding that the burden of proving entire fairness has shifted in an interested merger transaction is a careful judicial analysis of the factual circumstances of each case." Kahn v. Lynch, 638 A.2d at 1120.

The director defendants in this case may be able to secure the burden shifting benefit by demonstrating either sufficient independent director approval or fully informed shareholder approval. But that inquiry has been foreclosed by the Court of Chancery's grant of summary judgment and the present record does not permit this Court to resolve that issue.

The issue of the existence of a fully informed shareholder vote enforces the conclusion that dismissal of Emerald Partners' disclosure claims is inappropriate at this stage of the proceedings. Directors of Delaware corporations have a fiduciary duty to shareholders to exercise due care, good faith and loyalty whenever they communicate publicly or directly with shareholders about the corporation's affairs. When stockholder action is requested, directors are required to provide shareholders with all information that is material to the action being requested and "to provide a balanced, truthful account of all matters disclosed in the communications with shareholders."

The Court of Chancery did not decide the issue of materiality of the alleged proxy statement misstatements or omissions but focused, instead, on the statutory protection available to the directors in the context of due care claims. Since we conclude that the disclosure claims here alleged are not so categorized, the analysis falls short. Accordingly, we reverse the grant of summary judgment on the disclosure claims.

Although we reverse the Court of Chancery's grant of summary judgment as essentially premature on the present record, we note, for the guidance of the Court of Chancery and the parties, that the shield from liability provided by a certificate of incorporation provision adopted pursuant to 8 Del. C. §102(b)(7)[12] is in the nature of an affirmative defense. Defendants seeking exculpation under such a provision will normally bear the burden of establishing each of its elements. Here, the Court of Chancery incorrectly ruled that Emerald Partners was required to establish at trial that the individual defendants acted in bad faith or in breach of their duty of loyalty. To the contrary, the burden of demonstrating good faith, however slight it might be in given circumstances, is upon the party seeking the protection of the statute. Nonetheless, where the factual basis for a claim solely implicates a violation of the duty of care, this Court has indicated that the protections of such a charter provision may properly be invoked and applied. . . .

In sum, the grant of summary judgment in favor of the director defendants is reversed and remanded for proceedings consistent with this opinion. . . .

———————————

On remand, 11 years after the original complaint was filed in the case, the Court of Chancery conducted a trial on the entire fairness of the transaction.

---

12. The Court of Chancery found that at all relevant times, the individual defendants were protected by such a provision. May's certificate of incorporation provides:

> FIFTEENTH: A director (or an advisory director) of this Corporation shall not be personally liable to the Corporation or its stockholders for monetary damages for breach of fiduciary duty as a director, except for liability (i) for any breach of the director's duty of loyalty to the Corporation or its stockholders, (ii) for acts or omissions not in good faith or which involve intentional misconduct or a knowing violation of law, (iii) under Section 174 of [the] Delaware General Corporation Law, or (iv) for any transaction from which the director derived an improper personal benefit. . . .

Emerald Partners v. Berlin, 2001 WL 115340 (Del. Ch. 2001). The court's opinion extensively set out the facts concerning the process by which the outside directors negotiated the merger and arrived at the price, including finding the following:

> 1. Because Mr. Hall controlled both enterprises and Mr. Berlin worked for Mr. Hall, the decision whether or not May would pursue Hall's merger proposal would be made by the three nonaffiliated (outside), nonconflicted directors who constituted a majority of the board.
> 2. The three outside directors retained independent legal and financial counsel to advise them on whether to pursue the merger.
> 3. Mr. Hall understood that since this was a conflict-of-interest transaction, he should abstain from voting on it, and further he should "absent himself" from discussions about the transaction.
> 4. As the court stated, "[d]espite his professed sensitivity to the need for pro- cedural safeguards in negotiating what clearly would be a "conflict" transaction, Mr. Hall did not scrupulously observe the procedures to which he had committed to adhere. . . . Thus, despite contrary representations, Messrs. Hall and Berlin attended some of the board meetings where the proposed merger was discussed. On occasion they also conferred with Bear Stearns, the financial advisor [the independent directors had] retained for May. The non-affiliated directors also fell short of procedural nirvana, as they evidently did not insist that Mr. Hall absent himself at all times from the deliberating process. They also failed to ~~arms length~~ *arms length transaction* have themselves constituted as a 'special committee' by formal board resolution. *Nonetheless, and despite these procedural lapses, the credible evidence shows that Messrs. Florence, Sebastian, and Strauss at all times did act as if they were a formally created 'special committee,' and that on the advice of their financial and legal advisors they negotiated the merger terms in a good faith, arm's length, and adversarial manner."*
> 5. Mr. Hall had originally proposed a price of $85 to $105 million for May's purchase of the Hall companies. The price as eventually negotiated was $28.6 million, payable in May Corporation stock, which Bear Stearns opined was a fair price to pay. The unaffiliated directors extracted many other concessions from Mr. Hall concerning the structure of the transaction in the process of negotiating the purchase.

Emerald Partners v. Berlin, 2001 WL 115340, *5-*9 (Del. Ch. 2001) (emphasis added).

Having found as a matter of fact that the unaffiliated directors had acted in good faith, at arm's length, and in an adversarial manner, the court's opin- ion (by Vice Chancellor Jacobs) found it unnecessary to issue a ruling on the entire fairness of the transaction. Instead, the court held that the defendants had sustained their affirmative burden, as described by the Delaware Supreme Court in the case you just read, of showing that the exculpation provisions in Article Fifteen of May's certificate of incorporation barred plaintiffs' claims, since it found that the facts established that there were no violations of law; the outside directors received no personal benefits from the transaction, nor were they beholden to Mr. Hall, and thus they were independent and not act- ing under a conflict of interest; and that the outside directors had operated in good faith. *Emerald Partners*, 2001 WL at *22. As Vice Chancellor Jacobs put it, "[i]n summary, the non-affiliated director-defendants have carried their bur- den of establishing that Article Fifteenth of May's Certificate of Incorporation governs the plaintiff's money damage claims in this lawsuit, and that none of

478   11.   Directors' and Shareholders' Duty of Loyalty

Article Fifteenth's exceptions are applicable to the conduct that underlies those claims. Because the only relief that the plaintiff seeks is money damages, these defendants are exculpated from liability on all of the plaintiff's claims." *Emerald Partners*, 2001 WL at *27.

Not so fast. In a third opinion in the case, the Delaware Supreme Court reversed again, stating that:

> In Malpiede v. Townson, 780 A.2d 1075 (Del. 2001), we held that when the standard of review *ab initio* is the business judgment rule, properly raising the existence of a valid exculpatory Section 102(b)(7) provision in the corporate charter "entitled director defendants to dismissal of any claims for [monetary] damages against them that are based *solely* on alleged breaches of the board's duty of care." The rationale of our holding in *Malpiede* explains why an entire fairness analysis can never be avoided in any challenged transaction that requires an application of the entire fairness standard of judicial review *ab initio* at trial—as we held in our last *Emerald Partners* opinion—notwithstanding the existence of a Section 102(b)(7) provision. The category of transactions that require judicial review pursuant to the entire fairness standard *ab initio* do so because, by definition, the inherently interested nature of those transactions are inextricably intertwined with issues of loyalty. . . .

Emerald Partners v. Berlin, 787 A.2d 85, 92 (Del. 2001).

But the court noted,

> [a] determination that a transaction must be subjected to an entire fairness analysis is not an implication of liability. Therefore, when entire fairness is the applicable standard of judicial review, this Court has held that injury or damages becomes a proper focus only *after* a transaction is determined *not* to be entirely fair. *A fortiori*, the exculpatory effect of a Section 102(b)(7) provision only becomes a proper focus of judicial scrutiny after the director's potential personal liability for the payment of monetary damages has been established. Accordingly, although a Section 102(b)(7) charter provision may provide exculpation for directors against the payment of monetary damages that is attributed exclusively to violating the duty of care, even in a transaction that requires the entire fairness review standard *ab initio*, it cannot eliminate an entire fairness analysis by the Court of Chancery.

Emerald Partners, 787 A.2d at 92.

At this point, 15 years into the litigation, one can imagine the Court of Chancery becoming a bit weary of this particular case. Some of that weariness can be seen in the court's initial discussion of a serious tactical error the plaintiffs' lawyers made after the second remand. The parties had agreed that the original trial record would constitute the record on remand and that the parties would proceed by submitting post-trial briefs, to be followed by oral argument. And yet, although the evidentiary record remained unchanged and the Court of Chancery had issued extensive findings of fact in its 2001 opinion,

> Emerald, nonetheless, devoted much of its post-trial brief on remand to attacking, and attempting to relitigate, almost every fact that was found adversely to it. It is noteworthy that Emerald's post-trial brief on remand predicates its entire fairness arguments on the version of the facts Emerald contends the Court should find, as distinguished from the facts that the Court actually found. The inescapable inference is that Emerald (implicitly) was conceding that it could not prevail on

the entire fairness issues unless the original factual findings were changed. [While Emerald's counsel denied making any such concession at oral argument], one would have expected Emerald to have made, at the very least, alternative arguments predicated on the original findings, which it did not do. Accordingly, to the extent this Court adheres to its original findings, the analytical utility of Emerald's brief is limited.

Emerald Partners v. Berlin, 2003 WL 21003437, *2 (Del. Ch. 2003).

Then, adhering to its original findings of fact, Vice Chancellor Jacobs explicitly reviewed the merger under the entire fairness standard, which requires an examination of the fairness of the price (fair price) and of the fairness and independence of the process of negotiation (fair dealing). Emphasizing the facts set out above about the process of the negotiation and the price (as well as expert testimony on the price issues), the Court of Chancery once again concluded that the defendants remain entitled to judgment in their favor on all claims. Emerald Partners v. Berlin, 2003 WL 21003437, *27, *38 (Del. Ch. 2003). Whether the Delaware Supreme Court will now let this case conclude remains to be seen.

One of the central issues in any case concerning a transaction in which one or more directors have conflicts of interest is whether the directors who made the decision to approve the transaction were either "interested" in the transaction or lacked "independence." Whether a director is "interested" in a transaction goes to whether that director is on both sides of the transaction or can expect to receive a material financial benefit from the transaction not generally shared by the corporation or its shareholders. Thus, an agreement to hire a board member to represent the company in litigation would be a transaction in which that board member was "interested," since that board member is on both sides of the transaction. An agreement to hire a board member's law firm to represent the company in litigation would necessitate an evaluation of whether the retainer was "material" to the law firm and thus "financially material" to the board member/lawyer, since that is a transaction in which the board member can expect to receive a financial benefit, but the board member as an individual is not on both sides of the transaction. The "independence" of a director involves an inquiry into whether that director's decision resulted from being controlled by or economically beholden to another director who is interested in the transaction. In the above case, while Mr. May clearly was interested in the transaction, Mr. Berlin lacked independence, because he worked for Mr. May and was thus economically beholden to Mr. May — and would presumably act in Mr. May's interest, not necessarily in the corporation's interest, in order to keep his job. The following Problem further tests these important concepts of "interest" and "independence."

PROBLEM 11-1

The California Public Employees' Retirement System (CalPERS) is the largest public pension fund in the United States, with assets of over $130 billion. CalPERS has invested in over 1,600 companies and is widely known as one of the most active institutional investors in the United States. For many years, CalPERS has promoted its vision of good corporate governance through shareholder proposals, public relations, government lobbying, and shareholder lawsuits.

In 2000, CalPERS targeted Lone Star Steakhouse & Saloon (Lone Star) as needing corporate governance reform and placed Lone Star on a Corporate Governance Focus List. Lone Star, with Jamie Coulter as its CEO, had first sold its stock to the public in 1992. Lone Star had a predilection for engaging in transactions with other businesses that Coulter owned and for larding its board with directors who worked for various other Coulter enterprises. In the latter half of the 1990s, Lone Star's stock price languished. Perceiving a connection between the poor stock performance and Lone Star's lack of a disinterested and independent board of directors, CalPERS submitted the following shareholder proposal to amend Lone Star's bylaws:

> RESOLVED, that the stockholders of Lone Star Steakhouse & Saloon, Inc. (the "Company") amend the Company's bylaws to require that, at the earliest practical date, a majority of the Board be comprised of Independent Directors. For purposes of this proposal, the term "Independent Director" shall mean a director who:
>
> (1) has not been employed by the Company in an executive capacity within the last five years;
>
> (2) is not, and is not affiliated with a company that is, an advisor or consultant to the Company, or a significant customer or supplier of the company;
>
> (3) has no personal services contract(s) with the Company or the Company's senior management;
>
> (4) is not affiliated with a not-for-profit entity that receives significant contributions from the Company;
>
> (5) within the last five years, has not had any business relationship with the Company that the Company has been required to disclose under the Securities and Exchange Commission disclosure regulations;
>
> (6) is not employed by a public company at which an executive officer of the Company serves as a director;
>
> (7) has not had a relationship described in (1) through (6) above with any affiliate of the Company; and
>
> (8) is not a member of the immediate family of any person described in (1) through (7) above.

Although the shareholders approved this resolution, Lone Star did not change its board of directors. The next year, an individual shareholder (Guy Adams) ran for a seat on the board of directors. In a striking measure of shareholder dissatisfaction, Adams prevailed over incumbent management's objection.[1]

During the long decline of the company's stock price, the board of directors of Lone Star had "repriced" employee and director stock options five times. A stock option gives an employee the right, but not the obligation, to purchase a specified number of shares of the corporation at a fixed price (called the

---

1. Adams retained the seat for only one year, but he managed to initiate many corporate governance reforms, including the removal of Lone Star's poison pill and the addition of three independent directors to Lone Star's board. Stephanie D. Smith, *One Investor's Story; Tired of overpaid, underperforming CEOs? What you can learn from Guy Adams*, Money, Oct. 1, 2002.

"exercise price" or "strike price") that is generally equal to the value of the shares at the time the option is granted (the "market price"). Options are designed to provide employees and directors with incentives to increase the company's stock price. As the market price of the company's shares increase, the option to purchase shares at a fixed price below the market price becomes increasingly valuable. On the other hand, when a company's stock price declines, the exercise price is higher than the market price, and the options are said to be "under water." Since the holders of stock options profit only when the market price exceeds the exercise price, "under water" options have limited incentive effects.

The practice of repricing stock options is designed to reinvigorate the incentive effects of the options and reduce the temptation for employees to seek new options elsewhere. When a company's stock price has declined, resetting the strike price so that it is equal to the new market price can provide fresh incentives for managers to increase the stock's market price. On the other hand, many people view the repricing of stock options as a reward to managers for poor performance, and stock options became a frequent target of corporate governance reforms in the late 1990s. As a result of those efforts, accounting for repriced options was changed in March 2000, when the Financial Accounting Standards Board required companies that reprice options to record a compensation expense if the market price subsequently rises above the strike price of the repriced options.

Unfortunately, from CalPERS' perspective, all of Lone Star's repricing decisions were made prior to the new accounting interpretation. So CalPERS took a different tack and sued the board of directors for a breach of the duty of loyalty.

The repricing of employee stock options had been approved by a stock options committee consisting of three of the directors. The repricing of nonemployee director stock options was approved by Coulter and John White, the executive vice president and treasurer of Lone Star. No option holder participated in the decision to reprice his own options, but CalPERS suggested that the nonemployee directors on the stock options committee approved the repricing of employee options in exchange for the employees (Coulter and White) agreeing to reprice the directors' options.

What sort of evidence would you find relevant in evaluating CalPERS' claim for a breach of the duty of loyalty?

B.   MAJORITY (OR CONTROLLING) SHAREHOLDERS

Conflict-of-interest transactions very often arise in a context where a majority shareholder is making decisions that affect the interests of minority shareholders. Quite often these are instances where a parent company enters into a transaction with its controlled subsidiary. (A "parent" company is simply a separately incorporated company that owns stock in another separately incorporated company. If the parent company owns 100 percent of the stock of the subsidiary, the subsidiary is called a "wholly owned subsidiary." If the parent company owns less than 100 percent of the stock of the subsidiary, the subsidiary is called a "partially owned subsidiary.") Equally as often these transactions involve a merger or acquisition; thus, some background on mergers and acquisitions is necessary to understand the cases that follow.

Lawyers talking about mergers and acquisitions tend to divide the world into two categories of transactions: "friendly" and "hostile." Friendly deals are those where the board of directors of two companies agree that a business combination makes sense, and each board passes a resolution adopting a plan to permit the combination and, where required, disseminates a proxy disclosure document to put the proposal to a shareholder vote. The specifics of the various ways in which these combinations can be structured and which shareholders get voting rights are discussed in Chapter 14. As a general matter, the shareholders of a company being sold almost always have voting rights, while the shareholders of a company buying another company often do not. Hostile deals are those where the board of directors of a company to be acquired, called the "target" company, resists the acquisition. When that happens, the would-be acquiring company can bypass the board entirely and make an offer directly to the company's shareholders to buy voting control. This offer is called a "tender offer," because it is an offer to shareholders for them to "tender" their shares to the acquiring company or person for a specified amount of money. Tender offers are extensively regulated by federal securities laws, but the important point here is that if an acquiring company can buy control of 51 percent of shares of a company, it can replace the board of directors in a special meeting or in a consent proceeding, and then have the new board agree to be acquired. If the tender offeror can buy control of 90 percent of the company, it can then "cash out" the remaining shareholders in a procedure called a "short-form" merger, where the remaining shareholders are given notice after the fact that they are being given cash for their shares. There are various defensive measures companies can take to thwart a tender offer, as discussed in Chapter 15. In a "well-armored" company it may not be possible to successfully complete a hostile acquisition through use of a tender offer, but in many cases the tender offer possibility acts as the backdrop against which negotiations about a merger takes place.

The following case sets out some general principles about the content of a majority shareholder's fiduciary duties. It also introduces some of the procedures that majority shareholders might want to follow to "cleanse" transactions of the taint of a conflict of interest. In addition, the case illustrates the power that the threat of engaging in a tender offer gives to a would-be acquiring company, in this case the majority shareholder.

KAHN v. LYNCH COMMUNICATION SYSTEMS, INC.

638 A.2d 1110
Supreme Court of Delaware
April 5, 1994

HOLLAND, Justice.

This is an appeal by the plaintiff-appellant, Alan R. Kahn ("Kahn"), from a final judgment of the Court of Chancery which was entered after a trial. The action, instituted by Kahn in 1986, originally sought to enjoin the acquisition of the defendant-appellee, Lynch Communication Systems, Inc. ("Lynch"), by the defendant-appellee, Alcatel U.S.A. Corporation ("Alcatel"), pursuant to a tender offer and cash-out merger. Kahn amended his complaint to seek monetary damages after the Court of Chancery denied his request for a preliminary injunction. The Court of Chancery subsequently certified Kahn's action as a class action on behalf of all Lynch shareholders, other than the named defendants, who tendered their stock in the merger, or whose stock was acquired through the merger.

A three-day trial was held April 13-15, 1993. Kahn alleged that Alcatel was a controlling shareholder of Lynch and breached its fiduciary duties to Lynch and its shareholders. According to Kahn, Alcatel dictated the terms of the merger; made false, misleading, and inadequate disclosures; and paid an unfair price.

The Court of Chancery concluded that Alcatel was, in fact, a controlling shareholder that owed fiduciary duties to Lynch and its shareholders. It also concluded that Alcatel had not breached those fiduciary duties. Accordingly, the Court of Chancery entered judgment in favor of the defendants.

Kahn has raised three contentions in this appeal. Kahn's first contention is that the Court of Chancery erred by finding that "the tender offer and merger were negotiated by an independent committee," and then placing the burden of persuasion on the plaintiff, Kahn. Kahn asserts the uncontradicted testimony in the record demonstrated that the committee could not and did not bargain at arm's length with Alcatel. Kahn's second contention is that Alcatel's Offer to Purchase was false and misleading because it failed to disclose threats made by Alcatel to the effect that if Lynch did not accept its proposed price, Alcatel would institute a hostile tender offer at a lower price. Third, Kahn contends that the merger price was unfair. Alcatel contends that the Court of Chancery was correct in its findings, with the exception of concluding that Alcatel was a controlling shareholder.

This Court has concluded that the record supports the Court of Chancery's finding that Alcatel was a controlling shareholder. However, the record does not support the conclusion that the burden of persuasion shifted to Kahn. Therefore, the burden of proving the *entire* fairness of the merger transaction remained on Alcatel, the controlling shareholder. Accordingly, the judgment of the Court of Chancery is reversed. The matter is remanded for further proceedings in accordance with this opinion.

FACTS

Lynch, a Delaware corporation, designed and manufactured electronic telecommunications equipment, primarily for sale to telephone operating companies. Alcatel, a holding company, is a subsidiary of Alcatel (S.A.), a French company involved in public telecommunications, business communications, electronics, and optronics. Alcatel (S.A.), in turn, is a subsidiary of Compagnie Generale d'Electricite ("CGE"), a French corporation with operations in energy, transportation, telecommunications and business systems.

In 1981, Alcatel acquired 30.6 percent of Lynch's common stock pursuant to a stock purchase agreement. As part of that agreement, Lynch amended its certificate of incorporation to require an 80 percent affirmative vote of its shareholders for approval of any business combination. In addition, Alcatel obtained proportional representation on the Lynch board of directors and the right to purchase 40 percent of any equity securities offered by Lynch to third parties. The agreement also precluded Alcatel from holding more than 45 percent of Lynch's stock prior to October 1, 1986. By the time of the merger which is contested in this action, Alcatel owned 43.3 percent of Lynch's outstanding stock; designated five of the eleven members of Lynch's board of directors; two of three members of the executive committee; and two of four members of the compensation committee.

In the spring of 1986, Lynch determined that in order to remain competitive in the rapidly changing telecommunications field, it would need to obtain fiber optics technology to complement its existing digital electronic capabilities. Lynch's management identified a target company, Telco Systems, Inc. ("Telco"), which possessed both fiber optics and other valuable technological assets. The record reflects that Telco expressed interest in being acquired by Lynch. Because of the supermajority voting provision, which Alcatel had negotiated when it first purchased its shares, in order to proceed with the Telco combination Lynch needed Alcatel's consent. In June 1986, Ellsworth F. Dertinger ("Dertinger"), Lynch's CEO and chairman of its board of directors, contacted Pierre Suard ("Suard"), the chairman of Alcatel's parent company, CGE, regarding the acquisition of Telco by Lynch. Suard expressed Alcatel's opposition to Lynch's acquisition of Telco. Instead, Alcatel proposed a combination of Lynch and Celwave Systems, Inc. ("Celwave"), an indirect subsidiary of CGE engaged in the manufacture and sale of telephone wire, cable and other related products.

Alcatel's proposed combination with Celwave was presented to the Lynch board at a regular meeting held on August 1, 1986. Although several directors expressed interest in the original combination which had been proposed with Telco, the Alcatel representatives on Lynch's board made it clear that such a combination would not be considered before a Lynch/Celwave combination. According to the minutes of the August 1 meeting, Dertinger expressed his opinion that Celwave would not be of interest to Lynch if Celwave was not owned by Alcatel.

At the conclusion of the meeting, the Lynch board unanimously adopted a resolution establishing an Independent Committee, consisting of Hubert L. Kertz ("Kertz"), Paul B. Wineman ("Wineman"), and Stuart M. Beringer ("Beringer"), to negotiate with Celwave and to make recommendations concerning the appropriate terms and conditions of a combination with Celwave. On October 24, 1986, Alcatel's investment banking firm, Dillon, Read & Co., Inc. ("Dillon Read") made a presentation to the Independent Committee. Dillon Read expressed its views concerning the benefits of a Celwave/Lynch combination and submitted a written proposal of an exchange ratio of 0.95 shares of Celwave per Lynch share in a stock-for-stock merger. [In a stock-for-stock merger, the consideration that the Celwave shareholders would receive for selling their company would be Lynch stock. The exchange ratio reflects the relative values of the companies and of their stock.]

However, the Independent Committee's investment advisors, Thomson McKinnon Securities Inc. ("Thomson McKinnon") and Kidder, Peabody & Co. Inc. ("Kidder Peabody"), reviewed the Dillon Read proposal and concluded that the 0.95 ratio was predicated on Dillon Read's overvaluation of Celwave. Based upon this advice, the Independent Committee determined that the exchange ratio proposed by Dillon Read was unattractive to Lynch. The Independent Committee expressed its unanimous opposition to the Celwave/Lynch merger on October 31, 1986.

Alcatel responded to the Independent Committee's action on November 4, 1986, by withdrawing the Celwave proposal. Alcatel made a simultaneous offer *alt acted then tried to acquire Lynch.*

to acquire the entire equity interest in Lynch, constituting the approximately 57 percent of Lynch shares not owned by Alcatel. The offering price was $14 cash per share.

On November 7, 1986, the Lynch board of directors revised the mandate of the Independent Committee. It authorized Kertz, Wineman, and Beringer to negotiate the cash merger offer with Alcatel. At a meeting held that same day, the Independent Committee determined that the $14 per share offer was inadequate. The Independent Committee's own legal counsel, Skadden, Arps, Slate, Meagher & Flom ("Skadden Arps"), suggested that the Independent Committee should review alternatives to a cash-out merger with Alcatel, including a "white knight" third party acquiror, a repurchase of Alcatel's shares, or the adoption of a shareholder rights plan.

On November 12, 1986, Beringer, as chairman of the Independent Committee, contacted Michiel C. McCarty ("McCarty") of Dillon Read, Alcatel's representative in the negotiations, with a counteroffer at a price of $17 per share. McCarty responded on behalf of Alcatel with an offer of $15 per share. When Beringer informed McCarty of the Independent Committee's view that $15 was also insufficient, Alcatel raised its offer to $15.25 per share. The Independent Committee also rejected this offer. Alcatel then made its final offer of $15.50 per share.

At the November 24, 1986 meeting of the Independent Committee, Beringer advised its other two members that Alcatel was "ready to proceed with an unfriendly tender at a lower price" if the $15.50 per share price was not recommended by the Independent Committee and approved by the Lynch board of directors. Beringer also told the other members of the Independent Committee that the alternatives to a cash-out merger had been investigated but were impracticable.[3] After meeting with its financial and legal advisors, the Independent Committee voted unanimously to recommend that the Lynch board of directors approve Alcatel's $15.50 cash per share price for a merger with Alcatel. The Lynch board met later that day. With Alcatel's nominees abstaining, it approved the merger.

ALCATEL DOMINATED LYNCH CONTROLLING SHAREHOLDER STATUS

This Court has held that "a shareholder owes a fiduciary duty only if it owns a majority interest in or *exercises control* over the business affairs of the corporation." Ivanhoe Partners v. Newmont Mining Corp., Del. Supr., 535 A.2d 1334, 1344 (1987) (emphasis added). With regard to the exercise of control, this Court has stated:

> [A] shareholder who owns less than 50% of a corporation's outstanding stocks does not, without more, become a controlling shareholder of that corporation, with a concomitant fiduciary status. For a dominating relationship to exist in the absence of controlling stock ownership, a plaintiff must allege domination by a minority shareholder through actual control of corporation conduct.

3. The minutes reflect that Beringer told the Committee the "white knight" alternative "appeared impractical with the 80% approval requirement"; the repurchase of Alcatel's shares would produce a "highly leveraged company with a lower book value" and was an alternative "not in the least encouraged by Alcatel"; and a shareholder rights plan was not viable because of the increased debt it would entail.

If not a majority control, then exercised control over business affairs

Citron v. Fairchild Camera & Instrument Corp., Del. Supr., 569 A.2d 53, 70 (1989) (quotations and citation omitted).

Alcatel held a 43.3 percent minority share of stock in Lynch. Therefore, the threshold question to be answered by the Court of Chancery was whether, despite its minority ownership, Alcatel exercised control over Lynch's business affairs. Based upon the testimony and the minutes of the August 1, 1986 Lynch board meeting, the Court of Chancery concluded that Alcatel did exercise control over Lynch's business decisions. . . . The record supports the Court of Chancery's factual finding that Alcatel dominated Lynch.

At the August 1 meeting, Alcatel opposed the renewal of compensation contracts for Lynch's top five managers. According to Dertinger, Christian Fayard ("Fayard"), an Alcatel director, told the board members, "[y]ou must listen to us. We are 43 percent owner. You have to do what we tell you." The minutes confirm Dertinger's testimony. They recite that Fayard declared, "you are pushing us very much to take control of the company. Our opinion is not taken into consideration."

Although Beringer and Kertz, two of the independent directors, favored renewal of the contracts, according to the minutes, the third independent director, Wineman, admonished the board as follows:

> Mr. Wineman pointed out that the vote on the contracts is a "watershed vote" and the motion, due to Alcatel's "strong feelings," might not carry if taken now. Mr. Wineman clarified that "you [management] might win the battle and lose the war." With Alcatel's opinion so clear, Mr. Wineman questioned "if management wants the contracts renewed under these circumstances." He recommended that management "think twice." Mr. Wineman declared: "I want to keep the management. I can't think of a better management." Mr. Kertz agreed, again advising consideration of the "critical" period the company is entering.

The minutes reflect that the management directors left the room after this statement. The remaining board members then voted not to renew the contracts.

At the same meeting, Alcatel vetoed Lynch's acquisition of the target company, which, according to the minutes, Beringer considered "an immediate fit" for Lynch. Dertinger agreed with Beringer, stating that the "target company is extremely important as they have the products that Lynch needs now." Nonetheless, Alcatel prevailed. The minutes reflect that Fayard advised the board: "Alcatel, with its 44% equity position, would not approve such an acquisition as . . . it does not wish to be diluted from being the main shareholder in Lynch." From the foregoing evidence, the Vice Chancellor concluded:

> . . . Alcatel did control the Lynch board, at least with respect to the matters under consideration at its August 1, 1986 board meeting. The interplay between the directors was more than vigorous discussion, as suggested by defendants. The management and independent directors disagreed with Alcatel on several important issues. However, when Alcatel made its position clear, and reminded the other directors of its significant stockholdings, Alcatel prevailed. Dertinger testified that Fayard "scared [the non-Alcatel directors] to death." While this statement undoubtedly is an exaggeration, it does represent a first-hand view of how the board operated. I conclude that the non-Alcatel directors deferred to Alcatel because of its position as a significant stockholder and not because they decided in the exercise of their own business judgment that Alcatel's position was correct [citation omitted].

The record supports the Court of Chancery's underlying factual finding that "the non-Alcatel [independent] directors deferred to Alcatel because of its position as a significant stockholder and not because they decided in the exercise of their own business judgment that Alcatel's position was correct." The record also supports the subsequent factual finding that, notwithstanding its 43.3 percent minority shareholder interest, Alcatel did exercise actual control over Lynch by dominating its corporate affairs. The Court of Chancery's legal conclusion that Alcatel owed the fiduciary duties of a controlling shareholder to the other Lynch shareholders followed syllogistically as the logical result of its cogent analysis of the record.

ENTIRE FAIRNESS REQUIREMENT DOMINATING INTERESTED SHAREHOLDER

A controlling or dominating shareholder standing on both sides of a transaction, as in a parent-subsidiary context, bears the burden of proving its entire fairness. Weinberger v. UOP, Inc., Del. Supr., 457 A.2d 701, 710 (1983). *See* Rosenblatt v. Getty Oil Co., Del. Supr., 493 A.2d 929, 937 (1985). The demonstration of fairness that is required was set forth by this Court in *Weinberger*:

> The concept of fairness has two basic aspects: fair dealing and fair price. The former embraces questions of when the transaction was timed, how it was initiated, structured, negotiated, disclosed to the directors, and how the approvals of the directors and the stockholders were obtained. The latter aspect of fairness relates to the economic and financial considerations of the proposed merger, including all relevant factors: assets, market value, earnings, future prospects, and any other elements that affect the intrinsic or inherent value of a company's stock. However, the test for fairness is not a bifurcated one as between fair dealing and price. All aspects of the issue must be examined as a whole since the question is one of entire fairness.

Weinberger v. UOP, Inc., 457 A.2d at 711 (citations omitted).

The logical question raised by this Court's holding in *Weinberger* was what type of evidence would be reliable to demonstrate entire fairness. That question was not only anticipated but also initially addressed in the *Weinberger* opinion. *Id.* at 709-10 n.7. This Court suggested that the result "could have been entirely different if UOP had appointed an independent negotiating committee of its outside directors to deal with Signal at arm's length," because "fairness in this context can be equated to conduct by a theoretical, wholly independent, board of directors." *Id.* Accordingly, this Court stated, "a showing that the action taken was as though each of the contending parties had in fact exerted its bargaining power against the other at arm's length is strong *evidence* that the transaction meets the test of fairness." *Id.* (emphasis added). . . .

Once again, this Court holds that the exclusive standard of judicial review in examining the propriety of an interested cash-out merger transaction by a controlling or dominating shareholder is entire fairness. Weinberger v. UOP, Inc., 457 A.2d at 710-11. The initial burden of establishing entire fairness rests upon the party who stands on both sides of the transaction. *Id.* However, an approval of the transaction by an independent committee of directors or an informed majority of minority shareholders shifts the burden of proof on the issue of fairness from the controlling or dominating shareholder to the challenging shareholder-plaintiff. *See* Rosenblatt v. Getty Oil Co., 493 A.2d at 937-38. Nevertheless, even when an interested cash-out merger transaction receives the informed approval of a majority of minority stockholders or an independent committee of disinterested directors, an entire fairness analysis is the only proper standard of judicial review. *See id.*

INDEPENDENT COMMITTEES INTERESTED MERGER TRANSACTIONS

. . . In *Weinberger*, this Court noted that "[p]articularly in a parent-subsidiary context, a showing that the action taken was as though each of the contending parties had *in fact* exerted its bargaining power against the other at arm's length is strong evidence that the transaction meets the test of fairness." 457 A.2d at 709-10 n.7 (emphasis added). *Accord* Rosenblatt v. Getty Oil Co., 493 A.2d at 937-38 & n.7. In *Rosenblatt*, this Court pointed out that "[an] independent bargaining structure, while not conclusive, is strong evidence of the fairness" of a merger transaction. Rosenblatt v. Getty Oil Co., 493 A.2d at 938 n.7.

The same policy rationale which requires judicial review of interested cash-out mergers exclusively for entire fairness also mandates careful judicial scrutiny of a special committee's real bargaining power before shifting the burden of proof on the issue of entire fairness. A recent decision from the Court of Chancery articulated a two-part test for determining whether burden shifting is appropriate in an interested merger transaction. Rabkin v. Olin Corp., Del. Ch., C.A. No. 7547 (Consolidated), Chandler, V.C., 1990 WL 47648, slip op. at 14-15 (Apr. 17, 1990), *reprinted in* 16 Del. J. Corp. L. 851, 861-62 (1991), *aff'd*, Del. Supr., 586 A.2d 1202 (1990). In *Olin*, the Court of Chancery stated:

> The mere existence of an independent special committee . . . does not itself shift the burden. At least two factors are required. First, the majority shareholder must not dictate the terms of the merger. Rosenblatt v. Getty Oil Co., Del. Ch., 493 A.2d 929, 937 (1985). Second, the special committee must have real bargaining power that it can exercise with the majority shareholder on an arms length basis.

Id., slip op. at 14-15, 16 Del. J. Corp. L. at 861-62. This Court expressed its agreement with that statement by affirming the Court of Chancery decision in *Olin* on appeal.

LYNCH'S INDEPENDENT COMMITTEE

In the case *sub judice*, the Court of Chancery observed that although "Alcatel did exercise control over Lynch with respect to the decisions made at the August 1, 1986 board meeting, it does not necessarily follow that Alcatel also controlled the terms of the merger and its approval." This observation is theoretically accurate, as this opinion has already stated. Weinberger v. UOP, Inc., 457 A.2d at 709-10 n.7. However, the performance of the Independent Committee merits careful judicial scrutiny to determine whether Alcatel's demonstrated pattern of domination was effectively neutralized so that "each of the contending parties had in fact exerted its bargaining power against the other at arm's length." *Id.* The fact that the same independent directors had submitted to Alcatel's demands on August 1, 1986 was part of the basis for the Court of Chancery's finding of Alcatel's domination of Lynch. Therefore, the Independent Committee's ability to bargain at arm's length with Alcatel was suspect from the outset.

The Independent Committee's original assignment was to examine the merger with Celwave which had been proposed by Alcatel. The record reflects that the Independent Committee effectively discharged that assignment and, in fact, recommended that the Lynch board reject the merger on Alcatel's terms. Alcatel's response to the Independent Committee's adverse recommendation was not the pursuit of further negotiations regarding its Celwave proposal, but rather its response was an offer to buy Lynch. That offer was consistent with Alcatel's August 1, 1986 expressions of an intention to dominate Lynch, since an acquisition would effectively eliminate once and for all Lynch's remaining vestiges of independence.

The Independent Committee's second assignment was to consider Alcatel's proposal to purchase Lynch. The Independent Committee proceeded on that task with full knowledge of Alcatel's demonstrated pattern of domination. The Independent Committee was also obviously aware of Alcatel's refusal to negotiate with it on the Celwave matter.

BURDEN OF PROOF SHIFTED COURT OF CHANCERY'S FINDING

The Court of Chancery began its factual analysis by noting that Kahn had "attempted to shatter" the image of the Independent Committee's actions as having "appropriately simulated" an arm's length, third-party transaction. The Court of Chancery found that "to some extent, [Kahn's attempt] was successful." The Court of Chancery gave credence to the testimony of Kertz, one of the members of the Independent Committee, to the effect that he did not believe that $15.50 was a fair price but that he voted in favor of the merger because he felt there was no alternative.

The Court of Chancery also found that Kertz understood Alcatel's position to be that it was ready to proceed with an unfriendly tender offer at a lower price if Lynch did not accept the $15.50 offer, and that Kertz perceived this to be a threat by Alcatel. The Court of Chancery concluded that Kertz ultimately decided that, "although $15.50 was not fair, a tender offer and merger at that price would be better for Lynch's stockholders than an unfriendly tender offer at a significantly lower price." The Court of Chancery determined that "Kertz failed either to satisfy himself that the offered price was fair or oppose the merger."

In addition to Kertz, the other members of the Independent Committee were Beringer, its chairman, and Wineman. Wineman did not testify at trial. Beringer was called by Alcatel to testify at trial. Beringer testified that at the time of the Committee's vote to recommend the $15.50 offer to the Lynch board, he thought "that *under the circumstances*, a price of $15.50 was fair and should be accepted" (emphasis added).

Kahn contends that these "circumstances" included those referenced in the minutes for the November 24, 1986 Independent Committee meeting: "Mr. Beringer added that Alcatel is 'ready to proceed with an unfriendly tender at a lower price' if the $15.50 per share price is not recommended to, and approved by, the Company's Board of Directors." In his testimony at trial, Beringer verified, albeit reluctantly, the accuracy of the foregoing statement in the minutes: "[Alcatel] *let us know* that they were giving serious consideration to making an unfriendly tender" (emphasis added). . . .

According to the Court of Chancery, the Independent Committee rejected three lower offers for Lynch from Alcatel and then accepted the $15.50 offer "after being advised that [it] was fair and after considering the absence of alternatives." The Vice Chancellor expressly acknowledged the impracticability of Lynch's Independent Committee's alternatives to a merger with Alcatel:

> Lynch was not in a position to shop for other acquirors, since Alcatel could block any alternative transaction. Alcatel also made it clear that it was not interested in having its shares repurchased by Lynch. The Independent Committee decided that a stockholder rights plan was not viable because of the increased debt it would entail.

Nevertheless, based upon the record before it, the Court of Chancery found that the Independent Committee had "appropriately simulated a third-party transaction, where negotiations are conducted at arms-length and there is no compulsion to reach an agreement." The Court of Chancery concluded that the Independent Committee's actions "as a whole" were "sufficiently well informed . . . and aggressive to simulate an arms-length transaction," so that the burden of proof as to entire fairness shifted from Alcatel to the contending Lynch shareholder, Kahn. The Court of Chancery's reservations about that finding are apparent in its written decision.

THE POWER TO SAY NO, THE PARTIES' CONTENTIONS, ARM'S LENGTH BARGAINING

The Court of Chancery properly noted that limitations on the alternatives to Alcatel's offer did not mean that the Independent Committee should have agreed to a price that was unfair:

> The power to say no is a significant power. It is the duty of directors serving on [an independent] committee to approve only a transaction that is in the best interests of the public shareholders, to say no to any transaction that is not fair to those shareholders and is not the best transaction available. It is not sufficient for such directors to achieve the best price that a fiduciary will pay if that price is not a fair price.

(Quoting In re First Boston, Inc. Shareholders Litig., Del. Ch., C.A. 10338 (Consolidated), Allen, C., 1990 WL 78836, slip op. at 15-16 (June 7, 1990)). . . . Kahn contends the record reflects that the conduct of Alcatel deprived the Independent Committee of an effective "power to say no." Kahn argues that Alcatel not only threatened the Committee with a hostile tender offer in the event its $15.50 offer was not recommended and approved, but also directed the affairs of Lynch for Alcatel's benefit in such a way as to make it impossible for Lynch to continue as a public company under Alcatel's control without injury to itself and its minority shareholders. In support of this argument, Kahn relies upon another proceeding wherein the Court of Chancery has been previously presented with factual circumstances comparable to those of the case *sub judice*, albeit in a different procedural posture. *See* American Gen. Corp. v. Texas Air Corp., Del. Ch., C.A. Nos. 8390, 8406, 8650 & 8805, Hartnett, V.C., 1987 WL 6337 (Feb. 5, 1987), *reprinted in* 13 Del. J. Corp. L. 173 (1988).

In *American General,* in the context of an application for injunctive relief, the Court of Chancery found that the members of the Special Committee were "truly independent and . . . performed their tasks in a proper manner," but it also found that "at the end of their negotiations with [the majority shareholder] the Committee members were issued an ultimatum and told that they must accept the $16.50 per share price or [the majority shareholder] would proceed with the transaction without their input." *Id.*, slip op. at 11-12, 13 Del. J. Corp. L. at 181. The Court of Chancery concluded based upon this evidence that the Special Committee had thereby lost "its ability to negotiate in an arms-length manner" and that there was a reasonable probability that the burden of proving entire fairness would remain on the defendants if the litigation proceeded to trial. *Id.*, slip op. at 12, 13 Del. J. Corp. L. at 181.

Alcatel's efforts to distinguish *American General* are unpersuasive. Alcatel's reliance on *Braunschweiger* is also misplaced. In *Braunschweiger,* the Court of Chancery pointed out that "[p]laintiffs do not allege that [the management-affiliated merger partner] ever used the threat of a hostile takeover to influence the special committee." Braunschweiger v. American Home Shield Corp., slip op. at 13, 17 Del. J. Corp. L. at 219. Unlike *Braunschweiger,* in this case the coercion was extant and directed to a specific price offer which was, in effect, presented in the form of a "take it or leave it" ultimatum by a controlling share-holder with the capability of following through on its threat of a hostile takeover.

ALCATEL'S ENTIRE FAIRNESS BURDEN DID NOT SHIFT TO KAHN

A condition precedent to finding that the burden of proving entire fairness has shifted in an interested merger transaction is a careful judicial analysis of the factual circumstances of each case. Particular consideration must be given to evidence of whether the special committee was truly independent, fully informed, and had the freedom to negotiate at arm's length. Weinberger v. UOP, Inc., Del. Supr., 457 A.2d 701, 709-10 n.7 (1983). *See also* American Gen. Corp. [*supra*], Hartnett, V.C., 1987 WL 6337, slip op. at 11 (Feb. 5, 1987), *reprinted in* 13 Del. J. Corp. L. 173, 181 (1988). "Although perfection is not possible," unless the controlling or dominating shareholder can demonstrate that it has not only formed an independent committee but also replicated a process "as though each of the contending parties had in fact exerted its bargaining power at arm's length," the burden of proving entire fairness will not shift. *Weinberger*, 457 A.2d at 709-10 n.7. *See also* Rosenblatt v. Getty Oil Co., Del. Supr., 493 A.2d 929, 937-38 (1985). . . .

The Court of Chancery's determination that the Independent Committee "appropriately simulated a third-party transaction, where negotiations are conducted at arm's-length and there is no compulsion to reach an agreement," is not supported by the record. Under the circumstances present in the case *sub judice,* the Court of Chancery erred in shifting the burden of proof with regard to entire fairness to the contesting Lynch shareholder-plaintiff, Kahn. The record reflects that the ability of the Committee effectively to negotiate at arm's length was compromised by Alcatel's threats to proceed with a hostile tender offer if the $15.50 price was not approved by the Committee and the Lynch board. The fact that the Independent Committee rejected three initial offers, which were well below the Independent Committee's estimated valuation for Lynch and were not combined with an explicit threat that Alcatel was "ready to proceed" with a hostile bid, cannot alter the conclusion that any semblance of arm's length bargaining ended when the Independent Committee surrendered to the ultimatum that accompanied Alcatel's final offer. *See* Rabkin v. Philip A. Hunt Chem. Corp., Del. Supr., 498 A.2d 1099, 1106 (1985).

CONCLUSION

Accordingly, the judgment of the Court of Chancery is reversed. This matter is remanded for further proceedings consistent herewith, including a redetermination of the entire fairness of the cash-out merger to Kahn and the other Lynch minority shareholders with the burden of proof remaining on Alcatel, the dominant and interested shareholder.

C.   RATIFICATION

Ratification is a doctrine derived from agency law, where it serves to make the principal responsible for some prior act of the agent. Restatement (Second) of Agency §82. The distinctive feature of ratification is that it applies in circumstances where the original action could not have bound the principal, either because the actor was not an agent or because the action was not authorized or apparently authorized.

Before an act may be ratified, several conditions must be met. Most important, the principal must have knowledge of all material facts at the time of ratification. Restatement (Second) of Agency §91. Even if all of the conditions for ratification are met, certain transactions are not susceptible to ratification on public policy grounds. These include transactions that are illegal or fraudulent, which are treated as simply void.

The doctrine of ratification has been criticized on the ground that it gives the principal the option to accept or reject actions of the agent. The third party who dealt with the agent is bound by the ratification but cannot bind the principal absent ratification. While courts impose limits on the length of time that may elapse between the agent's action and the principal's ratification, it is at least theoretically possible for a principal to evaluate the actions of the agent, accepting "winning" actions and rejecting "losing" actions.

Despite these concerns about fairness to third parties, the argument in favor of ratification rests largely on fairness to those same parties. When a transaction is properly ratified, any defects in authority relating to the original transaction are cured. In other words, the ratification "relates back" to the original actions. This is especially beneficial to the third party when the original actions are tortious because attempting to replicate those actions at a later date is obviously undesirable.

In the corporate context, ratification is an important aspect of the law governing conflict-of-interest transactions. This is not true ratification (retroactive authorization of an action by an agent or purported agent), since director or shareholder approval of a conflict-of-interest transaction can take place before or after the transaction, and in some cases the transaction to be ratified was authorized. Yet shareholders stand in the place of principals, and managers and directors are their "agents." At common law, interested transactions were voidable, and this caused great uncertainty for third parties. In many instances, such uncertainty would cause third parties to refrain from engaging in transactions. This worked to the detriment of the corporation and its shareholders because interested transactions can be beneficial. The doctrine of ratification allows shareholders to approve interested transactions. And as we see below, in some instances, independent directors are also allowed to approve interested transactions on behalf of the shareholders.

1. Director Ratification

According to DGCL §144(a)(1), a conflict-of-interest transaction can be authorized by a majority of disinterested directors. *See also* Model Act §§8.61(b)(1) and 8.62. As the following case demonstrates, in a challenged transaction the courts will carefully scrutinize the actions of the disinterested directors to determine if they are, in fact, acting in a fully independent way, and that determination will affect the standard of review that will be applied to evaluate the challenged transaction.

KAHN v. TREMONT CORP.

694 A.2d 422
Supreme Court of Delaware
June 10, 1997

WALSH, Justice.

This is an appeal by a plaintiff-shareholder, Alan R. Kahn ("Kahn"), from a decision of the Court of Chancery which approved the purchase by Tremont Corporation ("Tremont") of 7.8 million shares of the Common Stock of NL Industries, Inc. ("NL"). The shares, constituting 15% of NL's outstanding stock, were purchased from Valhi, Inc. ("Valhi"), a corporation which was 90 percent owned by a trust for the family of Harold C. Simmons ("Simmons"). In turn, Valhi was the owner of a majority of NL's outstanding stock and controlled Tremont through the ownership of 44% of its outstanding shares.

Kahn alleges that Simmons effectively controlled the three related companies and, through his influence, structured the purchase of NL shares in a manner which benefited himself at the expense of Tremont. Following a six-day trial, the Court of Chancery concluded that due to Simmons' status as a controlling shareholder, the transaction must be evaluated under the entire fairness standard of review and not the more deferential business judgment rule. Nevertheless, the court found that Tremont's utilization of a Special Committee of disinterested directors was sufficient to shift the burden on the fairness issue to Kahn. With the burden shifted, the court concluded that both the price and the process were fair to Tremont.

Kahn has raised two contentions in this appeal: (i) that the court erred in its burden of proof allocation regarding the entire fairness of the transaction; and (ii) that the circumstances surrounding the purchase of NL shares indicate that the process was tainted and the price unfair to Tremont. After careful review of the record, we conclude that under the circumstances the Special Committee did not operate in an independent or informed manner and, therefore, the Court of Chancery erred in shifting the burden of persuasion to Kahn. Accordingly, the judgment of the Court of Chancery is reversed and the matter remanded for a new fairness determination with the burden of proof upon the defendants.

I

The lengthy presentation before the Court of Chancery requires a full exposition of the factual background of the dispute for analysis on appeal. Tremont is a Delaware corporation with its principal executive offices located in Denver, Colorado. Through its subsidiaries, Tremont produces titanium sponge, ingot and mill products. NL is a New Jersey corporation which derives a majority of its earnings from the manufacture and sale of titanium dioxide ("TiO_2"), a chemical used to impart whiteness or opacity. NL conducts this business through its European subsidiary Krones, which accounts for 85% to 90% of NL's total revenue. Valhi is also a Delaware corporation which, through subsidiary stock ownership, is engaged in a variety of businesses, including the production and sale of hardware, forest products, refined sugar, and the fast food restaurant business.

The individual defendants, collectively the board of directors of Tremont, are Susan E. Alderton, Richard J. Boushka, J. Landis Martin, Glenn R. Simmons, Harold C. Simmons, Michael A. Snetzer, Thomas P. Stafford and Avy H. Stein. Aside from their service on the Tremont board, several defendants hold influential positions with other Simmons' controlled entities. Harold Simmons is chairman of the board of Valhi, NL, and Contran, and the CEO of Contran and Valhi. J. Landis Martin is both the president and CEO of NL and Tremont. Susan E. Alderton serves as the vice president and treasurer of Tremont and NL. Glenn R. Simmons is the vice chairman of the board of Valhi as well as the vice chairman of the board and vice president of Contran. Michael A. Snetzer is the president of Valhi and Contran and a director of NL and Contran.

Kahn alleges that the defendants willingly participated in a series of improper transactions, beginning in 1990, which were orchestrated by Simmons for his own benefit. Specifically, he argues that the purchase of NL shares by Tremont was the final step in a series of transactions whereby Simmons was able to shift liquidity from several of his controlled companies to Valhi. Under the theory advanced by Kahn, two preceding transactions, a repurchase program and a "Dutch auction," were initiated in order to artificially inflate the price of NL shares. By increasing NL's per share price, Simmons was able to divest himself, at the expense of Tremont, of the stock in a failing company for above market prices.

In late 1990, NL's board believed that the current market price of NL's stock, then selling between $10 and $11 per share, was significantly undervalued. Accordingly, on October 2, 1990, the board authorized a repurchase program in the open market for up to five million shares. On the prior day NL stock had closed at $10.12 per share. Over the first three months of the program, through January 10, 1991, NL repurchased almost two million shares, at a total cost of over $22 million and an average price of approximately $11 per share.

Satisfied with this response, NL suspended its repurchases from January through May of 1991. From May to July 1991, however, NL resumed buying and purchased 733,700 shares on the open market for a total cost of $10 million or approximately $13.50 a share. The repurchase program was again suspended from August of 1991 to September 11, 1991. Following this brief hiatus, NL once again reinstated its open-market repurchases and continued to repurchase shares into early 1992. All told, NL repurchased over 3 million of its own shares at an average price of $12 per share.

In June of 1991, NL shares were trading at or above $15 per share. At this point NL, as the result of selling a large block of Lockheed stock, was holding approximately $500 million in cash to be used for investment purposes. In August 1991, with the market price of the stock at $16, NL's management decided that it would be advantageous for the company to buy additional NL shares beyond the five million already authorized in the share repurchase program. Accordingly, on August 6, 1991, the NL board voted to approve a Dutch auction self-tender offer for 10 million shares of NL.

Under the Dutch auction mechanism, each shareholder of NL would decide how many, if any, shares to tender and at what price within a designated price range. After the expiration of the auction period, NL would determine the lowest uniform price, within a preset range of $14.50 to $17.50, that would enable it to purchase 10 million shares. All of the shares tendered at or below the sale price would be purchased at the sale price, subject to proration. In the event that more than 10 million shares were tendered at or below the sale price, NL had the option to purchase an additional 1.3 million shares.

On the date the Dutch auction was announced, Valhi owned approximately 68% of the 63.4 million outstanding shares of NL. Valhi tendered all of its shares, at $16, recognizing that with proration it would sell, at most, approximately 10 million shares. At the close of the Dutch auction, $16 per share proved to be the lowest price within the range at which NL could purchase the shares. On September 12, 1991, NL accepted for purchase 11,268,024 shares, 10,928,750 of which were acquired from Valhi. Shortly following the close of the Dutch auction, NL's stock price fell from $16 to around $13.50.

Upon completion of the Dutch auction, Valhi had sold 10.9 million shares of NL and had reduced its ownership interest in the company from 68% to 62%. If Valhi could sell an additional 7.8 million shares of NL and reduce its ownership interest to below 50%, it would be able to reap two significant benefits. First, it would receive a tax savings of approximately $11.8 million on its proceeds from the Dutch auction, a potential savings of $1.52 per share. Secondly, Valhi would be in a position to deconsolidate NL from its financial statements, thereby improving its access to capital markets. In order to obtain these benefits, however, Valhi needed to sell 7.8 million shares of NL, amounting to 15% of NL's outstanding stock, by the end of calendar year 1991.

To explore the prospect of a further sale of NL shares, Snetzer, Valhi's President, contacted two potential purchasers, RCM Capital and Keystone Inc. Although both maintained significant holdings of NL shares, neither was interested in further purchases. Snetzer also contacted Salomon Brothers and requested an opinion concerning the marketability of the stock. Snetzer was advised by Salomon Brothers that its equity syndicate groups in the U.S. and Europe, as well as its private equity people, were in agreement that Valhi would incur an illiquidity discount of 20%, or greater, against NL's then market price in order to sell this unregistered stock in a series of private transactions. Snetzer did not retain Salomon to negotiate a sale because in his view Valhi was unwilling to sell the block of NL shares at that price.

Finding the alternatives unacceptable, Valhi decided to approach Tremont, which had $100 million in excess liquidity and was in the process of searching for a productive investment opportunity. Snetzer was of the opinion that an "all in the family" transaction would be more desirable since it had the potential to yield additional benefits for both companies. As a 44% owner of Tremont, Valhi would be more likely to accept an appropriate discount from market because it would still own an indirect 44% interest in the shares. In addition, a lower discount from market might be acceptable to Tremont because its management had access to better information concerning NL's business prospects than any unrelated buyers whom Salomon had considered. As a better informed purchaser, Tremont would be less susceptible to risk than would be a stranger and might be willing to pay a price closer to market. Based on this reasoning, on September 18, 1991, Snetzer wrote to Landis Martin, the President and CEO of Tremont, to propose the sale of 7.8 million shares of NL stock.

After speaking with Snetzer, Martin wrote to Tremont's three outside directors, Richard Boushka, Thomas Stafford, and Avy Stein, asking them to formulate an appropriate response to Valhi's offer. The three men were thereafter designated by the Tremont board as a Special Committee for the purpose of considering the proposal and recommending a course of action. Although the three men were deemed "independent" for purposes of this transaction, all had significant prior business relationships with Simmons or Simmons' controlled companies.

Stein, a lawyer, was affiliated with the law firm which represented Simmons on several of his corporate takeovers and had worked closely with Martin. In 1984 Stein left the law firm to organize and promote various business ventures. Over the next five years, Martin invested in projects which Stein was promoting despite their poor performance. In October of 1988, Stein's business ventures had all but dried up when Martin, then at NL, offered Stein a consulting position at $10,000 a month and bonuses to be paid at Martin's discretion. Stein remained in this position for one year, earning bonuses totaling $325,000, before taking a position with two subsidiaries of Continental Bank, N.A. Stafford was employed by NL in connection with Simmons' proxy contest to acquire control of Lockheed and received $300,000 in fees. Boushka was initially named to Simmons' slate of directors in connection with the Lockheed proxy contest and was paid a fee of $20,000.

Of the three Special Committee members, Stein was the most closely connected to management. Nevertheless, he assumed the role of chairman of the Special Committee and directed its operations. Stafford and Boushka deferred to Stein in the selection of both the financial and legal advisors for the Special Committee. The Court of Chancery noted that Stein's selection of advisors was not reassuring.

In choosing a financial advisor, the Special Committee considered several banking firms, both national and regional. In the end, at Stein's recommendation, the Special Committee retained Continental Partners ("Continental"), a company with whom Stein was affiliated. Continental is a wholly-owned subsidiary of Continental bank which, in prior years, had earned significant fee income from Simmons-related companies. The record also reflects that Martin, not a member of the Special Committee, signed the retainer agreement with

the defendants to the plaintiff through the use of a well functioning committee of independent directors. Kahn v. Lynch Communication Sys., Del. Supr., 638 A.2d 1110, 1117 (1994). Regardless of where the burden lies, when a controlling shareholder stands on both sides of the transaction the conduct of the parties will be viewed under the more exacting standard of entire fairness as opposed to the more deferential business judgment standard. *Id.* at 1116.

Entire fairness remains applicable even when an independent committee is utilized because the underlying factors which raise the specter of impropriety can never be completely eradicated and still require careful judicial scrutiny. *Weinberger,* 457 A.2d at 710. This policy reflects the reality that in a transaction such as the one considered in this appeal, the controlling shareholder will continue to dominate the company regardless of the outcome of the transaction. Citron v. E.I. Du Pont de Nemours & Co., Del. Ch., 584 A.2d 490, 502 (1990). The risk is thus created that those who pass upon the propriety of the transaction might perceive that disapproval may result in retaliation by the controlling shareholder. *Id.* Consequently, even when the transaction is negotiated by a special committee of independent directors, "no court could be certain whether the transaction fully approximate[d] what truly independent parties would have achieved in an arm's length negotiation." *Id.* Cognizant of this fact, we have chosen to apply the entire fairness standard to "interested transactions" in order to ensure that all parties to the transaction have fulfilled their fiduciary duties to the corporation and all its shareholders. *Kahn,* 638 A.2d at 1110.

Having established the appropriate legal standard by which the sale of NL stock will be reviewed, we turn to the issue of which party bears the burden of proof. Delaware has long adhered to the principle that the controlling or dominant shareholder is initially allocated the burden of proving the transaction was entirely fair. *Id.* at 1117. In *Rosenblatt,* however, we stated that "approval of a [transaction], as here, by an informed vote of a majority of the minority shareholders, while not a legal prerequisite, shifts the burden of proving the unfairness of the transaction entirely to the plaintiffs." *Rosenblatt,* 493 A.2d at 937. To obtain the benefit of burden shifting, the controlling shareholder must do more than establish a perfunctory special committee of outside directors. Rabkin v. Olin Corp., Del. Ch., C.A. No. 7547 (Consolidated), Chandler, V.C., 1990; *reprinted in* 16 Del. J. Corp. L. 851, 861-62, 1990 WL 47648 (1990), *aff'd,* Del. Supr., 586 A.2d 1202 (1990). Rather, the committee must function in a manner which indicates that the controlling shareholder did not dictate the terms of the transaction and that the committee exercised real bargaining power "at an arms-length." *Id.*

Here, Tremont, with Valhi's approval, established a Special Committee consisting of three outside directors. In evaluating the composition of Tremont's Special Committee, the Court of Chancery confessed to "having reservations concerning the establishment of the Special Committee and the selection of its advisors." The court's reservations arose from two main concerns. First, Stein was the dominant member of the Special Committee and played a key role in the negotiations. The Chancellor questioned the Special Committee's decision to leave the bulk of the work in the hands of one "who had a long and personally beneficial relationship with Mr. Martin [and Simmons' controlled companies]."

The court's second concern was prompted by its recognition that in complicated financial transactions such as this, professional advisors have the ability to influence directors who are anxious to make the right decision but who are often *in terra cognito.* As the Chancellor noted, "the selection of professional advisors for the Special Committee doesn't give comfort; it raises questions." Notably, Tremont's General Counsel suggested the name of an appropriate legal counsel to the Special Committee, and that individual was promptly retained. The Special Committee chose as its financial advisor a bank which had lucrative past dealings with Simmons-related companies and had been affiliated with Stein through his employment with a connected bank.

Despite these reservations and the appearance of conflict, the Chancellor concluded that the Special Committee's advisors satisfied their professional obligations to the Special Committee. The Chancellor further concluded that the Special Committee had discharged its duties in an informed and independent manner. These findings were sufficient, in the Chancellor's view, to shift to the plaintiff the burden of proving that the transaction was unfair.

In our view, the Court of Chancery's determination that the Special Committee of Tremont's outside directors was fully informed, active and appropriately simulated an arms length transaction, is not supported by the record. It is clear that Boushka and Stafford abdicated their responsibility as committee members by permitting Stein, the member whose independence was most suspect, to perform the Special Committee's essential functions. In particular, Stafford's absence from all meetings with advisors or fellow committee members rendered him ill-suited as a defender of the interests of minority shareholders in the dynamics of fast moving negotiations. Similarly, the circumstances surrounding the retaining of the Special Committee's advisors, as well as the advice given, cast serious doubt on the effectiveness of the Special Committee.

In our view, the Special Committee established to negotiate the purchase of the block of NL stock did not function independently. All three directors had previous affiliations with Simmons or companies which he controlled and, as a result, received significant financial compensation or influential positions on the boards of Simmons' controlled companies. Of the three directors, Stein was arguably the one most beholden to Simmons. In 1988 Stein was paid $10,000 a month as a consultant to NL and received over $325,000 in bonuses. The Special Committee's advisors did little to bolster the independence of the principals. The financial advisor, Continental Partners, was recommended by Stein and quickly retained by the full Special Committee. In the past, an affiliate bank of Continental had derived significant fees from Simmons controlled companies and at the time of the transaction was affiliated with Stein's current employer. In addition to being recommended by the General Counsel for NL and Tremont, the Special Committee's legal advisor had previously been retained by Valhi in connection with a convertible debt offering and by NL with respect to a proposed merger with Valhi.

From its inception, the Special Committee failed to operate in a manner which would create the appearance of objectivity in Tremont's decision to purchase the NL stock. As this Court has previously stated in defining director independence: "[i]t is the care, attention and sense of individual responsibility to the performance of one's duties . . . that generally touches on independence." *Aronson v. Lewis,* Del. Supr., 473 A.2d 805, 816 (1984). The record amply demonstrates that neither Stafford nor Boushka possessed the "care, attention and sense of responsibility" necessary to afford them the status of independent directors. The result was that Stein, arguably the least detached member of the Special Committee, became, de facto, a single member committee — a tenuous role. Stein conducted all negotiations over price and ancillary terms of the proposed purchase with Martin, and did so without the participation of the remaining two directors. "If a single member committee is to be used, the member should, like Caesar's wife, be above reproach." Lewis v. Fuqua, Del. Ch., 502 A.2d 962, 967 (1985).

The record is replete with examples of how the lack of the Special Committee's independence fostered an atmosphere in which the directors were permitted to default on their obligation to remain fully informed. Most notable was the failure of all three directors to attend the informational meetings with the Special Committee's advisors. These meetings were scheduled so that the Special Committee could explore, through the exchange of ideas with its advisors, the validity of the Valhi proposal and what terms the board should demand in order to make the purchase more beneficial to Tremont. Although Boushka had requested an independent analysis with respect to the future of the TiO$_2$ market, and one was ordered, the report was not read prior to the Special Committee's October 30 vote on the purchase of the NL stock. The failure of the individual directors to fully participate in an active process severely limited the exchange of ideas and prevented the Special Committee as a whole from acquiring critical knowledge of essential aspects of the purchase. In sum, we conclude that the Special Committee did not operate in a manner which entitled the defendants to shift from themselves the burden which encumbers a controlled transaction. *Accord Kahn,* 638 A.2d at 1110. . . .

IV

Although the Chancellor made extensive findings incident to his fair price analysis he did so in a procedural construct which required Kahn to prove unfairness of price. In resolving issues of valuation the Court of Chancery undertakes a mixed determination of law and fact. Kahn v. Household Acquisition Corp., Del. Supr., 591 A.2d 166, 175 (1991). We recognize the thoroughness of the Chancellor's fair price analysis and the considerable deference due his selection from among the various methodologies offered by competing experts. *Lynch Communication,* 669 A.2d at 87. But here, the process is so intertwined with price that under *Weinberger*'s unitary standard a finding that the price negotiated by the Special Committee might have been fair does not save the result. *Cf. Lynch Communication Systems,* 669 A.2d 79.

Arguably, as the Chancellor found, the resulting price might be deemed to be at the lowest level in a broad range of fairness. But this does not satisfy the *Weinberger* test. Although often applied as a bifurcated or disjunctive test, the concept of entire fairness requires the court to examine all aspects of the transaction in an effort to determine whether the deal was entirely fair. *Weinberger,* 457 A.2d at 711. When assigned the burden of persuasion, this test obligates the directors, or their surrogates, to present evidence which demonstrates that the cumulative manner by which it discharged all of its fiduciary duties produced a fair transaction. . . .

In our recent decision in Kahn v. Lynch Communication, we were confronted with a situation in which the actions of the majority shareholder dominated the negotiation process and stripped the independent committee of its ability to negotiate in an arms-length manner. After concluding that the Court of Chancery erred in shifting the burden of proof with regard to entire fairness to the controlling shareholder, we remand the matter to the Court of Chancery for "a redetermination of the entire fairness . . . with the burden of proof remaining on Alcatel, the dominant and interested shareholder." *Kahn,* 638 A.2d at 1122. A similar course is appropriate here. It is the responsibility of the Court of Chancery to make the requisite factual determinations under the appropriate standards, which underlie the concept of entire fairness. Whether the defendants, shouldering the burden of proof, will be able to demonstrate entire fairness is, in the first instance, a task committed to the Chancellor.

In the event the Court of Chancery determines that the defendants have not demonstrated the entire fairness of the disputed transaction, we assume that it will grant appropriate relief within its broad equitable authority. *Weinberger,* 457 A.2d at 714. Reversed and remanded.

2. *Disinterested Shareholder Ratification*

According to DGCL §144(a)(2), a conflict-of-interest transaction is not void or voidable if the facts of the conflict are fully disclosed and the transaction is "specifically approved in good faith by a vote of the shareholders." While the statute doesn't say that the shareholders must be disinterested—that is, no shares are held by a party with the conflict of interest—subsequent Delaware cases show that it is disinterested shareholder approval that is necessary, at a minimum, for shareholder ratification to be effective. And yet, as the next case demonstrates, the effect of shareholder ratification differs depending on whether or not there is a controlling shareholder. This case is an excellent summary of current Delaware Supreme Court precedent, and it deserves careful study.

In re WHEELABRATOR TECHNOLOGIES INC.
SHAREHOLDERS LITIGATION

663 A.2d 1194
Court of Chancery of Delaware
May 18, 1995

JACOBS, Vice Chancellor.

This shareholder class action challenges the September 7, 1990 merger (the "merger") of Wheelabrator Technologies, Inc. ("WTI") into a wholly-owned subsidiary of Waste Management, Inc. ("Waste"). The plaintiffs are shareholders of WTI. The named defendants are WTI and the eleven members of WTI's board of directors at the time the merger was negotiated and approved.[1]

The plaintiffs claim that WTI and the director defendants breached their fiduciary obligation to disclose to the class material information concerning

---

1. Three of the eleven individual director defendants, Paul M. Montrone, Rodney C. Gilbert, and Paul M. Meister, were all members of WTI's management. Four directors, Dean L. Buntrock, William P. Hulligan, Phillip B. Rooney, and Donald F. Flynn were officers of Waste Management. The remaining four directors, Michael D. Dingman, Gerald J. Lewis, Thomas P. Stafford, and Edward Montgomery, were outside directors.

the merger. The plaintiffs also claim that in negotiating and approving the merger, the director defendants breached their fiduciary duties of loyalty and care. The defendants deny that they breached any duty of disclosure. They further contend that because the merger was approved by a fully informed shareholder vote, that vote operates as a complete defense to, and extinguishes, the plaintiffs' fiduciary claims.

This is the Opinion of the Court on the defendants' motion for summary judgment. For the reasons elaborated below, the Court concludes that: (1) the plaintiffs have failed to adduce evidence sufficient to defeat summary judgment on their duty of disclosure claim, and that (2) the fully informed shareholder vote approving the merger operated to extinguish the plaintiffs' duty of care claims, but not their duty of loyalty claim. Accordingly, the defendants' summary judgment motion is granted in part and denied in part.

I. Procedural Background

On April 5, 1990, the plaintiffs commenced these class actions (which were later consolidated) challenging the then-proposed merger with Waste. After expedited discovery, the plaintiffs moved for a preliminary injunction. That motion was denied, In re Wheelabrator Technologies, Inc. Shareholders Litig., Del. Ch., Cons. C.A. No. 11495, Jacobs, V.C., 1990 WL 131351 (Sept. 6, 1990) ("*Wheelabrator I*"), and the merger was approved by WTI's shareholders, specifically, by a majority of WTI's shareholders other than Waste. On July 22, 1991, the plaintiffs filed a Second Amended Consolidated Class Action Complaint, which the defendants moved to dismiss pursuant to Chancery Court Rule 12(b)(6). That motion was denied in part and granted in part. In re Wheelabrator Technologies, Inc. Shareholders Litig., Del. Ch., Cons. C.A. No. 11495, Jacobs, V.C., 1992 WL 212595 (Sept. 1, 1992). As a result of that ruling, all but three claims alleged in the complaint were dismissed.

The first remaining claim is Count I of the complaint, which alleges that the defendants violated their duty to disclose all material facts related to the merger in the proxy statement issued in connection with the transaction. More specifically, plaintiffs allege that (i) the proxy statement falsely represented that the merger negotiations lasted one week, whereas in fact agreement on all essential merger terms had been reached on the first day; (ii) the proxy statement disclosed that WTI's negotiators had successfully extracted concessions from Waste, whereas in fact Waste had dictated the merger terms to WTI; and (iii) the proxy statement disclosed that WTI's board had carefully considered the merger agreement before approving and recommending it to shareholders, whereas in fact the board did not consider the matter carefully before it acted.

Count III alleges that the defendants breached their duty of care by failing adequately to investigate alternative transactions, neglecting to consider certain nonpublic information regarding certain of Waste's potential legal liabilities, failing to appoint a committee of independent directors to negotiate the merger, and failing adequately to consider the merger terms.

Count IV alleges that the defendants breached their duty of loyalty, in that a majority of WTI's eleven directors had a conflict of interest that caused them not to seek or obtain the best possible value for the company's shareholders in the merger.

On December 30, 1992, the defendants filed the pending summary judgment motion seeking dismissal of these claims. Following discovery and briefing, that motion was argued on March 3, 1995.

II. RELEVANT FACTS

WTI, a publicly held Delaware corporation headquartered in New Hampshire, is engaged in the business of developing and providing refuse-to-energy services. Waste, a Delaware corporation with principal offices in Illinois, provides waste management services to national and international commercial, industrial, and municipal customers.

In August 1988, Waste and WTI entered into a transaction (the "1988 transaction") to take advantage of their complementary business operations. In the 1988 transaction, Waste acquired a 22% equity interest in WTI in exchange for certain assets that Waste sold to WTI. The two companies also entered into other agreements that concerned WTI's rights to ash disposal, the purchase of real estate for future refuse-to-energy facilities, and other business development opportunities. As a result of the 1988 transaction, Waste became WTI's largest (22%) stockholder and was entitled to nominate four of WTI's eleven directors.

Over the next two years, Waste and WTI periodically discussed other ways to reduce perceived inefficiencies by coordinating their operations. Those discussions intensified in December 1989, when Waste acquired a refuse-to-energy facility in West Germany. That acquisition raised concerns that the four Waste designees to WTI's board of directors might have future conflicts of interest if WTI later decided to enter the West German market.

Prompted by these and other concerns, Waste began, in December 1989, to consider either acquiring a majority equity interest in WTI or, alternatively, divesting all of its WTI stock. After several discussions, both companies agreed that Waste would increase its equity position in WTI. On March 22, 1990, Waste proposed a stock-for-stock, market-to-market (*i.e.* no premium) exchange in which Waste would become WTI's majority stockholder. WTI declined that proposal, and insisted on a transaction in which its shareholders would receive a premium above the current market price of their shares.

The following day, March 23, 1990, representatives of WTI and Waste met in New York City. Accompanying WTI's representatives were members of WTI's investment banking firm, Lazard Freres. At that meeting, Waste's representatives expressed Waste's interest in acquiring an additional 33% of WTI, thereby making Waste the owner of 55% of WTI's outstanding shares. The parties ultimately agreed on that concept. They also agreed to structure the transaction as a stock-for-stock merger that would be conditioned upon the approval of a majority of WTI's disinterested stockholders, *i.e.*, a majority of WTI's stockholders other than Waste. Waste agreed to pay a 10% premium for the additional shares required to reach the 55% equity ownership level. Finally, it was agreed that the merger would involve no "lockup," breakup fees, or other arrangements that would impede WTI from considering alternative transactions.

During the following week, additional face-to-face meetings and telephone conversations took place between the two companies' representatives. Those negotiations resulted in five "ancillary agreements" that gave WTI certain funding and business opportunity options, as well as licenses to use certain Waste-owned intellectual property.

On March 30, 1990, agreement on the final merger exchange ratio was reached. The parties agreed that WTI shareholders would receive 0.574 shares of WTI stock plus 0.469 shares of Waste stock for each of their pre-merger WTI shares. That same day, March 30, 1990, WTI's board of directors held a special meeting to consider the merger agreement. All board members attended except the four Waste designees, who had recused themselves. Also present were WTI's "in-house" and outside counsel, and representatives of Lazard Freres and Salomon Brothers. The WTI board members reviewed copies of the draft merger agreement and materials furnished by the investment bankers concerning the financial aspects of the transaction. The directors also heard presentations from the investment bankers and from legal counsel, who opined that the transaction was fair. A question and answer session followed.

The seven board members present then voted unanimously to approve the merger and to recommend its approval by WTI's shareholders. After that vote, the four Waste-designated board members joined the meeting, and the full board then voted unanimously to approve and recommend the merger.

On July 30, 1990, WTI and Waste disseminated a joint proxy statement to WTI shareholders, disclosing the recommendation of both boards of directors that their shareholders approve the transaction. At a special shareholders meeting held on September 7, 1990, the merger was approved by a majority of WTI shareholders other than Waste.

III. The Parties' Contentions

The defendants seek the dismissal of plaintiffs' remaining disclosure claim on the ground that it has no evidentiary support. The defendants further contend that the effect of the fully informed shareholder vote approving the merger was to ratify the directors' actions in negotiating and approving the merger, and thereby extinguish the plaintiffs' claims that those actions constituted breaches of fiduciary duty.

The plaintiffs respond that they have raised genuine issues of material fact that preclude the grant of summary judgment on their disclosure claim. They further argue that even if the disclosure claim were dismissed, that would not result in the extinguishment of their breach of loyalty claim. Plaintiffs maintain that the only effect of shareholder ratification would be to impose upon them the burden of proving that the merger was unfair to the corporation, with entire fairness being the applicable standard of judicial review. . . .

IV. The Disclosure Claim

[The Court first analyzed the plaintiffs' disclosure claims and ruled against the plaintiffs, finding there was insufficient evidentiary support for the plaintiffs' contentions.]

For the foregoing reasons, summary judgment will be granted dismissing the remaining duty of disclosure claim.

V. The Fiduciary Duty Claims

In rejecting the disclosure claim, the Court necessarily has determined that the merger was approved by a fully informed vote of a majority of WTI's disinterested stockholders. That determination requires the Court to confront the defendants' argument that that vote constituted shareholder ratification which operated as a complete defense to, and consequently extinguished, the claims that the defendants breached their fiduciary duties of care and loyalty.

The plaintiffs do not dispute that if the WTI shareholder vote was fully informed, it operated to extinguish their due care claim in this case. They avidly insist, however, that that vote could not, as a legal matter, extinguish their duty of loyalty claim. Plaintiffs argue that because the merger was an "interested" transaction subject to the entire fairness standard of review, the sole effect of shareholder ratification was to shift to plaintiffs the burden of proving that the merger was unfair.

I conclude, for the reasons next discussed, that (1) the effect of the informed shareholder vote was to extinguish the plaintiffs' due care claim; (2) that vote did not operate either to extinguish the duty of loyalty claim (as defendants contend), or to shift to the plaintiffs the burden of proving that the merger was unfair (as plaintiffs contend); and (3) the effect of the shareholder vote in this case is to invoke the business judgment standard, which limits review to issues of gift or waste with the burden of proof resting upon the plaintiffs. Because the parties have not yet been heard on the question of how the business judgment standard would apply to these facts, summary judgment with respect to the duty of loyalty claim must be denied.

A. THE DUTY OF CARE CLAIM

As noted, the plaintiffs concede that if the WTI shareholder vote was fully informed, the effect of that informed vote would be to extinguish the claim that the WTI board failed to exercise due care in negotiating and approving the merger. Given the ratification holding of Smith v. Van Gorkom, Del. Supr., 488 A.2d 858, 889-90 (1985), that concession is not surprising. In *Van Gorkom*, the defendant directors argued that the shareholder vote approving a challenged merger agreement "had the legal effect of curing any failure of the board to reach an informed business judgment in its approval of the merger." *Id.* at 889. Accepting that legal principle (but not its application to the facts before it), the Supreme Court stated:

> The parties tacitly agree that a discovered failure of the Board to reach an informed business judgment constitutes a voidable, rather than a void, act. Hence, the merger can be sustained, notwithstanding the infirmity of the Board's actions, if its approval by majority vote of the shareholders is found to have been based on an informed electorate.

Id. at 889.

Accordingly, summary judgment dismissing the plaintiffs' due care claim will be granted. That leaves for decision the legal effect of the informed shareholder vote on the duty of loyalty claims alleged in Count IV of the complaint.

B. THE DUTY OF LOYALTY CLAIM

The defendants contend that the informed shareholder approval of the WTI-Waste merger also operated to extinguish the claim that the directors' approval of the merger violated their duty of loyalty to WTI and its stockholders. The plaintiffs counter that a fully informed shareholder vote cannot, as a matter of law, operate to extinguish a duty of loyalty claim. At most, plaintiffs argue, the informed shareholder vote in this case would only shift to the plaintiff the burden of showing that the merger was unfair. Having considered the relevant authorities, and the law on this subject generally, I conclude that neither side's position is correct.

1.

I begin with the candid observation that the defendants' "claim extinguishment" argument is squarely supported by two decisions of this Court, one handed down in this very case. *Wheelabrator I, supra,* Mem. Op. at 19-20; Weiss v. Rockwell, Int'l. Corp., Del. Ch., C.A. No. 8811, Jacobs, V.C. (July 19, 1989), *aff'd per curiam,* Del. Supr., 574 A.2d 264 (1990).

In *Weiss,* this Court dismissed a fiduciary duty of loyalty claim that the directors of Rockwell International had approved a charter amendment creating a new class of super-voting stock for the sole purpose of entrenching themselves in office. Citing *Van Gorkom,* this Court held, without extended analysis, that the fully informed shareholder approval of the amendment extinguished the duty of loyalty claim. *Weiss, supra,* Letter Op. at 10. The Supreme Court affirmed that dismissal without comment in a *per curiam* opinion. 574 A.2d 264 (1990). In *Wheelabrator I,* this Court, citing *Van Gorkom* and *Weiss,* denied the plaintiffs' motion for a preliminary injunction against the merger at issue here, on the ground (*inter alia*) that if WTI's shareholders approved the merger, that ratifying vote would extinguish the plaintiffs' so-called "*Revlon*" claim.

In *Weiss* and *Wheelabrator I,* this Court reached that result by extending to a duty of loyalty claim the "extinguishment" doctrine applied to a duty of care claim in *Van Gorkom.* Although this Court did not articulate the propriety of that extension in doctrinal or policy terms, the result it reached was informed by the Supreme Court's statement in *Van Gorkom* that:

> where a majority of fully informed stockholders ratify action *of even interested directors,* an attack on the ratified transaction normally must fail.

488 A.2d at 890 (emphasis added). That language suggested that the Supreme Court would endorse the application of its "claim extinguishment" doctrine to duty of loyalty claims.

Not surprisingly, the defendants here argue that *Weiss* and *Wheelabrator I* impel the Court to reach the same result, that is to conclude that the plaintiffs' duty of loyalty claims were automatically extinguished by virtue of shareholder ratification. My difficulty with the defendants' position is that since 1990 the law has changed, and there is now significant reason to conclude that *Wheelabrator I* and *Weiss* would not be regarded as good law today. Not only has the Delaware Supreme Court never endorsed the view adopted in those cases, the decisions that postdate *Weiss* and *Wheelabrator I* persuasively indicate that the Supreme Court would not hold that shareholder approval of board action claimed to violate the fiduciary duty of loyalty would operate automatically to extinguish a duty of loyalty claim.

2.

The question of whether or not shareholder ratification should operate to extinguish a duty of loyalty claim cannot be decided in a vacuum, divorced from the broader issue of what generally are the legal consequences of a fully-informed shareholder approval of a challenged transaction. The Delaware case law addressing that broader topic is not reducible to a single clear rule or unifying principle. Indeed, the law in that area might be thought to lack coherence because the decisions addressing the effect of shareholder "ratification" have fragmented that subject into three distinct compartments, only one of which involves "claim extinguishment."

The basic structure of stockholder ratification law is, at first glance, deceptively simple. Delaware law distinguishes between acts of directors (or management) that are "void" and acts that are "voidable." As the Supreme Court stated in Michelson v. Duncan, 407 A.2d 211, 218-19 (1979):

> The essential distinction between voidable and void acts is that the former are those which may be found to have been performed in the interest of the corporation but beyond the authority of management, as distinguished from acts which are *ultra vires,* fraudulent, or waste of corporate assets. The practical distinction, for our purposes, is that voidable acts are susceptible to cure by shareholder approval while void acts are not.

One possible reading of *Michelson* is that all "voidable" acts are "susceptible to cure by shareholder approval." Under that reading, shareholder ratification might be thought to constitute a "full defense" (407 A.2d at 219) that would automatically extinguish all claims challenging such acts as a breach of fiduciary duty. Any such reading, however, would be overbroad, because the case law governing the consequences of ratification does not support that view and, in fact, is far more complex.

The Delaware Supreme Court has found shareholder ratification of "voidable" director conduct to result in claim-extinguishment in only two circumstances. The first is where the directors act in good faith, but exceed the board's de jure authority. In that circumstance, *Michelson* holds that "a validly accomplished shareholder ratification relates back to cure otherwise unauthorized acts of officers and directors." 407 A.2d at 219. The second circumstance is where the directors fail "to reach an informed business judgment" in approving a transaction. *Van Gorkom,* 488 A.2d at 889.

Except for these two situations, no party has identified any type of board action that the Delaware Supreme Court has deemed "voidable" for claim extinguishment purposes. More specifically, no Supreme Court case has held that shareholder ratification operates automatically to extinguish a duty of loyalty claim. To the contrary, the ratification cases involving duty of loyalty claims have uniformly held that the effect of shareholder ratification is to alter the standard of review, *or* to shift the burden of proof, *or* both. Those cases further frustrate any effort to describe the "ratification" landscape in terms of a simple rule.

The ratification decisions that involve duty of loyalty claims are of two kinds: (a) "interested" transaction cases between a corporation and its directors (or between the corporation and an entity in which the corporation's directors are also directors or have a financial interest), and (b) cases involving a transaction between the corporation and its controlling shareholder.

Regarding the first category, 8 Del. C. §144(a)(2) pertinently provides that an "interested" transaction of this kind will not be voidable if it is approved in good faith by a majority of disinterested stockholders. Approval by fully informed, disinterested shareholders pursuant to §144(a)(2) invokes "the business judgment rule and limits judicial review to issues of gift or waste with the burden of proof upon the party attacking the transaction." Marciano v. Nakash, Del. Supr., 535 A.2d 400, 405 n.3 (1987). The result is the same in "interested" transaction cases not decided under §144:

> Where there has been independent shareholder ratification of interested director actions, the objecting stockholder has the burden of showing that no person of ordinary sound business judgment would say that the consideration received for the options was a fair exchange for the options granted.

Michelson, 407 A.2d at 224 (quoting Kaufman v. Shoenberg, Del. Ch., 91 A.2d 786, 791 (1952), at 791); *see also* Gottlieb v. Heyden Chem. Corp., Del. Supr., 91 A.2d 57, 59 (1952); and Citron v. E.I. Du Pont de Nemours & Co., 584 A.2d 490, 501 (citing authorities reaching the same result in mergers involving fiduciaries that were not controlling stockholders).

The second category concerns duty of loyalty cases arising out of transactions between the corporation and its controlling stockholder. Those cases involve primarily parent-subsidiary mergers that were conditioned upon receiving "majority of the minority" stockholder approval. In a parent-subsidiary merger, the standard of review is ordinarily entire fairness, with the directors having the burden of proving that the merger was entirely fair. Weinberger v. UOP, Inc., 457 A.2d 701, 703. But where the merger is conditioned upon approval by a "majority of the minority" stockholder vote, and such approval is granted, the standard of review remains entire fairness, but the burden of demonstrating that the merger was unfair shifts to the plaintiff. Kahn v. Lynch Communication Sys. Del. Supr., 638 A.2d 1110 (1994); Rosenblatt v. Getty Oil Co., 493 A.2d 929, 937-38 (1985); *Weinberger,* at 710; *Citron,* at 502. That burden-shifting effect of ratification has also been held applicable in cases involving mergers with a de facto controlling stockholder, and in a case involving a transaction other than a merger [where there was a controlling shareholder]. . . .

To repeat: in only two circumstances has the Delaware Supreme Court held that a fully-informed shareholder vote operates to extinguish a claim: (1) where the board of directors takes action that, although not alleged to constitute *ultra vires,* fraud, or waste, is claimed to exceed the board's authority; and (2) where it is claimed that the directors failed to exercise due care to adequately inform themselves before committing the corporation to a transaction. In no case has the Supreme Court held that stockholder ratification automatically extinguishes a claim for breach of the directors' duty of loyalty. Rather, the operative effect of shareholder ratification in duty of loyalty cases has been either to change the standard of review to the business judgment rule, with the burden of proof resting upon the plaintiff, *or* to leave "entire fairness" as the review standard, but shift the burden of proof to the plaintiff. Thus, the Supreme Court ratification decisions do not support the defendants' position.

That being the present state of the law, the question then becomes whether there exists a policy or doctrinal basis that would justify extending the claim-extinguishing effect of shareholder ratification to cases involving duty of loyalty claims. *Van Gorkom* does not articulate a basis, and the parties have suggested none. The defendants rely solely upon the argument that *Weiss* and *Wheelabrator I* continue to be good law. That position requires this Court to revisit these decisions.

3.

As earlier noted, *Weiss* and *Wheelabrator I* are the sole authorities upon which the defendants' "claim extinguishment" argument rests. In those cases this Court extended *Van Gorkom* (which validated the extinguishment of a duty of care claim) to extinguish a duty of loyalty claim. Plausible as that extension might have been in 1989 and 1990 when *Weiss* and *Wheelabrator I* were decided, later Supreme Court decisions persuasively indicate that that view is no longer tenable.

In Kahn v. Lynch Communication Sys., *supra*, an "interested" cash out merger between a corporation and its de facto controlling stockholder was challenged as a breach of the directors' duty of loyalty. Had *Weiss* or *Wheelabrator I* been viewed as the correct ratification rule, the Supreme Court could have stated that the effect of shareholder ratification would be to extinguish the duty of loyalty claim. Instead, however, the Supreme Court held that in an interested merger with a controlling stockholder, the applicable judicial review standard is entire fairness, and shareholder ratification merely shifts the burden of proof on the fairness issue from the controlling stockholder to the challenging plaintiff. 638 A.2d at 1117. The *Kahn* Court disclaimed any suggestion that shareholder ratification obviates further judicial review, by noting that "the unchanging nature of the underlying 'interested' transaction requires careful scrutiny." *Id.* at 1116.

Stroud v. Grace, [606 A.2d 75, 85 (Del. 1992)], is similarly instructive. There, as in *Weiss*, the claim was that certain charter amendments proposed by the board whose members were also the corporation's controlling stockholders, were unfair and a breach of the directors' duty of loyalty to the minority stockholders. The charter amendments were found to have been approved by the fully-informed vote of a majority of the minority stockholders. Had *Weiss* (which was also a charter amendment case) been viewed as the correct approach, the Supreme Court could simply have held, without further analysis, that the duty of loyalty claims were extinguished by the informed shareholder vote. But, the Court did not do that. It ruled that the ratifying vote "[shifted] the burden of proof to the [plaintiffs] to prove that the transaction was unfair," 606 A.2d at 90, and then proceeded to consider the plaintiffs' claim that the charter amendments were unfair because (*inter alia*) they were intended to interfere with the shareholder franchise.

From these decisions I conclude that in duty of loyalty cases arising out of transactions with a controlling shareholder, our Supreme Court would reject the proposition that the Delaware courts will have no reviewing function in cases where the challenged transaction is approved by an informed shareholder vote. *Kahn* makes explicit the Supreme Court's concern that even an informed shareholder vote may not afford the minority sufficient protection to obviate the judicial oversight role. Even if the ratified transaction does not involve a controlling stockholder, the result would not be to extinguish a duty of loyalty claim. In such cases the Supreme Court has held that the effect of shareholder ratification is to make business judgment the applicable review standard and shift the burden of proof to the plaintiff stockholder. None of these authorities holds that shareholder ratification operates automatically to extinguish a duty of loyalty claim.

For these reasons, and in the absence of any policy or doctrinal basis to conclude otherwise, I find that insofar as *Weiss* and *Wheelabrator I* hold that shareholder ratification extinguishes a duty of loyalty claim, those cases would not be regarded today as good law. If the contrary view is to prevail, its source must be the Delaware Supreme Court, which is the only Court that can author- itatively rationalize and bring needed coherence to this important area of our corporate law. Accordingly, the defendants' "claim extinguishment" argument, in the duty of loyalty context, must be rejected.

C. THE APPROPRIATE REVIEW STANDARD AND BURDEN OF PROOF

Having determined what effect shareholder ratification does *not* have, the Court must now determine what effect it does have. The plaintiffs argue that their duty of loyalty claim is governed by the entire fairness standard, with ratification operating only to shift the burden on the fairness issue to the plaintiffs. That is incorrect, because this merger did not involve an interested and controlling stockholder.

In both *Kahn* and *Stroud,* the Supreme Court determined that the effect of a fully informed shareholder vote was to shift the burden of proof within the entire fairness standard of review. *Kahn,* 638 A.2d at 1117; *Stroud,* 606 A.2d at 90. Crit- ical to the result in those cases was that the transaction involved a de facto (*Kahn, supra*) or de jure (*Stroud, supra*) controlling stockholder. That circumstance brought those cases within the purview of the ratification doctrine articulated in *Rosenblatt, supra*, Bershad v. Curtiss-Wright-Corp., Del. Supr., 535 A.2d 840 (1987), and Citron v. E.I. Du Pont de Nemours & Co., *supra*, all involving mergers between a corporation and its majority stockholder-parent. The partic- ipation of the controlling interested stockholder is critical to the application of the entire fairness standard because, as *Kahn* and *Stroud* recognize, the potential for process manipulation by the controlling stockholder, and the concern that the controlling stockholder's continued presence might influence even a fully informed shareholder vote, justify the need for the exacting judicial scrutiny and procedural protection afforded by the entire fairness form of review.

In this case, there is no contention or evidence that Waste, a 22% stockholder of WTI, exercised de jure or de facto control over WTI. Therefore, neither the holdings of or policy concerns underlying *Kahn* and *Stroud* are implicated here. Accordingly, the review standard applicable to this merger is business judgment, with the plaintiffs having the burden of proof.[8]

---

8. That result is reached not only by process of elimination but also by application of 8 Del. C. §144(a)(1). That statute provides that when a majority of fully informed, disinterested directors (even if less than a quorum) approve a transaction in which other directors are interested, the transaction will not be void or voidable by reason of the conflict of interest. Under §144(a)(1), a ratifying disinterested director vote has the same procedural effect as a ratifying disinterested shareholder vote under §144(a)(2). *See Marciano,* 535 A.2d at 405, n.3. Here, it is undisputed that

The final question concerns the proper application of that review standard to the facts at bar. Because no party has yet been heard on that subject, that issue cannot be determined on this motion. Its resolution must await further proceedings, which counsel may present (if they so choose) on a supplemental motion for summary judgment. . . .

For the foregoing reasons, the defendants' motion for summary judgment (1) is granted as to the disclosure claim, (2) is granted as to the duty of care claim, and (3) is denied as to the duty of loyalty claims. Counsel shall submit an appropriate implementing form of order.

PROBLEM 11-2

One has to wonder what the Western Union Corporation's business model is these days, when instant communication doesn't exactly bring to mind sending a telegram. Indeed, the company went into involuntary bankruptcy in 1991. Eventually a bankruptcy plan was devised, and the major assets of the company, which are its money transfer business, were sold in 1995 to Bennett Lebow and various entities controlled by Mr. Lebow. Upon purchasing the assets, Mr. Lebow set up the New Valley Corporation, capitalizing it with three separate classes of stock — Class A Preferred, Class B Preferred, and Common. Mr. Lebow, and entities controlled by him, own 61.1 percent of the Class A Senior Preferred shares; 11.3 percent of the Class B Preferred Shares, and 43.1 percent of the company's common shares. The Class A shares have a liquidation preference four times that of Class B.

As of 1999, New Valley was not reaching new heights of prosperity, and indeed its common stock price was languishing in the $6 to $7 per share range. At the same time, the company had an unpaid dividend arrearage owed to Class A holders of $234.6 million and a $172.9 million dividend arrearage owed to the Class B holders. Thus, the common shares would not be paying dividends in the near future, one could surmise. Contemplating this situation, the board of New Valley determined that market analysts were having a hard time determining New Valley's true value because of its complicated capital structure. Thus, a recapitalization was in order. Under the recapitalization plan that the board approved, the Class A and Class B shares' accrued and unpaid dividends would be wiped out. Each Class A share would be reclassified and changed into 20 common shares and one warrant to purchase an additional share for $12.50 (above the market price, clearly). (A "warrant" is a long-term option to buy the common stock of a corporation granted by the corporation.) Each Class B share would be reclassified and changed into one-third of a common share and warrants to purchase five additional shares at $12.50 per share. Each common share would be converted to one-tenth of a common share and three-tenths of a warrant to purchase a share for $12.50.

The plan was approved and recommended by a committee of the board made up of outside directors. In order to be adopted, the plan was put to a vote that required that a simple majority of all three classes approve it. After the plan was

---

the merger was approved by the fully informed vote of WTI's disinterested directors. Those directors were fully aware of both the obvious conflict of the Waste designees and of the conflict of three other directors, created by the prospect of accelerated stock options and of future employment.

publicly announced, in connection with the filing of the proxy statement with the SEC in preparation for the vote, Class A shares rose in value dramatically while Class B shares lost half of their value. At a special shareholders' meeting held in May 1999, each voting class approved the plan. The votes in favor of the plan were 82.7 percent of the outstanding Class A shares, 68.8 percent of the outstanding Class B shares, and 53.2 percent of the old common shares. After the recapitalization was effected, the common shares still traded well below the warrant price of $12.50, and the warrants themselves traded at $.50 per warrant.

Former holders of Class B shares are interested in evaluating whether they have a cause of action against the board for breach of the duty of loyalty, and/or for various disclosure violations. They point to the market reaction as evidence that the plan unfairly favored Class A shareholders at the expense of Class B shareholders. They also contend that the proxy statement contained the following material misrepresentations or omissions:

1.   It failed to disclose the projected value of the new common stock despite the fact that the board had that projection;
2.   It failed to estimate the value of the warrants, despite the fact that the board had that estimate;
3.   It failed to disclose that the investment banker who gave the fairness opinion anticipates getting further work from Lebow-related entities.

How do you advise the Class B shareholders? What additional information do you need prior to giving advice? Who would have the burden of proof in the litigation, and what would that party have to prove? How does the shareholder vote affect your analysis?

D.   CORPORATE OPPORTUNITIES

In addition to general cases of self-dealing, courts have identified other contexts in which the duty of loyalty is relevant. One of these is the diversion of corporate opportunities for the benefit of a corporate director or manager. These cases involve competition between the corporation and the director or manager. As an initial matter, the plaintiff claiming redress under the "corporate opportunity" doctrine must prove that the opportunity was a corporate opportunity. Courts have identified three tests of corporate opportunity:

(1) The "interest or expectancy" test, which precludes acquisition by corporate officers of the property of a business opportunity in which the corporation has a 'beachhead' in the sense of a legal or equitable interest or expectancy growing out of a preexisting right or relationship; (2) the "line of business" test, which characterizes an opportunity as corporate whenever a managing officer becomes involved in an activity intimately or closely associated with the existing or prospective activities of the corporation; and (3) the "fairness" test, which determines the existence of a corporate opportunity by applying ethical standards of what is fair and equitable under the circumstances.

Miller v. Miller, 222 N.W.2d 71 (Minn. 1974).

The American Law Institute has proposed the following definition of a "corporate opportunity":

> (1) Any opportunity to engage in a business activity of which a director or senior executive becomes aware, either:
>
>> (A) In connection with the performance of functions as a director or senior executive, or under circumstances that should reasonably lead the director or senior executive to believe that the person offering the opportunity expects it to be offered to the corporation; or
>>
>> (B) Through the use of corporate information or property, if the resulting opportunity is one that the director or senior executive should reasonably be expected to believe would be of interest to the corporation; or
>
> (2) Any opportunity to engage in a business activity of which a senior executive becomes aware and knows is closely related to a business in which the corporation is engaged or expects to engage.[1]

American Law Institute, Principles of Corporate Governance §5.05 (1992).

While a number of courts have embraced the ALI formulation, it is not clear that this definition yields results different from the common law definitions. The potentially more important innovation from the ALI relates to the process that must occur before a manager or directors can take advantage of a corporate opportunity. Traditionally, courts would not allow managers to take a corporate opportunity for themselves unless they could prove that the corporation consented or was unable to take advantage of the opportunity, for example, because of a lack of cash. This latter justification has caused courts no end of difficulties. The main problem is that even a corporation that is low on cash may be able to raise money to take advantage of an opportunity if the opportunity is sufficiently attractive. In addition, as noted by the Maine Supreme Court, "Often, the injection of financial ability into the equation will unduly favor the inside director or executive who has command of the facts relating to the finances of the corporation. Reliance on financial ability will also act as a disincentive to corporate executives to solve corporate financing and other problems." Northeast Harbor Golf Club, Inc. v. Harris, 661 A.2d 1146, 1149 (Me. 1995). In the face of this difficult judgment, the ALI suggests a mandatory disclosure regime:

> (a) *General Rule.* A director or senior executive may not take advantage of a corporate opportunity unless:
>
>> (1) The director or senior executive first offers the corporate opportunity to the corporation and makes disclosure concerning the conflict of interest and the corporate opportunity;
>>
>> (2) The corporate opportunity is rejected by the corporation; and
>>
>> (3) Either:
>>
>>> (A) The rejection of the opportunity is fair to the corporation;
>>>
>>> (B) The opportunity is rejected in advance, following such disclosure, by disinterested directors or, in the case of a senior executive who is

---

1. Note that §5.05(2) establishes a broader definition of "corporate opportunity" for senior executives than §5.05(1) establishes for outside directors.

not a director, by a disinterested superior, in a manner that satisfies the standards of the business judgment rule; or

   (C) The rejection is authorized in advance or ratified, following such disclosure, by disinterested shareholders and the rejection is not equivalent to a waste of corporate assets.

While a few courts have embraced the ALI's approach, most courts still struggle with these questions on a case-by-case basis.

The Delaware legislature has offered a new twist on the corporate opportunity doctrine, adopting the following as the new §122(17):

> Every corporation created under this chapter shall have power to: . . .
>
>   (17) Renounce, in its certificate of incorporation or by action of its board of directors, any interest or expectancy of the corporation in, or in being offered an opportunity to participate in, specified business opportunities or specified classes or categories of business opportunities that are presented to the corporation or one or more of its officers, directors or stockholders.

While this statute awaits adjudication, in Broz v. Cellular Information Systems, Inc., the Delaware Supreme Court tackles the most difficult aspect of the corporate opportunity doctrine — namely, whose opportunity is it?

BROZ v. CELLULAR INFORMATION SYSTEMS, INC.

673 A.2d 148
Supreme Court of Delaware
March 22, 1996

VEASEY, Chief Justice.

In this appeal, we consider the application of the doctrine of corporate opportunity. The Court of Chancery decided that the defendant, a corporate director, breached his fiduciary duty by not formally presenting to the corporation an opportunity which had come to the director individually and independent of the director's relationship with the corporation. Here the opportunity was not one in which the corporation in its current mode had an interest or which it had the financial ability to acquire, but, under the unique circumstances here, that mode was subject to change by virtue of the impending acquisition of the corporation by another entity.

We conclude that, although a corporate director may be shielded from liability by offering to the corporation an opportunity which has come to the director independently and individually, the failure of the director to present the opportunity does not necessarily result in the improper usurpation of a corporate opportunity. We further conclude that, if the corporation is a target or potential target of an acquisition by another company which has an interest and ability to entertain the opportunity, the director of the target company does not have a fiduciary duty to present the opportunity to the target company. Accordingly, the judgment of the Court of Chancery is reversed.

Robert F. Broz ("Broz") is the President and sole stockholder of RFB Cellular, Inc. ("RFBC"), a Delaware corporation engaged in the business of providing cellular telephone service in the Midwestern United States. At the time of the conduct at issue in this appeal, Broz was also a member of the board of directors of plaintiff below-appellee, Cellular Information Systems, Inc. ("CIS"). CIS is a publicly held Delaware corporation and a competitor of RFBC.

The conduct before the Court involves the purchase by Broz of a cellular telephone service license for the benefit of RFBC.[1] The license in question, known as the Michigan-2 Rural Service Area Cellular License ("Michigan-2"), is issued by the Federal Communications Commission ("FCC") and entitles its holder to provide cellular telephone service to a portion of northern Michigan. CIS brought an action against Broz and RFBC for equitable relief, contending that the purchase of this license by Broz constituted a usurpation of a corporate opportunity properly belonging to CIS, irrespective of whether or not CIS was interested in the Michigan-2 opportunity at the time it was offered to Broz.

The principal basis for the contention of CIS is that PriCellular, Inc. ("PriCellular"), another cellular communications company which was contemporaneously engaged in an acquisition of CIS, was interested in the Michigan-2 opportunity. CIS contends that, in determining whether the Michigan-2 opportunity rightfully belonged to CIS, Broz was required to consider the interests of PriCellular insofar as those interests would come into alignment with those of CIS as a result of PriCellular's acquisition plans.

After trial, the Court of Chancery agreed with the contentions of CIS and entered judgment against Broz and RFBC. The court held that: (1) irrespective of the fact the Michigan-2 opportunity came to Broz in a manner wholly independent of his status as a director of CIS, the Michigan-2 license was an opportunity that properly belonged to CIS; (2) due to an alignment of the interests of CIS and PriCellular arising out of PriCellular's efforts to acquire CIS, Broz breached his fiduciary duty by failing to consider whether the opportunity was one in which PriCellular would be interested; (3) despite the fact that CIS was aware of the opportunity and expressed no interest in pursuing it, Broz was required formally to present the transaction to the CIS board prior to seizing the opportunity for his own; and (4) absent formal presentation to the board, Broz' acquisition of Michigan-2 constituted an impermissible usurpation of a corporate opportunity. The trial court imposed a constructive trust on the agreement to purchase Michigan-2 and directed that the right to purchase the license be transferred to CIS. From this judgment, Broz and RFBC appeal.

Broz contends that the Court of Chancery erred in holding that he breached his fiduciary duties to CIS and its stockholders. Specifically, Broz asserts that he was under no obligation formally to present the corporate opportunity to the CIS Board of Directors. Broz further contends that PriCellular had

---

1. The Court recognizes that the actual purchase of the Michigan-2 license was consummated by RFBC as a corporate entity, rather than by Broz acting as an individual for his own benefit. Broz is, however, the sole party in interest in RFBC and all actions taken by RFBC, including the acquisition of Michigan-2, are accomplished at the behest of Broz. Therefore, insofar as the purchase of Michigan-2 is concerned, the Court will not distinguish between the actions of Broz and those of RFBC in analyzing Broz' alleged breach of fiduciary duty.

not consummated its acquisition of CIS at the time of his decision to purchase Michigan-2, and that, accordingly, he was not obligated to consider the interests of PriCellular. We agree with Broz and hold that: (1) the determination of whether a corporate fiduciary has usurped a corporate opportunity is fact-intensive and turns on, *inter alia*, the ability of the corporation to make use of the opportunity and the company's intent to do so; (2) while presentation of a purported corporate opportunity to the board of directors and the board's refusal thereof may serve as a shield to liability, there is no per se rule requiring presentation to the board prior to acceptance of the opportunity; and (3) on these facts, Broz was not required to consider the interests of PriCellular in reaching his determination whether or not to purchase Michigan-2.

II. FACTS

Broz has been the President and sole stockholder of RFBC since 1992. RFBC owns and operates an FCC license area, known as the Michigan-4 Rural Service Area Cellular License ("Michigan-4"). The license entitles RFBC to provide cellular telephone service to a portion of rural Michigan. Although Broz' efforts have been devoted primarily to the business operations of RFBC, he also served as an outside director of CIS at the time of the events at issue in this case. CIS was at all times fully aware of Broz' relationship with RFBC and the obligations incumbent upon him by virtue of that relationship.

In April of 1994, Mackinac Cellular Corp. ("Mackinac") sought to divest itself of Michigan-2, the license area immediately adjacent to Michigan-4. To this end, Mackinac contacted Daniels & Associates ("Daniels") and arranged for the brokerage firm to seek potential purchasers for Michigan-2. In compiling a list of prospects, Daniels included RFBC as a likely candidate. In May of 1994, David Rhodes, a representative of Daniels, contacted Broz and broached the subject of RFBC's possible acquisition of Michigan-2. Broz later signed a confidentiality agreement at the request of Mackinac, and received the offering materials pertaining to Michigan-2.

Michigan-2 was not, however, offered to CIS. Apparently, Daniels did not consider CIS to be a viable purchaser for Michigan-2 in light of CIS' recent financial difficulties. The record shows that, at the time Michigan-2 was offered to Broz, CIS had recently emerged from lengthy and contentious Chapter 11 proceedings. Pursuant to the Chapter 11 Plan of Reorganization, CIS entered into a loan agreement that substantially impaired the company's ability to undertake new acquisitions or to incur new debt. In fact, CIS would have been unable to purchase Michigan-2 without the approval of its creditors.

The CIS reorganization resulted from the failure of CIS' rather ambitious plans for expansion. From 1989 onward, CIS had embarked on a series of cellular license acquisitions. In 1992, however, CIS' financing failed, necessitating the liquidation of the company's holdings and reduction of the company's total indebtedness. During the period from early 1992 until the time of CIS' emergence from bankruptcy in 1994, CIS divested itself of some fifteen separate cellular license systems. CIS contracted to sell four additional license areas on

May 27, 1994, leaving CIS with only five remaining license areas, all of which were outside of the Midwest.

On June 13, 1994, following a meeting of the CIS board, Broz spoke with CIS' Chief Executive Officer, Richard Treibick ("Treibick"), concerning his interest in acquiring Michigan-2. Treibick communicated to Broz that CIS was not interested in Michigan-2. Treibick further stated that he had been made aware of the Michigan-2 opportunity prior to the conversation with Broz, and that any offer to acquire Michigan-2 was rejected. After the commencement of the PriCellular tender offer, in August of 1994, Broz contacted another CIS director, Peter Schiff ("Schiff"), to discuss the possible acquisition of Michigan-2 by RFBC. Schiff, like Treibick, indicated that CIS had neither the wherewithal nor the inclination to purchase Michigan-2. In late September of 1994, Broz also contacted Stanley Bloch ("Bloch"), a director and counsel for CIS, to request that Bloch represent RFBC in its dealings with Mackinac. Bloch agreed to represent RFBC, and, like Schiff and Treibick, expressed his belief that CIS was not at all interested in the transaction. Ultimately, all the CIS directors testified at trial that, had Broz inquired at that time, they each would have expressed the opinion that CIS was not interested in Michigan-2.[5]

On June 28, 1994, following various overtures from PriCellular concerning an acquisition of CIS, six CIS directors entered into agreements with PriCellular to sell their shares in CIS at a price of $2.00 per share. These agreements were contingent upon, *inter alia*, the consummation of a PriCellular tender offer for all CIS shares at the same price. Pursuant to their agreements with PriCellular, the CIS directors also entered into a "standstill" agreement which prevented the directors from engaging in any transaction outside the regular course of CIS' business or incurring any new liabilities until the close of the PriCellular tender offer. On August 2, 1994, PriCellular commenced a tender offer for all outstanding shares of CIS at $2.00 per share. The PriCellular tender offer mirrored the standstill agreements entered into by the CIS directors.

PriCellular's tender offer was originally scheduled to close on September 16, 1994. At the time the tender offer was launched, however, the source of the $106,000,000 in financing required to consummate the transaction was still in doubt. PriCellular originally planned to structure the transaction around bank loans. When this financing fell through, PriCellular resorted to a junk bond offering. PriCellular's financing difficulties generated a great deal of concern among the CIS insiders whether the tender offer was, in fact, viable. Financing difficulties ultimately caused PriCellular to delay the closing date of the tender offer from September 16, 1994 until October 14, 1994 and then again until November 9, 1994.

On August 6, September 6 and September 21, 1994, Broz submitted written offers to Mackinac for the purchase of Michigan-2. During this time period, PriCellular also began negotiations with Mackinac to arrange an option for the purchase of Michigan-2. PriCellular's interest in Michigan-2 was fully disclosed to CIS' chief executive, Treibick, who did not express any interest in Michigan-2,

5. We assume arguendo that informal contacts and individual opinions of board members are not a substitute for a formal process of presenting an opportunity to a board of directors. Nevertheless, in our view such a formal process was not necessary under the circumstances of this case in order for Broz to avoid liability. These contacts with individual board members do, however, tend to show that Broz was not acting surreptitiously or in bad faith.

and was actually incredulous that PriCellular would want to acquire the license. Nevertheless, CIS was fully aware that PriCellular and Broz were bidding for Michigan-2 and did not interpose CIS in this bidding war.

In late September of 1994, PriCellular reached agreement with Mackinac on an option to purchase Michigan-2. The exercise price of the option agreement was set at $6.7 million, with the option remaining in force until December 15, 1994. Pursuant to the agreement, the right to exercise the option was not transferrable to any party other than a subsidiary of PriCellular. Therefore, it could not have been transferred to CIS. The agreement further provided that Mackinac was free to sell Michigan-2 to any party who was willing to exceed the exercise price of the Mackinac-PriCellular option contract by at least $500,000. On November 14, 1994, Broz agreed to pay Mackinac $7.2 million for the Michigan-2 license, thereby meeting the terms of the option agreement. An asset purchase agreement was thereafter executed by Mackinac and RFBC.

Nine days later, on November 23, 1994, PriCellular completed its financing and closed its tender offer for CIS. Prior to that point, PriCellular owned no equity interest in CIS. Subsequent to the consummation of the PriCellular tender offer for CIS, members of the CIS board of directors, including Broz, were discharged and replaced with a slate of PriCellular nominees. On March 2, 1995, this action was commenced by CIS in the Court of Chancery.

At trial in the Court of Chancery, CIS contended that the purchase of Michigan-2 by Broz constituted the impermissible usurpation of a corporate opportunity properly belonging to CIS. Thus, CIS asserted that Broz breached his fiduciary duty to CIS and its stockholders. CIS admits that, at the time the opportunity was offered to Broz, the board of CIS would not have been interested in Michigan-2, but CIS asserts that Broz usurped the opportunity nevertheless. CIS claims that Broz was required to look not just to CIS, but to the articulated business plans of PriCellular, to determine whether PriCellular would be interested in acquiring Michigan-2. Since Broz failed to do this and acquired Michigan-2 without first considering the interests of PriCellular in its capacity as a potential acquiror of CIS, CIS contends that Broz must be held to account for breach of fiduciary duty.

In assessing the contentions of the parties in light of the facts of record, the Court of Chancery concluded:

> (1) that [CIS] . . . could have legitimately required its director [Broz] to abstain from the Mackinac transaction out of deference to its own interests in extending an offer, despite the fact that it came to such director in a wholly independent way (that is, the transaction is one that falls quite close to the core transactions that the corporation was formed to engage in); (2) that by no later than the time by which Price had extended the public tender offer, the circumstances of the company had changed so that it was quite plausibly in the corporation's interest and financially feasible for it to pursue the Mackinac transaction; (3) that in such circumstances as existed at the latest after October 14, 1994 (date of PriCellular's option contract on Michigan 2 RSA) it was the obligation of Mr. Broz as a director of CIS to take the transaction to the CIS board for its formal action; and (4) the after the fact testimony of directors to the effect that they would not have been interested in pursuing this transaction had it been brought to the board, is not helpful to defendant, in my opinion, because most of them did not know at that time of PriCellular's interest in the property and how it related to PriCellular's plan for CIS.

Based on these conclusions, the court held that:

> even though knowledge of the availability of the Michigan 2 RSA license and its associated assets came to Mr. Broz wholly independently of his role on the CIS board, that opportunity was within the core business interests of CIS at the relevant times; that at such time CIS would have had access to the financing necessary to compete for the assets that were for sale; and that the CIS board of directors were not asked to and thus did not consider whether such action would have been in the best interests of the corporation. In these circumstances I conclude that Mr. Broz as a director of CIS violated his duty of loyalty to CIS by seizing this opportunity without formally informing the CIS board fully about the opportunity and facts surrounding it and by proceeding to acquire rights for his benefit without the consent of the corporation. . . .

IV. APPLICATION OF THE CORPORATE OPPORTUNITY DOCTRINE

The doctrine of corporate opportunity represents but one species of the broad fiduciary duties assumed by a corporate director or officer. A corporate fiduciary agrees to place the interests of the corporation before his or her own in appropriate circumstances. In light of the diverse and often competing obligations faced by directors and officers, however, the corporate opportunity doctrine arose as a means of defining the parameters of fiduciary duty in instances of potential conflict. The classic statement of the doctrine is derived from the venerable case of Guth v. Loft, Inc. In *Guth*, this Court held that:

> if there is presented to a corporate officer or director a business opportunity which the corporation is financially able to undertake, is, from its nature, in the line of the corporation's business and is of practical advantage to it, is one in which the corporation has an interest or a reasonable expectancy, and, by embracing the opportunity, the self-interest of the officer or director will be brought into conflict with that of the corporation, the law will not permit him to seize the opportunity for himself.

The corporate opportunity doctrine, as delineated by *Guth* and its progeny, holds that a corporate officer or director may not take a business opportunity for his own if: (1) the corporation is financially able to exploit the opportunity; (2) the opportunity is within the corporation's line of business; (3) the corporation has an interest or expectancy in the opportunity; and (4) by taking the opportunity for his own, the corporate fiduciary will thereby be placed in a position inimicable to his duties to the corporation. The Court in *Guth* also derived a corollary which states that a director or officer may take a corporate opportunity if: (1) the opportunity is presented to the director or officer in his individual and not his corporate capacity; (2) the opportunity is not essential to the corporation; (3) the corporation holds no interest or expectancy in the opportunity; and (4) the director or officer has not wrongfully employed the resources of the corporation in pursuing or exploiting the opportunity.

Thus, the contours of this doctrine are well established. It is important to note, however, that the tests enunciated in *Guth* and subsequent cases provide guidelines to be considered by a reviewing court in balancing the equities of an individual case. No one factor is dispositive and all factors must be taken into account insofar as they are applicable. Cases involving a claim of usurpation of a corporate opportunity range over a multitude of factual settings. Hard and fast rules are not easily crafted to deal with such an array of complex situations. . . . In the instant case, we find that the facts do not support the conclusion that Broz misappropriated a corporate opportunity.

We note at the outset that Broz became aware of the Michigan-2 opportunity in his individual and not his corporate capacity. As the Court of Chancery found, "Broz did not misuse proprietary information that came to him in a corporate capacity nor did he otherwise use any power he might have over the governance of the corporation to advance his own interests." This fact is not the subject of serious dispute. In fact, it is clear from the record that Mackinac did not consider CIS a viable candidate for the acquisition of Michigan-2. Accordingly, Mackinac did not offer the property to CIS. In this factual posture, many of the fundamental concerns undergirding the law of corporate opportunity are not present (*e.g.*, misappropriation of the corporation's proprietary information). The burden imposed upon Broz to show adherence to his fiduciary duties to CIS is thus lessened to some extent. Nevertheless, this fact is not dispositive. The determination of whether a particular fiduciary has usurped a corporate opportunity necessitates a careful examination of the circumstances, giving due credence to the factors enunciated in *Guth* and subsequent cases.

We turn now to an analysis of the factors relied on by the trial court. First, we find that CIS was not financially capable of exploiting the Michigan-2 opportunity. Although the Court of Chancery concluded otherwise, we hold that this finding was not supported by the evidence. The record shows that CIS was in a precarious financial position at the time Mackinac presented the Michigan-2 opportunity to Broz. Having recently emerged from lengthy and contentious bankruptcy proceedings, CIS was not in a position to commit capital to the acquisition of new assets. Further, the loan agreement entered into by CIS and its creditors severely limited the discretion of CIS as to the acquisition of new assets and substantially restricted the ability of CIS to incur new debt.

The Court of Chancery based its contrary finding on the fact that PriCellular had purchased an option to acquire CIS' bank debt. Thus, the court reasoned, PriCellular was in a position to exercise that option and then waive any unfavorable restrictions that would stand in the way of a CIS acquisition of Michigan-2. The trial court, however, disregarded the fact that PriCellular's own financial situation was not particularly stable. PriCellular was unable to finance the acquisition of CIS through conventional bank loans and was forced to use the more risky mechanism of a junk bond offering to raise the required capital. Thus, the court's statement that "PriCellular had other sources of financing to permit the funding of that purchase" is clearly not free from dispute. Moreover, as discussed *infra*, the fact that PriCellular had available sources of financing is immaterial to the analysis. At the time that Broz was required to decide whether to accept the Michigan-2 opportunity, PriCellular had not yet acquired CIS, and any plans to do so were wholly speculative. Thus, contrary to the Court of Chancery's finding, Broz was not obligated to consider the contingency of a PriCellular acquisition of CIS and the related contingency of PriCellular thereafter waiving restrictions on the CIS bank debt. Broz was required to consider the facts only as they existed at the time he determined to accept the Mackinac offer and embark on his efforts to bring the transaction to fruition.

Second, while it may be said with some certainty that the Michigan-2 opportunity was within CIS' line of business, it is not equally clear that CIS had a cognizable interest or expectancy in the license. Under the third factor laid down by this Court in *Guth*, for an opportunity to be deemed to belong to the fiduciary's corporation, the corporation must have an interest or expectancy in that opportunity. As this Court stated in Johnston v. Greene, 121 A.2d 919, 924 (1956), "[f]or the corporation to have an actual or expectant interest in any specific property, there must be some tie between that property and the nature of the corporate business." Despite the fact that the nature of the Michigan-2 opportunity was historically close to the core operations of CIS, changes were in process. At the time the opportunity was presented, CIS was actively engaged in the process of divesting its cellular license holdings. CIS' articulated business plan did not involve any new acquisitions. Further, as indicated by the testimony of the entire CIS board, the Michigan-2 license would not have been of interest to CIS even absent CIS' financial difficulties and CIS' then current desire to liquidate its cellular license holdings. Thus, CIS had no interest or expectancy in the Michigan-2 opportunity.

Finally, the corporate opportunity doctrine is implicated only in cases where the fiduciary's seizure of an opportunity results in a conflict between the fiduciary's duties to the corporation and the self-interest of the director as actualized by the exploitation of the opportunity. In the instant case, Broz' interest in acquiring and profiting from Michigan-2 created no duties that were inimicable to his obligations to CIS. Broz, at all times relevant to the instant appeal, was the sole party in interest in RFBC, a competitor of CIS. CIS was fully aware of Broz' potentially conflicting duties. Broz, however, comported himself in a manner that was wholly in accord with his obligations to CIS. Broz took care not to usurp any opportunity which CIS was willing and able to pursue. Broz sought only to compete with an outside entity, PriCellular, for acquisition of an opportunity which both sought to possess. Broz was not obligated to refrain from competition with PriCellular. Therefore, the totality of the circumstances indicates that Broz did not usurp an opportunity that properly belonged to CIS.

A. Presentation to the Board:

In concluding that Broz had usurped a corporate opportunity, the Court of Chancery placed great emphasis on the fact that Broz had not formally presented the matter to the CIS board. The court held that "in such circumstances as existed at the latest after October 14, 1994 (date of PriCellular's option contract on Michigan 2 RSA) it was the obligation of Mr. Broz as a director of CIS to take the transaction to the CIS board for its formal action. . . . " In so holding, the trial court erroneously grafted a new requirement onto the law of corporate opportunity, *viz.*, the requirement of formal presentation under circumstances where the corporation does not have an interest, expectancy or financial ability.

The teaching of *Guth* and its progeny is that the director or officer must analyze the situation *ex ante* to determine whether the opportunity is one rightfully belonging to the corporation. If the director or officer believes, based on one of the factors articulated above, that the corporation is not entitled to the opportunity, then he may take it for himself. Of course, presenting the opportunity to the board creates a kind of "safe harbor" for the director, which removes the specter of a *post hoc* judicial determination that the director or officer has improperly usurped a corporate opportunity. Thus, presentation avoids the possibility that an error in the fiduciary's assessment of the situation will create future liability for breach of fiduciary duty. It is not the law of Delaware that presentation to the board is a necessary prerequisite to a finding that a corporate opportunity has not been usurped. . . .

Thus, we hold that Broz was not required to make formal presentation of the Michigan-2 opportunity to the CIS board prior to taking the opportunity for his own. In so holding, we necessarily conclude that the Court of Chancery erred in grafting the additional requirement of formal presentation onto Delaware's corporate opportunity jurisprudence.

B. Alignment of Interests Between CIS and PriCellular:

In concluding that Broz usurped an opportunity properly belonging to CIS, the Court of Chancery held that "[f]or practical business reasons CIS' interests with respect to the Mackinac transaction came to merge with those of PriCellular, even before the closing of its tender offer for CIS stock." Based on this fact, the trial court concluded that Broz was required to consider PriCellular's prospective, post-acquisition plans for CIS in determining whether to forego the opportunity or seize it for himself. Had Broz done this, the Court of Chancery determined that he would have concluded that CIS was entitled to the opportunity by virtue of the alignment of its interests with those of PriCellular.

We disagree. Broz was under no duty to consider the interests of PriCellular when he chose to purchase Michigan-2. As stated in *Guth*, a director's right to "appropriate [an] . . . opportunity depends on the circumstances existing at the time it presented itself to him without regard to subsequent events." *Guth*, 5 A.2d at 513. At the time Broz purchased Michigan-2, PriCellular had not yet acquired CIS. Any plans to do so would still have been wholly speculative. Accordingly, Broz was not required to consider the contingent and uncertain plans of PriCellular in reaching his determination of how to proceed.

Whether or not the CIS board would, at some time, have chosen to acquire Michigan-2 in order to make CIS a more attractive acquisition target for PriCellular or to enhance the synergy of any combined enterprise, is speculative. The trial court found this to be a plausible scenario and therefore found that, pursuant to the factors laid down in Guth, CIS had a valid interest or expectancy in the license. This speculative finding cuts against the statements made by CIS' Chief Executive and the entire CIS board of directors and ignores the fact that CIS still lacked the wherewithal to acquire Michigan-2, even if one takes into account the possible availability of PriCellular's financing. Thus, the fact of PriCellular's plans to acquire CIS is immaterial and does not change the analysis.

In reaching our conclusion on this point, we note that certainty and predictability are values to be promoted in our corporation law. Broz, as an active participant in the cellular telephone industry, was entitled to proceed in his own economic interest in the absence of any countervailing duty. The right of a director or officer to engage in business affairs outside of his or her fiduciary capacity would be illusory if these individuals were required to consider every potential, future occurrence in determining whether a particular business strategy would implicate fiduciary duty concerns. In order for a director to engage meaningfully in business unrelated to his or her corporate role, the director must be allowed to make decisions based on the situation as it exists at the time a given opportunity is presented. Absent such a rule, the corporate fiduciary would be constrained to refrain from exploiting any opportunity for fear of liability based on the occurrence of subsequent events. This state of affairs would unduly restrict officers and directors and would be antithetical to certainty in corporation law.

V. Conclusion

The corporate opportunity doctrine represents a judicially crafted effort to harmonize the competing demands placed on corporate fiduciaries in a modern business environment. The doctrine seeks to reduce the possibility of conflict between a director's duties to the corporation and interests unrelated to that role. In the instant case, Broz adhered to his obligations to CIS. We hold that the Court of Chancery erred as a matter of law in concluding that Broz had a duty formally to present the Michigan-2 opportunity to the CIS board. We also hold that the trial court erred in its application of the corporate opportunity doctrine under the unusual facts of this case, where CIS had no interest or financial ability to acquire the opportunity, but the impending acquisition of CIS by PriCellular would or could have caused a change in those circumstances.

Therefore, we hold that Broz did not breach his fiduciary duties to CIS. Accordingly, we reverse the judgment of the Court of Chancery holding that Broz diverted a corporate opportunity properly belonging to CIS and imposing a constructive trust.

CHAPTER
12

Litigation to Enforce Directors' Duties

A. THE DEMAND REQUIREMENT

When directors breach their fiduciary duties, often it is the company itself that
is directly harmed and should have the right to enforce a claim. But a company
acts through its directors and officers—the very people who have breached
their fiduciary duties. Of course, we cannot expect the directors and officers to
sue themselves. Recognizing this problem, courts of equity gave shareholders
the right to sue in such cases. A shareholder suit of this type is known as "derivative litigation," a designation acknowledging that the shareholders' claim is not
a claim of direct harm, but a claim that is derived from harm to the corporation. We have seen derivative litigation in prior chapters. For example, Brehm
v. Eisner involved litigation against the Disney company for excessive executive compensation, and Kahn v. Sullivan challenged Occidental Petrolum's
charitable contributions; both were brought as derivative actions.

The courts have described derivative claims as being two actions combined
in one. The first action is a suit by the shareholders against the corporation to
compel the corporation to sue. In derivative litigation, therefore, the corporation is a nominal defendant, even though the real defendants are the directors.
The second action is by the corporation against the directors, and the shareholders are, in a sense, only the nominal plaintiffs. They are suing on behalf of
the corporation.

Because the claim belongs to the corporation—not the shareholders—any
recovery goes to the corporation. This feature of derivative litigation introduces
a potential problem: why would any shareholder bear all of the costs of litigation
with the prospect of receiving only a portion of the benefits (equal to the shareholder's ownership interest in the corporation)? In most cases, the answer is
simple: the shareholders themselves would not sue under those circumstances.

This was a real problem for the courts of equity, which recognized the potential benefits from derivative litigation. Not only could such litigation provide
compensation to an injured corporation, but the fear of litigation could deter
future breaches of fiduciary duty. In short, the courts of equity wanted to
encourage derivative claims . . . at least, *meritorious* derivative claims.

To address the incentive problem, courts of equity decided that they would
award attorneys' fees for successful lawsuits. This mechanism for encouraging derivative litigation has profound effects on the frequency and efficacy of

claims. The obvious implication is that the shareholders are not the real party in interest: the attorneys have assumed that role.

Providing incentives to attorneys, however, can be a dangerous thing. Attorneys may be less concerned about the merits of the claim than they are about its settlement value. And, of course, no case would settle under this regime without an agreement on behalf of the defendants to pay fees for the plaintiffs' attorneys. Unmeritorious claims — commonly known as "strike suits" — became the next challenge.

The courts decided to meet that challenge by erecting various procedural obstacles: (1) plaintiffs must have been shareholders at the time of the alleged breach of duty ("contemporaneous ownership" rule); (2) plaintiffs must remain shareholders throughout the litigation ("standing requirement"); (3) shareholders must "demand" that the board of directors take action before the shareholder assumes control of the litigation ("demand requirement"); and (4) once a derivative claim is filed, the court must approve any settlement. The standing requirement has been embraced by the Delaware courts as a matter of common law. *See* Lewis v. Anderson, 477 A.2d 1040, 1046 (Del. 1984). The other three requirements are embodied in Chancery Rule 23.1, which provides:

> In a derivative action brought by 1 or more shareholders or members to enforce a right of a corporation or of an unincorporated association, the corporation or association having failed to enforce a right which may properly be asserted by it, the complaint shall allege that the plaintiff was a shareholder or member at the time of the transaction of which the plaintiff complains or that the plaintiff's share or membership thereafter devolved on the plaintiff by operation of law. The complaint shall also allege with particularity the efforts, if any, made by the plaintiff to obtain the action the plaintiff desires from the directors or comparable authority and the reasons for the plaintiff's failure to obtain the action or for not making the effort. The action shall not be dismissed or compromised without the approval of the Court, and notice by mail, publication or otherwise of the proposed dismissal or compromise shall be given to shareholders or members in such manner as the Court directs; except that if the dismissal is to be without prejudice or with prejudice to the plaintiff only, then such dismissal shall be ordered without notice thereof if there is a showing that no compensation in any form has passed directly or indirectly from any of the defendants to the plaintiff or plaintiff's attorney and that no promise to give any such compensation has been made.

The idea behind these procedures was that good derivative suits would work their way through the obstacles, while bad derivative suits would falter. Of course, whether this aspiration would be realized would depend in large part on the manner in which the courts enforced the procedures. By far the most important decisions in this regard relate to the demand requirement.

The Delaware courts have not interpreted the demand requirement as mandatory. In some instances, the courts have been willing to "excuse" demand. These are cases in which directors — as a result of some conflict of interest — would not be willing to act upon a demand. The courts describe those as cases in which a demand would be futile.

While this exception to the demand requirement might seem sensible enough at first blush, the effect of "demand futility" on derivative litigation has become the subject of persistent debate. The source of the controversy is the fact that Delaware courts review claims differently depending on whether demand is excused or has already been refused by the board of directors. If a plaintiff makes a demand and the board of directors refuses to act, the Delaware courts review the board's decision to refuse the demand. In other words, the case becomes a "wrongful refusal" case. Moreover, in deciding wrongful refusal cases, the Delaware courts have held that by making a demand, a shareholder tacitly acknowledges the board's independence and concedes the board's capacity to evaluate that demand. As a result, the court reviews the board's decision to refuse the demand under the deferential business judgment rule.

By contrast, if a plaintiff bypasses the board of directors and argues that a demand would be futile, the Delaware courts may scrutinize the case more carefully, as described in Aronson v. Lewis, 473 A.2d 805 (Del. 1984). The facts of that case are rather mundane: a stockholder of Meyers Parking System challenged certain transactions (namely, an employment agreement and interest-free loans) between the company and a 47 percent stockholder, who was also a director and officer of the company. The Court of Chancery refused to grant the defendant directors' motion to dismiss for failure to make a demand, holding that the plaintiff's allegations raised a "reasonable inference that the business judgment rule is not applicable for purposes of considering a pre-suit demand pursuant to Rule 23.1." In deciding whether a "reasonable inference" exists, the court examined the challenged transactions (that is, the employment agreement and the interest-free loans). If these transactions did not receive the protection of the business judgment rule, the court reasoned, then the directors who approved the transactions would become potentially liable for a breach of their fiduciary duty. As a result, they would not be capable of impartially considering a stockholder's demand.

In an interlocutory appeal, the defendants argued that the Court of Chancery had been too lax in its interpretation of the demand requirement. Observing that the board of directors is central to the management structure of a Delaware corporation, the defendants argued that the demand requirement could not be waived merely because the directors had approved the challenged transactions. If this were the standard, then demand would be waived in almost every case. Of course, the plaintiff countered by arguing that the board of directors was incapable of entertaining a demand with requisite impartiality because all of the directors had been selected for the board by the stockholder whose transactions were being challenged. These are all entirely predictable arguments, but the Delaware Supreme Court decided to seize the opportunity to revisit the standard for determining demand futility.

The supreme court began with the cardinal precept of Delaware corporate law that "directors, rather than shareholders, manage the business and affairs of the corporation." The demand requirement acknowledges the board's central role, but "where officers and directors are under an influence which sterilizes their discretion, they cannot be considered proper persons to conduct litigation on behalf of the corporation." Aronson, 473 A.2d at 814. The question thus became under what circumstances would a board's discretion become sterilized? It would require something more than approval of the challenged transaction (for this would disqualify almost every board, and the demand requirement would become meaningless). Instead, the court offered the following standard:

Our view is that in determining demand futility the Court of Chancery in the proper exercise of its discretion must decide whether, under the particularized facts alleged, a reasonable doubt is created that: (1) the directors *are* disinterested and independent [*or*] (2) the challenged transaction *was* otherwise the product of a valid exercise of business judgment. (Emphasis added.)

The easiest way for a plaintiff to meet this standard is to show that a majority of the directors were interested in the challenged transaction. Unfortunately for many plaintiffs, such a showing does not fit the facts. The following statements from *Aronson* highlight the difficulty of making such a showing:

- [E]ven proof of majority ownership of a company does not strip the directors of the presumptions of independence, and that their acts have been taken in good faith and in the best interests of the corporation. There must be coupled with the allegation of control such facts as would demonstrate that through personal or other relationships the directors are beholden to the controlling person.

- [I]t is not enough to charge that a director was nominated by or elected at the behest of those controlling the outcome of a corporate election. That is the usual way a person becomes a corporate director. It is the care, attention and sense of individual responsibility to the performance of one's duties, not the method of election, that generally touches on independence.

- Plaintiff's final argument is the incantation that demand is excused because the directors otherwise would have to sue themselves, thereby placing the conduct of the litigation in hostile hands and preventing its effective prosecution. . . . Its acceptance would effectively abrogate Rule 23.1 and weaken the managerial power of directors. Unless facts are alleged with particularity to overcome the presumptions of independence and a proper exercise of business judgment, in which case the directors could not be expected to sue themselves, a bare claim of this sort raises no legally cognizable issue under Delaware corporate law.

Initially, *Aronson* offered plaintiffs a Hobson's choice: make a demand and bring a wrongful refusal case under the business judgment rule, or avoid the demand and hope to show that the board of directors was interested. In the ensuing years, the Delaware courts have loosened the standards for demand futility somewhat. The case below, In re the Limited Derivative Litigation, is an excellent example of the modern application of the *Aronson* standards.

All of this should be read in contrast to the Model Business Corporation Act ("Model Act"), which has short-circuited the drama over demand futility by adopting a universal demand requirement, under which plaintiffs must always first bring demand to the board that it initiate derivative litigation for breach of fiduciary duty. *See* Model §7.42. If, after 90 days, the board has not acted, then the plaintiffs (who are, in every case, shareholders) can initiate litigation. *See* Model Act §7.42(2). The drafters of the Model Act adopted a universal demand approach for two reasons. First, they envision it as a sort of alternative dispute resolution mechanism. Thus, by bringing demand to the board, the board would have the opportunity to recognize problems with the actions they have taken and to take steps to address the plaintiffs' concerns without litigation. Second, given how much time in litigation is spent on the question of whether demand is required or excused, the drafters felt that eliminating that potential issue would save time and money and streamline the process of litigation.

In re THE LIMITED, INC. SHAREHOLDERS LITIGATION
2002 WL 537692 (unpublished)
Court of Chancery of Delaware
March 27, 2002

NOBLE, Vice Chancellor. . . .

Pending is a motion to dismiss the First Amended Consolidated Derivative Complaint ("Complaint") in a shareholder derivative suit brought on behalf of The Limited, Inc. ("The Limited" or the "Company"). The defendants are The Limited, the nominal defendant, and each of the twelve members of the Company's Board of Directors (the "Board"). The plaintiffs allege that the Company's directors committed corporate waste and breached their fiduciary duties of loyalty and due care by rescinding a Contingent Stock Redemption Agreement (the "Redemption Agreement") and funding in part with monies made available as the result of the rescission of the Redemption Agreement a self-tender offer that they also assert resulted in no consideration to the Company.

Defendants have moved to dismiss the Complaint on the basis that plaintiffs failed to meet the pre-suit demand requirements of Court of Chancery Rule 23.1. They also seek dismissal of the Complaint under Court of Chancery Rule 12(b)(6) for failure to state an actionable claim for corporate waste or breach of fiduciary duty.

I. BACKGROUND

A. THE PARTIES

Common stockholder plaintiffs Rochelle Phillips, Miriam Shapiro and Peter Sullivan bring this derivative action on behalf of The Limited, against the Company and each of its directors. The plaintiffs' allegations stem from The Limited's authorization of a self-tender offer for up to 15 million shares of its stock and the rescission of an agreement that included a call option to purchase 18.75 million shares of common stock from a trust set up for the benefit of Leslie H. Wexner's ("Mr. Wexner") children. Mr. Wexner is The Limited's founder as well as its President, Chief Executive Officer, and Chairman.

The Limited, a Delaware corporation based in Columbus, Ohio, is a specialty retailer operating more than 3,000 stores nationwide. In addition to being the Company's top executive, Mr. Wexner, one of the individual defendant-directors, is also its largest shareholder, owning or controlling approximately twenty-five percent of The Limited's outstanding stock at the time of the challenged transactions. Also named as a defendant in the Complaint is Abigail S. Wexner ("Mrs. Wexner"), Mr. Wexner's wife, who has served on the Board since 1997.

The remaining ten members of The Limited's Board named as defendants are Raymond Zimmerman ("Zimmerman"), Allan R. Tessler ("Tessler"), Claudine B. Malone ("Malone"), Eugene M. Freedman ("Freedman"), Martin Trust ("Trust"), Kenneth B. Gilman ("Gilman"), David T. Kollat ("Kollat"), E. Gordon Gee ("Gee"), Donald B. Shackelford ("Shackelford"), and Leonard A. Schlesinger ("Schlesinger").

B. THE SELF-TENDER

On May 3, 1999, The Limited announced that the Board had authorized the repurchase of up to 15 million shares of the Company's outstanding common stock, [approximately 6 percent of The Limited's 228,165,712 shares then outstanding], through a Dutch auction tender offer. Under the terms of the tender offer, the Company agreed to repurchase those shares at a premium over their pre-announcement closing price.[7] Mr. Wexner agreed that neither he nor any of his affiliates would participate in the tender.

This decision, according to the Company, was based in large part on the purportedly large amount of excess cash and cash equivalents generated by the Company's operations, an amount more than $660 million. The Board concluded that the stock repurchase was the most attractive method for utilizing the Company's excess cash and would demonstrate to the stockholders how much confidence it had in The Limited's business. Shortly after the expiration of the self-tender, The Limited announced that it had acquired 15,000,000 shares at a total cost to the Company of $750 million, $90 million more than the $660 million of cash and cash equivalents it had on hand.

C. THE CONTINGENT STOCK REDEMPTION AGREEMENT

When it made public its decision to conduct a self-tender offer, The Limited also announced that it had agreed to rescind the Redemption Agreement, an agreement it had entered into in 1996 with Mr. Wexner in both his individual capacity and as trustee of The Wexner Children's Trust (the "Children's Trust").

Under the Redemption Agreement, the Children's Trust acquired the right, through January 30, 2006, to require the Company to redeem [to buy from them] all or a portion of the 18.75 million shares of common stock it held at $18.75 per share, a put option. The Redemption Agreement also provided the Company with a six-month window, commencing on July 31, 2006, to redeem all or part of the remaining shares still held by the Children's Trust at $25.07 per share, a call option.

During the term of the Redemption Agreement, The Limited was required to retain $350 million in a restricted cash account in order to satisfy its obligations under the agreement should either of the options be triggered. In other words, the $350 million was to remain in this restricted account until the year 2006 to cover The Limited's potential obligations under the Redemption Agreement.

II. CONTENTIONS

The Complaint asserts claims of corporate waste and breaches of the fiduciary duties of loyalty and due care in connection with the challenged transactions described above.

Plaintiffs' due care and corporate waste claims rest on the relationship between the rescission of the Redemption Agreement and the self-tender. Plaintiffs allege that the only reason for structuring the transactions in this manner

---

7. The self-tender price was between $50 and $55 per share. This, plaintiffs indicate, represented a significant premium over the $43.75 pre-announcement closing price.

was to enable Mr. Wexner to avoid the terms of the Redemption Agreement which, they assert, had become particularly unfavorable to him.[12] Plaintiffs argue that these transactions lacked any legitimate business purpose other than to benefit Mr. Wexner at the Company's expense and came without a corresponding benefit to the Company. Plaintiffs also allege a breach of the fiduciary duty of loyalty on the basis that at least half of the Board had a disqualifying self-interest in the transactions or lacked independence in approving the challenged transactions due to their personal or professional relationships with Mr. Wexner.

Plaintiffs claim that the absence of impartiality on the part of a majority of the Board rendered any demand futile. Specifically, plaintiffs maintain they have pled particularized facts raising a reasonable doubt that a majority of the twelve-member Board was disinterested and independent at the time that their initial complaint was filed. In this respect, plaintiffs argue that they have alleged particularized facts demonstrating that a majority of the twelve-member Board stood to gain from the now challenged transactions or were economically beholden to Mr. Wexner (who, they allege, had a disqualifying self-interest). Additionally, the plaintiffs assert that they have alleged particularized facts raising a reasonable doubt as to whether the challenged transactions resulted from the exercise of sound business judgment.

Defendants respond by asserting that this action should be dismissed for two reasons. First, defendants argue that plaintiffs have failed to meet the pre-suit demand requirements of Court of Chancery Rule 23.1. Specifically, they contend that plaintiffs have failed to plead particularized facts as to why demand on the Board should be excused. Second, defendants argue that plaintiffs have not sufficiently alleged an actionable corporate waste claim or a breach of fiduciary duty claim and that the Complaint should be dismissed under Court of Chancery Rule 12(b)(6) for failure to state a claim for which this Court can grant relief.

III. Analysis

A. DEMAND FUTILITY

Court of Chancery Rule 23.1 provides that where a plaintiff initiates a shareholder derivative action without first making a demand on the company's board, the complaint must allege with particularity the reasons justifying the plaintiff's failure to do so.

In most situations, the board of directors has sole authority to initiate or to refrain from initiating legal actions asserting rights held by the corporation. This authority is subject to the limited exception, defined in Chancery Rule 23.1, permitting stockholders to initiate a derivative suit to enforce unasserted

---

12. By May 1999, the month in which The Limited announced the two challenged transactions, the price of the Company's stock was trading at more than $40 per share, significantly higher than the call price that the Company could have paid during the six-month window to exercise its option in 2006. Had the Company been empowered in May 1999 to force the Trust to sell it its shares, the Company could have purchased the Trust's 18.75 million shares for approximately $25 per share, thus realizing a savings of more than $15 per share from its then over $40 trading price. This equates to roughly $280,000,000.

rights of the corporation without the board's approval where they can show either that the board wrongfully refused the plaintiff's pre-suit demand to initiate the suit or, if no demand was made, that such a demand would be a futile gesture and is therefore excused.

The "heavy burden" of pleading demand futility is a substantive component of a plaintiff's case and, as such, the failure to meet either of the two showings prescribed by our Supreme Court in Aronson v. Lewis ends a court's inquiry before it can even address the merits of the challenged transaction. "Under Aronson v. Lewis, demand is considered futile and, therefore, excused only if the particularized facts alleged in the complaint create a reasonable doubt that: 1) the directors are disinterested and independent; or 2) the challenged transaction was otherwise the product of a valid exercise of business judgment." In this case, plaintiffs assert that their failure to make a demand should be excused because their Complaint raises a reasonable doubt as to both of the *Aronson* factors. Thus, I turn to consideration of the first prong of *Aronson*.

The plaintiffs argue that they have sufficiently alleged with particularity facts raising a reasonable doubt as to whether a majority of the directors on The Limited's Board were disinterested and independent.

To meet the first prong of the *Aronson* test and adequately show the futility of a pre-suit demand, a plaintiff must plead particularized facts sufficiently demonstrating that the defendant directors had a financial interest in the challenged transaction, that they were motivated by a desire to retain their positions on the board or within the company (an entrenchment motive), or that they were dominated or controlled by a person interested in the transaction.

In conducting this analysis, *Aronson* and its progeny limit the scope of my inquiry under Rule 23.1 to the allegations of the Complaint. For the reasons discussed below, I find that the plaintiffs have alleged sufficient particularized facts to raise a reasonable doubt as to the disinterestedness or independence of at least six of The Limited's twelve directors.

1. Director Disinterestedness

The Complaint alleges that the challenged transactions were approved by the Board for the sole or primary reason of enabling Mr. Wexner to negotiate a rescission of the Redemption Agreement affecting the Trust which he controlled. "Directorial interest exists whenever divided loyalties are present, or a director either has received, or is entitled to receive, a personal financial benefit from the challenged transaction which is not equally shared by the stockholders." Because Mr. Wexner, in his individual capacity and as trustee for the Trust, negotiated the Redemption Agreement at its creation, an agreement that was for the benefit of his children, the Complaint has alleged sufficiently particularized facts creating a reasonable doubt as to his disinterestedness in connection with the Company's rescission of that agreement. Mrs. Wexner similarly stood to benefit from the rescission of the Redemption Agreement, thereby creating a reasonable doubt as to her disinterestedness as a director in the approval of the rescission.

With respect to the remaining ten directors, however, the Complaint is devoid of any allegations suggesting the presence of any financial interest in the challenged transactions that would suffice for purposes of the first prong of *Aronson*. At issue with these directors are the plaintiffs' allegations challenging their independence (*i.e.*, whether they were so beholden to Mr. Wexner as to create a reasonable doubt about their independence). The independence of these directors will be discussed next.

2. *Director Independence*

Independence, the *Aronson* Court held, means that a director's decision is based on the corporate merits of the subject matter before the board rather than extraneous considerations or influences. To establish lack of independence, a plaintiff meets his burden by showing that the directors are either beholden to the controlling shareholder or so under its influence that their discretion is sterilized.

The Court in ascertaining the sufficiency of a complaint challenging a director's loyalty does not apply an objective "reasonable director standard"; instead, the Court must apply a "subjective 'actual person' test to determine whether a *particular* director[ ] . . . lacks independence because he is controlled by another."

The plaintiffs do not seriously contest the independence of four of The Limited's directors. The only allegations in the Complaint with respect to Zimmerman, Tessler, Malone, and Freedman are that each had been a director of The Limited for a number of years predating the challenged transactions. Allegations as to one's position as a director and the receipt of director's fees, without more, however, are not enough for purposes of pleading demand futility. As such, I find that the plaintiffs have not met their burden of raising, through allegations of particularized facts, a reasonable doubt as to the independence of Zimmerman, Tessler, Malone, or Freedman.

The Complaint states that Shackelford, a director of The Limited since 1975, was also a director of Intimate Brands, Inc., The Limited's 84% owned subsidiary, which is allegedly dependent upon The Limited for significant revenues. Shackelford's compensation from his role as a director of The Limited, alone, does not create a reasonable doubt as to that director's independence. Similarly, the receipt of director's fees from a subsidiary does not, in the absence of other facts suggesting a lack of independence, demonstrate a reasonable doubt as to that director's loyalty. Accordingly, I find that plaintiffs have failed to rebut the presumption as to Shackelford's independence as well.

The Complaint alleges that Kollat, a director of The Limited since 1976, is a principal of Audio Environments ("Audio"), a company supplying in-store music to The Limited's stores, from which Audio receives $400,000 annually in revenue. This Court has previously considered the potential impact on a director's independence from a business relationship between the director's employer (in which the director may have an interest) and the company on whose board the directors sits. "Although it has been held that a director whose small law firm received $1,000,000 in legal fees from the corporation was potentially beholden to the CEO, [a] plaintiff [who has failed to] allege[ ] particular facts indicating that [the money] allegedly paid to [the director] or his firm was so material as to taint [the director's] judgment . . . [fails] to create a reasonable doubt about his independence." The Complaint is devoid of any allegations asserting (or from which an inference can reasonably be drawn, for that matter) that the $400,000 annual revenue that Audio receives from its dealings with The Limited and its affiliates was material to Audio's business. Moreover, the Complaint does not allege how Kollat, as "a principal," may have benefited from any portion of those revenues. Accordingly, the plaintiffs have also failed to plead particularized facts raising a reasonable doubt as to Kollat's independence.

Gilman has served as a director since 1990. Since 1997, his principal employment has been as vice chairman and chief administrative officer of The Limited for which, during the years 1996–1998, he averaged $1.8 million in salary and bonuses. It is reasonable to infer that compensation of this magnitude is material to him. Moreover, as a general matter, compensation from one's principal employment is "typically of great consequence" to the employee. Because of Mr. Wexner's holdings of The Limited and his position, as chairman, chief executive officer, and director, these allegations of particularized facts raise a reasonable doubt as to Gilman's independence from Mr. Wexner's will.

Trust's status is similar to that of Gilman. Trust is a long-time (since 1978) director of the The Limited. His principal employment is as president and chief executive officer of a wholly-owned subsidiary of The Limited. His average compensation from that position, which can reasonably be inferred to be material to him, over the four-year period preceding the filing of the Complaint, was approximately $1.8 million. Again, these particularized facts generate a reasonable doubt as to whether Trust is able to make decisions about Mr. Wexner's interests that are independent from his control.

Schlesinger became a director of The Limited in 1996. He provided consulting services to The Limited and one of its wholly-owned subsidiaries for which, during the years 1996-1998, he received average annual compensation of $150,000. His principal occupation was as a senior administrative officer of Brown University. Thus, I must determine whether, on these particularized facts, it is appropriate to conclude that average annual consulting fees of $150,000 would be material to Schlesinger and that he was "beholden" to Mr. Wexner because of a desire to continue with those consulting services. I am satisfied that it is reasonable to infer from these allegations that continued annual compensation in excess of $150,000 would be material to Schlesinger, a senior university official, and that Schlesinger was beholden to Wexner for the continuation of the consulting services. Accordingly, plaintiffs have met their pleading burden for raising a reasonable doubt as to Schlesinger's independence.

Gee, who has been a director since 1991, was president of The Ohio State University, Mr. Wexner's alma mater, from 1990 to 1997. He subsequently became president of Brown University, a position he left before the Complaint was filed. Gee, as the result of nominations by Mr. Wexner, serves on the boards of both The Limited and a subsidiary of The Limited. These facts, whether viewed singly or cumulatively, do not support any inference questioning Gee's independence. Gee, however, while president of Ohio State, successfully solicited from Wexner a $25 million grant to establish The Wexner Center for the Arts. Furthermore, Gee, while president of Brown, is alleged to have continued to solicit Mr. Wexner for donations.

Thus, the question as to Gee becomes: if a director is the head of a charitable or educational institution, under what circumstances may his independence be called into question by the charitable giving of the allegedly dominating person, in this instance, Mr. Wexner?

This Court has considered this question previously. In Lewis v. Fuqua, the independence of Governor Terry Sanford was evaluated. He served with J.B. Fuqua, the allegedly controlling person, on both the board of Fuqua Industries, Inc. and the Board of Trustees of Duke University of which Governor

Sanford was then the president. Governor Sanford and Fuqua had a lengthy history of political, social and business relationships. Fuqua was a generous benefactor to Duke, [donating $10 million to Duke University]. The Court concluded that all of these facts, taken together, supported the conclusion that there was reasonable doubt of Governor Sanford's independence from the domination of Fuqua.

This conclusion may be contrasted with the determination in *Disney* that the independence of Father O'Donovan had not been sufficiently called into question. Father O'Donovan was the president of Georgetown University and served as a director of The Walt Disney Company. The allegedly dominating person, Mr. Eisner, the chairman of Disney, had given $1 million to Georgetown University, which was the alma mater of one of his children. The Court in *Disney* focused on two critical distinctions from the analysis in Lewis v. Fuqua: (i) Governor Sanford had "numerous political and financial dealings" with Fuqua; no such relationship was alleged between Father O'Donovan and Mr. Eisner; and (ii) both Fuqua and Governor Sanford served together as directors (or trustees) of both Duke and Fuqua Industries. Mr. Eisner, in comparison, had no formal relationship with Georgetown University.

Thus, unlike the relationship between Governor Sanford and Fuqua, Gee and Mr. Wexner are not alleged to have had lengthy political and financial dealings and they do not serve together on multiple boards. Furthermore, while Gee, as president of Brown University, may have solicited Mr. Wexner for donations, the Complaint does not allege that he was successful. Moreover, Gee left his position at Brown and the Complaint does not suggest any continuing need or desire to solicit Mr. Wexner for charitable donations.

However, the determination of whether a particular director is "beholden" to an allegedly controlling person is not limited to the power to affect the director in the future. One may feel "beholden" to someone for past acts as well. It may reasonably be inferred that Mr. Wexner's gift of $25 million to Ohio State was, even for a school of that size, a significant gift. While the gift was not to Gee personally, it was a positive reflection on him and his fundraising efforts as university president to have successfully solicited such a gift. In this context, even though there can be no "bright line" test, a gift of that magnitude can reasonably be considered as instilling in Gee a sense of "owingness" to Mr. Wexner. For that reason, I conclude that the plaintiffs have successfully alleged a reasonable doubt as to Gee's independence from Mr. Wexner's domination.[41]

Thus, six of the twelve directors of The Limited are either interested (Mr. Wexner and Mrs. Wexner) in the challenged transactions or subject to a reasonable doubt about their independence (Gilman, Trust, Schlesinger and Gee) from Mr. Wexner's domination. Although that, of course, is not a majority of the directors, where the challenged actions are those of a board consisting of an even number of directors, plaintiffs meet their burden of demonstrating the futility of making demand on the board by showing that half of the board was either interested or not independent. Accordingly, defendants' motion under Court of Chancery Rule 23.1 is denied.

---

41. I recognize that charitable giving to educational institutions, particularly one's alma mater, is to be encouraged. That, however, is not the issue here. The issue is whether such an extraordinary gift makes it reasonable to question Gee's independence. I conclude that it does.

With the determination that demand is excused, I now turn to consideration of defendants' application under Court of Chancery Rule 12(b)(6)'s more lenient pleading standards.

For the reasons set forth above, I am satisfied that the Complaint states a claim for breach of the duty of loyalty. The challenged transactions were approved by a unanimous board of twelve; six of those directors were either interested or subject to disqualifying doubts about their independence. As set forth below, the challenged transactions, while perhaps not constituting corporate waste, appear unfair to the stockholders. Thus, because the challenged transactions were not approved by a majority of independent and disinterested directors, the Complaint states a loyalty claim that survives a challenge under Court of Chancery Rule 12(b)(6).

Although the challenged transactions may be questioned because of doubts about the loyalty of the directors approving them, it does not necessarily follow that they constitute corporate waste.

For plaintiffs' waste claim to survive, the Complaint, under the liberal pleading standards of Court of Chancery Rule 12(b)(6), must show that the transactions were "effected on terms 'that no person of ordinary, sound business judgment could conclude represent a fair exchange.'" Plaintiffs' burden has also been described as requiring a showing that "the [transactions] in question either served no corporate purpose or [were] so completely bereft of consideration that [they] effectively constituted a gift."

I will first analyze the corporate waste claim for the two transactions separately, followed by a consideration of the two transactions taken together.

1. Rescission of the Redemption Agreement

By its terms, the Redemption Agreement required The Limited to maintain, untouched, a cash account of $350 million until 2006 to cover its potential obligations under the agreement. Because the price of the stock had risen appreciably since the creation of the Redemption Agreement, the plaintiffs allege that the rescission "destroyed a valuable option worth hundreds of millions of dollars to the Company. . . . without a corresponding benefit to the Company, . . . the only benefit accruing to [Mr.] Wexner and the [Children's] Trust, which no longer faced the prospect of being forced to sell shares below market value."

It is true that had the terms of the Redemption Agreement empowered the Company to trigger its call on May 3, 1999, the date of the Company's announcement, then Mr. Wexner, as trustee, would have been obligated to sell the Trust's 18,750,000 shares at approximately $15 below the shares' trading price at that time. The Company's call option, however, could not have been exercised until 2006, almost seven years after the date of The Limited's announcement. By that time, it is anyone's guess as to whether The Limited's stock would have continued to climb in value, whether it would have fallen below its May 1999 trading levels, or whether it would have fallen below either the put option price or the call option price. Any future benefit that the Company might have enjoyed had rescission not been effectuated, therefore, is speculation and conjecture.

The Company argues that rescinding the Redemption Agreement freed up $350 million in cash reserves that it was required to maintain. Freeing up such a substantial amount of otherwise stagnant and untouchable capital, in light of the stock market's volatility and unpredictability, it argues, is well within the realm of reason. That the plaintiffs assess the intrinsic value of the Redemption Agreement to have been between $350 and $550 million based on the Black-Scholes model is not dispositive. If the stock price had fallen below $18.75 at any time prior to 2006, the Company would have been open to the risk that Mr. Wexner would exercise the Children's Trust's put rights (which he would have arguably been under a duty to do), thereby requiring the Company to expend substantial monies from its reserve to purchase the stock at a premium to market. It is well-settled that " '[c]ourts are ill-fitted to attempt to weigh the 'adequacy' of consideration under the waste standard or, *ex post*, to judge appropriate degrees of business risk.' " Thus, the plaintiffs have failed to allege facts supporting a claim that rescission of the Redemption Agreement "served no corporate purpose or was so completely bereft of consideration that it effectively constituted a gift."

2. The Self-Tender Offer

The Board's purported justification for the self-tender was that " 'a significant share repurchase would be the most desirable use for [the Company's] excess cash' and 'it would demonstrate to the Company stockholders the Company's confidence in its business.' " Plaintiffs assert that the Board's stated goals for this transaction could have been achieved by alternative means less costly to the Company. Specifically, the Complaint alleges that the Company could have avoided paying a premium of more than 15% for its shares by effectuating "an open market purchase at the prevailing market price given the large daily volume of trading in the Company's stock." This, plaintiffs aver, "would have saved the Company well over $90 million." The Limited could also have used its "significant excess cash to pay a dividend to shareholders . . . [meaning that] the Company could have shared the benefits of its excess cash with all of its shareholders . . . [as opposed to only a relatively small number of individuals benefiting from] a self tender."

"Directors are guilty of corporate waste only when they authorize an exchange that is so one sided that no business person of ordinary, sound judgment could conclude that the corporation has received adequate consideration." That the Complaint identifies viable alternatives to the Board's decision here is not enough — it is precisely this kind of judicial after-the-fact evaluation that the business judgment rule seeks to prevent. Even the plaintiffs cannot dispute that the vehicle of a self-tender offer is a well-accepted option for corporate boards wanting to manage mounting cash reserves. Thus, because "reasonable, informed minds might disagree on the question, . . . a reviewing court will not attempt to itself evaluate the wisdom of the bargain or the adequacy of the consideration." Accordingly, I find that the plaintiffs have failed to allege that the Self-Tender is the basis for a viable corporate waste claim.

3. The Rescission and the Self-Tender Offer Together

It is the plaintiffs' position that "the two transactions *taken together* served no business purpose other than to benefit [Mr.] Wexner." At the time that these two transactions were announced, The Limited had more than $660 million in cash and cash equivalents on hand. The Complaint alleges that "[t]he only reason for a $750 million — as opposed to $500 million or $600 million — Self Tender, was to create an artificial 'need' to rescind the Redemption Agreement, and, thereby, allow [Mr.] Wexner to escape from the Redemption Agreement at the Company's expense."

The plaintiffs have failed to demonstrate that the Company received no benefit in exchange from these two transactions or that these transactions, taken together, served no corporate purpose. For one, Mr. Wexner promised not to participate in the Company's self-tender. Having done this, Mr. Wexner forfeited his ability to partake in the more than 15% premium offered by the Company for its shares. Moreover, rescinding the Redemption Agreement allowed the Company to manage the otherwise untouchable $350 million that would have been locked up by the terms of that agreement for another six to seven years. While the plaintiffs point out that The Limited only needed an additional $90 million in cash to cover its self-tender offer, nothing changes the fact that $260 million in liquid funds is a valuable asset for any company. As discussed in more detail above, the rescission of the Redemption Agreement protected the Company from a potentially costly liability that might have befallen it had the shares declined in value in the future. Considering that these transactions conferred upon all of The Limited's shareholders, excluding Mr. Wexner and his affiliates, an opportunity to reap the benefits of a more than 15% premium for their shares, while at the same time demonstrating to the market and those individuals declining to tender their shares the Board's confidence in the Company's stock, I am unwilling to find that the two transactions, viewed together, "served no corporate purpose." As such, even after accepting all of the plaintiffs' well-pled factual allegations and according them the benefit of all reasonable inferences, I find that the Complaint does not state a claim for corporate waste.

D. DUTY OF CARE

Plaintiffs, without much enthusiasm, also allege that the challenged transactions are the product of the directors' breach of their duty of care. The Complaint does not allege gross negligence or the insufficiency of the information upon which the Board based its decision.[64] Thus, the duty of care claim will be dismissed.

IV. CONCLUSION

For the foregoing reasons, defendants' motion to dismiss under Chancery Court Rule 23.1 is denied; defendants' motion under Chancery Court Rule 12(b)(6)

---

64. "[I]n making business decisions, directors must consider all material information reasonably available, and the directors' process is actionable only if grossly negligent." Brehm v. Eisner,

to dismiss plaintiffs' duty of care claim and corporate waste claim is granted. Otherwise, defendants' motion to dismiss is denied.

B.   DIRECT VERSUS DERIVATIVE CLAIMS

We have examined the procedural rules governing derivative litigation, but when is a claim a derivative claim and when is it a direct claim? The answer to this question is not always as simple as it might sound, as the following case shows.

TOOLEY v. DONALDSON, LUFKIN & JENRETTE, INC.
2003 WL 203060 (slip opinion)
Court of Chancery of Delaware
January 21, 2003

CHANDLER, J.

Plaintiff stockholders originally brought this class action suit to enjoin a delay in the closing of a tender offer in the proposed merger between Donaldson, Lufkin & Jenrette, Inc. ("DLJ") and Credit Suisse Group. They planned to tender their shares and alleged that the DLJ board members breached their fiduciary duties by wrongfully agreeing to a 22-day delay in the closing. Plaintiffs further alleged that they were harmed by this delay because of the lost time value of the consideration paid for their shares at the close of the tender offer.

The tender offer closed and plaintiffs' shares were cashed out on November 2, 2000. The merger has been consummated and plaintiffs continue to seek damages for the lost time value of their $90 per share that was occasioned by the postponed closing. Defendants have now moved to dismiss the complaint for lack of standing.

I. STATEMENT OF FACTS

Plaintiffs are former stockholders of DLJ, a Delaware corporation that provides various investment and banking services to institutional, governmental and

---

746 A.2d at 259. The only allegation in the Complaint speaking to the directors' alleged breaches of care states that:

> A Special Committee was apparently formed the very day the transaction was approved, solely to "rubber stamp" the transaction, without adequate deliberation, without adequate advice from independent legal counsel and independent financial advisors, without adequate consideration of the cost to the Company, and without any genuine exploration of alternative means through which the Company's excess cash could be used to benefit shareholders (without causing forfeiture of the valuable right). The Special Committee [also failed to] negotiate the transaction with [Mr.] Wexner. Such general and conclusory allegations, however, fail to support the inference that the Board breached its duty of care. Moreover, these allegations involve only the Special Committee, upon which, as of yet, Defendants have not relied.

individual clients. Before its acquisition by Credit Suisse Group, DLJ's largest stockholder was AXA Financial, Inc., owning approximately 71% of DLJ. AXA Financial, in turn, is majority-owned (approximately 60%) by its parent, AXA. All the individual defendants are former directors of DLJ.

On August 30, 2000, AXA Financial announced that Credit Suisse Group and DLJ had entered into a $13.4 billion merger agreement. The merger agreement was between Credit Suisse Group, Diamond Acquisition Corporation,[2] and DLJ, and expressly disavowed any third-party beneficiaries to the contract. According to this agreement, DLJ's public minority would receive $90 cash per DLJ share in a first-step tender offer to the DLJ public stockholders, and AXA Financial would subsequently receive the cash and stock combination equivalent of $90 per share. The first-step tender offer was intended to expire 20 days after its commencement, unless the offer was extended.

The merger agreement provided for two main types of extensions for the tender offer period. The first, a five-day extension, could be invoked without DLJ's consent if payment obligations were not satisfied, or as required by the SEC, or if more than 10% but less than 20% of all outstanding DLJ shares were tendered. The second type of extension allowed Credit Suisse Group to extend the offer under various enumerated conditions, one of which included an agreement between DLJ and Credit Suisse Group to postpone acceptance of DLJ stock for payment. Credit Suisse Group used both of these options to extend its tender offer.

Credit Suisse Group began its Tender Offer on September 8, 2000. This offer was set to expire on October 5, 2000. Credit Suisse then invoked a five-day extension of the offer, announced on October 6, 2000. At the end of this first extension, the parties agreed upon a second extension of the offer in a letter agreement. This letter agreement amended various terms of the merger agreement and extended the tender offer until November 2, 2000, a date 22 days later than the first extension date. In the letter agreement, Credit Suisse Group also removed several contingencies set forth in the merger agreement, such as material adverse changes and representations and warranties, by deeming them satisfied by DLJ. The tender offer closed on November 2, 2002, and the public minority shareholders were cashed out for $90 per share.

Plaintiffs filed this class action complaint, alleging that the second extension was not authorized by the merger agreement, lacked consideration, and was wrongfully approved "solely to accommodate the administrative needs of AXA Financial." Plaintiffs contend this was a breach of the DLJ board members' fiduciary duties, namely a breach of their duty of loyalty, because the board had a duty to proceed with the tender offer so that the DLJ shareholders would receive cash for their shares as soon as possible. Instead, the closing of the tender offer was delayed by 22 days. Plaintiffs contend they were injured because they lost the time value of the cash paid for their shares. In essence, plaintiffs' entire complaint rests upon the assertion not that the merger consideration was unfair, but that it was received 22 days later than initially agreed because of a wrongfully granted extension.

---

2. Diamond Acquisition Corporation was a wholly owned subsidiary of Credit Suisse Group, formed to effect the merger. For purposes of this opinion, I treat Diamond Acquisition the same as Credit Suisse Group.

II. Direct or Derivative Nature of the Claim

Defendants move to dismiss the complaint for lack of standing. They argue that, even if there was a breach of fiduciary duty by the board members, the complaint alleges, at most, a derivative claim. Therefore, plaintiffs lost standing to pursue the claim, pursuant to Chancery Court Rule 23.1, when their shares were cashed out. Once DLJ shareholders were cashed out, they would lose standing to sue on behalf of the corporation. Additionally, defendants assert that plaintiffs suffered no special injury resulting from the 22-day delay because this delay fell equally upon all shareholders and did not injure any contractual right of the shareholder separate from the corporation. Thus, because defendants contend that the complaint fails to allege a direct claim, they assert that plaintiffs' standing to bring this suit was extinguished when plaintiffs were cashed out. Thus, the complaint (they argue) should be dismissed.

Plaintiffs disagree and assert that the complaint alleges special injury, because only the tendered minority shares were subject to the 22-day delay in the closing of the tender offer. Plaintiffs reason that although the extension had a direct adverse economic impact on the class, the extension of the tender offer actually benefited AXA Financial, the majority shareholder, by accommodating its administrative needs. Thus, plaintiffs conclude, they have alleged the requisite special injury required to bring a direct suit, and the complaint cannot be dismissed for lack of standing.

Because plaintiffs are no longer DLJ stockholders, their standing to bring this suit depends upon whether it is direct or derivative in nature. A direct action seeks compensation for a special injury different from injury to the corporation or other shareholders. A derivative action seeks compensation for injury to the corporation.

According to Rule 23.1, derivative actions may only be maintained by shareholders of a corporation. Thus, standing to bring a derivative action is extinguished when a shareholder sells its shares in the corporation, even if the shareholder initially had standing to bring the suit. In such situations, the derivative suit can no longer be maintained by the shareholder, and the suit is traditionally dismissed.

In order to bring a *direct* claim, a plaintiff must have experienced some "special injury."[5] A special injury is a wrong that "is separate and distinct from that suffered by other shareholders, . . . or a wrong involving a contractual right of a shareholder, such as the right to vote, or to assert majority control, which exists independently of any right of the corporation."[6] Suits alleging special injuries may be maintained as a direct action, even though the same wrong injures the corporation as well. Additionally, shareholders do not lose standing to bring suit to recover for special injuries when their shares in the corporation are sold.

The Court will independently examine the nature of the wrong alleged and any potential relief to make its own determination of the suit's classification.[8] This determination is for the Court to make based upon the body of the complaint; plaintiffs' designation of the suit is not binding.

---

5. Lipton v. News Int'l., 514 A.2d 1075, 1079 (Del. 1986).

6. Moran v. Household Int'l, Inc., 490 A.2d 1059, 1070 (Del. Ch. 1985), *aff'd*, 500 A.2d 1346 (Del. 1986).

8. Kramer v. Western Pacific Indus., Inc., 546 A.2d 348, 352 (Del. 1988).

Here, it is clear that plaintiffs have no separate contractual right to bring a direct claim, and they do not assert contractual rights under the merger agreement. First, the merger agreement specifically disclaims any persons as being third party beneficiaries to the contract. Second, any contractual shareholder right to payment of the merger consideration did not ripen until the conditions of the agreement were met. The agreement stated that Credit Suisse Group was not required to accept any shares for tender, or could extend the offer, under certain conditions — one condition of which included an extension or termination by agreement between Credit Suisse Group and DLJ. Because Credit Suisse Group and DLJ *did* in fact agree to extend the tender offer period, any right to payment plaintiffs could have did not ripen until this newly negotiated period was over. The merger agreement only became binding and mutually enforceable at the time the tendered shares ultimately were accepted for payment by Credit Suisse Group. It is at that moment in time, November 3, 2000, that the company became bound to purchase the tendered shares, making the contract mutually enforceable. DLJ stockholders had no individual contractual right to payment until November 3, 2000, when their tendered shares were accepted for payment. Thus, they have no contractual basis to challenge a delay in the closing of the tender offer up until November 3.[11] Because this is the date the tendered shares were accepted for payment, the contract was not breached and plaintiffs do not have a contractual basis to bring a direct suit.

The only other type of special injury that would provide the stockholder plaintiffs with a basis to bring a direct claim is one that is separate and distinct from the injury suffered by the other shareholders or the corporation. Here, plaintiffs, as a class, allege that their injury is the lost time value of their $90 per share caused by the 22-day extension. They allege that this injury is different from both the non-tendering shareholders and the majority DLJ shareholder (*i.e.*, AXA Financial). As the argument goes, the injury is different from the non-tendering shareholders for the simple reason that the non-tendering shareholders did not tender their shares in the offer, so any delay in its closing was irrelevant to them. Similarly, the majority stockowner, AXA Financial, allegedly did not lose the time value of its money when the tender offer was extended because it was not subject to the tender offer either. Further, they allege, AXA Financial actually benefited from this extension because it was agreed upon solely to accommodate its administrative needs.

This argument is logically flawed, however. A delay in one step of the merger must logically lead to a delay in the subsequent steps of the staged merger because of the domino effect of the steps leading up to its closing. Although neither the non-tendering stockholders nor AXA Financial tendered their shares in the tender offer, it is not plausible that they did not suffer a similar delay in receiving the consideration paid for their shares. Neither the non-tendering stockholders nor AXA Financial could be cashed out until the tendering shareholders were cashed out. Thus, any 22-day delay occasioned by

---

11. Aside from this, it is notable that the merger agreement contained a much later termination date of March 31, 2001. This is the date on which the merger agreement would expire by its own terms, if the merger had not yet been consummated. The agreement anticipated various contingencies that could lead to delays in the consummation of the merger. Thus, it should not have surprised plaintiffs that a delay could have occurred, as it did here. Further, as compared to the final March 31, 2001, termination date contained in the merger agreement — a date over four months after the tender offer period actually closed — a delay of only 22 days hardly seems unexpected or unreasonable.

an extension of the tender offer would also result in a similar delay for the second step of the merger — the step that included both the minority stockholders and AXA Financial. Because this delay affected all DLJ shareholders equally, plaintiffs' injury was not a special injury, and this action is, thus, a derivative action at most. Accordingly, plaintiffs no longer have standing to bring this suit and it must be dismissed.

III. Conclusion

For the foregoing reasons, defendants' motion to dismiss the complaint for lack of standing is granted. An Order has been entered in accordance with this Memorandum Opinion.

C. SPECIAL LITIGATION COMMITTEES

In most cases where demand is properly excused, the company would still like to take control of the litigation. This is done by appointing a special litigation committee (SLC) (which sometimes might require expanding the size of the board and appointing new, disinterested directors), and then delegating power to the SLC to determine if it is in the company's best interest to proceed with the litigation. It would not be surprising to learn that it is the rare case in which the SLC recommends proceeding with the ligitation.

In Zapata Corp. v. Maldonado, 430 A.2d 779 (Del. 1980), the Delaware Supreme Court articulated the principles that Delaware courts use to evaluate a SLC's decision to terminate litigation. *Zapata* first came to the Delaware courts as a demand futility case. Several years after commencement of the case, a number of the defendant directors had been replaced by outside directors. The board of Zapata created an independent investigation committee (Committee), comprised of two outside directors, to determine whether continued litigation was in the best interests of the corporation. The Committee examined not only the Delaware litigation but related litigation arising out of the same matter in New York and Texas.

Following an investigation, the Committee concluded that all of the pending derivative lawsuits should be dismissed, and the company subsequently moved for summary judgment. The District Court for the Southern District of New York granted Zapata's motion, applying its interpretation of Delaware law, under which the Committee's action would be evaluated under the business judgment rule. Prior to the Delaware litigation in *Zapata* itself, most courts reviewed actions by SLCs under the business judgment rule, virtually ensuring the dismissal of every derivative claim subject to SLC review.

Contrary to the federal court in New York, the Delaware Court of Chancery denied Zapata's motion and held that the business judgment rule did not confer power "to a corporate board of directors to terminate a derivative suit." This conclusion is undoubtedly correct. As noted by the Delaware Supreme Court in reviewing this decision, the business judgment rule does not create authority. The authority, if any exists, emanates from Delaware General Corporation Law (DGCL) §141(a). The business judgment rule, by contrast, "evolved to give recognition and deference to directors' business expertise when exercising their managerial power under §141(a)." The issue with respect to SLCs, therefore, was whether the business judgment rule dictated deference.

To speak of deference to an SLC in this context may seem to be putting the cart in front of the horse. After all, the shareholder had properly initiated a derivative lawsuit. Why should the board have any continuing role? The supreme court addresses this question as follows:

> At the risk of stating the obvious, the problem is relatively simple. If, on the one hand, corporations can consistently wrest bona fide derivative actions away from well-meaning derivative plaintiffs through the use of the committee mechanism, the derivative suit will lose much, if not all, of its generally-recognized effectiveness as an intra-corporate means of policing boards of directors. If, on the other hand, corporations are unable to rid themselves of meritless or harmful litigation and strike suits, the derivative action, created to benefit the corporation, will produce the opposite, unintended result. It thus appears desirable to us to find a balancing point where bona fide stockholder power to bring corporate causes of action cannot be unfairly trampled on by the board of directors, but the corporation can rid itself of detrimental litigation.

430 A.2d at 786.

Assuming the board retains a continuing oversight role, the question becomes: When, if at all, should an authorized board committee be permitted to cause litigation, properly initiated by a derivative stockholder in his own right, to be dismissed? The federal court in New York had held that an authorized board committee could dismiss litigation as long as it passed muster under the business judgment rule, but the Delaware Supreme Court found this standard too lax. In a foreshadowing of standards later employed in the hostile takeover context, the court reasoned:

> We are not satisfied, however, that acceptance of the "business judgment" rationale at this stage of derivative litigation is a proper balancing point. While we admit an analogy with a normal case respecting board judgment, it seems to us that there is sufficient risk in the realities of a situation like the one presented in this case to justify caution beyond adherence to the theory of business judgment.
>
> The context here is a suit against directors where demand on the board is excused. We think some tribute must be paid to the fact that the lawsuit was properly initiated. It is not a board refusal case. . . .
>
> Moreover, notwithstanding our conviction that Delaware law entrusts the corporate power to a properly authorized committee, we must be mindful that directors are passing judgment on fellow directors in the same corporation and fellow directors, in this instance, who designated them to serve both as directors and committee members. The question naturally arises whether a "there but for the grace of God go I" empathy might not play a role. And the further question arises whether inquiry as to independence, good faith and reasonable investigation is sufficient safeguard against abuse, perhaps subconscious abuse.
>
> We thus steer a middle course between those cases which yield to the independent business judgment of a board committee and this case as determined below which would yield to unbridled plaintiff stockholder control. . . . The Court should apply a two-step test to the motion.
>
> First, the Court should inquire into the independence and good faith of the committee and the bases supporting its conclusions. Limited discovery may be ordered to facilitate such inquiries. The corporation should have the burden of

proving independence, good faith and a reasonable investigation, rather than presuming independence, good faith and reasonableness. If the Court determines either that the committee is not independent or has not shown reasonable bases for its conclusions, or, if the Court is not satisfied for other reasons relating to the process, including but not limited to the good faith of the committee, the Court shall deny the corporation's motion. If, however, the Court is satisfied under Rule 56 standards that the committee was independent and showed reasonable bases for good faith findings and recommendations, the Court may proceed, in its discretion, to the next step.

The second step provides, we believe, the essential key in striking the balance between legitimate corporate claims as expressed in a derivative stockholder suit and a corporation's best interests as expressed by an independent investigating committee. The Court should determine, applying its own independent business judgment, whether the motion should be granted. This means, of course, that instances could arise where a committee can establish its independence and sound bases for its good faith decisions and still have the corporation's motion denied. The second step is intended to thwart instances where corporate actions meet the criteria of step one, but the result does not appear to satisfy its spirit, or where corporate actions would simply prematurely terminate a stockholder grievance deserving of further consideration in the corporation's interest. The Court of Chancery of course must carefully consider and weigh how compelling the corporate interest in dismissal is when faced with a non-frivolous lawsuit. The Court of Chancery should, when appropriate, give special consideration to matters of law and public policy in addition to the corporation's best interests.

If the Court's independent business judgment is satisfied, the Court may proceed to grant the motion, subject, of course, to any equitable terms or conditions the Court finds necessary or desirable.

430 A.2d at 787-788.

The notion that courts should apply their "own independent business judgment" was viewed as quite innovative. In the wake of *Zapata*, courts outside Delaware reconsidered the standards used to evaluate actions by special litigation committees. Some courts remain deferential to SLC actions, *see* Houle v. Low, 556 N.E.2d 51 (Mass. 1990) (upholding such actions as long as they are "reasoned and principled"), while other courts view such decisions with great suspicion and employ standards of review similar to *Zapata. See* Alford v. Shaw, 358 S.E.2d 323 (N.C. 1987) (holding that *Zapata*-like standards should be employed in both demand-excused and demand-refused cases). The following is a recent Delaware case applying the *Zapata* standards in an unusual context. The case summarizes important developments in Delaware law governing SLCs. Moreover, it raises important questions about the role of SLCs in derivative litigation. As you read the case, consider whether the Delaware courts have properly extended the teachings of *Zapata*.

In re ORACLE CORP. DERIVATIVE LITIGATION

824 A.2d 917
Court of Chancery of Delaware
June 17, 2003

STRINE, Vice Chancellor.

In this opinion, I address the motion of the special litigation committee ("SLC") of Oracle Corporation to terminate this action, "the Delaware Derivative Action," and other such actions pending in the name of Oracle against certain Oracle directors and officers. These actions allege that these Oracle directors engaged in insider trading while in possession of material, non-public information showing that Oracle would not meet the earnings guidance it gave to the market for the third quarter of Oracle's fiscal year 2001. The SLC bears the burden of persuasion on this motion and must convince me that there is no material issue of fact calling into doubt its independence. This requirement is set forth in Zapata Corp. v. Maldonado and its progeny.

The question of independence "turns on whether a director is, *for any substantial reason*, incapable of making a decision with only the best interests of the corporation in mind." That is, the independence test ultimately "focus[es] on impartiality and objectivity." In this case, the SLC has failed to demonstrate that no material factual question exists regarding its independence.

During discovery, it emerged that the two SLC members — both of whom are professors at Stanford University — are being asked to investigate fellow Oracle directors who have important ties to Stanford, too. Among the directors who are accused by the derivative plaintiffs of insider trading are: (1) another Stanford professor, who taught one of the SLC members when the SLC member was a Ph.D. candidate and who serves as a senior fellow and a steering committee member alongside that SLC member at the Stanford Institute for Economic Policy Research or "SIEPR"; (2) a Stanford alumnus who has directed millions of dollars of contributions to Stanford during recent years, serves as Chair of SIEPR's Advisory Board and has a conference center named for him at SIEPR's facility, and has contributed nearly $600,000 to SIEPR and the Stanford Law School, both parts of Stanford with which one of the SLC members is closely affiliated; and (3) Oracle's CEO, who has made millions of dollars in donations to Stanford through a personal foundation and large donations indirectly through Oracle, and who was considering making donations of his $100 million house and $170 million for a scholarship program as late as August 2001, at around the same time period the SLC members were added to the Oracle board. Taken together, these and other facts cause me to harbor a reasonable doubt about the impartiality of the SLC.

It is no easy task to decide whether to accuse a fellow director of insider trading. For Oracle to compound that difficulty by requiring SLC members to consider accusing a fellow professor and two large benefactors of their university of conduct that is rightly considered a violation of criminal law was unnecessary and inconsistent with the concept of independence recognized by our law. The possibility that these extraneous considerations biased the inquiry of the SLC is too substantial for this court to ignore. I therefore deny the SLC's motion to terminate.

I. FACTUAL BACKGROUND

A. SUMMARY OF THE PLAINTIFFS' ALLEGATIONS

The Delaware Derivative Complaint centers on alleged insider trading by four members of Oracle's board of directors — Lawrence Ellison, Jeffrey Henley,

Donald Lucas, and Michael Boskin (collectively, the "Trading Defendants"). Each of the Trading Defendants had a very different role at Oracle.

Ellison is Oracle's Chairman, Chief Executive Officer, and its largest stockholder, owning nearly twenty-five percent of Oracle's voting shares. By virtue of his ownership position, Ellison is one of the wealthiest men in America. By virtue of his managerial position, Ellison has regular access to a great deal of information about how Oracle is performing on a week-to-week basis. Henley is Oracle's Chief Financial Officer, Executive Vice President, and a director of the corporation. Like Ellison, Henley has his finger on the pulse of Oracle's performance constantly. Lucas is a director who chairs Oracle's Executive Committee and its Finance and Audit Committee. Although the plaintiffs allege that Lucas's positions gave him access to material, non-public information about the company, they do so cursorily. On the present record, it appears that Lucas did not receive copies of week-to-week projections or reports of actual results for the quarter to date. Rather, his committees primarily received historical financial data. Boskin is a director, Chairman of the Compensation Committee, and a member of the Finance and Audit Committee. As with Lucas, Boskin's access to information was limited mostly to historical financials and did not include the week-to-week internal projections and revenue results that Ellison and Henley received.

According to the plaintiffs, each of these Trading Defendants possessed material, non-public information demonstrating that Oracle would fail to meet the earnings and revenue guidance it had provided to the market in December 2000. In that guidance, Henley projected—subject to many disclaimers, including the possibility that a softening economy would hamper Oracle's ability to achieve these results—that Oracle would earn 12 cents per share and generate revenues of over $2.9 billion in the third quarter of its fiscal year 2001 ("3Q FY 2001"). Oracle's 3Q FY 2001 ran from December 1, 2000 to February 28, 2001.

The plaintiffs allege that this guidance was materially misleading and became even more so as early results for the quarter came in. To start with, the plaintiffs assert that the guidance rested on an untenably rosy estimate of the performance of an important new Oracle product, its "Suite 11i" systems integration product that was designed to enable a business to run all of its information systems using a complete, integrated package of software with financial, manufacturing, sales, logistics, and other applications features that were "inter-operable." The reality, the plaintiffs contend, was that Suite 11i was riddled with bugs and not ready for prime time. As a result, Suite 11i was not in a position to make a material contribution to earnings growth.

In addition, the plaintiffs contend more generally that the Trading Defendants received material, non-public information that the sales growth for Oracle's other products was slowing in a significant way, which made the attainment of the earnings and revenue guidance extremely difficult. This information grew in depth as the quarter proceeded, as various sources of information that Oracle's top managers relied upon allegedly began to signal weakness in the company's revenues. These signals supposedly included a slowdown in the "pipeline" of large deals that Oracle hoped to close during the quarter and weak revenue growth in the first month of the quarter.

During the time when these disturbing signals were allegedly being sent, the Trading Defendants engaged in the following trades:

- On January 3, 2001, Lucas sold 150,000 shares of Oracle common stock at $30 per share, reaping proceeds of over $4.6 million. These sales constituted 17% of Lucas's Oracle holdings.
- On January 4, 2001, Henley sold one million shares of Oracle stock at approximately $32 per share, yielding over $32.3 million. These sales represented 7% of Henley's Oracle holdings.
- On January 17, 2001, Boskin sold 150,000 shares of Oracle stock at over $33 per share, generating in excess of $5 million. These sales were 16% of Boskin's Oracle holdings.
- From January 22 to January 31, 2001, Ellison sold over 29 million shares at prices above $30 per share, producing over $894 million. Despite the huge proceeds generated by these sales, they constituted the sale of only 2% of Ellison's Oracle holdings.

Into early to mid-February, Oracle allegedly continued to assure the market that it would meet its December guidance. Then, on March 1, 2001, the company announced that rather than posting 12 cents per share in quarterly earnings and 25% license revenue growth as projected, the company's earnings for the quarter would be 10 cents per share and license revenue growth only 6%. The stock market reacted swiftly and negatively to this news, with Oracle's share price dropping as low as $15.75 before closing at $16.88 — a 21% decline in one day. These prices were well below the above $30 per share prices at which the Trading Defendants sold in January 2001.

Oracle, through Ellison and Henley, attributed the adverse results to a general weakening in the economy, which led Oracle's customers to cut back sharply on purchases. Because (the company claimed) most of its sales close in the late days of quarters, the company did not become aware that it would miss its projections until shortly before the quarter closed. The reasons given by Ellison and Henley subjected them to sarcastic rejoinders from analysts, who noted that they had only recently suggested that Oracle was better-positioned than other companies to continue to deliver growth in a weakening economy.

B. THE PLAINTIFFS' CLAIMS IN THE DELAWARE DERIVATIVE ACTION

The plaintiffs make two central claims in their amended complaint in the Delaware Derivative Action. First, the plaintiffs allege that the Trading Defendants breached their duty of loyalty by misappropriating inside information and using it as the basis for trading decisions. This claim rests its legal basis on the venerable case of Brophy v. Cities Service Co., 70 A.2d 5 (Del. Ch. 1949). Its factual foundation is that the Trading Defendants were aware (or at least possessed information that should have made them aware) that the company would miss its December guidance by a wide margin and used that information to their advantage in selling at artificially inflated prices.

Second, as to the other defendants — who are the members of the Oracle board who did not trade — the plaintiffs allege a *Caremark* violation, in the sense that the board's indifference to the deviation between the company's December guidance and reality was so extreme as to constitute subjective bad faith.

Oracle's failure to meet its earnings and revenue guidance, and the sales by the Trading Defendants, inevitably generated a spate of lawsuits. Several derivative actions were filed in the state and federal courts of California. Those actions are, in substance, identical to the Delaware Derivative Action. Those suits have now all been stayed in deference to the SLC's investigation and the court's ruling on this motion.

Federal class actions were also filed, and the consolidated complaint in those actions formed the basis for much of the amended complaint in the Delaware Derivative Action. By now, the "Federal Class Action" has been dismissed for failure to state a claim upon which relief can be granted for the third time; this time the order addressing the second amended complaint dismissed the Federal Class Action with prejudice.

D. THE FORMATION OF THE SPECIAL LITIGATION COMMITTEE

On February 1, 2002, Oracle formed the SLC in order to investigate the Delaware Derivative Action and to determine whether Oracle should press the claims raised by the plaintiffs, settle the case, or terminate it. Soon after its formation, the SLC's charge was broadened to give it the same mandate as to all the pending derivative actions, wherever they were filed. The SLC was granted full authority to decide these matters without the need for approval by the other members of the Oracle board.

E. THE MEMBERS OF THE SPECIAL LITIGATION COMMITTEE

Two Oracle board members were named to the SLC. Both of them joined the Oracle board on October 15, 2001, more than a half a year after Oracle's 3Q FY 2001 closed. The SLC members also share something else: both are tenured professors at Stanford University.

Professor Hector Garcia-Molina is Chairman of the Computer Science Department at Stanford and holds the Leonard Bosack and Sandra Lerner Professorship in the Computer Science and Electrical Engineering Departments at Stanford. A renowned expert in his field, Garcia-Molina was a professor at Princeton before coming to Stanford in 1992. Garcia-Molina's appointment at Stanford represented a homecoming of some sort, because he obtained both his undergraduate and graduate degrees from Stanford.

The other SLC member, Professor Joseph Grundfest, is the W.A. Franke Professor of Law and Business at Stanford University. He directs the University's well-known Directors' College and the Roberts Program in Law, Business, and Corporate Governance at the Stanford Law School. Grundfest is also the principal investigator for the Law School's Securities Litigation Clearinghouse. Immediately before coming to Stanford, Grundfest served for five years as a Commissioner of the Securities and Exchange Commission. Like Garcia-Molina, Grundfest's appointment at Stanford was a homecoming, because he obtained his law degree and performed significant post-graduate work in economics at Stanford. As will be discussed more specifically later, Grundfest also serves as a steering committee member and a senior fellow of the Stanford

Institute for Economic Policy Research, and releases working papers under the "SIEPR" banner.

For their services, the SLC members were paid $250 an hour, a rate below that which they could command for other activities, such as consulting or expert witness testimony. Nonetheless, during the course of their work, the SLC members became concerned that (arguably scandal-driven) developments in the evolving area of corporate governance as well as the decision in Telxon v. Meyerson, 802 A.2d 257 (Del. 2002), might render the amount of their compensation so high as to be an argument against their independence. Therefore, Garcia-Molina and Grundfest agreed to give up any SLC-related compensation if their compensation was deemed by this court to impair their impartiality.

F. THE SLC MEMBERS ARE RECRUITED TO THE BOARD

The SLC members were recruited to the board primarily by defendant Lucas, with help from defendant Boskin. The wooing of them began in the summer of 2001. Before deciding to join the Oracle board, Grundfest, in particular, did a good deal of due diligence. His review included reading publicly available information, among other things, the then-current complaint in the Federal Class Action.

Grundfest then met with defendants Ellison and Henley, among others, and asked them some questions about the Federal Class Action. The claims in the Federal Class Action are predicated on facts that are substantively identical to those on which the claims in the Delaware Derivative Action are based. Grundfest received answers that were consistent enough with what he called the "exogenous" information about the case to form sufficient confidence to at least join the Oracle board. Grundfest testified that this did not mean that he had concluded that the claims in the Federal Class Action had no merit, only that Ellison's and Henley's explanations of their conduct were plausible. Grundfest did, however, conclude that these were reputable businessmen with whom he felt comfortable serving as a fellow director, and that Henley had given very impressive answers to difficult questions regarding the way Oracle conducted its financial reporting operations.

G. THE SLC'S ADVISORS

The most important advisors retained by the SLC were its counsel from Simpson Thacher & Bartlett LLP. Simpson Thacher had not performed material amounts of legal work for Oracle or any of the individual defendants before its engagement, and the plaintiffs have not challenged its independence. National Economic Research Advisors ("NERA") was retained by the SLC to perform some analytical work. The plaintiffs have not challenged NERA's independence.

H. THE SLC'S INVESTIGATION AND REPORT

The SLC's investigation was, by any objective measure, extensive. The SLC reviewed an enormous amount of paper and electronic records. SLC counsel interviewed seventy witnesses, some of them twice. SLC members participated in several key interviews, including the interviews of the Trading Defendants.

Importantly, the interviewees included all the senior members of Oracle's management most involved in its projection and monitoring of the company's financial performance, including its sales and revenue growth. These interviews combined with a special focus on the documents at the company bearing on these subjects, including e-mail communications.

The SLC also asked the plaintiffs in the various actions to identify witnesses the Committee should interview. The Federal Class Action plaintiffs identified ten such persons and the Committee interviewed all but one, who refused to cooperate. The Delaware Derivative Action plaintiffs and the other derivative plaintiffs declined to provide the SLC with any witness list or to meet with the SLC.

During the course of the investigation, the SLC met with its counsel thirty-five times for a total of eighty hours. In addition to that, the SLC members, particularly Professor Grundfest, devoted many more hours to the investigation.

In the end, the SLC produced an extremely lengthy Report totaling 1,110 pages (excluding appendices and exhibits) that concluded that Oracle should not pursue the plaintiffs' claims against the Trading Defendants or any of the other Oracle directors serving during the 3Q FY 2001. The bulk of the Report defies easy summarization. I endeavor a rough attempt to capture the essence of the Report in understandable terms, surfacing some implicit premises that I understand to have undergirded the SLC's conclusions. Here goes.

Having absorbed a huge amount of material regarding Oracle's financial condition during the relevant period, the flow of information to top Oracle executives, Oracle's business and its products, and the general condition of the market at that time, the SLC concluded that even a hypothetical Oracle executive who possessed all information regarding the company's performance in December and January of 3Q FY 2001 would not have possessed material, non-public information that the company would fail to meet the earnings and revenue guidance it provided the market in December. Although there were hints of potential weakness in Oracle's revenue growth, especially starting in mid-January 2001, there was no reliable information indicating that the company would fall short of the mark, and certainly not to the extent that it eventually did. . . . [The SLC also extensively evaluated various other elements of the insider trading claims under federal securities law and found them to be without merit — for instance, that the defendants did not act with scienter.]

Of course, the amount of the proceeds each of the Trading Defendants generated was extremely large. By selling only two percent of his holdings, Ellison generated nearly a billion dollars, enough to flee to a small island nation with no extradition laws and to live like a Saudi prince. But given Oracle's fundamental health as a company and his retention of ninety-eight percent of his shares, Ellison (the SLC found) had no need to take desperate — or, for that matter, even slightly risky — measures. The same goes for the other Trading Defendants; there was simply nothing special or urgent about their financial circumstances in January 2001 that would have motivated (or did motivate, in the SLC's view) the Trading Defendants to cash out because they believed that Oracle would miss its earnings guidance. And, of course, the SLC found that none of them possessed information that indicated that Oracle would, in fact, miss its mark for 3Q FY 2001.

For these and other reasons, the SLC concluded that the plaintiffs' allegations that the Trading Defendants had breached their fiduciary duty of loyalty by using inside information about Oracle to reap illicit trading gains were without merit. The SLC also determined that, consistent with this determination, there was no reason to sue the other members of the Oracle board who were in office as of 3Q FY 2001. Therefore, the SLC determined to seek dismissal of the Delaware Derivative Action and the other derivative actions.

II. The SLC Moves to Terminate

Consistent with its Report, the SLC moved to terminate this litigation. The plaintiffs were granted discovery focusing on three primary topics: the independence of the SLC, the good faith of its investigative efforts, and the reasonableness of the bases for its conclusion that the lawsuit should be terminated. Additionally, the plaintiffs received a large volume of documents comprising the materials that the SLC relied upon in preparing its Report.

III. The Applicable Procedural Standard

In order to prevail on its motion to terminate the Delaware Derivative Action, the SLC must persuade me that: (1) its members were independent; (2) that they acted in good faith; and (3) that they had reasonable bases for their recommendations. If the SLC meets that burden, I am free to grant its motion or may, in my discretion, undertake my own examination of whether Oracle should terminate and permit the suit to proceed if I, in my oxymoronic judicial "business judgment," conclude that procession is in the best interests of the company. This two-step analysis comes, of course, from *Zapata*.

In this case, the plaintiffs principally challenge the SLC's independence and the reasonableness of its recommendation. For reasons I next explain, I need examine only the more difficult question, which relates to the SLC's independence.

IV. Is the SLC Independent?

A. The Facts Disclosed in the Report

In its Report, the SLC took the position that its members were independent. In support of that position, the Report noted several factors including:

- the fact that neither Grundfest nor Garcia-Molina received compensation from Oracle other than as directors;
- the fact that neither Grundfest nor Garcia-Molina were on the Oracle board at the time of the alleged wrongdoing;
- the fact that both Grundfest and Garcia-Molina were willing to return their compensation as SLC members if necessary to preserve their status as independent;
- the absence of any other material ties between Oracle, the Trading Defendants, and any of the other defendants, on the one hand, and Grundfest and Garcia-Molina, on the other; and

- the absence of any material ties between Oracle, the Trading Defendants, and any of the other defendants, on the one hand, and the SLC's advisors, on the other.

Noticeably absent from the SLC Report was any disclosure of several significant ties between Oracle or the Trading Defendants and Stanford University, the university that employs both members of the SLC. In the Report, it was only disclosed that:

- defendant Boskin was a Stanford professor;
- the SLC members were aware that Lucas had made certain donations to Stanford; and
- among the contributions was a donation of $50,000 worth of stock that Lucas donated to Stanford Law School after Grundfest delivered a speech to a venture capital fund meeting in response to Lucas's request. It happens that Lucas's son is a partner in the fund and that approximately half the donation was allocated for use by Grundfest in his personal research.

B. THE "STANFORD" FACTS THAT EMERGED DURING DISCOVERY

In view of the modesty of these disclosed ties, it was with some shock that a series of other ties among Stanford, Oracle, and the Trading Defendants emerged during discovery. Although the plaintiffs have embellished these ties considerably beyond what is reasonable, the plain facts are a striking departure from the picture presented in the Report.

Before discussing these facts, I begin with certain features of the record — as I read it — that are favorable to the SLC. Initially, I am satisfied that neither of the SLC members is compromised by a fear that support for the procession of this suit would endanger his ability to make a nice living. Both of the SLC members are distinguished in their fields and highly respected. Both have tenure, which could not have been stripped from them for making a determination that this lawsuit should proceed.

Nor have the plaintiffs developed evidence that either Grundfest or Garcia-Molina have fundraising responsibilities at Stanford. Although Garcia-Molina is a department chairman, the record is devoid of any indication that he is required to generate contributions. And even though Grundfest heads up Stanford's Directors' College, the plaintiffs have not argued that he has a fundraising role in that regard. For this reason, it is important to acknowledge up front that the SLC members occupy positions within the Stanford community different from that of the University's President, deans, and development professionals, all of whom, it can be reasonably assumed, are required to engage heavily in the pursuit of contributions to the University. . . .

With this question in mind, I begin to discuss the specific ties that allegedly compromise the SLC's independence, beginning with those involving Professor Boskin.

1. *Boskin*

Defendant Michael J. Boskin is the T.M. Friedman Professor of Economics at Stanford University. During the Administration of President George H.W. Bush, Boskin occupied the coveted and important position of Chairman of the President's Council of Economic Advisors. He returned to Stanford after this government service, continuing a teaching career there that had begun many years earlier.

During the 1970s, Boskin taught Grundfest when Grundfest was a Ph.D. candidate. Although Boskin was not Grundfest's advisor and although they do not socialize, the two have remained in contact over the years, speaking occasionally about matters of public policy.

Furthermore, both Boskin and Grundfest are senior fellows and steering committee members at the Stanford Institute for Economic Policy Research, which was previously defined as "SIEPR." According to the SLC, the title of senior fellow is largely an honorary one. According to SIEPR's own web site, however, "[s]enior fellows actively participate in SIEPR research and participate in its governance."

Likewise, the SLC contends that Grundfest went MIA as a steering committee member, having failed to attend a meeting since 1997. The SIEPR web site, however, identifies its steering committee as having the role of "advising the director [of SIEPR] and guiding [SIEPR] on matters pertaining to research and academics." Because Grundfest allegedly did not attend to these duties, his service alongside Boskin in that capacity is, the SLC contends, not relevant to his independence.

That said, the SLC does not deny that both Boskin and Grundfest publish working papers under the SIEPR rubric and that SIEPR helps to publicize their respective works. Indeed, as I will note later in this opinion, Grundfest, in the same month the SLC was formed, addressed a meeting of some of SIEPR's largest benefactors—the so-called "SIEPR Associates." The SLC just claims that the SIEPR affiliation is one in which SIEPR basks in the glow of Boskin and Grundfest, not the other way around, and that the mutual service of the two as senior fellows and steering committee members is not a collegial tie of any significance.

With these facts in mind, I now set forth the ties that defendant Lucas has to Stanford.

2. Lucas

As noted in the SLC Report, the SLC members admitted knowing that Lucas was a contributor to Stanford. They also acknowledged that he had donated $50,000 to Stanford Law School in appreciation for Grundfest having given a speech at his request. About half of the proceeds were allocated for use by Grundfest in his research.

But Lucas's ties with Stanford are far, far richer than the SLC Report lets on. To begin, Lucas is a Stanford alumnus, having obtained both his undergraduate and graduate degrees there. By any measure, he has been a very loyal alumnus.

In showing that this is so, I start with a matter of some jousting between the SLC and the plaintiffs. Lucas's brother, Richard, died of cancer and by way of his will established a foundation. Lucas became Chairman of the Foundation and serves as a director along with his son, a couple of other family members, and some non-family members. A principal object of the Foundation's beneficence has been Stanford. The Richard M. Lucas Foundation has given $11.7 million to Stanford since its 1981 founding. Among its notable contributions, the Foundation funded the establishment of the Richard M. Lucas Center for Magnetic Resonance Spectroscopy and Imaging at Stanford's Medical School. Donald Lucas was a founding member and lead director of the Center.

The SLC Report did not mention the Richard M. Lucas Foundation or its grants to Stanford. In its briefs on this motion, the SLC has pointed out that Donald Lucas is one of nine directors at the Foundation and does not serve on its Grant Review Committee. Nonetheless, the SLC does not deny that Lucas is Chairman of the board of the Foundation and that the board approves all grants.

Lucas's connections with Stanford as a contributor go beyond the Foundation, however. From his own personal funds, Lucas has contributed $4.1 million to Stanford, a substantial percentage of which has been donated within the last half-decade. Notably, Lucas has, among other things, donated $424,000 to SIEPR and approximately $149,000 to Stanford Law School. Indeed, Lucas is not only a major contributor to SIEPR, he is the Chair of its Advisory Board. At SIEPR's facility at Stanford, the conference center is named the Donald L. Lucas Conference Center.

From these undisputed facts, it is inarguable that Lucas is a very important alumnus of Stanford and a generous contributor to not one, but two, parts of Stanford important to Grundfest: the Law School and SIEPR.

With these facts in mind, it remains to enrich the factual stew further, by considering defendant Ellison's ties to Stanford.

3. Ellison

There can be little doubt that Ellison is a major figure in the community in which Stanford is located. The so-called Silicon Valley has generated many success stories, among the greatest of which is that of Oracle and its leader, Ellison. One of the wealthiest men in America, Ellison is a major figure in the nation's increasingly important information technology industry. Given his wealth, Ellison is also in a position to make — and, in fact, he has made — major charitable contributions.

Some of the largest of these contributions have been made through the Ellison Medical Foundation, which makes grants to universities and laboratories to support biomedical research relating to aging and infectious diseases. Ellison is the sole director of the Foundation. Although he does not serve on the Foundation's Scientific Advisory Board that sifts through grant applications, he has reserved the right — as the Foundation's sole director — to veto any grants, a power he has not yet used but which he felt it important to retain. The Scientific Advisory Board is comprised of distinguished physicians and scientists from many institutions, but not including Stanford.

Although it is not represented on the Scientific Advisory Board, Stanford has nonetheless been the beneficiary of grants from the Ellison Medical Foundation — to the tune of nearly $10 million in paid or pledged funds. Although the Executive Director of the Foundation asserts by way of an affidavit that the grants are awarded to specific researchers and may be taken to another institution if the researcher leaves, the grants are conveyed under contracts between the Foundation and Stanford itself and purport by their terms to give Stanford the right (subject to Foundation approval) to select a substitute principal investigator if the original one becomes unavailable.

During the time Ellison has been CEO of Oracle, the company itself has also made over $300,000 in donations to Stanford. Not only that, when Oracle established a generously endowed educational foundation — the Oracle Help Us Help Foundation — to help further the deployment of educational technology in schools serving disadvantaged populations, it named Stanford as the "appointing authority," which gave Stanford the right to name four of the Foundation's seven directors. Stanford's acceptance reflects the obvious synergistic benefits that might flow to, for example, its School of Education from the University's involvement in such a foundation, as well as the possibility that its help with the Foundation might redound to the University's benefit when it came time for Oracle to consider making further donations to institutions of higher learning.

Taken together, these facts suggest that Ellison (when considered as an individual and as the key executive and major stockholder of Oracle) had, at the very least, been involved in several endeavors of value to Stanford.

Beginning in the year 2000 and continuing well into 2001 — the same year that Ellison made the trades the plaintiffs contend were suspicious and the same year the SLC members were asked to join the Oracle board — Ellison and Stanford discussed a much more lucrative donation. The idea Stanford proposed for discussion was the creation of an Ellison Scholars Program modeled on the Rhodes Scholarship at Oxford. The proposed budget for Stanford's answer to Oxford: $170 million. The Ellison Scholars were to be drawn from around the world and were to come to Stanford to take a two-year interdisciplinary graduate program in economics, political science, and computer technology. During the summer between the two academic years, participants would work in internships at, among other companies, Oracle.

The omnipresent SIEPR was at the center of this proposal, which was put together by John Shoven, the Director of SIEPR. Ellison had serious discussions and contact with SIEPR around the time Shoven's proposal first surfaced. Indeed, in February 2001, Ellison delivered a speech at SIEPR — at which he was introduced by defendant Lucas. In a CD-ROM that contains images from the speech, Shoven's voice-over touts SIEPR's connections with "some of the most powerful and prominent business leaders."

As part of his proposal for the Ellison Scholars Program, Shoven suggested that three of the four Trading Defendants — Ellison, Lucas, and Boskin — be on the Program board. In the hypothetical curriculum that Shoven presented to Ellison, he included a course entitled "Legal Institutions and the Modern Economy" to be taught by Grundfest. Importantly, the Shoven proposal included a disclaimer indicating that listed faculty members may not have been consulted, and Grundfest denies that he was. The circumstances as a whole make that denial credible, although there is one confounding factor.

Lucas, who was active in encouraging Ellison to form a program of this kind at Stanford, testified at his deposition that he had spoken to Grundfest about the proposed Ellison Scholars Program "a number of years ago," Lucas seems to recall having asked Grundfest if he would be involved with the yet-to-be created Program, but his memory was, at best, hazy. At his own deposition, Grundfest was confronted more generically with whether he had heard of the Program and had agreed to teach in it if it was created, but not with whether he had discussed the topic with Lucas.

Candidly, this sort of discrepancy is not easy to reconcile on a paper record. My conclusion, however, is that Grundfest is being truthful in stating that he had not participated in shaping the Shoven proposal, had not agreed to teach in the Program, and could not recall participating in any discussions about the Program.

That said, I am not confident that Grundfest was entirely unaware, in 2001 and/or 2002 of the possibility of such a program or that he did not have a brief conversation with Lucas about it before joining the Oracle board. Nor am I convinced that the discussions about the Ellison Scholars Program were not of a very serious nature, indeed, the record evidence persuades me that they were serious. To find otherwise would be to conclude that Ellison is a man of more than ordinary whimsy, who says noteworthy things without caring whether they are true.

I say that because Ellison spoke to two of the nation's leading news outlets about the possibility of creating the Ellison Scholars Program. According to the Wall Street Journal, Ellison was considering the possibility of donating $150 million to either Harvard or Stanford for the purpose of creating an interdisciplinary (political science, economics, and technology) academic program. And, according to Fortune, Ellison said in an interview with *Fortune* correspondent Brent Schlender: "[O]ne of the other philanthropic things I'm doing is talking to Harvard and Stanford and MIT about creating a research program that looks at how technology impacts [*sic*] economics, and in turn how economics impacts the way we govern ourselves." It is significant that the latter article was published in mid-August 2001 — around the same time that the SLC members were considering whether to join the Oracle board and within a calendar year of the formation of the SLC itself. Importantly, these public statements supplement other private communications by Stanford officials treating the Ellison Scholars Program as an idea under serious consideration by Ellison.

Ultimately, it appears that Ellison decided to abandon the idea of making a major donation on the Rhodes Scholarship model to Stanford or any other institution. At least, that is what he now says by affidavit. According to Shoven of SIEPR, the Ellison Scholars Program idea is going nowhere now, and all talks with Ellison have ceased on that front.

Given the nature of this case, it is natural that there must be yet another curious fact to add to the mix. This is that Ellison told the Washington Post in an October 30, 2000 article that he intended to leave his Woodside, California home — which is worth over $100 million — to Stanford upon his death. In an affidavit, Ellison does not deny making this rather splashy public statement. But, he now (again, rather conveniently) says that he has changed his testamentary intent. Ellison denies having "bequeathed, donated or otherwise conveyed the Woodside property (or any other real property that I own) to Stanford University." And, in the same affidavit, Ellison states unequivocally that he has no intention of ever giving his Woodside compound (or any other real property) to Stanford. Shortly before his deposition in this case, Grundfest asked Ellison about the Woodside property and certain news reports to the effect that he was planning to give it to Stanford. According to Grundfest, Ellison's reaction to his inquiry was one of "surprise." Ellison admitted to Grundfest that he said something of that sort, but contended that whatever he said was merely a "passing" comment. Plus, Ellison said, Stanford would, of course, not want his $100 million home unless it came with a "dowry" — *i.e.*, an endowment to support what is sure to be a costly maintenance budget. Stanford's Vice President for Development, John Ford, claimed that to the best of his knowledge Ellison had not promised anyone at Stanford that he would give Stanford his Woodside home. . . .

C. THE SLC'S ARGUMENT

The SLC contends that even together, these facts regarding the ties among Oracle, the Trading Defendants, Stanford, and the SLC members do not impair the SLC's independence. In so arguing, the SLC places great weight on the fact that none of the Trading Defendants have the practical ability to deprive either Grundfest or Garcia-Molina of their current positions at Stanford. Nor, given their tenure, does Stanford itself have any practical ability to punish them for taking action adverse to Boskin, Lucas, or Ellison — each of whom, as we have seen, has contributed (in one way or another) great value to Stanford as an institution. As important, neither Garcia-Molina nor Grundfest are part of the official fundraising apparatus at Stanford; thus, it is not their on-the-job duty to be solicitous of contributors, and fundraising success does not factor into their treatment as professors.

In so arguing, the SLC focuses on the language of previous opinions of this court and the Delaware Supreme Court that indicates that a director is not independent only if he is dominated and controlled by an interested party, such as a Trading Defendant. The SLC also emphasizes that much of our jurisprudence on independence focuses on economically consequential relationships between the allegedly interested party and the directors who allegedly cannot act independently of that director. Put another way, much of our law focuses the bias inquiry on whether there are economically material ties between the interested party and the director whose impartiality is questioned, treating the possible effect on one's personal wealth as the key to the independence inquiry. Putting a point on this, the SLC cites certain decisions of Delaware courts concluding that directors who are personal friends of an interested party were not, by virtue of those personal ties, to be labeled non-independent.

More subtly, the SLC argues that university professors simply are not inhibited types, unwilling to make tough decisions even as to fellow professors and large contributors. What is tenure about if not to provide professors with intellectual freedom, even in non-traditional roles such as special litigation committee members? No less ardently — but with no record evidence that reliably supports its ultimate point — the SLC contends that Garcia-Molina and Grundfest are extremely distinguished in their fields and were not, in fact, influenced by the facts identified heretofore. Indeed, the SLC argues, how could they have been influenced by many of these facts when they did not learn them until the post-Report discovery process? If it boils down to the simple fact that both share with Boskin the status of a Stanford professor, how material can this be when there are 1,700 others who also occupy the same position?

D. THE PLAINTIFFS' ARGUMENTS

The plaintiffs confronted these arguments with less nuance than was helpful. Rather than rest their case on the multiple facts I have described, the plaintiffs chose to emphasize barely plausible constructions of the evidence, such as that Grundfest was lying when he could not recall being asked to participate in the Ellison Scholars Program. From these more extreme arguments, however, one can distill a reasoned core that emphasizes what academics might call the "thickness" of the social and institutional connections among Oracle, the Trading Defendants, Stanford, and the SLC members. These connections, the plaintiffs argue, were very hard to miss — being obvious to anyone who entered the SIEPR facility, to anyone who read the *Wall Street Journal, Fortune,* or the *Washington Post,* and especially to Stanford faculty members interested in their own university community and with a special interest in Oracle. Taken in their totality, the plaintiffs contend, these connections simply constitute too great a bias-producing factor for the SLC to meet its burden to prove its independence.

Even more, the plaintiffs argue that the SLC's failure to identify many of these connections in its Report is not an asset proving its independence, but instead a fundamental flaw in the Report itself, which is the document in which the SLC is supposed to demonstrate its own independence and the reasonableness of its investigation. By failing to focus on these connections when they were obviously discoverable and when it is, at best, difficult for the court to believe that at least some of them were not known by the SLC — *e.g.,* Boskin's role at SIEPR and the fact that the SIEPR Conference Center was named after Lucas — the SLC calls into doubt not only its independence, but its competence. If it could not ferret out these things, by what right should the court trust its investigative acumen?

In support of its argument, the plaintiffs note that the Delaware courts have adopted a flexible, fact-based approach to the determination of directorial independence. This test focuses on whether the directors, for any substantial reason, cannot act with only the best interests of the corporation in mind, and not just on whether the directors face pecuniary damage for acting in a particular way.

E. THE COURT'S ANALYSIS OF THE SLC'S INDEPENDENCE

Having framed the competing views of the parties, it is now time to decide.

I begin with an important reminder: the SLC bears the burden of proving its independence. It must convince me.

But of what? According to the SLC, its members are independent unless they are essentially subservient to the Trading Defendants — *i.e.,* they are under the "domination and control" of the interested parties. If the SLC is correct and this is the central inquiry in the independence determination, they would win. Nothing in the record suggests to me that either Garcia-Molina or Grundfest are dominated and controlled by any of the Trading Defendants, by Oracle, or even by Stanford.

But, in my view, an emphasis on "domination and control" would serve only to fetishize much-parroted language, at the cost of denuding the independence inquiry of its intellectual integrity. Take an easy example. Imagine if two brothers were on a corporate board, each successful in different businesses and not dependent in any way on the other's beneficence in order to be wealthy. The brothers are brothers, they stay in touch and consider each other family, but each is opinionated and strong-willed. A derivative action is filed targeting a transaction involving one of the brothers. The other brother is put on a special litigation committee to investigate the case. If the test is domination and control, then one brother could investigate the other. Does any sensible person think that is our law? I do not think it is.

And it should not be our law. Delaware law should not be based on a reductionist view of human nature that simplifies human motivations on the lines of the least sophisticated notions of the law and economics movement. *Homo sapiens* is not merely *homo economicus.* We may be thankful that an array of other motivations exist that influence human behavior; not all are any better than greed or avarice, think of envy, to name just one. But also think of motives like love, friendship, and collegiality, think of those among us who direct their behavior as best they can on a guiding creed or set of moral values.[47]

Nor should our law ignore the social nature of humans. To be direct, corporate directors are generally the sort of people deeply enmeshed in social institutions. Such institutions have norms, expectations that, explicitly and implicitly, influence and channel the behavior of those who participate in their operation. Some things are "just not done," or only at a cost, which might not be so severe as a loss of position, but may involve a loss of standing in the institution. In being appropriately sensitive to this factor, our law also cannot assume — absent some proof of the point — that corporate directors are, as a general matter, persons of unusual social bravery, who operate heedless to the inhibitions that social norms generate for ordinary folk.

For all these reasons, this court has previously held that the Delaware Supreme Court's teachings on independence can be summarized thusly:

> At bottom, the question of independence turns on whether a director is, *for any substantial reason*, incapable of making a decision with only the best interests of the corporation in mind. That is, the Supreme Court cases ultimately focus on impartiality and objectivity.

This formulation is wholly consistent with the teaching of *Aronson*, which defines independence as meaning that "a director's decision is based on the corporate merits of the subject before the board rather than extraneous considerations or influences." As noted by Chancellor Chandler recently, a director may be compromised if he is beholden to an interested person. Beholden in this sense does not mean just owing in the financial sense, it can also flow out of "personal or other relationships" to the interested party. . . .

1. The Contextual Nature of the Independence Inquiry Under Delaware Law

In examining whether the SLC has met its burden to demonstrate that there is no material dispute of fact regarding its independence, the court must bear in mind the function of special litigation committees under our jurisprudence. Under Delaware law, the primary means by which corporate defendants may obtain a dismissal of a derivative suit is by showing that the plaintiffs have not met their pleading burden under the test of Aronson v. Lewis, [473 A.2d 805 (Del. 1985),] or the related standard set forth in Rales v. Blasband [, 634 A.2d 927 (Del. 1993)]. In simple terms, these tests permit a corporation to terminate a derivative suit if its board is comprised of directors who can impartially consider a demand.

Special litigation committees are permitted as a last chance for a corporation to control a derivative claim in circumstances when a majority of its directors cannot impartially consider a demand. By vesting the power of the board to determine what to do with the suit in a committee of independent directors, a

---

47. In an interesting work, Professor Lynn Stout has argued that there exists an empirical basis to infer that corporate directors are likely to be motivated by altruistic impulses and not simply by a concern for their own pocketbooks. *See* Lynn A. Stout, *In Praise of Procedure: An Economic and Behavioral Defense of* Smith v. VanGorkom *and the Business Judgment Rule*, 96 Nw. U.L. Rev. 675, 677-78 (2002).

corporation may retain control over whether the suit will proceed, so long as the committee meets the standard set forth in *Zapata*. . .

Thus, in assessing the independence of the Oracle SLC, I necessarily examine the question of whether the SLC can independently make the difficult decision entrusted to it: to determine whether the Trading Defendants should face suit for insider trading-based allegations of breach of fiduciary duty. An affirmative answer by the SLC to that question would have potentially huge negative consequences for the Trading Defendants, not only by exposing them to the possibility of a large damage award but also by subjecting them to great reputational harm. To have Professors Grundfest and Garcia-Molina declare that Oracle should press insider trading claims against the Trading Defendants would have been, to put it mildly, "news." Relatedly, it is reasonable to think that an SLC determination that the Trading Defendants had likely engaged in insider trading would have been accompanied by a recommendation that they step down as fiduciaries until their ultimate culpability was decided.

The importance and special sensitivity of the SLC's task is also relevant for another obvious reason: investigations do not follow a scientific process like an old-fashioned assembly line. The investigators' mindset and talent influence, for good or ill, the course of an investigation. Just as there are obvious dangers from investigators suffering from too much zeal, so too are dangers posed by investigators who harbor reasons not to pursue the investigation's targets with full vigor.

The nature of the investigation is important, too. Here, for example, the SLC was required to undertake an investigation that could not avoid a consideration of the subjective state of mind of the Trading Defendants. Their credibility was important, and the SLC could not escape making judgments about that, no matter how objective the criteria the SLC attempted to use.

Therefore, I necessarily measure the SLC's independence contextually, and my ruling confronts the SLC's ability to decide impartially whether the Trading Defendants should be pursued for insider trading. This contextual approach is a strength of our law, as even the best minds have yet to devise across-the-board definitions that capture all the circumstances in which the independence of directors might reasonably be questioned. By taking into account all circumstances, the Delaware approach undoubtedly results in some level of indeterminacy, but with the compensating benefit that independence determinations are tailored to the precise situation at issue.

Likewise, Delaware law requires courts to consider the independence of directors based on the facts known to the court about them specifically, the so-called "subjective 'actual person' standard."

That said, it is inescapable that a court must often apply to the known facts about a specific director a consideration of how a reasonable person similarly situated to that director would behave, given the limited ability of a judge to look into a particular director's heart and mind. This is especially so when a special litigation committee chooses, as was the case here, to eschew any live witness testimony, a decision that is, of course, sensible lest special litigation committee termination motions turn into trials nearly as burdensome as the derivative suit the committee seeks to end. But with that sensible choice came an acceptance of the court's need to infer that the special litigation committee members are persons of typical professional sensibilities.

2. The SLC Has Not Met Its Burden to Demonstrate the Absence of a Material Dispute of Fact About Its Independence

Using the contextual approach I have described, I conclude that the SLC has not met its burden to show the absence of a material factual question about its independence. I find this to be the case because the ties among the SLC, the Trading Defendants, and Stanford are so substantial that they cause reasonable doubt about the SLC's ability to impartially consider whether the Trading Defendants should face suit. The concern that arises from these ties can be stated fairly simply, focusing on defendants Boskin, Lucas, and Ellison in that order, and then collectively.

As SLC members, Grundfest and Garcia-Molina were already being asked to consider whether the company should level extremely serious accusations of wrongdoing against fellow board members. As to Boskin, both SLC members faced another layer of complexity: the determination of whether to have Oracle press insider trading claims against a fellow professor at their university. Even though Boskin was in a different academic department from either SLC member, it is reasonable to assume that the fact that Boskin was also on faculty would—to persons possessing typical sensibilities and institutional loyalty—be a matter of more than trivial concern. Universities are obviously places of at-times intense debate, but they also see themselves as communities. In fact, Stanford refers to itself as a "community of scholars." To accuse a fellow professor—whom one might see at the faculty club or at interdisciplinary presentations of academic papers—of insider trading cannot be a small thing—even for the most callous of academics.

As to Boskin, Grundfest faced an even more complex challenge than Garcia-Molina. Boskin was a professor who had taught him and with whom he had maintained contact over the years. Their areas of academic interest intersected, putting Grundfest in contact if not directly with Boskin, then regularly with Boskin's colleagues. Moreover, although I am told by the SLC that the title of senior fellow at SIEPR is an honorary one, the fact remains that Grundfest willingly accepted it and was one of a select number of faculty who attained that status. And, they both just happened to also be steering committee members. Having these ties, Grundfest (I infer) would have more difficulty objectively determining whether Boskin engaged in improper insider trading than would a person who was not a fellow professor, had not been a student of Boskin, had not kept in touch with Boskin over the years, and who was not a senior fellow and steering committee member at SIEPR.

In so concluding, I necessarily draw on a general sense of human nature. It may be that Grundfest is a very special person who is capable of putting these kinds of things totally aside. But the SLC has not provided evidence that that is the case. In this respect, it is critical to note that I do not infer that Grundfest would be less likely to recommend suit against Boskin than someone without these ties. Human nature being what it is, it is entirely possible that Grundfest would in fact be tougher on Boskin than he would on someone with whom he did not have such connections. The inference I draw is subtly, but importantly, different. What I infer is that a person in Grundfest's position would find it difficult to assess Boskin's conduct without pondering his own association with Boskin and their mutual affiliations. Although these connections might produce bias in either a tougher or laxer direction, the key inference is that these connections would be on the mind of a person in Grundfest's position, putting him in the position of either causing serious legal action to be brought against a person with whom he shares several connections (an awkward thing) or not doing so (and risking being seen as having engaged in favoritism toward his old professor and SIEPR colleague).

The same concerns also exist as to Lucas. For Grundfest to vote to accuse Lucas of insider trading would require him to accuse SIEPR's Advisory Board Chair and major benefactor of serious wrongdoing — of conduct that violates federal securities laws. Such action would also require Grundfest to make charges against a man who recently donated $50,000 to Stanford Law School after Grundfest made a speech at his request.

And, for both Grundfest and Garcia-Molina, service on the SLC demanded that they consider whether an extremely generous and influential Stanford alumnus should be sued by Oracle for insider trading. Although they were not responsible for fundraising, as sophisticated professors they undoubtedly are aware of how important large contributors are to Stanford, and they share in the benefits that come from serving at a university with a rich endowment. A reasonable professor giving any thought to the matter would obviously consider the effect his decision might have on the University's relationship with Lucas, it being (one hopes) sensible to infer that a professor of reasonable collegiality and loyalty cares about the well-being of the institution he serves.

In so concluding, I give little weight to the SLC's argument that it was unaware of just how substantial Lucas's beneficence to Stanford has been. I do so for two key reasons. Initially, it undermines, rather than inspires, confidence that the SLC did not examine the Trading Defendants' ties to Stanford more closely in preparing its Report. The Report's failure to identify these ties is important because it is the SLC's burden to show independence. In forming the SLC, the Oracle board should have undertaken a thorough consideration of the facts bearing on the independence of the proposed SLC members from the key objects of the investigation.

The purported ignorance of the SLC members about all of Lucas's donations to Stanford is not helpful to them for another reason: there were too many visible manifestations of Lucas's status as a major contributor for me to conclude that Grundfest, at the very least, did not understand Lucas to be an extremely generous benefactor of Stanford. It is improbable that Grundfest was not aware that Lucas was the Chair of SIEPR's Advisory Board, and Grundfest must have known that the Donald L. Lucas Conference Center at SIEPR did not get named that way by coincidence. And, in February 2002 — incidentally, the same month the SLC was formed — Grundfest spoke at a meeting of "SIEPR Associates," a group of individuals who had given $5,000 or more to SIEPR. Although it is not clear if Lucas attended that event, he is listed — in the same publication that reported Grundfest's speech at the Associates' meeting — as one of SIEPR's seventy-five "Associates." Combined with the other obvious indicia of Lucas's large contributor status (including the $50,000 donation Lucas made to Stanford Law School to thank Grundfest for giving a speech) and Lucas's obviously keen interest in his alma mater, Grundfest would have had to be extremely insensitive to his own working environment not to have considered Lucas an extremely generous alumni benefactor of Stanford, and at SIEPR and the Law School in particular.

Garcia-Molina is in a somewhat better position to disclaim knowledge of how generous an alumnus Lucas had been. Even so, the scope of Lucas's activities and their easy discoverability gives me doubt that he did not know of the relative magnitude of Lucas's generosity to Stanford. Furthermore, Grundfest comprised half of the SLC and was its most active member. His non-independence is sufficient alone to require a denial of the SLC's motion.

In concluding that the facts regarding Lucas's relationship with Stanford are materially important, I must address a rather odd argument of the SLC's. The argument goes as follows. Stanford has an extremely large endowment. Lucas's contributions, while seemingly large, constitute a very small proportion of Stanford's endowment and annual donations. Therefore, Lucas could not be a materially important contributor to Stanford and the SLC's independence could not be compromised by that factor.

But missing from that syllogism is any acknowledgement of the role that Stanford's solicitude to benefactors like Lucas might play in the overall size of its endowment and campus facilities. Endowments and buildings grow one contribution at a time, and they do not grow by callous indifference to alumni who (personally and through family foundations) have participated in directing contributions of the size Lucas has. Buildings and conference centers are named as they are as a recognition of the high regard universities have for donors (or at least, must feign convincingly). The SLC asks me to believe that what universities like Stanford say in thank you letters and public ceremonies is not in reality true; that, in actuality, their contributors are not materially important to the health of those academic institutions. This is a proposition that the SLC has not convinced me is true, and that seems to contradict common experience.

Nor has the SLC convinced me that tenured faculty are indifferent to large contributors to their institutions, such that a tenured faculty member would not be worried about writing a report finding that a suit by the corporation should proceed against a large contributor and that there was credible evidence that he had engaged in illegal insider trading. The idea that faculty members would not be concerned that action of that kind might offend a large contributor who a university administrator or fellow faculty colleague (*e.g.*, Shoven at SIEPR) had taken the time to cultivate strikes me as implausible and as resting on a narrow-minded understanding of the way that collegiality works in institutional settings.

In view of the ties involving Boskin and Lucas alone, I would conclude that the SLC has failed to meet its burden on the independence question. The tantalizing facts about Ellison merely reinforce this conclusion. The SLC, of course, argues that Ellison is not a large benefactor of Stanford personally, . . . and that, in any event, the SLC was ignorant of any negotiations between Ellison and Stanford about a large contribution. For these reasons, the SLC says, its ability to act independently of Ellison is clear.

I find differently. The notion that anyone in Palo Alto can accuse Ellison of insider trading without harboring some fear of social awkwardness seems a stretch. That being said, I do not mean to imply that the mere fact that Ellison is worth tens of billions of dollars and is the key force behind a very important social institution in Silicon Valley disqualifies all persons who live there from being independent of him. Rather, it is merely an acknowledgement of the simple fact that accusing such a significant person in that community of such serious wrongdoing is no small thing.

Given that general context, Ellison's relationship to Stanford itself contributes to my overall doubt, when heaped on top of the ties involving Boskin and Lucas. During the period when Grundfest and Garcia-Molina were being added to the Oracle board, Ellison was publicly considering making extremely large contributions to Stanford. Although the SLC denies knowledge of these public statements, Grundfest claims to have done a fair amount of research before joining the board, giving me doubt that he was not somewhat aware of the possibility that Ellison might bestow large blessings on Stanford. This is especially so when I cannot rule out the possibility that Grundfest had been told by Lucas about, but has now honestly forgotten, the negotiations over the Ellison Scholars Program.

Furthermore, the reality is that whether or not Ellison eventually decided not to create that Program and not to bequeath his house to Stanford, Ellison remains a plausible target of Stanford for a large donation. This is especially so in view of Oracle's creation of the Oracle Help Us Help Foundation with Stanford and Ellison's several public indications of his possible interest in giving to Stanford. And, while I do not give it great weight, the fact remains that Ellison's medical research foundation has been a source of nearly $10 million in funding to Stanford. Ten million dollars, even today, remains real money. . . .

As an alternative argument, the SLC contends that neither SLC member was aware of Ellison's relationship with Stanford until after the Report was completed. Thus, this relationship, in its various facets, could not have compromised their independence. Again, I find this argument from ignorance to be unavailing. An inquiry into Ellison's connections with Stanford should have been conducted before the SLC was finally formed and, at the very least, should have been undertaken in connection with the Report. In any event, given how public Ellison was about his possible donations it is difficult not to harbor troublesome doubt about whether the SLC members were conscious of the possibility that Ellison was pondering a large contribution to Stanford. In so concluding, I am not saying that the SLC members are being untruthful in saying that they did not know of the facts that have emerged, only that these facts were in very prominent journals at the time the SLC members were doing due diligence in aid of deciding whether to sign on as Oracle board members. The objective circumstances of Ellison's relations with Stanford therefore generate a reasonable suspicion that seasoned faculty members of some sophistication — including the two SLC members — would have viewed Ellison as an active and prized target for the University. The objective circumstances also require a finding that Ellison was already, through his personal Foundation and Oracle itself, a benefactor of Stanford.

Taken in isolation, the facts about Ellison might well not be enough to compromise the SLC's independence. But that is not the relevant inquiry. The pertinent question is whether, given *all* the facts, the SLC has met its independence burden.

When viewed in that manner, the facts about Ellison buttress the conclusion that the SLC has not met its burden. Whether the SLC members had precise knowledge of all the facts that have emerged is not essential, what is important is that by any measure this was a social atmosphere painted in too much vivid Stanford Cardinal red for the SLC members to have reasonably ignored it. Summarized fairly, two Stanford professors were recruited to the Oracle board in summer 2001 and soon asked to investigate a fellow professor and two benefactors of the University. On Grundfest's part, the facts are more substantial, because his connections — through his personal experiences, SIEPR, and the Law School — to Boskin and to Lucas run deeper.

It seems to me that the connections outlined in this opinion would weigh on the mind of a reasonable special litigation committee member deciding whether to level the serious charge of insider trading against the Trading Defendants. As indicated before, this does not mean that the SLC would be less inclined to find such charges meritorious, only that the connections identified would be on the mind of the SLC members in a way that generates an unacceptable risk of bias. That is, these connections generate a reasonable doubt about the SLC's impartiality because they suggest that material considerations other than the best interests of Oracle could have influenced the SLC's inquiry and judgments.

Before closing, it is necessary to address two concerns. The first is the undeniable awkwardness of opinions like this one. By finding that there exists too much doubt about the SLC's independence for the SLC to meet its *Zapata* burden, I make no finding about the subjective good faith of the SLC members, both of whom are distinguished academics at one of this nation's most prestigious institutions of higher learning. Nothing in this record leads me to conclude that either of the SLC members acted out of any conscious desire to favor the Trading Defendants or to do anything other than discharge their duties with fidelity. But that is not the purpose of the independence inquiry.

That inquiry recognizes that persons of integrity and reputation can be compromised in their ability to act without bias when they must make a decision adverse to others with whom they share material affiliations. To conclude that the Oracle SLC was not independent is not a conclusion that the two accomplished professors who comprise it are not persons of good faith and moral probity, it is solely to conclude that they were not situated to act with the required degree of impartiality. *Zapata* requires independence to ensure that stockholders do not have to rely upon special litigation committee members who must put aside personal considerations that are ordinarily influential in daily behavior in making the already difficult decision to accuse fellow directors of serious wrongdoing.

Finally, the SLC has made the argument that a ruling against it will chill the ability of corporations to locate qualified independent directors in the academy. This is overwrought. If there are 1,700 professors at Stanford alone, as the SLC says, how many must there be on the west coast of the United States, at institutions without ties to Oracle and the Trading Defendants as substantial as Stanford's? Undoubtedly, a corporation of Oracle's market capitalization could have found prominent academics willing to serve as SLC members, about whom no reasonable question of independence could have been asserted.

Rather than form an SLC whose membership was free from bias-creating relationships, Oracle formed a committee fraught with them. As a result, the SLC has failed to meet its *Zapata* burden, and its motion to terminate must be denied. Because of this reality, I do not burden the reader with an examination of the other *Zapata* factors. In the absence of a finding that the SLC was independent, its subjective good faith and the reasonableness of its conclusions would not be sufficient to justify termination. Without confidence that the SLC was impartial, its findings do not provide the assurance our law requires for the dismissal of a derivative suit without a merits inquiry.

V. CONCLUSION

The SLC's motion to terminate is DENIED. IT IS SO ORDERED.

[handwritten margin note: Is the derivative action an umbrella? then there can be various charges therein?]

TYCO: A CASE STUDY

One of the most dramatic of the corporate governance failures of 2002 was at Tyco International, Ltd. (Tyco), where the chief executive officer, L. Dennis Kozlowski, and the chief financial officer, Mark H. Swartz, were alleged to have masterminded a grand-style looting of the company without any significant "push-back" from the Tyco board. Kozlowski had for some time been a darling of the financial press, prominently featured in articles in the Wall Street Journal with headlines such as "In the Lead: How Some CEOs Get the Energy to Work Those Endless Days," and "CEO's Guide to Survival: Shared Traits of Leadership Help Chiefs of Sunbeam, Polaroid and Tyco Endure." The latter article, about the CEOs who were able to survive scandals at their companies, noted that nearly $50 billion of Tyco's $88.5 market capitalization disappeared in late 1999, when the SEC questioned the company's accounting practices, but that because of "a storehouse of credibility," Kozlowski had survived the "flap." Yet, in a prophetic turn of phrase, the article ended with a quote from Kozlowski stating that "[w]hen bad news becomes water torture—bad news followed by bad news by bad news—that's when CEOs lose credibility." Joann S. Lublin, *CEOs' Guide to Survival*, Wall St. J. (Feb. 27, 2001). And yet, by 2002 bad news was being followed by bad news and being followed by further bad news at Tyco, as Kozlowski and two other executives and one director were indicted for tax evasion, securities fraud, and embezzlement.

[handwritten margin note: unless in class notes.]

In the following paragraphs, the derivative plaintiffs describe their complaints against Kozlowski and others, including their auditors at PricewaterhouseCoopers LLP, and also describe why plaintiffs believe demand is futile:

Verified Stockholders' First Consolidated and Amended Derivative Complaint Summary of the Derivative Action

¶*1.*   This is a stockholders' derivative action brought on behalf of nominal defendant Tyco against the directors who served on Tyco's board of directors (the "Board") during the acts complained of herein, namely L. Dennis Kozlowski ("Kozlowski"), Mark H. Swartz ("Swartz"), Michael A. Ashcroft, Joshua M. Berman, John F. Fort, III, Richard S. Bodman, Stephen W. Foss, Wendy E. Lane, Jams S. Pasman, Jr., W. Peter Slusser, and Joseph F. Welch (collectively, the "Director Defendants"). This action is also brought against Mark A. Belnick ("Belnick"), Frank Walsh ("Walsh"), and against PricewaterhouseCoopers, LLP ("PwC") and PricewaterhouseCoopers LLP (Bermuda) ("PwC-US" and "PwC-Bermuda") (collectively "PwC") by Plaintiffs, who are now and, at all times relevant, have been shareholders of Tyco, for breach of defendants' fiduciary duties of loyalty and candor, gross mismanagement, and waste of corporate assets. Plaintiffs seek to recover, on behalf of the Company, *inter alia,* damages Tyco suffered as a result of defendants' knowing, reckless or grossly negligent failure to prevent financial abuse through the unfettered use of Tyco corporate assets for the personal benefit of certain Tyco executives.

*[handwritten margin note: derivative action charges *]*

¶2. In May of 2002, it was first disclosed that defendant Kozlowski was indicted for tax evasion as a result of alleged dealings with certain art collectors, who participated in a scheme to ship Kozlowski empty boxes to New Hampshire to avoid New York state sales tax estimated at approximately $1 million.

¶3. It was uncovered during the investigation that Kozlowski was actually a much bigger thief—it turned out that Kozlowski and his cronies were bilking Tyco out of hundreds of millions of dollars. Although his $6,000 shower curtain and vodka-spewing, life-sized, ice replica of Michelangelo's David were embarrassing enough, on September 12, 2002, Kozlowski, the former CFO Swartz, and Belnick (collectively the "Criminal Defendants") were indicted. Kozlowski and Swartz were charged with running a criminal enterprise within Tyco's executive suite, and charged with pilfering $170 million directly from the Company and for pocketing an additional $430 million through tainted stock sales.

¶4. The more that the Criminal Defendants were paid in reward for Tyco's soaring stock price, the more they spent on luxuries, and the more they allegedly stole. Apparently, the Criminal Defendants operated under the belief that they and the Company were one, and that they could take whatever they wanted whenever they wanted it. Of greater concern is why the Board or PwC did not disabuse them of this notion.

¶5. Most disturbing from the perspective of Board oversight, Kozlowski's misdeeds were remarkable for their absolute brazenness, not for their financial trickery. The crimes that Kozlowski and Swartz are charged with are not much more complicated than taking bags of cash from the Company—they simply borrowed tens of millions of dollars from the Company, and forgave the loans. This begs the obvious questions: Where was the Board? Where was PwC?

¶6. In fact, the Director Defendants, and thus the entire Board, was comprised by direct financial entanglements with the Criminal Defendants. Throughout Kozlowski's term as Chairman and CEO, he funneled both his personal funds and Tyco money to the Director Defendants in a series of related party transactions, including aircraft leases, real estate purchases and professional service contracts. As a result, the individual defendants were personally financially beholden to Kozlowski. In the most extreme example, Walsh, Tyco's former "lead director," conspired with Kozlowski to receive an undisclosed $20 million finder's fee—a transaction which has since resulted in Walsh's criminal conviction. PwC was also compromised by financial ties to Tyco and its management extending far beyond PwC's role as the independent auditor. PwC received nearly twice as much compensation for non-audit services from Tyco than it did for its auditing work. Much of these non-audit services involved either tax consulting or due diligence for Tyco's string of acquisitions, work which brought PwC into intimate engagement with Kozlowski's machinations.

¶7. As discussed herein, defendants caused Tyco to engage in actions that were *ultra vires* under relevant law. These activities, which caused Tyco to engage in behavior that was not sanctioned by law or corporate charter, reveals how seriously the Director Defendants' independence was compromised, and also demonstrates why demand on the Board is excused in this litigation.

¶8. From 1997 through 2001, the Criminal Defendants abused Tyco loan and relocation programs, dipping into one or the other for hundreds of millions in interest-free funds. As discussed herein, the Board and PwC were actually aware of or, in the alternative, were reckless or grossly negligent in not being aware of such abuses.

¶9. Tyco failed to disclose in any flings with the Untied States Securities and Exchange Commission ("SEC") the misuse of these programs or a host of other self-dealing transactions described herein.

¶10. In the end, the Board's failure to stop the orgy of getting and spending devastated Tyco's share price, resulting in a $90 billion drop in Tyco's stock.

¶11. Numerous federal and state investigations have been instituted and numerous shareholder lawsuits have been filed against Tyco and certain of its directors and/or officers.

¶12. Tyco has been harmed by, *inter alia*, the damages and expenses resulting from the federal securities class actions filed against the Company, investigations by the SEC, the New Hampshire Bureau of Securities, the Manhattan District Attorney's office and Florida, criminal indictments of Tyco's top executives, the downgrade of Tyco's credit rating, and its damaged reputation in the marketplace.

Overview of Self-Dealing Transactions
Abuse of KELP Loans

¶38. From 1996 through the first half of 2002, the Board permitted Kozlowski and Swartz to grant to themselves and their cronies hundreds of millions of dollars of low interest and no-interest loans from Tyco. Most of these loans were taken through abuse of Tyco's Key Employee Corporate Loan Program (the "KELP").

¶39. According to Tyco's proxy statements, the KELP, established by Tyco in 1983, and subsequently amended, was "designed to encourage ownership of Tyco common shares by executives and other key employees." The KELP ostensibly was designed to provide low interest loans to enable Tyco executives and employees to pay taxes due as a result of the vesting of ownership of shares granted under Tyco's restricted share ownership plan. The KELP itself, as filed with the SEC, explicitly described this narrow purpose:

> Under the Program, loan proceeds may be used for the payment of federal income taxes due upon the vesting of Company common stock from time to time under the 1983 Restricted Stock Ownership Plans for Key Employees, and to refinance other existing outstanding loans for such purpose.

¶40. Kozlowski and Swartz gave themselves hundreds of millions of dollars in KELP loans which they used for purposes not legitimately authorized by the KELP.

¶41. From 1997 to 2002, Kozlowski took an aggregate of approximately $270 million from Tyco that he charged as KELP loans — even though he only used approximately $29,000,000 of those funds to cover taxes due as a result of the vesting of his Tyco stock.

¶42. Kozlowski improperly took and used the remaining $242 million of supposed KELP loans — or roughly ninety percent of the approximately $270 million he had taken from Tyco — for impermissible and unauthorized purposes, including funding his extravagant lifestyle. For example, with his KELP loans, Kozlowski amassed millions of dollars in art, yachts, and estate jewelry, as well as an apartment on Park Avenue and an estate in Nantucket. He also used the KELP to fund his personal investments and business ventures.

¶43.   During that same time period, from 1997 to 2002, Swartz took an aggregate of approximately $85,000,000 dollars from Tyco that he charged as KELP loans — even though he only used approximately $13,000,000 worth of those funds to cover taxes due from the vesting of his Tyco stock.

¶44.   Swartz improperly took and used the remaining $72,000,000 of supposed KELP loans — or roughly eight-five percent — for impermissible and unauthorized purposes. For example, Swartz funded millions of dollars of his personal investments, business ventures, real estate holdings and trusts.

Abuse of Tyco's RLP

¶45.   The Board also permitted the Criminal Defendants to abuse Tyco's relocation loan program ("RLP"). This interest-free loan program, established by Tyco in 1995, was designed to assist Tyco employees who were required to relocate from New Hampshire to New York, when Tyco moved its corporate offices from New Hampshire to New York City, and, subsequently, to assist Tyco employees who were required to relocate to Boca Raton, Florida when Tyco moved some of its U.S. staff there. The RLP did not provide for relocation loans for moves to any other location.

¶46.   From 1996 to 2002, Kozlowski received Tyco relocation loans aggregating approximately $46,000,000. Kozlowski used $18,000,000 of those loans to purchase a waterfront compound in Boca Raton. Kozlowski used the remaining $28,000,000 of purported "relocation loans" for purposes which were not within the scope of the RLP.

¶47.   For example, Kozlowski used approximately $21,000,000 of "relocation" loans for various other purposes, including the purchase of prestigious properties in New Hampshire, Nantucket, and Connecticut. Kozlowski even used approximately $7,000,000 of Tyco's funds to purchase a Park Avenue apartment for his estranged wife, from whom he had been separated for many years and whom he subsequently divorced.

¶48.   Swartz borrowed more than $32,000,000 under the RLP. With those funds, he purchased a $6,500,000 apartment on New York City's Upper East Side and a $17,000,000 waterfront compound in Boca Raton. Swartz used the remaining $9,000,000 for purposes that were not authorized by the RLP, including the purchase of a yacht and the funding of real estate investments.

¶49.   From 1998 to 2002, Belnick received Tyco RLP loans of over $14 million.

¶50.   For years prior to his employment at Tyco, Belnick maintained his professional office in midtown Manhattan — only blocks from Tyco's headquarters at the time. When Belnick joined Tyco he received a loan of approximately $4 million to "relocate" to New York City — even though he was ineligible for the plan because he had not previously worked for Tyco (let alone worked for Tyco's New Hampshire headquarters, as required by the terms of the plan) and already owned a house in Westchester County, a suburb just outside of New York

City. Belnick used the loan to buy and renovate a new apartment on Central Park West in Manhattan.

¶51.   Belnick used the remaining $10,000,000 dollars in loans to purchase a ski chalet in Park City, Utah, although Belnick already owned a $2,000,000 property in Utah. In September of 2001, Belnick received the vast majority of the loan, pursuant to a promissory note with TME, a subsidiary of Tyco. The loan was ostensibly granted under the RLP to assist Belnick with his "relocation" to Park City, Utah. Tyco never had a corporate presence in Utah — let alone a loan program that paid for employees to relocate there.

Kozlowski and Swartz Stole Tens of Millions of Dollars Through Self-Engineered Forgiveness of Tyco Loans and Improper Bonus Plans

¶53.   The Board knew or were reckless or grossly negligent in not knowing that the Criminal Defendants were authorizing tens of millions of dollars of their KELP and RLP loans to be forgiven and written off Tyco's books. Kozlowski and Swartz also directed the acceleration of the vesting of Tyco common stock for their benefit.

¶54.   In August of 1999, Kozlowski authorized, and Swartz caused to be recorded in Tyco's books and records, a $25,000,000 loan forgiveness against Kozlowski's outstanding KELP balance and a $12,500,000 credit against Swartz's outstanding KELP balance. Although the KELP loan forgiveness was tantamount to a $37,500,000 payment from Tyco to Kozlowski and Swartz, these transactions were never disclosed to investors as part of Kozlowski's or Swartz's executive compensation in Tyco's Form 10-K annual reports and proxy statements.

¶55.   In September of 2000, the Board knew or were reckless or grossly negligent in not knowing, that Kozlowski, through TME, engineered a program whereby Tyco covertly forgave tens of millions of dollars of "relocation loans" that he, Swartz, and others owed. To receive these benefits, all that each RLP loan recipient had to do was execute a letter agreement in which they promised not to disclose the loan forgiveness "to anyone other than [their] financial, tax or legal advisors."

¶56.   Under the September 2000 relocation loan forgiveness program, Kozlowski received $32,976,068 in forgiven relocation loans and Swartz received $16,610,687 in forgiven relocation loans. Although the relocation loan forgiveness was tantamount to an additional $49,586,755 payment from Tyco to Kozlowski and Swartz, these transactions were never disclosed to investors as part of Kozlowski's or Swartz's executive compensation in Tyco's annual reports on Form 10-K and proxy statements.

Undisclosed Related Party Transactions with Tyco

¶62.   In 2000, the Board knew, or were reckless or grossly negligent in not knowing, that Kozlowski arranged for TME to purchase his house in New Hampshire for $4.5 million — three times the property's apparent fair market value. The Board knew, or were reckless or grossly negligent in not knowing, that this self-dealing had not been disclosed to investors.

¶63.   In 2000, in the midst of soaring prices for residential real estate in New York City, Kozlowski purchased a Park Avenue apartment from Tyco for the same price that Tyco had paid for it eighteen months earlier, without a contemporaneous appraisal justifying the absence of any increase in market value. This related party transaction which the Board should have been aware of was also concealed from investors.

¶*64.*   Swartz also engaged in undisclosed transactions with Tyco or its subsidiaries, which the Board knew, or were reckless in not knowing, were not disclosed to Tyco shareholders. For example, in 1995, Swartz sold his New Hampshire real estate to a Tyco subsidiary for $305,000. When Tyco sold that property to a third party in early 1997, Tyco obtained a far lower price for it than it had paid to Swartz earlier.

¶*65.*   Kozlowski enjoyed numerous and extensive perquisites from Tyco that the Board knowingly, recklessly or in gross negligence, concealed from investors. For example, in 2000, Kozlowski caused Tyco to purchase in Kozlowski's name (as nominee) an apartment on Fifth Avenue in New York City (for which Tyco paid over $31,000,000). In 2001, after a major renovation to that apartment, Kozlowski moved into the Fifth Avenue apartment and lived there rent-free.

¶*66.*   Kozlowski also directed millions of dollars of charitable contributions in his own name using Tyco funds — including contributions to Seton Hall University, Nantucket Historical Association, Berwick Academy, and Columbia University. Moreover Kozlowski used Tyco corporate aircraft for personal use at little to no cost.

¶*67.*   Swartz also received numerous perquisites from Tyco that the Board know, or were reckless or grossly negligent in not knowing, were not disclosed to investors. In 2000, for example, Swartz caused Tyco to purchase an apartment in Swartz's name on New York City's Upper East Side. Swartz then moved into the apartment and lived there rent-free — a perquisite worth in excess of $18,000 a month. Swartz also used Tyco's corporate aircraft for his own personal use at little to no cost.

The Board's Lack of Independence
Frank Walsh

¶*98.*   Walsh was a personal friend of Kozlowski and had served as a Tyco director for several years; in the late 1990s, he was the Chairman of the Board's Compensation Committee, and by early 2001 he had been appointed Lead Director, making him the principal conduit for communications between the Company's management and the Board.

¶*99.*   From 1996 to 2002, Tyco leased an aircraft from Stockwood, Inc., in which Walsh has a controlling interest. Stockwood, Inc. submitted and was paid for invoices totaling $2,490,319 for that lease.

¶*100.*   Stockwood VII, Inc., in which Walsh also has a controlling interest, provided pilot services to the Company. For the period 1996 to 2002, Stockwood VII, Inc. submitted and was paid for invoices totaling $1,077,071. Tyco renewed that agreement annually to October 31, 2000, and signed a new agreement beginning in January 2001, which ended in February 2002.

¶*101.*   In 2000, Walsh learned of Tyco's interest in acquiring the CIT Group ("CIT") — a company in which Walsh held 50,000 shares. Walsh offered to assist in Tyco's acquisition by arranging a meeting between Kozlowski and Albert R. Gamper, Jr. ("Gamper"), the Chief Executive Officer of CIT.

¶*102.* After the first meeting between Kozlowski and Gamper, Kozlowski proposed to pay Walsh an investment banking or finder's commission for his services if the transaction was successfully completed.

¶*103.* Despite serving as the purported Lead Director and acting with independence, Walsh advocated and voted in favor of the proposed CIT transaction without disclosing his expected financial gain. *oucH!!*

¶*104.* The terms and conditions of the Tyco/CIT merger were set forth in the Agreement and Plan of Merger dated March 12, 2001. In the section of the Agreement and Plan of Merger that contained the representations and warranties of Tyco, Tyco represented that, other than Lehman Brothers and Goldman, Sachs & Co. (the investment bankers that represented Tyco in the Tyco/CIT merger):

> . . . there is no investment banker, broker, finder *or other intermediary* that has been retained by or is authorized to act on behalf of [Tyco] who might be entitled to any fee or commission from [Tyco] . . . in connection with the transactions contemplated by this Agreement. (Emphasis added.)

¶*105.* On April 13, 2001, Tyco filed with the SEC a registration statement on Form S-4 (the "Registration Statement") for the securities related to the contemplated merger between Tyco and CIT. The Agreement and Plan of Merger was incorporated by reference in, and attached to, the Registration Statement.

¶*106.* In his capacity as a director of Tyco, Walsh signed the Registration Statement. At the time that he signed, Walsh knew that the Registration Statement contained a material misrepresentation regarding the payment of a "finder's fee" because he knew that he stood to obtain a $20 million fee if the transaction was consummated.

¶*107.* After the transaction was consummated, pursuant to his prior agreement with Kozlowski to receive a fee, Kozlowski caused Tyco to pay Walsh a $20 million "finder's fee" in the form of $10 million in cash and a $10 million charitable contribution to a foundation chosen by Walsh.

¶*108.* Ultimately, Walsh plead guilty to criminal violations of New York's General Business Law, returned $20 million to Tyco and paid a $2.5 million fine. Walsh, however, has not compensated Tyco for the severe damage to its business reputation or otherwise paid for the multiple criminal and civil investigations of the Company that were, in part, a direct result of his illegal actions.

¶*109.* On January 16, 2002, the Board met informally to discuss Kozlowski's plan to realize tens of billions of dollars in shareholder value by breaking up the company into four parts — each a multi-billion dollar entity in its own right — and selling billions of other assets. The Board also added Walsh's finder's fee issue to the agenda for that meeting.

¶*110.* The directors reviewed the facts and circumstances relating to the Walsh payment at the January 16 meeting and gave Walsh the opportunity to explain himself. Walsh was then excused from the discussion, and upon his return was told that it was the unanimous review of the Board that the money should be returned. Walsh responded by gathering up his papers, saying "adios" to the other directors, and walking out of the meeting.

John Fort

¶*111.*   In April, 1996, Fort sold Kozlowski a property at 59 Harbor Road, Rye, New Hampshire, where Fort had resided while CEO of Tyco. Immediately prior to the closing in April 1996, Fort was notified that the actual purchaser would be the GV Realty Trust, which Kozlowski represented as his own realty trust in which he was the sole beneficiary. Although GV Realty Trust was owned by Kozlowski, he caused Tyco to book the purchase to a general ledger Tyco account. Before the end of the year, the entry was reversed and transferred to Kozlowski's personal KELP loan account.

Michael Ashcroft

¶*113.*   On October 24, 1997, after the Tyco/ADT merger, Tyco purchased Ashcroft's Florida residence at 471 East Alexander Palm Road for more than $2,500,000. Ashcroft claimed that he understood at the time that he was selling the property to Kozlowski personally, and did not know until more than two years later that the purchaser of the property was the new Tyco subsidiary, ADT. Ashcroft claims to have inquired some months later of Swartz whether the transaction should be disclosed in the Company's proxy and that Swartz informed him that because Tyco explored competitive alternatives prior to purchasing his property, it did not consider the transaction reportable. Prosecutors investigated this activity and have recently shown renewed interest in Ashcroft's dealings with Kozlowski.

Richard Bodman

¶*114.*   Kozlowski invested $5 million in a private stock fund managed by Richard Bodman, according to a November 6, 2002 Wall Street Journal article.

Stephen Foss

¶*115.*   In May 2001, Tyco entered into a two-year lease agreement with Foss to lease a Cessna Citation aircraft for a minimum monthly lease payment of $38,000·for 20 hours of flight time. For the period May 2001 to May 2002, Tyco paid Foss a total of $570,000. N.H. Helicopters, Inc., of which Foss is the president, also provided pilot services to Tyco pursuant to a two-year agreement commencing on the same date. For the period May 2001 to May 2002, Tyco paid N.H. Helicopters, Inc. a total of $181,101.24. On July 25, 2002, after Kozlowski's resignation, both agreements were amended to terminate on September 30, 2002.

Joshua Berman

¶*116.*   Tyco has disclosed that Berman's firm, Kramer Levin, had received fees of $2 million per year from Tyco. Berman, in turn, personally benefitted because the legal fees paid by Tyco enhanced his compensation at Kramer Levin. The Wall Street Journal reported on June 12, 2002, that "Paul S. Pearlman, managing partner of Kramer Levin, said that Mr. Berman's compensation formula — until 2000 — was based on a formula that included, among other factors, how much Tyco business he brought to the law firm."

The New York Relocation

¶*131.* As a result of the RLP, Kozlowski was able to:

a. Rent a lavish Fifth Avenue apartment (817 Fifth Avenue, New York City), with annual rental of $264,000, paid for by the Company, from 1997 to 2001. The General Relocation Program would not have permitted this benefit;

b. Purchase with interest free loans in 2000—at depreciated book value and without appraisals—a Company-owned $7 million apartment at 60 Park Avenue, previously acquired by the Company at his behest. Kozlowski never occupied the apartment, but rather deeded it to his ex-wife a few months after the purchase. (Kozlowski repaid $5,118,125 of the loan on this apartment and then simply forgave the remainder of his own loan balance ($1,893,544) within a few months of the purchase.) On or about May 29, 2000, Kozlowski obtained $7,011,669 from Tyco for the purchase of property from Tyco. This purchase price was the same price Tyco had bought the apartment for 18 months earlier;

c. Sell his New Hampshire home to Tyco in 2000 for an amount significantly in excess of its market value. Kozlowski sold his house at 10 Runnymede, North Hampton, New Hampshire to the Company without appraisals for $4.5 million, an amount approximately three times its market value. After an appraisal in March 2002 valued the New Hampshire property at $1,500,000, Tyco wrote down the carrying value of the property to the appraised value and charged Kozlowski's $3,049,576 overpayment to expense. After the sale of 10 Runnymede Drive to the Company, Kozlowski reportedly continued to make personal use of the property by permitting his ex-wife to reside there for two years, without a lease and without even reimbursement to the Company of expenses; and

d. Purchase a second, more extravagant apartment on Fifth Avenue (950 Fifth Avenue, New York) in 2001 for $16.8 million and expend $3 million improvements. Kozlowski then caused Tyco to spend $11 million in furnishings for that apartment. He purchased and decorated the apartment with extravagant appointments and furnishings, including: a shower curtain for $6,000; a dog umbrella stand for $15,000; a sewing basket for $6,300; a traveling toilette box for $17,100; a gilt metal wastebasket for $2,200; coat hangers for $2,900; two sets of sheets for $5,960; a notebook for $1,650; and a pincushion for $445.

Tyco's Contractual Arrangement with PwC

¶*259.* In addition to its independent auditor role, PwC also provides significant on-going consulting services to Tyco. In 2001, PwC was paid $3.6 million for design and implementation of a financial information system, $18.1 million for tax-related services, $9.8 million non-financial audit services, and $6.5 million for statutory audit work in non-U.S. countries.

¶*260.* For many years, executives in PwC-US' Boston office, including auditors Scalzo and John O'Connor, served (and continue to serve) as Tyco's auditors. According to an October 10, 2002 article in Bloomberg News, Scalzo served as the lead PwC partner for PwC's Tyco account.

¶*261.* PwC's non-audit work has raised concerns in the investment community. A February 22, 2002 article in The Boston Globe noted that the Marco Consulting Group ("Marco"), a Chicago investment consultant holding 6.3 million Tyco shares, urged Tyco to cease hiring PwC for the non-audit services it provided to Tyco for millions of dollars in consulting fees. Marco noted that in 2001 PwC received more than three times more for consulting work than it did for audit work. Marco consultant Greg Kincszewski was quoted as stating "[t]his has to raise a question, *how independent is the audit?*" [Emphasis added.]

¶262.   An article in the September 20, 2002 edition of the New Hampshire Business Review entitled "Corporate Governance: Who Should We Trust?" noted that in a study of 17 company's [*sic*] in New Hampshire or with strong New Hampshire ties, Tyco was one of seven companies that paid its auditor more for consulting work than for auditing services. In fact, Tyco came in second place, paying PwC 76% more for consulting work. Interestingly, the article also noted that with respect to director pay " . . . no one comes close to Tyco, which rewarded directors with nearly $400,000 apiece."

¶263.   In the 2002 Tyco Annual Report, Tyco reported that it intended to maintain the highly lucrative consulting fees paid to PwC.

¶264.   PwC's relationship with Tyco can charitably be described as cozy. This is evidenced when one looks at Tyco's Bermuda office. According to a February 22, 2002 article in The Boston Globe, the head of Tyco's Bermuda Office is Glen Miskiewicz, a financial controller, who was previously employed by PwC. The Boston Globe further noted that "[h]olding its annual meeting in this elegant vacation spot [Bermuda] seems to undermine Tyco's recent efforts to increase communication with investors."

Investigation into PwC'S Conduct Is Continuing

¶265.   Although PwC has attempted to "whitewash" official investigations of its conduct with respect to Tyco, PwC's activities are in fact still under active scrutiny. For example, an October 15, 2002 article in The Boston Globe quoted PwC spokesman David Nestor as stating "[w]e've been in contact with the Manhattan district attorney's office, and they've assured us they don't intend to seek an indictment against [PwC], and they're not presently considering any indictments against any individuals at the firm.

¶266.   However, the same article further reported that Manhattan Assistant District Attorney Moscow stated that, although his office was not presently considering pressing charges against PwC or individual auditors, "[t]he investigation is ongoing."

¶267.   In addition, an October 1, 2002 article in the Newark Star-Ledger stated that "[a] senior official from the SEC said the relationship between Tyco and [PwC] could merit further scrutiny from agency investigators." The SEC official, who requested anonymity, said agency investigators would want to know, *inter alia*, the substance of any discussions between PwC and Tyco executives in connection with the secret payments.

¶268.   Experts have noted that PwC's activities with respect to Tyco are, at a minimum, highly questionable. For example, an October 1, 2002 article in the New York Daily News stated:

> In the case of [PwC], *experts said independent auditors should have noticed when more than half of an improper $96 million bonus program was booked against a tax account rather than as a general expense.*

"One of the things auditors look for are sizable items in the wrong place," said Jacob Frenkel, a former federal prosecutor and SEC enforcer now at the law firm Smith Gambrell & Russell. "*It's probably correct that hiding the bonuses in a deferred tax account is a clear misstatement.*"

¶269.   Similarly, a September 30, 2002 Business Week article quoted Columbia University securities law professor John Coffee as stating "*You would think if the auditors could spot anything, it would be the loans* [to corporate executives]." [Emphasis added.]

¶270.   A September 30, 2002 article in the Wall Street Journal underscores the gravamen of PwC's failure to uncover the wrongful conduct and advise the Tyco Board of the same:

> Typically, accounting experts say, employee bonuses are accounted for as part of general and administrative expenses. *But Tyco's filing says the TyCom bonus was booked in three different accounts totaling $97.4 million — slightly larger figure than the bonus payments, which Tyco didn't explain.* About $44.6 million of the total was booked as part of the TyCom offering expense, which some accounting experts said was incorrect but at least resulted in a similar bottom-line effect as the proper accounting treatment.
>
> The other $52.8 million, however, doesn't appear to have been counted as an expense at all, according to three accounting experts who reviewed Tyco's filing. Instead, *Tyco seems to have hidden the sum in two different reserve accounts that had been previously established on the balance sheet for unrelated purposes.* The majority of the money, $41 million, was booked against "Accrued Federal Income Tax," the filing says, in effect reducing sums that Tyco had put aside to pay its federal corporate taxes.
>
> "*This looks like blatant misstatement of both the income statement and the balance sheet,*" said Charles Mulford, an accounting professor at Georgia Institute of Technology in Atlanta, who reviewed the Tyco report but isn't involved in the case. Based on the filing, Mr. Mulford said the maneuver appears to have improperly inflated Tyco's pretax income by $52.8 million in the period, the fourth quarter of fiscal 2000. For that quarter, Tyco reported net income of $1.1 billion before the TyCom gain.
>
> Mr. Mulford called *dipping into the income-tax kitty particularly "egregious," and said "it would be very surprising if it wasn't picked up by the auditors."*
>
> Lynn Turner, a former chief accountant at the Securities and Exchange Commission who also reviewed the filing, went even further, saying "*this is called fraud.*" As for the auditors, he asked: "*How the hell do you do that and not have PricewaterhouseCoopers find it?*" Mr. Turner said auditors typically look closely at such items as tax accountants and big one-time gains, and should have spotted the bonus payments tucked in there. . . .
>
> Relations between Tyco's new management and PricewaterhouseCoopers are at a delicate stage, in part over this issue, according to a person close to Tyco. *This person said auditors at PricewaterhouseCoopers had access to information from which they could have known about loan forgiveness. They would also have been in a position to know that the board was required to approve the related tax-payment portion of the bonuses.* . . .
> [Emphasis added.]

¶271.   An October 14, 2002 article in Business Week entitled "Is The Avalanche Headed for Pricewaterhouse? Investigators Are Digging Into The

Firm's Tyco Dealings" also noted the baffling nature of PwC's willful blindness, and also provides great insight into how PwC's dual roles compromised its ability to provide adequate audit services:

> . . . *Especially outrageous to such critics as former SEC Chief Accountant Lynn E. Turner is PwC's failure to flag nearly $100 million in forgiven executive loans that Tyco booked against the gain from the partial initial public offering of a subsidiary in 2000. "Auditors must look at these large adjustments, because that is where we find the fraud has always been committed," says Turner.*
>
> *But PwC's relationship with Tyco went far beyond auditing the company's books. Reducing its tax bill has long been a key Tyco strategy for boosting earnings, and PwC was deeply involved in that effort.* According to its 2001 proxy statement, in addition to $13 million PwC earned in 2001 for auditing Tyco, the firm was paid even more —$18 million — for tax work. For that hefty fee, a Tyco spokesman says, "PwC helped Tyco with its U.S. tax planning, and the review and preparation of non-U.S. tax returns in more than 80 countries." In addition, Tyco says, "PwC reviews the Tyco tax department's analysis of our tax rate every quarter."
>
> What tax work PwC was doing and how that affected its audits is of particular interest because Tyco has been based in the tax haven of Bermuda since 1997. It also has dozens of subsidiaries in other offshore tax havens. These moves saved the company hundreds of millions in U.S. taxes, providing it a major competitive advantage. Tyco says this structure saved the company $600 million in taxes in 2001 alone.
>
> *Although it is common practice among accounting firms to serve as both auditor and tax adviser, the dual role has given rise to a chorus of critics. And for PwC, wearing both hats at scandal-ridden Tyco risks at least an appearance of conflict of interest.* That could further complicate life for PwC and its CEO, Samuel A. Di-Piazza Jr. Critics of the practice argue that tax work often involves helping companies take advantage of legal stratagems to cut their tax bills. A company must then estimate its tax bill and set up reserves to pay its taxes. A company that is sure its estimated tax savings would come through might reserve very little against the unlikely chance the savings would not occur. *The accuracy of those estimated savings and reserves are then reviewed by the auditor, which in Tyco's case was the same firm, PwC. "You are auditing the validity of a product that you're selling," complains John L. Buckley, Democratic counsel to the House Ways & Means Committee. "It is a gross conflict of interest."*
>
> While it's not known whether PwC did anything wrong because of its dual role, it clearly raises questions about its work After reading a recent SEC filing by Tyco outlining its internal probe of the former CEO, Lynn Turner says that $41 million of a $96 million loan-forgiveness scheme was charged to the balance sheet account for "accrued federal income tax." *Says Turner: "I can't understand how they missed that one."*
>
> *Now, as Tyco's new management attempts to untangle the company's myriad problems, that potential conflict may be coming into sharper focus.* Tyco's new CEO, Edward D. Breen Jr., announced on Sept. 25 that the company would be raising its expected tax rate for 2002 to 22% from the extremely low 18.5% used by prior management. *That will cut earnings of $160 million this year. "It would seem PwC gave Tyco overly aggressive advice," says Prudential Securities Inc. analyst Nicholas P. Heymann.*

Demand Allegations

¶391.   Plaintiffs have not made any demand on the Director Defendants to institute this action since such demand would be a futile and useless act for the following reasons:

(a) The violation of the federal securities laws or other laws, including income-tax evasion or keeping false books or records, cannot constitute legitimate business judgments or good faith conduct of the Company's business. Since these acts constitute violations of the federal securities and other laws including the Bermuda 1981 Companies Act, and breaches of the fiduciary duties owed by Tyco's Board of Directors, these acts are *ultra vires* and incapable of ratification by the Director Defendants. The acts of the Director Defendants in causing Tyco to violate the federal securities and other laws are per se not defensible by any alleged independent business judgment since they constitute illegal acts under such laws;

(b) The Director Defendants have for some time been aware of or recklessly or in gross negligence ignored the wrongs forming the basis for the claims alleged herein and the materiality of such wrongs, but have chosen not to protect Tyco or seek to recover amounts due to it and have failed to take action with respect to these claims because any such action would require them to sue themselves, their families, or their friends and business associates. Prior to the wrongs alleged herein, the Director Defendants also knew, or recklessly or in gross negligence, ignored defendant Kozlowski's and other Tyco executives' misuse of corporate funds, but failed to take any reasonable or adequate steps to remedy the known problems;

(c) The Director Defendants are not independent for the following reasons:

(1) The Board was firmly entrenched and tightly affiliated with defendant Kozlowski. According to Tyco's 2002 Proxy Statement, six of the Director Defendants have been affiliated with Tyco and defendant Kozlowski, either as Tyco or Former Tyco directors for periods between 10 and 20 years. Each of these defendants is closely affiliated with Tyco and is beholden to Tyco for the continuation of their positions;

(2) The Board's Compensation Committee, composed of defendants Foss, Pasman and Slusser, approved all of the policies under which compensation is awarded to Tyco's CEO, defendant Kozlowski and other executives. Tyco's 2002 Proxy Statement describes the duties of the Compensation Committee as follows:

> "The Compensation Committee approves all of the policies under which compensation is paid or awarded to Tyco's Chief Executive Officer, reviews and, as required, approves such policies for executive officers and key managers, and has oversight of the administration of executive compensation programs."

In view of these duties, Foss, Pasman and Slusser either knew or were reckless in not knowing of Kozlowski's and other executives' use of corporate funds for their own personal benefit.

(3) The Audit Committee, which was specifically charged with oversight of financial reporting and supervising of PwC, knew or were reckless in not knowing of the wrongdoing alleged herein;

(4) Defendants Berman and Swartz are Tyco employees and defendant Fort was former Tyco's Chairman and CEO until 1992. Defendant Ashcroft was Chairman and CEO of ADT until it merged with former Tyco in July 1997. Defendants Pasman and Slusser also became Tyco board members when former Tyco merged with ADT in July 1997. Each of these

individuals is closely affiliated with Tyco and was beholden to Tyco and defendant Kozlowski for the continuation of their positions.

(d) Demands to prosecute the claims stated herein were sent to the Tyco Board on February 18, 2002 and June 24, 2002, and yet no action has been taken by the Director Defendants to address the breaches of fiduciary duty at the Board level;

(e) Tyco has agreed to indemnify its directors and officers against liability for acts and omissions in the performance of their duties and maintains insurance policies to cover the costs of indemnification, which policies exclude claims brought by Tyco against its directors. Therefore, the Director Defendants are disabled from complying with any demand to sue themselves because it would result in the loss of their insurance coverage;

(f) The Director Defendants participated in, acquiesced in and/or approved the wrongs alleged herein and did so in affirmative violation of their duties to Tyco and its stockholders and have permitted the wrongs alleged and/or have remained inactive although they have long had knowledge of or were reckless or grossly negligent in ignoring those wrongs. The Director Defendants, therefore, participated in a long-term continuing course of corporate misconduct, mismanagement and waste of corporate assets;

(g) Because of their participation of the mismanagement of Tyco, the Director Defendants are in no position to prosecute this action. Each of them is in an irreconcilable conflict of interest regarding the prosecution of this action, and cannot exercise the requisite independence to make good faith business judgments;

(h) The Director Defendants cannot defend their actions by any alleged "independent" business judgment since each of them is responsible for the wrongs alleged, and have acted knowingly or recklessly or with gross negligence, and each would be required to sue himself or herself;

(i) The Director Defendants cannot defend their actions by any alleged "independent" business judgment in seeking to have this action dismissed or by not bringing this action against themselves, because it would undoubtedly be to the benefit of Tyco to seek recovery of the damages caused by the Director Defendants and to assert these derivative claims; and

(j) Defendants Berman and Fort, as Tyco employees, and defendants Swartz, Ashcroft, Pasman, and Slusser, as former Tyco or ADT employees, and the members of the Compensation Committee and the Audit Committee engaged in the wrongdoing and also constitute a majority of the Board of Directors who are not independent. As the persons primarily responsible for the wrongs complained of herein or beholden to defendant Kozlowski for their jobs with Tyco, they would be required to take legal action against themselves. Courts have specifically excused the demand requirement in circumstances such as this one where a corporation's officers and directors will themselves be defendants in a derivative action. Since defendants Swartz, Berman, Fort, Ashcroft, Pasman, and Slusser and the members of the Compensation Committee and the Audit Committee constitute a majority of the Director Defendants, and thus, they would be able to prevent the Board from taking any action against them.

QUESTIONS

(1)   Have plaintiffs adequately alleged that demand is futile?

(2)   Of what relevance is it to the derivative action that Tyco had hired an attorney, David Bois, to investigate these same allegations when they were made in press reports, and that 25 lawyers and 100 accountants spent 65,000 hours analyzing Tyco's corporate governance problems and financial accounts prior to any derivative actions having been filed?

(3)   How would you advise the company to proceed to respond to this complaint? What arguments would you emphasize, or what procedural steps would you advise the company to take?

CHAPTER

13

Oppression of Minority Shareholders

We have examined various methods of allocating control among shareholders in a closely held corporation, but even the best corporate planners cannot prevent conflict. The potential for conflict is especially acute when one or more shareholders owns a controlling interest in the corporation. This situation raises the possibility of "minority oppression."

From the earliest reported cases involving shareholder disputes, courts have consistently held that the will of the majority of the shareholders governs business corporations in all actions within the bounds of the corporate charter. Nevertheless, Courts are cognizant of the possibility that majority rule will lead to unfair results for minority shareholders. In the early 1800s, courts used a trust metaphor — in which directors were analogous to trustees and shareholders were analogous to beneficiaries of a trust — to impose on directors a fiduciary duty to serve *all* of the stockholders, not just to a select group. The clash of majority rule and universal fidelity resulted in an accommodation in which courts allowed directors to implement the will of the majority subject to limitations imposed through the doctrine of *ultra vires* and prohibitions against fraud and illegality.

Courts used this framework to adjudicate cases that today would often be resolved using the doctrine of minority oppression. Over the course of the nineteenth century, courts slowly changed their approach toward cases brought by minority shareholders. Having concluded that minority shareholders were beneficiaries in a trust relationship, courts were willing to override the usual binding effect of majority rule in certain circumstances. While the most important of those circumstances was labeled "fraud," this became an elastic concept in the hands of equity judges. Even when later judges became less willing to attach the label of "fraud" to actions of majority shareholders, however, they continued to redress the concerns of minority shareholders, increasingly under the rubric of "minority oppression."

Our study of minority oppression is split into three parts. In the first Section we explore the plight of the minority shareholder, which is the impetus for providing an oppression remedy. Observing the minority shareholder's precarious position, we ask, "What — if anything — should the law do to protect the minority shareholder against harm imposed by the majority shareholder?" As we will see, different states have different responses to this question, but most states have concluded that some action is necessary. This leads to the second Section, where we examine various possible remedies for minority oppression, including the traditional remedy of dissolution and the most common modern remedy — the buyout. As we will see, however, courts and legislatures have developed a wide range of other options. Third, we contemplate the possible meanings of "oppression" and consider whether the various definitions produce disparate results in litigated cases.

A.   THE PLIGHT OF THE MINORITY SHAREHOLDER

Traditional corporation laws contemplate centralized control in the board of directors and majority rule, but close corporations are characterized by shareholder participation in management and by the lack of a public market for the corporation's shares. When traditional corporation laws are applied to close corporations, minority shareholders are vulnerable to harm at the hands of the majority. In the classic oppression scenario, a majority shareholder terminates the minority shareholder's employment and refuses to declare dividends. Thus cut off from any financial benefit from his or her equity investment, the minority shareholder might attempt to exit, but the absence of a public market for the corporation's shares combined with the presence of a majority shareholder who has already manifested some hostility to minority shareholders may foreclose this option. Unless, of course, the minority shareholder is willing to sell to the majority. Given the circumstances, however, one would not expect the price of such a sale to reflect the true value of the minority's shares (in the absence of oppression). In short, the minority shareholder in a closely held corporation is easily stuck.

What is the proper response to the minority shareholder's plight? The courts of Massachusetts and Delaware have developed two very different responses. In the absence of legislative guidance, the Massachusetts courts have taken it upon themselves to craft a common law of minority oppression. In the well-known case of Donahue v. Rodd Electrotype Company of New England, 328 N.E.2d 505 (Mass. 1975), the Supreme Judicial Court of Massachusetts held that majority shareholders in a closely held corporation owe each another a heightened fiduciary duty comparable to the duty that partners owe to one another. Quoting Meinhard v. Salmon, the Court described this as a duty of "strict good faith."

The underlying facts of *Donahue* involved a repurchase of shares owned by the founder of Rodd Electrotype Company. The repurchase was authorized by the founder's sons, who remained majority shareholders. The purpose of the repurchase was to distribute assets of the company so that the 77-year-old founder could retire. The only problem with the plan was that Joseph Donahue — a longtime minority shareholder in the company — also wanted to sell his shares, but there was no ready market, and the majority shareholders were unwilling to accommodate him. The Massachusetts court held that the failure to repurchase Donahue's shares constituted a breach of duty by the controlling shareholders. In the process, the court fashioned an "equal opportunity" rule: "If the stockholder whose shares were purchased was a member of the controlling group, the controlling stockholders must cause the corporation to offer each stockholder an equal opportunity to sell a ratable number of his shares to the corporation at an identical price."

The Delaware Supreme Court responded to *Donahue* (18 years after the Massachusetts court spoke!) in Nixon v. Blackwell, 626 A.2D 1366 (Del. 1993). The Delaware Court went out of its way to address the issue: "Whether there should be any special, judicially-created rules to 'protect' minority stockholders of closely-held Delaware corporations." The answer was resoundingly negative:

> The case at bar points up the basic dilemma of minority stockholders in receiving fair value for their stock as to which there is no market and no market valuation. It is not difficult to be sympathetic, in the abstract, to a stockholder who finds himself or herself in that position. A stockholder who bargains for stock in a closely-held corporation and who pays for those shares (unlike the plaintiffs in this case who acquired their stock through gift) can make a business judgment whether to buy into such a minority position, and if so on what terms. One could bargain for definitive provisions of self-ordering permitted to a Delaware corporation through the certificate of incorporation or by-laws. . . . Moreover, in addition to such mechanisms, a stockholder intending to buy into a minority position in a Delaware corporation may enter into definitive stockholder agreements, and such agreements may provide for elaborate earnings tests, buy-out provisions, voting trusts, or other voting agreements.
>
> The tools of good corporate practice are designed to give a purchasing minority stockholder the opportunity to bargain for protection before parting with consideration. It would do violence to normal corporate practice and our corporation law to fashion an ad hoc ruling which would result in a court-imposed stockholder buy-out for which the parties had not contracted.

The Delaware Supreme Court was not the only court with reservations about *Donahue*. Indeed, only one year after deciding *Donahue*, the Massachusetts Supreme Judicial Court reconsidered its position in Wilkes v. Springside Nursing Home, Inc., 370 Mass. 842 (Mass. 1976), stating:

> [W]e are concerned that untempered application of the strict good faith standard enunciated in *Donahue* . . . will result in the imposition of limitations on legitimate action by the controlling group in a close corporation which will unduly hamper its effectiveness in managing the corporation in the best interests of all concerned.

Wilkes involved a corporation with four shareholders, each of whom owned an equal number of shares. According to the court, the four men had an understanding that

> each would be a director . . . and each would participate actively in the management and decision making involved in operating the corporation. It was, further, the understanding and intention of all the parties that, corporate resources permitting, each would receive money from the corporation in equal amounts as long as each assumed an active and ongoing responsibility for carrying a portion of the burdens necessary to operate the business.

The corporation operated in apparent harmony for 14 years, when two of the shareholders came to cross purposes over a property transaction. This dispute ultimately led to the isolation of one of the shareholders (Wilkes), who decided to exit. Before Wilkes could work out an amicable separation, the other three shareholders discontinued his salary and refused to reelect him as a director or officer of the company. Examining Wilkes' claim in light of *Donahue*, the court reasoned:

> [W]hen minority stockholders in a close corporation bring suit against the majority alleging a breach of the strict good faith duty owed to them by the majority, we must carefully analyze the action taken by the controlling stockholders in the individual case. It must be asked whether the controlling group can demonstrate a legitimate business purpose for its action. In asking this question, we acknowledge the fact that the controlling group in a close corporation must have some room to maneuver in establishing the business policy of the corporation. It must have a large measure of discretion, for example, in declaring or withholding dividends, deciding whether to merge or consolidate, establishing the salaries of corporate officers, dismissing directors with or without cause, and hiring and firing corporate employees.
>
> When an asserted business purpose for their action is advanced by the majority, however, we think it is open to minority stockholders to demonstrate that the same legitimate objective could have been achieved through an alternative course of action less harmful to the minority's interest. If called on to settle a dispute, our courts must weigh the legitimate business purpose, if any, against the practicability of a less harmful alternative.

Even under this less stringent application of fiduciary duty, the court held that the majority shareholders in *Wilkes* had breached their fiduciary duty: "It is an inescapable conclusion from all the evidence that the action of the majority stockholders here was a designed 'freeze out' for which no legitimate business purpose has been suggested."

The Delaware Supreme Court also had an opportunity to respond to *Wilkes*. In Riblet Products Corporation v. Nagy, 683 A.2d 37 (Del. 1996), the Court considered a claim by a minority shareholder (Nagy), who was also the chief executive officer of his corporation. The lawsuit arose after Nagy was fired, in breach of his employment contract. Although the Delaware court could have ignored *Wilkes* — as the court noted, "Nagy does not allege that his termination amounted to a wrongful freeze out of his stock interest in Riblet, nor does he contend that he was harmed as a stockholder by being terminated" — it stated emphatically, "*Wilkes* has not been adopted as Delaware law." As illustrated by *Nixon* and *Riblet*, minority shareholders are more vulnerable in Delaware than in any other state.

The case below is a recent example of the Massachusetts courts at work. As you read *Leslie*, consider whether the judge has remained true to the policies that animated the *Donahue* and *Wilkes* decisions. Contrast the Massachusetts and Delaware approaches and strive to understand why these two states take such different approaches.

LESLIE v. BOSTON SOFTWARE COLLABORATIVE, INC.

14 Mass. L. Rptr. 379
Superior Court of Massachusetts
February 12, 2002

VAN GESTEL, Justice.

This matter is before the Court, after a jury-waived trial, for findings of fact, rulings of law and an order for judgment.

FINDINGS OF FACT

In 1993, Mark Khayter ("Khayter"), Robert F. Goulart ("Goulart") and Dennis J. Leslie ("Leslie") entered into a simple partnership known as Boston Software Collaborative. Shortly thereafter, in September of 1994, the partnership business was incorporated in Massachusetts as Boston Software Collaborative, Inc. ("BSC"). BSC remains a corporation today.

When the partnership was established, Khayter, Goulart and Leslie each contributed $200 as start-up money.

From its inception to at least April 26, 2000, Leslie was an employee of BSC. Until June 12, 2000, he held the positions of treasurer and a director, and he at all times has been an approximately one-third shareholder.

Khayter at all times has been the president and chief executive officer of BSC, and at all times has been a director and an approximately one-third shareholder.

Goulart at all times has been the clerk of BSC, and he assumed the role of treasurer in June of 2000. He also at all times has been a director and an approximately one-third shareholder.

For tax purposes, BSC has elected to be treated as an S Corporation.

The corporate records for BSC are casual and somewhat incomplete. It is unclear, for example, whether any by-laws were ever formally adopted, although an unsigned version of a common form of by-laws — with the place for the name of the corporation to which they apply left blank — was proffered by the defendants over objection. Also, a reading of the minutes of shareholders' and directors' meetings exhibits a somewhat simplistic approach. The minutes seem more like notes of a club meeting than the formalized recording of corporate action.

Even the exact number of shares outstanding and the identity of all the shareholders is not without its uncertainty. In addition to Khayter, Goulart and Leslie, it appears that at least one other person, named Michael Bronshvayg ("Bronshvayg"), owns an inconsequentially small number of shares, and there is the possibility that a man named J. Houghton ("Houghton") may also own a still smaller number of shares. Both Bronshvayg and Houghton are employees of BSC, but not directors or officers.

BSC, in any event, is and always has been a closely-held corporation. It has a small number of shareholders, with Khayter, Goulart and Leslie each holding nearly one-third of the shares, and collectively holding in excess of 97% of all outstanding shares; there is no ready market for the BSC stock; and there is substantial majority shareholder participation in the management, direction and operations of the corporation. All of the shareholders, at least until Leslie's termination in June of 2000, were employees; and Khayter, Goulart and Leslie were, until that same time, the only directors.

Each of Khayter, Goulart and Leslie brought different skills and talents to BSC. All three were software engineers, of apparently somewhat different technical skills. Khayter seems to be the most technically proficient; Goulart's abilities are best expressed in the marketing area; and Leslie had an appetite, and some skills, for administrative and office management functions. Thus, at the start at least, they complemented each other for the general benefit of the business.

The method of compensation of the three principals created friction as the company grew. The nature of the product BSC provides is technical services in software engineering by its employees, including the principals, and by independent consultants to outside customers in need of such services for special projects. Clients, for the most part, are billed on hourly rates, and much of the work is performed physically at client sites. The analogy to a small- or medium-sized law firm is apt in many respects.

Up until early 1999, the great bulk of the compensation for the principals was allocated based upon the billings for their services. Since Leslie was doing more of the administrative and management work in the office, this scheme tended to put Leslie at the low end of the compensation ladder because office work did not result in billable hours. For example, the salaries and other compensation, not counting "distributions" which were equal for each principal, for the period from fiscal 1995 through fiscal 1998, were as follows:

	Fiscal 1995	Fiscal 1996	Fiscal 1997	Fiscal 1998
Khayter	$160,052	$148,195	$264,618	$151,180
Goulart	$171,990	$190,904	$265,785	$224,000
Leslie	$50,091	$144,382	$163,793	$103,338

Each of the principals received equal "distributions" in each of the fiscal years from 1995 through 1999 in the following amounts: 1995— $60,000; 1996—$80,000; 1997—$89,280; 1998—$47,500; and 1999—$62,000.[4]

For the fiscal years from 1995 through 1998, the principals averaged per year the following numbers of billable hours charged to clients: Khayter—2,065; Goulart—2036; and Leslie—876.

Again, over the four fiscal years from 1995 through 1998, the total revenues brought to BSC on time and materials billing for each of the three principals were: Khayter—$788,497; Goulart—$889,565; and Leslie—$296,749.

In late 1998, there was a possibility of selling BSC. At about that time, the principals agreed to change to a compensation scheme that essentially equalized their total compensation without reference to billable hours, as well as their distribution. Under this plan each of the principals was to be paid at a rate of about $157,000 per year, before any distributions. Khayter and Goulart insist that this plan was only to stay in effect for about six months until the company was sold. Leslie disagrees. In any event, the plan was still in operation until the spring of 2000, and Leslie never did agree to change it.

Friction began to emerge between Leslie, on the one hand, and Khayter and Goulart, on the other. There were issues over compensation, technical proficiency, economic contributions, employee dissatisfaction and customer complaints. Essentially, Leslie felt under-compensated because he contributed more to the non-billable, office administration end of the business. Khayter and Goulart felt that they worked harder, billed more and were technically much more proficient that Leslie and, therefore, were properly compensated at a higher level.

Credible examples of complaints about Leslie from employees and customers were presented. For the most part, at least on an incident-by-incident basis,

---

4. It is not wholly clear what the "distributions" were intended to be. They were called different things by each principal. They seem somewhat like distributions of year-end profits in a partnership, although they were not always paid just at year-end; or they may be like dividends in a corporation.

these were not matters of the magnitude that would ordinarily be seen as a justification for terminating a partner in a partnership or a shareholder in a closely held corporation.

For example, a number of employees complained that Leslie spent too much time working on personal matters while at the office, particularly emphasizing the work he did when he was in the process of building a new home in New Hampshire. Also, Leslie has an obviously brusque approach that employees found unpleasant. Some said he swore too much or at inappropriate times, and others reported on crude ethnic slurs that he tended to use.

One young employee was critical of Leslie's direction to her that she should not wear farmer-type overalls to work because "she looked like a New Hampshire hick." She was from New Hampshire. This same employee was upset that Leslie moved her desk because, he said, she was talking too much to fellow workers and was a distraction. Again from this employee, there was recited an occasion when Leslie, while driving her to a train station, first pleasantly reported to her about a raise in pay and then burst into a profanity-laced discourse about the company and another employee in particular. She felt intimidated and when she arrived home telephoned Goulart, asking for assistance.

In the late fall of 1999, three key employees threatened to quit BSC because of their concerns about working with Leslie or in a company run by him. They did not quit after discussing the matter with Goulart and receiving additional compensation.

There was a complaint in April 2000, revealed in a series of e-mails with one employee, about the timing of deposits into employees' 401(k) plans. Leslie's response to a fairly innocuous question was:

> Who the hell do you think your [sic] talking too [sic]! First of all don't take that tone of an e-mail with me . . . I have been administering the 401k for years and no one, not even you gets to talk to me in this manner. Your [sic] god damn money was sent out with everyone else's and if they haven't credited into your account we will look into it and find out what the issue is. If your [sic] having a bad day, get over it . . . Don't ever send me another e-mail like this again.

The customer complaints were generally in the nature of observations that Leslie was being billed as a senior software engineer but did not demonstrate commensurate skills, that his work took too much time to complete or was such that the customers did not want him to be assigned to their projects.

As noted above, by the end of 1999, the company not having been sold, Khayter and Goulart were anxious to return to the former time-and-materials, hourly billing method of compensation, and Leslie resisted. Finally, Khayter instructed Leslie to direct the office manager to make the change. Leslie, however, did not follow those instructions.

Leslie, in the spring of 2000, had been confiding many of his concerns about the company, its financial affairs and its future to Donald Follansbee ("Follansbee"), the new head of marketing for BSC. Near the end of April 2000, Leslie had told Follansbee of the possibility that he might leave the company. Apparently, on the evening of April 25, 2000, Leslie and his wife talked extensively about his future with BSC, and Leslie remained up the entire night considering the situation. Then, at 7:07 A.M. on April 26, 2000, Leslie sent an e-mail to

Follansbee that read as follows:

> Your [sic] Stuck With Me . . .
> After all that aggravation I have to go through, my wife insists that I stay.
> She reserves the right to shoot Bob and (or) Mark at a moments [sic] notice or at
> a minimum to severely injure them for what they are putting her through.
> But they are not going to take my vacation without a fight.

Later that day, Follansbee sent an e-mail to Khayter and Goulart that included
Leslie's e-mail to him. Follansbee's e-mail read:

> I received this message this morning and wanted to forward it on to you. As we
> discussed last night I will plan to be at BSC all day on Friday. I have not sent this
> message through the BSC server. Millennium and Mediaone were used. I have
> also switched off my BSC phone because I have several messages already from
> Dennis and I really do not want to get into a discussion over this.

Khayter and Goulart made a joint telephone call to Leslie late in the day on
April 26, 2000. They advised Leslie that he was being put on unpaid leave, that
he should not come to the BSC offices, that he should not communicate with
BSC personnel, and that he should appear at the offices of Palmer & Dodge,
the company's counsel, on Friday, April 28, 2000, for a meeting to discuss the
situation. They also told Leslie not to bring his gun to the meeting.

Leslie had a permit to carry a firearm and apparently did so from time to
time. On one occasion, for example, when BSC was located at 294 Washington
Street in Boston, Leslie had to go over to the post office in Post Office Square.
Because he could not bring his gun with him, he put it in the drawer of the
woman then acting as office manager. She protested that it made her nervous
to have the gun there, but he declined to remove it.

Khayter and Goulart were concerned about the shooting threat in Leslie's
April 26, 2000 e-mail to Follansbee. Leslie claims it was a "joke" and, in any
event, he did not expect Follansbee to forward the e-mail on to anyone. Khayter
and Goulart considered the shooting threat to be the final step in an expanding
deterioration of their relationship with Leslie and, thus, put him on unpaid
leave.

At the meeting at Palmer & Dodge on April 28, 2000, only the three principals were present. No lawyers were included in the conversation. Khayter
and Goulart presented Leslie with a document, prepared by a Palmer & Dodge
lawyer, entitled "Separation Agreement and Release." In essence, the document, in return for Leslie's termination of employment with BSC and a release
of all claims against it, offered Leslie: severance of 10 weeks pay, or less if he got
another job before that; a relationship with BSC in a consulting capacity if BSC
chose to do so; the possibility that BSC "may attempt" to locate and provide
contract opportunities for Leslie; payment of his accumulated vacation time at
his current hourly rate; and continuance of his medical insurance at least until
December 31, 2000. Leslie did not accept the proposal.

A modified proposal, not significantly more generous in terms, was later
tendered by Khayter and Goulart and also not accepted by Leslie.

On June 6, 2000, Leslie received notice of a June 12, 2000 shareholders
meeting to take place at Palmer & Dodge. The purpose for the meeting was

said to be: (1) the removal of Leslie as the company's 401(k) trustee; (2) the appointment of Goulart as the company's 401(k) trustee; and (3) the removal of Leslie as a director of BSC. A proxy accompanied the notice.

Leslie did not attend the shareholders' meeting, but he did send in his proxy, which he signed and dated June 8, 2000. In his proxy, Leslie voted in favor of his own removal as the company's 401(k) trustee and the appointment of Goulart to take over that position. He voted against his removal from the board of directors. The minutes of the meeting reflect that the first two questions — Leslie's removal and Goulart's appointment as 401(k) trustee — carried with 276,000 in favor and 24,000 abstaining. The vote to remove Leslie as a director carried with 184,000 in favor, 92,000 against and 24,000 abstaining.

The shareholders' meeting minutes recite that the meeting lasted five minutes, beginning at 4:15 P.M. and adjourning at 4:20 P.M.

Also on June 12, 2000, there was a BSC directors meeting. Leslie, however, never received notice of that meeting. Its minutes recite that the meeting lasted for 10 minutes, beginning at 4:00 P.M. and adjourning at 4:10 P.M. Leslie, thus, was still a director as of the time of, and throughout, this meeting.

There were two items voted on at the directors meeting: (1) to remove Leslie as treasurer of BSC; and (2) to appoint Goulart as treasurer. Khayter and Goulart each are recorded as voting in favor, and Leslie, who was not there, is designated as "Abstained (not present)."

Leslie, aside from a distribution of $62,000 for fiscal year 1999, and being paid for his accumulated vacation, has received no further compensation payments from BSC since his termination, and no dividends or other distributions have been paid to him since that time.

Although he is said to be unemployed currently, Leslie earned between $190,000 and $230,000 in software consulting income since June of 2000.

Shortly after Leslie was terminated at BSC, Khayter and Goulart increased their personal compensation by almost the amount previously being paid in compensation to Leslie. As a result, they each started earning at a rate of approximately $240,000 per year. Also in September 2000, Khayter and Goulart, for the first time, included themselves in the employee bonus plan. As a result, they each received an additional $45,000. They also, like Leslie, cashed out their accumulated vacation pay.

There have been no further "distributions" since those made in fiscal year 1999, and the company now appears to be experiencing a time of reduced income and profits because of the current economic slowdown.

Leslie complains that, in addition to the foregoing and despite the tempered economic conditions, Khayter and Goulart are mismanaging the BSC business. He cites four things in particular: (1) raises given to certain employees; (2) expenditures to establish a presence in the Atlanta, Georgia market; (3) increasing employee benefits to give them short- and long-term disability, life insurance and dental care; and (4) moving the BSC offices from 31 Milk Street to 50 Congress Street in Boston.

Leslie also claims that the compensation currently being paid to Khayter and Goulart is excessive. On this latter point, BSC presented an expert witness skilled in assessing and advising on competitiveness and fairness in executive compensation. The Court found that while the expert was fully qualified, his testimony was of only moderate assistance because, mostly, what he did was examine information from outside website data bases, particularly that of an entity called the Economic Research Institute or "ERI." The data base of ERI seems thorough and extensive. It suggests — and the expert's additional research seems to corroborate — that Khatyer's and Goulart's current compensation falls within the mid-point to slightly higher than the mid-point of executives performing their kind of work for companies of BSC's size and earnings.

Additionally, the Court observes Leslie's August 4, 2000 e-mail in which he recommended that Follansbee be made CEO and compensated at a rate that ultimately would be higher than that now being paid to Khayter and Goulart.

Standing alone, Khayter's and Goulart's compensation is reasonable, and the Court so finds.

The Complaint is structured somewhat differently from the norm. It has two sections: one is designated Direct Action; the other is called Derivative Action. Nothing is called a "count."

In the Direct Action section, Leslie, on his own behalf, charges the defendants with: A — failure to pay dividends; B — wrongful termination; and C — freeze-out.

In the Derivative Action section, Leslie complains and seeks judgment derivatively in favor of BSC against Khayter and Goulart for waste of corporate assets and breach of fiduciary duty.

[Only the Direct Action section will be discussed in this excerpted version of the opinion.]

RULINGS OF LAW

BSC is a close corporation established under the laws of the Commonwealth. Donahue v. Rodd Electrotype Co. of New England, Inc., 367 Mass. 578, 586 (1975). It is "typified by: (1) a small number of stockholders; (2) no ready market for the corporate stock; and (3) substantial majority stockholder participation in the management, direction and operations of the corporation." *Id.*

Thus, BSC "bears a striking resemblance to a partnership." *Id.* . . .

Leslie, here, finds himself in the position of a frozen-out minority shareholder. He is "cut off from all corporation-related revenues [and] must either suffer [his] losses or seek a buyer for [his] shares. . . . [He] . . . anticipated that his salary from his position with the corporation would be his livelihood. Thus, he cannot afford to wait passively." *Id.* at 591.

Despite the [language of *Donahue*], the duties placed on shareholders in a close corporation are not meant to impose a straitjacket on legitimate corporate activity. The fiduciary duty imposed does not limit "legitimate action by the controlling group in a close corporation" that is taken to manage the corporation "in the best interests of all concerned." Wilkes v. Springside Nursing Home, Inc., 370 Mass. 842, 851 (1976).

"The controlling group in a close corporation must have some room to maneuver in establishing the business policy of the corporation." *Wilkes,* 370 Mass. at 851. This Court must, therefore, carefully analyze the action taken by Khayter and Goulart in this case. The overriding question to be determined is "whether the[y] . . . can demonstrate a legitimate business purpose for [their] action." *Id.* In this regard, Khayter and Goulart "must have a large measure of discretion, for example, in declaring or withholding dividends, . . . establishing the salaries of corporate officers, dismissing directors with or without cause, and hiring and firing corporate employees." *Id.*

"When an asserted business purpose for their action is advanced by the majority, . . . it is open to the minority . . . to demonstrate that the same legitimate objective could have been achieved through an alternative course of action less harmful to the minority's interest." *Wilkes,* 370 Mass. at 851-52. This Court must, therefore, "weigh the legitimate business purpose, if any, against the practicability of a less harmful alternative." *Wilkes,* 370 Mass. at 852.

DIRECT ACTION

Here, the majority — Khayter and Goulart — terminated Leslie's employment, removed him as company treasurer, voted him off the board of directors and since have paid him no dividends or distributions. Leslie was hardly a model employee. At the same time, as a founder and a nearly one-third minority shareholder, he was entitled to the utmost good faith and fair dealing. That he did not receive.

With an ordinary employee, not entitled to partner-like treatment, the termination of Leslie was justified. Given Leslie's enhanced status as an owner, however, Khayter and Goulart did not act in a manner demonstrating the utmost good faith.

In any event, to this Court, after weighing the situation, there appear to have been less harmful alternatives open to Khayter and Goulart than the blunt course they followed. For example, Leslie's administrative functions could have been modified such that he could have been insulated from direct contact with the BSC employees by using Follansbee as the intermediary. Leslie could have been encouraged — and assisted — in becoming more extensively involved in off-site, time-and-materials billing projects. He could have been directed to take courses and training to upgrade his technical skills. Other incentives through the use of creative compensation techniques could have been explored. Clearly, there was no demonstrated need to force him off the board of directors and thereby cut off his access and knowledge about the day-to-day affairs of the company. In short, Khayter and Goulart did not have to so completely, fully and abruptly bring Leslie's participation to a complete halt without first making a serious attempt to solve the problem in other ways.

The resolution proposed at the Palmer & Dodge meeting on April 28, 2000, can hardly be seen as a serious effort to resolve a complex corporate issue among people who were duty bound to treat each other as partners. Ten weeks' severance pay, some accrued vacation, and a non-binding suggestion of the possibility of getting some work as a consultant in return for total termination of employment and a general release do not fit any reasonable definition of acting with the "utmost good faith and loyalty" by Khayter and Goulart to their "partner," Leslie.

"Equitable remedies are flexible tools to be applied with a focus on fairness and justice." Demoulas v. Demoulas, 428 Mass. 555, 580 (1998).

What then is appropriate by way of an equitable solution for Leslie? Even he, in his opposition to a motion in limine to exclude expert valuation testimony, concedes that returning him to his former position at BSC is not a desirable remedy. He said in that opposition: "This forced continuance of the corporate marriage would most likely result in future litigation such that it is not a remedy that will resolve the damage done nor prevent further similar damage in the future."

At the same time, the case law does not support, nor does this Court think it a proper equitable resolution on the facts presented, a compelled buy-out of Leslie's shares by BSC or Khayter and Goulart at some artificially determined value. Here, unlike in *Demoulas*, 428 Mass. 555, or Crowley v. Communications for Hospitals, Inc., 30 Mass. App. Ct. 751 (1991), none of the stockholders has received any monetary benefit from the purchase or sale of their shares.

Leslie's participation as an employee is, like the fallen egg, broken beyond repair. His return to BSC, as such, would not be in the best interest of the corporation or any of its shareholders, including Leslie himself.

In exercising its "broad powers to determine the appropriate relief 'to remedy the wrong complained of and make the [judgment] effective,'" *Demoulas*, 428 Mass. at 591, three things need attention by the Court: (1) fair compensation to Leslie for his loss of employment; (2) fair compensation to Leslie for any amounts received by Khayter and Goulart in the nature of a dividend; and (3) provision for Leslie, for so long as he remains a shareholder, to be able to monitor the management of BSC and participate in the returns to shareholders, without interfering unduly therein.

Because Leslie's reinstatement as an employee is unworkable, he is entitled to a fair severance award. In assaying what is fair, the Court has considered what he was making by way of compensation as an employee when terminated, as well as the $190,000 to $230,000 he made in the period following June 2000. Under all of the circumstances, this Court considers and awards severance for the period from May 1, 2000 through December 31, 2000, at Leslie's annual rate of $157,000 per year, which here amounts to $104,667.

Additionally, this Court concludes that the $45,000 "employee bonus" payments that Khayter and Goulart awarded themselves at the end of fiscal 1999, are nothing more than distributions or dividends of the kind previously made to shareholders. Consequently, Leslie is entitled to an equal payment of $45,000.

Also, hereafter any payments made to Khayter or Goulart that are not the functional equivalent of salary for work actually performed, as opposed to net profits of BSC, and exclusive of reasonable payments in lieu of vacation and reasonable benefits, should be made in an equal amount, and at the same time, to Leslie.

Finally, Leslie should be reinstated as a full voting member of the BSC board of directors so that he may be as fully aware as that position reasonably permits about the management and operation of BSC, and so that he may constructively participate in that management insofar as a director may properly do so.

It is to be observed that none of the foregoing is meant to compel the payment of any dividends by BSC. The directors of the corporation retain their wide discretion with regard to the decision whether to declare any dividends at all, as well as the amount of any such dividends. What must not be done is to make payments only to the majority shareholders, payments having different names or styles but being in reality dividends. . . .

ORDER FOR JUDGMENT

Based upon the foregoing findings of fact and rulings of law, the Court *ORDERS* the entry of judgment in favor of the plaintiff Dennis J. Leslie, individually, against Boston Software Collaborative, Inc. only, in the amount of $149,667, together with costs and interest at the statutory rate from May 1, 2000.

The Court further *ORDERS* judgment against all defendants: that hereafter, for so long as Dennis F. Leslie remains a shareholder, any payments made to Mark Khayter or Robert F. Goulart that are not the functional equivalent of compensation for work actually performed, as opposed to net profits of Boston Software Collaborative, Inc., and exclusive of reasonable payments in lieu of vacations and reasonable benefits, shall be made in an equal amount, and at the same time, to Dennis J. Leslie; and that Dennis J. Leslie shall be reinstated forthwith as a member of the Board of Directors of Boston Software Collaborative, Inc.

Judgment shall be entered for the defendants dismissing all of the derivative claims brought by Dennis J. Leslie on behalf of Boston Software Collaborative, Inc. . . .

PROBLEM 13-1

Like many Internet companies in the late 1990s, Mirror Image Internet, Inc. (MII) was losing money from its operations and desperately needed additional financing to stay alive. Formed in 1997 as a wholly owned subsidiary of Mirror AB, a Swedish company (Mirror), MII found several willing investors in March 1999. Xcelera Inc. invested $1.75 million in exchange for a 62.5 percent interest, and Plenteous Corp. (along with two other smaller investors) contributed $250,000 in exchange for minority interests in MII. In addition to the usual control rights associated with common stock, Xcelera and Plenteous obtained the right (voting together) to elect four directors to MII's board. Mirror retained the right to elect one director.

Almost immediately, Xcelera asserted its control by initiating a series of three stock issuances. The first two transactions — in April and July 1999, respectively — involved the sale of additional shares of common stock by MII to Xcelera. The shares sold to Xcelera in the March round of investments were priced at approximately $516 per share. In these two subsequent investment rounds, Xcelera caused MII to issue the additional shares at the same price. The minority shareholders unsuccessfully attempted to block the investments, then later tried to subscribe for a prorata share, asserting an "implied" contractual right to maintain their ownership interests in MII. In the end, Xcelera purchased all of the new shares of stock, thereby increasing its ownership interest in the company to 91.8 percent.

The third transaction involved an issuance of convertible preferred stock to Xcelera in November 1999. Each share of such stock was convertible into three shares of common stock. If the price of the preferred shares were converted into a price for common shares, each share of common stock would have sold for $4,260.

Within weeks of consummating the preferred stock transaction, MII announced a strategic alliance with Hewlett-Packard (HP) under which HP would invest $32 million in MII. In the wake of this announcement, the price of Xcelera's publicly traded stock rose from $67 to $160. Two months later, after well-known technology analyst George Gilder publicly touted MII's technology, Xcelera's stock price rose to $190.

The minority shareholders in MII claimed that no business reasons supported the three issuances of additional shares of MII stock to Xcelera. The sole purpose of these transactions, they claimed, was to increase Xcelera's ownership interest in MII at the expense of the minority shareholders.

If you were representing the minority shareholders, what facts would be most relevant to your claim of minority oppression (breach of fiduciary duty)?

B. REMEDIES FOR MINORITY OPPRESSION

We have just seen how courts have responded to the problem of minority oppression. Legislatures also have played a role by adopting special close corporation statutes. While corporation statutes have long allowed for judicial dissolution of a corporation in cases of illegality and fraud, many modern statutes also provide for judicial dissolution based on "oppressive conduct" by the majority shareholder. Indeed, this is now the most common ground for dissolution in litigated cases.

Legislatures also have provided additional remedies as alternatives to dissolution. The most common alternate remedy is the buyout, which is now available in half of the states. Moreover, courts have become increasingly willing to use buyouts as a relief, even if it is not provided by statute. Model Business Corporation Act (Model Act) §14.34 permits the corporation or the shareholders to purchase the shares of a shareholder petitioning for dissolution. The purpose of §14.34 is to ensure that minority shareholders do not use judicial dissolution strategically.

In addition to buyouts, many statutes now authorize appointment of a custodian or provisional director. Others allow for canceling or altering the charter, the bylaws, or a corporate resolution; directing or prohibiting any act of the corporation, shareholders, directors, officers, or other persons; selling all the property and franchises of the corporation to a single purchaser; and paying dividends or damages. Finally, some statutes simply empower courts to provide any equitable relief that the court deems appropriate.

Under Model Act §14.30, shareholders may seek judicial dissolution if (a) directors and shareholders are deadlocked and irreparable injury to the corporation is threatened or the business and affairs of the corporation can no longer be conducted to the advantage of the shareholders; (b) control persons are engaging in illegal, oppressive, or fraudulent conduct; (c) shareholders cannot elect directors for two consecutive years; and (d) corporate assets are being misapplied or wasted. Model Act §14.32 allows the court to appoint a receiver or custodian to the corporation. A receiver is responsible for winding up and liquidating the corporation. A custodian manages the corporation and is responsible largely for staying the course. In addition, as noted above,

Model Act §14.34 permits the court to order a buyout upon the election of the nonpetitioning shareholders.

The following case explores issues relating to remedies for minority oppression. *Naito* is a well-publicized Oregon case in which the trial court imposed a multifaceted remedy in an attempt to ensure the long-term viability of a large, family-owned corporation.

NAITO v. NAITO

35 P.3d 1068
Court of Appeals of Oregon
November 14, 2001

EDMONDS, P.J.

Plaintiffs are four shareholders of H. Naito Corporation (the corporation) and the spouses of three of them. In this action, they assert a number of claims against the corporation and four of its directors, who include the controlling shareholder. Defendants appeal a judgment that was based on the trial court's finding that the corporation and the controlling shareholder had acted oppressively toward plaintiffs. . . . As a remedy, the court ordered defendants to elect one of the plaintiffs to the corporation's board, required the corporation to pay dividends of $710,000 for every year that its net income is at least $1.3 million, and imposed various requirements concerning its future corporate structure. . . . Plaintiffs cross-appeal in several respects. On the appeal, we vacate the judgment and remand for modification. We affirm on the cross-appeal.

Because the claims in this case are equitable, we state the facts as we find them on de novo review, giving appropriate weight to the trial court's credibility findings. The case involves a family business that has played a prominent role in Portland for many years. All of the current shareholders are members of the family. Hide Naito (Hide), the founder, was a Japanese immigrant who came to this country in the early part of the twentieth century. In 1921, he started H. Naito Gifts, a small shop in downtown Portland that sold merchandise imported from Japan. Hide gradually expanded the business to additional locations and began selling at wholesale as well as retail. In 1938, he opened his own warehouse in what is now known as the Old Town area of Portland. During World War II, Hide and his family moved to Salt Lake City, thus avoiding internment, but the business essentially collapsed. Hide and his son Samuel Naito (Sam) reestablished the business in the years following the war. His younger son, William Naito (Bill), later joined them in the business. The wholesale business sold Asian giftware to thousands of gift shops and larger retailers around the country; at some point, the wholesale part of the business came to dominate the enterprise. The business was incorporated in 1958 as the Norcrest China Company. Hide continued working in it until a few years before his death in 1989, although Bill and Sam owned the controlling stock by 1980. Bill was the president when he died in May 1996. Sam is currently the president and chief executive officer. . . .

Over the years, Sam and Bill held various titles in the corporation, but in practice they owned the only voting stock and ran the business together after Hide's role declined. Sam focused his efforts on the retail side of the business, while

Bill managed and developed the real estate interests and dealt with the corporation's various lenders. Their relationship was both close and contentious; they frequently argued with each other, but they also relied on each other and made all significant decisions jointly. Bill was the driving force behind the riskier decisions. Some members of Sam's family and, to some extent, Sam himself, resented what they saw as Bill's attempts to dominate Sam, to denigrate his ability, and to push him into ventures that he might have preferred to avoid.

Sam and Bill had significantly different approaches to corporate decisions. Although each tended to ruminate about issues, and neither made up his mind quickly, Bill tended to take risks while Sam was more cautious. [The company's most visible] projects were primarily Bill's ideas, and each was a risky venture that involved a new direction for the corporation. Although each project proved to be successful, many members of the Naito family, including some of Bill's and Sam's children, were not comfortable with what they referred to as Bill's "empire building." Bill also played a more prominent role in Portland civic life and received more publicity than did Sam; some in the family thought that Bill wanted to give the impression that he was bright and creative while Sam simply plodded along. Over the years, these and other issues led to resentments between Bill and his family and Sam and his family, resentments that affected the parties after Bill died.

Sam's and Bill's goals for the corporation emphasized the growth of its overall value rather than immediate returns; they also tried to avoid receiving income in ways that required paying taxes. Thus, neither of them received a large salary. Rather, much of their compensation came in various other ways, including loans and other forms that were not immediately taxable. Sam's wife, Mary Naito (Mary), and Bill's wife, Millicent Naito (Micki), each worked for the business for over 15 years without receiving any salary, in part to avoid paying additional social security taxes. Mary was still working at the time of trial. Salaries for children working in the business were generally well below market rates for comparable positions, although they could receive informal compensation, such as living at McCormick Pier for little or no rent. The fringe benefits that the corporation provided to its employees, including members of the Naito family, were modest at best. The only corporate dividend came in 1982. Employment with the corporation was, as a practical matter, the only way that shareholders could receive any immediate benefit from their shares. Before Bill's death, there was a general understanding in the family that any member of the third generation who wanted employment in the family business would receive it.

The corporation has two classifications of stock. There are presently 1,000 shares of class A stock, which have full voting rights. At Bill's death, Sam and Bill each owned 500 of those shares. Bill's shares passed to Micki, subject to a provision of the buy-sell agreement that we discuss below. There are also 29,380 shares of class B stock, which have no voting rights but are otherwise equal to the class A stock. At the time of Bill's death, Sam and his family and Bill and his family each owned one-half of the class B shares. The third generation received shares by gifts from Hide and from their respective fathers. Each child now owns or controls significant amounts of Class B stock, as do Sam and Micki.

Sam and Mary have three children: Ron Naito, Larry Naito, and Verne Naito. Ron is a physician who does not take an active role in the business. When Bill died, Larry was the general manager of [one of the company's businesses]. He worked for that entity throughout the liability phase of this litigation, but his employment terminated before the remedies phase began. Verne is a certified public accountant. Before Bill's death, he had not worked for the corporation in any significant way.

Bill and Micki have four children: Robert Naito (Bob), Steven Naito, Anne Naito-Campbell, and Kenneth Naito (Ken). Bob worked with his father in the real estate side of the family corporation, including handling relationships with its lenders, for about 20 years. He also operated an ice cream store. . . . Beginning in 1994, he spent two years with another enterprise, but he returned to employment with the corporation a short time before Bill's death. Steve is a lawyer who had not worked for the corporation in any significant way before Bill's death. Anne began working [for the company] shortly after college. In early 1998, she moved to the corporate headquarters to work in public relations. After Bill's death, and before she became a plaintiff in this case, she represented the corporation in various civic organizations. Ken worked [for the company] for many years but now owns and operates restaurants in Washington state.

A problem that underlies many of the issues in this case is the question of what role that the members of the third generation of Naitos will play in the business and what benefits they will receive from it, given that generation's multiplicity of interests. These issues existed before Bill's death. After his death, a series of events occurred that have resulted in Sam and one of his sons effectively running the business, with other members of the third generation working either in subordinate positions or having no role and receiving almost no benefits. The basic issue that we must decide is whether those events constituted an unlawful oppression of the minority shareholders that entitles plaintiffs to a remedy and, if so, what is the appropriate remedy.

Under the buy-sell agreement that Sam and Bill executed in 1980, the surviving brother upon the death of the other was entitled to purchase five class A shares from the estate of the other at a price established in accordance with the agreement. The agreement also requires the surviving brother's estate to sell those shares back to the holder or holders of the decedent brother's class A shares upon the surviving brother's death. The effect of the agreement, thus, is to give the surviving brother effective control of the corporation but to reestablish equal control between the families when the surviving brother dies. When Sam and Bill made the agreement in 1980, their children had either just entered the work force or were not yet in it.

Bill's death in 1996 came at one of the corporation's most difficult times. It had lost $3.3 million in the fiscal year ending June 30, 1996. . . . Although the corporation's books showed significant retained earnings, primarily, if not exclusively, from its retail operations, it was short of cash and heavily indebted. . . .

After Bill died, there was a family meeting in June 1996. Although he had not yet received the controlling Class A shares, Sam was in effective control of the corporation. Although he promised at the meeting to operate the business fairly to everyone and suggested that it might begin paying dividends, Sam did not generally involve Bill's family in his decisions. Rather, he, Mary and Verne believed that he had to defend himself from what they perceived as Bill's family's desire to dominate him as they believed Bill had done before his death. Two issues triggered the disputes that eventually led to this litigation. First, Steve asked for a job assisting Bob in the real estate part of the business in the summer of 1996. Despite the corporation's practice of providing employment to family members, Sam refused Steve's request unless Verne also came to work in a position comparable to Bob's role. Second, Micki failed to deliver the five controlling Class A shares to Sam, despite Sam's exercise of his option to purchase them under the buy-sell agreement. In addition, she refused to give her personal guaranty to replace Bill's guaranty, as the corporation's lender had requested.

Members of the family held several meetings, with varying attendance, to discuss these and other issues relating to the future of the corporation. The meetings did not resolve anything but, instead, solidified factions among the shareholders. The firmest divisions were between Micki, Bob, and Steve (everyone began to refer to them as "MBS") and Sam and Verne. The divisions became particularly evident after meetings on August 16 and August 23, 1996, to discuss Steve's employment. At those meetings, Steve indicated that Micki would refuse to convey the five controlling shares because of technical flaws in Sam's exercise of his rights under the buy-sell agreement. Bob and Steve told Sam that he was not up to the task of running the business and that he should step aside so that they could operate it. To Sam and Verne, those statements were both insulting and an attempt to keep Sam in Bill's shadow. MBS also sought to divide the company's assets among the shareholders rather than keeping the business together, as Sam preferred. Over the next two years, MBS insisted that the corporation take several business decisions that Sam opposed. As it turned out, those decisions would not necessarily have been advantageous.

Sam refused to provide Micki a stipend in recognition of Bill's service to the company and her years of unpaid employment. All of Bill's family believed that Micki deserved a stipend and that Bill and Sam had had an understanding that their widows would receive such compensation. In April 1997, the board of directors decided to pay Micki $3,000 a month. That decision came almost a year after Bill's death, and Bill's family believed that the amount was not enough. Moreover, there was no promise that the stipend would continue indefinitely. Those feelings continued after the board raised the amount to $5,000 in May 1998.

Sam also refused to place Micki on the corporation's board, despite her ownership of almost half of the voting shares. In support of his refusal, Sam pointed to some confusion about whether Micki wanted to be a director or preferred to have Bob or Steve represent her on the board. In Sam's mind, having either Bob or Steve on the board was out of the question. It is clear, however, that Sam made no effort to resolve the confusion in a way that could have resulted in Micki's presence on the board; rather, he used it as an excuse to keep her off.

From late 1996 through early 1998, Sam and Verne made a number of significant decisions that both cemented Sam's control and contributed to a turnaround in the corporation's financial condition. In October 1996, Sam, the sole remaining director, chose Larry and Verne to replace Bill on the board of directors. At the same time, Sam began gradually to reduce Bob's role in business operations, in part by taking advantage of the lack of clarity of Bob's role after his return to the business. Early in 1997, Sam finally received the five Class A shares that the agreement required Micki to sell him, thus giving him a majority of the voting stock and control of the corporation. By that time, Sam and Bob were communicating primarily by written notes, although their desks were only 10 feet from each other. [Bob resigned in March 1997.]

At the June 1997 shareholder's meeting, Sam used his voting control to elect a board that consisted of himself, Larry, Ken, Verne, and two new outside directors, David Kobos and John Rees.[18] Steve voted Micki's shares for Sam, Kobos, and Rees and against Larry, Ken, and Verne. The reconstituted board actively examined the issues that Sam and Verne presented to it. However, Sam and Verne established the board's agenda and, while the board tweaked their proposals, it did not question the underlying directions that Sam and Verne suggested. That characterization is particularly applicable to proposals concerning the relationship between the corporation and its shareholders.

Also at the June 1997 shareholders' meeting, the shareholders adopted a change in corporate governance that gave voting rights to the Class B shares if the Class A shares were deadlocked. As ORS 60.441 required, the Class B shareholders voted on the change; MBS voted against it, while all other shareholders who were present, including Ken and Anne, voted in favor of the change. Under the change, if there was a deadlock on any issue that was appropriate for shareholder decision, as was likely to occur after Sam died, the Class B shareholders would be able to vote on it rather than having the deadlock continue. Given the alignment of the Class B shareholders at the time of the change, the likelihood was that any resolution would not favor MBS.[19]

At the end of July 1997, Verne came to work full-time for the corporation as Sam's second in command. The terms of his contract, which the board approved after discussing and modifying the original proposal, included a salary that was closer to market level than the corporation had previously paid family members, along with significant severance payments if his employment were terminated. Sam's salary also increased so that it was closer to the market level. Finally, in September 1998 the board appointed Sam as president and Verne as vice-president and secretary, while at the same time removing all other officers from office. Thus, Verne, as the only other officer, would be in charge of the corporation after Sam's death or resignation, while the severance provision would make it costly for the other shareholders to terminate his employment, as everyone anticipated that they would want to do. . . .

The corporation reported a substantial profit for the fiscal year ending June 30, 1997, and it remained profitable throughout 1998 and 1999. . . .

In spring 1998, Anne asked Sam for a loan from the corporation to help with her family's financial needs. Although the corporation had previously loaned money to a number of family members, Sam refused her request. After some discussion, he offered instead to buy 100 shares of her Class B stock for $1,000 per share, telling her that the price was the actual value of the stock. The purchase took place in June 1998. After Anne intervened in this action as a plaintiff, she came to believe that the price was too low and that the effect of the sale was to give Sam's family a permanent majority of the Class B shares, thus giving it control of the corporation if a deadlock of the Class A shares occurred after Sam's death. Sam and Anne ultimately agreed that she could

---

18. Sam chose the outside directors because of their areas of expertise, Kobos in retail business and Rees in real estate. Rees subsequently resigned and was replaced by James Meyer.

19. Among the third generation's members, only Verne and Bob are interested in running the corporation. The parties agree, however, that neither has any hope of receiving the support of a majority of the current Class B shareholders.

repurchase the shares for the price that he paid, and Anne borrowed money from Micki for the purpose.

In May 1998, after the refinancing, the board declared a dividend of $2 per share. At Sam and Verne's suggestion, Verne also began developing a stock repurchase program as the method of getting money to the complaining shareholders. Their explanation for taking that approach, rather than simply declaring a larger dividend, was that MBS had once suggested a repurchase plan and that some shareholders did not want the effect of double taxation from paying personal income tax on a dividend after the corporation had paid a corporate income tax on the profits that had made the dividend possible. Sam and Verne are the only shareholders whom defendants have identified as having that concern. On May 20, 1998, plaintiffs filed this law suit, including claims against Sam for the breach of fiduciary duties owed to the minority shareholders. In August 1998, Sam and the corporation filed their answer, and in September 1998, Anne and her husband moved to intervene as plaintiffs.

Meanwhile, Verne spent some time developing a repurchase plan, which was the subject of board discussions. In January 1999, immediately before the beginning of the trial of this case and after plaintiffs had formally requested the payment of a dividend, the board adopted such a plan. Under that plan, the board created a fund of $3 million to be used for purchasing shares at $1,100 per share for Class B shares and $1,320 for Class A shares. . . .

The trial court divided the trial into liability and remedies phases. In February 1999, the court made extensive oral findings of fact at the end of the liability phase of the trial. It found that some of defendants' actions, particularly the failure to pay adequate dividends, constituted oppression of the plaintiff shareholders. In reaching that conclusion, it focused on the exclusion of plaintiffs from employment or other involvement with the corporation and on the corporation's failure to provide them any alternative financial benefit. Those actions also included what the court considered to be an excessively low offering price in the stock repurchase plan and the delay in providing Micki a stipend and then in only a very low amount. The court recognized that many of Sam's actions could be supported as reasonable business decisions when viewed in isolation, but it found that their net effect was to remove plaintiffs from any participation in the business of the corporation and sharing of its income. The court then examined the corporation's dividend policy in light of what it concluded were the essential criteria discussed in Zidell v. Zidell, Inc., 277 Or. 413, 560 P.2d 1086 (1977). It ruled that, although Kobos and Meyer exercised independent judgment on the proposals that Sam and Verne made, they did not set their own agenda but instead went along with Sam's and Verne's oppressive dividend proposals. The court did not believe that the stock redemption plan was independently oppressive, but it reasoned that the plan was unfair in light of the dividend policy and the other factors in the case.

Between the court's findings at the close of the liability phase of the case in February 1999 and the beginning of the remedies phase of trial in late May, both the board and the shareholders made significant decisions. At a board meeting on March 22, 1999, Sam proposed a special dividend of $24 per share, or a total of $729,120. That amount still provided for a capital budget of $5 million for the next year. Larry sought a dividend of between $1.25 million and $1.5 million. After discussion, and with Larry abstaining, the board declared a dividend of $25, per share, or a total of $759,500. The board then unanimously adopted a dividend policy that it would follow in the future. Under the policy, management would recommend a dividend each year. The shareholders would then have an opportunity to give their opinions to a committee of directors who were not members of the Naito family. After that committee made its recommendation, the board would determine the amount of the dividend, if any. The board also resolved that, for the years 1999 through 2001, the dividend would be at least $500,000, provided that the corporation's net profit was at least $1.87 million.

The board also adopted an offer to purchase shares, with a pool that totaled $2.25 million. That amount represented the original $3 million pool less the approximate amount of the special dividend. The price for the offer was to be determined based on an appraisal of the corporation. The board appointed Kobos and Meyer as a committee to select the appraisers. It then increased Micki's stipend to $8,000 per month, subject to reduction only if the corporation's financial circumstances required a reduction of the same percentage in Sam's and Verne's salaries. When Larry suggested adding Micki to the board, both Sam and Kobos said that that action would not be advisable during the pending litigation. The board also proposed repealing the provision for the Class B shares to vote if the Class A shares were deadlocked; Sam stated that he would vote in favor of the repeal, and the matter was referred to the shareholders. . . .

At the annual shareholders' meeting on May 10, 1999, all of the Class A shares and a majority of the Class B shares voted to repeal the authority for Class B shares to vote in case of a deadlock. Ron and Ken did not attend, and Larry abstained. Sam then nominated a slate of directors that replaced Larry with a third non shareholder director, who was unknown to the other shareholders. Sam voted his controlling shares in favor of the slate that he had nominated, while Micki abstained. The rest of the meeting consisted of an extensive discussion of the preparation for the new repurchase proposal and of the company's business affairs. . . .

At the conclusion of the remedies phase of the trial, the court found, in light of the amount of dividends that had been declared, the low price in the stock repurchase proposal, and the economic circumstances of the parties, that the amendment of the bylaws to permit Class B shares to vote on a deadlock violated the implied duty of good faith and fair dealing under Bill's and Sam's buy-sell agreement. As a result of that change, the holder of Micki's Class A shares would not have received the 50 percent voting rights that the agreement contemplated on Sam's death. Based on that conclusion, the court ordered that Sam pay Micki's attorney fees related to her claim under that agreement.

The court then turned to the issue of dividends. It noted that the corporation had over $11 million in cash available, that it had future capital needs for maintenance and expansion, and that there was $3 million available to fund a stock repurchase plan that could be used instead for dividends. In that regard, the court stated its belief that, generally, a real estate company's net income is unrealistically reduced by depreciation, a reduction that does not reflect economic reality, and that, therefore, there is more cash available for dividends than might otherwise be apparent. Based on those findings, the court ordered the corporation to pay dividends of $710,000 per year for each of the five years beginning in 2000, so long as it had $1.3 million in net profits from the previous year.

In its judgment, the court also enjoined Sam for a period of five years from voting his Class A shares in ways that would affect the rights of Micki's Class A shares, unless Micki or her successor consented. It also enjoined the corporation from issuing additional Class A shares without her consent. It retained jurisdiction for five years for issues concerning dividends, the estate planning of Class A shareholders, and amendments to the articles of incorporation concerning Class A shares. It authorized an award of attorney fees to Micki. Finally, it dismissed all of plaintiffs' other claims with prejudice.

On appeal, defendants challenge the judgment in its entirety. . . .

We turn to the primary issue on appeal: whether plaintiffs have proved their claim of majority oppression of minority shareholder interests. Much of the law in this regard is well-established. Majority or other controlling shareholders owe fiduciary duties of loyalty, good faith, fair dealing, and full disclosure to the minority. Directors owe similar duties to the corporation. At least in closely held corporations, conduct that violates those duties is likely to be oppressive under ORS 60.661(2)(b),[27] thus authorizing a court to dissolve the corporation or order some lesser remedy. As we noted in [Chiles v. Robertson, 94 Or. App. 604, 619 (1989)], the heart of a corporate fiduciary's duty is an attitude, not a rule. "The fiduciary best fulfills its duties if it approaches them with the attitude of seeking the beneficiary's interests rather than the personal interests of the fiduciary."

Plaintiffs' principal argument is that they have been excluded from all participation in the corporation and all other benefits of owning their stock. Plaintiffs have certainly shown that they do not have the involvement in or the influence on corporate policy that they once had. What they do not fully accept, however, is that the diminution in their role is the result of the terms of the buy-sell agreement between Sam and Bill. Bob, Steve, and, to a lesser extent, Micki, did not fully accept that under the terms of the buy-sell agreement Bill's death changed the power relationships in the corporation. Their use of a technical excuse to delay delivering the five control shares and their actions at the August meetings provoked a response from Sam that led to a breakdown of relations. Their insistence thereafter that the corporation take actions that Sam did not want to take — some of which would, in fact, have had negative results [—was] the problem. Viewing a number of the actions about which plaintiffs complain in the context in which they occurred answers plaintiffs' claim that Sam's earlier actions were oppressive. Sam had the legal right to exercise the authority that the buy-sell agreement gave him after Bill's death. In light of MSB's challenge to that authority, it is not surprising that Sam did not want Steve to work with Bob, at least unless Sam could have Verne as his supporter. It is also not surprising that Sam began to withdraw responsibilities from Bob and that their relationship deteriorated. Bob's resignation was the result of his deteriorating relationship with Sam and of his own action in responding to a bank request in a way that supported Micki and harmed the corporation. We are not persuaded that Sam's actions in those regards are the kind of conduct that the law treats as oppressive conduct against minority interests.

---

27. ORS 60.661(2)(b) provides that a circuit court may dissolve a corporation in a proceeding brought by a shareholder if it is established that "[t]he directors or those in control of the corporation have acted, are acting or will act in a manner that is illegal, oppressive or fraudulent."

In the same manner, the decision to allow Class B shareholders to break a deadlock after Sam's death was a practical solution to a real problem. That action did not ensure that Sam's family would control the corporation after his death. Anne and Ken, two of Bill's children, voted for the change, while the relationship between Ron and Larry, on the one hand, and Verne, on the other, was such that it was unlikely that they would constitute a solid block for any future decisions. Rather, it was probable that the Class B shareholders could form a variety of alliances and that those alliances could cross family lines. In this light, Sam's subsequent purchase of 100 of Anne's Class B shares was unlikely to affect the future balance of power. Again, we are not persuaded that plaintiffs have carried their burden in regard to those decisions. Finally, the delay in giving Micki a stipend, and the amount once the corporation gave it, may be evidence of Sam's unwillingness to deal generously with her or to abide by an agreement with Bill, but it is not oppression of her in her capacity as a shareholder.

By early 1998, however, the financial picture of the corporation had changed. The financial justifications for the minority shareholders not receiving benefits from their ownership interests began to lose force. Attempts to divide the corporation's assets among the parties had foundered and continued to founder, in large part because of the hard line that Sam and Verne took in the negotiations. At the same time, the corporation was profitable and, after the Montgomery Park refinancing, it had substantial cash reserves with no limitations on paying dividends other than providing prudent reserves for its future business needs. Although the corporation faced significant expenditures for deferred maintenance and capital projects, it had over $5 million in retained earnings after allowing for those expenditures. At the time, the corporation did not contemplate any new ventures that would call for extraordinary resources.

Under these circumstances, there was no justification in 1998 for failing to make a significant distribution to the shareholders beyond the token dividends that the corporation declared. Rather than issuing dividends that reflected the value of the corporation, the board adopted a stock repurchase plan that would permit dissident shareholders to sell some of their shares to the corporation. On appeal, defendants justify their decision by arguing that certain shareholders had expressed an interest in selling their shares and that others did not want the double taxation effect of a dividend. The evidence does not support either contention. At most, the evidence is that Ken suggested that a regular dividend *combined with* some way for shareholders to liquidate some of their shares might resolve the parties' problem. Anne's attorney also indicated that she would accept a redemption of *all* of her shares as an "exit" strategy, but there was no indication that any minority shareholder would agree to dilute his or her interests by participating in a partial buy-out. As to the second argument, that some shareholders wanted to avoid double taxation of their dividends, the evidence shows that that concern applied only to Sam and Verne themselves.

The repurchase plan that the board adopted shortly before the trial began was limited to a $3 million fund with no suggestion that additional amounts would follow. That amount was too small for the corporation to purchase all of the shares that any shareholder except Micki owned. Thus, any shareholder other than Micki who accepted the offer would receive money that might be subject to tax as regular income. Because Sam and Verne did not intend to sell any of their shares, the sale would increase their proportionate interest in the corporation and reduce the interest of a shareholder who sold. If Micki sold her Class A shares, Sam's heirs would continue to control the corporation after Sam's death. If any shareholder sold Class B shares, Verne and Sam's heirs would be more likely to prevail in any deadlock. Thus, the repurchase plan would have, in effect, frustrated the purpose of returning the ownership interests to parity at the time of Sam's death. Finally, we agree with the trial court that the offering price in the plan was, at best, on the low end of a reasonable range.

This offer, with all its problems, was the only way that the corporation provided for the minority shareholders to receive any substantial value from their shares. We conclude that the repurchase offer did not constitute a good faith effort on the part of the board to provide a reasonable portion of the corporation's income to the shareholders, nor does it justify the failure to pay adequate dividends. By failing to provide for adequate dividends or other financial benefits on reasonable terms, Sam acted for his own self-interest in derogation of the interests of the minority shareholders and therefore failed to act with the fiduciary attitude that we described in *Chiles*.

Defendants argue that there is no evidence that a majority of the board shared whatever motives Sam and Verne had and that, as a result, it is improper to attribute their actions to the board as a whole. They point out that the board, not the controlling shareholder, has the authority to declare a dividend and that the court in *Zidell* focused on the actions of the directors, not of the shareholders, in determining whether the corporation's dividend policy was oppressive. Defendants conclude that, because the board actively participated in the challenged decisions, and because a majority of the board did not share Sam's and Verne's animus towards plaintiffs, it necessarily follows that the board's decisions were made in good faith and are beyond challenge. However, the Supreme Court, in its opinion in *Zidell*, emphasized the fiduciary duties of "those in control of corporation affairs," including that decisions concerning dividends be made in good faith and reflect "legitimate business purposes rather than the private interests of those in control." 277 Or. at 418. In *Zidell*, the corporate boards consisted of the two controlling shareholders and a former shareholder who was aligned with them. There was, thus, no distinction between the directors and those in control of the corporations.

Here, the board consists of Sam and Verne, two non aligned shareholders, and two non shareholders. However, Sam and Verne were the driving force behind the board's decision to pay only nominal dividends and to focus instead on a share repurchase plan. Sam and Verne developed the structure of that plan. The other directors played only minor roles in deciding either the general direction or the details of that decision. As with other board actions, Sam and Verne set the agenda and provided most of the information on which the board acted. . . . Consequently, we reject defendants' argument that the board's adoption of Sam's and Verne's proposal insulates the corporation and Sam from liability.

We turn to the question of the appropriate remedy. In their cross-appeal plaintiffs challenge the trial court's decision to order increased dividends and argue, rather, that the appropriate remedy is a divisive reorganization. . . . In this case, we do not believe that the oppressive conduct is so egregious that it requires the drastic remedy of a compulsory purchase or divisive reorganization. The record indicates that the business is being run well under Sam's control. We agree with the trial court that the proper remedy is to keep the business together for the benefit of all the shareholders but to require it to pay reasonable dividends. . . .

By February 1998, when it became possible to declare dividends, Sam and Verne were in day-to-day control of the corporation. For various reasons, many of which we have described, they were hostile to MBS. Although Anne had generally supported Sam, once she intervened in this case they immediately extended that hostility to her. Their only attempt to provide substantial benefits to the minority shareholders consisted of a stock repurchase program that, as structured, was more beneficial to their interests than to the minority interests. Although the corporation had the financial capability to pay substantial dividends out of current profits, Sam and Verne supported only what were, in fact, token dividends. . . .

Although we agree with the trial court that increased dividends are the appropriate remedy, we believe that the trial court failed to give adequate weight to the board's determination at its March 22, 1999, meeting of how to determine the amount of those dividends. Courts are generally reluctant to interfere with the exercise of business discretion by the officers and directors of a corporation. Although courts will not ignore corporate misconduct, it is not their role to second-guess business decisions that are within the range of reasonableness. The policy that the board adopted at the March meeting established a procedure that involves significant consultation with plaintiffs and the other minority shareholders for determining the amount of future dividends, and it promises a minimum payment if the corporation achieves a designated level of profitability. Determining what is an adequate dividend requires an exercise of business judgment based on considerations that include the corporation's future needs and likely future profitability. Determining those factors involves predicting such matters as changing market conditions, probable capital and maintenance requirements, future corporate opportunities, civic projects, and many other things that go toward the success of a business. The people who are usually in the best position to exercise that judgment, and who have the responsibility for doing so, are the corporation's management and directors. The trial court rejected the board's policy and, instead, applying its own view of the corporation's needs, required the corporation to pay larger dividends based on a smaller profit than the board had promised. In doing so, the court improperly substituted its judgment for that of the board.

The fact that we approve the policy adopted by the board in March 1999 does not, however, mean that there is no continuing role for the trial court. In light of the years of hostility between the parties and our finding of oppression, it is important to ensure that the policy works as the board apparently intended it to work. For that reason, the trial court on remand will modify the judgment by deleting the current provision concerning dividends and replacing it with a provision requiring defendants to adhere to the dividend policy adopted on March 22, 1999, for a period of five fiscal years, beginning with fiscal 2000, and retaining continuing jurisdiction over the implementation of that policy.[35]

---

35. We emphasize that the essential aspect of the board's policy, in our view, is its provision for a committee of non-shareholder directors to recommend the amount of a dividend and for minority shareholders to participate in that committee's decision. That procedure provides a formal mechanism for the board to take the minority shareholders' interests into account in

On appeal, judgment vacated and remanded with instructions to enter judgment limited to requiring defendants, for five consecutive fiscal years of defendant corporation beginning with fiscal year 2000, to implement in good faith the dividend policy adopted on March 22, 1999, and retaining jurisdiction to enforce the judgment; affirmed on cross-appeal.

C.   THE MEANING OF "OPPRESSION"

"Oppression" normally is not defined by the modern state corporate law statutes, thus leaving the task to courts. As we have already seen, courts have defined it in various ways. Some of the most common definitions include: (a) burdensome, harsh, and wrongful conduct that is a visible departure from standards of fair dealing; (b) a breach of the duty of fair dealing, which is enhanced in the close corporation setting; and/or (c) frustration of the reasonable expectations of the minority shareholder. Kiriakides v. Atlas Food Systems & Services, Inc. deals with the tension among the various definitions of "oppression" that have been adopted by state courts. The court observes that a "reasonable expectations" approach views the problem through the minority shareholder's eyes, while an approach that focuses on "burdensome, harsh, and wrongful conduct" focuses on the actions of the majority shareholder. While reading the case, consider whether the result would differ depending on the standard selected.

KIRIAKIDES v. ATLAS FOOD SYSTEMS & SERVICES, INC.
541 S.E.2d 257
Supreme Court of South Carolina
January 29, 2001

Toal, Justice.

FACTS

This is a case in which respondents, minority shareholders in a closely held family corporation, claim the majority shareholders have acted in a manner which is fraudulent, oppressive and unfairly prejudicial. They seek a buyout of their shares under South Carolina's judicial dissolution statutes. A rather detailed recitation of the facts is necessary to an understanding of the plaintiffs' claims.

---

setting dividends. It does not prevent the board from basing its decision on dividends, or on other matters relating to the corporation's business, on its view of the best interests of the business as a whole. Aside from the board's stated intention to provide dividends of at least $500,000 if the corporation's income is at least $1.87 million, the policy does not commit the board to any particular level of dividend. If the board carries out this policy as intended, we would not anticipate any further breaches of fiduciary duty in this respect. In order to ensure that the policy does provide the protection to plaintiffs that we believe it will, the judgment will require the board to adhere to it for five years and will provide for the trial court to retain jurisdiction during that period to ensure proper implementation of the policy.

Respondents are 72-year-old John Kiriakides and his 74-year-old sister Louise Kiriakides. John and Louise are the minority shareholders in the family business, Atlas Food Systems & Services, Inc. (Atlas). Petitioners are their older brother, 88-year-old Alex Kiriakides, Jr., and the family business and its subsidiaries, Marica Enterprises, Ltd. (MEL), and Marica, Inc. (Marica).

Atlas is a food vending service which provides refreshments to factories and other businesses. The business began prior to World War II but slowed down while Alex was away during the war. After the war, Alex, John, and their father Alex, Sr., began working together to build the family business. Alex, Sr. died in 1949. Atlas was incorporated in 1956. Currently, Alex is the majority stockholder, owning 57.68%; John owns 37.7%, and Louise owns 3%.

Throughout Atlas' history, Alex has been in charge of the financial and corporate affairs of the family business; he has had overall control and is Chairman of the Board of Directors. John is also on the three member Board. In 1986, John became President of Atlas, after years of running client relations and field operations. Two of Alex' children are also employed by Atlas, his son Alex III, and his daughter Mary Ann. Alex III is (since John's departure as discussed below) President and is on the Board; Mary Ann is a CPA who performs accounting and financial functions; their brother Michael worked for Atlas in the past, but is no longer employed there.

For years, Atlas operated as a prototypical closely held family corporation. Troubles developed, however, in 1995, when a rift began between Alex and John. The initial dispute arose over property owned by John and Alex in Greenville. Alex convinced John to transfer his interest in the property to his son Alex III for a price less than it was worth. John signed the deed prepared by Alex believing he was conveying only a small portion of his interest in the property to Alex III. After discovering his entire interest had been transferred to Alex III, John became distrustful of Alex and began requesting documents and records concerning the family business. The relationship between the two became very strained. Several subsequent incidents served to heighten the tension.

In December 1995, the Board and shareholders of Atlas decided to convert Atlas from a subchapter C corporation to a subchapter S corporation. However, in March 1996, Alex, without bringing a vote, unilaterally determined the company would remain a C corporation. Later, in mid-1996, a dispute arose over Atlas' contract to purchase a piece of commercial property. Notwithstanding the contract, John, Alex III and William Freitag (Senior Vice President of Finance and Administration) decided not to go through with the sale. Alex however, without consulting or advising John, elected to go through with the sale. When John learned of Alex' decision, he became extremely upset and allegedly advised Alex III he was quitting his job as President. The next day, Alex III made plans with managers to continue operations in John's absence; John, however, went to the Atlas office in Greenville and visited Atlas offices in Columbia, Orangeburg and Charleston.

The following Monday, John went to work at Atlas doing "business as usual." He was told later that day (by Alex' son Michael) that management was planning John would no longer be President of Atlas. John circulated a memo indicating he intended to remain President; Alex III replied in a memo prepared with the aid of his father, refusing to allow John to continue as president of the company. The following day, Alex refused to allow John to stay on as president of Atlas, and designated Alex III as President. John was offered, but refused a position as a consultant.

In September 1996, Atlas offered to purchase John's interest in Atlas, MEL and K Enterprises, for one million dollars, plus the cancellation of $800,000 obligations owed by John. John refused this offer, believing it too low. John filed this suit in November 1996, seeking to obtain corporate records. The complaint was subsequently amended, naming Louise as a plaintiff, and adding claims for fraud under the judicial dissolution statute. The complaint sought an accounting, a buyout of John and Louise's shares, and damages for fraud. The trial was bifurcated on the issues of liability and damages.

After a five day hearing, the referee found Alex had engaged in fraud in numerous respects, and found Atlas had engaged in conduct which was fraudulent, oppressive and unfairly prejudicial toward John and Louise. The referee held a buyout was the appropriate remedy under S.C. Code Ann. §33-14-300(2)(ii) and §33-14-310(d)(4)[, the South Carolina statute that permits a court to order a buyout of shares rather than dissolving the corporation]. The referee found that, at the bifurcated damages hearing, it would be determined whether John and Louise had suffered any damages from the fraud in this regard. The Court of Appeals affirmed in result. . . .

LAW/ANALYSIS . . .

3. BUYOUT DUE TO OPPRESSIVE CONDUCT

a. Oppression Under S.C. Code Ann. §33-14-300

The referee found that, taken together, the majority's actions were "illegal, fraudulent, oppressive or unfairly prejudicial," justifying a buyout of John and Louise's interests under S.C. Code Ann. §33-14-300(2)(ii) and §33-14-310(d)(4).[16] Accordingly, the referee held a buyout was in order. . . .

The Court of Appeals affirmed the referee's holdings. In making this ruling, the Court of Appeals defined the statutory terms "oppressive" and "unfairly prejudicial" as follows:

> 1) A visible departure from the standards of fair dealing and a violation of fair play on which every shareholder who entrusts his money to a company is entitled to rely; or
> 2) A breach of the fiduciary duty of good faith and fair dealing; or
> 3) Whether the reasonable expectations of the minority shareholders have been frustrated by the actions of the majority; or
> 4) A lack of probity and fair dealing in the affairs of a company to the prejudice of some of its members; or
> 5) A deprivation by majority shareholders of participation in management by minority shareholders.

---

16. Section 33-14-300(2)(ii) permits a court to order dissolution if it is established by a shareholder that "the directors or those in control of the corporation have acted, are acting, or will act in a manner that is illegal, fraudulent, oppressive, or unfairly prejudicial either to the corporation or to any shareholder (whether in his capacity as a shareholder, director, or officer of the corporation)." Section 33-14-310(d)(4) permits a court to make such order or grant such relief, other than dissolution, as in its discretion is appropriate, including providing for the purchase at their fair value of shares of any shareholder, either by the corporation or by other shareholders.

Atlas contends the Court of Appeals' definitions of oppressive, unfairly prejudicial conduct are beyond the scope of our judicial dissolution statute. We agree. In our view, the Court of Appeals' broad view of oppression is contrary to the legislative intent and is an unwarranted expansion of section 33-14-300.

South Carolina's judicial dissolution statute was amended in 1963 in recognition of the growing trend toward protecting minority shareholders from abuses by those in the majority. . . . [17] The official comment to section 33-14-300 provides:

> The application of these grounds for dissolution to specific circumstances obviously involves judicial discretion in the application of a general standard to concrete circumstances. The court should be cautious in the application of these grounds so as to limit them to genuine abuse rather than instances of acceptable tactics in a power struggle for control of a corporation.

Although the terms "oppressive" and "unfairly prejudicial" are not defined in section 33-14-300, the comment to S.C. Code Ann. §33-18-400 (1990), which allows shareholders in a statutory close corporation to petition for relief on the grounds of oppressive, fraudulent, or unfairly prejudicial conduct provides:

> No attempt has been made to define oppression, fraud, or unfairly prejudicial conduct. These are elastic terms whose meaning varies with the circumstances presented in a particular case, and it is felt that existing case law provides sufficient guidelines for courts and litigants.

Given the Legislature's deliberate exclusion of a set definition of oppressive and unfairly prejudicial conduct, we find the Court of Appeals' enunciation of rigid tests is contrary to the legislative intent.

Under the Court of Appeals' holding, a finding of fraudulent/oppressive conduct may be based upon any one of its alternative definitions. We do not believe the Legislature intended such a result. In particular, we do not believe the Legislature intended a court to judicially order a corporate dissolution solely upon the basis that a party's "reasonable expectations" have been frustrated by majority shareholders. To examine the "reasonable expectations" of minority shareholders would require the courts of this state to microscopically examine the dealings of closely held family corporations, the intentions of majority and minority stockholders in forming the corporation and thereafter, the history of

---

17. Prior to 1963, dissolution could be based only upon illegal, fraudulent or oppressive conduct. In an attempt to afford minority shareholders greater protection, the legislature amended the statute in 1963 to include "unfairly prejudicial" conduct. The statute, as amended, "broadens the scope of actionable conduct by providing the frozen-out minority shareholder a right of action based on conduct by the majority shareholders which might not rise to the level of fraud." Joshua Henderson, Buyout Remedy for Oppressed Minority Shareholders, 47 S.C. L. Rev. 195, 199 (Autumn 1995) (hereinafter Henderson). This trend arose due to the nationwide epidemic of unfair treatment of minority shareholders. See F.H. O'Neal, Oppression of Minority Stockholders: Protecting Minority Rights, 35 Clev. St. L. Rev. 121 (1986-87). . . . Prof. O'Neal observed: Unfair treatment of holders of minority interests in family companies and other closely held corporations by persons in control of those corporations is so widespread that it is a national business scandal. The amount of litigation growing out of minority shareholder oppression—actual, fancied or fabricated—has grown tremendously in recent years, and the flood of litigation shows no sign of abating. *Id.* at 121.

family dealings, and the like. We do not believe the Legislature, in enacting section 33-14-300, intended such judicial interference in the business philosophies and day to day operating practices of family businesses.

In adopting the "reasonable expectations" approach, the Court of Appeals cited the North Carolina case of Meiselman v. Meiselman, 309 N.C. 279, 307 S.E.2d 551 (N.C. 1983). In *Meiselman*, a minority shareholder in a family-owned close corporation was "frozen out" of the family corporation in much the same fashion as John and Louise claim they have been frozen out of Atlas. The minority shareholder brought an action requesting a buyout of his interests under N.C.G.S. §55-125.1(a)(4), which permits a North Carolina court to liquidate assets when it is *"reasonably necessary for the protection of the rights or interests of the complaining shareholders."* (Emphasis supplied).

In holding the minority shareholder was entitled to relief, the *Meiselman* court noted that the trial court had focused on the conduct of the majority shareholder, using standards of "oppression," "overreaching," "unfair advantage," and the like. The Court found this was error because the North Carolina statute in question required the trial court to focus on the plaintiff's "rights and interests," his "reasonable expectations," in the corporate defendants, and determine whether those rights or interests were in need of protection. The focus in *Meiselman*, based upon the language of the North Carolina statute, was upon the interests of the minority shareholder, as opposed to the conduct of the majority.

Unlike the North Carolina statute in *Meiselman*, section 33-14-300 does not place the focus upon the "rights or interests" of the complaining shareholder but, rather, specifically places the focus upon the actions of the majority, *i.e.*, whether they "have acted, are acting, or will act in a manner that is illegal, fraudulent, oppressive, or unfairly prejudicial either to the corporation or to any shareholder." Given the language of our statute, a "reasonable expectations" approach is simply inconsistent with our statute. . . .

Although several jurisdictions have adopted "reasonable expectations" as a guide to the meaning of "oppression," it has been noted by one commentator that "no court has adopted the reasonable expectations test without the assistance of a statute." Ralph A. Peeples, The Use and Misuse of the Business Judgment Rule in the Close Corporation, 60 Notre Dame L. Rev. 456, 505 (1985). One criticism of the "reasonable expectations" approach is that it "ignores the expectations of the parties other than the dissatisfied shareholder." See Lerner v. Lerner Corp., 132 Md. App. 32, 750 A.2d 709, 722 (Md. 2000) (citing Robert W. Hillman, The Dissatisfied Participant in the Solvent Business Venture: A Consideration of the Relevant Permanence of Partnerships and Close Corporations., 67 Minn. L. Rev. 1, 75-78 (1982)). One recent commentator has suggested that a pure "reasonable expectations" approach overprotects the minority's interests. Douglas K. Moll, Shareholder Oppression in Close Corporations: The Unanswered Question of Perspective, 53 Vand. L. Rev. 749, 826 (April 2000) (hereinafter Moll). Similarly, it has been suggested that the reasonable expectations approach is "based on false premises, invites fraud, and is an unnecessary invasion of the rights of the majority." J.C. Bruno, Reasonable Expectations: A Primer on an Oppressive Standard, 71 Mich. B.J. 434 (May 1992). We find adoption of the "reasonable expectations" standard is inconsistent with section 33-14-300, which places an emphasis not upon the minority's expectations but, rather, on the actions of the majority. We decline to adopt such an expansive approach to oppressive conduct in the absence of a legislative mandate.[24] We find, consistent with the Legislature's comment to section 33-18-400, that the terms "oppressive" and "unfairly prejudicial" are elastic terms whose meaning varies with the circumstances presented in a particular case. . . .

We find a case-by-case analysis, supplemented by various factors which may be indicative of oppressive behavior, to be the proper inquiry under S.C. Code §33-14-300.[25] Accordingly, the Court of Appeals' opinion is modified to the extent it adopted a "reasonable expectations" approach.

b. Oppression Under Circumstances of This Case

The question remains whether the conduct of Atlas toward John and Louise was "oppressive" and "unfairly prejudicial" under the factual circumstances presented. We find this case presents a classic example of a majority "freeze-out," and that the referee properly found Atlas had engaged in conduct which was fraudulent, oppressive and unfairly prejudicial. Accordingly, the referee properly ordered a buyout of their shares. . . .

The particular problems encountered by those in the close corporation setting was noted in *Meiselman*, 307 S.E.2d at 559:

> The right of the majority to control the enterprise achieves a meaning and has an impact in close corporations that it has in no other major form of business organization under our law. Only in the close corporation does the power to manage carry with it the de facto power to allocate the benefits of ownership arbitrarily among the shareholders and to discriminate against a minority whose investment is imprisoned in the enterprise. The essential basis of this power in the close corporation is the inability of those so excluded from the benefits of proprietorship to withdraw their investment at will.

This unequal balance of power often leads to a "squeeze out" or "freeze out"[28] of the minority by the majority shareholders. In the close corporation, a shareholder

> [F]aces a potential danger the shareholder of a public corporation generally avoids — the possibility of harm to the fair value of the shareholder's investment. At its extreme, this harm manifests itself as the classic freeze out where the minority shareholder faces a trapped investment and an indefinite exclusion form participation in business returns. The position of the close corporation shareholder, therefore, is uniquely precarious.

---

24. If the legislature wishes to afford such expansive rights to minority shareholders, it may amend the statute to include language similar to the statutes in North Carolina, California, and New York.

25. We [believe] that the best approach to the statutory definition of oppressive conduct may well be a case-by-case analysis, augmented by factors or typical patterns of majority conduct which tend to be indicative of oppression, such as exclusion from management, withholding of dividends, paying excessive salaries to majority shareholders, and analogous activities. In this regard, we note that we do not hold that a court may never consider the parties' reasonable expectations, or the other items enumerated by the Court of Appeals, as factors in assessing oppressive conduct; such factors, however, are not to be utilized as the sole test of oppression under South Carolina law.

28. "Freeze out" is often used as a synonym for "squeeze out." The term squeeze out means the use by some of the owners or participants in a business enterprise of strategic position, inside information, or powers of control, or the utilization of some legal device or technique, to eliminate from the enterprise one or more of its owners or participants. 2 F. Hodge O'Neal & Robert B. Thompson, O'Neal's Oppression of Minority Shareholders, §1.01 at 1 (2d ed.1999).

Moll, 53 Vand. L. Rev. at 790-91. Common freeze out techniques include the termination of a minority shareholder's employment, the refusal to declare dividends, the removal of a minority shareholder from a position of management, and the siphoning off of corporate earnings through high compensation to the majority shareholder. Often, these tactics are used in combination. In a public corporation, the minority shareholder can escape such abuses by selling his shares; there is no such market, however, for the stock of a close corporation. . . .

The present case presents a classic situation of minority "freeze out." The referee considered the following factors: 1) Alex' unilateral action to deprive Louise of the benefits of ownership in her shares in Atlas, and subsequent reduction in her distributions based upon the reduced number of shares, 2) Alex' conduct in depriving John and Louise of the 21% interest of Marica stock, 3) the fact that there is no prospect of John and Louise receiving any financial benefit from their ownership of Atlas shares, 4) the fact that Alex and his family continue to receive substantial benefit from their ownership in Atlas, 5) the fact that Atlas has substantial cash and liquid assets, very little debt and that, notwithstanding its ability to declare dividends, it has indicated it would not do so in the foreseeable future, 6) the fact that Alex, majority shareholder in total control of Atlas, is totally estranged from John and Louise, 7) Atlas' extremely low buyout offers to John and Louise, and 8) the fact that Atlas is not appropriate for a public stock offering at the present time.

These factors, when coupled with the referee's findings of fraud, present a textbook example of a "freeze out" situation. Short of a buyout of their shares, it is unlikely John and Louise will ever receive any benefit from their ownership interests in Atlas. We find the referee properly concluded the totality of the circumstances demonstrated that the majority had acted "oppressively" and "unfairly prejudicially" to John and Louise. Accordingly, we affirm the referee's finding that a buyout of John and Louise's shares is the appropriate remedy under the circumstances of this case.

We are constrained to note that this case cries out for settlement between the parties. In fact, both parties conceded both in brief and at oral argument before this Court that a buyout is in order; it is at this point simply a matter of price. It is patent from the record before us that Atlas has an abundance of cash and liquid assets which would permit a buyout. Given the parties' ages and the need for a resolution of this matter, we simply cannot fathom why an amicable settlement cannot be reached between the parties.

. . . [T]he Court of Appeals' opinion is affirmed in result as modified and the case remanded to the referee to determine a valuation of John and Louise's shares, and to ascertain any damages suffered as a result of Alex' fraud.

PROBLEM 13-2

Billings Generation, Inc. (BGI) was a closely held Montana corporation specializing in the development of cogeneration power plants. BGI had five equal shareholders, and each shareholder served on the company's board of directors. All of the shareholders had also served as officers of BGI, until two of the shareholders — James Sletteland and Ron Blendu — were removed by a vote of the other three directors.

BGI entered into a partnership with a subsidiary of Exxon to "acquire, design, construct, invest in, own, maintain, develop, improve, manage and otherwise operate a qualified cogeneration or small power production facility under the Public Utility Regulatory Policy Act (PURPA) to be constructed and developed near Billings, Montana." In connection with this project, two of BGI's remaining officers performed legal services and charged the partnership $633,000 over the course of nearly three years. They used an hourly billing rate of $225 per hour.

Sletteland brought a derivative suit (as a shareholder of BGI) against the two BGI officers in an attempt to recover excessive legal fees. Unfortunately for Sletteland, the partnership agreement expressly allowed the hiring of the two BGI officers for legal services. Moreover, BGI's partner was authorized to approve the legal fees and did so. Finally, it appeared that the legal fees were reasonable given the complexity of the project. In short, Sletteland's claim was rejected.

The more interesting claim, for present purposes, was the officers' counterclaim, which objected to the timing of Sletteland's suit. They argued that Sletteland breached his *fiduciary duties as a minority shareholder* of BGI by attempting to derail the partnership's efforts to refinance some of its indebtedness. For reasons that need not be detailed here, the partnership had a relatively small window of time during which the refinancing was attractive. And according to BGI's partner, "where fraud has been alleged against the senior officers of [BGI], underwriters are unlikely to take up the bonds until the litigation is resolved." The refinancing ultimately failed, and according to the BGI officers, the delay caused by Sletteland's lawsuit was a major cause of the failure.

Should minority shareholders owe fiduciary duties to majority shareholders? Even if such duties exist, would you apply them when a minority shareholder brings a lawsuit for oppression, as in this case? If the standards for minority oppression claims are too easily met, do we run the risk of encouraging "majority oppression"?

CHAPTER
14

Friendly Mergers and Acquisitions

As everyone who reads the newspaper knows, companies don't exist in isolation, nor are they immune from combining and splitting apart into new configurations through various techniques. Particularly when the value of stocks being traded in the capital markets is rising, there is an increase in mergers and acquisitions activity, because the stock of an acquiring company can be used as the consideration for the purchase of another company.

As discussed in Chapter 11, lawyers tend to divide business combinations into two categories: "friendly" and "hostile." Recall that friendly deals are those where the boards of directors of two companies agree that a business combination makes sense, while hostile acquisitions take place notwithstanding the resistance of one company's board. Since there are mechanisms for effecting hostile acquisitions, such as the use of a tender offer (or a tender offer conditioned on receiving proxy authority to overcome some types of defenses), not all "friendly" deals are in fact marked by real friendliness. In some instances a board will agree to a takeover plan because it knows that the acquiror will be able take control anyway, particularly if the company does not have effective anti-takeover devices in place. The Lotus Company agreed to be acquired by IBM, notwithstanding initial resistance, when IBM's lawyers pointed out that under the Lotus Company's charter, the shareholders could act on consent pursuant to Delaware General Corporation Law (DGCL) §228, and thus IBM could simply buy a majority of Lotus's stock, act on consent to replace the board, and have the new board agree to the acquisition.

Overwhelmingly, though, friendly deals predominate in the market for corporate control: less than 2 percent of completed transactions in an average year arise as hostile acquisitions. Yet some of the most contested legal issues involve hostile acquisitions, in part because they often sharply raise the issue of whether the board or the shareholders should have the power to make fundamental decisions about a company's future. Both friendly and hostile deals involve the same fiduciary duties we have seen previously (loyalty, care, good faith, disclosure), but because the factual circumstances in which they come into play are different in friendly rather than hostile deals, and the legal analysis of whether there has been a breach differs in the two situations, we will look at each separately.

A. STRUCTURING AN ACQUISITION

There are three ways to structure an acquisition under state statutory law: as a merger or consolidation; as a purchase of the assets and liabilities of the selling company; or as a purchase of 100 percent of the stock of the selling company. While the ultimate effect of using any one of these three mechanisms may be essentially equivalent in any given case—*A* corporation acquires *B* corporation—there are different implications for a number of important issues depending on which form is used. Thus, there will be important differences in tax treatment; which shareholders get voting rights to approve or disapprove of the combination; whether all of the liabilities of the acquired firm get transferred to the acquiring firm; and what remedies there are for dissenting shareholders. This is an area of corporate law where form predominates over substance, and which form is used matters a great deal.

Merger or Consolidation. A merger under state law is a procedure where one company is entirely "merged into" another by operation of law. *See* DGCL §251; Model Business Corporation Act (Model Act) §11.02. (It is called a "merger" when the surviving company is one of the two companies that entered into the process; it is called a "consolidation" when two companies use the statutory merger procedure to combine to form a new company altogether.) In a merger or consolidation, all of the assets and all of the liabilities of the company being merged out of existence transfer automatically upon (a) both boards adopting a resolution approving a plan of merger; (b) the shareholders that have voting rights approving the merger; and (c) the company filing the plan of merger with the secretary of state in the state of incorporation. The consideration used by the acquiring company to pay the selling company may be stock of the acquiring company, bonds, cash, securities of another company (such as a parent corporation), or some combination of these. *See* DGCL §251(b); Model Act §11.02(c)(3). If stocks or bonds constitute at least 50 percent of the merger consideration, this is a nontaxable transaction for the acquiring corporation, for the selling corporation, and for the seller's shareholders. If cash is more than 50 percent of the consideration, the transaction is taxable.

Because a merger or consolidation can involve fundamental changes in the company in which a shareholder is invested, shareholders are given voting rights to approve the merger—at least some shareholders are given such rights some of the time. The shareholders of the selling company in a merger (the company that will merge out of existence) are always given voting rights to approve or disapprove of the merger unless it is a "short form merger," described below. *See* DGCL §251(c); Model Act §11.04(b). In some cases shareholders of the buying company (the company that will survive the merger) are given voting rights, but only if the charter of the surviving company will be amended by the merger; the rights or privileges attached to shares of the surviving company will be changed by the merger; or the surviving company is going to issue new shares of stock equal to 20 percent or more of the common stock outstanding prior to the merger in order to pay for the merger. *See* DGCL §251(f); Model Act §11.04(g). The theory behind these limitations on acquiring shareholders' voting rights is that shareholders' votes should be required only "if the transaction fundamentally alters the character of the enterprise or substantially reduces the shareholders' participation in voting or profit distribution." Official Comment, Model Act, §11.04. It is only when there are amendments to the charter, changes to the features of the shares or vote dilution greater than 20 percent that the transaction is treated as fundamentally altering the character of the company in which the acquiring company's shareholders are invested.

Even these voting rights for an acquiring company's shareholders can be eliminated in some cases, however, by using what is called a "triangular" merger structure. In a triangular merger, the surviving company establishes a wholly owned subsidiary (the parent company owns 100 percent of the stock) and capitalizes the subsidiary with the merger consideration, which can include the parent's stock, cash, bonds, or some combination of stock, cash, and bonds. *See* DGCL §251(b); Model Act §11.02(c)(3). The subsidiary and the selling company then enter into a merger agreement, which both boards of directors approve, and the selling company's shareholders vote on the plan. Now the only shareholder of the acquiror that might have voting rights is the parent company itself, which has already approved the transaction by virtue of its board's approval, thus eliminating the time, expense, and uncertainty of a shareholder vote.

Finally, there is also what is known as a "short-form" merger. In this event, where a parent company owns 90 percent or more of the stock of a subsidiary, the parent can merge the subsidiary into itself using simplified procedures, and without a shareholder vote. *See* DGCL §253; Model Act §11.05. The simplified procedures include notifying minority shareholders of the subsidiary that the merger has occurred, offering them the merger consideration for their shares that the parent has determined is fair, and notifying dissenting shareholders who do not believe the merger consideration is fair of their rights to a procedure called an "appraisal" to determine what fair consideration should have been. We discuss appraisal proceedings in more detail below. Generally the appraisal method is considered to be a procedure that is unfavorable for dissenting shareholders, at least under Delaware law.

Purchase of Assets. A purchase of assets under state law is exactly what it sounds like — that is, it is a negotiated transaction to purchase specified assets and liabilities of another company. *See* DGCL §271; Model Act §12.02. Unlike a merger, the selling company's assets and liabilities don't all transfer automatically as a matter of law; rather, the liabilities that are assumed by the purchasing company and those that remain with the selling company are subject to negotiation. This is one of the advantages of a sale of assets: there can be more flexibility in which liabilities are transferred. (A caveat here is that many states are developing a doctrine of "successor liability," which permits tort claims to be asserted against the successor company notwithstanding whatever contractual arrangements were made by the two companies. In fact, the Model Act permits such claims to be asserted against shareholders of the selling company, pro rata, for five years after the sale of assets. *See* Model Act §14.07.) The procedure for accomplishing the transaction is as follows: as with a merger, both boards of directors adopt resolutions authorizing the transaction. If the selling company is selling substantially all of its assets, then its shareholders have the right to vote to approve the sale. *See* DGCL §271(a); Model Act §12.02(a). If, however, the selling company is selling part but not substantially all of its assets, then its shareholders do not have voting rights. The purchasing company's shareholders don't have voting rights in an asset purchase transaction (except, under the Model Act, if the company will issue shares greater than 20 percent of outstanding shares before the purchase in exchange for the assets to be a purchased).

See Model Act §6.21(f). In Model Act jurisdictions, dissenting shareholders in the selling company have appraisal rights (discussed below) except if their shares are publicly traded and they are receiving either cash or publicly traded shares. *See* Model Act §13.02(b). In Delaware dissenting shareholders don't have appraisal rights. A sale of assets for cash is a taxable transaction for the selling shareholders (the cash will be treated as a dividend), while a sale of assets for stock is nontaxable.

Once the shareholders have approved the sale, the assets (and liabilities as agreed to in negotiations between the two companies) are transferred in exchange for the merger consideration. At the same time, the selling board adopts a resolution dissolving the corporation, paying any creditors that have not agreed to the substitution of a new debtor, cancelling the outstanding stock, and distributing the rest of the merger consideration to the selling shareholders.

Purchase of stock. A purchase of the stock of a company can occur in a friendly transaction, with the support of the target board, but also can occur in a hostile transaction. In both cases, an acquirer gains control of a majority or even all the shares of a company by making an offer directly to shareholders to purchase their shares for a premium — that is, at an above-market price. As mentioned before, this is called a "tender offer," which is regulated by federal securities law. Shareholders decide individually whether to participate in the tender offer, so this is not a case like a merger or sale of assets where a majority of shareholders acting as a group must approve the transaction for it to go forward. If enough individual shareholders tender their shares, an acquirer can gain control of a majority of shares and thus control the company. This is how a tender offer mechanism is used in a hostile acquisition to go over the board's authority and directly to the shareholders — although modern acquisitions practice has developed strategies called "rights plans" or "poison pills" for the board to use to prevent a tender offer from being successful in some cases. (This issue is discussed in more detail in the next chapter, but you will see it referred to below as the board's ability to "just say no.")

The mechanism of the tender offer is used in a variety of contexts, including "self-tenders" by a corporation of its own stock, or a tender offer by a controlling shareholder, such as a parent corporation, as the first step in "squeezing out" or "cashing out" minority shareholders. In this latter case, the controlling shareholder will first launch a tender offer for as many shares as necessary, usually hoping to get above a 90 percent shareholding interest. After the controlling shareholder gets above 90 percent ownership, it can then do a short-form merger to cash out the remaining minority shareholders. If the controlling shareholder doesn't get above a 90 percent ownership interest because not enough shareholders tender their shares, the controlling shareholder will still be in a controlling position and can then effect a regular cash-out merger of the minority shareholders by "persuading" the controlled board of the subsidiary company to adopt a resolution approving an agreement to merge with the parent company. This agreement to merge would then be put to a shareholders' vote in the subsidiary, and if a majority of the minority shareholders vote for the merger, it will go forward. You will see this technique in a number of the cases below. (You have seen it, in fact, in a number of cases you have read concerning the directors' or majority shareholder's fiduciary duty of loyalty.

Recall, for instance, Kahn v. Lynch Communication Systems, Inc., and In re Wheelabrator Technologies Inc. Shareholders Litigation in Chapter 11.)

Appraisal. As indicated above, when shareholders' interests are being fundamentally affected by a business combination, they are given rights to approve or disapprove the transaction. Shareholders who are given voting rights under state law are usually also given the right to challenge the price at which their shares were purchased in a proceeding known as an "appraisal." *See* DGCL §262; Model Act §13.02. One important exception to this generalization is when selling shareholders have the right to vote on a merger but start out with stock of a publicly held company and end up with stock of another publicly held company. Then there are no appraisal rights. The theory behind this exception is that if shareholders do not like the transaction, they can sell their shares in the market. Moreover, shareholders in a short-form merger are given appraisal rights even though they don't have voting rights. When shareholders do have appraisal rights, in order to assert them they must vote against the transaction, notify the company within a specified period of time that they might assert their appraisal rights, and then actually assert their rights within the time specified in the controlling statute. *See* DGCL §262(d); Model Act §13.22(b)(2)(ii).

In the following case study, you can see some of the tactical issues that are involved in utilizing various of these statutory approaches to structure an acquisition. Moreover, in the contract provisions included in the case study, you will also see some ways that deals get "protected" from interlopers during the considerable amount of time that can elapse between two boards deciding on a business combination and the transaction closing. We'll see additional examples of those "deal protection devices" in later cases.

DAIMLER-CHRYSLER: A CASE STUDY

One of the most celebrated mergers of all time occurred in 1998, when "Big Three" automaker Chrysler Corporation combined with German powerhouse Daimler Benz AG.[1] Although negotiated and publicized as a "merger of equals," it became apparent fairly quickly after the merger was consummated that Daimler was in control of the combined company.[2] This case study explores the issues that drove the negotiations and examines the contracts that ultimately led to one of the biggest corporate combinations in history.

Prelude to Merger: The Kerkorian Threat

On December 14, 1990, Chrysler Corp. announced that Beverly Hills billionaire Kirk Kerkorian had accumulated 22 million shares of its common stock. The stake represented 9.8 percent of Chrysler's 224 million shares outstanding and was purchased at a total cost of $272 million. Kerkorian was then Chrysler's largest shareholder.

Kerkorian stated in an SEC filing that the shares, purchased through Kerkorian's investment firm, Tracinda Corp., were acquired for investment purposes

---

1. "AG" is short for Aktiengesellschaft, the German equivalent of a publicly traded corporation in the United States.
2. For an entire book dedicated to this thesis, see Bill Vlasic & Bradley A. Stertz, *Taken for a Ride* (2001).

only and resulted from the high regard he held for Chrysler's then CEO and chairman, Lee Iacocca. Upon learning of Kerkorian's purchases on December 14, 1990, Iacocca called a special meeting of Chrysler's board. The board reacted quickly by strengthening Chrysler's poison pill, reducing the trigger from 20 percent to 10 percent. Chrysler officials maintained that the move was simply precautionary, while Kerkorian's spokesman called it an overreaction.

In the period following Kerkorian's initial investment until November 1994, Kerkorian's participation in Chrysler's affairs was muted. It appeared that he would stick to his declared intention to remain a passive investor, as he remained quiet and simply maintained his holdings by purchasing enough shares from new offerings to remain at 9.8 percent.

Chrysler's performance during this time was poor, as the company weathered the economic downturn of the early 1990s. In March 1991, Chrysler cut the 30-cent quarterly dividend in half and engaged in other cost-cutting measures to help minimize losses. However, the automaker's fortunes turned around in 1992 as the economy strengthened. Chrysler was poised with a new lineup of vehicles, including the Dodge Viper, the Jeep Grand Cherokee, and a trio of midsize sedans.

In 1992 Iacocca's relationship with Kerkorian blossomed as Iacocca stepped down from his post. Chrysler appointed Robert J. Eaton, a former GM executive, as his successor. Before retiring, Iacocca complained privately that he was being treated shabbily by the board by being forced to move on too quickly. Kerkorian responded by issuing a letter to Chrysler's board threatening to seek board representation to rectify concerns over "Mr. Iacocca's continued leadership role in the company." However, after a meeting with Iacocca, Eaton, and another board member, Kerkorian became convinced that "the interests of Chrysler's shareholders [were] being well represented" and dropped his threat to take a more active role in Chrysler's management. In exchange the board acknowledged that Iacocca would represent Kerkorian's interest on the board.

In November 1994, Kerkorian again began to feel dissatisfied with Chrysler's stock performance. This time he pointed the finger at Chrysler's cash stockpile. In a filing with the SEC and a letter to Chrysler's board, Kerkorian detailed his proposals for increasing the value of his investment, which included instituting a stock repurchase program, effecting a 2-for-1 stock split, and raising the quarterly dividend. He also declared his intention to increase his stake in Chrysler to 15 percent. Accordingly, he asked Chrysler's board to redeem its poison pill takeover defense, which had a 10 percent threshold. This move focused attention on the cash stockpile Chrysler was amassing, which, at the time of Kerkorian's announcement, was approximately $6.6 billion. Chrysler was intent on saving at least $7.5 billion to continue its aggressive product development through the next economic downturn. Many of Chrysler's large investors supported Kerkorian's push for a stock repurchase and an increased dividend.

The Chrysler board met on December 1, 1994, to respond to Kerkorian's proposals. The board appeased Kerkorian by raising Chrysler's quarterly dividend 60 percent —from 25 cents to 40 cents—by announcing a $1 billion stock buyback program, and by raising its poison pill threshold from 10 percent to 15 percent. Chrysler was able to approve these measures and still remain on track to reach its $7.5 billion cash goal by the end of 1995. The move was pleasing overall to Kerkorian, although he continued to hold out hope for a stock split. He subsequently purchased an additional 4 million shares, raising his total share in the company to 10.16 percent. Despite the actions taken by the board, the stock price languished, dropping to a low of $38.25 in late March 1995.

On April 12, 1995, Kerkorian and Iacocca tendered an unsolicited bid for Chrysler at $55 a share. Kerkorian's plan amounted to a leveraged buyout with $12 to $13 billion in loans, $2 billion from Kerkorian's continued equity holdings, another $3 billion from additional equity partners, and $5.5 billion from Chrysler's cash. The $55-a-share offering price represented a 40 percent premium over market price.

Reaction to the offer was mostly negative. Auto workers and management spoke out against Kerkorian's proposal to use up the majority of Chrysler's cash cushion; however, a few institutional investors appeared to embrace the offer. Whatever support Kerkorian may have had initially was withdrawn when it was discovered that he did not have financing arranged prior to launching the bid. He was unable to gain financial backing from banks who do business with Chrysler, because they were concerned, under pressure from Chrysler, about the proposed use of Chrysler's cash.

Kerkorian then shifted his focus to mounting a possible proxy fight. He sent a letter to Robert Eaton proposing that the board let the shareholders vote on his offer, or, alternatively, let them vote on the idea of raising the annual dividend to $5 per share. Kerkorian purchased an additional 1.9 million shares in the open market at $50 to $52, pushing his share of the company to 14.1 percent.

After these transactions, both sides attempted to curry favor with investors in preparation for an increasingly likely proxy fight. On September 5, 1995, Kerkorian hired former Chrysler CFO and board member Jerome B. York to serve as Tracinda Corporation's vice chairman. The move gave Kerkorian a legitimate candidate through which he could pursue board representation. Along with Kerkorian's increased stake in the company, the hiring of York also reestablished Kerkorian's credibility. Chrysler countered by doubling the stock repurchase program to $2 billion and by sending Eaton to meet with Chrysler's big investors. Chrysler even took out newspaper and magazine ads defending the company's record. York countered Chrysler's posturing by focusing attention on Chrysler's vehicle quality problems.

On October 25, 1995, in a letter to Eaton, York demanded a seat on Chrysler's board. York's demand also included a proposal to add two board seats to be filled by persons mutually agreed upon. The letter also asked Chrysler to appoint a committee of outside directors to examine Chrysler's cash management policy, adopt an anti-greenmail bylaw, require shareholder approval of any issuance of blank check preferred stock, and to raise the poison pill threshold from 15 percent to 20 percent. Chrysler's board met the following week and responded by commissioning a 90-day review of its corporate governance policies and board membership.

On February 8, 1996, Kerkorian signed a five-year standstill agreement that prohibited him from purchasing Chrysler shares in exchange for a board seat, filled by Kerkorian aide James D. Aljian; an increase in the stock repurchase program to $3 billion; an increased dividend; and an end to the feud between Iacocca and Chrysler involving his stock options. The agreement appears to have been motivated by findings made during the 90-day review. York said that after visiting other shareholders, it became clear that a settlement was something investors wanted. As agreed, Chrysler boosted the quarterly dividend again on May 16, 1996, to 70 cents. In addition, Chrysler declared a 2-for-1 stock split.

Consolidating Power at Daimler-Benz

At the same time Chrysler was settling with Kerkorian, Daimler's CEO, Jürgen Schrempp, was battling to establish control of his company. Unlike Robert Eaton, however, Schrempp's opponent was inside the company. Helmut Werner was the CEO of Mercedes-Benz, the powerful automobile subsidiary of Daimler. While Schrempp was forced to answer to Daimler's shareholders—including, most significantly, Deutsche Bank—Werner answered to Schrempp, at least nominally. In reality, he had insulated himself from Schrempp and had become the most powerful executive in the company. Schrempp felt the need for change.

At the beginning of 1996, Daimler was in trouble. The company's woes were caused primarily by some unwise acquisitions during the 1980s. When Schrempp assumed office in 1995, his first task was to slash jobs. This did not endear Schrempp to German labor, which held half of the seats on Daimler's supervisory board. (By law, the supervisory board of a German corporation must be equally divided between management representatives and labor representatives, with management having the tie-breaking vote.) Schrempp concluded that retrenchment was the only path to safety.

Schrempp also decided to streamline Daimler's cumbersome governance system. As a corporation, Daimler was managed by a supervisory board and a management board. Schrempp controlled the management board, but the supervisory board was led by Hilmar Kopper, the head of Deutsche Bank, which was Daimler's largest shareholder. (Many German corporations have large banks as substantial shareholders. Some commentators have argued that this concentration of ownership is useful in mitigating the agency costs that inevitably arise in the corporate context.)

But Daimler was not just a corporation, it was a conglomerate, a holding company with numerous subsidiary businesses each reporting to Schrempp. The problem—from Schrempp's standpoint—was that he was required to answer to Kopper and other members of the supervisory board, but the operational decisions were made by Werner and his counterparts at Daimler's other subsidiaries. Within months of taking office, therefore, Schrempp resolved to merge Mercedes into Daimler, thus consolidating control of the most important assets of the company and removing Werner as a rival.

As one would expect, Werner did not go along with this plan quietly. The first battle occurred in the management board, which consisted of eight members, including Schrempp and Werner. After multiple meetings and some backroom negotiations, Schrempp convinced the members of the management board of the merits of his proposal, which prevailed by a 7-to-1 vote (with Werner dissenting). The battle then moved to the supervisory board, but with the management board's approval and Kopper's support, Schrempp made fast work of the supervisory board. Werner resigned, and leadership of the company belonged to Schrempp.

The Search for a Deal

In the wake of this extended battle with Kerkorian, Chrysler's management felt the need to do some forward thinking. Perceiving the trend toward consolidation in the automobile industry, Eaton decided that Chrysler must seek a strategic partner. At the same time, Schrempp was searching for ways to double Daimler's revenues. Further conglomeration was not the answer; after all, he had spent the first part of his tenure overseeing the retrenchment from failed conglomeration efforts. Instead, Schrempp concluded that Daimler must expand its automobile operations by manufacturing not only premium cars but also cars for the masses.

It didn't take long for the companies to find each other. Under Schrempp's predecessor, the two companies had entertained briefly the idea of forming a strategic partnership, but both sides had concluded that the timing was wrong. When Schrempp approached Chrysler in 1997, however, he found a receptive audience. Over the next several months, the parties spoke informally and then more seriously about a merger. Finally, on May 7, 1998, they publicly announced the merger.

Constructing the Deal

Moving from the idea of a merger to the details of a merger is a protracted and sometimes painful process. The business combination agreement that the parties signed on May 7 described the obligations of each party in some detail, thus providing the framework for the transaction. Of course, other contracts and regulatory filings were required to execute the plan, but the combination agreement provided the basic form. The following paragraphs summarize a few of the issues that occupied the parties during their negotiations.

Headquarters. When the parties initiated merger discussions, they left open the question of where the company would be headquartered. This might be viewed as one of the most important decisions to be made, at least for the ongoing health of the combined company. When the time came to actually make the decision, Schrempp insisted that the company reside in Germany. According to *Taken for a Ride*,

> Schrempp knew there was no way he could merge Daimler and Chrysler as an American corporation. His supervisory board would not accept it, his employees would not accept it, and Germany would not accept it. Schrempp's global perspective and ambitions had their limits. He could bring Chrysler into the fold but could never move Daimler out of Germany. In Germany, companies are governed by "codetermination," in which half the members of the supervisory board are elected representatives of the labor force. Codetermination was an absolute tenet of German democracy, one that even Schrempp could not overcome.

Id. at 201.

General Structure. The transaction contemplated three parties: Daimler, Chrysler, and Oppenheim AG, which was referred to as "Newco" in the combination agreement. Newco was formed as a wholly owned subsidiary of Daimler specifically to facilitate this transaction. Newco was to play three critical roles: (1) it would acquire shares of Daimler common stock (as well as American depository shares[3] representing Daimler stock) through an exchange offer; (2) it

---

3. "American depositary shares" (ADSs) are securities that are created by non-U.S. companies to facilitate ownership and trading of the company's shares by U.S. investors. The shares are issued by a U.S. commercial bank, which acts as the depositary, and the shares represent a bundle of control and financial rights that are associated with underlying shares of a company's stock. The underlying shares are held by a correspondent bank in the home country of the company. ADSs are evidenced by physical certificates called American depositary receipts or ADRs.

would acquire shares of Chrysler through an exchange offer; and (3) it would merge with Daimler to create the new Daimler-Chrysler.

Once the shareholders of Daimler and Chrysler approved the merger (on the topic of shareholder approval, see below), Newco was committed to offer an exchange of one share of its own common stock for one "ordinary share" of Daimler stock. In addition, Newco offered to exchange one Newco ADS for one Daimler-Benz ADS. These exchanges together would consolidate all of the ordinary shares of Daimler in Newco and turn the former shareholders of Daimler into shareholders of Newco. In addition, Newco would change its name to "Daimler Chrysler Aktiengesellschaft."

"As promptly as possible following the date" of the combination agreement, Newco was to appoint an exchange agent in the United States who would form and hold all of the stock of a Delaware corporation known as "Chrysler Merger Sub." Immediately after consummation of the exchange offer discussed above, Chrysler Merger Sub would be merged into Chrysler, with Chrysler remaining as the surviving company. The terms of that merger would require the conversion of shares of Chrysler common stock into the right to receive Newco ADSs.

Meanwhile, the exchange agent would become the sole shareholder of the surviving company (Chrysler). This was to be only temporary, of course, as the parties wanted Chrysler and Daimler to be consolidated into the same firm. As soon as possible after the merger became effective, therefore, Newco would issue its own ordinary shares to the exchange agent — these are the shares that would underlie the Newco ADSs — and the exchange agent would in turn transfer all shares of Chrysler common stock to Newco.

The most difficult aspect of the merger agreement is the provision that dictates the value of Chrysler shares under the exchange just described. Prior to the Chrysler merger, the former shareholders of Daimler would be 100 percent owners of Newco. After the Chrysler merger, the former shareholders of Daimler and the former shareholders of Chrysler would share ownership of Newco. Their relative ownership interests would be dictated by the relative values of the two companies, which were negotiated in the merger talks.

The thing that makes the valuation provision so complicated is the lag time between the date of the negotiations and the date of the exchange. Between those two dates, the market values of the two companies could be affected by myriad factors. The valuation provision attempts to anticipate and account for changes. Of course, the currency here is Newco shares. Under the exchange offer, every ordinary share of Daimler was worth one share of Newco. The relative values of Daimler and Chrysler, therefore, were dictated by the exchange rate of Chrysler shares for Newco shares. The combined effect of the merger and the exchange offer was that (1) Newco owned all of the shares of Chrysler *and* all of the shares of Daimler; and (2) the former shareholders of Chrysler and Daimler together owned all of the shares of Newco.

Only one step remained to complete the transaction: the merger of Daimler into Newco, with Newco (which, as noted above, had been renamed "Daimler Chrysler Aktiengesellschaft") as the surviving corporation. Under the German stock corporation law — like under corporation law in the United States — Newco succeeded to all rights, assets, liabilities, and obligations of Daimler by operation of law. As part of the merger, all shareholders who still held shares of Daimler (that is, those who did not exchange their shares pursuant to the exchange offer) would automatically become shareholders of Newco at the same one-to-one conversion rate that prevailed in the exchange offer.

Shareholder Approval. Two shareholders needed to be convinced. On the Chrysler side, Tracinda Corporation still controlled a substantial percentage of Chryslers shares. On the Daimler side, Deutsche Bank AG was a substantial shareholder and creditor. In addition to these major shareholders, the parties needed to obtain the approval of at least 90 percent of the outstanding shares of each company to qualify for the favorable pooling-of-interests accounting treatment.[4]

The combination agreement required Chrysler to hold a special shareholder meeting "as promptly as practicable after the F-4 Registration Statement is declared effective under the Securities Act." Daimler, in turn, was required to schedule a shareholder meeting "so that the vote necessary to obtain the Chrysler Stockholder Approval occurs simultaneously with the Daimler-Benz Stockholder Approval."

Post-Merger Governance Structure. With the decision to form the new company in Germany, a host of other corporate governance issues fell into place automatically. In accordance with German company law, the new company would have a two-tiered governance structure comprised of a supervisory board (*Aufsichtsrat*) and a management board (*Vorstand*). Under the German Co-determination Law of 1976, half of the supervisory board must be comprised of representatives elected by the company's employees. In addition, the combination agreement specifies that the remaining representatives would be divided equally between Daimler and Chrysler. The parties also agreed that the chairman of Newco's supervisory board would be the then-current chairman of Daimler's supervisory board.

Control over the management board was also dictated by the combination agreement:

> The Management Board (*Vorstand*) of Newco AG shall consist of 18 members. In general, 50% of such members shall be those designated by Chrysler, and 50% of such members shall be those designated by Daimler-Benz, and there will be two additional members with responsibility for Daimler-Benz's non-automotive businesses.

Deal Protection Devices. As in any well-constructed merger, the combination agreement provided various mechanisms to increase the likelihood that the transaction would actually be consummated. The most conspicuous provision of the combination agreement in this regard was the "no-shop" clause, which prohibited both parties from soliciting, initiating, or encouraging the making of a takeover proposal or participating in discussions regarding a takeover proposal. This included a prohibition on furnishing information to prospective acquirors. An exception arises "if the party's Board of Directors (or the Management Board (*Vorstand*) in the case of Daimler-Benz) determines in good faith,

---

4. As its description implies, the effect of "pooling of interests" accounting is to treat two merged entities as if they had never been separate. This approach allows the company that survives a merger to carry forward all assets at their historical cost. Contrast this to "purchase" accounting, which treats a merger as a purchase of one entity by another and thus revalues the assets of the acquired entity. Although many companies found "pooling of interests" accounting more favorable, the Financial Accounting Standards Board eliminated it as an option in 2001.

after receiving the advice of outside counsel, that its failure to do so may result in a breach of its fiduciary duties to its stockholders under applicable law." This is the provision commonly known as a "fiduciary out."

Conclusion

The creation of Daimler-Benz was completed on November 17, 1998, when the company's shares began trading on the New York Stock Exchange. The shareholders of both corporations had overwhelmingly approved the combination (98 percent for Chrysler and 99 percent for Daimler). A short time after the shareholder meetings, Standard & Poors announced that Chrysler would be removed from the S&P 500 stock index and the new Daimler-Benz would not be selected to replace it—only American companies are allowed in this club. The stock prices of both Chrysler and Daimler fell on this news in anticipation of index funds selling their shares. Within a short time after the combination, it became apparent that this was not the "merger of equals" that Robert Eaton had demanded, but a takeover by Schrempp. This revelation led to a class-action lawsuit by institutions who had been investors in Chrysler and a separate lawsuit by Kerkorian. Both lawsuits claimed that Daimler had misrepresented the deal. Daimler-Chrysler settled the class action claims for $300 million in August 2003, but Kerkorian's claim was still pending as this case study went to press. Kerkorian is seeking $8 billion in damages.

Questions

(1)   In a transaction of this size and complexity, how do the parties assure themselves that there are no "skeletons on the closet"? For example, how does each party know that the other is not hiding a potentially large liability? What specific kinds of future liabilities must be considered in structuring the agreement?

(2)   In the wake of highly publicized accounting scandals, wouldn't the parties be concerned about the possibility that the other side is fabricating or materially misstating its financial statements? What kinds of provisions may be included in the merger agreement to protect against this concern?

(3)   What issues arise with respect to compliance with the various laws governing both companies? Does Chrysler simply trust Daimler to ensure that all of the requirements of German law are met? And vice versa?

(4)   The parties included in the combination agreement an obligation on all sides to use "reasonable best efforts" to consummate the transaction. Why would the parties think such a provision necessary or useful?

B. FIDUCIARY DUTIES IN FRIENDLY TRANSACTIONS

As in any transaction in which the directors make decisions that affect the shareholders of the company, directors authorizing a merger, sale of assets, or sale of stock must fulfill their fiduciary duties of care and loyalty in evaluating and approving the transaction, and they must generally act in good faith. They also must fulfill their fiduciary and federal securities law duties to disclose all material facts to the shareholders in the proxy statement soliciting shareholders' votes, or in the notice the company sends out describing the transaction, as in a short-form merger. Recall, for instance, that Smith v. Van Gorkam was a friendly sale of the Trans Union company to a company controlled by Jay Pritzker. In that case there were not only violations of the selling directors' duty of care in determining the sale price of the transaction, but also violations of the directors' duty to disclose to the shareholders important facts about how the sale price had been determined. Even where shareholders don't have voting rights, as in a short-form merger, directors have a duty of full disclosure, including disclosure about dissenting shareholders' right to an appraisal, since without full disclosure shareholders may not know that there's a problem with the price of the transaction and that they should seek an appraisal.

The content of directors' duties, as in other contexts we've seen, is affected by whether the transaction is an arm's length transaction between two unrelated companies, or is a conflict-of-interest transaction. Oddly enough, the content of directors' duties is also affected by whether the directors use a purely negotiated merger transaction or a tender offer transaction, as you will see in In re Pure Resources, Inc., 808 A.2d 421 (Del. Ch. 2002), below. Smith v. Van Gorkam is a paradigmatic example of an arm's length transaction and thus involved the duties of care and disclosure. Many times mergers occur between two companies that are already "related" through stock ownership, however, as in a parent/subsidiary transaction; or between companies with directors with substantial stock ownership on both sides of the transaction or with common directors on both boards. In these types of cases the directors' duty of loyalty is also implicated, so the burden shifts to the directors initially to demonstrate the entire fairness of the transaction.

1. Entire Fairness Review

The following case, Weinberger v. UOP, which you've seen referred to extensively in earlier chapters, provides a discussion of these fiduciary duty issues by the Delaware Supreme Court en banc. While this is a relatively old decision (1983), clearly its analysis is still vital, and thus it bears careful attention. Weinberger is important not only for its analysis of the duty of loyalty issues, here inherent in a negotiated merger between a parent/controlling shareholder and its minority-owned subsidiary, but also for its discussion of the remedy of appraisal for shareholders who don't agree with a transaction, and therefore vote against it. Note in particular the court's discussion of the "exclusivity" of the appraisal remedy. We'll return to that issue in Section D of this chapter.

WEINBERGER v. UOP, INC.
457 A.2d 701
Supreme Court of Delaware (en banc)
February 1, 1983

MOORE, Justice.

This post-trial appeal was reheard en banc from a decision of the Court of Chancery. It was brought by the class action plaintiff below, a former shareholder of UOP, Inc., who challenged the elimination of UOP's minority shareholders by a cash-out merger between UOP and its majority owner, The Signal Companies, Inc. Originally, the defendants in this action were Signal, UOP, certain officers and directors of those companies, and UOP's investment banker, Lehman Brothers Kuhn Loeb, Inc. The present Chancellor held that the terms of the merger were fair to the plaintiff and the other minority shareholders of UOP. Accordingly, he entered judgment in favor of the defendants. [This appeal followed.] . . .

I.

The facts found by the trial court, pertinent to the issues before us, are supported by the record, and we draw from them as set out in the Chancellor's opinion.

Signal is a diversified, technically based company operating through various subsidiaries. Its stock is publicly traded on the New York, Philadelphia and Pacific Stock Exchanges. UOP, formerly known as Universal Oil Products Company, was a diversified industrial company engaged in various lines of business, including petroleum and petro-chemical services and related products, construction, fabricated metal products, transportation equipment products, chemicals and plastics, and other products and services including land development, lumber products and waste disposal. Its stock was publicly held and listed on the New York Stock Exchange.

In 1974 Signal sold one of its wholly-owned subsidiaries for $420,000,000 in cash. *See* Gimbel v. Signal Companies, Inc., Del. Ch., 316 A.2d 599, *aff'd*, Del. Supr., 316 A.2d 619 (1974). While looking to invest this cash surplus, Signal became interested in UOP as a possible acquisition. Friendly negotiations ensued, and Signal proposed to acquire a controlling interest in UOP at a price of $19 per share. UOP's representatives sought $25 per share. In the arm's length bargaining that followed, an understanding was reached whereby Signal agreed to purchase from UOP 1,500,000 shares of UOP's authorized but unissued stock at $21 per share.

This purchase was contingent upon Signal making a successful cash tender offer for 4,300,000 publicly held shares of UOP, also at a price of $21 per share. This combined method of acquisition permitted Signal to acquire 5,800,000 shares of stock, representing 50.5% of UOP's outstanding shares. The UOP board of directors advised the company's shareholders that it had no objection to Signal's tender offer at that price. Immediately before the announcement of the tender offer, UOP's common stock had been trading on the New York Stock Exchange at a fraction under $14 per share.

The negotiations between Signal and UOP occurred during April 1975, and the resulting tender offer was greatly oversubscribed. However, Signal limited its total purchase of the tendered shares so that, when coupled with the stock bought from UOP, it had achieved its goal of becoming a 50.5% shareholder of UOP.

Although UOP's board consisted of thirteen directors, Signal nominated and elected only six. Of these, five were either directors or employees of Signal. The sixth, a partner in the banking firm of Lazard Freres & Co., had been one of Signal's representatives in the negotiations and bargaining with UOP concerning the tender offer and purchase price of the UOP shares.

However, the president and chief executive officer of UOP retired during 1975, and Signal caused him to be replaced by James V. Crawford, a long-time employee and senior executive vice president of one of Signal's wholly-owned subsidiaries. Crawford succeeded his predecessor on UOP's board of directors and also was made a director of Signal.

By the end of 1977 Signal basically was unsuccessful in finding other suitable investment candidates for its excess cash, and by February 1978 considered that it had no other realistic acquisitions available to it on a friendly basis. Once again its attention turned to UOP.

The trial court found that at the instigation of certain Signal management personnel, including William W. Walkup, its board chairman, and Forrest N. Shumway, its president, a feasibility study was made concerning the possible acquisition of the balance of UOP's outstanding shares. This study was performed by two Signal officers, Charles S. Arledge, vice president (director of planning), and Andrew J. Chitiea, senior vice president (chief financial officer). Messrs. Walkup, Shumway, Arledge and Chitiea were all directors of UOP in addition to their membership on the Signal board.

Arledge and Chitiea concluded that it would be a good investment for Signal to acquire the remaining 49.5% of UOP shares at any price up to $24 each. Their report was discussed between Walkup and Shumway who, along with Arledge, Chitiea and Brewster L. Arms, internal counsel for Signal, constituted Signal's senior management. In particular, they talked about the proper price to be paid if the acquisition was pursued, purportedly keeping in mind that as UOP's majority shareholder, Signal owed a fiduciary responsibility to both its own stockholders as well as to UOP's minority. It was ultimately agreed that a meeting of Signal's executive committee would be called to propose that Signal acquire the remaining outstanding stock of UOP through a cash-out merger in the range of $20 to $21 per share.

The executive committee meeting was set for February 28, 1978. As a courtesy, UOP's president, Crawford, was invited to attend, although he was not a member of Signal's executive committee. On his arrival, and prior to the meeting, Crawford was asked to meet privately with Walkup and Shumway. He was then told of Signal's plan to acquire full ownership of UOP and was asked for his reaction to the proposed price range of $20 to $21 per share. Crawford said he thought such a price would be "generous," and that it was certainly one which should be submitted to UOP's minority shareholders for their ultimate consideration. He stated, however, that Signal's 100% ownership could cause internal problems at UOP. He believed that employees would have to be given some assurance of their future place in a fully-owned Signal subsidiary. Otherwise, he feared the departure of essential personnel. Also, many of UOP's key employees had stock option incentive programs which would be wiped out by a merger. Crawford therefore urged that some adjustment would have to be made, such as providing a comparable incentive in Signal's shares, if after the merger he was to maintain his quality of personnel and efficiency at UOP.

Thus, Crawford voiced no objection to the $20 to $21 price range, nor did he suggest that Signal should consider paying more than $21 per share for the minority interests. Later, at the executive committee meeting the same factors were discussed, with Crawford repeating the position he earlier took with Walkup and Shumway. Also considered was the 1975 tender offer and the fact that it had been greatly oversubscribed at $21 per share. For many reasons, Signal's management concluded that the acquisition of UOP's minority shares provided the solution to a number of its business problems.

Thus, it was the consensus that a price of $20 to $21 per share would be fair to both Signal and the minority shareholders of UOP. Signal's executive committee authorized its management "to negotiate" with UOP "for a cash acquisition of the minority ownership in UOP, Inc., with the intention of presenting a proposal to [Signal's] board of directors . . . on March 6, 1978." Immediately after this February 28, 1978 meeting, Signal issued a press release stating:

> The Signal Companies, Inc. and UOP, Inc. are conducting negotiations for the acquisition for cash by Signal of the 49.5 per cent of UOP which it does not presently own, announced Forrest N. Shumway, president and chief executive officer of Signal, and James V. Crawford, UOP president.
>
> Price and other terms of the proposed transaction have not yet been finalized and would be subject to approval of the boards of directors of Signal and UOP, scheduled to meet early next week, the stockholders of UOP and certain federal agencies.

The announcement also referred to the fact that the closing price of UOP's common stock on that day was $14.50 per share.

Two days later, on March 2, 1978, Signal issued a second press release stating that its management would recommend a price in the range of $20 to $21 per share for UOP's 49.5% minority interest. This announcement referred to Signal's earlier statement that "negotiations" were being conducted for the acquisition of the minority shares.

Between Tuesday, February 28, 1978 and Monday, March 6, 1978, a total of four business days, Crawford spoke by telephone with all of UOP's non-Signal, *i.e.*, outside, directors. Also during that period, Crawford retained Lehman Brothers to render a fairness opinion as to the price offered the minority for its stock. He gave two reasons for this choice. First, the time schedule between the announcement and the board meetings was short (by then only three business days) and since Lehman Brothers had been acting as UOP's investment banker for many years, Crawford felt that it would be in the best position to respond on such brief notice. Second, James W. Glanville, a long-time director of UOP and a partner in Lehman Brothers, had acted as a financial advisor to UOP for many years. Crawford believed that Glanville's familiarity with UOP, as a member of its board, would also be of assistance in enabling Lehman Brothers to render a fairness opinion within the existing time constraints.

Crawford telephoned Glanville, who gave his assurance that Lehman Brothers had no conflicts that would prevent it from accepting the task. Glanville's immediate personal reaction was that a price of $20 to $21 would certainly be fair, since it represented almost a 50% premium over UOP's market price. Glanville sought a $250,000 fee for Lehman Brothers' services, but Crawford thought this too much. After further discussions Glanville finally agreed that Lehman Brothers would render its fairness opinion for $150,000.

During this period Crawford also had several telephone contacts with Signal officials. In only one of them, however, was the price of the shares discussed. In a conversation with Walkup, Crawford advised that as a result of his communications with UOP's non-Signal directors, it was his feeling that the price would have to be the top of the proposed range, or $21 per share, if the approval of UOP's outside directors was to be obtained. But again, he did not seek any price higher than $21.

Glanville assembled a three-man Lehman Brothers team to do the work on the fairness opinion. These persons examined relevant documents and information concerning UOP, including its annual reports and its Securities and Exchange Commission filings from 1973 through 1976, as well as its audited financial statements for 1977, its interim reports to shareholders, and its recent and historical market prices and trading volumes. In addition, on Friday, March 3, 1978, two members of the Lehman Brothers team flew to UOP's headquarters in Des Plaines, Illinois, to perform a "due diligence" visit, during the course of which they interviewed Crawford as well as UOP's general counsel, its chief financial officer, and other key executives and personnel.

As a result, the Lehman Brothers team concluded that "the price of either $20 or $21 would be a fair price for the remaining shares of UOP." They telephoned this impression to Glanville, who was spending the weekend in Vermont.

On Monday morning, March 6, 1978, Glanville and the senior member of the Lehman Brothers team flew to Des Plaines to attend the scheduled UOP directors meeting. Glanville looked over the assembled information during the flight. The two had with them the draft of a "fairness opinion letter" in which the price had been left blank. Either during or immediately prior to the directors' meeting, the two-page "fairness opinion letter" was typed in final form and the price of $21 per share was inserted.

On March 6, 1978, both the Signal and UOP boards were convened to consider the proposed merger. Telephone communications were maintained between the two meetings. Walkup, Signal's board chairman, and also a UOP director, attended UOP's meeting with Crawford in order to present Signal's position and answer any questions that UOP's non-Signal directors might have. Arledge and Chitiea, along with Signal's other designees on UOP's board, participated by conference telephone. All of UOP's outside directors attended the meeting either in person or by conference telephone.

First, Signal's board unanimously adopted a resolution authorizing Signal to propose to UOP a cash merger of $21 per share as outlined in a certain merger agreement and other supporting documents. This proposal required that the merger be approved by a majority of UOP's outstanding minority shares voting at the stockholders meeting at which the merger would be considered, and that the minority shares voting in favor of the merger, when coupled with Signal's 50.5% interest would have to comprise at least two-thirds of all UOP shares. Otherwise the proposed merger would be deemed disapproved.

UOP's board then considered the proposal. Copies of the agreement were delivered to the directors in attendance, and other copies had been forwarded earlier to the directors participating by telephone. They also had before them UOP financial data for 1974-1977, UOP's most recent financial statements, market price information, and budget projections for 1978. In addition they had Lehman Brothers' hurriedly prepared fairness opinion letter finding the price of $21 to be fair. Glanville, the Lehman Brothers partner, and UOP director, commented on the information that had gone into preparation of the letter.

Signal also suggests that the Arledge-Chitiea feasibility study, indicating that a price of up to $24 per share would be a "good investment" for Signal, was discussed at the UOP directors' meeting. The Chancellor made no such finding, and our independent review of the record, detailed *infra,* satisfies us by a preponderance of the evidence that there was no discussion of this document at UOP's board meeting. Furthermore, it is clear beyond peradventure that nothing in that report was ever disclosed to UOP's minority shareholders prior to their approval of the merger.

After consideration of Signal's proposal, Walkup and Crawford left the meeting to permit a free and uninhibited exchange between UOP's non-Signal directors. Upon their return a resolution to accept Signal's offer was then proposed and adopted. While Signal's men on UOP's board participated in various aspects of the meeting, they abstained from voting. However, the minutes show that each of them "if voting would have voted yes."

On March 7, 1978, UOP sent a letter to its shareholders advising them of the action taken by UOP's board with respect to Signal's offer. This document pointed out, among other things, that on February 28, 1978 "both companies had announced negotiations were being conducted."

Despite the swift board action of the two companies, the merger was not submitted to UOP's shareholders until their annual meeting on May 26, 1978. In the notice of that meeting and proxy statement sent to shareholders in May, UOP's management and board urged that the merger be approved. The proxy statement also advised:

> The price was determined after *discussions* between James V. Crawford, a director of Signal and Chief Executive Officer of UOP, and officers of Signal which took place during meetings on February 28, 1978, and in the course of several subsequent telephone conversations. (Emphasis added.)

In the original draft of the proxy statement the word "negotiations" had been used rather than "discussions." However, when the Securities and Exchange Commission sought details of the "negotiations" as part of its review of these materials, the term was deleted and the word "discussions" was substituted. The proxy statement indicated that the vote of UOP's board in approving the merger had been unanimous. It also advised the shareholders that Lehman Brothers had given its opinion that the merger price of $21 per share was fair to UOP's minority. However, it did not disclose the hurried method by which this conclusion was reached.

As of the record date of UOP's annual meeting, there were 11,488,302 shares of UOP common stock outstanding, 5,688,302 of which were owned by the minority. At the meeting only 56%, or 3,208,652, of the minority shares were voted. Of these, 2,953,812, or 51.9% of the total minority, voted for the merger, and 254,840 voted against it. When Signal's stock was added to the minority shares voting in favor, a total of 76.2% of UOP's outstanding shares approved the merger while only 2.2% opposed it.

By its terms the merger became effective on May 26, 1978, and each share of UOP's stock held by the minority was automatically converted into a right to receive $21 cash.

II.

A.

A primary issue mandating reversal is the preparation by two UOP directors, Arledge and Chitiea, of their feasibility study for the exclusive use and benefit of Signal. This document was of obvious significance to both Signal and UOP. Using UOP data, it described the advantages to Signal of ousting the minority at a price range of $21-$24 per share. Mr. Arledge, one of the authors, outlined the benefits to Signal: [Handwritten comments of Mr. Arledge are indicated in parentheses.]

PURPOSE OF THE MERGER

1) Provides an outstanding investment opportunity for Signal — (Better than any recent acquisition we have seen.)
2) Increases Signal's earnings.
3) Facilitates the flow of resources between Signal and its subsidiaries — (Big factor — works both ways.)
4) Provides cost savings potential for Signal and UOP.
5) Improves the percentage of Signal's "operating earnings" as opposed to "holding company earnings."
6) Simplifies the understanding of Signal.
7) Facilitates technological exchange among Signal's subsidiaries.
8) Eliminates potential conflicts of interest.

Having written those words, solely for the use of Signal, it is clear from the record that neither Arledge nor Chitiea shared this report with their fellow directors of UOP. We are satisfied that no one else did either. This conduct hardly meets the fiduciary standards applicable to such a transaction. While Mr. Walkup, Signal's chairman of the board and a UOP director, attended the March 6, 1978 UOP board meeting and testified at trial that he had discussed the Arledge-Chitiea report with the UOP directors at this meeting, the record does not support this assertion. Perhaps it is the result of some confusion on Mr. Walkup's part. In any event Mr. Shumway, Signal's president, testified that he made sure the Signal outside directors had this report prior to the March 6, 1978 Signal board meeting, but he did not testify that the Arledge-Chitiea report was also sent to UOP's outside directors.

Mr. Crawford, UOP's president, could not recall that any documents, other than a draft of the merger agreement, were sent to UOP's directors before the March 6, 1978 UOP meeting. Mr. Chitiea, an author of the report, testified that it was made available to Signal's directors, but to his knowledge it was not circulated to the outside directors of UOP. He specifically testified that he "didn't share" that information with the outside directors of UOP with whom he served. . . .

Actually, it appears that a three-page summary of figures was given to all UOP directors. Its first page is identical to one page of the Arledge-Chitiea report, but this dealt with nothing more than a justification of the $21 price. Significantly, the contents of this three-page summary are what the minutes reflect Mr. Walkup told the UOP board. However, nothing contained in either the minutes or this three-page summary reflects Signal's study regarding the $24 price.

The Arledge-Chitiea report speaks for itself in supporting the Chancellor's finding that a price of up to $24 was a "good investment" for Signal. It shows that a return on the investment at $21 would be 15.7% versus 15.5% at $24 per share. This was a difference of only two-tenths of one percent, while it meant over $17,000,000 to the minority. Under such circumstances, paying UOP's minority shareholders $24 would have had relatively little long-term effect on Signal, and the Chancellor's findings concerning the benefit to Signal, even at a price of $24, were obviously correct. Levitt v. Bouvier, Del. Supr., 287 A.2d 671, 673 (1972).

Certainly, this was a matter of material significance to UOP and its shareholders. Since the study was prepared by two UOP directors, using UOP information for the exclusive benefit of Signal, and nothing whatever was done to disclose it to the outside UOP directors or the minority shareholders, a question of breach of fiduciary duty arises. This problem occurs because there were common Signal-UOP directors participating, at least to some extent, in the UOP board's decision-making processes without full disclosure of the conflicts they faced.[7]

B.

In assessing this situation, the Court of Chancery was required to:

> examine what information defendants had and to measure it against what they gave to the minority stockholders, in a context in which "complete candor" is required. In other words, the limited function of the Court was to determine whether defendants had disclosed all information in their possession germane to the transaction in issue. And by "germane" we mean, for present purposes, information such as a reasonable shareholder would consider important in deciding whether to sell or retain stock.
>
> . . . Completeness, not adequacy, is both the norm and the mandate under present circumstances.

Lynch v. Vickers Energy Corp., Del. Supr., 383 A.2d 278, 281 (1977) (*Lynch I*). This is merely stating in another way the long-existing principle of Delaware law that these Signal designated directors on UOP's board still owed UOP and its shareholders an uncompromising duty of loyalty. The classic language of Guth v. Loft, Inc., Del. Supr., 5 A.2d 503, 510 (1939), requires no embellishment:

> A public policy, existing through the years, and derived from a profound knowledge of human characteristics and motives, has established a rule that demands

---

7. Although perfection is not possible, or expected, the result here could have been entirely different if UOP had appointed an independent negotiating committee of its outside directors to deal with Signal at arm's length. *See, e.g.,* Harriman v. E.I. duPont de Nemours & Co., 411 F. Supp. 133 (D. Del.1975). Since fairness in this context can be equated to conduct by a theoretical, wholly independent, board of directors acting upon the matter before them, it is unfortunate that this course apparently was neither considered nor pursued. Johnston v. Greene, Del. Supr., 121 A.2d 919, 925 (1956). Particularly in a parent-subsidiary context, a showing that the action taken was as though each of the contending parties had in fact exerted its bargaining power against the other at arm's length is strong evidence that the transaction meets the test of fairness. Getty Oil Co. v. Skelly Oil Co., Del. Supr., 267 A.2d 883, 886 (1970); Puma v. Marriott, Del. Ch., 283 A.2d 693, 696 (1971).

of a corporate officer or director, peremptorily and inexorably, the most scrupulous observance of his duty, not only affirmatively to protect the interests of the corporation committed to his charge, but also to refrain from doing anything that would work injury to the corporation, or to deprive it of profit or advantage which his skill and ability might properly bring to it, or to enable it to make in the reasonable and lawful exercise of its powers. The rule that requires an undivided and unselfish loyalty to the corporation demands that there shall be no conflict between duty and self-interest.

Given the absence of any attempt to structure this transaction on an arm's length basis, Signal cannot escape the effects of the conflicts it faced, particularly when its designees on UOP's board did not totally abstain from participation in the matter. There is no "safe harbor" for such divided loyalties in Delaware. When directors of a Delaware corporation are on both sides of a transaction, they are required to demonstrate their utmost good faith and the most scrupulous inherent fairness of the bargain. Gottlieb v. Heyden Chemical Corp., Del. Supr., 91 A.2d 57, 57-58 (1952). The requirement of fairness is unflinching in its demand that where one stands on both sides of a transaction, he has the burden of establishing its entire fairness, sufficient to pass the test of careful scrutiny by the courts. . . .

There is no dilution of this obligation where one holds dual or multiple directorships, as in a parent-subsidiary context. Levien v. Sinclair Oil Corp., Del. Ch., 261 A.2d 911, 915 (1969). Thus, individuals who act in a dual capacity as directors of two corporations, one of whom is parent and the other subsidiary, owe the same duty of good management to both corporations, and in the absence of an independent negotiating structure (see note 7, *supra*), or the directors' total abstention from any participation in the matter, this duty is to be exercised in light of what is best for both companies. Warshaw v. Calhoun, Del. Supr., 221 A.2d 487, 492 (1966). The record demonstrates that Signal has not met this obligation.

C.

The concept of fairness has two basic aspects: fair dealing and fair price. The former embraces questions of when the transaction was timed, how it was initiated, structured, negotiated, disclosed to the directors, and how the approvals of the directors and the stockholders were obtained. The latter aspect of fairness relates to the economic and financial considerations of the proposed merger, including all relevant factors: assets, market value, earnings, future prospects, and any other elements that affect the intrinsic or inherent value of a company's stock. . . . However, the test for fairness is not a bifurcated one as between fair dealing and price. All aspects of the issue must be examined as a whole since the question is one of entire fairness. However, in a non-fraudulent transaction we recognize that price may be the preponderant consideration outweighing other features of the merger. Here, we address the two basic aspects of fairness separately because we find reversible error as to both.

D.

Part of fair dealing is the obvious duty of candor required by *Lynch I*, *supra*. . . . With the well-established Delaware law on the subject, and the Court of Chancery's findings of fact here, it is inevitable that the obvious conflicts posed by Arledge and Chitiea's preparation of their "feasibility study," derived from UOP information, for the sole use and benefit of Signal, cannot pass muster.

The Arledge-Chitiea report is but one aspect of the element of fair dealing. How did this merger evolve? It is clear that it was entirely initiated by Signal. The serious time constraints under which the principals acted were all set by Signal. It had not found a suitable outlet for its excess cash and considered UOP a desirable investment, particularly since it was now in a position to acquire the whole company for itself. For whatever reasons, and they were only Signal's, the entire transaction was presented to and approved by UOP's board within four business days. Standing alone, this is not necessarily indicative of any lack of fairness by a majority shareholder. It was what occurred, or more properly, what did not occur, during this brief period that makes the time constraints imposed by Signal relevant to the issue of fairness.

The structure of the transaction, again, was Signal's doing. So far as negotiations were concerned, it is clear that they were modest at best. Crawford, Signal's man at UOP, never really talked price with Signal, except to accede to its management's statements on the subject, and to convey to Signal the UOP outside directors' view that as between the $20-$21 range under consideration, it would have to be $21. The latter is not a surprising outcome, but hardly arm's length negotiations. Only the protection of benefits for UOP's key employees and the issue of Lehman Brothers' fee approached any concept of bargaining.

As we have noted, the matter of disclosure to the UOP directors was wholly flawed by the conflicts of interest raised by the Arledge-Chitiea report. All of those conflicts were resolved by Signal in its own favor without divulging any aspect of them to UOP. . . .

Finally, the minority stockholders were denied the critical information that Signal considered a price of $24 to be a good investment. Since this would have meant over $17,000,000 more to the minority, we cannot conclude that the shareholder vote was an informed one. Under the circumstances, an approval by a majority of the minority was meaningless. *Lynch I*, 383 A.2d at 279, 281; Cahall v. Lofland, Del. Ch., 114 A. 224 (1921).

Given these particulars and the Delaware law on the subject, the record does not establish that this transaction satisfies any reasonable concept of fair dealing, and the Chancellor's findings in that regard must be reversed.

E.

Turning to the matter of price, plaintiff also challenges its fairness. His evidence was that on the date the merger was approved the stock was worth at least $26 per share. In support, he offered the testimony of a chartered investment analyst who used two basic approaches to valuation: a comparative analysis of the premium paid over market in ten other tender offer-merger combinations, and a discounted cash flow analysis.

. . . [The Court then rejected prior Delaware case law that had used only one method of valuing stock, holding that] a more liberal approach must include proof of value by any techniques or methods which are generally considered acceptable in the financial community and otherwise admissible in court. . . .

The plaintiff has not sought an appraisal, but rescissory damages of the type contemplated by Lynch v. Vickers Energy Corp., Del. Supr., 429 A.2d 497, 505-06 (1981) (*Lynch II*). In view of the approach to valuation that we announce today, we see no basis in our law for *Lynch II*'s exclusive monetary formula for relief. On remand the plaintiff will be permitted to test the fairness of the $21 price by the standards we herein establish, in conformity with the principle applicable to an appraisal — that fair value be determined by taking "into account all relevant factors" [*see* 8 Del. C. §262(h), *supra*]. In our view this includes the elements of rescissory damages if the Chancellor considers them susceptible of proof and a remedy appropriate to all the issues of fairness before him. To the extent that *Lynch II*, 429 A.2d at 505-06, purports to limit the Chancellor's discretion to a single remedial formula for monetary damages in a cash-out merger, it is overruled.

While a plaintiff's monetary remedy ordinarily should be confined to the more liberalized appraisal proceeding herein established [taking into account "all relevant factors" in determining the value of shares, as required under DGCL §262(h)], we do not intend any limitation on the historic powers of the Chancellor to grant such other relief as the facts of a particular case may dictate. The appraisal remedy we approve may not be adequate in certain cases, particularly where fraud, misrepresentation, self-dealing, deliberate waste of corporate assets, or gross and palpable overreaching are involved. Cole v. National Cash Credit Association, Del. Ch., 156 A. 183, 187 (1931). Under such circumstances, the Chancellor's powers are complete to fashion any form of equitable and monetary relief as may be appropriate, including rescissory damages. Since it is apparent that this long completed transaction is too involved to undo, and in view of the Chancellor's discretion, the award, if any, should be in the form of monetary damages based upon entire fairness standards, *i.e.*, fair dealing and fair price.

Obviously, there are other litigants, like the plaintiff, who abjured an appraisal and whose rights to challenge the element of fair value must be preserved. Accordingly, the quasi-appraisal remedy we grant the plaintiff here will apply only to: (1) this case; (2) any case now pending on appeal to this Court; (3) any case now pending in the Court of Chancery which has not yet been appealed but which may be eligible for direct appeal to this Court; (4) any case challenging a cash-out merger, the effective date of which is on or before February 1, 1983; and (5) any proposed merger to be presented at a shareholders' meeting, the notification of which is mailed to the stockholders on or before February 23, 1983. Thereafter, the provisions of 8 Del. C. §262, as herein construed, respecting the scope of an appraisal and the means for perfecting the same, shall govern the financial remedy available to minority shareholders in a cash-out merger. Thus, we return to the well established principles of Stauffer v. Standard Brands, Inc., Del. Supr., 187 A.2d 78 (1962) and David J. Greene & Co. v. Schenley Industries, Inc., Del. Ch., 281 A.2d 30 (1971), mandating a stockholder's recourse to the basic remedy of an appraisal.

The judgment of the Court of Chancery, finding both the circumstances of the merger and the price paid the minority shareholders to be fair, is reversed. The matter is remanded for further proceedings consistent herewith. Upon remand the plaintiff's post-trial motion to enlarge the class should be granted.

Reversed and Remanded.

PROBLEM 14-1

General Cigar is a Delaware corporation with its executive offices in New York. It is a leading manufacturer of premium, high-end cigars. These cigars sell for $10.00 or more per cigar, are kept under the controlled humidity formerly reserved for art museums, and are described in catalogues with the kind of prose formerly reserved for fine wines, such as:

> The [Brand X] is blended exclusively for us by Carlos Fuente, Jr., using 4-to 5-year-old aged Dominican tobacco taken from the finest and most fertile plants. The distinctive flavor of this cigar, with hints of licorice and chocolate, comes from its wrapper, grown on a private estate in Ecuador owned by the Oliva family, where this proprietary wrapper leaf is grown for the Fuente Family exclusively for our cigars. The leaf is taken from the higher primings and matures slowly by sunlight filtered through the region's natural cloud covering.

General Cigar went public in 1997, using a dual class capitalization, with 13.6 million shares of publicly traded Class A common stock outstanding, and 13.4 million shares of Class B common stock outstanding. The Class B shares are not publicly traded. Class A shares have one vote per share, and Class B shares have 10 votes per share. Notwithstanding the voting disparity, the company's certificate of incorporation provides for equal consideration in the event of a sale or merger. At the time of the facts at issue, four members of the Cullman family — Edgar M. Cullman, Sr., Edgar M. Cullman, Jr., Susan R. Cullman, and John L. Ernst (a nephew of Edgar, Sr., and cousin of the other Cullmans) — owned 162 shares of Class A and 9.9 million shares of Class B stock. This constituted 67 percent of the voting power in the corporation. Each of the Cullmans is a member of General Cigar's 11-person board of directors.

In the early fall of 1999, a European cigar company, Swedish Match, approached the Cullmans and expressed an interest in buying out all of the Class A public shareholders and all of the Class B shares not owned by the Cullmans. With the assistance of another board member, Peter Solomon, and his financial advising firm, Peter J. Solomon & Co., the Cullmans arrived at an understanding with Swedish Match that they would sell Swedish Match one-third of their Class B shares for $15.00 per share; immediately after that sale General Cigar would cash out the public, unaffiliated shareholders for $15.00 per share in a cash-out merger; Cullman Sr. and Cullman Jr. would retain their positions as chairman and CEO of the surviving company for three years and have the power to appoint a majority of the board; and if the transaction did not go forward, the Cullmans would not vote for any other transaction for a period of one year. Even after the proposed sale the Cullman group would continue to have voting control over the company because of the disproportionate 10:1 voting strength of the Class B shares the Cullmans would retain.

Once the negotiations reached agreement on these points, General Cigar appointed a special committee consisting of three outside directors, Dan W. Lufkin, Thomas C. Israel, and Frances T. Vincent, Jr., to decide if the transaction was advisable. The committee had independent legal advice from Wachtell, Lipton, Rosen & Katz, and had independent financial advice from Deutsche

Bank Securities. In early January of 2000 the special committee received copies of the proposed agreements and then, based on advice from their legal and financial advisers, negotiated directly with Swedish Match. As a result of their negotiation, the purchase price for the publicly owned class A and B shares was increased from $15.00 to $15.25 per share, and the length of time the Cullmans would not vote for an alternative transaction was increased from 12 months to 18 months. On January 19, 2000, the special committee unanimously recommended approval of the transaction. That same day, the General Cigar board also unanimously recommended approval. Approval of the merger required that a majority of the unaffiliated shareholders of Class A stock, voting separately as a class, vote in favor of the transaction. In April a majority of the unaffiliated Class A shareholders voted for the transaction.

Assume that a number of Class A stockholders who voted against the transaction come to you for advice on challenging the merger. They suggest the following facts about directors Lufkin, Israel and Vincent. Directors Israel, and Vincent had long-standing (15-year) business relationships with the Cullmans, including as board members of General Cigar or its predecessors since 1986. Director Lufkin was a founder of Donaldson, Lufkin & Jenrette (DLJ), a securities firm, and lead underwriter in the company's IPO, earning a substantial fee as a result. The stockholders contend that Director Lufkin couldn't possibly hope to attract any future General Cigar business if he voted against the merger. In addition, Class A shareholders challenge the independence of other directors. Director Barnet, they claim, has a financial interest in the merger because he will be a director in the surviving company. Director Bernbach has a consulting agreement with General Cigar for $75,000 per year, and the Class A shareholders assert that this agreement would not be extended if Director Bernbach voted against the merger. Director Solomon has an interest in the transaction because his company stands to gain $3.3 million if the merger is consummated.

How do you analyze whether or not to proceed with this case? Who will have the burden of proof, and what will the burden be? What additional facts do you need to advise Class A stockholders on whether to challenge this transaction?

2. *The Tender Offer Context*

The following case discusses in elegant detail a perplexing feature of Delaware corporate law: the content of fiduciary duties, even in a parent/controlling shareholder and subsidiary/minority shareholder context, is fundamentally affected by whether the transaction uses a negotiated merger structure or a tender offer structure. This case also examines, as in other cases you've seen, the use of a special committee to negotiate on behalf of the minority shareholders. Although Delaware law does not require using such a committee, clearly having such a committee helps the board to show that there was fair dealing as part of an entire fairness analysis. Yet, as the following case shows, the special committee must be an active, independent body, with independent legal and financial advisors, if its involvement is going to be successful in showing fair dealing.

In re PURE RESOURCES, INC. SHAREHOLDERS LITIGATION
808 A.2d 421
Delaware Court of Chancery
October 7, 2002

STRINE, Vice Chancellor.

This is the court's decision on a motion for preliminary injunction. The lead plaintiff in the case holds a large block of stock in Pure Resources, Inc., 65% of the shares of which are owned by Unocal Corporation. The lead plaintiff and its fellow plaintiffs seek to enjoin a now-pending exchange offer (the "Offer") by which Unocal hopes to acquire the rest of the shares of Pure in exchange for shares of its own stock.

The plaintiffs believe that the Offer is inadequate and is subject to entire fairness review, consistent with the rationale of Kahn v. Lynch Communication Systems, Inc. and its progeny. Moreover, they claim that the defendants, who include Unocal and Pure's board of directors, have not made adequate and non-misleading disclosure of the material facts necessary for Pure stockholders to make an informed decision whether to tender into the Offer.

By contrast, the defendants argue that the Offer is a non-coercive one that is accompanied by complete disclosure of all material facts. As such, they argue that the Offer is not subject to the entire fairness standard, but to the standards set forth in cases like Solomon v. Pathe Communications Corp., standards which they argue have been fully met.

In this opinion, I conclude that the Offer is subject, as a general matter, to the *Solomon* standards, rather than the *Lynch* entire fairness standard. I conclude, however, that many of the concerns that justify the *Lynch* standard are implicated by tender offers initiated by controlling stockholders, which have as their goal the acquisition of the rest of the subsidiary's shares [either in the tender offer itself, or in combination with a later short-form merger]. These concerns should be accommodated within the *Solomon* form of review, by requiring that tender offers by controlling shareholders be structured in a manner that reduces the distorting effect of the tendering process on free stockholder choice and by ensuring minority stockholders a candid and unfettered tendering recommendation from the independent directors of the target board. In this case, the Offer for the most part meets this standard, with one exception that Unocal may cure.

But I also find that the Offer must be preliminarily enjoined because material information relevant to the Pure stockholders' decision-making process has not been fairly disclosed. Therefore, I issue an injunction against the Offer pending an alteration of its terms to eliminate its coercive structure and to correct the inadequate disclosures.

I

These are the key facts as I find them for purposes of deciding this preliminary injunction motion.

A.

Unocal Corporation is a large independent natural gas and crude oil exploration and production company with far-flung operations. In the United States, its most important operations are currently in the Gulf of Mexico. Before May 2000, Unocal also had operations in the Permian Basin of western Texas and southeastern New Mexico. During that month, Unocal spun off its Permian Basin unit and combined it with Titan Exploration, Inc. Titan was an oil and gas company operating in the Permian Basin, south central Texas, and the central Gulf Coast region of Texas. It also owned mineral interests in the southern Gulf Coast.

The entity that resulted from that combination was Pure Resources, Inc. Following the creation of Pure, Unocal owned 65.4% of Pure's issued and outstanding common stock. The remaining 34.6% of Pure was held by Titan's former stockholders, including its managers who stayed on to run Pure. The largest of these stockholders was Jack D. Hightower, Pure's Chairman and Chief Executive Officer, who now owns 6.1% of Pure's outstanding stock before the exercise of options. As a group, Pure's management controls between a quarter and a third of the Pure stock not owned by Unocal, when options are considered.

B.

Several important agreements were entered into when Pure was formed. The first is a Stockholders Voting Agreement. That Agreement requires Unocal and Hightower to vote their shares to elect to the Pure board five persons designated by Unocal (so long as Unocal owns greater than 50% of Pure's common stock), two persons designated by Hightower, and one person to be jointly agreed upon by Unocal and Hightower. Currently, the board resulting from the implementation of the Voting Agreement is comprised as follows:

UNOCAL DESIGNEES:

- Darry D. Chessum—Chessum is Unocal's Treasurer and is the owner of one share of Pure stock.
- Timothy H. Ling—Ling is President, Chief Operating Officer, and director of Unocal. He owns one share of Pure stock.
- Graydon H. Laughbaum, Jr.—Laughbaum was an executive for 34 years at Unocal before retiring at the beginning of 1999. For most of the next three years, he provided consulting services to Unocal. Laughbaum owns 1,301 shares of Pure stock.
- HD Maxwell—Maxwell was an executive for many years at Unocal before 1992. Maxwell owns one share of Pure stock.
- Herbert C. Williamson, III—Williamson has no material ties to Unocal. He owns 3,364 shares of Pure stock.

HIGHTOWER DESIGNEES:

- Jack D. Hightower—As mentioned, he is Pure's CEO and its largest stockholder, aside from Unocal.

- George G. Staley — Staley is Pure's Chief Operating Officer and also a large stockholder, controlling 625,261 shares.

JOINT DESIGNEE OF UNOCAL AND HIGHTOWER:

- Keith A. Covington — Covington's only tie to Unocal is that he is a close personal friend of Ling, having gone to business school with him. He owns 2,401 Pure shares.

As part of the consideration it received in the Titan combination, Unocal extracted a "Business Opportunities Agreement" ("BOA") from Titan. So long as Unocal owns at least 35% of Pure, the BOA limits Pure to the oil and gas exploration and production business in certain designated areas, which were essentially co-extensive with the territories covered by Titan and the Permian Basin operations of Unocal as of the time of the combination. The BOA includes an acknowledgment by Pure that it has no business expectancy in opportunities outside the limits set by the contract. This limitation is not reciprocal, however.

By contrast, the BOA expressly states that Unocal may compete with Pure in its areas of operation. Indeed, it implies that Pure board members affiliated with Unocal may bring a corporate opportunity in Pure's area of operation to Unocal for exploitation, but may not pursue the opportunity personally.

Another protection Unocal secured in the combination was a Non-Dilution Agreement. That Agreement provides Unocal with a preemptive right to maintain its proportionate ownership in the event that Pure issues new shares or undertakes certain other transactions.

Finally, members of Pure's management team entered into "Put Agreements" with Unocal at the time of the combination. The Put Agreements give the managers — including Hightower and Staley — the right to put their Pure stock to Unocal upon the occurrence of certain triggering events — among which would be consummation of Unocal's Offer.

The Put Agreements require Unocal to pay the managers the "per share net asset value" or "NAV" of Pure, in the event the managers exercise their Put rights within a certain period after a triggering event. One triggering event is a transaction in which Unocal obtains 85% of Pure's shares, which could include the Offer if it results in Unocal obtaining that level of ownership. The NAV of Pure is determined under a complex formula dependent largely on Pure's energy reserves and debt. Notably, Pure's NAV for purposes of the Put Agreement could fall below or exceed the price of a triggering transaction, but in the latter event the triggering transaction would provide the Put holders with the right to receive the higher NAV. Although it is not clear whether the Put holders can tender themselves into the Offer in order to create a triggering transaction and receive the higher of the Offer price or the NAV, it is clear that the Put Agreements can create materially different incentives for the holders than if they were simply holders of Pure common stock.

In addition to the Put Agreements, senior members of Pure's management team have severance agreements that will (if they choose) be triggered in the event the Offer succeeds. In his case, Hightower will be eligible for a severance payment of three times his annual salary and bonus, or nearly four million dollars, an amount that while quite large, is not substantial in comparison to the economic consequences of the treatment of his equity interest in Pure.

Staley has a smaller, but similar package, and the economic consequences of the treatment of his equity also appear to be more consequential than any incentive to receive severance.

II.

A.

With these agreements in mind, I now turn to the course of events leading up to Unocal's offer.

From its formation, Pure's future as an independent entity was a subject of discussion within its board. Although Pure's operations were successful, its status as a controlled subsidiary of another player in the oil and gas business suggested that the day would come when Pure either had to become wholly-owned by Unocal or independent of it.

This reality was made manifest as Pure's management undertook to expand its business. On several occasions, this resulted in requests by Pure for limited waivers of the BOA to enable Pure to take advantage of opportunities beyond the areas designated in that contract. Unocal granted these waivers in each case. Another aspect of this subject also arose, as Unocal considered re-entering areas of geographical operation core to Pure's operations. Concerns arose in the minds of Unocal's lawyers about the extent to which the BOA could truly protect those Unocal officers (*i.e.*, Chessum and Ling) who sat on the Pure board from claims of breach of fiduciary duty in the event that Unocal were to pursue, for example, an opportunity in the Permian Basin. Because Unocal owed an indemnification obligation to Chessum and Ling and because it would be difficult to get officers to serve on subsidiary boards if Unocal did not back them, Unocal obviously was attentive to this uncertainty. Stated summarily, some, if not all, the complications that the BOA was designed to address remained a concern — a concern that would be eradicated if Unocal purchased the rest of Pure.

The aggressive nature of Pure's top management also fed this furnace. Hightower is an assertive deal-maker with plans to make Pure grow. To his mind, Unocal should decide on a course of action: either let Pure expand as much it could profitably do or buy the rest of Pure. In one of the negotiations over a limited waiver of the BOA, Hightower put this choice to Unocal in more or less these terms.

During the summer of 2001, Unocal explored the feasibility of acquiring the rest of Pure. On behalf of Unocal, Pure directors Maxwell and Laughbaum collected non-public information about Pure's reserves, production capabilities, and geographic assets and reported back to Unocal. This was done with the permission of Pure's management. By September 2001, it appeared that Unocal might well propose a merger, but the tragic events of that month and other more mundane factors resulted in the postponement of any proposal. Unocal's Chief Financial Officer informed Hightower of Unocal's decision not to proceed and that "all evaluation work on such a transaction ha[d] ceased."

That last statement was only fleetingly true. The record contains substantial evidence that Unocal's management and board soon renewed their consideration of taking Pure private. Pure director Ling knew that this renewed evaluation was going on, but it appears that he never shared that information with his fellow Pure directors. Nor did Unocal ever communicate to Pure that its September 2001 representation that all evaluation work had ceased was no longer correct. Nonetheless, during this period, Unocal continued to have access to non-public information from Pure.

Supplementing the pressure for a transaction that was generated by Hightower's expansion plans was a specific financing vehicle that Hightower sought to have the Pure board pursue. In the spring of 2002, Pure's management began seriously considering the creation of a "Royalty Trust." The Royalty Trust would monetize the value of certain mineral rights owned by Pure by selling portions of those interests to third parties. This would generate a cash infusion that would reduce Pure's debt and potentially give it capital to expand. By August of 2002, Hightower was prepared to push hard for this transaction, subject to ensuring that it could be accounted for on a favorable basis with integrity and would not have adverse tax effects.

For its part, Unocal appears to have harbored genuine concerns about the transaction, in addition to its shared concern about the accounting and tax implications of the Royalty Trust. Among its worries was that the Royalty Trust would simply inflate the value of the Put rights of management by delivering Pure (and increasing its NAV) without necessarily increasing its stock price. The Royalty Trust also complicated any future acquisition of Pure because the formation of the Trust would leave Unocal entangled with the third-parties who invested in it, who might be classified as holding a form of equity in Pure.

Although the record is not without doubt on the point, it appears that the Pure board decided to pursue consideration of the Royalty Trust during mid-August 2002. During these meetings, however, Chessum raised a host of issues that needed to be resolved favorably before the board could ultimately agree to consummate a Royalty Trust transaction. The plaintiffs argue that Chessum was buying time and trying to throw sand in the gears. Although I believe Unocal was worried about the transaction's effect, I am not prepared to say that Chessum's concerns were illegitimate. Indeed, many of them were shared by Hightower. Nonetheless, what is more evident is that the Royalty Trust discussions put pressure on Unocal to decide whether to proceed with an acquisition offer and that the Royalty Trust was likely not the method of financing that Unocal would use if it wholly owned Pure.

I infer that Hightower knew this. Simultaneous with pushing the Royalty Trust, Hightower encouraged Unocal to make an offer for the rest of Pure. Hightower suggested that Unocal proceed by way of a tender offer, because he believed that his Put rights complicated the Pure board's ability to act on a merger proposal.

B.

Despite his entreaties, Hightower was surprisingly surprised by what came next, as were the members of the Pure board not affiliated with Unocal. On August 20, 2002, Unocal sent the Pure board a letter that stated in pertinent part that:

> It has become clear to us that the best interests of our respective stockholders will be served by Unocal's acquisition of the shares of Pure Resources that we do not already own. . . .

Unocal recognizes that a strong and stable on-shore, North America production base will facilitate the execution of its North American gas strategy. The skills and technology required to maximize the benefits to be realized from that strategy are now divided between Union Oil and Pure. Sound business strategy calls for bringing those assets together, under one management, so that they may be deployed to their highest and best use. For those reasons, we are not interested in selling our shares in Pure. Moreover, if the two companies are combined, important cost savings should be realized and potential conflicts of interest will be avoided.

Consequently, our Board of Directors has authorized us to make an exchange offer pursuant to which the stockholders of Pure (other than Union Oil) will be offered 0.6527 shares of common stock of Unocal for each outstanding share of Pure common stock they own in a transaction designed to be tax-free. Based on the $34.09 closing price of Unocal's shares on August 20, 2002, our offer provides a value of approximately $22.25 per share of Pure common stock and a 27% premium to the closing price of Pure common stock on that date.

Unocal's offer is being made directly to Pure's stockholders. . . .

Our offer will be conditioned on the tender of a sufficient number of shares of Pure common stock such that, after the offer is completed, we will own at least 90% of the outstanding shares of Pure common stock and other customary conditions. . . . Assuming that the conditions to the offer are satisfied and that the offer is completed, we will then effect a "short form" merger of Pure with a subsidiary of Unocal as soon as practicable thereafter. In this merger, the remaining Pure public stockholders will receive the same consideration as in the exchange offer, except for those stockholders who choose to exercise their appraisal rights.

We intend to file our offering materials with the Securities and Exchange Commission and commence our exchange offer on or about September 5, 2002. Unocal is not seeking, and as the offer is being made directly to Pure's stockholders, Delaware law does not require approval of the offer from Pure's Board of Directors. We, however, encourage you to consult with your outside counsel as to the obligations of Pure's Board of Directors under the U.S. tender offer rules to advise the stockholders of your recommendation with respect to our offer [as required under Rule 14D-9]. . . .

Unocal management asked Ling and Chessum to make calls to the Pure board about the Offer. In their talking points, Ling and Chessum were instructed to suggest that any Special Committee formed by Pure should have powers "limited to hiring independent advisors (bank and lawyers) and to coming up with a recommendation to the Pure shareholders as to whether or not to accept UCL's offer; any greater delegation is not warranted."

The next day the Pure board met to consider this event. Hightower suggested that Chessum and Ling recuse themselves from the Pure board's consideration of the Offer. They agreed to do so. After that, the Pure board voted to establish a Special Committee comprised of Williamson and Covington to respond to the Unocal bid. Maxwell and Laughbaum were omitted from the Committee because of their substantial employment histories with Unocal. Despite their work with Unocal in assessing the advisability of a bid for Pure in 2001, however, Maxwell and Laughbaum did not recuse themselves generally from the Pure board's process of reacting to the Offer. Hightower and Staley were excluded from the Committee because there were circumstances in which the Put Agreements could provide them with incentive to support the procession of the Offer, not because the Offer was at the most favorable price, but because it would trigger their right to receive a higher price under the NAV formula in the Put Agreements.

The precise authority of the Special Committee to act on behalf of Pure was left hazy at first, but seemed to consist solely of the power to retain independent advisors, to take a position on the offer's advisability on behalf of Pure, and to negotiate with Unocal to see if it would increase its bid. Aside from this last point, this constrained degree of authority comported with the limited power that Unocal had desired.

During the early days of its operation, the Special Committee was aided by company counsel, Thompson & Knight, and management in retaining its own advisors and getting started. Soon, though, the Special Committee had retained two financial advisors and legal advisors to help it.

For financial advisors, the Special Committee hired Credit Suisse First Boston ("First Boston"), the investment bank assisting Pure with its consideration of the Royalty Trust, and Petrie Parkman & Co., Inc., a smaller firm very experienced in the energy field. The Committee felt that the knowledge that First Boston had gleaned from its Royalty Trust work would be of great help to the Committee, especially in the short time frame required to respond to the Offer, which was scheduled to expire at midnight on October 2, 2002.

For legal advisors, the Committee retained Baker Botts and Potter Anderson & Corroon. Baker Botts had handled certain toxic tort litigation for Unocal and was active as lead counsel in representing an energy consortium of which Unocal is a major participant in a major piece of litigation. Nonetheless, the Committee apparently concluded that these matters did not materially compromise Baker Botts' ability to act aggressively towards Unocal.

After the formation of the Special Committee, Unocal formally commenced its Offer, which had these key features:

- An exchange ratio of 0.6527 of a Unocal share for each Pure share.
- A non-waivable majority of the minority tender provision, which required a majority of shares not owned by Unocal to tender. Management of Pure, including Hightower and Staley, are considered part of the minority for purposes of this condition, not to mention Maxwell, Laughbaum, Chessum, and Ling.
- A waivable condition that a sufficient number of tenders be received to enable Unocal to own 90% of Pure and to effect a short-form merger under 8 Del. C. §253.
- A statement by Unocal that it intends, if it obtains 90%, to consummate a short-form merger as soon as practicable at the same exchange ratio.

As of this time, this litigation had been filed and a preliminary injunction hearing was soon scheduled. Among the issues raised was the adequacy of the Special Committee's scope of authority.

Thereafter, the Special Committee sought to, in its words, "clarify" its authority. The clarity it sought was clear: the Special Committee wanted to be delegated the full authority of the board under Delaware law to respond to the Offer. With such authority, the Special Committee could have searched for alternative transactions, speeded up consummation of the Royalty Trust, evaluated the feasibility of a self-tender, and put in place a shareholder rights plan (*a.k.a.*, poison pill) to block the Offer.

What exactly happened at this point is shrouded by invocations of privilege. But this much is clear. Having recused themselves from the Pure board process before, Chessum and Ling reentered it in full glory when the Special Committee asked for more authority. Chessum took the lead in raising concerns and engaged Unocal's in-house and outside counsel to pare down the resolution proposed by the Special Committee. After discussions between Counsel for Unocal and the Special Committee, the bold resolution drafted by Special Committee counsel was whittled down to take out any ability on the part of the Special Committee to do anything other than study the Offer, negotiate it, and make a recommendation on behalf of Pure in the required 14D-9.

The record does not illuminate exactly why the Special Committee did not make this their Alamo. It is certain that the Special Committee never pressed the issue to a board vote and it appears that the Pure directors never seriously debated the issue at the board table itself. The Special Committee never demanded that Chessum and Ling recuse themselves from consideration of this issue, much less Maxwell and Laughbum.

At best, the record supports the inference that the Special Committee believed some of the broader options technically open to them under their preferred resolution (*e.g.*, finding another buyer) were not practicable. As to their failure to insist on the power to deploy a poison pill — the by-now *de rigeur* tool of a board responding to a third-party tender offer — the record is obscure. The Special Committee's brief suggests that the Committee believed that the pill could not be deployed consistently with the Non-Dilution Agreement protecting Unocal, but nowhere indicates how Unocal's contractual right to preserve its 65% position precluded a rights plan designed solely to keep it at that level. The Special Committee also argues that the pill was unnecessary because the Committee's ability to make a negative recommendation — coupled with Hightower's and Staley's by-then apparent opposition to the Offer — were leverage and protection enough.

My ability to have confidence in these justifications has been compromised by the Special Committee's odd decision to invoke the attorney-client privilege as to its discussion of these issues. Because the Committee delegated to its legal advisors the duty of negotiating the scope of the Committee's authority and seems to have acquiesced in their acceptance of defeat at the hands of Unocal's lawyers, invocation of the privilege renders it impossible for me know what really went on.

The most reasonable inference that can be drawn from the record is that the Special Committee was unwilling to confront Unocal as aggressively as it would have confronted a third-party bidder. No doubt Unocal's talented counsel made much of its client's majority status and argued that Pure would be on uncertain legal ground in interposing itself — by way of a rights plan — between Unocal and Pure's stockholders. Realizing that Unocal would not stand for this broader authority and sensitive to the expected etiquette of subsidiary-parent relations, the Pure board therefore decided not to vote on the issue, and the Special Committee's fleeting act of boldness was obscured in the rhetoric of discussions about "clarifying its authority."

Contemporaneous with these events, the Special Committee met on a more or less continuous basis. On a few occasions, the Special Committee met with Unocal and tried to persuade it to increase its offer. On September 10, for example, the Special Committee asked Unocal to increase the exchange ratio from 0.6527 to 0.787. Substantive presentations were made by the Special Committee's financial advisors in support of this overture.

After these meetings, Unocal remained unmoved and made no counteroffer. Therefore, on September 17, 2002, the Special Committee voted not to recommend the Offer, based on its analysis and the advice of its financial advisors. The Special Committee prepared the 14D-9 on behalf of Pure, which contained the board's recommendation not to tender into the Offer. Hightower and Staley also announced their personal present intentions not to tender, intentions that if adhered to would make it nearly impossible for Unocal to obtain 90% of Pure's shares in the Offer.

During the discovery process, a representative of the lead plaintiff, which is an investment fund, testified that he did not feel coerced by the Offer. The discovery record also reveals that a great deal of the Pure stock held by the public is in the hands of institutional investors.

III. The Plaintiffs' Demand for a Preliminary Injunction

A. THE MERITS

The plaintiffs advance an array of arguments, not all of which can be dealt with in the time allotted to me for decision. . . .

Distilled to the bare minimum, the plaintiffs argue that the Offer should be enjoined because: (i) the Offer is subject to the entire fairness standard and the record supports the inference that the transaction cannot survive a fairness review; (ii) in any event, the Offer is actionably coercive and should be enjoined on that ground; and (iii) the disclosures provided to the Pure stockholders in connection with the Offer are materially incomplete and misleading. . . .

B. THE PLAINTIFFS' SUBSTANTIVE ATTACK ON THE OFFER

1.

The primary argument of the plaintiffs is that the Offer should be governed by the entire fairness standard of review. In their view, the structural power of Unocal over Pure and its board, as well as Unocal's involvement in determining the scope of the Special Committee's authority, make the Offer other than a voluntary, non-coercive transaction. In the plaintiffs' mind, the Offer poses the same threat of (what I will call) "inherent coercion" that motivated the Supreme Court in Kahn v. Lynch Communication Systems, Inc., 638 A.2d 1110 (Del. 1994) to impose the entire fairness standard of review on any interested merger involving a controlling stockholder, even when the merger was approved by an independent board majority, negotiated by an independent special committee, and subject to a majority of the minority vote condition.

In support of their argument, the plaintiffs contend that the tender offer method of acquisition poses, if anything, a greater threat of unfairness to minority stockholders and should be subject to the same equitable constraints. More case-specifically, they claim that Unocal has used inside information from Pure to foist an inadequate bid on Pure stockholders at a time advantageous to Unocal. Then, Unocal acted self-interestedly to keep the Pure Special Committee from obtaining all the authority necessary to respond to the Offer. As a result, the plaintiffs argue, Unocal has breached its fiduciary duties as majority stock-holder, and the Pure board has breached its duties by either acting on behalf of Unocal (in the case of Chessum and Ling) or by acting supinely in response to Unocal's inadequate offer (the Special Committee and the rest of the board). Instead of wielding the power to stop Unocal in its tracks and make it really negotiate, the Pure board has taken only the insufficient course of telling the Pure minority to say no.

In response to these arguments, Unocal asserts that the plaintiffs misunder-stand the relevant legal principles. Because Unocal has proceeded by way of an exchange offer and not a negotiated merger, the rule of *Lynch* is inapplicable. Instead, Unocal is free to make a tender offer at whatever price it chooses so long as it does not: i) "structurally coerce" the Pure minority by suggesting explicitly or implicitly that injurious events will occur to those stockholders who fail to tender; or ii) mislead the Pure minority into tendering by concealing or misstat-ing the material facts. This is the rule of law articulated by, among other cases, Solomon v. Pathe Communications Corp., 672 A.2d 35 (Del. 1996). Because Unocal has conditioned its Offer on a majority of the minority provision and intends to consummate a short-form merger at the same price, it argues that the Offer poses no threat of structural coercion and that the Pure minority can make a voluntary decision. Because the Pure minority has a negative recom-mendation from the Pure Special Committee and because there has been full disclosure (including of any material information Unocal received from Pure in formulating its bid), Unocal submits that the Pure minority will be able to make an informed decision whether to tender. For these reasons, Unocal asserts that no meritorious claim of breach of fiduciary duty exists against it or the Pure directors.

2.

This case therefore involves an aspect of Delaware law fraught with doctrinal tension: what equitable standard of fiduciary conduct applies when a controlling shareholder seeks to acquire the rest of the company's shares? In considering this issue, it is useful to pause over the word "equitable" and to capture its full import.

The key inquiry is not what statutory procedures must be adhered to when a controlling stockholder attempts to acquire the rest of the company's shares. Controlling stockholders counseled by experienced lawyers rarely trip over the legal hurdles imposed by legislation.

Nor is the doctrine of independent legal significance of relevance here. That doctrine stands only for the proposition that the mere fact that a transaction cannot be accomplished under one statutory provision does not invalidate it if a different statutory method of consummation exists. Nothing about that doctrine alters the fundamental rule that inequitable actions in technical con-formity with statutory law can be restrained by equity. [*See* Schnell v. Chris-Craft Indus., Inc., 285 A.2d 437, 439 (Del.1971) ("[I]nequitable action does not become permissible simply because it is legally possible.").]

This is not to say that the statutory method by which a controlling stockholder proceeds is not relevant to determining the equitable standard of conduct that a court must apply. To the contrary, the structure and statutory rubric employed to consummate transactions are highly influential to courts shaping the com-mon law of corporations. There are good reasons why this is so. A statute's own terms might foreclose (explicitly or implicitly) the application of traditional concepts of fiduciary duty, thereby requiring judges to subordinate default principles of the common law to the superior mandate of legislation.[14] The relevant statutory technique might also be one that does not foreclose common law equitable review altogether, but that has certain characteristics that influence the judiciary's formulation of the extent and nature of the duties owed by the fiduciaries involved in the transaction. Much of the judicial carpentry in the corporate law occurs in this context, in which judges must supplement the broadly enabling features of statutory corporation law with equitable principles sufficient to protect against abuse and unfairness, but not so rigid as to stifle useful transactions that could increase the shareholder and societal wealth generated by the corporate form.

In building the common law, judges forced to balance these concerns cannot escape making normative choices, based on imperfect information about the world. This reality clearly pervades the area of corporate law implicated by this case. When a transaction to buy out the minority is proposed, is it more important to the development of strong capital markets to hold controlling stockholders and target boards to very strict (and litigation-intensive) standards of fiduciary conduct? Or is more stockholder wealth generated if less rigorous protections are adopted, which permit acquisitions to proceed so long as the majority has not misled or strong-armed the minority? Is such flexibility in fact beneficial to minority stockholders because it encourages liquidity-generating tender offers to them and provides incentives for acquirers to pay hefty premiums to buy control, knowing that control will be accompanied by legal rules that permit a later "going private" transaction to occur in a relatively non-litigious manner?

At present, the Delaware case law has two strands of authority that answer these questions differently. In one strand, which deals with situations in which controlling stockholders negotiate a merger agreement with the target board to buy out the minority, our decisional law emphasizes the protection of minority stockholders against unfairness. In the other strand, which deals with situations when a controlling stockholder seeks to acquire the rest of the company's shares through a tender offer followed by a short-form merger under 8 Del. C. §253, Delaware case precedent facilitates the free flow of capital between willing buyers and willing sellers of shares, so long as the consent of the sellers is not procured by inadequate or misleading information or by wrongful compulsion.

These strands appear to treat economically similar transactions as categorically different simply because the method by which the controlling stockholder proceeds varies. This disparity in treatment persists even though the two basic methods (negotiated merger versus tender offer/short-form merger) pose similar threats to minority stockholders. Indeed, it can be argued that the distinction in approach subjects the transaction that is more protective of minority

---

14. *See, e.g.*, In re Unocal Exploration Corp. S'holders Litig., 793 A.2d 329, 338 & n.26 (Del. Ch. 2000) (stating that when controlling stockholder consummates a short-form merger under 8 Del. C. §253 that is not proceeded by any prior transaction subject to entire fairness review, plaintiff is relegated to the appraisal remedy in the absence of "fraud, gross overreaching, or other such wrongful conduct" or misdisclosures; otherwise, the statute's authorization of a simplified procedure for effecting such mergers would be undermined by the imposition of an equitable requirement of fair process), *aff'd sub nom.*, Glassman v. Unocal Exploration Corp., 777 A.2d 242 (Del. 2001) (same).

stockholders when implemented with appropriate protective devices—a merger negotiated by an independent committee with the power to say no and conditioned on a majority of the minority vote—to more stringent review than the more dangerous form of a going private deal—an unnegotiated tender offer made by a majority stockholder. The latter transaction is arguably less protective than a merger of the kind described, because the majority stockholder-offeror has access to inside information, and the offer requires disaggregated stockholders to decide whether to tender quickly, pressured by the risk of being squeezed out in a short-form merger at a different price later or being left as part of a much smaller public minority. This disparity creates a possible incoherence in our law.

3.

To illustrate this possible incoherence in our law, it is useful to sketch out these two strands. I begin with negotiated mergers. In Kahn v. Lynch Communication Systems, Inc., the Delaware Supreme Court addressed the standard of review that applies when a controlling stockholder attempts to acquire the rest of the corporation's shares in a negotiated merger pursuant to 8 Del. C. §251. The Court held that the stringent entire fairness form of review governed regardless of whether: i) the target board was comprised of a majority of independent directors; ii) a special committee of the target's independent directors was empowered to negotiate and veto the merger; and iii) the merger was made subject to approval by a majority of the disinterested target stockholders. . . . [The Court then described the rationale of *Lynch*.]

The policy balance struck in *Lynch* continues to govern negotiated mergers between controlling stockholders and subsidiaries. If anything, later cases have extended the rule in *Lynch* to a broader array of transactions involving controlling shareholders. [*See, e.g.*, Emerald Partners v. Berlin, 787 A.2d 85, 93 n.52 (Del. 2001); Kahn v. Tremont Corp., 694 A.2d 422, 428 (Del. 1997).]

4.

The second strand of cases involves tender offers made by controlling stockholders—*i.e.*, the kind of transaction Unocal has proposed. The prototypical transaction addressed by this strand involves a tender offer by the controlling stockholder addressed to the minority stockholders. In that offer, the controlling stockholder promises to buy as many shares as the minority will sell but may subject its offer to certain conditions. For example, the controlling stockholder might condition the offer on receiving enough tenders for it to obtain 90% of the subsidiary's shares, thereby enabling the controlling stockholder to consummate a short-form merger under 8 Del. C. §253 at either the same or a different price.

As a matter of statutory law, this way of proceeding is different from the negotiated merger approach in an important way: neither the tender offer nor the short-form merger requires any action by the subsidiary's board of directors. The tender offer takes place between the controlling shareholder and the minority shareholders so long as the offering conditions are met. And, by the explicit terms of §253, the short-form merger can be effected by the controlling stockholder itself, an option that was of uncertain utility for many years because it was unclear whether §253 mergers were subject to an equitable requirement of fair process at the subsidiary board level. That uncertainty was recently resolved in Glassman v. Unocal Exploration Corp., 777 A.2d 242 (Del. 2001), an important recent decision, which held that a short-form merger was not reviewable in an action claiming unfair dealing, and that, absent fraud or misleading or inadequate disclosures, could be contested only in an appraisal proceeding that focused solely on the adequacy of the price paid.

Before *Glassman*, transactional planners had wondered whether the back-end of the tender offer/short-form merger transaction would subject the controlling stockholder to entire fairness review. *Glassman* seemed to answer that question favorably from the standpoint of controlling stockholders, and to therefore encourage the tender offer/short-form merger form of acquisition as presenting a materially less troublesome method of proceeding than a negotiated merger.

Why? Because the legal rules that governed the front end of the tender offer/short-form merger method of acquisition had already provided a more flexible, less litigious path to acquisition for controlling stockholders than the negotiated merger route. Tender offers are not addressed by the Delaware General Corporation Law ("DGCL"), a factor that has been of great importance in shaping the line of decisional law addressing tender offers by controlling stockholders — but not, as I will discuss, tender offers made by third parties.

Because no consent or involvement of the target board is statutorily mandated for tender offers, our courts have recognized that "[i]n the case of totally voluntary tender offers . . . courts do not impose any right of the shareholders to receive a particular price. Delaware law recognizes that, as to allegedly voluntary tender offers (in contrast to cash-out mergers), the determinative factors as to voluntariness are whether coercion is present, or whether there are materially false or misleading disclosures made to stockholders in connection with the offer." Solomon v. Pathe Communications Corp., 672 A.2d 35, 39 (Del. 1996) (citations and quotations omitted). In two recent cases, this court has followed *Solomon*'s articulation of the standards applicable to a tender offer, and held that the "Delaware law does not impose a duty of entire fairness on controlling stockholders making a non-coercive tender or exchange offer to acquire shares directly from the minority holders."

The differences between this approach, which I will identify with the *Solomon* line of cases, and that of *Lynch* are stark. To begin with, the controlling stockholder is said to have no duty to pay a fair price, irrespective of its power over the subsidiary. Even more striking is the different manner in which the coercion concept is deployed. In the tender offer context addressed by *Solomon* and its progeny, coercion is defined in the more traditional sense as a wrongful threat that has the effect of forcing stockholders to tender at the wrong price to avoid an even worse fate later on, a type of coercion I will call structural coercion. The inherent coercion that *Lynch* found to exist when controlling stockholders seek to acquire the minority's stake is not even a cognizable concern for the common law of corporations if the tender offer method is employed.

This latter point is illustrated by those cases that squarely hold that a tender [offer] is not actionably coercive if the majority stockholder decides to: (i) condition the closing of the tender offer on support of a majority of the minority and (ii) promise that it would consummate a short-form merger on the same terms as the tender offer. In those circumstances, at least, these cases can be read to bar a claim against the majority stockholder even if the price offered is below what would be considered fair in an entire fairness hearing ("fair price") or an appraisal action ("fair value"). That is, in the tender offer context, our courts consider it sufficient protection against coercion to give effective veto power over the offer to a majority of the minority. Yet that very same protection is considered insufficient to displace fairness review in the negotiated merger context.

5.

[The court first discusses the power of the board of directors to interject defenses, such as a "poison pill," to prevent a third-party tender offer, subject to fiduciary duty review, and the debate among academics about whether this is a proper role for the board of directors.]

What is clear, however, is that Delaware law has not regarded tender offers as involving a special transactional space, from which directors are altogether excluded from exercising substantial authority. To the contrary, much Delaware jurisprudence during the last twenty years has dealt with whether directors acting within that space comported themselves consistently with their duties of loyalty and care. It therefore is by no means obvious that simply because a controlling stockholder proceeds by way of a tender offer that either it or the target's directors fall outside the constraints of fiduciary duty law.

In this same vein, the basic model of directors and stockholders adopted by our [mergers and acquisitions] case law is relevant. Delaware law has seen directors as well-positioned to understand the value of the target company, to compensate for the disaggregated nature of stockholders by acting as a negotiating and auctioning proxy for them, and as a bulwark against structural coercion. Relatedly, dispersed stockholders have been viewed as poorly positioned to protect and, yes, sometimes, even to think for themselves.

6.

Because tender offers are not treated exceptionally in the third-party context, it is important to ask why the tender offer method should be consequential in formulating the equitable standards of fiduciary conduct by which courts review acquisition proposals made by controlling stockholders. Is there reason to believe that the tender offer method of acquisition is more protective of the minority, with the result that less scrutiny is required than of negotiated mergers with controlling stockholders?

Unocal's answer to that question is yes and primarily rests on an inarguable proposition: in a negotiated merger involving a controlling stockholder, the controlling stockholder is on both sides of the transaction. That is, the negotiated merger is a self-dealing transaction, whereas in a tender offer, the controlling stockholder is only on the offering side and the minority remain free not to sell.

As a formal matter, this distinction is difficult to contest. When examined more deeply, however, it is not a wall that can bear the full weight of the *Lynch/Solomon* distinction. In this regard, it is important to remember that the overriding concern of *Lynch* is the controlling shareholders have the ability to take retributive action in the wake of rejection by an independent board, a special committee, or the minority shareholders. That ability is so influential that the usual cleansing devices that obviate fairness review of interested transactions cannot be trusted.

The problem is that nothing about the tender offer method of corporate acquisition makes the 800-pound gorilla's [the controlling shareholder's] retributive capabilities less daunting to minority stockholders. Indeed, many commentators would argue that the tender offer form is more coercive than a merger vote. In a merger vote, stockholders can vote no and still receive the transactional consideration if the merger prevails. In a tender offer, however, a non-tendering shareholder individually faces an uncertain fate. That stockholder could be one of the few who holds out, leaving herself in an even more thinly traded stock with little hope of liquidity and subject to a §253 merger at a lower price or at the same price but at a later (and, given the time value of money, a less valuable) time. The 14D-9 warned Pure's minority stockholders of just this possibility. For these reasons, some view tender offers as creating a prisoner's dilemma — distorting choice and creating incentives for stockholders to tender into offers that they believe are inadequate in order to avoid a worse fate. But whether or not one views tender offers as more coercive of shareholder choice than negotiated mergers with controlling stockholders, it is difficult to argue that tender offers are materially freer and more reliable measures of stockholder sentiment. . . .

[S]ome of the other factors that are said to support fairness review of negotiated mergers involving controlling stockholders also apply with full force to tender offers made by controlling stockholders. The informational advantage that the controlling stockholder possesses is not any different; in this case, for example, Unocal was able to proceed having had full access to non-public information about Pure. The tender offer form provides no additional protection against this concern.

Furthermore, the tender offer method allows the controlling stockholder to time its offer and to put a bull rush on the target stockholders. Here, Unocal studied an acquisition of Pure for nearly a year and then made a "surprise" offer that forced a rapid response from Pure's Special Committee and the minority stockholders.

Likewise, one struggles to imagine why subsidiary directors would feel less constrained in reacting to a tender offer by a controlling stockholder than a negotiated merger proposal. Indeed, an arguably more obvious concern is that subsidiary directors might use the absence of a statutory role for them in the tender offer process to be less than aggressive in protecting minority interests, to wit, the edifying examples of subsidiary directors courageously taking no position on the merits of offers by a controlling stockholder. Or, as here, the Special Committee's failure to demand the power to use the normal range of techniques available to a non-controlled board responding to a third-party tender offer.

For these and other reasons that time constraints preclude me from explicating, I remain less than satisfied that there is a justifiable basis for the distinction between the *Lynch* and *Solomon* lines of cases. Instead, their disparate teachings reflect a difference in policy emphasis that is far greater than can be explained by the technical differences between tender offers and negotiated mergers, especially given Delaware's director-centered approach to tender offers made by third-parties, which emphasizes the vulnerability of disaggregated stockholders absent important help and protection from their directors.

7.

The absence of convincing reasons for this disparity in treatment inspires the plaintiffs to urge me to apply the entire fairness standard of review to Unocal's offer. Otherwise, they say, the important protections set forth in the *Lynch* line of cases will be rendered useless, as all controlling stockholders will simply choose to proceed to make subsidiary acquisitions by way of a tender offer and later short-form merger. [Although "troubled by the imbalance in Delaware law exposed by the *Solomon/Lynch* line of cases," the Court determined that *Salomon* applied.]

8.

To be more specific about the application of *Solomon* in these circumstances, it is important to note that the *Solomon* line of cases does not eliminate the fiduciary duties of controlling stockholders or target boards in connection with tender offers made by controlling stockholders. Rather, the question is the contextual extent and nature of those duties, a question I will now tentatively, and incompletely, answer.

The potential for coercion and unfairness posed by controlling stockholders who seek to acquire the balance of the company's shares by acquisition requires some equitable reinforcement, in order to give proper effect to the concerns undergirding *Lynch*. In order to address the prisoner's dilemma problem, our law should consider an acquisition tender offer by a controlling stockholder non-coercive only when: 1) it is subject to a non-waivable majority of the minority tender condition; 2) the controlling stockholder promises to consummate a prompt §253 merger at the same price if it obtains more than 90% of the shares; and 3) the controlling stockholder has made no retributive threats. . . .

The informational and timing advantages possessed by controlling stockholders also require some countervailing protection if the minority is to truly be afforded the opportunity to make an informed, voluntary tender decision. In this regard, the majority stockholder owes a duty to permit the independent directors on the target board both free rein and adequate time to react to the tender offer, by (at the very least) hiring their own advisors, providing the minority with a recommendation as to the advisability of the offer, and disclosing adequate information for the minority to make an informed judgment. For their part, the independent directors have a duty to undertake these tasks in good faith and diligently, and to pursue the best interests of the minority.

When a tender offer is non-coercive in the sense I have identified and the independent directors of the target are permitted to make an informed recommendation and provide fair disclosure, the law should be chary about superimposing the full fiduciary requirement of entire fairness upon the statutory tender offer process. Here, the plaintiffs argue that the Pure board breached its fiduciary duties by not giving the Special Committee the power to block the Offer by, among other means, deploying a poison pill. Indeed, the plaintiffs argue that the full board's decision not to grant that authority is subject to the entire fairness standard of review because a majority of the full board was not independent of Unocal.

That argument has some analytical and normative appeal, embodying as it does the rough fairness of the goose and gander rule.[49] I am reluctant, however,

---

49. Management-side lawyers must view this case, and the recent *Digex* case, *see* In re Digex Inc. S'holders Litig., 789 A.2d 1176 (Del. Ch. 2000), as boomerangs. Decades after their invention, tools designed to help management stay in place are now being wielded by minority stockholders.

to burden the common law of corporations with a new rule that would tend to compel the use of a device [the poison pill] that our statutory law only obliquely sanctions and that in other contexts is subject to misuse, especially when used to block a high value bid that is not structurally coercive. When a controlling stockholder makes a tender offer that is not coercive in the sense I have articulated, therefore, the better rule is that there is no duty on its part to permit the target board to block the bid through use of the pill. Nor is there any duty on the part of the independent directors to seek blocking power. But it is important to be mindful of one of the reasons that make a contrary rule problematic — the awkwardness of a legal rule requiring a board to take aggressive action against a structurally non-coercive offer by the controlling stockholder that elects it. This recognition of the sociology of controlled subsidiaries puts a point on the increased vulnerability that stockholders face from controlling stockholder tenders, because the minority stockholders are denied the full range of protection offered by boards in response to third party offers. This factor illustrates the utility of the protective conditions that I have identified as necessary to prevent abuse of the minority.

9.

Turning specifically to Unocal's Offer, I conclude that the application of these principles yields the following result. The Offer, in its present form, is coercive because it includes within the definition of the "minority" those stockholders who are affiliated with Unocal as directors and officers. It also includes the management of Pure, whose incentives are skewed by their employment, their severance agreements, and their Put Agreements. This is, of course, a problem that can be cured if Unocal amends the Offer to condition it on approval of a majority of Pure's unaffiliated stockholders. Requiring the minority to be defined exclusive of stockholders whose independence from the controlling stockholder is compromised is the better legal rule (and result). Too often, it will be the case that officers and directors of controlled subsidiaries have voting incentives that are not perfectly aligned with their economic interest in their stock and who are more than acceptably susceptible to influence from controlling stockholders. Aside, however, from this glitch in the majority of the minority condition, I conclude that Unocal's Offer satisfies the other requirements of "non-coerciveness." Its promise to consummate a prompt §253 merger is sufficiently specific,[51] and Unocal has made no retributive threats.

Although Unocal's Offer does not altogether comport with the above-described definition of non-coercive, it does not follow that I believe that the plaintiffs have established a probability of success on the merits as to their claim that the Pure board should have blocked that Offer with a pill or other measures. Putting aside the shroud of silence that cloaked the board's (mostly, it seems, behind the scenes) deliberations, there appears to have been at least a

---

I note that the current situation can be distinguished from *Digex,* insofar as in that case the controlling stockholder forced the subsidiary board to take action only beneficial to it, whereas here the Pure board simply did not interpose itself between Unocal's Offer and the Pure minority.

51. A note is in order here. I believe Unocal's statement of intent to be sufficiently clear as to expose it to potential liability in the event that it were to obtain 90% and not consummate the short-form merger at the same price (*e.g.*, if it made the exchange ratio in the short-form merger less favorable). The promise of equal treatment in short-form merger is what renders the tender decision less distorting.

rational basis to believe that a pill was not necessary to protect the Pure minority against coercion, largely, because Pure's management had expressed adamant opposition to the Offer. Moreover, the board allowed the Special Committee a free hand: to recommend against the Offer — as it did; to negotiate for a higher price — as it attempted to do; and to prepare the company's 14D-9 — as it did.

For all these reasons, therefore, I find that the plaintiffs do not have a probability of success on the merits of their attack on the Offer, with the exception that the majority of the minority condition is flawed.

C. THE PLAINTIFFS' DISCLOSURE CLAIMS

As their other basis for attack, the plaintiffs argue that neither of the key disclosure documents provided to the Pure stockholders — the S-4 Unocal issued in support of its Offer and the 14D-9 Pure filed in reaction to the Offer — made materially complete and accurate disclosure. The general legal standards that govern the plaintiffs' disclosure claims are settled.

In circumstances such as these, the Pure stockholders are entitled to disclosure of all material facts pertinent to the decisions they are being asked to make. In this case, the Pure stockholders must decide whether to take one of two initial courses of action: tender and accept the Offer if it proceeds or not tender and attempt to stop the Offer. If the Offer is consummated, the non-tendering stockholders will face two subsequent choices that they will have to make on the basis of the information in the S-4 and 14D-9: to accept defeat quietly by accepting the short-form merger consideration in the event that Unocal obtains 90% and lives up to its promise to do an immediate short-form merger or seek to exercise the appraisal rights described in the S-4. I conclude that the S-4 and the 14D-9 are important to all these decisions, because both documents state that Unocal will effect the short-form merger promptly if it gets 90%, and shareholders rely on those documents to provide the substantive information on which stockholders will be asked to base their decision whether to accept the merger consideration or to seek appraisal. . . .

The plaintiffs advance a plethora of disclosure claims, only the most important of which can be addressed in the time frame available to me. I therefore address them in order of importance, as I see them.

1.

First and foremost, the plaintiffs argue that the 14D-9 is deficient because it does not disclose *any* substantive portions of the work of First Boston and Petrie Parkman on behalf of the Special Committee, even though the bankers' negative views of the Offer are cited as a basis for the board's own recommendation not to tender. Having left it to the Pure minority to say no for themselves, the Pure board (the plaintiffs say) owed the minority the duty to provide them with material information about the value of Pure's shares, including, in particular, the estimates and underlying analyses of value developed by the Special Committee's bankers. This duty is heightened, the plaintiffs say, because the Pure minority is subject to an immediate short-form merger if the Offer proceeds as Unocal hopes, and will have to make the decision whether to seek appraisal in those circumstances.

In response, the Pure director-defendants argue that the 14D-9 contains a great deal of financial information, including the actual opinions of First

Boston and Petrie Parkman. They also note that the S-4 contains historical financial information about Pure's results as well as certain projections of future results. As such, they claim that disclosure of more detailed information about the banker's views of value, while interesting, would not have been material. Furthermore, the Special Committee argues that disclosure could be injurious to the minority. Because the Special Committee still hopes to secure a better price at the negotiating table, they are afraid that disclosure of their bankers' range of values will hamper their bargaining leverage. Finally, the director-defendants cite Delaware case law that indicates that a summary of the results of the actual valuation analyses conducted by an investment banker ordinarily need not be disclosed.

This is a continuation of an ongoing debate in Delaware corporate law, and one I confess to believing has often been answered in an intellectually unsatisfying manner. Fearing stepping on the SEC's toes and worried about encouraging prolix disclosures, the Delaware courts have been reluctant to require informative, succinct disclosure of investment banker analyses in circumstances in which the bankers' views about value have been cited as justifying the recommendation of the board. But this reluctance has been accompanied by more than occasional acknowledgment of the utility of such information, an acknowledgment that is understandable given the substantial encouragement Delaware case law has given to the deployment of investment bankers by boards of directors addressing mergers and tender offers.

These conflicting impulses were manifested recently in two Supreme Court opinions. In one, Skeen v. Jo-Ann Stores, Inc., 750 A.2d 1170 (Del. 2000), the Court was inclined towards the view that a summary of the bankers' analyses and conclusions was not material to a stockholders' decision whether to seek appraisal. In the other, McMullin v. Beran, 765 A.2d 910 (Del. 2000), the Court implied that information about the analytical work of the board's banker could well be material in analogous circumstances.

In my view, it is time that this ambivalence be resolved in favor of a firm statement that stockholders are entitled to a fair summary of the substantive work performed by the investment bankers upon whose advice the recommendations of their board as to how to vote on a merger or tender rely. I agree that our law should not encourage needless prolixity, but that concern cannot reasonably apply to investment bankers' analyses, which usually address the most important issue to stockholders — the sufficiency of the consideration being offered to them for their shares in a merger or tender offer. Moreover, courts must be candid in acknowledging that the disclosure of the banker's "fairness opinion" alone and without more, provides stockholders with nothing other than a conclusion, qualified by a gauze of protective language designed to insulate the banker from liability. . . .

When controlling stockholders make tender offers, they have large informational advantages that can only be imperfectly overcome by the special committee process, which almost invariably involves directors who are not involved in the day-to-day management of the subsidiary. The retention of financial advisors by special committees is designed to offset some of this asymmetry, and it would seem to be in full keeping with that goal for the minority stockholders to be given a summary of the core analyses of these advisors in circumstances in which the stockholders must protect themselves in the voting or tender process. That this can be done without great burden is demonstrated by the many transactions in which meaningful summary disclosure of bankers' opinions are made, either by choice or by SEC rule [in certain going-private transactions, where it is required].

For all these reasons, I conclude that the plaintiffs have shown a reasonable probability of success on their claim that the 14D-9 omits material information regarding the First Boston and Petrie Parkman analyses.

2.

The plaintiffs' next claim is easier to resolve. In the 14D-9, the following statement appears:

> On September 11, 2002, Pure's board of directors held a telephonic meeting to discuss the Special Committee's request for a clarification of its purposes, powers, authority and independence. After discussion, Pure's board of directors adopted clarifying resolutions.

This statement is an inaccurate and materially misleading summary of the Pure board's rejection of the Special Committee's request for broader authority. No reasonable reader would know that the Special Committee sought to have the full power of the Pure board delegated to it — including the power to block the Offer through a rights plan — and had been rebuffed. No reasonable reader would know that Chessum and Ling (who just a few pages earlier in the 14D-9 had recused themselves from the Pure board's response to the Offer) had reinserted themselves into the process with Unocal's legal advisors and had beaten back this fit of assertiveness by the Special Committee.

The Pure stockholders would find it material to know that the Special Committee had been denied the powers they sought. As important, they are entitled to a balanced and truthful recitation of events, not a sanitized version that is materially misleading. The plaintiffs have established a probability of success on this issue. . . .

4.

The S-4 contains a section discussing the "Key Factors" motivating Unocal's decision to extend the Offer. The plaintiffs contend that this discussion is materially incomplete and misleading in at least two respects. First, the plaintiffs note that the S-4 has an extensive section on minimizing conflicts of interest, which dilates on the constraints that the BOA imposes on Pure. The plaintiffs argue, and I agree, that the discussion omits any acknowledgement of a very real motivating factor for Unocal's offer — to eliminate the potential exposure to liability Chessum and Ling faced if Unocal began to compete with Pure in Pure's core areas of operation. The record evidence supports the inference that this was a material concern of Unocal. In order for the disclosure that was made not to be misleading, this concern of Unocal's should be disclosed as well.

The plaintiffs' second contention is similar. In its board deliberations on the Offer, Unocal considered a management presentation indicating that Pure was considering "alternative funding vehicles not optimum to Unocal." This appears to be a reference to the Royalty Trust. Although this was highlighted as a concern for its own board, Unocal omitted this motivation from the S-4. This subject is material because the Royalty Trust is an important transaction that could be highly consequential to Pure's future if the Offer does not succeed.

The fact that the Royalty Trust's consideration is one of the motivations for Unocal to buy Pure now might factor into a stockholder's determination of whether Unocal has really put its best bid on the table. Moreover, it is necessary to make the rest of the disclosures regarding Unocal's motives not misleading.

5.

The plaintiffs advance an array of additional and cursorily argued disclosure claims. These claims either have been addressed by supplemental disclosures required by the SEC, do not involve materially important issues, or are too inadequately developed to sustain an injunction application.

IV. IRREPARABLE INJURY AND THE BALANCE OF HARMS

This court has recognized that irreparable injury is threatened when a stockholder might make a tender or voting decision on the basis of materially misleading or inadequate information. Likewise, the possibility that structural coercion will taint the tendering process also gives rise, in my view, to injury sufficient to support an injunction. The more tailored relief of an injunction also has the advantage of allowing a restructured Offer to proceed, potentially obviating the need for a complex, after-the-fact, damages case.

The defendants would have me deny the request for an injunction on the factual ground that the Offer cannot succeed if Hightower and his fellow managers, as well as the lead plaintiff, live up to their expressed desire not to tender. This may have some basis in fact, although it seems more reliably so only as to the waivable 90% condition, rather than the non-waivable majority of the minority condition. In any event, I am not prepared to gamble when a injunction can be issued that can be lifted in short order if Unocal and the Pure board respond to the concerns addressed in this opinion.

That is, although I recognize that this court rightly hesitates to deny stockholders an opportunity to accept a tender offer, I believe that the risks of an injunction are outweighed by the need for adequate disclosure and to put in place a genuine majority of the *unaffiliated* minority condition. Thus, I conclude that the balance of the hardships favors the issuance of a preliminary injunction.

V. CONCLUSION

For all these reasons, the plaintiffs' motion for a preliminary injunction is hereby granted, and the consummation of the Offer is hereby enjoined. IT IS SO ORDERED, and the parties shall submit a more complete preliminary injunction order for entry within the next 48 hours.

C. SHAREHOLDERS' RIGHTS TO VOTE

The general rules on when shareholders have a right to vote to approve a transaction were set out in Section B and thus do not need to be repeated here.

Generally, it is clear in a merger which shareholders have voting rights and which do not. Thus, the planning issue that arises is to structure the transaction in such a way that a shareholder vote can be avoided where the outcome of the vote seems doubtful or just needlessly expensive or time-consuming. The time factor is of particular importance, because a shareholder vote must be preceded by the issuance of a proxy statement, and the shareholders must have at least 20 business days to consider the proxy statement prior to the vote, according to SEC rules. Effectively, then, a month is required for a shareholder vote, during which time another company may come forward to try to engage in a different transaction with one of the merger partners, including a hostile transaction. Thus, transactions can often be structured as a triangular merger (or reverse triangular merger) in order to avoid a shareholder vote because of the time factor, and in order to protect the deal. (There are other "deal protection" devices you've seen above, including "no-shop" provisions and "window-shop" provisions designed to discourage merger partners from testing the water to determine if another company will come forward with a better price.)

With a sale of assets transaction, however, the question of whether the selling shareholders get a vote is occasionally problematic and depends on whether the assets being sold are "substantially all" of the assets of the company. The Model Act has adopted a fairly clear rule, which states that neither voting rights nor appraisal rights are available if the company will be left with at least 25 percent of its presale assets and either 25 percent of after-tax operating income or 25 percent of revenues. Model Act §12.02(a). The Delaware analysis is less precise, since the courts have defined "substantially all" assets through common law adjudication. The Delaware courts emphasize a disjunctive qualitative/quantitative test that looks at both the quantitative importance of the assets being sold to the company or their qualitative importance. In the leading case, the Delaware Chancery Court stated that "all or substantially all" of the assets are involved if the sale is of assets "quantitatively vital to the operation of the corporation and is out of the ordinary and substantially affects the existence and purpose of the corporation." Gimbel v. Signal Cos., 316 A.2d 599, 606 (Del. Ch. 1974)). The following Problem explores the meaning of selling "substantially all" of the assets of the company under Delaware law.

PROBLEM 14-2

Apple Computer is in the business of manufacturing and selling personal computers (PCs), bundled with Apple's proprietary operating system, MacOS. Known primarily for its Macintosh, PowerPC, and iMac computers, Apple is a distant and struggling second in the PC market to the behemoth Microsoft.

Since 1994, Apple has been the largest shareholder in another Silicon Valley company named Exponential, owning just under 10 percent of Exponential's voting shares. Exponential designs and markets the PowerPC microprocessing chips (CPUs) that IBM, Apple, and Motorola have jointly developed to serve as the "brains" for their PCs. In October 1996, Exponential and Apple entered into an agreement setting forth the terms by which Exponential would "design, develop, prototype and test" a new generation of PowerPC CPUs and sell them to Apple. Under the terms of that agreement, the new chips were to have been available as of April 1997.

In late March 1997, Exponential's CEO wrote to Apple to inform it that Exponential would not meet its April deadline and that the new CPUs would not be available until September at the earliest. This news was not well received at Apple, and although the facts are not clear about what happened next, two things are clear. First, Exponential sued Apple under the agreement (perhaps of the view that the best defense is a good offense), claiming that Apple's post-March refusal to work out the development problems between the two companies and Apple's refusal to allow Exponential to sell its product to manufacturers of Apple clones had effectively put Exponential out of business. Second, Exponential sent its shareholders a letter stating that it was closing its San Jose facility and would soon decide whether to close its only other facility in Austin, Texas; and that it would be seeking a buyer for the 45 patents it owned. Soon thereafter Exponential sold its patents to S3, a graphics chip maker, for $10 million.

Apple contends that since this sale of patents is a sale of substantially all of Exponential's assets, its shareholders have a right to vote under DGCL §271. Exponential replies that its breach of contract action against Apple (including claims of breach of fiduciary duty and intentional interference with prospective economic advantage), in which it seeks damages of $500 million is a valuable corporate asset, and thus its sale of all of its patents is not a sale of substantially all of its assets.

What additional facts do you need to analyze Apple's claim that Exponential violated DGCL §271? How would you advise Apple to proceed? How would you advise Exponential in this situation?

D. THE APPRAISAL REMEDY

As we've seen in Weinberger v. UOP, a majority shareholder (usually a parent company) has the power to "cash out" the minority shareholders (usually a subsidiary), using either a merger or a short-form merger. (This could also be structured as a sale of assets, although that would not be as common.) The question then arises: what protects the minority shareholder in this situation from being cashed out at a price that is unfair? As always, the law relies on the constraints of fiduciary duty — the board that approves either the merger or the short-form merger must act in good faith, consistent with its duties of loyalty, due care, and full disclosure. Moreover, even if the board acts consistent with those duties, the shareholders may have a remedy if they believe that the price at which they were cashed out does not represent "fair value" for their shares. This remedy is a specific type of proceeding called an "appraisal." *See* DGCL §262; Model Act §13.02.

While you've seen language in Weinberger v. UOP stating that appraisal is the "exclusive" remedy for dispossessed shareholders in a cash-out merger, in fact appraisal is only the exclusive remedy when price is the only issue. So where plaintiffs claim that the price at which they were cashed out is unfair *and* that there were other breaches (of fiduciary duty in the process of deciding on a merger, or of disclosure duties in proxy solicitations to approve the merger, for instance), then plaintiffs may bring an equitable action to try to stop the merger or an action for equitable damages such as rescission after the fact, or they may initiate fiduciary duty litigation. There is one sense in which an appraisal proceeding really is exclusive, however, and that is that only the fairness of the price can be litigated in an appraisal action. So if plaintiffs in an appraisal proceeding uncover breaches of fiduciary duty through discovery, they will be forced into parallel litigation.

The perils of this "parallel litigation" procedure are well illustrated in a convoluted litigation in Delaware, Cinerama, Inc. v. Technicolor (also referred to as Cede & Co. v. Technicolor after the name of the depositary company, Cede & Co., in whose name many shares of stock owned by institutions and brokerage firms are held). As of 2003, this 20-year litigation had produced six published opinions by the Delaware Supreme Court; seven published opinions of the Delaware Court of Chancery; a spontaneous recusal by a Delaware Chancellor, who was apparently fed up with the latest Supreme Court remand; numerous unpublished interim orders, and one can only imagine how many discovery orders. As the chancery court recognized in denying an interlocutory appeal of its order setting out trial procedures in 2001 for the second trial in the appraisal action,

> [t]he long history of the dispute between these parties is well known not only to the parties, but also to all those who are familiar with Delaware corporate law. As Cinerama continues to battle its seemingly eternal adversary, Technicolor, the present appraisal proceeding is all that remains after almost two decades of fierce litigation. As these parties launch their final campaign, the conflict between them not only appears to sustain both combatants, but has in part come to define them.

Cede v. Technicolor, 2001 WL 515106 (Del. Ch. 2001).

The *Cinerama* litigation began in 1983 as an appraisal proceeding, but the plaintiffs, Cinerama, who were minority shareholders in the target company, Technicolor, Inc., soon uncovered information leading them to believe that at least some members of the board had breached their fiduciary duties. Their claim was that two of Technicolor's board members, including its chief executive officer, had secretly been negotiating with executives of the potential acquirer, MacAndrews & Forbes Group, Inc., and giving them information on how to structure a winning bid, and that the "tainted" board members had pushed the transaction on the Technicolor board without disclosing these facts. Further, plaintiffs claimed, the process the board had used to determine the price at which to sell Technicolor was not adequate. In the litigation, because the alleged breaches were uncovered after the plaintiffs had already begun an appraisal proceeding and because price is the only permissible issue in an appraisal proceeding, the Delaware Supreme Court allowed both a personal liability action and an appraisal action to go forward in the court of chancery, in parallel, and consolidated through trial. Timing problems in the parallel actions have perhaps caused the Delaware Supreme Court to regret that ruling: the court ultimately upheld a finding of entire fairness by the board (finding that the conflict of interest by two members of the board did not "taint" the entire board's procedures) but based its "fair price" part of the entire fairness analysis on the chancery court's opinion in the appraisal action that the price paid to cash out the minority was about $2.00 per share *higher* than the value of the shares. Unfortunately, when the appraisal ruling on the fair value of the stock came to the Delaware Supreme Court for review, it was reversed. Thus, as of 2003 the *Cinerama* case has gone back for a second trial in the appraisal action. If in this trial the Chancery Court finds the price was unfair, the Delaware Supreme Court might have to re-evaluate its entire fairness opinion!

Appraisal as a remedy is not very satisfactory to many potential plaintiffs for reasons in addition to the limited nature of the proceeding, however, particularly in Delaware, which is perhaps why fewer than 10 percent of eligible shareholders ever seek appraisal. (The following analysis draws upon the excellent work of Professors Klein and Coffee in William A. Klein & John C. Coffee, Jr, *Business Organization and Finance: Legal and Economic Principles* (8th ed. 2002)). First, appraisal actions are individual actions, not class actions, so shareholders must exercise the initiative to perfect their appraisal rights on their own. While the court may ultimately consolidate the individual actions, this can be a formidable obstacle, particularly to an out-of-state shareholder. In contrast, a claim of breach of fiduciary duty can be asserted by a single shareholder representing the interests of all shareholders in a class action. Second, dissenters must initially bear all of the costs of litigation, and while the court may ultimately assess costs against the company, it need not. Third, shareholders do not get paid until the end of the litigation, and while the court has the power to award reasonable interest, the amount of interest awarded may be far less than the amount of money the shareholder could have earned on the same amount of money invested elsewhere. Finally, the shareholder receives no dividends (if the consideration was stock in a privately held company) and has no voting rights during the appraisal proceeding.

The Model Act attempts to ameliorate some of these difficulties. Probably most important to shareholders, the company must pay dissenters the merger consideration at the beginning of the litigation if the dissenter deposits the shares with the company. *See* Model Act §13.24. In addition to payment, the company is asked to provide additional information so the shareholder can decide whether to settle the action. If within 60 days the shareholder has not decided to settle the action, the corporation must institute, and pay for, an appraisal proceeding. *See* Model Act §13.30(a). Ultimately the court may assess costs against the dissenters, but at least under this procedure it is the company that is out of pocket for the costs of litigation during the pendency of the proceeding.

The following case explores an issue that has generated substantial litigation over the past decade — namely, whether a court that is determining the value of a minority shareholder's claim should apply a discount to reflect the lack of marketability or lack of control of a minority stake in a privately held company. At first glance, this issue may seem arcane and uninteresting, but whether a discount is applied makes a substantial difference in the price paid to minority shareholders. Moreover, this issue goes to the heart of the appraisal remedy: what is its ultimate purpose? Perhaps predictably, courts have differed in their approach to this fundamental question, as ably discussed by the Supreme Court of Colorado.

PUEBLO BANCORPORATION v. LINDOE, INC.

63 P.3d 353
Supreme Court of Colorado (en banc)
January 21, 2003

Justice RICE delivered the Opinion of the Court.

In this dissenter's rights action, Petitioner, Pueblo Bancorporation, appeals the court of appeals' reversal of the trial court's determination of the fair value of the shares owned by Lindoe, Inc., a minority shareholder in Pueblo Bancorporation. The parties do not disagree over the value of Pueblo Bancorporation; the only issue is whether the trial court, in assigning a specific "fair value" to Lindoe's shares, should apply a discount to reflect the shares' lack of marketability. The trial court applied such a discount, but the court of appeals reversed and held, as a matter of law, no marketability discount may be applied. We granted certiorari to resolve a conflict in the court of appeals regarding the meaning of "fair value." We hold that "fair value" under the Colorado dissenters' rights statute means the shareholder's proportionate ownership interest in the value of the corporation. Therefore, no marketability discount may be applied. The court of appeals decision is affirmed.

I. FACTS AND PROCEDURAL HISTORY

Petitioner, Pueblo Bancorporation ("Holding Company"), a Colorado corporation, is a bank holding company whose principal asset is The Pueblo Bank and Trust, a commercial bank with several branches throughout southeastern Colorado. In November of 1997, Holding Company had 114,217 outstanding shares, owned by thirty-eight shareholders—including twenty-nine individuals, two corporations, and seven retirement trusts.

One of Holding Company's corporate shareholders was Respondent, Lindoe, Inc. Lindoe, which is also a bank holding company, first purchased shares in 1988 and has since acquired additional shares as they became available. By November of 1997, Lindoe owned 6,525 (5.71%) of Holding Company's outstanding shares and was its sixth-largest shareholder.

This dispute was set in motion by a change in federal tax law. Prior to 1997, Holding Company was taxed as a corporation under subchapter C of the Internal Revenue Code. I.R.C. §1361(a)(2). The earnings of a C corporation are subject to double taxation; earnings are taxed once at the corporate level and then taxed a second time at the individual level when distributed to shareholders. In contrast, corporations which qualify under subchapter S of the Internal Revenue Code are not generally subject to double taxation; corporate earnings are not taxed at the corporate level but pass through to the shareholders, who pay tax on the corporate income according to their proportionate ownership interest in the entity. I.R.C. §1363. There are narrow restrictions on the types of corporations that may qualify as S corporations, and prior to 1997, Holding Company could not qualify. However, in 1997, because of certain changes to the rules governing S corporations, Holding Company became eligible to elect S corporation status.

Because of the opportunity to eliminate the double tax, Holding Company's board of directors sought to convert the company into an S corporation. However, they faced two potential obstacles. First, under the Code, an S corporation cannot have a corporation as a shareholder. I.R.C. §1361(b)(1)(B). Several of Holding Company's shareholders, including Lindoe, would not qualify to hold stock in Holding Company if it were an S corporation. Second, an election to become an S corporation requires the unanimous approval of its shareholders; a single dissenting vote can block the conversion. I.R.C. §1362(a)(2).

To avoid both of these potential pitfalls, Holding Company devised a plan to accomplish the conversion through merger. Holding Company created a second corporation, Pueblo Bancorp Merger Corporation (Merger Corp.), which was organized as an S corporation. Three of Holding Company's directors served as directors of Merger Corp. and the officers of the two entities were the same. The two companies entered into a merger agreement, subsequently approved by the shareholders of both companies. The resulting entity was an S corporation which continued operating under the name Pueblo Bancorporation; however, only those shareholders who could legally own shares in an S corporation were eligible to remain shareholders of the surviving corporation. Shareholders, such as Lindoe, that were ineligible to receive shares of the surviving entity received a cash payout in exchange for their Holding Company stock.

After an appraisal of the value of its shares, Holding Company offered $341 per share to the cashed out shareholders. Several shareholders accepted the amount and tendered their stock. Lindoe, however, chose to dissent and seek a higher amount. Pursuant to the procedure set out in Colorado's dissenters' rights statute, Lindoe sent a notice to Holding Company rejecting Holding Company's fair value determination and providing its own estimate of fair value: $775 per share. Disputing Lindoe's estimate, Holding Company initiated this action in order to obtain the court's determination of the fair value of Lindoe's shares.

The trial to determine fair value was a classic battle of experts. Holding Company's expert concluded that Holding Company, as an entity, was worth $72.9 million, or $638 per share. Lindoe provided two valuation experts whose estimates regarding the value of Holding Company ranged from $82.8 million to $88.5 million, a per share value of $725 to $775. The primary source of disagreement throughout the proceeding was whether the court should apply a minority or marketability discount to determine the fair value of Lindoe's shares.[2] Holding Company's expert, arguing that the court must apply both a minority and marketability discount in order to accurately reflect the value of Lindoe's shares, applied both discounts to arrive at his final opinion that the shares had a fair value of $344 per share. Lindoe's experts argued that application of discounts was inappropriate; the fair value of the shares in their opinion was between $725 and $775 per share.

The trial court first determined the value of Holding Company as an entity by combining the opinions of two of the experts. It concluded that the enterprise value of Holding Company was $76,087,723, or $666.16 per share. On the issue of discounts, the court was persuaded by Holding Company and applied both a minority discount and a marketability discount to arrive at its fair value determination of $362.03. Because Lindoe had already received $341 for its shares, the court entered judgment in favor of Lindoe in the amount of $137,220.75 ($21.03 times 6,525, the number of shares held by Lindoe).

On appeal, the primary issue, as it was in the trial court, was whether it was appropriate to apply a minority or marketability discount. The court of appeals

---

2. The distinction between a minority discount and a marketability discount is important. A minority discount adjusts the value of specific minority shares to reflect the fact that the shares lack sufficient voting power to control corporate decisions and policies. A marketability discount adjusts the value of specific shares to reflect the fact that there is no ready trading market for the shares. Because there are a small number of potential buyers of closely-held corporate stock, a shareholder may be unable to secure a willing buyer if he decides to cash out of his investment. *See* Edwin T. Hood *et al., Valuation of Closely Held Business Interests*, 65 UMKC L. Rev. 399, 438 (1997).

sided with Lindoe and reversed the trial court, holding that the court erred in applying the discounts. Pueblo Bancorporation v. Lindoe, Inc., 37 P.3d 492 (Colo. App. 2001).

We granted certiorari to resolve a conflict in the court of appeals regarding the question of whether a marketability discount may be applied in determining "fair value" under the Colorado dissenters' rights statute.[3]

II. ANALYSIS

Under Colorado's dissenters' rights statute, a dissenting shareholder must follow certain procedures in order to receive the fair value of his shares. First, upon majority shareholder approval of certain corporate actions, the dissenting shareholder must notify the company of his intention to demand dissenters' rights. Upon receiving notice, the company must pay the dissenting shareholder the amount which the company estimates to be the fair value of the dissenter's shares. If the dissenting shareholder is dissatisfied with the company's estimate of fair value, he must provide his own estimate and demand payment in that amount from the company. Upon receiving such a demand from the dissenting shareholder, the company must either pay the amount of the dissenter's estimate or commence a proceeding for a judicial determination of fair value.

Throughout the entire process, the statutory standard of value to which a dissenting shareholder is entitled is "fair value":

> "Fair Value," with respect to a dissenter's shares, means the value of the shares immediately before the effective date of the corporate action to which the dissenter objects, excluding any appreciation or depreciation in anticipation of the corporate action except to the extent that exclusion would be inequitable.

§7-113-101(4), 2 C.R.S. (2002).

This case requires us to determine what the General Assembly meant by "fair value." . . .

Because we are unable to resolve the meaning of "fair value" by reference to the plain language of the statute, and because of the conflicting interpretations of the term found in prior case law, it is the role of this court to determine the meaning of this statutory phrase. Of course, if the legislature disapproves of our interpretation, it has the power to amend the statute to make its intention clear.

In our view, the term "fair value" could reasonably be subject to one of three interpretations. One possible interpretation, urged by Lindoe, is that fair value requires the court to value the dissenting shares by looking at what they represent: the ownership of a certain percentage of the corporation. In this case, the trial court found that Holding Company, as an entity, was worth $76.1 million. Lindoe owned 5.71 percent of Holding Company and therefore, under this view, Lindoe is entitled to 5.71 percent of Holding Company's value, or just

3. We granted certiorari review only on the issue of whether a marketability discount may be applied. We do not review the court of appeals' conclusion that a minority discount should not be applied in determining fair value.

over $4.3 million. Because the proper measure of value is the shareholder's proportionate interest in the value of the entity, discounts at the shareholder level are inapplicable.

Another interpretation of fair value is to value the dissenters' specific allotment of shares, just as one would value the ownership of a commodity. Under this view, although Lindoe's shares represent ownership of 5.71 percent of Holding Company, the "fair value" of its ownership interest is only the amount a willing buyer would pay to acquire the shares. In effect, this interpretation reads fair value as synonymous with fair market value. An investor who wants to buy a minority allotment of shares in a closely-held corporation would discount the price he was otherwise willing to pay for the shares because the shares are a minority interest in the company and are a relatively illiquid investment. Likewise, under this interpretation, the trial court should usually apply minority and marketability discounts.

The third possible interpretation of fair value is a case-by-case approach which allows the trial court to adapt the meaning of fair value to the specific facts of the case. In some circumstances, fair value of a dissenter's shares will mean his proportionate interest in the corporation; in other cases it will mean the fair market value of specific shares valued as a commodity.

For the reasons set forth below, we first hold that the meaning of "fair value" is a question of law, not an issue of fact to be opined on by appraisers and decided by the trial court on a case-by-case basis.

Next, we conclude that fair value must have a definitive meaning; either it is the shareholder's proportionate ownership interest in the corporation or it is the value of the shareholder's specific allotment of shares. We conclude that the legislature chose the term "fair value" for a reason and therefore it must mean something different than "fair market value." To determine the precise meaning of "fair value," we consider the purpose underlying the dissenters' rights statute and the interpretation of "fair value" provided by courts and commentators from around the country.

Finally, we hold that the proper interpretation of fair value is the shareholder's proportionate interest in the value of the corporation. Therefore, a marketability discount should not be applied at the shareholder level to determine the "fair value" of the dissenter's shares.

A. THE ERROR OF A CASE-BY-CASE APPROACH

Holding Company urges this court to adopt a case-by-case approach to the meaning of "fair value." This approach would leave the decision of whether to apply a marketability discount in the discretion of the trial court. . . .

A case-by-case interpretation of "fair value" results in a definition that is too imprecise to be useful to the business community. . . .

We conclude that a case-by-case approach to the definition of "fair value" is untenable. "Fair value" must have a definitive meaning; either it is the value of the shareholder's proportionate interest in the value of the corporation as an entity, or it is the value of the specific shares in the hands of that particular shareholder. To the extent [that prior cases] embraced a case-by-case determination of the meaning of "fair value," they are overruled.

We now turn to the language and purpose of the statute to determine which of these two interpretations the legislature intended.

B. FAIR VALUE DOES NOT MEAN FAIR MARKET VALUE

The interpretation of "fair value" advocated by Holding Company reads the term as synonymous with "fair market value." Under a fair market value standard a marketability discount should be applied because the court is, by definition, determining the price at which a specific allotment of shares would change hands between a willing buyer and a willing seller. However, in a dissenters' rights action, the dissenting shareholder is not in the same position as a willing seller on the open market — he is an unwilling seller with little or no bargaining power. We are convinced that "fair value" does not mean "fair market value."

In the sixty year history of Colorado's dissenters' rights statute, the measure of compensation has changed from "value" to "fair value," but the legislature has never required that dissenters be paid "fair market value" for their shares.

Fair market value is typically defined as the price at which property would change hands between a willing buyer and a willing seller when neither party is under an obligation to act. If the General Assembly intended to create a fair market value measure for the price of a dissenter's shares, it knew how to provide it; the phrase has been used many times in a wide variety of other statutes.

We conclude that if the General Assembly intended a dissenter to receive the fair market value for his shares, it would have said so. . . .

Although the plain language of the statute is ambiguous, we conclude that "fair value" is not synonymous with "fair market value." To determine the precise meaning of the term, we next consider the purpose of the statute and the interpretation of "fair value" provided by courts and commentators around the country.

C. "FAIR VALUE" MEANS THE SHAREHOLDER'S PROPORTIONATE OWNERSHIP INTEREST IN THE CORPORATION

We hold that the proper interpretation of fair value is the shareholder's proportionate ownership interest in the value of the corporation, without discounting for lack of marketability. This view is consistent with the underlying purpose of the dissenters' rights statute and the strong national trend against applying discounts.

1. *Purpose of the Dissenters' Rights Statute*

Historically, the dissenters' rights statutes were intended to compensate minority shareholders for the loss of their veto power and to provide liquidity for dissenting shareholders who found themselves trapped in an involuntarily altered investment. *See* Barry M. Wertheimer, *The Purpose of the Shareholders' Appraisal Remedy*, 65 Tenn. L. Rev. 661 (1998); Mary Siegel, *Back to the Future: Appraisal Rights in the Twenty-First Century*, 32 Harv. J. on Legis. 79, 93-97 (1995).

In recent years, the purpose of modern dissenters' rights statutes has been vigorously debated by commentators. The consensus that has developed among courts and commentators is that the modern dissenters' rights statute exists to protect minority shareholders from oppressive conduct by the majority.

The necessity of a dissenters' rights statute for protection of minority shareholders is illustrated by examining the situations in which the remedy is typically used today. The original concern of the appraisal remedy was for shareholders who were trapped in a post-merger investment that did not resemble their original investment. Today, financial practice and legal environments have changed such that mergers are often used solely to cash out minority shareholders.

In a typical cash-out merger, a corporation creates a shell company which is owned by the corporation's majority shareholders. The original corporation and the shell company merge and only the majority shareholders continue as shareholders of the surviving company; the minority shareholders are involuntarily cashed out of their investment.

The dissenters' rights statute serves as the primary assurance that minority shareholders will be properly compensated for the involuntary loss of their investment. The remedy protects the minority shareholders *ex ante*, by deterring majority shareholders from engaging in wrongful transactions, and *ex post*, by providing adequate compensation to minority shareholders.

In this case, the sole purpose of the merger between Holding Company and Merger Corp. was to cash out minority shareholders, such as Lindoe, who did not qualify to hold stock in an S corporation. The time and price at which Lindoe was cashed out was determined entirely by Holding Company.

The purpose of the dissenters' rights statute would best be fulfilled through an interpretation of "fair value" which ensures minority shareholders are compensated for what they have lost, that is, their proportionate ownership interest in a going concern. A marketability discount is inconsistent with this interpretation; it injects unnecessary speculation into the appraisal process and substantially increases the possibility that a dissenting shareholder will be under-compensated for his ownership interest. An interpretation of "fair value" that gives minority shareholders "less than their proportionate share of the whole firm's fair value would produce a transfer of wealth from the minority shareholders to the shareholders in control. Such a rule would inevitably encourage corporate squeeze-outs." In re Valuation of Common Stock of McLoon Oil Co., 565 A.2d 997 (Me. 1989).

2. *The National Trend*

The interpretation of fair value which we adopt today is the clear majority view. It has been adopted by most courts that have considered the issue, the authors of the Model Business Corporation Act, and the American Law Institute.

a. Other Jurisdictions

Our interpretation of "fair value" is consistent with the interpretation adopted by most courts that have considered the issue. The interpretation of other states is especially persuasive for two reasons. First, the language of the Colorado statute, because it was based on the Model Act, is nearly identical to the language of dissenters' rights statutes around the country. . . .

Second, we believe that one of the purposes of the MBCA was to facilitate a degree of national uniformity among state corporate law. Because the General Assembly enacted Colorado's corporate code based largely on the Model Act, we presume that it intended, to some degree, to place Colorado's corporate law in step with the law of other states. Holding Company's interpretation of "fair value" conflicts with the interpretation adopted by most courts that have already considered the issue.

In the leading case regarding discounts, Cavalier Oil Corp. v. Harnett, 564 A.2d 1137 (Del. 1989), the Delaware Supreme Court held that discounts should not be used in determining the "fair value" of a dissenters' shares. In that case, the majority shareholders of a closely-held Delaware corporation, in order to consolidate ownership of the company, approved a short-form merger. The dissenting shareholder, who owned just 1.5 percent of the company's outstanding shares, exercised his dissenters' rights. In determining the fair value of his shares, the Delaware Court of Chancery refused to apply a discount at the shareholder level. The supreme court affirmed:

> [T]he appraisal process is not intended to reconstruct a pro forma sale but to assume that the shareholder was willing to maintain his investment position, however slight, had the merger not occurred. Discounting individual share holdings injects into the appraisal process speculation on the various factors which may dictate the marketability of minority shareholdings. More important, to fail to accord to a minority shareholder the full proportionate value of his shares imposes a penalty for lack of control, and unfairly enriches the majority shareholders who may reap a windfall from the appraisal process by cashing out a dissenting shareholder, a clearly undesirable result.

Cavalier, 564 A.2d at 1145.

Since *Cavalier,* courts across the country have considered the issue of marketability discounts and have generally followed Delaware's lead. Of the jurisdictions with "fair value" statutes, courts in fifteen states have held that a marketability discount should not be applied in determining fair value.

In addition, five state legislatures have already adopted the 1999 amendments to the MBCA's fair value definition which explicitly prohibit minority and marketability discounts.

Finally, several other states, while not specifically addressing the issue of marketability discounts, have expressed the view that the proper interpretation of "fair value" is the shareholder's proportionate interest of the corporation as a going concern, not the specific stock valued as a commodity.

In contrast, only six states with "fair value" statutes have clearly concluded that fair value may include marketability discounts.

The clear majority trend is to interpret fair value as the shareholder's proportionate ownership of a going concern and not to apply discounts at the shareholder level. The interpretation urged by Holding Company would position Colorado among a shrinking minority of jurisdictions in the country. We decline to do so. Although corporate law varies widely among the states, we believe there is some benefit to a consistent interpretation of the same statutory language from one jurisdiction to the next.

b. The 1999 Amendments to the Model Business Corporation Act

We also find the recent amendments to the Model Business Corporation Act to be persuasive. In 1999, the MBCA amended its definition of fair value to reflect the national trend against discounts in fair value appraisals. "Fair value," according to the amended definition:

> means the value of the corporation's shares determined: . . .
>
>   (iii) without discounting for lack of marketability or minority status except, if appropriate, for amendments to the articles pursuant to section 13.02(a)(5).

Model Bus. Corp. Act 3d §13.01(4)(iii) (1984) (amended 1999). The commentary to the 1999 amendments makes clear that the change was an adoption of the "more modern view that appraisal should generally award a shareholder his or her proportional interest in the corporation after valuing the corporation as a whole, rather than the value of the shareholder's shares when valued alone." MBCA §13.01 official cmt. 2.

The MBCA has long been the source of Colorado's corporate law, including the dissenters' rights statute. Colorado's first dissenters' rights statute was enacted in 1941 and has undergone numerous revisions since that time. Since 1958, when Colorado adopted the first Model Business Corporation Act, the corporate code of this state has been largely modeled after the amendments and revisions to the Model Act.

In 1984, the Revised Model Business Corporation Act was published. The General Assembly followed suit in 1993 by repealing the entire Corporate Code and enacting, in large part, the 1984 Act. The current version of Colorado's dissenters' rights statute, although amended in 1996, remains substantially the same as the 1984 Model Act. The most important part of the statute for the purpose of this case, the definition of "fair value," is nearly identical to the definition found in the 1984 Model Act.

Holding Company argues that because the General Assembly has not adopted the 1999 MBCA amendments we should infer that it has rejected them. We are not persuaded. It has been less than four years since the MBCA was amended, too short a period of time to infer intent from legislative inaction. Because the legislature has consistently relied on the MBCA when fashioning the corporate laws of this state we find the views of the MBCA on this issue to be persuasive.

c. The American Law Institute

Finally, we are persuaded by the recommendations of the American Law Institute regarding the interpretation of "fair value." The ALI has endorsed the national trend of interpreting fair value as the proportionate share of a going concern "without any discount for minority status or, absent extraordinary circumstances, lack of marketability." A.L.I., *Principles of Corporate Governance: Analysis and Recommendations* §7.22(a) (1994). To determine fair value, the trial court must determine the aggregate value for the firm as an entity, and then simply allocate that value pro rata in accordance with the shareholders' percentage ownership. A.L.I. §7.22 cmt. *d.* . . .

III. CONCLUSION

We hold that the term "fair value," for the purpose of Colorado's dissenters' rights statute, means the dissenting shareholder's proportionate interest in the corporation valued as a going concern. The trial court must determine the value of the corporate entity and allocate the dissenting shareholder his proportionate ownership interest of that value, without applying a marketability discount at the shareholder level. The court of appeals decision is affirmed.

Justice KOURLIS dissenting.

In my view, defining "fair value" so to extinguish the possibility of marketability discounts in dissenters' rights actions represents a policy decision that the

General Assembly must make. Our statute is, as the majority notes, ambiguous. Colorado courts, with the exception of the court of appeals' decision in this case, have never interpreted the language of the statute as precluding trial courts from considering a marketability discount in valuing dissenters' shares. We must presume that the General Assembly is aware of those cases.

Despite the national trend to eliminate the marketability discount and the 1999 amendments to the Model Business Corporations Act ("MBCA"), also eliminating marketability discounts, the Colorado General Assembly has made no movement to change the Colorado statute. In my view, we cannot infer from any legislative history surrounding the dissenters' rights statute that the General Assembly has or would mandatorily exclude the use of marketability discounts in arriving at valuation.

Hence, absent a clear legislative declaration, an interpretation of the term "fair value" that essentially gives a shareholder more money for its shares because of a merger than the shareholder would have received immediately prior to the corporate action does not, in my view, comport with the language of the statute or with this state's prior case law. . . .

CHAPTER
15

Defending Against Hostile Takeovers

As discussed in previous chapters, mergers and acquisitions can either be negotiated transactions between the managements of two corporations, called "friendly" transactions, or they can be "hostile" transactions, in which one company is taken over by another company or by a determined bidder in spite of the target company's board's resistance. Much business lawyering seeks to ensure that companies can engage in friendly transactions with limited interference from shareholders. When possible, and when consistent with intelligent tax planning, this is acheived by structuring a transaction so that shareholders do not have a vote. At the same time, business lawyers also work to create governance structures that give companies the tools they need to resist being taken over in hostile transactions. This is done either by adopting defense mechanisms called "poison pills," which limit the ability of a potential acquiror to purchase shares, or by enacting charter amendment provisions that create staggered boards or supermajority voting requirements — both of which effectively limit the voting power of shareholders. As you will see below, the Delaware courts have been more sympathetic to tender offer restrictions than to voting restrictions, although in both instances management's power to defend against unwanted takeovers is broad, subject to fiduciary duty constraints.

In order to understand the following cases, some introduction to the context is in order. Some defensive techniques, called "shark repellents," may be adopted in advance of any identified threat. These may include adopting a staggered board, which in Delaware means it will take two years to secure a majority coalition on the board because of the "for-cause" removal implications of a staggered board; or adopting supermajority shareholder voting requirements for fundamental transactions, such as approving a merger or sale of substantially all assets. There are other defensive techniques that boards can use in response to a specific takeover attempt. One of the most important of these are poison pills, which you will see being implemented in many of the cases in this chapter. Poison pills usually involve the distribution of "rights" to existing shareholders pursuant to Delaware General Corporation Law (DGCL) §157. These rights allow the shareholders to buy shares of the acquiring company ("flip-over pills") or the target company ("flip-in pills") at a deep discount — typically half price — if any bidder acquires a certain percentage of the target's shares (called the "trigger"), usually 10 or 15 percent, without the board's approval. If the rights are triggered, the bidder's stake will immediately be diluted as existing shareholders exercise their rights to buy shares at bargain basement prices, which would then require the bidder to buy substantially more shares to take control.

Poison pills make it virtually impossible to buy control in a tender offer because it is prohibitively expensive unless the target board approves of the acquisition. As a result, no bidder ever goes above the "trigger." Poison pills are the most important arrow in a company's quiver of defenses, because they can be adopted by the board in response to an identified threat; and they can be "redeemed" (eliminated) by the board by paying a nominal amount to the shareholders to allow a merger with a favored acquisition partner. Poison pills force would-be acquirors to either negotiate with the board of directors or engage in a proxy fight to elect a board that is committed to replacing the board of directors and then redeeming the pill. In Delaware, however, if the board is staggered, two annual elections are needed to take majority control of the target's board, because staggering the board implies a "for cause" limitation on removal of board members; thus even a proxy fight requires two years. The combination of a pill and a staggered board is a powerful anti-takeover device, and it is probably for this reason that as of 1998, 59 percent of public companies in the United States had staggered boards, as did 82 percent of companies going public for the first time in 2001. *See* Lucian Bebchuk, John Coates & Guhan Subramanian, *The Powerful Antitakeover Force of Staggered Boards: Theory, Evidence and Policy*, 54 Stan. L. Rev. 887, 888 (2002).

In the face of an identified takeover attempt, the adoption of any of these techniques raises stark fiduciary duty issues, and one central question: was the board acting in the corporation's and shareholders' best interest by acting to remain independent, or was it acting to entrench itself—that is, to perpetuate itself in office? This question arises when a board adopts defensive measures because of the target shareholders' presumed financial interests in allowing a free-flowing market for corporate control. Target shareholders typically receive takeover premiums (increases) of between 40 percent (in friendly deals) and 50 percent (in hostile bids) for their shares, as compared to the pre-bid market price. If a shareholder holds stock in Intel, let's say, at $100.00 per share, she will typically be paid between $140 and $150 per share if a takeover of Intel goes forward. So when a board takes defensive actions to rebuff a takeover, those defenses may prevent shareholders from getting a takeover premium for their shares.

Ironically, in practice one effect of takeover defenses in some cases is to enhance the ultimate financial result for the target shareholders. In some cases, the effect of a board taking defensive action is that another bidder enters the fray, or management is given more leverage in negotiating with the first bidder, forcing that bidder to offer more money. The ultimate impact of defensive measures in those cases is that the company is sold for a higher price, and the shareholders get a higher premium, as the above data on takeover premiums show—that prices in hostile takeovers are higher than prices in negotiated takeovers. Yet where there is a staggered board and a pill, the effect of these takeover defenses is often to cause the attempted acquiror to give up. The firm remains independent, which obviously means the target shareholders are denied a premium.

In current mergers and acquisitions practice, boards of directors know that whatever defensive measures they take will be tested in litigation, since litigation is an inevitable part of hostile acquisitions and attempted hostile acquisitions. Thus, fiduciary duty litigation has an important role to play in providing a forum in which the courts evaluate the central question: is the board acting in the corporation's best interests by adopting defensive measures, given the increased likelihood the takeover will fail and there will be no premium, or is the board acting simply to entrench themselves and maintain their positions? You'll see that this question is the subtext in just about every case you read in this area.

A. A BRIEF HISTORY OF HOSTILE TAKEOVERS

In order to understand this kind of litigation and these cases, it is useful to know something about hostile takeovers in the United States. One underlying issue in many of these decisions is where to locate power in the corporation — in the shareholders or in management. A more encompassing issue, evident in many of the Delaware decisions, is whether we ought to consider corporations simply as vehicles to maximize shareholder wealth, in which case hostile tender offers would presumably flourish, or whether we ought to consider corporations more as social entities with relationships to employees, creditors, communities, and shareholders that can be undermined by hostile takeovers and some of the resulting dislocations. This consideration comes into focus only upon learning the history of hostile takeovers in the 1980s, when many of these first cases arose.

The legal procedures that permit hostile takeovers are either a tender offer or a proxy contest. In a tender offer, a "bidder" offers to buy enough shares in the "target" company directly from existing shareholders to exert voting control and uses that control to elect its own directors. The tender offer is an offer to buy shares at a premium, and is made to all shareholders in their individual capacity. As such, the offer bypasses the board completely and may not need a majority of shareholders to agree to sell to be successful. (If a potential acquiror already owns 14 percent of a company, the acquiror can make a tender offer for an additional 37 percent of the company's shares and thus end up owning 51 percent of the company.) Federal securities law regulates the tender offer process pursuant to amendments to the so-called '34 Act, principally found in §§13(d) and 14(d) of the Williams Act. These statutory provisions seek to reduce some coercive aspects of tender offers by regulating the timing of tender offers (they must stay open for 20 days), by regulating the disclosure a tender offeror and target must provide to shareholders, and by providing certain rules to ensure fairness. These rules include requirements that bidders must buy shares *pro rata* from shareholders rather than buying shares on a first-come, first-served basis, and that bidders must pay every shareholder who tenders the highest price in the tender offer. This protects shareholders who tender early from missing out on later, higher tender offer prices. The focus of these regulations is to slow down the process, to provide shareholders with enough information to be able to make an intelligent decision about tendering or not, and to some extent to reduce the incentives shareholders might otherwise feel to tender early so as not to miss out on a tender offer premium.

In a proxy contest, as you've seen in previous chapters, a suitor seeks proxy voting authority from enough shareholders to put its slate of directors in power on the board. In this procedure, the potential acquiror bypasses the board, but needs to persuade a majority of shareholders to vote for the acquiror's slate in order to be successful. Of the two, hostile tender offers are the more secure: if the acquiror can arrange the financing necessary to purchase 51 percent of the shares at a premium, it can be certain to be successful in taking over another company, assuming majority voting rules and a board that is not staggered. Moreover, since the tender offeror sets the conditions for actually purchasing shares in the tender offer, the offeror will be under no obligation to purchase shares if the requisite number of shareholders refuse to tender. As you will see, legislatures have acted to make hostile acquisitions by tender offer much more difficult, as compared to the situation in the early 1980s, as has the poison pill, so proxy contests have assumed more importance at least as a theoretical mechanism to effect a hostile takeover.

Tender offers permitting hostile takeovers have existed for decades but were not used with any regularity until a period beginning in the late 1970s, and dramatically increasing in a period beginning in about 1985. This market shift seems to have been fueled primarily by a shift in norms among investment bankers as to whether it was proper to provide funding for a hostile tender offer to effect a takeover. As Professors Gilson and Black have stated,

> Until 1975, no major investment banking firm would participate in a hostile takeover attempt. But once Morgan Stanley, the most conservative of the leading firms, legitimized hostile takeovers by participating in a hostile tender offer for International Nickel in 1975, the conduct of parties to acquisitions moved farther and farther from the image of "gentlemen" conducting business in a restrained and courteous fashion. Increasingly, the dominant metaphor was war.

Ronald J. Gilson & Bernard S. Black, *The Law and Finance of Corporate Acquisitions* (2d ed. 1995).

Many of the hostile takeovers of the late 1980s were quite different from earlier waves of takeovers, in that the suitor didn't seek to acquire a company in order to run it better than existing management or to create a conglomerate of unrelated products. Rather, hostile takeovers in the late 1980s were often "bust-up" takeovers, in which a company was purchased at a premium and then the different subsidiaries or operating divisions were sold to pay off the debt incurred in buying the company. (That debt would be incurred in buying target shares at a premium in the tender offer to shareholders.)

The takeovers of the late 1980s were also different in the way they were financed. The new financing mechanism, called "high-yield bonds" or "junk bonds," allowed many of these hostile takeovers to go forward with very little money of the purchaser in the deal—often 10 percent or even less—and lots of debt. The market for junk bonds were the creation of Michael Milken, of Drexel, Burnham Lambert, a now-defunct securities firm. These bonds were high-yield because they were high-risk, having repayments dependent on companies with an uncertain future. However, they provided a way to raise much larger amounts of money than banks would typically provide in their lending. As a result of the existence of junk bond financing, the size of transactions increased, and the ratio of debt to equity increased. When RJR Nabisco was taken over by Kohlberg, Kravis Roberts (KKR) in 1989, after a bruising fight with the then-CEO Ross Johnson, who sought control, the ultimate price paid for the company was $24.8 billion, well beyond the financing capacity of most acquirors in prior decades. Because these transactions exhibited highly leveraged financial structures, they were called "LBOs," or leveraged buyouts; if management was buying out the company in a leveraged transaction it was called an "MBO," or management buyout, which creates special fiduciary duty issues because of the inherent conflict of interest. Perhaps needless to say, takeover specialists such as T. Boone Pickens, KKR, or Forstmann, Little ended up making a lot of money by engaging in bust-up takeovers, and were either villifed or venerated, depending on one's perspective, in movies such as "Wall Street" (roughly based on Michael Milken and Ivan Boesky); "Barbarians at the Gate" (the story of the RJR Nabisco takeover); and "Other People's Money" (depicting takeover specialists generally).

In about 1990, this type of takeover activity cooled. Junk bonds dried up as a financing mechanism when Michael Milken was indicted in 1990 and then went to jail in 1991 for numerous violations of federal securities laws, and his firm declared bankruptcy. State anti-takeover legislation, which had been passed in many states in the mid-1980s, was upheld against constitutional commerce clause and preemption attacks in the late 1980s; many states then enacted strong anti-takeover legislation, described briefly below. Moreover, there was an economic downturn in 1990-1992, which depressed mergers and acquisitions as bankruptcies replaced deals at the center of high-stakes business practices.

Law professors and legal commentators continue to debate whether the transactions of the 1980s were "good" for society or not. Many economists would say that these bust-up takeovers in the 1980s were simply necessary divestitures of unrelated businesses and subsidiaries, that allowed companies to unwind the conglomerates that had been put together in the 1960s and 1970s. Those conglomerates, it is argued, had too many disparate units in too many different businesses and thus were underperforming the market. If existing management saw the value of "deconglomerization," assets could be sold without a bust-up takeover, but if existing management didn't see this strategic necessity, a hostile takeover would be necessary to wrest control from management and put these assets to their highest-value use. Many politicians, managers, labor advocates, and reporters saw the social dislocations these takeovers caused, the jobs lost, and the communities affected by corporate downsizing or by relocations outside of the United States and felt that the social costs were too high to justify whatever economic benefits these types of takeovers produced.

In response, most states enacted protective legislation in the late 1980s to make hostile takeovers more difficult. The first type of state legislation imposed disclosure obligations in addition to those in the Williams Act, and created state regulatory agencies that had to approve takeover bids. But in 1982, the U.S. Supreme Court held that this type of statute was an unconstitutional interference with interstate commerce. Edgar v. MITE Corp., 457 U.S. 624 (1982). In response, state legislatures passed "second-generation" protective legislation that has, so far, withstood constitutional challenge. *See* CTS Corp. v. Dynamics Corp., 481 U.S. 69 (1987) (Indiana's control share statute is not preempted by the Williams Act, nor does it violate the Commerce Clause); Amanda Acquisition Corp. v. Universal Foods, 877 F.2d 496 (7th Cir. 1989) (Easterbrook, J.) (same result regarding Wisconsin's moratorium statute). These statutes take a number of forms, but for purposes of this discussion, it is only necessary to highlight their impact, which was twofold: they essentially shut down some of the most coercive tender offers, and they rendered hostile takeovers using tender offers rather than proxy contests virtually impossible in many states. And if the statutes hadn't done that, poison pills would have. Thus, in combination with opinions in Delaware upholding the legality of poison pills, by the end of the 1980s the power of the board to fend off hostile takeovers was well established, although not unlimited.

And yet takeovers, both hostile and friendly, flourished from 1993 until the stock market began to decline in 2000. Each year from 1995 through 1999 records were broken regarding the value of negotiated deals. These deals were valued at $1.75 trillion in 1999, up from $1.65 trillion in 1998. Hostile takeovers occurred as well during this period, notwithstanding state legislative impediments and companies' adoption of shark repellents and poison pills. Thus, in 1995 there were nearly 70 hostile takeover bids, compared to 88 hostile takeover bids in 1988, the peak year for hostile takeovers in the 1980s. As Professor Coates puts it, "At a minimum, the roaring mergers and acquisitions market [of the late 1990s] shows that defenses are not major impediments to the movement of assets to 'higher valuing users' via the market for corporate control." John C. Coates IV, *Takeover Defenses in the Shadow of the Pill: A Critique of the Scientific Evidence*, 79 Tex. L. Rev. 271 (2000). And a robust mergers and acquisitions market is not just a U.S. phenomenon: worldwide, the value of mergers and acquisitions in 1999 was $3.4 trillion, a 40 percent increase from the previous record of $2.5 trillion in 1998. Cross-border mergers were also on the rise during this period: the dollar value of cross-border mergers in 1999, $1.1 trillion, was almost double the value of cross-border mergers in 1998 and accounted for nearly 33 percent of the value of all worldwide deals.

Takeovers in the 1990s were different from those of the 1980s, however. First, a majority were not cash acquisitions, which the acquirer financed with junk bonds. Rather, given soaring stock prices, 55 percent of acquirors used shares of their company's stock as the consideration in share-for-share exchanges. A second difference from the 1980 takeovers is that many of these transactions were strategic acquisitions in which an acquiror sought to increase its size or expand its business operations by acquiring other companies in the same or a related field. Acquiring lots of small phone companies (and one large one, MCI) is how WorldCom grew from a small, start-up phone company based in Clinton, Mississippi, to an industry behemoth, servicing 20 percent of consumers' telephone needs and 50 percent of Internet traffic in the United States at the time of its bankruptcy in 2002. So, unlike the acquisitions of the 1960s and 1970s, these acquisitions for the most part did not create conglomerates of unrelated businesses within the same corporate structure; they were acquisitions of related businesses. And unlike in the 1980s, these acquisitions did not lead to "busting up" the companies being purchased. While many of the 1990s mergers and acquisitions led to layoffs from "synergies" — that is, companies could eliminate overlapping or redundant operations — takeovers didn't lead to the same hostility and political response as did takeovers in the 1980s. Perhaps this is because states had already passed protective legislation giving the board the power to ward off unsolicited tender offers. Perhaps it was because 50 percent of Americans were stockholders by the 1990s, either directly or through their pension funds, and were happy with what their stock portfolios were doing in the period from 1992 through 2000. In any case, political debate about takeovers in the 1990s in the United States was just about nonexistent.

Yet within the corporation and the corporate governance relationship, questions about the distribution of powers between shareholders and directors to respond to hostile takeover attempts, and about directors' fiduciary duties, remain central. You will see these questions developed in the cases set out below. The first series of cases, Unocal Corp. v. Mesa Petroleum Co. and its progeny, evaluates defensive measures that boards take to determine if those measures are consistent with the board's duties of care and loyalty to the corporation and its shareholders. Given the importance of poison pills as a particular defensive technique, we will look at the legitimacy of pills and the latest variations on them (so-called "dead hand" and "slow hand" pills), and then turn to other recent applications of *Unocal*. The second series of cases, the *Revlon* line, seeks to determine if there has been a change-of-control transaction and evaluates the board's duties once it is no longer defending the company against an unwanted suitor, but is actively selling the company. As you will see below, a quite different legal analysis obtains if the company is being sold versus being defended.

B. DELAWARE'S "INTERMEDIATE SCRUTINY" OF DEFENSIVE MEASURES

The following case sets out the analytic process the Delaware courts continue to use and refine to evaluate boards' uses of defensive measures. *Unocal* is generally considered to be one of the most innovative cases in the history of Delaware corporate law. Piecing together prior cases, it constructs a new method of analyzing defensive measures.

After *Unocal* was decided, the Securities and Exchange Commission promulgated Rule 14(d)-10, based on the authority of §14 of the '34 Act. Rule 14(d)-10 prohibits selective tender offers and requires all securities holders tendering into a tender to be paid the highest price paid to anyone in the tender offer. Thus, Rule 14(d)-10 now prohibits the selective self-tender upheld by the *Unocal* court. *Unocal* is still an extremely important case, however, since the process the court used to evaluate the Unocal board's defensive actions remains the process used in Delaware to analyze these types of cases.

UNOCAL CORP. v. MESA PETROLEUM CO.
493 A.2d 946
Supreme Court of Delaware
June 10, 1985

MOORE, Justice.

We confront an issue of first impression in Delaware — the validity of a corporation's self-tender for its own shares which excludes from participation a stockholder making a hostile tender offer for the company's stock.

The Court of Chancery granted a preliminary injunction to the plaintiffs, Mesa Petroleum Co., Mesa Asset Co., Mesa Partners II, and Mesa Eastern, Inc.

(collectively "Mesa"),[1] enjoining an exchange offer of the defendant, Unocal Corporation (Unocal) for its own stock. The trial court concluded that a selective exchange offer, excluding Mesa, was legally impermissible. We cannot agree with such a blanket rule. The factual findings of the Vice Chancellor, fully supported by the record, establish that Unocal's board, consisting of a majority of independent directors, acted in good faith, and after reasonable investigation found that Mesa's tender offer was both inadequate and coercive. Under the circumstances the board had both the power and duty to oppose a bid it perceived to be harmful to the corporate enterprise. On this record we are satisfied that the device Unocal adopted is reasonable in relation to the threat posed, and that the board acted in the proper exercise of sound business judgment. We will not substitute our views for those of the board if the latter's decision can be "attributed to any rational business purpose." Sinclair Oil Corp. v. Levien, Del. Supr., 280 A.2d 717, 720 (1971). Accordingly, we reverse the decision of the Court of Chancery and order the preliminary injunction vacated.

I.

On April 8, 1985, Mesa, the owner of approximately 13% of Unocal's stock, commenced a two-tier "front loaded" cash tender offer for 64 million shares, or approximately 37%, of Unocal's outstanding stock at a price of $54 per share. The "back-end" was designed to eliminate the remaining publicly held shares by an exchange of securities purportedly worth $54 per share. However, pursuant to an order entered by the United States District Court for the Central District of California on April 26, 1985, Mesa issued a supplemental proxy statement to Unocal's stockholders disclosing that the securities offered in the second-step merger would be highly subordinated, and that Unocal's capitalization would differ significantly from its present structure. Unocal has rather aptly termed such securities "junk bonds."

Unocal's board consists of eight independent outside directors and six insiders. It met on April 13, 1985, to consider the Mesa tender offer. Thirteen directors were present, and the meeting lasted nine and one-half hours. The directors were given no agenda or written materials prior to the session. However, detailed presentations were made by legal counsel regarding the board's obligations under both Delaware corporate law and the federal securities laws. The board then received a presentation from Peter Sachs on behalf of Goldman Sachs & Co. (Goldman Sachs) and Dillon, Read & Co. (Dillon Read) discussing the bases for their opinions that the Mesa proposal was wholly inadequate. Mr. Sachs opined that the minimum cash value that could be expected from a sale or orderly liquidation for 100% of Unocal's stock was in excess of $60 per share. In making his presentation, Mr. Sachs showed slides outlining the valuation techniques used by the financial advisors, and others, depicting recent business combinations in the oil and gas industry. The Court of Chancery found that the Sachs presentation was designed to apprise the directors of the scope of the analyses performed rather than the facts and numbers used in reaching the conclusion that Mesa's tender offer price was inadequate.

---

1. T. Boone Pickens, Jr., is President and Chairman of the Board of Mesa Petroleum and President of Mesa Asset and controls the related Mesa entities.

Mr. Sachs also presented various defensive strategies available to the board if it concluded that Mesa's two-step tender offer was inadequate and should be opposed. One of the devices outlined was a self-tender by Unocal for its own stock with a reasonable price range of $70 to $75 per share. The cost of such a proposal would cause the company to incur $6.1-6.5 billion of additional debt, and a presentation was made informing the board of Unocal's ability to handle it. The directors were told that the primary effect of this obligation would be to reduce exploratory drilling, but that the company would nonetheless remain a viable entity.

The eight outside directors, comprising a clear majority of the thirteen members present, then met separately with Unocal's financial advisors and attorneys. Thereafter, they unanimously agreed to advise the board that it should reject Mesa's tender offer as inadequate, and that Unocal should pursue a self-tender to provide the stockholders with a fairly priced alternative to the Mesa proposal. The board then reconvened and unanimously adopted a resolution rejecting as grossly inadequate Mesa's tender offer. Despite the nine and one-half hour length of the meeting, no formal decision was made on the proposed defensive self-tender.

On April 15, the board met again with four of the directors present by telephone and one member still absent. This session lasted two hours. Unocal's Vice President of Finance and its Assistant General Counsel made a detailed presentation of the proposed terms of the exchange offer. A price range between $70 and $80 per share was considered, and ultimately the directors agreed upon $72. The board was also advised about the debt securities that would be issued, and the necessity of placing restrictive covenants upon certain corporate activities until the obligations were paid. The board's decisions were made in reliance on the advice of its investment bankers, including the terms and conditions upon which the securities were to be issued. Based upon this advice, and the board's own deliberations, the directors unanimously approved the exchange offer. Their resolution provided that if Mesa acquired 64 million shares of Unocal stock through its own offer (the Mesa Purchase Condition), Unocal would buy the remaining 49 percent outstanding for an exchange of debt securities having an aggregate par value of $72 per share. The board resolution also stated that the offer would be subject to other conditions that had been described to the board at the meeting, or which were deemed necessary by Unocal's officers, including the exclusion of Mesa from the proposal (the Mesa exclusion). Any such conditions were required to be in accordance with the "purport and intent" of the offer.

Unocal's exchange offer was commenced on April 17, 1985, and Mesa promptly challenged it by filing this suit in the Court of Chancery. On April 22, the Unocal board met again and was advised by Goldman Sachs and Dillon Read to waive the Mesa Purchase Condition as to 50 million shares. This recommendation was in response to a perceived concern of the shareholders that, if shares were tendered to Unocal, no shares would be purchased by either offeror. The directors were also advised that they should tender their own Unocal stock into the exchange offer as a mark of their confidence in it.

Another focus of the board was the Mesa exclusion. Legal counsel advised that under Delaware law Mesa could only be excluded for what the directors reasonably believed to be a valid corporate purpose. The directors' discussion centered on the objective of adequately compensating shareholders at the "back-end" of Mesa's proposal, which the latter would finance with "junk bonds." To include Mesa would defeat that goal, because under the proration aspect of the exchange offer (49%) every Mesa share accepted by Unocal would displace one held by another stockholder. Further, if Mesa were permitted to tender to Unocal, the latter would in effect be financing Mesa's own inadequate proposal. . . .

[After hearings on Mesa's motion for a temporary restraining order (TRO) and preliminary injunction (PI), and subsequent to the Delaware Supreme court posing questions of fact for the chancery court to consider in its hearing for a PI,] the Vice Chancellor issued an unreported opinion on May 13, 1985 granting Mesa a preliminary injunction. Specifically, the trial court noted that "[t]he parties basically agree that the directors' duty of care extends to protecting the corporation from perceived harm whether it be from third parties or shareholders." The trial court also concluded in response to the second inquiry in the Supreme Court's May 2 order, that "[a]lthough the facts, . . . do not appear to be sufficient to prove that Mesa's principle objective is to be bought off at a substantial premium, they do justify a reasonable inference to the same effect."

As to the third and fourth questions posed by this Court, the Vice Chancellor stated that they "appear to raise the more fundamental issue of whether directors owe fiduciary duties to shareholders who they perceive to be acting contrary to the best interests of the corporation as a whole." While determining that the directors' decision to oppose Mesa's tender offer was made in a good faith belief that the Mesa proposal was inadequate, the court stated that the business judgment rule does not apply to a selective exchange offer such as this.

On May 13, 1985 the Court of Chancery certified this interlocutory appeal to us as a question of first impression, and we accepted it on May 14. The entire matter was scheduled on an expedited basis.

II.

The issues we address involve these fundamental questions: Did the Unocal board have the power and duty to oppose a takeover threat it reasonably perceived to be harmful to the corporate enterprise, and if so, is its action here entitled to the protection of the business judgment rule?

Mesa contends that the discriminatory exchange offer violates the fiduciary duties Unocal owes it. Mesa argues that because of the Mesa exclusion the business judgment rule is inapplicable, because the directors by tendering their own shares will derive a financial benefit that is not available to *all* Unocal stockholders. Thus, it is Mesa's ultimate contention that Unocal cannot establish that the exchange offer is fair to *all* shareholders, and argues that the Court of Chancery was correct in concluding that Unocal was unable to meet this burden.

Unocal answers that it does not owe a duty of "fairness" to Mesa, given the facts here. Specifically, Unocal contends that its board of directors reasonably and in good faith concluded that Mesa's $54 two-tier tender offer was coercive and inadequate, and that Mesa sought selective treatment for itself. Furthermore, Unocal argues that the board's approval of the exchange offer was made in good faith, on an informed basis, and in the exercise of due care. Under these circumstances, Unocal contends that its directors properly employed this device to protect the company and its stockholders from Mesa's harmful tactics.

III.

We begin with the basic issue of the power of a board of directors of a Delaware corporation to adopt a defensive measure of this type. Absent such authority, all other questions are moot. Neither issues of fairness nor business judgment are pertinent without the basic underpinning of a board's legal power to act.

The board has a large reservoir of authority upon which to draw. Its duties and responsibilities proceed from the inherent powers conferred by 8 Del. C. §141(a), respecting management of the corporation's "business and affairs." Additionally, the powers here being exercised derive from 8 Del. C. §160(a), conferring broad authority upon a corporation to deal in its own stock. From this it is now well established that in the acquisition of its shares a Delaware corporation may deal selectively with its stockholders, provided the directors have not acted out of a sole or primary purpose to entrench themselves in office. Cheff v. Mathes, Del. Supr., 199 A.2d 548, 554 (1964); [other citations].

Finally, the board's power to act derives from its fundamental duty and obligation to protect the corporate enterprise, which includes stockholders, from harm reasonably perceived, irrespective of its source. Thus, we are satisfied that in the broad context of corporate governance, including issues of fundamental corporate change, a board of directors is not a passive instrumentality.

Given the foregoing principles, we turn to the standards by which director action is to be measured. In Pogostin v. Rice, Del. Supr., 480 A.2d 619 (1984), we held that the business judgment rule, including the standards by which director conduct is judged, is applicable in the context of a takeover. Id. at 627. The business judgment rule is a "presumption that in making a business decision the directors of a corporation acted on an informed basis, in good faith and in the honest belief that the action taken was in the best interests of the company." Aronson v. Lewis, Del. Supr., 473 A.2d 805, 812 (1984) (citations omitted). A hallmark of the business judgment rule is that a court will not substitute its judgment for that of the board if the latter's decision can be "attributed to any rational business purpose." Sinclair Oil Corp. v. Levien, Del. Supr., 280 A.2d 717, 720 (1971).

When a board addresses a pending takeover bid it has an obligation to determine whether the offer is in the best interests of the corporation and its shareholders. In that respect a board's duty is no different from any other responsibility it shoulders, and its decisions should be no less entitled to the respect they otherwise would be accorded in the realm of business judgment. There are, however, certain caveats to a proper exercise of this function. Because of the omnipresent specter that a board may be acting primarily in its own interests, rather than those of the corporation and its shareholders, there is an enhanced duty which calls for judicial examination at the threshold before the protections of the business judgment rule may be conferred.

This Court has long recognized that:

> We must bear in mind the inherent danger in the purchase of shares with corporate funds to remove a threat to corporate policy when a threat to control is

involved. The directors are of necessity confronted with a conflict of interest, and an objective decision is difficult.

Bennett v. Propp, Del. Supr., 187 A.2d 405, 409 (1962). In the face of this inherent conflict directors must show that they had reasonable grounds for believing that a danger to corporate policy and effectiveness existed because of another person's stock ownership. Cheff v. Mathes, 199 A.2d at 554-55. However, they satisfy that burden "by showing good faith and reasonable investigation. . . . " *Id.* at 555. Furthermore, such proof is materially enhanced, as here, by the approval of a board comprised of a majority of outside independent directors who have acted in accordance with the foregoing standards. *See* Aronson v. Lewis, 473 A.2d at 812, 815. . . .

IV.

A.

In the board's exercise of corporate power to forestall a takeover bid our analysis begins with the basic principle that corporate directors have a fiduciary duty to act in the best interests of the corporation's stockholders. As we have noted, their duty of care extends to protecting the corporation and its owners from perceived harm whether a threat originates from third parties or other shareholders. But such powers are not absolute. A corporation does not have unbridled discretion to defeat any perceived threat by any Draconian means available.

The restriction placed upon a selective stock repurchase is that the directors may not have acted solely or primarily out of a desire to perpetuate themselves in office. *See* Cheff v. Mathes, 199 A.2d at 556; Kors v. Carey, 158 A.2d at 140. Of course, to this is added the further caveat that inequitable action may not be taken under the guise of law. Schnell v. Chris-Craft Industries, Inc., Del. Supr., 285 A.2d 437, 439 (1971). The standard of proof established in Cheff v. Mathes . . . is designed to ensure that a defensive measure to thwart or impede a takeover is indeed motivated by a good faith concern for the welfare of the corporation and its stockholders, which in all circumstances must be free of any fraud or other misconduct. Cheff v. Mathes, 199 A.2d at 554-55. However, this does not end the inquiry.

B.

A further aspect is the element of balance. If a defensive measure is to come within the ambit of the business judgment rule, it must be reasonable in relation to the threat posed. This entails an analysis by the directors of the nature of the takeover bid and its effect on the corporate enterprise. Examples of such concerns may include: inadequacy of the price offered, nature and timing of the offer, questions of illegality, the impact on "constituencies" other than shareholders (*i.e.*, creditors, customers, employees, and perhaps even the community generally), the risk of nonconsummation, and the quality of securities being offered in the exchange. While not a controlling factor, it also seems to us that a board may reasonably consider the basic stockholder interests at stake, including those of short term speculators, whose actions may have fueled the coercive aspect of the offer at the expense of the long term investor.[11] Here, the threat posed was viewed by the Unocal board as a grossly inadequate two-tier coercive tender offer coupled with the threat of greenmail.

Specifically, the Unocal directors had concluded that the value of Unocal was substantially above the $54 per share offered in cash at the front end. Furthermore, they determined that the subordinated securities to be exchanged in Mesa's announced squeeze out of the remaining shareholders in the "back-end" merger were "junk bonds" worth far less than $54. It is now well recognized that such offers are a classic coercive measure designed to stampede shareholders into tendering at the first tier, even if the price is inadequate, out of fear of what they will receive at the back end of the transaction. Wholly beyond the coercive aspect of an inadequate two-tier tender offer, the threat was posed by a corporate raider with a national reputation as a "greenmailer."[13]

In adopting the selective exchange offer, the board stated that its objective was either to defeat the inadequate Mesa offer or, should the offer still succeed, provide the 49% of its stockholders, who would otherwise be forced to accept "junk bonds," with $72 worth of senior debt. We find that both purposes are valid.

However, such efforts would have been thwarted by Mesa's participation in the exchange offer. First, if Mesa could tender its shares, Unocal would effectively be subsidizing the former's continuing effort to buy Unocal stock at $54 per share. Second, Mesa could not, by definition, fit within the class of shareholders being protected from its own coercive and inadequate tender offer.

Thus, we are satisfied that the selective exchange offer is reasonably related to the threats posed. It is consistent with the principle that "the minority stockholder shall receive the substantial equivalent in value of what he had before." Sterling v. Mayflower Hotel Corp., Del. Supr., 93 A.2d 107, 114 (1952). *See also* Rosenblatt v. Getty Oil Co., Del. Supr., 493 A.2d 929, 940 (1985). This concept of fairness, while stated in the merger context, is also relevant in the area of tender offer law. Thus, the board's decision to offer what it determined to be

---

11. There has been much debate respecting such stockholder interests. One rather impressive study indicates that the stock of over 50 percent of target companies, who resisted hostile takeovers, later traded at higher market prices than the rejected offer price, or were acquired after the tender offer was defeated by another company at a price higher than the offer price. *See* Lipton, [*Takeover Bids in the Target's Boardroom*, 35 Bus. Law. 101,] 106-109, 132-133. Moreover, an update by Kidder Peabody & Company of this study, involving the stock prices of target companies that have defeated hostile tender offers during the period from 1973 to 1982 demonstrates that in a majority of cases the target's shareholders benefitted from the defeat. The stock of 81% of the targets studied has, since the tender offer, sold at prices higher than the tender offer price. When adjusted for the time value of money, the figure is 64%. *See* Lipton & Brownstein, *supra* ABA Institute at 10. The thesis being that this strongly supports application of the business judgment rule in response to takeover threats. There is, however, a rather vehement contrary view. *See* Easterbrook & Fischel, [The Proper Rule of a Target's Management in Responding to a Tender Offer, 94 Harv. L. Rev. 1161, 1739-1745 (1981)].

13. The term "greenmail" refers to the practice of buying out a takeover bidder's stock at a premium that is not available to other shareholders in order to prevent the takeover. The Chancery Court noted that "Mesa has made tremendous profits from its takeover activities although in the past few years it has not been successful in acquiring any of the target companies on an unfriendly basis." Moreover, the trial court specifically found that the actions of the Unocal board were taken in good faith to eliminate both the inadequacies of the tender offer and to forestall the payment of "greenmail."

the fair value of the corporation to the 49% of its shareholders, who would otherwise be forced to accept highly subordinated "junk bonds," is reasonable and consistent with the directors' duty to ensure that the minority stockholders receive equal value for their shares.

V.

Mesa contends that it is unlawful, and the trial court agreed, for a corporation to discriminate in this fashion against one shareholder. It argues correctly that no case has ever sanctioned a device that precludes a raider from sharing in a benefit available to all other stockholders. However, as we have noted earlier, the principle of selective stock repurchases by a Delaware corporation is neither unknown nor unauthorized. Cheff v. Mathes, 199 A.2d at 554; 8 Del. G.C.L. §160. The only difference is that heretofore the approved transaction was the payment of "greenmail" to a raider or dissident posing a threat to the corporate enterprise. All other stockholders were denied such favored treatment, and given Mesa's past history of greenmail, its claims here are rather ironic.

However, our corporate law is not static. It must grow and develop in response to, indeed in anticipation of, evolving concepts and needs. Merely because the General Corporation Law is silent as to a specific matter does not mean that it is prohibited. In the days when *Cheff, Bennett, Martin* and *Kors* were decided, the tender offer, while not an unknown device, was virtually unused, and little was known of such methods as two-tier "front-end" loaded offers with their coercive effects. Then, the favored attack of a raider was stock acquisition followed by a proxy contest. Various defensive tactics, which provided no benefit whatever to the raider, evolved. Thus, the use of corporate funds by management to counter a proxy battle was approved. Litigation, supported by corporate funds, aimed at the raider has long been a popular device.

More recently, as the sophistication of both raiders and targets has developed, a host of other defensive measures to counter such ever mounting threats has evolved and received judicial sanction. These include defensive charter amendments and other devices bearing some rather exotic, but apt, names: Crown Jewel, White Knight, Pac Man, and Golden Parachute. Each has highly selective features, the object of which is to deter or defeat the raider.

Thus, while the exchange offer is a form of selective treatment, given the nature of the threat posed here the response is neither unlawful nor unreasonable. If the board of directors is disinterested, has acted in good faith and with due care, its decision in the absence of an abuse of discretion will be upheld as a proper exercise of business judgment.

To this Mesa responds that the board is not disinterested, because the directors are receiving a benefit from the tender of their own shares, which because of the Mesa exclusion, does not devolve upon *all* stockholders equally. *See* Aronson v. Lewis, Del. Supr., 473 A.2d 805, 812 (1984). However, Mesa concedes that if the exclusion is valid, then the directors and all other stockholders share the same benefit. The answer of course is that the exclusion is valid, and the directors' participation in the exchange offer does not rise to the level of a disqualifying interest.

Nor does this become an "interested" director transaction merely because certain board members are large stockholders. As this Court has previously noted, that fact alone does not create a disqualifying "personal pecuniary interest" to defeat the operation of the business judgment rule. Cheff v. Mathes, 199 A.2d at 554.

Mesa also argues that the exclusion permits the directors to abdicate the fiduciary duties they owe it. However, that is not so. The board continues to owe Mesa the duties of due care and loyalty. But in the face of the destructive threat Mesa's tender offer was perceived to pose, the board had a supervening duty to protect the corporate enterprise, which includes the other shareholders, from threatened harm.

Mesa contends that the basis of this action is punitive, and solely in response to the exercise of its rights of corporate democracy. Nothing precludes Mesa, as a stockholder, from acting in its own self-interest. However, Mesa, while pursuing its own interests, has acted in a manner which a board consisting of a majority of independent directors has reasonably determined to be contrary to the best interests of Unocal and its other shareholders. In this situation, there is no support in Delaware law for the proposition that, when responding to a perceived harm, a corporation must guarantee a benefit to a stockholder who is deliberately provoking the danger being addressed. There is no obligation of self-sacrifice by a corporation and its shareholders in the face of such a challenge.

Here, the Court of Chancery specifically found that the "directors' decision [to oppose the Mesa tender offer] was made in the good faith belief that the Mesa tender offer is inadequate." Given our standard of review under Levitt v. Bouvier, Del. Supr., 287 A.2d 671, 673 (1972), and Application of Delaware Racing Association, Del. Supr., 213 A.2d 203, 207 (1965), we are satisfied that Unocal's board has met its burden of proof. Cheff v. Mathes, 199 A.2d at 555.

VI.

In conclusion, there was directorial power to oppose the Mesa tender offer, and to undertake a selective stock exchange made in good faith and upon a reasonable investigation pursuant to a clear duty to protect the corporate enterprise. Further, the selective stock repurchase plan chosen by Unocal is reasonable in relation to the threat that the board rationally and reasonably believed was posed by Mesa's inadequate and coercive two-tier tender offer. Under those circumstances the board's action is entitled to be measured by the standards of the business judgment rule. Thus, unless it is shown by a preponderance of the evidence that the directors' decisions were primarily based on perpetuating themselves in office, or some other breach of fiduciary duty such as fraud, over-reaching, lack of good faith, or being uninformed, a Court will not substitute its judgment for that of the board.

In this case that protection is not lost merely because Unocal's directors have tendered their shares in the exchange offer. Given the validity of the Mesa exclusion, they are receiving a benefit shared generally by all other stockholders except Mesa. In this circumstance the test of Aronson v. Lewis, 473 A.2d at 812, is satisfied. If the stockholders are displeased with the action of their elected representatives, the powers of corporate democracy are at their disposal to turn the board out. Aronson v. Lewis, Del. Supr., 473 A.2d 805, 811 (1984). *See also* 8 Del. C. §§141(k) and 211(b).

With the Court of Chancery's findings that the exchange offer was based on the board's good faith belief that the Mesa offer was inadequate, that the board's action was informed and taken with due care, that Mesa's prior activities justify a reasonable inference that its principle objective was greenmail, and implicitly, that the substance of the offer itself was reasonable and fair to the corporation and its stockholders if Mesa were included, we cannot say that the Unocal directors have acted in such a manner as to have passed an "unintelligent and unadvised judgment." The decision of the Court of Chancery is therefore REVERSED, and the preliminary injunction is VACATED.

C.   POISON PILLS AND VARIATIONS

Poison pills give the board substantial leverage in negotiations with potential acquirors. As set out above, the effect of triggering a pill is to change the capital structure of the target firm and to dilute the holdings of a potential acquiror, making it prohibitively expensive to buy control of a firm in the face of board opposition backed up by a pill. The pill can be "redeemed" — that is, eliminated — by the directors by purchasing them back from the shareholders at a nominal amount. Thus, poison pills give potential acquirors two options: they can either negotiate with the target board and convince the directors to redeem the pill and go forward with a merger — often by raising the amount of money per share of the offer; or they can engage in a proxy contest to nominate a board of directors committed to redeeming the pill.

This "ballot box" alternative to negotiating with the target board would seem to offer a real alternative to potential acquirors and thus to pose a threat to boards determined to stay independent. As a result, stronger variations of the pill were developed — the so-called "dead hand" and "slow hand" pills. In fact, though, if a company has a staggered board in its charter and is either incorporated in Delaware or has a for-cause limitation on removing directors, then the ballot box alternative imposes significant delay, requiring two annual elections before an acquiror is able to take control. Thus, stronger pills may not have been necessary, since few bidders want to take the economic risk of such a long delay before taking control. The following case evaluates the legality of these later variations of the pill. It is important for that evaluation, as well as for its substantial review of the first Delaware case to uphold the legality of pills generally, Moran v. Household International, Inc.

QUICKTURN DESIGN SYSTEMS, INC. v. MENTOR GRAPHICS CORP.
721 A.2d 1281
Supreme Court of Delaware
December 31, 1998

HOLLAND, Justice.

This is an expedited appeal from a final judgment entered by the Court of Chancery. The dispute arises out of an ongoing effort by Mentor Graphics Corporation ("Mentor"), a hostile bidder, to acquire Quickturn Design Systems, Inc. ("Quickturn"), the target company. The plaintiffs-appellees are

Mentor and an unaffiliated stockholder of Quickturn. The named defendants-appellants are Quickturn and its directors.

In response to Mentor's tender offer and proxy contest to replace the Quickturn board of directors, as part of Mentor's effort to acquire Quickturn, the Quickturn board enacted two defensive measures. First, it amended the Quickturn shareholder rights plan ("Rights Plan") by adopting a "no hand" feature of limited duration (the "Delayed Redemption Provision" or "DRP"). Second, the Quickturn board amended the corporation's by-laws to delay the holding of any special stockholders meeting requested by stockholders for 90 to 100 days after the validity of the request is determined (the "Amendment" or "By-Law Amendment"). Mentor filed actions for declarative and injunctive relief in the Court of Chancery challenging the legality of both defensive responses by Quickturn's board. The Court of Chancery conducted a trial on the merits. It determined that the By-Law Amendment is valid. It also concluded, however, that the DRP is invalid on fiduciary duty grounds.

In this appeal, Quickturn argues that the Court of Chancery erred in finding that Quickturn's directors breached their fiduciary duty by adopting the Delayed Redemption Provision. We have concluded that, as a matter of Delaware law, the Delayed Redemption Provision was invalid. Therefore, on that alternative basis, the judgment of the Court of Chancery is affirmed.

STATEMENT OF FACTS

THE PARTIES

Mentor (the hostile bidder) is an Oregon corporation, headquartered in Wilsonville, Oregon, whose shares are publicly traded on the NASDAQ national market system. Mentor manufactures, markets, and supports electronic design automation ("EDA") software and hardware. It also provides related services that enable engineers to design, analyze, simulate, model, implement, and verify the components of electronic systems. Mentor markets its products primarily for large firms in the communications, computer, semiconductor, consumer electronics, aerospace, and transportation industries.

Quickturn, the target company, is a Delaware corporation, headquartered in San Jose, California. Quickturn has 17,922,518 outstanding shares of common stock that are publicly traded on the NASDAQ national market system. Quickturn invented, and was the first company to successfully market, logic emulation technology, which is used to verify the design of complex silicon chips and electronics systems. Quickturn is currently the market leader in the emulation business, controlling an estimated 60% of the worldwide emulation market and an even higher percentage of the United States market. Quickturn maintains the largest intellectual property portfolio in the industry, which includes approximately twenty-nine logic emulation patents issued in the United States, and numerous other patents issued in foreign jurisdictions. Quickturn's customers include the world's leading technology companies, among them

Intel, IBM, Sun Microsystems, Texas Instruments, Hitachi, Fujitsu, Siemens, and NEC.

Quickturn's board of directors consists of eight members, all but one of whom are outside, independent directors. All have distinguished careers and significant technological experience. Collectively, the board has more than 30 years of experience in the EDA industry and owns one million shares (about 5%) of Quickturn's common stock.

Since 1989, Quickturn has historically been a growth company, having experienced increases in earnings and revenues during the past seven years. Those favorable trends were reflected in Quickturn's stock prices, which reached a high of $15.75 during the first quarter of 1998, and generally traded in the $15.875 to $21.25 range during the year preceding Mentor's hostile bid. Since the spring of 1998, Quickturn's earnings, revenue growth, and stock price levels have declined, largely because of the downturn in the semiconductor industry and more specifically in the Asian semiconductor market. Historically, 30%-35% of Quickturn's annual sales (approximately $35 million) had come from Asia, but in 1998, Quickturn's Asian sales declined dramatically with the downturn of the Asian market.[5] Management has projected that the negative impact of the Asian market upon Quickturn's sales should begin reversing itself sometime between the second half of 1998 and early 1999.

Quickturn-Mentor Patent Litigation

Since 1996, Mentor and Quickturn have been engaged in patent litigation that has resulted in Mentor being barred from competing in the United States emulation market. Because its products have been adjudicated to infringe upon Quickturn's patents, Mentor currently stands enjoined from selling, manufacturing, or marketing its emulation products in the United States. Thus, Mentor is excluded from an unquestionably significant market for emulation products. . . .

Mentor's Interest in Acquiring Quickturn

Mentor began exploring the possibility of acquiring Quickturn. If Mentor owned Quickturn, it would also own the patents, and would be in a position to "unenforce" them by seeking to vacate Quickturn's injunctive orders against Mentor in the patent litigation. The exploration process began when Mr. Bernd Braune, a Mentor senior executive, retained Arthur Andersen ("Andersen") to advise Mentor how it could successfully compete in the emulation market. The result was a report Andersen issued in October 1997, entitled "PROJECT VELOCITY" and "Strategic Alternatives Analysis." The Andersen report identified several advantages and benefits Mentor would enjoy if it acquired Quickturn.

In December 1997, Mentor retained Salomon Smith Barney ("Salomon") to act as its financial advisor in connection with a possible acquisition of Quickturn. Salomon prepared an extensive study which it reviewed with Mentor's senior executives in early 1998. The Salomon study concluded that although a

---

5. By the summer of 1998, Quickturn's stock price had declined to $6 per share. On August 11, 1998, the closing price was $8.00. It was in this "trough" period that Mentor, which had designs upon Quickturn since the fall of 1997, saw an opportunity to acquire Quickturn for an advantageous price.

Quickturn acquisition could provide substantial value for Mentor, Mentor could not afford to acquire Quickturn at the then-prevailing market price levels. Ultimately, Mentor decided not to attempt an acquisition of Quickturn during the first half of 1998.

After Quickturn's stock price began to decline in May 1998, however, Gregory Hinckley, Mentor's Executive Vice President, told Dr. Walden Rhines, Mentor's Chairman, that "the market outlook being very weak due to the Asian crisis made it a good opportunity" to try acquiring Quickturn for a cheap price. Mr. Hinckley then assembled Mentor's financial and legal advisors, proxy solicitors, and others, and began a three month process that culminated in Mentor's August 12, 1998 tender offer.

Mentor Tender Offer and Proxy Contest

On August 12, 1998, Mentor announced an unsolicited cash tender offer for all outstanding common shares of Quickturn at $12.125 per share, a price representing an approximate 50% premium over Quickturn's immediate pre-offer price, and a 20% discount from Quickturn's February 1998 stock price levels. Mentor's tender offer, once consummated, would be followed by a second step merger in which Quickturn's nontendering stockholders would receive, in cash, the same $12.125 per share tender offer price.

Mentor also announced its intent to solicit proxies to replace the board at a special meeting. Relying upon Quickturn's then-applicable by-law provision governing the call of special stockholders meetings, Mentor began soliciting agent designations from Quickturn stockholders to satisfy the by-law's stock ownership requirements to call such a meeting.[11]

Quickturn Board Meetings

Under the Williams Act, Quickturn was required to inform its shareholders of its response to Mentor's offer no later than ten business days after the offer was commenced. During that ten day period, the Quickturn board met three times, on August 13, 17, and 21, 1998. During each of those meetings, it considered Mentor's offer and ultimately decided how to respond.

The Quickturn board first met on August 13, 1998, the day after Mentor publicly announced its bid. All board members attended the meeting, for the purpose of evaluating Mentor's tender offer. The meeting lasted for several hours. Before or during the meeting, each board member received a package that included (i) Mentor's press release announcing the unsolicited offer; (ii) Quickturn's press release announcing its board's review of Mentor's offer; (iii) Dr. Rhines's August 11 letter to Mr. Antle; (iv) the complaints filed by Mentor against Quickturn and its directors; and (v) copies of Quickturn's then-current Rights Plan and by-laws.

The Quickturn board first discussed retaining a team of financial advisors to assist it in evaluating Mentor's offer and the company's strategic alternatives. The board discussed the importance of selecting a qualified investment bank,

---

11. The applicable by-law (Article II, §2.3) authorized a call of a special stockholders meeting by shareholders holding at least 10% of Quickturn's shares. In their agent solicitation, Mentor informed Quickturn stockholders that Mentor intended to call a special meeting approximately 45 days after it received sufficient agent designations to satisfy the 10% requirement under the original by-law. The solicitation also disclosed Mentor's intent to set the date for the special meeting, and to set the record date and give formal notice of that meeting.

and considered several investment banking firms. Aside from Hambrecht & Quist ("H & Q"), Quickturn's long-time investment banker, other firms that the board considered included Goldman Sachs & Co. and Morgan Stanley Dean Witter. Ultimately, the board selected H & Q, because the board believed that H & Q had the most experience with the EDA industry in general and with Quickturn in particular.

During the balance of the meeting, the board discussed for approximately one or two hours (a) the status, terms, and conditions of Mentor's offer; (b) the status of Quickturn's patent litigation with Mentor; (c) the applicable rules and regulations that would govern the board's response to the offer required by the Securities Exchange Act of 1934 (the "34 Act"); (d) the board's fiduciary duties to Quickturn and its shareholders in a tender offer context; (e) the scope of defensive measures available to the corporation if the board decided that the offer was not in the best interests of the company or its stockholders; (f) Quickturn's then-current Rights Plan and special stockholders meeting by-law provisions; (g) the need for a federal antitrust filing; and (h) the potential effect of Mentor's offer on Quickturn's employees. The board also instructed management and H & Q to prepare analyses to assist the directors in evaluating Mentor's offer, and scheduled two board meetings, August 17, and August 21, 1998.

The Quickturn board next met on August 17, 1998. That meeting centered around financial presentations by management and by H & Q. Mr. Keith Lobo, Quickturn's President and CEO, presented a Medium Term Strategic Plan, which was a "top down" estimate detailing the economic outlook and the company's future sales, income prospects and future plans (the "Medium Term Plan"). The Medium Term Plan contained an optimistic (30%) revenue growth projection for the period 1998-2000. After management made its presentation, H & Q supplied its valuation of Quickturn, which relied upon a "base case" that assumed management's 30% revenue growth projection. On that basis, H & Q presented various "standalone" valuations based on various techniques, including a discounted cash flow ("DCF") analysis. Finally, the directors discussed possible defensive measure, but took no action at that time.

The Quickturn board held its third and final meeting in response to Mentor's offer on August 21, 1998. Again, the directors received extensive materials and a further detailed analysis performed by H & Q. The focal point of that analysis was a chart entitled "Summary of Implied Valuation." That chart compared Mentor's tender offer price to the Quickturn valuation ranges generated by H & Q's application of five different methodologies.[14] The chart showed that Quickturn's value under all but one of those methodologies was higher than Mentor's $12.125 tender offer price.

Quickturn's Board Rejects Mentor's Offer as Inadequate

After hearing the presentations, the Quickturn board concluded that Mentor's offer was inadequate, and decided to recommend that Quickturn shareholders reject Mentor's offer. The directors based their decision upon: (a) H &

---

14. The five methodologies and the respective price ranges were: Historical Trading Range ($6.13-$21.63); Comparable Public Companies ($2.55-$15.61); Comparable M & A Transactions ($6.00-$31.36); Comparable Premiums Paid ($9.54-$10.72); and Discounted Cash Flow Analysis ($11.88- $57.87).

Q's report; (b) the fact that Quickturn was experiencing a temporary trough in its business, which was reflected in its stock price; (c) the company's leadership in technology and patents and resulting market share; (d) the likely growth in Quickturn's markets (most notably, the Asian market) and the strength of Quickturn's new products (specifically, its Mercury product); (e) the potential value of the patent litigation with Mentor; and (f) the problems for Quickturn's customers, employees, and technology if the two companies were combined as the result of a hostile takeover.

Quickturn's Defensive Measures

At the August 21 board meeting, the Quickturn board adopted two defensive measures in response to Mentor's hostile takeover bid. First, the board amended Article II, §2.3 of Quickturn's by-laws, which permitted stockholders holding 10% or more of Quickturn's stock to call a special stockholders meeting. The By-Law Amendment provides that if any such special meeting is requested by shareholders, the corporation (Quickturn) would fix the record date for, and determine the time and place of, that special meeting, which must take place not less than 90 days nor more than 100 days after the receipt and determination of the validity of the shareholders' request.

Second, the board amended Quickturn's shareholder Rights Plan by eliminating its "dead hand" feature and replacing it with the Deferred Redemption Provision, under which no newly elected board could redeem the Rights Plan for six months after taking office, if the purpose or effect of the redemption would be to facilitate a transaction with an "Interested Person" (one who proposed, nominated or financially supported the election of the new directors to the board).[15] Mentor would be an Interested Person under this definition.

The effect of the By-Law Amendment would be to delay a shareholder-called special meeting for at least three months. The effect of the DRP would be to delay the ability of a newly-elected, Mentor-nominated board to redeem the Rights Plan or "poison pill" for six months, in any transaction with an Interested Person. Thus, the combined effect of the two defensive measures would be to delay any acquisition of Quickturn by Mentor for at least nine months. . . .

QUICKTURN'S DELAYED REDEMPTION PROVISION

At the time Mentor commenced its bid, Quickturn had in place a Rights Plan that contained a so-called "dead hand" provision. That provision had a limited "continuing director" feature that became operative only if an insurgent that owned more than 15% of Quickturn's common stock successfully waged a proxy contest to replace a majority of the board. In that event, only the "continuing

_____

15. The amended Rights Plan pertinently provides that: "[I]n the event that a majority of the Board of Directors of the Company is elected by stockholder action at an annual or special meeting of stockholders, then until the 180th day following the effectiveness of such election (including any postponement or adjournment thereof), the Rights shall not be redeemed if such redemption is reasonably likely to have the purpose or effect of facilitating a Transaction with an Interested Person." An "Interested Person" is defined under the amended Rights Plan as "any Person who (i) is or will become an Acquiring Person if such Transaction were to be consummated or an Affiliate or Associate of such a Person, and (ii) is, or directly or indirectly proposed, nominated or financially supported, a director of [Quickturn] in office at the time of consideration of such Transaction who was elected at an annual or special meeting of stockholders."

directors" (those directors in office at the time the poison pill was adopted) could redeem the rights.

During the same August 21, 1998 meeting at which it amended the special meeting by-law, the Quickturn board also amended the Rights Plan to eliminate its "continuing director" feature, and to substitute a "no hand" or "delayed redemption provision" into its Rights Plan. The Delayed Redemption Provision provides that, if a majority of the directors are replaced by stockholder action, the newly elected board cannot redeem the rights for six months if the purpose or effect of the redemption would be to facilitate a transaction with an "Interested Person."

It is undisputed that the DRP would prevent Mentor's slate, if elected as the new board majority, from redeeming the Rights Plan for six months following their election, because a redemption would be "reasonably likely to have the purpose or effect of facilitating a Transaction" with Mentor, a party that "directly or indirectly proposed, nominated or financially supported" the election of the new board. Consequently, by adopting the DRP, the Quickturn board built into the process a six month delay period in addition to the 90 to 100 day delay mandated by the By-Law Amendment.

COURT OF CHANCERY INVALIDATES DELAYED REDEMPTION PROVISION

When the board of a Delaware corporation takes action to resist a hostile bid for control, the board of directors' defensive actions are subjected to "enhanced" judicial scrutiny. Unocal Corp. v. Mesa Petroleum Co., Del. Supr., 493 A.2d 946, 955 (1985). For a target board's actions to be entitled to business judgment rule protection, the target board must first establish that it had reasonable grounds to believe that the hostile bid constituted a threat to corporate policy and effectiveness; and second, that the defensive measures adopted were "proportionate," that is, reasonable in relation to the threat that the board reasonably perceived. Id.. The Delayed Redemption Provision was reviewed by the Court of Chancery pursuant to that standard.

The Court of Chancery found: "the evidence, viewed as a whole, shows that the perceived threat that led the Quickturn board to adopt the DRP, was the concern that Quickturn shareholders might mistakenly, in ignorance of Quickturn's true value, accept Mentor's inadequate offer, and elect a new board that would prematurely sell the company before the new board could adequately inform itself of Quickturn's fair value and before the shareholders could consider other options." The Court of Chancery concluded that Mentor's combined tender offer and proxy contest amounted to substantive coercion. Having concluded that the Quickturn board reasonably perceived a cognizable threat, the Court of Chancery then examined whether the board's response — the Delayed Redemption Provision — was proportionate in relation to that threat.

In assessing a challenge to defensive measures taken by a target board in response to an attempted hostile takeover, enhanced judicial scrutiny requires an evaluation of the board's justification for each contested defensive measure and its concomitant results. The Court of Chancery found that the Quickturn board's "justification or rationale for adopting the Delayed Redemption Provision was to force any newly elected board to take sufficient time to become familiar with Quickturn and its value, and to provide shareholders the opportunity to consider alternatives, before selling Quickturn to *any* acquiror." The Court of Chancery concluded that the Delayed Redemption Provision could not pass the proportionality test. Therefore, the Court of Chancery held that "the DRP cannot survive scrutiny under *Unocal* and must be declared invalid."

DELAYED REDEMPTION PROVISION VIOLATES FUNDAMENTAL DELAWARE LAW

In this appeal, Mentor argues that the judgment of the Court of Chancery should be affirmed because the Delayed Redemption Provision is invalid as a matter of Delaware law. According to Mentor, the Delayed Redemption Provision, like the "dead hand" feature in the Rights Plan that was held to be invalid in [Carmody v. Toll Brothers, Inc., 1988 WL 418896 (Del. Ch. 1998)], will impermissibly deprive any newly elected board of both its statutory authority to manage the corporation under 8 Del. C. §141(a) and its concomitant fiduciary duty pursuant to that statutory mandate. We agree.

Our analysis of the Delayed Redemption Provision in the Quickturn Rights Plan is guided by the prior precedents of this Court with regard to a board of directors authority to adopt a Rights Plan or "poison pill." In *Moran*, this Court held that the "inherent powers of the Board conferred by 8 Del. C. §141(a) concerning the management of the corporation's 'business and affairs' provides the Board additional authority upon which to enact the Rights Plan." Moran v. Household International, Inc., Del. Supr., 500 A.2d 1346, 1353 (1985), *citing* Unocal Corp. v. Mesa Petroleum Co., Del. Supr., 493 A.2d 946, 953 (1985). Consequently, this Court upheld the adoption of the Rights Plan in *Moran* as a legitimate exercise of business judgment by the board of directors. In doing so, however, this Court also held "the rights plan is not absolute":

> When the Household Board of Directors is faced with a tender offer and a request to redeem the Rights [Plan], they will not be able to arbitrarily reject the offer. They will be held to the same fiduciary standards any other board of directors would be held to in deciding to adopt a defensive mechanism, the same standards as they were held to in originally approving the Rights Plan.

Id. at 1354.

In *Moran*, this Court held that the "ultimate response to an actual takeover bid must be judged by the Directors' actions at the time and nothing we say relieves them of their fundamental duties to the corporation and its shareholders." Moran v. Household International, Inc., 500 A.2d at 1357. Consequently, we concluded that the use of the Rights Plan would be evaluated when and if the issue arises.

One of the most basic tenets of Delaware corporate law is that the board of directors has the ultimate responsibility for managing the business and affairs of a corporation. Section 141(a) requires that any limitation on the board's authority be set out in the certificate of incorporation. The Quickturn certificate of incorporation contains no provision purporting to limit the authority of the board in any way. The Delayed Redemption Provision, however, would prevent a newly elected board of directors from *completely* discharging its fundamental management duties to the corporation and its stockholders for six months.

While the Delayed Redemption Provision limits the board of directors' authority in only one respect, the suspension of the Rights Plan, it nonetheless restricts the board's power in an area of fundamental importance to the shareholders — negotiating a possible sale of the corporation. Therefore, we hold that the Delayed Redemption Provision is invalid under Section 141(a), which confers upon any newly elected board of directors *full* power to manage and direct the business and affairs of a Delaware corporation.

In discharging the statutory mandate of Section 141(a), the directors have a fiduciary duty to the corporation and its shareholders. Revlon, Inc. v. MacAndrews & Forbes Holdings, Inc., Del. Supr., 506 A.2d 173, 179 (1986); Aronson v. Lewis, Del. Supr., 473 A.2d 805, 811 (1984); Guth v. Loft, Inc., Del. Supr., 23 Del. Ch. 255, 5 A.2d 503, 510 (1939). This unremitting obligation extends equally to board conduct in a contest for corporate control. Mills Acquisition Co. v. Macmillan, Inc., Del. Supr., 559 A.2d 1261, 1280 (1989); Smith v. Van Gorkom, Del. Supr., 488 A.2d 858, 872-73 (1985). The Delayed Redemption Provision prevents a newly elected board of directors from completely discharging its fiduciary duties to protect fully the interests of Quickturn and its stockholders.

This Court has recently observed that "although the fiduciary duty of a Delaware director is unremitting, the exact course of conduct that must be charted to properly discharge that responsibility will change in the specific context of the action the director is taking with regard to either the corporation or its shareholders." Malone v. Brincat, Del. Supr., 722 A.2d 5 (1998). This Court has held "[t]o the extent that a contract, or a provision thereof, purports to require a board to act *or not act* in such a fashion as to limit the exercise of fiduciary duties, it is invalid and unenforceable." *See* Paramount Communications, Inc. v. QVC Network, Inc., 637 A.2d at 51 (emphasis added). The Delayed Redemption Provision "tends to limit in a substantial way the freedom of [newly elected] directors' decisions on matters of management policy." Abercrombie v. Davies, Del. Ch., 123 A.2d 893, 899 (1956), *rev'd on other grounds,* Del. Supr., 130 A.2d 338 (1957).

Therefore, "it violates the duty of each [newly elected] director to exercise his own best judgment on matters coming before the board." *Id.*

In this case, the Quickturn board was confronted by a determined bidder that sought to acquire the company at a price the Quickturn board concluded was inadequate. Such situations are common in corporate takeover efforts. In *Revlon*, this Court held that no defensive measure can be sustained when it represents a breach of the directors' fiduciary duty. *A fortiori*, no defensive measure can be sustained which would require a new board of directors to breach its fiduciary duty. In that regard, we note Mentor has properly acknowledged that in the event its slate of directors is elected, those newly elected directors will be required to discharge their unremitting fiduciary duty to manage the corporation for the benefit of Quickturn and its stockholders.

CONCLUSION

The Delayed Redemption Provision would prevent a new Quickturn board of directors from managing the corporation by redeeming the Rights Plan to facilitate a transaction that would serve the stockholders' best interests, even under circumstances where the board would be required to do so because of its fiduciary duty to the Quickturn stockholders. Because the Delayed Redemption Provision impermissibly circumscribes the board's statutory power under Section 141(a) and the directors' ability to fulfill their concomitant fiduciary duties, we hold that the Delayed Redemption Provision is invalid. On that alternative basis, the judgment of the Court of Chancery is affirmed.

PROBLEM 15-1

After the *Quickturn* decision dashed the hopes of dead-hand and slow-hand pill advocates, creative lawyers' minds turned to developing second-generation post-*Quickturn* bylaws provisions that might be legal in Delaware. One such bylaw, proposed by Professor John Coates (former partner at the law firm of Wachtell, Lipton, which created the idea of the poison pill) and Bradley Faris, an attorney at Latham and Watkins, reads as follows:

SPECIAL MEETING BYLAW

RESOLVED, that Section(s) _____ of the Bylaws of the Company be and hereby is/are amended to read as follows:

1.1   Call of Special Meetings Generally. Special meetings of stockholders for any purpose or purposes may be called:

> (a) at any time by the board of directors of the Company (the "Board"), or
> (b) by a committee of the Board duly designated by the Board whose powers and authority, as expressly provided in a resolution of the Board, include the power to call such meetings.

1.2   Call of Special Meetings Upon Receipt of Qualified Tender Offer. Notwithstanding any other provision of these bylaws to the contrary, at any time from and after the commencement and prior to the termination or withdrawal of ("during the pendency of") a Qualified Tender Offer (as defined in section 1.5), a special meeting of stockholders for any purpose or purposes may be called by a demand in writing by stockholders of record owning five (5%) percent of the issued and outstanding shares of common stock, par value $_____ per share, of the Company ("Shares"). The Board shall determine a place and time for such special meeting, provided that such place shall be within the United States (exclusive of Alaska and Hawaii) and such time shall be no more than forty-five (45) calendar days after the receipt of such demand. The record date for such special meeting shall be ten (10) calendar days prior to the time for such special meeting.

1.3   Nominations of Persons for Election at Special Meetings Upon Receipt of Qualified Tender Offer. Notwithstanding any provision of these bylaws to the contrary, nominations of persons for election to the Board may be made at any special meeting of stockholders called pursuant to the terms of section 1.2, (a) by or at the direction of the Board and (b) by any stockholder of the Company entitled to vote at such meeting, without compliance with any advance notice or disclosure provision of these bylaws.

1.4   Restrictions on Bylaw Amendments during Qualified Tender Offer. Notwithstanding any provision of these bylaws to the contrary, during the pendency of a Qualified Tender Offer (as defined in section 1.5), each provision of each of the Company's bylaws may be modified or repealed only by action of stockholders of the Company, and not by action of the Board or any committee thereof.

1.5 Qualified Tender Offer Defined. "Qualified Tender Offer" shall mean any tender offer for any or all of the Shares, provided that such tender offer shall (a) disclose the person making such offer's commitment to consummate, within one year of the closing of such tender offer, a merger, liquidation or similar transaction pursuant to which holders of Shares outstanding upon consummation thereof shall receive the same type and amount of consideration as offered in the tender offer, (b) offer consideration with a current market value at least equal to [125%] of the market price of the Shares on the fifth business day preceding first public announcement or publication of the Qualified Tender Offer, and (c) be subject to no condition other than (1) there shall have been validly tendered and not properly withdrawn prior to the expiration of the offer a number of Shares which represent at least a majority of all Shares, on a fully diluted basis, on the date of purchase, (2) expiration or termination of any waiting period under the Hart-Scott-Rodino Antitrust Improvements Act of 1976 applicable to the purchase of the Company's shares of stock pursuant to the offer, and (3) other conditions customary at the time of the offer for corporations of a similar size and in a similar line of business as the Company, negotiated with and agreed to by the target corporation on an arm's-length basis, including without limitation conditions relating to (i) legal or administrative proceedings, (ii) governmental action or enactment or application of statutes or regulations, (iii) extraordinary changes in economic or political conditions, (iv) extraordinary actions or transactions by the Company with respect to its capitalization, and (v) agreement with the Company on an alternative transaction.

1.6 Modification or Repeal Only by Stockholders; Severability. Notwithstanding any other provision of these bylaws, sections 1.1, 1.2, 1.3, 1.4, 1.5 and 1.6 may be modified or repealed only by action of the stockholders of the Company and not by action of the Board or any committee thereof. The illegality, invalidity, or unenforceability of this section 1.6 or any of sections 1.1, 1.2, 1.3, 1.4 or 1.5 shall not in any way affect or impair the legality, validity, or enforceability of any other section of these bylaws.

What does this by-law accomplish for shareholders? Is it likely to be upheld by the Delaware courts? Why or why not? Assume your client is an institutional investor that wants to sponsor a shareholder resolution under Rule 14a-8 proposing this bylaw amendment to one of the companies in its portfolio. What arguments might a company use to exclude this resolution? Assume further that your client asks you what types of charter provisions it should evaluate in choosing the company to target. What advice do you give?

D. REFINING "INTERMEDIATE SCRUTINY"

The *Unocal* process of analysis is often referred to as an "enhanced scrutiny" or "intermediate scrutiny" standard, because the board isn't given the benefit of the business judgment rule at the outset but also isn't under a burden to prove the entire fairness of the transaction at the outset. Rather, the court employs a two-step analysis: (1) the board must show that it had reasonable grounds to believe there was a threat to an important corporate policy from an offer (the "threat analysis"); and (2) the board must show that the means used to defend against that threat were proportionate to the threat (the "proportionality review").

The threat analysis involves an inquiry into the same issues that arise under the business judgment rule — did the board act in good faith and pursuant to a reasonable investigation in determining that there was a threat posed to the shareholders or to an important corporate policy by the takeover bid? The only difference lies in the burden of proof, which is shifted to the defendant in *Unocal* cases. Subsequent decisions suggest that burden-shifting here does not affect the outcome of the cases, as directors almost always prevail on this part of the analysis. Particularly if they have financial advisers opine that the price of a takeover bid is too low, the directors will be able to show that the takeover bid is a threat to shareholders: a price that is too low is always a threat to the shareholders.

The more innovative and controversial aspect of *Unocal* was the proportionality review. This part of the analysis seems to contemplate a substantive review of board decisions by the court. Perhaps driven by the same deference that animates the business judgment rule, the Delaware Supreme Court has, until recently, been reluctant to second-guess directors' actions, notwithstanding the "enhanced" scrutiny under *Unocal*. That has not stopped the court from tinkering with the proportionality review. In Unitrin, Inc. v. American General Corp., 651 A.2d 1361 (Del. 1995), the court held that the proportionality review required two levels of inquiry. At the first level, the court would determine whether the challenged defensive action was "coercive" or "preclusive." A defensive measure is "coercive" if it is "aimed at 'cramming down' on its shareholders a management-sponsored alternative" to an outside bid, and a defensive measure is "preclusive" if it prevents any bidder from being able to successfully take over the company, including by using a proxy contest.

If the board's action is neither coercive nor preclusive, the court must still evaluate the action to determine whether it falls within the "range of reasonableness." In other words, a defensive action constitutes a breach of fiduciary duty if it is unreasonable in light of the threat posed by a bid, even if it is not so extreme as to be coercive or preclusive. At this stage of the inquiry, however, the court is again deferential to the board. In the words of the *Unitrin* court:

> The *ratio decidendi* for the "range of reasonableness" standard is a need of the board of directors for latitude in discharging its fiduciary duties to the corporation and its shareholders when defending against perceived threats. The concomitant requirement is for judicial restraint. Consequently, if the board of directors' defensive response is not draconian (preclusive or coercive) and is within a "range of reasonableness," a court must not substitute its judgment for the board's.

According to the *Unocal* court, the two steps in the analysis are a "threshold" to be crossed on the way to the business judgment rule. If the defendants carry their burden, therefore, the plaintiffs theoretically have the opportunity to show that there is some other reason to rebut the business judgment rule. As noted by Vice-Chancellor Strine in In re Gaylord Container Corp. S'holders Litig., 753 A.2d 462, 475-476 (Del. Ch. 2000), this structure simply does not make sense:

> It is not at all apparent how a plaintiff could meet this burden in a circumstance where the board met its burden under *Unocal*. To the extent that the plaintiff

has persuasive evidence of disloyalty (for example, that the board acted in a self-interested or bad-faith fashion), this would fatally undercut the board's *Unocal* showing. Similarly, it is hard to see how a plaintiff could rebut the presumption of the business judgment rule by demonstrating that the board acted in a grossly careless manner in a circumstance where the board had demonstrated that it had acted reasonably and proportionately. Least of all could a plaintiff show that the board's actions lacked a rational business purpose in a context where the board had already demonstrated that those actions were reasonable, *i.e.*, rational.

More recently, the *Unocal* standard has undergone some more renovation. In MM Companies v. Liquid Audio, Inc., 2003 WL 58969 (Del. 2003), the court added another level to the proportionality review. The case involved a board expansion similar to *Blasius* (see Chapter 6):

> The *Blasius* compelling justification standard of enhanced judicial review is based upon accepted and well-established legal tenets. This Court and the Court of Chancery have recognized the substantial degree of congruence between the rationale that led to the *Blasius* "compelling justification" enhanced standard of judicial review and the logical extension of that rationale *within* the context of the *Unocal* enhanced standard of judicial review. Both standards recognize the inherent conflicts of interest that arise when a board of directors acts to prevent shareholders from effectively exercising their right to vote either contrary to the will of the incumbent board members generally or to replace the incumbent board members in a contested election. . . .
>
> This case presents a paragon of when the compelling justification standard of *Blasius* must be applied within *Unocal*'s requirement that any defensive measure be proportionate and reasonable in relation to the threat posed. The *Unocal* standard of review applies because the Liquid Audio board's action was a "defensive measure taken in response to some threat to corporate policy and effectiveness which touches upon issues of control." The compelling justification standard of *Blasius* also had to be applied *within* an application of the *Unocal* standard to that specific defensive measure because the primary purpose of the Board's action was to interfere with or impede the effective exercise of the shareholder franchise in a contested election for directors. . . .
>
> When the *primary purpose* of a board of directors' defensive measure is to interfere with or impede the effective exercise of the shareholder franchise in a contested election for directors, the board must first demonstrate a compelling justification for such action as a condition precedent to any judicial consideration of reasonableness and proportionality.

And that leads us to the most recent pronouncement of the Delaware Supreme Court under *Unocal*. In this much anticipated case, the court considered the combined effect of (1) stockholder voting agreements, pursuant to which two individuals holding 65 percent of the voting power of a target company's stock irrevocably agreed to vote in favor of a proposed merger; (2) a provision of the merger agreement, expressly authorized under Delaware General Corporation Law §251(c)), requiring the board of directors of the target company to submit the proposed merger for a stockholder vote regardless of whether the board of directors continued to recommend the merger; and (3) the omission of a so-called "fiduciary out" clause, which would allow the target company to withdraw from the merger agreement if the board of directors concluded that its fiduciary duties required such action. In a rare occurrence, the court reached a divided decision, with two justices dissenting. As you read the case, consider whether the court has fulfilled the aspirations of *Unocal*.

OMNICARE, INC. v. NCS HEALTHCARE, INC.
818 A.2d 914
Supreme Court of Delaware
April 4, 2003

HOLLAND, Justice.

NCS Healthcare, Inc. ("NCS"), a Delaware corporation, was the object of competing acquisition bids, one by Genesis Health Ventures, Inc. ("Genesis"), a Pennsylvania corporation, and the other by Omnicare, Inc. ("Omnicare"), a Delaware corporation. . . .

THE PARTIES

The defendant, NCS, is a Delaware corporation headquartered in Beachwood, Ohio. NCS is a leading independent provider of pharmacy services to long-term care institutions including skilled nursing facilities, assisted living facilities and other institutional healthcare facilities. NCS common stock consists of Class A shares and Class B shares. The Class B shares are entitled to ten votes per share and the Class A shares are entitled to one vote per share. The shares are virtually identical in every other respect.

The defendant Jon H. Outcalt is Chairman of the NCS board of directors. Outcalt owns 202,063 shares of NCS Class A common stock and 3,476,086 shares of Class B common stock. The defendant Kevin B. Shaw is President, CEO and a director of NCS. At the time the merger agreement at issue in this dispute was executed with Genesis, Shaw owned 28,905 shares of NCS Class A common stock and 1,141,134 shares of Class B common stock.

The NCS board has two other members, defendants Boake A. Sells and Richard L. Osborne. Sells is a graduate of the Harvard Business School. He was Chairman and CEO at Revco Drugstores in Cleveland, Ohio from 1987 to 1992, when he was replaced by new owners. Sells currently sits on the boards of both public and private companies. Osborne is a full-time professor at the Weatherhead School of Management at Case Western Reserve University. He has been at the university for over thirty years. Osborne currently sits on at least seven corporate boards other than NCS.

The defendant Genesis is a Pennsylvania corporation with its principal place of business in Kennett Square, Pennsylvania. It is a leading provider of health-care and support services to the elderly. The defendant Geneva Sub, Inc., a wholly owned subsidiary of Genesis, is a Delaware corporation formed by Genesis to acquire NCS.

The plaintiffs in the class action own an unspecified number of shares of NCS Class A common stock. They represent a class consisting of all holders of Class A common stock. As of July 28, 2002, NCS had 18,461,599 Class A shares and 5,255,210 Class B shares outstanding.

Omnicare is a Delaware corporation with its principal place of business in Covington, Kentucky. Omnicare is in the institutional pharmacy business, with annual sales in excess of $2.1 billion during its last fiscal year. Omnicare purchased 1000 shares of NCS Class A common stock on July 30, 2002. . . .

FACTUAL BACKGROUND

The parties are in substantial agreement regarding the operative facts. They disagree, however, about the legal implications. This recitation of facts is taken primarily from the opinion by the Court of Chancery.

NCS SEEKS RESTRUCTURING ALTERNATIVES

Beginning in late 1999, changes in the timing and level of reimbursements by government and third-party providers adversely affected market conditions in the health care industry. As a result, NCS began to experience greater difficulty in collecting accounts receivables, which led to a precipitous decline in the market value of its stock. NCS common shares that traded above $20 in January 1999 were worth as little as $5 at the end of that year. By early 2001, NCS was in default on approximately $350 million in debt, including $206 million in senior bank debt and $102 million of its $5\frac{3}{4}\%$ Convertible Subordinated Debentures (the "Notes"). After these defaults, NCS common stock traded in a range of $0.09 to $0.50 per share until days before the announcement of the transaction at issue in this case.

NCS began to explore strategic alternatives that might address the problems it was confronting. As part of this effort, in February 2000, NCS retained UBS Warburg, L.L.C. to identify potential acquirers and possible equity investors. UBS Warburg contacted over fifty different entities to solicit their interest in a variety of transactions with NCS. UBS Warburg had marginal success in its efforts. By October 2000, NCS had only received one non-binding indication of interest valued at $190 million, substantially less than the face value of NCS's senior debt. This proposal was reduced by 20% after the offeror conducted its due diligence review.

NCS FINANCIAL DETERIORATION

In December 2000, NCS terminated its relationship with UBS Warburg and retained Brown, Gibbons, Lang & Company as its exclusive financial advisor. During this period, NCS's financial condition continued to deteriorate. In April 2001, NCS received a formal notice of default and acceleration from the trustee for holders of the Notes. As NCS's financial condition worsened, the Noteholders formed a committee to represent their financial interests (the "Ad Hoc Committee"). At about that time, NCS began discussions with various investor groups regarding a restructuring in a "pre-packaged" bankruptcy. NCS did not receive any proposal that it believed provided adequate consideration for its stakeholders. At that time, full recovery for NCS's creditors was a remote prospect, and any recovery for NCS stockholders seemed impossible.

OMNICARE'S INITIAL NEGOTIATIONS

In the summer of 2001, NCS invited Omnicare, Inc. to begin discussions with Brown Gibbons regarding a possible transaction. On July 20, Joel Gemunder,

Omnicare's President and CEO, sent Shaw a written proposal to acquire NCS in a bankruptcy sale under Section 363 of the Bankruptcy Code. This proposal was for $225 million subject to satisfactory completion of due diligence. NCS asked Omnicare to execute a confidentiality agreement so that more detailed discussions could take place.

In August 2001, Omnicare increased its bid to $270 million, but still proposed to structure the deal as an asset sale in bankruptcy. Even at $270 million, Omnicare's proposal was substantially lower than the face value of NCS's outstanding debt. It would have provided only a small recovery for Omnicare's Noteholders and no recovery for its stockholders. In October 2001, NCS sent Glen Pollack of Brown Gibbons to meet with Omnicare's financial advisor, Merrill Lynch, to discuss Omnicare's interest in NCS. Omnicare responded that it was not interested in any transaction other than an asset sale in bankruptcy.

There was no further contact between Omnicare and NCS between November 2001 and January 2002. Instead, Omnicare began secret discussions with Judy K. Mencher, a representative of the Ad Hoc Committee. In these discussions, Omnicare continued to pursue a transaction structured as a sale of assets in bankruptcy. In February 2002, the Ad Hoc Committee notified the NCS board that Omnicare had proposed an asset sale in bankruptcy for $313,750,000.

NCS INDEPENDENT BOARD COMMITTEE

In January 2002, Genesis was contacted by members of the Ad Hoc Committee concerning a possible transaction with NCS. Genesis executed NCS's standard confidentiality agreement and began a due diligence review. Genesis had recently emerged from bankruptcy because, like NCS, it was suffering from dwindling government reimbursements.

Genesis previously lost a bidding war to Omnicare in a different transaction. This led to bitter feelings between the principals of both companies. More importantly, this bitter experience for Genesis led to its insistence on exclusivity agreements and lock-ups in any potential transaction with NCS.

NCS FINANCIAL IMPROVEMENT

NCS's operating performance was improving by early 2002. As NCS's performance improved, the NCS directors began to believe that it might be possible for NCS to enter into a transaction that would provide some recovery for NCS stockholders' equity. In March 2002, NCS decided to form an independent committee of board members who were neither NCS employees nor major NCS stockholders (the "Independent Committee"). The NCS board thought this was necessary because, due to NCS's precarious financial condition, it felt that fiduciary duties were owed to the enterprise as a whole rather than solely to NCS stockholders.

Sells and Osborne were selected as the members of the committee, and given authority to consider and negotiate possible transactions for NCS. The entire four member NCS board, however, retained authority to approve any transaction. The Independent Committee retained the same legal and financial counsel as the NCS board.

The Independent Committee met for the first time on May 14, 2002. At that meeting Pollack suggested that NCS seek a "stalking-horse merger partner" to obtain the highest possible value in any transaction. The Independent Committee agreed with the suggestion.

GENESIS INITIAL PROPOSAL

Two days later, on May 16, 2002, Scott Berlin of Brown Gibbons, Glen Pollack and Boake Sells met with George Hager, CFO of Genesis, and Michael Walker, who was Genesis's CEO. At that meeting, Genesis made it clear that if it were going to engage in any negotiations with NCS, it would not do so as a "stalking horse." As one of its advisors testified, "We didn't want to be someone who set forth a valuation for NCS which would only result in that valuation . . . being publicly disclosed, and thereby creating an environment where Omnicare felt to maintain its competitive monopolistic positions, that they had to match and exceed that level." Thus, Genesis "wanted a degree of certainty that to the extent [it] w[as] willing to pursue a negotiated merger agreement . . . , [it] would be able to consummate the transaction [it] negotiated and executed."

In June 2002, Genesis proposed a transaction that would take place outside the bankruptcy context. Although it did not provide full recovery for NCS's Noteholders, it provided the possibility that NCS stockholders would be able to recover something for their investment. As discussions continued, the terms proposed by Genesis continued to improve. On June 25, the economic terms of the Genesis proposal included repayment of the NCS senior debt in full, full assumption of trade credit obligations, an exchange offer or direct purchase of the NCS Notes providing NCS Noteholders with a combination of cash and Genesis common stock equal to the par value of the NCS Notes (not including accrued interest), and $20 million in value for the NCS common stock. Structurally, the Genesis proposal continued to include consents from a significant majority of the Noteholders as well as support agreements from stockholders owning a majority of the NCS voting power.

GENESIS EXCLUSIVITY AGREEMENT

NCS's financial advisors and legal counsel met again with Genesis and its legal counsel on June 26, 2002, to discuss a number of transaction-related issues. At this meeting, Pollack asked Genesis to increase its offer to NCS stockholders. Genesis agreed to consider this request. Thereafter, Pollack and Hager had further conversations. Genesis agreed to offer a total of $24 million in consideration for the NCS common stock, or an additional $4 million, in the form of Genesis common stock.

At the June 26 meeting, Genesis's representatives demanded that, before any further negotiations take place, NCS agree to enter into an exclusivity agreement with it. As Hager from Genesis explained it: "[I]f they wished us to continue to try to move this process to a definitive agreement, that they would need to do it on an exclusive basis with us. We were going to, and already had incurred significant expense, but we would incur additional expenses . . . , both internal and external, to bring this transaction to a definitive signing. We wanted them to work with us on an exclusive basis for a short period of time to see if we could reach agreement." On June 27, 2002, Genesis's legal counsel delivered a draft form of exclusivity agreement for review and consideration by NCS's legal counsel.

The Independent Committee met on July 3, 2002, to consider the proposed exclusivity agreement. Pollack presented a summary of the terms of a possible Genesis merger, which had continued to improve. The then-current Genesis proposal included (1) repayment of the NCS senior debt in full, (2) payment of par value for the Notes (without accrued interest) in the form of a combination of cash and Genesis stock, (3) payment to NCS stockholders in the form of $24 million in Genesis stock, plus (4) the assumption, because the transaction was to be structured as a merger, of additional liabilities to trade and other unsecured creditors.

NCS director Sells testified, Pollack told the Independent Committee at a July 3, 2002 meeting that Genesis wanted the Exclusivity Agreement to be the first step towards a completely locked up transaction that would preclude a higher bid from Omnicare:

A: [Pollack] explained that Genesis felt that they had suffered at the hands of Omnicare and others. I guess maybe just Omnicare. I don't know much about Genesis [sic] acquisition history. But they had suffered before at the 11:59:59 and that they wanted to have a pretty much bulletproof deal or they were not going to go forward.
Q: When you say they suffered at the hands of Omnicare, what do you mean?
A: Well, my expression is that that was related to—a deal that was related to me or explained to me that they, Genesis, had tried to acquire, I suppose, an institutional pharmacy, I don't remember the name of it. Thought they had a deal and then at the last minute, Omnicare outbid them for the company in a like 11:59 kind of thing, and that they were unhappy about that. And once burned, twice shy.

After NCS executed the exclusivity agreement, Genesis provided NCS with a draft merger agreement, a draft Noteholders' support agreement, and draft voting agreements for Outcalt and Shaw, who together held a majority of the voting power of the NCS common stock. Genesis and NCS negotiated the terms of the merger agreement over the next three weeks. During those negotiations, the Independent Committee and the Ad Hoc Committee persuaded Genesis to improve the terms of its merger.

The parties were still negotiating by July 19, and the exclusivity period was automatically extended to July 26. At that point, NCS and Genesis were close to executing a merger agreement and related voting agreements. Genesis proposed a short extension of the exclusivity agreement so a deal could be finalized. On the morning of July 26, 2002, the Independent Committee authorized an extension of the exclusivity period through July 31.

OMNICARE PROPOSES NEGOTIATIONS

By late July 2002, Omnicare came to believe that NCS was negotiating a transaction, possibly with Genesis or another of Omnicare's competitors, that would potentially present a competitive threat to Omnicare. Omnicare also came to believe, in light of a run-up in the price of NCS common stock, that whatever transaction NCS was negotiating probably included a payment for its stock. Thus, the Omnicare board of directors met on the morning of July 26 and, on the recommendation of its management, authorized a proposal to acquire NCS that did not involve a sale of assets in bankruptcy.

On the afternoon of July 26, 2002, Omnicare faxed to NCS a letter outlining a proposed acquisition. The letter suggested a transaction in which Omnicare would retire NCS's senior and subordinated debt at par plus accrued interest, and pay the NCS stockholders $3 cash for their shares. Omnicare's proposal, however, was expressly conditioned on negotiating a merger agreement, obtaining certain third party consents, and completing its due diligence.

Mencher saw the July 26 Omnicare letter and realized that, while its economic terms were attractive, the "due diligence" condition substantially undercut its strength. In an effort to get a better proposal from Omnicare, Mencher telephoned Gemunder and told him that Omnicare was unlikely to succeed in its bid unless it dropped the "due diligence outs." She explained this was the only way a bid at the last minute would be able to succeed. Gemunder considered Mencher's warning "very real," and followed up with his advisors. They, however, insisted that he retain the due diligence condition "to protect [him] from doing something foolish." Taking this advice to heart, Gemunder decided not to drop the due diligence condition.

Late in the afternoon of July 26, 2002, NCS representatives received voice-mail messages from Omnicare asking to discuss the letter. The exclusivity agreement prevented NCS from returning those calls. In relevant part, that agreement precluded NCS from "engag[ing] or particpat[ing] in any discussions or negotiations with respect to a Competing Transaction or a proposal for one." The July 26 letter from Omnicare met the definition of a "Competing Transaction."

Despite the exclusivity agreement, the Independent Committee met to consider a response to Omnicare. It concluded that discussions with Omnicare about its July 26 letter presented an unacceptable risk that Genesis would abandon merger discussions. The Independent Committee believed that, given Omnicare's past bankruptcy proposals and unwillingness to consider a merger, as well as its decision to negotiate exclusively with the Ad Hoc Committee, the risk of losing the Genesis proposal was too substantial. Nevertheless, the Independent Committee instructed Pollack to use Omnicare's letter to negotiate for improved terms with Genesis.

GENESIS MERGER AGREEMENT AND VOTING AGREEMENTS

Genesis responded to the NCS request to improve its offer as a result of the Omnicare fax the next day. On July 27, Genesis proposed substantially improved terms. First, it proposed to retire the Notes in accordance with the terms of the indenture, thus eliminating the need for Noteholders to consent to the transaction. This change involved paying all accrued interest plus a small redemption premium. Second, Genesis increased the exchange ratio for NCS common stock to one-tenth of a Genesis common share for each NCS common share, an 80% increase. Third, it agreed to lower the proposed termination fee in the merger agreement from $10 million to $6 million. In return for these concessions, Genesis stipulated that the transaction had to be approved by midnight the next day, July 28, or else Genesis would terminate discussions and withdraw its offer.

The Independent Committee and the NCS board both scheduled meetings for July 28. The committee met first. Although that meeting lasted less than an hour, the Court of Chancery determined the minutes reflect that the directors were fully informed of all material facts relating to the proposed transaction. After concluding that Genesis was sincere in establishing the midnight deadline, the committee voted unanimously to recommend the transaction to the full board.

The full board met thereafter. After receiving similar reports and advice from its legal and financial advisors, the board concluded that "balancing the potential loss of the Genesis deal against the uncertainty of Omnicare's letter, results in the conclusion that the only reasonable alternative for the Board of Directors is to approve the Genesis transaction." The board first voted to authorize the voting agreements with Outcalt and Shaw, for purposes of Section 203 of the Delaware General Corporation Law ("DGCL"). The board was advised by its legal counsel that "under the terms of the merger agreement and because NCS shareholders representing in excess of 50% of the outstanding voting power would be *required* by Genesis to enter into stockholder voting agreements contemporaneously with the signing of the merger agreement, and would agree to vote their shares in favor of the merger agreement, shareholder approval of the merger would be assured even if the NCS Board were to withdraw or change its recommendation. *These facts would prevent NCS from engaging in any alternative or superior transaction in the future.*" (emphasis added).

After listening to a *summary* of the merger terms, the board then resolved that the merger agreement and the transactions contemplated thereby were advisable and fair and in the best interests of all the NCS stakeholders. The NCS board further resolved to recommend the transactions to the stockholders for their approval and adoption. A definitive merger agreement between NCS and Genesis and the stockholder voting agreements were executed later that day. The Court of Chancery held that it was not a per se breach of fiduciary duty that the NCS board never read the NCS/Genesis merger agreement word for word.

NCS/GENESIS MERGER AGREEMENT

Among other things, the NCS/Genesis merger agreement provided the following:

- NCS stockholders would receive 1 share of Genesis common stock in exchange for every 10 shares of NCS common stock held;
- NCS stockholders could exercise appraisal rights under 8 Del. C. §262;
- NCS would redeem NCS's Notes in accordance with their terms;
- NCS would submit the merger agreement to NCS stockholders regardless of whether the NCS board continued to recommend the merger;
- NCS would not enter into discussions with third parties concerning an alternative acquisition of NCS, or provide non-public information to such parties, unless (1) the third party provided an unsolicited, bona fide written proposal documenting the terms of the acquisition; (2) the NCS board believed in good faith that the proposal was or was likely to result in an acquisition on terms superior to those contemplated by the NCS/Genesis merger agreement; and (3) before providing non-public information to that third party, the third party would execute a confidentiality agreement at least as restrictive as the one in place between NCS and Genesis; and
- If the merger agreement were to be terminated, under certain circumstances NCS would be required to pay Genesis a $6 million termination fee and/or Genesis's documented expenses, up to $5 million.

VOTING AGREEMENTS

Outcalt and Shaw, in their capacity as NCS stockholders, entered into voting agreements with Genesis. NCS was also required to be a party to the voting agreements by Genesis. Those agreements provided, among other things, that:

- Outcalt and Shaw were acting in their capacity as NCS stockholders in executing the agreements, not in their capacity as NCS directors or officers;
- Neither Outcalt nor Shaw would transfer their shares prior to the stockholder vote on the merger agreement;
- Outcalt and Shaw agreed to vote all of their shares in favor of the merger agreement; and
- Outcalt and Shaw granted to Genesis an irrevocable proxy to vote their shares in favor of the merger agreement.
- The voting agreement was specifically enforceable by Genesis.

The merger agreement further provided that if either Outcalt or Shaw breached the terms of the voting agreements, Genesis would be entitled to terminate the merger agreement and potentially receive a $6 million termination fee from NCS. Such a breach was impossible since Section 6 provided that the voting agreements were specifically enforceable by Genesis.

OMNICARE'S SUPERIOR PROPOSAL

On July 29, 2002, hours after the NCS/Genesis transaction was executed, Omnicare faxed a letter to NCS restating its conditional proposal and attaching a draft merger agreement. Later that morning, Omnicare issued a press release publicly disclosing the proposal.

On August 1, 2002, Omnicare filed a lawsuit attempting to enjoin the NCS/Genesis merger, and announced that it intended to launch a tender offer for NCS's shares at a price of $3.50 per share. On August 8, 2002, Omnicare began its tender offer. By letter dated that same day, Omnicare expressed a desire to discuss the terms of the offer with NCS. Omnicare's letter continued to condition its proposal on satisfactory completion of a due diligence investigation of NCS.

On August 8, 2002, and again on August 19, 2002, the NCS Independent Committee and full board of directors met separately to consider the Omnicare tender offer in light of the Genesis merger agreement. NCS's outside legal counsel and NCS's financial advisor attended both meetings. The board was unable to determine that Omnicare's expressions of interest were likely to lead to a "Superior Proposal," as the term was defined in the NCS/Genesis merger agreement. On September 10, 2002, NCS requested and received a waiver from Genesis allowing NCS to enter into discussions with Omnicare without first having to determine that Omnicare's proposal was a "Superior Proposal."

On October 6, 2002, Omnicare irrevocably committed itself to a transaction with NCS. Pursuant to the terms of its proposal, Omnicare agreed to acquire all the outstanding NCS Class A and Class B shares at a price of $3.50 per share in cash. As a result of this irrevocable offer, on October 21, 2002, the NCS board withdrew its recommendation that the stockholders vote in favor of the NCS/Genesis merger agreement. NCS's financial advisor withdrew its fairness opinion of the NCS/Genesis merger agreement as well.

GENESIS REJECTION IMPOSSIBLE

The Genesis merger agreement permits the NCS directors to furnish non-public information to, or enter into discussions with, "any Person in connection with an unsolicited bona fide written Acquisition Proposal by such person" that the board deems likely to constitute a "Superior Proposal." That provision has absolutely no effect on the Genesis merger agreement. Even if the NCS board "changes, withdraws or modifies" its recommendation, as it did, it must still submit the merger to a stockholder vote.

A subsequent filing with the Securities and Exchange Commission ("SEC") states: "the NCS independent committee and the NCS board of directors have determined to withdraw their recommendations of the Genesis merger agreement and recommend that the NCS stockholders vote against the approval and adoption of the Genesis merger." In that same SEC filing, however, the NCS board explained why the success of the Genesis merger had already been predetermined. "Notwithstanding the foregoing, the NCS independent committee and the NCS board of directors recognize that (1) the existing contractual obligations to Genesis currently prevent NCS from accepting the Omnicare irrevocable merger proposal; and (2) the existence of the voting agreements entered into by Messrs. Outcalt and Shaw, whereby Messrs. Outcalt and Shaw agreed to vote their shares of NCS Class A common stock and NCS Class B common stock in favor of the Genesis merger, ensure NCS stockholder approval of the Genesis merger." This litigation was commenced to prevent the consummation of the inferior Genesis transaction.

LEGAL ANALYSIS

DEAL PROTECTION DEVICES REQUIRE ENHANCED SCRUTINY

The dispositive issues in this appeal involve the defensive devices that protected the Genesis merger agreement. The Delaware corporation statute provides that the board's management decision to enter into and recommend a merger transaction can become final only when ownership action is taken by a vote of the stockholders. Thus, the Delaware corporation law expressly provides for a balance of power between boards and stockholders which makes merger transactions a shared enterprise and ownership decision. Consequently, a board of directors' decision to adopt defensive devices to protect a merger agreement may implicate the stockholders' right to effectively vote contrary to the initial recommendation of the board in favor of the transaction.

It is well established that conflicts of interest arise when a board of directors acts to prevent stockholders from effectively exercising their right to vote contrary to the will of the board. The "omnipresent specter" of such conflict may be present whenever a board adopts defensive devices to protect a merger agreement.[27] The stockholders' ability to effectively reject a merger agreement is likely to bear an inversely proportionate relationship to the structural and economic devices that the board has approved to protect the transaction. . . .

27. *See* Unocal Corp. v. Mesa Petroleum Co., 493 A.2d 946, 954 (Del. 1985).

There are inherent conflicts between a board's interest in protecting a merger transaction it has approved, the stockholders' statutory right to make the final decision to either approve or not approve a merger, and the board's continuing responsibility to effectively exercise its fiduciary duties at all times after the merger agreement is executed. These competing considerations require a threshold determination that board-approved defensive devices protecting a merger transaction are within the limitations of its statutory authority and consistent with the directors' fiduciary duties. [D]efensive devices adopted by the board to protect [a] merger transaction must withstand enhanced judicial scrutiny under the *Unocal* standard of review, even when that merger transaction does not result in a change of control. . . .

GENESIS' ONE DAY ULTIMATUM

The record reflects that two of the four NCS board members, Shaw and Outcalt, were also the *same* two NCS stockholders who combined to control a majority of the stockholder voting power. Genesis gave the four person NCS board less than twenty-four hours to vote in favor of its proposed merger agreement. Genesis insisted the merger agreement include a Section 251(c) clause, mandating its submission for a stockholder vote even if the board's recommendation was withdrawn. Genesis further insisted that the merger agreement omit any effective fiduciary out clause.

Genesis also gave the two stockholder members of the NCS board, Shaw and Outcalt, the same accelerated time table to personally sign the proposed voting agreements. These voting agreements committed them irrevocably to vote their majority power in favor of the merger and further provided in Section 6 that the voting agreements be specifically enforceable. Genesis also required that NCS execute the voting agreements.

Genesis' twenty-four hour ultimatum was that, *unless both* the merger agreement and the voting agreements were signed with the terms it requested, its offer was going to be withdrawn. According to Genesis' attorneys, these "were unalterable conditions to Genesis' willingness to proceed." Genesis insisted on the execution of the interlocking voting rights and merger agreements because it feared that Omnicare would make a superior merger proposal. The NCS board signed the voting rights and merger agreements, without any effective fiduciary out clause, to expressly guarantee that the Genesis merger would be approved, even if a superior merger transaction was presented from Omnicare or any other entity.

DEAL PROTECTION DEVICES

Defensive devices, as that term is used in this opinion, is a synonym for what are frequently referred to as "deal protection devices." Both terms are used interchangeably to describe any measure or combination of measures that are intended to protect the consummation of a merger transaction. Defensive devices can be economic, structural, or both.

Deal protection devices need not all be in the merger agreement itself. In this case, for example, the Section 251(c) provision in the merger agreement was combined with the separate voting agreements to provide a structural defense for the Genesis merger agreement against any subsequent superior transaction. Genesis made the NCS board's defense of its transaction absolute by insisting on the omission of any effective fiduciary out clause in the NCS merger agreement.

Genesis argues that stockholder voting agreements cannot be construed as deal protection devices taken by a board of directors because stockholders are entitled to vote in their own interest. . . .

In this case, the stockholder voting agreements were inextricably intertwined with the defensive aspects of the Genesis merger agreement. In fact, the voting agreements with Shaw and Outcalt were the linchpin of Genesis' proposed tripartite defense. Therefore, Genesis made the execution of those voting agreements a non-negotiable condition precedent to its execution of the merger agreement. In the case before us, the Court of Chancery held that the acts which locked-up the Genesis transaction were the Section 251(c) provision and "the execution of the *voting agreement* by Outcalt and Shaw."

With the assurance that Outcalt and Shaw would irrevocably agree to exercise their majority voting power in favor of its transaction, Genesis insisted that the merger agreement reflect the other two aspects of its concerted defense, *i.e.*, the inclusion of a Section 251(c) provision and the omission of any effective fiduciary out clause. Those dual aspects of the merger agreement would not have provided Genesis with a complete defense in the absence of the voting agreements with Shaw and Outcalt.

THESE DEAL PROTECTION DEVICES UNENFORCEABLE

In this case, the Court of Chancery correctly held that the NCS directors' decision to adopt defensive devices to *completely* "lock up" the Genesis merger mandated "special scrutiny" under the two-part test set forth in *Unocal*. . . . The record does not, however, support the Court of Chancery's conclusion that the defensive devices adopted by the NCS board to protect the Genesis merger were reasonable and proportionate to the threat that NCS perceived from the potential loss of the Genesis transaction.

. . . In this case, the Court of Chancery did not expressly address the issue of "coercion" in its *Unocal* analysis. It did find as a fact, however, that NCS's public stockholders (who owned 80% of NCS and overwhelmingly supported Omnicare's offer) will be forced to accept the Genesis merger because of the structural defenses approved by the NCS board. Consequently, the record reflects that any stockholder vote would have been robbed of its effectiveness by the impermissible coercion that predetermined the outcome of the merger without regard to the merits of the Genesis transaction at the time the vote was scheduled to be taken. Deal protection devices that result in such coercion cannot withstand *Unocal*'s enhanced judicial scrutiny standard of review because they are not within the range of reasonableness. . . .

The deal protection devices adopted by the NCS board were designed to coerce the consummation of the Genesis merger and preclude the consideration of any superior transaction. The NCS directors' defensive devices are not within a reasonable range of responses to the perceived threat of losing the Genesis offer because they are preclusive and coercive. Accordingly, we hold that those deal protection devices are unenforceable.

EFFECTIVE FIDUCIARY OUT REQUIRED

The defensive measures that protected the merger transaction are unenforceable not only because they are preclusive and coercive but, alternatively, they are unenforceable because they are invalid as they operate in this case. Given the specifically enforceable irrevocable voting agreements, the provision in the merger agreement requiring the board to submit the transaction for a stockholder vote and the omission of a fiduciary out clause in the merger agreement completely prevented the board from discharging its fiduciary responsibilities to the minority stockholders when Omnicare presented its superior transaction. "To the extent that a [merger] contract, or a provision thereof, purports to require a board to act or not act in such a fashion as to limit the exercise of fiduciary duties, it is invalid and unenforceable."[74] . . .

Under the circumstances presented in this case, where a cohesive group of stockholders with majority voting power was irrevocably committed to the merger transaction, "[e]ffective representation of the financial interests of the minority shareholders imposed upon the [NCS board] an affirmative responsibility to protect those minority shareholders' interests."[79] The NCS board could not abdicate its fiduciary duties to the minority by leaving it to the stockholders alone to approve or disapprove the merger agreement because two stockholders had already combined to establish a majority of the voting power that made the outcome of the stockholder vote a foregone conclusion.

The Court of Chancery noted that Section 251(c) of the Delaware General Corporation Law now permits boards to agree to submit a merger agreement for a stockholder vote, even if the Board later withdraws its support for that agreement and recommends that the stockholders reject it.[80] The Court of Chancery also noted that stockholder voting agreements are permitted by Delaware law. In refusing to certify this interlocutory appeal, the Court of Chancery stated "it is simply nonsensical to say that a board of directors abdicates its duties to manage the 'business and affairs' of a corporation under Section 141(a) of the DGCL by agreeing to the inclusion in a merger agreement of a term authorized by §251(c) of the same statute."

Taking action that is otherwise legally possible, however, does not *ipso facto* comport with the fiduciary responsibilities of directors in all circumstances. The synopsis to the amendments that resulted in the enactment of Section 251(c) in the Delaware corporation law statute specifically provides: "the amendments are not intended to address the question of whether such a submission requirement is appropriate in any particular set of factual circumstances." Section 251 provisions, like the no-shop provision examined in QVC, are "presumptively valid in the abstract."[82] Such provisions in a merger agreement may not, however, "validly define or limit the directors' fiduciary duties under Delaware law

---

74. Paramount Communications Inc. v. QVC Network Inc., 637 A.2d 34, 51 (Del. 1993).

79. McMullin v. Beran, 765 A.2d 910, 920 (Del. 2000).

80. Section 251(c) was amended in 1998 to allow for the inclusion in a merger agreement of a term requiring that the agreement be put to a vote of stockholders whether or not their directors continue to recommend the transaction. Before this amendment, Section 251 was interpreted as precluding a stockholder vote if the board of directors, after approving the merger agreement but before the stockholder vote, decided no longer to recommend it. *See* Smith v. Van Gorkom, 488 A.2d 858, 887-88 (Del. 1985).

82. Paramount Communications Inc. v. QVC Network Inc., 637 A.2d at 48.

or prevent the [NCS] directors from carrying out their fiduciary duties under Delaware law."[83]

Genesis admits that when the NCS board agreed to its merger conditions, the NCS board was seeking to assure that the NCS creditors were paid in full and that the NCS stockholders received the highest value available for their stock. In fact, Genesis defends its "bulletproof" merger agreement on that basis. We hold that the NCS board did not have authority to accede to the Genesis demand for an absolute "lock-up."

The directors of a Delaware corporation have a continuing obligation to discharge their fiduciary responsibilities, as future circumstances develop, after a merger agreement is announced. Genesis anticipated the likelihood of a superior offer after its merger agreement was announced and demanded defensive measures from the NCS board that *completely* protected its transaction.[84] Instead of agreeing to the absolute defense of the Genesis merger from a superior offer, however, the NCS board was required to negotiate a fiduciary out clause to protect the NCS stockholders if the Genesis transaction became an inferior offer. By acceding to Genesis' ultimatum for complete protection *in futuro,* the NCS board disabled itself from exercising its own fiduciary obligations at a time when the board's own judgment is most important, *i.e.* receipt of a subsequent superior offer. . . .

The NCS board was required to contract for an effective fiduciary out clause to exercise its continuing fiduciary responsibilities to the minority stockholders.[88] The issues in this appeal do not involve the general validity of either stockholder voting agreements or the authority of directors to insert a Section 251(c) provision in a merger agreement. In this case, the NCS board combined those two otherwise valid actions and caused them to operate in concert as an absolute lock up, in the absence of an effective fiduciary out clause in the Genesis merger agreement.

In the context of this preclusive and coercive lock up case, the protection of Genesis' contractual expectations must yield to the supervening responsibility of the directors to discharge their fiduciary duties on a continuing basis. The merger agreement and voting agreements, as they were combined to operate in concert in this case, are inconsistent with the NCS directors' fiduciary duties. To that extent, we hold that they are invalid and unenforceable.

CONCLUSION

With respect to the Fiduciary Duty Decision, the order of the Court of Chancery dated November 22, 2002, denying plaintiffs' application for a preliminary injunction is reversed. With respect to the Voting Agreements Decision, the

---

83. *Id.*

84. The marked improvements in NCS's financial situation during the negotiations with Genesis strongly suggests that the NCS board should have been alert to the prospect of competing offers or, as eventually occurred, a bidding contest.

88. *See* Paramount Communications Inc. v. QVC Network Inc., 637 A.2d at 42-43. Merger agreements involve an ownership decision and, therefore, cannot become final without stockholder approval. Other contracts do not require a fiduciary out clause because they involve business judgments that are within the *exclusive* province of the board of directors' power to manage the affairs of the corporation. *See* Grimes v. Donald, 673 A.2d 1207, 1214-15 (Del. 1996).

order of the Court of Chancery dated October 29, 2002 is reversed to the extent that decision permits the implementation of the Voting Agreements contrary to this Court's ruling on the Fiduciary Duty claims. With respect to the appeal to this Court of that portion of the Standing Decision constituting the order of the Court of Chancery dated October 25, 2002, that granted the motion to dismiss the remainder of the Omnicare complaint, holding that Omnicare lacked standing to assert fiduciary duty claims arising out of the action of the board of directors that preceded the date on which Omnicare acquired its stock, the appeal is dismissed as moot.

The mandate shall issue immediately.

VEASEY, Chief Justice, with whom STEELE, Justice, joins dissenting.

The beauty of the Delaware corporation law, and the reason it has worked so well for stockholders, directors and officers, is that the framework is based on an enabling statute with the Court of Chancery and the Supreme Court applying principles of fiduciary duty in a common law mode on a case-by-case basis. Fiduciary duty cases are inherently fact-intensive and, therefore, unique. This case is unique in two important respects. First, the peculiar facts presented render this case an unlikely candidate for substantial repetition. Second, this is a rare 3-2 split decision of the Supreme Court. . . .

The process by which this merger agreement came about involved a joint decision by the controlling stockholders and the board of directors to secure what appeared to be the only value-enhancing transaction available for a company on the brink of bankruptcy. The Majority adopts a new rule of law that imposes a prohibition on the NCS board's ability to act in concert with controlling stockholders to lock up this merger. The Majority reaches this conclusion by analyzing the challenged deal protection measures as isolated board actions. The Majority concludes that the board owed a duty to the NCS minority stockholders to refrain from acceding to the Genesis demand for an irrevocable lock-up notwithstanding the compelling circumstances confronting the board and the board's disinterested, informed, good faith exercise of its business judgment.

Because we believe this Court must respect the reasoned judgment of the board of directors and give effect to the wishes of the controlling stockholders, we respectfully disagree with the Majority's reasoning that results in a holding that the confluence of board and stockholder action constitutes a breach of fiduciary duty. The essential fact that must always be remembered is that this agreement and the voting commitments of Outcalt and Shaw concluded a lengthy search and intense negotiation process in the context of insolvency and creditor pressure where no other viable bid had emerged. Accordingly, we endorse the Vice Chancellor's well-reasoned analysis that the NCS board's action before the hostile bid emerged was within the bounds of its fiduciary duties under these facts.

We share with the Majority and the independent NCS board of directors the motivation to serve carefully and in good faith the best interests of the corporate enterprise and, thereby, the stockholders of NCS. It is now known, of course, after the case is over, that the stockholders of NCS will receive substantially more by tendering their shares into the topping bid of Omnicare than they would have received in the Genesis merger, as a result of the post-agreement

Omnicare bid and the injunctive relief ordered by the Majority of this Court. Our jurisprudence cannot, however, be seen as turning on such *ex post* felicitous results. Rather, the NCS board's good faith decision must be subject to a real-time review of the board action before the NCS-Genesis merger agreement was entered into.

AN ANALYSIS OF THE PROCESS LEADING TO THE LOCK-UP REFLECTS A QUINTESSENTIAL, DISINTERESTED AND INFORMED BOARD DECISION REACHED IN GOOD FAITH

The Majority has adopted the Vice Chancellor's findings and has assumed arguendo that the NCS board fulfilled its duties of care, loyalty, and good faith by entering into the Genesis merger agreement. Indeed, this conclusion is indisputable on this record. The problem is that the Majority has removed from their proper context the contractual merger protection provisions. The lock-ups here cannot be reviewed in a vacuum. A court should review the entire bidding process to determine whether the independent board's actions permitted the directors to inform themselves of their available options and whether they acted in good faith.

Going into negotiations with Genesis, the NCS directors knew that, up until that time, NCS had found only one potential bidder, Omnicare. Omnicare had refused to buy NCS except at a fire sale price through an asset sale in bankruptcy. Omnicare's best proposal at that stage would not have paid off all creditors and would have provided nothing for stockholders. The Noteholders, represented by the Ad Hoc Committee, were willing to oblige Omnicare and force NCS into bankruptcy if Omnicare would pay in full the NCS debt. Through the NCS board's efforts, Genesis expressed interest that became increasingly attractive. Negotiations with Genesis led to an offer paying creditors off and conferring on NCS stockholders $24 million — an amount infinitely superior to the prior Omnicare proposals.

But there was, understandably, a *sine qua non*. In exchange for offering the NCS stockholders a return on their equity and creditor payment, Genesis demanded certainty that the merger would close. If the NCS board would not have acceded to the Section 251(c) provision, if Outcalt and Shaw had not agreed to the voting agreements and if NCS had insisted on a fiduciary out, there would have been no Genesis deal! Thus, the only value-enhancing transaction available would have disappeared. NCS knew that Omnicare had spoiled a Genesis acquisition in the past, and it is not disputed by the Majority that the NCS directors made a reasoned decision to accept as real the Genesis threat to walk away.

When Omnicare submitted its conditional eleventh-hour bid, the NCS board had to weigh the economic terms of the proposal against the uncertainty of completing a deal with Omnicare. Importantly, because Omnicare's bid was conditioned on its satisfactorily completing its due diligence review of NCS, the NCS board saw this as a crippling condition, as did the Ad Hoc Committee. As a matter of business judgment, the risk of negotiating with Omnicare and losing Genesis at that point outweighed the possible benefits. The lock-up was indisputably a *sine qua non* to any deal with Genesis.

A lock-up permits a target board and a bidder to "exchange certainties."[97] Certainty itself has value. The acquirer may pay a higher price for the target if the acquirer is assured consummation of the transaction. The target company also benefits from the certainty of completing a transaction with a bidder because losing an acquirer creates the perception that a target is damaged goods, thus reducing its value. . . .

. . . If the creditors decided to force NCS into bankruptcy, which could have happened at any time as NCS was unable to service its obligations, the stockholders would have received nothing. The NCS board also did not know if the NCS business prospects would have declined again, leaving NCS less attractive to other bidders, including Omnicare, which could have changed its mind and again insisted on an asset sale in bankruptcy.

Situations will arise where business realities demand a lock-up so that wealth-enhancing transactions may go forward. Accordingly, any bright-line rule prohibiting lock-ups could, in circumstances such as these, chill otherwise permissible conduct.

OUR JURISPRUDENCE DOES NOT COMPEL THIS COURT TO INVALIDATE THE JOINT ACTION OF THE BOARD AND THE CONTROLLING STOCKHOLDERS

The Majority invalidates the NCS board's action by announcing a new rule that represents an extension of our jurisprudence. That new rule can be narrowly stated as follows: A merger agreement entered into after a market search, before any prospect of a topping bid has emerged, which locks up stockholder approval and does not contain a "fiduciary out" provision, is per se invalid when a later significant topping bid emerges. As we have noted, this bright-line, per se rule would apply regardless of (1) the circumstances leading up to the agreement and (2) the fact that stockholders who control voting power had irrevocably committed themselves, *as stockholders,* to vote for the merger. Narrowly stated, this new rule is a judicially-created "third rail" that now becomes one of the given "rules of the game," to be taken into account by the negotiators and drafters of merger agreements. In our view, this new rule is an unwise extension of existing precedent.

Although it is debatable whether *Unocal* applies — and we believe that the better rule in this situation is that the business judgment rule should apply[102] — we'll, nevertheless, assume arguendo — as the Vice Chancellor did — that *Unocal* applies. Therefore, under *Unocal* the NCS directors had the burden of going forward with the evidence to show that there was a threat to corporate policy and effectiveness and that their actions were reasonable in response to that threat. The Vice Chancellor correctly found that they reasonably perceived the threat that NCS did not have a viable offer from Omnicare — or anyone else — to pay off its creditors, cure its insolvency and provide some payment to stockholders. The NCS board's actions — as the Vice Chancellor correctly held — were reasonable in relation to the threat because the Genesis deal was

---

97. *See* Rand v. Western Air Lines, 1994 WL 89006 at *6 (Del. Ch.).

102. The basis for the *Unocal* doctrine is the "omnipresent specter" of the board's self-interest to entrench itself in office. Unocal Corp. v. Mesa Petroleum Co., 493 A.2d 946, 954 (Del. 1985). NCS was not plagued with a specter of self-interest. Unlike the *Unocal* situation, a hostile offer did not arise here until *after* the market search and the locked-up deal with Genesis.

the "only game in town," the NCS directors got the best deal they could from Genesis and—but for the emergence of Genesis on the scene—there would have been no viable deal.

The Vice Chancellor held that the NCS directors satisfied *Unocal*. . . . Indeed, he concluded—based on the undisputed record and his considerable experience—that: "The overall quality of testimony given by the NCS directors is among the strongest this court has ever seen. All four NCS directors were deposed, and each deposition makes manifest the care and attention given to this project by every member of the board." We agree fully with the Vice Chancellor's findings and conclusions, and we would have affirmed the judgment of the Court of Chancery on that basis.

In our view, the Majority misapplies the *Unitrin* concept of "coercive and preclusive" measures to preempt a proper proportionality balancing. Thus, the Majority asserts that "in applying *enhanced judicial scrutiny* to *defensive devices* designed to protect a merger agreement, . . . a court must . . . determine that those measures are not preclusive or coercive. . . . " Here, the deal protection measures were not adopted unilaterally by the board to fend off an existing hostile offer that threatened the corporate policy and effectiveness of NCS. They were adopted because Genesis—the "only game in town"—would not save NCS, its creditors and its stockholders without these provisions.

The Majority—incorrectly, in our view—relies on *Unitrin* to advance its analysis. The discussion of "draconian" measures in *Unitrin* dealt with unilateral board action, a repurchase program, designed to fend off an existing hostile offer by American General. In *Unitrin* we recognized the need to police preclusive and coercive actions initiated *by the board* to delay or retard an existing hostile bid so as to ensure that the stockholders can benefit from the board's negotiations with the bidder or others and to exercise effectively the franchise as the ultimate check on board action. *Unitrin* polices the effect of board action on existing tender offers and proxy contests to ensure that the board cannot permanently impose its will on the stockholders, leaving the stockholders no recourse to their voting rights.

The very measures the Majority cites as "coercive" were approved by Shaw and Outcalt through the lens of their independent assessment of the merits of the transaction. The proper inquiry in this case is whether the NCS board had taken actions that "have the effect of causing the stockholders to vote in favor of the proposed transaction for some reason other than the merits of that transaction."[109] Like the termination fee upheld as a valid liquidated damages clause against a claim of coercion in Brazen v. Bell Atlantic Corp., the deal protection measures at issue here were "an integral part of the merits of the transaction" as the NCS board struggled to secure—and did secure—the only deal available.[110]

Outcalt and Shaw were fully informed stockholders. As the NCS controlling stockholders, they made an informed choice to commit their voting power to the merger. The minority stockholders were deemed to know that when controlling stockholders have 65% of the vote they can approve a merger without

109. *Geier*, 671 A.2d at 1382-83.
110. 695 A.2d 43, 50 (Del. 1997).

the need for the minority votes. Moreover, to the extent a minority stock-holder may have felt "coerced" to vote for the merger, which was already a *fait accompli*, it was a meaningless coercion—or no coercion at all—because the controlling votes, those of Outcalt and Shaw, were already "cast." Although the fact that the controlling votes were committed to the merger "precluded" an overriding vote against the merger by the Class A stockholders, the pejorative "preclusive" label applicable in a *Unitrin* fact situation has no application here. Therefore, there was no meaningful minority stockholder voting decision to coerce.

In applying *Unocal* scrutiny, we believe the Majority incorrectly preempted the proportionality inquiry. In our view, the proportionality inquiry must account for the reality that the contractual measures protecting this merger agreement were necessary to obtain the Genesis deal. The Majority has not demonstrated that the director action was a disproportionate response to the threat posed. Indeed, it is clear to us that the board action to negotiate the best deal reasonably available with the only viable merger partner (Genesis) who could satisfy the creditors and benefit the stockholders, was reasonable in relation to the threat, by any practical yardstick.

AN ABSOLUTE LOCK-UP IS NOT A PER SE VIOLATION OF FIDUCIARY DUTY

We respectfully disagree with the Majority's conclusion that the NCS board breached its fiduciary duties to the Class A stockholders by failing to negotiate a "fiduciary out" in the Genesis merger agreement. What is the practical import of a "fiduciary out"? It is a contractual provision, articulated in a manner to be negotiated, that would permit the board of the corporation being acquired to exit without breaching the merger agreement in the event of a superior offer.

In this case, Genesis made it abundantly clear early on that it was willing to negotiate a deal with NCS but only on the condition that it would not be a "stalking horse." Thus, it wanted to be certain that a third party could not use its deal with NCS as a floor against which to begin a bidding war. As a result of this negotiating position, a "fiduciary out" was not acceptable to Genesis. The Majority Opinion holds that such a negotiating position, if implemented in the agreement, is invalid per se where there is an absolute lock-up. We know of no authority in our jurisprudence supporting this new rule, and we believe it is unwise and unwarranted. . . .

CONCLUSION

It is regrettable that the Court is split in this important case. One hopes that the Majority rule announced here—though clearly erroneous in our view—will be interpreted narrowly and will be seen as *sui generis*. By deterring bidders from engaging in negotiations like those present here and requiring that there must always be a fiduciary out, the universe of potential bidders who could reasonably be expected to benefit stockholders could shrink or disappear. Nevertheless, if the holding is confined to these unique facts, negotiators may be able to navigate around this new hazard.

Accordingly, we respectfully dissent.

PROBLEM 15-2

Gaylord Containers (Gaylord) manufactures container board and other paper products. Marvin A. Pomerantz, founder, chairman, and chief executive officer, held about 62 percent of the voting power, and the other directors and officers held about 12 percent. As a result of a bankruptcy reorganization, the company's Class B stock having ten votes per share would automatically convert to Class A stock having one vote per share, unless the stock price stayed at a prescribed level. If the conversion occurred, Mr. Pomerantz would then have about 12 percent of the voting power and the other directors and officers would have about 8 percent. The board took the following challenged actions when it concluded that the dual-class common stock structure would automatically convert to a single-class stock structure on July 31, 1995.

On June 12, 1995, the board adopted a shareholder rights plan (poison pill). The plan provided that when someone acquires 15 percent of Gaylord's common stock without the board's approval, all stockholders other than the acquiror would have a right to buy $100 worth of common stock for $50 for each share owned.

On July 7, 1995, the board issued a notice of a special stockholder meeting to be held on July 21. The purpose of the meeting was to vote on proposed charter and bylaw amendments providing that:

- stockholders may act only at a stockholder meeting, not by written consent;
- a special stockholder meeting may be called only by the board or the chairman of the board;
- a two-thirds supermajority vote is required to amend the bylaws and certain provisions of the charter; and
- the corporation elects to be governed by 8 Del. C. §203, which provides, among other things, that the corporation may not merge with a stockholder owning less than 85 percent of the corporation's stock without the board's approval.

In its proxy statement, the board explained that the purpose of the proposed charter and bylaw amendments was to increase the effectiveness of the shareholder rights plan by preventing a person who controlled a majority of the voting stock, but less than two-thirds, from circumventing the plan. The board disclosed that the proposed amendments would have an entrenching effect and that Mr. Pomerantz controlled sufficient votes to approve them.

Between July 18, 1995, and November 30, 1995, there were reports in the news media that other companies were interested in acquiring Gaylord.

A number of Gaylord's institutional shareholders would like to see these rumors materialize into an actual takeover. Thus, they sue the directors for breach of fiduciary duty, claiming that "the combined effect of the board's actions in the weeks before the impending drop in the board's voting power from 74 to 20 percent raises a fair inference that the board's primary purpose was entrenchment."

Analyze this case. How do you think the Delaware courts will respond, given their elaboration on *Unocal* in subsequent cases?

E. CHANGE-OF-CONTROL TRANSACTIONS

The following cases further refine the *Unocal* analysis but also introduce a new framework for evaluating directors' actions when there is a "change-of-control" transaction. Although it would seem to be obvious when a company is involved in a "change-of-control" transaction; thus, when "*Revlon* duties" attach, you will see in the subsequent cases that this seemingly obvious issue contains some interesting subtleties. These cases, in particular *Revlon* and Paramount v. Time, also explore some important issues about the nature of the public corporation as an economic entity or a social entity or some combination thereof; and about the relative distribution of power of shareholders versus directors in shaping the course of a company's future. As we've seen in prior chapters, shareholders are relatively constrained in what actions they can initiate in public corporations and in what decisions they can make. As you read these cases, ask yourself if these powers are augmented or constrained in the takeover context. Are the courts allowing directors to be too paternalistic towards shareholders by "protecting" them from tender offers at a price that is too low? If the price is really too low, won't the shareholders be able to understand that fact, and don't the directors have adequate means available to communicate that fact to the shareholders?

REVLON, INC. v. MACANDREWS
506 A.2d 173
Supreme Court of Delaware
March 13, 1986

MOORE, Justice.

In this battle for corporate control of Revlon, Inc. (Revlon), the Court of Chancery enjoined certain transactions designed to thwart the efforts of Pantry Pride, Inc. (Pantry Pride) to acquire Revlon. The defendants are Revlon, its board of directors, and Forstmann Little & Co. and the latter's affiliated limited partnership (collectively, Forstmann). The injunction barred consummation of an option granted Forstmann to purchase certain Revlon assets (the lock-up option), a promise by Revlon to deal exclusively with Forstmann in the face of a takeover (the no-shop provision), and the payment of a $25 million cancellation fee to Forstmann if the transaction was aborted. The Court of Chancery found that the Revlon directors had breached their duty of care by entering into the foregoing transactions and effectively ending an active auction for the company. The trial court ruled that such arrangements are not illegal per se under Delaware law, but that their use under the circumstances here was impermissible. We agree. *See* MacAndrews & Forbes Holdings, Inc. v. Revlon, Inc., Del. Ch., 501 A.2d 1239 (1985). Thus, we granted this expedited interlocutory appeal to consider for the first time the validity of such defensive measures in the face of an active bidding contest for corporate control. Additionally, we address for the first time the extent to which a corporation may consider the impact of a takeover threat on constituencies other than shareholders. *See* Unocal Corp. v. Mesa Petroleum Co., Del. Supr., 493 A.2d 946, 955 (1985).

In our view, lock-ups and related agreements are permitted under Delaware law where their adoption is untainted by director interest or other breaches of fiduciary duty. The actions taken by the Revlon directors, however, did not meet this standard. Moreover, while concern for various corporate constituencies is proper when addressing a takeover threat, that principle is limited by the requirement that there be some rationally related benefit accruing to the stockholders. We find no such benefit here. Thus, under all the circumstances we must agree with the Court of Chancery that the enjoined Revlon defensive measures were inconsistent with the directors' duties to the stockholders. Accordingly, we affirm.

I.

[The facts of the case, distilled to their essence, are as follows. This case arose from Pantry Pride's efforts, at the behest of Ronald O. Perelman, chairman and chief executive officer, to buy the Revlon company, whose chairman and CEO Michel C. Bergerac, wanted nothing to do with being sold. Pantry Pride's initial approach, on August 14, was to suggest a negotiated deal at $42-$43 per share, or a hostile tender offer at $45 per share. Revlon's 14-member board met, and on the advice of its investment bankers, concluded that $45 per share was an inadequate price. (Of the 14 members, only two were independent: six were members of senior management; two were major stockholders; and four had significant business relationships with Revlon.) Upon determining that the price was inadequate, the directors adopted a poison pill, and authorized a self-tender for 5 million of its 30 million outstanding shares. Pantry Pride responded on August 23 with a cash tender offer for 100 percent of outstanding shares at $47.50 per common share and $26.67 per preferred share, conditioned upon Pantry Pride getting financing and Revlon getting rid of its poison pill. Revlon responded on August 29 by starting its own tender offer, now for up to 10 million shares, offering to exchange each common share tendered for one senior subordinated note (the Note) of $47.50 principal at 11.75 percent interest, due 1995, and one-tenth of a share of $9.00 cumulative convertible preferred stock valued at $100 per share. The new Notes contained a promise (called a "covenant" in financial circles) that Revlon would not take on any additional debt, sell assets, or pay dividends unless approved by the independent members of the board. Pantry Pride remained determined to acquire Revlon, offering $50 per share in September, then $53 per share and $56.25 per share in early October, each offer conditioned on the board removing the poison pill.

Facing this determined acquiror, the Revlon board authorized management to try to shop the company to other potential acquirers, eventually bringing forth two competitors to Pantry Pride: Forstmann, Little and Adler & Shaykin — both "investment groups" engaged in buying and selling companies. At a time when Pantry Pride was offering $53 per share, Revlon's board unanimously agreed to be acquired by Forstmann at $56 per share. Forstmann agreed to take on the $475 million of debt Revlon had taken on to fund the self-tender, and in exchange Revlon would remove the poison pill and, significantly, would waive the Note covenants to allow the company to take on more debt or sell assets. When this news became public, the price of the Notes started to fall, and directors reported being "deluged" with angry Noteholders threatening litigation. Pantry Pride, Revlon, and Forstmann met to try to negotiate a solution. Negotiations then broke down, but not before Pantry Pride announced that it would engage in "fractional bidding" to outbid any Forstmann offer.

By this point in the fracas, Revlon had provided its confidential financial data to Forstmann, not Pantry Pride, so Forstmann was in a position to make a higher offer: $57.25 per share, with several conditions. These included Revlon's agreement to a lock-up option (a right to buy valuable Revlon divisions at a $100-$175 million discount if another acquiror got 40 percent of Revlon's shares), a no-shop provision, its agreement to waive the Note covenants and remove the pill, and its agreement to a $25 million cancellation fee. Forstmann also agreed to support the falling Note values by an exchange of new Notes. In response Pantry Pride announced a new tender offer, at $58 per share in cash, and brought an action to enjoin Revlon from performing any of its obligations under its contract with Forstmann.]

II.

To obtain a preliminary injunction, a plaintiff must demonstrate both a reasonable probability of success on the merits and some irreparable harm which will occur absent the injunction. Gimbel v. Signal Companies, Del. Ch., 316 A.2d 599, 602 (1974), *aff'd*, Del. Supr., 316 A.2d 619 (1974). Additionally, the Court shall balance the conveniences of and possible injuries to the parties. *Id.*

A.

We turn first to Pantry Pride's probability of success on the merits. The ultimate responsibility for managing the business and affairs of a corporation falls on its board of directors. In discharging this function the directors owe fiduciary duties of care and loyalty to the corporation and its shareholders. These principles apply with equal force when a board approves a corporate merger pursuant to 8 Del. C. §251(b), and of course they are the bedrock of our law regarding corporate takeover issues. While the business judgment rule may be applicable to the actions of corporate directors responding to takeover threats, the principles upon which it is founded—care, loyalty and independence—must first be satisfied.

If the business judgment rule applies, there is a "presumption that in making a business decision the directors of a corporation acted on an informed basis, in good faith and in the honest belief that the action taken was in the best interests of the company." Aronson v. Lewis, 473 A.2d [805, 812 (1984)]. However, when a board implements anti-takeover measures there arises "the omnipresent specter that a board may be acting primarily in its own interests, rather than those of the corporation and its shareholders. . . . " Unocal Corp. v. Mesa Petroleum Co., 493 A.2d at 954. This potential for conflict places upon the directors the burden of proving that they had reasonable grounds for believing there was a danger to corporate policy and effectiveness, a burden satisfied by a showing of good faith and reasonable investigation. *Id.* at 955. In addition, the directors must analyze the nature of the takeover and its effect on the corporation in order to ensure balance — that the responsive action taken is reasonable in relation to the threat posed. *Id.*

B.

The first relevant defensive measure adopted by the Revlon board was the Rights Plan, which would be considered a "poison pill" in the current language of corporate takeovers — a plan by which shareholders receive the right to be bought out by the corporation at a substantial premium on the occurrence of a stated triggering event. By 8 Del. C. §§141 and 122(13), the board clearly had the power to adopt the measure. *See* Moran v. Household International, Inc., 500 A.2d at 1351. Thus, the focus becomes one of reasonableness and purpose.

The Revlon board approved the Rights Plan in the face of an impending hostile takeover bid by Pantry Pride at $45 per share, a price which Revlon reasonably concluded was grossly inadequate. Lazard Freres had so advised the directors, and had also informed them that Pantry Pride was a small, highly leveraged company bent on a "bust-up" takeover by using "junk bond" financing to buy Revlon cheaply, sell the acquired assets to pay the debts incurred, and retain the profit for itself. In adopting the Plan, the board protected the shareholders from a hostile takeover at a price below the company's intrinsic value, while retaining sufficient flexibility to address any proposal deemed to be in the stockholders' best interests.

To that extent the board acted in good faith and upon reasonable investigation. Under the circumstances it cannot be said that the Rights Plan as employed was unreasonable, considering the threat posed. Indeed, the Plan was a factor in causing Pantry Pride to raise its bids from a low of $42 to an eventual high of $58. At the time of its adoption the Rights Plan afforded a measure of protection consistent with the directors' fiduciary duty in facing a takeover threat perceived as detrimental to corporate interests. Far from being a "show-stopper," as the plaintiffs had contended in *Moran,* the measure spurred the bidding to new heights, a proper result of its implementation. *See Moran,* 500 A.2d at 1354, 1356-67.

Although we consider adoption of the Plan to have been valid under the circumstances, its continued usefulness was rendered moot by the directors' actions on October 3 and October 12. At the October 3 meeting the board redeemed the Rights conditioned upon consummation of a merger with Forstmann, but further acknowledged that they would also be redeemed to facilitate any more favorable offer. On October 12, the board unanimously passed a resolution redeeming the Rights in connection with any cash proposal of $57.25 or more per share. Because all the pertinent offers eventually equalled or surpassed that amount, the Rights clearly were no longer any impediment in the contest for Revlon. This mooted any question of their propriety under *Moran* or *Unocal.*

C.

The second defensive measure adopted by Revlon to thwart a Pantry Pride takeover was the company's own exchange offer for 10 million of its shares. The directors' general broad powers to manage the business and affairs of the corporation are augmented by the specific authority conferred under 8 Del.

C. §160(a), permitting the company to deal in its own stock. However, when exercising that power in an effort to forestall a hostile takeover, the board's actions are strictly held to the fiduciary standards outlined in *Unocal*. These standards require the directors to determine the best interests of the corporation and its stockholders, and impose an enhanced duty to abjure any action that is motivated by considerations other than a good faith concern for such interests.

The Revlon directors concluded that Pantry Pride's $47.50 offer was grossly inadequate. In that regard the board acted in good faith, and on an informed basis, with reasonable grounds to believe that there existed a harmful threat to the corporate enterprise. The adoption of a defensive measure, reasonable in relation to the threat posed, was proper and fully accorded with the powers, duties, and responsibilities conferred upon directors under our law.

D.

However, when Pantry Pride increased its offer to $50 per share, and then to $53, it became apparent to all that the break-up of the company was inevitable. The Revlon board's authorization permitting management to negotiate a merger or buyout with a third party was a recognition that the company was for sale. The duty of the board had thus changed from the preservation of Revlon as a corporate entity to the maximization of the company's value at a sale for the stockholders' benefit. This significantly altered the board's responsibilities under the *Unocal* standards. It no longer faced threats to corporate policy and effectiveness, or to the stockholders' interests, from a grossly inadequate bid. The whole question of defensive measures became moot. The directors' role changed from defenders of the corporate bastion to auctioneers charged with getting the best price for the stockholders at a sale of the company.

III.

This brings us to the lock-up with Forstmann and its emphasis on shoring up the sagging market value of the Notes in the face of threatened litigation by their holders. Such a focus was inconsistent with the changed concept of the directors' responsibilities at this stage of the developments. The impending waiver of the Notes covenants had caused the value of the Notes to fall, and the board was aware of the noteholders' ire as well as their subsequent threats of suit. The directors thus made support of the Notes an integral part of the company's dealings with Forstmann, even though their primary responsibility at this stage was to the equity owners.

The original threat posed by Pantry Pride — the break-up of the company — had become a reality which even the directors embraced. Selective dealing to fend off a hostile but determined bidder was no longer a proper objective. Instead, obtaining the highest price for the benefit of the stockholders should have been the central theme guiding director action. Thus, the Revlon board could not make the requisite showing of good faith by preferring the noteholders and ignoring its duty of loyalty to the shareholders. The rights of the former already were fixed by contract. Wolfensohn v. Madison Fund, Inc., Del.

Supr., 253 A.2d 72, 75 (1969); Harff v. Kerkorian, Del. Ch., 324 A.2d 215 (1974). The noteholders required no further protection, and when the Revlon board entered into an auction-ending lock-up agreement with Forstmann on the basis of impermissible considerations at the expense of the shareholders, the directors breached their primary duty of loyalty.

The Revlon board argued that it acted in good faith in protecting the noteholders because *Unocal* permits consideration of other corporate constituencies. Although such considerations may be permissible, there are fundamental limitations upon that prerogative. A board may have regard for various constituencies in discharging its responsibilities, provided there are rationally related benefits accruing to the stockholders. *Unocal*, 493 A.2d at 955. However, such concern for non-stockholder interests is inappropriate when an auction among active bidders is in progress, and the object no longer is to protect or maintain the corporate enterprise but to sell it to the highest bidder.

Revlon also contended that by Gilbert v. El Paso Co., Del. Ch., 490 A.2d 1050, 1054-55 (1984), it had contractual and good faith obligations to consider the noteholders. However, any such duties are limited to the principle that one may not interfere with contractual relationships by improper actions. Here, the rights of the noteholders were fixed by agreement, and there is nothing of substance to suggest that any of those terms were violated. The Notes covenants specifically contemplated a waiver to permit sale of the company at a fair price. The Notes were accepted by the holders on that basis, including the risk of an adverse market effect stemming from a waiver. Thus, nothing remained for Revlon to legitimately protect, and no rationally related benefit thereby accrued to the stockholders. Under such circumstances we must conclude that the merger agreement with Forstmann was unreasonable in relation to the threat posed.

A lock-up is not per se illegal under Delaware law. Its use has been approved in an earlier case. Thompson v. Enstar Corp., Del. Ch., [1984 WL 8240] (1984). Such options can entice other bidders to enter a contest for control of the corporation, creating an auction for the company and maximizing shareholder profit. Current economic conditions in the takeover market are such that a "white knight" like Forstmann might only enter the bidding for the target company if it receives some form of compensation to cover the risks and costs involved. However, while those lock-ups which draw bidders into the battle benefit shareholders, similar measures which end an active auction and foreclose further bidding operate to the shareholders' detriment. . . .

The Forstmann option had a . . . destructive effect on the auction process. Forstmann had already been drawn into the contest on a preferred basis, so the result of the lock-up was not to foster bidding, but to destroy it. The board's stated reasons for approving the transactions were: (1) better financing, (2) noteholder protection, and (3) higher price. As the Court of Chancery found, and we agree, any distinctions between the rival bidders' methods of financing the proposal were nominal at best, and such a consideration has little or no significance in a cash offer for any and all shares. The principal object, contrary to the board's duty of care, appears to have been protection of the noteholders over the shareholders' interests.

While Forstmann's $57.25 offer was objectively higher than Pantry Pride's $56.25 bid, the margin of superiority is less when the Forstmann price is adjusted for the time value of money. In reality, the Revlon board ended the auction in return for very little actual improvement in the final bid. The principal benefit went to the directors, who avoided personal liability to a class of creditors to whom the board owed no further duty under the circumstances. Thus, when a board ends an intense bidding contest on an insubstantial basis, and where a significant by-product of that action is to protect the directors against a perceived threat of personal liability for consequences stemming from the adoption of previous defensive measures, the action cannot withstand the enhanced scrutiny which *Unocal* requires of director conduct.

In addition to the lock-up option, the Court of Chancery enjoined the no-shop provision as part of the attempt to foreclose further bidding by Pantry Pride. The no-shop provision, like the lock-up option, while not per se illegal, is impermissible under the *Unocal* standards when a board's primary duty becomes that of an auctioneer responsible for selling the company to the highest bidder. The agreement to negotiate only with Forstmann ended rather than intensified the board's involvement in the bidding contest.

It is ironic that the parties even considered a no-shop agreement when Revlon had dealt preferentially, and almost exclusively, with Forstmann throughout the contest. After the directors authorized management to negotiate with other parties, Forstmann was given every negotiating advantage that Pantry Pride had been denied: cooperation from management, access to financial data, and the exclusive opportunity to present merger proposals directly to the board of directors. Favoritism for a white knight to the total exclusion of a hostile bidder might be justifiable when the latter's offer adversely affects shareholder interests, but when bidders make relatively similar offers, or dissolution of the company becomes inevitable, the directors cannot fulfill their enhanced *Unocal* duties by playing favorites with the contending factions. Market forces must be allowed to operate freely to bring the target's shareholders the best price available for their equity. Thus, as the trial court ruled, the shareholders' interests necessitated that the board remain free to negotiate in the fulfillment of that duty. . . .

V.

In conclusion, the Revlon board was confronted with a situation not uncommon in the current wave of corporate takeovers. A hostile and determined bidder sought the company at a price the board was convinced was inadequate. The initial defensive tactics worked to the benefit of the shareholders, and thus the board was able to sustain its *Unocal* burdens in justifying those measures. However, in granting an asset option lock-up to Forstmann, we must conclude that under all the circumstances the directors allowed considerations other than the maximization of shareholder profit to affect their judgment, and followed a course that ended the auction for Revlon, absent court intervention, to the ultimate detriment of its shareholders. No such defensive measure can be sustained when it represents a breach of the directors' fundamental duty of care. In that context the board's action is not entitled to the deference accorded it by the business judgment rule. The measures were properly enjoined. The decision of the Court of Chancery, therefore, is
Affirmed.

PARAMOUNT COMMUNICATIONS, INC. v. TIME, INC.

571 A.2d 1140
Supreme Court of Delaware
March 9, 1990

HORSEY, Justice.

Paramount Communications, Inc. ("Paramount") and two other groups of plaintiffs ("Shareholder Plaintiffs"), shareholders of Time Incorporated ("Time"), a Delaware corporation, separately filed suits in the Delaware Court of Chancery seeking a preliminary injunction to halt Time's tender offer for 51% of Warner Communication, Inc.'s ("Warner") outstanding shares at $70 cash per share. The court below consolidated the cases and, following the development of an extensive record, after discovery and an evidentiary hearing, denied plaintiffs' motion. . . . On the same day, plaintiffs filed in this Court an interlocutory appeal, which we accepted on an expedited basis. . . . The principal ground for reversal, asserted by all plaintiffs, is that Paramount's June 7, 1989 uninvited all-cash, all-shares, "fully negotiable" (though conditional) tender offer for Time triggered duties under Unocal Corp. v. Mesa Petroleum Co., Del. Supr., 493 A.2d 946 (1985), and that Time's board of directors, in responding to Paramount's offer, breached those duties. As a consequence, plaintiffs argue that in our review of the Time board's decision of June 16, 1989 to enter into a revised merger agreement with Warner, Time is not entitled to the benefit and protection of the business judgment rule.

Shareholder Plaintiffs also assert a claim based on Revlon v. MacAndrews & Forbes Holdings, Inc., Del. Supr., 506 A.2d 173 (1986). They argue that the original Time-Warner merger agreement of March 4, 1989 resulted in a change of control which effectively put Time up for sale, thereby triggering *Revlon* duties. Those plaintiffs argue that Time's board breached its *Revlon* duties by failing, in the face of the change of control, to maximize shareholder value in the immediate term.

Applying our standard of review, we affirm the Chancellor's ultimate finding and conclusion under *Unocal*. . . .

I

Time is a Delaware corporation with its principal offices in New York City. Time's traditional business is publication of magazines and books; however, Time also provides pay television programming through its Home Box Office, Inc. and Cinemax subsidiaries. In addition, Time owns and operates cable television franchises through its subsidiary, American Television and Communication Corporation. During the relevant time period, Time's board consisted of sixteen directors. Twelve of the directors were "outside," nonemployee directors. . . .

As early as 1983 and 1984, Time's executive board began considering expanding Time's operations into the entertainment industry. In 1987, Time established a special committee of executives to consider and propose corporate strategies for the 1990s. The consensus of the committee was that Time should move ahead in the area of ownership and creation of video programming. This expansion, as the Chancellor noted, was predicated upon two considerations:

first, Time's desire to have greater control, in terms of quality and price, over the film products delivered by way of its cable network and franchises; and second, Time's concern over the increasing globalization of the world economy. Some of Time's outside directors, especially Luce and Temple, had opposed this move as a threat to the editorial integrity and journalistic focus of Time.[4] Despite this concern, the board recognized that a vertically integrated video enterprise to complement Time's existing HBO and cable networks would better enable it to compete on a global basis.

In late spring of 1987, a meeting took place between Steve Ross, CEO of Warner Brothers, and Nicholas, [CEO] of Time. Ross and Nicholas discussed the possibility of a joint venture between the two companies through the creation of a jointly-owned cable company. Time would contribute its cable system and HBO. Warner would contribute its cable system and provide access to Warner Brothers Studio. The resulting venture would be a larger, more efficient cable network, able to produce and distribute its own movies on a worldwide basis. Ultimately the parties abandoned this plan, determining that it was impractical for several reasons, chief among them being tax considerations.

On August 11, 1987, Gerald M. Levin, Time's vice chairman and chief strategist, wrote J. Richard Munro a confidential memorandum in which he strongly recommended a strategic consolidation with Warner. In June 1988, Nicholas and Munro sent to each outside director a copy of the "comprehensive long-term planning document" prepared by the committee of Time executives that had been examining strategies for the 1990s. The memo included reference to and a description of Warner as a potential acquisition candidate.

Thereafter, Munro and Nicholas held meetings with Time's outside directors to discuss, generally, long-term strategies for Time and, specifically, a combination with Warner. Nearly a year later, Time's board reached the point of serious discussion of the "nuts and bolts" of a consolidation with an entertainment company. On July 21, 1988, Time's board met, with all outside directors present. The meeting's purpose was to consider Time's expansion into the entertainment industry on a global scale. Management presented the board with a profile of various entertainment companies in addition to Warner, including Disney, 20th Century Fox, Universal, and Paramount.

Without any definitive decision on choice of a company, the board approved in principle a strategic plan for Time's expansion. The board gave management the "go-ahead" to continue discussions with Warner concerning the possibility of a merger. With the exception of Temple and Luce, most of the outside directors agreed that a merger involving expansion into the entertainment field promised great growth opportunity for Time. Temple and Luce remained unenthusiastic about Time's entry into the entertainment field. The board's consensus was that a merger of Time and Warner was feasible, but only if Time controlled the board of the resulting corporation and thereby preserved a management committed to Time's journalistic integrity. To accomplish this goal,

---

4. The primary concern of Time's outside directors was the preservation of the "Time Culture." They believed that Time had become recognized in this country as an institution built upon a foundation of journalistic integrity. Time's management made a studious effort to refrain from involvement in Time's editorial policy. Several of Time's outside directors feared that a merger with an entertainment company would divert Time's focus from news journalism and threaten the Time Culture.

the board stressed the importance of carefully defining in advance the corporate governance provisions that would control the resulting entity. Some board members expressed concern over whether such a business combination would place Time "*in play*." The board discussed the wisdom of adopting further defensive measures to lessen such a possibility.[5]

Of a wide range of companies considered by Time's board as possible merger candidates, Warner Brothers, Paramount, Columbia, M.C.A., Fox, MGM, Disney, and Orion, the board, in July 1988, concluded that Warner was the superior candidate for a consolidation. Warner stood out on a number of counts. Warner had just acquired Lorimar and its film studios. Time-Warner could make movies and television shows for use on HBO. Warner had an international distribution system, which Time could use to sell films, videos, books and magazines. Warner was a giant in the music and recording business, an area into which Time wanted to expand. None of the other companies considered had the musical clout of Warner. Time and Warner's cable systems were compatible and could be easily integrated; none of the other companies considered presented such a compatible cable partner. Together, Time and Warner would control half of New York City's cable system; Warner had cable systems in Brooklyn and Queens; and Time controlled cable systems in Manhattan and Queens. Warner's publishing company would integrate well with Time's established publishing company. Time sells hardcover books and magazines, and Warner sells softcover books and comics. Time-Warner could sell all of these publications and Warner's videos by using Time's direct mailing network and Warner's international distribution system. Time's network could be used to promote and merchandise Warner's movies.

In August 1988, Levin, Nicholas, and Munro, acting on instructions from Time's board, continued to explore a business combination with Warner. By letter dated August 4, 1988, management informed the outside directors of proposed corporate governance provisions to be discussed with Warner. The provisions incorporated the recommendations of several of Time's outside directors.

From the outset, Time's board favored an all-cash or cash and securities acquisition of Warner as the basis for consolidation. Bruce Wasserstein, Time's financial advisor, also favored an outright purchase of Warner. However, Steve Ross, Warner's CEO, was adamant that a business combination was only practicable on a stock-for-stock basis. Warner insisted on a stock swap in order to preserve its shareholders' equity in the resulting corporation. Time's officers, on the other hand, made it abundantly clear that Time would be the acquiring corporation and that Time would control the resulting board. Time refused to permit itself to be cast as the "acquired" company.

Eventually Time acquiesced in Warner's insistence on a stock-for-stock deal, but talks broke down over corporate governance issues. Time wanted Ross' position as a co-CEO to be temporary and wanted Ross to retire in five years. Ross, however, refused to set a time for his retirement and viewed Time's proposal as indicating a lack of confidence in his leadership. Warner considered it

---

5. Time had in place a panoply of defensive devices, including a staggered board, a "poison pill" preferred stock rights plan triggered by an acquisition of 15% of the company, a fifty-day notice period for shareholder motions, and restrictions on shareholders' ability to call a meeting or act by consent.

vital that their executives and creative staff not perceive Warner as selling out to Time. Time's request of a guarantee that Time would dominate the CEO succession was objected to as inconsistent with the concept of a Time-Warner merger "of equals." Negotiations ended when the parties reached an impasse. Time's board refused to compromise on its position on corporate governance. Time, and particularly its outside directors, viewed the corporate governance provisions as critical for preserving the "Time Culture" through a pro-Time management at the top.

Throughout the fall of 1988 Time pursued its plan of expansion into the entertainment field; Time held informal discussions with several companies, including Paramount. Capital Cities/ABC approached Time to propose a merger. Talks terminated, however, when Capital Cities/ABC suggested that it was interested in purchasing Time or in controlling the resulting board. Time steadfastly maintained it was not placing itself up for sale.

Warner and Time resumed negotiations in January 1989. The catalyst for the resumption of talks was a private dinner between Steve Ross and Time outside director, Michael Dingman. Dingman was able to convince Ross that the transitional nature of the proposed co-CEO arrangement did not reflect a lack of confidence in Ross. Ross agreed that this course was best for the company and a meeting between Ross and Munro resulted. Ross agreed to retire in five years and let Nicholas succeed him. Negotiations resumed and many of the details of the original stock-for-stock exchange agreement remained intact. In addition, Time's senior management agreed to long-term contracts.

Time insider directors Levin and Nicholas met with Warner's financial advisors to decide upon a stock exchange ratio. Time's board had recognized the potential need to pay a premium in the stock ratio in exchange for dictating the governing arrangement of the new Time-Warner. Levin and outside director Finkelstein were the primary proponents of paying a premium to protect the "Time Culture." The board discussed premium rates of 10%, 15% and 20%. Wasserstein also suggested paying a premium for Warner due to Warner's rapid growth rate. The market exchange ratio of Time stock for Warner stock was .38 in favor of Warner. Warner's financial advisors informed its board that any exchange rate over .400 was a fair deal and any exchange rate over .450 was "one hell of a deal." The parties ultimately agreed upon an exchange rate favoring Warner of .465. On that basis, Warner stockholders would have owned approximately 62% of the common stock of Time-Warner.

On March 3, 1989, Time's board, with all but one director in attendance, met and unanimously approved the stock-for-stock merger with Warner. Warner's board likewise approved the merger. The agreement called for Warner to be merged into a wholly-owned Time subsidiary with Warner becoming the surviving corporation. The common stock of Warner would then be converted into common stock of Time at the agreed upon ratio. Thereafter, the name of Time would be changed to Time-Warner, Inc.

The rules of the New York Stock Exchange required that Time's issuance of shares to effectuate the merger be approved by a vote of Time's stockholders. The Delaware General Corporation Law required approval of the merger by a majority of the Warner stockholders. Delaware law did not require any vote by Time stockholders. The Chancellor concluded that the agreement was the product of "an arms-length negotiation between two parties seeking individual advantage through mutual action."

The resulting company would have a 24-member board, with 12 members representing each corporation. The company would have co-CEO's, at first Ross and Munro, then Ross and Nicholas, and finally, after Ross' retirement, by Nicholas alone. The board would create an editorial committee with a majority of members representing Time. A similar entertainment committee would be controlled by Warner board members. A two-thirds supermajority vote was required to alter CEO successions but an earlier proposal to have supermajority protection for the editorial committee was abandoned. Warner's board suggested raising the compensation levels for Time's senior management under the new corporation. Warner's management, as with most entertainment executives, received higher salaries than comparable executives in news journalism. Time's board, however, rejected Warner's proposal to equalize the salaries of the two management teams.

At its March 3, 1989 meeting, Time's board adopted several defensive tactics. Time entered an automatic share exchange agreement with Warner. Time would receive 17,292,747 shares of Warner's outstanding common stock (9.4%) and Warner would receive 7,080,016 shares of Time's outstanding common stock (11.1%). Either party could trigger the exchange. Time sought out and paid for "confidence" letters from various banks with which it did business. In these letters, the banks promised not to finance any third-party attempt to acquire Time. Time argues these agreements served only to preserve the confidential relationship between itself and the banks. The Chancellor found these agreements to be inconsequential and futile attempts to "dry up" money for a hostile takeover. Time also agreed to a "no-shop" clause, preventing Time from considering any other consolidation proposal, thus relinquishing its power to consider other proposals, regardless of their merits. Time did so at Warner's insistence. Warner did not want to be left "on the auction block" for an unfriendly suitor, if Time were to withdraw from the deal.

Time's board simultaneously established a special committee of outside directors, Finkelstein, Kearns, and Opel, to oversee the merger. The committee's assignment was to resolve any impediments that might arise in the course of working out the details of the merger and its consummation.

Time representatives lauded the lack of debt to the United States Senate and to the President of the United States. Public reaction to the announcement of the merger was positive. Time-Warner would be a media colossus with international scope. The board scheduled the stockholder vote for June 23; and a May 1 record date was set. On May 24, 1989, Time sent out extensive proxy statements to the stockholders regarding the approval vote on the merger. In the meantime, with the merger proceeding without impediment, the special committee had concluded, shortly after its creation, that it was not necessary either to retain independent consultants, legal or financial, or even to meet. Time's board was unanimously in favor of the proposed merger with Warner; and, by the end of May, the Time-Warner merger appeared to be an accomplished fact.

On June 7, 1989, these wishful assumptions were shattered by Paramount's surprising announcement of its all-cash offer to purchase all outstanding shares of Time for $175 per share. The following day, June 8, the trading price of

Time's stock rose from $126 to $170 per share. Paramount's offer was said to be "fully negotiable."[8]

Time found Paramount's "fully negotiable" offer to be in fact subject to at least three conditions. First, Time had to terminate its merger agreement and stock exchange agreement with Warner, and remove certain other of its defensive devices, including the redemption of Time's shareholder rights. Second, Paramount had to obtain the required cable franchise transfers from Time in a fashion acceptable to Paramount in its sole discretion. Finally, the offer depended upon a judicial determination that section 203 of the General Corporate Law of Delaware (The Delaware Anti-Takeover Statute) was inapplicable to any Time-Paramount merger. While Paramount's board had been privately advised that it could take months, perhaps over a year, to forge and consummate the deal, Paramount's board publicly proclaimed its ability to close the offer by July 5, 1989. Paramount executives later conceded that none of its directors believed that July 5th was a realistic date to close the transaction.

On June 8, 1989, Time formally responded to Paramount's offer. Time's chairman and CEO, J. Richard Munro, sent an aggressively worded letter to Paramount's CEO, Martin Davis. Munro's letter attacked Davis' personal integrity and called Paramount's offer "smoke and mirrors." Time's nonmanagement directors were not shown the letter before it was sent. However, at a board meeting that same day, all members endorsed management's response as well as the letter's content.

Over the following eight days, Time's board met three times to discuss Paramount's $175 offer. The board viewed Paramount's offer as inadequate and concluded that its proposed merger with Warner was the better course of action. Therefore, the board declined to open any negotiations with Paramount and held steady its course toward a merger with Warner. . . . During the course of their June meetings, Time's outside directors met frequently without management, officers or directors being present. At the request of the outside directors, corporate counsel was present during the board meetings and, from time to time, the management directors were asked to leave the board sessions. During the course of these meetings, Time's financial advisors informed the board that, on an auction basis, Time's per share value was materially higher than Warner's $175 per share offer.[9] After this advice, the board concluded that Paramount's $175 offer was inadequate.

At these June meetings, certain Time directors expressed their concern that Time stockholders would not comprehend the long-term benefits of the Warner merger. Large quantities of Time shares were held by institutional investors. The board feared that even though there appeared to be wide support for the Warner transaction, Paramount's cash premium would be a tempting prospect to these investors. In mid-June, Time sought permission from the New York Stock Exchange to alter its rules and allow the Time-Warner merger to proceed without stockholder approval. Time did so at Warner's insistence. The New

8. Subsequently, it was established that Paramount's board had decided as early as March 1989 to move to acquire Time. However, Paramount management intentionally delayed publicizing its proposal until Time had mailed to its stockholders its Time-Warner merger proposal along with the required proxy statements.
9. Time's advisors estimated the value of Time in a control premium situation to be significantly higher than the value of Time in other than a sale situation.

York Stock Exchange rejected Time's request on June 15; and on that day, the value of Time stock reached $182 per share.

The following day, June 16, Time's board met to take up Paramount's offer. The board's prevailing belief was that Paramount's bid posed a threat to Time's control of its own destiny and retention of the "Time Culture." Even after Time's financial advisors made another presentation of Paramount and its business attributes, Time's board maintained its position that a combination with Warner offered greater potential for Time. Warner provided Time a much desired production capability and an established international marketing chain. Time's advisors suggested various options, including defensive measures. The board considered and rejected the idea of purchasing Paramount in a "Pac Man" defense.[10] The board considered other defenses, including a recapitalization, the acquisition of another company, and a material change in the present capitalization structure or dividend policy. The board determined to retain its same advisors even in light of the changed circumstances. The board rescinded its agreement to pay its advisors a bonus based on the consummation of the Time-Warner merger and agreed to pay a flat fee for any advice rendered. Finally, Time's board formally rejected Paramount's offer.

At the same meeting, Time's board decided to recast its consolidation with Warner into an outright cash and securities acquisition of Warner by Time; and Time so informed Warner. Time accordingly restructured its proposal to acquire Warner as follows: Time would make an immediate all-cash offer for 51% of Warner's outstanding stock at $70 per share. The remaining 49% would be purchased at some later date for a mixture of cash and securities worth $70 per share. To provide the funds required for its outright acquisition of Warner, Time would assume 7-10 billion dollars worth of debt, thus eliminating one of the principal transaction-related benefits of the original merger agreement. Nine billion dollars of the total purchase price would be allocated to the purchase of Warner's goodwill.

Warner agreed but insisted on certain terms. Warner sought a control premium and guarantees that the governance provisions found in the original merger agreement would remain intact. Warner further sought agreements that Time would not employ its poison pill against Warner and that, unless enjoined, Time would be legally bound to complete the transaction. Time's board agreed to these last measures only at the insistence of Warner. For its part, Time was assured of its ability to extend its efforts into production areas and international markets, all the while maintaining the Time identity and culture. The Chancellor found the initial Time-Warner transaction to have been negotiated at arms length and the restructured Time-Warner transaction to have resulted from Paramount's offer and its expected effect on a Time shareholder vote.

On June 23, 1989, Paramount raised its all-cash offer to buy Time's outstanding stock to $200 per share. Paramount still professed that all aspects of the offer were negotiable. Time's board met on June 26, 1989 and formally rejected Paramount's $200 per share second offer. The board reiterated its belief that, despite the $25 increase, the offer was still inadequate. The Time board maintained that the Warner transaction offered a greater long-term value for the

---

10. In a "Pac Man" defense, Time would launch a tender offer for the stock of Paramount, thus consuming its rival. Moran v. Household Intern., Inc., Del. Supr., 500 A.2d 1346, 1350 n.6 (1985).

stockholders and, unlike Paramount's offer, did not pose a threat to Time's survival and its "culture." Paramount then filed this action in the Court of Chancery.

II

The Shareholder Plaintiffs first assert a *Revlon* claim. They contend that the March 4 Time-Warner agreement effectively put Time up for sale, triggering *Revlon* duties, requiring Time's board to enhance short-term shareholder value and to treat all other interested acquirors on an equal basis. The Shareholder Plaintiffs base this argument on two facts: (i) the ultimate Time-Warner exchange ratio of .465 favoring Warner, resulting in Warner shareholders' receipt of 62% of the combined company; and (ii) the subjective intent of Time's directors as evidenced in their statements that the market might perceive the Time-Warner merger as putting Time up "for sale" and their adoption of various defensive measures.

The Shareholder Plaintiffs further contend that Time's directors, in structuring the original merger transaction to be "takeover-proof," triggered *Revlon* duties by foreclosing their shareholders from any prospect of obtaining a control premium. In short, plaintiffs argue that Time's board's decision to merge with Warner imposed a fiduciary duty to maximize immediate share value and not erect unreasonable barriers to further bids. Therefore, they argue, the Chancellor erred in finding: that Paramount's bid for Time did not place Time "for sale"; that Time's transaction with Warner did not result in any transfer of control; and that the combined Time-Warner was not so large as to preclude the possibility of the stockholders of Time-Warner receiving a future control premium.

Paramount asserts only a *Unocal* claim in which the shareholder plaintiffs join. Paramount contends that the Chancellor, in applying the first part of the *Unocal* test, erred in finding that Time's board had reasonable grounds to believe that Paramount posed both a legally cognizable threat to Time shareholders and a danger to Time's corporate policy and effectiveness. Paramount also contests the court's finding that Time's board made a reasonable and objective investigation of Paramount's offer so as to be informed before rejecting it. Paramount further claims that the court erred in applying *Unocal*'s second part in finding Time's response to be "reasonable." Paramount points primarily to the preclusive effect of the revised agreement which denied Time shareholders the opportunity both to vote on the agreement and to respond to Paramount's tender offer. Paramount argues that the underlying motivation of Time's board in adopting these defensive measures was management's desire to perpetuate itself in office.

The Court of Chancery posed the pivotal question presented by this case to be: Under what circumstances must a board of directors abandon an in-place plan of corporate development in order to provide its shareholders with the option to elect and realize an immediate control premium? As applied to this case, the question becomes: Did Time's board, having developed a strategic plan of global expansion to be launched through a business combination with Warner, come under a fiduciary duty to jettison its plan and put the corporation's future in the hands of its shareholders?

While we affirm the result reached by the Chancellor, we think it unwise to place undue emphasis upon long-term versus short-term corporate strategy. Two key predicates underpin our analysis. First, Delaware law imposes on a board of directors the duty to manage the business and affairs of the corporation. 8 Del. C. §141(a). This broad mandate includes a conferred authority to set a corporate course of action, including time frame, designed to enhance corporate profitability. Thus, the question of "long-term" versus "short-term" values is largely irrelevant because directors, generally, are obliged to chart a course for a corporation which is in its best interests without regard to a fixed investment horizon. Second, absent a limited set of circumstances as defined under *Revlon*, a board of directors, while always required to act in an informed manner, is not under any per se duty to maximize shareholder value in the short term, even in the context of a takeover. In our view, the pivotal question presented by this case is: "Did Time, by entering into the proposed merger with Warner, put itself up for sale?" A resolution of that issue through application of *Revlon* has a significant bearing upon the resolution of the derivative *Unocal* issue.

A.

We first take up plaintiffs' principal *Revlon* argument, summarized above. In rejecting this argument, the Chancellor found the original Time-Warner merger agreement not to constitute a "change of control" and concluded that the transaction did not trigger *Revlon* duties. The Chancellor's conclusion is premised on a finding that "[b]efore the merger agreement was signed, control of the corporation existed in a fluid aggregation of unaffiliated shareholders representing a voting majority — in other words, in the market." The Chancellor's findings of fact are supported by the record and his conclusion is correct as a matter of law. However, we premise our rejection of plaintiffs' *Revlon* claim on different grounds, namely, the absence of any substantial evidence to conclude that Time's board, in negotiating with Warner, made the dissolution or break-up of the corporate entity inevitable, as was the case in *Revlon*.

Under Delaware law there are, generally speaking and without excluding other possibilities, two circumstances which may implicate *Revlon* duties. The first, and clearer one, is when a corporation initiates an active bidding process seeking to sell itself or to effect a business reorganization involving a clear break-up of the company. *See, e.g.*, Mills Acquisition Co. v. Macmillan, Inc., Del. Supr., 559 A.2d 1261 (1988). However, *Revlon* duties may also be triggered where, in response to a bidder's offer, a target abandons its long-term strategy and seeks an alternative transaction involving the breakup of the company. Thus, in *Revlon*, when the board responded to Pantry Pride's offer by contemplating a "bust-up" sale of assets in a leveraged acquisition, we imposed upon the board a duty to maximize immediate shareholder value and an obligation to auction the company fairly. If, however, the board's reaction to a hostile tender offer is found to constitute only a defensive response and not an abandonment of the corporation's continued existence, *Revlon* duties are not triggered, though *Unocal* duties attach.

The plaintiffs insist that even though the original Time-Warner agreement may not have worked "an objective change of control," the transaction made a "sale" of Time inevitable. Plaintiffs rely on the subjective intent of Time's board of directors and principally upon certain board members' expressions of concern that the Warner transaction *might* be viewed as effectively putting Time up for sale. Plaintiffs argue that the use of a lock-up agreement, a no-shop clause, and so-called "dry-up" agreements prevented shareholders from obtaining a control premium in the immediate future and thus violated *Revlon*.

We agree with the Chancellor that such evidence is entirely insufficient to invoke *Revlon* duties; and we decline to extend *Revlon*'s application to corporate transactions simply because they might be construed as putting a corporation either "in play" or "up for sale." The adoption of structural safety devices alone does not trigger *Revlon*. Rather, as the Chancellor stated, such devices are properly subject to a *Unocal* analysis.

Finally, we do not find in Time's recasting of its merger agreement with Warner from a share exchange to a share purchase a basis to conclude that Time had either abandoned its strategic plan or made a sale of Time inevitable. The Chancellor found that although the merged Time-Warner company would be large (with a value approaching approximately $30 billion), recent takeover cases have proven that acquisition of the combined company might nonetheless be possible. In re Time Incorporated Shareholder Litigation, Del. Ch., C.A. No. 10670, Allen, C. (July 14, 1989), slip op. at 56. The legal consequence is that *Unocal* alone applies to determine whether the business judgment rule attaches to the revised agreement. . . .

B.

We turn now to plaintiffs' *Unocal* claim. We begin by noting, as did the Chancellor, that our decision does not require us to pass on the wisdom of the board's decision to enter into the original Time-Warner agreement. That is not a court's task. Our task is simply to review the record to determine whether there is sufficient evidence to support the Chancellor's conclusion that the initial Time-Warner agreement was the product of a proper exercise of business judgment.

We have purposely detailed the evidence of the Time board's deliberative approach, beginning in 1983-84, to expand itself. Time's decision in 1988 to combine with Warner was made only after what could be fairly characterized as an exhaustive appraisal of Time's future as a corporation. After concluding in 1983-84 that the corporation must expand to survive, and beyond journalism into entertainment, the board combed the field of available entertainment companies. By 1987 Time had focused upon Warner; by late July 1988 Time's board was convinced that Warner would provide the best "fit" for Time to achieve its strategic objectives. The record attests to the zealousness of Time's executives, fully supported by their directors, in seeing to the preservation of Time's "culture," *i.e.*, its perceived editorial integrity in journalism. We find ample evidence in the record to support the Chancellor's conclusion that the Time board's decision to expand the business of the company through its March 3 merger with Warner was entitled to the protection of the business judgment rule. *See* Aronson v. Lewis, Del. Supr., 473 A.2d 805, 812 (1984).

The Chancellor reached a different conclusion in addressing the Time-Warner transaction as revised three months later. He found that the revised agreement was defense-motivated and designed to avoid the potentially disruptive effect that Paramount's offer would have had on consummation of the proposed merger were it put to a shareholder vote. Thus, the court declined to apply the traditional business judgment rule to the revised transaction and instead analyzed the Time board's June 16 decision under *Unocal*. The court ruled that *Unocal* applied to all director actions taken, following receipt of Paramount's hostile tender offer, that were reasonably determined to be defensive. Clearly that was a correct ruling and no party disputes that ruling.

In *Unocal*, we held that before the business judgment rule is applied to a board's adoption of a defensive measure, the burden will lie with the board to prove (a) reasonable grounds for believing that a danger to corporate policy and effectiveness existed; and (b) that the defensive measure adopted was reasonable in relation to the threat posed. *Unocal*, 493 A.2d 946. Directors satisfy the first part of the *Unocal* test by demonstrating good faith and reasonable investigation. We have repeatedly stated that the refusal to entertain an offer may comport with a valid exercise of a board's business judgment. *See, e.g., Macmillan*, 559 A.2d at 1285 n.35; *Van Gorkom*, 488 A.2d at 881; Pogostin v. Rice, Del. Supr., 480 A.2d 619, 627 (1984).

Unocal involved a two-tier, highly coercive tender offer. In such a case, the threat is obvious: shareholders may be compelled to tender to avoid being treated adversely in the second stage of the transaction. In subsequent cases, the Court of Chancery has suggested that an all-cash, all-shares offer, falling within a range of values that a shareholder might reasonably prefer, cannot constitute a legally recognized "threat" to shareholder interests sufficient to withstand a *Unocal* analysis. AC Acquisitions Corp. v. Anderson, Clayton & Co., Del. Ch., 519 A.2d 103 (1986); *see* Grand Metropolitan, PLC v. Pillsbury Co., Del. Ch., 558 A.2d 1049 (1988); City Capital Associates v. Interco, Inc., Del. Ch., 551 A.2d 787 (1988). In those cases, the Court of Chancery determined that whatever threat existed related only to the shareholders and only to price and not to the corporation.

From those decisions by our Court of Chancery, Paramount and the individual plaintiffs extrapolate a rule of law that an all-cash, all-shares offer with values reasonably in the range of acceptable price cannot pose any objective threat to a corporation or its shareholders. Thus, Paramount would have us hold that only if the value of Paramount's offer were determined to be clearly inferior to the value created by management's plan to merge with Warner could the offer be viewed — objectively — as a threat.

Implicit in the plaintiffs' argument is the view that a hostile tender offer can pose only two types of threats: the threat of coercion that results from a two-tier offer promising unequal treatment for nontendering shareholders; and the threat of inadequate value from an all-shares, all-cash offer at a price below what a target board in good faith deems to be the present value of its shares. *See, e.g., Interco*, 551 A.2d at 797; *see also* BNS, Inc. v. Koppers, D. Del., 683 F. Supp. 458 (1988). Since Paramount's offer was all-cash, the only conceivable "threat," plaintiffs argue, was inadequate value. We disapprove of such a narrow and rigid construction of *Unocal*, for the reasons which follow.

Plaintiffs' position represents a fundamental misconception of our standard of review under *Unocal* principally because it would involve the court in substituting its judgment as to what is a "better" deal for that of a corporation's board of directors. . . . The usefulness of *Unocal* as an analytical tool is precisely its flexibility in the face of a variety of fact scenarios. *Unocal* is not intended as an abstract standard; neither is it a structured and mechanistic procedure of appraisal. Thus, we have said that directors may consider, when evaluating the threat posed by a takeover bid, the "inadequacy of the price offered, nature and timing of the offer, questions of illegality, the impact on 'constituencies' other than shareholders . . . the risk of nonconsummation, and the quality of securities being offered in the exchange." 493 A.2d at 955. The open-ended analysis mandated by *Unocal* is not intended to lead to a simple mathematical exercise: that is, of comparing the discounted value of Time-Warner's expected trading price at some future date with Paramount's offer and determining which is the higher. Indeed, in our view, precepts underlying the business judgment rule militate against a court's engaging in the process of attempting to appraise and evaluate the relative merits of a long-term versus a short-term investment goal for shareholders. To engage in such an exercise is a distortion of the *Unocal* process and, in particular, the application of the second part of *Unocal*'s test, discussed below.

In this case, the Time board reasonably determined that inadequate value was not the only legally cognizable threat that Paramount's all-cash, all-shares offer could present. Time's board concluded that Paramount's eleventh hour offer posed other threats. One concern was that Time shareholders might elect to tender into Paramount's cash offer in ignorance or a mistaken belief of the strategic benefit which a business combination with Warner might produce. Moreover, Time viewed the conditions attached to Paramount's offer as introducing a degree of uncertainty that skewed a comparative analysis. Further, the timing of Paramount's offer to follow issuance of Time's proxy notice was viewed as arguably designed to upset, if not confuse, the Time stockholders' vote. Given this record evidence, we cannot conclude that the Time board's decision of June 6 that Paramount's offer posed a threat to corporate policy and effectiveness was lacking in good faith or dominated by motives of either entrenchment or self-interest.

Paramount also contends that the Time board had not duly investigated Paramount's offer. Therefore, Paramount argues, Time was unable to make an informed decision that the offer posed a threat to Time's corporate policy. Although the Chancellor did not address this issue directly, his findings of fact do detail Time's exploration of the available entertainment companies, including Paramount, before determining that Warner provided the best strategic "fit." In addition, the court found that Time's board rejected Paramount's offer because Paramount did not serve Time's objectives or meet Time's needs. Thus, the record does, in our judgment, demonstrate that Time's board was adequately informed of the potential benefits of a transaction with Paramount. We agree with the Chancellor that the Time board's lengthy pre-June investigation of potential merger candidates, including Paramount, mooted any obligation on Time's part to halt its merger process with Warner to reconsider Paramount. Time's board was under no obligation to negotiate with Paramount. *Unocal*, 493 A.2d at 954-55; *see also Macmillan*, 559 A.2d at 1285 n.35. Time's failure to negotiate cannot be fairly found to have been uninformed. The evidence supporting this finding is materially enhanced by the fact that twelve of Time's sixteen board members were outside independent directors. *Unocal*, 493 A.2d at 955; Moran v. Household Intern., Inc., Del. Supr., 500 A.2d 1346, 1356 (1985).

We turn to the second part of the *Unocal* analysis. The obvious requisite to determining the reasonableness of a defensive action is a clear identification of the nature of the threat. As the Chancellor correctly noted, this "requires an evaluation of the importance of the corporate objective threatened; alternative methods of protecting that objective; impacts of the 'defensive' action, and other relevant factors." In re: Time Incorporated Shareholder Litigation, Del. Ch., 1989 WL 79880 (July 14, 1989). It is not until both parts of the *Unocal* inquiry have been satisfied that the business judgment rule attaches to defensive actions of a board of directors. *Unocal,* 493 A.2d at 954. As applied to the facts of this case, the question is whether the record evidence supports the Court of Chancery's conclusion that the restructuring of the Time-Warner transaction, including the adoption of several preclusive defensive measures, was a *reasonable response* in relation to a perceived threat.

Paramount argues that, assuming its tender offer posed a threat, Time's response was unreasonable in precluding Time's shareholders from accepting the tender offer or receiving a control premium in the immediately foreseeable future. Once again, the contention stems, we believe, from a fundamental mis-understanding of where the power of corporate governance lies. Delaware law confers the management of the corporate enterprise to the stockholders' duly elected board representatives. 8 Del. C. §141(a). The fiduciary duty to manage a corporate enterprise includes the selection of a time frame for achievement of corporate goals. That duty may not be delegated to the stockholders. *Van Gorkom,* 488 A.2d at 873. Directors are not obliged to abandon a deliberately conceived corporate plan for a short-term shareholder profit unless there is clearly no basis to sustain the corporate strategy. *See, e.g., Revlon,* 506 A.2d 173.

Although the Chancellor blurred somewhat the discrete analyses required under *Unocal,* he did conclude that Time's board reasonably perceived Paramount's offer to be a significant threat to the planned Time-Warner merger and that Time's response was not "overly broad." We have found that even in light of a valid threat, management actions that are coercive in nature or force upon shareholders a management-sponsored alternative to a hostile offer may be struck down as unreasonable and nonproportionate responses. *Macmillan,* 559 A.2d 1261; *AC Acquisitions Corp.,* 519 A.2d 103.

Here, on the record facts, the Chancellor found that Time's responsive action to Paramount's tender offer was not aimed at "cramming down" on its share-holders a management-sponsored alternative, but rather had as its goal the carrying forward of a pre-existing transaction in an altered form. Thus, the response was reasonably related to the threat. The Chancellor noted that the revised agreement and its accompanying safety devices did not preclude Paramount from making an offer for the combined Time-Warner company or from changing the conditions of its offer so as not to make the offer depen-dent upon the nullification of the Time-Warner agreement. Thus, the response was proportionate. We affirm the Chancellor's rulings as clearly supported by the record. Finally, we note that although Time was required, as a result of Paramount's hostile offer, to incur a heavy debt to finance its acquisition of Warner, that fact alone does not render the board's decision unreasonable so long as the directors could reasonably perceive the debt load not to be so injurious to the corporation as to jeopardize its well being.

C. CONCLUSION

Applying the test for grant or denial of preliminary injunctive relief, we find plaintiffs failed to establish a reasonable likelihood of ultimate success on the merits. Therefore, we AFFIRM.

Problem 15-3

One of the unresolved interpretive issues concerning Paramount v. Time and its progeny is whether *Paramount* means that a board can "just say no" in the face of an all-cash for all-shares tender offer and refuse to redeem the poison pill, essentially putting the bidder to the time and expense of a proxy contest; or whether there are fiduciary duty limits on the board's refusal.

Consider the facts of the following recent case:

Wallace Computer Services is a computer services and supply company whose major new product is an advanced computer system that can provide multiple versions of business forms for businesses with many branch offices. The company is incorporated in Delaware. It has a classified board and a poison pill. Moore Computer is a Canadian company that prints and delivers business forms. In February 1995 Moore Computer incorporated a subsidiary in New York for the purpose of making a tender offer for all of the outstanding shares of Wallace stock.

After Moore's "friendly" approach and suggestion of a business combination were rebuffed, Moore announced its intention to commence an all-cash tender offer at $56 for all outstanding shares of Wallace common stock, conditioned on (a) the valid tender of a majority of all outstanding shares of Wallace common stock, on a fully diluted basis as of the date of purchase; and (b) the Wallace board redeeming Wallace's poison pill. This price represented a 27 percent premium above the market price of the shares.

Upon Moore's announcement, Wallace engaged Goldman Sachs to advise it on the tender offer price. Goldman Sachs reviewed both publicly and privately available financial data and interviewed top executives and operations executives at Wallace. Based on that analysis, it concluded that the tender offer price was inadequate. In part, this conclusion was based on the fact that Wallace had achieved record financial results in the prior fiscal year and quarter, which it believed was just the beginning of its receiving the benefits of its capital expenditure plan for a new computer system. Goldman Sachs also believed that a reorganization or recapitalization plan that Wallace could adopt would produce current value to the shareholders that could exceed $56 per share.

Meanwhile, nearly 75 percent of Wallace shareholders had tendered into the offer. Nonetheless, the board determined the offer was inadequate and refused to redeem the pill. May the board "just say no" under these circumstances?

PARAMOUNT COMMUNICATIONS INC. v. QVC NETWORK INC.
637 A.2d 34
Supreme Court of Delaware
December 9, 1993

VEASEY, Chief Justice.

In this appeal we review an order of the Court of Chancery dated November 24, 1993 (the "November 24 Order"), preliminarily enjoining certain defensive measures designed to facilitate a so-called strategic alliance between Viacom Inc. ("Viacom") and Paramount Communications Inc. ("Paramount") approved by the board of directors of Paramount (the "Paramount Board" or the "Paramount directors") and to thwart an unsolicited, more valuable, tender offer by QVC Network Inc. ("QVC"). In affirming, we hold that the sale of control in this case, which is at the heart of the proposed strategic alliance, implicates enhanced judicial scrutiny of the conduct of the Paramount Board under Unocal Corp. v. Mesa Petroleum Co., Del. Supr., 493 A.2d 946 (1985), and Revlon, Inc. v. MacAndrews & Forbes Holdings, Inc., Del. Supr., 506 A.2d 173 (1986). We further hold that the conduct of the Paramount Board was not reasonable as to process or result.

QVC and certain stockholders of Paramount commenced separate actions (later consolidated) in the Court of Chancery seeking preliminary and permanent injunctive relief against Paramount, certain members of the Paramount Board, and Viacom. This action arises out of a proposed acquisition of Paramount by Viacom through a tender offer followed by a second-step merger (the "Paramount-Viacom transaction"), and a competing unsolicited tender offer by QVC. The Court of Chancery granted a preliminary injunction. QVC Network, Inc. v. Paramount Communications Inc., Del. Ch., 635 A.2d 1245, Jacobs, V.C. (1993), (the "Court of Chancery Opinion"). We affirmed by order dated December 9, 1993. Paramount Communications Inc. v. QVC Network Inc., Del. Supr., Nos. 427 and 428, 1993, 637 A.2d 828, Veasey, C.J. (Dec. 9, 1993) (the "December 9 Order").

The Court of Chancery found that the Paramount directors violated their fiduciary duties by favoring the Paramount-Viacom transaction over the more valuable unsolicited offer of QVC. The Court of Chancery preliminarily enjoined Paramount and the individual defendants (the "Paramount defendants") from amending or modifying Paramount's stockholder rights agreement (the "Rights Agreement"), including the redemption of the Rights, or taking other action to facilitate the consummation of the pending tender offer by Viacom or any proposed second-step merger, including the Merger Agreement between Paramount and Viacom dated September 12, 1993 (the "Original Merger Agreement"), as amended on October 24, 1993 (the "Amended Merger Agreement"). Viacom and the Paramount defendants were enjoined from taking any action to exercise any provision of the Stock Option Agreement between Paramount and Viacom dated September 12, 1993 (the "Stock Option Agreement"), as amended on October 24, 1993. The Court of Chancery did not grant preliminary injunctive relief as to the termination fee provided for the benefit of Viacom in Section 8.05 of the Original Merger Agreement and the Amended Merger Agreement (the "Termination Fee").

Under the circumstances of this case, the pending sale of control implicated in the Paramount-Viacom transaction required the Paramount Board to act on an informed basis to secure the best value reasonably available to the stockholders. Since we agree with the Court of Chancery that the Paramount directors violated their fiduciary duties, we have AFFIRMED the entry of the order of the Vice Chancellor granting the preliminary injunction and have REMANDED these proceedings to the Court of Chancery for proceedings consistent herewith. . . .

I. FACTS

The Court of Chancery Opinion contains a detailed recitation of its factual findings in this matter. Court of Chancery Opinion, 635 A.2d 1245, 1246-1259. Only a brief summary of the facts is necessary for purposes of this opinion. The following summary is drawn from the findings of fact set forth in the Court of Chancery Opinion and our independent review of the record.

Paramount is a Delaware corporation with its principal offices in New York City. Approximately 118 million shares of Paramount's common stock are outstanding and traded on the New York Stock Exchange. The majority of Paramount's stock is publicly held by numerous unaffiliated investors. Paramount owns and operates a diverse group of entertainment businesses, including motion picture and television studios, book publishers, professional sports teams, and amusement parks.

There are 15 persons serving on the Paramount Board. Four directors are officer-employees of Paramount: Martin S. Davis ("Davis"), Paramount's Chairman and Chief Executive Officer since 1983; Donald Oresman ("Oresman"), Executive Vice-President, Chief Administrative Officer, and General Counsel; Stanley R. Jaffe, President and Chief Operating Officer; and Ronald L. Nelson, Executive Vice President and Chief Financial Officer. Paramount's 11 outside directors are distinguished and experienced business persons who are present or former senior executives of public corporations or financial institutions.

Viacom is a Delaware corporation with its headquarters in Massachusetts. Viacom is controlled by Sumner M. Redstone ("Redstone"), its Chairman and Chief Executive Officer, who owns indirectly approximately 85.2 percent of Viacom's voting Class A stock and approximately 69.2 percent of Viacom's nonvoting Class B stock through National Amusements, Inc. ("NAI"), an entity 91.7 percent owned by Redstone. Viacom has a wide range of entertainment operations, including a number of well-known cable television channels such as MTV, Nickelodeon, Showtime, and The Movie Channel. Viacom's equity co-investors in the Paramount-Viacom transaction include NYNEX Corporation and Blockbuster Entertainment Corporation.

QVC is a Delaware corporation with its headquarters in West Chester, Pennsylvania. QVC has several large stockholders, including Liberty Media Corporation, Comcast Corporation, Advance Publications, Inc., and Cox Enterprises Inc. Barry Diller ("Diller"), the Chairman and Chief Executive Officer of QVC, is also a substantial stockholder. QVC sells a variety of merchandise through a televised shopping channel. QVC has several equity co-investors in its proposed combination with Paramount including BellSouth Corporation and Comcast Corporation.

Beginning in the late 1980s, Paramount investigated the possibility of acquiring or merging with other companies in the entertainment, media, or communications industry. Paramount considered such transactions to be desirable, and perhaps necessary, in order to keep pace with competitors in the rapidly evolving field of entertainment and communications. Consistent with its goal of strategic expansion, Paramount made a tender offer for Time Inc. in 1989, but was ultimately unsuccessful. *See* Paramount Communications, Inc. v. Time Inc., Del. Supr., 571 A.2d 1140 (1990) (*"Time-Warner"*).

Although Paramount had considered a possible combination of Paramount and Viacom as early as 1990, recent efforts to explore such a transaction began at a dinner meeting between Redstone and Davis on April 20, 1993. Robert Greenhill ("Greenhill"), Chairman of Smith Barney Shearson Inc. ("Smith Barney"), attended and helped facilitate this meeting. After several more meetings between Redstone and Davis, serious negotiations began taking place in early July.

It was tentatively agreed that Davis would be the chief executive officer and Redstone would be the controlling stockholder of the combined company, but the parties could not reach agreement on the merger price and the terms of a stock option to be granted to Viacom. With respect to price, Viacom offered a package of cash and stock (primarily Viacom Class B nonvoting stock) with a market value of approximately $61 per share, but Paramount wanted at least $70 per share.

Shortly after negotiations broke down in July 1993, two notable events occurred. First, Davis apparently learned of QVC's potential interest in Paramount, and told Diller over lunch on July 21, 1993, that Paramount was not for sale. Second, the market value of Viacom's Class B nonvoting stock increased from $46.875 on July 6 to $57.25 on August 20. QVC claims (and Viacom disputes) that this price increase was caused by open market purchases of such stock by Redstone or entities controlled by him.

On August 20, 1993, discussions between Paramount and Viacom resumed when Greenhill arranged another meeting between Davis and Redstone. After a short hiatus, the parties negotiated in earnest in early September, and performed due diligence with the assistance of their financial advisors, Lazard Freres & Co. ("Lazard") for Paramount and Smith Barney for Viacom. On September 9, 1993, the Paramount Board was informed about the status of the negotiations and was provided information by Lazard, including an analysis of the proposed transaction.

On September 12, 1993, the Paramount Board met again and unanimously approved the Original Merger Agreement whereby Paramount would merge with and into Viacom. The terms of the merger provided that each share of Paramount common stock would be converted into 0.10 shares of Viacom Class A voting stock, 0.90 shares of Viacom Class B nonvoting stock, and $9.10 in cash. In addition, the Paramount Board agreed to amend its "poison pill" Rights Agreement to exempt the proposed merger with Viacom. The Original Merger Agreement also contained several provisions designed to make it more difficult for a potential competing bid to succeed. We focus, as did the Court of Chancery, on three of these defensive provisions: a "no-shop" provision (the "No-Shop Provision"), the Termination Fee, and the Stock Option Agreement.

First, under the No-Shop Provision, the Paramount Board agreed that Paramount would not solicit, encourage, discuss, negotiate, or endorse any competing transaction unless: (a) a third party "makes an unsolicited written, bona fide proposal, which is not subject to any material contingencies relating to financing"; and (b) the Paramount Board determines that discussions or negotiations with the third party are necessary for the Paramount Board to comply with its fiduciary duties.

Second, under the Termination Fee provision, Viacom would receive a $100 million termination fee if: (a) Paramount terminated the Original Merger Agreement because of a competing transaction; (b) Paramount's stockholders did not approve the merger; or (c) the Paramount Board recommended a competing transaction.

The third and most significant deterrent device was the Stock Option Agreement, which granted to Viacom an option to purchase approximately 19.9 percent (23,699,000 shares) of Paramount's outstanding common stock at $69.14 per share if any of the triggering events for the Termination Fee occurred. In addition to the customary terms that are normally associated with a stock option, the Stock Option Agreement contained two provisions that were both unusual and highly beneficial to Viacom: (a) Viacom was permitted to pay for the shares with a senior subordinated note of questionable marketability instead of cash, thereby avoiding the need to raise the $1.6 billion purchase price (the "Note Feature"); and (b) Viacom could elect to require Paramount to pay Viacom in cash a sum equal to the difference between the purchase price and the market price of Paramount's stock (the "Put Feature"). Because the Stock Option Agreement was not "capped" to limit its maximum dollar value, it had the potential to reach (and in this case did reach) unreasonable levels.

After the execution of the Original Merger Agreement and the Stock Option Agreement on September 12, 1993, Paramount and Viacom announced their proposed merger. In a number of public statements, the parties indicated that the pending transaction was a virtual certainty. Redstone described it as a "marriage" that would "never be torn asunder" and stated that only a "nuclear attack" could break the deal. Redstone also called Diller and John Malone of Tele-Communications Inc., a major stockholder of QVC, to dissuade them from making a competing bid.

Despite these attempts to discourage a competing bid, Diller sent a letter to Davis on September 20, 1993, proposing a merger in which QVC would acquire Paramount for approximately $80 per share, consisting of 0.893 shares of QVC common stock and $30 in cash. QVC also expressed its eagerness to meet with Paramount to negotiate the details of a transaction. When the Paramount Board met on September 27, it was advised by Davis that the Original Merger Agreement prohibited Paramount from having discussions with QVC (or anyone else) unless certain conditions were satisfied. In particular, QVC had to supply evidence that its proposal was not subject to financing contingencies. The Paramount Board was also provided information from Lazard describing QVC and its proposal.

On October 5, 1993, QVC provided Paramount with evidence of QVC's financing. The Paramount Board then held another meeting on October 11, and decided to authorize management to meet with QVC. Davis also informed the Paramount Board that Booz-Allen & Hamilton ("Booz-Allen"), a management consulting firm, had been retained to assess, *inter alia,* the incremental earnings potential from a Paramount-Viacom merger and a Paramount-QVC merger. Discussions proceeded slowly, however, due to a delay in Paramount signing a confidentiality agreement. In response to Paramount's request for information, QVC provided two binders of documents to Paramount on October 20.

On October 21, 1993, QVC filed this action and publicly announced an $80 cash tender offer for 51 percent of Paramount's outstanding shares (the "QVC tender offer"). Each remaining share of Paramount common stock would be converted into 1.42857 shares of QVC common stock in a second-step merger. The tender offer was conditioned on, among other things, the invalidation of the Stock Option Agreement, which was worth over $200 million by that point.[5] QVC contends that it had to commence a tender offer because of the slow pace of the merger discussions and the need to begin seeking clearance under federal antitrust laws.

Confronted by QVC's hostile bid, which on its face offered over $10 per share more than the consideration provided by the Original Merger Agreement, Viacom realized that it would need to raise its bid in order to remain competitive. Within hours after QVC's tender offer was announced, Viacom entered into discussions with Paramount concerning a revised transaction. These discussions led to serious negotiations concerning a comprehensive amendment to the original Paramount-Viacom transaction. In effect, the opportunity for a "new deal" with Viacom was at hand for the Paramount Board. With the QVC hostile bid offering greater value to the Paramount stockholders, the Paramount Board had considerable leverage with Viacom.

At a special meeting on October 24, 1993, the Paramount Board approved the Amended Merger Agreement and an amendment to the Stock Option Agreement. The Amended Merger Agreement was, however, essentially the same as the Original Merger Agreement, except that it included a few new provisions. One provision related to an $80 per share cash tender offer by Viacom for 51 percent of Paramount's stock, and another changed the merger consideration so that each share of Paramount would be converted into 0.20408 shares of Viacom Class A voting stock, 1.08317 shares of Viacom Class B nonvoting stock, and 0.20408 shares of a new series of Viacom convertible preferred stock. The Amended Merger Agreement also added a provision giving Paramount the right not to amend its Rights Agreement to exempt Viacom if the Paramount Board determined that such an amendment would be inconsistent with its fiduciary duties because another offer constituted a "better alternative." Finally, the Paramount Board was given the power to terminate the Amended Merger Agreement if it withdrew its recommendation of the Viacom transaction or recommended a competing transaction.

Although the Amended Merger Agreement offered more consideration to the Paramount stockholders and somewhat more flexibility to the Paramount Board than did the Original Merger Agreement, the defensive measures designed to make a competing bid more difficult were not removed or modified. In particular, there is no evidence in the record that Paramount sought to use its newly-acquired leverage to eliminate or modify the No-Shop Provision, the Termination Fee, or the Stock Option Agreement when the subject of amending the Original Merger Agreement was on the table.

Viacom's tender offer commenced on October 25, 1993, and QVC's tender offer was formally launched on October 27, 1993. Diller sent a letter to the Paramount Board on October 28 requesting an opportunity to negotiate with Paramount, and Oresman responded the following day by agreeing to meet. The meeting, held on November 1, was not very fruitful, however, after QVC's proposed guidelines for a "fair bidding process" were rejected by Paramount on the ground that "auction procedures" were inappropriate and contrary to Paramount's contractual obligations to Viacom.

On November 6, 1993, Viacom unilaterally raised its tender offer price to $85 per share in cash and offered a comparable increase in the value of the securities

---

5. By November 15, 1993, the value of the Stock Option Agreement had increased to nearly $500 million based on the $90 QVC bid. *See* Court of Chancery Opinion, 635 A.2d 1245, 1271.

being proposed in the second-step merger. At a telephonic meeting held later that day, the Paramount Board agreed to recommend Viacom's higher bid to Paramount's stockholders.

QVC responded to Viacom's higher bid on November 12 by increasing its tender offer to $90 per share and by increasing the securities for its second-step merger by a similar amount. In response to QVC's latest offer, the Paramount Board scheduled a meeting for November 15, 1993. Prior to the meeting, Oresman sent the members of the Paramount Board a document summarizing the "conditions and uncertainties" of QVC's offer. One director testified that this document gave him a very negative impression of the QVC bid.

At its meeting on November 15, 1993, the Paramount Board determined that the new QVC offer was not in the best interests of the stockholders. The purported basis for this conclusion was that QVC's bid was excessively conditional. The Paramount Board did not communicate with QVC regarding the status of the conditions because it believed that the No-Shop Provision prevented such communication in the absence of firm financing. Several Paramount directors also testified that they believed the Viacom transaction would be more advantageous to Paramount's future business prospects than a QVC transaction. Although a number of materials were distributed to the Paramount Board describing the Viacom and QVC transactions, the only quantitative analysis of the consideration to be received by the stockholders under each proposal was based on then-current market prices of the securities involved, not on the anticipated value of such securities at the time when the stockholders would receive them.

The preliminary injunction hearing in this case took place on November 16, 1993. On November 19, Diller wrote to the Paramount Board to inform it that QVC had obtained financing commitments for its tender offer and that there was no antitrust obstacle to the offer. On November 24, 1993, the Court of Chancery issued its decision granting a preliminary injunction in favor of QVC and the plaintiff stockholders. This appeal followed.

II. APPLICABLE PRINCIPLES OF ESTABLISHED DELAWARE LAW

The General Corporation Law of the State of Delaware (the "General Corporation Law") and the decisions of this Court have repeatedly recognized the fundamental principle that the management of the business and affairs of a Delaware corporation is entrusted to its directors, who are the duly elected and authorized representatives of the stockholders. 8 Del. C. §141(a); Aronson v. Lewis, Del. Supr., 473 A.2d 805, 811-12 (1984); Pogostin v. Rice, Del. Supr., 480 A.2d 619, 624 (1984). Under normal circumstances, neither the courts nor the stockholders should interfere with the managerial decisions of the directors. The business judgment rule embodies the deference to which such decisions are entitled. *Aronson*, 473 A.2d at 812.

Nevertheless, there are rare situations which mandate that a court take a more direct and active role in overseeing the decisions made and actions taken by directors. In these situations, a court subjects the directors' conduct to enhanced scrutiny to ensure that it is reasonable. The decisions of this Court have clearly established the circumstances where such enhanced scrutiny will be applied.

E.g., Unocal, 493 A.2d 946; Moran v. Household Int'l, Inc., Del. Supr., 500 A.2d 1346 (1985); *Revlon,* 506 A.2d 173; Mills Acquisition Co. v. Macmillan, Inc., Del. Supr., 559 A.2d 1261 (1989); Gilbert v. El Paso Co., Del. Supr., 575 A.2d 1131 (1990). The case at bar implicates two such circumstances: (1) the approval of a transaction resulting in a sale of control, and (2) the adoption of defensive measures in response to a threat to corporate control.

A. THE SIGNIFICANCE OF A SALE OR CHANGE OF CONTROL

When a majority of a corporation's voting shares are acquired by a single person or entity, or by a cohesive group acting together, there is a significant diminution in the voting power of those who thereby become minority stockholders. Under the statutory framework of the General Corporation Law, many of the most fundamental corporate changes can be implemented only if they are approved by a majority vote of the stockholders. Such actions include elections of directors, amendments to the certificate of incorporation, mergers, consolidations, sales of all or substantially all of the assets of the corporation, and dissolution. 8 Del. C. §§211, 242, 251-258, 263, 271, 275. Because of the overriding importance of voting rights, this Court and the Court of Chancery have consistently acted to protect stockholders from unwarranted interference with such rights.

In the absence of devices protecting the minority stockholders, stockholder votes are likely to become mere formalities where there is a majority stockholder. For example, minority stockholders can be deprived of a continuing equity interest in their corporation by means of a cash-out merger. *Weinberger* [v. UOP, Inc., 457 A.2d 701, 703 (Del. 1983)]. Absent effective protective provisions, minority stockholders must rely for protection solely on the fiduciary duties owed to them by the directors and the majority stockholder, since the minority stockholders have lost the power to influence corporate direction through the ballot. The acquisition of majority status and the consequent privilege of exerting the powers of majority ownership come at a price. That price is usually a control premium which recognizes not only the value of a control block of shares, but also compensates the minority stockholders for their resulting loss of voting power.

In the case before us, the public stockholders (in the aggregate) currently own a majority of Paramount's voting stock. Control of the corporation is not vested in a single person, entity, or group, but vested in the fluid aggregation of unaffiliated stockholders. In the event the Paramount-Viacom transaction is consummated, the public stockholders will receive cash and a minority equity voting position in the surviving corporation. Following such consummation, there will be a controlling stockholder who will have the voting power to: (a) elect directors; (b) cause a break-up of the corporation; (c) merge it with another company; (d) cash-out the public stockholders; (e) amend the certificate of incorporation; (f) sell all or substantially all of the corporate assets; or (g) otherwise alter materially the nature of the corporation and the public stockholders' interests. Irrespective of the present Paramount Board's vision of a long-term strategic alliance with Viacom, the proposed sale of control would provide the new controlling stockholder with the power to alter that vision.

Because of the intended sale of control, the Paramount-Viacom transaction has economic consequences of considerable significance to the Paramount stockholders. Once control has shifted, the current Paramount stockholders will have no leverage in the future to demand another control premium. As a result, the Paramount stockholders are entitled to receive, and should receive, a control premium and/or protective devices of significant value. There being no such protective provisions in the Viacom-Paramount transaction, the Paramount directors had an obligation to take the maximum advantage of the current opportunity to realize for the stockholders the best value reasonably available.

B. THE OBLIGATIONS OF DIRECTORS IN A SALE OR CHANGE OF CONTROL TRANSACTION

The consequences of a sale of control impose special obligations on the directors of a corporation.[13] In particular, they have the obligation of acting reasonably to seek the transaction offering the best value reasonably available to the stockholders. The courts will apply enhanced scrutiny to ensure that the directors have acted reasonably. The obligations of the directors and the enhanced scrutiny of the courts are well-established by the decisions of this Court. The directors' fiduciary duties in a sale of control context are those which generally attach. In short, "the directors must act in accordance with their fundamental duties of care and loyalty." Barkan v. Amsted Indus., Inc., Del. Supr., 567 A.2d 1279, 1286 (1989). As we held in *Macmillan:*

> It is basic to our law that the board of directors has the ultimate responsibility for managing the business and affairs of a corporation. In discharging this function, the directors owe fiduciary duties of care and loyalty to the corporation and its shareholders. *This unremitting obligation extends equally to board conduct in a sale of corporate control.*

559 A.2d at 1280 (emphasis supplied) (citations omitted).

In the sale of control context, the directors must focus on one primary objective — to secure the transaction offering the best value reasonably available for the stockholders — and they must exercise their fiduciary duties to further that end. The decisions of this Court have consistently emphasized this goal. *Revlon,* 506 A.2d at 182 ("The duty of the board . . . [is] the maximization of the company's value at a sale for the stockholders' benefit."); *Macmillan,* 559 A.2d at 1288 ("[I]n a sale of corporate control the responsibility of the directors is to get the highest value reasonably attainable for the shareholders."); *Barkan,* 567 A.2d at 1286 ("[T]he board must act in a neutral manner to encourage the highest possible price for shareholders.").

In pursuing this objective, the directors must be especially diligent. *See* Citron v. Fairchild Camera and Instrument Corp., Del. Supr., 569 A.2d 53, 66

---

13. We express no opinion on any scenario except the actual facts before the Court, and our precise holding herein. Unsolicited tender offers in other contexts may be governed by different precedent. For example, where a potential sale of control by a corporation is not the consequence of a board's action, this Court has recognized the prerogative of a board of directors to resist a third party's unsolicited acquisition proposal or offer. *See Pogostin,* 480 A.2d at 627; *Time-Warner,* 571 A.2d at 1152; Bershad v. Curtiss-Wright Corp., Del. Supr., 535 A.2d 840, 845 (1987); *Macmillan,* 559 A.2d at 1285 n.35. The decision of a board to resist such an acquisition, like all decisions of a properly-functioning board, must be informed, *Unocal,* 493 A.2d at 954-55, and the circumstances of each particular case will determine the steps that a board must take to inform itself, and what other action, if any, is required as a matter of fiduciary duty.

(1989) (discussing "a board's active and direct role in the sale process"). In particular, this Court has stressed the importance of the board being adequately informed in negotiating a sale of control: "The need for adequate information is central to the enlightened evaluation of a transaction that a board must make." *Barkan*, 567 A.2d at 1287. This requirement is consistent with the general principle that "directors have a duty to inform themselves, prior to making a business decision, of all material information reasonably available to them." *Aronson*, 473 A.2d at 812. *See also* Cede & Co. v. Technicolor, Inc., Del. Supr., 634 A.2d 345, 367 (1993); Smith v. Van Gorkom, Del. Supr., 488 A.2d 858, 872 (1985). Moreover, the role of outside, independent directors becomes particularly important because of the magnitude of a sale of control transaction and the possibility, in certain cases, that management may not necessarily be impartial. *See Macmillan*, 559 A.2d at 1285 (requiring "the intense scrutiny and participation of the independent directors").

Barkan teaches some of the methods by which a board can fulfill its obligation to seek the best value reasonably available to the stockholders. 567 A.2d at 1286-87. These methods are designed to determine the existence and viability of possible alternatives. They include conducting an auction, canvassing the market, etc. Delaware law recognizes that there is "no single blueprint" that directors must follow. *Id.* at 1286-87; *Citron*, 569 A.2d at 68; *Macmillan*, 559 A.2d at 1287.

In determining which alternative provides the best value for the stockholders, a board of directors is not limited to considering only the amount of cash involved, and is not required to ignore totally its view of the future value of a strategic alliance. *See Macmillan*, 559 A.2d at 1282 n.29. Instead, the directors should analyze the entire situation and evaluate in a disciplined manner the consideration being offered. Where stock or other non-cash consideration is involved, the board should try to quantify its value, if feasible, to achieve an objective comparison of the alternatives. In addition, the board may assess a variety of practical considerations relating to each alternative, including:

> [an offer's] fairness and feasibility; the proposed or actual financing for the offer, and the consequences of that financing; questions of illegality; . . . the risk of non-consum[m]ation; . . . the bidder's identity, prior background and other business venture experiences; and the bidder's business plans for the corporation and their effects on stockholder interests.

Macmillan, 559 A.2d at 1282 n.29. These considerations are important because the selection of one alternative may permanently foreclose other opportunities. While the assessment of these factors may be complex, the board's goal is straightforward: Having informed themselves of all material information reasonably available, the directors must decide which alternative is most likely to offer the best value reasonably available to the stockholders.

C. ENHANCED JUDICIAL SCRUTINY OF A SALE OR CHANGE OF CONTROL TRANSACTION

Board action in the circumstances presented here is subject to enhanced scrutiny. Such scrutiny is mandated by: (a) the threatened diminution of the current stockholders' voting power; (b) the fact that an asset belonging to public stockholders (a control premium) is being sold and may never be available again; and (c) the traditional concern of Delaware courts for actions which impair or impede stockholder voting rights. . . . In *Macmillan,* this Court held:

> When *Revlon* duties devolve upon directors, this Court will continue to exact an enhanced judicial scrutiny at the threshold, as in *Unocal,* before the normal presumptions of the business judgment rule will apply. 559 A.2d at 1288. The *Macmillan* decision articulates a specific two-part test for analyzing board action where competing bidders are not treated equally:
>
>> In the face of disparate treatment, the trial court must first examine whether the directors properly perceived that shareholder interests were enhanced. In any event the board's action must be reasonable in relation to the advantage sought to be achieved, or conversely, to the threat which a particular bid allegedly poses to stockholder interests.

Id. See also Roberts v. General Instrument Corp., Del. Ch., C.A. No. 11639, 1990 WL 118356, Allen, C. (Aug. 13, 1990), *reprinted at* 16 Del. J. Corp. L. 1540, 1554 ("This enhanced test requires a judicial judgment of reasonableness in the circumstances.").

The key features of an enhanced scrutiny test are: (a) a judicial determination regarding the adequacy of the decisionmaking process employed by the directors, including the information on which the directors based their decision; and (b) a judicial examination of the reasonableness of the directors' action in light of the circumstances then existing. The directors have the burden of proving that they were adequately informed and acted reasonably.

Although an enhanced scrutiny test involves a review of the reasonableness of the substantive merits of a board's actions, a court should not ignore the complexity of the directors' task in a sale of control. There are many business and financial considerations implicated in investigating and selecting the best value reasonably available. The board of directors is the corporate decision-making body best equipped to make these judgments. Accordingly, a court applying enhanced judicial scrutiny should be deciding whether the directors made a reasonable decision, not a perfect decision. If a board selected one of several reasonable alternatives, a court should not second-guess that choice even though it might have decided otherwise or subsequent events may have cast doubt on the board's determination. Thus, courts will not substitute their business judgment for that of the directors, but will determine if the directors' decision was, on balance, within a range of reasonableness. *See Unocal,* 493 A.2d at 955-56; *Macmillan,* 559 A.2d at 1288; *Nixon,* 626 A.2d at 1378.

D. *REVLON* AND *TIME-WARNER* DISTINGUISHED

The Paramount defendants and Viacom assert that the fiduciary obligations and the enhanced judicial scrutiny discussed above are not implicated in this case in the absence of a "break-up" of the corporation, and that the order granting the preliminary injunction should be reversed. This argument is based on their erroneous interpretation of our decisions in *Revlon* and *Time-Warner.*

In *Revlon,* we reviewed the actions of the board of directors of Revlon, Inc. ("Revlon"), which had rebuffed the overtures of Pantry Pride, Inc. and had instead entered into an agreement with Forstmann Little & Co. ("Forstmann") providing for the acquisition of 100 percent of Revlon's outstanding stock by

Forstmann and the subsequent break-up of Revlon. Based on the facts and circumstances present in *Revlon*, we held that "[t]he directors' role changed from defenders of the corporate bastion to auctioneers charged with getting the best price for the stockholders at a sale of the company." 506 A.2d at 182. We further held that "when a board ends an intense bidding contest on an insubstantial basis, . . . [that] action cannot withstand the enhanced scrutiny which *Unocal* requires of director conduct." *Id.* at 184.

It is true that one of the circumstances bearing on these holdings was the fact that "the break-up of the company . . . had become a reality which even the directors embraced." *Id.* at 182. It does not follow, however, that a "break-up" must be present and "inevitable" before directors are subject to enhanced judicial scrutiny and are required to pursue a transaction that is calculated to produce the best value reasonably available to the stockholders. In fact, we stated in *Revlon* that "when bidders make relatively similar offers, or dissolution of the company becomes inevitable, the directors cannot fulfill their enhanced *Unocal* duties by playing favorites with the contending factions." *Id.* at 184 (emphasis added). *Revlon* thus does not hold that an inevitable dissolution or "break-up" is necessary.

The decisions of this Court following *Revlon* reinforced the applicability of enhanced scrutiny and the directors' obligation to seek the best value reasonably available for the stockholders where there is a pending sale of control, regardless of whether or not there is to be a break-up of the corporation. In *Macmillan*, this Court held:

> We stated in *Revlon*, and again here, that *in a sale of corporate control* the responsibility of the directors is to get the highest value reasonably attainable for the shareholders.

559 A.2d at 1288 (emphasis added). In *Barkan*, we observed further:

> We believe that the general principles announced in *Revlon*, in *Unocal* [*supra*] and in *Moran* [*supra*] govern this case and every case in which a *fundamental change of corporate control* occurs or is contemplated.

567 A.2d at 1286 (emphasis added).

Although *Macmillan* and *Barkan* are clear in holding that a change of control imposes on directors the obligation to obtain the best value reasonably available to the stockholders, the Paramount defendants have interpreted our decision in *Time-Warner* as requiring a corporate break-up in order for that obligation to apply. The facts in *Time-Warner*, however, were quite different from the facts of this case, and refute Paramount's position here. In *Time-Warner*, the Chancellor held that there was no change of control in the original stock-for-stock merger between Time and Warner because Time would be owned by a fluid aggregation of unaffiliated stockholders both before and after the merger:

> If the appropriate inquiry is whether a change in control is contemplated, the answer must be sought in the specific circumstances surrounding the transaction. Surely under some circumstances a stock for stock merger could reflect a transfer of corporate control. That would, for example, plainly be the case here if Warner were a private company. But where, as here, the shares of both constituent corporations are widely held, corporate control can be expected to remain unaffected by

a stock for stock merger. This in my judgment was the situation with respect to the original merger agreement. When the specifics of that situation are reviewed, it is seen that, aside from legal technicalities and aside from arrangements thought to enhance the prospect for the ultimate succession of [Nicholas J. Nicholas, Jr., then president of Time], neither corporation could be said to be acquiring the other. *Control of both remained in a large, fluid, changeable and changing market.*

The existence of a control block of stock in the hands of a single shareholder or a group with loyalty to each other does have real consequences to the financial value of "minority" stock. The law offers some protection to such shares through the imposition of a fiduciary duty upon controlling shareholders. *But here, effectuation of the merger would not have subjected Time shareholders to the risks and consequences of holders of minority shares. This is a reflection of the fact that no control passed to anyone in the transaction contemplated.* The shareholders of Time would have "suffered" dilution, of course, but they would suffer the same type of dilution upon the public distribution of new stock.

Paramount Communications Inc. v. Time Inc., Del. Ch., No. 10866, 1989 WL 79880, Allen, C. (July 17, 1989), *reprinted at* 15 Del. J. Corp. L. 700, 739 (emphasis added). Moreover, the transaction actually consummated in *Time-Warner* was not a merger, as originally planned, but a sale of Warner's stock to Time.

In our affirmance of the Court of Chancery's well-reasoned decision, this Court held that "The Chancellor's findings of fact are supported by the record and *his conclusion is correct as a matter of law.*" 571 A.2d at 1150 (emphasis added). Nevertheless, the Paramount defendants here have argued that a break-up is a requirement and have focused on the following language in our *Time-Warner* decision:

> However, we premise our rejection of plaintiffs' *Revlon* claim on different grounds, namely, the absence of any substantial evidence to conclude that Time's board, in negotiating with Warner, made the dissolution or break-up of the corporate entity inevitable, as was the case in *Revlon.*
>
> Under Delaware law there are, generally speaking and *without excluding other possibilities*, two circumstances which may implicate *Revlon* duties. The first, and clearer one, is when a corporation *initiates an active bidding process seeking to sell itself* or to effect a business reorganization involving a clear break-up of the company. However, *Revlon* duties may also be triggered where, in response to a bidder's offer, a target abandons its long-term strategy and seeks an alternative transaction involving the breakup of the company.

Id. at 1150 (emphasis added) (citation and footnote omitted).

The Paramount defendants have misread the holding of *Time-Warner.* Contrary to their argument, our decision in *Time-Warner* expressly states that the two general scenarios discussed in the above-quoted paragraph are not the *only* instances where "*Revlon* duties" may be implicated. The Paramount defendants' argument totally ignores the phrase "without excluding other possibilities." Moreover, the instant case is clearly within the first general scenario set forth in *Time-Warner.* The Paramount Board, albeit unintentionally, had "initiate[d] an active bidding process seeking to sell itself" by agreeing to sell control of the corporation to Viacom in circumstances where another potential acquiror (QVC) was equally interested in being a bidder.

The Paramount defendants' position that *both* a change of control *and* a break-up are *required* must be rejected. Such a holding would unduly restrict the application of *Revlon,* is inconsistent with this Court's decisions in *Barkan* and *Macmillan,* and has no basis in policy. There are few events that have a more significant impact on the stockholders than a sale of control or a corporate break-up. Each event represents a fundamental (and perhaps irrevocable) change in the nature of the corporate enterprise from a practical standpoint. It is the significance of *each* of these events that justifies: (a) focusing on the directors' obligation to seek the best value reasonably available to the stockholders; and (b) requiring a close scrutiny of board action which could be contrary to the stockholders' interests.

Accordingly, when a corporation undertakes a transaction which will cause: (a) a change in corporate control; *or* (b) a break-up of the corporate entity, the directors' obligation is to seek the best value reasonably available to the stockholders. This obligation arises because the effect of the Viacom-Paramount transaction, if consummated, is to shift control of Paramount from the public stockholders to a controlling stockholder, Viacom. Neither *Time-Warner* nor any other decision of this Court holds that a "break-up" of the company is essential to give rise to this obligation where there is a sale of control.

III. Breach of Fiduciary Duties by Paramount Board

We now turn to duties of the Paramount Board under the facts of this case and our conclusions as to the breaches of those duties which warrant injunctive relief.

A. The Specific Obligations of the Paramount Board

Under the facts of this case, the Paramount directors had the obligation: (a) to be diligent and vigilant in examining critically the Paramount-Viacom transaction and the QVC tender offers; (b) to act in good faith; (c) to obtain, and act with due care on, all material information reasonably available, including information necessary to compare the two offers to determine which of these transactions, or an alternative course of action, would provide the best value reasonably available to the stockholders; and (d) to negotiate actively and in good faith with both Viacom and QVC to that end.

Having decided to sell control of the corporation, the Paramount directors were required to evaluate critically whether or not all material aspects of the Paramount-Viacom transaction (separately and in the aggregate) were reasonable and in the best interests of the Paramount stockholders in light of current circumstances, including: the change of control premium, the Stock Option Agreement, the Termination Fee, the coercive nature of both the Viacom and QVC tender offers,[18] the No Shop Provision, and the proposed disparate use of the Rights Agreement as to the Viacom and QVC tender offers, respectively.

18. Both the Viacom and the QVC tender offers were for 51 percent cash and a "back-end" of various securities, the value of each of which depended on the fluctuating value of Viacom and QVC stock at any given time. Thus, both tender offers were two-tiered, front-end loaded, and coercive. Such coercive offers are inherently problematic and should be expected to receive particularly careful analysis by a target board. *See Unocal,* 493 A.2d at 956.

These obligations necessarily implicated various issues, including the questions of whether or not those provisions and other aspects of the Paramount-Viacom transaction (separately and in the aggregate): (a) adversely affected the value provided to the Paramount stockholders; (b) inhibited or encouraged alternative bids; (c) were enforceable contractual obligations in light of the directors' fiduciary duties; and (d) in the end would advance or retard the Paramount directors' obligation to secure for the Paramount stockholders the best value reasonably available under the circumstances.

The Paramount defendants contend that they were precluded by certain contractual provisions, including the No-Shop Provision, from negotiating with QVC or seeking alternatives. Such provisions, whether or not they are presumptively valid in the abstract, may not validly define or limit the directors' fiduciary duties under Delaware law or prevent the Paramount directors from carrying out their fiduciary duties under Delaware law. To the extent such provisions are inconsistent with those duties, they are invalid and unenforceable. *See Revlon,* 506 A.2d at 184-85.

Since the Paramount directors had already decided to sell control, they had an obligation to continue their search for the best value reasonably available to the stockholders. This continuing obligation included the responsibility, at the October 24 board meeting and thereafter, to evaluate critically both the QVC tender offers and the Paramount-Viacom transaction to determine if: (a) the QVC tender offer was, or would continue to be, conditional; (b) the QVC tender offer could be improved; (c) the Viacom tender offer or other aspects of the Paramount-Viacom transaction could be improved; (d) each of the respective offers would be reasonably likely to come to closure, and under what circumstances; (e) other material information was reasonably available for consideration by the Paramount directors; (f) there were viable and realistic alternative courses of action; and (g) the timing constraints could be managed so the directors could consider these matters carefully and deliberately.

B. THE BREACHES OF FIDUCIARY DUTY BY THE PARAMOUNT BOARD

The Paramount directors made the decision on September 12, 1993, that, in their judgment, a strategic merger with Viacom on the economic terms of the Original Merger Agreement was in the best interests of Paramount and its stockholders. Those terms provided a modest change of control premium to the stockholders. The directors also decided at that time that it was appropriate to agree to certain defensive measures (the Stock Option Agreement, the Termination Fee, and the No-Shop Provision) insisted upon by Viacom as part of that economic transaction. Those defensive measures, coupled with the sale of control and subsequent disparate treatment of competing bidders, implicated the judicial scrutiny of *Unocal, Revlon, Macmillan,* and their progeny. We conclude that the Paramount directors' process was not reasonable, and the result achieved for the stockholders was not reasonable under the circumstances.

When entering into the Original Merger Agreement, and thereafter, the Paramount Board clearly gave insufficient attention to the potential consequences of the defensive measures demanded by Viacom. The Stock Option Agreement had a number of unusual and potentially "draconian" provisions, including the Note Feature and the Put Feature. Furthermore, the Termination Fee, whether or not unreasonable by itself, clearly made Paramount less attractive to other bidders, when coupled with the Stock Option Agreement. Finally, the No-Shop Provision inhibited the Paramount Board's ability to negotiate with other potential bidders, particularly QVC, which had already expressed an interest in Paramount.

Throughout the applicable time period, and especially from the first QVC merger proposal on September 20 through the Paramount Board meeting on November 15, QVC's interest in Paramount provided the opportunity for the Paramount Board to seek significantly higher value for the Paramount stockholders than that being offered by Viacom. QVC persistently demonstrated its intention to meet and exceed the Viacom offers, and frequently expressed its willingness to negotiate possible further increases.

The Paramount directors had the opportunity in the October 23-24 time frame, when the Original Merger Agreement was renegotiated, to take appropriate action to modify the improper defensive measures as well as to improve the economic terms of the Paramount-Viacom transaction. Under the circumstances existing at that time, it should have been clear to the Paramount Board that the Stock Option Agreement, coupled with the Termination Fee and the No-Shop Clause, were impeding the realization of the best value reasonably available to the Paramount stockholders. Nevertheless, the Paramount Board made no effort to eliminate or modify these counterproductive devices, and instead continued to cling to its vision of a strategic alliance with Viacom. Moreover, based on advice from the Paramount management, the Paramount directors considered the QVC offer to be "conditional" and asserted that they were precluded by the No-Shop Provision from seeking more information from, or negotiating with, QVC.

By November 12, 1993, the value of the revised QVC offer on its face exceeded that of the Viacom offer by over $1 billion at then current values. This significant disparity of value cannot be justified on the basis of the directors' vision of future strategy, primarily because the change of control would supplant the authority of the current Paramount Board to continue to hold and implement their strategic vision in any meaningful way. Moreover, their uninformed process had deprived their strategic vision of much of its credibility. *See Van Gorkom,* 488 A.2d at 872; Cede v. Technicolor, 634 A.2d at 367; Hanson Trust PLC v. ML SCM Acquisition Inc., 2d Cir., 781 F.2d 264, 274 (1986).

When the Paramount directors met on November 15 to consider QVC's increased tender offer, they remained prisoners of their own misconceptions and missed opportunities to eliminate the restrictions they had imposed on themselves. Yet, it was not "too late" to reconsider negotiating with QVC. The circumstances existing on November 15 made it clear that the defensive measures, taken as a whole, were problematic: (a) the No-Shop Provision could not define or limit their fiduciary duties; (b) the Stock Option Agreement had become "draconian"; and (c) the Termination Fee, in context with all the circumstances, was similarly deterring the realization of possibly higher bids. Nevertheless, the Paramount directors remained paralyzed by their uninformed belief that the QVC offer was "illusory." This final opportunity to negotiate on the stockholders' behalf and to fulfill their obligation to seek the best value reasonably available was thereby squandered.

IV. Viacom's Claim of Vested Contract Rights

Viacom argues that it had certain "vested" contract rights with respect to the No-Shop Provision and the Stock Option Agreement. In effect, Viacom's argument is that the Paramount directors could enter into an agreement in violation of their fiduciary duties and then render Paramount, and ultimately its stockholders, liable for failing to carry out an agreement in violation of those duties. Viacom's protestations about vested rights are without merit. This Court has found that those defensive measures were improperly designed to deter potential bidders, and that such measures do not meet the reasonableness test to which they must be subjected. They are consequently invalid and unenforceable under the facts of this case.

The No-Shop Provision could not validly define or limit the fiduciary duties of the Paramount directors. To the extent that a contract, or a provision thereof, purports to require a board to act or not act in such a fashion as to limit the exercise of fiduciary duties, it is invalid and unenforceable. *Cf.* Wilmington Trust v. Coulter, 200 A.2d at 452-54. Despite the arguments of Paramount and Viacom to the contrary, the Paramount directors could not contract away their fiduciary obligations. Since the No-Shop Provision was invalid, Viacom never had any vested contract rights in the provision.

As discussed previously, the Stock Option Agreement contained several "draconian" aspects, including the Note Feature and the Put Feature. While we have held that lock-up options are not per se illegal, *see Revlon,* 506 A.2d at 183, no options with similar features have ever been upheld by this Court. Under the circumstances of this case, the Stock Option Agreement clearly is invalid. Accordingly, Viacom never had any vested contract rights in that Agreement.

Viacom, a sophisticated party with experienced legal and financial advisors, knew of (and in fact demanded) the unreasonable features of the Stock Option Agreement. It cannot be now heard to argue that it obtained vested contract rights by negotiating and obtaining contractual provisions from a board acting in violation of its fiduciary duties. As the Nebraska Supreme Court said in rejecting a similar argument in ConAgra, Inc. v. Cargill, Inc., 222 Neb. 136, 382 N.W.2d 576, 587-88 (1986), "To so hold, it would seem, would be to get the shareholders coming and going." Likewise, we reject Viacom's arguments and hold that its fate must rise or fall, and in this instance fall, with the determination that the actions of the Paramount Board were invalid.

V. Conclusion

The realization of the best value reasonably available to the stockholders became the Paramount directors' primary obligation under these facts in light of the change of control. That obligation was not satisfied, and the Paramount Board's process was deficient. The directors' initial hope and expectation for a strategic alliance with Viacom was allowed to dominate their decisionmaking process to the point where the arsenal of defensive measures established at the outset was perpetuated (not modified or eliminated) when the situation was dramatically altered. QVC's unsolicited bid presented the opportunity for significantly greater value for the stockholders and enhanced negotiating leverage for the directors. Rather than seizing those opportunities, the Paramount directors chose to wall themselves off from material information which was reasonably available and to hide behind the defensive measures as a rationalization for refusing to negotiate with QVC or seeking other alternatives. Their view of the strategic alliance likewise became an empty rationalization as the opportunities for higher value for the stockholders continued to develop.

It is the nature of the judicial process that we decide only the case before us — a case which, on its facts, is clearly controlled by established Delaware law. Here, the proposed change of control and the implications thereof were crystal clear. In other cases they may be less clear. The holding of this case on its facts, coupled with the holdings of the principal cases discussed herein where the issue of sale of control is implicated, should provide a workable precedent against which to measure future cases.

For the reasons set forth herein, the November 24, 1993, Order of the Court of Chancery has been AFFIRMED, and this matter has been REMANDED for proceedings consistent herewith, as set forth in the December 9, 1993, Order of this Court.

F.   STATE ANTI-TAKEOVER LEGISLATION

As hostile takeover activity accelerated in the 1980s, the states responded with various types of legislation to make takeovers more difficult or to preclude certain acquisition techniques. These legislative approaches include the following.

Other Constituency Statutes. "Other constituency statutes" make it clear that in the exercise of their fiduciary duties, when considering defensive measures, directors may consider the potential impact of a takeover not only on shareholders, but also on employees, creditors, consumers, and communities. It's questionable whether this fundamentally differs from the common law approach set out in *Unocal*, in which the Delaware court acknowledged the power of the board to consider other constituents, so long as that consideration is ultimately related to shareholders' interest. Two-thirds of the states now have other constituency statutes. Delaware does not, but essentially provides the same broad discretion to directors through its decisions, in particular Paramount v. Time, Inc.

Moratorium Statutes. "Moratorium statutes," enacted in Delaware, New York, and 28 other states, impose a moratorium on any "business combination" where the bidder buys a specified level of the target's stock, unless the merger was initially approved by the target's board. (*See* DGCL §203.) In Delaware, the "trigger" is 15 percent of the stock and the moratorium is three years unless the bidder acquires 85 percent of the stock at the same time it crosses the 15 percent threshold, in which case the statute doesn't apply. The purpose of this statutory exception was to prevent particularly coercive tender offers, the "two-step, front-loaded cash tender offer" at issue in *Unocal*. As you saw in that case, the concern was that since shareholders would be concerned that the consideration they'd get in the second step would be stock of the bidder or junk bonds, they'd be coerced into tendering even if they didn't believe that the price was fair. In New York, the "trigger" is 20 percent of the stock; the moratorium is five years; and the term "business combination" includes not only mergers, as in Delaware, but also liquidations or substantial sales of assets. The purpose of this broad definition of "business combination" is to make it impossible for bidders to engage in "bust-up" takeovers for five years after acquiring control.

Control Share Statutes. "Control share" statutes typically provide that a majority of disinterested shareholders must approve the acquisition of a control block of shares, usually 20 percent. (*See* Ohio Gen. Corp. Law §1701.831.) Corporations may "opt out" of this statute, however. Another variation is Indiana's, in which an acquiror may cross the 20 percent threshold but loses voting rights unless a majority of disinterested shares (neither the bidder's nor target management's shares) grants them back. This statute was upheld in CTS Corp. v. Dynamics Corp., 481 U.S. 69 (1987), set out below.

Fair Price Statutes. "Fair price" statutes require either a supermajority vote for the second step in a two-step merger between the target and an "interested party" (purchaser of 10 percent of shares or more), or require that the price paid in the second step be as high as the highest price paid in the first step. (*See* Md. Gen. Corp. Law §§3-601-3-603 (1986). Corporations may "opt out" of this statute with a charter amendment approved by supermajority vote.

Pennsylvania's Anti-Takeover Legislation. Pennsylvania has struck out on its own and has passed a particularly stringent statute. First, its "other constituency" statute provides that the interests of shareholders should not predominate in the decision about whether to participate in a business combination. (*See* Pa. C.S.A. §511(d).) Second, its "fair value" statute provides that if anyone buys 20 percent of the firm's stock, every other shareholder can "put" their stock to the bidder — that is, sell it on demand, at a fair price, taking into account any control premium paid in the acquisition of 20 percent of shares or more. (*See* 15 Pa. C.S.A. §2541 (1988).) Pennsylvania also has a "disgorgement" statute, which requires that anyone who purchases 20 percent or more of a company's shares and then resells them within 18 months must give any profits to the corporation. (*See* Pa. B.C.L. §2571.)

The importance of these legislative restrictions is often blunted because the ability of a company to quickly adopt a poison pill effectively prevents bidders from using two-tier, front-end loaded tender offers anyway. That is, a poison pill will block a tender offeror from acquiring more than 14.9 percent of shares, irrespective of whether the company has in place fair price provisions or business combination statutes, since acquiring more than 14.9 percent of shares will trigger most pills, making the acquisition economically infeasible. Still, the following case, concerning a control share statute, is well worth reading, both because of its clear overview of federal tender offer regulation and because of the rather philosophical discussion by the court majority of the nature of the corporation. Notice as well Justice White's view in dissent that state anti-takeover legislation that impedes tender offers undermines federal securities law protection of *individual* investors' interests in selling their shares at a premium. Is Justice White correct in suggesting that protecting shareholders as a group from coercive tender offers, which was the purported purpose of Indiana's statute, undermines protection of shareholders as individuals? We see that in voting, shareholders only have power as a group. In selling, ought federal regulation to focus on shareholders' individual interests, as Justice White contends? Or does tender offer regulation that affects buying control of a company raise different policy concerns than those raised by individuals' decisions to buy or sell in the market?

CTS CORP. v. DYNAMICS CORP. OF AMERICA
Supreme Court of the United States
481 U.S. 69
April 21, 1987

Justice POWELL delivered the opinion of the Court.

[This case presents] the questions whether the Control Share Acquisitions Chapter of the Indiana Business Corporation Law, Ind. Code §23-1-42-1 *et seq.* (Supp.1986), is pre-empted by the Williams Act, 82 Stat. 641 454, as amended, 15 U.S.C. §§78m(d)-(e) and 78n(d)-(f) (1982 ed. and Supp. III), or violates the Commerce Clause of the Federal Constitution, Art. I, §8, cl. 3.

I

A

On March 4, 1986, the Governor of Indiana signed a revised Indiana Business Corporation Law, Ind. Code §23-1-17-1 *et seq.* (Supp. 1986). That law included the Control Share Acquisitions Chapter (Indiana Act or Act). Beginning on August 1, 1987, the Act will apply to any corporation incorporated in Indiana, §23-1-17-3(a), unless the corporation amends its articles of incorporation or bylaws to opt out of the Act, §23-1-42-5. Before that date, any Indiana corporation can opt into the Act by resolution of its board of directors. §23-1-17-3(b). The Act applies only to "issuing public corporations." The term "corporation" includes only businesses incorporated in Indiana. *See* §23-1-20-5. An "issuing public corporation" is defined as:

"a corporation that has:
"(1) one hundred (100) or more shareholders;
"(2) its principal place of business, its principal office, or substantial assets within Indiana; and
"(3) either:
"(A) more than ten percent (10%) of its shareholders resident in Indiana;
"(B) more than ten percent (10%) of its shares owned by Indiana residents; or
"(C) ten thousand (10,000) shareholders resident in Indiana." §23-1-42-4(a).

The Act focuses on the acquisition of "control shares" in an issuing public corporation. Under the Act, an entity acquires "control shares" whenever it acquires shares that, but for the operation of the Act, would bring its voting power in the corporation to or above any of three thresholds: 20%, 33⅓%, or 50%. §23-1-42-1. An entity that acquires control shares does not necessarily acquire voting rights. Rather, it gains those rights only "to the extent granted by resolution approved by the shareholders of the issuing public corporation." §23-1-42-9(a). Section 23-1-42-9(b) requires a majority vote of all disinterested[2] shareholders holding each class of stock for passage of such a resolution. The practical effect of this requirement is to condition acquisition of control of a corporation on approval of a majority of the pre-existing disinterested shareholders.

The shareholders decide whether to confer rights on the control shares at the next regularly scheduled meeting of the shareholders, or at a specially scheduled meeting. The acquiror can require management of the corporation to hold such a special meeting within 50 days if it files an "acquiring person statement," requests the meeting, and agrees to pay the expenses of the meeting. *See* §23-1-42-7. If the shareholders do not vote to restore voting rights to the shares, the corporation may redeem the control shares from the acquiror at fair market value, but it is not required to do so. §23-1-42-10(b). Similarly, if the acquiror does not file an acquiring person statement with the corporation, the corporation may, if its bylaws or articles of incorporation so provide, redeem the shares at any time after 60 days after the acquiror's last acquisition. §23-1-42-10(a).

B

On March 10, 1986, appellee Dynamics Corporation of America (Dynamics) owned 9.6% of the common stock of appellant CTS Corporation, an Indiana corporation. On that day, six days after the Act went into effect, Dynamics announced a tender offer for another million shares in CTS; purchase of those shares would have brought Dynamics' ownership interest in CTS to 27.5%. Also on March 10, Dynamics filed suit in the United States District Court for the Northern District of Illinois, alleging that CTS had violated the federal securities laws in a number of respects no longer relevant to these proceedings. On March 27, the board of directors of CTS, an Indiana corporation, elected to be governed by the provisions of the Act, *see* §23-1-17-3.

Four days later, on March 31, Dynamics moved for leave to amend its complaint to allege that the Act is pre-empted by the Williams Act, 15 U.S.C. §§78m(d)-(e) and 78n(d)-(f) (1982 ed. and Supp. III), and violates the Commerce Clause, Art. I, §8, cl. 3. [The U.S. District Court granted a preliminary injunction to Dynamics, finding both that the Indiana statute was preempted by the Williams Act and that it violated the Commerce Clause. The Seventh Circuit affirmed on both grounds.]

II

The first question . . . is whether the Williams Act pre-empts the Indiana Act. As we have stated frequently, absent an explicit indication by Congress of an intent to pre-empt state law, a state statute is pre-empted only

---

2. "Interested shares" are shares with respect to which the acquiror, an officer, or an inside director of the corporation "may exercise or direct the exercise of the voting power of the corporation in the election of directors." §23-1-42-3. . . .

" 'where compliance with both federal and state regulations is a physical impossibility . . . ,' Florida Lime & Avocado Growers, Inc. v. Paul, 373 U.S. 132, 142-143 (1963), or where the state 'law stands as an obstacle to the accomplishment and execution of the full purposes and objectives of Congress.' Hines v. Davidowitz, 312 U.S. 52, 67 (1941). . . . " Ray v. Atlantic Richfield Co., 435 U.S. 151, 158 (1978).

Because it is entirely possible for entities to comply with both the Williams Act and the Indiana Act, the state statute can be pre-empted only if it frustrates the purposes of the federal law.

A

Our discussion begins with a brief summary of the structure and purposes of the Williams Act. Congress passed the Williams Act in 1968 in response to the increasing number of hostile tender offers. Before its passage, these transactions were not covered by the disclosure requirements of the federal securities laws. *See* Piper v. Chris-Craft Industries, Inc., 430 U.S. 1, 22 (1977). The Williams Act, backed by regulations of the SEC, imposes requirements in two basic areas. First, it requires the offeror to file a statement disclosing information about the offer, including: the offeror's background and identity; the source and amount of the funds to be used in making the purchase; the purpose of the purchase, including any plans to liquidate the company or make major changes in its corporate structure; and the extent of the offeror's holdings in the target company. *See* 15 U.S.C. §78n(d)(1) (incorporating §78m(d)(1) by reference); 17 CFR §§240.13d-1, 240.14d-3 (1986).

Second, the Williams Act, and the regulations that accompany it, establish procedural rules to govern tender offers. For example, stockholders who tender their shares may withdraw them while the offer remains open, and, if the offeror has not purchased their shares, any time after 60 days from commencement of the offer. 15 U.S.C. §78n(d)(5); CFR §240.14d-7(a)(1) (1986) as amended, 51 Fed. Reg. 25873 (1986). The offer must remain open for at least 20 business days. 17 CFR §240.14e-1(a) (1986). If more shares are tendered than the offeror sought to purchase, purchases must be made on a pro rata basis from each tendering shareholder. 15 U.S.C. §78n(d)(6); 17 CFR §240.14(8) (1986). Finally, the offeror must pay the same price for all purchases; if the offering price is increased before the end of the offer, those who already have tendered must receive the benefit of the increased price. §78n(d)(7).

B

The Indiana Act differs in major respects from the Illinois statute that the Court considered in Edgar v. MITE Corp., 457 U.S. 624 (1982). After reviewing the legislative history of the Williams Act, Justice White, joined by Chief Justice Burger and Justice Blackmun (the plurality), concluded that the Williams Act struck a careful balance between the interests of offerors and target companies, and that any state statute that "upset" this balance was pre-empted. *Id.*, at 632-634.

The plurality then identified three offending features of the Illinois statute. Justice White's opinion first noted that the Illinois statute provided for a 20-day precommencement period. During this time, management could disseminate its views on the upcoming offer to shareholders, but offerors could not publish their offers. The plurality found that this provision gave management "a powerful tool to combat tender offers." *Id.*, at 635. This contrasted dramatically with the Williams Act; Congress had deleted express precommencement notice provisions from the Williams Act. According to the plurality, Congress had determined that the potentially adverse consequences of such a provision on shareholders should be avoided. Thus, the plurality concluded that the Illinois provision "frustrate[d] the objectives of the Williams Act." *Ibid.* The second criticized feature of the Illinois statute was a provision for a hearing on a tender offer that, because it set no deadline, allowed management " 'to stymie indefinitely a takeover,' " *id.*, at 637 (quoting MITE Corp. v. Dixon, 633 F.2d 486, 494 (CA7 1980)). The plurality noted that " 'delay can seriously impede a tender offer,' " 457 U.S., at 637 (quoting Great Western United Corp. v. Kidwell, 577 F.2d 1256, 1277 (CA5 1978) (Wisdom, J.)), and that "Congress anticipated that investors and the takeover offeror would be free to go forward without unreasonable delay," 457 U.S. at 639. Accordingly, the plurality concluded that this provision conflicted with the Williams Act. The third troublesome feature of the Illinois statute was its requirement that the fairness of tender offers would be reviewed by the Illinois Secretary of State. Noting that "Congress intended for investors to be free to make their own decisions," the plurality concluded that " '[t]he state thus offers investor protection at the expense of investor autonomy — an approach quite in conflict with that adopted by Congress.' " *Id.*, at 639-640 (quoting MITE Corp. v. Dixon, *supra*, at 494).

C

As the plurality opinion in *MITE* did not represent the views of a majority of the Court, we are not bound by its reasoning. We need not question that reasoning, however, because we believe the Indiana Act passes muster even under the broad interpretation of the Williams Act articulated by Justice White in *MITE*. As is apparent from our summary of its reasoning, the overriding concern of the *MITE* plurality was that the Illinois statute considered in that case operated to favor management against offerors, to the detriment of shareholders. By contrast, the statute now before the Court protects the independent shareholder against the contending parties. Thus, the Act furthers a basic purpose of the Williams Act, " 'plac[ing] investors on an equal footing with the takeover bidder,' " Piper v. Chris-Craft Industries, Inc., 430 U.S., at 30, 97 S. Ct., at 943 (quoting the Senate Report accompanying the Williams Act, S. Rep. No. 550, 90th Cong., 1st Sess., 4 (1967)).

The Indiana Act operates on the assumption, implicit in the Williams Act, that independent shareholders faced with tender offers often are at a disadvantage. By allowing such shareholders to vote as a group, the Act protects them from the coercive aspects of some tender offers. If, for example, shareholders believe that a successful tender offer will be followed by a purchase of nontendering shares at a depressed price, individual shareholders may tender their shares — even if they doubt the tender offer is in the corporation's best interest — to protect themselves from being forced to sell their shares at a depressed price. As the SEC explains: "The alternative of not accepting the tender offer is virtual assurance that, if the offer is successful, the shares will have to be sold in the lower priced, second step." Two-Tier Tender Offer Pricing and

Non-Tender Offer Purchase Programs, SEC Exchange Act Rel. No. 21079 (June 21, 1984), [1984 Transfer Binder] CCH Fed. Sec. L. Rep. ¶83,637, p.86,916 (footnote omitted) (hereinafter SEC Release No. 21079). *See* Lowenstein, *Pruning Deadwood in Hostile Takeovers: A Proposal for Legislation*, 83 Colum. L. Rev. 249, 307-309 (1983). In such a situation under the Indiana Act, the shareholders as a group, acting in the corporation's best interest, could reject the offer, although individual shareholders might be inclined to accept it. The desire of the Indiana Legislature to protect shareholders of Indiana corporations from this type of coercive offer does not conflict with the Williams Act. Rather, it furthers the federal policy of investor protection.

In implementing its goal, the Indiana Act avoids the problems the plurality discussed in *MITE*. Unlike the *MITE* statute, the Indiana Act does not give either management or the offeror an advantage in communicating with the shareholders about the impending offer. The Act also does not impose an indefinite delay on tender offers. Nothing in the Act prohibits an offeror from consummating an offer on the 20th business day, the earliest day permitted under applicable federal regulations, *see* 17 CFR §240.14e-1(a) (1986). Nor does the Act allow the state government to interpose its views of fairness between willing buyers and sellers of shares of the target company. Rather, the Act allows *shareholders* to evaluate the fairness of the offer collectively.

D

The Court of Appeals based its finding of pre-emption on its view that the practical effect of the Indiana Act is to delay consummation of tender offers until 50 days after the commencement of the offer. 794 F.2d, at 263. As did the Court of Appeals, Dynamics reasons that no rational offeror will purchase shares until it gains assurance that those shares will carry voting rights. Because it is possible that voting rights will not be conferred until a shareholder meeting 50 days after commencement of the offer, Dynamics concludes that the Act imposes a 50-day delay. This, it argues, conflicts with the shorter 20-business-day period established by the SEC as the minimum period for which a tender offer may be held open. 17 CFR §240.14e-1 (1986). We find the alleged conflict illusory.

The Act does not impose an absolute 50-day delay on tender offers, nor does it preclude an offeror from purchasing shares as soon as federal law permits. If the offeror fears an adverse shareholder vote under the Act, it can make a conditional tender offer, offering to accept shares on the condition that the shares receive voting rights within a certain period of time. The Williams Act permits tender offers to be conditioned on the offeror's subsequently obtaining regulatory approval. *E.g.*, Interpretive Release Relating to Tender Offer Rules, SEC Exchange Act Rel. No. 34-16623 (Mar. 5, 1980), 3 CCH Fed. Sec. L. Rep. ¶24,284I, p.17,758, quoted in MacFadden Holdings, Inc. v. JB Acquisition Corp., 802 F.2d 62, 70 (CA2 1986). There is no reason to doubt that this type of conditional tender offer would be legitimate as well.

Even assuming that the Indiana Act imposes some additional delay, nothing in *MITE* suggested that *any* delay imposed by state regulation, however short, would create a conflict with the Williams Act. The plurality argued only that the offeror should "be free to go forward without *unreasonable* delay." 457 U.S., at 639, 102 S. Ct., at 2639 (emphasis added). In that case, the Court was confronted with the potential for indefinite delay and presented with no persuasive reason why some deadline could not be established. By contrast, the Indiana Act provides that full voting rights will be vested — if this eventually is to occur — within 50 days after commencement of the offer. This period is within the 60-day period Congress established for restitution of withdrawal rights in 15 U.S.C. §78n(d)(5). We cannot say that a delay within that congressionally determined period is unreasonable.

Finally, we note that the Williams Act would pre-empt a variety of state corporate laws of hitherto unquestioned validity if it were construed to pre-empt any state statute that may limit or delay the free exercise of power after a successful tender offer. State corporate laws commonly permit corporations to stagger the terms of their directors. *See* Model Business Corp. Act §37 (1969 draft) in 3 Model Business Corp. Act Ann. (2d ed. 1971) (hereinafter Model Act); American Bar Foundation, Revised Model Business Corp. Act §8.06 (1984 draft) (1985) (hereinafter RMBCA). By staggering the terms of directors, and thus having annual elections for only one class of directors each year, corporations may delay the time when a successful offeror gains control of the board of directors. Similarly, state corporation laws commonly provide for cumulative voting. *See* 1 Model Act §33, ¶4; RMBCA §7.28. By enabling minority shareholders to assure themselves of representation in each class of directors, cumulative voting provisions can delay further the ability of offerors to gain untrammeled authority over the affairs of the target corporation. *See* Hochman & Folger, *Deflecting Takeovers: Charter and By-Law Techniques*, 34 Bus. Law. 537, 538-539 (1979).

In our view, the possibility that the Indiana Act will delay some tender offers is insufficient to require a conclusion that the Williams Act pre-empts the Act. The longstanding prevalence of state regulation in this area suggests that, if Congress had intended to pre-empt all state laws that delay the acquisition of voting control following a tender offer, it would have said so explicitly. The regulatory conditions that the Act places on tender offers are consistent with the text and the purposes of the Williams Act. Accordingly, we hold that the Williams Act does not pre-empt the Indiana Act.

III

As an alternative basis for its decision, the Court of Appeals held that the Act violates the Commerce Clause of the Federal Constitution. We now address this holding. On its face, the Commerce Clause is nothing more than a grant to Congress of the power "[t]o regulate Commerce . . . among the several States . . . ," Art. I, §8, cl. 3. But it has been settled for more than a century that the Clause prohibits States from taking certain actions respecting interstate commerce even absent congressional action. *See, e.g.,* Cooley v. Board of Wardens, 12 How. 299, 13 L. Ed. 996 (1852). The Court's interpretation of "these great silences of the Constitution," H.P. Hood & Sons, Inc. v. Du Mond, 336 U.S. 525, 535 (1949), has not always been easy to follow. Rather, as the volume and complexity of commerce and regulation have grown in this country, the Court has articulated a variety of tests in an attempt to describe the difference between those regulations that the Commerce Clause permits and those regulations that it prohibits. *See, e.g.,* Raymond Motor Transportation, Inc. v. Rice, 434 U.S. 429, 441, n.15 (1978).

A

The principal objects of dormant Commerce Clause scrutiny are statutes that discriminate against interstate commerce. *See, e.g.*, Lewis v. BT Investment Managers, Inc., 447 U.S. 27, 36-37 (1980); Philadelphia v. New Jersey, 437 U.S. 617, 624 (1978). *See generally* Regan, *The Supreme Court and State Protectionism: Making Sense of the Dormant Commerce Clause*, 84 Mich. L. Rev. 1091 (1986). The Indiana Act is not such a statute. It has the same effects on tender offers whether or not the offeror is a domiciliary or resident of Indiana. Thus, it "visits its effects equally upon both interstate and local business," Lewis v. BT Investment Managers, Inc., *supra*, 447 U.S., at 36.

Dynamics nevertheless contends that the statute is discriminatory because it will apply most often to out-of-state entities. This argument rests on the contention that, as a practical matter, most hostile tender offers are launched by offerors outside Indiana. But this argument avails Dynamics little. "The fact that the burden of a state regulation falls on some interstate companies does not, by itself, establish a claim of discrimination against interstate commerce." Exxon Corp. v. Governor of Maryland, 437 U.S. 117, 126 (1978). *See* Minnesota v. Clover Leaf Creamery Co., 449 U.S. 456 (1981) (rejecting a claim of discrimination because the challenged statute "regulate[d] even-handedly . . . without regard to whether the [commerce came] from outside the State"); Commonwealth Edison Co. v. Montana, 453 U.S. 609, 619 (1981) (rejecting a claim of discrimination because the "tax burden [was] borne according to the amount . . . consumed and not according to any distinction between in-state and out-of-state consumers"). Because nothing in the Indiana Act imposes a greater burden on out-of-state offerors than it does on similarly situated Indiana offerors, we reject the contention that the Act discriminates against interstate commerce.

B

This Court's recent Commerce Clause cases also have invalidated statutes that may adversely affect interstate commerce by subjecting activities to inconsistent regulations. *E.g.*, Brown-Forman Distillers Corp. v. New York State Liquor Authority, 476 U.S. 573, 583-584 (1986); Edgar v. MITE Corp., 457 U.S., at 642 (plurality opinion of White, J.); Kassel v. Consolidated Freightways Corp., 450 U.S. 662, 671 (1981) (plurality opinion of Powell, J.). *See* Southern Pacific Co. v. Arizona, 325 U.S. 761, 774 (1945) (noting the "confusion and difficulty" that would attend the "unsatisfied need for uniformity" in setting maximum limits on train lengths); Cooley v. Board of Wardens, *supra*, 12 How., at 319 (stating that the Commerce Clause prohibits States from regulating subjects that "are in their nature national, or admit only of one uniform system, or plan of regulation"). The Indiana Act poses no such problem. So long as each State regulates voting rights only in the corporations it has created, each corporation will be subject to the law of only one State. No principle of corporation law and practice is more firmly established than a State's authority to regulate domestic corporations, including the authority to define the voting rights of shareholders. *See* Restatement (Second) of Conflict of Laws §304 (1971) (concluding that the law of the incorporating State generally should "determine the right of a shareholder to participate in the administration of the affairs of the corporation"). Accordingly, we conclude that the Indiana Act does not create an impermissible risk of inconsistent regulation by different States.

C

The Court of Appeals did not find the Act unconstitutional for either of these threshold reasons. Rather, its decision rested on its view of the Act's potential to hinder tender offers. We think the Court of Appeals failed to appreciate the significance for Commerce Clause analysis of the fact that state regulation of corporate governance is regulation of entities whose very existence and attributes are a product of state law. As Chief Justice Marshall explained:

> "A corporation is an artificial being, invisible, intangible, and existing only in contemplation of law. Being the mere creature of law, it possesses only those properties which the charter of its creation confers upon it, either expressly, or as incidental to its very existence. These are such as are supposed best calculated to effect the object for which it was created." Trustees of Dartmouth College v. Woodward, 4 Wheat. 518, 636, 4 L. Ed. 518 (1819).

See First National Bank of Boston v. Bellotti, 435 U.S. 765, 822-824 (1978) (Rehnquist, J., dissenting). Every State in this country has enacted laws regulating corporate governance. By prohibiting certain transactions, and regulating others, such laws necessarily affect certain aspects of interstate commerce. This necessarily is true with respect to corporations with shareholders in States other than the State of incorporation. Large corporations that are listed on national exchanges, or even regional exchanges, will have shareholders in many States and shares that are traded frequently. The markets that facilitate this national and international participation in ownership of corporations are essential for providing capital not only for new enterprises but also for established companies that need to expand their businesses. This beneficial free market system depends at its core upon the fact that a corporation — except in the rarest situations — is organized under, and governed by, the law of a single jurisdiction, traditionally the corporate law of the State of its incorporation.

These regulatory laws may affect directly a variety of corporate transactions. Mergers are a typical example. In view of the substantial effect that a merger may have on the shareholders' interests in a corporation, many States require supermajority votes to approve mergers. *See, e.g.,* 2 Model Act §73 (requiring approval of a merger by a majority of all shares, rather than simply a majority of votes cast); RMBCA §11.03 (same). By requiring a greater vote for mergers than is required for other transactions, these laws make it more difficult for corporations to merge. State laws also may provide for "dissenters' rights" under which minority shareholders who disagree with corporate decisions to take particular actions are entitled to sell their shares to the corporation at fair market value. *See, e.g.,* 2 Model Act §§80, 81; RMBCA §13.02. By requiring the corporation to purchase the shares of dissenting shareholders, these laws may inhibit a corporation from engaging in the specified transactions.[12]

---

12. Numerous other common regulations may affect both nonresident and resident shareholders of a corporation. Specified votes may be required for the sale of all of the corporation's assets. *See* 2 Model Act §79; RMBCA §12.02. The election of directors may be staggered over a period

It thus is an accepted part of the business landscape in this country for States to create corporations, to prescribe their powers, and to define the rights that are acquired by purchasing their shares. A State has an interest in promoting stable relationships among parties involved in the corporations it charters, as well as in ensuring that investors in such corporations have an effective voice in corporate affairs.

There can be no doubt that the Act reflects these concerns. The primary purpose of the Act is to protect the shareholders of Indiana corporations. It does this by affording shareholders, when a takeover offer is made, an opportunity to decide collectively whether the resulting change in voting control of the corporation, as they perceive it, would be desirable. A change of management may have important effects on the shareholders' interests; it is well within the State's role as overseer of corporate governance to offer this opportunity. The autonomy provided by allowing shareholders collectively to determine whether the takeover is advantageous to their interests may be especially beneficial where a hostile tender offer may coerce shareholders into tendering their shares.

Appellee Dynamics responds to this concern by arguing that the prospect of coercive tender offers is illusory, and that tender offers generally should be favored because they reallocate corporate assets into the hands of management who can use them most effectively.[13] *See generally* Easterbrook & Fischel, *The Proper Role of a Target's Management in Responding to a Tender Offer*, 94 Harv. L. Rev. 1161 (1981). As indicated *supra,* at 1646, Indiana's concern with tender offers is not groundless. Indeed, the potentially coercive aspects of tender offers have been recognized by the SEC, *see* SEC Release No. 21079, p.86,916, and by a number of scholarly commentators, *see, e.g.,* Bradley & Rosenzweig, *Defensive Stock Repurchases*, 99 Harv. L. Rev. 1377, 1412-1413 (1986); Macey & McChesney, *A Theoretical Analysis of Corporate Greenmail*, 95 Yale L.J. 13, 20-22 (1985); Lowenstein, 83 Colum. L. Rev., at 307-309. The Constitution does not require the States to subscribe to any particular economic theory. We are not inclined

---

of years to prevent abrupt changes in management. *See* 1 Model Act §37; RMBCA §8.06. Various classes of stock may be created with differences in voting rights as to dividends and on liquidation. *See* 1 Model Act §15; RMBCA §6.01(c). Provisions may be made for cumulative voting. *See* 1 Model Act §33, ¶4; RMBCA §7.28; n.9, *supra*. Corporations may adopt restrictions on payment of dividends to ensure that specified ratios of assets to liabilities are maintained for the benefit of the holders of corporate bonds or notes. *See* 1 Model Act §45 (noting that a corporation's articles of incorporation can restrict payment of dividends); RMBCA §6.40 (same). Where the shares of a corporation are held in States other than that of incorporation, actions taken pursuant to these and similar provisions of state law will affect all shareholders alike wherever they reside or are domiciled.

Nor is it unusual for partnership law to restrict certain transactions. For example, a purchaser of a partnership interest generally can gain a right to control the business only with the consent of other owners. *See* Uniform Partnership Act §27, 6 U.L.A. 353 (1969); Uniform Limited Partnership Act §19 (1916 draft), 6 U.L.A. 603 (1969); Revised Uniform Limited Partnership Act §§702, 704 (1976 draft), 6 U.L.A. 259, 261 (Supp. 1986). These provisions — in force in the great majority of the States — bear a striking resemblance to the Act at issue in this case.

13. It is appropriate to note when discussing the merits and demerits of tender offers that generalizations usually require qualification. No one doubts that some successful tender offers will provide more effective management or other benefits such as needed diversification. But there is no reason to *assume* that the type of conglomerate corporation that may result from repetitive takeovers necessarily will result in more effective management or otherwise be beneficial to shareholders. The divergent views in the literature — and even now being debated in the Congress — reflect the reality that the type and utility of tender offers vary widely. Of course, in many situations the offer to shareholders is simply a cash price substantially higher than the market price prior to the offer.

"to second-guess the empirical judgments of lawmakers concerning the utility of legislation," Kassel v. Consolidated Freightways Corp., 450 U.S., at 679 (Brennan, J., concurring in judgment). In our view, the possibility of coercion in some takeover bids offers additional justification for Indiana's decision to promote the autonomy of independent shareholders. . . .

D

Dynamics' argument that the Act is unconstitutional ultimately rests on its contention that the Act will limit the number of successful tender offers. There is little evidence that this will occur. But even if true, this result would not substantially affect our Commerce Clause analysis. We reiterate that this Act does not prohibit any entity — resident or nonresident — from offering to purchase, or from purchasing, shares in Indiana corporations, or from attempting thereby to gain control. It only provides regulatory procedures designed for the better protection of the corporations' shareholders. We have rejected the "notion that the Commerce Clause protects the particular structure or methods of operation in a . . . market." Exxon Corp. v. Governor of Maryland, 437 U.S., at 127. The very commodity that is traded in the securities market is one whose characteristics are defined by state law. Similarly, the very commodity that is traded in the "market for corporate control" — the corporation — is one that owes its existence and attributes to state law. Indiana need not define these commodities as other States do; it need only provide that residents and nonresidents have equal access to them. This Indiana has done. Accordingly, even if the Act should decrease the number of successful tender offers for Indiana corporations, this would not offend the Commerce Clause.

IV

On its face, the Indiana Control Share Acquisitions Chapter evenhandedly determines the voting rights of shares of Indiana corporations. The Act does not conflict with the provisions or purposes of the Williams Act. To the limited extent that the Act affects interstate commerce, this is justified by the State's interests in defining the attributes of shares in its corporations and in protecting shareholders. Congress has never questioned the need for state regulation of these matters. Nor do we think such regulation offends the Constitution. Accordingly, we reverse the judgment of the Court of Appeals.

Justice SCALIA, concurring in part and concurring in the judgment.

I join Parts I, III-A, and III-B of the Court's opinion. However, having found, as those Parts do, that the Indiana Control Share Acquisitions Chapter neither "discriminates against interstate commerce," *ante,* at 1649, nor "create[s] an impermissible risk of inconsistent regulation by different States," *ante,* at 1649, I would conclude without further analysis that it is not invalid under the dormant Commerce Clause. While it has become standard practice at least since Pike v. Bruce Church, Inc., 397 U.S. 137 (1970), to consider, in addition to these factors, whether the burden on commerce imposed by a state statute "is clearly excessive in relation to the putative local benefits," *id.,* at 142, such an inquiry is ill suited to the judicial function and should be undertaken rarely if at all. This case is a good illustration of the point. Whether the control shares statute "protects shareholders of Indiana corporations," Brief for Appellant in No. 86-97, p.88, or protects incumbent management seems to me a highly debatable question, but it is extraordinary to think that the constitutionality of the Act should depend on the answer. Nothing in the Constitution says that the protection of entrenched management is any less important a "putative local benefit" than the protection of entrenched shareholders, and I do not know what qualifies us to make that judgment — or the related judgment as to how effective the present statute is in achieving one or the other objective — or the ultimate (and most ineffable) judgment as to whether, given importance-level x, and effectiveness-level y, the worth of the statute is "outweighed" by impact-on-commerce z. . . .

I also agree with the Court that the Indiana Control Share Acquisitions Chapter is not pre-empted by the Williams Act, but I reach that conclusion without entering into the debate over the purposes of the two statutes. The Williams Act is governed by the antipre-emption provision of the Securities Exchange Act of 1934, 15 U.S.C. §78bb(a), which provides that nothing it contains "shall affect the jurisdiction of the securities commission (or any agency or officer performing like functions) of any State over any security or any person insofar as it does not conflict with the provisions of this chapter or the rules and regulations thereunder." Unless it serves no function, that language forecloses pre-emption on the basis of conflicting "purpose" as opposed to conflicting "provision." Even if it does not have literal application to the present case (because, perhaps, the Indiana agency responsible for securities matters has no enforcement responsibility with regard to this legislation), it nonetheless refutes the proposition that Congress meant the Williams Act to displace *all* state laws with conflicting purpose. And if any are to survive, surely the States' corporation codes are among them. It would be peculiar to hold that Indiana could have pursued the purpose at issue here through its blue-sky laws, but cannot pursue it through the State's even more sacrosanct authority over the structure of domestic corporations. Prescribing voting rights for the governance of state-chartered companies is a traditional state function with which the Federal Congress has never, to my knowledge, intentionally interfered. I would require far more evidence than is available here to find implicit pre-emption of that function by a federal statute whose provisions concededly do not conflict with the state law.

I do not share the Court's apparent high estimation of the beneficence of the state statute at issue here. But a law can be both economic folly and constitutional. The Indiana Control Share Acquisitions Chapter is at least the latter. I therefore concur in the judgment of the Court.

Justice WHITE, with whom Justice BLACKMUN and Justice STEVENS join as to Part II, dissenting.

The majority today upholds Indiana's Control Share Acquisitions Chapter, a statute which will predictably foreclose completely some tender offers for stock in Indiana corporations. I disagree with the conclusion that the Chapter is neither pre-empted by the Williams Act nor in conflict with the Commerce Clause. The Chapter undermines the policy of the Williams Act by effectively preventing minority shareholders, in some circumstances, from acting in their own best interests by selling their stock. In addition, the Chapter will substantially burden the interstate market in corporate ownership, particularly if other States follow

Indiana's lead as many already have done. The Chapter, therefore, directly inhibits interstate commerce, the very economic consequences the Commerce Clause was intended to prevent. The opinion of the Court of Appeals is far more persuasive than that of the majority today, and the judgment of that court should be affirmed.

I

The Williams Act expressed Congress' concern that individual investors be given sufficient information so that they could make an informed choice on whether to tender their stock in response to a tender offer. The problem with the approach the majority adopts today is that it equates protection of individual investors, the focus of the Williams Act, with the protection of shareholders as a group. Indiana's Control Share Acquisitions Chapter undoubtedly helps protect the interests of a majority of the shareholders in any corporation subject to its terms, but in many instances, it will effectively prevent an individual investor from selling his stock at a premium. Indiana's statute, therefore, does not "furthe[r] the federal policy of *investor* protection," *ante*, at 1646 (emphasis added), as the majority claims.

In discussing the legislative history of the Williams Act, the Court, in Piper v. Chris-Craft Industries, Inc., 430 U.S. 1 (1977), looked to the legislative history of the Williams Act and concluded that the Act was designed to protect individual investors, not management and not tender offerors: "The sponsors of this legislation were plainly sensitive to the suggestion that the measure would favor one side or the other in control contests; however, they made it clear that the legislation was designed solely to get needed information to the investor, the constant focal point of the committee hearings." *Id.*, at 30-31. The Court specifically noted that the Williams Act's legislative history shows that Congress recognized that some "takeover bids . . . often serve a useful function." *Id.*, at 30. As quoted by the majority, *ante*, at 1645, the basic purpose of the Williams Act is " 'plac[ing] *investors* on an equal footing with the takeover bidder.' " *Piper, supra*, at 30 (emphasis added).

The Control Share Acquisitions Chapter, by design, will frustrate individual investment decisions. Concededly, the Control Share Acquisitions Chapter allows the majority of a corporation's shareholders to block a tender offer and thereby thwart the desires of an individual investor to sell his stock. In the context of discussing how the Chapter can be used to deal with the coercive aspects of some tender offers, the majority states: "In such a situation under the Indiana Act, the shareholders as a group, acting in the corporation's best interest, could reject the offer, although individual shareholders might be inclined to accept it." *Ante*, at 1646. I do not dispute that the Chapter provides additional protection for Indiana corporations, particularly in helping those corporations maintain the status quo. But it is clear to me that Indiana's scheme conflicts with the Williams Act's careful balance, which was intended to protect individual investors and permit them to decide whether it is in their best interests to tender their stock. As noted by the plurality in *MITE,* "Congress . . . did not want to deny shareholders 'the opportunities which result from the competitive bidding for a block of stock of a given company,' namely, the opportunity to sell shares for a premium over their market price. 113 Cong. Rec. 24666 (1967) (remarks of Sen. Javits)." Edgar v. MITE Corp., 457 U.S. 624, 633, n.9.

The majority claims that if the Williams Act pre-empts Indiana's Control Share Acquisitions Chapter, it also pre-empts a number of other corporate-control provisions such as cumulative voting or staggering the terms of directors. But this view ignores the fundamental distinction between these other corporate-control provisions and the Chapter: unlike those other provisions, the Chapter is designed to prevent certain tender offers from ever taking place. It is transactional in nature, although it is characterized by the State as involving only the voting rights of certain shares. "[T]his Court is not bound by '[t]he name, description or characterization given [a challenged statute] by the legislature or the courts of the State,' but will determine for itself the practical impact of the law." Hughes v. Oklahoma, 441 U.S. 322, 336 (1979) (quoting Lacoste v. Louisiana Dept. of Conservation, 263 U.S. 545, 550 (1924)). The Control Share Acquisitions Chapter will effectively prevent minority shareholders in some circumstances from selling their stock to a willing tender offeror. It is the practical impact of the Chapter that leads to the conclusion that it is pre-empted by the Williams Act.

II

Given the impact of the Control Share Acquisitions Chapter, it is clear that Indiana is directly regulating the purchase and sale of shares of stock in interstate commerce. Appellant CTS' stock is traded on the New York Stock Exchange, and people from all over the country buy and sell CTS' shares daily. Yet, under Indiana's scheme, any prospective purchaser will be effectively precluded from purchasing CTS' shares if the purchaser crosses one of the Chapter's threshold ownership levels and a majority of CTS' shareholders refuse to give the purchaser voting rights. This Court should not countenance such a restraint on interstate trade.

The United States, as *amicus curiae*, argues that Indiana's Control Share Acquisitions Chapter "is written as a restraint on the *transferability* of voting rights in specified transactions, and it could not be written in any other way without changing its meaning. Since the restraint on the transfer of voting rights is a restraint on the transfer of shares, the Indiana Chapter, like the Illinois Act [in *MITE*], restrains 'transfers of stock by stockholders to a third party.'" Brief for Securities and Exchange Commission and United States as *Amici Curiae* 26. I agree. The majority ignores the practical impact of the Chapter in concluding that the Chapter does not violate the Commerce Clause. The Chapter is characterized as merely defining "the attributes of shares in its corporations," *ante,* at 1652. The majority sees the trees but not the forest. . . .

Unlike state blue sky laws, Indiana's Control Share Acquisitions Chapter regulates the purchase and sale of stock of Indiana corporations in interstate commerce. Indeed, as noted above, the Chapter will inevitably be used to block interstate transactions in such stock. Because the Commerce Clause protects the "interstate market" in such securities, Exxon Corp. v. Governor of Maryland, 437 U.S. 117 (1978), and because the Control Share Acquisitions Chapter substantially interferes with this interstate market, the Chapter clearly conflicts with the Commerce Clause.

With all due respect, I dissent.

CHAPTER
16

Fraud and Insider Trading Under Federal Securities Law

In Chapter 7, we examined the federal securities law that applies to proxy communications with shareholders and saw that there is a private cause of action for any material misstatement or omission in a proxy communication under section 14(a) of the Exchange Act and Rule 14a-9. The purpose of that cause of action is to encourage companies to provide full and accurate disclosure to shareholders in conjunction with every proxy solicitation. Yet many statements companies make are not made in the context of proxy solicitations; they are general statements to the press, to securities analysts, and to the public. Beyond Rule 14a-9, other sections of the federal securities laws have as their goal ensuring that companies' statements to the capital markets generally embody full and fair disclosure.

By far the most important of these other sections is section 10(b) of the Exchange Act, and Rule 10b-5 promulgated thereunder. Together these create a cause of action for fraud for any material misstatement or omission in connection with the purchase or sale of securities that has caused damages. Liability under section 10(b) and Rule 10b-5 reaches not only statements contained in required disclosure documents such as quarterly and annual reports, but also every public statement a company's authorized agent makes, such as in a press release, news conference, or response to reporters' questions. Pick up any newspaper in the United States and you can read about either the SEC or private investors as a class suing a company for securities fraud — for instance, because the financial statements overstate revenues by a few billion dollars — and the odds are overwhelming that a violation of section 10(b) and Rule 10b-5 has been alleged. This chapter begins with an examination of the more important elements of a cause of action for fraud generally under section 10(b) and Rule 10b-5. We then move on to look at a specific species of fraud under Section 10(b) and Rule 10b-5: insider trading. Bear in mind that a detailed examination of these topics is beyond the scope of this casebook, but you can look forward to such an examination by taking an upper-level securities class.

A.   SECTION 10(b) AND RULE 10b-5

Section 10 of the Securities Exchange Act of 1934, 15 U.S.C. §78j, provides in relevant part:

> It shall be unlawful for any person, directly or indirectly, by the use of any means or instrumentality of interstate commerce or of the mails, or of any facility of any national securities exchange . . .
>
> (b) To use or employ, in connection with the purchase or sale of any security . . . any manipulative or deceptive device or contrivance in contravention of such rules and regulations as the Commission may prescribe as necessary or appropriate in the public interest or for the protection of investors.

Rule 10b-5, 17 C.F.R. §240.10b-5 (2000), provides:

> It shall be unlawful for any person, directly or indirectly, by the use of any means or instrumentality of interstate commerce, or of the mails or of any facility of any national securities exchange,
>
> (a) to employ any device, scheme, or artifice to defraud,
>
> (b) to make any untrue statement of a material fact or to omit to state a material fact necessary in order to make the statements made, in the light of the circumstances under which they were made, not misleading, or
>
> (c) to engage in any act, practice, or course of business which operates or would operate as a fraud or deceit upon any person, in connection with the purchase or sale of any security.

Based on this statutory and regulatory language, the elements of a cause of action are a (1) misstatement or omission of a (2) material fact on which the plaintiff (3) relied (4) in connection with the (5) purchase or sale of securities, causing (6) damages. We will discuss all but the damages element below.

Traditionally, courts treated Rule 10b-5 as primarily about disclosure, not about corporate governance or enforcing fiduciary duties. In Santa Fe v. Green, for example, the majority shareholders in a short-form merger notified plaintiffs that their shares would be purchased for $150 per share. As part of the disclosure document notifying the minority shareholders of the merger and of their appraisal rights, the majority shareholders told the minority they had obtained independent appraisals of the company's physical assets (land, timber, buildings, and machinery), which showed those assets were worth $640 per share. The minority shareholders sued under section 10(b) and Rule 10b-5, claiming that the use of the short-form merger procedure was a scheme or an artifice to defraud the minority of the fair value of their shares. The U.S. Supreme Court rejected the minority's claim, stating that "our cases have rejected the view that a breach of fiduciary duty by majority stockholders, without any deception, misrepresentation, or nondisclosure, violates the statute and the Rule." Santa Fe v. Green, 430 U.S. 462, 467 (1977).

More recently, courts seem to have started to come to view section 10(b)/Rule 10b-5 as an important mechanism regulating corporate governance insofar as disclosure brings to light conflicts of interest and enhances shareholder power.

This development, which is shown in the insider trading case below (United States v. O'Hagan) and in the *Zandford* case, will also likely be seen as the courts start to interpret Sarbanes-Oxley, which explicitly federalizes some aspects of corporate governance. Thus, while in this Section we explore some of the more important technical requirements of a cause of action under section 10(b)/Rule 10b-5, the larger issue on which to focus is how this cause of action mitigates conflicts between managers and shareholders.

1.   *Misstatements and Omissions*

In order to demonstrate liability under section 10(b) and Rule 10b-5, plaintiffs must first show that the defendant misstated a material fact or omitted to state a material fact necessary to make the statements that were made not misleading. For instance, if a company states that "to date, the FDA has not disapproved any drug that we are developing," it would be a material omission not to also state, "but we have been advised that the FDA staff is recommending that approval be denied of our most promising drug," if those were the circumstances. Thus, although the first statement is literally true, it would be held to be a half-truth if not elaborated upon in the manner indicated.

By far the most difficult issues that arise with respect to this element of a cause of action under section 10(b) and Rule 10b-5 concern omissions, since "silence, absent a duty to speak, is not misleading under Rule 10b-5." Basic Inc. v. Levinson, 485 U.S. 224, 239 n.17 (1988). The question arises, then, when is there a duty to speak — that is, a duty to disclose a fact that was omitted? Such a duty can arise to avoid half-truths, as in the example in the paragraph above. A duty to speak may arise because a company is selling new securities and thus needs to file a disclosure document (a "prospectus") under the Securities Act of 1933. The contents of the prospectus will be specified by line-item instructions in Regulation S-K (which contains integrated instructions for disclosure documents under both the '33 Act and the '34 Act). Prospectus disclosure is also guided by Rule 408, which requires any additional disclosure necessary to make the statements not misleading that are made in response to line-item disclosure under Regulation S-K. When a public company files quarterly reports or annual reports, again, Regulation S-K sets out the required disclosure, and again there is a requirement to avoid half-truths. If a company is buying back its own stock, there is a duty to disclose all material information that might affect the value of the stock in order to avoid liability, because a company has a fiduciary duty to its shareholders to disclose material information when it buys securities from them. Or in the context of a proxy statement, either in advance of the annual meeting or in conjunction with a merger, there is a duty to speak. Thus, there are very many points in time when there is a duty to speak, and failure to speak (an omission) will create liability.

Yet, as the following case indicates, at least until Sarbanes-Oxley was passed we did not have a "real time" disclosure regimen requiring immediate disclosure of every material event. Rather, prior to Sarbanes-Oxley, the SEC had promulgated Form 8-K, which specified certain material events that needed to be disclosed within 15 days, such as a change in control of the registrant, the acquisition or disposition of major assets not in the ordinary course of business, or a bankruptcy filing. Form 8-K also specified certain events, such as a change in accountant or resignation of a director, that needed to be disclosed within five days. Sarbanes-Oxley has directed the SEC to develop rules to identify which kinds of material changes in the financial condition or operations of the issuer must be disclosed "on a rapid and current basis," section 409 of Sarbanes-Oxley, 15 U.S.C. §78m(l). Section 409 moves capital market regulation in the direction of "continuous disclosure," as defined in the following case. While the holding of this case may be undermined in some circumstances by the regulations the SEC develops, it is still a good overview of the duty to disclose and thus is worth studying notwithstanding section 409.

GALLAGHER v. ABBOTT LABORATORIES

269 F.3d 806
United States Court of Appeals, Seventh Circuit
October 17, 2001

EASTERBROOK, Circuit Judge.

Year after year the Food and Drug Administration inspected the Diagnostic Division of Abbott Laboratories, found deficiencies in manufacturing quality control, and issued warnings. The Division made efforts to do better, never to the FDA's satisfaction, but until 1999 the FDA was willing to accept Abbott's promises and remedial steps. On March 17, 1999, the FDA sent Abbott another letter demanding compliance with all regulatory requirements and threatening severe consequences. This could have been read as more saber rattling — Bloomberg News revealed the letter to the financial world in June, and Abbott's stock price did not even quiver — but later developments show that it was more ominous. By September 1999 the FDA was insisting on substantial penalties plus changes in Abbott's methods of doing business. On September 29, 1999, after the markets had closed, Abbott issued a press release describing the FDA's position, asserting that Abbott was in "substantial" compliance with federal regulations, and revealing that the parties were engaged in settlement talks. Abbott's stock fell more than 6%, from $40 to $37.50, the next business day. On November 2, 1999, Abbott and the FDA resolved their differences, and a court entered a consent decree requiring Abbott to remove 125 diagnostic products from the market until it had improved its quality control and to pay a $100 million civil fine. Abbott took an accounting charge of $168 million to cover the fine and worthless inventory. The next business day Abbott's stock slumped $3.50, which together with the earlier drop implied that shareholders saw the episode as costing Abbott (in cash plus future compliance costs and lost sales) more than $5 billion. (Neither side has used the capital asset pricing model or any other means to factor market movements out of these price changes, so we take them at face value.)

Plaintiffs in these class actions under §10(b) of the Securities Exchange Act of 1934, and the SEC's Rule 10b-5 contend that Abbott committed fraud by deferring public revelation. The classes comprise all buyers of Abbott's securities between March 17 and November 2. (One class consists of persons who bought securities in ALZA, a firm that Abbott proposed to acquire through an exchange of securities and whose market price thus tracked Abbott's. For simplicity we treat these plaintiffs as purchasers of Abbott stock.) The district judge dismissed the complaints under Fed. R. Civ. P. 12(b)(6) for failure to state a claim on which relief may be granted. The market's non-reaction to Bloomberg's disclosure shows, the judge thought, that the FDA's letter was not by itself material or that the market price had earlier reflected the news; only later developments contained material information, which Abbott disclosed in September and November. Moreover, the judge concluded, plaintiffs had not identified any false or fraudulent statement by Abbott, as opposed to silence in the face of bad news. We are skeptical that these shortcomings justify dismissal for failure to state a claim on which relief may be granted; the judge's reasons seem more akin to an invocation of Fed. R. Civ. P. 9(b), which requires fraud to be pleaded with particularity, or the extra pleading requirements for securities cases created by the Private Securities Litigation Reform Act of 1995. But it is not necessary to decide whether Rule 12(b)(6), Rule 12(c), Rule 9(b), or the Reform Act supplies the best basis of decision. Nor is it necessary to decide whether the news was "material" before the FDA's negotiating position stiffened, to decide whether Abbott acted with the state of mind necessary to support liability under Rule 10b-5, or to address other potential stumbling blocks. What sinks plaintiffs' position is their inability to identify any false statement — or for that matter any truthful statement made misleading by the omission of news about the FDA's demands.

Much of plaintiffs' argument reads as if firms have an absolute duty to disclose all information material to stock prices as soon as news comes into their possession. Yet that is not the way the securities laws work. We do not have a system of continuous disclosure. Instead firms are entitled to keep silent (about good news as well as bad news) unless positive law creates a duty to disclose. Until the Securities Act of 1933 there was no federal regulation of corporate disclosure. The 1933 Act requires firms to reveal information only when they issue securities, and the duty is owed only to persons who buy from the issuer or an underwriter distributing on its behalf; every other transaction is exempt under §4. (No member of either class contends that he purchased securities from Abbott, or an underwriter on Abbott's behalf, between March 17 and November 2.) Section 13 of the Securities Exchange Act of 1934, 15 U.S.C. §78m, adds that the SEC may require issuers to file annual and other periodic reports — with the emphasis on *periodic* rather than continuous. Section 13 and the implementing regulations contemplate that these reports will be snapshots of the corporation's status on or near the filing date, with updates due not when something "material" happens, but on the next prescribed filing date.

Regulations implementing §13 require a comprehensive annual filing, the Form 10-K report, and less extensive quarterly supplements on Form 10-Q. The supplements need not bring up to date everything contained in the annual 10-K report; counsel for the plaintiff classes conceded at oral argument that nothing in Regulation S-K (the SEC's list of required disclosures) requires either an updating of Form 10-K reports more often than annually, or a disclosure in a quarterly Form 10-Q report of information about the firm's regulatory problems. The regulations that provide for disclosures on Form 10-Q tell us *which* items in the annual report must be updated (a subset of the full list), and how often (quarterly).

Many proposals have been made to do things differently — to junk this combination of sale-based disclosure with periodic follow-up and replace it with a system under which *issuers* rather than *securities* are registered and disclosure must be continuous. *E.g.*, American Law Institute, *Federal Securities Code* xxvii-xxviii, §602 & commentary (1978); Securities and Exchange Commission, *Report of the Advisory Committee on the Capital Formation and Regulatory Process* 9-14, 36-38 (1996). Regulation S-K goes some distance in this direction by defining identical items of disclosure for registration of stock and issuers' subsequent reports, and by authorizing the largest issuers to use their annual 10-K reports as the kernels of registration statements for new securities. But Regulation S-K does not replace periodic with continuous disclosure, and the more ambitious proposals to do this have not been adopted.

The ALI's proposal, for example, was embraced by the SEC, *see* 1933 Act Release No. 6242 (Sept. 18, 1980); 1933 Act Release No. 6377 (Jan. 31, 1982), but never seriously pursued, and revisions of Regulation S-K satisfied many of the original supporters of the ALI's proposal. The advisory committee report, prepared by a distinguished group of scholars and practitioners under the leadership of Commissioner Steven M.H. Wallman, did not persuade the SEC's other members and was not taken up by the agency as a legislative plan or even as the basis of a demonstration project. Whatever may be said for and against these proposals, they must be understood as projects for legislation (and to a limited extent for the use of the SEC's rulemaking powers); judges have no authority to scoop the political branches and adopt continuous disclosure under the banner of Rule 10b-5. *Especially* not under that banner, for Rule 10b-5 condemns only fraud, and a corporation does not commit fraud by standing on its rights under a periodic-disclosure system. The Supreme Court has insisted that this judicially created right of action be used only to implement, and not to alter, the rules found in the text of the 1933 and 1934 Acts.

Trying to locate some statement that was either false or materially misleading because it did not mention the FDA's position, plaintiffs pointed in the district court to several reports filed or statements made by Abbott before November 2, 1999. All but two of these have fallen by the wayside on appeal. What remain are Abbott's Form 10-K annual report for 1998 filed in March 1999 and an oral statement that Miles White, Abbott's CEO, made at the annual shareholders' meeting the next month.

Plaintiffs rely principally on Item 303(a)(3)(ii) of Regulation S-K, which provides that registration statements and annual 10-K reports must reveal

> any known trends or uncertainties that have had or that the registrant reasonably expects will have a material favorable or unfavorable impact on net sales or revenues or income from continuing operations.

The FDA's letter, and its negotiating demands, are within this description, according to the plaintiff classes. We shall assume that this is so. The 10-K report did state that Abbott is "subject to comprehensive government regulation" and that "[g]overnment regulatory actions can result in . . . sanctions." Plaintiffs say that this is too general in light of the FDA's letter and Abbott's continuing inability to satisfy the FDA's demands. Again we shall assume that plaintiffs are right. But there is a fundamental problem: The 10-K report was filed on March 9, 1999, and the FDA's letter is dated March 17, eight days later. Unless Abbott had a time machine, it could not have described on March 9 a letter that had yet to be written.

Attempting to surmount this temporal problem, plaintiffs insist that Abbott had a "duty to correct" the 10-K report. Yet a statement may be "corrected" only if it was *in*correct when made, and nothing said as of March 9 was incorrect . . . .

As for White's statements at the annual meeting: he said very little that was concrete (as opposed to puffery), and everything concrete was true. White said, for example:

> The outcome [of our efforts] has been growth more than five times faster than the diagnostics market. We expect this trend to continue for the foreseeable future, due to the unprecedented state of our new product cycle. By supplementing our internal investment with opportunistic technology acquisitions, Abbott's diagnostics pipeline is fuller than ever before.

The statement about past performance was accurate, and the plaintiffs have not given us any reason to doubt that White honestly believed that similar growth would continue, or that White honestly believed "Abbott's diagnostics pipeline [to be] fuller than ever before." Even with the benefit of hindsight these statements cannot be gainsaid. Here is where Rule 9(b) pinches: Plaintiffs have done nothing to meet the requirements for pleading fraud with respect to the annual meeting, even if it were possible (which we doubt) to treat as "fraud" the predictive components in White's boosterism.

Affirmed.

2.   *Materiality Requirement/Reliance*

We have already seen the definition of a "material" fact or omission in Chapters 6 and 7: a fact a reasonable investor would consider significant in the total mix of information available about a company. We have also already seen that this definition is quite fact- and context-specific, and that in recent years the parameters of what "reasonable investors" want to know about a company are expanding from financial information, which is presumably always material, to social and environmental information in some instances.

One of the more interesting problems in securities regulation and section 10(b)/Rule 10b-5 causes of action concerns the materiality of speculative or future facts. After all, an investment today in a company is an indication of the investor's view of the company's future, and any reasonable investor would want that view to be as informed as management's view concerning current trends, risks, and business developments that might affect the future of the company. The following case, Basic Inc. v. Levinson, sets out the process of analysis for determining whether speculative future events are material. This case is also of major importance in understanding the scope of section 10(b)/Rule 10b-5's reliance requirement, so that part of the opinion is also included. To understand the significance of the discussion of reliance, some context is in order.

Under the common law of fraud, plaintiffs must show that they relied upon a material misstatement of fact to their economic detriment. Section 10(b) was enacted to expand the scope of the common law cause of action for fraud, though, because in the early 1930s common law remedies were thought to have been inadequate to protect investors during the Roaring Twenties. Two related problems with the common law reliance element are discussed in Basic

Inc. v. Levinson: first, while reliance is an element of a plaintiffs' case in a face-to-face transaction, what sort of reliance must be proved in a "market" transaction (on an Exchange or over NASDAQ)? Also, section 10(b) expanded the scope of the common law cause of action for fraud beyond misstatements of fact to omissions to state necessary facts. But how can one "rely" on an omission? Basic Inc. v. Levinson's "fraud on the market" theory addresses the first problem, and the Court's discussion of Affiliated Ute Citizens v. United States summarizes its prior resolution of the second problem.

BASIC INC. v. LEVINSON

485 U.S. 224, 108 S. Ct. 978
Supreme Court of the United States
March 7, 1988

Justice BLACKMUN.

This case requires us to apply the materiality requirement of §10(b) of the Securities Exchange Act of 1934 (1934 Act), 48 Stat. 881, as amended, 15 U.S.C. §78a *et seq.*, and the Securities and Exchange Commission's Rule 10b-5, 17 CFR §240.10b-5 (1987), promulgated thereunder, in the context of preliminary corporate merger discussions. We must also determine whether a person who traded a corporation's shares on a securities exchange after the issuance of a materially misleading statement by the corporation may invoke a rebuttable presumption that, in trading, he relied on the integrity of the price set by the market.

I

Prior to December 20, 1978, Basic Incorporated was a publicly traded company primarily engaged in the business of manufacturing chemical refractories for the steel industry. As early as 1965 or 1966, Combustion Engineering, Inc., a company producing mostly alumina-based refractories, expressed some interest in acquiring Basic, but was deterred from pursuing this inclination seriously because of antitrust concerns it then entertained. . . . In 1976, however, regulatory action opened the way to a renewal of Combustion's interest. The "Strategic Plan," dated October 25, 1976, for Combustion's Industrial Products Group included the objective: "Acquire Basic Inc. $30 million." . . .

Beginning in September 1976, Combustion representatives had meetings and telephone conversations with Basic officers and directors, including petitioners here [members of the board of directors], concerning the possibility of a merger. During 1977 and 1978, Basic made three public statements denying that it was engaged in merger negotiations.[4] On December 18, 1978, Basic

---

4. On October 21, 1977, after heavy trading and a new high in Basic stock, the following news item appeared in the Cleveland Plain Dealer:

> "[Basic] President Max Muller said the company knew no reason for the stock's activity and that no negotiations were under way with any company for a merger. He said Flintkote recently denied Wall Street rumors that it would make a tender offer of $25 a share for control of the Cleveland-based maker of refractories for the steel industry." App. 363.

asked the New York Stock Exchange to suspend trading in its shares and issued a release stating that it had been "approached" by another company concerning a merger. *Id.*, at 413. On December 19, Basic's board endorsed Combustion's offer of $46 per share for its common stock, *id.*, at 335, 414-416, and on the following day publicly announced its approval of Combustion's tender offer for all outstanding shares.

Respondents are former Basic shareholders who sold their stock after Basic's first public statement of October 21, 1977, and before the suspension of trading in December 1978. Respondents brought a class action against Basic and its directors, asserting that the defendants issued three false or misleading public statements and thereby were in violation of §10(b) of the 1934 Act and of Rule 10b-5. Respondents alleged that they were injured by selling Basic shares at artificially depressed prices in a market affected by petitioners' misleading statements and in reliance thereon.

The District Court adopted a presumption of reliance by members of the plaintiff class upon petitioners' public statements that enabled the court to conclude that common questions of fact or law predominated over particular questions pertaining to individual plaintiffs. *See* Fed. Rule Civ. Proc. 23(b)(3). The District Court therefore certified respondents' class. On the merits, however, the District Court granted summary judgment for the defendants. It held that, as a matter of law, any misstatements were immaterial: there were no negotiations ongoing at the time of the first statement, and although negotiations were taking place when the second and third statements were issued, those negotiations were not "destined, with reasonable certainty, to become a merger agreement in principle." . . .

The United States Court of Appeals for the Sixth Circuit affirmed the class certification, but reversed the District Court's summary judgment, and remanded the case. 786 F.2d 741 (1986). The court reasoned that while petitioners were under no general duty to disclose their discussions with Combustion, any statement the company voluntarily released could not be " 'so incomplete as to mislead.' " *Id.*, at 746, quoting SEC v. Texas Gulf Sulphur Co., 401 F.2d 833, 862 (2d Cir. 1968) (en banc). In the Court of Appeals' view, Basic's statements that no negotiations where taking place, and that it knew of no corporate developments to account for the heavy trading activity, were misleading. With respect to materiality, the court rejected the argument that preliminary merger discussions are immaterial as a matter of law, and held that "once a statement is made denying the existence of any discussions, even discussions that might not have been material in absence of the denial

---

On September 25, 1978, in reply to an inquiry from the New York Stock Exchange, Basic issued a release concerning increased activity in its stock and stated that

> "management is unaware of any present or pending company development that would result in the abnormally heavy trading activity and price fluctuation in company shares that have been experienced in the past few days." *Id.*, at 401.

On November 6, 1978, Basic issued to its shareholders a "Nine Months Report 1978." This Report stated:

> "With regard to the stock market activity in the Company's shares we remain unaware of any present or pending developments which would account for the high volume of trading and price fluctuations in recent months." *Id.*, at 403.

are material because they make the statement made untrue." 786 F.2d, at 749.

The Court of Appeals joined a number of other Circuits in accepting the "fraud-on-the-market theory" to create a rebuttable presumption that respondents relied on petitioners' material misrepresentations, noting that without the presumption it would be impractical to certify a class under Federal Rule of Civil Procedure 23(b)(3). *See* 786 F.2d, at 750-751.

We granted certiorari, 479 U.S. 1083 (1987), to resolve the split, *see* Part III, *infra,* among the Courts of Appeals as to the standard of materiality applicable to preliminary merger discussions, and to determine whether the courts below properly applied a presumption of reliance in certifying the class, rather than requiring each class member to show direct reliance on Basic's statements.

II

The 1934 Act was designed to protect investors against manipulation of stock prices. *See* S. Rep. No. 792, 73d Cong., 2d Sess., 1-5 (1934). Underlying the adoption of extensive disclosure requirements was a legislative philosophy: "There cannot be honest markets without honest publicity. Manipulation and dishonest practices of the market place thrive upon mystery and secrecy." H.R. Rep. No. 1383, 73d Cong., 2d Sess., 11 (1934). This Court "repeatedly has described the 'fundamental purpose' of the Act as implementing a 'philosophy of full disclosure.'" Santa Fe Industries, Inc. v. Green, 430 U.S. 462, 477-478 (1977), quoting SEC v. Capital Gains Research Bureau, Inc., 375 U.S. 180, 186 (1963).

Pursuant to its authority under §10(b) of the 1934 Act, 15 U.S.C. §78j, the Securities and Exchange Commission promulgated Rule 10b-5. Judicial interpretation and application, legislative acquiescence, and the passage of time have removed any doubt that a private cause of action exists for a violation of §10(b) and Rule 10b-5, and constitutes an essential tool for enforcement of the 1934 Act's requirements. *See, e.g.,* Ernst & Ernst v. Hochfelder, 425 U.S. 185, 196 (1976); Blue Chip Stamps v. Manor Drug Stores, 421 U.S. 723, 730 (1975).

The Court previously has addressed various positive and common-law requirements for a violation of §10(b) or of Rule 10b-5. *See, e.g.,* Santa Fe Industries, Inc. v. Green, *supra* ("manipulative or deceptive" requirement of the statute); Blue Chip Stamps v. Manor Drug Stores, *supra* ("in connection with the purchase or sale" requirement of the Rule); Dirks v. SEC, 463 U.S. 646 (duty to disclose); Chiarella v. United States, 445 U.S. 222 (1980) (same); Ernst & Ernst v. Hochfelder, *supra* (scienter). *See also* Carpenter v. United States, 484 U.S. 19 (1987) (confidentiality). The Court also explicitly has defined a standard of materiality under the securities laws, *see* TSC Industries, Inc. v. Northway, Inc., 426 U.S. 438 (1976), concluding in the proxy-solicitation context that "[a]n omitted fact is material if there is a substantial likelihood that a reasonable shareholder would consider it important in deciding how to vote." *Id.,* at 449. Acknowledging that certain information concerning corporate developments could well be of "dubious significance," *id.,* at 448, the Court was careful not to set too low a standard of materiality; it was concerned that a minimal standard might bring an overabundance of information within its reach, and lead management "simply to bury the shareholders in an avalanche of trivial information—a result that is hardly conducive to informed decisionmaking." *Id.*, at 448-449. It further explained that to fulfill the materiality requirement "there must be a substantial likelihood that the disclosure of the omitted fact would have been viewed by the reasonable investor as having significantly altered the 'total mix' of information made available." *Id.*, at 449. We now expressly adopt the *TSC Industries* standard of materiality for the §10(b) and Rule 10b-5 context.

III

The application of this materiality standard to preliminary merger discussions is not self-evident. Where the impact of the corporate development on the target's fortune is certain and clear, the *TSC Industries* materiality definition admits straightforward application. Where, on the other hand, the event is contingent or speculative in nature, it is difficult to ascertain whether the "reasonable investor" would have considered the omitted information significant at the time. Merger negotiations, because of the ever-present possibility that the contemplated transaction will not be effectuated, fall into the latter category.

A

Petitioners urge upon us a Third Circuit test for resolving this difficulty. . . . Under this approach, preliminary merger discussions do not become material until "agreement-in-principle" as to the price and structure of the transaction has been reached between the would-be merger partners. *See* Greenfield v. Heublein, Inc., 742 F.2d 751, 757 (3d Cir. 1984), *cert. denied*, 469 U.S. 1215 (1985). By definition, then, information concerning any negotiations not yet at the agreement-in-principle stage could be withheld or even misrepresented without a violation of Rule 10b-5.

Three rationales have been offered in support of the "agreement-in-principle" test. The first derives from the concern expressed in *TSC Industries* that an investor not be overwhelmed by excessively detailed and trivial information, and focuses on the substantial risk that preliminary merger discussions may collapse: because such discussions are inherently tentative, disclosure of their existence itself could mislead investors and foster false optimism. *See* Greenfield v. Heublein, Inc., 742 F.2d, at 756; Reiss v. Pan American World Airways, Inc., 711 F.2d 11, 14 (2d Cir. 1983). The other two justifications for the agreement-in-principle standard are based on management concerns: because the requirement of "agreement-in-principle" limits the scope of disclosure obligations, it helps preserve the confidentiality of merger discussions where earlier disclosure might prejudice the negotiations; and the test also provides a usable, bright-line rule for determining when disclosure must be made. *See* Greenfield v. Heublein, Inc., 742 F.2d, at 757; Flamm v. Eberstadt, 814 F.2d 1169, 1176-1178 (7th Cir. 1987).

None of these policy-based rationales, however, purports to explain why drawing the line at agreement-in-principle reflects the significance of the information upon the investor's decision. The first rationale, and the only one connected to the concerns expressed in *TSC Industries*, stands soundly rejected, even by a Court of Appeals that otherwise has accepted the wisdom of the agreement-in-principle test. "It assumes that investors are nitwits, unable to appreciate — even when told — that mergers are risky propositions up until the closing." Flamm v. Eberstadt, 814 F.2d, at 1175. Disclosure, and not paternalistic withholding of accurate information, is the policy chosen and expressed by Congress. We have recognized time and again, a "fundamental purpose" of the various Securities Acts, "was to substitute a philosophy of full disclosure for the philosophy of *caveat emptor* and thus to achieve a high standard of business ethics in the securities industry." SEC v. Capital Gains Research Bureau, Inc., 375 U.S., at 186. . . . The role of the materiality requirement is not to "attribute to investors a child-like simplicity, an inability to grasp the probabilistic significance of negotiations," Flamm v. Eberstadt, 814 F.2d, at 1175, but to filter out essentially useless information that a reasonable investor would not consider significant, even as part of a larger "mix" of factors to consider in making his investment decision. TSC Industries, Inc. v. Northway, Inc., 426 U.S., at 448-449.

The second rationale, the importance of secrecy during the early stages of merger discussions, also seems irrelevant to an assessment whether their existence is significant to the trading decision of a reasonable investor. To avoid a "bidding war" over its target, an acquiring firm often will insist that negotiations remain confidential, *see, e.g.*, In re Carnation Co., Exchange Act Release No. 22214, 33 S.E.C. Docket 1025 (1985), and at least one Court of Appeals has stated that "silence pending settlement of the price and structure of a deal is beneficial to most investors, most of the time." Flamm v. Eberstadt, 814 F.2d at 1177.

We need not ascertain, however, whether secrecy necessarily maximizes shareholder wealth — although we note that the proposition is at least disputed as a matter of theory and empirical research — for this case does not concern the *timing* of a disclosure; it concerns only its accuracy and completeness. We face here the narrow question whether information concerning the existence and status of preliminary merger discussions is significant to the reasonable investor's trading decision. Arguments based on the premise that some disclosure would be "premature" in a sense are more properly considered under the rubric of an issuer's duty to disclose. The "secrecy" rationale is simply inapposite to the definition of materiality.

The final justification offered in support of the agreement-in-principle test seems to be directed solely at the comfort of corporate managers. A bright-line rule indeed is easier to follow than a standard that requires the exercise of judgment in the light of all the circumstances. But ease of application alone is not an excuse for ignoring the purposes of the Securities Acts and Congress' policy decisions. Any approach that designates a single fact or occurrence as always determinative of an inherently fact-specific finding such as materiality must necessarily be overinclusive or underinclusive. In *TSC Industries* this Court explained: "The determination [of materiality] requires delicate assessments of the inferences a 'reasonable shareholder' would draw from a given set of facts and the significance of those inferences to him. . . . " 426 U.S., at 450. . . .

We therefore find no valid justification for artificially excluding from the definition of materiality information concerning merger discussions, which would otherwise be considered significant to the trading decision of a reasonable investor, merely because agreement-in-principle as to price and structure has not yet been reached by the parties or their representatives.

B

The Sixth Circuit explicitly rejected the agreement-in-principle test, as we do today, but in its place adopted a rule that, if taken literally, would be equally insensitive, in our view, to the distinction between materiality and the other elements of an action under Rule 10b-5:

> When a company whose stock is publicly traded makes a statement, as Basic did, that "no negotiations" are underway, and that the corporation knows of "no reason for the stock's activity," and that "management is unaware of any present or pending corporate development that would result in the abnormally heavy trading activity," information concerning ongoing acquisition discussions becomes material *by virtue of the statement denying their existence.* . . .

786 F.2d, at 748-749 (emphasis in original).

This approach, however, fails to recognize that, in order to prevail on a Rule 10b-5 claim, a plaintiff must show that the statements were *misleading* as to a *material* fact. It is not enough that a statement is false or incomplete, if the misrepresented fact is otherwise insignificant.

C

Even before this Court's decision in *TSC Industries,* the Second Circuit had explained the role of the materiality requirement of Rule 10b-5, with respect to contingent or speculative information or events, in a manner that gave that term meaning that is independent of the other provisions of the Rule. Under such circumstances, materiality "will depend at any given time upon a balancing of both the indicated probability that the event will occur and the anticipated magnitude of the event in light of the totality of the company activity." SEC v. Texas Gulf Sulphur Co., 401 F.2d, at 849. Interestingly, neither the Third Circuit decision adopting the agreement-in-principle test nor petitioners here take issue with this general standard. Rather, they suggest that with respect to preliminary merger discussions, there are good reasons to draw a line at agreement on price and structure.

In a subsequent decision, the late Judge Friendly, writing for a Second Circuit panel, applied the *Texas Gulf Sulphur* probability/magnitude approach in the specific context of preliminary merger negotiations. After acknowledging that materiality is something to be determined on the basis of the particular facts of each case, he stated:

> "Since a merger in which it is bought out is the most important event that can occur in a small corporation's life, to wit, its death, we think that inside information, as regards a merger of this sort, can become material at an earlier stage than would be the case as regards lesser transactions—and this even though the mortality rate of mergers in such formative stages is doubtless high." SEC v. Geon Industries, Inc., 531 F.2d 39, 47-48 (2d Cir. 1976).

We agree with that analysis.

Whether merger discussions in any particular case are material therefore depends on the facts. Generally, in order to assess the probability that the event will occur, a factfinder will need to look to indicia of interest in the trans-action at the highest corporate levels. Without attempting to catalog all such possible factors, we note by way of example that board resolutions, instructions to investment bankers, and actual negotiations between principals or their intermediaries may serve as indicia of interest. To assess the magnitude of the transaction to the issuer of the securities allegedly manipulated, a factfinder will need to consider such facts as the size of the two corporate entities and of the potential premiums over market value. No particular event or factor short of closing the transaction need be either necessary or sufficient by itself to render merger discussions material.[17]

As we clarify today, materiality depends on the significance the reasonable investor would place on the withheld or misrepresented information. The fact-specific inquiry we endorse here is consistent with the approach a number of courts have taken in assessing the materiality of merger negotiations. Because the standard of materiality we have adopted differs from that used by both courts below, we remand the case for reconsideration of the question whether a grant of summary judgment is appropriate on this record.

IV

A

We turn to the question of reliance and the fraud-on-the-market theory. Succinctly put:

> "The fraud on the market theory is based on the hypothesis that, in an open and developed securities market, the price of a company's stock is determined by the available material information regarding the company and its business. . . . Misleading statements will therefore defraud purchasers of stock even if the purchasers do not directly rely on the misstatements. . . . The causal connection between the defendants' fraud and the plaintiffs' purchase of stock in such a case is no less significant than in a case of direct reliance on misrepresentations." Peil v. Speiser, 806 F.2d 1154, 1160-1161 (3d Cir. 1986).

Our task, of course, is not to assess the general validity of the theory, but to consider whether it was proper for the courts below to apply a rebuttable presumption of reliance, supported in part by the fraud-on-the-market theory. *Cf.* the comments of the dissent, *post,* at 994-995.

This case required resolution of several common questions of law and fact concerning the falsity or misleading nature of the three public statements made by Basic, the presence or absence of scienter, and the materiality of the misrepresentations, if any. In their amended complaint, the named plaintiffs alleged

---

17. To be actionable, of course, a statement must also be misleading. Silence, absent a duty to disclose, is not misleading under Rule 10b-5. "No comment" statements are generally the functional equivalent of silence. *See* In re Carnation Co., Exchange Act Release No. 22214, 33 S.E.C. Docket 1025 (1985). *See also* New York Stock Exchange Listed Company Manual §202.01, reprinted in 3 CCH Fed. Sec. L. Rep. ¶23,515 (1987) (premature public announcement may properly be delayed for valid business purpose and where adequate security can be maintained); American Stock Exchange Company Guide §§401-405, reprinted in 3 CCH Fed. Sec. L. Rep. ¶¶23,124A-23,124E (1985) (similar provisions).

that in reliance on Basic's statements they sold their shares of Basic stock in the depressed market created by petitioners. *See* Amended Complaint in No. C79-1220 (ND Ohio), ¶¶27, 29, 35, 40; *see also id.*, ¶33 (alleging effect on market price of Basic's statements).

Requiring proof of individualized reliance from each member of the proposed plaintiff class effectively would have prevented respondents from proceeding with a class action, since individual issues then would have overwhelmed the common ones. The District Court found that the presumption of reliance created by the fraud-on-the-market theory provided "a practical resolution to the problem of balancing the substantive requirement of proof of reliance in securities cases against the procedural requisites of [Federal Rule of Civil Procedure] 23." The District Court thus concluded that with reference to each public statement and its impact upon the open market for Basic shares, common questions predominated over individual questions, as required by Federal Rules of Civil Procedure 23(a)(2) and (b)(3).

Petitioners and their *amici* complain that the fraud-on-the-market theory effectively eliminates the requirement that a plaintiff asserting a claim under Rule 10b-5 prove reliance. They note that reliance is and long has been an element of common-law fraud, and argue that because the analogous express right of action includes a reliance requirement, *see, e.g.*, §18(a) of the 1934 Act, as amended, 15 U.S.C. §78r(a), so too must an action implied under §10(b).

We agree that reliance is an element of a Rule 10b-5 cause of action. *See* Ernst & Ernst v. Hochfelder, 425 U.S., at 206 (quoting Senate Report). Reliance provides the requisite causal connection between a defendant's misrepresentation and a plaintiff's injury. There is, however, more than one way to demonstrate the causal connection. Indeed, we previously have dispensed with a requirement of positive proof of reliance, where a duty to disclose material information had been breached [an omission case], concluding that the necessary nexus between the plaintiffs' injury and the defendant's wrongful conduct had been established. *See* Affiliated Ute Citizens v. United States, 406 U.S., at 153-154. Similarly, we did not require proof that material omissions or misstatements in a proxy statement decisively affected voting, because the proxy solicitation itself, rather than the defect in the solicitation materials, served as an essential link in the transaction. *See* Mills v. Electric Auto-Lite Co., 396 U.S. 375, 384-385 (1970).

The modern securities markets, literally involving millions of shares changing hands daily, differ from the face-to-face transactions contemplated by early fraud cases, and our understanding of Rule 10b-5's reliance requirement must encompass these differences.[22]

"In face-to-face transactions, the inquiry into an investor's reliance upon information is into the subjective pricing of that information by that investor. With the presence of a market, the market is interposed between seller and buyer and, ideally, transmits information to the investor in the processed form of a market price. Thus the market is performing a substantial part of the valuation process performed by the investor in a face-to-face transaction. The market is acting as the

---

22. Actions under Rule 10b-5 are distinct from common-law deceit and misrepresentation claims, *see* Blue Chip Stamps v. Manor Drug Stores, 421 U.S. 723, 744-745 (1975), and are in part designed to add to the protections provided investors by the common law, *see* Herman & MacLean v. Huddleston, 459 U.S. 375, 388-389 (1983).

unpaid agent of the investor, informing him that given all the information available to it, the value of the stock is worth the market price." In re LTV Securities Litigation, 88 F.R.D. 134, 143 (ND Tex. 1980).

B

Presumptions typically serve to assist courts in managing circumstances in which direct proof, for one reason or another, is rendered difficult. *See, e.g.,* 1 D. Louisell & C. Mueller, *Federal Evidence* 541-542 (1977). The courts below accepted a presumption, created by the fraud-on-the-market theory and subject to rebuttal by petitioners, that persons who had traded Basic shares had done so in reliance on the integrity of the price set by the market, but because of petitioners' material misrepresentations that price had been fraudulently depressed. Requiring a plaintiff to show a speculative state of facts, *i.e.,* how he would have acted if omitted material information had been disclosed, *see* Affiliated Ute Citizens v. United States, 406 U.S., at 153-154 or if the misrepresentation had not been made, *see* Sharp v. Coopers & Lybrand, 649 F.2d 175, 188 (3d Cir. 1981), would place an unnecessarily unrealistic evidentiary burden on the Rule 10b-5 plaintiff who has traded on an impersonal market. *Cf.* Mills v. Electric Auto-Lite Co., 396 U.S., at 385.

Arising out of considerations of fairness, public policy, and probability, as well as judicial economy, presumptions are also useful devices for allocating the burdens of proof between parties. *See* E. Cleary, McCormick on Evidence 968-969 (3d ed. 1984); *see also* Fed. Rule Evid. 301 and Advisory Committee Notes, 28 U.S.C. App., p.685. The presumption of reliance employed in this case is consistent with, and, by facilitating Rule 10b-5 litigation, supports, the congressional policy embodied in the 1934 Act. In drafting that Act, Congress expressly relied on the premise that securities markets are affected by information, and enacted legislation to facilitate an investor's reliance on the integrity of those markets:

> "No investor, no speculator, can safely buy and sell securities upon the exchanges without having an intelligent basis for forming his judgment as to the value of the securities he buys or sells. The idea of a free and open public market is built upon the theory that competing judgments of buyers and sellers as to the fair price of a security brings [*sic*] about a situation where the market price reflects as nearly as possible a just price. Just as artificial manipulation tends to upset the true function of an open market, so the hiding and secreting of important information obstructs the operation of the markets as indices of real value." H.R. Rep. No. 1383 at 11.

See Lipton v. Documation, Inc., 734 F.2d 740, 748 (CA 11 1984.)

The presumption is also supported by common sense and probability. Recent empirical studies have tended to confirm Congress' premise that the market price of shares traded on well-developed markets reflects all publicly available information, and, hence, any material misrepresentations. It has been noted that "it is hard to imagine that there ever is a buyer or seller who does not rely on market integrity. Who would knowingly roll the dice in a crooked crap game?" Schlanger v. Four-Phase Systems Inc., 555 F. Supp. 535, 538 (S.D.N.Y. 1982). Indeed, nearly every court that has considered the proposition has concluded that where materially misleading statements have been disseminated into an impersonal, well-developed market for securities, the reliance of individual plaintiffs on the integrity of the market price may be presumed. Commentators generally have applauded the adoption of one variation or another of the fraud-on-the-market theory. An investor who buys or sells stock at the price set by the market does so in reliance on the integrity of that price. Because most publicly available information is reflected in market price, an investor's reliance on any public material misrepresentations, therefore, may be presumed for purposes of a Rule 10b-5 action.

Any showing that severs the link between the alleged misrepresentation and either the price received (or paid) by the plaintiff, or his decision to trade at a fair market price, will be sufficient to rebut the presumption of reliance. For example, if petitioners could show that the "market makers" were privy to the truth about the merger discussions here with Combustion, and thus that the market price would not have been affected by their misrepresentations, the causal connection could be broken: the basis for finding that the fraud had been transmitted through market price would be gone. Similarly, if, despite petitioners' allegedly fraudulent attempt to manipulate market price, news of the merger discussions credibly entered the market and dissipated the effects of the misstatements, those who traded Basic shares after the corrective statements would have no direct or indirect connection with the fraud. . . .

V

The judgment of the Court of Appeals is vacated, and the case is remanded to that court for further proceedings consistent with this opinion.

It is so ordered.

Justice WHITE, with whom Justice O'CONNOR joins, concurring in part and dissenting in part. I join Parts I-III of the Court's opinion, as I agree that the standard of materiality we set forth in TSC Industries, Inc. v. Northway, Inc., 426 U.S. 438, 449 (1976), should be applied to actions under §10(b) and Rule 10b-5. But I dissent from the remainder of the Court's holding because I do not agree that the "fraud-on-the-market" theory should be applied in this case.

I

Even when compared to the relatively youthful private cause-of-action under §10(b), *see* Kardon v. National Gypsum Co., 69 F. Supp. 512 (E.D. Pa. 1946), the fraud-on-the-market theory is a mere babe.[1] Yet today, the Court embraces this theory with the sweeping confidence usually reserved for more mature legal doctrines. In so doing, I fear that the Court's decision may have many adverse, unintended effects as it is applied and interpreted in the years to come. . . .

1. The earliest Court of Appeals case adopting this theory cited by the Court is Blackie v. Barrack, 524 F.2d 891 (CA 9 1975), *cert. denied*, 429 U.S. 816, 97 S. Ct. 57, 50 L. Ed. 2d 75 (1976). Moreover, widespread acceptance of the fraud-on-the-market theory in the Courts of Appeals cannot be placed any earlier than five or six years ago. *See ante*, at 991, n.24; Brief for Securities and Exchange Commission as *Amicus Curiae* 21, n.24.

B.

But even as the Court attempts to limit the fraud-on-the-market theory it endorses today, the pitfalls in its approach are revealed by previous uses by the lower courts of the broader versions of the theory. Confusion and contradiction in court rulings are inevitable when traditional legal analysis is replaced with economic theorization by the federal courts.

In general, the case law developed in this Court with respect to §10(b) and Rule 10b-5 has been based on doctrines with which we, as judges, are familiar: common-law doctrines of fraud and deceit. *See, e.g.*, Santa Fe Industries, Inc. v. Green, 430 U.S. 462, 471-477 (1977). Even when we have extended civil liability under Rule 10b-5 to a broader reach than the common law had previously permitted, *see ante*, at 991, n.22, we have retained familiar legal principles as our guideposts. *See, e.g.*, Herman & MacLean v. Huddleston, 459 U.S. 375, 389-390 (1983). The federal courts have proved adept at developing an evolving jurisprudence of Rule 10b-5 in such a manner. But with no staff economists, no experts schooled in the "efficient-capital-market hypothesis," no ability to test the validity of empirical market studies, we are not well equipped to embrace novel constructions of a statute based on contemporary microeconomic theory.

The "wrong turns" in those Court of Appeals and District Court fraud-on-the-market decisions which the Court implicitly rejects as going too far should be ample illustration of the dangers when economic theories replace legal rules as the basis for recovery. Yet the Court today ventures into this area beyond its expertise, beyond—by its own admission—the confines of our previous fraud cases. *See ante*, at 989-990. Even if I agreed with the Court that "modern securities markets . . . involving millions of shares changing hands daily" require that the "understanding of Rule 10b-5's reliance requirement" be changed, *ibid.*, I prefer that such changes come from Congress in amending §10(b). The Congress, with its superior resources and expertise, is far better equipped than the federal courts for the task of determining how modern economic theory and global financial markets require that established legal notions of fraud be modified. In choosing to make these decisions itself, the Court, I fear, embarks on a course that it does not genuinely understand, giving rise to consequences it cannot foresee.[5]

For while the economists' theories which underpin the fraud-on-the-market presumption may have the appeal of mathematical exactitude and scientific certainty, they are—in the end—nothing more than theories which may or may not prove accurate upon further consideration. Even the most earnest advocates of economic analysis of the law recognize this. *See, e.g.*, Easterbrook, Afterword: Knowledge and Answers, 85 Colum. L. Rev. 1117, 1118

5. For example, Judge Posner in his Economic Analysis of Law §15.8, pp.423-424 (3d ed. 1986), submits that the fraud-on-the-market theory produces the "economically correct result" in Rule 10b-5 cases but observes that the question of damages under the theory is quite problematic. Notwithstanding the fact that "[a]t first blush it might seem obvious," the proper calculation of damages when the fraud-on-the-market theory is applied must rest on several "assumptions" about "social costs" which are "difficult to quantify." *Ibid.* Of course, answers to the question of the proper measure of damages in a fraud-on-the-market case are essential for proper implementation of the fraud-on-the-market presumption. Not surprisingly, the difficult damages question is one the Court expressly declines to address today. *Ante*, at 992, n.27.

(1985). Thus, while the majority states that, for purposes of reaching its result it need only make modest assumptions about the way in which "market professionals generally" do their jobs, and how the conduct of market professionals affects stock prices, *ante,* at 991, n.23, I doubt that we are in much of a position to assess which theories aptly describe the functioning of the securities industry.

Consequently, I cannot join the Court in its effort to reconfigure the securities laws, based on recent economic theories, to better fit what it perceives to be the new realities of financial markets. I would leave this task to others more equipped for the job than we.

C.

At the bottom of the Court's conclusion that the fraud-on-the-market theory sustains a presumption of reliance is the assumption that individuals rely "on the integrity of the market price" when buying or selling stock in "impersonal, well-developed market[s] for securities." *Ante,* at 991-992. Even if I was prepared to accept (as a matter of common sense or general understanding) the assumption that most persons buying or selling stock do so in response to the market price, the fraud-on-the-market theory goes further. For in adopting a "presumption of reliance," the Court *also* assumes that buyers and sellers rely — not just on the market price — but on the "*integrity*" of that price. It is this aspect of the fraud-on-the-market hypothesis which most mystifies me.

To define the term "integrity of the market price," the majority quotes approvingly from cases which suggest that investors are entitled to "'rely on the price of a stock as a reflection of its value.'" *Ante,* at 990 (quoting Peil v. Speiser, 806 F.2d 1154, 1161 (3d Cir. 1986)). But the meaning of this phrase eludes me, for it implicitly suggests that stocks have some "true value" that is measurable by a standard other than their market price. While the scholastics of medieval times professed a means to make such a valuation of a commodity's "worth," I doubt that the federal courts of our day are similarly equipped.

Even if securities had some "value" — knowable and distinct from the market price of a stock — investors do not always share the Court's presumption that a stock's price is a "reflection of [this] value." Indeed, "many investors purchase or sell stock because they believe the price *inaccurately* reflects the corporation's worth." *See* Black, *Fraud on the Market: A Criticism of Dispensing with Reliance Requirements in Certain Open Market Transactions,* 62 N.C. L. Rev. 435, 455 (1984) (emphasis added). If investors really believed that stock prices reflected a stock's "value," many sellers would never sell, and many buyers never buy (given the time and cost associated with executing a stock transaction). As we recognized just a few years ago: "[I]nvestors act on inevitably incomplete or inaccurate information, [consequently] there are always winners and losers; but those who have 'lost' have not necessarily been defrauded." Dirks v. SEC, 463 U.S. 646, 667, n.27 (1983). Yet today, the Court allows investors to recover who can show little more than that they sold stock at a lower price than what might have been.

I do not propose that the law retreat from the many protections that §10(b) and Rule 10b-5, as interpreted in our prior cases, provide to investors. But any extension of these laws, to approach something closer to an investor insurance scheme, should come from Congress, and not from the courts. . . .

PROBLEM 16-1

If ever there was a ironically named corporation, it was the Aqua Vie Beverage Corporation (AVBC). "Aqua Vie" means "water life," and yet the water the company tried to sell had no life: in particular, no shelf life. The company was formed in order to produce and market a new product, a lightly flavored, non-sparkling spring water. The problem was, after about 60 days, the water in bottles on the store shelves turned brown. AVBC tried to change the production process in various ways, but to no avail. And, not surprisingly, no one flocked to buy brown, chemically flavored spring water. And so Aqua Vie, the company, died young: it was forced to recall all of the product it had distributed and to pay back its national distributors for their costs. As a result it ran out of money, but not before finding itself on the wrong side of a lawsuit claiming securities fraud under section 10(b)/Rule 10b-5.

Plaintiffs in the lawsuit had purchased 3,000 shares of stock in the over-the-counter market at $4.00 per share, based in part on industry publications that had described AVBC's product as "promising, if speculative." At the time of the plaintiffs' purchase, AVBC's financial statements, audited by Deloitte & Touche, had included certain "reserves" of money to pay for potential future costs, including the costs of product recalls. "Reserves" are bookkeeping entries that are subtracted from operating income. A company selling products at retail will establish reserves for a number of future contingencies, such as the costs of product repairs for products under warranty; the costs of returns; the costs of dealer incentives necessary to sell old products to make room for new; and the costs of product liability litigation. Because the amount of the reserve for the cost of product recalls was wildly low, the financial statements ended up overstating the income of the company. Plaintiffs ultimately alleged that at the time the financial statements were issued, AVBC's chief of quality control had already sounded an alarm, warning the CEO and other top executives that there was an "instability" in the product formula and suggesting that a product recall would be necessary.

The defendants in the case — the company, its officers and directors, and Deloitte & Touche — defended with an interesting "reliance" argument. They pointed out that the Basic v. Levinson presumption of reliance is, as the Court stated, based on the proposition "that where materially misleading statements have been disseminated into an impersonal, well-developed market for securities, the reliance of individual plaintiffs on the integrity of the market price may be presumed." Basic v. Levinson, 485 U.S. 224, 247 (1988). These stocks were not trading in an efficient market, defendants pointed out; they were being traded over the counter, in a thinly traded, illiquid market. Stocks in that market are listed in "pink sheets" that circulate daily and contain "bid" and "ask" prices (bids to buy shares and what someone is asking to sell shares). The pink sheets do not include trading information, such as the volume of sales or the prices investors are actually paying. Thus, defendants argued, because this market is not efficient, the presumption of reliance should not be available, and plaintiffs should have to prove that they actually relied upon the financial statements — the allegedly material misstatement of facts — in choosing to make their purchase.

How should a court respond to this argument? If it is accepted, what difficulties do the plaintiffs face?

3. Scienter Requirement

One of the most important bulwarks against liability under section 10(b)/Rule 10b-5 is the requirement that plaintiffs allege, and eventually prove, that the defendant's misstatement or omission of material fact was made with "scienter" — that is, with an intent to deceive. *See* Ernst & Ernst v. Hockfelder, 425 U.S. 185, 193 (1976). *Ernst & Ernst* involved a company, First Securities, whose president, Leston B. Nay, defrauded investors for decades by encouraging them to invest in "escrow funds" that paid a high rate of return. In fact, there were no such funds, but rather a variation on a Ponzi scheme: as long as Nay could continue to get new investors, he could pay out high rates of returns to prior investors and skim generous funds off the top for himself, and everyone was happy. Events eventually caused the scheme to unravel, as these schemes invariably do, and Nay committed suicide, leaving a note that described the firm as bankrupt and the escrow accounts as "spurious." Plaintiffs brought a cause of action against Nay's estate and against First Securities' accountants, Ernst & Ernst, claiming the accountants aided and abetted Nay's securities fraud by their negligent failure to uncover odd rules at First Securities, including that only Nay could open the mail. Had Ernst & Ernst conducted a proper audit, the fraud would have been discovered decades earlier, plaintiffs claimed, and their funds would not have been depleted.

The Court rejected the SEC's argument that negligent behavior could suffice to set out a cause of action under section 10(b)/Rule 10b-5:

> Section 10(b) makes unlawful the use or employment of "any manipulative or deceptive device or contrivance" in contravention of Commission rules. The words "manipulative or deceptive" used in conjunction with "device or contrivance" strongly suggest that §10(b) was intended to proscribe knowing or intentional misconduct.
>
> In its *Amicus curiae* brief, however, the Commission contends that nothing in the language "manipulative or deceptive device or contrivance" limits its operation to knowing or intentional practices. In support of its view, the Commission cites the overall congressional purpose in the 1933 and 1934 Acts to protect investors against false and deceptive practices that might injure them. . . . The Commission then reasons that since the "effect" upon investors of given conduct is the same regardless of whether the conduct is negligent or intentional, Congress must have intended to bar all such practices and not just those done knowingly or intentionally. The logic of this effect-oriented approach would impose liability for wholly faultless conduct where such conduct results in harm to investors, a result the Commission would be unlikely to support. But apart from where its logic might lead, the Commission would add a gloss to the operative language of the statute quite different from its commonly accepted meaning. . . . The argument simply ignores the use of the words "manipulative," "device," and "contrivance" terms that make unmistakable a congressional intent to proscribe a type of conduct quite different from negligence. Use of the word "manipulative" is especially significant. It is and was virtually a term of art when used in connection with securities markets. It connotes intentional or willful conduct designed to deceive or defraud investors by controlling or artificially affecting the price of securities.

Ernst & Ernst v. Hockfelder, 425 U.S. 185, 193 (1976).

The *Ernst & Ernst* Court left open whether recklessness would suffice to show scienter under section 10(b)/Rule 10b-5, *id.* at 193 n.12, but the federal circuit courts of appeals have found recklessness to be sufficient to set out a cause of action under section 10(b)/Rule 10b-5 as well. *See* Hollinger v. Titan Capital Corp., 914 F.2d 1564, 1568 n.6 (9th Cir. 1990) (citing opinions from every circuit holding that recklessness is sufficient).

Notwithstanding the requirement to plead that defendants acted with scienter, and the general requirement under the Federal Rules of Civil Procedure to allege fraud with particularity, *see* Rule 9(b), Fed. R. Civ. P., in December 1995 Congress amended the federal securities laws to make it more difficult to bring claims under section 10(b)/Rule 10b-5. These amendments were made in response to the perception that there was too much securities litigation in the United States, and this was undermining U.S. economic competitiveness. Ironically, this perception was fueled by high technology firms in California, which also fueled the technology stock price bubble that burst starting in March of 2000, wiping out 70 percent of the value of the "technology-heavy" NASDAQ trading market. The 1995 amendments, called the Private Securities Litigation Reform Act of 1995, did not purport to change the scienter requirement under section 10(b)/Rule 10b-5, but amended the pleading requirements, requiring plaintiffs to state facts that provide a "strong inference" that the defendants acted with the required mental state to set out a cause of action. The following Problem sets out some of the facts a labor union pension fund alleged in a recent case to plead a "strong inference" of the intent to defraud necessary to state a cause of action under section 10(b)/Rule 10b-5. (These are fact-intensive cases, as reflected in the length of this Problem.)

PROBLEM 16-2

On June 27, 1994, an air carrier named America West filed for Chapter 11 bankruptcy reorganization. Several investors, including TPG Limited Partnership and Continental Airlines, were involved in the reorganization plan. In return for an equity investment to help bring the carrier out of bankruptcy, the investors received several million shares of Class A and Class B stock, as well as warrants to purchase Class B common stock. Class A stock, which was not publicly traded, entitled the shareholder to 50 votes per share, whereas publicly traded Class B common stock entitled the shareholder to one vote per share. Under the reorganization plan, TPG obtained nearly 800,000 shares of Class A stock, more than 5 million shares of Class B stock, and approximately 1.5 million warrants to purchase additional Class B stock. Consequently, TPG held 49 percent of the Class A stock, and Continental held 8.3 percent of the Class A stock. Both TPG and Continental entered into a stockholder's agreement with America West, which contained a "lock-up" provision requiring that the investors retain two shares of Class B publicly traded stock for every share of Class A stock until May 20, 1998. Class A stock could be converted to Class B stock at any point.

On January 1, 1994, Defendant William A. Franke became chief executive officer (CEO) of America West. Plaintiff, the airline mechanics' pension fund, alleges that aircraft maintenance deteriorated dramatically during his term as CEO and later as president of the company. Plaintiff asserts that Franke instituted a policy known as "don't gold plate the plane" (that is, maintenance workers should only do the minimum) and discontinued "open-door" and "self-disclosure" practices with the Federal Aviation Administration (FAA).

In December 1995, America West fired 375 aircraft mechanics, half of the maintenance work force, and outsourced its maintenance to a company called Tramco. In an internal e-mail dated June 22, 1998, an FAA officer described the "maintenance saga" that began in December 1995. The FAA officer stated that "Tramco was not properly doing maintenance" and that the FAA was fighting an "ongoing battle to educate [the] upper management" of America West that it "was, in fact, responsible for oversight." The FAA began an aggressive enforcement program, which included inspections, warning letters, and meetings. Throughout 1996 and 1997, the FAA continued to conduct inspections, find violations, and issue warnings to America West regarding its maintenance operations. In a meeting with America West, the FAA described these maintenance issues as a "systematic problem." America West's "incident rate," which is the number of safety-related incidents per 100,000 departures, was above average for the industry in the second and third quarters of 1997. By the fourth quarter of 1997, the number of Service Difficulty Reports (SDRs), which are maintenance problems that could have safety implications, had increased from 50 to 80 per quarter, in contrast to other major carriers' average of 40 SDRs per quarter.

Of some comfort to the traveling public, perhaps, America West's maintenance issues led to operational problems, including canceled or delayed flights and slower maintenance cycles, and resulted in sublevel performance compared to the S & P index of other airline stocks. For example, America West suffered a third-quarter loss of $45.7 million in 1996. During this quarter, the company's stock fell to $11¼, half the previous value of the shares. By October 1997, the stock was trading at about $14 to $15 per share.

The low-altitude performance of America West's stock obviously affected both its shareholders and the officers who held stock options. In response, plaintiff alleges that TPG and Continental decided to raise the stock price by May 20, 1998, the date on which they could freely sell their publicly traded stock under the stockholder's agreement. Plaintiff alleges that, under the influence of TPG and Continental, America West redoubled its efforts to push the stock price higher by peppering the market with false statements about the company's outlook, launching a campaign to secure favorable recommendations from analysts by misinforming them stating that operational problems had been fixed, and representing that the improved financial returns were due to exceptionally efficient management rather than unsafe maintenance practices. Plaintiff also alleges that, in its statements and financial documents, America West overstated its operating income by under-reporting maintenance and repairs expenses, including by failing to establish adequate financial reserves for deferred maintenance expenses.

By failing to perform required inspections and routine maintenance, America West allegedly achieved artificially high utilization rates (that is, the number of hours flown by an aircraft per day), which in turn increased their revenues. Plaintiff alleges that America West, TPG, and Continental all knew that America West would eventually bear the brunt of these deferred costs.

Plaintiff also alleges that TPG and Continental caused America West to repurchase its own stock as a "manipulative device designed to further inflate its price." During the second and third quarters of 1998, America West spent $87 million repurchasing 4.2 million shares on the open market. In total, America West spent nearly $100 million repurchasing 4.9 million shares.

Plaintiff asserts that the scheme to raise the stock price succeeded by overstating the company's operating income, ignoring maintenance and operational problems, failing to inform investors and the public of its ongoing structural problems, and repurchasing publicly traded stock. By December 30, 1997, the stock hit $18⅞, its highest price in 17 months. By March 10, 1998, America West stock reached $27¼, the highest price since its bankruptcy reorganization. By April 21, 1998, America West's stock soared to an all-time high of $31⁵/₁₆. In the 1997 Annual Report released on May 4, 1998, Franke and Goodmanson, president of America West, stated that America West had "produced the best financial results in its history and realized substantial improvements in its operational performance." The report also emphasized that "safety will continue to be a foremost priority."

From April 23, 1998, to May 6, 1998, several high-ranking America West "insiders," including outside directors Bollenbach, Fraser, and Ryan, sold 101,000 shares at as high as $30⁹/₁₆ per share, netting $3 million in proceeds. As noted earlier, under the stockholder's agreement, TPG and Continental could begin selling their publicly traded Class B stock, without selling any of their supervoting Class A stock, beginning on May 20, 1998. On May 28, 1998, TPG sold approximately 99 percent of its Class B stock (1,613,586 shares) at approximately $27¾ per share, totaling over $44 million. On June 22, 1998, Continental sold all of its Class B stock (317,140 shares) at $28⅛ per share, totaling over $8.9 million. By the end of July 1998, insiders had sold 2.4 million shares for over $67 million.

And yet, by May 1998, America West had begun secret settlement negotiations with the FAA. In a June 15, 1998, meeting, Goodmanson verbally promised FAA officials that America West would resolve its maintenance problems. The terms of the agreement were discussed in a series of meetings held on June 16, 18, and 24, 1998. On June 23, 1998, the day after Continental sold its Class B stock, the Wall Street Journal reported that "America West face[d] the prospect of substantial federal sanctions for failing to properly oversee the work of outside maintenance contractors on its jetliners. The [FAA] is seeking to impose at least $1 million in civil penalties." The article also stated that separate from the prospect of sanctions "the FAA put America West on its 'watch list' June 9 because of labor unrest among maintenance workers and flight attendants. . . . The airline spokeswoman said the enhanced surveillance hasn't turned up any 'significant maintenance or operational problems.'"

On June 24, 1998, the Knight-Ridder Tribune Business News published an article titled "America West Brass Calls FAA Scrutiny 'Routine.'" In the article, Goodmanson stated that the increased surveillance was "routine FAA procedure" when an airline is involved in labor negotiations, and reiterated that "no significant maintenance or operating problems had been discovered." Plaintiffs allege that these types of reassurances kept the stock value high.

On July 14, 1998, the FAA and America West reached a settlement agreement under which the company agreed to pay $5 million for violating the FAA's aircraft inspection and maintenance rules. The agreement stated that "[b]oth the FAA and America West recognize that organizational changes are required to ensure that America West can conduct such operations at the highest level of safety." Yet America West continued to reassure the public and its investors that the FAA's actions would not have a negative impact on the company. Goodmanson and other America West officers assured multiple money and portfolio managers, shareholders, and analysts that America West did not anticipate any major increase in maintenance costs or the cost of oversights. On the day that the settlement agreement was announced, American West issued a statement that "problems cited have been fully addressed" and "that the settlement agreement's provisions will not have a material adverse effect on the Company's operations or financial results." In a July 21, 1998, conference call with analysts, managers, investors, and shareholders, Goodmanson stated that America West was "not anticipating any major increase in maintenance costs or the cost of oversights going forward as a result of [the FAA settlement]." That same day, America West issued a release titled "America West Reports 80% Increase in Second Quarter Earnings; The Best Quarterly Results in Company History." Plaintiff alleges that the operating income was once again overstated by approximately 10 percent because its financial statements didn't accurately reflect the future costs of deferred maintenance, which artificially depressed America West's operating costs, inflated its operating income, and misled investors.

Notwithstanding its public relations campaign, America West's stock began to decline in late July. The stock value dropped from $29 per share on July 22, 1998, to $21⁵/₁₆ on August 4, 1998. The following day, America West announced a new program authorizing the repurchase of up to 5 million shares. In the company's release regarding the new program, Franke stated that it reflected America West's belief that its stock was "an attractive investment."

On September 3, 1998, however, America West announced that it would not meet third-quarter earnings estimates because of unsatisfactory operational performance. America West revealed that it was in the process of (1) purchasing two additional spare airplanes, (2) increasing the number of cities (from four to thirteen) where overnight maintenance capabilities would be available, (3) increasing its inventory of spare parts, and (4) hiring more than 100 mechanics. The stock immediately fell over six points, from the previous day's $20⁵/₁₆ per share, to $14 per share on September 3, 1998. The stock continued to fall, reaching a low of $9⁵/₈ in early October 1998.

Immediately after the September 3, 1998, announcement, analysts slashed the forecast for America West's third and fourth quarters of 1998. Oppenheimer downgraded America West because of "operational disruptions" that were "negatively affecting dispatch reliability, on-time performance and therefore earnings." DLJ Securities issued a report stating that the cause of America West's earnings deficiencies appeared to be "100% operational" and that these problems were the result of ongoing labor issues and "a far more smothering presence of the [FAA] on the 'property' than we had understood." The report noted that "[t]wo disturbing aspects of yesterday's announcement . . . were the fact that the current scenario is reminiscent of operationally-related earnings shortfalls in 1996, and that we had no inkling from the company of the problems. . . ."

Has the plaintiff pleaded facts sufficient to show a strong inference that the defendants acted with an intent to deceive the market or with recklessness about whether the market would be deceived? Was the information about the FAA concerns and actions material? What, if any, were the company's material misstatements or omissions?

4. *"In Connection with" Requirement*

While it would seem to be obvious whether a misstatement or omission was made "in connection with" a purchase or sale of securities, the *Zandford* case and United States v. O'Hagan, are expanding the definition of when a misstatement or omission is in connection with a purchase or sale of securities. In both cases, the expansion changes the focus of the section 10(b)/Rule 10b-5 violation to enforcing fiduciary duties, as you'll see below.

SECURITIES & EXCHANGE COMMN. v. ZANDFORD

535 U.S. 813
Supreme Court of the United States
June 3, 2002

JUSTICE STEVENS delivered the opinion of the Court.

The Securities and Exchange Commission (SEC) filed a civil complaint alleging that a stockbroker violated both §10(b) of the Securities Exchange Act of 1934 and the SEC's Rule 10b-5, by selling his customer's securities and using the proceeds for his own benefit without the customer's knowledge or consent. The question presented is whether the alleged fraudulent conduct was "in connection with the purchase or sale of any security" within the meaning of the statute and the rule.

I

Between 1987 and 1991, respondent was employed as a securities broker in the Maryland branch of a New York brokerage firm. In 1987, he persuaded William Wood, an elderly man in poor health, to open a joint investment account for himself and his mentally retarded daughter. According to the SEC's complaint, the "stated investment objectives for the account were 'safety of principal and income.'" The Woods granted respondent discretion to manage their account and a general power of attorney to engage in securities transactions for their benefit without prior approval. Relying on respondent's promise to "conservatively invest" their money, the Woods entrusted him with $419,255. Before Mr. Wood's death in 1991, all of that money was gone.

In 1991, the National Association of Securities Dealers (NASD) conducted a routine examination of respondent's firm and discovered that on over 25 separate occasions, money had been transferred from the Woods' account to accounts controlled by respondent. In due course, respondent was indicted in the United States District Court for the District of Maryland on 13 counts of wire fraud in violation of 18 U.S.C. §1343. The first count alleged that respondent sold securities in the Woods' account and then made personal use of the proceeds. Each of the other counts alleged that he made wire transfers between Maryland and New York that enabled him to withdraw specified sums from the Woods' accounts. Some of those transfers involved respondent writing checks to himself from a mutual fund account held by the Woods, which required liquidating securities in order to redeem the checks. Respondent was convicted on all counts, sentenced to prison for 52 months, and ordered to pay $10,800 in restitution.

After respondent was indicted, the SEC filed a civil complaint in the same District Court alleging that respondent violated §10(b) and Rule 10b-5 by engaging in a scheme to defraud the Woods and by misappropriating approximately $343,000 of the Woods' securities without their knowledge or consent. The SEC moved for partial summary judgment after respondent's criminal conviction, arguing that the judgment in the criminal case estopped respondent from contesting facts that established a violation of §10(b). Respondent filed a motion seeking discovery on the question whether his fraud had the requisite "connection with" the purchase or sale of a security. The District Court refused to allow discovery and entered summary judgment against respondent. It enjoined him from engaging in future violations of the securities laws and ordered him to disgorge $343,000 in ill-gotten gains.

The Court of Appeals for the Fourth Circuit reversed the summary judgment and remanded with directions for the District Court to dismiss the complaint. It first held that the wire fraud conviction, which only required two findings — (1) that respondent engaged in a scheme to defraud and (2) that he used interstate wire communications in executing the scheme — did not establish all the elements of a §10(b) violation. Specifically, the conviction did not necessarily establish that his fraud was "in connection with" the sale of a security.[2] The court then held that the civil complaint did not sufficiently allege the necessary connection because the sales of the Woods' securities were merely incidental to a fraud that "lay in absconding with the proceeds" of sales that were conducted in "a routine and customary fashion." Respondent's "scheme was simply to steal the Woods' assets" rather than to engage "in manipulation of a particular security." Ultimately, the court refused "to stretch the language of the securities fraud provisions to encompass every conversion or theft that happens to involve securities." Adopting what amounts to a "fraud on the market" theory of the statute's coverage, the court held that without some "relationship to market integrity or investor understanding," there is no violation of §10(b).

---

2. A summary of the evidence in the Court of Appeals' opinion affirming the judgment in respondent's criminal case supports the conclusion that the verdict did not necessarily determine that the fraud was connected with the sale of a security:

"The Government presented ample direct and circumstantial evidence showing that Zandford had engaged in a scheme to defraud the Woods. It showed that: (1) Zandford had systematically transferred large sums of money from the Woods' account to his own accounts over a nineteen month period; (2) prior to November 1987, the Woods had no relationship with Zandford; (3) Zandford, and not the Woods, benefited from the money transfers; (4) the Woods were vulnerable victims due to their physical and mental limitations; (5) the personal services agreement, the loan, and the vintage car restoration business were not only contrary to the Woods' stated investment objectives, but they violated the rules of NASD and those of Zandford's employer that prohibited brokers from engaging in such arrangements; and (6) vehicles owned as part of the vintage car restoration business were titled in the name of Zandford's girlfriend as opposed to the Woods' names. Additional evidence showing a scheme to defraud included Zandford's failure to disclose to his employer the existence of the agreements and personal loans; his failure to report on his taxes or bank loan applications that he received income from acting as the personal representative; and his failure to disclose on his taxes his involvement in a vintage car restoration business. Zandford's contention that there is insufficient evidence supporting that he had engaged in a scheme to defraud the Woods is meritless."

We granted the SEC's petition for a writ of certiorari to review the Court of Appeals' construction of the phrase "in connection with the purchase or sale of any security." Because the Court of Appeals ordered the complaint dismissed rather than remanding for reconsideration, we assume the allegations contained therein are true and affirm that disposition only if no set of facts would entitle petitioner to relief. We do not reach the question whether the record supports the District Court's grant of summary judgment in the SEC's favor — a question that requires all potential factual disputes to be resolved in respondent's favor. We merely hold that the allegations of the complaint, if true, entitle the SEC to relief; therefore, the Court of Appeals should not have directed that the complaint be dismissed.

II

Section 10(b) of the Securities Exchange Act makes it "unlawful for any person . . . [t]o use or employ, in connection with the purchase or sale of any security . . . , any manipulative or deceptive device or contrivance in contravention of such rules and regulations as the [SEC] may prescribe." Rule 10b-5, which implements this provision, forbids the use, "in connection with the purchase or sale of any security," of "any device, scheme, or artifice to defraud" or any other "act, practice, or course of business" that "operates . . . as a fraud or deceit." Among Congress' objectives in passing the Act was "to insure honest securities markets and thereby promote investor confidence" after the market crash of 1929. United States v. O'Hagan, 521 U.S. 642, 658 (1997). More generally, Congress sought "'to substitute a philosophy of full disclosure for the philosophy of *caveat emptor* and thus to achieve a high standard of business ethics in the securities industry.'" Affiliated Ute Citizens of Utah v. United States, 406 U.S. 128, 151 (1972) (quoting SEC v. Capital Gains Research Bureau, Inc., 375 U.S. 180, 186 (1963)).

Consequently, we have explained that the statute should be "construed 'not technically and restrictively, but flexibly to effectuate its remedial purposes.'" 406 U.S., at 151 (quoting *Capital Gains Research Bureau, Inc.,* 375 U.S., at 195). In its role enforcing the Act, the SEC has consistently adopted a broad reading of the phrase "in connection with the purchase or sale of any security." It has maintained that a broker who accepts payment for securities that he never intends to deliver, or who sells customer securities with intent to misappropriate the proceeds, violates §10(b) and Rule 10b-5. *See, e.g.,* In re Bauer, 26 S.E.C. 770, 1947 WL 24474 (1947); In re Southeastern Securities Corp., 29 S.E.C. 609, 1949 WL 36491 (1949). This interpretation of the ambiguous text of §10(b), in the context of formal adjudication, is entitled to deference if it is reasonable. For the reasons set forth below, we think it is. While the statute must not be construed so broadly as to convert every common-law fraud that happens to involve securities into a violation of §10(b), neither the SEC nor this Court has ever held that there must be a misrepresentation about the value of a particular security in order to run afoul of the Act.

The SEC claims respondent engaged in a fraudulent scheme in which he made sales of his customer's securities for his own benefit. Respondent submits that the sales themselves were perfectly lawful and that the subsequent misappropriation of the proceeds, though fraudulent, is not properly viewed as having the requisite connection with the sales; in his view, the alleged scheme is not materially different from a simple theft of cash or securities in an investment account. We disagree.

According to the complaint, respondent "engaged in a scheme to defraud" the Woods beginning in 1988, shortly after they opened their account, and that scheme continued throughout the 2-year period during which respondent made a series of transactions that enabled him to convert the proceeds of the sales of the Woods' securities to his own use. The securities sales and respondent's fraudulent practices were not independent events. This is not a case in which, after a lawful transaction had been consummated, a broker decided to steal the proceeds and did so. Nor is it a case in which a thief simply invested the proceeds of a routine conversion in the stock market. Rather, respondent's fraud coincided with the sales themselves.

Taking the allegations in the complaint as true, each sale was made to further respondent's fraudulent scheme; each was deceptive because it was neither authorized by, nor disclosed to, the Woods. With regard to the sales of shares in the Woods' mutual fund, respondent initiated these transactions by writing a check to himself from that account, knowing that redeeming the check would require the sale of securities. Indeed, each time respondent "exercised his power of disposition for his own benefit," that conduct, "without more," was a fraud. United States v. Dunn, 268 U.S. 121, 131 (1925). In the aggregate, the sales are properly viewed as a "course of business" that operated as a fraud or deceit on a stockbroker's customer.

Insofar as the connection between respondent's deceptive practices and his sale of the Woods' securities is concerned, the case is remarkably similar to Superintendent of Ins. of N.Y. v. Bankers Life & Casualty Co., 404 U.S. 6 (1971). In that case the directors of Manhattan Casualty Company authorized the sale of the company's portfolio of treasury bonds because they had been "duped" into believing that the company would receive the proceeds of the sale. We held that "Manhattan was injured as an investor through a deceptive device which deprived it of any compensation for the sale of its valuable block of securities." Id., at 10. In reaching this conclusion, we did not ask, as the Fourth Circuit did in this case, whether the directors were misled about the value of a security or whether the fraud involved "manipulation of a particular security." In fact, we rejected the Second Circuit's position in Superintendent of Ins. of N.Y. v. Bankers Life & Casualty Co., 430 F.2d 355, 361 (C.A. 2 1970), that because the fraud against Manhattan did not take place within the context of a securities exchange it was not prohibited by §10(b). We refused to read the statute so narrowly, noting that it "must be read flexibly, not technically and restrictively." Id., at 12. Although we recognized that the interest in " 'preserving the integrity of the securities markets,' " was one of the purposes animating the statute, we rejected the notion that §10(b) is limited to serving that objective alone.

Like the company directors in *Bankers Life*, the Woods were injured as investors through respondent's deceptions, which deprived them of any compensation for the sale of their valuable securities. They were duped into believing respondent would "conservatively invest" their assets in the stock market and that any transactions made on their behalf would be for their benefit for the " 'safety of principal and income.' " The fact that respondent misappropriated the proceeds of the sales provides persuasive evidence that he had violated §10(b) when he made the sales, but misappropriation is not an essential element of the offense. Indeed, in *Bankers Life*, we flatly stated that it was "irrelevant" that "the proceeds of the sale that were due the seller were misappropriated." 404 U.S., at 10. It is enough that the scheme to defraud and the sale of securities coincide.

The Court of Appeals below distinguished *Bankers Life* on the ground that it involved an affirmative misrepresentation, whereas respondent simply failed to inform the Woods of his intent to misappropriate their securities. We are not persuaded by this distinction. Respondent was only able to carry out his fraudulent scheme without making an affirmative misrepresentation because the Woods had trusted him to make transactions in their best interest without prior approval. Under these circumstances, respondent's fraud represents an even greater threat to investor confidence in the securities industry than the misrepresentation in *Bankers Life*. Not only does such a fraud prevent investors from trusting that their brokers are executing transactions for their benefit, but it undermines the value of a discretionary account like that held by the Woods. The benefit of a discretionary account is that it enables individuals, like the Woods, who lack the time, capacity, or know-how to supervise investment decisions, to delegate authority to a broker who will make decisions in their best interests without prior approval. If such individuals cannot rely on a broker to exercise that discretion for their benefit, then the account loses its added value. Moreover, any distinction between omissions and misrepresentations is illusory in the context of a broker who has a fiduciary duty to her clients.

More recently, in Wharf (Holdings) Ltd. v. United Int'l Holdings, Inc., 532 U.S. 588 (2001), our decision that the seller of a security had violated §10(b) focused on the secret intent of the seller when the sale occurred. The purchaser claimed "that Wharf sold it a security (the option) while secretly intending from the very beginning not to honor the option." *Id.*, at 597. Although Wharf did not specifically argue that the breach of contract underlying the complaint lacked the requisite connection with a sale of securities, it did assert that the case was merely a dispute over ownership of the option, and that interpreting §10(b) to include such a claim would convert every breach of contract that happened to involve a security into a violation of the federal securities laws. *Id.*, at 596. We rejected that argument because the purchaser's claim was not that the defendant failed to carry out a promise to sell securities; rather, the claim was that the defendant sold a security while never intending to honor its agreement in the first place. *Id.*, at 596-597. Similarly, in this case the SEC claims respondent sold the Woods' securities while secretly intending from the very beginning to keep the proceeds. In *Wharf*, the fraudulent intent deprived the purchaser of the benefit of the sale whereas here the fraudulent intent deprived the seller of that benefit, but the connection between the deception and the sale in each case is identical.

In United States v. O'Hagan, 521 U.S. 642 (1997), we held that the defendant had committed fraud "in connection with" a securities transaction when he used misappropriated confidential information for trading purposes. We reasoned that "the fiduciary's fraud is consummated, not when the fiduciary gains the confidential information, but when, without disclosure to his principal, he uses the information to purchase or sell securities. The securities transaction and the breach of duty thus coincide. This is so even though the person or entity defrauded is not the other party to the trade, but is, instead, the source of the nonpublic information." *Id.*, at 655-656. The Court of Appeals distinguished

O'Hagan by reading it to require that the misappropriated information or assets not have independent value to the client outside the securities market. We do not read *O'Hagan* as so limited. In the chief passage cited by the Court of Appeals for this proposition, we discussed the Government's position that "[t]he misappropriation theory would not . . . apply to a case in which a person defrauded a bank into giving him a loan or embezzled cash from another, and then used the proceeds of the misdeed to purchase securities," because in that situation "the proceeds would have value to the malefactor apart from their use in a securities transaction, and the fraud would be complete as soon as the money was obtained." 521 U.S., at 656. Even if this passage could be read to introduce a new requirement into §10(b), it would not affect our analysis of this case, because the Woods' securities did not have value for respondent apart from their use in a securities transaction and the fraud was not complete before the sale of securities occurred.

As in *Bankers Life, Wharf,* and *O'Hagan,* the SEC complaint describes a fraudulent scheme in which the securities transactions and breaches of fiduciary duty coincide.[4] Those breaches were therefore "in connection with" securities sales within the meaning of §10(b). Accordingly, the judgment of the Court of Appeals is reversed, and the case is remanded for further proceedings consistent with this opinion.

It is so ordered.

5.   *Purchaser-Seller Requirement*

THE WHARF (HOLDINGS) LTD. v. UNITED INTL. HOLDINGS, INC.

532 U.S. 588
Supreme Court of the United States
May 21, 2001

Justice BREYER delivered the opinion of the Court.

This securities fraud action focuses upon a company that sold an option to buy stock while secretly intending never to honor the option. The question before us is whether this conduct violates §10(b) of the Securities Exchange Act of 1934, which prohibits using "any manipulative or deceptive device or contrivance" "in connection with the purchase or sale of any security." We conclude that it does.

I

Respondent United International Holdings, Inc., a Colorado-based company, sued petitioner The Wharf (Holdings) Limited, a Hong Kong firm, in Colorado's Federal District Court. United said that in October 1992 Wharf had

---

4. Contrary to the Court of Appeals' prediction, our analysis does not transform every breach of fiduciary duty into a federal securities violation. If, for example, a broker embezzles cash from a client's account or takes advantage of the fiduciary relationship to induce his client into a fraudulent real estate transaction, then the fraud would not include the requisite connection to a purchase or sale of securities. Likewise if the broker told his client he was stealing the client's assets, that breach of fiduciary duty might be in connection with a sale of securities, but it would not involve a deceptive device or fraud.

sold it an option to buy 10% of the stock of a new Hong Kong cable television system. But, United alleged, at the time of the sale Wharf secretly intended not to permit United to exercise the option. United claimed that Wharf's conduct amounted to a fraud "in connection with the . . . sale of [a] security," prohibited by §10(b), and violated numerous state laws as well. A jury found in United's favor. The Court of Appeals for the Tenth Circuit upheld that verdict. And we granted certiorari to consider whether the dispute fell within the scope of §10(b).

The relevant facts, viewed in the light most favorable to the verdict winner, United, are as follows. In 1991, the Hong Kong Government announced that it would accept bids for the award of an exclusive license to operate a cable system in Hong Kong. Wharf decided to prepare a bid. Wharf's chairman, Peter Woo, instructed one of its managing directors, Stephen Ng, to find a business partner with cable system experience. Ng found United. And United sent several employees to Hong Kong to help prepare Wharf's application, negotiate contracts, design the system, and arrange financing.

United asked to be paid for its services with a right to invest in the cable system if Wharf should obtain the license. During August and September 1992, while United's employees were at work helping Wharf, Wharf and United negotiated about the details of that payment. Wharf prepared a draft letter of intent that contemplated giving United the right to become a co-investor, owning 10% of the system. But the parties did not sign the letter of intent. And in September, when Wharf submitted its bid, it told the Hong Kong authorities that Wharf would be the system's initial sole owner, although Wharf would also "consider" allowing United to become an investor.

In early October 1992, Ng met with a United representative, who told Ng that United would continue to help only if Wharf gave United an enforceable right to invest. Ng then orally granted United an option with the following terms: (1) United had the right to buy 10% of the future system's stock; (2) the price of exercising the option would be 10% of the system's capital requirements minus the value of United's previous services (including expenses); (3) United could exercise the option only if it showed that it could fund its 10% share of the capital required for at least the first 18 months; and (4) the option would expire if not exercised within six months of the date that Wharf received the license. The parties continued to negotiate about how to write documents that would embody these terms, but they never reduced the agreement to writing.

In May 1993, Hong Kong awarded the cable franchise to Wharf. United raised $66 million designed to help finance its 10% share. In July or August 1993, United told Wharf that it was ready to exercise its option. But Wharf refused to permit United to buy any of the system's stock. Contemporaneous internal Wharf documents suggested that Wharf had never intended to carry out its promise. For example, a few weeks before the key October 1992 meeting, Ng had prepared a memorandum stating that United wanted a right to invest that it could exercise if it was able to raise the necessary capital. A handwritten note by Wharf's Chairman Woo replied, "No, no, no, we don't accept that." In September 1993, after meeting with the Wharf board to discuss United's investment in the cable system, Ng wrote to another Wharf executive, "How do we get out?" In December 1993, after United had filed documents with the Securities and Exchange Commission (SEC) representing that United was negotiating the acquisition of a 10% interest in the cable system, an internal Wharf memo stated that "[o]ur next move should be to claim that our directors got quite *upset* over these representations. . . . Publicly, we *do not* acknowledge [United's] opportunity" to acquire the 10% interest. In the margin of a December 1993 letter from United discussing its expectation of investing in the cable system, Ng wrote, "[B]e careful, must deflect this! [H]ow?" Other Wharf documents referred to the need to "back ped[al]," and "stall."

These documents, along with other evidence, convinced the jury that Wharf, through Ng, had orally sold United an option to purchase a 10% interest in the future cable system while secretly intending not to permit United to exercise the option, in violation of §10(b) of the Securities Exchange Act and various state laws. The jury awarded United compensatory damages of $67 million and, in light of "circumstances of fraud, malice, or willful and wanton conduct," punitive damages of $58.5 million on the state-law claims. As we have said, the Court of Appeals upheld the jury's award. And we granted certiorari to determine whether Wharf's oral sale of an option it intended not to honor is prohibited by §10(b).

II . . .

To succeed in a Rule 10b-5 suit, a private plaintiff must show that the defendant used, in connection with the purchase or sale of a security, one of the four kinds of manipulative or deceptive devices to which the Rule refers, and must also satisfy certain other requirements not at issue here.

In deciding whether the Rule covers the circumstances present here, we must assume that the "security" at issue is not the cable system stock, but the option to purchase that stock. That is because the Court of Appeals found that Wharf conceded this point. . . . Consequently, we must decide whether Wharf's secret intent not to honor the option it sold United amounted to a misrepresentation (or other conduct forbidden by the Rule) in connection with the sale of the option.

Wharf argues that its conduct falls outside the Rule's scope for two basic reasons. First, Wharf points out that its agreement to grant United an option to purchase shares in the cable system was an oral agreement. And it says that §10(b) does not cover oral contracts of sale. Wharf points to *Blue Chip Stamps*, in which this Court construed the Act's "purchase or sale" language to mean that only "actual purchasers and sellers of securities" have standing to bring a private action for damages. *See* 421 U.S., at 730-731. Wharf notes that the Court's interpretation of the Act flowed in part from the need to protect defendants against lawsuits that "turn largely on which oral version of a series of occurrences the jury may decide to credit." *Id.*, at 742, 95 S. Ct. 1917. And it claims that an oral purchase or sale would pose a similar problem of proof and thus should not satisfy the Rule's "purchase or sale" requirement.

Blue Chip Stamps, however, involved the very different question whether the Act protects a person who did not actually buy securities, but who might have done so had the seller told the truth. The Court held that the Act does not cover such a potential buyer, in part for the reason that Wharf states.

But United is not a potential buyer; by providing Wharf with its services, it actually bought the option that Wharf sold. And *Blue Chip Stamps* said nothing to suggest that oral purchases or sales fall outside the scope of the Act. Rather, the Court's concern was about "the abuse potential and proof problems inherent in suits by investors who neither bought nor sold, but asserted they would have traded absent fraudulent conduct by others." *United States v. O'Hagan,* 521 U.S. 642, 664, 117 S. Ct. 2199, 138 L. Ed. 2d 724 (1997). Such a "potential purchase" claim would rest on facts, including the plaintiff's state of mind, that might be "totally unknown and unknowable to the defendant," depriving the jury of "the benefit of weighing the plaintiff's version against the defendant's version." *Blue Chip Stamps, supra,* at 746, 95 S. Ct. 1917. An actual sale, even if oral, would not create this problem, because both parties would be able to testify as to whether the relevant events had occurred.

Neither is there any other convincing reason to interpret the Act to exclude oral contracts as a class. The Act itself says that it applies to "any contract" for the purchase or sale of a security. Oral contracts for the sale of securities are sufficiently common that the Uniform Commercial Code and statutes of frauds in every State now consider them enforceable. See U.C.C. §8-113 (Supp. 2000) ("A contract . . . for the sale or purchase of a security is enforceable whether or not there is a writing signed or record authenticated by a party against whom enforcement is sought"). Any exception for oral sales of securities would significantly limit the Act's coverage, thereby undermining its basic purposes. . . .

Second, Wharf argues that a secret reservation not to permit the exercise of an option falls outside §10(b) because it does not "relat[e] to the value of a security purchase or the consideration paid"; hence it does "not implicate [§10(b)'s] policy of full disclosure." But even were it the case that the Act covers only misrepresentations likely to affect the value of securities, Wharf's secret reservation was such a misrepresentation. To sell an option while secretly intending not to permit the option's exercise is misleading, because a buyer normally presumes good faith. For similar reasons, the secret reservation misled United about the option's value. Since Wharf did not intend to honor the option, the option was, unbeknownst to United, valueless.

Finally, Wharf supports its claim for an exemption from the statute by characterizing this case as a "disput[e] over the ownership of securities." Wharf expresses concern that interpreting the Act to allow recovery in a case like this one will permit numerous plaintiffs to bring federal securities claims that are in reality no more than ordinary state breach-of-contract claims — actions that lie outside the Act's basic objectives. United's claim, however, is not simply that Wharf failed to carry out a promise to sell it securities. It is a claim that Wharf sold it a security (the option) while secretly intending from the very beginning not to honor the option. And United proved that secret intent with documentary evidence that went well beyond evidence of a simple failure to perform. Moreover, Wharf has not shown us that its concern has proved serious as a practical matter in the past. Nor does Wharf persuade us that it is likely to prove serious in the future.

For these reasons, the judgment of the Court of Appeals is
Affirmed.

B. INSIDER TRADING

1. The Classical Theory

The classical theory of insider trading is concerned with corporate insiders' unfair use of corporate information to make a profit at the expense of outsiders who couldn't possibly, by dint of hard work, discover the information. For instance, if a person studied all of the available public information about data warehousing companies and decided that she thought Company A was well positioned to get a large contract that the U.S. Post Office just announced it would be awarding, she would have no legal duty to disclose that analysis prior to buying Company A's stock. (This assumes that the investor is not an employee or director or other fiduciary of Company A.) And if Company A did get the contract and the stock price went up, she can go out and celebrate without fear of an unpleasant future meeting with the SEC or an assistant U.S. attorney. But if an employee of Company A has just heard through the corporate grapevine that the company got the U.S. Post Office contract, she would have a legal duty to disclose that information prior to trading, or to abstain from trading.

This proposition, that an insider with knowledge of material nonpublic information is prohibited from trading in the company's stock, was derived initially from the duties of full disclosure required of any agent under state fiduciary duty law and then imported into federal securities law. (The following discussion is based on Richard W. Painter, Kimberly D. Krawiec & Cynthia A. Williams, *Don't Ask, Just Tell: Insider Trading After* United States v. O'Hagan, 84 Va. L. Rev. 153 (1988).) At first these federal decisions were limited to face-to-face transactions. For instance, in Speed v. Transamerica Corp., 99 F. Supp. 808, 828-829 (D. Del. 1951), the court held that "[i]t is unlawful [under Rule 10b-5] for an insider, such as a majority stockholder, to purchase the stock of minority stockholders without disclosing material facts affecting the value of the stock, known to the majority stockholder by virtue of his inside position." Beginning in 1961 the SEC began to take the position that a similar "disclose or abstain" rule applied in open market transactions, *see* Cady, Roberts & Co., 40 S.E.C. 907 (1961), as did the federal courts. One of the most important of these federal decisions, which you'll see discussed in the case below, was SEC v. Texas Gulf Sulpher, 401 F.2d 833 (2d Cir. 1968) (en banc). In that case, the Texas Gulf Sulpher company had geological reports indicating huge, easily extractable mineral deposits of extremely valuable minerals on land it owned (and on neighboring pieces it was busily buying up). The company continued to downplay the finds, or deny them altogether, even as word started to leak out and reporters started asking questions. Meanwhile a number of insiders were also busily buying the company's stock, surmising that when the true state of the facts became known the stock price would increase. Finding a violation of section 10(b) and Rule 10b-5, the Second Circuit en banc held that "anyone in possession of material inside information must either disclose it to the investing public, or . . . must abstain from trading." SEC v. Texas Gulf Sulpher, *supra*. The source of this duty to disclose is the fiduciary duty of full disclosure the insiders, as agents, owe to the shareholders, as principals. This has come to be called the "classical" theory of insider trading liability, and it specifically targets trading activity by people inside the firm: officers, directors, and employees. In contrast, the "misappropriation theory," to be examined in the next section, prohibits some people outside the firm from trading without disclosure of material, nonpublic information where that information has been misappropriated in violation of fiduciary duties to the source of the information — such as a law clerk trading on information gained in a clerkship.

The following case presents a case of insider trading under the classical theory, but addresses one of the unresolved issues: is it enough to show that the insider "possessed" material nonpublic information when trading, or must a plaintiff or the government show that the insider actually used the information in deciding to trade? While that question might seem murky, the court below provides a clear articulation of both the issue and the answer. The case involves the materiality of forward-looking information, so serves as a good review of that issue as well.

UNITED STATES v. SMITH

155 F.3d 1051
United States Court of Appeals, Ninth Circuit
August 25, 1998

O'SCANNLAIN, Circuit Judge.

In this appeal from an insider securities trading conviction, we must decide difficult evidentiary issues involving an illegal interception of voicemail, as well as whether internal corporate earnings projections may constitute "material" inside information and whether conviction requires proof of actual use of that inside information.

I

PDA Engineering, Inc. ("PDA") was, in 1993, a software design firm with headquarters in Orange County, California. Shares in PDA were publicly traded on the National Association of Securities Dealers Exchange (commonly referred to as "NASDAQ"). Richard Smith served as PDA's Vice President for North American Sales and worked in PDA's Nashville, Tennessee, office. By early 1993, after nearly three years with PDA, Smith had accumulated 51,445 shares of PDA stock.

In a series of transactions between June 10 and June 18, 1993, Smith liquidated his entire position in PDA. In addition to selling his own shares, Smith "sold short"[1] 25,000 shares on July 8, and another 10,000 shares on July 20. Smith's parents also sold and sold short a total of 12,000 shares.

---

1. "Short selling is a device whereby the speculator sells stock which he does not own, anticipating that the price will decline and that he will thereby be enabled to 'cover,' or make delivery of the stock sold, by purchasing it at the lesser price. If the decline materializes, the short seller realizes as a profit the differential between the sales price and the lower purchase or covering price." Louis Loss & Joel Seligman, *Fundamentals of Securities Regulation* 699 (3d ed. 1988) (quoting Stock Exchange Practices, Report of Comm. on Banking & Currency, S. Rep. No. 1455, 73d Cong., 2d Sess. 50-51 (1934)) (internal quotation marks omitted).

Amidst this flurry of sales activity, on June 19, Smith telephoned Angela Bravo de Rueda ("Bravo"), an employee in the Los Angeles office of PDA, and left her the following voicemail message:

> Hi, Angie, Rich. . . . I talked to Tom last night after I left you some messages and he and Lou discovered that there was about a million and a half dollar mistake in the budget, so now we're back at ground zero and we've got to scramble for the next few days. Anyway, finally I sold all my stock off on Friday and I'm going to short the stock because I know its going to go down a couple of points here in the next week as soon as Lou releases the information about next year's earnings. I'm more concerned about this year's earnings actually.

Unbeknownst to either Smith or Bravo, another Los Angeles-based PDA employee, Linda Alexander-Gore ("Gore"), guessed correctly Bravo's voicemail password and accessed Bravo's mailbox. When Gore encountered Smith's message, she forwarded it to her own mailbox. In order to retrieve it, she then called her own voicemail from her home telephone, played the message, and recorded it with a handheld audiotape recorder. [The Court observed in a footnote that "[t]he record does not reveal the precise reason for Gore's curiosity.] After recording the message, Gore approached a co-worker, Robert Phillips ("Phillips"). She informed him of the general nature of the communication and provided him with a copy of the recording.

Phillips listened to the message and telephoned the United States Attorney's Office for the Central District of California, where he spoke to Assistant United States Attorney Bart Williams ("Williams"). Phillips told Williams that he believed he had information, in the form of an audiotape, that indicated possible criminal activity. He played the tape for Williams approximately four times and attempted to answer several questions about the contents of the recording. He informed Williams that he believed that the speaker on the tape was Smith and that the references in the message to "Tom" and "Lou" were probably to Tom Curry and Lou Delmonico, both corporate officers at PDA. Phillips offered to send Williams a copy of the tape itself, but Williams declined. Phillips never spoke to Williams again.

Williams referred the matter to Special Agent Maura Kelly ("Kelly") of the Federal Bureau of Investigation ("FBI"). Kelly contacted the Pacific Regional Office of the Securities and Exchange Commission ("SEC") and relayed to a staff attorney that an "anonymous informant had told [Williams] about insider trading in the stock of a company called PDA Engineering by a person named Richard Smith and that the anonymous informant had a tape of a conversation involving an individual purporting to be Smith discussing insider trading." In November 1993, the SEC issued a formal order of investigation against Smith. Over the course of the ensuing eight months, the SEC obtained documentary evidence from various sources and deposed a number of witnesses. Sometime during the seventh month of its eight-month investigation (in July 1994), the SEC obtained via administrative subpoena an audiotape copy of the recorded voicemail message.

In September 1994, the SEC referred the matter back to the United States Attorney in Los Angeles for possible criminal prosecution. Throughout the next eighteen months, the United States Attorney's Office and the FBI conducted substantial additional investigation, during which they interviewed fifteen individuals and subpoenaed sixteen additional boxes of documents.

Smith was indicted on eleven counts of insider trading in violation of §10(b) of the Securities Exchange Act of 1934, 15 U.S.C. §78j(b), and SEC Rule 10b-5, 17 C.F.R. §240.10b-5, and on one count of obstruction of justice in violation of 18 U.S.C. §1505. Smith moved to suppress the evidence supporting the eleven insider trading counts and to dismiss the indictment as a whole, including the obstruction-of-justice count. After an extensive hearing, the district court suppressed the voicemail message itself, but refused to exclude the remainder of the government's evidence, concluding that it was not "derived from" the initial illegal recording. Although the court granted Smith's motion to dismiss the obstruction count, it denied his motion to dismiss with respect to the insider trading counts.

After a week-long trial, a jury returned guilty verdicts on all eleven insider trading counts. Smith filed a motion for judgment of acquittal or, in the alternative, for a new trial. The district court denied the motion, and Smith appealed.

Smith's contentions on appeal are essentially these: (1) that the government's evidence of insider trading was "derived from" an illegal wiretap and, therefore, should have been excluded pursuant to 18 U.S.C. §2515; (2) that the information he possessed was forward-looking, or "soft," information, and hence was not "material" within the meaning of Rule 10b-5; and (3) that the district court erroneously instructed the jury that it could convict Smith based upon his mere possession, as opposed to his use, of inside information.

II

[The court first determined that the tape of the voicemail had been properly excluded by the district court but that the evidence that had been developed independently was not required to be suppressed.]

III

[The court first set out the text of section 10(b) and Rule 10b-5.] A violation of Rule 10b-5 comprises four elements: a (1) misleading (2) statement or omission (3) of a "material" fact (4) made with scienter. *See* SEC v. Fehn, 97 F.3d 1276, 1289 (9th Cir. 1996). Under the "classical theory" of insider trading liability, a violation of Rule 10b-5 occurs "when a corporate insider trades in the securities of his corporation on the basis of material, nonpublic information." United States v. O'Hagan, 521 U.S. 642, 651 (1997); *accord* SEC v. Clark, 915 F.2d 439, 443 (9th Cir. 1990) ("[A] person violates Rule 10b-5 by buying or selling securities on the basis of material nonpublic information if . . . he is an insider of the corporation in whose shares he trades.") (quoting Barbara Bader Aldave, *Misappropriation: A General Theory of Liability for Trading on Nonpublic Information,* 13 Hofstra L. Rev. 101, 101-02 (1984)).

Smith contends that the information upon which he traded consisted of "forecasts of future sales and revenue." This "soft," forward-looking information, he insists, cannot, as a matter of law, constitute "material" information within the meaning of Rule 10b-5 and, consequently, cannot give rise to insider trading liability. Smith complains that the district court employed an erroneous understanding of materiality (*i.e.*, as including "soft" information) when it refused to dismiss the indictment, denied his motions for judgment of acquittal and new trial, and instructed the jury. He urges reversal on all three grounds.

. . . Smith does not contend that the information he possessed falls outside the Basic Inc. v. Levenson definition of materiality — that a reasonable investor would not have considered it useful or significant.[20] Rather, he argues that "[t]his Circuit has set limits on the type of information that may be considered material as a matter of law." Specifically, Smith says, "this Court has repeatedly held that forecasts of future sales and revenue are too speculative to constitute material facts." Smith contends that both the government's indictment and its proof at trial centered on his possession of "soft" information in the form of quarterly revenue projections. For instance, Smith points out, the indictment alleged that Smith knew in April 1993 that PDA "actually *expected* to realize" roughly 16% percent less in revenues for the fiscal year's fourth quarter than it had projected (a shortfall of approximately $2.3 million), and that Smith knew in June 1993 (in light of revised sales figures) that PDA "actually *expected*" to come up about 12% short. The government's evidence at trial, Smith maintains, mirrored the allegations in the indictment. Specifically, it elicited testimony from Smith's supervisor that Smith knew, both in April and in June, that PDA *was not likely* to meet fourth quarter revenue projections. When Smith traded on the basis of his knowledge of a fourth-quarter shortfall, the government's case went, he violated §10(b) and Rule 10b-5.

In support of his contention that "soft" information cannot, as a matter of law, be "material" within the meaning of Rule 10b-5, Smith invokes a handful of Ninth Circuit cases — In re Worlds of Wonder Securities Litigation, 35 F.3d 1407 (9th Cir. 1994), In re VeriFone Securities Litigation, 11 F.3d 865 (9th Cir. 1993), In re Lyondell Petrochemical Co. Securities Litigation, 984 F.2d 1050 (9th Cir. 1993), and In re Convergent Technologies Securities Litigation, 948 F.2d 507 (9th Cir. 1991) — and a recent First Circuit decision, Glassman v. Computervision Corp., 90 F.3d 617 (1st Cir. 1996). These cases, however, cannot bear the weight of the extreme interpretation with which Smith has saddled them. The decisions Smith cites stand for a more modest proposition, namely, that, *in the circumstances presented in those individual cases,* the disputed information was not sufficiently certain or significant to be considered material. We have never held — nor even hinted — that forward-looking information or intra-quarter data cannot, *as a matter of law,* be material. Nor has any other court for that matter, at least to the best of our knowledge. Indeed, both the Supreme Court's landmark decision in *Basic* and preexisting Ninth Circuit authority confirm that so-called "soft" information can, under the proper circumstances, be "material" within the meaning of Rule 10b-5. In *Basic* — the very case that announced the governing standard for Rule 10b-5 materiality — the Supreme Court dealt specifically with preliminary merger negotiations, events it dubbed "contingent or speculative in nature." *Id.* at 232, 108 S. Ct. 978. And although

---

20. Indeed, to do so would, as the SEC argues, "defy logic and experience." After all, investors are concerned, perhaps above all else, with the future cash flows of the companies in which they invest. Surely, the average investor's interest would be piqued by a company's internal projections of economic downturn.

the *Basic* Court acknowledged that its decision did not concern "earnings forecasts or projections" per se, *id.* at 232 n.9, 108 S. Ct. 978, it expressly adopted a "fact-intensive inquiry" to govern the materiality of "contingent or speculative information or events," *id.* at 238-40, 108 S. Ct. 978. It held that, with respect to forward-looking information, materiality "will depend at any given time upon a balancing of both the indicated probability that the event will occur and the anticipated magnitude of the event in light of totality of the company activity." *Id.* at 238, 108 S. Ct. 978 (quoting *Texas Gulf Sulphur,* 401 F.2d at 849). The Court's fact-specific approach fatally undermines Smith's claim that forward-looking information cannot, *as a matter of law,* be material. Likewise, only recently, in *Fehn,* 97 F.3d 1276, we specifically invoked the *Basic* standard for "determining the materiality of a corporate event that has not yet occurred." *Id.* at 1291. . . .

There is, quite simply, no case law to support Smith's blanket assertion that forward-looking statements cannot, as a matter of law, constitute "material" information within the meaning of Rule 10b-5. Indeed, both the Supreme Court and this court have held to the contrary and have observed that determining materiality requires a nuanced, case-by-case approach. Consequently, we reject Smith's contentions that the district court erred (1) in refusing to dismiss the indictment, (2) in denying his motion for a judgment of acquittal, and (3) in instructing the jury based upon the *Basic* definition of materiality.

IV

With respect to Smith's state of mind, the district court instructed the jury as follows:

> In order for you to find the defendant guilty on [the insider trading counts] of the indictment, the government must prove a causal relationship between the material nonpublic information in the defendant's possession and the defendant's trading.
>
> That is, the government must prove that the defendant sold or sold short PDA stock because of material nonpublic information that he knowingly possessed. It is not sufficient that the government proves that the defendant sold or sold short PDA stock while knowingly in possession of the material nonpublic information. However, the government need not prove that the defendant sold or sold short PDA stock solely because of the material nonpublic information. It is enough if the government proves that such inside information was a significant factor in defendant's decision to sell or sell short PDA stock.

Although he accedes in much of the instruction, Smith objects to the final two sentences, arguing that they "confused the jury" by providing that the government need only demonstrate that the inside information was a "significant factor" in his decision to trade, and not "the reason." The government and the SEC counter by arguing that, in fact, the district court's instruction "exceeded the requirements of existing law." They insist that there is no "causation" element to an insider trading prosecution. Rather, they contend, "[w]hen a corporate insider like Smith has information relating to his company that he knows (or is reckless in not knowing) to be material and nonpublic and he trades in the company's stock, he violates the antifraud provisions of the federal securities laws, *whether or not the information is a factor in his decision to trade.*"

In other words, the government contends, it needed only to prove that Smith knowingly *possessed* material nonpublic information, not that he actually *used* the information in deciding to buy or sell.

A

Although the use-possession debate has attracted a good deal of attention from academic commentators, very few courts (and none in this circuit) have addressed the issue head on. In support of their proposed "possession-only" standard, the government and the SEC rely principally upon dictum from a Second Circuit case, United States v. Teicher, 987 F.2d 112, 119 (2d Cir. 1993). The court in *Teicher* suggested, without squarely deciding, that proof of "knowing possession" is sufficient to sustain an insider trading prosecution and that the government need not affirmatively prove that the investor used the information in formulating his trade. For support, the court pointed to "a number of factors." *Id.* at 120. First, it asserted that the SEC has "consistently endorsed" a knowing-possession standard, and that the agency's interpretation of Rule 10b-5 in that respect is "entitled to some consideration." *Id.* Second, the court found the less exacting knowing-possession standard to be more consistent with the language of §10(b) and Rule 10b-5, both of which require only that a deceptive trade practice be conducted "in connection with" the purchase or sale of a security. *See id.* Third, the court observed that a knowing-possession standard "comports with the oft-quoted maxim that one with a fiduciary or similar duty to hold material nonpublic information in confidence must either 'disclose or abstain' with regard to trading." *Id.* (quoting Chiarella v. United States, 445 U.S. 222, 227 (1980)). Finally, the *Teicher* court pointed to what it believed to be the probable, yet subtle (indeed perhaps unconscious), effect that inside information has on traders:

> Because the advantage [an inside trader has over other traders] is in the form of information, it exists in the mind of the trader. Unlike a loaded weapon which may stand ready but unused, material information can not lay idle in the human brain.

Id. at 120-121.

Despite the Second Circuit's thoughtful analysis, we believe that the weight of authority supports a "use" requirement. Perhaps most significantly, the Supreme Court has consistently suggested, albeit in dictum, that Rule 10b-5 requires that the government prove causation in insider trading prosecutions. Indeed, just last Term, in United States v. O'Hagan, 521 U.S. 642 (1997), the Court indicated that an insider trading suspect must actually use the information to which he is privy, observing that "[u]nder the 'traditional' or 'classical theory' of insider trading liability, §10(b) and Rule 10b-5 are violated when a corporate insider trades in the securities of his corporation *on the basis of* material, nonpublic information." *Id.* 117 S. Ct. at 2207 (emphasis added). The *O'Hagan* Court was even more explicit in a separate portion of the opinion: "[T]he fiduciary's fraud is consummated, not when the fiduciary gains the confidential information, but when, without disclosure to his principal, he *uses the information* to purchase or sell securities." *Id.* 117 S. Ct. at 2209 (emphasis added). The Court's earlier decisions sound a similar theme. *See, e.g.*, Dirks v. SEC, 463 U.S. 646, 653 n.10 (1983) (referring to "duty that insiders owe . . . not to trade on inside information"); *id.* at 654 (referring to "duty to disclose before trading on material nonpublic information"); *id.* at 658-59 (referring to "trad[ing] on" inside information); *id.* at 662 (observing that "a purpose of the securities laws was to eliminate 'use of inside information for personal advantage'"; quoting In re Cady, Roberts & Co., 40 S.E.C. 907, 912 n.15 (1961)); *Chiarella*, 445 U.S. at 226 (referring to "the unfairness of allowing a corporate insider to take advantage of [inside] information by trading without disclosure"); *id.* at 229, 100 S. Ct. 1108 (observing that "[t]he federal courts have found violations of §10(b) where corporate insiders used undisclosed information for their own benefit").

In addition to suggestions from the Supreme Court, the only court of appeals squarely to consider the causation issue concluded that Rule 10b-5 does, in fact, entail a "use" requirement. *See* SEC v. Adler, 137 F.3d 1325, 1337-39 (11th Cir. 1998). In reaching its decision, the Eleventh Circuit pointed out that the SEC's position with regard to causation has not been nearly as "consistent" as the Second Circuit implied in *Teicher;* rather, it has "fluctuat[ed] over time." *Id.* at 1336. Although the SEC's current policy appears to be that "Rule 10b-5 does not require a showing that an insider sold his securities for the purpose of taking advantage of material non-public information," In re Sterling Drug, Inc., Fed. Sec. L. Rep. (CCH) ¶81,570, at 80,295 (April 18, 1978), such has not always been the case. In fact, in the not-too-distant past, the SEC concluded that an essential element of an insider trading violation was that the inside information "be a factor in [the insider's] decision to effect the transaction." In re Investors Management Co., Fed. Sec. L. Rep. (CCH) ¶78,163, at 80,514 (July 29, 1971). Of course, the fact that the SEC's position with respect to the causation issue has flip-flopped is not fatal to its claim to deference. *See* NLRB v. Local Union No. 103, 434 U.S. 335, 351 (1978) ("An administrative agency is not disqualified from changing its mind; and when it does, the courts . . . should not approach the statutory construction issue de novo and without regard to the administrative understanding of the statutes."). Nor, however, is the agency's about-face irrelevant to our inquiry. *See* Skidmore v. Swift & Co., 323 U.S. 134, 140 (1944) (listing "consistency with earlier and later pronouncements" as a pertinent consideration in determining the persuasiveness of an agency ruling).

The *Adler* court also thought a "use" requirement more consistent with the language of §10(b) and Rule 10b-5, which emphasizes "manipulat[ion]," "decept[ion]," and "fraud." We agree. By focusing exclusively upon the phrase "in connection with," the Second Circuit, we think, lost sight of the law's main thrust. After all, §10(b) and Rule 10b-5 do not just prohibit certain unspecified acts "in connection with" the purchase or sale of securities; rather, they prohibit the employment of "manipulative" and "deceptive" trading practices in connection with those transactions. This court has expressly held that "scienter" is a necessary element of an insider trading violation, *see* SEC v. Fehn, 97 F.3d 1276, 1289 (9th Cir. 1996), and has defined scienter as "a mental state embracing intent to deceive, manipulate, or defraud," Hollinger v. Titan Capital Corp., 914 F.2d 1564, 1568 (9th Cir. 1990) (quoting Ernst & Ernst v. Hochfelder, 425 U.S. 185, 193 (1976)). As the Supreme Court put the matter in *Dirks*, "[i]t is not enough that an insider's conduct results in harm to investors; rather a violation [of Rule 10b-5] may be found only where there is 'intentional or willful conduct designed to deceive or defraud investors.'" *Dirks*, 463 U.S.

at 663 n.23 (quoting *Ernst & Ernst,* 425 U.S. at 199). Like our colleagues on the Eleventh Circuit, we are concerned that the SEC's "knowing possession" standard would not be — indeed, could not be — strictly limited to those situations actually involving intentional fraud.[25] For instance, an investor who has a preexisting plan to trade, and who carries through with that plan after coming into possession of material nonpublic information, does not intend to defraud or deceive; he simply intends to implement his pre-possession financial strategy. The SEC suggests that the requisite intent to defraud is inherent in the act of trading while in possession of inside information:

> A corporate insider who trades knowing that he has inside information not available to persons on the other sides of his trades knows that those persons, to whom he owes a fiduciary duty, are at a disadvantage and will be making their decisions on the basis of incomplete information.

The SEC's position, however, rests upon a faulty premise. The persons with whom a hypothetical insider trades are not at a "disadvantage" at all provided the insider does not "use" the information to which he is privy. That is to say, if the insider merely possesses and does not use, the two parties are trading on a level playing field; if the insider merely possesses and does not use, *both* individuals are "making their decisions on the basis of incomplete information." It is the insider's use, not his possession, that gives rise to an informational advantage and the requisite intent to defraud.

Moreover, with respect to our colleagues on the Second Circuit, we do not believe that the "oft-quoted maxim" of "disclose or abstain," *Teicher,* 987 F.2d at 120 (citing *Chiarella,* 445 U.S. at 227, 100 S. Ct. 1108), supports a knowing-possession standard. The trouble with "oft-quoted maxims," of course, is that they rarely, if ever, capture the complexity of the idea that they are supposed to represent. "Disclose or abstain" is no exception. It was absolutely clear both in *Chiarella,* upon which the *Teicher* court relied for its "disclose or abstain" citation, and in *Cady, Roberts,* upon which *Chiarella* relied, that the suspected inside traders had, in fact, *used* inside information in consummating their trades. Indeed, in *Cady, Roberts,* the wellspring of the "disclose or abstain" principle, the SEC premised its decision, at least in part, on the proposition that "[a] significant purpose of the Exchange Act was to eliminate the idea that the *use* of inside information for personal advantage was a normal emolument of corporate office." *Cady, Roberts,* 40 S.E.C. at 912 n.15 (emphasis added). Consequently, understood in its proper context, we believe that the latter half of the maxim "disclose *or abstain*" enjoins not *all* trading, but trading *on the basis of material nonpublic information.*

We do not take lightly the SEC's argument that a "use" requirement poses difficulties of proof. . . . We appreciate that a "use" requirement renders criminal prosecutions marginally more difficult for the government to prove. The difficulties, however, are by no means insuperable. It is certainly not necessary that the government present a smoking gun in every insider trading

---

25. In fact, a knowing-possession standard would, we think, go a long way toward making insider trading a strict liability crime. In view of the statutorily authorized ten-year prison sentence that may accompany an insider trading conviction, *see* 15 U.S.C. §78ff(a), any construction of Rule 10b-5 that de facto eliminates the mens rea requirement should be disfavored, *see* United States v. United States Gypsum Co., 438 U.S. 422, 436-38 (1978).

prosecution. (Not that a smoking gun will always be beyond the government's reach; consider, for instance, that in this case Bravo might herself have gone to the authorities with Smith's statement that "I'm going to short the stock because I know its going to go down a couple of points here in the next week as soon as Lou releases the information about next year's earnings.") Any number of types of circumstantial evidence might be relevant to the causation issue. Suppose, for instance, that an individual who has never before invested comes into possession of material nonpublic information and the very next day invests a significant sum of money in substantially out-of-the-money call options.[26] We are confident that the government would have little trouble demonstrating "use" in such a situation, or in other situations in which unique trading patterns or unusually large trading quantities suggest that an investor had used inside information.

Consequently, we reject the government's proffered "knowing possession" standard for insider trading violations as contrary [to] the weight of existing authority. Rather, we hold that Rule 10b-5 requires that the government (or the SEC, as the case may be) demonstrate that the suspected inside trader actually used material nonpublic information in consummating his transaction.

B

Smith contends that the district court's instructions in this case were insufficient as a matter of law. Specifically, he complains that "a jury instruction which allows the government to obtain a conviction *without* proof that the defendant traded in stock *'because of'* the material nonpublic information' that he possessed, effectively wipes out the scienter requirement as defined by this Court and the Supreme Court." As a legal matter, he is correct. The trouble for Smith lies not in the law but in the facts, because the district court in this case *did* require proof of causation. It specifically instructed the jury that "the government must prove that the defendant sold or sold short PDA stock *because of* material nonpublic information that he knowingly possessed" and cautioned that "[i]t is *not* sufficient that the government proves that the defendant sold or sold short PDA stock while knowingly in possession of the material nonpublic information." In other words, even under the more rigorous "use" standard that we adopt today, Smith has nothing to complain about. We must therefore reject Smith's challenge to the district court's state-of-mind instruction.

V

For the foregoing reasons, the district court's decision is affirmed in all respects.

---

26. "An 'out-of-the-money' call option allows a person purchasing the option to buy stock during a limited period in the future at a fixed price (the 'strike price'). That price is higher than the current market price. Thus, the option holder essentially is betting that the market price will rise over the strike price within the limited time period. The time period limitations make such investments extremely speculative." United States v. Grossman, 843 F.2d 78, 81 n.1 (2d Cir. 1988).

2.   *The Misappropriation Theory*

Since the law of insider trading has been treated as a species of a section 10(b) and Rule 10b-5, there have been serious difficulties in defining who beyond insiders is under a duty to abstain or disclose. This is because "silence, absence a duty to disclose, is not deceptive," Basic, Inc. v. Levinson, 485 U.S. 224, 239 n.17 (1988), and deception (scienter) is part of the cause of action under Section 10(b) and Rule 10b-5. For insiders, the duty to disclose arises from the fiduciary duty that every agent owes his or her principal — here, the shareholders of the company or persons about to be shareholders. But "outsiders" to a company, such as a company's outside counsel, owe fiduciary duties to the company, not to the shareholders individually. And the farther you go "outside" the company, the more attenuated any potential claims of a fiduciary duty-based duty to disclose become. What duty might a law clerk have to the shareholders of a company, when aware of an opinion being drafted that may have an impact on the company's share price? Clearly there is a fiduciary duty to the judge for whom the clerk works, but not to the shareholders of a company that may be affected by the judge's ruling. What duty might a hairdresser have, when a CEO's husband tells him that the CEO's company is just about to purchase another company? These questions present gaps in the law of insider trading where an outsider having no fiduciary duty to the trading partner, either a purchaser or seller, may be able to trade on material, nonpublic information without liability under section 10(b)/Rule 10b-5.

Until 1980, a number of courts and the SEC interpreted section 10(b) and Rule 10b-5 not to distinguish between insiders and outsiders, but rather to impose on anyone in possession of material, nonpublic information an obligation either to disclose that information or refrain from trading. Although *Texas Gulf Sulpher* had involved insiders, the language it used could be more broadly construed to prohibit anyone from trading on the basis of material, nonpublic information. *See* SEC v. Texas Gulf Sulpher, 401 F. 2d 833, 848 (2d Cir. 1968) (in discussing the obligations of corporate insiders, the court stated that "anyone in possession of material inside information must either disclose it to the investing public, or . . . must abstain from trading). In 1980, though, the Supreme Court rejected this "equality of access" theory of insider trading in Chiarella v. United States, 445 U.S. 222 (1980). *Chiarella* involved an employee of a financial printer who worked on tender offer documents. Mr. Chiarella was able to determine from those documents which companies were going to be the targets in hostile takeover attempts, and he bought stock in those companies before the tender offers were publicly announced. (It is typical to either leave the names blank in such sensitive documents until the final printing, or to use false names that get replaced at the last moment, but Mr. Chiarella was able to figure out the true targets from other information in the documents. Ultimately he made $30,000 from the appreciation in the stock he bought.) The Second Circuit had upheld his conviction for insider trading, but the Supreme Court reversed, rejecting the equality of access theory of insider trading:

> When an allegation of fraud is based upon nondisclosure, there can be no fraud
> absent a duty to speak. . . . The element required to make silence fraudulent — a
> duty to disclose — is absent in this case. No duty could arise from petitioner's

relationship with the sellers of the target company's securities, for petitioner had no prior dealings with them. He was not their agent, he was not a fiduciary, he was not a person in whom the sellers had placed their trust and confidence. He was, in fact, a complete stranger who dealt with the sellers only through impersonal market transactions. We cannot affirm petitioner's conviction without recognizing a general duty between all participants in market transactions to forgo actions based on material, nonpublic information. Formulation of such a broad duty, which departs radically from the established doctrine that duty arises from a specific relationship between two parties, should not be undertaken absent some explicit evidence of congressional intent.

Chiarella v. United States, 445 U.S. 222, 235 (1980).

A concurrence in *Chiarella* by Justice Stevens discussed with some approval an alternative theory of liability, which has come to be known as the misappropriation theory of insider trading, although Justice Stevens recognized that the misappropriation theory could not be the basis on which to uphold the conviction against Mr. Chiarella because it had not been presented at trial. Under this theory, the deception necessary to ground liability consists of fraud on the source of the information. *Chiarella*, 445 U.S. at 238. The fraud in *Chiarella*, under this theory, consisted of Mr. Chiarella's misappropriating the information the acquiring companies had entrusted to his employer and using it for his personal financial gain. And yet, the misappropriation theory was dictum discussed in a concurrence, so it hardly provided a clear answer to the question of who beyond insiders must disclose material nonpublic information or abstain from trading.

The following case, after 25 years of lower court development and SEC endorsement of the misappropriation theory post-*Chiarella,* provides the Supreme Court's ultimate endorsement of the theory. Note that this theory grounds liability on deception based on a breach of fiduciary duty between an agent (*e.g.*, the law clerk, in the previous example) and a principal (*e.g.*, the judge), not on a breach of a fiduciary duty of disclosure between a company insider and the buyer and seller of stock. As such, notice the extent to which securities liability here reinforces core concepts of the principal/agent relationship and the fiduciary duties inherent in that relationship.

UNITED STATES v. O'HAGAN

521 U.S. 642
Supreme Court of the United States
June 25, 1997

Justice GINSBURG delivered the opinion of the Court.

This case concerns the interpretation and enforcement of §10(b) . . . of the Securities Exchange Act of 1934, and [the rule] made by the Securities and Exchange Commission pursuant [thereto], Rule 10b-5. . . . [W]e address and resolve [this issue]: (1) Is a person who trades in securities for personal profit, using confidential information misappropriated in breach of a fiduciary duty to the source of the information, guilty of violating §10(b) and Rule 10b-5? Our answer to the . . . question is yes. . . .

I

Respondent James Herman O'Hagan was a partner in the law firm of Dorsey & Whitney in Minneapolis, Minnesota. In July 1988, Grand Metropolitan PLC (Grand Met), a company based in London, England, retained Dorsey & Whitney as local counsel to represent Grand Met regarding a potential tender offer for the common stock of the Pillsbury Company, headquartered in Minneapolis. Both Grand Met and Dorsey & Whitney took precautions to protect the confidentiality of Grand Met's tender offer plans. O'Hagan did no work on the Grand Met representation. Dorsey & Whitney withdrew from representing Grand Met on September 9, 1988. Less than a month later, on October 4, 1988, Grand Met publicly announced its tender offer for Pillsbury stock.

On August 18, 1988, while Dorsey & Whitney was still representing Grand Met, O'Hagan began purchasing call options for Pillsbury stock. Each option gave him the right to purchase 100 shares of Pillsbury stock by a specified date in September 1988. Later in August and in September, O'Hagan made additional purchases of Pillsbury call options. By the end of September, he owned 2,500 unexpired Pillsbury options, apparently more than any other individual investor. O'Hagan also purchased, in September 1988, some 5,000 shares of Pillsbury common stock, at a price just under $39 per share. When Grand Met announced its tender offer in October, the price of Pillsbury stock rose to nearly $60 per share. O'Hagan then sold his Pillsbury call options and common stock, making a profit of more than $4.3 million.

The Securities and Exchange Commission (SEC or Commission) initiated an investigation into O'Hagan's transactions, culminating in a 57-count indictment. The indictment alleged that O'Hagan defrauded his law firm and its client, Grand Met, by using for his own trading purposes material, nonpublic information regarding Grand Met's planned tender offer. According to the indictment, O'Hagan used the profits he gained through this trading to conceal his previous embezzlement and conversion of unrelated client trust funds. O'Hagan was charged with 20 counts of mail fraud, in violation of 18 U.S.C. §1341; 17 counts of securities fraud, in violation of §10(b) of the Securities Exchange Act of 1934 (Exchange Act), and SEC Rule 10b-5; 17 counts of fraudulent trading in connection with a tender offer, in violation of §14(e) of the Exchange Act, and SEC Rule 14e-3(a); and 3 counts of violating federal money laundering statutes. A jury convicted O'Hagan on all 57 counts, and he was sentenced to a 41-month term of imprisonment.

A divided panel of the Court of Appeals for the Eighth Circuit reversed all of O'Hagan's convictions. Liability under §10(b) and Rule 10b-5, the Eighth Circuit held, may not be grounded on the "misappropriation theory" of securities fraud on which the prosecution relied. . . . Judge Fagg, dissenting, stated that he would recognize and enforce the misappropriation theory. . . .

Decisions of the Courts of Appeals are in conflict on the propriety of the misappropriation theory under §10(b) and Rule 10b-5. . . . We granted certiorari and now reverse the Eighth Circuit's judgment.

II

We address . . . the Court of Appeals' reversal of O'Hagan's convictions under §10(b) and Rule 10b-5. Following the Fourth Circuit's lead, *see* United States

v. Bryan, 58 F.3d 933, 943-959 (1995), the Eighth Circuit rejected the misappropriation theory as a basis for §10(b) liability. We hold, in accord with several other Courts of Appeals,[3] that criminal liability under §10(b) may be predicated on the misappropriation theory.[4]

A . . .

Under the "traditional" or "classical theory" of insider trading liability, §10(b) and Rule 10b-5 are violated when a corporate insider trades in the securities of his corporation on the basis of material, nonpublic information. Trading on such information qualifies as a "deceptive device" under §10(b), we have affirmed, because "a relationship of trust and confidence [exists] between the shareholders of a corporation and those insiders who have obtained confidential information by reason of their position with that corporation." Chiarella v. United States, 445 U.S. 222, 228 (1980). That relationship, we recognized, "gives rise to a duty to disclose [or to abstain from trading] because of the 'necessity of preventing a corporate insider from . . . tak[ing] unfair advantage of . . . uninformed . . . stockholders.'" *Id.*, at 228-229. The classical theory applies not only to officers, directors, and other permanent insiders of a corporation, but also to attorneys, accountants, consultants, and others who temporarily become fiduciaries of a corporation. *See* Dirks v. SEC, 463 U.S. 646, 655, n.14 (1983).

The "misappropriation theory" holds that a person commits fraud "in connection with" a securities transaction, and thereby violates §10(b) and Rule 10b-5, when he misappropriates confidential information for securities trading purposes, in breach of a duty owed to the source of the information. Under this theory, a fiduciary's undisclosed, self-serving use of a principal's information to purchase or sell securities, in breach of a duty of loyalty and confidentiality, defrauds the principal of the exclusive use of that information. In lieu of premising liability on a fiduciary relationship between company insider and purchaser or seller of the company's stock, the misappropriation theory premises liability on a fiduciary-turned-trader's deception of those who entrusted him with access to confidential information.

The two theories are complementary, each addressing efforts to capitalize on nonpublic information through the purchase or sale of securities. The classical theory targets a corporate insider's breach of duty to shareholders with whom the insider transacts; the misappropriation theory outlaws trading on the basis of nonpublic information by a corporate "outsider" in breach of a duty owed not to a trading party, but to the source of the information. . . .

In this case, the indictment alleged that O'Hagan, in breach of a duty of trust and confidence he owed to his law firm, Dorsey & Whitney, and to its

---

3. *See, e.g.*, United States v. Chestman, 947 F.2d 551, 566 (C.A. 2 1991) (en banc), *cert. denied*, 503 U.S. 1004 (1992); SEC v. Cherif, 933 F.2d 403, 410 (C.A. 7 1991), *cert. denied*, 502 U.S. 1071 (1992); SEC v. Clark, 915 F.2d 439, 453 (C.A. 9 1990).

4. Twice before we have been presented with the question whether criminal liability for violation of §10(b) may be based on a misappropriation theory. In Chiarella v. United States, 445 U.S. 222, 235-237 (1980), the jury had received no misappropriation theory instructions, so we declined to address the question. In Carpenter v. United States, 484 U.S. 19, 24 (1987), the Court divided evenly on whether, under the circumstances of that case, convictions resting on the misappropriation theory should be affirmed.

client, Grand Met, traded on the basis of nonpublic information regarding Grand Met's planned tender offer for Pillsbury common stock. This conduct, the Government charged, constituted a fraudulent device in connection with the purchase and sale of securities.

B

We agree with the Government that misappropriation, as just defined, satisfies §10(b)'s requirement that chargeable conduct involve a "deceptive device or contrivance" used "in connection with" the purchase or sale of securities. We observe, first, that misappropriators, as the Government describes them, deal in deception. A fiduciary who "[pretends] loyalty to the principal while secretly converting the principal's information for personal gain," "dupes" or defrauds the principal. *See* Aldave, *Misappropriation: A General Theory of Liability for Trading on Nonpublic Information*, 13 Hofstra L. Rev. 101, 119 (1984).

We addressed fraud of the same species in Carpenter v. United States, 484 U.S. 19 (1987), which involved the mail fraud statute's proscription of "any scheme or artifice to defraud," 18 U.S.C. §1341. Affirming convictions under that statute, we said in *Carpenter* that an employee's undertaking not to reveal his employer's confidential information "became a sham" when the employee provided the information to his co-conspirators in a scheme to obtain trading profits. 484 U.S., at 27. A company's confidential information, we recognized in *Carpenter,* qualifies as property to which the company has a right of exclusive use. *Id.,* at 25-27. The undisclosed misappropriation of such information, in violation of a fiduciary duty, the Court said in *Carpenter,* constitutes fraud akin to embezzlement — " 'the fraudulent appropriation to one's own use of the money or goods entrusted to one's care by another.' " *Id.,* at 27 (quoting Grin v. Shine, 187 U.S. 181, 189 (1902)). *Carpenter*'s discussion of the fraudulent misuse of confidential information, the Government notes, "is a particularly apt source of guidance here, because [the mail fraud statute] (like Section 10(b)) has long been held to require deception, not merely the breach of a fiduciary duty."

Deception through nondisclosure is central to the theory of liability for which the Government seeks recognition. As counsel for the Government stated in explanation of the theory at oral argument: "To satisfy the common law rule that a trustee may not use the property that [has] been entrusted [to] him, there would have to be consent. To satisfy the requirement of the Securities Act that there be no deception, there would only have to be disclosure." [S]*ee generally* Restatement (Second) of Agency §§390, 395 (1958) (agent's disclosure obligation regarding use of confidential information).[6]

The misappropriation theory advanced by the Government is consistent with Santa Fe Industries, Inc. v. Green, 430 U.S. 462 (1977), a decision underscoring that §10(b) is not an all-purpose breach of fiduciary duty ban; rather, it trains

___

6. Under the misappropriation theory urged in this case, the disclosure obligation runs to the source of the information, here, Dorsey & Whitney and Grand Met. Chief Justice Burger, dissenting in *Chiarella,* advanced a broader reading of §10(b) and Rule 10b-5; the disclosure obligation, as he envisioned it, ran to those with whom the misappropriator trades. 445 U.S., at 240 ("a person who has misappropriated nonpublic information has an absolute duty to disclose that information or to refrain from trading"); *see also id.,* at 243, n.4. The Government does not propose that we adopt a misappropriation theory of that breadth.

on conduct involving manipulation or deception. In contrast to the Government's allegations in this case, in *Santa Fe Industries*, all pertinent facts were disclosed by the persons charged with violating §10(b) and Rule 10b-5; therefore, there was no deception through nondisclosure to which liability under those provisions could attach. Similarly, full disclosure forecloses liability under the misappropriation theory: Because the deception essential to the misappropriation theory involves feigning fidelity to the source of information, if the fiduciary discloses to the source that he plans to trade on the nonpublic information, there is no "deceptive device" and thus no §10(b) violation — although the fiduciary-turned-trader may remain liable under state law for breach of a duty of loyalty.[7]

We turn next to the §10(b) requirement that the misappropriator's deceptive use of information be "in connection with the purchase or sale of [a] security." This element is satisfied because the fiduciary's fraud is consummated, not when the fiduciary gains the confidential information, but when, without disclosure to his principal, he uses the information to purchase or sell securities. The securities transaction and the breach of duty thus coincide. This is so even though the person or entity defrauded is not the other party to the trade, but is, instead, the source of the nonpublic information. A misappropriator who trades on the basis of material, nonpublic information, in short, gains his advantageous market position through deception; he deceives the source of the information and simultaneously harms members of the investing public.

The misappropriation theory targets information of a sort that misappropriators ordinarily capitalize upon to gain no-risk profits through the purchase or sale of securities. Should a misappropriator put such information to other use, the statute's prohibition would not be implicated. The theory does not catch all conceivable forms of fraud involving confidential information; rather, it catches fraudulent means of capitalizing on such information through securities transactions.

The Government notes another limitation on the forms of fraud §10(b) reaches: "The misappropriation theory would not . . . apply to a case in which a person defrauded a bank into giving him a loan or embezzled cash from another, and then used the proceeds of the misdeed to purchase securities." In such a case, the Government states, "the proceeds would have value to the malefactor apart from their use in a securities transaction, and the fraud would be complete as soon as the money was obtained." In other words, money can buy, if not anything, then at least many things; its misappropriation may thus be viewed as sufficiently detached from a subsequent securities transaction that §10(b)'s "in connection with" requirement would not be met.

Justice Thomas' charge that the misappropriation theory is incoherent because information, like funds, can be put to multiple uses misses the point. The Exchange Act was enacted in part "to insure the maintenance of fair and honest markets," 15 U.S.C. §78b, and there is no question that fraudulent uses of confidential information fall within §10(b)'s prohibition if the fraud is "in connection with" a securities transaction. It is hardly remarkable that a rule

---

7. Where, however, a person trading on the basis of material, nonpublic information owes a duty of loyalty and confidentiality to two entities or persons — for example, a law firm and its client — but makes disclosure to only one, the trader may still be liable under the misappropriation theory.

suitably applied to the fraudulent uses of certain kinds of information would be stretched beyond reason were it applied to the fraudulent use of money.

Justice Thomas does catch the Government in overstatement. Observing that money can be used for all manner of purposes and purchases, the Government urges that confidential information of the kind at issue derives its value *only* from its utility in securities trading. Substitute "ordinarily" for "only," and the Government is on the mark.[8] . . .

The misappropriation theory comports with §10(b)'s language, which requires deception "in connection with the purchase or sale of any security," not deception of an identifiable purchaser or seller. The theory is also well tuned to an animating purpose of the Exchange Act: to insure honest securities markets and thereby promote investor confidence. *See* 45 Fed. Reg. 60412 (1980) (trading on misappropriated information "undermines the integrity of, and investor confidence in, the securities markets"). Although informational disparity is inevitable in the securities markets, investors likely would hesitate to venture their capital in a market where trading based on misappropriated nonpublic information is unchecked by law. An investor's informational disadvantage vis-à-vis a misappropriator with material, nonpublic information stems from contrivance, not luck; it is a disadvantage that cannot be overcome with research or skill.

In sum, considering the inhibiting impact on market participation of trading on misappropriated information, and the congressional purposes underlying §10(b), it makes scant sense to hold a lawyer like O'Hagan a §10(b) violator if he works for a law firm representing the target of a tender offer, but not if he works for a law firm representing the bidder. The text of the statute requires no such result. The misappropriation at issue here was properly made the subject of a §10(b) charge because it meets the statutory requirement that there be "deceptive" conduct "in connection with" securities transactions. . . .

The judgment of the Court of Appeals for the Eighth Circuit is reversed, and the case is remanded for further proceedings consistent with this opinion.

It is so ordered.

Justice SCALIA, concurring in part and dissenting in part.

. . . I do not agree . . . with Part II of the Court's opinion, containing its analysis of respondent's convictions under §10(b) and Rule 10b-5.

I do not entirely agree with Justice THOMAS's analysis of those convictions either, principally because it seems to me irrelevant whether the Government's theory of why respondent's acts were covered is "coherent and consistent." It is true that with respect to matters over which an agency has been accorded adjudicative authority or policymaking discretion, the agency's action must be supported by the reasons that the agency sets forth, but I do not think an

---

8. Justice Thomas' evident struggle to invent other uses to which O'Hagan plausibly might have put the nonpublic information is telling. It is imaginative to suggest that a trade journal would have paid O'Hagan dollars in the millions to publish his information. Counsel for O'Hagan hypothesized, as a nontrading use, that O'Hagan could have "misappropriat[ed] this information of [his] law firm and its client, deliver[ed] it to [Pillsbury], and suggest[ed] that [Pillsbury] in the future . . . might find it very desirable to use [O'Hagan] for legal work." But Pillsbury might well have had large doubts about engaging for its legal work a lawyer who so stunningly displayed his readiness to betray a client's confidence. Nor is the Commission's theory "incoherent" or "inconsistent" for failing to inhibit use of confidential information for "personal amusement . . . in a fantasy stock trading game."

agency's unadorned application of the law need be, at least where (as here) no *Chevron* deference is being given to the agency's interpretation, *see* Chevron U.S.A. Inc. v. Natural Resources Defense Council, Inc., 467 U.S. 837 (1984). In point of fact, respondent's actions either violated §10(b) and Rule 10b-5, or they did not — regardless of the reasons the Government gave. And it is for us to decide.

While the Court's explanation of the scope of §10(b) and Rule 10b-5 would be entirely reasonable in some other context, it does not seem to accord with the principle of lenity we apply to criminal statutes (which cannot be mitigated here by the Rule, which is no less ambiguous than the statute). In light of that principle, it seems to me that the unelaborated statutory language: "[t]o use or employ, in connection with the purchase or sale of any security . . . any manipulative or deceptive device or contrivance," §10(b), must be construed to require the manipulation or deception of a party to a securities transaction.

Justice THOMAS, with whom The Chief Justice joins, concurring in the judgment in part and dissenting in part.

Today the majority upholds respondent's convictions for violating §10(b) of the Securities Exchange Act of 1934, and Rule 10b-5 promulgated thereunder, based upon the Securities and Exchange Commission's "misappropriation theory." Central to the majority's holding is the need to interpret §10(b)'s requirement that a deceptive device be "use[d] or employ [ed], in connection with the purchase or sale of any security." Because the Commission's misappropriation theory fails to provide a coherent and consistent interpretation of this essential requirement for liability under §10(b), I dissent. . . .

I

I do not take issue with the majority's determination that the undisclosed misappropriation of confidential information by a fiduciary can constitute a "deceptive device" within the meaning of §10(b). Nondisclosure where there is a pre-existing duty to disclose satisfies our definitions of fraud and deceit for purposes of the securities laws.

Unlike the majority, however, I cannot accept the Commission's interpretation of when a deceptive device is "use[d] . . . in connection with" a securities transaction. Although the Commission and the majority at points seem to suggest that *any* relation to a securities transaction satisfies the "in connection with" requirement of §10(b), both ultimately reject such an overly expansive construction and require a more integral connection between the fraud and the securities transaction. The majority states, for example, that the misappropriation theory applies to undisclosed misappropriation of confidential information "for securities trading purposes," thus seeming to require a particular intent by the misappropriator in order to satisfy the "in connection with" language. The Commission goes further, and argues that the misappropriation theory satisfies the "in connection with" requirement because it "depends on an *inherent* connection between the deceptive conduct and the purchase or sale of a security."

The Commission's construction of the relevant language in §10(b), and the incoherence of that construction, become evident as the majority attempts to describe why the fraudulent theft of information falls under the Commission's misappropriation theory, but the fraudulent theft of money does not. The majority correctly notes that confidential information "qualifies as property to which the company has a right of exclusive use." It then observes that the "undisclosed misappropriation of such information, in violation of a fiduciary duty, . . . constitutes fraud akin to embezzlement— the fraudulent appropriation to one's own use of the money or goods entrusted to one's care by another." So far the majority's analogy to embezzlement is well taken, and adequately demonstrates that undisclosed misappropriation can be a fraud on the source of the information.

What the embezzlement analogy does not do, however, is explain how the relevant fraud is "use[d] or employ[ed], in connection with" a securities transaction. And when the majority seeks to distinguish the embezzlement of funds from the embezzlement of information, it becomes clear that neither the Commission nor the majority has a coherent theory regarding §10(b)'s "in connection with" requirement.

Turning first to why embezzlement of information supposedly meets the "in connection with" requirement, the majority asserts that the requirement "is satisfied because the fiduciary's fraud is consummated, not when the fiduciary gains the confidential information, but when, without disclosure to his principal, he uses the information to purchase or sell securities. The securities transaction and the breach of duty thus coincide."

The majority later notes, with apparent approval, the Government's contention that the embezzlement of funds used to purchase securities would *not* fall within the misappropriation theory. The misappropriation of funds used for a securities transaction is not covered by its theory, the Government explains, because "the proceeds would have value to the malefactor apart from their use in a securities transaction, and the fraud would be complete as soon as the money was obtained."

Accepting the Government's description of the scope of its own theory, it becomes plain that the majority's explanation of how the misappropriation theory supposedly satisfies the "in connection with" requirement is incomplete. The touchstone required for an embezzlement to be "use[d] or employ[ed], in connection with" a securities transaction is not merely that it "coincide" with, or be consummated by, the transaction, but that it is *necessarily* and *only* consummated by the transaction. Where the property being embezzled has value "apart from [its] use in a securities transaction"—even though it is in fact being used in a securities transaction—the Government contends that there is no violation under the misappropriation theory.

My understanding of the Government's proffered theory of liability, and its construction of the "in connection with" requirement, is confirmed by the Government's explanation during oral argument:

"*Court*:   What if I appropriate some of my client's money in order to buy stock? . . .
"*Court*:   Have I violated the securities laws?
"*Counsel*:   I do not think that you have.
"*Court*:   Why not? Isn't that in connection with the purchase of securit[ies] just as much as this one is?
"*Counsel*:   It's not just as much as this one is, because in this case it is the use of the information that enables the profits, pure and simple. There would be no opportunity to engage in profit—

"*Court*:   Same here. I didn't have the money. The only way I could buy this stock was to get the money. . . .
"*Counsel*:   The difference . . . is that once you have the money you can do anything you want with it. In a sense, the fraud is complete at that point, and then you go on and you can use the money to finance any number of other activities, but *the connection is far less close than in this case, where the only value of this information for personal profit for respondent was to take it and profit in the securities markets by trading on it.* . . .
"*Court*:   So what you're saying is, is in this case the misappropriation can only be of relevance, or is of substantial relevance, is with reference to the purchase of securities.
"*Counsel*:   Exactly.
"*Court*:   When you take the money out of the accounts you can go to the racetrack, or whatever.
"*Counsel*:   That's exactly right, and because of that difference, [there] can be no doubt that this kind of misappropriation of property is in connection with the purchase or sale of securities. "Other kinds of misappropriation of property may or may not, but this is a unique form of fraud, unique to the securities markets, in fact, because *the only way in which respondent could have profited through this information is by either trading on it or by tipping somebody else to enable their trades.*"

As the above exchange demonstrates, the relevant distinction is not that the misappropriated information *was* used for a securities transaction (the money example met that test), but rather that it could *only* be used for such a transaction.

The Government's construction of the "in connection with" requirement — and its claim that such requirement precludes coverage of financial embezzlement — also demonstrates how the majority's described distinction of financial embezzlement is incomplete. Although the majority claims that the fraud in a financial embezzlement case is complete as soon as the money is obtained, and before the securities transaction is consummated, that is not uniformly true, and thus cannot be the Government's basis for claiming that such embezzlement does not violate the securities laws. It is not difficult to imagine an embezzlement of money that takes place via the mechanism of a securities transaction — for example where a broker is directed to purchase stock for a client and instead purchases such stock — using client funds — for his own account. The unauthorized (and presumably undisclosed) transaction is the very act that constitutes the embezzlement and the "securities transaction and the breach of duty thus coincide." What presumably distinguishes monetary embezzlement for the Government is thus that it is not *necessarily* coincident with a securities transaction, not that it *never* lacks such a "connection."

Once the Government's construction of the misappropriation theory is accurately described and accepted — along with its implied construction of §10(b)'s "in connection with" language — that theory should no longer cover cases, such as this one, involving fraud on the source of information where the source has no connection with the other participant in a securities transaction. It seems obvious that the undisclosed misappropriation of confidential information is not necessarily consummated by a securities transaction. In this case, for example, upon learning of Grand Met's confidential takeover plans, O'Hagan could have done any number of things with the information: He could have sold it to a newspaper for publication; he could have given or sold the information to Pillsbury itself; or he could even have kept the information and used it solely for his personal amusement, perhaps in a fantasy stock trading game.

Any of these activities would have deprived Grand Met of its right to "exclusive use" of the information and, if undisclosed, would constitute "embezzlement" of Grand Met's informational property. Under *any* theory of liability, however, these activities would not violate §10(b) and, according to the Commission's monetary embezzlement analogy, these possibilities are sufficient to preclude a violation under the misappropriation theory even where the informational property *was* used for securities trading. That O'Hagan actually did use the information to purchase securities is thus no more significant here than it is in the case of embezzling money used to purchase securities. In both cases the embezzler *could have* done something else with the property, and hence the Commission's necessary "connection" under the securities laws would not be met.[2] If the relevant test under the "in connection with" language is whether the fraudulent act is *necessarily* tied to a securities transaction, then the misappropriation of confidential information used to trade no more violates §10(b) than does the misappropriation of funds used to trade. As the Commission concedes that the latter is not covered under its theory, I am at a loss to see how the same theory can coherently be applied to the former.

The majority makes no attempt to defend the misappropriation theory as set forth by the Commission. Indeed, the majority implicitly concedes the indefensibility of the Commission's theory by acknowledging that alternative uses of misappropriated information exist that do not violate the securities laws and then dismissing the Government's repeated explanations of its misappropriation theory as mere "overstatement." Having rejected the Government's description of its theory, the majority then engages in the "imaginative" exercise of constructing its own misappropriation theory from whole cloth. Thus, we are told, if we merely "[s]ubstitute 'ordinarily' for 'only'" when describing the degree of connectedness between a misappropriation and a securities transaction, the Government would have a winner. Presumably, the majority would similarly edit the Government's brief to this Court to argue for only an "ordinary," rather than an " *inherent* connection between the deceptive conduct and the purchase or sale of a security."

I need not address the coherence, or lack thereof, of the majority's new theory, for it suffers from a far greater, and dispositive, flaw: It is not the theory offered by the Commission. Indeed, as far as we know from the majority's opinion, this new theory has *never* been proposed by the Commission, much less adopted by rule or otherwise. . . .

In upholding respondent's convictions under the new and improved misappropriation theory, the majority also points to various policy considerations underlying the securities laws, such as maintaining fair and honest markets, promoting investor confidence, and protecting the integrity of the securities markets. But the repeated reliance on such broad-sweeping legislative purposes reaches too far and is misleading in the context of the misappropriation theory.

---

2. Indeed, even if O'Hagan or someone else thereafter used the information to trade, the misappropriation would have been complete before the trade and there should be no §10(b) liability. The most obvious real-world example of this scenario would be if O'Hagan had simply tipped someone else to the information. The mere act of passing the information along would have violated O'Hagan's fiduciary duty and, if undisclosed, would be an "embezzlement" of the confidential information, regardless of whether the tippee later traded on the information.

It reaches too far in that, regardless of the overarching purpose of the securities laws, it is not illegal to run afoul of the "purpose" of a statute, only its letter. The majority's approach is misleading in this case because it glosses over the fact that the supposed threat to fair and honest markets, investor confidence, and market integrity comes not from the supposed fraud in this case, but from the mere fact that the information used by O'Hagan was nonpublic.

As the majority concedes, because "the deception essential to the misappropriation theory involves feigning fidelity to the source of information, if the fiduciary discloses *to the source* that he plans to trade on the nonpublic information, there is no 'deceptive device' and thus no §10(b) violation." Indeed, were the source expressly to authorize its agents to trade on the confidential information — as a perk or bonus, perhaps — there would likewise be no §10(b) violation. Yet in either case — disclosed misuse or authorized use — the hypothesized "inhibiting impact on market participation," would be identical to that from behavior violating the misappropriation theory: "Outsiders" would still be trading based on nonpublic information that the average investor has no hope of obtaining through his own diligence.[6]

The majority's statement that a "misappropriator who trades on the basis of material, nonpublic information, in short, *gains his advantageous market position through deception; he deceives the source of the information and simultaneously harms members of the investing public*," thus focuses on the wrong point. Even if it is true that trading on nonpublic information hurts the public, it is true whether or not there is any deception of the source of the information.[7] Moreover, as we have repeatedly held, use of nonpublic information to trade is not itself a violation of §10(b). Rather, it is the use of fraud "in connection with" a securities transaction that is forbidden. Where the relevant element of fraud has no impact on the integrity of the subsequent transactions as distinct from the nonfraudulent element of using nonpublic information, one can reasonably question whether the fraud was used in connection with a securities transaction. And one can likewise question whether removing that aspect of fraud, though perhaps laudable, has anything to do with the confidence or integrity of the market.

The absence of a coherent and consistent misappropriation theory and, by necessary implication, a coherent and consistent application of the statutory "use or employ, in connection with" language, is particularly problematic in the

---

6. That the dishonesty aspect of misappropriation might be eliminated via disclosure or authorization is wholly besides the point. The dishonesty in misappropriation is in the relationship between the fiduciary and the principal, not in any relationship between the misappropriator and the market. No market transaction is made more or less honest by disclosure to a third-party principal, rather than to the market as a whole. As far as the market is concerned, a trade based on confidential information is no more "honest" because some third party may know of it so long as those on the other side of the trade remain in the dark.

7. The majority's statement, by arguing that market advantage is gained "through" deception, unfortunately seems to embrace an error in logic: Conflating causation and correlation. That the misappropriator may both deceive the source and "simultaneously" hurt the public no more shows a causal "connection" between the two than the fact that the sun both gives some people a tan and "simultaneously" nourishes plants demonstrates that melanin production in humans causes plants to grow. In this case, the only element common to the deception and the harm is that both are the result of the same antecedent cause — namely, using nonpublic information. But such use, even for securities trading, is not illegal, and the consequential deception of the source follows an entirely divergent branch of causation than does the harm to the public. The trader thus "gains his advantageous market position *through*" the use of nonpublic information, whether or not deception is involved; the deception has no effect on the existence or extent of his advantage.

context of this case. The Government claims a remarkable breadth to the delegation of authority in §10(b), arguing that "the very aim of this section was to pick up unforeseen, cunning, deceptive devices that people might cleverly use in the securities markets." As the Court aptly queried, "[t]hat's rather unusual, for a criminal statute to be that open-ended, isn't it?" Unusual indeed. Putting aside the dubious validity of an open-ended delegation to an independent agency to go forth and create regulations criminalizing "fraud," in this case we do not even have a formal regulation embodying the agency's misappropriation theory. Certainly Rule 10b-5 cannot be said to embody the theory — although it deviates from the statutory language by the addition of the words "any person," it merely repeats, unchanged, §10(b)'s "in connection with" language. Given that the validity of the misappropriation theory turns on the construction of that language in §10(b), the regulatory language is singularly uninformative.

Because we have no regulation squarely setting forth some version of the misappropriation theory as the Commission's interpretation of the statutory language, we are left with little more than the Commission's litigating position or the majority's completely novel theory that is not even acknowledged, much less adopted, by the Commission. As we have noted before, such positions are not entitled to deference and, at most, get such weight as their persuasiveness warrants. Yet I find wholly unpersuasive a litigating position by the Commission that, at best, embodies an inconsistent and incoherent interpretation of the relevant statutory language and that does not provide any predictable guidance as to what behavior contravenes the statute. That position is no better than an ad hoc interpretation of statutory language and in my view can provide no basis for liability.

PROBLEM 16-3

The Young Presidents Organization (YPO) was formed in 1950 in New York City with a simple aspiration: "Let's become better presidents by learning from each other." In March 1999, Keith Kim was the CEO of a troubled potato chip manufacturer called Granny Goose Foods, Inc., and he decided to take this "learning" in a new and unexpected direction.

When Kim's Northern California chapter of YPO departed for their annual retreat in Snowmass, Colorado, one member was missing. The CEO of Meridian Data was immersed in merger talks with Quantum Corporation and could not get away. He asked the YPO moderator to explain his absence to the other members but asked them to keep the information confidential.

Of course, the members of YPO were expected to keep information like this confidential as a matter of course. The "Principles" of Kim's local chapter stated: "We operate in an atmosphere of absolute confidentiality. Nothing discussed in this forum will be discussed with outsiders. Confidentiality, in all ways and for always." In addition, all members signed a "Confidentiality Commitment" that contained the following provision:

> I understand that to achieve the level of trust necessary to ensure the interchange we all seek in the Forum, all information shared by the membership must be held in absolute confidence. . . . I understand that no Forum business can be discussed with anyone outside the Forum, including spouses, "significant others," other YPO, or non-YPO members. . . . I understand that breaking this

contract will result in being asked to resign from the Forum. Most important, I understand that I have a major moral and ethical responsibility to my Forum friends, who have entrusted me with their most personal feelings, problems, and issues. To break this trust is to destroy all that the Forum can mean to its members.

Despite the emphasis on confidentiality, Kim decided to use the information he learned on the plane for personal gain. Over the ensuing three days, Kim purchased 187,300 shares of Meridian stock for between $2.00 and $4.12 per share. He also told his business partner, his brother, and his brother-in-law about the merger negotiations, and all of them purchased shares of Meridian.

About one week later, Meridian announced that it was being acquired by Quantum, and its share price increased to $7.56. Kim made a profit of $832,627 on an investment of $583,360. Kim's "tippees" also fared well: his business partner made $200,885; his brother made $27,469; and his brother-in-law made $13,492. Shortly thereafter, Kim was arrested and charged with wire fraud and securities fraud.

Under the reasoning of *O'Hagan*, would Kim be guilty of insider trading for misappropriation of confidential information? Does Rule 10b5-2 make your decision any easier? Would Kim's tippees be guilty of insider trading?

C.   REGULATION FD

Although Congress and the SEC have for the most part regulated insider trading through section 10(b) and Rule 10b-5, it has not done so entirely. In 1984, Congress enacted the Insider Trading Sanctions Act of 1984, which makes it illegal to trade options and other derivative securities in circumstances where it would be illegal to trade in the underlying security. Insider Trading Sanctions Act of 1984, Pub. L. No. 98-376, 98 Stat. 1264, 1265 (codified in scattered subsections of 15 U.S.C. §78). In 1988 Congress amended the Exchange Act to provide a remedy for contemporaneous traders against "any person who violates any provision of this title or the rules or regulations thereunder by purchasing or selling a security while in possession of material, nonpublic information." Section 20A of the 1934 Act, enacted as the Insider Trading and Securities Fraud Enforcement Act of 1988. Moreover, in Rule 14e-3 the SEC prohibited most trading on the basis of material, nonpublic information about a pending tender offer (a direct response to *Chiarella*). (The potential tender offeror may continue to buy securities up to the 5 percent "trigger" of section 13(d), which then requires public disclosure of the purchases and the purpose of the purchases — that is, whether they are for investment or as the first step in a takeover attempt.) And in section 16 of the Exchange Act Congress specifically addressed insider trading by requiring insiders to disgorge any profits from "short-swing" sales in their company's stock — that is, a purchase followed within six months by a sale or vice versa. Securities Exchange Act of 1934, §16, 15 U.S.C. §78p (1994).

Probably the most controversial action taken by the SEC to regulate the trading on material, nonpublic information is Regulation Fair Disclosure (Reg. FD), promulgated in 1999. Regulation FD states that if a company discloses material, nonpublic information to brokers or dealers, investment advisers, investment companies, securities analysts, or large shareholders, it must publicly disclose the same information either simultaneously, in the case of intentional disclosure, or promptly, in the case of nonintentional disclosure. The purpose of Regulation FD is to create a level playing field, and stop the selective disclosure of material, nonpublic information to securities professionals in conference calls, conversations between institutional investors and the company, and similar nonpublic formats. Conference calls between companies and securities analysts and other market professionals were a regular feature of communications between companies and the market prior to Regulation FD. Selective disclosure to market professionals were not violations of insider trading law under existing Supreme Court precedent prior to Regulation FD because of a loophole left by Dirks v. SEC, 463 U.S. 646 (1983). In that case, the Supreme Court had analyzed the potential liability of Raymond Dirks, an officer of a broker-dealer firm, who had received information (making him a "tippee") from company insiders ("tippers") suggesting massive fraud at the company. Dirks had investigated the information, discussing it with other broker-dealers and with clients along the way, and was ultimately successful in bringing the fraud to light—and was then prosecuted by the SEC for his efforts. The Court in *Dirks* exonerated Dirks, holding that "tippee" liability is a derivative form of liability, and depends on whether the insider/tipper breached a duty owed to shareholders. *Dirks*, 463 U.S. at 654. If the insider disclosed the information without breaching a fiduciary duty to the company or personally benefitting—such as when a company insider discusses the company with securities analysts and other market professionals—there is no breach by the tipper and thus no derivative breach by the tippee. This interpretation of *Dirks* had allowed selective disclosure to market professionals to flourish, leading the SEC to enact Regulation FD.

Regulation FD is controversial precisely because it keeps information from the market by keeping it from securities professionals. As you read the following consent judgment in an SEC proceeding, consider whether the goal of fairness to "the market" is advanced by Regulation FD, whether that benefit is worth the cost of decreased information to market professionals and thus to the market generally, and whether there are alternative ways the SEC could have regulated selective disclosure.

IN THE MATTER OF SECURE COMPUTING CORP. & JOHN McNULTY

Administrative Proceeding File No. 3-10948
November 25, 2002

ORDER INSTITUTING CEASE-AND-DESIST PROCEEDINGS, MAKING FINDINGS, AND IMPOSING A CEASE-AND-DESIST ORDER PURSUANT TO SECTION 21C OF THE SECURITIES EXCHANGE ACT OF 1934

I.

The Securities and Exchange Commission ("Commission") deems it appropriate that public cease-and-desist proceedings be, and hereby are, instituted pursuant to Section 21C of the Securities Exchange Act of 1934 ("Exchange

Act") against Secure Computing Corporation ("Secure" or the "Company") and John McNulty ("McNulty") (collectively, the "Respondents"), to determine whether Secure and McNulty, respectively, violated and caused violations of Section 13(a) of the Exchange Act and Regulation FD.

II.

In anticipation of the institution of these proceedings, Respondents have submitted an Offer of Settlement ("Offer") which the Commission has determined to accept. Solely for the purpose of these proceedings and any other proceedings brought by or on behalf of the Commission, or to which the Commission is a party, and without admitting or denying the findings herein, except as to the Commission's jurisdiction over them and the subject matter of these proceedings, Respondents consent to the entry of the Order Instituting Cease-and-Desist Proceedings, Making Findings, and Imposing a Cease-and-Desist Order Pursuant to Section 21C of the Securities Exchange Act of 1934, as set forth below.

III.

On the basis of this Order and the Respondents' Offer, the Commission finds that:

A. Nature of Proceeding

1. In early March 2002, Secure Computing Corporation, a Silicon Valley software company, and its Chief Executive Officer ("CEO"), John McNulty, disclosed material non-public information about a significant contract to two portfolio managers at two institutional advisers in violation of Regulation FD, which requires disclosures of material, non-public information to be made to the marketplace as a whole. Following the disclosures, Secure announced the contract to the public in a press release issued after the close of the stock markets. However, investors who sold Secure stock prior to the Company's press release were denied information that may have affected their investment decisions.

B. Respondents

2. Secure is a Delaware corporation with its principal place of business in San Jose, California. The Company's common stock is registered with the Commission pursuant to Section 12(g) of the Exchange Act and is quoted on the NASDAQ Stock Market under the symbol "SCUR." The company reported revenue of $52.5 million for the year ended December 31, 2001.

3. McNulty, 55, has been the CEO and Chairman of the Board of Secure since July 1999. He also served as President and Chief Operating Officer between May 1999 and approximately July 1999.

C. Background

4. Secure is a Silicon Valley software company specializing in Internet security-related products.

5. In early 2002, Secure entered into an original equipment manufacturing ("OEM") agreement with one of the nation's largest computer networking companies (the "buyer"). The buyer agreed to bundle one of Secure's products

(the "product") with the buyer's network systems. Neither the buyer nor Secure made any public announcement of the arrangement. The agreement required the buyer's consent before Secure could announce the deal. The buyer's consent was contingent upon its sales force selling the product to "beta" customers who would test the product and provide feedback and customer testimonials that could be used in a press release.

6. Later in 2002, the buyer posted an electronic user manual containing technical information about the product on the buyer's website for use by its sales force and beta customers.

7. In early March 2002, Secure held an executive staff meeting, in which McNulty participated by telephone. At that meeting, Secure executives expressed concern that news of the OEM agreement might begin to leak to the public because the buyer's sales force was selling the product to beta customers. As a result, Secure management decided to press the buyer to proceed with a public announcement of the OEM agreement as soon as possible.

8. On March 6, at the buyer's request, Secure posted a page on its own website providing information and software downloads for the buyer's sales force and for customers who were evaluating the product. Secure's main website page did not reference the deal or provide a link to this web address. As of March 6, 2002, McNulty knew that neither the buyer nor Secure had issued a public announcement of the OEM agreement.

D. McNulty's March 6 Disclosures

9. Secure actively promotes its stock to institutional investors through in-person presentations and a program of conference calls with broker-dealers, investment advisers and other organizations. McNulty plays a key role in these promotions, making many of the presentations and conference calls.

10. On Wednesday, March 6, McNulty conducted a conference call with a portfolio manager at an investment advisory firm. A salesperson at a brokerage firm that follows Secure arranged and attended the call. McNulty took the call from his home. In addition, Secure's Director of Investor Relations ("IR Director") participated in the conference call from her office.

11. During the call, McNulty was asked questions concerning the product. McNulty then asked the IR Director whether he could discuss something that had been posted on the Company's and its new partner's website; at that point, McNulty did not identify the buyer by name. The IR Director, apparently unaware that McNulty was referring to the deal with the buyer, confirmed that he could.

12. McNulty then told the portfolio manager and brokerage firm salesperson that Secure had entered into a deal with the buyer to sell the product, identifying the buyer by name. McNulty also said that there was information on both Secure's and the buyer's websites and provided the Secure web page address describing the buyer's integration of the product. As McNulty spoke, the IR Director recognized that the OEM agreement had not been publicly announced and that McNulty should not be discussing the subject, but she did not interrupt McNulty.

13. McNulty's disclosure was the first time the salesperson from the brokerage firm had heard about the OEM agreement regarding the product. While still on the call, the salesperson looked up the web page and then e-mailed the Secure web page address to the brokerage firm's sales force.

14. The conference call ended around 11:00 A.M. (PST). As soon as the call ended, the IR Director attempted to reach McNulty and left him a voicemail message informing him that he had disclosed nonpublic information during the conference call.

15. Before he listened to the IR Director's voicemail message, McNulty received an e-mail message from a managing partner of the brokerage firm asking about the deal. McNulty sent an e-mail response providing Secure's web page address for the product integration. McNulty further wrote, "There won't be a[n] announcement/press release until [the buyer] has some customer references — bottom line though it ain't bad!!!!!!"

16. Shortly after sending the e-mail response — at approximately noon PST — McNulty retrieved the IR Director's voicemail message. McNulty then telephoned the managing partner of the brokerage firm and requested that the information be kept confidential.

17. Secure made no general public announcement of the software agreement on March 6. Secure's stock closed at $17.40 per share on that day, an increase of 8% over the previous day's close, on trading volume that was more than double that of the day before.

E. McNulty's March 7 Disclosure

18. On the morning of March 7, trading volume in Secure's stock rose significantly, and Secure received several calls from investors and analysts inquiring into rumors about an OEM deal. Secure's management (including McNulty) determined that it would have to issue a press release as soon as possible, and set about trying to obtain the buyer's consent to a public announcement. Secure did not inform the buyer of Secure's prior disclosure. The buyer did not agree to the issuance of a press release.

19. Meanwhile, also on March 7, McNulty conducted conference calls with four additional institutional investors. On March 7, at around 10:15 A.M. (PST), during the fourth call, a portfolio manager of another institutional advisory firm asked McNulty about the OEM agreement with the buyer. McNulty confirmed that Secure had a deal with the buyer under which the buyer would integrate Secure's product into the buyer's product. McNulty further explained that the deal had not yet been publicized because the buyer needed to obtain customer references first, but that he anticipated an announcement shortly.

20. Secure's stock price closed at $18.55 per share on March 7, a 7% rise from March 6 on volume that was 130% higher.

F. The March 7 Public Announcement

21. On March 7 at 1:40 P.M. (PST), following the market close, Secure issued a press release announcing the OEM agreement. On the day following the press release, Friday, March 8, the stock price rose another 7% on continued high volume. The following Monday, March 11, the stock price continued to rise, closing at $21.81 — the highest close since early January 2002. All told, Secure's stock price rose 35% between March 5 and March 11. Secure did not issue any other significant announcements during this period.

G. Secure Violated, and McNulty Caused the Violation of, Regulation FD

22. The information that Secure and McNulty selectively disclosed concerning the OEM agreement on March 6 and 7 was material and nonpublic.

23. The March 6 disclosures were nonintentional. Thus, Secure needed to make prompt public disclosure of the information concerning the OEM agreement. However, on March 7, three hours before issuing a press release, Secure and McNulty again selectively disclosed the information. The March 7 selective disclosure violated Regulation FD because Secure and McNulty failed to make simultaneous public disclosure of the information to the public.

24. Secure violated, and McNulty was a cause of Secure's violation of, Section 13(a) of the Exchange Act and Regulation FD.

IV.

In view of the foregoing, the Commission deems it appropriate to impose the sanctions specified in the Respondents' Offer.
ACCORDINGLY, IT IS HEREBY ORDERED:

A. Pursuant to Section 21C of the Exchange Act, Respondent Secure shall cease and desist from committing or causing any violations and any future violations of Section 13(a) of the Exchange Act and Regulation FD; and
B. Pursuant to Section 21C of the Exchange Act, Respondent McNulty shall cease and desist from causing any violations and any future violations of Section 13(a) of the Exchange Act and Regulation FD.

By the Commission (Commissioner Campos dissenting as to the lack of a penalty).
Jonathan G. Katz
Secretary

PROBLEM 16-4

One of the concerns about Regulation FD is that it reduces, rather than expands, the amount of information made available to securities analysts and the market. Thus, when analysts call a company to ask questions company officials may refuse to answer, citing Reg. FD, rather than disclose negative trends or conclusions to market professionals generally. This dynamic has been observed by analysts at the Calvert family of funds, among others. Calvert is one of the oldest "socially responsible investment" (SRI) mutual fund companies, with a range of different mutual funds that are designed to help investors "achieve financial security while helping to build a sustainable world and protect our quality of life." Currently it manages $8.5 billion in assets. Like most SRI funds, Calvert screens the companies in which it invests for both their financial performance and their social performance, evaluating a broad range of issues and information concerning companies' "triple-bottom line" (economic, environmental, and social impacts).

One source of data that is particularly useful to SRI analysts in evaluating environmental performance is the Toxic Release Inventory (TRI). TRI is a federal statute that since 1986 has required manufacturing companies to report annually on the levels of specified toxic chemicals that they've released. TRI reporting is done facility by facility and chemical by chemical, so SRI analysts need to perform significant work to aggregate reports in order to develop an accurate assessment of a company's environmental practices. After Reg. FD was promulgated, Calvert analysts had a number of experiences of calling specific companies to ask questions like "Why do your TRI data show a 40% increase in emissions over the last year?," or "Why are your facilities in X state showing a significant increase in emissions?," and having the companies refuse to answer the questions, citing Reg. FD. Some companies even refuse to answer more general questions now, such as what their safety policies are or what steps they take to produce their TRI data. Although Calvert's policy is to ask companies to disclose their answers publicly, not just to Calvert, that seems to be part of the problem, because under Reg. FD if the information is material and it is disclosed to one analyst it must be disclosed generally and companies prefer non-disclosure of negative information when possible. Prior to Reg. FD more companies would answer these questions. The strategy of using Reg. FD as a shield against disclosure may be counterproductive with SRI firms, since analysts assume that it is primarily poor performers who refuse to answer. Still, the phenomenon raises the general question of whether Reg. FD has advanced its own policy goals, or whether it is unintentionally inhibiting them.

What does it say about the materiality of environmental information that a company refuses to answer questions about its TRI data, citing Reg. FD? What time frame should be used to determine the materiality of environmental information, given the long latency of some environmental harms and the long-term risks those harms pose to companies and their shareholders? Is there any way to revise Reg. FD to advance the goal of inhibiting selective disclosure without suffering the "chilling effect"? Should analysts who work hard to synthesize data that is generally available, such as TRI data, in order to ask probing questions be rewarded with answers without imposing a general disclosure obligation on the company? If such select disclosure is allowed, how does one avoid the conflicts of interest that led to Reg. FD in the first place — that is, favored analysts being given at mid-quarter more information on financial projections or significant corporate developments?

Table of Cases

Index

References are to page numbers.